THE CAMBRIDGE
HISTORY OF JUDAISM

VOLUME VIII

THE CAMBRIDGE HISTORY OF JUDAISM

FOUNDING EDITORS

W. D. Davies†

L. Finkelstein†

ALREADY PUBLISHED

Volume 1 *Introduction: The Persian Period*
Edited by W. D. Davies and Louis Finkelstein
1984, 978 0 521 21880 1

Volume 2 *The Hellenistic Age*
Edited by W. D. Davies and Louis Finkelstein
1989, 978 0 521 21929 7

Volume 3 *The Early Roman Period*
Edited by William Horbury, W. D. Davies and John Sturdy
1999, 978 0 521 24377 3

Volume 4 *The Late Roman-Rabbinic Period*
Edited by Steven T. Katz
2006, 978 0 521 77248 8

Volume 7 *The Early Modern World, 1500–1815*
Edited by Jonathan Karp and Adam Sutcliffe
2018, 978 0 521 88904 9

THE CAMBRIDGE
HISTORY OF JUDAISM

VOLUME VIII

THE MODERN WORLD, 1815–2000

VOLUME EDITORS

MITCHELL B. HART

TONY MICHELS

CAMBRIDGE
UNIVERSITY PRESS

CAMBRIDGE
UNIVERSITY PRESS

University Printing House, Cambridge CB2 8BS, United Kingdom

One Liberty Plaza, 20th Floor, New York, NY 10006, USA

477 Williamstown Road, Port Melbourne, VIC 3207, Australia

314-321, 3rd Floor, Plot 3, Splendor Forum, Jasola District Centre, New Delhi - 110025, India

79 Anson Road, #06-04/06, Singapore 079906

Cambridge University Press is part of the University of Cambridge.

It furthers the University's mission by disseminating knowledge in the pursuit of education, learning and research at the highest international levels of excellence.

www.cambridge.org
Information on this title: www.cambridge.org/9781108790451
DOI: 10.1017/9781139019828

First published 2017
First paperback edition 2019

A catalogue record for this publication is available from the British Library

Library of Congress Control Number: 77085704

Library of Congress Cataloging in Publication data
(Revised for volume 8)
Main entry under title:
The Cambridge History of Judaism / Edited by W.D. Davies and Louis Finkelstein
ISBN 978-0-521-21880-1 (hardback)
1. Judaism – History
1. Davies, W.D. 11. Finkelstein, Louis
296'.09'01 BM165

ISBN 978-0-521-76953-2 Hardback
ISBN 978-1-108-79045-1 Paperback

CONTENTS

ACKNOWLEDGMENTS

This volume has been over a decade in the making. We must begin therefore by thanking all the contributors not only for their work but also for their patience and understanding. We'd like to thank and acknowledge David Rechter at the University of Oxford, whose input at the outset of this project was invaluable. Thank you to Athan Biss and Gregory Jones-Katz for their invaluable help with manuscript preparation. We would also like to thank Laura Macy, freelance copy-editor working with Out of House Publishing, for helping to bring the manuscript through the final crucial stage to publication. Her editorial work was invaluable and greatly appreciated.

Mitch Hart would like to acknowledge the generous support of Mr. Alexander Grass and his family, sponsors of the Alexander Grass Chair in Jewish History at the University of Florida. And as always, my greatest thanks to Nina Caputo, who has also lived with this project for over a decade.

With much gratitude, Tony Michels would like to thank Rebecca Michels for her support.

INTRODUCTION

MITCHELL B. HART AND TONY MICHELS

I

Most scholars work on the assumption that they can recognize modernity in the broadest sense when they see it: modernization often functions as a catch-all phrase, implicitly conveying a series of large-scale forces that worked to transform society, with Northern and Western Europe functioning as their origin and cradle. A standard list would include the Enlightenment, mercantilism/early capitalism, absolutism and the strengthening of centralized authority, along with a whole host of related developments that came into play as indirect outgrowths of these major forces – industrialization, urbanization, secularization, increasing religious tolerance (or at least moves towards this), social and economic mobility, and the gradual, often painful, inclusion of previously marginalized or excluded groups into the political and cultural commonwealth.

The debate surrounding the onset of "Jewish modernity" reaches back into the nineteenth century, and the many and various ways in which Jews became modern, or didn't, now form a staple of scholarly research. The beginnings of Jewish modernity on a substantial scale have often been situated in the last decades of the eighteenth century in Europe, associated with the rise of the Jewish Enlightenment (Haskalah) in Germany, the granting of civic emancipation to the Jews in France at the outset of the Revolution, and the subsequent emancipation of Jews in other parts of Europe in the wake of Napoleon's conquests. By way of contrast, 1815 marks the beginning of a period of reaction: for most Jews, part of the downfall of the Napoleonic system was a return to subordinate status. But this once-regnant notion of the Haskalah as the "big bang" of Jewish modernization has been questioned as different strands of modernization are

We would like to acknowledge the contribution of Dr. David Rechter of the University of Oxford, who was involved at the early stages of this project, both in the selection of the themes for essays and in the writing of this introduction. His input is greatly appreciated.

I

scrutinized – religious, intellectual, secular, political, cultural, economic – in different regions.

No matter when we might date its beginnings, it has become clear that we are dealing not with the smooth rise of Jewish modernity, of integration and acculturation, but rather an endlessly complex process of back and forth, success and failure, mutual accommodation and rejection. Rather than re-engage directly with the by-now venerable debate about the beginnings of Jewish modernity, we see this volume as an opportunity, following Lord Acton's dictum, to make problems rather than periods the focus of attention.[1] Since modernity does not "begin," the search for its origins can easily degenerate into a specious undertaking. A degree of self-reflexivity is called for, as it is not sufficient merely to invoke the categories "modern" and "modernity" without further ado. As an historian of the American Revolution has written: "Making modernity their grail gives historians [among others] a strong incentive to discover telltale signs of its emergence."[2] Two points are important here: First, scholars in Jewish Studies have for some time now been aware of the varying ways in which Jews became modern, and this awareness is reflected in this volume. Second, while each Jewry established its own particular relationship to the processes and demands of modernity, it is nonetheless possible to identify similarities and continuities that span time and space, connecting the experience of Jews across political and cultural borders; this too will find expression in the essays found here.

This volume on "modern Judaism," then, poses questions not so much about when the Jews became modern (although this is inevitably addressed), but how and why they did or did not do so. While aware of the perils of being overly prescriptive, we have asked contributors to deal with both the material and ideal spheres. In other words, these essays take account of the ideas and ideologies that shaped Jewish life in the two centuries under consideration, while also conveying a sense of the political, social, economic, and institutional infrastructures that both acted on these ideas and were acted upon by them. In the end, though, we remain keenly aware of the difficulties posed by a project that appears to assume something called 'modernity' – and by extension, Jewish modernity – and

---

[1] The *locus classicus* of this debate is Michael Meyer, "Where Does Modern Jewish History Begin?," *Judaism* 23 (1975): 329–338.

[2] Jack Rakove, "Drink Hard, Play Hard and Simply Vanish," *London Review of Books*, 23, no. 7 (2001): 32. Cited in David Rechter, "Western and Central European Jewry in the Modern Period: 1750–1933," *The Oxford Handbook of Jewish Studies*, eds. Martin Goodman, Jeremy Cohen, and David Sorkin (Oxford: Oxford University Press, 2002), p. 383.

then sets out to find innumerable examples of it. We might argue that this very epistemological and methodological discomfort, a heightened self-reflexivity, is a constitutive aspect of modernity itself. As the sociologist Anthony Giddens has put it, "Modernity turns out to be enigmatic at its core, and there seems no way in which this enigma can be 'overcome'. We are left with questions where once there appeared to be answers, and … it is not only philosophers who realize this. A general awareness of the phenomenon filters into anxieties which press in on everyone."[3]

II

One of the key themes that reappears in these essays is that of the question of Jewish identity: what did it, and what does it mean to be a Jew within states and societies in which internal, communal, and external mechanisms of control and compulsion are vanishing? Without drawing too rigid of a line between pre-modern and modern along these lines, we can say that this question of identity – the very notion of Jewishness as a potential problem or question to be addressed by Jews themselves – is a fundamentally modern question insofar as it comes to affect immediately not just isolated individuals such as Uriel de Costa or Baruch Spinoza, but potentially every Jew.

Modernity is, in part then, the breakdown of the almost total control of the Jewish community – rabbinic and communal authorities – over the individual, the disappearance of the ability or power of the community to enforce belonging, to impose identity, through a set of compulsive measures. This was itself a product of the emergence of the modern nation-state, with its appropriation and centralization of power and coercion together with the shift from collective to individual rights and duties as the hallmark of the subject or citizen.

Modernity for the Jews will mean a reorientation of the relationship between Jews – at the individual and collective levels – and the government, between Jews and the State. The rise of the modern state, built on the ideals of individual rights, and the civic equality of all citizens, demanded a revolutionary shift in thinking about the relationship between the Jews and the State. This, in turn, would produce dramatic shifts in the relationship between the Jews and other groups within society. And,

---

[3] Anthony Giddens, *The Consequences of Modernity* (Stanford: Stanford University Press, 1990), p. 49. Giddens, however, does draw too rigid a distinction in this regard between modern and pre-modern mentalities and societies, and thus we are not suggesting that pre-modern (and pre-modern Jewish) societies were not also self-reflexive.

just as important, it demanded and produced revolutionary changes in the internal structure of the Jewish community.

The emergence over time of individual autonomy vis-à-vis the organized Jewish community and Judaism as a set of commandments and obligations meant that the individual Jew was increasingly free to choose what it meant to be a Jew. Jewish identity, then, becomes a question, a challenge or problem, a matter of individual decision over the course of a lifetime. This does not mean that there are no "objective" factors involved here. One is either born into a Jewish family or one is not; one is either raised as a self-conscious Jew or one is not. Thus, with the exception of those who converted to Judaism and joined a Jewish community, Jewish identity continued to be a matter in part of descent or biology, as well as familial and communal ties. And these are, indisputably, very powerful forces. But these are the elements that are continuous with the traditional past. What is different, what helps us begin to distinguish the modern from what came before, is the matter of choice: the choice of what sort of Jew to be within an increasingly wide and varied range of religious, cultural, and social possibilities, or even to sever all or most ties to one's own Jewish past and present.

III

A volume on the history of Jews in the modern world, in this case one composed of essays by forty authors, must raise the question of narrative unity and coherence. Can there be such a thing as "a history" of the Jews? Can we legitimately speak of something such as "modern Jewish history" in anything but nominalist terms? Do 'the Jews' exist as a coherent thing in any sense other than when they are brought together in a volume such as this? While the series in which this volume appears bears the title *The Cambridge History of Judaism*, we recognize, as have others before us of course, the enormous gap between the complex and multifaceted reality of the past and the work that historians do to bring this reality into a more or less coherent and understandable story. Moreover, the essays in this volume range well beyond the strictly religious, and so "the history of Judaism" can be perhaps misleading. Indeed, some of the essays here barely touch on Judaism, qua religion, at all. So we are speaking of Jews or Jewishness as much as Judaism, of the complex and complicated mix of forces and developments over the past two hundred and more years that went into producing a 'modern Jewish identity' – or more accurately, modern Jewish identities.

Thus, we conceive of the "Judaism" of this volume's title in the broadest possible terms: the book aims to offer a portrait of Jewish civilization and its relationships with the surrounding world over roughly the past two centuries. Given that diversity is at the heart of the modern Jewish experience, such a portrayal will of necessity be constructed from numerous themes, approaches, narratives and episodes. Indeed, it would be futile to attempt to encompass the entirety of "modern Judaism" in a strictly systematic fashion in a single volume. We're confident, however, that the result is not a mere eclecticism without a discernible connecting thread. Rather, our approach is grounded in the conviction that the essays in this volume present a composite picture of a complex and variegated Jewish society or societies. Our goal was not to put together an encyclopedia on a grand scale; we did not strive for comprehensiveness. A volume such as this by its nature conveys large amounts of information, but contributors accomplish this by means of argument and informed narrative, in the context of ideas and perspectives, not as a form of vulgar factology.

The field of Jewish Studies has experienced exponential growth in recent decades, and given the plethora and sheer variety of modern source materials, it is well beyond the powers of any given individual to master the field(s). Developments both within the Jewish world and in numerous academic disciplines make this a propitious time for a new modern *Cambridge History of Judaism*. As noted above, it was one of our working assumptions that a volume such as this neither can be, nor should strive to be, comprehensive. Inevitably, even with some forty chapters, it will give short shrift or ignore certain aspects of modern Jewish life. In devising the structure and contents, we have made particular choices regarding what deserves extended analysis and what might be addressed only in passing, if at all. It is also necessary to note that there were a number of thematic essays that we wanted, and even solicited, but for one reason or another were unable in the end to secure. Thus, there are notable gaps.

Many of the individual chapter themes will be self-evident to readers with a modicum of familiarity with modern Jewish history: emancipation, national identity, religious reform, social, cultural, and economic integration and/or assimilation, mass migration and mobility, antisemitism, Zionism and the State of Israel. All these, along with other now normative themes, constitute a significant part of the volume. But we have also made choices that reflect important shifts in recent scholarship, both within Jewish Studies and within the larger academy. Many previously unheard, or indeed unimagined, movements have gained traction and now enjoy institutional and intellectual support, demanding integration into any new account of modern Jewry. We imposed no methodological or theoretical demands on individual contributors, and readers will note a wide range of approaches. Some may be dissatisfied that recent particular innovations or trends in critical scholarship did not receive adequate attention. Nonetheless, we hope that part of what this volume can contribute to a wider intellectual audience is, at the least, a demonstration of the potential utility of approaches for the study of the Jews and Judaism(s) in the modern context.

Recently, for example, Jewish scholars have turned towards post-colonial studies, and particularly scholarship focused on Southeast Asia, to shed light on European Jewry in the nineteenth and twentieth centuries. The essays in *Orientalism and the Jews* (2005) and more recently, *Colonialism and the Jews* (2017), demonstrate how the insights of post-colonial scholarship might be applied to the Jewish case.[4] Contributions along such lines serve to introduce these ideas and methods to many in the field of Jewish Studies. Regardless of whether or not they become convinced of the utility of such an approach to the Jewish past, students of modern Jewry are at a disadvantage if they remain unaware of the ideas themselves, and that post-colonial studies has now made inroads into Jewish studies. In a similar vein, the need to take account of the postmodern turn in Jewish Studies, and in scholarship more broadly, makes a volume such as this timely. Postmodernity is a subject in and of itself, an unavoidable component of the development of scholarship and intellectual life in the second half of the twentieth century; inevitably, it has consequences for how we conceive and narrate Jewish modernity, and we encouraged contributors to incorporate aspects of the postmodern perspective in their essays when appropriate. A new history of modern Judaism must demonstrate awareness of, and engagement with, postmodernity, while at the same time resisting its less persuasive positions and demands. It is necessary to steer a course between, on the one hand, the wilds of a postmodernist fragmentation that denies the very existence of any collective "Jewish experience" and, on the other, an older ethnocentric dispensation that viewed Jewish history and culture as a unitary field and accordingly minimized the substantial differences between scattered Jewish societies. Surely, not all or perhaps even most of the essays here engage directly with this or other recent intellectual developments; but we hope that those that do suggest the possibility and need for further work in this direction.

It is worth noting that many of the most significant developments over the past few centuries, developments that have undoubtedly had a hand in making Jews modern, are not addressed here in any systematic way: revolutionary changes in transportation and communication, in food production and distribution, medicine and hygiene, and the myriad other realms that transformed the lives of everyone over time, Jews included. These, we might say, are the undergirdings of the more particular shifts or changes

---

[4] Ivan Davidson Kalmar and Derek Penslar, eds., *Orientalism and the Jews* (Waltham, MA: Brandeis University Press, 2005); Ethan B. Katz, Lisa Moses Leff, and Maud S. Mandel, eds., *Colonialism and the Jews* (Bloomington: Indiana University Press, 2017).

within the Jewish communities explored in these essays. In a number of cases individual Jews figured prominently in the creation of these revolutionary shifts or changes that in turn produced "modernity": for example, the medical research that resulted in identifying the cause of and developing a cure for certain diseases; the research in physics that resulted, inter alia, in the discovery of nuclear weapons and energy; the development of the modern department store; the invention of mass advertising, and the emergence of a host of new scientific and scholarly disciplines such as anthropology, sociology, and psychoanalysis that purported to make sense of these enormous changes. The stories of these individuals are certainly worth telling. However, one could argue that it was and is the enormous effects, the collective benefits and dangers that resulted from their work that in the end is vastly more important for the story of Jewish modernity.

IV

The Cambridge History of Judaism series offers students and scholars exemplary scholarship, "snapshots" of the best of contemporary work. In the case of Volume Eight, we would hope that, in so doing, it comes to play a significant role in shaping the field's understanding of itself. It will, we hope, help determine how students of modern Jewish life grasp the general contours of the modern Jewish experience. At the same time, it strives to guide the direction of future research. Thus, we sought to pay due attention to popular and material cultural expressions of Jewishness; to non-traditional or alternative forms of religious expression; and to the methodological insights that come from disciplines such as gender and body studies, none of which have occupied much space in most comprehensive histories of modern Jewry to date. All, however, have contributed greatly to the dynamics of modern Jewish life, influencing the new and different ways in which historians, literary critics, religious and cultural studies scholars tell the story of Jews and modernity. *The Cambridge History of Judaism* is an ideal forum, we believe, for writing these innovations into the normative or mainstream narrative of the modern Jewish world.

Inevitably, as we've remarked, there are major gaps in areas covered in this volume. We have tried to be comprehensive geographically and thematically, but we recognize that the volume lacks essays in a number of crucial areas. Thus, there is no essay devoted specifically to the involvement of Jews, or the representation of Jews, in European popular culture – theater, song, film, and television – while we do have essays on this theme for the American and Middle Eastern contexts. Nor is there an essay devoted to Jews and art, or Jews and music. Again, such gaps reflect only a lack of space, not a judgment about the relative significance of these subjects.

Part I, *History and Geography*, lays the foundation for what follows by presenting a series of interlocking surveys that address the history of diverse areas of Jewish settlement. The loose organizing principle for Part II is the magnetic pole of emancipation, broadly conceived; chapter themes here are grouped around the challenges posed by and to this elemental feature of Jewish life in the modern period. Our intent here is not to imply that emancipation was the sole determinant of Jewish modernity. Rather, it allows for a flexible approach that does not fixate on the role or importance of emancipation, but uses it as a plausible and convenient framework to generate an appropriately wide choice of themes. Building on these, Part III adopts a thematic approach organized around the category "culture," with the goal of casting a wide net in terms of perspectives, concepts and topics. Part IV then focuses on the twentieth century, offering readers a sense of the dynamic nature of Judaism and Jewish identities and affiliations. Surely there will be overlap between sections, as it is neither possible nor desirable to attempt to maintain rigid boundaries when it comes to matters as fluid and dynamic as cultural and intellectual expression and influence. Indeed, it is one of the goals of this volume to explore the variety of ways in which Jews have reinvented and reinvigorated Judaism, Jewish cultural expression, and Jewish forms of community over the past two hundred years. It is imperative to keep in mind that while this is not an attempt to compile an exhaustive catalog, the choice of themes ought not to appear scattershot. Its intent has been the construction of a stimulating and challenging wide-lens portrait. Collectively, these chapters offer a window on to the breadth and depth of Jewish societies and their manifold engagements with aspects of the modern world.

PART I

HISTORY AND GEOGRAPHY

CHAPTER I

CENTRAL AND WESTERN EUROPE

ROBIN JUDD

In 1824, Itzig Behrend, a Jewish dealer of grain, cattle, and wool, and his son, Abraham, entered into a long, stormy relationship with neighbors over a home. The elder Behrend lived in Grove, a small village in the German state of Hesse-Kassel. His son, Abraham, apprenticed himself to a tinsmith and sought to live in the slightly larger neighboring city of Rodenberg. After his apprenticeship, Abraham and Itzig paid full price (1,105 thalers) for a Rodenberg house, which previously had been owned by a Christian burgher. Not wanting a Jew to occupy a home that once had belonged to a non-Jew, the local burghers tried to prevent Abraham from moving in. The Behrends appealed to the administration in Kassel, which initially supported their right of residence but later recanted. Abraham recognized that he would be unable to sway the authorities, and so he and his father purchased a second house, which they planned to tear down and rebuild.[1] The principal magistrate again took issue with Abraham's plan, this time refusing residence on the basis that neither Behrend paid local community taxes. Abraham was in luck. Hessian policies implemented a decade earlier had lifted the payment of some local community taxes. Abraham finally received permission to build a house in which he could reside.

Fourteen years later, Abraham's younger brother, Israel, similarly decided to settle in Rodenberg. He now moved into the original home that the Behrend family had purchased but never lived in. Unlike his brother, the younger Behrend encountered no obstacles. "Times had changed," recalled the father, "and he could move in with no trouble."[2]

The Behrend family story, while not unique, neatly illustrates several important themes in modern Western and Central European Jewish history.

---

[1] Behrend's chronicle does not clarify why they purchased a house that they would destroy. It is possible that they were worried that Abraham would be refused residence rights if he moved into an intact home. It is also likely that the house was in disrepair.

[2] Itzig Behrend, "Itzig Behrend," in *Jewish Life in Germany: Memoirs from Three Centuries*, ed. Monika Richarz, trans. Stella P. Rosenfeld and Sidney Rosenfeld (Bloomington: Indiana University Press, 1991), 48–49.

First, the narrative offers a nuanced example of integration. Itzig Behrend's sons chose to live in a community that was larger and had more resources than the town in which their father lived. They gradually embraced novel crafts and built new homes. They adopted some of the characteristics of the majority, intentionally or inadvertently influenced the environment in which they lived, and used the changing judicial systems to fight for what they perceived to be the privileges and rights owed to them. Second, the Behrend family slowly moved from exclusion to semi-inclusion; their story was lodged in a twisted narrative of emancipation, which included shifting state and municipal policies concerning citizenship and participation, changing legal understandings of the religious other and his community, and varying notions of the Jew, Judaism, and the local Jewish community. Finally, despite the fact that the elder Behrend never moved from Hesse-Kassel, he and his family simultaneously identified with several different geographic and cultural communities: including, but not limited to, those of Grove, Rodenberg, Hesse-Kassel, the French Empire, Prussia, and the local and regional Jewish communities.

The multiple national and local identities of Jews, the dramatically shifting notions and implications of toleration and intolerance, and the movement between absorption and influence constitute some of the key tensions and markers of modern Jewish history. These themes may be used to explore the history of Jews in Western and Central Europe between 1800 and 1945.[3] While such an analysis offers only a snapshot of the Jewish experience and, by definition, bypasses many key moments and mundane experiences of everyday Jewish life, these themes lend insight into the multiple variations and transformations of Jewish communal life during the nineteenth and twentieth centuries. They offer a historical interpretation of modern Jewish history that can be approached in spatial and temporal terms, highlighting the instants when political borders played both significant and insignificant roles.[4] They also serve as a corrective, illuminating not only the ways in which Western and Central European Jewish history was uneven but also how its actors operated as members of the minority in a pluralistic landscape.

Between 1800 and 1939, the Jews of Western and Central Europe constituted an increasingly urban, albeit geographically diverse, portrait. They varied from the acculturated bourgeoisie of cosmopolitan Paris, to the religiously traditional townlets of Galicia, to pockets of cattle traders in

[3] To keep this essay as manageable as possible, I have chosen to take my analysis through 1945 only.

[4] Moshe Rosman, "Jewish History across Borders," in *Rethinking European Jewish History*, eds. Jeremy Cohen and Moshe Rosman (Oxford: Littman Library of Jewish Civilization, 2009), 17.

agricultural Bavaria. The majority of Jews lived in Austria-Hungary, the German states, France, and the Netherlands, with substantial Jewish communities also existing in Italy, Switzerland, and Belgium.[5]

Western and Central European Jews saw their populations rise and fall in the nineteenth and early twentieth centuries, in relative proportion to the larger non-Jewish populace. Between 1814 and 1900, when Europe's population more than doubled, Jews also experienced dramatic demographic growth. In 1820, for example, Jews in the German states numbered 223,000; by 1900, they totaled 520,000. France also saw an increase. The French state estimated in 1820 that 50,000 Jews resided within its national geographic boundaries (including the regions of Alsace and Lorraine); that number came closer to 115,000 by 1900.[6] Galicia witnessed a meteoric rise. Its Jewish population increased from nearly 200,000 at the beginning of the nineteenth century to 800,000 at its end. Diminishing infant mortality- and increasing life expectancy rates played a large role in this population upsurge.[7] The low numbers of Jewish deaths occasioned by violence also shaped the population data.[8] Most important, Jewish migrations resulted in Jewish population growth. Between 1890 and 1914, nearly 30 percent of all Eastern European Jews changed their place of residence; this would have a major impact on the size of Western and Central European Jewish communities.

When Europe's population began to decrease in the early twentieth century, Western and Central European Jewish communities analogously witnessed a declining birthrate. During the last decade of the nineteenth

[5] According to Salo Baron, Jewish population demographics were as follows: in Austria-Hungary (1800/25: 568,000; 1900: 2,069,000), the German states (1820–25: 223,000; 1900: 520,000; and 1933 504,000), France (1820: 50,000, including Alsace and Lorraine; 1900: 115,000, excluding Alsace-Lorraine; 1936: 260,000, including Alsace and Lorraine), and the Netherlands (1820: 45,000; 1900: 104,000; 1933: 112,000). He and others have also noted that historians can be somewhat confident in Jewish population statistics from the nineteenth century, because it was then that increasing numbers of countries conducted regular censuses and maintained records of Jewish communal membership. Salo W. Baron, "Population," *Encyclopedia Judaica*, v. 13, 884 and 889–892.

[6] France's total population numbered 30,000,000 in 1820 and 38,961,000 in 1900. The total population of what would become Germany was 26,624,000 in 1820 and 56,367,000 in 1900.

[7] Advancements in medicine, technology, public health, and food production led to this low infant mortality rate; Jewish historians imagine that Jewish familial cohesiveness and the proliferation of confessional charitable societies played significant roles in shaping population rates.

[8] Until World War I, most of the great European battles took place outside of territories densely inhabited by Jews.

century, the surplus of Jewish births over Jewish deaths began to narrow. Alarmed, Jewish social scientists warned that their once thriving populations would perish if Jewish immigration ceased.[9] They had reason to worry. Between 1911 and 1924, for example, the Prussian Jewish population experienced a surplus of 18,252 deaths, whose losses were compensated only by the influx of Jews from Eastern Europe.[10]

Among other things, the demographic information for European Jews during the nineteenth and early twentieth centuries highlights Jews' multiple geographic ties. Jewish transnationalism in Europe seeped across state, regional, and local borders. European Jews physically moved across cities and states. Even more of them participated in the social networks, cultural identities, and economic involvements that connected them and their institutions in several spaces. Jews who remained in a single space also experienced a multiplicity of geographic and national identities. Their communities were the product of migrations and they too took part in cross-regional networks.

During the nineteenth and twentieth centuries, Central and Western European Jews experienced these multiple geographic identities in several ways: through Jewish immigration and migration, urbanization, and the construction of supra-national, national and local allegiances. These processes became inexorably linked to narratives of emancipation, acculturation, economic diversification, and identity construction, thus highlighting the very complex and messy characteristics of modern Jewish life.

A PEOPLE OF THE CITY AND TOWN: JEWISH URBANIZATION AND MIGRATION

Despite the fact that for much of the nineteenth century Western and Central European Jews resided in small towns, Jewish urbanization served as a significant trend of modern Jewish life. In 1815, for example, only 20,000 Jews lived in large German speaking cities. By 1850, the number of Jews in major cities had doubled.[11] Dresden's Jewish population grew

---

[9] Felix A. Theilhaber, *Der Untergang der deutschen Juden* (Munich: E. Reinhardt, 1911), particularly 20–26.

[10] The total Prussian population saw a small increase in the number of births over the number of deaths.

[11] Steven M. Lowenstein, "The Beginning of Integration," in *Jewish Daily Life in Germany 1618–1945*, ed. Marion A. Kaplan (Oxford: Oxford University Press, 2005), 100–101. Scholars also have pointed out the ways in which Jewish neighborhood and residence patterns shifted in the nineteenth century. See, for example, Věra Leininger, *Auszug aus dem Ghetto: Rechtsstellung und Emanzipationsbemühungen der Juden in Prag in der ersten Hälfte des 19. Jahrhunderts* (Singapore: Kuda Api Press, 2006).

from 1,000 Jews in the early nineteenth century to 2,300 in 1886, to 4,300 in 1913, and to over 6,000 in 1925. The Parisian Jewish population similarly increased exponentially. In 1789, it only contained somewhere around 500–800 individuals; by 1851, the community had grown to over 10,000 Jews and by 1861, the Parisian Jewish population numbered somewhere around 26,000.[12]

Emancipation, economic shifts, and state growth motivated Jewish urbanization and Jewish migration across Western and Central Europe. Many Jews moved to nineteenth-century cities because they now received the consent to do so, a shift rooted in late eighteenth-century processes of modern nation-state building and the consolidation of state power. As new nation-states incorporated their territories, they began to make significant changes to policies concerning Jewish residents. Several communities lifted centuries-old anti-Jewish restrictions against movement, trade, and settlement. These constraints included the medieval "De non tolerandis Judaeis" pledge, which promised Christians that Jews would only receive the right to settle in the outskirts of cities. The repeal of this policy allowed for Jewish migrants to begin moving to the cities in considerable number. When, in 1847, the city of Leipzig allowed for Jews to settle there, it became one of the major hubs of German-Jewish life. Leipzig's small Jewish community numbered fewer than 200 in 1847 but its population grew to 1,739 in 1871, 3,179 in 1880, 7,676 Jews in 1905, and 13,032 in 1925.[13] Vienna saw a similar transformation. Before the city lifted its residence restrictions in 1848, it only permitted 179 Jews to reside within the city's borders. After 1848, thousands of Jewish families from Bohemia, Hungary, and Romania left their villages and towns to settle in the capital city and enjoy its economic, cultural, and social opportunities. By 1857, Jews made

---

[12] Paris saw tremendous growth in this period more generally. It went from 546,000 residents in 1801 to 1,696,000 in 1861. Michael Graetz, *The Jews in Nineteenth-Century France: From the French Revolution to the Alliance Israelite Universelle*, trans. Jane Marie Todd (Stanford: Stanford University Press, 1996), 42–43. Jewish urban history has witnessed a significant boom in the past three decades. See, for example, Anthony Kauders, *German Politics and the Jews: Düsseldorf and Nuremberg, 1910–1933* (Oxford: Oxford University Press, 1996); Shulamit S. Magnus, *Jewish Emancipation in a German City: Cologne, 1798–1871* (Stanford: Stanford University Press, 1997); Ezra Mendelsohn, ed., *People of the City: Jews and the Urban Challenge* (New York and Oxford: Oxford University Press, 1999); and Saskia Coenen Snyder, *Building a Public Judaism: Synagogues and Jewish Identity in Nineteenth Century Europe* (Cambridge and London: Harvard University Press, 2013).

[13] Gesellschaft für Christlich-Jüdische Zusammenarbeit Dresden, *Juden in Sachsen: Ihr Leben und Leiden* (Dresden: Evangelische Verlagsanstalt, 1994), 29–31.

up 1–3 percent of the population, by 1880 they constituted 10 percent of all Viennese residents, and by 1890 that number climbed to 12 percent.[14]

In addition to lifting residence restrictions, Western and Central European nation-states also abolished, to varying degrees, some of the corporate privileges and constraints directed at the semiautonomous Jewish communities. Hoping to solidify state power and to hasten or prevent Jewish acculturation, municipal and state governments increasingly repealed poll taxes, encouraged (if not mandated) professional diversification, prohibited the use of Hebrew or Yiddish in communal documents, encouraged the creation of Jewish schools, reorganized Jewish communal structures, and, in some cases, extended the rights of citizenship.

Each state's emancipatory narrative was distinct. German state governments, for example, began to politically integrate their inhabitants in the late eighteenth century; but until unification in 1871, the thirty-eight German states independently determined varying standards for membership and political participation, and they each treated Jewish political integration differently. Some governments granted Jews full civic rights. Other states extended certain rights during periods of openness, only to repeal them during conservative phases; a third group continuously resisted yielding to Jews any civic freedoms.[15] The Habsburg Monarchy offered a slightly different example. It lifted a series of legal discriminations against Jews in the 1780s. Now able to acquire land and marry without first taking a special exam, Jews were expected to professionalize, refused the right to use Hebrew and Yiddish in public and communal records, and forced to adopt German-sounding personal and family names. In 1867, the year of the compromise between Austria and Hungary, the Austro-Hungarian Empire extended full civic equality to its Jews. French Jews received their emancipatory rights nearly eighty years before their Jewish co-religionists in the Austro-Hungarian Empire, but their narrative of political integration was similarly circuitous. In the aftermath of 1789, the revolutionary

---

[14] Habsburg Jews also migrated to other urban centers within the Monarchy, namely Budapest, Prague, and Brünn. Steven Beller, *Vienna and the Jews, 1867–1938: A Cultural History* (Cambridge: Cambridge University Press, 1991), 166. Also see, Marsha L. Rozenblit, *The Jews of Vienna, 1867–1914: Assimilation and Identity* (Albany: State University of New York Press, 1984).

[15] On German-Jewish emancipation, see, Arno Herzig, "The Process of Emancipation from the Congress of Vienna to the Revolution of 1848/1849," *Leo Baeck Institute Yearbook* 37 (1992): 61–69; Werner E. Mosse, "From 'Schutzjuden' to 'Deutsche Staatsbürger Jüdischen Glaubens': The Long and Bumpy Road of Jewish Emancipation in Germany," in *Paths of Emancipation: Jews, States, and Citizenship*, eds. Pierre Birnbaum and Ira Katznelson (Princeton: Princeton University Press, 1995), 59–93.

state extended emancipatory rights to its Jews in two stages: the *Sephardim* in 1790 and the *Ashkenazim* in 1791. However, the granting of citizenship to Jews did not put an end to concern over Jewry's integration or their political worthiness. Instead, after a series of public interrogations over Jewish allegiances, the French Empire enacted a series of three legal measures aimed to integrate Jews into French society (1808). The first two decrees set up centralized, hierarchical organizations (consistories) under the jurisdiction of the French Ministry of Religions that would organize and oversee Jewish communal life. The third and most far-reaching of the rulings, the so-called Infamous Decree, presumed Jews – particularly the Ashkenazim in the Alsace region – guilty of chicanery unless proven innocent. This law restricted Jewish commerce and money lending for a period of ten years. It remained in effect until 1818, when Louis XVIII chose not to renew it.

Emancipation redistributed the Jewish populations of Europe. Emancipation in France encouraged Jews to migrate to the cities and towns, such as Strasbourg or Paris, where previously there had been few or no Jews.[16] In the German states, where emancipation took place unevenly, the emancipation of Jews in one locale would frequently encourage migration from an area where anti-Jewish restrictions remained in place.[17] Philip Tuchmann's parents, for example, moved their family from Ühlfeld, where Jews lacked citizenship rights, to Dessau, which had emancipated its Jews. "It was a great undertaking for my father to leave his place of birth ..." Tuchmann remembered. "He hoped, however, that in Dessau he had made a good choice ... the authorities and citizens of Dessau were already completely enlightened and the Jews there enjoyed the same esteem as everyone else."[18]

Tuchmann's story illuminates the ways in which Jews could use the erratic nature of emancipation to seek out the privileges they desired. While not all Jews favored emancipatory changes, Tuchmann's father moved to an area that promised him the rights of citizenship. Across geographic, generational, religious, and gender divides, other Jews who desired political

---

[16] During the first decades of the nineteenth century, the larger cities of the region (Strasbourg, Colmar, and Mulhouse) restricted Jewish settlement until emancipation, which therefore resulted in a minimal number of Jewish settlements. Simon Schwarzfuchs, "Alsace and Southern Germany: the Creation of a Border," in *Jewish Emancipation Reconsidered: the French and German Models*, eds. Michael Brenner, Vicki Caron, and Uri R. Kaufmann (Tübingen: Mohr Siebeck, 2003), 10.

[17] Steven Lowenstein, *The Mechanics of Change: Essays in the Social History of German Jewry* (Atlanta: Brown Judaic Studies, 1992).

[18] "Philipp Tuchmann," in *Jewish Life in Germany: Memoirs from Three Centuries*, 108–109.

integration similarly attempted to meet emancipation's demands. Many of them sought out new economic opportunities and entered what professions were available to them.

Thousands of European Jews, such as Phillip Tuchmann's father or the younger Behrends with whom this essay began, needed to migrate in order to take advantage of these economic opportunities. Upon his arrival in Dessau, for example, the elder Tuchmann expanded his hops business several times, something he was unable to accomplish in Ühlfeld. He sold fuels, produced products on which breweries relied,[19] and, once his sons came of age, co-founded a lumber business. Each of Behrend's sons left Grove to apprentice and work elsewhere. Of the three, the oldest, Philipp, traveled the furthest. He first apprenticed with a dyer and then a print-cutter in Oldenorf. He then made his way to Berlin, then Hamburg, then Lorraine, then Paris, and finally to Lyon.

Jewish migration, then, could be pulled and not pushed. The growth of the Jewish community of Cologne, a city located on the Rhine River, was illustrative of this phenomenon. As Shulamit Magnus has shown, Jews were not enticed to move there because they were fleeing discrimination elsewhere. The city's early Jewish migrants originated from nearby locations under French rule that, like Cologne, had extended citizenship rights to its Jewish minority. Instead, Cologne attracted Jews because of the opportunities available in trade, banking, and the liberal professions.[20] Vienna, Budapest, and Paris also demonstrated migration patterns of economic betterment. Even before it formally allowed Jewish residence in 1848, Vienna housed a large, unofficial Jewish population, which was involved with the textile trade. Viennese Jews would later make up a significant percentage of the capital city's journalists, lawyers, doctors, merchants, artists, and businessmen. Theodor Herzl, the chief architect of political Zionism, exemplified this trend. Born and raised in Budapest, he moved with his family to Vienna, where he attended university and established his career, later going temporarily to Paris, where he was the correspondent for the liberal daily newspaper, *Neue Freie Presse*. Paris similarly served as the home for the French Jewish economic and intellectual elite, attracting the great wholesaling and banking families, such as the Rothschilds and Foulds, as well as acclaimed writers and politicians, including the family of the future French Prime Minister, Léon Blum. Like Cologne and Vienna, the French city attracted many more penniless Jews than wealthy ones.[21] At

---

[19] These included honey, syrup, drying racks, and pitch.

[20] Magnus, *Jewish Emancipation in a German City*.

[21] In the early 1800s, the German states housed nearly 10,000 Jews who were classified as *Bettlejuden* ("Beggar Jews").

the turn of the nineteenth century, only 12 percent of Parisian Jews could be considered bourgeoisie;[22] by 1872, however, that percentage had grown to 66 percent.[23] Many Jews would go to towns and cities to eke out a livelihood, frequently turning to the established local Jewish communal authorities for assistance.

Western and Central European cities and large towns also offered Jews spaces for acculturation, religious reform, and/or escape.[24] Until the middle of the 1800s, most European-speaking Jews followed the priorities, practices, and beliefs of pre-modern Jewry. By mid-century, increasing numbers of Western and Central European Jews started to support change. They gradually violated the Sabbath, ignored Jewish dietary laws, and ceased worshiping at synagogue regularly. Some embraced modifications with little self-reflection. Others consciously articulated a desire for a reassessment of their religious practices and ideologies. The towns and cities, rather than the countryside villages, offered spaces where such reforms could be embraced. In the German-speaking world, Berlin, Hamburg, Frankfurt, and Vienna served as centers for the Jewish religious reform movement, a transformative undertaking that took place alongside emancipation and state growth.

In addition to shedding some of their external religious particularities and pursuing new economic opportunities, those Jews who desired integration mimicked the cultural mores of the growing middle class. Jews became patrons of the theater, classical music, and the opera. They pursued secondary school and university educations. While the majority of Western and Central European Jews did not matriculate at universities, thousands of Jewish (male and later female) students flocked to Berlin, Vienna, Breslau, and Paris;[25] the number of Jewish men who matriculated at Prussian universities, for example, grew from 1,134 in 1886 to 1,356 in

---

[22] This was a smaller percentage than that of the non-Jewish population.

[23] Paula E. Hyman, *The Jews of Modern France* (Berkeley: University of California Press, 1998), 62–63. Also see Graetz, *The Jews in Nineteenth-Century France* and Zosa Szajkowki, *Jews and the French Revolutions of 1789, 1830, and 1848* (New York: Ktav Publishing House, 1970).

[24] Marion Kaplan argues that movement to the cities may have actually limited Jewish and non-Jewish interaction since the urban environment would have been foreign to the new Jewish arrivals. Marion Kaplan, "Friendships on the Margins: Jewish Social Relations in Imperial Germany," *Central European History* 34.4 (2001): 480.

[25] Interestingly, universities were open to Jewish students before secondary schools. In the German-speaking world, compulsory schooling ranged from 1816 to 1870; in France, the Guizot law of 1833 mandated universal public education (although it made it neither compulsory nor free). Jewish women entered the universities more slowly.

1911.[26] Eduard Silbermann, who was born in 1851 in Kolmsdorf (Upper Franconia) to the owner of a dry goods business, was illustrative of this trend. Silbermann's mother desired that her children be educated, and she insisted that the family leave Kolmsdorf for Bamberg, the nearest large-size city. Her husband refused. Not only did Bamberg's Jews lack emancipatory rights, but he was unsure that he would be able to create a sufficient livelihood for himself there. The family moved instead to Bishberg, the closest mid-size city, where Eduard and his brothers could attend grade school. After 1861, when Jews received the right of free movement in Bamberg, the Silbermann family moved there. Eduard attended Gymnasium (upper level schooling) and later studied law, eventually serving as president of the Senate of the Higher Regional Court in Munich.[27] Rabbi Moses Seligmann experienced a different trajectory. He turned to general studies only after he completed his rabbinic education at the yeshiva in Frankfurt am Main. He took his Gymnasium exams in Speyer, and then studied at the Universities of Heidelberg and Munich. When he was unable to obtain a rabbinic post in Bavaria, he immigrated to Paris, where he remained for a number of years before returning to Germany.[28]

Despite his circuitous path toward a rabbinic post, Seligmann wanted his son to have similar educational opportunities and made certain that Caesar attended both the Gymnasium and the university. The younger Seligmann threw himself into his studies, but, unlike his father, he created a social circle that was almost exclusively made up of non-Jews. Rabbi Seligmann expressed concern over his son's non-Jewish cohort. In his view, his son would always "remain the Jew" in the eyes of non-Jews. Germans, he alleged, would never cease to express "*rischus* (hostility toward Jews)."[29] Seligmann's point of view was simplistic; however, it tapped into a formative characteristic of nineteenth-century Central and Western European life, namely the emerging understanding of the Jew as an "other" and the wide range of actions that emerged from such assumptions.

THE JEWISH QUESTION

Over the course of the mid- to late nineteenth century, antisemitism increasingly served as one lens through which an individual could view

---

[26] Marion A. Kaplan, "As Germans and as Jews in Imperial Germany," in *Jewish Daily Life in Germany, 1618–1945*, ed. Marion A. Kaplan (Oxford: Oxford University Press, 2005), 211.

[27] "Eduard Silbermann" in *Jewish Life in Germany: Memoirs from Three Centuries*, 89–93.

[28] "Moses Seligmann," in *Jewish Life in Germany: Memoirs from Three Centuries*, 143.

[29] "Moses Seligmann," 147.

his or her world. Modern antisemitism had its origins in the dramatic social, political, and economic rearrangements at this time. It articulated a concern with the particularity of Jews, championed the removal of supposed Jewish deviance from society, expressed a longing to return to a "utopian" past, and pushed for immigration controls. It worried about alleged conspiracies to control the world; the supposed disproportionate minority representation of Jews in commerce, journalism, and the arts; and Jewish alleged bloodthirstiness. Over the course of the late nineteenth and early twentieth centuries, some radical anti-Semites revived the medieval charge that Jews ritually killed Christian children to use their blood for the Passover Matzah;[30] others, similarly influenced by the pre-occupation with blood, warned that Jews could harm European civilization through Jewish–Christian procreation and worried that intermarriage threatened a nation's strength. Antisemitism's claims were inherently contradictory, resulting in what historian Derek Penslar has called, a "double helix of intersecting paradigms."[31] On the one hand, anti-Jewish campaigns painted Jews as powerful manipulators who maliciously integrated into the non-Jewish world and then used their influence in cunning ways. On the other hand, they depicted Jews as social savages, unlearned in the ways of culture and unworthy of integration. These clusters materialized in antisemitism's counter-intuitive claim that Jews were both unable to socially and politically integrate and that they had acculturated so successfully that they could disguise themselves among their compatriots. These binary constellations took other forms as well: antisemitic literature simultaneously portrayed the Jew as dandy and as slovenly; as the supersexualized, violent male Jew and as the emasculated, feminized male-child; as the occidental sexualized Jewish temptress and as the desexualized materialistic Jewess.

The Jews of Western and Central Europe did not experience these charges universally. Instead, antisemitism's particular characteristics and actions were refracted by local and regional contexts. While comparatively speaking, Jews in Germany faced fewer legal discriminatory measures than their Austro-Hungarian or Russian co-religionists, several German states and municipalities enshrined discrimination by excluding Jews from certain judiciary, military, or university posts. Many German social clubs and informal social settings rejected Jewish participation, and Germany witnessed the rise of special interest groups and political parties whose platforms revolved around anti-Jewish rhetoric. German antisemitic political

[30] "Verein zur Abwehr des Antisemitismus," *Ergänzung zum Antisemiten-Spiegel: Die Antisemiten im Lichte des Christenthums, des Rechtes und der Wissenschaft* (Berlin, 1903).
[31] Derek Penslar, *Shylock's Children: Economics and Jewish Identity in Modern Europe* (Berkeley: University of California Press, 2001), 13; generally see 11–49.

parties organized effectively and quickly; by the early 1890s, the main-stream German Conservative Party feared that it would lose support if it did not embrace antisemitism's tenets. In 1892, it adopted the Tivoli program, demanding, "a Christian authority for the Christian people and Christian teachers for Christian pupils." Tivoli, the exclusion of Jews from some social clubs, and the late nineteenth-century successes of antisemitic political parties contributed toward making antisemitism tolerable, if not reputable, in the German speaking world.[32]

In his study of the Breslau Jewish community, historian Till van Rahden demonstrates the way in which antisemitism increasingly served as a "cultural code" within the Silesian capital. After 1878, when a portion of the Protestant bourgeoisie recanted its support of the liberal parties and began to support Breslau's conservative movement, Breslau's "anti-Semitic mood of society" became particularly charged. The local Catholic press, which already had demonstrated antisemitic beliefs, intensified its anti-Jewish coverage, and several local papers took on anti-Jewish views. Interestingly, while antisemitism proliferated in the political arena, Van Rahden shows that it did not prevent Breslau Jews from achieving a high level of integration.[33] Antisemitism, then, was practiced and experienced unevenly.

German and French antisemitic circles shared several racial, economic, and social concerns, thus underscoring transnational "cross-fertilization" of antisemitism.[34] Yet, both were lodged within particular historical contexts and cultures. French political antisemitism was typified by two cultural milieus: royal right-wing antisemitism and radical left-leaning anti-Jewish hatred. The former was rooted in conservative Roman Catholic and Protestant circles that yearned for the restoration of the monarchy, Church, and nobility. The false accusation of the Jewish army officer, Alfred Dreyfus, of spying for Germany epitomized French right-wing antisemitism. For anti-Semites, Dreyfus's alleged actions proved the existence of Jewish treachery. The affair split the French nation, quickly extending beyond discussions of the Jews' role in the polity to concern the rightful place of the army and monarchy in the nation-state. Eventually, the

---

[32] Shulamit Volkov, "Antisemitism as a Cultural Code: Reflections on the History and Historiography of Antisemitism in Imperial Germany," *Leo Institute Year Book* 23.1 (1978): 25–46.

[33] Till van Rahden, "Intermarriage, the New Woman, and the Situational Ethnicity of Breslau Jews, 1870s to 1920s," *Leo Baeck Institute Yearbook* 46 (2001): 125–150; Till van Rahden, *Jews and Other Germans: Civil Society, Religious Diversity, and Urban Politics in Breslau, 1860–1925* (Madison: University of Wisconsin Press, 2008).

[34] Shelley Baranowski, *Nazi Empire: German Colonialism and Imperialism from Bismarck to Hitler* (Cambridge: Cambridge University Press, 2010), 26.

French government acquitted Dreyfus, discrediting the conservative establishments. Despite the acquittal, the Dreyfus affair continued to linger.[35]

Like German antisemitism, French antisemitism was not solely a right-wing phenomenon. French left-wing antisemitism originated in anarchist and socialist groups. Blaming the Jews for the misery of the French underclass, left-wing French anti-Semites expressed concern that Jewish emancipation had ironically resulted in the creation of a new circle of autocrats who ruled the French polity and economy. Warning that Jewish families, such as the Rothschilds, posed a particular danger to French society and culture, they called for the exclusion of Jews from certain cultural and social arenas, as well as immigration restrictions.

MULTIPLE GEOGRAPHIES: EASTERN EUROPEAN IMMIGRATION AND TRANSNATIONAL TIES

Anxiety over Jewish immigration was a major characteristic of nineteenth- and twentieth-century Jewish life and was grounded in the arrival of millions of Jews who came permanently or temporarily to Western and Central European cities. Increasing antisemitism, economic hardships, the revolution in Russia of 1905, and the exclusionary violence of the pogroms led to the migration of more than 2.5 million Jews from Eastern Europe. Of these, approximately 350,000 immigrated to Western Europe.[36] According to an 1891 report in the Warsaw Jewish newspaper, *Hazfirah,* "almost all the Jews living in the southern provinces of Russia have been seized by the urge to leave. ..."[37] In her memoirs, Henriette Hildesheimer Hirsch remembered the thousands of refugees who arrived in Berlin. Her father, she recalled, "worked most intensely after the terrible pogroms in Russia. Throngs of helpless, completely ruined Jews came to German without any means ... Often refugees came to us who had nothing in hand except a note that said, 'Hildesheimer, Berlin.'"[38]

[35] Pierre Birnbaum, *Anti-Semitism in France: A Political History from Leon Blum to the Present,* trans. Miriam Kochan (Oxford: Oxford University Press, 1992), 147–77 and Martin Johnson, *The Dreyfus Affair: Honour and Politics in the Belle Epoque* (New York: Macmillan, 1999).

[36] It is important to note that Jews were not only migrating to Western and Central Europe, but Jews within Western and Central Europe were also leaving the continent. Posen and Bavaria, for example, saw its population decline in the early and mid-nineteenth century because of overseas emigration.

[37] *Hazfirah,* "On the Latest Wave of Emigration," in *Jew in the Modern World: A Documentary History,* eds. Paul Mendes-Flohr and Jehuda Reinharz (New York and Oxford: Oxford University Press, 2011), 395.

[38] "Henriette Hirsch, née Hildesheimer," in *Jewish Life in Germany: Memoirs from Three Centuries,* 177.

Eastern European Jews also fled to Central and Western Europe during World War I with the establishment of the Eastern front, which extended between the Austro-Hungarian Empire, Bulgaria and Germany on one side and the Russian Empire and Romania on the other. The Eastern Front included territories that were home to millions of Jews. While many of those Jews fled to other parts of Eastern Europe, thousands of them escaped to Central European cities. Frederick Andermann's grandmother, father, and uncles and aunts, for example, fled to Vienna from Czernowitz (southwestern Ukraine). "Conditions were difficult," he recalled, "and food was hard to obtain. Despite this, life in Vienna was exciting."[39]

Migration characterized nineteenth- and twentieth-century European Jewish life, but Jews experienced an assortment of national projects and allegiances even when they did not move from place to place or serve as hosts to migrants. In her memoir, *The Education of Fanny Lewald*, the Jewish-born writer, Fanny Lewald, neatly described the multiple geographic allegiances and ambivalences her Königsberg family experienced when French troops invaded her East Prussian city in 1809. In contrast to the East Prussian city's draconian restrictions on its Jews, the French emancipated the Jewish residents. It "was natural, therefore," she wrote, "that among many Jews the question arose whether freedom under a foreign ruler was not preferable to serfdom under a native royal family." Lewald's father, she remembered, "knew the value of the French Revolutionary reforms quite well as they concerned the Jews ... and felt a sympathy for Napoleon"; moreover, her grandfather had been imprisoned in the late 1700s, a victim of anti-Jewish sentiment and restrictions. Despite all this, her father was "completely German."[40] For the next decade, the family lived with daily ambivalence. They quietly disparaged the French and swore their allegiance to the Prussian state, but they sang French songs, befriended French soldiers, and enjoyed the by-products of French emancipation. Later, the Lewald family's geographic circle would widen when it experienced another occupation, namely that of the Russian troops. With the arrival of the Russian forces, they housed another group of soldiers, learned a few Russian words, and used Russian booty in the family's exchange and banking business.

---

[39] Frederick Andermann, "Czernowitz Memoirs," ME 1550 Leo Back Institute, Center for Jewish History (New York), 12.

[40] Fanny Lewald, *The Education of Fanny Lewald: An Autobiography*. ed. and trans. Hanna Ballin Lewis (Albany: State University of New York Press, 1992), 14–15.

Alsace, home to one of the oldest Jewish communities in Europe, offers a similar example.[41] Ceded to France by the Holy Roman Empire in 1648, the region became Haut-Rhin and Bas-Rhin in the aftermath of the 1789 French Revolution. Its community of approximately 30,000 Jews was granted emancipation in 1791, although Jews were only admitted to Strasbourg in 1792. The target of a series of regeneration efforts, Alsatian Jews served as one of the centers of French Jewish life and saw some fluidity between the French and German borders.[42] In 1871, those communities suddenly became part of a newly unified confederation of German states. When France lost the Franco-Prussian War, Prussia assumed control over the regions of Haut-Rhin and Bas-Rhin (with the exception of the city of Belfort), which became the imperial territory of Elsaß-Lothringen.[43] According to the Treaty of Frankfurt, individuals born and residing in Elsaß-Lothringen faced a choice: remain in the region, and become German, or elect French citizenship, petition, and migrate. Moreover, the thousands of Alsatians and Lorrainers who had emigrated from the region to other parts of France or abroad were also required to affirm their French citizenship or face being assigned a German nationality. Thousands of French Jews left the region. In 1900, in the area of Moselle (Lorraine) annexed by Germany, there were 7,015 Jews, as compared to the 8,571 Jews who lived there in 1870. In his 1886 novel, *La vie Juive*, the French Jewish writer, León Cahun, highlighted the negative impact of migration on French Jewish life when he described that the village schoolteacher, Anselme, stopped attending synagogue regularly when he moved with his family to Paris.[44] Jean Richard Bloch's ...*et Compagnie* also tells the story of Alsatian displacement. The novel follows the Simlers, a Jewish family of cloth manufacturers, who, in 1871, leave Alsace for western France, where they experience economic success and social isolation.[45] The Alsatian Jewish story would change again after the First World War when the Treaty

---

[41] Vicki Caron, *Between France and Germany: The Jews of Alsace-Lorraine, 1871–1918* (Stanford: Stanford University Press, 1988) and Ruth Harris, *Dreyfus: Politics, Emotion and the Scandal of the Century* (New York: Henry Holt and Company, 2010), 73–104.

[42] Schwarzfuchs, "Alsace and Southern Germany."

[43] Robert I. Giesburg, *The Treaty of Frankfurt: A Study in Diplomatic History, September 1870–September 1873* (Philadelphia: University of Pennsylvania Press, 1966), 1–36.

[44] Hyman, *The Jews of Modern France*, 54.

[45] Jean Richard-Bloch, ...*et Compagnie* (Paris, 1937). My appreciation to Lauren Henry, whose study of Alsatian and Algerian Jews introduced me to this text. Lauren Henry, "'Attached in Heart and Soul': Alsatian Migration, Disjuncture and Exile in French-Language Literature after 1871" (Unpublished).

of Versailles ceded the regions to France and more Jewish immigrants came to the region.

Such a phenomenon was not limited to individual nation-states. The disparate communities of Austro-Hungary, which were encompassed into the growing empire at different times, offer an example that extends into the twentieth century and cuts across several geographic nation-states. The Jews of the Habsburg Empire embraced a range of radically different identities. As Marsha Rozenblit has shown, the supra-national state allowed Jews to separate the ethnic, political, and cultural components of their identity. They were Jewish in an ethnic sense, Austrian by political loyalty, and German, Czech, or Polish by cultural affiliation. By the end of the nineteenth century, some Jews in the Czech lands had adopted Czech language and culture, while many acculturating Moravian and Bohemian Jews affiliated with German culture and spoke German. Modernizing Jews in Galicia adopted Polish culture; most Hungarian Jews learned the Magyar language. Jewish behavior, writes Rozenblit,

ranged from militant affirmations of Jewish ethnic pride, to the simple assumption of ethnic difference, to indifference, even hostility, to the issue. No matter how they understood their Jewish ethnicity, however, they did not feel as strong a need as Jews in Germany or France to insist that they fully belonged to the national communities whose culture they had adopted. This tripartite identity proved comfortable to the Jews, who appreciated the opportunity the multinational state gave them to be patriotic citizens, adherents of German, Czech, or Polish culture, and Jews all at the same time.[46]

CROSS REGIONAL NETWORKS AND JEWISH INTERNATIONALISM

Whether they were migrants or remained in one locale, many nineteenth- and twentieth-century European Jews participated in social, political, and economic networks that extended beyond local geographic borders. Mass education, the explosion of the public sphere, new forms of communication, and developments in mass politics encouraged new international ties among Jewish communities. Exposed to a continuous flow of economic, ideological, and social transfers, Jews took part in self-defense efforts, cross-regional associational lives, and international movements.[47]

[46] Marsha L. Rozenblit, *Reconstructing a National Identity: The Jews of Habsburg Austria During World War I* (Oxford: Oxford University Press, 2001), 23. Also see Rozenblit, *The Jews of Vienna, 1867–1914*.

[47] One of the cross-regional networks not discussed here concerned the businesses created by Jewish families across towns, cities, and states. Fanny Lewald's father's business was

While Jewish communities had always been international because of their supra-local nature, the nineteenth century witnessed the expression of what Abigail Green has termed, "religious internationalism," self-defense movements that focused on religious causes. According to Green, just as Jews, Protestants, and Catholics had once exhibited their faith by attending religious services, they now supported foreign religious causes, participated in directed philanthropic giving, and read religious newspapers' coverage of international matters.[48]

The Damascus and Mortara affairs each played a significant role in developing this new form of Jewish religious internationalism. When the Jews of Damascus were accused of ritual murder after a Capuchin monk and his servant disappeared in 1840, Western and Central European Jews intervened. Rather than quietly appealing to a few non-Jewish notables as they had done during past moments of conflict, Jewish leaders engaged in mass political action. They lobbied their governmental officials, covered the affair in local Jewish presses, and organized a delegation to the Middle East headed by Moses Montefiore, a British Jew, and Adolphe Crémieux, vice president of the Central Consistory. Many European Jews who were not politically active expressed their solidarity in other ways. Jews in the Alsatian town of Haguenau, for example, included the Jews of Damascus in their memorial book, a list of (mostly) European Jewish victims of persecution that dated back several centuries.[49]

The Mortara affair garnered similar responses. In 1858, the Catholic Church seized Edgar Mortara, a six-year old Italian Jewish child, when church officials learned that the Mortara family's former nanny had secretly baptized the boy. Church authorities maintained that Jewish parents could not raise a Catholic child and it yielded secular authority to prevent the return of Edgar to his family. Italian Jews and Jewish communities across Europe and the United States protested; like during the Damascus affair, they wrote newspaper articles and editorials, lobbied governmental officials, and sent delegates.[50] The affair also led to the creation of several defense organizations, including the Alliance Israélite Universelle, a Jewish

---

based in Königsberg, for example, but it had ties to her oldest uncle in St. Petersburg and her cousin in Warsaw. Lewald, *The Education of Fanny Lewald*, 22.

[48] Abigail Green, "Nationalism and the 'Jewish International' Religious Internationalism in Europe and the Middle East c.1840–c.1880," *Comparative Studies in Society and History* 50 (2008), 536. Also see, Abigail Green, *Moses Montefiore: Jewish Liberator, Imperial Hero* (Cambridge, MA: Harvard University Press, 2010).

[49] Hyman, *The Jews of Modern France*, 81.

[50] David I. Kertzer, *The Kidnapping of Edgardo Mortara* (New York: Vintage Books, 1998). Jews would later respond similarly during the Dreyfus Affair.

defense organization founded in Paris in 1860. The Alliance fought oppressive and discriminating laws and political disabilities; defended Jews in those countries where they were subject to persecution; and spread French culture and learning through schools throughout the French empire.

As the campaigns to defend the Jews of Damascus and return Edgar Mortara to his parents suggest, Jews increasingly became involved in diverse forms of mass politics that had international dimensions. They fused philanthropic measures, supra-local allegiances, and self-defense. Toward the end of the nineteenth century, an additional significant example emerged, namely the development of several modes of Jewish nationalism, which attempted to respond to the rise of acculturation and antisemitism in Western Europe and the growth of poverty and pogroms in Eastern Europe. It was within this context that Zionism developed.

Formulated by Theodor Herzl, Political Zionism affirmed the supranational nature of Jews, holding that all Jews shared a common legacy and tradition.[51] Political Zionists asserted that no matter where Jews resided, they constituted a single nation that would never escape antisemitism and they were responsible for building an autonomous Jewish homeland. In late August 1897 the first group of Zionists met in Basel to discuss these views. Herzl recorded, "Were I to sum up the Basel Congress in a word, it would be this ... At Basel I founded the Jewish State."[52] Over the course of the late nineteenth century and the first decades of the twentieth century, several varieties of Jewish nationalism emerged. They included Cultural Zionism, which called for a group of Hebrew-speakers to develop a spiritual center in the Land of Israel, Socialist Zionism, which sought to blend Jewish nationalism with utopian socialism, Marxist Zionism, which united class struggle and nationalism, and Mizrahi, which hoped to stem the secularism of other established varieties of Jewish nationalism.

There had been a few local precedents for Jewish nationalism, including the work of Zvi Hirsch Kalischer, a Prussian rabbi (1798–1874), who had embraced a collective return of the Jews to Palestine in order to bring about the divine salvation of the Jewish people. Kalischer and other early advocates of Jewish nationalism attracted few devotees and matters were not to change significantly over the course of the late nineteenth and early twentieth century. Zionism continued to draw suspicion, rather than allure, from many Jews. When Theodore Herzl published *The Jewish State: Attempt at*

---

[51]   Herzl had long been interested in the "Jewish Question," but the Dreyfus Affair and the successful Vienna mayoral election of anti-Semite Karl Lueger intensified his desire to contend with the problem of contemporary antisemitism.

[52]   Quoted in Yoram Hazony, *The Jewish State: The Struggle for Israel's Soul* (New York: Basic Books, 2001), 123.

a Modern Solution of the Jewish Question (1896), the volume was met with ridicule. Many Eastern European Jewish political activists praised Herzl; most Western and Central European Jews, however, favored emancipation and acculturation, rather than a movement that highlighted Jewish international distinctiveness or supra-national allegiance.

Despite its limited appeal, Zionism began to grow in Central Europe, attracting adherents among Eastern European Jewish immigrants or young Jews. Sammy Groenemann fell in the latter category. Twenty-five years old when he attended his first Zionist conference in Berlin, Gronemann and his young colleagues established a newspaper and worked to convince German Jews of Zionism's appeal. He remembered how conventional German Jewry received him.

And now a young person, scarcely fully fledged, came along and wanted to teach them that all these views, with which they had grown up and on which rested their entire position concerning all problems, were absurd. He demanded of those who fearfully attempted to hide their Jewishness and gave it asylum in the synagogue, that they declare themselves openly as Jews and prove their solidarity with all Jews everywhere. That must have seemed unappealing and dangerous to them.[53]

Although the majority of German Jews opposed Jewish nationalism, by 1914 there were almost 10,000 members of German Zionist organizations.

French Zionism deviated slightly from its German counterpart. It also engendered disapproval from the native French Jewish population, gained support from immigrant Jewish circles, and witnessed the creation of *Hovevei Zion* (Lovers of Zion) societies in its capital city, but it did not reach the moderate level of support attained in Germany. By World War I, there were only 1,000 French Zionist supporters. Unlike German Zionism, the French Zionist movement was perceived as a cause that attracted immigrant support only. This was due both to its large number of immigrant supporters and also to the fact that its newspapers, pamphlets, and letters bore the imprint of its émigré authors. The international Zionist movement published materials in German, but not in the French language. This meant that French Zionists had to produce all of their own materials, which came to reflect their own immigrant French character and therefore did not appeal to many French Jews. French Zionism, however, became increasingly significant after World War I. The First World War transformed Jewish communities, such as those in France, which had already been dramatically shaken by the great nineteenth-century historical process of migration, urbanization, transnationalism, secularization, and politicization.

[53] "Sammy Gronemann," in *Jewish Life in Germany: Memoirs from Three Centuries*, 260.

WORLD WAR I AND ITS IMPACT

World War I and its aftermath radically altered European politics, culture, society, and geography. At the war's end, European economies were destroyed, millions of people were dead or missing, and long-standing political empires had been devastated. The Jewish communities of Europe were hardly immune from the war's devastation or its aftershocks. Instead, the interwar period witnessed an intensification of the phenomena that had come to characterize modern Jewish life: the competing identities of Jews, the radically shifting notions and implications of toleration and intolerance, and the fluidity between Jewish integration and Jewish influence.

Jews continued to negotiate disparate – sometimes competing – national projects and identities into, through, and after World War I. Central and Western European Jews patriotically immersed themselves in civic and national projects. Central and Western European Jews served in unprecedented numbers during the First World War both because the militaries were increasingly open to their participation and because Jewish men were motivated to fight for social acceptance and masculine pride.[54] 275,000 Jews enlisted in the Austro-Hungary army and 100,000 Jews served in the German army. The French military saw a similar contribution from its Jewish population, so that it was unsurprising when, in August 1914, the newspaper, *L'Univers Israélite*, announced that it would be temporarily suspending publication "since our editor and all our subeditors have joined, or will shortly join, their battle stations …"[55] What was unprecedented was the number of immigrant Jews living in France who enlisted, namely 8,500 of the 30,000, resulting in the further integration of immigrant Jews into French Jewish life. While a sizeable French immigrant Jewish population opposed the war, those immigrants avoided a public critique of the fighting since opposition would have risked their amnesty in France. Instead, the Federation of Jewish Socialists was emblematic of Jewish immigrant groups when it proclaimed, "If we are not yet Frenchmen in law, we are so in heart and soul, and our most sacred duty is to put ourselves at once at the disposal of that great and noble nation in order to participate in her defense."[56]

With the Paris Peace Conference of 1919, interwar Jews encountered disparate national movements, which underpinned the new states that had

---

[54] Derek J. Penslar, *Jews and the Military: A History* (Princeton: Princeton University Press, 2013).

[55] Cited in Emmanuel de Roux, "Exhibition Honours Jewish Soldiers in First World War," *The Guardian*, October 24, 2002, www.theguardian.com/education/2002/oct/24/highereducation.news.

[56] Hyman, *The Jews of Modern France*, 134.

emerged from the Ottoman, Austro-Hungarian, and German Empires. The 564,000 German Jews living in the newly established Weimar Republic promoted a wide range of national allegiances. Some enthusiastically embraced the new Republic; ostensibly based on democratic and universalist principles, Weimar Germany lifted all remaining legal discriminatory measures against the Jews. It enshrined a constitution that accommodated competing political ideologies, mutually antagonist social pressures, and democratic, participatory values. The Jewish industrialist Walter Rathenau, who became foreign minister in 1922, presented himself as hyper-patriotic, and, as such, offered a contrast to the allegation that Jews were disloyal.[57] Other German Jews supported Germany's socialist revolution and expressed ambivalence about the Republic. A minority remained monarchists. Edwin Landau, who returned home to West Prussia after the war ended, could not envision himself as a Republican. He remembered, "the monarchy was still too much in my blood. I needed some time to accustom myself to everything and to free myself from old ideas."[58] He negotiated his German allegiances by forming a local chapter of the *Reichsbund jüdischer Frontsoldaten*, a group of Jewish former World War I front-soldiers.

In the aftermath of the First World War, European Jews frequently found themselves in nation-states with which they may not have felt an allegiance. Weimar Jewry now held 627 fewer Jewish communities then it had encompassed during the Kaiserreich. Those Jewish circles ostensibly had new national allegiances. In the Free City of Danzig (established in 1920), for example, German-speaking Jews felt a continued allegiance and kinship with Germany, yet they joined their non-Jewish German-speaking compatriots in running the independent city in order to guarantee that the Poles not find a pretext for intervention. As antisemitism in the Free City increased, they found their allegiances tested.

The Jewish communities of the former Austro-Hungarian Empire experienced similar challenges. Consider the Jews of Czechoslovakia, who, before the War, had lived in the Austro-Hungarian Empire. Czechoslovakia was founded in 1918. With its creation, the new nation-state encompassed disparate Jews from Bohemia, Moravia, and Silesia. These Jewish communities lacked a common culture, language, level of religious observance, or demography. The 1921 Czechoslovakian census made this disparity clear. 336,420 Czechoslovak nationals formally identified as being part of the Israelite religion. Of those Jews, the majority (180,616) professed

---

[57] Shulamit Volkov, *Walther Rathenau: Weimar's Fallen Statesman* (New Haven: Yale University Press, 2012).

[58] "Edwin Landau," in *Jewish Life in Germany: Memoirs from Three Centuries*, 307.

to being members of the Jewish nationality. 73,371 defined themselves as members of the Czech nationality, 49,123 as Germans, 29,473 as Magyars, 3,751 as Russians, 74 as Poles, and 112 belonging to other nationalities. Interestingly, 100 people professed no religion but identified as members of the Jewish nationality. The city of Czernowitz (Tschernowitz) offers a similar example. In the aftermath of World War I, Czernowitz became Cernauti when Bukovina came under Romanian control.[59] In his memoirs of the interwar town, Frederick Andermann recalled the very German-centered identity of the Jews in his circle: even though other Jews spoke Yiddish and embraced more observant life styles, "newspapers, books, conferences were in German despite the Romanian authority … and the cultural centre remained Vienna, rather than Bucharest."[60] Many Jews remained Austro-Hungarian royalists; a minority adopted postures of Romanian patriotism.

In addition to creating new nation-states, the representatives at the 1919 Paris Peace Conference articulated a novel vision for the place of religious, racial, and linguistic minorities in state and society. The Minorities Treaties were agreed upon between the British Empire, France, Italy, Japan, and the United States on the one hand and the fourteen newly created or expanded states in Europe and the Middle East on the other hand. They guaranteed minorities the rights to equal treatment and protection by the state; to establish and oversee religious, educational, and social welfare institutions for their minority group; and to use minority languages for certain public purposes. The Minorities Treaties would impact Jews, but it was not created explicitly for them. Some Jews were unabashedly enthusiastic about the Treaties; others questioned its value, meaning, implications, and whether it could guarantee Jewish safety. Future events would legitimate those concerns. Efforts to invoke the Treaties in order to stop the threatened expulsion of Galician Jewish war refugees from Vienna or the *numerous clausus* in Hungarian universities failed. One of the only successful uses of the Treaties took place in May 1933 when Franz Bernheim and representatives of the Comité des Délégations Juives petitioned the League of Nations on behalf of the Jews of German Upper Silesia (subsequently known as the Bernheim Petition). Bernheim had lost his job because of racial discrimination and complained that Nazi anti-Jewish legislation was being applied to Upper Silesia, an area protected by the Minorities

---

[59] It would later become Chernovtsy (Russia) in 1940 and it has been Chernivtsi (Ukraine) since 1991.
[60] Andermann, "Czernowitz Memoirs."

Treaties. The Bernheim Petition forced a temporary suspension of Nazi anti-Jewish legislation in German Upper Silesia.[61]

The early twentieth century witnessed increasing charges of Jewish disloyalty. The enthusiasm Jews expressed during, into, and after the war concerning disparate national and civic projects was not always reciprocated. As World War I dragged on, Jews found themselves as objects of suspicion, evidenced by the Prussian War Ministry's 1916 census of Jewish participation in the war effort. Hinting that Jews were cowardly, the census sought to determine how many Jewish soldiers actually served on the front line.[62] When Edwin Landau returned home from the front, he came to realize how deep German distrust was of Jews. He remembered, "One thing was certain ... If we Jewish soldiers had thought that by our participation in the war we would gain the love of our fellow citizens, then we were mistaken. ..."[63]

German interwar antisemitism built upon the anti-Jewish themes that had been articulated during the war. Anti-Semites blamed Jews for Germany's defeat and for the internal revolutions that followed, reproached Jews for Germany's financial devastation, and accused Eastern European Jewish immigrants (*Ostjuden*) of seizing the jobs of unemployed Germans. Antisemitism pervaded the written and spoken realms and shaped behavior on Germany's streets where paramilitary groups, ex-soldiers, and street thugs lashed out against Jewish bystanders. In 1923, for example, mobs rioted in the Scheunenviertel area of Berlin, a neighborhood heavily populated by Eastern European immigrants.[64]

German antisemitism intensified over the course of the 1920s and early 1930s, typified by the growing role of the National Socialists. While the earlier 1919 iteration of the National Socialist Party, the German Workers Party, was a small, relatively insignificant group in southern Germany, it began to successfully, albeit slowly, transition from a group of rabble-rousers into a political party in 1925. The Nazis labored to attract followers from all regions and social groups and worked to construct a party program and bureaucracy. Central to the Nazi ideology was the dehumanization of Jews, whom Hitler and other Nazi leaders referred to as "cancer," "parasites," and "cockroaches." According to Hitler's worldview, Jews were

[61] Carole Fink, *Defending the Rights of Others: The Great Powers, the Jews, and International Minority Protection, 1878–1938* (Cambridge: Cambridge University Press, 2004).
[62] The census revealed that 80 percent of all Jewish soldiers served on the front lines, a much higher proportion than the general population.
[63] "Edwin Landau," in *Jewish Life in Germany: Memoirs from Three Centuries*, 307.
[64] See Avraham Barkai, "Under the Lengthening Shadow of Antisemitism," in *German-Jewish History in Modern Times*, vol. 4, ed. Michael A. Meyer (New York: Columbia University Press, 1998), 46–55.

inhuman but were disguised in human form. They were allegedly engaged in an apocalyptic battle against human beings. According to historian Saul Friedländer, the Nazis embraced a "redemptive anti-Semitism" that called for the victory over the Jews in a quasi-religious mission.[65]

It has been a truism to look at the radical National Socialist politics of the late 1920s and early 1930s as an inevitability of some kind: perhaps that they foreshadowed the Nazis' legislative restrictions or their genocidal atrocities. Certain historians have proposed that antisemitism's deep roots in the German psyche allowed for, if not encouraged, "willing execution-ers" to later murder millions of Jews.[66] Such assumptions, while tempting in their simplicity, are unsuitable. As scholars have shown, these readings use hindsight as the lens through which historical events are understood. Interwar antisemitism was neither linear nor direct. To use the famous terminology of Karl Schleunes, it assumed a "twisted road" to genocidal politics of the National Socialists and their collaborators.[67] German anti-semitism and the Nazi rise to power were nonlinear developments. German antisemitism, like the Republic in which it was lodged, was shaped by liberal, tolerant, and reformist motivations, as well as by illiberal, anti-reformist, and intolerant impulses.

While several French historians have minimized the role antisemitism played in the interwar years and have asserted that the Dreyfus Affair and Vichy Regime were aberrations in French history,[68] scholars such as Pierre Birnbaum and Paula Hyman have asserted its significance.[69] In the after-math of the First World War, social discrimination against Jews became increasingly common in France, and French antisemitic publications and pundits blamed Jews for the economic depression, immigration, and the emergence of the Popular Front, an alliance of left-wing movements (including the French Communist Party) that came to power during the

[65] Saul Friedländer, *Nazi Germany and the Jews: The Years of Persecution, 1933–1939* (New York: Harper Collins, 1998), 3.

[66] Daniel J. Goldhagen, *Hitler's Willing Executioners: Ordinary Germans and the Holocaust* (New York: Knopf, 1996) and Hans Mommsen. "The Reaction of the German Population to Anti-Jewish Persecution and the Holocaust," in *Lessons and Legacies: The Meaning of the Holocaust in a Changing World*, ed. Peter Hayes (Evanston: Northwestern University Press, 1991), 141–154.

[67] Karl A. Schleunes, *The Twisted Road to Auschwitz: Nazi Policy toward German Jews, 1933–1939* (Urbana: University of Illinois Press, 1970).

[68] See, for example, Eugen Weber, "Reflections on the Jews in France," in *The Jews in Modern France*, eds. Frances Malino and Bernard Wasserstein (Waltham: Brandeis University Press, 1985).

[69] See, for example, Birnbaum, *Anti-Semitism in France* and Paula E. Hyman, *From Dreyfus To Vichy: The Remaking of French Jewry, 1906–1939* (New York: Columbia University Press, 1979).

1930s. The decade before the Second World War witnessed sporadic attacks on Jewish businesses in Alsace Lorraine and on Jews in immigrant Jewish neighborhoods. The mob violence that ensued during the 1934 Stavisky affair served as one example of these sporadic attacks. In 1933, the municipal bonds issued by the credit organization founded by Serge Alexandrew Stavisky, a Russian Jew who lived in France, were discovered to be worthless. The following year, Stavisky was found dead, having left behind losses that equaled approximately eighteen million contemporary dollars. The affair that ensued threatened to destabilize the Third Republic. Stavisky's close involvement with many financial leaders and political insiders led to the resignation of premier Camille Chautemps, who was accused by the right-wing opposition of having orchestrated Stavisky's death. The new premier dismissed a number of Parisian politicians, including the prefect of the Paris police who had been known for his right-wing sympathies. The affair encouraged antisemitic fantasies of Jewish political and economic nefariousness and served as one cause of widespread riots in Paris on February 6, 1934.[70] That affair and other events like it suggest that interwar French antisemitism helped lay the groundwork for the Vichy regime and, like in Germany, offered a "cultural code," which allowed Europeans to position themselves with other groups in the political arena and to insist on their own political prestige.[71]

Paradoxically, at the same time when Jews experienced growing discrimination, economic losses, and violence in Central and Eastern Europe, they also became increasingly productive in the cultural sphere. In Germany, the hyper assimilation of an earlier generation and post-war antisemitism encouraged the creation of a specifically modern German-Jewish culture that focused on Jewish ethnic and religious legacies. Scholars such as Gershom Scholem, Martin Buber, and Franz Rosenzweig challenged the Judaism of their middle-class parents and called for new forms of Jewish involvement and education. Franz Kafka's oft-reproduced "Letter to his Father" typified the disdain the younger generation had for its parents: "But what sort of Judaism was it that I got from you? ... It was indeed, so far as I could see, a mere nothing, a joke – not even a joke."[72] In France, young Jews created Jewish organizations that broke with the exclusively religious framework encouraged by the native Jewish establishment. The Union Universelle de la Jeunesse Juive (Universal Union of Jewish Youth, UUJJ) was the first

---

[70] William Brustein, *Roots of Hate: Anti-Semitism in Europe before the Holocaust* (Cambridge: Cambridge University Press, 2003), p. 202; Paul F. Jankowski, *Stavisky: A Confidence Man in the Republic of Virtue* (Ithaca and New York: Cornell University Press, 2002).

[71] Volkov, "Antisemitism as a Cultural Code."

[72] Franz Kafka, *The Basic Kafka* (New York: Simon and Schuster, 1979), 215.

non-Zionist organization to support an understanding of French Jewish identity that rested on ethnic and historical components.[73]

The growth of European Zionism in the aftermath of the First World War served as another example of interwar Jewish cultural and political production. While most German, Austrian, and French Jewish groups formally opposed Zionism, Zionism increasingly enticed young Central and Western European Jews who were attracted by its youth movements, scouting associations, study groups, and athletic associations. The Fifth Aliyah (1929–1939) witnessed more than 250,000 Jews coming to Palestine, the majority of whom originated from Germany and Austria. The German-speaking Jewish emigrants settled in Palestine's few urban areas; over half went to Tel Aviv, which grew from 4,000 inhabitants in 1921 to 135,000 in 1935.[74] The Jews who immigrated to Palestine were clearly in the minority, however, during the 1920s and 1930s, an increasing number of European Jews adopted a more conciliatory tone towards the Zionist project. In 1925, for example, French rabbis formed a charitable institution, *Oeuvre Palestinienne*, which supported a religious rebirth of Eretz-Israel. Zionists also began to gain political support in local Jewish communal politics. In 1925, Zionists won a majority of seats on the board of the Viennese *Israelitsche Kultusgemeinde*. While those who voted for local Zionist groups in Jewish communal elections or migrated to Palestine were in the minority, European Jews increasingly supported the Zionist project during the 1930s.

At the dawn of World War II, the Jewish communities of Western and Central Europe constituted vibrant, disparate, urban populations that continued to struggle over the meaning of their Jewish identities. The Nazi-orchestrated attempted genocide of European Jews and the physical devastation of the war itself would threaten the extinction of these Jewish communities and change them irrevocably.

GENOCIDE AND ITS IMMEDIATE AFTERMATH

Between 1933 and 1945, the Nazis and their collaborators deprived European Jews of their civic rights, property, dignity, and lives. The Nazis murdered millions of Jews during the Holocaust, destroying Jewish communities that had developed on European soil during the previous hundreds of years.

With their accession to power in 1933, the Nazi government utilized propaganda and legislation to ostracize and denigrate Jews. It created 110

---

[73] Vicki Caron makes clear that French Jews were not only split on the immigrant/native divide, but within those groups as well.

[74] By 1936 more than 5,000 Jews from France and North Africa had settled in Palestine.

camps for political opponents, criminals, "asocial elements," and so-called inferior races; passed national legislation that sought to remove Jews from public life; and tacitly approved the random physical attacks of Jews by its Brownshirts (members of the Nazi paramilitary group, SA). Historian Marion Kaplan has shown that these laws, and the ways in which the public interpreted them, were not always consistent. Anti-Jewish promulgations were executed rapidly and then stopped (the April 1933 boycotts, for example, were canceled almost immediately); some promulgations were vague, while others were unequivocal.[75]

Nazi persecution resulted in the transformation of relationships between Jews and non-Jews. Neighbors, friends, employers, clients, even spouses and children, gradually distanced themselves from Jews and excluded them from German social life. German non-Jews, argues Kaplan, watched as German Jews lost their businesses and practices, financially benefited from Jews' professional and economic downfalls, made it difficult for Jews to interact socially, and witnessed and/or read about the beatings, incarcerations, and murders of Jews. They not only witnessed the outcasting of Jews, but they also participated in it. This involvement led to what Kaplan refers to as Jewry's "social death," a necessary step in the Final Solution. Just two weeks after the Nazis implemented legislation limiting Jewish participation in German public life, Willy Cohn described this process: "The way we Jews are being treated now, we have never been treated like this before. True, we are not being killed, but we are being tortured mentally, and our ability to make a living is being systematically throttled."[76] Cohn's diaries make clear that he and his fellow Jews experienced their ostracism unevenly. The profession, gender, age, and place of residence influenced how Jews perceived of their exclusion and whether they chose to flee. While three-fifths of German Jews did emigrate, this entailed a difficult and costly process. Other Jews focused on daily survival, which distracted them from thinking about fleeing. They preserved Jewish organizations and networks, continued to marry and raise families, created schools and social welfare institutions, and learned skills necessary for emigration.

As Germany started to occupy its European neighbors, the Nazis utilized ghettos and camps to confine and, later, systematically murder Jews, Roma, Poles, and other ethnic groups in Eastern Europe. The German invasion of Poland on September 1, 1939, and the ensuing Second World War, brought with it the public beatings, humiliation, torture, and shootings of Jews.

---

[75] Marion A. Kaplan, *Between Dignity and Despair: Jewish Life in Nazi Germany* (Oxford: Oxford University Press, 1999).

[76] Willy Cohn, *No Justice in Germany: The Breslau Diaries, 1933–1941*, ed. Norbert Conrads and trans. Kenneth Kronenberg (Stanford: Stanford University Press, 2012), 6.

The ghettos were sites of tremendous brutality, and millions of Jews died of starvation, illness, and beatings even before the Nazis implemented their two-pronged "final solution," which relied on killing centers and mobile killing units. The organized massive killings of Jews by the *Einsatzgruppen* and killing centers followed the launch of Operation Barbarossa, the June 22, 1941 German invasion of the Soviet Union.

Recent scholarship has found that Germany established far more camps and ghettos than had been previously assumed. Between 1933 and 1945, the Nazis created approximately 42,500 ghettos and camps throughout Europe; they spanned from German-controlled France, into and across Germany, to Russia. These camps varied in their size, configuration, administration, and purpose. They included prisoner of war camps, "care-centers" (where camp staff killed babies after their birth or forced pregnant women to abort), brothels, forced labor camps, and "killing centers."[77] The Nazis murdered approximately six million Jews during the Holocaust; they devastated the Jewish communities and cultures that had flourished in Europe for hundreds of years.

The war's end found hundreds of thousands of Jews scattered across Europe – in camps, in hiding, with the partisans, and in unfamiliar towns and cities. As scholars have shown, place of origin, war experiences, post-war journeys, age, gender, and health all would influence the processes of identity construction that these post-war Jews would undergo.[78] The period following liberation witnessed the very beginning of this development. In the months following the Allies' victory, European Jews moved from place to place and experienced unexpected entanglements with a wide range of groups.

Liberation of the killing centers began as early as July 1944, when the Soviets entered the Majdanek camp, and the liberation of Jews continued into May 1945. Hundreds of thousands of Jews, including thousands of children, found themselves homeless and stateless; even if they were

---

[77] Geoffrey P. Megargee, ed., *The United States Holocaust Memorial Museum Encyclopedia of Camps and Ghettos, 1933–1945, vol. 1: Early Camps, Youth Camps, and Concentration Camps and Subcamps under the SS-Business Administration Main Office (WVHA)* (Bloomington: Indiana University Press, 2009) and Martin Dean and Geoffrey P. Mengargee eds, *The United States Holocaust Memorial Museum Encyclopedia of Camps and Ghettos, 1933–1945, vol. 2: Ghettos in German Occupied Eastern Europe* (Bloomington: Indiana University Press, 2012).

[78] See, for example, Atina Grossmann, *Jews, Germans, and Allies: Close Encounters in Occupied Germany* (Princeton: Princeton University Press, 2009); Maud S. Mandel, *In the Aftermath of Genocide: Armenians and Jews in Twentieth Century France* (Durham: Duke University Press, 2003); and Tara Zahra, *The Lost Children: Reconstructing Europe's Families after World War II* (Cambridge: Cambridge University Press, 2011).

sufficiently healthy to travel, there were few places where they could go. Restrictive immigration laws persisted in the United States and Canada, and the State of Israel would not be founded until 1948. Many of the nearly 250,000 "displaced persons" (DPs) lived in the DP camps established for them by the allies in Germany, Italy, and Austria. They began journeys to find loved ones, return to what they hoped would be home, leave the domiciles they realized they had lost, flee the Soviets, move from one DP camp to the next, or migrate legally or illegally to another place altogether. After her liberation, for example, Judith Magyar Isaacson, her mother, and aunt, went from a hotel in Leipzig's bombed-out district, to a former SS camp, to a small apartment in a town nearby. When the Russian Army began approaching Leipzig, Isaacson's new American boyfriend drove her and her mother to Berneck-am-Fichtelgebirge, a resort town in Bavaria where they lived in a "charming house" requisitioned by her boyfriend, Ike, from a former Nazi official.[79] Lala Fishman, who had spent the war years passing as a non-Jew, similarly fled from Poland into Germany; after living in a DP camp, she moved to a nearby apartment.[80] Fishman was not alone. Thousands of DPs entered the American zone from Eastern Europe after liberation. They included survivors who had been freed in Germany but initially returned to their hometowns and survivors who had been sent to Poland from the Soviet Union and then fled to the American zone. As these Jewish refugees moved from place to place, they experienced a wide range of unexpected encounters.

In the immediate aftermath of liberation, European Jews interacted with a variety of individuals: they intermingled with other Jews, non-Jewish Europeans, Allied soldiers, and non-governmental organization workers. Members of these different heterogeneous groups lived as neighbors; they interacted with one another on the streets and shopped in the same markets. They frequented the same theaters and concert halls. Several had sexual relationships with one another. As Atina Grossman has shown, these sites of interaction in Germany were unexpected. Many Germans had assumed that Jews would never again live on German soil. Instead, occupied Germany served as the "unlikely, unloved, and reluctant host" to thousands of its past victims.[81] In the aftermath of the Second World War, Jews did not merely reside in Germany but they coexisted with Germans in unforeseen ways.

---

[79] Judith Magyar Isaacson, *Seed of Sarah: Memoirs of a Survivor* (Urbana and Chicago: University of Illinois Press, 1991), 127.

[80] Lala Fishman and Steven Weingartner, *Lala's Story: A Memoir of the Holocaust* (Evanston: Northwestern University Press, 1998).

[81] Grossmann, *Jews, Germans, and Allies*, 1.

European Jews also spent extensive time with American, British, and Canadian soldiers. At the war's end, the soldiers found themselves unexpectedly responsible for assisting the DPs in a variety of ways. Among other things, they organized the collection of necessary goods for European Jews, helped to settle Jewish refugees in the various DP camps, advocated on behalf of the Jewish DPs, set up makeshift hospitals, established Jewish centers, led or participated in religious services, helped to trace missing relatives and loved ones, provided lifecycle counseling and pastoral care, and led Zionist youth activities. Their intimacy with the DP population frequently ran afoul of the non-fraternization policies and some of the earliest opponents of the non-fraternization policy were Jewish soldiers and chaplains.

The arrival of NGOs, such as the Jewish Joint Distribution committee, added an additional dimension to the networks Jews created in immediate post-war Europe. In France, the Joint's goals were threefold: to establish an emergency relief program to supply money, food, and clothing to those survivors most in need, to build a support network for children uprooted or orphaned during the war, and to rebuild French Jewish economic stability so that the community would be able to care for its own long-term needs.[82] Throughout Europe, humanitarian workers focused on the care of displaced children, who became symbols of wartime dislocation and post-war reconstruction.[83]

In December 1945, it was clear that the Jewish communities of Europe had been irrevocably changed; it was less certain that the surviving remnant of European Jewry would re-establish itself on the soil that it had inhabited for hundreds of years. Over the course of the 1940s, the core of international Jewish life shifted from Europe to two new centers: North America, which had begun to receive Jewish immigrants in large numbers at the end of the nineteenth century, and the state of Israel, which, after its founding in 1948, opened its doors to all Jews who wished to 'return' there. The Holocaust, however, did not put an end to Jewish life in Europe. Instead, over the course of the second half of the twentieth century, European countries saw the flourishing of diverse Jewish communities, many of whom began attracting émigrés from other parts of the world. Despite these new communities' dissimilarities, they witnessed several of the phenomena that had characterized Jewish life. They persisted in acculturating to changing societal norms while simultaneously influencing the societies in which they lived; they continued to be shaped by shifting

---

[82] Maud S. Mandel, "Philanthropy or Cultural Imperialism? The Impact of American Jewish Aid in Post-Holocaust France," *Jewish Social Studies* 9.1 (2002), 53–94.

[83] Tara Zahra terms the disputes over displaced children a "psychological Marshall Plan."

notions and implications of toleration and intolerance, while also becoming complicit tolerant and intolerant actors; and they remained engaged in negotiating a messy maze of competing national projects and narratives.

SELECT BIBLIOGRAPHY

Beller, Steven. *Vienna and the Jews, 1867–1938: A Cultural History*. Cambridge: Cambridge University Press, 1991.

Birnbaum, Pierre. *Anti-Semitism in France: A Political History from Leon Blum to the Present*. Translated by Miriam Kochan. Oxford: Oxford University Press, 1992.

and Ira Katznelson, eds. *Paths of Emancipation: Jews, States, and Citizenship*. Princeton: Princeton University Press, 1995.

Caron, Vicki. *Between France and Germany: The Jews of Alsace-Lorraine, 1871–1918*. Stanford: Stanford University Press, 1988.

Cohen, Jeremy and Moshe Rosman, eds. *Rethinking European Jewish History*. Oxford: Oxford University Press, 2009.

Fink, Carole. *Defending the Rights of Others: The Great Powers, the Jews, and International Minority Protection, 1878–1938*. Cambridge: Cambridge University Press, 2004.

Friedländer, Saul. *Nazi Germany and the Jews: The Years of Persecution, 1933–1939*. New York: Harper and Row, 1998.

Graetz, Michael. *The Jews in Nineteenth-Century France: From the French Revolution to the Alliance Israelite Universelle*. Translated by Jane Marie Todd. Stanford: Stanford University Press, 1996.

Grossmann, Atina. *Jews, Germans, and Allies: Close Encounters in Occupied Germany*. Princeton: Princeton University Press, 2009.

Hyman, Paula E. *From Dreyfus To Vichy: The Remaking of French Jewry, 1906–1939*. New York: Columbia University Press, 1979.

The Jews of Modern France. Berkeley: University of California Press, 1998.

Judd, Robin. *Contested Rituals: Circumcision, Kosher Butchering, and Jewish Political Life in Germany, 1843–1933*. Ithaca: Cornell University Press, 2007.

Kaplan, Marion A. *Between Dignity and Despair: Jewish Life in Nazi Germany*. Oxford: Oxford University Press, 1999.

ed. *Jewish Daily Life in Germany 1618–1945*. Oxford: Oxford University Press, 2005.

Kertzer, David I. *The Kidnapping of Edgardo Mortara*. New York: Vintage Books, 1998.

Lewald, Fanny. *The Education of Fanny Lewald: An Autobiography*. Edited and translated by Hanna Ballin Lewis. Albany: State University of New York Press, 1992.

Lowenstein, Steven M. *The Mechanics of Change: Essays in the Social History of German Jewry*. Atlanta: Brown Judaic Studies, 1992.

Magnus, Shulamit S. *Jewish Emancipation in a German City: Cologne, 1798–1871*. Stanford: Stanford University Press, 1997.

Mandel, Maud S. *In the Aftermath of Genocide: Armenians and Jews in Twentieth Century France*. Durham: Duke University Press, 2003.

Penslar, Derek J. *Shylock's Children: Economics and Jewish Identity in Modern Europe*. Berkeley: University of California Press, 2001.

Jews and the Military: A History. Princeton: Princeton University Press, 2013.

Richarz, Monika ed. *Jewish Life in Germany: Memoirs from Three Centuries*. Translated by Stella P. Rosenfeld and Sidney Rosenfeld. Bloomington: Indiana University Press, 1991.

Rozenblit, Marsha L. *Reconstructing a National Identity: The Jews of Habsburg Austria during World War I*. Oxford: Oxford University Press, 2001.

Schleunes, Karl A. *The Twisted Road to Auschwitz: Nazi Policy toward German Jews, 1933–1939*. Urbana: University of Illinois Press, 1970.

Van Rahden, Till. *Jews and Other Germans: Civil Society, Religious Diversity, and Urban Politics in Breslau, 1860–1925*. Trans. Marcus Brainard. Madison: University of Wisconsin Press, 2008.

Volkov, Shulamit. "Antisemitism as a Cultural Code: Reflections on the History and Historiography of Antisemitism in Imperial Germany." *Leo Institute Year Book* 23, no. 1 (1978): 25–46.

Zahra, Tara. *The Lost Children: Reconstructing Europe's Families after World War II*. Cambridge: Cambridge University Press, 2011.

CHAPTER 2

RUSSIAN AND SOVIET JEWRY

OLGA LITVAK

I

Like the history of Jewish settlement in North America, the history of
Russian Jewry is implicated in the imperial expansion of Europe. Russian
Jewry was not born, but made by an act of *raison d'état*, in the last quarter
of the long eighteenth century. Before the architects of partition (1772–
1795), Frederick II of Prussia (r. 1740–1786), Catherine II (r. 1762–1796)
and the Habsburg emperor, Joseph II (r. 1765–1790), set about putting an
end to the "nonsensical disordering" of Polish sovereignty, Jewish residence
on Russian territory had been officially proscribed.[1] Through Poland's diplomatic dismemberment Russia acquired an ethnic and confessional frontier of bewildering social complexity. While most of the population was
divided between Catholicism and Eastern Orthodoxy, peasants and landowners, the region was also home to German-speaking urban Protestants
and Islamicized free-holding Tatars as well as to the largest concentration
of Jews – most of whom made a living from local trade in agricultural
goods and the economic administration of Polish estates – in the world.[2]
Stretching from the Baltic to the Black Sea where Russia's Polish possessions merged with the southern frontier that Catherine II wrested from the
Ottomans in 1774, the Jewish landscape of Russia's western borderlands
grew continually more diverse. By the beginning of the nineteenth century, the Russian empire had roughly one million Jewish subjects, divided
between the provinces of Central or Congress Poland, Lithuania-Belarus
and southeastern Ukraine. Among them were Warsaw's commercial elites
and Vilna's venerable Talmudists whose students warmed the back benches
of study houses throughout the northwest, small-town householders

[1] On the political justification of partition, see Larry Wolff, *Inventing Eastern Europe: The
Map of Civilization on the Mind of Enlightenment* (Stanford: Stanford University Press,
1994), 17–49. The quotation appears on p. 18.
[2] On the place of the western borderlands in Russian imperial geography, see Dominic
Lieven, *Empire: The Russian Empire and Its Rivals* (New Haven: Yale University Press,
2001), 201–230.

and their sharp-witted wives running taverns and other concessions in the private towns of the Polish nobility, Hasidic rebbes holding court in the Podolian hinterland, mystics, provincial philosophers, free-thinkers, preachers, midwives, matchmakers, traveling players, rich, poor, and everything in between. There were densely settled and highly differentiated Jewish settlements in White Russia as well as tiny, isolated communities of village Jews in Volhynia. Despite official restrictions on Jewish residence, a small number of wealthy and well-connected merchants had even begun, in the first years after partition, to filter into the Russian interior, drawn especially to the two imperial capitals, Moscow and St. Petersburg. People united in law by a common confession and educated in the same principles of faith in the God of Israel were, in fact, divided by class conflicts and regional loyalties, to say nothing of customs, accents, songs, clothes, recipes, sensibilities and jokes. Theoretically normative Judaism remained elusive in practice; the imaginary person known to historians as the "traditional Eastern European Jew" existed more in the breach than in reality.[3]

The greatest challenge facing the imperial authorities lay in administering this sizeable and heterogeneous population, whose religion represented an object of nearly pathological suspicion to the Orthodox emperors and their servitors. In an unprecedented act of political largesse and enlightened tolerance, Catherine actively rejected the Russian precedent of total exclusion and undertook to integrate her new Jewish subjects into the empire's estate structure. Unlike the Habsburgs and the Prussians – the other two partitioning powers that assumed responsibility for substantial proportions of the Jewish residents of the Polish-Lithuanian Commonwealth – Romanov Russia had no medieval tradition of Jewry law. The "ingathering of Russian Jewry" was, from the beginning, a modern colonial project.[4] New imperial affinities, social interests, and cultural styles clashed with long-standing local identities, not always to the benefit of the former. The Polish-Lithuanian past, still visible in the picturesque ruins of noble mansions and castles and in the figures of dispossessed and unreconstructed Polish aristocrats, continued to haunt imperial Russian-Jewish history in the form of the mythology of the shtetl, the Jewish market town that lived in the shadow of the magnates' great estates and a poignant sign of unresolved and conflicted feelings about the tenuous, unfinished, and improbable construction of modern Russian Jewry.

[3] On the diversity of Russian-Jewish experience and expression during the imperial period, see ChaeRan Y. Freeze and Jay M. Harris, eds. *Everyday Jewish Life in Imperial Russia, 1772–1914* (Hanover, NH: Brandeis University Press, 2013).

[4] See John D. Klier, *Russia Gathers Her Jews: The Origins of Russia's Jewish Question, 1772–1825* (DeKalb: Illinois University Press, 1984).

Catherine's most salient achievement lay in legalizing Jewish residence in the Russian Empire. Although restricted to the western provinces (which included the important addition of New Russia at the southwestern tip of the empire), the Pale of Jewish Settlement, first defined in Catherinian legislation, represented a significant innovation in Russian jurisprudence.[5] In a country where the vast majority of the population was considered personal chattel of a very small privileged minority, confinement to the Pale was neither a sign of extraordinary oppression nor an especially notable symptom of Russia's alleged legal backwardness. Given the Orthodox intransigence of her predecessors, Catherine's Jews might have considered themselves fortunate to have been neither expelled nor summarily enserfed.

The new privilege of legal residence went hand-in-hand with administrative leveling, of a kind. Following Catherine, imperial law devolved most of the responsibility for governing Jews in the collective onto the Jewish "community" (Rus. *obshchestvo*), but also made provisions for individual Jews to join the municipal corporations in the towns where they lived. This system of "dual jurisdiction" translated Jewish personal status both into the terms of a state-recognized confession, signified by responsibilities and taxes owed by the individual to the local Jewish community, *and* to the juridical category of the estate, signified by various civil terms of social ascription to which every subject of the tsar belonged. Like their Orthodox counterparts, therefore, individual Jews could aspire to various ranks, such as "town dwellers" (Rus. *meshchane*), "merchants" (Rus. *kuptsy*), and "honored citizens" (Rus. *pochetnye grazhdane*).[6] Some of these categories, attained in various ways in exchange for state service or financial considerations, came with additional personal privileges – including residence beyond the Pale – denied to Jews *en masse*. In many cases, the rewards of rank vitiated confessional responsibility and compromised Jewish collective discipline. During the pre-reform period, such tensions acquired their greatest urgency under the impact of taxation and with the introduction of military recruitment, exacted from the community and implemented by Jewish leadership, made up of local "notables" whose own financial interests lay in cooperating with the regime even when they were attempting to intercede with the authorities on behalf of their co-religionists. The Jewish *obshchestvo* in imperial Russia was not a representative democracy and, contrary to anti-semitic fantasies of Jewish power – frequently offered up to the delectation of the Russian reading public by renegades from Jewish

[5] See Richard Pipes, "Catherine II and the Jews," *Soviet Jewish Affairs* 5 (1975): 3–20.

[6] On the pre-reform estate system and the social meaning of rank, see Gregory L. Freeze, "The Soslovie (Estate) Paradigm and Russian Social History," *The American Historical Review* 91 (1986): 11–36.

communal authority – hardly dedicated to the programmatic defense of Jewish "interest," even in the unlikely possibility that any common cause could be distilled from the palpable reality of Jewish differences.[7]

To the contrary, under the imperial system of provincial self-government, potential victims of internal corruption, which is to say, most people, often had good reason to distrust their own officially appointed or officially sanctioned leadership. While the effects of such distrust produced a thin stream of unbelief (few societies can tolerate more than a small number of skeptics), it galvanized a much greater current of desire for personal and collective sanctity. Under the circumstances, a communal ideal based on voluntary – rather than compulsory or formal – membership, and one that rendered religious power contingent upon the accrual of spiritual benefits to the believer, stood to gain many more recruits than downright apostasy from Judaism. Thus it happened that one of the earliest beneficiaries of increasing popular resentment toward the Jewish power structure and the gradual desacralization of the kehillah was Hasidism, a movement whose adherents were bound to each other and to their rebbe by affective ties, patronage networks, and the assurance of pastoral care.

Enabled by the ambiguities of "dual jurisdiction," the Russian conquest of Poland was followed, in short order, by the Hasidic conquest of Polish-Jewish society.[8] Imperial attempts to police the boundaries of confessional jurisdiction actually weakened the relationship between self and society and inadvertently provided the Hasidic mythology of collective rupture and inner renewal with sufficient purchase to supplant the established institutional structure of Jewish communal life in the name of a utopian return to a state of "perfect faith."[9] In the short term, the dissemination of Hasidic populism during the first four decades of the nineteenth century may be read as a conservative revolution, a characteristically modern

---

[7] The charge against Jewish communal authority as a plot against Christians, a staple motif in the Russian mythology of Jewish power, was first issued by the apostate Jacob Brafman in his *Book of the Kahal* (Rus. *Kniga kagala*, 1869). On its appropriation into the discourse of Russian Judeophobia, see Steven Lukashevich, *Ivan Aksakov, 1823–1886: A Study in Russian Thought and Politics* (Cambridge, MA: Harvard University Press, 1965), 96–106. Russian Judeophobia followed the pattern set by the policy of "dual jurisdiction": Aksakov, like many other Russian conservatives, were prepared to entertain the social integration of Jewish individuals but feared "Jewry" in the collective.

[8] See Glenn Dynner, *Men of Silk: The Hasidic Conquest of Polish Jewish Society* (Oxford: Oxford University Press, 2006).

[9] On the Hasidic ideal of "perfect (alt. innocent) faith," see Benjamin Brawn, "Shuvah shel 'haemunah hatemimah': tfisat haemunah haharedit vetsmihatah bemeah ha-19," in *'Al haemunah: 'iyunim bemusag haemunah ubetoldotav bemasoret hayehudit*, ed. Moshe Halbertal, et al. (Jerusalem: Keter, 2005), 403–443.

attempt to shore up the connection between the intimate and the cosmic. But viewed through the wide-angle lens of historical perspective, Hasidism may also be seen as symptomatic of the increasing importance of a distinction between public confession and personal religion that had a transformative and lasting effect on the development of Jewish thought.[10] For all of their differences, the Hasidic rebbe shared with the reforming German rabbi the self-appointed role of "caretaker of the soul" (Ger. *Seelssorger*), charged with the "sacralization of life" rather than with the rabbinic prerogative of expounding Talmudic law.[11] Consistent with the shift from communal to congregational autonomy among contemporary German Jews, Hasidism thus entered into the bloodstream of Jewish culture not as a vestige of unregenerate Polish-Jewish medievalism but as a direct consequence of the shocks of modernization under the Russians. The first of these to be experienced not by the few but by the many was administered by the government of Nicholas I (r. 1825–1855).

II

Nicholas I inherited the principle of "dual jurisdiction" from his predecessors. The innovative character of his policies lay, rather, in its energetic application.[12] Like Catherine II and Alexander I (r. 1801–1825), Nicholas I was prepared to encourage the integration of Jewish individuals into the Russian estate structure, even as his infamous conscription policy gave additional discretionary powers to the Jewish *obshchestvo*. The introduction of "official enlightenment" allocated government funds for higher education in order to facilitate Jewish entry into Russian universities (this privilege actually went back to the Statute of 1804). Additional money was dispensed for an ambitious plan to resettle Jewish "townsmen" on the land and for the creation of two rabbinic seminaries, one in Vilna and one in Zhitomir, dedicated to training a modern Jewish rabbinate to steer the course of confessional reform. Furthermore, Nicholas continued to confer the benefits of privileged status on Jewish merchants who held government monopolies; this kind of social co-optation, already in evidence during the

---

[10] See Leora Batnitzky, *How Judaism Became a Religion: An Introduction to Modern Jewish Thought* (Princeton: Princeton University Press, 2011).

[11] On the evolution of the modern German rabbinate, see David Sorkin, *The Transformation of German Jewry, 1780–1840* (Oxford: Oxford University Press, 1987). The quotations appear on p. 137 and p. 90, respectively.

[12] For the fullest treatment of Nicholaevan Jewish policy, see Michael F. Stanislawski, *Tsar Nicholas I and the Jews: The Transformation of Jewish Society in Russia, 1825–1855* (Philadelphia: Jewish Publication Society, 1983).

reigns of Catherine II and Alexander I, expanded the rising class of Jewish notables, legally resident in Moscow and St. Petersburg, self-educated but with prodigious cultural aspirations on behalf of their children, many of whom went on to universities, distinguished careers in the liberal professions and, in some notable instances, philanthropy and Jewish public service. But even as Nicholaevan incentives fostered social mobility, the legal consolidation of the Pale of Settlement in 1835 tightened the restrictions on residence that maintained the collective existence of Russian Jewry. Suspicious of any public institution that was even nominally independent of the government, Nicholas formally abolished Jewish self-government in 1844. Nevertheless, the Jewish *obshchestvo* continued to function as an instrument of tax collection; moreover, being charged by the government with implementing the conscription law enacted in 1827, its actual reach into the lives of ordinary people grew longer.

The conscription decree replaced the traditional privilege of purchasing the collective exemption of Jews from military duty with a personal obligation to serve, a duty to which all of Russia's non-privileged estates were subject. The "lower ranks," defined by their liability to corporal punishment and their exclusion from serf ownership, included all townsmen (Rus. *meshchane*) and serfs, whether they were bound to the state or privately owned by the clergy or the nobility. The government levied its recruit quotas in the same way it levied taxes – in the collective. This meant that, like the peasant *mir* and the town assembly, the Jewish *obshchestvo* had to hand over a certain proportion of its adult male population into the jurisdiction of the Russian army, an institution that was a kind of legal estate in its own right. The term of service was twenty-five years. Recruits were expected to be fully socialized into military life and had little success reintegrating into their former communities, should they have been lucky enough to survive and return. Most pre-reform soldiers lived and died in the military.[13]

After the Napoleonic Wars, Alexander I had first attempted to turn state peasants into a separate estate of military colonists or cantonists; Nicholas I embraced this idea with enthusiasm but – following an 1831 uprising in the cantons – worried about giving armed peasants too much independence. Integrating Alexander's original military settlements into the hierarchical structure of the standing army, Nicholas attached cantonist battalions to each of the regiments stationed throughout the empire. These battalions functioned as military schools for soldiers' sons who were born into the military estate; but Nicholas also saw cantonist battalions as

---

[13] On the pre-reform army, see Elise Kimerling-Wirtschafter, *From Serf to Russian Soldier* (Princeton: Princeton University Press, 1990).

potential educational institutions for other children whose birth and social station placed them at the margins of imperial law. Orphans, vagrants, children of prisoners, and of Polish nobles (dispossessed or imprisoned for participating in the Polish revolt of 1831) often ended up in cantonist ranks until they were old enough to enter regular military service. Nicholas also permitted Jewish communities to draft boys, aged twelve to eighteen, for entry into cantonist battalions, in place of adult recruits.[14]

Insofar as the Nicholaevan army symbolized the disciplinary function of the state, cantonist battalions provided a model training ground for the creation of Russian subjects. To that end, Nicholas (who saw in Russian Orthodoxy an effective means of ensuring social stability and political loyalty) actively promoted the conversion of Jewish cantonists. In principle, Jewish society might have dodged the threat of conversion entirely, since the military exhibited no marked preference for taking Jewish children in place of Jewish adults and provided no special dispensation for communities that were prepared to fulfill their recruitment obligation in this way. Adult Jewish soldiers in Russian ranks were not subject to conversionary pressure. Unlike Jewish minors, Jewish soldiers were frequently stationed near Jewish communities and officially relieved of their duties during the Jewish holidays. Nevertheless, military records show that approximately 70,000 Jews entered the Nicholaevan army as children. About two thirds converted. Jewish memory today generally holds Nicholas accountable for this calamity. But in the lion's share of cases, Jewish communal leaders obviously *elected* to draft children instead of adults.[15]

In hindsight, it is easy to see this complicity with Nicholas's conversionary program as a deplorable moral lapse; but, specific cases aside, it is difficult to escape the conclusion that the decision to draft minors was anything but ethically irresponsible or, worse, deliberately malicious. To begin with, Jews married young; by the time they were of draft age, many Jewish men were already fathers and husbands. It would have been unthinkable to break up families, deprive women and children of a crucial source of support, and throw more people on the limited resources of public charity. Second, in view of the unanticipated explosion of the Russian-Jewish population during the half-century after partition, it is not unreasonable to

---

[14] On cantonist battalions, see Elise Kimerling [Wirtschafter], "Soldiers' Children, 1719–1856: A Study in Social Engineering in Imperial Russia," *Forschungen zur osteuropäischen Geschichte* 30 (1982): 61–136 and Richard Pipes, "The Russian Military Colonies, 1810–1831," *The Journal of Modern History* 22 (1950): 205–219.

[15] On the social impact of the cantonist provision, see Yohanan Petrovsky-Shtern, *Jews in the Russian Army, 1827–1917: Drafted into Modernity* (Cambridge: Cambridge University Press, 2009), 90–128.

suppose that many Jewish families had an increasingly large and unsustainable number of mouths to feed. Horrifying though this is, the conscription of a child might have lightened a family's economic burden; the decision to cooperate with Jewish authorities or to resist – with uncertain results – was driven by a fine calculus of desperation. Finally, Jewish communal leaders were subject to social pressures that made them gravitate toward the poor and the marginal in their search of recruits. Jewish literature naturally stresses the most dramatic cases of orphans, the sole providers of their widowed mothers, being drafted in place of the well-fed offspring of a town's wealthiest and most fertile Jewish families. Of course, conscription could also function as a way to circumscribe the disruptive effects of adolescent rebellion. There are, not surprisingly, fewer such tales among the horror stories of the notorious era of *rekrutchina*. We do not know how many fifteen-year-olds ended up being drafted because they showed a disturbing proclivity to smoke on the Sabbath, flirt with unsuspecting Jewish virgins, read forbidden books or taunt their elders in the synagogue. In any event, few Jewish cantonists returned home to tell their side of the story.[16]

Nicholaevan conscription policy destabilized Jewish society on a scale that was entirely disproportionate to the number of Jewish recruits who ended up serving in the pre-reform army. Seventy thousand is not a small number but even by the most conservative estimate it was hardly more than three percent of the population. The primary source of class conflict and general resentment of all legally constituted Jewish authority, recruitment became a touchstone for fears of collective dissolution, family breakdown and the erosion of faith. Such anxieties escalated in the 1840s, when "official enlightenment" began to enlist recruits for its new Jewish schools. Many people were prepared to see the school as the logical extension of the barracks. "School service (Rus. *shkol'naia povinnost'*) was established on the same basis as military service and drew on the same population for recruits."[17] Exemption from conscription, a privilege that accompanied university matriculation or enrollment at one of the two rabbinical academies opened by the state in 1843, made the prospect of education highly attractive. Stipends and uniforms provided irresistible economic incentives for poorer families. Although there were far fewer of them than of Jewish soldiers – with whom they frequently identified – the graduates of Nicholas's Jewish schools shook up existing Jewish hierarchies to a far greater extent than victims of *rekrutchina*. "Official enlightenment"

---

[16] On the tension between the memory of Nicholaevan *rekrutchina* and its history, see Olga Litvak, *Conscription and the Search for Modern Russian Jewry* (Bloomington: Indiana University Press, 2006).

[17] P. S. Marek, *Ocherki po istorii prosveshcheniia evreev v Rossii* (Moscow: Trud, 1909), 80–81.

served as a laboratory for the crystallization of Jewish high culture, akin to Hasidic populism in its rivalry with the Jewish establishment.

On the one hand, the extension of government support to an alternative Jewish elite, who made their way back into the Jewish community as "crown rabbis," teachers, censors, school inspectors, physicians, and other professionals, served to institutionalize a new kind of Jewish intellectual life alongside more traditional frameworks of Jewish sociability and Jewish learning. On the other hand, the purveyors of this new culture, except in a small number of big cities (Vilna, Odessa, Warsaw, St. Petersburg, Riga) remained largely isolated from small-town Jewish society, where Hasidism made rapid inroads. The charisma of Hasidic rebbes was immune to the kind of animus directed against communal authorities and freshly minted "Nicholaevan patriots" who defended Jewish honor to the government but insisted that the tsar acted in the best interests of his Jewish subjects. If anything, the pressure of impossible choices between immediate practical benefits and fear of apostasy made Jewish parents even more likely to seek out spiritual guidance and direct access to the sources of divine blessing, the special purview of the tsaddik. In some instances, desperate (or hopeful) Hasidim went so far as to attribute to their rebbes the power of annulling the evil decrees (Heb. *gzerot*) that forced Jewish children into the uniforms of students and soldiers. In fact, the pious needed only to be patient; the God of history was on their side.

III

In the last two years of the Nicholaevan reign, conscription quotas were stepped up throughout the empire; the tsar was fighting a ruinous naval war in the Crimea and the military resources of the empire were considerably strained. Under pressure to meet mounting obligations, Jewish communities began to make use of recruit-catchers (Yid. *khappers*) to detain any eligible male who might be traveling without the necessary exemption papers. The odious spectacle of homegrown thugs in the employ of Jewish authorities exacerbated long-standing popular grievances and became the focus of a blistering critique of Jewish power. At the same time, secular social networks, cemented at state educational institutions, pushed new elites to the fore. In larger towns within the Pale – Odessa, Vilna, Warsaw, and even places like Minsk, Berdichev and Zhitomir – as well as in the two capitals, Moscow and St. Petersburg, Nicholaevan privilege and the expansion of the Russian economy contributed to the growth of Jewish "society" in the interstices between the confessional community and the estate structures that governed Russian life. The word *obshchestvo*, now paired with the adjective "educated," acquired a resonance that was in direct competition with the term's conventional, widely held meaning. Among the beneficiaries of imperial privilege and "official enlightenment," Russian-speaking Jewish professionals such as doctors, notaries, bookkeepers, and teachers, as well as merchants, private bankers, and tax farmers were enthusiastic patrons of Italian opera and German spas.[18] They were also readers of Yiddish novels, subscribers to Hebrew newspapers and founders of Jewish philanthropic organizations.[19] Institutions that were ostensibly dedicated to the improvement of the Jewish masses were patronized largely by people who were bent on self-improvement. Private initiative took over the "official enlightenment" project, gradually scuttled by the government along with Nicholaevan *rekrutchina* and the drafting of minors.

The social, economic, and cultural disparities between Jewish "educated society" and the masses of Jews eking out a living in the small towns of the Pale – bridged at the margins by the provincial middling classes – continued to expand over the course of the period between the emancipation of the serfs in 1861 and Russia's first revolution in 1905. Instead of abolishing the Pale, the state extended the privileges of emancipation from the Jewish communal regime to new categories of Jews, such as merchants with sufficient capital to enroll in the first guild (1859), university graduates holding advanced degrees, particularly doctors and lawyers (1861), craftsmen such as brewers, mechanics, and distillers (1865), army veterans (1867), and, finally, pharmacists and veterinarians as well as university graduates without advanced degrees (1879). Inaugurated by Alexander II (r. 1855–1881) and more or less in force throughout the rest of the imperial period, the policy of "partial emancipation" combined with the effects of capitalism, to deepen the cleavages that rent the texture of Jewish life.[20] By the end of the period, Russian-Jewish public activists lamented that the "traditional unity of the Jews has been in the realm of myth for a long time. The history

---

[18] See Steven J. Zipperstein, *The Jews of Odessa: A Cultural History, 1794–1881* (Stanford: Stanford University Press, 1986).

[19] On the middle-class audience of modern Jewish literature, see Alyssa P. Quint, "'Yiddish Literature for the Masses?': A Reconsideration of Who Read What in Jewish Eastern Europe," *AJS Review* 29 (2005): 61–89. On the rise of private Jewish philanthropy, see Brian Horowitz, *Jewish Philanthropy and Enlightenment in Late-Tsarist Russia* (Seattle: University of Washington Press, 2009) and Natan M. Meir, *Kiev, Jewish Metropolis: A History, 1859–1914* (Bloomington: Indiana University Press, 2010), 211–260.

[20] On the politics of social emancipation, see Benjamin I. Nathans, *Beyond the Pale: The Jewish Encounter with Late Imperial Russia* (Berkeley: University of California Press, 2002), 23–80.

of the disintegration of this unity is exceedingly depressing."[21] The only real wonder is whether it had ever existed.

Freed by law to reconstruct their Jewish lives on a strictly voluntary basis and to promote the personal ideal of self-improvement as the path to social success, the emancipated avant-garde of Russian Jewry exemplified the success of the few at the expense of the many. Although the world beyond the Pale continued to expand, the benefits of imperial emancipation always remained highly partial. While the allure of *embourgeoisement* raised the stakes on heroic personal achievement (in finance or education) anxieties about the ever-present threat of a drop in status sharpened the distinction between self-made Russian Jews and unreconstructed Russian Jewry. The discrepancy between the rising tide of social, economic, and cultural expectations and the realities of tightening economic competition and potential proletarianization nurtured a restless provincial culture torn between resentment and entitlement. The government's apparent intransigence about abolishing the Pale began to be viewed as an intractable obstacle to Jewish civic integration and material well-being.

Private discontent and articulate despair played out on the pages of the Jewish press. The resentment of the few gathered unprecedented cultural momentum. Conservatives in Vilna and radicals in Odessa were equally ill at ease with the implications of partial emancipation for the future of Russian Jewry. For the first time, the press openly debated the ambiguities of Jewish confessional/civic status alongside Russia's other "accursed questions."[22] As Alexander's reign grew to its explosive conclusion, the program of personal emancipation and its counterpart – a historicist faith in gradual collective improvement – had given way to messianic visions of renewal and an apocalyptic faith in the redemptive potential of violence. The inner tensions of the Great Reforms acquired the lineaments of national crisis.

Emancipation fundamentally transformed the peasant economy in ways that destabilized age-old patterns of exchange, particularly on the western frontier, the most dynamic sector of industrial development in the empire. There were additional opportunities for work beyond agriculture; but the new class of migrant laborers now had to contend with seasonal unemployment, and an unstable, unregulated labor market. Many more people were now beyond the immediate mechanisms of social control that the government had had at its disposal during the era of serfdom. Despite its reputation as a police-state, watched over by the notorious Third Section, the

[21] G. B. Sliozberg, quoted in "Otchet o soveshchanii evreiskikh obshchestvennykh deiatelei," *Evreiskii mir* 1 no. 11–12 (1909), 35–37.
[22] See John D. Klier, *Imperial Russia's Jewish Question, 1855–1881* (Cambridge: Cambridge University Press, 1995).

Russian empire remained profoundly under-governed, with a local police force that was comparatively tiny, as well as inefficient and corrupt. The prospect of civil disturbance had raised its ugly head more than once in the immediate post-emancipation period; however, most peasant unrest remained limited, confined to skirmishes related to the misunderstanding of the terms of the emancipation decree (the idea of emancipation without land presented a particular problem). Traditional political judgment, based on a fundamental respect for the patriarchal authority of the tsar, remained unshaken, despite the best efforts of Russian populists and *zemstvo* officials to introduce a greater sense of individual autonomy and respect for Western legal principles. But in the wake of a disturbing wave of revolutionary terrorism in St. Petersburg, the irruption of anti-Jewish economic violence in the borderlands betokened a sea-change in the nature of social disorder in the empire. The state's response finally discredited the sedulously cultivated self-image of the Romanovs as reforming tsars; tarred with the brush of antisemitism, neither the government of Alexander III (r. 1881–1894) nor that of his heir, Nicholas II (r. 1894–1917), could sustain the myth of autocratic liberalism. Violence, in turn, helped to crystallize the emancipation anxieties of Jewish "educated society" into a new political ideology.[23]

The 1881 assassination of Alexander II by a radical populist group known as the People's Will brought into focus the contradictions implicit in the concept of a reforming autocracy. The government of the tsar-liberator lifted the lid off Nicholaevan repression and destabilized traditional hierarchies without attempting to build social consensus. The abolition of serfdom created the conditions for free labor, without providing basic economic protections against the risks of underemployment. The mitigation of censorship restrictions and the introduction of public trials encouraged open discussion and galvanized civil discourse; but in the absence of civil liberties, let alone the guarantee of equality before the law, the political irrelevance of Russia's vibrant public sphere was all the more galling. Such contradictions created a breeding ground for ideological extremism and acts of deliberate provocation; before their discovery of Marxism during the 1890s, largely in train of disappointed hopes in peasant revolution, Russian radicals vested their political energies in the oppositional instincts of the *narod*. The People's Will – already responsible for a number of prior attacks on high officials – expected that the assassination of the tsar would

---

[23] For an account of the conditions that led up to 1881, see I. Michael Aronson, *Troubled Waters: Origins of the 1881 Anti-Jewish Pogroms in Russia* (Pittsburgh: University of Pittsburgh Press, 1990).

ignite a popular uprising against the autocracy.[24] What happened instead was something much more consistent with the temper of Alexander's unfinished revolution from above.

The southern borderland of the empire constituted Russia's emergent economic frontier. In the 1860s, southwestern Ukraine began to attract seasonal labor; migrant workers, unmoored from their local villages, rode the rails of the recently constructed rail system in search of work. The spring of 1881 was an exceptionally bad time. In the immediate aftermath of the assassination, the authority of the autocracy seemed temporarily suspended; there were rumors of a new emancipation law, this time with provisions for the redistribution of land. Idle migrant workers, buoyed by the customary revelry of the Easter season and incited by gossip about Jewish responsibility for the murder of the tsar (fueled, undoubtedly, by the fact that the People's Will counted a number of Jewish students among its members) began to travel from town to town, attacking Jewish property. Before the autocracy was able to move in troops and subdue the rioters, the so-called southern tempests had grown into a full-fledged three-day bender which resulted in the destruction of millions of rubles worth of property. A few people were physically injured but hundreds more were left homeless and destitute.

After the dust finally settled, the government instituted a judicial inquiry which resulted in a small number of prosecutions, but it was difficult to round up all of the culprits because they were not local men; the question of responsibility hung in the air and poisoned the atmosphere even further. Officials in the Ministry of the Interior understood that the phenomenon of pogroms – as the riots came infamously to be known – was symptomatic of modern social instability rather than a vestige of traditional religious prejudice. In fact, they attributed pogroms to social, rather than theological, causes: revolutionary "agitation" among the quiescent peasantry and "Jewish exploitation" of the countryside. To the extent that this etiology took into account the importance of changing relationships between the city and the country that would continue to test the legitimacy of the autocracy throughout the late imperial period, it was not altogether misguided. But, of course, the administration missed the forest for the trees and, having sought refuge in blaming the victim, refused to take any responsibility for the general state of immiseration and insecurity that led to violence in the first place.

---

[24] On Russian populism, see the classic account by Franco Venturi, *Roots of Revolution: A History of the Populist and Socialist Movements in Nineteenth-Century Russia* (Chicago: University of Chicago Press, 1983).

While it was true that revolutionary terrorism did its part to undermine the authority of the regime and implicitly encouraged the popular recourse to force, the pogroms constituted a fundamentally reactionary response to economic conditions that were the direct result of unserfment. As every generation of Russian radicals discovered to its own chagrin, peasants were immune to revolutionary propaganda. It was also true that things were much more volatile in the Pale than elsewhere because the density of Jewish settlement and traditional Jewish concentration in the distribution and processing of agricultural goods made Jewish middlemen look like exploiters of both peasant producers and urban consumers. But it was also true that, more than anywhere else in Russia, in the Pale of Settlement these conditions were the direct result of government policy, which restricted Jewish economic activity and confined the Jewish population to the Pale. Moreover, Jewish livelihood suffered just as much, if not more, from the same economic pressures that contributed to the ostensible "exploitation" of peasants. And, as bad as pogroms were for Russian Jewry, they were even worse for the autocracy.

Instead of doing anything to alleviate poverty and reduce economic insecurity in ways that might have promoted a greater sense of public investment and political faith in the good will of the autocracy, the government prescribed another course of repressive counter-measures. Designed to reverse the effects of political unrest and to curtail the exponential growth of free trade in the Pale, the May Laws and the *numerus clausus* aimed at keeping both Jews and peasants backward. Initially enacted as a series of "emergency measures," the May Laws aimed at clearing Russian villages of Jewish traders in order to render the reality of Jewish economic life more consistent with the legal status of Jews as "townsmen" while protecting peasants from the depredations of the money market. Like many similarly ambitious administrative measures, the May Laws proved largely unenforceable, but the persistence of humiliating and troublesome regulations – not to mention the ever-present threat of what the historian Shimon Dubnow famously called "legal pogroms" waged by the police against people who were caught traveling without residence permits – further undermined Jewish livelihood and Jewish security.

In the last quarter of the nineteenth century, the quality of Russian-Jewish life continued to erode not so much because of the threat or scale of physical anti-semitic violence – there was not another pogrom in Russia for twenty years – but mostly because counterproductive government policies and the depredations of capitalism combined to make conditions in the Pale of Settlement more and more unbearable. With the introduction of quotas on Jewish attendance at universities (the *numerus clausus*), leaving the Pale became more difficult, just as it was becoming more urgent.

Like the May Laws, the *numerus clausus* was observed mostly in the breach; but the moral and financial costs involved in evading an unjust and hated law had a dispiriting effect on Jewish public culture and undermined any residual respect for an oppressive and hostile regime. Ironically, the law that was meant to reduce the number of Jews in the revolutionary student movement probably drove more Jewish twenty-year-olds into the arms of Russian radicals even when they started out just wanting to go to medical school. And, in the final analysis, the *numerus clausus* did nothing to stem the tide of Jews entering Russian institutions of higher learning; there is strong evidence that rates of Jewish attendance were actually *on the rise* during the era of counter-reforms.[25]

Did the pogroms fundamentally alter the course of Russian-Jewish history? For many years, Jewish scholarship said yes, positioning the pogroms as the dividing line between the liberal and postliberal phase of Russian-Jewish history. Pointing to the beginning of mass migration and to the rise of Zionism after the so-called crisis of 1881–1882, consensus has long upheld the proposition that the profound shock of the "southern tempests" put an end to the hopes of Jewish emancipation and forced Russian Jews to seek a solution to the Jewish Question not just beyond the Pale but beyond the imperial frontier altogether, across the Atlantic, as well as in the once-and-future homeland of the Jewish nation.[26] In the past twenty years or so, the picture has grown more complicated. For one thing, both Jewish nationalism and the great Jewish migration had their roots in the contradictions of the Great Reforms, rather than in the reactionary political climate of the early 1880s. As a matter of fact, Jewish migration from the Russian empire, much like every other case of mass migration in history, had a distinctly secular, economic profile.[27] The first Russian Jews to cross the border came from the northwestern region of the Pale.[28] Jewish Lithuania experienced no pogrom violence, but it was subject, during the 1870s, to a series of bad harvests and devastating epidemics that arguably had a more profound effect on the decision to move than did pogroms in the south, a region known for greater economic opportunity and greater instability as well. Moreover, Jewish migration began internally, spurred by the opening

---

[25] On the impact of the *numerus clausus,* see Nathans, *Beyond the Pale*, 257–310.

[26] See Jonathan Frankel, "The Crisis of 1881–1882 as a Turning Point in Modern Jewish History," in *The Legacy of Jewish Migration: 1881 and Its Impact*, ed. David Berger (New York: Columbia University Press, 1983), 9–22.

[27] For this argument, see Simon Kuznets, "Immigration of Russian Jews to the Unites States: Background and Structure," *Perspectives in American History* 9 (1975): 35–124.

[28] On Jewish migration from Lithuania, see Cormac Ó Gráda, *Jewish Ireland in the Age of Joyce: A Socioeconomic History* (Princeton: Princeton University Press, 2006), 9–29.

of the imperial frontier to the west and to the south; before people were prepared to move to New York, they moved to Odessa, Warsaw, Kiev, and Lodz. By the last decade of the nineteenth century, a third of Russia's Jewish population lived in twelve of the largest cities in the empire, connected to transnational markets by the railroad.[29] Contrary to the iconic image of the sheltered domestic idyll of the shtetl destroyed by pogroms and uprooted by emigration, the *habitus* of late imperial Russian Jewry was predominantly urban, economically competitive, socially flexible and culturally resilient. The contradictions of Russian-Jewish life admitted both precociously modern rates of divorce *and* inveterately conservative religious sensibilities.[30]

As for the discovery of Jewish nationalism, that too predates the pogroms. Jewish nationalism had its roots in the critique of secularization and in the general sense of cultural pessimism that set in during the 1870s, when the government began to pull back from its commitment to the education of Russian Jewry. With such efforts increasingly in private hands, Jewish intellectuals began to question the historical inevitability of improvement. Deprived of government patronage, Jewish writers found themselves in the highly uncomfortable position of having to minister to the needs of the Jewish middle-class, chiefly by way of the Jewish press; no Jewish newspaper could afford to stay in business unless it successfully courted the tastes of the middle-class subscriber. The vagaries of Jewish consumers clashed with the Romantic mission of Jewish intellectuals as the unacknowledged legislators of Jewish values and the producers of Jewish knowledge. After two decades of emancipation, the providential reconciliation between individual self-improvement and collective progress seemed no longer imminent. "I ask myself," mused Judah Leib Levin in the pointedly titled "Questions of Our Time"

> What can be the advantage of this century
> That it should consider itself so worthy of praise?
> Has it really scaled such great heights,
> Filling all things with the light of the mind;

[29] The cities were Warsaw, Ekaterinoslav, Lodz, Dvinsk, Lublin, Kovno, Zhitomir, Elizavetgrad, Kishinev, Kremenetz, Odessa, and Mogilev. On the impact of internal migration, see Richard H. Rowland, "Geographical Patterns of the Jewish Population in the Pale of Settlement of Late Imperial Russia," *Jewish Social Studies* 48 (1986): 207–234.

[30] On the divorce rates and on the importance of female agency, see ChaeRan Y. Freeze, *Jewish Marriage and Divorce in Imperial Russia* (Hanover, NH: Brandeis University Press, 2002), 201–242. On popular reading tastes as a reflection of Russian-Jewish cultural conservatism, see Zeev Gries, *The Book in the Jewish World, 1700–1900*, trans. Jeffrey M. Green (Oxford and Portland, OR: Littman Library of Jewish Civilization, 2007).

Its leaders and sages – all of them superior,
In knowledge, enlightened and in principles, pure?
Or is it all a mirage, a trick of the eyes –
A gleam of sunlight on rotting wood, a flash of
    foam upon the waters?[31]

No longer content to wait upon "this blessed nineteenth century," Jewish intellectuals began to argue that the nation's future had to be wrested from the past by an act of sovereign human will.

Thus, although the pogroms certainly imparted a sense of urgency to the unresolved dilemmas of time and conscience, fear of violence and the prospect of proletarianization did not disconfirm the liberal *telos* of modern Russian-Jewish culture. When the pogroms came, converts to Zionism were already well primed to receive anti-Jewish violence as nothing short of a personal revelation about the all-important *now*. A caesura in the passage of historical time, the pogrom marked an opening for the possibility of Jewish renewal, conceived under the Nietzschean sign of eternal return:

7 May [1881]. It is good for me to have been afflicted. […] For have I not now experienced at least this once in my own life, the feelings that my fathers had felt all the days of their lives? For if they lived all their days in fear and confusion, why should I not share a bit in that sensation of horror which was for them lifelong? Am I not their son? Their troubles are dear to me and I shall suffer for their dignity … My mind is now at rest, for I have chanced to know and to feel the life of my people in the course of the Exile … It is good for me to have been afflicted.[32]

The logic of Zionism, articulated here by M. L. Lilienblum, depended less on the contemporary threat of antisemitism – to which there were always any number of possible responses – and more on the capacity of modern Hebrew literature to generate a sense of national crisis, powerful enough to counteract the corrosive effects of rational skepticism, social alienation and gender trouble.[33] Committed to the memory of "traditional Jewish unity," Jewish nationalists hoped that they could get history to go in reverse, toward a lost collective ideal. But the real problem, confronting both Russian reactionaries and the "Lovers of Zion," – the organization that Lilienblum co-founded with the Odessa physician, L. S. Pinsker – was that the genie of Jewish emancipation, however reluctantly released, could not be driven back into the bottle.

---

[31] *Hashahar* 9 (1878): 133–134.
[32] M. L. Lilienblum, "Derekh teshuvah [1899]," in *Ktavim otobiografiyyim*, ed. Shlomo Breiman (Jerusalem: Mosad-bialik, 1970), 2, 188–189.
[33] See Benjamin Nathans, "A Hebrew Drama: Lilienblum, Dubnow and the Idea of Crisis in East European Jewish History," *Simon Dubnow Institute Yearbook* 5 (2006): 211–227.

IV

For Russian Jewry, the twentieth century opened with the bloody drama of another pogrom, set this time in the Bessarabian town of Kishinev. In many ways, the events that unfolded there in the spring of 1903 anticipated the main themes of Russian-Jewish history between the years of Russia's first revolution in 1905 and the formation of the Soviet Union in 1923 – physical violence, the disruption of the economy, displacement and impoverishment, political mobilization. But for contemporary observers, the Kishinev pogrom revealed not the future of the Jews but the parlous state of the autocracy. In Kishinev, tsarist authorities faced the dire consequences of an escalating crisis of legitimacy the effects of which would be felt throughout the country just two years later.

What precisely happened in Kishinev? While the actual course of events is not much in dispute, the underlying causes, particularly the role of the government, have generated considerable controversy.[34] A relatively large provincial town with a highly volatile economy, prone to periodic downturns and chronic underemployment, and home to an ethnically and religiously diverse population, Kishinev incubated a particularly virulent brand of Russian Orthodox nationalism, on the rise throughout the southwestern provinces. Stoked by the chauvinistic rhetoric of the local paper and set off by a nearby case of blood libel, the pogrom ultimately took the form of a three-day riot that, unlike the "southern tempests" of 1881–1882, also claimed a number of Jewish lives. Fifty Jewish people were killed but a much greater number was injured; significantly, there were also a number of rape cases. As in 1881–1882, extensive property damage left thousands homeless and penniless. A series of copycat riots followed throughout the southwest.

Once again, the provincial government appeared powerless to anticipate disorder or to stop events in their tracks; Cossack forces rode in after three days but the show of Russian authority failed to make an impression on the rioters. Local officials reported being afraid for their own lives. Jewish educated society reacted with outrage and even went so far as to blame the Russian police of fomenting the pogrom, an accusation of conspiracy which continued to reverberate in Russian-Jewish scholarship for years. The abject spectacle of Jewish victimhood mobilized the Russian-Jewish socialist party, otherwise known as the Bund, to call for self-defense. Bundists began to organize a Jewish militia in preparedness for future outbreaks. There was a public outcry abroad as well, ignited by reports and pictures

---

[34] For a thoughtful discussion of the "legacy" of Kishinev, see Edward H. Judge, *Easter in Kishinev: Anatomy of a Pogrom* (New York: New York University Press, 1992), 134–146.

published in newspapers in London and New York. Very quickly Kishinev became an international event, a symbol of endemic Russian antisemitism, political backwardness, and administrative inefficiency.[35]

In Russian-Jewish history, Kishinev signifies the translation of ideology into politics.[36] Before 1903, the nationalist movement could not compete with the prestige of the Russian Social Democratic Party; the latter was better organized, more disciplined, more ideologically coherent and attracted many more Jewish members then the Zionists, discredited by the floundering diplomatic efforts of Theodor Herzl and a number of serious internal disputes. The Bund, the Jewish party affiliated with the RSDP, enjoyed strong support among Jewish working people throughout Eastern Europe. While Zionism did not become a mass movement until the inter-war period, the reaction to Kishinev provided a rallying point for Jewish nationalist leadership, centered in nearby Odessa, and endowed the Zionist program with a powerful sense of its own inevitability, a quality that Ber Borochov famously termed "elemental" (Rus. *stikhiinost*).[37] After Herzl died in 1904, Russian Zionists – particularly Borochov, the founder of the Marxist Poalei Zion and Vladimir Jabotinsky whose fame was directly linked to Kishinev and who spearheaded the right-wing Revisionist split – assumed a leading role in the Zionist movement.[38] Borochov, born in 1881, and Jabotinsky, born in 1880, represented the "generation of 1905," a cohort whose political coming-of-age was marked by Kishinev and the ensuing ordeal of Russia's first revolution.[39]

The year 1905 brought Russia its first constitution and its first experiment with representative government, forced by a short-lived compromise between state and society, from a deeply reactionary Nicholas II who wanted nothing so much as to drag the country back into the seventeenth century, the age of patriarchal obedience and Orthodox humility. Following the announcement of the October Manifesto, the empire faced

---

[35] See Judge, *Easter in Kishinev*, 76–106.

[36] See Jonathan Frankel, *Prophecy and Politics: Socialism, Nationalism and the Russian Jews, 1862–1917* (Cambridge: Cambridge University Press, 1981), 134–170 and Litvak, "The Poet in Hell: H. N. Bialik and the Genealogy of the Kishinev Pogrom," *Jewish Studies Quarterly* 12 (2005): 101–128.

[37] See Frankel, *Prophecy and Politics*, 329–364 and Mitchell Cohen, *Zion and State: Nation, Class and the Shaping of Modern Israel* (New York: Basil Blackwell, 1987), 85–104.

[38] Cohen, *Zion and State*, 134–148 and Michael Stanislawski, *Zionism and the Fin de Siècle: Cosmopolitanism and Nationalism from Nordau to Jabotinsky* (Berkeley: University of California Press, 2001), esp. 178–202.

[39] See Scott Ury, "The Generation of 1905 and the Politics of Despair: Alienation, Friendship, Community," in *The Revolution of 1905 and Russia's Jews*, ed. Stefani Hoffman and Ezra Mendelsohn (Philadelphia: University of Pennsylvania Press, 2008), 96–110.

nearly two years of violent urban disorder. Companies of professing patriots attacked students, revolutionaries, and Jews, in the name of Holy Rus'
and the sacred person of the tsar. Pogroms became so frequent throughout
the Pale of Settlement that many Russian provincial newspapers began
carrying a special daily column dedicated to reporting the outbreaks. In
Odessa alone more than 3,000 people were killed before order was finally
restored by the beginning of 1907; the death toll for the entire empire ran
into the tens of thousands.[40] In most cases, it proved difficult to distinguish
between counter-revolutionary violence and ethnic conflict. By this point,
antisemitism was fast becoming a salient feature in the ideological repertoire of the Russian right-wing.

Russian radicals, Bundists, and Zionists organized self-defense militia units but these had limited effect; street fighting was fierce and only
claimed additional lives. To quell the disorder, the Ministry of the Interior
began an anti-revolutionary campaign. Many Russian socialists, a substantial proportion of whom were Jewish, ended up on the gallows and in exile
in Siberia. Those who managed to escape with their lives fled to America
and to Palestine, changing forever the character of Jewish political culture
in both places.[41] Back in Russia, Jewish politics likewise began to penetrate smaller provincial towns, largely through the popular press; there
were now, for the first time in the life of the empire, two Yiddish dailies
that boasted mass circulation, a development that proved crucial in the
politicization of Jewish daily life in the last years before the First World
War. As a matter of fact, increasing awareness of the Jewish people – the
narod – as an historical actor with collective rights also helped to transform
the character of metropolitan Jewish culture.

Jewish organizational life blossomed after the Revolution of 1905.[42]
Countless provincial societies, modeled after similar institutions established first in St. Petersburg, were dedicated to the pursuit of local history
and ethnography, the cultivation of literary, artistic, and musical tastes,
as well as to public discussion of critical contemporary questions. Jewish
philanthropists in St. Petersburg sponsored activities of this kind on a
much larger scale; the most famous Russian-Jewish collective project was
Sh. An-sky's Ethnographic Expedition of 1912. Artifacts and materials that

---

[40] For a snapshot of pogrom violence during the Revolution of 1905, see Robert Weinberg,
The Revolution of 1905 in Odessa: Blood on the Steps (Bloomington: Indiana University
Press, 1993), 164–187 and Scott Ury, *Barricades and Banners: The Revolution of 1905 and
the Transformation of Warsaw Jewry* (Stanford: Stanford University Press, 2012).

[41] Frankel, *Prophecy and Politics*, 365–547.

[42] For a description, see Jeffrey Veidlinger, *Jewish Public Culture in the Late Russian Empire*
(Bloomington: Indiana University Press, 2009).

An-sky collected in turn inspired modernist experiments in Jewish visual, musical, and literary expression. At the same time, the work of cultural self-recognition contributed to the rise of Jewish civic consciousness and an open identification with the Jewish masses. Russian-Jewish elites now rejected partial emancipation as a matter of principle.[43]

Even as official Russian life became increasingly conservative and openly anti-semitic, Jewish liberals were more and more prepared to use parliamentary and judicial institutions to insist on Jewish civil rights but also on the historic privileges of Jewish collective institutions. Jewish attorneys successfully defended Mendel Beilis, tried on charges of ritual murder in 1913.[44] Jewish deputies in the Duma supported Jewish cultural and educational autonomy, while advocating the abolition of the Pale, a bitter reminder of the seemingly immovable obstacle of "dual jurisdiction." Despite the efforts of the emancipated few, however, it would take another revolution as well as a world war to ensure the emancipation of the many. That said, when the war came in 1914, the cultural orientation of Russian Jewish elites and the political literacy of the masses proved an asset in the fight for the reconstitution of Jewish communal life and for the mobilization of resources to stave off the immediate threats of starvation, disease, and homelessness.[45]

Between the outbreak of the First World War and the end of the Russian Civil War, in 1921, Russian Jewry was caught up in the crossfire of continuous military conflict. This understatement poorly captures the *tsuris* that afflicted the Jewish residents of the former Pale of Settlement for seven horrific years. To begin with, in 1915, masses of Jewish civilians were expelled from their homes by Russian military authorities (who were motivated largely by fears of espionage rather than concerns for the safety of people who found themselves on the front lines), not, of course, without violence; this was the initial indication of a wide-spread refugee problem that eventually led to the internal collapse of the Pale.[46] For the first time in Russia's history, there were substantial numbers of Jewish people in the interior of the country. As the war progressed, many former

[43] See Christoph Gassenschmidt, *Jewish Liberal Politics in Tsarist Russia, 1900–1914* (New York: New York University Press, 1995).
[44] See Robert Weinberg, *Blood Libel in Late Imperial Russia: The Ritual Murder Trial of Mendel Beilis* (Bloomington: Indiana University Press, 2014).
[45] See Andrew N. Koss, "*World War One and the Remaking of Jewish Vilna, 1914–1918*" (PhD thesis, Stanford University, 2010).
[46] On the evacuations, see Eric Lohr, *Nationalizing the Russian Empire: The Campaign against Enemy Aliens during World War I* (Cambridge, MA: Harvard University Press, 2003), 137–165.

Jewish subjects of the tsar came under German occupation authorities, who imposed a semblance of order but could do nothing to alleviate the prospect of overcrowding, illness, and impoverishment. In retrospect, the refugee problem turned out to be only the flower of war; the fruits were still to follow.

After the fall of the Romanov Empire in 1916, peace broke out in liberated Ukraine and brought forth the possibility of ethnic coopera- tion; but the newly established Jewish-Ukrainian republic had a short shelf life. Within a year, the Civil War had come south. Mobilized by the prospect of a Bolshevik victory, armed defenders of the old regime, con- sisting mostly of roving warlords and their followers living off the land, began to attack whatever remained of Jewish settlements. Their motive was chiefly economic but also punitive. Enraged reactionaries blamed Jews for the Revolution. The steady cycle of anti-semitic murder, rape, and dispossession that claimed upwards of 50,000 lives in just over three years endowed the word pogrom with an entirely unprecedented kind of daily horror.[47]

The end of the war found Russian Jewry in pieces. Divided among the sovereign states formed by the Versailles settlement, the post-war Russian- Jewish population consisted of several Jewries living on territories of the former Pale of Settlement and Habsburg Galicia that now constituted autonomous nation-states, under the nominal protection of the League of Nations. A large proportion ended up in independent Poland, which was home to roughly three million Jews, but there were also substantial Jewish minorities in Lithuania and Latvia, and smaller ones in Romania, Bulgaria and Estonia.[48] As a result of the demographic and economic collapse of the Pale during World War I and the Russian Civil War, the Russian interior, including Moscow and St. Petersburg (renamed Petrograd during the war and Leningrad in 1924) had an unprecedented number of Jews. Together with the surviving Jewish populations of Ukraine and Belorussia, adjoined to the Soviet Union in 1923, this group formed the demographic basis of Soviet Jewry, the heir perforce of the unfinished imperial attempt at mak- ing Russian Jews.

[47] On the transition from the brief interlude of Ukrainian independence to the nightmare of the Civil War, see Henry Abramson, *A Prayer for the Government: Ukrainians and Jews in Revolutionary Times, 1917–1920* (Cambridge, MA: Ukrainian Research Institute of Harvard University, 1999) and Oleg Budnitskii, *Russian Jews between Reds and Whites, 1917–1920* (Philadelphia: University of Pennsylvania Press, 2011).

[48] For a survey of the post-war demographic dispersion of Russian Jewry, see Ezra Mendelsohn, *The Jews of East Central Europe between the World Wars* (Bloomington: Indiana University Press, 1987).

V

Jewish emancipation in Russia was the work of the Provisional Government, which took power following the tsar's abdication in February of 1917. Within weeks of its installation, in anticipation of a Constituent Assembly, the Provisional Government abolished all legislative restrictions based on religion and national origins; this may have been the most durable political legacy of a regime that lasted all of seven months. In the interim between February and October 1917, Jewish activists glimpsed a "wider perspective" for the fulfillment of their particular projects of collective revival; February represented the "consummation" of the struggle not only for the emancipation of the Jews but for the cultural emancipation of Judaism.[49] By far the largest proportion of Russian Jews leaned toward some form of cultural autonomy within the framework of a democratic federation; few shared the ruthless cosmopolitanism of the Bolsheviks. Even the Jewish left inclined to other parties. In the elections to the Constituent Assembly, held in November 1917, most Jewish votes went either to the Mensheviks or to Jewish parties.[50] The Civil War considerably radicalized Russian-Jewish convictions although committed Jewish CP members still represented a tiny, if very visible, minority, of the Bolshevik government. Many new recruits joined the security forces. But all Jewish Bolsheviks, including Lev Trotsky, the commander of the Red Army and probably the most famous Russian Jew in the world, had disavowed whatever Jewish affiliations they may have had and considered themselves Bolsheviks first and last.

The much-discussed leftward turn of Russian Jewry is really not hard to understand; the violence of the Civil War had a great deal more to do with it than anything like the proverbial association between Jews and radicalism.[51] Although the Red Army was also responsible for some of the anti-Jewish violence in the Ukraine, the pogrom never became part of its ideology. Under Bolshevik rule, antisemitism was officially proscribed as a treasonous offense, punishable by the ultimate penalty. The White forces saw the killing of Jews as part of their battle for Holy Russia; anticipating Hitler, they equated Judaism with Bolshevism. Even apolitical Jews were prepared not only to flee this kind of ideological and physical terror but

---

[49] Kenneth B. Moss, *Jewish Renaissance in the Russian Revolution* (Cambridge, MA: Harvard University Press, 2009), 23.

[50] Baruch Gurevitz, *National Communism in the Soviet Union, 1918–1928* (Pittsburgh: University of Pittsburgh Press, 1980), 24–42. Statistical information on the Jewish electorate appears on p. 37, fn. 4.

[51] For an attempt to analyze this connection, see Robert J. Brym, *The Jewish Intelligentsia and Russian Marxism: A Sociological Study of Intellectual Radicalism and Ideological Divergence* (Houndmills: Palgrave Macmillan, 1978).

to fight against it in Red Army ranks. The Red Army formed a revolutionary avant-garde. Military service opened the door into the party and into
the security apparatus. Given the connection between antisemitism and
Russian reaction, it is not surprising that Jews were prepared to engage in
the unsavory work of ridding the fragile state of its internal enemies. It is
more difficult to remember, after the age of Stalin, that the defenders of
Russia's Old Regime, were not very nice people either. Their unconsciona-
ble treatment of Jewish civilians – including the most vulnerable members
of the population, children, women, the elderly, the sick, and the poor –
during the Civil War did not exactly endear Jews to the memory of the
tsars. An abstract commitment to social justice and ideological purity was,
in many cases, mixed with the very human and more immediate motive of
revenge. Given the escalation of the political temper of the times, it may
be just as surprising that *more* Jews did not join the Bolshevik assault on
the imperial past as that some chose to do so. At any rate, throughout the
Soviet period, Jews who joined the *party* remained in the minority; but
the Soviet *state* continued to command some form of loyalty on the part
of the majority almost until its demise in 1989. This distinction between
state and party is key to understanding the formation of Soviet-Jewish
consciousness.

In the 1920s, the newly established Soviet Union of Socialist
Republics explicitly declared its commitment both to the emancipation
of the individual and to the support of national self-determination. In
the "affirmative action state," nation building was a matter of public
policy.[52] During the interwar period, the Soviet Union was the only
state in Europe that not only outlawed antisemitism but committed
some of its overstretched resources to maintaining Jewish public life,
defined in accordance with the ideological norms of Soviet secularization. The Jewish Section of the Communist Party was charged both
with the active suppression of Jewish clericalism and the regeneration of
Jewish mass culture in the former territories of the Pale.[53] Throughout
Belorussia and Ukraine there were now institutions devoted to Jewish
scholarship, literature, music, and art, as well as Jewish-Soviet schools,
clubs, and workers' cooperatives. All of this activity took place in the
new Soviet Yiddish, purged of Hebraic spelling and openly religious
references. The Jewish Section of the Communist Party sponsored a

---

[52] Terry Martin, *The Affirmative Action Empire: Nations and Nationalism in the Soviet
Union, 1923–1939* (Ithaca: Cornell University Press, 2001).

[53] See Zvi Y. Gitelman, *Jewish Nationality and Soviet Politics: The Jewish Section of the
CPSU, 1917–1930* (Princeton: Princeton University Press, 1972).

wide range of Yiddish periodicals and tried to encourage the creation of a new Soviet-Yiddish literature for the masses.[54]

The project of Jewish collective regeneration never quite took off, although Soviet-Yiddish elementary schools played an important role in the Sovietization of provincial Jewry. Even before it was effectively killed by Stalin, the party-led Soviet-Jewish renaissance remained a small subculture, confined to the "Soviet Jewish folk intelligentsia," increasingly despondent about the prospect of national "dispersion."[55] Indeed, most Soviet Jews – like many of their counterparts among the other national minorities of the USSR – saw their path to success in the embrace of radical emancipation by the state and the journey beyond the former Pale. Soviet Jews overwhelmingly chose to live in Moscow rather than in the Red shtetl and to send their children to Russian universities instead of local trade schools and Yiddish-speaking agricultural settlements. Increasingly literate in the language of the state, Soviet Jews embraced the classics of Soviet literature, many of them written by Jewish virtuosi of Russian verse and prose. While the literary intermarriage between the Jewish Ilya Il'f and the Ukrainian Evgeny Petrov (both came from Odessa) produced not one, but two, modernist masterpieces that became the living scripture of Soviet Jewry (*The Twelve Chairs*, 1928 and *The Golden Calf*, 1931), Soviet-Yiddish, written for the masses, remained at the margins of popular taste.

Soviet culture continued to reflect the persistence of regional differences, increasingly mapped onto class distinctions (which no one in the Soviet Union would ever admit existed) between provincial, poor, and less well-educated Yiddish speakers in the small towns of Belorussia and Ukraine and metropolitan Russian-speaking Jews, professionalized, upwardly mobile, integrated into the Soviet technological elite and living in Leningrad and Moscow.[56] To some extent, then, the polarizing effects of "dual jurisdiction" persisted into the Soviet period. But, notwithstanding the more obvious markers of Jewish origins among the former (such as language use and the persistence of religious customs such as circumcision, synagogue attendance, and kashrut), even the latter imbibed a sense of Jewish pride, mixed with powerful feelings of nostalgia, from the works of Russia's twentieth-century Jewish avant-garde.[57]

For the masses, the pull of integration into Soviet life in the 1920s and 1930s was very strong. Along with movement into white-collar and

[54] See David Shneer, *Yiddish and the Creation of Soviet Jewish Culture, 1918–1930* (Cambridge: Cambridge University Press, 2004).

[55] Shneer, *Yiddish and the Creation of Soviet Jewish Culture,* 201.

[56] On the provincialization of Soviet Jewry, see Elissa Bemporad, *Becoming Soviet Jews: The Bolshevik Experiment in Minsk* (Bloomington: Indiana University Press, 2013).

[57] See Alice Nakhimovsky, *Russian-Jewish Literature and Identity: Jabotinsky, Babel, Grossman, Galich, Roziner, Markish* (Baltimore: Johns Hopkins University Press, 1992).

technical occupations, Soviet Jewry displayed impressive rates of inter-marriage, signs of the rapid effects of secularization all along the Soviet ethnic frontier.[58] Cast against the remnants of life in the imperial "prison house of nations" and contrasted with the contemporary resurgence of anti-semitic reaction in the avowedly democratic nations that bordered the Soviet Union, the ideal of the *homo sovieticus* inspired feelings of allegiance to the state that would become increasingly significant on the eve of the Second World War. In 1938, it was arguably safer to be a secular Jew in Red Moscow than a pious Jew in the Lithuanian Jerusalem or any other East Central European city, where the ominous presence of black and brown shirts threatened the security of all Jews, regardless of their religious or political convictions.

World War II, known in the Soviet Union as the Great Patriotic War, marked a high point in the process of Jewish socialization. Often treated as a variation on the theme of Eastern European Jewish victimhood in the Holocaust, Soviet-Jewish history does not easily fit into this paradigm.[59] Unlike their counterparts in occupied Poland and nearly everywhere else in East Central Europe, Soviet Jews were never stripped of their citizenship. Even though the Nazis certainly collapsed their enemy status as Bolsheviks with their racial status as Jews, Soviet Jews survived, fought, and died under the hammer and sickle. In fact, they were inclined to be more loyal to the state as a result of the war and to enjoy many of the benefits that Soviet citizenship conferred on defenders of the fatherland. By contrast, the wartime process of counter-emancipation of European Jewry turned out to be permanent. Actually, this crucial distinction – despite many important differences, not least the relative scale of death and destruc-tion – brings the Soviet-Jewish experience closer to the American-Jewish experience as combatants in the war than it does to the legal "destruction of European Jewry"[60] in Germany and in the allied and occupied territories in the Nazi orbit.

There is a certain Soviet logic in official reluctance, after the war, to highlight what historians of Soviet Jewry call the "ethnic" aspect of Soviet-Jewish suffering; the controversial repression of the Holocaust "on Soviet soil" was not entirely a product of official antisemitism but also a consequence of the exclusive claims of Soviet military identity

[58] See Mordechai Altschuler, *Soviet Jewry on the Eve of the Holocaust: A Social and Demographic Profile* (New York and Oxford: Berghahn Books, 1998).

[59] See Zvi Y. Gitelman, "Politics and the Historiography of the Holocaust in the Soviet Union," in *Bitter Legacy: Confronting the Holocaust in the USSR*, ed. Gitelman (Bloomington: Indiana University Press, 1997), 14–42.

[60] Raul Hilberg, *The Destruction of the European Jews* (Chicago: Quadrangle Books, 1961).

on Jewish veterans, the most outspoken representatives of Soviet-Jewish wartime memory. Their powerful sense of belonging speaks to the success of Soviet-Jewish integration through combat and on the frontlines (again, this is not at all unlike the Americanization of Jewish GIs during World War II). It is surely significant that Jewish resentment of Soviet forgetting of the Holocaust became a serious issue not so much for the patriarchs and matriarchs of the wartime generation but for their children, alienated from the regime by the post-war state. Of course, Jewish veterans themselves often revisited their memories in light of their confrontation with the atrocities of Stalinism. The most famous case of this process of ideological revision is that of the Soviet-Jewish journalist and writer, Vassily Grossman (1905–1964); the contrast between his wartime diaries and his war novel *Life and Fate* (written after the war and published abroad in 1959) exemplifies the ambiguous afterlife of Soviet-Jewish patriotism.

How did Soviet Jewry live through the war? To begin with, hundreds of thousands Jewish men and women served in the Soviet military as well as in partisan units in Nazi-occupied territories. Casualty rates ran very high but they were no higher for Jewish soldiers than they were for anyone else. After the invasion of the Soviet Union in 1941, Jewish civilians in Belorussia and the Ukraine faced round-ups and murder at the hands of commando units (often staffed by local collaborators as well as by German soldiers); the most infamous of these shootings, and the largest, occurred at a place called Babi Yar. But the Soviet army also evacuated a large number of people from the eastern front; many Jews survived the war in Soviet Central Asia. Throughout the Soviet Union, Jewish men, women, and children tried to bear the common prospect of starvation, disease, and possible German victory as best they could. Jewish writers, poets, journalists, musicians, artists – the entire Jewish culture front – participated in the Soviet war effort. Uncovering and reporting the extent of Nazi crimes against the Jews became a regular feature of Soviet newspapers. Soviet photographers, many of them Jewish, supplied some of the earliest documentation of Nazi killing fields.[61] The Soviet Jewish Anti-Fascist Committee mobilized the Yiddishist intelligentsia as well as famous Jewish members of the Russian-speaking mainstream. Feelings of rage, defiance, and despair linked explicitly to Jewish "life and fate" at the hands of the Nazis legitimately merged with implacable Soviet hatred of the enemy. Ilya Ehreburg, notably ambivalent about his Jewish origins during the 1920s, experienced

---

[61] See David Shneer, *Through Soviet Jewish Eyes: Photography, War and the Holocaust* (New Brunswick, NJ: Rutgers University Press, 2011).

a kind of genealogical epiphany: "I grew up in a Russian city [Moscow],"
he confessed in 1941,

My mother tongue is Russian. I am a Russian writer. Like all Russians, I am now
defending my homeland. But Hitler and his followers have reminded me of something else: my mother's name was Hannah. I am a Jew. I say this with pride. Hitler
hates us more than anyone. And this is a credit to us [Jews].[62]

Ehrenburg's many Jewish readers had more reason than anyone else in the
USSR to take Hitler personally and to embrace the Soviet struggle against
fascism as their own righteous cause. This wartime legacy of Soviet-Jewish
patriotism made the pathological temper of the post-war campaign against
"Zionist cosmopolitans" that much harder to bear. The post-war state had
reneged on its contract with Russian Jewry.[63]

As the Cold War gained political traction, antisemitism began to play an
increasingly prominent role in Soviet state ideology and Soviet social life; its
resurgence marked the end of the heroic period of Jewish emancipation. In the
late twenties to early thirties, Stalin had gradually shut down the Soviet project
of Jewish regeneration; the Yiddish press was curtailed, Yiddish institutions
were closed, as was the Jewish Section of the CSPU. Like many of the other
leaders of newly proscribed deviations from the Stalinist principle "nationalist
in form, socialist in content," the Soviet Yiddish establishment underwent a
radical purge. Some of the most prominent people were dismissed from their
positions, arrested, and shot. But a number of prominent Soviet Yiddishists
survived the Great Terror (1937–1938) to play a visible role in Stalin's anti-
fascist campaign; some even attained very high rank. Moreover, the fate of the
Yiddishist intelligentsia did not have an adverse impact on Jewish social and
economic mobility; a great many Jewish "specialists" and Party members perished in the Terror, along with other prominent figures of various ethnic background (Georgian communists, for instance), but not because they were Jews.

Immediately after the war, however, the ideological attack on Yiddish
took a distinctly anti-Jewish turn. The 1948 murder of Solomon Mikhoels,
director of the State Yiddish Theatre and the head of the Anti-Fascist
Committee served as a sign of things to come: the shooting of Soviet-
Yiddish poets in 1952, the so-called Doctors' Plot, and Stalin's plan to
deport the Jewish population to the Soviet Far East. Fortunately, the Great
Leader died in 1953. Under Khrushchev, manifestations of antisemitism
at the level of social policy and in Soviet discourse became much less dramatic but much more insidious, often linked to ostensible "economic

[62] "To the Jews," in *An Anthology of Jewish-Russian Literature*, ed. Maxim D. Shrayer (Armonk, NY: M. E. Sharpe, 2007), 21, 532. Translation slightly altered.
[63] See Amir Weiner, *Making Sense of War: The Second World War and the Fate of the Bolshevik Revolution* (Princeton: Princeton University Press, 2001), 231–363.

crimes." For the first time in the history of the USSR, anti-semitic measures began to effect the Soviet-Jewish population as a whole. Khrushchev
and Brezhnev revived the counter-reform policies of Alexander III and
Nicholas II, compromising emancipation.

The change was linked to shifting Cold War alliances, aimed against
Israel and the US, and to domestic nationalities policy, specifically the co-
optation of native elites by the state at the expense of local minorities. Even
more oppressive than the constant barrage of transparently anti-semitic
rhetoric in the daily papers, was the introduction of quotas on Jewish university attendance and the attempt to limit Jewish professional advancement, especially in the sciences and the humanities, where technical
experts, known in Soviet parlance as "engineers," of Jewish origin had been
very prominent during the 1920s and 1930s. Combined with the general
climate of economic stagnation, which set in during the late 1960s–1970s,
these limitations on access to educational and career opportunities, not to
mention housing, durable goods, and other perks of a privileged Soviet
life, undermined the economic future of Soviet Jewry and undercut Jewish
faith in the Soviet state. Social gaps continued to widen; alienation from
the regime grew in Jewish circles at an even faster rate than among the
general population. In the 1960s, Russian intellectuals began to identify
the Soviet-Jewish condition with their own internal exile from Soviet society. Yevgeny Yevtushenko's belated lament for the forgotten Jewish dead of
Babi Yar became the anthem of the entire dissident movement. Despite the
official taboo on the memory of Jewish suffering, Yevtushenko promised,
on behalf of all Russian poets, "Nothing in me shall ever forget!"

> The "Internationale," let it thunder
> when the last anti-semite on earth
>   is buried forever.
> In my blood there is no Jewish blood.
> In their callous rage, all anti-semites
> must hate me now as a Jew.
> For that reason
>   I am a true Russian![64]

After 1967, the anti-semitic proposition that all Jews were traitors to
the Soviet government who secretly harbored Zionist sympathies became
something of a self-fulfilling prophecy as more and more Jewish families
began to consider emigration and the renunciation of Soviet citizenship. In
the *perestroika* period and in the unstable early years of the FSU, Russian
Jews, once again, sought economic and political emancipation with their

---

[64] "Babi yar (1961)," trans. George Reavey, *Twentieth-Century Russian Poetry: Silver and
Steel*, ed. Albert C. Todd and Max Hayward (New York: Doubleday, 1993), 807.

feet. Nearly a century after the great migration of the nineteenth century had come to an end, there is, once again, a Russian-Jewish Diaspora, spread across the Americas, Israel, and Western Europe.[65]

In the Diaspora, the Russianness of Soviet Jews has become, paradoxically, more visible than their Jewishness. Soviet Jews elect to speak Russian at home, embrace Russian literature as a source of intellectual pride and moral inspiration and remain, for the most part, resolutely secular. The failure of the late Soviet state to command the loyalty of Soviet-Jewish baby boomers and their children did not vitiate the success of the Soviet experiment in Jewish Russification. Much like post-expulsion Iberian Jews who combined Castilian high culture with a commitment to the preservation of Jewish ethnicity, even second-generation Soviet Jews find it difficult to assimilate the categories of personal ascription that characterize Jews belonging in their host societies. On the one hand, Soviet Jews are likely to reject a normative confessional commitment to religious observance; for the most part, they treat ritual performance as a signifier of heritage rather than an ethical obligation or a spiritual duty to God. Many of them, again much like Iberian-Jewish transplants, bear the cultural imprint of a mixed religious background and combine Jewish self-assertion with the rudiments of Christian (here, Russian-Orthodox) belief.[66] For Jewish Americans, Soviet-Jewish syncretism violates the basic distinction between Judaism and Christianity. In Israel, the high rates of intermarriage among Soviet-Jewish immigrants and their resistance to formal conversion to obtain the benefits of citizenship – a bargain that seems, strikingly, to recall the "political sacrament" of conversion to Orthodoxy demanded by the imperial government – presents a serious challenge to a state that claims to be integrally Jewish. While Americans and Israelis insist on seeing Soviet Jews as *marranos* seeking only to return to Judaism, Soviet Jews exhibit all of the complicated identity issue of *conversos*, who were similarly reluctant to throw their former selves overboard upon rejoining the Jewish fold. The comparison is rich in possibilities; but what Soviet-Jewish emancipation from the normative claims of both religion and nationalism will mean for the history of Judaism remains an open question.

---

[65] See Larissa Remennick, *Russian Jews on Three Continents: Identity, Integration and Conflict* (New Brunswick, NJ: Transaction, 2007).

[66] On Soviet-Jewish conversions to Russian Orthodoxy, see Judith Deutsch Kornblatt, *Doubly Chosen: Jewish Identity, the Soviet Intelligentsia and the Russian Orthodox Church* (Madison: University of Wisconsin Press, 2001).

SELECT BIBLIOGRAPHY

Aronson, I. Michael. *Troubled Waters: Origins of the 1881 Anti-Jewish Pogroms in Russia.* Pittsburgh: University of Pittsburgh Press, 1990.

Avrutin, Eugene M. *Jews and the Imperial State: Identification Politics in Tsarist Russia.* Ithaca, NY: Cornell University Press, 2010.

Bemporad, Elissa. *Becoming Soviet Jews: The Bolshevik Experiment in Minsk.* Bloomington: Indiana University Press, 2013.

Budnitskii, Oleg. *Russian Jews between Reds and Whites, 1917–1920.* Philadelphia: University of Pennsylvania Press, 2011.

Frankel, Jonathan. *Prophecy and Politics: Socialism, Nationalism and the Russian Jews, 1862–1917.* Cambridge: Cambridge University Press, 1981.

Freeze, ChaeRan Y. *Jewish Marriage and Divorce in Imperial Russia.* Hanover, NH: Brandeis University Press, 2002.

and Jay M. Harris, eds. *Everyday Jewish Life in Imperial Russia, 1772–1914.* Hanover, NH: Brandeis University Press, 2013.

Fürst, Juliane, "Born Under the Same Star: Refuseniks, Dissidents and Late Socialist Society." In *The Jewish Movement in the Soviet Union,* ed. Yaacov Ro'I, 137–163. Washington, DC: Woodrow Wilson Center Press, 2012.

Gitelman, Zvi Y. *Jewish Nationality and Soviet Politics: The Jewish Section of the CPSU, 1917–1930.* Princeton: Princeton University Press, 1972.

Judge, Edward H. *Easter in Kishinev: Anatomy of a Pogrom.* New York: New York University Press, 1992.

Klier, John D. *Imperial Russia's Jewish Question, 1855–1881.* Cambridge: Cambridge University Press, 1995.

Russia Gathers Her Jews: The Origins of the "Jewish Question" in Russia, 1772–1825. DeKalb: Northern Illinois University Press, 1986.

Litvak, Olga. *Conscription and the Search for Modern Russian Jewry.* Bloomington: Indiana University Press, 2006.

Haskalah: The Romantic Movement in Judaism. New Brunswick, NJ: Rutgers Rutgers University Press, 2012.

Meir, Natan, M. *Kiev, Jewish Metropolis: A History, 1859–1914.* Bloomington: Indiana University Press, 2010.

Mendelsohn, Ezra. *Class Struggle in the Pale: The Formative Years of the Jewish Workers' Movement in Tsarist Russia.* Cambridge: Cambridge University Press, 1970.

Moss, Kenneth B. *Jewish Renaissance in the Russian Revolution.* Cambridge, MA: Harvard University Press, 2009.

Nathans, Benjamin I. *Beyond the Pale: The Jewish Encounter with Late Imperial Russia.* Berkeley: University of California Press, 2002.

Petrovsky-Shtern, Yohanan. *Jews in the Russian Army, 1827–1917: Drafted into Modernity.* Cambridge: Cambridge University Press, 2009.

Pipes, Richard. "Catherine II and the Jews," *Soviet-Jewish Affairs* 5 (1975): 3–20.

Quint, Alyssa P. "'Yiddish Literature for the Masses?': A Reconsideration of Who Read What in Jewish Eastern Europe," *AJS Review* 29 (2005): 61–89.

Remennick, Larissa. *Russian Jews on Three Continents: Identity, Integration and Conflict.* New Brunswick, NJ: Transaction Press, 2007.

Shneer, David. *Yiddish and the Creation of Soviet Jewish Culture, 1918–1930*. Cambridge: Cambridge University Press, 2004.

Sicher, Ephraim. *Jews in Russian Literature after the October Revolution: Writers and Artists between Hope and Apostasy*. Cambridge: Cambridge University Press, 1996.

Stampfer, Shaul. *Lithuanian Yeshivas of the Nineteenth Century: Creating a Tradition of Learning*. Oxford: Littman Library of Jewish Civilization, 2012.

Stanislawski, Michael F. *Tsar Nicholas I and the Jews: The Transformation of Jewish Society in Russia, 1825–1855*. Philadelphia: The Jewish Publication Society, 1983.

Zionism and the Fin de Siècle: Cosmopolitanism and Nationalism from Nordau to Jabotinsky. Berkeley: University of California Press, 2001.

Ury, Scott. *Barricades and Banners: The Revolution of 1905 and the Transformation of Warsaw Jewry*. Stanford: Stanford University Press, 2012.

Veidlinger, Jeffrey. *Jewish Public Culture in the Late Russian Empire*. Bloomington: Indiana University Press, 2009.

Zipperstein, Steven J. *The Jews of Odessa: A Cultural History, 1794–1881*. Stanford: Stanford University Press, 1986.

CHAPTER 3

POLAND

SCOTT URY

INTRODUCTION

Extending from the German border in the west to the Russian lands in the east and from the Baltic sea in the north to the Carpathian Mountains in the south, Poland – in its various shapes and sizes – has stood at the heart of Europe for centuries. One reflection of Poland's centrality over the ages is the critical place and role of the Jews of Poland. Indeed, throughout the nineteenth and the first half of the twentieth-centuries, Poland was home to the largest Jewish community in the world. The centrality of the Jews of Poland continued throughout the Second World War and even after the war as Holocaust survivors and other members of the Polish-Jewish and Polish Catholic Diasporas repeatedly turned to Poland as the *terra sancta* of Jewish and Polish histories and cultures. This key role in the collective memories and histories of two vibrant and active diaspora communities that longed for their respective narratives of national liberation, rehabilitation, and honor has repeatedly placed Poland and its Jewish residents at the center of a series of ongoing debates in Poland, Israel, the United States, and other lands. As a result, Poland – both as an actual territory and as a symbolic home – continues to serve as a lightning rod for a variety of key issues in Jewish and European histories, memories and collectivities: empires and nations, war and destruction, totalitarianism and democracy, liberation and redemption.

For these reasons, an understanding of Jewish society and culture in nineteenth- and twentieth-century Poland is critical for students and scholars of modern Jewish history, as well as those interested in the development of Eastern Europe, if not the entire European continent. Moreover, while initial encounters with the modern state, movements for religious revival, attempts at cultural and social integration, the impact of industrialization and urbanization, and the advent of modern political movements characterize the experience of many European Jewish communities in the nineteenth century, few communities passed through these events and developments more intensely than Jews in Polish lands. The same can also be said of key aspects of the twentieth century, however brief and horrific it was, especially in Eastern Europe. Ultimately, the experiences of modern war, the challenges of minority politics in the era of the nation-state, genocide, confrontations with totalitarian systems, the transition to democracy and the long-awaited entrance of Poland (and other parts of Eastern Europe) into a radically reconfigured Europe has inseparably bound the Jews of Poland to Polish society and to the course of the twentieth century.

This chapter discusses these and other questions through a chronological analysis of the course of Jewish history and changes in Jewish society in Polish lands from the late eighteenth century to today. Beginning with an analysis of Jewish society on the eve of the great partitions, the chapter continues by examining interactions between Jews and the imperial state, internal developments in the realm of Jewish society and religion, and larger social and political changes that took place toward the end of the nineteenth century. After a discussion of the impact of World War I, the article continues by looking at the trials and tribulations of Polish Jewry in the interwar era, with a particular emphasis on the educational and political realms. This analysis of the interwar era is followed by an overview of the developments during the period of German occupation during World War II and the implementation of Nazi policies in Poland. The penultimate section addresses the experiences of Jews immediately after the Holocaust and during the Communist era. The article concludes with a brief discussion of the parallel transformations of Polish and Jewish societies after the dramatic fall of Communism in 1989.

While intended as an overview for students, non-specialists, and interested readers, the essay revolves around several thematic and methodological points that will also be of interest to scholars. First, this chapter repeatedly places "the Jews of Poland" in a particular historical and geographic space, that of Polish lands. Unlike many works in the past, Jews are framed and portrayed as being "of Poland" and not just "in Poland."[1] Secondly, despite the fact that "the end" of Polish Jewry (the Holocaust) is clear to all, this essay attempts to avoid historical teleology. As incomprehensible and tragic as the events of the Second World War were, the essay is not meant to be read as a prelude to a pre-destined disaster, but, rather, as a historical summary of two-hundred years of Jewish life in Polish lands. Another critical aspect of this essay is one of identification

---

[1] On this point, see Adam Teller and Magda Teter, "Borders and Boundaries in the Historiography of the Jews in the Polish-Lithuanian Commonwealth," *Polin* 22 (2010): 3–46; and, Israel Bartal and Scott Ury, "Jews and Their Neighbours: Isolation, Confrontation and Influence," in *Jews and Their Neighbours since 1750*, eds. Israel Bartal, Antony Polonsky, and Scott Ury (Oxford: Littman, 2012), 3–30.

and terminology. As Poland ceased to exist as an independent political entity for most of the nineteenth century, many Jews were not sure if they themselves were "Russian Jews," "Polish Jews," "Poles of the Mosaic Faith," or just Jews. Therefore, I have tried to avoid pre-determining later historical phenomena associated with terms like "Poland" and "Polish Jewry" and prefer to employ more exact terminology like "Polish lands" and "the Jews of Poland." My hope is that such linguistic practices will help elucidate many of the tensions that characterized the path of Poland's Jews from partitions to post-Communism. Lastly, as part of larger transformations regarding the study of Polish and East European Jewry since 1989, much of this essay rests on scholarship written since the fall of Communism and penned by authors from the three major centers of research on Polish Jewry: Poland, the United States, and Israel. As such, this essay on "The Jews of Poland" reflects a new generation of scholarship that has come of age since the dramatic conclusion of the twentieth century.

"THOSE WERE THE DAYS!": THE JEWS OF THE POLISH-LITHUANIAN COMMONWEALTH

Although Jewish and Polish legends of pride and prejudice often claim over a thousand years of Jewish history in Polish lands, sources documenting a continuous Jewish presence in Polish lands date back to the late eleventh or the early twelfth centuries. In the centuries that followed, Jewish communities began to grow as a result of several factors. First, many Jews from German-speaking lands migrated (some would say fled) eastward in response to growing tensions between Christians and Jews and restrictive regulations in Western European lands. In response to this wave of Jewish migration eastward, Polish magnates and other rulers offered privileges and rights that were beneficial for Jewish newcomers. Outlined in the 1264 Statute of Kalisz granted to the Jews by Duke Bolesław the Pious, different privileges (royal and later noble) regularly granted new Jewish communities and their members a range of religious, residential, and economic rights that made settling in Poland a tempting offer for many Jews. Although privileges varied, they often granted Jews the right to settle, trade, and practice their religion. Many Jewish communities were also granted the right to construct houses of worship, cemeteries, and other physical institutions that lent a sense of presence and permanence to Jewish life in Polish lands.

As a result of these and other factors, the Jewish population of early modern Poland grew rapidly from some 100,000–150,000 in 1660 to approximately 600,000–750,000 in 1764–1765 (roughly 5–7 percent of a total population of some 11 million residents). Most of the Jews who settled in Polish lands did so in towns or cities. Due to these demographic patterns, Jews made up close to 50 percent of the urban population in both royal and privately owned towns as well as towns owned by the Catholic Church. Moreover, while roughly one-third of the Jewish population lived in the Commonwealth's western half, the vast majority of Jews settled in the eastern and southeastern parts of the Polish-Lithuanian Commonwealth. These settlement patterns were augmented by occupational trends that found some one-third of the Jews concentrated in either domestic or international commerce, and another third in some aspect of the lucrative alcohol trade. Alongside those Jews who lived in cities, roughly 25 percent of the Commonwealth's Jewish population lived in small towns with relatively few Jews, usually around two families each. Many of these small town or rural Jews worked as leaseholders or innkeepers on noble estates where they performed economic functions that connected the nobles to the peasantry such as administering noble lands, collecting dues, and managing various pre-modern means of production.[2]

In addition to being granted freedom of religious practice, economic activity and movement, Jews were also granted the right to organize and administer internal communal affairs on the local, regional, and inter-communal level. Local Jewish communal matters were administered by the *kahal* (community) which was responsible for religious and educational affairs as well as collecting taxes. The *kahal* also appointed judges who ruled on internal Jewish matters. The *kahal* wielded additional influence by employing communal officials such as rabbis, scribes, cantors, and ritual slaughterers. Local Jewish communal bodies also had the right to administer punitive measures such as writs of exclusion, acts of public shaming, and even physical violence. Despite its oligarchical character and dominance by the communal elite, the *kahal*'s officers rotated monthly. Together, distinctive residential patterns, occupational structure and communal organizations lent a sense of community to Jewish residents as well as a sense of difference from their neighbors in early modern Poland.[3]

The political, financial, and legal concerns of local Jewish communities were usually represented to the ruling powers by regional and national Jewish bodies. While initially created to assist with the collection of taxes and other administrative matters, inter-communal bodies quickly became

---

[2] On these developments, see Gershon David Hundert, *Jews in Poland-Lithuania in the Eighteenth Century: A Genealogy of Modernity* (Berkeley: University of California Press, 2004), 21–31; and Glenn Dynner, *Yankel's Tavern: Jews, Liquour and Life in the Kingdom of Poland* (New York: Oxford University Press, 2013).

[3] Hundert, *Jews in Poland-Lithuania*, 79–98.

symbols and bastions of Jewish authority, autonomy, and power. Founded at some time in the second half of the sixteenth century, the Council of Four Lands (*Va'ad Arba Aratsot*) and the Council of the Land of Lithuania (*Va'ad Medinat Lita*) were responsible for a wide range of political, judicial, and administrative activities. Inter-communal councils met twice a year at commercial fairs in Lublin and Jarosław and included representatives of the different regional councils. As a result of this high level of political sophistication, some observers– including the Jewish historian and political activist Simon Dubnow– have pointed to these bodies as early modern predecessors to the national politics that characterized Jewish society in early twentieth-century Eastern Europe.[4]

Thus, while the Jews were a distinct community in Polish lands, they were, in many senses, also integral parts of the variegated society that composed the early modern Polish-Lithuanian Commonwealth. Key economic roles, ongoing political activities, and the institutionalization of local rights not only made Jews part of Poland, but also ensured that Poland was part of the Jews' social, political, economic, legal, and intellectual worlds. In this and other cases, influence was often a two-way street. Moreover, while the collapse of the feudal order and the entry into the nineteenth century are often seen as the harbingers of a new set of radically different, inherently modern dilemmas regarding the nature, direction, and borders of Jewish society and its tension-filled relationship to Polish society, the sense of a distinctly Polish-Jewish culture and society struck roots among many Jewish residents of the Polish-Lithuanian Commonwealth and continued for generations among many of their descendants.

"ALL THE KING'S HORSES": THE PARTITIONS OF POLAND, THE END OF THE FEUDAL ORDER AND THE TRIALS OF THE LONG NINETEENTH CENTURY

The three major partitions of the Polish-Lithuanian Commonwealth in 1772, 1793, and 1795 marked not only the final days of the Commonwealth but also the end of the early modern paradise that Jews and Poles had created for themselves in Eastern Europe. No longer the masters of their own domains, the residents of the Commonwealth had to contend with the centralizing desires and bureaucratic machinations of the three partitioning powers: Austria, Prussia, and Russia. Ongoing encounters with official attempts at social reform and the bureaucratic need for order

---

[4] Simon Dubnow, "Autonomism: The Basis of the National Program," in *Nationalism and History: Essays on Old and New Judaism*, ed. Koppel S. Pinson (Philadelphia: Jewish Publication Society, 1958), 137–138.

would color Jewish society, culture, and politics in Polish territories for the better part of what is often referred to as the long nineteenth century, from 1772 to 1914.

Early indications of how governmental reform would contribute to fundamental changes in Jewish society appeared already in the final years of the Polish-Lithuanian Commonwealth. Frustrated with administrative inefficiency as well as charges of Jewish corruption, the Polish government decided to abolish the inter-communal Jewish councils in 1764. This drive to eradicate the institutions, mechanisms and practices that helped create and sustain Jewish communal autonomy fueled intense debates during the Four Year Sejm (legislative assembly) of 1788–1792 regarding the future shape of both Polish and Jewish societies. Through legal protests, political pressure and, at times, eruptions of popular violence, members of the urban and merchant classes in Warsaw and other cities demanded that additional restrictions be placed on Jewish residency and economic activity. Jewish leaders responded by submitting petitions to the Sejm Committee for Jewish Affairs and its Committee for Towns. These acts of intercession failed, and non-Christians were deprived of most political rights in towns and municipalities. That said, none of the reforms advocated by the various Sejm committees succeeded in changing the social or estate system in any significant way.[5]

Although a religious and spiritual movement at its core, the growth of Hasidism in Polish lands was also influenced by the collapse of the feudal order. Born in or around the year 1700, Yisrael ben Eliezer enjoyed a certain degree of prominence in the last third of his life as the leader of a movement of Jewish religious revival and reform that would become known as Hasidism. Based in the center of Międybóż, ben Eliezer was widely perceived as a faith healer as well as the leader of a circle of spiritually pious men known as Hasidim and was referred to by many as the *Ba'al Shem Tov* (the *Besht*, the Master of the Good Name). While scholars, such as Moshe Rosman and Immanuel Etkes, debate the extent to which the *Besht* actually created Hasidism, it is widely agreed upon that his image and teachings, as collected and canonized in the incredibly popular *Shivhei ha-Besht*, were later used to construct a new movement of Jewish religion and society that swept the Jews of Poland like a wildfire.[6] Thanks to

---

[5] Artur Eisenbach, *The Emancipation of the Jews in Poland, 1780–1870*, trans. Janina Dorosz, ed. Antony Polonsky (Oxford: Basil Blackwell, 1991), 111–112.

[6] On these academic debates, see Immanuel Etkes, *Ba`al ha-shem: ha-Besht: Magyah, mistikah, hanhagah* (Jerusalem: Shazar Center, 2000); and, Moshe (Murray) Rosman, *Founder of Hasidism: A Quest for the Historical Ba'al Shem Tov* (Berkeley: University of California Press, 1996).

studies by David Assaf, Glenn Dynner, and Marcin Wodziński, one can now trace the Hasidic "conquest" of Jewish towns and communities in the late eighteenth and early nineteenth centuries.[7] Starting with the second generation of Hasidic leaders and centering around the figure of Dov Ber the *maggid* of Mezeritch (d. 1772), Hasidism was transformed from a myriad of circles of pious men into the dominant religious, social, and political movement in Polish lands. While scholars debate whether the movement took off due to spiritual innovations (such as intense prayer sessions, a reappraisal of Talmudic study, and new forms of community that revolved around more intimate circles and experiences) or due to institutional and political changes, few question the sudden rise and newfound supremacy of Hasidism in Polish lands, including Galicia. One sign of Hasidism's incredible popularity was that the main Jewish opponent of Hasidism, Elijah the Gaon of Vilna and his supporters, the *misnagdim* (the opponents), made little headway in Polish territories. In fact, the religious and social divides between these two camps often mark the very divide between the Jews of Poland and those in Lithuanian lands.

In addition to helping give rise to the new movement of Hasidism, the institutional vacuum created by larger political changes also helped produce a new Jewish economic elite. The transition from a feudal economy based on cooperation between Jews and nobles to an economy grounded in commercial trade and government contracts gave birth to a new set of entrepreneurs among Jews in Polish centers with strong ties to Jewish communities elsewhere. Providing supplies to armies struggling against the Napoleonic invasions and procuring credit for government projects proved to be profitable endeavors for entrepreneurs like Jadyta (Yehudis) Jakubowicz of Warsaw, her husband Szmul Jakubowicz (Zbytkower), Benjamin and Simon Symons, and others. Together, these Jewish merchants and traders quickly became key figures in the Polish economy and leaders of the newly reconfigured Polish-Jewish society of the early nineteenth century.[8]

While Dynner has argued that many of these new elites supported the rise of Hasidism, they also advocated Jewish integration into Polish

---

[7] David Assaf, *The Regal Way: The Life and Times of Rabbi Israel of Ruzhin* (Stanford: Stanford University Press, 2002); Glenn Dynner, *Men of Silk: The Hasidic Conquest of Polish Jewish Society* (New York: Oxford University Press, 2006); and, Marcin Wodziński, *Haskalah and Hasidism in the Kingdom of Poland: A History of Conflict* (Oxford-Portland, OR: Littman, 2005).

[8] On this new class of Jewish entrepreneurs, see Cornelia Aust, "Between Amsterdam and Warsaw: Commercial Networks of the Ashkenazic Mercantile Elite in Central Europe," *Jewish History* 27, no. 1 (2013): 41–71.

society as well as different government efforts to reform Jewish society.[9] Those supporting Jewish integration gained ground between 1795 and 1807 when large parts of central Poland fell under Prussian rule. During this period, Prussian authorities implemented reforms and attempted to regulate Jewish society in the spirit of the German Enlightenment. As part of these efforts, Jews in Poland were granted legal rights including those of residency and employment. Often, these rights were conditional upon the success of various efforts to reform the Jews and integrate them into the reigning administrative, social and economic systems. These and related patterns continued between 1807 and 1815 after these areas fell under French administrative rule and the region became known as the Duchy of Warsaw. This spirit of enlightenment and reform continued during the years of the Kingdom of Poland (1815–1830) when central Poland maintained a relatively autonomous status under Russian protection. During this period, attempts to reform Jewish religious and economic practices led to increased taxes on kosher slaughter and a ban on Jewish inn-keeping.[10] As part of these reform efforts, Jewish communal autonomy was abolished in 1822 in Congress Poland and in 1815 in the Prussian Grand Duchy of Posen.

Although not always successful, these early reforms were supported by a small group of Jewish reformers that included Menahem Mendel Lefin of Satanów, Joseph Perl of the Galician town of Tarnopol, Antoni Eisenbaum of Warsaw, and others. Together, these and other Jews formed the early supporters of the Jewish Enlightenment, the Haskalah, in Polish lands. During the period of the Four Year Sejm, Lefin and the French-educated Jacques Calmanson prepared proposals for legislative reforms. Although still a small minority among local Jews, these early Jewish enlighteners found support among their Christian interlocutors like the Freemason and anti-clericalist Stanisław Potocki and the leading ideologue and politician Stanisław Staszic. That said, while both sides agreed that Jewish society was in need of reform and improvement, significant divides remained regarding how much reform was necessary and what means were to be used to enforce these measures.

In 1826, the Warsaw Rabbinic School was established and was administered by the local maskil Antoni Eisenbaum. A stalwart of the Haskalah in Polish lands, Eisenbaum also ran the first Polish Jewish journal, the government-supported bilingual Polish and Yiddish weekly, *Dostrzegacz*

---

[9] See Dynner, *Men of Silk*, 89–116.

[10] Stefan Kieniewicz, "The Jews of Warsaw, Polish Society, and the Partitioning Powers, 1795–1861," in *From Shtetl to Socialism: Studies from POLIN*, ed. Antony Polonsky (London: Littman, 1993), 90. Also see Dynner, *Yankel's Tavern*.

Nadwiślański / Der beobakhter an der Vayksel (The Observer on the Vistula), which was published between December 1823 and September 1824. Ultimately, the actions of Eisenbaum and other members of this early generation of Jewish enlighteners (maskilim) helped create the language, concepts, and institutions that would enable future generations of Jews (and Poles) to imagine and search for the common ground necessary to reform both Polish and Jewish societies.

This movement towards reform and inter-ethnic solidarity was bolstered further during the Polish Uprising of 1830–1831. While the majority of Poland's Jews remained neutral in the struggle between Polish aspirations for self-determination and Russian desires to maintain control over the empire, several hundred Jews decided to join the Polish National Guard and were required to adopt European dress and shave their beards in order to do so. Moreover, some 1,000 Jews participated in the pro-Polish Civil Guard, which was supported by Warsaw's Jewish community. Despite these and other acts of solidarity, the Uprising was defeated and the Russian Empire soon re-asserted its control over Congress Poland. In response to the insurrection, local Polish autonomy was abolished, the Polish army was disbanded, and Russian administrators began to run the ten Russian provinces of Russian Poland.[11]

Despite these restrictive measures, the period between the two Polish insurrections – 1831 and 1863 – was a one of significant economic, civic, and political development. These changes often led to new pressures for increased Jewish integration into wider social and political frameworks. Here, as well, integration was regularly conditioned upon the Jews' ability to shed their old habits and to begin contributing to, taking part in, and become parts of Polish society. While freedom came in a variety of shapes and sizes, it also demanded a price: change. Two aspects of Jewish society that reformers deemed particularly problematic at the time were the over-concentration of Jews in urban environments and their continued practice of ostensibly unproductive professions. In 1840, for example, over 85 percent of Jews lived in towns where they accounted for some 40 percent of the Congress Kingdom's urban population.[12] Attempts to reform the Jews included memoranda submitted by the leader of the Jewish Enlightenment Jakub Tugenhold in 1836 and again in 1851 to establish a vocational school in Warsaw where young Jews would learn "useful trades" and become blacksmiths, upholsters, locksmiths, and other types of craftsmen. As part of these plans for occupational reform, a Jewish orphanage established in Warsaw provided vocational training between 1841 and 1861.

---

[11] Eisenbach, *The Emancipation of the Jews*, 252–255 and 294.
[12] Eisenbach, *The Emancipation of the Jews*, 264.

Later, the Society for the Encouragement of Jews in the Polish Kingdom, established by Mathias Rosen and others in 1860, continued such efforts aimed at the professional "productivization" of the Jews of Poland.[13] Despite these efforts by government officials, Polish reformers and their Jewish supporters, reform projects were not as drastic as parallel efforts undertaken in Russia's Pale of Settlement. For instance, the conscription act implemented in the Kingdom of Poland in 1843 was far less severe than the one implemented in Russian territories by Tsar Nicholas I in 1827.[14]

Government and reformist efforts to recast Jewish communal structures and occupational profile continued after the Revolutions of 1848, which left central Poland relatively untouched. An official decree in 1848 continued the policy of removing Jews from rural areas and prohibiting them from participating in so-called harmful occupations such as inn-keeping. An additional ruling in 1851 forbade Jews from engaging in the slaughter and trade of meat in villages. Such restrictions were matched by limitations preventing Jews from joining guilds and employing Christian servants as well as those that prohibited them from working as municipal lawyers, pharmacists, physicians, and other public servants. The ongoing mixture of coercion and reform was best expressed in the decree of 1851, which demanded that Jews abandon traditional Jewish dress and adopt so-called Christian attire.[15] In this and other cases, reformers, enlighteners and defenders of the Jewish people repeatedly asked if a Jew could become a member of Polish society and, if so, how and at what price.

The ascension of Tsar Alexander II to the Russian throne in 1855 brought a new era of reform to the empire. Anticipation of far-reaching changes grew among many Jews in the Congress Kingdom and among members of other groups across the empire. At the time, the growing circle of bourgeois Jews were among the most hopeful. By the mid-nineteenth century, a new class of Jewish industrialists and merchants had begun to coalesce in Lodz, Warsaw, and other centers. Although they often started their careers in industries like tobacco factories and sugar production, many moved on to more modern endeavors like railroad construction and large-scale finance. Members of this new class of Jewish industrialists and financiers were often centered around family relations, and prominent families like the Rosens and the Nathansons in Warsaw were not only influential in local industry and business, but also in Jewish affairs and even in non-Jewish philanthropies and related activities. For example, the sugar

[13] Eisenbach, *The Emancipation of the Jews*, 401.
[14] Wodziński, *Haskalah and Hasidism in the Kingdom of Poland*, 37.
[15] Eisenbach, *The Emancipation of the Jews*, 377–378 and 380.

magnate and financier Mathias Bersohn of Warsaw created a museum in 1853 and hosted a Polish literary salon in his home on Elektoralna Street.[16]

Encouraged by the economic elite and hopeful of the reforms implemented by the "Tsar Liberator" Alexander II, a new generation of Jewish intellectuals and activists began to grow in this period. Openly advocating cooperation between Poles and Jews in the economic, social, and political realms, Jakub Tugenhold, Abraham Stern, and others worked to reform Jewish society. Together, they advocated the end of Jewish communal separation, the institution of a secular educational program for Jews, the adoption of more "productive" occupations, and increased loyalty to the state and the monarch. These activities were very often grounded in and drew strength from new institutions of enlightenment and reform like the Warsaw Rabbinic Academy, the "German" (or Progressive) synagogue on Daniłowiczowska Street in Warsaw that was established in 1802, and a similar institution in Lodz founded in the 1840s. However, unlike earlier generations, such reform-minded sentiments were not limited to small circles. Over the course of its thirty-five years of operation, the Warsaw Rabbinic Academy matriculated over 1,200 candidates, who together formed a new generation of Jewish leaders in Poland. Although centered in Warsaw, advocates of the Jewish Enlightenment could also be found in the movement's other center, the city of Zamość as well as smaller towns like Płock, Kalisz and Częstochowa and the new industrial center of Lodz.[17] This new generation of leaders also included members of the rabbinate like the young Markus Jastrow, the preacher of the "German" synagogue on Daniłowiczowska Street, and Dov Beer Meisels, the rabbi of Warsaw since 1856, both of whom supported educational, social, and political cooperation between Poles and Jews.[18] The goal of social integration was similarly supported by leaders of Warsaw's organized Jewish community (*gmina*) like Mathias Rosen and Hilary Nussbaum, who called for an end to governmental restrictions regarding Jews and claimed that Jews could be productive, law abiding members of Polish society who deserved to be viewed and welcomed as equals. Despite such fervent calls for integration, it would be an over-simplification to claim that these reformers wished to erase all differences between Poles and Jews. In most cases they envisioned some hybrid state in which Jews would maintain certain aspects of their Jewish religion, culture, and a distinctly Jewish sense of self but would also be accepted as members of Polish society.

---

[16] Eisenbach, *The Emancipation of the Jews*, 388–389.
[17] Wodziński, *Haskalah and Hasidism in the Kingdom of Poland*, 43–45, 46, and 49.
[18] Eisenbach, *The Emancipation of the Jews*, 390.

The condition of the Jews and their place in Polish society were frequently discussed in the burgeoning Polish public sphere. Thanks, in part,
to relaxed censorship regulations, forums like the Polish newspaper *Gazeta
Warszawska* (The Warsaw Gazette) began to debate the status and place
of Jews in Polish society. In addition to responding to these debates with
spirited defenses, Jewish activists petitioned the government to permit the
establishment of a Jewish journal in Polish. Under the stewardship of the
maskil Daniel Neufeld, *Jutrzenka: Tygodnik dla Izraelitów polskich* (The
Dawn: A Weekly for Polish Israelites) was published between 1861 and
1863. The paper soon became a platform to promote the construction of
a common ground for Poles, Jews, and those who viewed themselves as
representatives of the new community that would soon become known
as Polish Jews. Widespread changes that many had long waited for and
worked toward seemed to be taking shape in Warsaw, Lodz, and other
centers.

The social and ideological movement toward some form of Polish-
Jewish rapprochement (if not community) gained ground in the years
preceding the January Insurrection of 1863.[19] In a moment later immortal-
ized in a painting by the Polish-Jewish painter Aleksander Lesser, Jastrow
and Meisels participated alongside representatives of the Protestant and
Catholic communities in the funeral for five victims of anti-government
demonstrations in Warsaw in 1861. After being arrested and then deported
for their actions, Jastrow and Meisels both returned to Warsaw and took
part in the Polish Insurrection of January 1863. Although Jastrow and
Meisels represent prominent cases of Jewish solidarity with a burgeoning sense of Poland and Polishness, many other Jews threw their support
behind the Polish uprising and nation.[20] At the same time, there were
many Jews who preferred to remain neutral in the struggle for Polish
independence, others who believed that the imperial system was the best
option for minorities like the Jews, and a third group that began to search
for an autonomous, Jewish-oriented solution to the problems posed by
the growing tensions between empires and nations. Like the Uprising of
1830–1831, the Insurrection of 1863 was defeated by Russian forces and the
imperial punishment was swift and sometimes deadly. Russian authorities
responded by abolishing the autonomous status of the Kingdom of Poland,
implementing restrictions upon the use of the Polish language and the

[19] See, for example, Magdalena Opalski and Israel Bartal, *Poles and Jews: A Failed
Brotherhood* (Hanover, NH: Brandeis University Press, 1992).
[20] See Theodore R. Weeks, *From Assimilation to Antisemitism: The 'Jewish Question' in
Poland, 1850–1914* (Dekalb, IL: Northern Illinois University Press, 2006), 45–48.

dissemination of Polish culture, and undertaking other measures designed to thwart Polish efforts towards independence.

Despite these measures, the decades leading up to World War I were a time of economic, industrial, and demographic growth in Polish lands. The overall population of central Poland almost doubled in this period, from over five million in 1865 to close to nine million by 1897. The Jewish population rose similarly at this time, from some 700,000 in 1865 to over 1,200,000 by the end of the nineteenth century. While the percentage of Jews among the general population grew relatively little from some 13.5 percent to roughly 14.5 percent, the second half of the nineteenth century witnessed the growth of new Jewish centers in cities like Lodz and Warsaw. The Jewish population in Lodz skyrocketed from approximately 10,000 residents in 1869 to almost 100,000 in 1897 and to some 170,000 on the eve of the First World War. A major textile center that grew dramatically in the second half of the nineteenth century, Lodz attracted Jewish, Polish, and German migrants. While many poor Jewish migrants settled in the new suburb of Bałuty (which was created in the 1850s by two Jewish entrepreneurs), other Jewish residents of Lodz became part of the new class of industrialists, including members of the Poznański family. During this period, the number of Jews in Warsaw grew almost threefold, from over 70,000 in 1864 to more than 210,000 by the end of the century.[21] As a result of these demographic changes, cities like Lodz and Warsaw had substantial Jewish populations that represented around one-third of the total residents. Smaller cities and centers had even higher percentages of Jews. By the turn of the century, Jews made up over 50 percent of the population of Lublin and Siedlce, over 40 percent of the inhabitants of Radom and Będzin, and over 30 percent of the residents of Kalisz and Piotrków. The exact source of this demographic growth is debated by researchers. Some claim that there was a sharp rise in the number of Jews who immigrated from the Russian Pale of Settlement, the so-called *Litvakes*, to these new centers in Polish lands. Others maintain that the rising Jewish urban population was due to internal migration from nearby towns and relatively high birth rates. Either way, the Jews of Poland were widely identified with these new cities and many other aspects of modern society.

Far-reaching demographic, technological, and social transformations changed the rhythm of daily life and often led to increased tensions in

[21] For these and other statistics, see Stephen D. Corrsin, "Aspects of Population Change and Acculturation in Jewish Warsaw at the End of the Nineteenth Century: The Censuses of 1882 and 1897," in *The Jews in Warsaw: A History*, ed. Władysław Bartoszewski and Antony Polonsky (Oxford: Basil Blackwell, 1991), 214.

Lodz, Warsaw, and other centers. Thus, while traditional Jewish historiography has long seen the pogroms of 1881–1882 as specifically anti-Jewish acts, more recent studies have attempted to place them within the context of break-neck urbanization, rapid demographic growth, and the quick pace of modernization that characterized wide parts of the Russian Empire.[22] Polish observers at the time were keen to point out the fact that the violence of 1881–1882 did not spread from the Russian Empire's southwestern regions to its Polish territories. One glaring exception was the anti-Jewish violence that broke out in Warsaw on Christmas Day 1881. Originating in the Holy Cross Church in Warsaw's Old Town, rumors and chaos soon led to assaults, looting, and acts of murder in Jewish neighborhoods nearby. While the number of casualties was relatively low by contemporary standards, some two thousand Jewish homes were damaged. Although shocking, many Polish and Jewish leaders attributed the violence to government forces or provocateurs, and not to local Poles.[23] Visions of Polish-Jewish harmony and hopes for a better world continued to dominate the imagination of large parts of the Polish and Jewish intelligentsia.

The growth of these new Jewish centers also changed the nature of Jewish society, culture, and community. After years of government restrictions, Jewish communal institutions were allowed to expand their activities in the decades leading up to World War I, and the communal board (*gmina*) administered a much wider range of religious, social and educational activities than in the past. Inspired by the spirit of Polish Positivism, the legally recognized communal organizations created new, large-scale philanthropic and educational projects throughout this period. Ludwik Natanson, President of Warsaw's organized Jewish community from 1871 to 1896, helped create a Jewish hospital, established a vocational school, and helped found the city's reformed synagogue on Tłomackie Street.

While the official *gmina* served as the focus of Jewish communal affairs, its position was soon challenged by a new wave of cultural institutions, political movements and communal activists that began to demand a different style and form of Jewish leadership and community in the late nineteenth and early twentieth-centuries. As the tsarist government relaxed censorship

[22] Compare, for example, S. M. Dubnow, *History of the Jews in Russia and Poland*, 2 (Philadelphia: Jewish Publication Society, 1918), esp. 249–251 and 259–261, to I. Michael Aronson, *Troubled Waters: The Origins of the 1881 Anti-Jewish Pogroms in Russia* (Pittsburgh: University of Pittsburgh Press, 1991); and Hans Rogger, "Conclusion and Overview," in *Pogroms: Anti-Jewish Violence in Modern Russian History*, ed. John D. Klier and Shlomo Lambroza (Cambridge: Cambridge University Press, 1992), 314–372.
[23] See Weeks, *From Assimilation to Antisemitism*, 74–86.

restrictions on newspapers and other publications, Warsaw became a thriving center of Jewish dailies and weeklies in several languages. By 1906, the city was home to five Yiddish dailies (*Der veg, Idishes tageblat, Der telegraf, Di naye tsaytung,* and *Unzer leben*), three Hebrew newspapers (*Ha-tsefirah, Ha-yom,* and *Ha-tsofeh*) and one Polish-language Jewish daily (*Nowa Gazeta).* All together, these publications had a combined distribution of over 100,000 copies daily. Moreover, it is unclear how many people read each specific newspaper as many were passed from hand to hand and others were read aloud in semi-public forums. These newspapers helped lay the foundations for the leading Yiddish dailies that would dominate Jewish culture and society for the next three and a half decades.

Many of the same young people who supported and led the Jewish press were also involved in other cultural affairs, including the newly legalized realm of Jewish theater. Here, too, large population centers were able to support new cultural projects including at least four Yiddish theaters in Warsaw and one in Lodz. Although less popular than theater in Yiddish, Jewish troupes also performed in Hebrew. Many Jews also frequented Jewish theater in Polish as well as the general Polish theater. Together with other public institutions and organizations, the Yiddish theater and the new Jewish dailies transformed the nature of urban society and culture for hundreds of thousands of Jews in Lodz, Warsaw, and other centers.[24]

Another new base of institutional and communal power among Jews in the former Congress Poland were the political organizations that began to appear and take shape in the region. The rapid industrialization and the growth of a new class of Jewish workers gave rise to socialist and revolutionary organizations among Jews. Founded in Vilna in 1897, the General Union of Jewish Workers in Lithuania, Poland, and Russia (the Bund), attracted many supporters in Warsaw, Lodz, Białystok, and other industrial centers. Their activities were illegal up to 1905 and, as a result, remained limited to secret meetings and sporadic public activities. That said, a core of several thousand members that sought to raise the consciousness of Jewish and non-Jewish workers had already coalesced. Proto-Zionist organizations like *Hibat Zion* (Lovers of Zion) also gained footholds in different centers including Białystok and Warsaw, which served as a center of *Hibat Zion* activity under the leadership of Shaul Pinhas Rabinowitz (*Shef'er*). Less hostile towards the tsarist regime and its empire, Zionist activities remained limited to fundraising for Jewish settlements in Palestine and educational activities. Still other Jews like the young Yitzhak Tabenkin and

---

[24] On these and related developments, see Scott Ury, *Barricades and Banners: The Revolution of 1905 and the Transformation of Warsaw Jewry* (Stanford: Stanford University Press, 2012), 141–171.

Nahum Nir-Rafalkes were attracted to organizations like Poale-Zion which advocated Ber Borochov's synthesis of Jewish nationalism and socialism. Other Jews gravitated towards distinctly non-Jewish organizations like the Polish Socialist Party (PPS), the Social Democracy of the Kingdom of Poland and Lithuania (SDKPiL) and smaller revolutionary organizations that thrived between the legal and illegal realms.

Many of these social, cultural, and political forces came to a head in and around the Revolution of 1905. Like many other residents of Russian Poland, tens, if not hundreds, of thousands of Jews joined the various protests against the tsarist regime. Although early protests against conscription for the Russo-Japanese War were often organized by the Bund, the Polish Socialist Party, the SDKPiL, and other revolutionary organizations, the level of commitment of Jewish participants to the ideals espoused by these organizations remains debated. Indeed, once the government instituted semi-democratic reforms like those outlined by the October Manifesto in 1905, many of the same Jewish residents who had earlier supported revolutionary parties began to place their support behind newly legalized political organizations (Jewish, Polish, and Polish-Jewish) that advocated Jewish participation in democratic processes like the elections to the Russian State Dumas. The elections to the First and Second Dumas in 1906 and 1907 were marked by an increased sense of conflict between Jews and Poles, and often degenerated into angry competition between two competing voting blocs rooted in ethnic differences. Tensions between Poles and Jews were exacerbated by the decision of the Polish National Democratic Movement (ND, *Endecja*) to implement anti-Jewish rhetoric throughout early electoral campaigns. These tensions and fears were further inflamed in the summer and fall of 1906 when anti-Jewish pogroms broke out in the Polish cities of Białystok and Siedlce. Although estimates regarding the exact number of victims vary, some eighty people were killed in the Białystok pogrom in early June, and approximately thirty in the Siedlce pogrom in September of that year.[25] Conflict between Poles and Jews was exacerbated further in the elections to the Fourth Duma in 1912. Humiliated by the election in Warsaw of a Jewish-backed socialist representative, the Polish National Democrats responded by implementing an economic boycott of Jewish shops and businesses. As in other cases, this boycott was enforced through threats and even acts of violence. Unlike the crisis of 1881–1882, by 1912 it was hard for observers to claim that open calls for and repeated acts of anti-Jewish violence were mere aberrations or the work of provocateurs. Once a key, albeit enigmatic, part

[25] Ury, *Barricades and Banners*, 214–271.

of Polish society, the Jews, the Jewish Question, and antisemitic attitudes had now become integral, central parts of Polish politics and society.[26] The hopeful visions that characterized the dreams and desires of Polish and Jewish reformers throughout the nineteenth century repeatedly clashed, crashed, and collapsed as Polish and Jewish societies entered a twentieth century grounded in distinctly modern means of political organization, thinking, and action.

These electoral battles were followed by the outbreak of World War I in August 1914. Much of the fighting during World War I took place in the lands between Germany and Russia, and, as a result, had disastrous effects on the Jews of Poland as well as those in the Russian Empire's Pale of Settlement. Frustrated by repeated defeats at the hands of German and Austrian armies, Russian forces either expelled or encouraged the flight of hundreds of thousands of Jews in Polish lands, the eastern Kresy region and Galicia.[27] These actions often came in response to rumors that Jews had sided with the invading German or Austrian forces. While estimates vary, scholars place the number of Jewish refugees at the time between 250,000 and 450,000. Additionally, hundreds, if not in the thousands of prominent Jews were kidnapped and held ransom by Russian troops. Disastrous, haphazard, and violent, the Russian retreat in 1915 created room for the arrival of German troops and the implementation of German administrative rule over much of what was once Russian Poland. Relative to the tsarist administration, German occupiers seemed rather benevolent. Jews were granted widespread political rights and, with the help of German Jewish reformers, new institutions were permitted to remold Polish Jewry. Educational, political and social projects grew during the period of German military rule and many helped pave the way for the unprecedented Jewish political and cultural revival in interwar Poland. As was often case in Eastern Europe, one person's invasion was another's moment of liberation.

"THE BEST OF TIMES, THE WORST OF TIMES": THE INTERWAR ERA

After over a hundred years of imperial rule, Poland gained political independence in 1918 along with the other nation-states of East Central Europe as a result of the Peace of Versailles and the Paris Peace Conference. Like many of the other newly minted nations, the advent of an independent Polish state was seen by many as the arrival of a new era in the history

---

[26] Weeks, *From Assimilation to Antisemitism*, 149–169.

[27] See, Alexander Victor Prusin, *Nationalizing a Borderland: War, Ethnicity, and Anti-Jewish Violence in East Galicia, 1914–1920* (Tuscaloosa: University of Alabama Press, 2005).

of the Polish nation. At the same time, independence created a series of dilemmas for many of Poland's approximately thirty million residents. With independent Poland's newly expanded borders, roughly 35 percent of its citizens were not ethnic Poles. In addition to Germans, Ukrainians, and Belorussians, there were some three million Jews who made up over 10 percent of the general population. Once again, Jews were disproportionately represented in urban regions where they numbered over 30 percent in Poland's larger cities like Lodz, Lwów, and Warsaw. As a result of these and related factors, Poland and other newly independent states were forced to sign the Minorities Treaty. Designed to protect the civil, religious, and cultural rights of national minorities, the Minorities Treaty and attitudes toward the document reflect both the blessings and curses of the interwar era, if not nationalism itself.[28]

Conflicts between Polish desires for independence and the place and status of Jews and other minorities in the independent nation-state began almost immediately with the early battles surrounding Polish independence between 1918 and 1921. As Polish forces advanced against Bolshevik and Ukrainian armies in the east, Jews in provincial centers and cities throughout the borderlands region were repeatedly accused of collaboration with hostile forces. In some cases, these charges degenerated to assaults and violence against local Jews including pogroms in cities such as Vilna, Pinsk, and Lwów.[29]

Although the anti-Jewish assaults associated with Polish battles for independence were viewed by some as the unfortunate side effect of battles for national liberation, a series of anti-Jewish measures adopted by the Polish Sejm (Parliament) between the two World Wars proved more difficult to rationalize. In 1919 the Polish Sejm passed the Sunday Rest Law. Ostensibly designed to re-enforce the Catholic nature of Polish society and to guarantee at least one day of rest for workers, the law adversely affected the ability of most Jews to earn a living and was seen by many as an anti-Jewish measure masquerading as labor reform. While it is not clear how effective authorities were in enforcing the law, the Sunday Rest Law colored the atmosphere in interwar Poland. Some fifteen years later, the Sejm passed another law that affected Jewish life, the 1936 ban on kosher slaughter. Like similar measures in Germany in 1933 and Italy in 1938, supporters of the ban claimed the need to protect animals from religious barbarism.[30] The anti-slaughter act was paralleled by the introduction of

---

[28] See Ezra Mendelsohn, *Zionism in Poland: The Formative Years, 1915–1926* (New Haven: Yale University Press, 1981); and Ezra Mendelsohn, *The Jews of East Central Europe between the World Wars* (Bloomington: Indiana University Press, 1983).

[29] Mendelsohn, *Zionism in Poland*, 88–91.

[30] Mendelsohn, *The Jews of East Central Europe between the World Wars*, 43 and 73–74.

quotas regarding the percentage of Jewish students allowed to study in Polish universities. As a result of these *numerus clausus*, the percentage of Jewish students in Polish universities decreased dramatically from almost 25 percent in 1921–1922 to a little over 8 percent in 1938–1939.

This wave of anti-Jewish legislation was paralleled by increasingly hostile attitudes towards Jews in the social and political realms. The death of Poland's beloved leader Józef Piłsudski in 1935, the rise of the Nazi party in Germany, and the economic depression all contributed to a noticeable growth of nationalistic and antisemitic activities in the late 1930s. These developments included the rise of new, far-right parties like the Camp of National Unity (OZN), public campaigns to promote mass Jewish emigration from Poland, Church propaganda against the Jews, and organized economic boycotts of Jews and Jewish businesses. These and other actions often spilled over to the realm of violence including sporadic but repeated pogroms. Between 1935 and 1937, almost 1,300 Jews were wounded and "hundreds of Jews were killed" in over 150 different attacks in towns and villages in Poland.[31] By the late 1930s, the situation in Poland was indeed grave. That said, as bad as things were in Poland, most scholars do not view these developments as factors leading directly to the events that took place in Nazi-occupied Poland during World War II. Large parts of Polish society were becoming more and more hostile towards Jews in the late 1930s, but there was no policy of mass extermination.

Despite these and other difficulties, Jewish politics and culture thrived and some would even say reached their peak in interwar Poland. With some three million Jews, legally recognized rights to educational, cultural, and communal autonomy, and a relatively democratic political system, Jewish political parties, communal organizations, and cultural activities flourished in Poland. Jewish political parties operated across the ideological spectrum from the Bund and Poale Zion on the left, to the General Zionists and *Folkspartey* (People's Party) in the center, to the religious *Agudes Yisroel* and Revisionist Zionists in the conservative camp. Led by Yitzhak Grünbaum, the General Zionists were particularly successful in the Sejm elections of 1922 and 1928. In both elections, Grünbaum led electoral coalitions composed of different national groups in a Minorities' Bloc.[32] While the General Zionists were successful in the 1920s, the Revisionist Zionists led by Vladimir (Ze'ev) Jabotinsky began to gain popularity in the 1930s. The new party received almost 30,000 votes to the Zionist Congress of 1931 and close to 65,000 in 1933. By 1936, it boasted of some 450,000

---

[31] Mendelsohn, *The Jews of East Central Europe between the World Wars*, 74.
[32] Mendelsohn, *Zionism in Poland*, 213–222.

members in its New Zionist Organization.[33] Although less prominent on the national stage, *Agudes Yisroel* was influential in elections to Jewish community boards (kehillot). Similarly, the Bund was far more successful in local elections than on the national stage.

In addition to political parties, party-affiliated youth movements grew in interwar Poland. Committed to promoting youth culture, Zionist organizations like *Dror* (Freedom) and *Hashomer Hatzair* (The Young Guard) included between 70,000 and 100,000 members in 1939. Some contend that the growth of youth movements reflected a larger crisis among Jewish youth in Poland, and that this crisis led many young Jews to turn to youth movements for structure and guidance. Despite the economic, social, and political hardships that many faced, emigration to Palestine (aliyah) remained a relatively limited phenomenon. Between 1918 and 1942, approximately 139,000 Jews migrated to British Palestine out of a total Jewish population of some 3,000,000.[34]

As part of their efforts to respond to the needs of Jewish youth in Poland, different parties created educational institutions and networks. The nationally oriented, secular Central Yiddish School Organization (*Tsysho*) had 120 elementary schools, three high schools and two teacher seminaries. The secular Zionist *Tarbut* (Culture) school system was even more successful, educating over 40,000 students in Hebrew between 1934 and 1937.[35] And the religious *Khorev* and *Beis Yaakov* schools had some 100,000 students in the same period. Despite these statistics, between 60 and 70 percent of all Jewish students studied in Polish public schools and not in Jewish frameworks.[36]

In addition to cultural and educational projects that were politically aligned, Jewish culture thrived in interwar Poland. Although founded before World War I, two Yiddish papers published in Warsaw – *Haynt* and *Der moment* – reshaped everyday life for hundreds of thousands of Yiddish-readers. Alongside these two mainstays of modern Jewish culture, there were hundreds of other daily and weekly papers in Hebrew, Polish, and Yiddish. Primarily published in Yiddish with a growing number of Polish titles, Jewish dailies were part of a larger constellation of popular cultural institutions that included Jewish theaters with regular performances in Yiddish and in Polish. While scholars debate the nature and impact of the stark dichotomies of daily life in interwar Poland, the strange combination of social exclusion and political tension with communal autonomy

[33] Mendelsohn, *The Jews of East Central Europe between the World Wars*, 53–54 and 76–77.
[34] Mendelsohn, *Zionism in Poland*, 110–120 and 223–227.
[35] Mendelsohn, *Zionism in Poland*, 189–196.
[36] Mendelsohn, *The Jews of East Central Europe between the World Wars*, 65–66.

and national culture helped create an unprecedented period of political activity and cultural production among Jews in interwar Poland.

WORLD WAR II AND THE HOLOCAUST

Little reflects the influence of geo-politics on the history of the Jews in Poland more than the German–Soviet division and conquest of the Second Polish Republic in September of 1939. In little over a month, Germany conquered and then annexed large parts of western and northern Poland into the eastern territories of the Reich, thus placing over ten million Poles and some 600,000 Jews under direct German rule. A German civil administration known as the *Generalgouvernement* was implemented over the rest of Polish territories which included over ten million Poles and roughly 1.3–1.5 million Jews. As a result of the Molotov–Ribbentrop non-aggression pact, Soviet troops conquered large parts of eastern Poland in September of 1939 and some four to five million Poles and approximately 1.2 million Jews came under Soviet rule. The fate of Poland's Jewish citizens over the next five years very often depended on which of these administrative zones they belonged to.[37]

On September 21, 1939, Reinhard Heydrich sent a directive outlining German policy towards Jews in Polish territories. This order included the expulsion of Jews from northwestern districts and the countryside and their concentration in the *Generalgouvernement* and its cities, the establishment of Jewish communal councils (*Judenräte*), and exemptions for economically useful Jews. The head of the *Generalgouvernement*, Hans Frank, issued similar decrees and other rulings including: ordering all Jews over the age of ten to wear a white armband with a blue Star of David, the prohibition of Jews from changing their residence, and the creation of forced labor details for Jews.[38]

Although historians debate whether or not there was a direct connection between Heydrich's orders and later, more deadly, developments, Frank also decided to establish Jewish Councils throughout the *Generalgouvernement*. Often chosen by German officials and designed to assist authorities in their implementation of anti-Jewish policies, members of local councils hoped that their actions would somehow soften the blow of German rule. The Councils undertook activities that previously fell under the jurisdiction of municipal authorities including housing, health-care, employment, and sanitation. Jewish Councils also had their own Jewish police that

---

[37] Yehuda Bauer, *A History of the Holocaust* (New York-London: Franklin Watts, 1982), 146–147.

[38] Bauer, *A History of the Holocaust*, 147–150.

would play key roles in the deportation process and in the confiscation of Jewish property. Although leaders of local councils like Adam Czerniaków in Warsaw, Marek Biberstein in Kraków, and Dr. Joseph Parnes in Lwów did their best to serve the interests of their local Jewish communities, their influence was restricted by German authorities. In other cases, *Judenräte* leaders like Mordechai Chaim Rumkowski in Lodz, Jacob Gens in Vilna, and Efraim Barasz in Białystok were accused of working more closely with German authorities by supplying Jewish labor in an attempt to curry the Nazis' favor. Ultimately, leaders of the *Judenräte* were entrusted with the difficult decision of selecting which Jews would be deported and which remained in local ghettos.[39] As a result, their actions were sharply criticized after the war by Hannah Arendt in her study *Eichmann in Jerusalem*, and in the courts and streets of Israel surrounding the Kastner affair and the subsequent assassination of Rudolf Kastner in 1957.

While the Jewish Councils were established as a result of a direct order, the process of concentrating Jews in self-enclosed Jewish enclaves (ghettos) was often undertaken independently by local authorities. As a result, conditions varied greatly between different ghettos. The first ghetto was an open one established in the city of Piotrków Trybunalski in October 1939. This was followed by the creation of a sealed ghetto in the city of Lodz in May 1940. In the area under the jurisdiction of the *Generalgouvernement*, ghettos were established between November 1940 and May 1941 including those in Warsaw, and Lublin and Kraków. Larger ghettos like the ones in Lodz and Warsaw were very often sealed off from the surrounding region by fences or walls; smaller ghettos often had much more porous borders. In regions occupied by Soviet forces in 1939, ghettos were established after the German invasion on June 22, 1941. Although scholars agree that Jewish ghettos were established to help facilitate the separation of Jews from Europe and society, it remains unclear whether or not the process of ghettoization was intended as part of a Final Solution that was dedicated to a policy of mass murder. On the one hand, conditions in most ghettos included crowded living quarters, poor sanitation, and minimal food rations that led to outbreaks of epidemics, famine, and high mortality rates. Thus, in 1941 alone some 43,000 Jews (over 10 percent of the population) died in the Warsaw Ghetto from illness, starvation, and disease, in particular typhus. On the other hand, there is no direct evidence to date which demonstrates that the process of ghettoization was intended as the first phase in a larger policy of extermination. That said, once the process of ghettoization began, the concentration of large numbers of Jews

[39] Bauer, *A History of the Holocaust*, 155–167.

in tightly enclosed areas under the rule of Jewish Councils facilitated the actual process of mass murder.[40]

While it remains unclear exactly who gave the direct order to exterminate the Jews of Europe and when that decision was made, most historians agree that the process of mass murder began with the German invasion into Soviet-occupied Poland in June 1941. There on the eastern front, the *Einsatzgruppen* followed the invading German army and began killing entire Jewish communities *en masse*. Hundreds of thousands of Jews were killed in this manner. Some scholars contend that these killings laid the foundations for the actual plan to exterminate the Jews of Europe. In fact, soon thereafter at the Wannsee Conference in January 1942, the *Generalgouvernement* was chosen as the place where the "Final Solution" would be implemented. Following the creation of the first extermination camp with gas chambers in Chełmno in late 1941, additional extermination camps were constructed in Bełżec, Sobibór, and Treblinka in early 1942. Soon thereafter, massive deportations of Jews began throughout the *Generalgouvernement*. These actions included large-scale deportations of Jews from Lublin in March and April of 1942, from Kraków in May and June of 1942, from Radom in August 1942, and from Białystok in February 1943. As the largest Jewish center in the region, the deportation of some 300,000 Jews from Warsaw lasted approximately ten weeks, between late July and mid-September 1942. In the year and half between March 1942 and October 1943, approximately two million Polish Jews were sent to their deaths.

While many remained helpless in the face of these unprecedented and perhaps incomprehensible developments, small groups in different ghettos and other areas began to organize various forms of armed resistance. The place, role, and effectiveness of armed revolts is still debated, especially among historians in Israel. Starting in Vilna, armed resistance spread to other ghettos including those in Będzin, Białystok, Częstochowa, Kraków, Lwów and, in perhaps the most celebrated case, in Warsaw. All told, there were between fifty and a hundred cases of armed resistance by Jews in different ghettos in Poland. Other Jews joined partisan movements or fled to family camps in forests. In some cases, Jews joined non-Jewish partisan groups, usually Communist or pro-Soviet organizations. Jews also initiated and took part in uprisings in concentration camps. Members of the Jewish *sonderkommando* revolted in Treblinka, Sobibór, and Birkenau. While none of these actions reversed the process of extermination or the course of the war, they remain central to many Jewish and Israeli interpretations of the period as proof of the Jews' bravery, heroism, and honor.

---

[40] Bauer, *A History of the Holocaust*, 168–191.

While Jewish and Israeli historians often focus on acts of armed resistance by Jews, the actions of those Poles who helped save Jews are meticulously documented and recorded by Polish historians. Here, too, the exact number of Jews who survived the war either in hiding or with false papers remains debated, as do the number of Poles who risked their own lives by taking part in such actions. The consensus is that somewhere between 30,000 and 50,000 Jews survived the war in Poland and the vast remainder spent the war in the Soviet Union. Many of those who were in Poland were assisted by ethnic Poles, including some 4,000 Jews who were assisted by the Polish Government in Exile's Council for Aid to Jews (*Żegota*). While scholars debate whether these actions represent the height of humanity or its nadir, between some 350,000 and 380,000 Polish Jews, or between 8 and 14 percent of Poland's pre-war Jewish population, survived the war through these and other means.

"O, BRAVE NEW WORLD!": THE COMMUNIST ERA

As Polish society attempted to re-organize and reconstruct itself in wake of the destruction wreaked across Polish lands by German and then Soviet armies, some 230,000–300,000 Jews returned to Poland after the war. While the vast majority of these survivors were concerned with recreating their own lives, a vocal minority of activists who survived the war in the Soviet Union and other frameworks were deeply committed to the Communists' construction of the Polish People's Republic.

Part of the larger struggle over the fate of post-war Poland included a series of armed conflicts between supporters of the Polish national camp, on the one hand, and members of the pro-Soviet, Communist forces, on the other. These armed conflicts fed a larger sense of chaos that sometimes spilled over into anti-Jewish acts. Although the July 4, 1946 pogrom in Kielce is the best-known of the post-war pogroms, similar events took place in Kraków, Białystok, Częstochowa, and other locations. All told, approximately six-hundred Jews were killed in such acts of violence in 1945 and 1946. While scholars debate the causes, motive and actors involved in the wave of violence, few disagree about its impact on many of those Jews who had returned to their native realm, Poland.[41]

Although Zionist activists like Yitzhak (Antek) Zuckerman and Avraham (Adolf) Berman were active in Poland before the Kielce pogrom, the events in Kielce in the summer of 1946 set off a wave of organized Jewish emigration from Poland, mostly to British Mandate Palestine. In

---

[41] See David Engel, *Ben shihrur le-brihah: Nitsole ha-Sho'ah be-Polin veha-ma'avak 'al han-hagatam, 1944–1946* ('Am 'oved: Tel Aviv, 1996).

the following months, some 100,000 Jews left Poland. By 1950, between 170,000 and 250,000 Jews had fled Poland. As a result of this organized migration, approximately 80,000–90,000 Jews were left in Poland by the time the Communists consolidated power in Poland and the State of Israel was created in 1948.

Struggles between Jewish Communists, on the one hand, and supporters of the Jewish national movement, Zionism, on the other, would color the experiences of Polish Jewry throughout the Cold War. Of the Jews who remained in Poland, there was a core of dedicated Jewish Communists. However, there was also a much larger, silent majority of Jews who for a variety of reasons chose not to emigrate to various locations. As in other post-war Communist countries like Romania, Czechoslovakia and East Germany, some Jews achieved high levels of prominence in the pro-Soviet Polish People's Republic. Avraham Berman's brother Jakub was part of a troika of Polish leaders in Stalin's pro-Soviet regime, as was another Jew Hilary Minc. The role of these Jewish Communists in implementing and sustaining a pro-Stalinist regime in post-war Poland is hotly debated by scholars to this day, often through the prism of the *żydokomuna*.[42] While many point to the high number of Jews in key government positions and the disproportionate number of Jews involved with the Communist security apparatus, others argue that the Soviet Union successfully implemented pro-communist regimes throughout Eastern Europe without the support of these and other Jews. Either way, the myth of the *żydokomuna* remains a dominant motif in post-war Polish society and one that has colored the last seventy years of Polish Jewish history.[43]

Despite the commitment of high-ranking Jewish officials to Communist visions, Jewish institutions continued to function in Communist Poland. Authorities permitted Jewish cultural activities such as that of the Jewish Social and Cultural Society (TSKŻ), Yiddish theater, and for part of the period even Jewish schools. At the same time, Jewish culture and Jewish lives seemed particularly precarious in the wake of the Holocaust and under the long shadow of Soviet Stalinism. As a result, the Jewish population of Poland continued to dwindle through repeated waves of migration. After the rise of Władysław Gomułka to power in 1956, some 50,000 Jews (including 14,000 repatriates from the Soviet Union) left Poland for

---

[42] Roughly translated as Judeo–Communism, the myth of *żydokomuna* served as a unifying principle for a series of preconceptions regarding the connection between Jews and Communism, including the belief that Communism was created, or at the very least led, by Jews as part of a larger effort to dominate Polish society.

[43] See, Krystyna Kersten, *Polacy, Żydzi, komunizm: Anatomia półprawd, 1939–1968* (Warsaw: Niezależna Oficyna Wydawnicza, 1992).

Israel. While the "Gomulka Aliyah" of 1956 is rarely viewed as being motivated by anti-semitic attitudes, Gomułka's angry speech in 1968 in wake of
the tensions in the Middle East and student demonstrations in Poland led
to widespread protests and ultimately to large-scale anti-Jewish campaigns
in which Poland's Jews were often portrayed and attacked as a pro-Zionist
fifth column. As a result of these protests and government harassment of
Jews (which included expulsion from the party and loss of employment)
an additional wave of migration of Jews from Poland after 1968 included
between 13,000 and 25,000 Polish citizens of Jewish descent. Although
approximately 25 percent migrated to Israel, many sought refuge in third
countries including Scandinavian lands.[44]

"'TIS NEW TO THEE": POLAND AFTER COMMUNISM

Although the events of 1968 have long been viewed as the end of almost
a thousand years of Jewish life in Polish lands, developments taking place
since 1989 have cast doubts on what seems to have been the pre-mature
recitation of the *kaddish* for the Jews of Poland. The fall of Communism
led to a wave of social, cultural, political and economic transformations
as Poland returned to what many had long claimed was its rightful place
in "the heart of Europe." One part of this process was a widespread confrontation in Poland with some of the darker aspects of the country's past,
including the role played by many in the Nazis' efforts to exterminate the
Jews of Europe. Spurred, in part, by the debates surrounding Jan T. Gross's
books *Neighbors* and *Fear*, many in post-Communist Poland began asking
difficult questions about what it meant to be a Pole in the twenty-first century.[45] This larger process also influenced public opinion regarding Jews and
their place in Poland, and this, in turn, helped create an atmosphere open
to a renewal of Jewish culture in post-Communist Poland. This renaissance
included the rebirth of Jewish culture and institutions in Poland's major
cities including Warsaw, Kraków, and Wrocław. While annual Jewish festivals in Kraków and other cities introduce tens of thousands of Poles to
various aspects of Jewish culture from klezmer music to Israeli folk dancing,
synagogues, communal organizations, and other bodies continue to lend
institutional support to the rebirth of Jewish culture on Polish lands. In
many cases, these efforts are assisted by international Jewish organizations

[44] See, Alina Cała and Helena Datner, eds. *Dzieje Żydów w Polsce 1944–1968: Teksty źródłowe*
(Warsaw: Żydowski Instytut Historyczny, 1997).
[45] Jan T. Gross, *Fear: Anti-Semitism in Poland after Auschwitz* (New York: Random House,
2006); and Gross, *Neighbors: The Destruction of the Jewish Community of Jedwabne,
Poland* (New York: Penguin, 2002).

like the Joint Distribution Committee (JDC), the Lauder Foundation and even Chabad as well as communal activists from Poland and abroad. Together with these international Jewish organizations, the children of Jewish Communists, the descendants of Polish-Jewish "Marranos," and self-proclaimed Catholic-Jews have begun to reconstruct Jewish religious, social, and cultural life, as Poland and its New Jews return to the fold of Europe. Finally, while the very image of active synagogues, vibrant youth groups, and dynamic cultural events may strike Jewish tourists in Kraków and Israeli youth on their way to commemorative marches from Birkenau to Auschwitz as counter-intuitive – if not blasphemous – little attests to the history of Polish Jews more than the renaissance of Jewish life taking place in Poland since the fall of the Berlin Wall in November 1989.

SELECT BIBLIOGRAPHY

Aronson, I. Michael. *Troubled Waters: The Origins of the 1881 Anti-Jewish Pogroms in Russia.* Pittsburgh: University of Pittsburgh Press, 1991.

Assaf, David. *The Regal Way: The Life and Times of Rabbi Israel of Ruzhin.* Stanford: Stanford University Press, 2002.

Aust, Cornelia. "Between Amsterdam and Warsaw: Commercial Networks of the Ashkenazic Mercantile Elite in Central Europe," *Jewish History* 27, no. 1 (2013): 41–71.

Bacon, Gershon C. *The Politics of Tradition: Agudat Yisrael in Poland, 1916–1939.* Jerusalem: The Magnes Press, 1996.

Bartal Israel and Scott Ury. "Jews and Their Neighbours: Isolation, Confrontation and Influence." In *Jews and their Neighbours in Eastern Europe since 1750*, ed. Israel Bartal, Antony Polonsky, and Scott Ury, 3–30. POLIN, 24. Oxford: Littman, 2012.

Bauer, Yehuda. *A History of the Holocaust.* New York-London: Franklin Watts, 1982.

Cała, Alina and Helena Datner, eds. *Dzieje Żydów w Polsce 1944–1968: Teksty źródłowe.* Warsaw: Żydowski Instytut Historyczny, 1997.

Corrsin, Stephen D. "Aspects of Population Change and Acculturation in Jewish Warsaw at the End of the Nineteenth Century: The Censuses of 1882 and 1897." In *The Jews in Warsaw: A History*, ed. Władysław Bartoszewski and Antony Polonsky, 212–231. Oxford: Basil Blackwell, 1991.

Dubnow, Simon. "Autonomism: The Basis of the National Program." In Dubnow, *Nationalism and History: Essays on Old and New Judaism*, ed. Koppel S. Pinson, 131–142. Philadelphia: Jewish Publication Society, 1958.

History of the Jews in Russia and Poland, vol. 2. Philadelphia: Jewish Publication Society, 1918.

Dynner, Glenn. *Men of Silk: The Hasidic Conquest of Polish Jewish Society.* New York: Oxford University Press, 2006.

Yankel's Tavern: Jews, Liquour and Life in the Kingdom of Poland. New York: Oxford University Press, 2013.

Eisenbach, Artur. *The Emancipation of the Jews in Poland, 1780–1870*, trans. Janina Dorosz, ed. Antony Polonsky. Oxford: Basil Blackwell, 1991.

Encyclopedia of the Holocaust. Ed. Yisrael Gutman. New York: Macmillan.

Engel, David. *Ben shihrur le-brihah: Nitsole ha-Sho'ah be-Polin veha-ma'avak 'al hanhaga-tam, 1944–1946.* Tel Aviv: 'Am 'oved, 1996.

Engelking, Barbara and Jacek Leociak. *The Warsaw Ghetto: A Guide to the Perished City,* trans. Emma Harris. New Haven-London: Yale University Press, 2009.

Etkes, Immanuel. *Ba`al ha-shem: ha-Besht: magyah, mistikah, hanhagah.* Jerusalem: Shazar Center, 2000.

Gross, Jan Tomasz. *Fear: Anti-Semitism in Poland after Auschwitz.* New York: Random House, 2007.

Neighbors: The Destruction of the Jewish Community of Jedwabne, Poland. New York: Penguin, 2002.

Gutman, Yisrael, Ezra Mendelsohn, Jehuda Reinharz, and Chona Shmeruk, eds. *The Jews of Poland Between the Two World Wars.* Hanover-London: University Press of New England, 1989.

Hundert, Gershon David. *Jews in Poland-Lithuania in the Eighteenth Century: A Genealogy of Modernity.* Berkeley: University of California Press, 2004.

Kersten, Krystyna. *Polacy, Żydzi, komunizm: Anatomia półprawd, 1939–1968.* Warsaw: Niezależna Oficyna Wydawnicza, 1992.

Kieniewicz, Stefan. "The Jews of Warsaw, Polish Society, and the Partitioning Powers, 1795–1861." In *From Shtetl to Socialism: Studies from POLIN,* ed. Antony Polonsky, 83–102. London: Littman, 1993.

Marcus, Joseph. *Social and Political History of the Jews in Poland, 1919–1939.* Berlin: Mouton Publishers, 1983.

Mendelsohn, Ezra. *The Jews of East Central Europe between the World Wars.* Bloomington: Indiana University Press, 1983.

Zionism in Poland: The Formative Years. New Haven: Yale University Press, 1981.

Opalski, Magdalena and Israel Bartal. *Poles and Jews: A Failed Brotherhood.* Hanover, NH: Brandeis University Press, 1992.

Polonsky, Antony. *The Jews in Poland and Russia.* 3 vols. Oxford: Littman, 2010–2012.

Prusin, Alexander Victor. *Nationalizing a Borderland: War, Ethnicity, and Anti-Jewish Violence in East Galicia, 1914–1920.* Tuscaloosa: University of Alabama Press, 2005.

Rogger, Hans. "Conclusion and Overview." In *Pogroms: Anti-Jewish Violence in Modern Russian History,* ed. John D. Klier and Shlomo Lambroza, 314–372. Cambridge: Cambridge University Press, 1992.

Rosman, Moshe. *Founder of Hasidism: A Quest for the Historical Ba'al Shem Tov.* Berkeley: University of California Press, 1996.

The Lords' Jews: Magnate-Jewish Relations in the Polish-Lithuanian Commonwealth during the Eighteenth Century. Cambridge, MA: Harvard University Press, 1990.

Schatz, Jaff. *The Generation: The Rise and Fall of the Jewish Communists of Poland.* Berkeley-Los Angeles: University of California Press, 1991.

Shore, Marci. *Caviar and Ashes: A Warsaw Generation's Life and Death in Marxism, 1918–1968.* New Haven: Yale University Press, 2006.

Teller, Adam and Magda Teter. "Borders and Boundaries in the Historiography of the Jews in the Polish-Lithuanian Commonwealth." *Polin* 22 (2010): 3–46.

Ury, Scott. *Barricades and Banners: The Revolution of 1905 and the Transformation of Warsaw Jewry.* Stanford: Stanford University Press, 2012.

Weeks, Theodore R. *From Assimilation to Antisemitism: The 'Jewish Question' in Poland, 1850–1914.* Dekalb, IL: Northern Illinois University Press, 2006.

Weiser, Kalman (Keith). *Jewish People, Yiddish Nation: Noah Prylucki and the Folkists in Poland.* Toronto: University of Toronto Press, 2011.

Wodziński, Marcin. *Hasidism and Politics: The Kingdom of Poland, 1815–1864.* Oxford: Littman, 2016.

Haskalah and Hasidism in the Kingdom of Poland: A History of Conflict. Oxford-Portland, OR: Littman, 2005.

"Reform and Exclusion? Conceptions of the Reform of the Jewish Community during the Declining Years of the Polish Enlightenment." In *Jews and Their Neighbours since 1750*, ed. Israel Bartal, Antony Polonsky, and Scott Ury, 31–48. POLIN, 24. Oxford: Littman, 2012.

CHAPTER 4

THE BALKANS AND SOUTHEASTERN EUROPE

MATTHIAS B. LEHMANN

When the young Elijah Carmona, who would later become one of the most prolific authors of Judeo-Spanish novels and the editor of the satirical periodical *El Juguetón*, left his native Istanbul to look for work in Salonika and Izmir (his ambitions were frustrated in both cities), and when he went to Alexandria and Cairo in later years to find a way to publish his novels after he had run into problems with the censors in the capital, he relied on three overlapping networks: he carried letters of introduction to the local chief rabbi whom he would seek out for assistance; he made sure to bring letters of reference from the Alliance Israélite Universelle, the French organization that was running an extensive network of schools offering modern, Western education to Jews throughout the Ottoman Empire; and he had recourse to relatives and friends of the family.[1] Carmona's picaresque memoir highlights the repeated failures and mishaps he encountered on his way, and it certainly should not be taken at face value, but what is interesting is the way he seems seamlessly to navigate different kinship, secular, and religious networks (it is clear that he is not religiously observant himself). He is not "playing" the local rabbinate against the secularists of the Alliance – rather, he and his contemporaries inhabit a world in which the boundary between traditional and modern, rabbinic and Western networks is crossed easily and frequently. As this example illustrates, the "old" and the "new," the religious and the secular, "Orient" and "Occident" coexisted in an ongoing dialogue, and in myriad manifestations of ambiguity, throughout the late Ottoman period. Carmona's world was one of closely intertwined communities in the Ottoman (or formerly Ottoman) lands of southeastern Europe, Asia Minor, and the Levant, part of what Esther Benbassa and Aron Rodrigue have called the Eastern Sephardi *Kulturbereich*.[2]

---

[1] Elijah Carmona, *Como nació Eliyah Carmona, como se engrandeció y como se hizo director del "Juguetón"* (Istanbul, 1926), 32–40, 48–75.

[2] Esther Benbassa and Aron Rodrigue, *Sephardi Jewry* (Berkeley, 2000), xvii. Other general surveys of Ottoman Jewry and the Jews of the Balkans include Avigdor Levy, ed., *The Jews of the Ottoman Empire* (Princeton, 1994); Stanford Shaw, *The Jews of the Ottoman Empire and the Turkish Republic* (New York, 1991); Minna Rozen, *The Last Ottoman Century*

Throughout the early modern and modern periods, the Jews in the Ottoman Empire were a predominantly urban society. Though a fairly small minority of the overall population of the empire – just over 1 percent – Jews were a more significant and visible sector of the population in many big cities. In Salonika, one of the largest urban centers of the empire, they constituted almost half of the city's population of 160,000 as late as 1912,[3] and other major urban communities included Istanbul (about 47,000 Jews, or 4.44 percent of the city's population, in 1897, and over 50,000 in 1912), and Izmir and its environs (over 35,000 Jews in 1912).[4] According to an estimate based on census data from the end of the Ottoman period (from 1911–1912), about 25 percent of the 357,000 Ottoman Jews lived in the European provinces of the empire (the Balkans), 15 percent in the Istanbul province, and 15 percent in Western Anatolia (including the port city of Izmir); another 15 percent lived in Greater Syria, about 24 percent in Ottoman Iraq, and the remainder elsewhere in Anatolia.[5]

SIGNS OF CHANGE IN A WORLD OF TRADITION

The first manifestations of the social and cultural changes that would transform Ottoman Jewish society in the nineteenth century appeared within the world of rabbinic tradition. From the 1730s, Ottoman rabbis began to publish works in the vernacular language of the Ottoman Jews (Ladino), reaching out to a broader reading public and laying the foundations for the Judeo-Spanish public sphere that would emerge in the course of the nineteenth century. Authors like Jacob Huli (who published the *Me'am Lo'ez*, the classic of Ladino literature, in 1730) and Abraham Asa in the eighteenth century created a vernacular rabbinic literature that made traditional religious knowledge accessible to an audience hitherto all but excluded from rabbinic learning, and that facilitated new reading practices. One of the most important ways in which this new vernacular

and Beyond: The Jews of Turkey and the Balkans, 1808–1945, vol. 1 (Tel Aviv, 2005); Jacob Barnai, "The Jews in the Ottoman Empire," in *History of the Jews in the Islamic Countries, Part 2: From the Middle of the Nineteenth to the Middle of the Twentieth Century*, ed. Shmuel Ettinger (Jerusalem 1986) (Hebrew), 183–297. An important collection of primary sources in English translation is Julia Phillips Cohen and Sarah Abrevaya Stein, eds, *Sephardi Lives: A Documentary History, 1700–1950* (Stanford, 2014).

[3] K. E. Fleming, *Greece: A Jewish History* (Princeton, 2008), 67.

[4] These numbers, as well as the data that follows, come from Justin McCarthy, "Jewish Population in the Late Ottoman Period," in *The Jews of the Ottoman Empire*, ed. Avigdor Levy, 375–397 (Princeton, 1994), and Kemal Karpat, *Ottoman Population, 1830–1914* (Madison, 1985).

[5] The percentages here do not include noncitizens and Jews in Ottoman Arabia.

literature contributed to social change was its inclusion of women as a reading public for rabbinic educational writing. The *Pele Yo'ets*, one of the most popular rabbinic works in Ladino in the nineteenth century, spelled out an educational ideal that included a female audience alongside its male readers, and explicitly encouraged the establishment of study groups for women: "It is good for women, friends and relatives, to meet, one Sabbath at one home, another Sabbath at a different home, and for each group to appoint a woman who can read, and to spend the hour with [study]. One advantage is that they will look for ways to teach their daughters [how to read as well]." Women were now addressed directly and without recourse to a rabbinic, male intermediary, other than the author of the text himself. What is more, for some of the rabbinic authors, educating women and young girls was not restricted to the teaching of religious subjects: Isaac Amarachi and Joseph Sason, writing in the 1840s, encouraged their readers "to teach the daughters the holy tongue [Hebrew] and the language of the country in which one lives, and teach them to understand the prayers they say, and writing and calculus, and then teach them a profession, because idleness leads to promiscuity."[6]

Obviously not all women took advantage of the new possibilities opened up to them by vernacular rabbinic literature, just as not all men flocked to the study sessions or read the new volumes of Judeo-Spanish rabbinic writings and not all rabbis embraced such innovations. Still, the new Judeo-Spanish literature created a new reading public, facilitated individual, unsupervised reading, opened up new spaces for sociability, and even encouraged the teaching of "non-Jewish" languages and secular subjects, anticipating in a way the rise of modern schools under the auspices of organizations like the Alliance Israélite Universelle.

RISE OF A LEVANTINE MIDDLE CLASS AND THE ALLIANCE ISRAÉLITE UNIVERSELLE

Many of the earliest advocates of making Ottoman Jews modern – i.e., more "Western" – were members of a small elite of wealthy merchants and businessmen, the so-called *francos*, European Jews who had emigrated to the empire from Italy, often from the large Sephardi community and major Italian port city of Livorno. They established themselves in some of the major Ottoman trading hubs, including Istanbul, Izmir, Salonika, Alexandria, and Aleppo. It was not only their European background that led them to become advocates for reform, but also the fact that, though

---

[6] See Matthias B. Lehmann, *Ladino Rabbinic Literature and Ottoman Sephardic Culture* (Bloomington, 2005), 68–69, 131–133.

forming an economic elite in Ottoman cities, they were often excluded from the traditional power structures, so that the project of modernization was an opportunity to assert their own claim to political influence within the community. Among the best-known examples of this group was Moïse Allatini in Salonika, who wrote in a letter to the Austrian Jew Ludwig August Frankl in 1856 that "we wish with all our hearts that our emerging relationship might bring some benefit to our poor co-religionists of this city, who, by their numbers and their misery, by their crass ignorance and by their inferior position to people of other religions, have urgent need for help, support and enlightenment...." In Istanbul, Abraham Camondo – the "Rothschild of the East" who helped finance the Ottoman war effort during the Crimean War – played a similar role.[7]

Not all advocates of reform were *francos*, however. A good example is the Rozanes family in Rusçuk, on the Danube River. Abraham Rozanes (whose son, Solomon, would later pen one of the classical histories of Ottoman Jewry[8]) was a perfect example of an Ottoman maskil. Speaking several languages, he was also trained as a rabbinic scholar, as a *mohel* (circumciser) and *shohet* (ritual slaughterer). In the spirit of the Jewish Enlightenment, he undertook several attempts to establish a modern school in Rusçuk and finally succeeded with the opening of a new school in 1870. (The French Alliance would open its own modern school in Rusçuk three years later.) One of the teachers, a close associate of Rozanes in his efforts at reform and modernization, was Rabbi Menahem Farhi, another Ottoman maskil, who corresponded with Hebrew newspapers like *Ha-Magid*, *Ha-Levanon*, and *Ha-Tsfira*, as well as with Judah Alkalai, a Serbian rabbi who advocated the revival of Hebrew and a Jewish return to Palestine, and who is usually seen as a forerunner of religious Zionism.[9]

Opposition from the old elites arose against all of these initiatives. Controversies in many communities pitted those who promoted modern, European-style educational reform against a traditionalist faction of those who rejected any such move. Rabbinic literature of the time includes numerous polemics against the dangers of teaching foreign (i.e., European) languages and non-Jewish (i.e., secular, scientific) knowledge. Unlike the

---

[7] Aron Rodrigue, "The Beginnings of Westernization and Community Reform Among Istanbul's Jewry, 1854–65," in *Jews of the Ottoman Empire*, ed, Levy, 439–456. The quotation appears there, 441. See also idem, "Abraham de Camondo of Istanbul: The Transformation of Jewish Philanthropy," in *From East and West: Jews in a Changing Europe*, ed. Frances Malino and David Sorkin (Oxford, 1990), 46–56.

[8] Solomon Rozanes, *History of the Jews in Turkey and in the Middle East*, 6 vols (Tel Aviv, Sofia, Jerusalem, 1907–1945) (Hebrew).

[9] Zvi Keren, *The Jewish Community of Rusçuk* (Jerusalem, 2005) (Hebrew), 219–227.

situation in Central Europe, however, this struggle over modern education never generated the emergence of ideological camps, such as a Sephardi Orthodoxy or a Sephardi reform movement. By the time the French-based Alliance Israélite Universelle opened its first schools in the empire, in the 1860s, a compromise had emerged according to which the rabbis continued to teach Hebrew and religious subjects even in the modern schools under the auspices of the Alliance, whereas the core of the curriculum was decidedly European (in particular French) in orientation.

The conflicts between traditionalists and reformers should not be seen as a conflict between religious and secular elites, though. Different alliances were forged and broken. Some rabbis, like Jacob Avigdor in Istanbul, Abraham Gategno in Salonika, or Abraham Palache in Izmir, would sometimes appear in the sources as more sympathetic to educational reform than others. In the end, it is probably best to understand the controversies of the late nineteenth century not only in terms of an ideological-cultural clash between modernizers and traditionalists, but also as a political power struggle in which members of the old notable families, the new *franco* elite – usually under the protection of foreign consuls – and different factions within the rabbinate fought over influence and conflicting economic interests.[10]

A central role in the transformation of Ottoman Jewry was played by an organization established in Paris in 1860 in order to promote modern, westernizing education among non-European Jews and translating the universalist ideals of the French Revolution and the French imperial "civilizing mission" into an idiom of international Jewish solidarity: the Alliance Israélite Universelle.[11] In its heyday on the eve of the First World War, the number of Alliance schools, from Morocco in the West to Iran in the East, had expanded from just three in 1865 to 183, teaching 43,700 pupils, in 1913.[12] It was primarily through its network of schools that the Alliance left its imprint on Eastern Sephardi Jewry. By 1911, a majority of the school-age population of Jews in Ottoman Turkey attended an Alliance school (the percentage was lower in Istanbul, about 35 percent, and Izmir,

[10] The struggles between advocates of modern education and their opponents are discussed in Aron Rodrigue, *French Jews, Turkish Jews: The Alliance Israélite Universelle and the Politics of Jewish Schooling in Turkey, 1860–1925* (Bloomington, 1990); Rozen, *Last Ottoman Century*.

[11] On the Alliance's work in the Ottoman Empire see Rodrigue, *French Jews, Turkish Jews*; Lisa Moses Leff, *Sacred Bonds of Solidarity: The Rise of Internationalism in Nineteenth-Century France* (Stanford, 2006).

[12] Aron Rodrigue, *Jews and Muslims: Images of Sephardi and Eastern Jewries in Modern Times* (Seattle, 2003), 15.

14 percent, where other European schools attracted many children especially of the wealthier classes). It is true that many of the poorer families could not always afford to keep their children in an Alliance school, but nonetheless between a fifth and one third of all those who attended a school run by the Alliance completed the full program.[13] The teachers for the Alliance schools were recruited from the local communities, and a career with the French organization created an unprecedented opportunity for upward social mobility. After attending the *École normale israélite orientale* in Paris – there were schools for both boys and girls – the recruits from Alliance schools in North Africa and the Middle East would eventually return to teach at a school in the region, though usually not in their hometowns.[14]

Upon their return, these Alliance teachers were set to broadcast the "civilizing mission" of the strongly centralized French organization: instilling a sense of France "as our cultural mother," in the words of Leon Sciaky,[15] and representing an ideology that was shaped by a European discourse of emancipation that the French Jewish elites of the late nineteenth century had thoroughly internalized and which they now applied to what they considered to be their backward and uncivilized co-religionists in the "Orient." The Alliance ideology of "betterment" and "improvement," using the vocabulary familiar from earlier debates over the emancipation of Jews in Western Europe, and the tensions that arose when applying this set of ideas to the circumstances of the Jewish communities in the late Ottoman Empire, are illustrated well by the following declaration on the importance of teaching Jewish history in the 1890s:

We want the teachers to devote to Jewish history all their attention and zeal. Perhaps never before have Jews needed to know their past as much as now, the long and painful martyrdom of their ancestors and the frequent and bloody violence that marked their settlement in their different countries of adoption. How instructive is this history … it shows on the one hand that the same prejudices have always been nourished … On the other hand, one also sees in it how in the end human reason, the idea of tolerance and love always win out over hatred and superstition. … Jews should force themselves, always remaining faithful to their glorious past and attached to their faith, to surpass their compatriots in loyalty, courage, honesty and patriotism. It is here that lies the moral of Jewish history.[16]

---

[13] Rodrigue, *French Jews, Turkish Jews*, 92, 111, 115, 117.

[14] See Frances Malino, "'Adieu à ma maison': Sephardi Adolescent Identities, 1932–36," *Jewish Social Studies* 15:1 (2008): 131–144.

[15] Leon Sciaky, *Farewell to Salonica* (Philadelphia, 2003; originally published 1946), 158.

[16] Quoted in Rodrigue, *French Jews, Turkish Jews*, 86.

Displaying the historicist sensibility of middle-class modernity, the Alliance's approach to the teaching of (post-biblical) Jewish history shows the tension between three elements of its mission, which coexisted uneasily but were hardly seen as contradictory at the time: the commitment to pan-Jewish solidarity expressed in the teaching of a common historical narrative of the Jewish people; the belief in human progress leading to tolerance and civilization, epitomized by the French Revolution and the Alliance itself; and, finally, the need to make the Jews of the Ottoman Empire into patriotic citizens of their homeland. It goes without saying that not every graduate from an Alliance school bought into the organization's ideology *tout court*. Still, the Alliancist language of modernity was extraordinarily successful in shaping public discourse in the Jewish communities of the Ottoman lands. It facilitated the rise of a Francophone Jewish middle class in cities throughout the empire and its successor states and came to define "modernity" in the Ottoman Jewish context.

EMANCIPATION IN AN OTTOMAN KEY

Wary of the apparent decline in Ottoman power, with military defeats and territorial losses creating an acute sense of crisis, members of the empire's ruling elite had begun to advocate for the reform and modernization of the Ottoman state by the late eighteenth century, a process that gained momentum by the mid-nineteenth century.

The myriad changes in the empire's administration, fiscal foundations, legal system, military organization, and the forging of a new national, "Ottoman" identity left their imprint on the Jewish subjects of the sultan. Partly advancing its own reforming agenda, partly responding to pressure from the European powers, the Sublime Porte (as the Ottoman government was known) initiated a series of legal changes that completely reshaped – at least in theory – the centuries-old patterns of relations between the state and its non-Muslim subjects. Until the mid-nineteenth century, Jews and the far more numerous Christian communities[17] were considered as "protected" subject communities, following the provisions of Islamic law that granted protection (*dhimma* [Ar.], *zimmet* [Tk.]) to the so-called people of the book, Christians and Jews, as long as they paid a special poll tax (*djizya* [Ar.], *cizye* [Tk.]) and abided by certain restrictions imposed under Islamic law. Unlike the Habsburg or Russian empires, the Ottoman state had been a multi-ethnic empire without a dominant ethnic group well into the nineteenth century, but a basic distinction existed between Muslims

---

[17] Rodrigue, *French Jews, Turkish Jews*, 26, cites numbers of 150,000 Jews vs. 2,000,000 Greeks and 2,400,000 Armenians in the mid-nineteenth century.

and non-Muslims. The officially recognized non-Muslim communities, called *millets* at least since the reforms of the nineteenth century, included the Jews, the Greeks (i.e., Greek Orthodox), and the Armenians, with other groups gaining (or demanding) such recognition in later decades.[18]

In the old order, the different religious communities enjoyed a great deal of internal autonomy (though there is debate as to how much of this autonomy was officially recognized by the Ottoman state), and religious minorities tended to occupy specific niches in the Ottoman economy. The separation between the different communities should not be exaggerated, to be sure: Jews and non-Jews spoke different languages, for example, but they still mingled in the same marketplace. Jews tended to live in proximity to one another, but nowhere were there separate, much less closed off Jewish quarters (as in Italy and Morocco). Likewise, Jews were, by and large, subject to the rules of rabbinic law, or halacha, and thus to the rabbinic authorities of their residence. Still it was common throughout Ottoman history to find Jews turn to Muslim sharia courts, even when the matter concerned an internal Jewish conflict.[19]

An early milestone in the modernization of the empire, the destruction of the Janissary corps in 1826 which paved the way for military, financial, and administrative reforms, incidentally spelled disaster for the Istanbul Jewish community: three of its leaders – the tax farmer Bekhor Isaac Carmona as well as the financiers Ezekiel Gabai and Isaiah Ajiman – who maintained business ties with the Janissary commanders were murdered and replaced by Armenian bankers. There had long been competition between the various religious minorities, and Greek and Armenian Christians had come to replace the Jews in their role as middlemen in the trade with the West and in other areas such as banking. By and large, the role that Jews played in the Ottoman economy was rather modest and there was widespread poverty in the Jewish communities. A fair number of individual Jews, however, continued to be successful and were part of a growing number of minority businessmen who sought and obtained protection from European consulates and thus gained a privileged position within the community that exempted them from taxes or placed them under consular jurisdiction. The *francos* were one example of this phenomenon.

[18] See Bernard Lewis, *The Jews of Islam* (Princeton, 1984); Benjamin Braude, "Foundation Myths of the Millet System," in *Christians and Jews in the Ottoman Empire*, eds. Benjamin Braude and Bernard Lewis, 2 vols (New York 1982), vol. 1, 69–88.

[19] Haim Gerber and Jacob Barnai, *The Jews of Izmir in the Nineteenth Century: Ottoman Documents from the Shar'i Court* (Jerusalem, 1984) (Hebrew).

The Ottoman legal and political reforms of the nineteenth century, collectively known as the Tanzimat,[20] transformed the status of the Jewish and other minority communities in a profound way. Some of the measures – especially the ones that affected the non-Muslim population of the empire – came in response to pressure from the European powers, which had discovered the protection of religious minorities under Ottoman rule as a convenient tool to assert their political influence in the empire. As historians have recently pointed out, however, the Tanzimat should not be seen as responding primarily to European pressure: the reforms also responded to the modernizing impulse of Ottoman elites themselves. The Hatt-ı şerif of Gülhane, or Rose Chamber Edict, of 1839, and later the reform edict of 1856 set out to transform the legitimizing ideology of the empire and declared the equality of all the subjects of the sultan, regardless of religion.

Effectively abolishing the principle of *dhimma*, the reforms of 1839 and 1856, along with the Ottoman law of citizenship of 1869, introduced the novel category of "Ottoman," which included Muslims and non-Muslims alike and juxtaposed them to non-Ottoman foreigners, including Muslims living beyond the realm of the sultan. At the same time, however, the non-Muslim subjects retained their corporate identity as the Greek, Armenian, or Jewish *millet* ("nation" or "community"), though they were expected to modernize just as the state itself was undergoing a process of legal and political reform. The Hatt-ı hümayun of 1856 declared that it was the sultan's intention

to renew and expand still further the newly instituted regulations with the aim of arriving at a state of affairs conforming to the dignity of my Empire and the position which it occupies among the civilized nations. ... I wish to augment by this the well-being and internal prosperity, the happiness of my subjects, who are all equal in my sight and are equally dear to me, and who are united by the cordial ties of patriotism....

Proclaiming the equality of all subjects, the 1856 edict abolished the poll tax – the most important symbol of the regime of *dhimma* – though it was replaced by a new "military exemption tax" (*bedel-i askeri*) imposed on all

[20] See, for example, M. Şükrü Hanioğlu, *A Brief History of the Late Ottoman Empire* (Princeton, 2008); Reşat Kasaba, ed., *The Cambridge History of Turkey, Volume 4: Turkey in the Modern World* (Cambridge, 2008); Donald Quataert, *The Ottoman Empire, 1700–1922* (Cambridge, 2000); Bernard Lewis, *The Emergence of Modern Turkey* (Oxford, 2002; first published 1961); İnalcık, Halil, ed., with Donald Quataert, *An Economic and Social History of the Ottoman Empire* (Cambridge, 1994); Robert Mantran, ed., *Histoire de l'Empire ottoman* (Paris, 1989).

THE BALKANS AND SOUTHEASTERN EUROPE

non-Muslims. Despite embracing the principle of equality, however, the edict also stipulated that

all the privileges and spiritual immunities accorded from ancient times by my ancestors to all Christian communities or to other non-Muslim rites established within my Empire, are confirmed ... Each Christian community and other non-Muslim rite will ... be obliged to proceed ... with an examination of its present immunities and privileges, and to discuss them and submit to my Sublime Porte those reforms required by the process of enlightenment and by the times.[21]

The latter provision engendered the reorganization – though undertaken reluctantly – of the Jewish communities, leading to a "constitution" for the Jewish *millet*, the *hahamhane nizamnamesi* of 1865, which considerably empowered the lay element. The state also sought to centralize the administration of the non-Muslim *millets*, and a Chief Rabbi – *hahambaşı* – had already been appointed in 1835, though his authority remained contested and his position was primarily political, serving as the intermediary between government and Jewish *millet* and as the "guarantor of the loyalty of the community."[22] With the Tanzimat, Jews gained access to Ottoman schools and could take positions in the Ottoman administration, and there were those who served in the army. A small elite came to occupy positions of authority in the new Tanzimat order, for example some of the leaders of the Istanbul community in the 1890s: David Molho Efendi, chief interpreter at the imperial divan, Isaac Molho, an admiral and supervisor of health in the Ottoman navy, and Leon Rosenthal, who was in charge of the imperial rugs in the sultan's palace.[23] Still, overall the Jews remained underrepresented in the state bureaucracy and the military.

The reform edicts of 1839 and 1856 raise the question whether the declaration of equality should be seen as the Ottoman version of a pan-European process leading towards the emancipation of the Jews. One difference is, of course, that Ottoman Jews gained legal equality alongside the far more numerous Christian communities, and that they were not the main target of the Ottoman legal reforms. By contrast, the Jews in most European countries were emancipated only after a lengthy and public debate about the virtues of granting civic rights to the Jews, and to the Jews specifically. Emancipation in the European context, moreover, was part of a larger discourse of "regeneration" and "moral improvement," trying to transform the economic role of the Jews all the while making them into loyal citizens

---

[21] For the English translation see Norman Stillman, *The Jews of Arab Lands: A History and Source Book* (Philadelphia, 1979), 357–360.
[22] Esther Benbassa, *Haim Nahum: A Sephardic Chief Rabbi in Politics* (Tuscaloosa, 1995), 35.
[23] Rozen, *The Last Ottoman Century*, 96–97.

of the state. In the Ottoman Empire, ironically enough, this discourse was represented primarily by European Jewish organizations like the Alliance, and not by the Ottoman state. The Jews of the Ottoman Empire were emancipated, then, in the context of a broader process of westernizing reform, but without an *ideology* of emancipation as in Europe.

In 1876, the Ottoman constitutionalist movement – represented by the "Young Ottoman" opposition – achieved a short-lived success: the promulgation of a constitution by the new sultan Abdülhamid II. An Ottoman parliament was elected – it included four Jewish deputies in its first session and six in the second. Abdülhamid did not relish the limits on sultanic power and following the disastrous Russo-Ottoman war of 1877–78, he suspended parliament and constitution and established an authoritarian regime that lasted for three decades, until the Young Turk Revolution of 1908.[24]

Despite its authoritarian character, however, the Hamidian period did not bring to an end the modernization of the empire. Now increasingly anti-Western and pan-Islamic in outlook, Abdülhamid's government continued the path of modernization that began in the Tanzimat era. Western economic encroachment only increased as Ottoman debt spun out of control after the war of 1877–78 and a new Public Debt Administration was established in 1881. Still, the investment in the "technical trappings of modernity" continued with "railways, the telegraph, factories, censuses, passports, steamships, world fairs, clock towers, and art-deco palaces."[25] Bureaucratic reform likewise advanced, and the state embarked on a major effort, from education to the control of the press through rigorous censorship, to forge a new ideology of pan-Islamism and Ottomanism to sustain the legitimacy of the regime.

The years of Hamidian rule, and later that of the Young Turks following the revolution of 1908, also saw an expansion of the industrial sector. The city of Salonika, with its major port and railroad connections both to Istanbul and to Europe, emerged as a particularly important place – and, given the Jewish plurality of its population, Jews were instrumental in the development of the Salonikan textile, tobacco, brick, and other industries as entrepreneurs and industrialists, as well as providing a large portion of the industrial workforce in the city. In Salonika, Jews continued to play

---

[24] On the Ottoman Empire under Abdülhamid see Kemal Karpat, *The Politicization of Islam: Reconstructing Identity, State, Faith, and Community in the Late Ottoman State* (Oxford, 2001); Selim Deringil, *The Well-Protected Domains: Ideology and the Legitimation of Power in the Ottoman Empire 1876–1909* (London, 1998); Minna Rozen, "The Hamidian Era Through the Jewish Looking Glass," *Turcica* 37 (2005): 113–154.

[25] Deringil, *Well-Protected Domains*, 171.

a central role in numerous aspects of the urban economy, including as porters who hauled everything from charcoal for heating to foodstuff like dried fruit, olives, salted fish, or oranges between the port and the city's markets. The new factories, in turn, created a growing working class, Jewish as well as Christian, and employed an expanding female work force: three quarters of the workers in Salonika's cotton-spinning mills were girls of twelve to eighteen years, working fifteen-hour days in the summer and ten hours in the winter.[26]

The westernization of an ever wider Jewish urban middle class, meanwhile, pursued apace in the schools of the Alliance, as well as in Ottoman schools. The ones who could afford it moved to new, more modern neighborhoods on the outskirts of the big cities like Istanbul, Salonika, or Izmir, where they joined the also westernized Christian and Muslim middle class. The result was a growing secularization, if not assimilation, and while Ottoman Jewish identity as an ethno-religious group was never challenged, adherence to the rules of rabbinic tradition declined. While this did not lead to the creation of a religious reform movement, the consequences were all too visible for the rabbinic leadership: The author of a moralizing book in Hebrew, the *Pele Yo'ets*, could still argue in the 1820s that it was better to live "in the domain of Islam where the flag of Torah flies high. Jews there live according to the Torah, and rabbis and communal leaders have the power to root out evil and maintain our faith." By the time that the author's son published a Judeo-Spanish adaptation of the work, in the early 1870s, he saw it fit to omit this assessment, and he lamented instead: "There are so many who take advantage of the freedom to discharge the yoke of the Torah and the commandments and commit transgressions in public, and all their intention is to imitate the [gentile] nations. ... In all times there were good and bad people ... [but] now they have removed the veil and transgress openly."[27]

The Young Turk rebellion in 1908, which led to the removal of Abdülhamid II the following year and to the restoration of the constitution, elections to parliament – four Jews, from the districts of Salonika, Istanbul, Baghdad, and Izmir sat in parliament for the ruling Committee of Union and Progress – and lifting of censorship, also had its echoes in the Jewish community. In 1908, the acting Chief Rabbi, Moshe Halevi, was removed – he had been in office since 1872 and was closely associated with the Hamidian regime – and replaced by Haim Nahum, the

---

[26] Donald Quataert, "The Industrial Working Class of Salonica, 1850–1912," in *Jews, Turks, Ottomans*, ed. Avigdor Levy (Syracuse, 2002), 194–211; idem, "Premières fumes d'usines," in *Salonique, 1850–1918*, ed. Gilles Veinstein (Paris, 1993), 177–194.

[27] Lehmann, *Ladino Rabbinic Literature*, 148, 152.

candidate representing the Alliancist camp within the community. This represented arguably the height of the Alliance's influence over Ottoman Jewry, but it was also the beginning of the end: under siege from nationalism, both within the community (the Zionist faction) and without (the rise of Turkish nationalism under the new government), the Alliance soon found itself on the defensive.[28]

JUDEO-SPANISH PUBLIC CULTURE

In his posthumously published memoirs, Sa'adi Halevi (1820–1903), a printer and publisher in Salonika, tells the story of how he established the Ladino newspaper, *La Epoca*, in the late 1870s.[29] Some elements of his narrative are certainly exaggerated and polemical, but what it represents well is the self-identity of the rising Jewish middle class of the late Ottoman (and early post-Ottoman) period, and its role in creating a new communicative space within which it could contest the traditional social and cultural order and advocate its own claim to modernity. Sa'adi's memoir is replete with references to the "ignorance" and "fanaticism" of the traditionalists, from Salonika's rabbis who placed him under a *herem*, or ban, to the mob that smashed the windows of his home and the gang of Jewish dock workers who once threatened to kill him and whom he only barely escaped. On the other hand, Sa'adi enjoyed support from Moïse Allatini, a Salonikan entrepreneur of *franco* origin, as well as from the members of the Cercle des Intimes, a philanthropic and cultural association in Salonika that was founded in 1873. In the end, Sa'adi managed to import a set of Hebrew characters for his printing press from Vienna and obtained the license to publish *La Epoca* from the imperial government in 1875.

Newspapers like *La Epoca* in Salonika, *El Tiempo* and *El Telegrafo* in Istanbul, or *El Meseret* and *La Voz del Pueblo* in Izmir played a crucial role as vehicles for shaping a Judeo-Spanish public culture in the cities of the Ottoman Empire.[30] While the newspapers represented at times competing

---

[28] Esther Benbassa, *Une diaspora sépharade en transition* (Paris, 1993); idem, *Haim Nahum: A Sephardic Chief Rabbi in Politics, 1892–1923*. See also Hasan Kayalı, "Jewish Representation in the Ottoman Parliaments," in *Jews of the Ottoman Empire*, ed. Levy, 507–517.

[29] "Mis memorias: como nació *La Epoca*," appeared in *La Epoca* in 28 installments between September 1907 and March 1908. This version was published and somewhat embellished by Sa'adi's sons. For Sa'adi's memoir see Aron Rodrigue and Sarah Abrevaya Stein, eds, *A Jewish Voice from Ottoman Salonica: The Ladino Memoir of Sa'adi Besalel a-Levi* (Stanford, 2012).

[30] On Ladino newspaper culture see Sarah Abrevaya Stein, *Making Jews Modern: The Yiddish and Ladino Press in the Russian and Ottoman Empires* (Bloomington, 2004); Olga

political camps they all shared the common outlook of a self-conscious modernity. News about Jewish communities from around the world, sections with practical advice on health, hygiene, or food, advertisements promoting Western and European-style goods from furniture to hats to pink pills against indigestion, were all designed to "make Jews modern," as the title of Sarah Stein's comparative work on the Ladino and Yiddish press aptly suggests.[31] The impressive number of different newspapers, some short-lived and others, like *El Tiempo* and *La Epoca*, published for decades and surviving into the interwar period, reached an ever growing Judeo-Spanish reading audience, though their reach, at least until the 1890s, should not be exaggerated.

Female readers were seen as an important audience, and many articles and advertisements were directed at them. The actual print run of the papers was often surprisingly small – a couple of hundred subscribers in the case of *La Epoca* – but the papers circulated beyond this rather small base as every single copy was shared by several people and newspapers were read aloud in the coffeehouses of Ottoman cities. This was common for non-Jewish newspapers as well, and it was a continuation of a reading practice that had first emerged with the rabbinic vernacular literature in the eighteenth and early nineteenth centuries. Ladino newspapers also published serialized novels which were often adaptations of foreign-language sources (mostly French, sometimes Hebrew and other languages) and which served the dual purpose of the newspapers themselves: to entertain – and to introduce their readers to European culture, transmitting the values, sentiments, and tastes of a Western readership yet transforming and adapting them for an Ottoman, Judeo-Spanish context.[32] Both the publication of newspapers and the publication of translated and adapted novels had their parallel in the world of Ottoman Turkish, Greek, Armenian, or Bulgarian readers in the Ottoman Empire. The first Ottoman novels, for example, appeared in Turkish written in Armenian script in the early 1850s, and the first official Ottoman newspaper appeared in 1831.[33]

According to Sa'adi's memoirs, support for the successful establishment of *La Epoca* came from the Cercle des Intimes (later renamed Club des Intimes), one of numerous voluntary associations that sprang up

Borovaya, *Modern Ladino Culture: Press, Belles Lettres, and Theater in the Late Ottoman Empire* (Bloomington, 2012), 23–136.

[31] See in particular chapters 4 and 6 in Stein, *Making Jews Modern*.

[32] Borovaya, *Modern Ladino Culture*, 139–165. Not all Ladino novels were adaptations of European works, to be sure, and there were plenty of original Ladino works as well, including those of Elijah Carmona (see above).

[33] Hanioğlu, *A Brief History of the Late Ottoman Empire*, 62, 98.

throughout the empire and which expanded even more once the authoritarian rule of Abdülhamid ended in 1908. Voluntary organizations such as burial societies and professional guilds (both Jewish and with mixed membership) had long existed in traditional Sephardi society. The nineteenth century saw the proliferation of a new type of association, which legitimized secular sociability, either for its own sake or in the service of a philanthropic or ideological cause. Some associations were similar to circles of maskilim in Eastern Europe, for example the Hevrat Dorshei ha-Haskalah established 1879 in Edirne, which maintained a reading room and subscribed to Hebrew periodicals. Numerous other associations were tied to the Alliance and its schools, for instance the Salonika Alliance Committee and the Regional Committee of the Alliance in Istanbul founded in 1863, and later an entire network of Alliancist alumni associations. Over time, various associations would take on competing political and ideological causes and thus represent the growing politicization of Judeo-Spanish public culture, in particular following the fall of the Hamidian regime in 1908. In Istanbul, for example, two competing associations of Alliance alumni were founded in 1910, the Alliancist *Amicale* and the Zionist *Agudat Crémieux*.[34] When Sultan Mehmed V visited Salonika in 1911, numerous Jewish organizations competed with one another as they designed and set up "triumphal arches" to highlight their modern outlook and their Ottoman patriotism.[35] Salonika, moreover, with its large number of Jewish industrial workers, saw the rise of socialist associations and newspapers, with the Workers' Socialist Federation of Salonika founded in 1909 and newspapers such as *Jurnal del Lavorador* (1909–10) and *Solidaridad Ovradera* (1911–12), which introduced socialist ideas to working class readers in Ladino.

Judeo-Spanish public culture existed in the multi-ethnic, multi-lingual context of the Ottoman Empire. Much to the chagrin of community leaders and journalists who wanted to see Ottoman Jews embrace Ottoman patriotism in response to the politics of the Tanzimat, few Jews knew much Turkish. Many certainly had sufficient command of the Turkish vernacular (or some other language spoken by their non-Jewish neighbors) to get by in the marketplace, but very few individuals were literate in Ottoman Turkish – which was, in any event, a language limited to a small elite and used in the state bureaucracy and Ottoman high culture. Greek was the language of high culture and trade in the Balkans, Arabic in

[34] Esther Benbassa, "Associational Strategies in Ottoman Jewish Society in the Nineteenth and Twentieth Centuries," in *Jews of the Ottoman Empire*, ed. Levy, 457–484.

[35] Julia Phillips Cohen, *Becoming Ottomans: Sephardi Jews and Imperial Citizenship in the Modern Era* (Oxford, 2014), 108–127.

Islamic religious education and, of course, throughout the Arab provinces, and increasingly it was French that emerged as a language of learning and cultural creativity, and even as a spoken language, among a cosmopolitan Ottoman middle class. This was also true for the Jews, many of whom had access to the Francophone schools of the Alliance. While some leading Sephardi intellectuals – ironically, many of them publishing in the Ladino press – denounced the Judeo-Spanish vernacular as a jargon and a sign of cultural backwardness, others defended the language which remained, in any event, the first language of most Jews in the Ottoman Empire and its successor states well into the interwar period. In the words of an often-quoted Alliance report from 1908, "Turkish is the borrowed suit; French is gala dress; Judeo-Spanish is the worn dressing gown in which one is most at ease."[36]

This linguistic difference of the Ottoman Jews should not be misread as cultural isolation, however. A good example of the multi-ethnic border crossings in the Ottoman city is the case of music: whereas Ottoman court music filtered into the musical traditions that could be heard in Greek or Armenian churches as well as in synagogues, Jewish, Greek, or Armenian musicians performed in the imperial court. A close association between Jewish musicians and Mevlevi dervishes is well documented, and in the early twentieth century, the gramophone and the *gazinos* (nightclubs) of the Ottoman cities became new venues of an intercultural Ottoman "music world."[37] Jews participated in all aspects of urban life in Ottoman cities, as they had for centuries. Some rose to hold prominent positions, like Abraham Ibn Zonana who was one of the founders of the Ottoman Red Crescent in 1869 or Elijah Cohen Bey who was an admiral and oculist at the imperial palace and the naval hospital.[38] Less respectably, some Ashkenazi immigrants from Eastern Europe played an important role in the white slave trade, for which Istanbul became a major crossroads alongside Buenos Aires in Argentina, and many young Eastern European Jewish girls ended up as prostitutes in the Ottoman capital. Social ills like prostitution were still denounced in the interwar period in Salonika, for example in the Ladino novel *Sochetá podrida* ("rotten society"), published in 1930.[39]

---

[36] Rodrigue, *Jews and Muslims*, 131.

[37] On Ottoman Jewish music and its modern legacy see Paméla Dorn Sezgin, "Hakhamim, Dervishes, and Court Singers: The Relationship of Ottoman Jewish Music to Classical Turkish Music," in *Jews of the Ottoman Empire*, ed. Levy, 585–632; Maureen Jackson, *Mixing Musics: Turkish Jewry and the Urban Landscape of a Sacred Song* (Stanford, 2013).

[38] Rozen, *Last Ottoman Century*, 97.

[39] Rıfat Bali, *The Jews and Prostitution in Constantinople, 1854–1922* (Istanbul, 2008).

OTTOMANISM AND ZIONISM

Jewish identity in the late Ottoman Empire and its successor states was negotiated in a complex web of competing narratives and national projects: first, the attempt to forge an Ottoman civic identity, or "Ottomanism," as an ideological basis legitimating the continued existence of the empire. Second, the various national movements that competed with and eventually succeeded this Ottomanist agenda, and the ensuing nation-building process in the newly independent states. Third, there was the claim of Zionism, or Jewish nationalism, which was greeted reluctantly in the Ottoman lands, but which emerged as an increasingly powerful force in particular as Jews confronted and resisted the claims of the new nation-states of southeastern Europe.

Ottomanism began as a corollary of the Tanzimat as it "transformed the subjects of the sultan into citizens of the state," predicated on the declaration of equality between Muslim and non-Muslim "Ottomans."[40] By and large, Ottomanism did not gain significant support from among the Christian *millets* and as it failed to curtail the nationalist movements that eroded Ottoman rule in the Balkans, and under the long regime of Abdülhamid II, Ottomanism became increasingly identified with Islamism, and with Turkish nationalism after the Young Turk Revolution in 1908. The Jews of the Ottoman Empire are often identified as the only (or the last) non-Muslim community to subscribe to Ottomanism, and the economic competition with Greeks or Armenians and the inherent tension between the Balkan nation-states and the Jews as a religious-ethnic minority residing in their midst would have given them good cause to prefer the old, imperial order. But, as Julia Cohen has shown, Jewish Ottomanism was also deliberately created and promoted by the empire's Jewish elites, propagated in Jewish schools and in the Ladino press.[41] While it is difficult to assess how much of this Jewish Ottomanism was a performance staged for the Ottoman public sphere, and how much of it was genuinely embraced by the Jewish public, the fact remains that thousands of Ottoman Sephardim voted with their feet and emigrated from the empire, especially after the turn of the twentieth century. Ottoman Jewish émigrés were adept at resisting and sometimes subverting the attempts of Ottoman and other governments to classify them in terms of national belonging, and they continued to rely on their connections in a wider Sephardi diaspora that transcended national boundaries.[42]

[40] Karpat, *The Politicization of Islam*, 12 and *passim*.

[41] Cohen, *Becoming Ottomans*.

[42] See Devi Mays, "Transplanting Cosmopolitans: The Migration of Sephardic Jews to Mexico, 1900–1934" (Ph.D. diss., Indiana University, Bloomington, 2013). For an

Jewish Ottomanism was predicated on a double myth: the myth of an age-old tradition of Jewish allegiance to the empire and of a special Muslim–Jewish (or Turkish–Jewish) relationship; and the myth of the benevolent welcome extended by the Ottoman sultans to the Jews expelled from Spain in 1492 as the founding moment of Ottoman Jewry. In 1892, Ottoman Jews commemorated the 400-year anniversary of their "arrival" in the Ottoman lands, a celebration that had first been proposed by a Jewish journalist in Izmir. As the celebratory rhetoric focused on the continued "hospitality" shown by the Ottomans to the Jews ever since 1492, it also betrayed a certain degree of anxiety on part of the Jews in the age of nationalism as it inadvertently represented the Jews as strangers, even centuries after their arrival on the shores of the empire. What is more, the rhetoric completely displaced the legacy of the Greek- and Arabic-speaking non-Sephardi Jews who had lived in the area long before the Ottomans arrived on the scene, and it undermined the notion of Ottoman "brotherhood" as it set the (Sephardi) Jews apart from Armenians and Greeks in their relation to the Ottoman state.[43] Interestingly, the official discourse – and the underlying, unarticulated anxiety – re-appeared in the 500-year celebrations in the Turkish Republic, held in 1992.[44]

Meanwhile, Jewish nationalism was making inroads into the Ottoman Jewish community. While it is true that organized Zionism did not gain much traction among the Eastern Sephardim until after the Young Turk revolution of 1908, there were local precedents for Jewish nationalism: the most well-known case was Rabbi Judah Alkalai in Zemun who advocated a collective return of the Jews to Palestine and the revival of Hebrew as the national Jewish language, or little known figures such as H. G. Nahmias, Marco Barukh, or Moshe Jacob Hay Altarats.[45] These individuals, and early Zionists especially in Bulgaria, explicitly cited the example of the various nationalist movements around them and advocated following the example of the Greeks, Serbs, or Bulgarians, whose elites were pursuing a

example of Ottoman Jews embracing their "Ottomanism" abroad see Julia Phillips Cohen, "Oriental by Design: Ottoman Jews, Imperial Style, and the Performance of Heritage," *American Historical Review* 119, no. 2 (2015): 364–398. On the broader question of citizenship in the wake of the Ottoman empire see Sarah Abrevaya Stein, *Extraterritorial Dreams: European Citizenship, Sephardi Jews, and the Ottoman Twentieth Century* (Chicago, 2016).

[43] Cohen, *Becoming Ottomans*, 45–62.

[44] See Marcy Brink-Danan, *Jewish Life in 21st-Century Turkey: The Other Side of Tolerance* (Bloomington, 2012).

[45] Norman Stillman, *Sephardi Religious Responses to Modernity* (Luxembourg, 1995), 49–64; Benbassa and Rodrigue, *Sephardi Jewry*, 117–120; Matthias Lehmann, "Jewish Nationalism in Ladino," *Jewish Studies Quarterly* 17 (2010): 146–159.

national cultural "renaissance." The political implications of Jewish nationalism, however, were problematic. A Jewish homeland in Palestine threatened to clash with the pan-Islamist Ottomanism of sultan Abdülhamid. Jewish nationalism, if equated with similar developments among Greeks or Armenians, also threatened to undermine the carefully crafted image of the Ottoman Jewish community as the most loyal *millet*, and it is thus not surprising that much of the Ottoman Jewish leadership rejected political Zionism.

As Esther Benbassa, Minna Rozen,[46] and others have shown, political and social tensions in the Eastern Sephardi communities of the early twentieth century were played out between the Alliancist elite (with the Ottoman Chief Rabbi Haim Nahum, elected in 1909, at their helm) and its opponents who allied themselves with the Zionists: the Hilfsverein der deutschen Juden, the German equivalent of the Alliance; the traditionalists among the religious leadership; the Ashkenazi community in Istanbul; the B'nai B'rith. The confrontation between the different camps was showcased, often in shrill tones, in the pages of the Ladino press, with the Alliance and the World Zionist Organization each sponsoring individual papers and journalists. It is important to recognize, however, that in many of these highly publicized conflicts the issues at hand had often little to do with an ideological clash over Jewish nationalism and more to do with questions of social inequality and political power in the community. In this sense, Zionism served a similar purpose as the advocacy of westernization had decades earlier, when a new elite challenged the established order of traditional Ottoman Jewry with its program of modern, Western-style education.

In the end, the history and success of Zionism among the Eastern Sephardi communities varied from place to place. Everywhere there was a tension between the expectation of the Jewish minorities to integrate and assimilate into the newly established nation-states of southeastern Europe and Turkey, and the persistence of a Jewish ethnic group identity epitomized by Zionism. In Bulgaria, the Zionist camp established its control over Jewish community politics quite solidly and drove out the Alliance and its schools from the Bulgarian Jewish community by the early twentieth century. Salonika, with its Jewish plurality, saw an unusually strong coalition of Revisionist and religious Zionists – one of its leaders, Abraham

---

[46] On Zionism in the Ottoman and post-Ottoman world see Esther Benbassa, *Une diaspora sépharade en transition*; idem, "Zionism in the Ottoman Empire at the End of the Nineteenth and the Beginning of the Twentieth Century," *Studies in Zionism* 11 (1990), 127–140; and numerous publications by the same author; Rozen, *Last Ottoman Century*.

Recanati, serving on Salonika's city council and as deputy mayor from 1929 to 1931 – confronting the non-Zionist socialists.[47]

IN THE AGE OF NATIONALISM

The encounter between Jews and Balkan nationalisms was everywhere an uneasy one, and it mirrored the tension inherent in the nation-building process throughout the region: "The liberal concept of the nation-state aimed to reconcile majoritarian ethnic rule with guarantees of individual rights. … In theory, assimilation of the minority to the majority was supposed in the long run to lead to a homogenization of the population."[48] Everywhere the violence and wars led to massive loss of life and the displacement of large numbers of civilians: one scholar has estimated that between five to seven million individuals migrated from territories lost by the Ottoman Empire to the remaining Ottoman lands between 1783 and 1913, and among these migrants were a significant number of Jews. The Balkan Wars of 1912–13 and World War I again led to the displacement of large numbers of Jews among the massive number of refugees on all sides.[49]

The problem is illustrated well by the Greek example. As a result of the Balkan War of 1912–13, Salonika, the city long known as the "Jerusalem of the Balkans," became a part of Greece.[50] At that point, 40 percent of the city's population was Jewish, 25 percent Muslim, and only 30 percent of its residents were Greek Orthodox. The political status of Salonika was controversial, too, with Bulgaria having its own designs on Macedonia and others demanding an international status for the cosmopolitan port city. Greek nationalism, on the other hand, had long been predicated on the *megáli idéa* aiming at a territorial restoration of the Byzantine Empire and seeing all Greeks – both in the kingdom that gained independence from the Ottomans in the 1830s and beyond its borders – as part of the Greek nation.

---

[47] Benbassa and Rodrigue, *Sephardi Jewry*, 140.

[48] Mark Mazower, *The Balkans* (New York, 2002), 116. See also Barbara Jelavich, *History of the Balkans*, 2 vols (Cambridge, 1983); L. Carl Brown, ed., *Imperial Legacy: The Ottoman Imprint on the Balkans and the Middle East* (New York, 1996); Rozen, *Last Ottoman Century*.

[49] Karpat, *Ottoman Population*; McCarthy, "Jewish Population"; Avigdor Levy, "The Siege of Edirne (1912–1913) as Seen by a Jewish Eyewitness: Social, Political, and Cultural Perspectives," in *Jews, Turks, Ottomans*, ed. Avigdor Levy (Syracuse, 2002), 153–193.

[50] See Fleming, *Greece*; Mark Mazower, *Salonica, City of Ghosts* (New York, 2005); Devin Naar, *Jewish Salonica: Between the Ottoman Empire and Modern Greece* (Stanford, 2016).

The presence of ethnic and religious minorities presented a challenge for the homogenization of the newly formed nation-states of the Balkans, and the large presence of Jews in Salonika – who were perceived as loyal to the old, Ottoman order – threatened the Greek claim to the city. At the same time, the national movements on the Balkans, including Greek national-ism, had perpetuated the Ottoman category of the *millet* as an ethno-religious group, and Greek national identity was closely intertwined with a Christian Orthodox religious identity. The dilemma how to integrate a group such as the Judeo-Spanish speaking Jews of Salonika thus presented a test that potentially undermined the foundation of the national ideology.

The great fire of 1917 that destroyed a large portion of Salonika's central districts and displaced about 60,000 people, presented an opportunity for the Greek state to radically remake the city. Making the city less "Ottoman" and more "modern," the urban topography was completely transformed, and thousands of Jews, who had inhabited the largely Jewish quarters in the town's center, were relocated to new areas on the outskirts – and thus marginalized symbolically. The major demographic shift, however, occurred after the First World War and the ensuing war between Greece and Turkey (1919–22), when the two countries agreed on a massive popula-tion transfer in the Treaty of Lausanne of 1923: 1.2 million Greek Orthodox Christians from Asia Minor were relocated to Greece, and up to half a mil-lion Muslims from Greece to Turkey. As most Greek Orthodox refugees streamed into Macedonia, the demographic balance changed radically: in Salonika, by 1926, 80 percent of the population were Greek Orthodox and only 15 to 20 percent Jewish.

The population transfer came at the end of a period of cataclysmic vio-lence. In Anatolia alone, some two million Muslims, 800,000 Armenians, and 500,000 Orthodox Christians had been killed in the years between 1915 and 1922. War, expulsions, and genocide (namely against the Armenians) were undoing the complex ethno-religious mix of Ottoman society, and the nation-states succeeding the empire, including Greece and Turkey, pursued an agenda of forging a homogeneous society. Among the peo-ple transferred from Salonika to Turkey in 1923 were the ten or twelve thousand Dönme, descendants of a group of Jews who had followed the seventeenth-century messianic figure Sabbatai Zevi when he converted to Islam in 1666. The Dönme were expelled from Salonika because they were considered Muslims; in Turkey, however, they were increasingly seen as "secret Jews," a product, as Marc Baer has shown, of the "ethnicized reli-gion" and racial thinking of early twentieth-century Turkish nationalism.[51]

---

[51] Marc David Baer, *The Dönme: Jewish Converts, Muslim Revolutionaries, and Secular Turks* (Stanford, 2010); on the population exchange of 1923, 142–154.

In Greece, tensions between Greeks and Jews engendered resentment, especially among the Greek refugees uprooted from Asia Minor, and anti-semitism became a fixture in the nationalist Greek press (and elsewhere in the Balkans) in the interwar period.[52] The problem continued to be how the Jews, as an ethnic and religious minority who had lived in the area for centuries yet, in the case of most Sephardim, continued to speak their own language, could ever become fully "Greek." In the words of the newspaper *Makedonía*, which became a mouthpiece of nationalist antise-mitic rhetoric, in 1929: "Either [the Jews] will acquire a Greek conscious-ness, identifying their interests and their expectations with ours, or they will seek a home elsewhere, because Thessaly is not in a position to nurse at its bosom people who are Greeks only in name." In 1931, nationalist agitation and suspicion of Jewish loyalty to the Greek nation-state led to violence: rioting in the poor Jewish Campbell neighborhood culminated with the burning and looting of Jewish homes and businesses. Worse, in the ensuing trial the court ruled that the perpetrators had been motivated by patriotism and were thus acquitted. The case only reinforced the notion that Jews could not, at least for some, really ever be Greek. In the end, of course, it was not Greek nationalism but the German occupation in 1941 that ended centuries of Jewish life in Salonika.[53]

The unraveling of the empire and its multi-ethnic legacy presented chal-lenges not only to the Christian nation-states, but also in Turkey proper (the Turkish Republic was established in October 1923).[54] Despite the secu-larization and westernization under the leadership of Kemal Atatürk, to be "Turkish" remained entangled with being Muslim (though secular), and making Jews Turkish proved no easier than making Jews Greek. As the old, Ottoman-style autonomy of the Jewish community was abolished, and foreign schools – including those of the Alliance – had to close their doors, the foundations of the Jewish community were undermined, while the full integration of the Jews into the new nation remained contentious. The Jews were a small minority, to be sure, and thus hardly seen as a threat to the building of a Turkish nation-state. Still, the 1920s and 1930s saw the

---

[52] See Rıfat Bali, "L'antisémitisme en Turquie de 1923 a nos jours," in idem, *Les relations entre Turcs et juifs dans la Turquie moderne* (Istanbul, 2001), 39–74; Rena Molho, "Popular Antisemitism and State Policy in Salonica during the City's Annexation to Greece, 1912–1919" and "La legislation anti-juive de Venizélos entre les deux guerres," in idem, *Salonica and Istanbul: Social, Political and Cultural Aspects of Jewish Life* (Istanbul, 2005), 217–241.

[53] Fleming, *Greece*, 94–100.

[54] Avner Levi, *History of the Jews in the Turkish Republic* (Jerusalem, 1992) (Hebrew); Avner Levi, *Türkiye Cumhuriyeti'nde Yahudiler* (Istanbul, 1992); Corry Guttstadt, *Die Türkei, die Juden und der Holocaust* (Berlin, 2008), 49–108.

growth of antisemitic propaganda in the nationalist press, with recurring accusations against Jews (and other minorities) of betrayal, disloyalty, and economic domination. One cause célèbre was the trial of Sami Günzberg, a Jew who became the official dentist of Atatürk and who was accused, in 1923, of being a spy, and his clinic a place for German army officers to consort with Muslim women. He was acquitted only in 1928. Another, rather bizarre, case involved a forged letter, allegedly signed by 300 Jewish notables, which numerous Turkish newspapers claimed had been sent to Madrid in 1926 to express Jewish identification with Spain. Antisemitic agitation met with some success, especially in Thrace where many of the Muslim refugees from Greece had settled and where pogroms against Jews in several towns erupted in the summer of 1934. Jews fled from the area, including the city of Edirne, to Istanbul after (apparently unfounded) rumors that the Turkish government had conspired to remove the Jews from this sensitive border region.

Government officials, including prime minister Inönü, repeatedly denied that antisemitism existed in Turkey, and, as Avner Levi has argued, in many instances anti-Jewish agitation (except in the case of the Thrace riots) was driven by a small number of intellectuals and journalists, rather than representing a widespread antisemitism. It is also noteworthy that, as the Turkish government seemed intent on driving out minorities from their prominent role in business or the professions, Jews were at times treated more favorably than Greeks or Armenians. When lawyers' licenses were reviewed in 1924, 58 percent of Jewish lawyers and 55 percent of their Muslim counterparts kept their license, but 75 percent of Armenian and Greek lawyers lost theirs.[55] The most persistent claim against the Jews that appeared in the Turkish press in those years was focused on the issue of language as they were denounced for continuing to speak Ladino (or French) rather than Turkish. This complaint echoed the Kemalist ideology according to which Turkish national identity was defined through the use of the Turkish language. The *Citizen, Speak Turkish!* (*Vatandaş Türkçe Konuş*) campaign initiated in 1928 reinforced the pressure especially on the non-Muslim minorities, in particular the Jews, to speak only Turkish in public, and the 1930s saw an intensification of the Turkification policy.[56]

When the Kingdom of Serbs, Croats, and Slovenes was formed at the end of World War I (Yugoslavia, as it was called after 1929), it straddled the centuries-old border that had separated the Ottoman from

[55] Levi, *Jews in the Turkish Republic*, 29–30, 48.
[56] Senem Aslan, "'Citizen, Speak Turkish!' A Nation in the Making," *Nationalism and Ethnic Politics* 13 (2007): 245–272.

the Habsburg Empire, and the new nation-state included Jewish communities as diverse as the Sephardi, Ladino-speaking communities of Belgrade and Sarajevo and the Ashkenazi, German and Yiddish-speaking communities – themselves split into a dominant reform-oriented "Neologue" community and the Orthodox – in Croatia, in particular Zagreb, and in the Vojvodina. The Jews of Yugoslavia thus mirrored the ethnic and linguistic diversity of the new kingdom. Their historical experiences varied greatly, from Croatia which had long been under Habsburg rule and where Jews were allowed to establish communities only in the late eighteenth century and Bosnia, which had been occupied by Austria in 1878, to the communities of Serbia which had lived under Ottoman rule and then experienced the long and bumpy road to emancipation in independent Serbia, marred by their expulsion from the Serbian countryside in the mid-nineteenth century and a series of blood libels in the 1860s.

Jews were a small minority in interwar Yugoslavia – about half a percent, though more prominent in Belgrade, Sarajevo, and Zagreb. As Emil Kerenji has argued, like Yugoslavia, Yugoslav Jewry had to be created. A central role in the process of forging a united, Yugoslav Jewish community was played by the leaders of the Zionist movement in Zagreb who, in order to assert their leadership over the Zionist movement in Yugoslavia, were "the first to imagine, at the turn of the century, the possibility of a unified Yugoslav Jewry" and "set out to forge a Serbo-Croatian speaking Jewry that would eventually become Yugoslav Jewry."[57] They did so by creating an associational life (the Bar Giora association) and publishing newspapers (*Židovska smotra* and, later, *Židov*) in Serbo-Croatian.[58]

Thus, on the eve of the Second World War, the Jewish communities of southeastern Europe and Asia Minor had begun their transformation from an Ottoman *millet* to a religious-ethnic minority in the new nation-states of the post-imperial order. The war, the mass murder of the Jews under German occupation in Greece and Yugoslavia, and eventually the wave of emigration from countries like Bulgaria or Turkey to the newly established state of Israel all but ended the centuries-long history of the Jewish communities in the Eastern Sephardi heartland.

[57] Emil Kerenji, "Jewish Citizens of Socialist Yugoslavia: Politics of Jewish Identity in a Socialist State, 1944–1974" (Ph.D. diss., University of Michigan, 2008), 47. On Yugoslav Jewry in general see Harriet Pass Freidenreich, *The Jews of Yugoslavia: A Quest for Community* (Philadelphia, 1979).
[58] Kerenji, "Jewish Citizens," 47–95.

THE END OF JUDEO-SPANISH HISTORY?

The fate of the Eastern Sephardim has long been all but absent from the historiography of the Holocaust. Yet, one of the largest Sephardi communities in the world, Salonika, was annihilated by the Nazis. Almost 90 percent of Greek Jewry (between 60,000 and 70,000; 50,000 from Salonika alone) was murdered in the Holocaust, as were about 80 percent of Yugoslav Jews (55,000–60,000).[59]

When the German occupying forces in Serbia came under attack from a communist-led uprising in the summer of 1941, the *Wehrmacht* began to detain "all communists, all those suspected as such, all Jews ..." as hostages. For every German soldier killed, one hundred Serbian hostages were to be shot. In the fall of 1941 – that is, some three months before Heydrich called the infamous Wannsee conference to establish the framework for the so-called final solution, the systematic extermination of all European Jews – firing squads of the *Wehrmacht* killed all adult male Jews in Serbia. In October 1941, a senior official of the German military administration in Serbia wrote in a letter to a friend:

In the last eight days I had 2,000 Jews and 200 Gypsies shot in accordance with the ratio 1:100 for bestially murdered German soldiers ... This is not a pretty business. At any rate, it has to be, if only to make clear what it means even to attack a German soldier, and, for the rest, the Jewish question solves itself most quickly this way.[60]

Later that year, the remaining Serbian Jews – mostly women and children – were concentrated in one camp in Zemun and in 1942, more than 6,000 were killed in gas vans. Up to 100 women and children were loaded into vans and gassed while crossing central Belgrade, being buried across the city in anonymous mass graves.

In the puppet state of Croatia that was created by Germany and Italy in 1941, including Bosnia with the large Jewish community of Sarajevo, it was the local fascist Ustasha regime that was responsible for the mass murder of the Jews. Between September and November 1941, the Jews of Sarajevo were brought to the Jasenovac concentration camp where they were killed. Croatian Jews were rounded up and handed over to the Germans for deportation.[61]

---

[59] On the Holocaust in the Eastern Sephardi heartland see Benbassa and Rodrigue, *Sephardi Jewry*, 164–184.

[60] Quoted in Christopher Browning, *The Origins of the Final Solution: the Evolution of Nazi Jewish Policy, September 1939–March 1942* (Lincoln and Jerusalem, 2004), 341.

[61] Benbassa and Rodrigue, *Sephardi Jewry*, 165, 172–3. On Sarajevo see Emily Greble, *Sarajevo, 1941–1945: Muslims, Christians, and Jews in Hitler's Europe* (Ithaca, 2011).

Germany occupied northern Greece, including Salonika, in 1941, and the previously Italian-controlled zone in the South in 1943.[62] At first, the "Rosenberg Sonderkommando" swept into Salonika to loot archives, books, and artifacts from the city's Jewish community for the planned Library for the Exploration of the Jewish Question in Frankfurt. On July 11, 1942, all Jewish men between the ages of 18 and 45 were ordered to Freedom Square in central Salonika where they were forced to do humiliating exercises under the burning sun and beaten if they collapsed. Thousands were drafted for slave labor. The systematic process of social exclusion, abuse and, eventually, deportation and murder had begun. In early 1943, the Jews of Salonika were forced into ghettos within in the city – most in the Baron de Hirsch neighborhood – and on March 15, 1943, the deportations to Auschwitz-Birkenau began. With the exception of those who had been able to escape to the Italian zone of Greece and a few hundred who were saved because they held Spanish and Italian citizenship, practically the entire Jewish community of Salonika was deported and killed. 48,974 Jews from northern Greece were sent to Auschwitz alone, where 37,386 were gassed immediately upon arrival.

In those areas that were annexed to Bulgaria, an ally of Nazi Germany, in Macedonia (Monastir and Skopje, for example) as well as Thrace, Jews were deported to Treblinka, even though those in Bulgaria proper were saved. Anti-Jewish legislation went into effect in early 1941 and, in response to German pressure, the Bulgarians committed to deport 20,000 Jews. When word got out, however, that Jews holding Bulgarian citizenship were going to be included in this number, a rare public protest ensued and the partial deportation from Bulgaria proper was stopped. Thus, with the exception of the Jews in Bulgaria, the Jewish communities of the Balkans were annihilated. A few thousand Jews survived as foreign citizens, joining the Greek or the Yugoslav partisans, or in hiding, but the centuries-old communities of the Eastern Sephardi heartland disappeared, with very small communities remaining today in cities like Salonika and Sarajevo. Even of the material legacy of centuries of Sephardi culture little is left: today, the campus of Salonika's Aristotle University extends on top of what used to be in its day the largest Jewish cemetery in Europe, destroyed in 1942.

The Jews of Turkey, which upheld what Corry Guttstadt has called a "one-sided neutrality" all the while maintaining good relations with Germany to almost the end of the war – were spared the violence of the Holocaust. Turkey took in a number of Jewish academics who had been expelled from German universities and who came to play an important role in the development of the new University of Istanbul. For the most

---

[62] On Greece see Fleming, *Greece*; Mark Mazower, *Inside Hitler's Greece* (New Haven, 1993), and Steven Bowman, *The Agony of Greek Jews, 1940–1945* (Stanford, 2009).

part, however, the Turkish government went to great lengths to restrict the influx of Jewish refugees from Europe and a secret government decree from August 1938 explicitly banned the entry of "foreign Jews who are subject to restrictions in their home country … regardless of their religious affiliation." Also visas for Jews in transit to Palestine were subject to severe restrictions. When Britain granted entry permits to Palestine for 5,000 Jewish orphans from Bulgaria, Hungary, and Romania in 1943, the Turkish authorities granted visas for only 75 children every ten days, with the proviso that new visas would only be issued once the previous group had left the country.[63] The war years left other scars as the Turkification policies of Atatürk's republic intensified. The infamous "capital tax" (*varlık vergisi*) of November 1942, was designed to force the Turkification of the economy and push out non-Muslim competition. The tax was applied unevenly to different religious-ethnic groups; according to one estimate, Muslims were taxed, on average, 5 percent, of their annual income, Greeks 156 percent, Jews 179 percent, and Armenians 232 percent. It was only in 1944 that the tax was repealed.[64]

After the war, the two communities that had survived World War II – in Bulgaria and in Turkey – as well as the small remnants of Greek or Yugoslav Jewry were reduced dramatically by a massive emigration to the new State of Israel. Today, only Turkey remains home to a relatively sizeable Jewish community, estimated anywhere from 18,000 to 25,000 individuals.[65] What is curious, however, is how the Sephardi Jews of the various Ottoman successor states have at times achieved only in their new Diaspora – in Israel, in the United States, and elsewhere – what remained so elusive during the nation-building processes of the late nineteenth and early twentieth centuries: the Sephardim of Greece have finally become "Greek Jews," the Jews of Istanbul and Izmir "Turkish Jewish," and those from Sofia "Bulgarian."[66] The new, post-factum "national" identity has

---

[63] Guttstadt, *Die Türkei, die Juden und der Holocaust*, 230, 249.

[64] These numbers in Benbassa and Rodrigue, *Sephardi Jewry*, 182. See Rıfat Bali, *The 'Varlık Vergisi' Affair* (Istanbul, 2005).

[65] Kerenji, "Jewish Citizens," argues that talking of a "remnant" community may be too final, or teleological, as there continues to be Jewish life in places like Belgrade, Sarajevo or, in Greece, in Athens and Salonika, and in rather more significant numbers, in Istanbul. On Istanbul, see Brink-Danan, *Jewish Life in 21st-Century Turkey*; Shaul Tuval, *The Jewish Community of Istanbul, 1948–1992* (Jerusalem, 2004) (Hebrew); on Salonika, Bea Lewkowicz, *The Jewish Community of Salonika* (London, 2006); on Ioannina, Annette Fromm, *We Are Few: Folklore and Ethnic Identity of the Jewish Community of Ioannina, Greece* (Lanham, 2008).

[66] Fleming, *Greece*; Guy Haskell, *From Sofia to Jaffa: The Jews of Bulgaria and Israel* (Detroit, 1994).

often – though not everywhere – obscured the historically much deeper-rooted common Judeo-Spanish heritage of these communities.

SELECT BIBLIOGRAPHY

Baer, Marc David. *The Dönme: Jewish Converts, Muslim Revolutionaries, and Secular Turks.* Stanford, 2010.

Bali, Rıfat. *Les relations entre Turcs et juifs dans la Turquie modern.* Istanbul, 2001.

Benbassa, Esther. *Haim Nahum: A Sephardic Chief Rabbi in Politics.* Tuscaloosa, 1995.
Une diaspora sépharade en transition. Paris, 1993.
and Aron Rodrigue. *Sephardi Jewry: A History of the Judeo-Spanish Community, 14th–20th Centuries.* Berkeley, 2000.

Borovaya, Olga. *Modern Ladino Culture: Press, Belles Lettres, and Theater in the Late Ottoman Empire.* Bloomington, 2012.

Bowman, Steven. *The Agony of Greek Jews, 1940–1945.* Stanford, 2009.

Braude, Benjamin and Bernard Lewis, eds. *Christians and Jews in the Ottoman Empire,* 2 vols. New York 1982.

Brink-Danan, Marcy. *Jewish Life in 21st-Century Turkey: The Other Side of Tolerance.* Bloomington, 2012.

Cohen, Julia Phillips. *Becoming Ottomans: Sephardi Jews and Imperial Citizenship in the Modern Era.* Oxford, 2014.
and Sarah Abrevaya Stein, eds. *Sephardi Lives: A Documentary History, 1700–1950.* Stanford, 2014.

Fleming, K. E. *Greece: A Jewish History.* Princeton, 2008.

Freidenreich, Harriet Pass. *The Jews of Yugoslavia: A Quest for Community.* Philadelphia, 1979.

Gerber, Haim and Jacob Barnai. *The Jews of Izmir in the Nineteenth Century: Ottoman Documents from the Shar'i Court.* Jerusalem, 1984 (Hebrew).

Greble, Emily. *Sarajevo, 1941–1945: Muslims, Christians, and Jews in Hitler's Europe.* Ithaca, 2011.

Guttstadt, Corry. *Die Türkei, die Juden und der Holocaust.* Berlin, 2008.

Haskell, Guy. *From Sofia to Jaffa: The Jews of Bulgaria and Israel.* Detroit, 1994.

Jackson, Maureen. *Mixing Musics: Turkish Jewry and the Urban Landscape of a Sacred Song.* Stanford, 2013.

Karmi, Ilan. *The Jewish Community of Istanbul in the Nineteenth Century.* Istanbul, 1996.

Keren, Zvi. *The Jewish Community of Rusçuk.* Jerusalem, 2005 (Hebrew).

Kerenji, Emil. "Jewish Citizens of Socialist Yugoslavia: Politics of Jewish Identity in a Socialist State, 1944–1974," Ph.D. diss., University of Michigan, 2008.

Leff, Lisa Moses. *Sacred Bonds of Solidarity: The Rise of Internationalism in Nineteenth-Century France.* Stanford, 2006.

Lehmann, Matthias B. *Ladino Rabbinic Literature and Ottoman Sephardic Culture.* Bloomington, 2005.

Levi, Avner. *History of the Jews in the Turkish Republic.* Jerusalem, 1992 (Hebrew).

Levy, Avigdor, ed. *The Jews of the Ottoman Empire.* Princeton, 1994.
Jews, Turks, Ottomans. Syracuse, 2002.

Mays, Devi. "Transplanting Cosmopolitans: The Migration of Sephardic Jews to Mexico, 1900–1934," Ph.D. diss., Indiana University, Bloomington, 2013.

Mazower, Mark. *Salonica, City of Ghosts*. New York, 2005.

Molho, Rena. *Salonica and Istanbul: Social, Political and Cultural Aspects of Jewish Life*. Istanbul, 2005.

Naar, Devin. *Jewish Salonica: Between the Ottoman Empire and Modern Greece*. Stanford, 2016.

Nahum, Henri. *Juifs de Smyrne, XIXe-XXe siècle*. Paris, 1997.

Rodrigue, Aron. *French Jews, Turkish Jews: The Alliance Israélite Universelle and the Politics of Jewish Schooling in Turkey, 1860–1925*. Bloomington, 1990.

   Jews and Muslims: Images of Sephardi and Eastern Jewries in Modern Times. Seattle, 2003.

   ed. *Ottoman and Turkish Jewry: Community and Leadership*. Bloomington, 1992.

Rodrigue, Aron and Sarah Abrevaya Stein, eds. *A Jewish Voice from Ottoman Salonica: The Ladino Memoir of Sa'adi Besalel a-Levi*. Stanford, 2012.

Rozen, Minna. *The Last Ottoman Century and Beyond: The Jews of Turkey and the Balkans, 1808–1945*. Tel Aviv, 2005.

Shaw, Stanford. *The Jews of the Ottoman Empire and the Turkish Republic*. New York, 1991.

Stein, Sarah Abrevaya. *Making Jews Modern: The Yiddish and Ladino Press in the Russian and Ottoman Empires*. Bloomington, 2004.

Tuval, Shaul. *The Jewish Community of Istanbul, 1948–1992*. Jerusalem, 2004 (Hebrew).

CHAPTER 5

GREAT BRITAIN, THE COMMONWEALTH, AND ANGLOPHONE JEWRY

ADAM MENDELSOHN

Writing late in the dreary Philadelphia winter of 1846, Issac Leeser, the prickly editor of America's first monthly Jewish newspaper boldly predicted a "hundred-fold increase" in Jewish immigration to "Great Britain, Australia, New Zealand, Hindoostan, South America, the West Indies, the United States, and Canada."[1] Perfect hindsight has dulled the shine of Leeser's prescience. Scarcely 15,000 Jews lived in the United States in 1840; fewer than five hundred in British Canada, and sixty lonely pioneers in hardscrabble New Zealand. It was still little more than a decade since Jewish chained migrants transported to Australia as convicts outnumbered their unfettered co-religionists in the antipodes. Ever the optimist, Leeser saw portents of change in a variety of unexpected places: in his ever more frequent encounters with scatterings of Jews in intrepid frontier towns during his extensive travels across an ever-growing nation, in the news he published of congregations sprouting in the distant outposts of the British Empire, and in newfound subscribers to his newspaper as far afield as Canada, England, the Caribbean, and New South Wales. Above all, he anticipated that the "milder laws of English-speaking nations" would have a magnetic effect on the Jews of Europe.[2] What Leeser recognized, however imperfectly, were the first signs of the flourishing of Jewish life in an expanding Anglophone Diaspora that offered Jews a distinct path to modernity.

There were some striking similarities between the challenges and opportunities that Jews faced in English-speaking countries over the course of the nineteenth century. Although British Jews and their colonial cousins were dissenters within an Anglican Empire, and retained a hierarchical pattern of religious organization that emulated the Established church, they were tied by more than language to Jews in the United States. The Jewish communities of the British Empire and America were confronted with and were forced to adapt to the challenges of voluntarism (the breakdown

---

[1] *Occident* (hereafter *Occ*) 4 (January 1847): 470.
[2] *Occ* 2 (March 1845): 571–572.

of communal authority and pressures for religious reform), a permissive and relatively accepting social environment (intermarriage, irreligion, and non-affiliation), and the considerable energies of proselytizing missionaries. Similarly, the strategies commonly adopted by Jewish communities across the English-speaking world to counter these perceived threats came to be drawn from a common repertoire. This is unsurprising given the circulation of books and newspapers, the movement of religious leaders, and the influence of transnational trends within the Church.

There was little cause for optimism, however, when Isaac Leeser first arrived in America as a teenager in 1824. Fewer than 6,000 Jews lived in the United States, most in port cities along the Atlantic seaboard. He arrived at a moment of transition. The scaffolding of the Sephardic Atlantic world – bonds of reciprocity and obligation among synagogues, colonial merchants, and port communities – was fraying, as Caribbean Jewry stagnated in size and the galloping western frontier increasingly became the locus of economic opportunity. The future looked uncertain as America's freedoms exposed the frailties of the American Jewish community. In several cities Jews were beginning to rebel against the hegemonic synagogue community, casting off an organizational model that had structured communal life since the colonial period. Social acceptance drew many away from rigorous religious observance; the rate of intermarriage nearly doubled in the decades after the Revolution.[3]

Jewish institutional life in Britain looked equally sclerotic in the first decades of the nineteenth century. Assailed by critics, the incumbent Chief Rabbi held limited authority and was regarded with indifference by many within his own community. The Board of Deputies of British Jews, in name the representative body of the community, was noteworthy for its lethargy rather than its leadership. The Jewish population of England was substantially larger than that of the United States – already more than 15,000 strong at the start of the century – but many were members of the substantial impoverished underclass of their host society.[4] The majority lived in London, then the most populous city in Europe, where they worked as hawkers, artisans, and petty shopkeepers. They shared their poverty and a surprising degree of social intercourse with their non-Jewish neighbors. For most, the tug of economic and social mobility was still

---

[3] Jonathan Sarna, *American Judaism: A History* (New Haven, 2004), 45, 54–55.

[4] Todd Endelman discusses a variety of population estimates in *The Jews of Georgian England, 1714–1830* (Ann Arbor, 1999), 172–173. Lipman estimates 20,000 to 25,000 Jews in 1800. Vivian Lipman, "The Anglo-Jewish Community in Victorian Society," in *Studies in the Cultural Life of the Jews in England*, ed. Dov Noy and Issachar Ben-Ami (Jerusalem, 1975), 151–159.

faint. The everyday experience of the Jewish poor was far removed from that of the small elite that fashioned itself into a communal aristocracy. Although Ashkenazim had made up the majority of the community since the mid-eighteenth century, they were outnumbered by Sephardim within this stratum that built its fortunes on trade, brokerage, and banking.[5]

There were, however, already signs of change. In the first decades of the century, Britain rediscovered its appetite for colonization, establishing settlement colonies at the Cape and antipodes, and steadily accumulating and consolidating territory and control in South Asia and the Far East.[6] The focus of the empire drifted decisively away from its old Caribbean moorings. This second British Empire presented a far larger set of opportunities to a wider swathe of Jews at home and abroad. Colonial demand stimulated metropolitan markets. Jews were fortuitously positioned in a number of marginal niches that were boosted by the imperial economy.[7] Directly and indirectly this aided the uneven upward mobility of Britain's Jewish lower classes, further enriched the Jewish elite, and attracted ever more immigrants to England and its colonial possessions.[8]

The imperial system provided a tempting prospect for would-be immigrants to the outposts of the British Empire, promising and often providing Jews with equal treatment before the law. The political opportunities available to Jews advanced more quickly in the colonies.[9] Even if Jews labored under political disabilities in England until 1871, by mid-century these restrictions were in effect an encumbrance only to the anglicized elite.[10] Although the State privileged the Anglican Church, Jews shared their

[5] The best single-volume study of the Jewish community is Todd Endelman, *The Jews of Britain, 1656 to 2000* (Berkeley, 2002). For its class structure in 1800 see pages 42–51.

[6] On this transition, see P. J. Marshall, "Britain without America – A Second Empire?" in *The Oxford History of the British Empire, Volume II: The Eighteenth Century*, ed. P. J. Marshall (Oxford, 1998), 576–594.

[7] On the economic impact of Empire on Britain, see B. R. Tomlinson, "Economics and Empire: The Metropolitan Context" in *The Oxford History of the British Empire, Volume III: The Nineteenth Century*, ed. Andrew Porter (Oxford, 1999), 31–51.

[8] For a useful summary of the changes within the Jewish economy see Vivian Lipman, *Social History of the Jews in England, 1850–1950* (London, 1954), 29–34.

[9] This issue is explored in Sheldon Godfrey and Judith Godfrey, *Search Out the Land* (Montreal, 1995); Israel Getzler, *Neither Toleration nor Favour* (Melbourne, 1971); Samuel Hurwitz and Edith Hurwitz, "The New World Sets an Example for the Old: The Jews of Jamaica and Political Rights, 1661–1831," *American Jewish Historical Quarterly* 55 (1965): 37–56.

[10] This point is made in Endelman, *Jews of Georgian England*, 277–280; Endelman, *The Jews of Britain*, 100–101; David Katz, *The Jews in the History of England, 1485–1850* (Oxford, 2002), 323.

secondary status with Catholics and dissenters. In practical terms these disabilities meant little in their daily commercial and personal transactions. Conversely, Jews often benefited from the pulse of millennialism that flowed through Victorian veins as well as the anti-popery that bled fervor from anti-Judaism.[11] While some imperial administrators harbored suspicions of Jews as a group, in practice and policy the Crown discriminated relatively rarely against Jews as individuals in the application of the law. If anything, colonial Jews benefited from similar legal and political structures, modeled on the metropolitan template, which governed the colonies, as well as the prevailing liberal principles of tolerance and fair-play. The empire also extended its protections to its Jewish subjects who traveled and traded abroad, an important advantage for merchants who operated in the Ottoman Empire, Persia, and China. At times Jews were useful for the empire, and empire was useful for Jews. In several instances they acted as subagents of imperialism – pushing for imperial action to serve their own interests – and on occasion as skillful manipulators of the power of precedent within the colonial system to advance their own rights.[12] The imperial mood also provided a measure of social sanction for international Jewish solidarity.[13]

From the mid-nineteenth century onwards, the Jewish population in Anglophone countries grew rapidly, aided by a tide of immigrants from Central and Eastern Europe seeking to improve their economic and social prospects. This migration was facilitated by technological innovation, but also by push factors that persuaded Jews that their prospects were brighter abroad.[14] Once numerically insignificant Jewish communities grew at a

[11] On the impact of millennialism in Britain, see Israel Finestein, *Anglo-Jewry in Changing Times: Studies in Diversity, 1840–1914* (London, 1999), 140–67; Katz, *Jews in the History of England*, 378–82; Mel Scult, *Millennial Expectations and Jewish Liberties* (Leiden, 1978).

[12] The Sydney Jewish community astutely referenced Jamaican precedent when appealing to the New South Wales Legislative Council for funds to defray building debts. See *Voice of Jacob* (hereafter *VoJ*), April 10, 1846; April 24, 1846; *Jewish Chronicle* (hereafter *JC*), March 5, 1847; *Report of the Committee of the Sydney Synagogue 1847* (Sydney, 1847). See also the appeal from the Jews of Tunis for the protection of the British Consul General in the *VoJ*, August 1, 1845; Moses Montefiore to the Earl of Clarendon, Foreign Office, April 10, 1856, London Committee of Deputies of the British Jews minute book, ACC/3121/B1/2, LMA; minutes of meeting, October 5, 1858, Board of Deputies Correspondence 1844–1860, ACC/3121/B1/1, LMA; *JC*, October 27, 1854.

[13] See Abigail Green, "Rethinking Sir Moses Montefiore: Religion, Nationhood, and International Philanthropy in the Nineteenth Century," *American Historical Review* 110 (June 2005): 631–658; Todd Endelman, "Communal Solidarity Among the Jewish Elite of Victorian London," *Victorian Studies* 28 (1985): 493 n. 6.

[14] On technological change and immigration see Daniel Headrick, *The Tools of Empire: Technology and European Imperialism in the Nineteenth Century* (New York, 1981),

jarring pace. By far the largest stream of immigrants made their way to the United States. By 1850, America was home to 50,000 Jews. A decade later, its Jewish population had more than doubled (and perhaps quadrupled).[15] By contrast fewer than 10,000 German Jews settled permanently in Britain during the entire Victoria period; of those that did, a higher proportion appear to have arrived with the resources, education, and experience needed to immediately establish their own businesses.[16] Although Britain attracted fewer immigrants – the Jewish population only reached 60,000 in 1880 – these figures conceal the vast number of transmigrants who stopped temporarily on their way to the United States and the colonies.[17] The existing communal infrastructure struggled to cope with this influx. Even Australia, separated by a lengthy and relatively expensive voyage from Europe, grew exponentially. Between 1840 and 1861, the total Australian Jewish population expanded roughly fivefold, in large part due to an onrush of immigrants attracted after the discovery of gold in New South Wales and Victoria.[18] This general pattern held true for South Africa, Canada, and New Zealand, albeit in smaller numbers. Only Jamaica, whose plantation economy struggled throughout the century, failed to grow at an equivalent rate.[19]

144–148; Robert Kubicek, "British Expansion, Empire, and Technological Change," in *The Oxford History of the British Empire, Volume III*, ed. Andrew Porter, 249–251; *JC*, February 24, 1854.

[15] On "German" immigration to the United States, see Avraham Barkai, *Branching Out: German-Jewish Immigration to the United States, 1820–1914* (New York, 1994); Hasia Diner, *A Time for Gathering: The Second Migration, 1820–1880* (Baltimore, 1992); Naomi W. Cohen, *Encounter with Emancipation: The German Jews in the United States 1830–1914* (Philadelphia, 1984).

[16] On German Jewish immigrants in England see Todd Endelman, "German-Jewish Settlement in Victorian England," in *Second Chance: Two Centuries of German-Speaking Jews in the United Kingdom*, ed. Werner Mosse (Tübingen, 1991), 37–56. For a comparison of those who settled in England with those who went to America, see 41–43. On the Jewish population of Britain at mid-century, see Petra Laidlaw, "Jews in the British Isles in 1851: Birthplaces, Residence and Migrations," *The Jewish Journal of Sociology* 53 (2011): 32–47. For the settlement patterns of immigrants see 41–43.

[17] Lloyd Gartner estimates that more than a million Jewish immigrants spent some time in Britain on their way to America. This form of stage migration may have been more typical in the 1840s and 1850s. Lloyd Gartner, *The Jewish Immigrant in England, 1870–1914* (London, 2001), ix, 17, 35, 38.

[18] For Australian Jewish population estimates see Hilary Rubinstein, *The Jews in Australia: A Thematic History. Volume One: 1788–1945* (Port Melbourne, Victoria, 1991), 90.

[19] There were roughly 451 Jews in British Canada in 1851, and 1,186 by 1860. The Jewish population of Quebec in 1861 was around 572. There are few reliable figures for the size

Initially scions of the Anglo-Jewish elite comprised a disproportionate share of early Jewish free settlers in Australia and the Cape. If these sons and daughters of privilege were somewhat insulated from the jolting downturns that periodically disrupted colonial growth, they were far from alone in profiting from empire. Colonial economies were remarkably open to enterprising immigrants. Although the rate of failure was high, settlers benefited from growing international demand for colonial produce and an expanding domestic market driven by immigration. The colonies provided a fluid economic and social environment, relatively free of entrenched competition and barriers to entry, enabling legions of Jewish settlers to transcend their humble antecedents. Just as colonies offered a venue for redemption, the colonial port city could provide cover for those with less salubrious ambitions. The flux of colonial communities and the inevitable delay in the verification of the bona fides of newcomers could be turned toward fraud. Scoundrels arriving from abroad were sometimes able to outpace their reputations and the law, leaving distressed creditors in every port.[20]

Jewish communities also grew in Britain's expanding eastern empire. These colonies attracted fewer settlers and therefore relied heavily on

of the South African Jewish population prior to the census of 1875, which found 375 Jews in the major urban centers of the Cape Colony. The diamond town of Kimberley, then outside British control, had around 120 Jews. Accordingly, Gideon Shimoni's estimate of 4,000 Jews in South Africa prior to the start of mass eastern European migration in the 1880s seems too high. Census figures from New Zealand record 61 Jews in 1848, 188 in 1858, 326 in 1861, 955 in 1864, 1,247 in 1867 before plateauing for the rest of the nineteenth century. One (of very few) estimates of the Jewish population of Jamaica calculated around 1,800 Jews on the island in 1871. In the mid-eighteenth century, the population was roughly 800. For the Canadian figures see Gerald Tulchinsky, *Taking Root: the Origins of the Canadian Jewish Community* (Hanover, NH, 1993), 50, 58. For South Africa, see Milton Shain, *The Roots of Antisemitism in South Africa* (Johannesburg, 1994), 11–12; Gideon Shimoni, *Community and Conscience: the Jews in Apartheid South Africa* (Hanover, NH, 2003), 2. For New Zealand, Lazarus Goldman, *The History of the Jews in New Zealand* (Wellington, 1958), 67, 92. For thorough estimates of the Jewish population in Jamaica in the eighteenth and early nineteenth century, see Eli Faber, *Jews, Slaves, and the Slave Trade* (New York, 1998), 58, 106–107, 186–220; Carol Holzberg, *Minorities and Power in a Black Society: The Jewish Community of Jamaica* (Lanham, MD, 1987), 20–21.

[20] The most notorious example of this was Isaac (Ikey) Solomon – supposedly the inspiration for Charles Dicken's Fagin – who escaped prison in England for New York (where he continued to dabble in fraud and forgery), Rio de Janeiro, and finally Hobart, where he rejoined his wife and eventually became a member of the synagogue. Solomon's saga is described with relish in John Levi and George Bergman, *Australian Genesis* (Adelaide, 1974), 122–141.

enterprising intermediaries to operate effectively. Major ports became multi-ethnic cities, home to conspicuous and successful trading diasporas. The Baghdadi Jews that settled in Bombay and Calcutta from the early decades of the nineteenth century onward proved particularly adroit at servicing the empire. Like camp-followers behind an advancing army, Baghdadis established trading posts in each of the new territories claimed by Britain in the East.[21] The Crown Colony of Aden, annexed by Britain in 1839, provides another illustrative example of the opportunities for Jews in the eastern empire. The port town's Jewish population grew from around 250 in 1839 (a third of the total population) to 1,070 three years later, drawing refugees and merchants attracted by the town's mercantile prospects. The port sat athwart the sea lanes to Asia and Australia, commanding the entrance of the Red Sea and trade routes with the Arabian Peninsula. As a trade depot and coaling station, the constant traffic of steamships offered employment for everyone from petty entrepreneurs selling cigarettes and trinkets to ships anchored at Steamer Point, merchants trading with England, China, India, and the United States, and Bene Israel stationed as civil servants and soldiers.[22] There were manifold ways of servicing the imperial project: in Port Said and Suez, the shunting yard of the British Empire, enterprising Jews pimped prostitutes to sailors and tourists bound for India, the Far East, and Australia.[23]

Other imperial cities also become nodes in Jewish sub-ethnic networks.[24] In the 1840s Manchester became home to an enclave of Jews from Aleppo, part of a larger self-sustaining Aleppine Diaspora that included colonies

---

[21] See Caroline Plüss, "Globalizing Ethnicity and Multi-local Identifications: The Parsee, Indian Muslim and Sephardic Trade Diasporas in Hong Kong," in *Diaspora Entrepreneurial Networks: Four Centuries of History*, ed. Ina Baghdiantz McCabe, Gelina Harlaftis and Ionna Pepelasis Minoglou (New York: Berg, 2005), 245–268; Chiara Betta, "The Trade Diaspora of Baghdadi Jews: From India to China's Treaty Ports, 1842–1937," in *Diaspora Entrepreneurial Networks*, ed. McCabe, Harlaftis and Minoglou, 269–285; Chen Zhilong, "Shanghai: A Window for Studying Sino-Indian Relations in the Era of Colonialism and Imperialism," in *India and China in the Colonial World*, ed. Madhavi Thampi (New Delhi, 2005), 33–51; Ruth Fredman Cernea, *Almost Englishmen: Baghdadi Jews in British Burma* (Lanham, MD, 2007), xv–xvi, 5.

[22] See Reuben Ahroni, *The Jews of the British Crown Colony of Aden: History, Culture, and Ethnic Relations* (Leiden, 1994), 34, 40–41, 46–56, 108, 111, 147, 319; Caesar Farah, *The Sultan's Yemen* (London, 2002), 120–125; Zaka Kour, *The History of Aden, 1839–72* (London, 1981), 15, 21, 26; *JC*, June 17, 1859. On Aden's place within the British Empire, see Robert Blyth, *The Empire of the Raj* (London, 2003).

[23] See Jacob Landau, *Jews in Nineteenth-Century Egypt* (New York, 1969), 37.

[24] On Ottoman Jews in Manchester, see Bill Williams, *The Making of Manchester Jewry, 1740–1875* (Manchester, 1976), 319–325.

in Calcutta, Cairo, Jamaica, and New York. The offshoots of this network maintained close ties with Aleppo, rejuvenated by a regular supply of new-comers and religious leaders, and supporting the mother community with a return flow of remittances.[25] Moroccan Jews had already established a sig-nificant presence in Gibraltar, Cairo, and Manchester by the late eighteenth century. In London, the wealthier members of this expatriate community joined the Sephardic establishment. Poorer immigrants became peddlers specializing in the sale of spices, rhubarb, and Moroccan slippers.[26] The imperial capital also became home to a cohort of successful colonial Jews who retired to England. The presence of these remade men in metropoli-tan Jewish society provided an alluring example to would-be immigrants, misrepresenting the prospect that awaited the majority who set off for the colonies. A striking number of those who returned to London as colo-nial worthies became supporters of communal and religious reform. Those who had spent decades in the West Indies, antipodes or at the Cape may have become inured of a less rigid religious environment and accustomed to exercising power within the Jewish community.[27]

Into the 1830s no single institution served the Jewish communities of this sprawling empire. This changed when two ineffectual institutions that had exercised limited authority beyond London were transformed by ambitious new leaders. The Board of Deputies of British Jews and the Chief Rabbinate sought to fill this vacuum by acting as the primary reli-gious and political representatives of Jews within the British Empire (and sometimes beyond), albeit within the parameters of politesse and whim imposed by their strong-willed and long-lived leaders. Led with endless

---

[25] See Yaron Harel, "The First Jews from Aleppo in Manchester: New Documentary Evidence," *AJS Review* 23.2 (1998): 196–199; David Sassoon, *A History of the Jews in Baghdad* (Letchwood, 1949), 209–210; Walter P. Zenner, "Streams of Immigration: Sephardic Immigration to Britain and the United States" in *From Iberia to Diaspora: Studies in Sephardic History and Culture*, ed. Yedida K. Stillman and Norman A. Stillman (Boston: Brill, 1999), 142; Walter P. Zenner, *A Global Community: The Jews from Aleppo, Syria* (Detroit: Wayne State University Press, 2000), 33–50; Harvey Goldberg, *Sephardi and Middle Eastern Jewries: History and Culture in the Modern Era* (Bloomington, 1996), 21.

[26] See Daniel Schroeter, *The Sultan's Jews* (Stanford, 2002), 55–76; Daniel Schroeter and Joseph Chetrit, "The Transformation of the Jewish Community of Essaouira (Mogador) in the Nineteenth and Twentieth Centuries," in *Sephardi and Middle Eastern Jewries: History and Culture in the Modern Era*, ed. Harvey Goldberg (Bloomington, 1996), 103.

[27] See Adam Mendelsohn, "Not the Retiring Kind: Jewish Colonials in England in the Mid-Nineteenth Century," in *Colonialism and the Jews*, ed. Ethan B. Katz, Lisa Moses Leff, and Maud S. Mandel (Bloomington: Indiana University Press, 2017), 81–100.

energy by Moses Montefiore, its President intermittently for a twenty-eight-year span beginning in 1835, the Board achieved, at least vicariously, attentive audiences at royal courts from Constantinople to St. Petersburg. His expeditions to Damascus, Rome, Russia, Morocco, and Palestine represented a novel form of Jewish solidarity and political intervention. These expeditions turned Montefiore into a Jewish folk hero across the Jewish world.[28] The Board also became – often reluctantly – a locus for fundraising and mobilization on behalf of communities hobbled by fire, flood, earthquake, plague, and war, or threatened by harsh imperial edict in North Africa, the Ottoman Empire, and Russian territories.[29] It also took on the role of agent and lobbyist on behalf of imperial Jewry, petitioning the Secretary of State for the Colonies on behalf of distant communities: for example, appealing for subventions for synagogues in Malta, Hobart, and Sydney; for the right to erect tabernacles in Gibraltar (a contentious matter given the risk of conflagration in a tinderbox town); and in protest against coerced conversions in Van Dieman's Land.[30]

By force of his personality and stature, Montefiore dominated the patrician Board's deliberations. Unsurprisingly its policies more often than not reflected his views and those of his allies. On occasion this led to acrimony, as when his long running and bitter feud with religious reformers spilled over into the Board's own meetings. The Board's internal shortcomings were less apparent to observers abroad.[31] To them the Board seemed to have the ear of the policymakers who administered the most powerful empire

---

[28] For Montefiore's life and career see Abigail Green, *Moses Montefiore: Jewish Liberator, Imperial Hero* (Cambridge, MA, 2010).

[29] These expeditions are discussed in detail in Sonia Lipman and Vivian Lipman, eds, *The Century of Moses Montefiore* (Oxford, 1985); D. De Sola Pool, "Some Relations of Gershom Kursheedt and Sir Moses Montefiore," *Proceedings of the American Jewish Historical Society* (hereafter *PAJHS*) 37 (1947): 213–220; *JC*, May 15, 1863. For fundraising on behalf of communities abroad, see *VoJ*, January 3 and February 28, 1845; *JC*, August 5, 1850; November 18, 1859; March 2, 1860; October 5, 1860; *Occ* 2 (February 1845) and 6 (December 1848). See also the numerous pleas sent to the Board of Deputies, ACC/3121/B1/1, LMA, Correspondence, 1844–1860.

[30] See Jacob Abeasis to the Board, November 11, 1851, ACC/3121/A/7 1851–1855; Minutes of meeting February 20, 1855, ACC/3121/A/7; Moses Sernya, Abraham Hassan, Haim Benobel to the Board, October 11, 1855, ACC/3121/A/8 1855–1858; Minutes of meetings, March 18, 1847 and November 8, 1848, ACC/3121/A/6, LMA. For the activities of the Board of Deputies, see Aubrey Newman, *The Board of Deputies of British Jews, 1760–1985: A Brief Survey* (London, 1987).

[31] A variety of these shortcomings are described in detail in Michael Clark, *Albion and Jerusalem: The Anglo-Jewish Community in the Post-Emancipation Era* (Oxford, 2009), 109–169.

in the world. So impressed were Jews in America that they sought to duplicate it, choosing in 1859 a name for their own new organization that revealed their inspiration: the Board of Delegates of American Israelites.[32] A handful of decades later, the Jews of India flirted with creating their own Board of Deputies to look after their interests, something that Jews in South Africa, Canada, and Australia later established in a variety of modified forms.

Much as Montefiore energized the Board, Nathan Marcus Adler reimagined the role of Chief Rabbi. Unlike his predecessor, who maintained infrequent contact with colonial congregations and exercised limited authority even within the Anglo-Jewish community, Adler arrived with broader ambitions.[33] When he assumed office in 1845 he became the first "Chief Rabbi of Great Britain and the Empire."[34] The new title was telling. Adler took his responsibilities toward his imperial fief seriously, seizing the opportunity presented by the gangly growth of Jewish communities across the empire to extend his authority overseas. He began to court the colonial congregations from the time he first took office, gathering statistical information on all the Ashkenazi synagogues and supplying each with a set of detailed proposals for improving schooling, worship, and communal organization, suggested with an eye to exerting his authority, constraining reformist tendencies, and standardizing religious practice. Adler corresponded frequently with the colonies and the United States, projecting the power of the Chief Rabbinate abroad, cajoling and prodding recalcitrant communities, answering queries on all manner of issues (everything from the procedure for slaughtering and selling kosher meat to Muslims in Cape Town, to the use of "the lately discovered soothing agent 'chloroform'" for

[32] See Bertram Korn, *The American Reaction to the Mortara Case, 1858–1859* (Cincinnati, 1957); Max Kohler, "The Board of Delegates of American Israelites, 1859–1878," *PAJHS* 29 (1925): 75–136; Allan Tarshish, "The Board of Delegates of American Israelites (1859–1878)," *PAJHS* 49 (September 1959): 16–32. For earlier examples of American Jewish efforts on behalf of international Jewry, see Hyman Grinstein, *The Rise of the Jewish Community of New York, 1654–1860* (Philadelphia, 1945), 420–422, 430–464; Joseph Jacobs, "The Damascus Affair of 1840 and the Jews of America," *PAJHS* 10 (1902): 119–128; Jonathan Sarna, *Jacksonian Jew: The two Worlds of Mordecai Noah* (New York, 1981), 61–76.

[33] The single slender surviving letter book left by Solomon Hirschell for the period 1826–1839 contains little correspondence with overseas congregations. See Letter Book, Chief Rabbi S Herschell, ENA 4160, Archives of the Jewish Theological Seminary.

[34] For Adler, see Steven Singer, "*Chief Rabbi Nathan Marcus Adler: Major Problems in his Career*" (MA thesis, Yeshiva University, 1974); Eugene Black, "The Anglicization of Orthodoxy: The Adlers, Father and Son," in *From East and West: Jews in a Changing Europe*, ed. Frances Malino and David Sorkin (Cambridge, MA, 1991), 295–313.

circumcision in Melbourne), and policing the boundaries of a fractious community.[35]

Whatever his shortcomings, Adler's strenuous efforts to establish authority over an unruly fief were instrumental in integrating and homogenizing Orthodoxy within the empire. Whereas previously colonial congregations operated almost entirely independently, they now received direction and instruction from London. Although the new Chief Rabbi's jurisdiction did not extend to the United States, the interests of Orthodox Jewry in Britain and America were intertwined in a number of areas. The Office of the Chief Rabbi, often in cooperation with the communal authorities in Holland, served as a clearing house for contributions from all over the Jewish world for the Jews of Palestine.[36] Adler was frequently required to act as an interlocutor and banker for the scores of immigrants who passed though England on their way to the New World. He occasionally served as an arm-twister for wives and families left in limbo by absent husbands.[37] Adler offered advice to American congregations seeking hazzans and American scholars seeking pulpits in England. He also answered questions of particular concern to American Jews, such as the permissibility of steamboat travel on the Sabbath, mixed synagogue choirs, and the reforms of Isaac Mayer Wise.[38] In these matters he often relied on the

[35] On average, Adler sent 1,000 letters a year. Most of these letters concerned congregational matters in Britain, but a significant number were sent to synagogues abroad. Letter register, Office of the Chief Rabbi, ACC/2805/01/01/088, LMA; Adler to the Reverend Rabinowitz, Cape Town, September 1859, ACC/2805/1/1/5, LMA; Jews' Hospital to Adler, February 12, 1857, ACC/2805/01/01/003, LMA; *VoJ*, July 31, 1846; Raymond Apple, "Rabbinic Responsa Relating to Australia: Abraham Eber Hirschowitz," *Australian Jewish Historical Society Journal* 9.6 (1984): 435; Porush, "Chief Rabbinate and Early Australian Jewry," 485–486; John Simon, "The Influence of the Chief Rabbinate of the United Kingdom on the South African Jewish Community," *Proceedings of the International Academic Conference of the Jewish Historical Society of England and the Institute of Jewish Studies* (London, 1996): 221–225.

[36] On cooperation with Holland, see Moshe Davis, *America and the Holy Land: With Eyes Toward Zion*, vol. 4 (Westport, CT, 1995), 97–99.

[37] For cases of abandonment and agunah, see Adler to I. Mars, August 6 and 20, 1852, ACC/2805/01/01/001; Adler to Isaacs, October 22, 1858, ACC/2805/1/1/5; Adler to unknown (letter number 8067), 1853, ACC/2805/01/01/001; A. I. Myers (New York) to Adler, March 9, 1855; Leah Green (New York) to Adler, September 24, 1855, ACC/2805/01/01/089, LMA.

[38] See Adler to the Wardens of Rodeph Shalom, March/April 1859, ACC/2805/1/1/5, LMA; Adler to A. L. Goldsmith (New York), September 1, 1846; Adler to Nussbaum (New York), October 13, 1846; Adler to Amsel Leo (New York), May 25, 1847, ACC/2805/01/01/088; Oppenheim (Cincinnati) to Adler, September 9, 1855; Oppenheim to Adler, September 28, 1856, ACC/2805/01/01/ 089, LMA.

coterie of hazzans who had left British pulpits for more lucrative positions in America.[39]

Although Nathan Marcus Adler brought considerably more energy to the role of Chief Rabbi than his predecessor his writ in the colonies was diluted by distance. Delay in the passage of letters provided colonial congregations with significant latitude while they waited months for responses to their questions. Local realities also demanded compromises. The embryonic Jewish communities in the settler colonies struggled to adapt to frontier settings. With a gender imbalance in New South Wales weighted at two men for every woman in 1841, the exclusion of the intermarried would doom the already foundering congregations.[40] This problem was not unique to Sydney and its surrounds, nor was it confined to poor members of the community. While intermarriage was the most visible compromise with local circumstances, much of the friction between hazzans and colonial congregations arose from apathy toward kashrut, mikvehs, and synagogue attendance. Many wealthy Jewish colonists had little patience for a meddlesome priest, particularly when they held power over his paycheck, and had functioned without the services of a hazzan for lengthy periods.

Even though far from London, many in the colonies felt a close affinity with metropolitan ways. The consecration of the York Street Synagogue in Sydney in 1844 was typical of this sense of attachment. The ceremony was based on the identical order of service used for the New Synagogue at Great St. Helen's in London.[41] The antipodean synagogue also derived the format of its service, organizational structure, and code of regulations directly from the Great Synagogue in London. The congregation, was, however, forced to bow to local pressures, lamenting that "from circumstances every ceremony and rite cannot be so strictly complied as in the Mother Country."[42] The community expected that its ties with England would be reciprocal: it took for granted that metropolitan Jewry would assist in the

[39] He also communicated with Abraham Rice and Max Lilienthal. See Adler to Rice, June 1858, ACC/2805/1/1/5, LMA; Adler to Lilienthal, August 13, 1846, ACC/2805/01/01/088, LMA. See also Adler to Morris Raphall, October 12, 1860, ACC/2805/1/1/6, LMA; Adler to S. M. Isaacs, September 18, 1856, ACC/2805/01/01/003, LMA; Adler's letter to Isaacs, Raphall, Fischel, Leeser, and De Sola, March 1858, is a letter of introduction for Jonah Bondi, ACC/2805/1/1/4, LMA.

[40] The statistic is cited in Kirsten McKenzie, *Scandal in the Colonies: Sydney and Cape Town 1820–1850* (Carlton, Victoria, 2004), 50.

[41] Israel Porush, "From Bridge Street to York Street," *Australian Jewish Historical Society Journal* 2.2 (1944): 62.

[42] *Report of the Committee of the Sydney Synagogue, 1845-5605, presented to the general meeting held on 28th September, 1845*, 3; Laws and Regulations of the New Synagogue, Sydney, 1845; *Occ* 5 (February 1848); see also Percy Marks, "The First Synagogue in Australia,"

outfitting of the new synagogue and library, and supply many essential religious articles.[43]

In Australia, South Africa, and Canada, Jewish settlers created a panoply of institutions from scratch, even as they coped with the difficulties begot of their distance from the mainsprings of Jewish life. Religious freedom presented a stern challenge to communal solidity in each of these contexts. As traditional powers of communal coercion decayed, synagogues scrambled to adapt. Congregations also contended with rival Jewish confraternities – clubs, societies, and fraternities – that promised an alternative secular space for fellowship. Jewish leaders in America and the British Empire also grappled with other implications of the evolving religious marketplace. In England, Nathan Marcus Adler (and those who followed him) struggled to contain demands for religious modernization, continuing his predecessor's campaign against the West London Synagogue of British Jews and struggling to contain further reformist inroads in Manchester and elsewhere. In reality, the powers of his office were limited, more often having to rely on suasion than on sanctions. Nonetheless, the trajectory of religious development in Britain and its empire diverged significantly from that of the United States. While synagogues proliferated (and competed) in larger American cities and Reform Judaism took firm root, there was much less religious dynamism across the Atlantic. Anglo-Jewry mimicked the formality and hierarchy of Anglicanism; Judaism in the United States imitated the creative destruction of American Protestantism. Change was curtailed by indifference and apathy, a more sedate rate of immigration, and constraints on the formation of new synagogues.

Despite these significant differences, synagogues from New Zealand to New York developed similar new ideas about religious leadership. Prior to the 1840s, the responsibilities of hazzans in the United States and the British Empire had largely been limited to leading prayer and performing a variety of duties that often included those of mohel and shochet. Drawing on innovations introduced in Central Europe, and influenced by the Christian milieu, Jewish innovators sought to transform the synagogue reader from a religious functionary who enjoyed limited authority and status into a "proper minister" who would supply "spiritual advice and guidance."[44] The new model minister was expected to perform the roles of preacher, pastor, and public figure. The keenest advocates of preaching on both sides of the Atlantic shared the conviction that pulpit instruction

Royal Australian Historical Society, 11, no. 4 (1925); Suzanne D. Rutland, *Edge of the Diaspora: Two Centuries of Jewish Settlement in Australian* (New York, 2001), 48–49.

[43] *VoJ*, November 25, 1842.

[44] *JC*, June 24, 1853; *Report of the Committee of the Sydney Synagogue*, 1847.

would address the ills that imperiled American and Anglo-Jewry. The introduction of regular vernacular sermons would restore "healthy religious sentiment" and "make religion lovely in the eyes of the multitude."[45] Ministerial responsibilities also shifted into the secular realm, reflecting the broad aspiration toward acceptance within the surrounding society. The model minister was expected to be the presentable and respectable public face of the community and its interlocutor with its Christian neighbors. The ideal hazzan would be the counterpart and coequal of the Christian clergyman. The model minister was expected to assume extensive pastoral obligations, becoming actively involved in communal advocacy, fundraising, and administration. This privileging of preaching and public service transformed the role of the hitherto humble hazzan.[46]

Hazzans with saleable skills – foremost the ability to produce elegant pulpit oratory – benefited from the emergence of an international ministerial marketplace. Those who could preach eloquently in English were a scarce commodity, and were able to pursue the opportunities for personal and financial advancement that the English-speaking Diaspora offered.[47] It was no coincidence that many of the pathbreaking preachers in America and the empire were also the pioneers of the English-language Jewish press. These religious leaders, the majority of whom had been born in continental Europe, were receptive to the innovations of their Central European colleagues. All of these men recognized the potential of the press to reach and teach the dispersed Jewish communities of England and the United States. Moreover, the press provided a vehicle to advance their ambitions as educators, preachers, and self-publicists. The press would amplify their sermons across America and the British Empire and provide them with a huge new audience. The *Jewish Chronicle*, the *Voice of Jacob*, and the *Occident* routinely publicized, recorded, summarized, and critiqued sermons delivered by a variety of preachers.[48]

A further factor in increased cooperation was the dramatic expansion of the missionary movement from the middle decades of the nineteenth century onward. The largest mission societies in the United States and Britain developed an international system of stations, subscribers, and

---

[45] *Occ* 6 (July 1848).

[46] For the transformation of the role of the rabbi see Steven Singer, "The Anglo-Jewish Ministry in Early Victorian London," *Modern Judaism* 5.3 (1985): 279–283.

[47] See Adam Mendelsohn, "The Sacrifices of the Isaacs: The Diffusion of New Models of Religious Leadership in the English-Speaking Jewish World," in *Transnational Traditions: New Perspectives on American Jewish History*, ed. Adam Mendelsohn and Ava Kahn (Detroit: Wayne State University Press, 2014).

[48] See *JC*, February 4 and May 6, 1842; *Occ* 3 (July 1845): 177–189; 4 (January 1847): 478–487.

sympathizers. Mission societies that focused on Jews were a small part of this much larger Protestant missionary enterprise. Measured in baptisms, missions aimed at Jews had very limited success, particularly given the resources expended.[49] Measured in terms of the agitation and anxiety that they aroused among Jewish communities, and the fevered efforts adopted to counteract their perceived menace, the equation is altered entirely. In the same way that foreign missionary activity created a shared sense of unease and vulnerability among Jews, the measures adopted to counteract the perceived missionary menace stimulated unprecedented cooperation between Jews across imperial and national boundaries. As mission societies and their Evangelical supporters increasingly thought and acted in global terms, American and Anglo-Jewry were forced to do the same.[50] Missions were engines for innovation within Anglophone Jewry, persuading Jewish communities from New South Wales to New York to mimic their methods.[51] In this way, missionaries were carriers of modernity, catalyzing cultural and social change within the Jewish communities they encountered. Jewish responses to missionary innovations in the areas of philanthropy, publishing, and schooling also had important implications for the integration of the English-speaking Jewish world.

Anglo-Jewry was the first to face sustained organized evangelizing, setting an important precedent in its response to the mission movement. When word circulated at the beginning of 1807 that the London Missionary Society planned to strategically site a free school in the East End of London, Chief Rabbi Solomon Hirschell – Adler's predecessor – delivered two sermons in the Great Synagogue cautioning parents against the perils of the conversionist classroom. His warning was reprinted and distributed as a pamphlet, and a delegation visited the Society to protest the plan.[52] Once these efforts to arrest the missionary enterprise failed, the communal elite

---

[49] Mel Scult, for example, calculated that each London Society convert between 1809 and 1816 cost the society £500 in total expenditure. Scult, *Millennial Expectations and Jewish Liberties*, 97.

[50] On the growth of the missionary movement see David W. Bebbington, *The Dominance of Evangelicalism: The Age of Spurgeon and Moody* (Downers Grove, IL: InterVarsity Press, 2005), 20, 45, 78–80, 109–111; Andrew Porter, *Religion versus Empire? British Protestant Missionaries and Overseas Expansion, 1700-1914* (Manchester: Manchester University Press, 2004), 136–162.

[51] Here I am extending Jonathan Sarna's arguments on the challenge and response dynamic between Jews and missionaries in the United States to the broader Anglophone world. See Jonathan Sarna, "The American Jewish Response to Nineteenth-Century Christian Missions" in *Essential Papers on Jewish–Christian Relations in the United States*, ed. Naomi Cohen (New York, 1990).

[52] Endelman, *Jews of Georgian England*, 236–242.

tested a tactic that later became characteristic of Jewish responses to missionary schooling throughout the Anglophone Diaspora: emulation. In effect, Jewish communities chose to compete with missionaries in the educational marketplace, a reflection of the withering of communal powers to compel parents to conform. Efforts to improve Jewish education for the poor in Manchester, Birmingham, and Liverpool in the 1840s were driven by similar motives.[53] The same trend appears to have held true in New South Wales where the Sydney Hebrew School, which catered primarily to the "humbler classes," was established shortly after active missionizing began in the city.[54]

The Jewish Sunday school also borrowed heavily from the Christian hymnbook.[55] The first Hebrew Sunday School opened in Philadelphia in March 1838, and was quickly copied with varying degrees of success across the United States.[56] The idea also gained traction elsewhere in the English-speaking Jewish world, unsurprising given the diffusion of evangelical Sunday schools in Britain and across the empire.[57] Over a period of two decades, Jewish Sunday and Sabbath schools opened in Montreal, Melbourne, Sydney, Geelong, Cape Town, St. Thomas, Kingston, and London.[58] The

[53] Williams, *Manchester Jewry*, 90, 95–97; Endelman, *Jews of Britain*, 86–87; Harvey W. Meirovich, "Ashkenazic Reactions to Conversionists, 1800–1850," *Transactions & Miscellanies (Jewish Historical Society of England)* 26 (1974–1978): 6–25, here 13–14; *VoJ*, February 21, 1845.

[54] *Report of the Sydney Hebrew School* (Sydney, 1859).

[55] Lance Sussman, *Isaac Leeser and the Making of American Judaism* (Detroit, 1995), 234–241.

[56] Dianne Ashton, *Rebecca Gratz: Women and Judaism in Antebellum America* (Detroit, 1997), 123, 142, 145, 147, 150; Karla Goldman, *Beyond the Synagogue Gallery: Finding a Place for Women in American Judaism* (Cambridge, 2001), 61–62; Jacob Rader Marcus, *United States Jewry, 1776–1985* (Detroit, 1993), 390–392; Cohen, *Encounter with Emancipation*, 71–72; Anne Boylan, *Sunday School: The Formation of an American Institution, 1790–1880* (New Haven, 1988), 135–146; Jonathan Sarna and Nancy Klein, *The Jews of Cincinnati* (Cincinnati, 1989), 42; Sussman, *Isaac Leeser*, 274n74; *Occ* (April 1850): 56; (November 1846): 390.

[57] Bebbington, *Dominance of Evangelicalism*, 103–105.

[58] Tulchinsky, *Taking Root*, 41–42; Rutland, *Edge of the Diaspora*, 69; Israel Porush, *The House of Israel: A Study of Sydney Jewry from its Foundation (1788) and a History of the Great Synagogue of Sydney, the Mother Congregation of Australian Jewry, Compiled on the Occasion of its Centenary (1878–1978)* (Melbourne: Hawthorn Press, 1977), 30–31; Joseph Aron and Judy Arndt, *The Enduring Remnant: The First 150 Years of the Melbourne Hebrew Congregation, 1841–1991* (Melbourne: Melbourne University Press, 1992), 266, 287; Adam Mendelsohn, "Tongue Ties: the Emergence of the English-language Diaspora in the mid-19th century," *American Jewish History* 93, no. 2 (2007): 178; Gustav Saron and Louis Hotz, ed., *The Jews in South Africa: A History* (Cape Town: Oxford University Press, 1955), 22; Louis Herrman, *The Cape Town Hebrew Congregation, 1841–1941: A Centenary History*

advances made in the provision of formal education – schools and the texts relied upon in the classroom – were supplemented by a drive to instruct and improve the broader Jewish public. A number of communal and religious leaders realized that since it was impossible to lower an impregnable intellectual portcullis around an increasingly integrated and acculturated Jewish community, it was essential to reach and teach Jews in new ways. Jewish editors and authors, including several pioneering female poets and novelists, experimented with new literary forms – the newspaper, novel, textbook, and tract – designed to supply the Jewish reading public with edifying and instructive literature.

Poor and undereducated Jews were seen as particularly vulnerable to the entreaties and propaganda of missionaries, if not to the lures of the gin-palace, casino, and theater. Popular education – which comported with a Victorian ethos of self-improvement – promised to be a panacea for a plethora of other communal ills. Some of these concerns reflected those of the middle-class society that Jews aspired to, and in increasing numbers, joined: temperance, labor unrest, and vice.[59] In America, England, and Jamaica advocates of communal reform pushed for the modernization and consolidation of communal welfare, pointing to the proliferation of voluntary charities and benevolent societies as evidence of unnecessary competition and redundancy.[60] In Britain this pressure culminated in the formation of the Jewish Board of Guardians in 1859. Jewish orphanages were created even more quickly in the United States, but lagged in Britain

(Cape Town, 1941), 51, 106–108; Jacob A. P. M. Andrade, *A Record of the Jews in Jamaica from the English Conquest to the Present Time* (Kingston: The Jamaica Times, 1941), 106–108; Judah Cohen, *Through the Sands of Time: A History of the Jewish Community of St. Thomas, U.S. Virgin Islands* (Hanover, NH, 2004), 70–72; *Report of the Sydney Jewish Sabbath School and Society for the Diffusion of Religious Knowledge* (Sydney, 1863).

[59] Se for example, *JC,* February 4, 1842. For similar views expressed in America, see *Occ* 3 (October 1845).

[60] For Henry Faudel's ambitious educational and charity reform scheme in London see Mordechai Rozin, *The Rich and the Poor: Jewish Philanthropy and Social Control in Nineteenth-Century London* (Brighton, 1999), 104–110; Vivian D. Lipman, *A century of social service, 1859-1959: The Jewish Board of Guardians* (London: Routledge and Kegan Paul, 1959), 21–22. For editorials in the *Jewish Chronicle* advocating the formation of the Board of Guardians see *JC,* October 22, 1857 and January 29, 1858. For efforts at welfare reform in Manchester in the 1840s and 1850s, see Williams, *Manchester Jewry,* 89–90, 146–147, 156, 171–173; Rainer Liedtke, *Jewish Welfare in Hamburg and Manchester, c.1850–1914* (Oxford, 1998), 72. For earlier schemes to reform the poor, see Endelman, *Jews of Georgian England,* 227–247. For Moses Nathan and Lewis Ashenheim's scheme to reorganize the Jewish relief system in Jamaica, see *First Fruits of the West,* 1.2 (March 1844); 1.5 (June 1844).

where existing institutions were adapted to meet the need demand from a population swollen by immigration.[61] Orphanages also sought to rescue Jewish children confined to workhouses and other institutions operating under a Christian ethos, an objective that assumed new urgency following the Mortara affair.[62]

Although Jewish charities and schools reflected local needs and impulses, similarities in educational and welfare reform point to common pressures and influences. These continuities should not be surprising given the overlapping challenges faced by Jews living in liberal societies, the growth of a Jewish middle class, and the broader trend toward the professionalization of organizational life. These homogenizing influences were strengthened by the pooling of intellectual resources among English-speaking Jewish communities. Communal leaders were inclined to dip into a shared repertoire of ideas – disseminated by newspapers and books – to find solutions to their common problems with missionaries and modernity.

The Jewish literary evanescence in English that started at mid-century – Bible translations, newspapers, textbooks, and tracts – created a cultural cargo that circulated within the Anglophone world. The proliferating Jewish schools, libraries, and literary associations deepened demand for works produced by Jewish presses. For Jews in America and the British Empire, the mass reading public and literary society provided new models of sociability and solidarity that had not existed before. Both reconfigured older Jewish norms to fit Victorian cultural forms, synthesizing a tradition of religious study with a modern ethos of self-improvement and mutual instruction. Just as the clubroom provided an alternative locus for Jewish affiliation outside of the synagogue, the shelf of books and stack of newspapers promised a novel form of Jewish association. The printed word could create an ethereal fellowship of letters freed from the constraints of geography.

Perhaps the innovation that had the most important consequences for the integration of the Anglophone Jewish world was the newspaper. The English-language Jewish press emerged at a time of massive expansion

---

[61] The Jews' Hospital (1806) and Jews' Orphan Asylum (1831) in London catered for Jewish orphans. In the United States, orphanages were opened in Philadelphia (1855), New Orleans (1855), New York (1860), Charleston (1860), Cleveland (1868). See Reena Friedman, *These Are Our Children: Jewish Orphanages in the United States, 1880–1925* (Hanover, NH, 1994), 1–5, 11, 200 n9; Lipman, *Jewish Board of Guardians*, 18, 50.

[62] Grinstein, *Jewish Community of New York*, 160–161; see also Mark Bauman, "Variations on the Mortara Case in Midnineteenth-Century New Orleans," *American Jewish Archives Journal* 55.2 (2003): 43–58.

of newspaper publishing.[63] A substantial litter of Jewish newspapers was born following the Damascus Affair, coinciding with a period of missionary triumphalism and expansionism.[64] Although Jewish publishers printed primarily for the local market, newspapers and books circulated widely. Here the press was aided by advances in the technologies of transportation and trade. In 1844 the London *Voice of Jacob* boasted of its subscribers at the "extreme side of the habitable globe."[65] The number of foreign subscribers does not reveal the full extent of readership. Newspapers passed through multiple hands as they were shared among communities and collected by literary societies. Their articles were often quoted at length in the local press.

Newspapers tied the dispersed outposts of English-speaking Jewry into a transnational intellectual and cultural community. This replicated a pattern within the broader English-speaking world. Periodicals modeled on familiar metropolitan publications sprouted wherever English-speakers gathered in numbers.[66] Imported American and English periodicals provided news and a degree of comfort for immigrants pining for a distant homeland.[67] The English-language Jewish newspapers that emerged in the early 1840s – *First Fruits of the West* in Kingston, Jamaica, the *Occident and American Jewish Advocate* in Philadelphia, the *Jewish Chronicle* and *Voice of Jacob* in London – and those that emerged later served a similar purpose for far-flung Jewish communities. Jewish emigrants from England, accustomed to reading both general and Jewish newspapers, carried a newspaper culture with them to the colonies. The prevalence of stage migration by Central European immigrants, which involved temporary stops in Britain

---

[63] For the number of newspapers published in London see *The Literary and Educational Year Book for 1859* (London, 1859), 112–115, 127, 129.

[64] The number of Jewish newspapers published worldwide doubled between 1841 and 1846. Leeser estimated in August 1846 that there were ten Jewish periodicals in Germany, two in France, three in England, one in Turkey, and one in Italy, besides his own in America. On the impact of the Damascus Affair on the Jewish press, see Jonathan Frankel, *The Damascus Affair: 'Ritual Murder', Politics, and the Jews in 1840* (Cambridge, 1997), 404–405; *Occ* 4 (August 1846).

[65] The newspaper also had subscribers in "the part of India bordering on China." *VoJ*, March 22 and May 10, 1844.

[66] See Alan Crown, "The Jewish Press, Community and Jewish Publishing in Australia," in *Noblesse Oblige: Essays in Honor of David Kessler OBE*, ed. Alan Crown (London, 1998), 38–39.

[67] One contemporary writer noted that "as the German demands his national beverages wherever he settles, so that Briton insists on his newspaper." Quoted in Simon Potter, "Webs, Networks, and Systems: Globalization and the Mass Media in the Nineteenth- and Twentieth-Century British Empire," *Journal of British Studies* 46 (July 2007): 627.

on the way to America or the colonies, aided this form of cultural transmission. Many British emigrants continued to read the English Jewish press, and some were later involved in the establishment and editing of Jewish newspapers in their new homes.[68]

The *Occident*, *Voice of Jacob*, *Jewish Chronicle*, and their descendants reported extensively on English-speaking Jewish communities around the world, relying on correspondents and each others' columns to supply news and gossip. In effect, the Jewish newspaper circulated a shared body of information. Newspapers provided much more than news, in many cases serving as the only connection between isolated communities and the broader Jewish world. Sharing newspapers and news forged a sense of shared identity. Jewish readers created an imagined bond with distant brethren, seeing themselves as participants in a global English-speaking Jewish community.[69] Newspapers also buttressed a sense of paternalistic obligation toward their eastern brethren, reinforced by the perceived political, material, and intellectual advantages of liberal Anglophone countries over North Africa, Eastern Europe, and the Ottoman Empire. In the nineteenth century, Eastern Jewry was seen to be vulnerable to the depredations of sophisticated American and British missionary organizations, needing outside assistance to counter the inducements proffered by evangelists. This international alms-race became particularly acute following the natural disasters that periodically struck Jewish populations in the major urban centers of the Near East. This frequent fundraising and mobilization on behalf of imperiled Jews abroad affirmed a sense of Anglophone solidarity and common cause as American, British, Australian, Jamaican, and South African Jewry collectively and collaboratively raised money for dispatch overseas. Fundraising for Zionist settlement in Palestine (and to support the fledgling State of Israel after 1948) would later play much the same role.

By the second half of the nineteenth century, several basic patterns of communal organization and trends toward acculturation and upward mobility were well entrenched among Jews within the British Empire. At the same time, Anglo-Jewry's cultural and economic hegemony within the Anglophone Diaspora was slipping. The American Jewish community overtook Anglo-Jewry in size; it now almost certainly outstripped its peer

---

[68] See, for example, the *Voice of Jacob, or the Hebrew's Monthly Miscellany* first published in Sydney in May 1842.

[69] This argument for the integrative role of the press relies on Potter, "Webs, Networks, and Systems," 621–625. See also Alan Lester, "British Settler Discourse and the Circuits of Empire," *History Workshop Journal* 54.1 (2002): 25; Simon Potter, ed., *Imperial Communication: Australia, Britain and the British Empire* (London, 2005).

in cultural output.[70] The United States was becoming a center of creativity in its own right, a new cultural and religious pole competing for influence with Britain in the Anglophone Jewish world. The shifting balance of power within the English-speaking Jewish world is abundantly evident through the prism of the Chief Rabbinate.

In November 1836, at the beginning of his career, Isaac Leeser wrote to Solomon Hirschell, the aging Chief Rabbi in London, imploring his "advice and counsel." Over seven pages, Leeser explained his reasons for petitioning Hirschell, whose reputation was "familiarly known" to American Jewry. Leeser was the young hazzan of Mikveh Israel in Philadelphia, one of the largest congregations in the United States. He described an unruly Jewish community: there was "no one … authorized to give an opinion in contested or uncertain points of law," "books for reference" were "but few" and "knowledge [not] as extensive as it should be." He complained that over the course of the five years he had served as hazzan at Mikveh Israel he had routinely been presented with problems "more complicated" than his limited religious "information was able to afford." He presented Hirschell with a list of questions: was it permissible to bury a child whose father was uncircumcised? What were the religious rights of the offspring of intermarried parents? (He reckoned the latter issue was of interest to "a third of all American families.") Leeser hoped to draw upon his counsel in future "from time to time." For the moment, he expected Hirschell to provide a summary of the relevant laws, and send his reply "in English that it may be extensively circulated."[71]

[70] Even though cultural output can only be imperfectly measured, the number of Jewish-related publications in the United States grew steadily from the 1830s onward. Robert Singerman's *Judaica Americana* lists 209 Jewish-related publications in the 1830s, 413 in the 1840s, 507 in the 1850s, and 565 in 1860s. (This method of measurement is used by Jonathan Sarna in "Jewish Culture comes to America," *Jewish Studies* 42 (2004): 47–48.) A similar calculation for Britain and its Empire reveals a different pattern, with publications spiking in the 1840s and 1850s – elevated by the polemical literature produced in response to the Damascus Affair, the Reform secession in London, and the emancipation debate in parliament – before declining substantially in the 1860s. Joseph Jacobs and Lucien Wolf list 82 discrete new publications produced in 1830s, 234 in 1840s, 202 in 1850s, and 113 in 1860s in their *Bibliotheca Anglo-Judaica* (London, 1888). The gross number of publications recorded should not be compared directly with those in Singerman. Singerman's criteria for inclusion are described in *Judaica Americana: A Bibliography of Publications to 1900*, vol. 1 (New York, 1990), xxviii.

[71] Isaac Leeser to Solomon Hirschell, November 4, 5596 (1836). The letter is partially transcribed in *Raynors Historical Collection Auctions Catalogue*, March 30, 2006: 22–23. This may not have been Leeser's first letter to Hirschell. Joseph Hertz mentions a letter sent from Leeser to Hirschell in 1834. See Joseph Hertz, *Jewish Translations of the Bible in English* (London, 1920), 13.

The Jewish world that Leeser departed in 1868 was strikingly different from that of three decades before. In the immediate post-bellum period, American Jewry appeared to be in rude good health, reinvigorated by immigration and economic opportunity. Lassitude was replaced with religious dynamism, albeit much of it directed toward the kinds of modernization of which the Orthodox Leeser disapproved.[72] Although its synagogue pulpits were still served by hazzans from Central Europe and Britain, for the first time an American seminary – one of Leeser's pet projects – trained rabbinical students.[73] Some of his other schemes to revitalize Jewish life had also borne fruit. This newfound vigor did not escape the notice of outsiders; the United States became a favored destination of Palestinian emissaries who collected funds to remit to the Holy Land.[74]

While an increasingly assertive and confident American community shouldered Anglo-Jewry aside in size and dynamism, several British institutions retained outsized sway in the Anglophone Diaspora into the twentieth century. The influence of the Board of Deputies of British Jews was sustained both by its access to Whitehall – the center of a hegemonic empire – and by the social and economic status of its patrician leadership. Similarly the Chief Rabbinate benefited from the centralized and hierarchical nature of the Anglo-Jewish establishment. Even as religious reformers and some Eastern European Jewish immigrants disputed the authority of his office, the Chief Rabbi could still claim to represent the vast majority of Jews in the British Empire, a position without parallel in the fragmented and disharmonious American religious marketplace. Nonetheless, the Office of the Chief Rabbi and its influence was transformed during these same decades. If Leeser's fawning epistle to Solomon Hirschell reflects the dependence and weakness of American Jewry at the birth of the Anglophone Diaspora, the careers of two of Hirschell's successors reveal a changing pattern of power within the English-speaking Jewish world.

From his appointment as Chief Rabbi in 1802 until his death in 1842, Solomon Hirschell maintained informal and infrequent contact with

---

[72] For the optimism of the immediate post-Civil War period, see Sarna, *American Judaism*, 124–125.

[73] Maimonides College failed in 1873. For a full description of the seminary and its antecedents, see Bertram Korn, *Eventful Years and Experiences: Studies in Nineteenth Century American Jewish History* (Cincinnati, 1954), 151–213.

[74] See Salo Baron, "Palestinian Emissaries in America, 1849–1879," *Jewish Social Studies* 5 (1943): 115–62, 225–92; Grinstein, *Rise of the Jewish Community of New York*, 440–447. For collection books detailing the extensive travels of two such emissaries, see "Palestine, miscellaneous material," microfilm 870, American Jewish Archives.

colonial congregations.[75] With limited authority and little inclination to use it, the Chief Rabbinate exercised almost no control over Jewish affairs in the broader British Empire.[76] Under his energetic and forceful replacement, the Chief Rabbinate underwent a dramatic transformation, replacing the lethargy that had characterized the latter years of Hirschell's tenure with vigorous action at home and abroad.[77] Adler's appointment was widely welcomed both within the empire and in America.[78] The colonial congregations looked to Adler as a source of practical assistance in their battle against irreligion and indifference. He was deluged with requests to sanction liturgical changes, to grant permission for conversions, and, most of all, to supply hazzans to fill empty pulpits. In effect, the Chief Rabbinate became a placement office for colonial congregations, a largely thankless task given the paucity of talented candidates. Typical was the complaint of one querulous colonist in Australia who wrote to the *Jewish Chronicle* to complain that without "properly qualified persons to perform religious duties" – an implied critique of Adler – children were "growing up with about as much knowledge of their faith as the Aborigines."[79]

Isaac Leeser initially looked to Adler to provide religious leadership, reacting with excitement to his appointment.[80] Although the new Chief Rabbi's writ did not extend to the United States, the interests of Orthodox Jewry in Britain and America were intertwined in a number of areas. The Chief Rabbi did not, however, play the close mentoring role that Leeser original envisaged in his letter to Solomon Hirschell. If anything, Adler's influence declined as American Jewry grew and prospered. Although far from self-sufficient, by mid-century the American Jewish community had already filled many of the wants detailed in Leeser's letter of 1836. More importantly, the community had begun to add its own innovations to

---

[75] The single slender surviving letter book left by Solomon Hirschell for the period 1826–1839 contains little correspondence with overseas congregations. See Letter Book, Chief Rabbi S Herschell, ENA 4160, Archives of the Jewish Theological Seminary.

[76] The only recorded instance of authority exercised in the antipodes occurred when Hirschell sent Aaron Levi, a dayan of the London Beth Din (and Talmud teacher to David Myer Isaacs), to solve an agunah problem in Hobart in 1830. It is unclear whether the absconding husband was a free settler or a transported convict. While in Australia, Levi sold prayerbooks and a Torah scroll to the community by subscription. *Report of the Committee of the Sydney Synagogue*, 1845, 4; Cecil Roth, "Rabbi Aaron Levy's Mission to Australia," *Australian Jewish Historical Society* 3 no. 1 (1949): 1–4.

[77] For Adler, see Singer, "*Chief Rabbi Nathan Marcus Adler*"; Black, "The Anglicization of Orthodoxy."

[78] See, for example, *Occ* 2 (March 1845); *JC*, July 10, 1846; *VoJ*, May 22, 1846.

[79] *JC*, April 20, 1860.

[80] See *Occ* 2 (March 1845); 4 (May 1846).

Anglophone Jewish life: the first Sunday school (1838); the first branch of the B'nai B'rith fraternal order (1843); the first mass subscription publication society (1845); and the first complete translation of the Bible into English (1853).

A letter received by Isaac Leeser from Geelong in Australia in 1856, exactly two decades after sending his own epistle to London, reveals a sizeable shift in the internal dynamics of the Anglophone Jewish world. Notably Harriet Levien, the young daughter of the town hotelier, chose to write to Leeser and not London to ask for advice and counsel. Although Geelong was certainly no center of Australian Jewish life – it had a temporary synagogue and only intermittent service from a hazzan – it was firmly within the bailiwick of the Chief Rabbi.[81] Yet Harriet preferred to put her questions to the Philadelphia hazzan, she wrote, rather "than to a stranger, for you are not such to me, although I am to you, as I have long been acquainted with you through your writings; indeed it was your 'Catechism for younger children' which first aroused in me the wish for a fuller knowledge of our law." Geelong, she complained, was a "small town" with "very few Jews, and none of them well acquainted with our religion (that is to say the Spirit of it although they may know some of the peculiar forms)." She had looked first to the Bible for answers to her religious questions but was left with further uncertainties. Could her brother expect the six men he employed on his farm "at a very high rate of wages" to work on the Sabbath? Was it permissible to "play chess, music, to dance" on the Festivals as some of her Jewish neighbors claimed? Did the menstrual laws described in Leviticus apply to her in the Antipodes? There was "much more" that she wanted to learn about Jewish law and eagerly hoped that he would answer her questions *"plainly* and *decisively."*[82]

Closer examination of Levien and her letter illuminates in microcosm several core features of the early Anglophone Diaspora. The Levien family were recent immigrants, drawn to this outpost of Empire by economic opportunity. Harriet's father traveled to Australia in 1840, following a sibling who had been transported for fraud: chained migration inspired the unfettered variety. Geelong had eleven Jews in 1848 but grew quickly in the 1850s with the discovery of gold in nearby Ballarat. Scores of fortune

[81] In 1856, the Chief Rabbi listed Geelong (along with Sydney, Melbourne, Port Adelaide, Launceston, Hobart Town, Wellington, Cape Town, Toronto, Montreal, and Calcutta) among the colonial congregations under his authority. See Office of the Chief Rabbi Letter Book ACC/2805/1/1/4, LMA.

[82] The letter is transcribed in George Bergman, "A Jewish Farmer's Religious Scruples: A Letter from Geelong (1856)," *Australian Jewish Historical Society Journal* 6.3 (1967): 157–161.

seekers flocked to these boom towns. Jacob Montefiore, a scion of the aristocratic Sephardic family, bought gold in Geelong for dispatch to London. Jewish clothiers in Melbourne (and their suppliers overseas) profited from the extravagant tastes of these new-made men. Some of the new settlers directed their wealth towards attaining the trappings of religious and social respectability. Geelong consecrated its first synagogue in June 1854, and Ballarat the following year. In Geelong, the synagogue denied privileged membership to men married to "women not of the Jewish faith" or living "publicly with women in a state of concubinage," surely a sign that such relationships were not uncommon.[83] Both synagogues sought to counteract irreligion and ignorance by appointing hazzans able to preach mellifluous sermons in English. Geelong was briefly served by Meyer Myers, then in his early twenties, who soon left Australia for a tempestuous pulpit career in St. Thomas, Kingston, and Boston.[84] Ballarat recruited his brother, Emanuel Myers, from London. He later served synagogues in Launceston, Melbourne, Montreal, New York, and Waco, Texas. Between these travels, he found time to reprint and claim partial credit for the catechism first published by his more distinguished father and uncle.

Although Harriet Levien was far from Philadelphia, her letter demonstrates the diffusion of the new English-language literature produced in large part to counteract missionary activity. Her Biblicism and choice of terminology suggest that she may have read Grace Aguilar's influential *The Spirit of Judaism*, edited and published by Leeser in Philadelphia in 1842. Alongside her Bible – perhaps Leeser's translation – Harriet was familiar with the catechism he produced for the students of the first Hebrew Sunday School in Philadelphia. Although it is not known whether Leeser ever responded, Harriet later organized a Sabbath school in Geelong modeled on the Hebrew Sunday School, where she and other young women taught classes of up to thirty children.[85] The United States had clearly become a center of creativity in its own right, a new cultural and religious pole competing for influence with Britain in the Anglophone Jewish world.

---

[83] Geelong had 99 Jews in 1857 and 128 in 1861. *JC*, September 11, 1857; January 20, 1860; March 21, 1862; February 10, 1865; August 18, 1876; Levi and Bergman, *Australian Genesis*, 241, 296, 304; Hilary Rubinstein, *The Jews in Victoria, 1835–1985* (Sydney, 1986), 15, 28–30, 134; Rutland, *Edge of the Diaspora*, 56; Aron and Arndt, *Enduring Remnant*, 177, 307.

[84] For Meyer Myers, see Robert P. Swierenga, *The Forerunners: Dutch Jewry in the North American Diaspora* (Detroit: Wayne State University Press, 1994), 169; Cohen, *Through the Sands of Time*, 95–102; *JC*, September 11, 1857; September 19, 1862; October 31, 1862.

[85] *JC*, December 29, 1854; June 22, 1866; October 8, 1873.

Even as the American upstart impinged on the Chief Rabbi's fiefdom in the 1850s, several structural factors conspired to further reduce the influence of the Chief Rabbi in the United States over the next decades. The growth of Reform Judaism ensured that many American congregations were uninterested, if not openly dismissive, of the prattlings of a distant Orthodox rabbi, however august his title. Eastern European immigrants were unlikely to look to the Chief Rabbi, and his brand of anglicized Orthodoxy, for religious leadership. As the generation of British-trained hazzans who filled American pulpits retired – Morris Raphall in 1865, Henry Abraham Henry in 1869, Samuel Isaacs in 1877, Sabato Morais in 1897 – the Chief Rabbi lost his network of sympathetic and influential acolytes. American Jewry also took its first steps toward training its own religious leaders – first Maimonides College, later Hebrew Union College and the Jewish Theological Seminary – eventually reducing its dependence on imported rabbis.

Perhaps the firmest indication of the altered internal dynamics of the Anglophone Diaspora was the appointment as Chief Rabbi of an American-trained rabbi who had served lengthy stints in New York and Johannesburg. Joseph Herman Hertz was born in Hungary in 1872, and immigrated with his parents to New York in 1883.[86] His intellectual talents were recognized early: at age 14 he joined the first class of rabbinical students at the Jewish Theological Seminary and he later studied for a doctorate at Columbia University. He formed a close attachment with the elderly Sabato Morais, a founder and teacher at the Seminary, and in 1894, became the first rabbi ordained by the institution.[87] Even before his graduation, Hertz was recruited by a synagogue in Syracuse, New York that had been impressed by his eloquent preaching. His thunderous sermons were to serve him well throughout his career. The young rabbi spent four years at Congregation Adath Yeshurun before swapping upstate New York for the excitement and financial rewards of Johannesburg.[88] This daring

---

[86] For brief biographies of Hertz, see Sefton Temkin, "Orthodoxy with Moderation: A Sketch of Joseph Herman Hertz," *Judaism* 24 (1975): 278–295; Israel Finestein, "Hertz, Joseph Herman (1872–1946)," *Oxford Dictionary of National Biography* (Oxford, 2004); Isidore Epstein, ed., *Joseph Herman Hertz, 1872–1946* (London, 1947): 74.

[87] See Joseph Hertz, "Sabato Morais – A Pupil's Tribute," in *The Jewish Theological Seminary Semi-Centennial Volume*, ed. Cyrus Adler (New York, 1939), 46–48. Abraham Karp, "A Century of Conservative Judaism in the United States," *American Jewish Year Book* 86 (1986): 10–11.

[88] He wrote to Meldola de Sola in Montreal that "Rather than bend the knee to the Baal of Reform Judaism, I was willing to exile myself to the ends of the earth, to a storm-center of materialism, away from the stimulating … atmosphere of books and men and movements. True, that financially my position leaves little to be desired, but *lo al halechem levado* [not by bread alone]." Quoted in Temkin, "Orthodoxy with Moderation," 283.

decision – in 1898 Johannesburg was still a rough gold-mining boomtown far from the centers of Jewish life – made his career.[89] The Johannesburg congregation actively sought an American to fill its pulpit, particularly one able to preach eloquently, serve as pastor to an immigrant Jewish community that was already 12,000 strong, and act as a figurehead able to speak on its behalf in the public square.[90]

In filling the last criterion, the Witwatersrand Old Hebrew Congregation got more than it bargained for. Hertz arrived in Johannesburg as the South African Republic prepared for war with the British Empire; his inflammatory orations demanding full political rights for Jews and other foreigners who had flocked to the Transvaal ensured his deportation when war broke out in October 1899. This minor episode, heralded as heroic at the time, established his fame and pro-British bona fides.[91] Hertz spent his temporary exile in England (where he met Solomon Schechter) and the United States, before returning to South Africa in 1901.[92] After a full decade in Johannesburg, Hertz accepted a pulpit in New York City. (This was not his first attempt to return to New York. In 1909 he unsuccessfully applied for the vacant chair in homiletics at the Jewish Theological Seminary. Solomon Schechter appointed Mordecai Kaplan instead.[93]) This stint proved short-lived: in February 1913, he was chosen as Chief Rabbi of the United Hebrew Congregations of the British Empire, a position he held until his death in 1946. Alongside his abiding celebrity, commanding

---

[89] For the early years of Jewish Johannesburg, see Mendel Kaplan and Marian Robertson, *Founders and Followers: Johannesburg Jewry, 1887–1915* (Cape Town, 1991). For the Jewish underworld in Johannesburg, see Charles Van Onselen, *Studies in the Social and Economic History of the Witwatersrand 1886–1914, Volume 1: New Babylon* (London, 1982). For the transnational criminal ties of this underworld, see Charles Van Onselen, *The Fox and the Flies* (New York, 2007).

[90] The job advertisement called for "Rabbinical diploma, university training and degree, Mohel, speak English, good appearance, under 45 years of age, married, fluent preacher, irreproachable character, be competent to lead in all humanitarian projects, and command the respect of all. American experience preferable, large sphere of labor, Congregation Orthodox but mixed choir." Quoted in Temkin, "Orthodoxy with Moderation," 284.

[91] See *JC*, August 4, 1899; December 22, 1899; February 9, 1900; April 20, 1900; May 11, 1900; September 27, 1901; December 22, 1911. Hertz was careful to keep the *Jewish Chronicle* well informed of his wartime activities.

[92] Schechter wrote to Cyrus Adler after meeting Hertz that he had "disagreed violently [with Hertz] on the Boer War, but if he is a sample of the kind of man your Seminary produces it must be a very fine institution indeed." Quoted in Temkin, "Orthodoxy with Moderation," 285 n. 26.

[93] Harvey Meirovich, *A Vindication of Judaism: The Polemics of the Hertz Pentateuch* (New York, 1998), 16–17.

pulpit presence and strong scholarly credentials, Hertz was chosen as a rabbi able to bridge the gulf between recent Eastern European immigrants and the established anglicized community.[94]

If Hertz's pulpit peregrinations exemplified the integration of the Anglophone Diaspora, his tenure as Chief Rabbi did much to strengthen the bonds between the Jews of America and those of the British Empire. In October 1920 he departed on an eleven-month tour of his colonial congregations. The trip was the first of its kind undertaken by a Chief Rabbi, a reflection of the growing wealth, size, and significance of the Jewish communities he visited in South Africa, Canada, Australia, and New Zealand.[95] The major publication project he undertook as editor and author – the first "exclusively Jewish" commentary on the Pentateuch in English – made a more lasting impression on Anglophone Jewry.

Hertz's commentaries, composed as extended homilies, bore the intellectual imprint of Sabato Morais and his other teachers at the Jewish Theological Seminary, as well as the influence of Solomon Schechter.[96] In a further sign of the changing nature of the Anglophone Diaspora, Hertz depended on the American market to ensure the success of his venture. Hertz made an "impassioned appeal" to Orthodox and Conservative rabbis in America to purchase and promote his text. A century before, it was Leeser who appealed to Adler to persuade British Jews to buy his Bible translation. Although initially a commercial failure in the United States after the final volume was printed in 1936, sales took off once the Pentateuch was published as a single volume. One estimate calculated that since 1945, 20,000 to 50,000 copies were distributed annually.[97] The Hertz Chumash "found its way into the pews of most congregations in English-speaking lands, and throughout the twentieth century, remained the most influential Jewish commentary upon the Bible in both Great Britain and the United States."[98] Much as the English-language Jewish literature

[94] When he spoke at Young Israel in New York, Hertz lectured in English on Friday evening and Yiddish on Saturday morning. See Jeffrey Gurock, "The Orthodox Synagogue," in *The American Synagogue: A Sanctuary Transformed*, ed. Jack Wertheimer (Hanover, NH, 1995), 56–57. For an account of his election as Chief Rabbi, see Geoffrey Alderman, *Modern British Jewry* (Press, 1992), 218–219.

[95] The trip is described by Hertz in *The First Pastoral Tour to the Jewish Communities of the British Overseas Dominions* (London, 1924).

[96] Meirovich describes this influence in more detail in *Vindication of Judaism*, 3–4, 12–18.

[97] Meirovich, *Vindication of Judaism*, 167–169. Soncino Press continues to sell the Chumash.

[98] David Ellenson, "A Vindication of Judaism: The Polemics of the Hertz Pentateuch: A Review Essay," *Modern Judaism* 21, 2001: 66. Meirovich contends that the "Hertz Commentary may well lay claim to the distinction of having almost

produced by Isaac Leeser, Abraham Benisch, and others soothed the birth-pangs of the Anglophone Diaspora and diffused a distinctive sensibility to all corners of the English-speaking world, the Hertz Chumash found an eager new audience in Eastern European immigrants (and their descendants) in the British Empire and United States. The volume served many as a primer in Jewish theology, traditional practice, and Jewish pride.[99]

The careers of Hirschell, Adler, and Hertz marked three stages in the life of the Anglophone Diaspora. The ineffectual and doddering Solomon Hirschell, with his imperfect English and limited interest in Jewish life within the British Empire, died just as the English-speaking Jewish world began to take shape. His successor, Nathan Adler, extended his authority overseas. He was unable, however, to secure lasting influence in the United States. Instead, cultural and religious innovations introduced in America were emulated within Adler's own backyard. Even in Geelong, Jews adopted American ideas to reinvigorate Jewish life. Joseph Hertz trained in America and assumed office on the eve of the First World War. The conflict entrenched the ascendance of the United States as a superpower and demonstrated the importance of its Jewish community as a source of largesse and political influence for the larger Jewish world. Although Anglo-Jewry was far from irrelevant – if anything, the Balfour Declaration and the British conquest of Jerusalem enhanced its influence – the star of American Jewry was rising within the Anglophone Diaspora. As Chief Rabbi, Hertz was forced to grapple with the tail-end and consequences of a tidal wave of Eastern European immigration that transformed Jewish communal life from Australia to America. Perhaps 150,000 Eastern European immigrants settled permanently in Britain between 1881 and 1914.[100] More than two million more made their way to the United States, cementing the primacy of American Jewry within the Jewish world. Yet wherever they settled within the Anglophone Diaspora, the cultural, political, religious, and social orientations of these Yiddish-speaking immigrants were far removed from the mores and cultural connections that bound English-speaking Jewish communities together. But for the rapid acculturation and *embourgeoisement* of the children of these immigrants in America, England, Canada, South Africa, and Australia, this influx might have created a lasting Yiddish-speaking Diaspora located in English-speaking lands that may

single-handedly given shape to the way in which English-speaking laymen the world over have understood their Judaism over the course of the past two generations." Meirovich, *Vindication of Judaism*, 2; Joseph Hertz, *The Pentateuch and Haftorahs* (London, 1936).

[99] See Meirovich, *Vindication of Judaism*, 182.
[100] Endelman, *Jews of Britain*, 127.

have rendered the Anglophone Diaspora of secondary significance. Instead, the Anglophone Diaspora was immeasurably strengthened by the anglicization of these immigrants.

Even as Hertz sought to keep the connections between English-speaking Jews alive through his travels and publishing, his efforts to foster solidarity encountered a challenge less familiar to his predecessors. By the time of the Hertz's tenure, colonial Jewish communities had developed characters distinct from that of Anglo-Jewry, borne of their locations and own histories. The development of Canadian Jewry, for example, was increasingly inflected by its proximity to the United States and the influence of its large Yiddish-speaking community in Montreal; Australian Jewry by its distance from Europe and America and the development of Australian identity; the South African Jewish community by the complex racial and political dynamics of its host society. As the constituent communities of the Anglophone Diaspora aged and, in most cases, expanded, Jews continued to share much in common with those elsewhere in the English-speaking Jewish world, but also embraced increasingly resonant local and national identities.[101]

Hertz died months after the end of the Second World War. In years immediately following the Holocaust, with Europe and its Jewish communities shattered and an exhausted Britain unwilling to sustain its presence in Palestine, American Jewry emerged as the vital center of the Jewish world.[102] Over the next decades, the Jewish communities of Australia, Canada, and South Africa, buoyed by an influx of Holocaust survivors, economic prosperity, social acceptance, and new-found confidence, sought to play a larger and more assertive role in international Jewish affairs as well. The political connections between these countries and the shared communal concerns of their Jews domestically (maintaining Jewish life in free and welcoming societies, counteracting antisemitism) and internationally (Israel, Soviet Jewry), revivified older bonds between Anglophone Jewish communities. Although the balance of power has shifted away from Anglo-Jewry over time, and new concerns and connections have replaced some of

[101] For the history of South African Jewry in the twentieth century, see Richard Mendelsohn and Milton Shain, *The Jews in South Africa: An Illustrated History* (Johannesburg, 2009). On Australia, see Hilary L. Rubinstein and W.D. Rubinstein, *The Jews in Australia: A Thematic History*, 2 vols (Port Melbourne, 1991) and Rutland, *Edge of the Diaspora*. On Canada, see Gerald Tulchinksy, *Canada's Jews: A People's Journey* (Toronto, 2008).

[102] For demographic data, see Sergio DellaPergola, "Changing Cores and Peripheries: Fifty Years in Socio-Demographic Perspective," in *Terms of Survival: The Jewish World Since 1945*, ed. Robert Wistrich (London, 1995), 16–17.

those that sustained the Anglophone Diaspora in the mid-nineteenth century, the Anglophone Diaspora as a whole has proved remarkably durable and flexible. From humble beginnings in the 1840s, the English-speaking Diaspora attained, out of good fortune and tragedy, a position of uncontested preeminence a century later.

SELECT BIBLIOGRAPHY

Alderman, Geoffrey. *Modern British Jewry*. Oxford, 1992.

Black, Eugene. *The Social Politics of Anglo-Jewry, 1880–1920*. Oxford, 1988.

Endelman, Todd. *The Jews of Britain, 1656 to 2000*. Berkeley, 2002.

Feldman, David. *Englishmen and Jews: Social Relations and Political Culture, 1840–1914*. New Haven, 1994.

Gartner, Lloyd. *The Jewish Immigrant in England, 1870–1914*. London, 2001.

Gerber, Jane, ed. *The Jews in the Caribbean*. Oxford, 2013.

Gilman, Sander and Milton Shain, ed. *Jewries at the Frontier: Accommodation, Identity, Conflict*. Champaign, IL, 1990.

Katz, David. *The Jews in the History of England, 1485–1850*. Oxford, 2002.

Kushner, Tony. *Anglo-Jewry Since 1066: Place, Locality, and Memory*. Manchester, UK, 2012.

Levi, John and George Bergman, *Australian Genesis: Jewish Convicts and Settlers 1788–1850*. Melbourne, 2001.

Levine, Stephen. *The New Zealand Jewish Community*. Lanham, MD 1999.

Lipman, Vivian D. *Social History of the Jews in England, 1850–1950*. London, 1954.

Mendelsohn, Richard and Milton Shain, *The Jews in South Africa: an Illustrated History*. Johannesburg, 2009.

Menkis, Richard and Norman Ravvin, ed. *The Canadian Jewish Studies Reader*. Calgary, 2004.

Roland, Joan. *Jews in British India: Identity in a Colonial Era*. Hanover, NH, 1989.

Rubinstein, Hilary. *The Jews in Australia: A Thematic History. Volume One: 1788–1945*. Port Melbourne, Victoria, 1990.

Rubinstein, W. D. *The Jews in Australia: A Thematic History. Volume Two: 1945 to the Present*. Port Melbourne, Victoria, 1990.

A History of the Jews in the English-Speaking World: Great Britain. New York, 1996.

Ruderman, David. *Jewish Enlightenment in an English Key: Anglo-Jewry's Construction of Modern Jewish Thought*. Princeton, 2000.

Rutland, Suzanne. *Edge of the Diaspora: Two Centuries of Jewish Settlement in Australia*. Sydney, 1997.

Tulchinsky, Gerald. *Canada's Jews: A People's Journey*. Toronto, 2008.

Taking Root: the Origins of the Canadian Jewish Community. Hanover, NH, 1993.

CHAPTER 6

THE UNITED STATES

HASIA DINER

The history of Judaism and the Jewish people in the United States from 1820 to 2000 involves a dramatic narrative of growth, change, diversification, and integration into the larger society. Beginning as a small relatively homogenous minority community, living obscurely on the margins of a profoundly Protestant American society, Jews moved themselves and their community into the center of American life, openly asserting their place in the nation. Over the course of the almost two hundred years under consideration here, American Jews profoundly changed the nature of Judaism and Jewish practice. In the 1820s nearly all of Jewish life took place within the boundaries of traditionally oriented synagogues whose style and substance differed little from what existed at the same time in Europe and whose rite had changed only in minor ways, over the course of the last centuries. By 2000, however, a highly variegated and constantly changing landscape of institutions, practices, and forms of identification characterized Jews and Judaism in America.

The history of Jews and Judaism in America pre-dates the 1820s; indeed Jews as individuals had been present in the North American colonies from the seventeenth century onward, and the eighteenth century saw the formation of communities and congregations. That history deserves to be told as well; however, less because of the miniscule numbers and the geographic limitation of those communities, but because of the lack of institutional variety and the absence of any kind of intra-Jewish competition or debate over the nature of community life, it stands outside of the basic trajectory of American Jewish life. Likewise Jews as Jews in the pre-1820 period by and large functioned with a kind of self-imposed obscurity that made them nearly invisible.

The larger history of Jewish life in America, from the 1820s onward, took its shape from five forces at work in American society which became increasingly pronounced in the nineteenth century. These factors constituted some of the basic characteristics of American social, political, and cultural life. In an increasingly democratized society, Jews claimed their citizenship. In a society that over time came to embrace the idea of religion as a force for good, even if it deviated from Protestantism, Jews could present their religion as worthy of respect. Similarly America, after the 1820s, became the world's most powerful magnet for a diverse immigration, which in turn ensured that no one group – Jews in this case – stood out for their foreignness. In a society profoundly divided by color and in which whiteness made for privilege, the Jews' racial identity, as perceived by others, opened up for them the basic protections of state and society. Finally, a nation bent on material acquisition and untrammeled economic expansion, provided a comfortable berth for a people with a long exposure to capitalism and the commercial life. These factors worked together creating a setting which gave American Jewish history its basic contours.

For their part, Jews in America, starting in the early nineteenth century, started to demand, often as manifested by their actions, the right to define the nature of the community and its institutions. Notoriously anarchic, Jewish communal forms reflected the "consent of the governed," as Jewish women and men created the kinds of institutions they wanted, rejected those that they did not want, and worried relatively little about the absence of homogeneity in practice or forms of identification.

1820–1870

From 1820 through the 1870s, an immigration of about 250,000 Jews, mostly from Central Europe, expanded the size of the Jewish population which had numbered about 1,500 at the time of the American Revolution. By the 1870s a transformative mass migration of Jews from Eastern Europe commenced. In the 1820s the first institutions of Jewish life outside the synagogue began to take shape and Jews in America could live as Jews removed from the orbit of congregational life. Schools and, charitable, mutual aid, and leisure time Jewish organizations came into being which had no connection to synagogues and which allowed individual Jewish women and men to function as Jews without belonging to a congregation. The 1843 founding of the B'nai B'rith in New York proved to be particularly noteworthy, as this fraternal organization eventually spread all over the United States, offering its members a range of Jewish services which obviated the need for synagogues, for those who felt so inclined.[1]

Similarly, this decade saw the proliferation of multiple synagogues in cities which previously had had only one. This increase reflected both the

---

[1] Leon Jick, *The Americanization of the Synagogue: 1820–1870* (Hanover, NH: University Press of New England, 1992); Deborah Dash Moore, *B'nai B'rith and the Challenge of Ethnic Identity* (Albany, NY: SUNY Press, 1981).

growth in the number of Jews and the arrival of Jews from new parts of Europe who preferred to worship in institutions that reflected their pre-migration styles. This meant that on some level synagogues in New York, Philadelphia, Baltimore, and elsewhere essentially competed with each other for members. Individuals disgruntled with one synagogue could handily move over to another at the same time that they could, and did, found new institutions as they saw fit.

Additionally, Jews began to settle and create the outlines of commu-nity in the trans-Appalachian west, with new hubs of Jewish life forming in Cincinnati, Pittsburgh, and elsewhere away from the eastern seaboard. The creation of a congregation in Cincinnati in 1819 marked the first such undertaking beyond the Appalachian Mountains, a harbinger of the conti-nental expansion of both the United States and the Jews. Over the course of the decades following the 1820s, just as the nation moved westward and came to include the entire North American continent, so too Jews and Jewish enclaves, larger and smaller, sprouted in every state and territory. In large measure due to the fact that itinerant peddlers, young men willing to go anywhere, served as the juggernauts of Jewish migration, Jews pen-etrated every region for commercial purposes and made possible Jewish life in every large city and in hundreds upon hundreds of small towns.

In those small towns Jews clustered in the field of small business and even in the large cities petty merchandising became the Jews' economic métier. While a handful of former peddlers became fabulously wealthy, emerging as magnates in the fields of finance and retailing, most of the men who had once sold from packs on their backs settled down to lives of modest comfort, operating small stores, some though not all of which specialized in clothing. In the smaller communities Jewish shopkeepers became asso-ciated with stable respectability, often belonging to the Masonic order and despite their status as religious outsiders, winning, particularly in the west, local political office. Jewish small business constituted a family affair, and wives and children of the merchants worked in the shops as well.

The 1820s also witnessed the first ideological challenge to traditional Judaism, with a short lived, but still historically notable, reform effort in Charleston, South Carolina. In the next decades efforts at reform would transform into a formal movement within Judaism named Reform. A rela-tively non-ideological movement, it came initially from the efforts of ordi-nary Jews in congregations across the country who wanted to add various accoutrements to the service that they found appealing, including mixed male–female seating, English language sermons, or a shorter service, all reflective of their acquisition of American tastes and sensibilities. Over time and particularly after the 1850s, when German-trained rabbis began to arrive in America, the movement assumed institutional form and rabbis began to offer ideological and/or theological justifications for the changes they advocated, for example, as to why certain prayers should be excised or why certain principles of the Judaic tradition ought to be rethought.[2]

Others, particularly such notables as the *hazzan*, or cantor, of Philadelphia's Mikveh Israel Congregation, Isaac Leeser, wanted no part of Reform, but instituted a variety of changes which he believed would reinvigorate traditional Judaism. Recognizing the increased American orientation of his members and other American Jews, Leeser instituted American-style translations of the Jewish prayerbook, the Bible, the Passover Haggadah, and a catechism to teach children the basics of Judaism; he introduced a sermon into his service, and even dressed himself in the robe of a Protestant minister, but advocated for the retention of tradition. He encouraged his congregant Rebecca Gratz to organize the first Jewish Sunday school, innovating by empowering a woman to manage a Jewish educational endeavor, but doing so in the name of keeping Judaism alive and intact in its traditional form.

Notably, throughout the entire era from the 1820s through the 1870s American Jewry tended to be poor in terms of its access to religious personnel. The first rabbi, Abraham Rice, did not arrive in the United States until 1840, and thereafter all rabbis who practiced in America derived from both European birth and training. In this "rabbi-less" period, hazzanim like Leeser served as rabbis. More commonly, lay men with some knowledge of the liturgy and the law stepped in and functioned in a rabbinic capacity. This period, therefore, could be considered the age of the laity.

Ordinary Jews in their communities decided on basic matters of how to organize Jewish life: whether they should secure the services of a rabbi, whether they should try to find someone to provide kosher meat, and the like. While some Jews always lived as outliers, with no connection to organized Jewish life, and blended into the American population, most Jews throughout this half century cobbled together a Jewish life for themselves, marrying within the community, ensuring the circumcision of their sons on the eighth day after birth, enjoying fellowship with other Jews, marking holy days, particularly the fall high holidays, and being buried in consecrated ground. They had little interest in the debates among rabbis, but rather had a fundamental idea as to what Judaism required of them and behaved accordingly as they could.

From the American side, the 1820s offered another important starting point. On the one hand, this decade witnessed the passage in 1824 of Maryland's "Jew Bill." A general move towards a more expansive franchise

[2] Alan Silverstein, *Alternatives to Assimilation: The Response of Reform Judaism to American Culture, 1840–1920* (Hanover, NH: University Press of England, 1994).

during this decade of "the common man," meant that the last of the lingering civil disabilities endured by Jews ceased to limit their access to public life. While over the course of the next few decades there would be incidents that would raise some questions as to the right of Judaism to exist in America as a legitimate religious persuasion, the trend pointed towards greater acceptance. During the Civil War, for example, Congress had authorized the Young Men's Christian Association to provide chaplaincy services to men serving in the army. The legislation decreed that a chaplain had to be a regularly ordained minister of a Christian denomination. When one company decided on a Jew, a non-ordained Hebrew teacher, to be its chaplain, the YMCA field worker protested vehemently against both the fact that the individual in question lacked ordination and because he was a Jew. A number of Jewish community leaders, through the Board of Delegates of American Israelites, founded by the B'nai B'rith, sought the intervention of President Abraham Lincoln, who met their demands and made sure that Jews could serve as chaplains and that Judaism would merit the same benefits that Christianity did.[3]

The increasing comfort that Jews perceived in American society as bearers of a religious tradition that put them decidedly into the minority can be briefly viewed from the point of view of synagogue exteriors. In the period before the 1820s, all synagogues looked like American houses of worship and they stood devoid of any symbols, lettering, or marking that drew attention to the Jewish function of the spaces therein. By the 1850s newly constructed synagogues began to put Hebrew letters on their outsides, boldly proclaiming that what went on inside differed from what went on in churches. By the 1860s and becoming much more dominant in the decades thereafter, American synagogues, which went through a major building boom, began to opt for the Moorish style of architecture with turrets, rose windows, onion-shaped domes, redolent of the Levant and utterly unlike other American religious structures. Jews clearly felt comfortable with the idea that passers-by, non-Jews, would know that these edifices differed from the houses of worship of the Methodists, Presbyterians, Episcopalians, and the like.

Americans in the main welcomed Jews into their communities. Public officials and members of the Protestant clergy typically attended the dedication of synagogues, thereby giving their stamp of approval to the anchoring of Jewish institutions into the edifice of community life. On Thanksgiving and other civic holidays rabbis and Protestant clergymen swapped pulpits, and non-Jews visited synagogues both to witness

---

[3] On the 1820s as a formative period see Hasia Diner, *A Time for Gathering: The Second Migration, 1820–1880* (Baltimore: Johns Hopkins University Press, 1992), 1–5.

something new and exotic and to proclaim America's religious tolerance. Simon Tuska, the first American born, though European educated, rabbi, actually penned a book in 1854, *Stranger in the Synagogue*, a kind of guide book for non-Jews who found themselves in a Jewish house of worship. The fact that a rabbi wrote such a book demonstrated the degree to which Americans increasingly thought of Jews in their midst as a fairly normal and non-problematic phenomenon.[4]

But a counter-theme also developed in this period. Notably, the 1820s also saw the escalation of organized evangelical activity targeting Jews as potential converts to Christianity. While some such efforts went on in the 1810s, missionaries founded the American Society for Meliorating the Condition of the Jews in 1823, bent on bringing Jews into the Christian fold. Evangelical endeavors left a profound mark on Jewish life in America, and many innovations – political, cultural, educational, and charitable – owed their origins to the project of Jewish communal leaders to undermine the missionaries' energies. Jews, for example, began to create Jewish hospitals, in part to counteract the missionaries who roamed municipal hospitals trying to get death-bed conversions from Jewish patients. Solomon Jackson launched the enterprise of American Jewish journalism in 1823 with his magazine, *Israel's Advocate*, an anti-missionary publication, and Rebecca Gratz's Sunday School derived its impetus in part from her and Isaac Leeser's fear that poor Jewish children proved to be particularly attractive targets of those bent on converting them to Christianity.[5]

By and large, the Jewish women and men of America in the years from the 1820s through the 1870s adapted to America in their personal and communal lives. They fulfilled what they considered to be their obligations as Jews at the same time that they embraced the nation. While most Americans of this period would never have seen a Jew, American society accommodated to them. Judaism increasingly came to be viewed as a religion that fit neatly into the fabric of American life, posing few problems for the overwhelmingly Protestant majority. Jews proved themselves to be hard working individuals who did little to disrupt American life, and they used their respectability to help fashion a Jewish communal life in the United States.[6]

---

[4] Simon Tuska, *Stranger in the Synagogue; or, The Rites and Ceremonies of the Jewish Worship, Described and Explained* (Rochester, NY: E. Darrow and Brother, 1854).

[5] Yaakov Ariel, *Evangelizing the Chosen People: Missions to the Jews in America, 1880–2000* (Chapel Hill: University of North Carolina Press, 2000).

[6] For an important figure of this period see Lance Sussman, *Isaac Leeser and the Making of American Judaism* (Detroit: Wayne State University Press, 1991); see also, Dianne Ashton, *Rebecca Gratz: Women and Judaism in Antebellum America* (Detroit: Wayne State University Press, 1997).

1870–1924

By the 1870s, a new era had commenced in the history of Jews and Judaism in the United States, one that was shaped by a number of overarching developments which essentially defined it in the history of Jews and Judaism in America. The 1870s launched a tidal wave of Jewish migration from Eastern Europe to the United States, bringing over about three million Jews, who constituted about one-third of European Jewry. By dint of sheer numbers, they transformed America into a significant spot on the world Jewish scene. The United States would maintain its significance thereafter. Additionally, the size of that migration made Eastern Europe the place of origin of nearly all American Jews. The descendants of those who had come from Central Europe in the previous half century and those who came from other places, the Ottoman Empire, for example, constituted negligible minorities in the Eastern European majority. Nearly all subsequent political, religious, economic, and cultural forces in American Jewish life emanated from these immigrants and their offspring.

The Eastern European Jewish immigrants exhibited some important differences from the earlier Jewish immigrants, and those differences impacted upon the structure of Jewish life in America. The immigrants of the late nineteenth and early twentieth centuries did not head out for the back roads and the small towns in pursuit of making a livelihood. They tended to remain overwhelmingly clustered in America's largest cities, and the majority of them chose to go no further than the major port of disembarkation, New York City. They did this less because of cultural or religious sensibilities than, mostly, because New York, and to a lesser degree Chicago and Philadelphia, offered the most reasonable way to make a living, namely in industrial work, the garment trade in particular. As urban workers who lived in densely packed neighborhoods they created a set of institutions and communal practices which also made them distinctive. Such institutions as the Jewish trade unions, Jewish socialist societies, the Yiddish press, and the Yiddish theater dominated this era and provided a dazzling array of venues and modes by which immigrant Jews engaged with each other and with their Jewishness.

In the 1870s American Jewry began to announce its religious distinctiveness and independence from Europe, with the founding of the Union of American Hebrew Congregations, in 1873, and two years later, in 1875, the founding of the Hebrew Union College in Cincinnati. Both the products in large measure of Isaac Mayer Wise, an immigrant rabbi from Bohemia, these two institutions reflected the rise of the Reform movement in the United States. The institutional vigor of the movement rose up from the activities of ordinary Jews who, as they settled in new communities and founded congregations, believed that they had the right to make changes in patterns of worship as those made sense to them. The number of rabbis could not keep up with the pace of Jewish population growth and Wise envisioned his school as a breeding ground for American-born rabbis, who spoke the language of the laity, both literally and figuratively. All later religious changes, whether stimulated by the Reform camp or by those on the more traditional side of the Judaic spectrum, spoke to American concerns and to an understanding that the Judaism of American Jewry had to be cast in terms that worked for it. American Jews, nearly all agreed, would not respond to a European-inflected Judaism.

The 1870s, on a different note, saw the first highly publicized and dramatic manifestation of antisemitism in America. While the 1877 refusal of the Grand Union Hotel in Saratoga Springs, New York, to accommodate the financier Joseph Seligman involved only him and his family, it functioned as a harbinger of increased anti-Jewish exclusion in places of public accommodation and made American Jews, regardless of class, aware of the divide between themselves and the Christian majority. Increasingly, from the 1870s through the 1920s, anti-Jewish behavior and sentiment reflected not the religious discomfort of Christians with Judaism but a racially inspired antisemitism that viewed Jews as different and defective. By the end of this period numerous colleges and universities began to institute quotas on Jewish students, trying to keep their numbers down lest the colleges become viewed as "too Jewish."

Of these three major changes, the period between the 1870s and 1924 took its shape mostly from the fact of the mass migration. This single overarching force dominated all others and left its mark on nearly all religious, cultural, political, and social developments among American Jews. The flood of Jewish immigrants from the Austro-Hungarian and Russian (and to a much smaller degree Ottoman) empires touched every aspect of American Jewry, in terms of both its inner life and its relationship with the larger society. The sheer volume of this Jewish migration, coming as it did during the most intense period of general immigration to the United States, accompanied by industrial development, urbanization, social unrest, and profound challenges to native-born Americans' belief that America ought to be a society of small town, white Protestants, meant that other Americans began to scrutinize the Jews as never before. The fact that journalists, reformers, public commentators, educators, and others wrote about the Jews, particularly the new immigrants, and analyzed how they lived, redounded upon the inner life of the Jewish communities.

Like the previous wave of Jewish immigrants, those from Eastern Europe arrived poor, though not destitute. In America they opted for crowded neighborhoods, where they lived among themselves, in relatively substandard housing. They found themselves subjected to both the vagaries of the American economy with its cycles of boom and bust and the social problems associated with poverty and urban life. Disease abounded in their enclaves, tuberculosis in particular, and women and men worked for relatively low wages in unsafe factories.

Men and women arrived in relatively equal number, and while young able-bodied workers predominated, about one-quarter of the immigrants tended to be either older adults or young children. Jews came as permanent immigrants, with no interest in going back to Europe, and in America they went about the business of finding work and creating community institutions that represented their sensibilities. A majority, both men and women, went to work in the garment industry, and by working in this field they, unlike most of the other immigrants of that era, worked for employers with whom they shared ties of ethnicity and community. The two labor unions that developed in this industry – the International Ladies' Garment Workers Union, founded in 1900, and the Amalgamated Clothing Workers' Union of 1914 – both saw Jewish workers in conflict with Jewish bosses, a fact that shaped much of the history of both unions and of the industry.

Particularly after 1905, large numbers of Jewish immigrants came to the United States already radicalized into socialist politics, and even those who never became socialists, before or after the migration, inhabited Jewish spaces in America very much impacted by socialism, a worldview which disdained religion. In 1897 the socialist Yiddish newspaper, the *Forverts*, the Jewish Daily Forward, began publication. By 1916 it sold almost a quarter of a million copies a day, making it the country's largest circulating foreign language newspaper. Even non-socialist Jews read it, and in doing so, whether reading the newspaper's news coverage, advice column, want-ads, theater criticism, or literary offerings, they were drawn into the world of socialism.

Not all supported radical ideologies, and many socialists participated in an array of communal projects. *Landsmanshaftn*, or home town societies, provided fellowship with men and women from the same town in Europe, while they also offered health and unemployment benefits. At times these societies became settings for religious life. The Lower East Side as well as similar enclaves such as Chicago's Maxwell Street neighborhood supported hundreds of small synagogues, storefronts mostly, known as *anshes* –men of – or *hevras* –fellowship groups – in which men gathered to worship with friends from back home, settings where they could hear familiar melodies. These enclaves also throbbed with Jewish street life and supported a vast Jewish commercial infrastructure of bakeries, butcher shops, cafes, and restaurants, all selling kosher (and non-kosher) food to the Jewish public. Jewish streets in these neighborhoods tended to be characterized by a vibrant street life, very different than what went on in the more refined American Jewish neighborhoods in the same cities.

Better-off American Jews with longer and deeper roots in the country took upon themselves the chore of caring for the newly arrived immigrants, hoping in the process to accomplish three ends: relieve the distress of the poor newcomers, to whom they felt a strong bond of kinship, and aid in their actual adjustments; ensure the immigrants' acquisition of American know-how; and lessen the obviousness of their foreign births, and in the process deflect attention away from Jews as an alien entity in America.

In late 1886, a group of traditional but comfortably American Jews opened the doors of the Jewish Theological Seminary in New York City. On the one hand, they did so in reaction to what they considered the excesses of Reform, which seemed to be shedding much of the substance of rabbinic Judaism, particularly as expressed in the Union of American Hebrew Congregations' 1885 Pittsburgh Platform in which the Reform movement announced that it rejected Jewish dietary laws, laws of Sabbath observance, and the notion of the Jews as a people, rather than just a religious community.

The founders of JTS worried about the arrival of so many Eastern European Jewish immigrants on two levels. They feared the influx into America of an Eastern-European-style Judaism replete with disorderly congregations where worshippers swayed in prayer, and with bearded rabbis, ignorant of English, old fashioned by American standards, who would represent Judaism to America very poorly. A few years earlier, in 1883, a group of these "old world" traditionalists on New York's Lower East Side had opened the Machazikai Talmud Torah, a European-style institution of learning with Yiddish as the language of instruction, and the same year that JTS commenced its work, the Etz Chaim Yeshiva opened, another school that its leaders hoped would resemble Jewish schools in Poland or Russia. By 1888, two years after the first students came to JTS, most of whom were young boys from immigrant Eastern European homes, a group of traditional Lower East Side congregations brought to America from Vilna, Lithuania, the Talmudic scholar Jacob Joseph to be the "chief rabbi" of the United States. To the JTS advocates this seemed antithetical to American norms, and they hoped that their school would produce rabbis who honored Jewish tradition but did so in elegant English and in synagogues that emphasized order and decorum.

Backers of JTS also recognized that the children of the immigrants would become American, with or without the intervention of Jewish organizations, and they hoped to provide the rising American-born generation with a model of educated, American, refined Judaism, which did not resemble the religious practices of the "old world." They fretted that the lure of American popular culture and the passion of socialism would both trump Judaism, and that the children of the immigrants would find little in tradition to keep them anchored in the Jewish community. The school served as the nucleus of the Conservative movement which took shape gradually over the course of the early twentieth century. In 1901 some of its alumni founded the Alumni Association of the Jewish Theological Seminary of America, which in 1901 would rename itself the Rabbinical Assembly. In the 1920s That body created a law committee intended to deliberate on the legal, or *halachic*, matters that vexed the rabbis and their congregants. In 1913 the various congregations that had loosely affiliated with JTS, often by virtue of having a JTS graduate as a rabbi, formed themselves into the United Synagogue. The partisans of this kind of Judaism envisioned it as the perfect vehicle for American Jews, one which they expected would blend American and western idioms and styles with Jewish tradition, unlike Reform, which by the end of the nineteenth century articulated a radical break with tradition, and Eastern European Orthodoxy, which asserted that little or nothing could change.

Likewise, in the 1890s a group of Jewish women, starting out in Chicago, came together in order to advance their own Jewish education. Those who created the National Council of Jewish Women came from the ranks of the successful, integrated business-class Jews whose parents or grandparents had migrated earlier in the century. They functioned comfortably in late nineteenth-century middle-class America, but they felt woefully inadequate when it came to knowing much about Judaism or Jewish history. Council, as the organization came to be known, provided these women, and their peers in other American cities as the organization spread, with fulfilling leisure-time activities. But the organization moved quickly away from this sole mission and began to take on the cause of the protection of Jewish immigrants. For example, concerned about the possibility that single immigrant Jewish girls would fall into the clutches of procurers, Council volunteered to be at Ellis Island and steer such young women to safe houses it had created – places where the girls would be protected until they made contact with friends and family already in the United States. Council set up training programs to provide these young women with marketable skills. NCJW also pressured immigration officials to provide kosher food to immigrants being detained at Ellis Island or any of the immigrant receiving stations, and it worked with railroad companies to ensure the safety of immigrants in transit out of New York. These represented just a few of the many NCJW concerns vis-à-vis the matter of Jewish immigration to America. While all along NCJW functioned as an avenue for the social pursuits of middle-class American Jewish women, it made recreation a vehicle to fulfill a social service function. The arrival of the immigrants, and the problems they faced, provided NCJW and other local and national Jewish organizations with a compelling concern.

Well-off American Jews devised projects and plans to solve problems they associated with the immigrants, considering themselves obligated as Jews to help their poor co-religionists at the same time that, witnessing the intensification of a racially based antisemitism in America, they worried that the conditions of life would worsen for all Jews, immigrant and native-born alike. Jacob Schiff, a banker, himself an immigrant from Germany, thought that one matter he could address involved the over-concentration of immigrant Jews in New York City. In an America that viewed cities as unnatural, and urban life as antithetical to national values, the fact that most Jews lived in cities, and one in particular, seemed to Schiff to be a problem calling for a solution. With likeminded other American Jews, he settled on two possible solutions. One involved using his not-inconsiderable contacts with American government officials to have Galveston, Texas designated a port of entry for immigrants and to steer passenger ships coming from Bremen, Hamburg, and the other Europe places where Jews boarded to Galveston rather than New York. Schiff hoped that those who landed in Galveston would fan out around the west, settling in small towns, and in some ways recapitulating the experiences of the pre-1870s immigrants. Secondly Schiff played an instrumental role in creating the Industrial Removal Office. This office served as a combined employment and relocation agency. Jews in New York who wanted to leave the city and try their luck elsewhere applied to the IRO, which matched them up with a smaller community that, using local Jews as agents, indicated how many immigrants they could accommodate with employment and housing and which skill those newcomers should possess. Schiff and the others involved with both plans at one and the same time believed that they served the immigrants and ameliorated their conditions, while simultaneously hoping to defuse growing antisemitism.[7]

1924–1948

The 1924 passage of the National Origins Act meant that mass Jewish immigration came to an end. While about 150,000 German, Austrian, and Czech Jewish refugees came to the United States in the 1930s, this did little to change the basic fabric of American Jewish life. Rather, the cessation of immigration led to the transformative reality that by 1930 a majority of

[7] Gerald Sorin, *A Time for Building: The Third Migration, 1880–1920* (Baltimore: Johns Hopkins University Press, 1992), 63–68.

American Jews had been born in the United States, a reality that reverberated in the religious, political, cultural, and social lives of these Jews and their children.

In the 1920s most Jews still earned a living as industrial workers and petty shopkeepers. By the end of World War II, the factory workers dwindled to an insignificant number, and those in business now operated more significant enterprises, while white-collar workers, managers, and professionals constituted the majority of American Jews by the middle of the 1940s. A flush time for American Jews, even those who still labored in factories did so under the protection of effective unions. Jews had the resources to fuel a building boom in synagogues, community centers, schools, resorts, summer camps, and philanthropic ventures directed heavily overseas to relieve Jewish distress in Eastern Europe and Palestine.

Although American Jews had always been deeply influenced by national and world events, three phenomena of the years 1924–1948 affected them deeply. The Great Depression of the 1930s influenced American Jews on several levels. It stalled, a bit, their economic mobility, and young Jews, in particular, who set their sights on careers in the professions found the limited opportunities of the era particularly bitter. More importantly, the exigencies of the economic crisis and the New Deal enacted by President Franklin Roosevelt brought Jews into the government as never before and into those circles of influence which constructed American policy. At the same time a visible minority of American Jews, mostly children of the immigrants, allied themselves with the Communist Party, seeing it as offering the best plan to end the country's economic and social distress.

More powerful than the Depression, the Holocaust in Europe, with the devastating loss of six million Jews at the hands of the Nazis, shocked American Jews, while the emergence of Jewish statehood in Israel in 1948 exhilarated them. But in these matters, American Jews stood on the sidelines, monitoring developments, using their political capital to make a difference, and dedicating the bulk of their philanthropic infrastructure to aid Jews in Europe and in the fledgling state.

The main internal developments reflected their rising middle-class Americanization. The Depression did not stem the migration of Jews out of older urban slums into more comfortable neighborhoods of second and third settlement begun in the 1920s.[8] Nor did it stem their movement out of the working class.[9]

---

[8] Louis Wirth, *The Ghetto* (Chicago: University of Chicago Press, 1927), 241–261.

[9] Deborah Dash Moore, *At Home in America: Second Generation New York Jews* (New York: Columbia University Press, 1981), 30. This period is well covered in Henry Feingold,

This era began with the passage of the National Origins Act, which, while not specifically aimed at Jews, affected them profoundly. At the end of World War II, however, legislative and judicial changes reduced discrimination against Jews and others. The 1945 passage of the Ives-Quinn anti-discrimination bill in New York State, the first act of its kind in the country, led to other states with large Jewish populations such as New Jersey and Massachusetts banning discrimination in employment and public accommodations based on race, religion, or national origin.[10] In 1948 the US Supreme Court, in the landmark case *Shelley v. Kramer*, invalidated the restrictive covenants which had barred Jews from buying houses in various neighborhoods and New York State passed the Fair Education Practices Act, outlawing discrimination in college and university admissions. Jews benefited from these laws and they and their organizations led the fight against discrimination, which worked for African Americans among others.[11]

American Jews increasingly moved, slowly, from the margins, although Jews continued to cluster in certain occupations and even in the realm of business, they tended to be concentrated in such fields as garment making and liquor distribution. Some achieved wide recognition as articulators of American culture, making movies, staging Broadway shows, and composing music, accepted by the general public as exemplars of the American popular culture. As teachers in public schools, they educated American children. They participated in civic affairs, particularly with the expansion of the federal government under the New Deal, crafting legislation that affected the lives of all Americans.

But in this era, more than any other, anti-Jewish behavior and rhetoric cast a shadow on American Jews. These peak years of American antisemitism saw widespread discrimination in housing and employment, and in places of leisure such as hotels and resorts. Jews reacted to the anti-semitism. Jewish agencies like the American Jewish Committee (founded in 1906), the Anti-Defamation League (1913), and the American Jewish Congress (1918) defended Jewish rights. They lobbied with legislators and testified in Congress against discrimination, issued propaganda to counter anti-Jewish stereotyping on the stage and in the press, and exposed the

A Time for Searching: Entering the Mainstream, 1920–1945 (Baltimore: Johns Hopkins University Press, 1992), 125–154.

[10] Stuart Svonkin, *Jews Against Prejudice: American Jews and the Fight for Civil Liberties* (New York: Columbia University Press, 1997), 89.

[11] *American Jewish Year Book, 5709, 1948–1949* (Philadelphia: Jewish Publication Society, 1949), 115.

nefarious goals of the Ku Klux Klan in America and the Nazis in Europe.[12] They worked behind the scenes, quietly, to get antisemitic publications withdrawn. Louis Marshall, of the American Jewish Committee, did this with automobile manufacturer Henry Ford, who in the 1920s reprinted the notorious antisemitic forgery, "The Protocols of the Elders of Zion."[13] Jewish organizations eschewed airing their fears publicly, considering noisy demonstrations and impassioned proclamations ways to aid the anti-Semites who craved publicity.

Most Jews confronted the realities of antisemitism privately. Some changed their names to pass in public. Some ceased to be Jewish. Most sought the comfort of Jewish spaces. For Jewish college students Hillel, founded in 1923 on the campus of the University of Illinois, offered a chance to interact with their Jewish peers, away from the hostility that pervaded college social spaces, particularly the fraternities, boardinghouses, and dormitories.

Most Jews lived in primarily Jewish neighborhoods. As Jews relocated further from the old neighborhoods they ended up living in more thoroughly Jewish neighborhoods than before. In 1920, 54 percent of New York's Jews lived in areas in which at least 40 percent of the population was Jewish. But by 1930, in the scattered Jewish enclaves around New York, 72 percent of them lived in such densely Jewish spaces.[14] Some may have done so because of discrimination in real estate, but for most, living in a Jewish enclave fit with a desire to be among fellow Jews. Exclusion from resorts and hotels caused pain to some, but most Jews preferred to spend leisure time with co-religionists. An elaborate New York Jewish culture of vacations in the Catskill Mountains evolved from simple bungalow colonies to elaborate resorts like Grossinger's and the Concord, where Jews sought pleasure with other Jews, ate Jewish-style food, and reveled in the entertainment which made this "borscht belt" famous.

The lack of appeal of Zionism, a political movement that emerged in the United States in the 1890s, as it did in Europe, demonstrated that American Jews did not consider antisemitism to be so potent a force in their lives as to warrant seriously thinking about relocating elsewhere where they would find less hostility. The movement, even at its height in the 1930s and early 1940s, during the years which saw the rise of Nazism and the horrors of the Holocaust, enrolled a slim minority of American

[12] Emanuel Celler, *You Never Leave Brooklyn: The Autobiography of Emanuel Celler* (New York: Day, 1953), 81.

[13] Charles Reznikoff, ed., *Louis Marshall, Champion of Liberty: Selected Papers and Addresses*, 2 vols (Philadelphia: Jewish Publication Society, 1957). See vol. I, 392.

[14] Moore, *At Home in America*, 30.

Jews in the various organizations which made up its institutional infra-structure, although most American Jews did support the idea of a Jewish homeland – not necessarily a politically sovereign entity – for Jews suffer-ing elsewhere. Those who affiliated with Zionism did so to help Jews in other places who faced persecution. American Jews did not see themselves, as they saw their European brethren, as living in exile.

Hitler's ascendance in Germany in 1933 and the reign of terror unleashed upon Jews there, and then in Austria, Czechoslovakia, and the rest of Europe after the German invasion of Poland in September 1939, pushed increasing numbers of American Jews into the Zionist camp. In 1938 the Reform movement, which had officially rejected the idea of the creation of a Jewish state, reversed course and expressed its support for a homeland. In May 1942 American Zionists met in New York at the Biltmore Hotel and, stirred by Abba Hillel Silver, demanded a sovereign Jewish state in Palestine as a war aim. Those present, and the masses of American Jews who did not formally join Zionist organizations, considered the creation of a Jewish homeland the only solution to Jewish suffering, which they themselves did not endure.[15]

American Zionism focused on philanthropy. Hadassah, the women's Zionist organization founded in 1912, enlisted the time, energy, financial resources, and loyalty of tens of thousands nationwide. Through the lead-ership of Henrietta Szold, it raised millions of dollars for health and welfare projects in Palestine. Hadassah, a mass membership organization, emerged by the 1920s as the largest Jewish organization in America, with 80,000 members in 1941. Its chapters, with weekly meetings and activities, gal-vanized Jewish women's communal lives. Hadassah's strength reflected its ability to provide a lived context for Jews in America. While aided might-ily in succoring other Jews, particularly through Youth Aliyah, founded in 1934 to rescue German Jewish children, Hadassah gave Jewish women a way to structure their American lives.[16]

It recognized that American Jews were on the move at home. Jewish geo-graphic shifts differed from previous patterns of mobility. Until the 1920s when Jews left a neighborhood, new Jewish immigrants replaced them. Now other, non-Jewish newcomers filled their spaces. In many cities,

---

[15] Melvin Urofsky, *American Zionism from Herzl to the Holocaust* (New York: Doubleday, 1975); Naomi Cohen, *American Jews and the Zionist Idea* (Hoboken, NJ: Ktav, 1975): Mark Raider, *The Emergence of American Zionism* (New York: New York University Press, 1998).

[16] There is no scholarly history of Hadassah or biography of Henrietta Szold. See Joan Dash, *Summoned to Jerusalem: The Life of Henrietta Szold* (New York: Harper and Row, 1970).

African Americans from the South moved in where Jews moved out. From the 1920s through the end of the 1940s Jews and Blacks overlapped in the same areas. But the Jews stood poised to leave, as African Americans arrived.[17]

The American-born children of the Eastern European immigrants differed from their parents in notable ways. Native-born English speakers, they knew and understood how to negotiate American institutions and considered themselves entitled to the full benefits of citizenship. Their Americanness led to the decline and ultimate demise of key institutions of the immigrant era, including the *landsmanshaft*,[18] the daily Yiddish press, and the Yiddish theater, as well as the small traditional congregations, *anshe* and *chevras*, based on European places of origin.

Synagogues became crucial community institutions, particularly at the era's end. The 1920s ushered in a synagogue-building boom, with new congregations forming in new neighborhoods or older congregations transplanting themselves as congregants moved. In the 1920s only about one-third of Jews belonged, yet by the early post-war period the number climbed to over half. However, of those who belonged, most attended sporadically, showing up typically at the high holidays, the anniversary of the death of a beloved to recite *kaddish*, or for life-cycle events of family and friends. Most Jews, members of synagogues included, did not strictly observe the Sabbath, and rabbis realized that Sabbath services competed with their members' need to make a living and their desire to enjoy leisure.

Competition provided the framework for Jewish religious life. Synagogues competed with other venues of Jewish life. Jewish community centers had evolved in the 1920s out of the old Young Men's Hebrew Associations, products of the 1880s and 1890s, coordinated on a national level by the Jewish Welfare Board. They provided places for Jews to create community life, as did B'nai B'rith lodges, Hadassah chapters, National Council of Jewish Women branches, Zionist organizations, chapters of the Jewish War Veterans and a panoply of other institutions where Jews met.[19] Synagogues also competed with the popular culture attractions of the larger society, including theater, movies, and shopping. Jewish religious

---

[17] Arnold Hirsch, *Making the Second Ghetto: Race and Housing in Chicago, 1940–1960* (Cambridge: Cambridge University Press, 1983), 4–5; Hillel Levine and Lawrence Harmon, *The Death of an American Jewish Community* (New York: Free Press, 1992), 33, 37, 53.

[18] Daniel Soyer, *Jewish Immigrant Associations and American Identity in New York, 1880–1939* (Cambridge: Harvard University Press, 1997), 191.

[19] Benjamin Rabinowitz, "The Young Men's Hebrew Associations," *Publications of the American Jewish Historical Society* 37 (1947): 222–323.

leaders recognized that Sabbath restrictions did not stop most Jews from such behaviors.

Until the 1920s a rough division marked Judaism in America. Most of the descendants of the mid-nineteenth-century immigrants from Central Europe opted for Reform. Until the end of the nineteenth century, as immigration continued from Germany and German Jews in America maintained a high fertility rate, Reform temples showed steady membership. Traditional congregations, those labeled "Orthodox," served those Eastern European Jews who did not embrace socialist secularism. Conservative Judaism, the product of the early twentieth century, remained too small to have a natural constituency.

By 1930, as Reform's numbers began to decline, the movement realized that it had to attract the descendants of the Eastern Europeans.[20] Simultaneously, a changed Reform rabbinate viewed Judaism differently than its predecessors. Many now came from Eastern European immigrant families. The best-known Reform rabbi of this era, Abba Hillel Silver, had been born in Lithuania and grew up on the Lower East Side, but, attracted to Reform, he received his ordination at Hebrew Union College.

Reform adopted changes to adapt to a new constituency. Congregations that had once acknowledged class hierarchies abolished family pews. Open seating fit a democratically oriented American Jewry that did not honor the old wealthy elite. Reform rabbis turned to the radio to address Jewish issues, projecting the image of an active rabbinic presence. Rabbi Harry Levi of Boston's old, prestigious Temple Israel, Abba Hillel Silver of Cleveland's The Temple, as well as rabbis in Milwaukee, Detroit, and St. Paul took to the airwaves.[21]

Jews familiar with traditional Judaism would have found the choreography of the classical Reform service alien, so Reform reintroduced the bar mitzvah ceremony, rejected by the movement earlier, and prayers once excised reappeared. More Hebrew could be heard in the liturgy. For the children and grandchildren of the Eastern European immigrants who saw Judaism as a social experience, the Reform temple as a formal space would have seemed jarring. Reform congregations accordingly enhanced synagogue sociability. Individual congregations established youth groups, and in 1939 the movement founded the National Federation of Temple Youth. Reform's renunciation of its previous opposition to Zionism put

---

[20] Union of American Hebrew Congregations, *Reform Judaism in the Large Cities* (New York: UAHC, 1931), 10.

[21] Leon Jick, "The Reform Synagogue," in *The American Synagogue: A Sanctuary Transformed*, ed. Jack Wertheimer (Hanover, NH: University Press of New England, 1987), 98–99.

it in line with the sentiments of the offspring of the Eastern Europeans. This coincided with the growing crisis in Europe and the fact that many Reform rabbis played key roles in the Zionist movement, including Rabbis Stephen Wise, Abba Hillel Silver, and James Heller, as well as Julian Mack, an active Reform layperson. In 1930, as a telling detail, the Reform movement's official hymnal added the Zionist anthem, "Hatikvah." In 1938 the Reform rabbis declared at their annual meeting in Columbus, Ohio, that they now supported the idea of a Jewish homeland, a rejection of the ideology of the 1885 Pittsburgh Platform.[22]

The Conservative movement also responded to the era's pressures, but differently. In 1919 only 22 congregations affiliated with Conservative Judaism. A decade later it rose to 229, almost equal to Reform. By the war's end, Conservatism emerged as the largest American Jewish denomination. It sought members among the successful Eastern European immigrants as they moved out of older neighborhoods. They primarily targeted the immigrants' children.

Conservative rabbis considered themselves traditional in terms of Jewish law, and the Rabbinical Assembly's Committee on Jewish Law deliberated carefully between 1928 and 1948, not sure how to mold tradition to American times. In these years "conservative" Conservatives, particularly Louis Ginsberg and Boaz Cohen, constituted the majority of the committee, and it issued few decisions that conflicted with traditional practice. Conservatism hesitated to proclaim its beliefs. It published a *Festival Prayerbook* in 1927, for use on Passover, Succoth, and Shevuot, times when few congregants sat in synagogue, but it abjured from issuing a high holiday or a Sabbath prayerbook until after World War II. It did not want to offend traditionalists, innovators, or the majority of American Jews who cared little about theology, yet cherished their identities as Jews. The movement wanted all to join.

Members of Conservative congregations liked the familiarity of the rite when it did not conflict with their American selves, preferring for example mixed male–female seating. They hoped these synagogues would socialize their progeny into Jewish life in ways that would not jeopardize their movement into the American middle class.[23] The synagogues courted young families, women, children, and teenagers, with special services, clubs, lectures, and programs to fit their interests. Some Conservative congregations became synagogue-centers, which in the 1920s and 1930s added such

---

[22] For a text of the Columbus Platform see, Mark Lee Raphael, *Jews and Judaism in the United States: A Documentary History* (New York: Behrman House, 1983), 205–207.

[23] David Kaufman, *Shul with a Pool: The "Synagogue-Center" in American Jewish History* (Hanover, NH: University Press of New England, 1999), 206–274.

facilities as swimming pools, gymnasia, meeting halls, and social rooms in order to attract potential members and give them a place to be Jewish.[24]

The synagogue-center idea in part emerged from the writings and activities of Mordecai Kaplan, who wrote arguably the most important book in American Jewish history, his *Judaism as a Civilization* (1934). Kaplan articulated in this book the basic ideas that reflected the reality of Jewish life in America. Its impact reflected the degree to which he so perfectly recognized the patterns of Jewish existence in America. While he found some, indeed much, of it problematic, he tapped the pulse of what American Jews did and thought. In this book, Kaplan posed the dilemma of his generation of American Jews. Born in Eastern Europe, Kaplan came to America as a child, and attended the Jewish Theological Seminary in its early years. He began his rabbinic career at an Orthodox congregation, but increasingly could not reconcile traditional Judaism with American ideals. In *Judaism as a Civilization*, in the innovative synagogue he founded, in the Society for the Advancement of Judaism, and in his long career at the Jewish Theological Seminary, he explored his crisis which he considered to be that of most educated American Jews.

American Jews, Kaplan argued, inhabited two competing civilizations, the Jewish and the American. These two had to achieve a harmony with each other for Judaism to retain the loyalty of its American adherents. Judaism could not survive unless it accommodated itself to America, and American Jews had the right to mold tradition to fit democratic values. They had to alter rituals and principles to make them consistent with America, while still serving a Jewish purpose. He coined the aphorism "*halacha* should have a vote, but not a veto" as he encouraged American Jews to create new forms and texts for worship. He rejected the Judaic principle of chosenness, which he believed in America came off as repugnant, jarring with notions of democracy and equality. Kaplan wanted Jewish communities to provide for the social and cultural needs of the masses. The idea of creating an "organic Jewish community" lay at the heart of his prescription for the future. Finally, Kaplan observed how America women no longer willingly accepted second-class citizenship, and two years after the passage of the women's suffrage amendment, Kaplan called his daughter Judith to the Torah to become the world's first bat mitzvah.

As a Zionist, Kaplan believed that the growing Jewish settlements in Palestine would provide American Jews with a positive model. Like Henrietta Szold he thought that the example of Jews in Palestine building

---

[24] Jack Wertheimer, "The Conservative Synagogue," in *The American Synagogue: A Sanctuary Transformed*, ed. Jack Wertheimer (Hanover, NH: University Press of New England, 1987), 121.

a new modern society would inspire American Jews and strengthen their Jewish loyalties.

Kaplan influenced many of his JTS students, some of whom helped him found Reconstructionism. In 1935 they commenced publication of *The Reconstructionist*, and in 1940 founded the Jewish Reconstructionist Foundation, which in 1941 issued a *New Haggadah* and in 1945 a Sabbath prayerbook, both of which excised references to chosenness, to the resurrection of the dead, and to the inevitable coming of the messiah. A group of Orthodox rabbis held a ceremony in 1945, burning copies of the books and issuing a *herem*, a writ of excommunication, against Kaplan for this heresy.[25]

Despite this drama, Orthodox congregations, rabbis, and institutions of learning also competed with the liberal branches for the next generation of American-born Jews of Eastern European parents. Orthodoxy's inner divisions, however, fostered less coherence in terms of how to relate to American conditions, and competition *within* Orthodoxy stymied its effectiveness.

Some within Orthodoxy embraced modernization and included in their congregations Jews who did not follow *halacha*. American-born, English-speaking, university-trained Orthodox rabbis, particularly the graduates of Yeshiva University, founded in 1925 under the leadership of Bernard Revel, served congregations which could easily have hired JTS graduates. Most members of the National Council of Young Israel (1924), Rabbinical Council of America, organized in 1935, and of the Union of Orthodox Congregations (OU), a product of the late nineteenth century, recognized that they had to compete with the other denominations.[26]

Orthodox synagogues in the areas of second and third settlement and in smaller cities did not all separate men and women during services and allowed non-observant men to hold office and share in ritual honors. Members of Orthodox congregations sent their children to public schools, and locally Orthodox rabbis cooperated with their Reform and Conservative counterparts. Nationally, rabbis of the three denominations worked together on the Synagogue Council of America, founded in 1926.[27] Many Orthodox congregations innovated with ancillary programs

[25] Mel Scult, *Judaism Faces the Twentieth Century: A Biography of Mordecai M. Kaplan* (Detroit: Wayne State University Press, 1993) and Jeffrey Gurock and Jacob J. Schachter, *A Modern Heretic and A Traditional Community: Mordecai M. Kaplan, Orthodoxy, and American Judaism* (New York: Columbia University Press, 1997).

[26] Jeffrey S. Gurock, *From Fluidity to Rigidity: The Religious Worlds of Conservative and Orthodox Jews in Twentieth Century America* (Ann Arbor: Jean and Samuel Frankel Center for Judaic Studies, 1998), 5–11.

[27] Gurock, "The Orthodox Synagogue," 64.

for young families, women, and children, and a few emerging Orthodox Jewish day-schools taught boys and girls together.[28] The appointment of Rabbi Joseph Soloveitchik to the Talmud faculty of Yeshiva University in 1939 heralded the rise of modern Orthodoxy.

But a countervailing force began. Some traditional rabbis eschewed modernization, separating themselves from the modernizers. Rabbis and their followers connected to a handful of yeshivot which came into being in the 1920s, starting with Rabbi Shraga Feivel Mendelowitz's Mesifta Torah V'daath Yeshiva, founded in 1921 in Brooklyn's Williamsburg neighborhood. In 1933 the Ner Israel Yeshiva opened its doors in Baltimore, Yeshiva Tifferth Jerusalem in 1937 in Manhattan, and Yeshiva Chaim Berlin in Brooklyn in 1939. These served as beach heads for a traditionalist, educationally oriented assault on American Orthodoxy's embrace of secular American society.[29] With the rise of Nazism in Germany the Breuer community fled to New York's Washington Heights where it built a full, largely self-sufficient Orthodox community, Khal Adas Jeshurun.

Starting in the early 1940s, a stream of European Orthodox congregations and rabbis made their way to America. Rabbis, heads of yeshivot, Hasidic rebbes, and their followers from Hungary and Lithuania arrived. In 1942 the Lubavticher rebbe arrived, bringing the Chabad movement to the United States, and in 1941 Rabbi Aaron Kotler of Kletzk, Poland, reorganized his yeshiva and community in Lakewood, New Jersey. Unlike the modernizers, these new Orthodox chose to self-segregate. They fled to the United States under duress and hoped to recreate as much as possible European traditions.[30]

1948–1968

In these two decades, American Jews created new communal practices which reflected the dominant themes of the post-war age: prosperity and affluence, suburbanization and acceptance, and the triumph of political liberalism, making this something of a "golden age." Jewish activities, undertaken particularly by Jewish women in new suburban communities,

---

[28] Jenna Weissman Joselit, *New York's Jewish Jews: The Orthodox Community in the Interwar Years* (Bloomington: Indiana University Press, 1990).

[29] Jeffrey S. Gurock, "Resistors and Accommodators: Varieties of Orthodox Rabbis in America, 1886–1983," *American Jewish Archives* 35, no. 2 (1983): 100–187; Gershon Kranzler, *Williamsburg* (New York: Feldheim, 1961); Charles Liebman, "Orthodoxy in American Jewish Life," *American Jewish Year Book* 66 (1965): 21–92.

[30] Oscar Handlin and Mary Handlin, "A Century of Jewish Immigration to the United States," *American Jewish Year Book* 50 (1949): 1–84.

fostered a middle-class Jewish consensus. Jews took pride in and supported the newly created, vulnerable, State of Israel. This era, which witnessed a "religious revival," emphasized the beneficent effect of religious
affiliation, and Judaism rhetorically joined the giants of Protestantism and
Catholicism to be thought of as a mainstream American faith.[31]

Jews rushed, with other white Americans, to the nation's suburban communities, made possible by post-war technology, economic expansion, and
federal and local social policy.[32] While in their homes they increasingly
observed less of Jewish law and ritual than previous generations, their
high levels of synagogue affiliation and their involvement in Jewish social
networks showed their loyalty to Judaism, however articulated. More
American Jews affiliated formally with synagogues and Jewish community
institutions than at any other time since the eighteenth century. At no time
before or after did as many children receive a structured Jewish education,
with up to 80 percent in some communities.[33] While critics, intellectuals,
and many rabbis scoffed at the quality of that education and the depth of
religiosity of suburban synagogues, the figures indicated that American
Jews opted for a Jewish life in an American idiom. Historians differ as to
the depth of that affiliation and the long-term impact of the patterns set in
motion in the suburban post-war era: some see a vibrant desire on the part
of American Jews to affiliate and be part of the Jewish world, while others
emphasize the influence of the intellectual criticism and later rejection of
suburban Judaism, and of the counterculture and general criticism of 1950s
America that became dominant in the latter part of the 1960s. Statements
that the religious commitment and Jewish intensity of the post-war period
amounted to not much more than shallow conformity depend much on
the prejudices of the observer and stand in stark contrast to the behavior
of American Jews of those years.

Amid that enjoyment they remembered the trauma of the Holocaust,
and they worked to change America by participating in the civil rights
struggle.[34] They made times, places, and ways to commemorate the
Holocaust and to weave references to it into their political and communal work.[35] Rabbi Joachim Prinz represented American Jewry among the

[31] Will Herberg, *Catholic–Protestant–Jew: An Essay in American Religious Sociology* (Garden City, NY: Doubleday, 1955).

[32] Kenneth T. Jackson, *Crabgrass Frontier: The Suburbanization of the United States* (Oxford: Oxford University Press, 1987).

[33] *American Jewish Year Book* 59 (1958): 116.

[34] Cheryl Greenberg, *Troubling the Waters: Black–Jewish Relations in the American Century* (Princeton: Princeton University Press, 2006), 74–113.

[35] Hasia Diner, *We Remember with Reverence and Awe: American Jews and the Myth of Silence After the Holocaust, 1945–1962* (New York: New York University Press, 2009), 18–85.

speakers at the 1963 March on Washington. The words of this refugee from Nazi Germany blended American Jewish thinking about the tragedy of the six million and post-war liberalism, as he declared, "When I lived under the Hitler regime, I learned many things." He had learned, he said, that discrimination against some endangered all.[36]

American Jews engaged on at all levels with civil rights organizations to push through legislation that changed much of American life. In the aftermath of World War II nearly all of organized Jewry actively supported the movement, emphasizing the Jewish component in their work.

American Jews lived with increasing levels of mobility, acceptance, and expanded opportunities. Suburbanization provided the dominant tendency of the period. New Jewish neighborhoods grew up around the large cities.[37] Some Jews opted for suburbs in new regions, particularly in and around Los Angeles and Miami.[38] In these places, Jewish builders and developers played a role in attracting Jews to the new communities.

Suburbanization impacted Jewish institutions. Synagogues, schools, and community centers, as well as stores selling specifically Jewish goods, followed the Jews, with a concomitant Jewish abandonment of the central city. The few Jews who immigrated from abroad did not cluster in the old neighborhoods. Holocaust survivors who arrived did not form their own neighborhoods,[39] nor did those who came, in small numbers, from Hungary in the late 1950s, when about 10,000 refugees arrived,[40] or the 1,000 who fled from Egypt in the early 1960s,[41] or the 4,000 from Cuba in the aftermath of the 1959 Revolution.[42]

Some Jews remained in the urban neighborhoods, generally the elderly and the poor, and they made up the dwindling membership of inner-city synagogues, the last consumers of the daily Yiddish press, such as the surviving but ailing *Tog-Morgen Zhurnal*, the *Forverts*, and for those on the far left, the *Freiheit*. Even some of these individuals had to move, as urban renewal projects demolished old poor Jewish neighborhoods.

Sociological studies found that Jews in the mid-1950s had moved to the ranks of professionals and managers. From 75 to 96 percent of those identified made a living in non-manual occupations, as opposed to 38 percent

---

[36] *American Jewish Year Book* 65 (1964): 18.

[37] Albert Gordon, *Jews in Suburbia* (Boston: Beacon Press, 1959), 6

[38] Deborah Dash Moore, *To the Golden Cities: Pursuing the American Jewish Dream in Miami and L.A.* (New York: Free Press, 1994), 23.

[39] *American Jewish Year Book* 52 (1951): 142–143.

[40] *American Jewish Year Book* 59 (1958): 98–99; 60 (1959): 19.

[41] *American Jewish Year Book* 61 (1960): 11.

[42] *American Jewish Year Book* 63 (1962): 146.

of all other Americans. As of 1953, one-sixth of American Jews over the age of 18 had graduated from college, far higher than the figure for the general population, which stood at one-twentieth.[43] Jews chose predominantly Jewish suburbs, and built up Jewish social lives. The formation of Jewish enclaves in Skokie, Illinois, Shaker Heights, Ohio, Newton, Massachusetts, and Silver Spring, Maryland, in turn attracted other Jews, eager to find a home in a good suburb with many Jews and Jewish amenities.

Suburban Jewish life tended to coalesce around synagogues, with an explosion in synagogue construction. Between 1945 and 1950 American Jews spent between $500 million and $600 million on religious buildings. Made up primarily of young families, with a husband who had been a soldier during the war, and a wife who did not work outside the home, and in which both had a relatively high level of American education, the synagogues and the suburbs manifested a high level of homogeneity.

More than half of all American Jews belonged to a synagogue, and many of these had never belonged to one before.[44] In deciding to join, American Jews emphasized the needs of their young children, having launched a "Jewish baby boom," which defined Jewish suburban life. While the Jewish spike in population never equaled that of non-Jews, it signaled an important communal agenda.[45] The Jewish denizens of America's suburbs expected synagogues to convey to their children a sense of Jewishness, socialize them into Jewish life, and enable them to mark Jewish life-cycle events.[46]

Community-wide Jewish schools, independent of synagogues, declined in favor of synagogue schools, which usually met one or two weekday afternoons and Sunday mornings. Schools prepared boys for bar mitzvah, an event which in this age of Jewish affluence allowed parents to proclaim their success. Girls started enrolling in equal number to boys, and by the late 1950s Reform and Conservative congregations began to offer girls a chance to demonstrate their learning and mark their coming of age with a bat mitzvah ceremony. Not as elaborate in ritual as the boys' event, it offered girls a chance to participate in public Judaism.

Children stood at the top of the Jewish communal agenda, and as a field Jewish education became more coordinated and professionalized. Before 1920 only four American cities – Boston, Detroit, Minneapolis, and Pittsburgh – maintained a central communal educational body. By

[43] *American Jewish Year Book* 56 (1955): 26–27.
[44] Edward Shapiro, *A Time for Healing : American Jewry Since World War Two* (Baltimore: Johns Hopkins University Press, 1992), 159.
[45] C. Bezalel Sherman, *The Jew Within American Society* (Detroit: Wayne State University Press, 1960), 90.
[46] *American Jewish Year Book* 58 (1957): 75.

1950 most communities, large and small, organized boards, or bureaus, of Jewish education, to bring higher standards to the enterprise of learning.[47] Additionally, "junior congregation" became a fixture of suburban synagogues. On Sabbath mornings boys and girls held their own services, guided by a teacher or assistant rabbi. The youngsters performed the ritual roles ordinarily undertaken by adult men.

Synagogues provided suburban Jews with loci to "be" Jewish, celebrate life cycle events and recreate with other Jews. Classes and clubs met in the synagogues: men's clubs, sisterhoods, teen groups, theatrical groups, Jewish Boy and Girl Scout troops, nursery schools. Synagogues had gift shops which sold ritual objects, many of them made in Israel.

American Jews were not particularly observant, however. Most did not follow the restrictions of the dietary laws or Sabbath, and few attended services on a weekly basis. Certainly Jews packed the sanctuaries on the high holidays, when Jews chose to be different than the people around them, staying away from their places of work and schools. Otherwise, they attended infrequently. While the Conservative movement experienced its special golden age, the other movements lagged. Actually, Orthodoxy experienced a new burst of life, and while it did not grow numerically in the 1950s and 1960s, it intensified internally in terms of the depth of observance, learning among its adherents, and the solidification of its infrastructure. Some of the post-World War II refugees considered American observance, even in Orthodox congregations, lax. In Brooklyn's Williamsburg, Crown Heights, and Boro Park, as well as in Lakewood, New Jersey and Monsey, in Rockland County, New York, they established all-Jewish, traditional communities, made up of adherents who had no interest in "fitting in" to America. They set a standard that gradually came to dominate more modern Orthodox institutions.

American Orthodox bodies now chided their members for weak levels of observance and learning. They also challenged the other branches of Judaism with a new zeal. In 1954, for example, Rabbi Oscar Fasman of the Hebrew Theological College of Chicago declared that Orthodoxy as an organized entity should not recognize the legitimacy of Conservative and Reform Judaism, and in 1958 the Orthodox Rabbinical Alliance recommended that Orthodox Jews in America not engage in activities which brought them in contact with non-Orthodox Jews.[48] The physical realities of the suburbs, however, slowed the spread of Orthodoxy. As automobile enclaves, with houses fairly spread far apart and rigid separation between residential and non-residential areas enforced by zoning, suburbs proved

---

[47] *American Jewish Year Book* 52 (1951): 97–109.
[48] *American Jewish Year Book* 56 (1955): 235.

inhospitable for people who one day a week were prohibited by religious law from driving.

Reform also lagged behind Conservatism in terms of drawing in the children and grandchildren of Eastern European immigrants, products of Jewish neighborhoods. Although few had grown up in synagogue-going families, they still found Reform inauthentic. The Central Conference of American Rabbis and the Union of American Hebrew Congregations continued to try to reclaim some more traditional practices. Under the leadership of Rabbi Maurice Eisendrath of the Union of American Hebrew Congregations and Rabbi Nelson Glueck, president of Hebrew Union College, Reform introduced even more elements of ritual practice once discarded as inappropriate to modern America; these included head coverings for men, prayer shawls, and the chanting of the *kiddush,* to welcome the Sabbath. Temples in the suburbs also added more days and hours to their religious school calendars. Reform did begin to grow. In 1940 U.A.H.C. claimed 265 congregations with 59,000 members, and by 1955, it had 520 with 255,000 members. By 1964 the number of temples climbed to 660.

Reform also played a pivotal role in leading organized American Judaism in its demonstrative advocacy of the liberal causes of the day: civil rights, church–state separation and, by 1964, opposition to the US war in Vietnam, in particular. In 1961 the movement opened the Religious Action Center in Washington, DC, from which it lobbied for causes it believed linked the Jewish tradition to liberal Americanism.[49]

But the Conservative movement emerged in the 1950s as the largest and fastest growing denomination, having struck a balance between Jewish law and post-war realities. It convinced a plurality of American Jews that by standing mid-way between Reform and Orthodoxy, it had none of the others' liabilities. It experienced great growth. At the end of World War II it included about 350 congregations. Between 1955 and 1957 the United Synagogue welcomed 131 new congregations to its ranks, and another 138 between 1957 and 1961. Suburban Jews found much in Conservatism appealing. The clubs, classes, and activities spoke to them and their children. In 1961 so many young people applied to the movement's Ramah summer camps that over 3,000 had to be rejected because of a lack of space.[50]

Conservative Judaism represented traditionalism in the suburbs, but without Orthodoxy's burdens. Men and women sat together during services, rabbis gave English sermons on timely topics, and congregations

[49] Jick, "The Reform Synagogue," 102–104.
[50] *American Jewish Year Book* 62 (1961): 129.

emphasized decorum and aesthetics. Conservative rabbis were thoroughly American. As of 1957 the Jewish Theological Seminary noted that more of its rabbinical students had graduated from Harvard College than from Yeshiva University.[51] In liturgical matters it opted for cosmetic changes, as witnessed in the *Sabbath and Daily Prayerbook,* issued in 1948 under the editorship of Hartford's Rabbi Morris Silverman. Anyone who actually knew Hebrew well could detect the minor alterations, but most could not. The traditional morning prayer in which Jewish men thanked God for not having "made me a non-Jew (*"goy"*) got rewritten as giving thanks for "having made me in his image." English texts accompanying Hebrew prayers stressed the compatibility of Judaism with American liberalism. The Silverman prayerbook tackled the idea of the "chosen people" by noting that the principle did not imply a belief in racial superiority. Instead it claimed that God had chosen the Jewish people to observe the commandments.[52]

The most significant changes made by the Conservative movement in the post-war era reflected suburban realities. In 1950 the Committee on Jewish Law and Standards of the Rabbinical Assembly ruled, with some dissent, that Jews might drive to synagogue on the Sabbath. Rather than excoriate congregants for their behavior, it sanctioned an already common practice. The Conservative movement in 1954 declared that women could be called to the Torah to recite the blessings over the sacred scrolls. By amending practices in place for over millennia, the Conservative movement recognized the reality that Jewish women played an increasingly defining role in Judaism in suburban America. In the suburbs, Jewish women facilitated much of Jewish life. Women's voluntarism made possible the libraries and gift shops, the schools and committees, and the social events which drew members to the institutions. They predominated in the adult Jewish education classes.[53] Beyond synagogues, Jewish women created and sustained communal organizations, laboring for the federations, the local Jewish fund raising bodies which collected money for international, national, and local Jewish needs, and for National Council of Jewish Women, Hadassah, ORT, the Brandeis Women's Clubs, and Pioneer Women, popular Jewish women's organizations which sustained Jewish community.

On the surface, it certainly seemed as though a harmonious, homogeneous, consensus-based American Jewry emerged during the post-war period.

---

[51] *American Jewish Year Book* 60 (1959): 54.
[52] *Sabbath and Festival Prayerbook* (Rabbinical Assembly and United Synagogue of America, 1948), vii, viii, x, 45.
[53] Albert Gordon, *Jews in Suburbia,* 78–79, 125.

1968–2000

Bold contrasts characterized the last decades of the twentieth century. Ushered in by the turbulence of the late 1960s with the upheavals in American culture, Jews simultaneously manifested greater commitment to the Jewish component of their lives than previously and yet many maintained fewer involvements with anything Jewish. The era's contradictions caused many to worry about the future of Judaism in America.

The vast majority of American Jews enjoyed a comfortable upper-middle-class economic status and benefited from more extensive education than the population as a whole. American Jews had a low birth rate and invested much in their children. They actively participated in the production of American culture, and in every area of American intellectual, economic, political, academic, and artistic endeavor, the names of American Jews surfaced as influential leaders of their fields. American Jews divided profoundly among themselves over Jewishness, Jewish identity, and the degree to which being Jewish mattered. For some among them Jewishness intensely defined who they were, and they talked about Jewish life boldly and exuberantly in public, parading their identity in front of other Americans in unprecedented ways; yet, for an increasing number Jewishness faded, becoming something of minor significance, devoid of personal meaning.

Starting in the middle of the 1960s American Jewish communal leaders expressed alarm over escalating levels of intermarriage.[54] Historically, family had imparted Jewish identity and socialized children into Jewishness, regardless of how articulated. But as increasing numbers of Jewish children, products of "mixed-marriages," were being raised in homes with a non-Jewish parent, community leaders fretted that the cement of Jewish life would crack.

Ironically in the last third of the twentieth century, as more Jews did intermarry and some drifted away from organized Jewish life, more non-Jews than ever chose to become Jewish. Mostly, the result of marriage to Jewish partners, the flow of converts into Judaism occurred at an unimagined pace. In 1954 about 3,000 converts a year entered the ranks of the Jewish people. At the end of the 1970s, the annual rate stood at 10,000. By the 1980s about 150,000 non-Jews had chosen Judaism.[55] Reform, which by the last decades of the twentieth century became the majority movement and whose members evinced high rates of intermarriage, responded first. The

---

[54] Robert Gordis, *Judaism in a Christian World* (New York: McGraw-Hill, 1966); *American Jewish Year Book* 71 (1970): 101.

[55] Joseph Rosenbloom, *Conversion to Judaism: From the Biblical Period to the Present* (New York: Behrman House, 1978); Paul Cowan and Rachel Cowan, *Mixed Blessings: Marriage Between Jews and Christians* (New York: Doubleday, 1987).

movement reached out to the intermarried, hoping the non-Jewish spouse would convert. It allowed individual rabbis to decide if they would offici-ate at a ceremony joining a Jew and a non-Jew and some congregations allowed the non-Jewish spouse to actively participate in synagogue life. Most boldly, in 1983 the Central Conference of American Rabbis decided to recognize as a Jew anyone who had *a* Jewish parent, mother or father, and who had received a Jewish education. As a major change in Jewish practice, which since the early part of the Common Era, accorded Jewish status to the child of a Jewish mother, this put Reform at odds with the other denominations. While the Reconstructionists, a small but growing branch, stood with the Reform,[56] the Conservative movement realized the extent of the trend and both held to *halachic* standards and tried to be wel-coming to the non-Jewish spouses of members and their children.

The biggest contrast and deepest divide of late twentieth-century Judaism involved that which separated Orthodoxy from liberal Judaism. For the Orthodox, about 7 to 9 percent of the American Jewish population, details of observance became increasingly more rigid. As they saw it, only strict adherence to the law could prevent intermarriage.[57] Among the Orthodox, those most observant set the standard and others had to react. The ultra-Orthodox challenged those observant Jews who partook of the larger cul-ture. Calling themselves "Torah True," they believed that American culture offered them nothing of value, except in as much as they hoped the state would protect their right to self-segregation.[58] Modern Orthodoxy, associ-ated with Yeshiva University, believed however that its adherents could, with great vigilance, bring together Western culture, secular learning, some increase in the public roles of women, a degree of co-operation with the liberal denominations with a deep commitment to normative practice and Torah study. But as the right wing, sometimes referred to as the "yeshiva world," grew larger and more strident, modern Orthodoxy felt compelled to respond by also turning more rightward.[59]

The more traditional flank of Orthodoxy splintered within itself, including a number of Hasidic sects – Bobover, Lubavitch, Satmar, Skver, Ger – distinctively marked by their clothing, their segregated communal

[56] On the denominalization of Reconstruction after 1968 see Charles Liebman, "Reconstructionism in American Life," *American Jewish Year Book* 71 (1970): 3–99.

[57] *American Jewish Year Book* 99 (1999): 54.

[58] Jerome Mintz, *Hasidic People: A Place in the New World* (Cambridge: Harvard University Press, 1992).

[59] Samuel Heilman, *Cosmopolitans and Parochials: Modern Orthodox Jews in America* (Chicago: University of Chicago Press, 1989); Heilman, *Defenders of the Faith: Inside Ultra-Orthodox Jewry* (New York: Shocken, 1992).

patterns, and their avoidance of contact with other American Jews. They lived primarily in their own communities, and in Boro Park, Crown Heights, and Williamsburg in Brooklyn and New Square in New York's Rockland County they dwelled by themselves. Because of their numerical concentration they exerted political clout, and since their leader could deliver *all* the community's votes, politicians courted them and tried to meet their demands.

One Jewish drama of the late twentieth century involved the life and death of Rabbi Menachem Mendel Schneeerson, the seventh Lubavitcher rebbe. Having arrived in the United States in 1942, he set about creating institutions to promote his particular brand of Judaism, and by the 1970s he and his followers planted Chabad houses all over America and the world. Inspired by the idea of outreach to non-observant Jews, by 1990 Chabad had planted itself in over 300 cities and on college campuses. It published books and magazines, transmitting the rebbe's talks and lessons over cable television and radio. When he died in 1994 some of his followers proclaimed him to have been the messiah, the anointed one, in whose wake would follow the prophesied "end of days." Lubavitch billboards appeared all over America. Bumper stickers exalting Schneerson sprouted on cars. Lubavitch missionaries approached Jews on the street, begging them to return to the "real" Jewish practice so as to hasten Schneeerson's resurrection from the dead.[60]

Contradictions of various sorts ran through late twentieth-century Jewish life. At one extreme, an untold number sustained no formal involvement with Judaism or Jewish life.[61] Although these individuals did not convert to Christianity, Judaism and Jewish culture did not define their lives. Yet surveys found that a majority of American Jews yearly attended a Passover seder and lit Hanukkah candles. Even those intermarrying often wanted to incorporate Jewish elements into their ceremonies and preferred to have a rabbi present.

Non-Orthodox Jews also manifested intense Jewish commitments, made great investments in Jewish life, and proposed innovations which they hoped would invigorate American Judaism. They paid attention to the trends in Jewish life and wrote and read a stream of popular books which attempted to assay the state of the Jews.[62] Many believed strongly

[60] Shaul Shimon Deutsch, *Larger than Life: The Life and Times of the Lubavitch Rebbe Rabbi Menachem Mendel Schneerson* (New York: Chasidic Historical Productions, 1995).

[61] Sidney Goldstein, *Jews on the Move: Implications for Jewish Identity* (Albany: State University of New York Press, 1995).

[62] Charles Silberman, *A Peculiar People: American Jews and their Lives Today* (New York: Summit Books, 1985); Leonard Fein, *Where Are We: The Inner Life of America's Jews* (New

that Judaism had to change and meet standards set by the larger society. Since in these years American society experienced a revolution in gender roles, so too, Jewish women in particular demanded that Judaism change to reflect new social realities. The movement of women into the rabbinate began in 1972 with the Hebrew Union College's ordination of Sally Preisand; this move was followed by the Reconstructionists in 1974. The Conservative movement followed suit in the late 1980s, admitting women to the Jewish Theological Seminary, and each year it and all the seminaries of the liberal movements graduated classes with women as rabbis and cantors. The effort to bring gender equality to Judaism demonstrated how much many Jews cared about Judaism.[63]

Individual American Jews also cared so much about their Jewishness that starting in the late 1960s they challenged existing practices, by creating their own institutions outside the established communal framework. Young people, advocates of a Jewish counterculture, sought new kinds of spiritual energy and created *havurot*, small independent fellowship groups without rabbis, emphasizing the equality of all members.[64]

The *havurah* movement emphasized spirituality, and this trend captured others as well. Some discovered the lore and knowledge of Kabbalah, mysticism born of the Middle Ages. Jews interested in exploring this and other forms of new spiritual practices founded retreat centers Elat Hayim in Pennsylvania and P'nai Or Religious Fellowship, founded by Zalman Schachter-Shalomi to bring about a renewal of Judaism through a bricolage of forms new and old, intrinsic and extrinsic to Judaism. In 1995 the National Center for Jewish Healing brought together Jews, clergy, and lay people from around the country interested in bringing matters of the spirit to matters of the flesh.[65]

The world of Jewish learning also changed. Until the late 1960s very little in the way of Jewish studies existed in American universities. In the late 1960s, Jewish college students began to demand courses on Jewish history,

York: Harper and Row, 1988); Samuel Heilman, *Portrait of American Jews: the Last Half of the Twentieth Century* (Seattle: University of Washington Press, 1995); Samuel Freedman, *Jew Versus Jew: The Struggle for the Soul of American Jewry* (New York: Simon and Schuster, 2000); J. J. Goldberg, *Jewish Power: Inside the American Jewish Establishment* (Reading, MA: Addison-Wesley, 1996); Jack Wertheimer, *A People Divided: Judaism in Contemporary America* (New York: Basic Books, 1993).

[63] Reena Sigman Friedman, "The Jewish Feminist Movement," in *Jewish American Voluntary Organizations*, ed. Michael Dobkowski (Westport, CT: Greenwood, 1986), 580.

[64] Riv-Ellen Prell, *Prayer and Community: The Havurah in American Judaism* (Detroit: Wayne State University Press, 1989).

[65] *American Jewish Year Book* 97 (1997): 206.

culture, and literature, and individual Jews with financial means decided to provide the necessary funds to colleges and universities, both public and private, to hire professors to teach Judaic subjects. A few dozen academics met in 1969 to create the Association for Jewish Studies, but by 2000 over a thousand professors and students come together annually at the AJS meetings to explore the Jewish experience.[66]

Late twentieth-century American Jewish innovations also involved a turn to the aesthetic. The revival of *klezmer* music, a form that seemingly had died out with the end of the immigrant generation, offered one such example. From the 1980s onward the explosion of Jewish film festivals in San Francisco, New York, Chicago, Washington, DC, even Raleigh-Durham, North Carolina and Portland, Maine – cities not historically associated with organized Jewish life – provided American Jews with a way to showcase their culture. Likewise, Jewish museums grew in number and vibrancy. In 1950 only two museums in America focused on the Jewish experience. In 1977 enough existed to lead to the creation of the Council of American Jewish Museums, which by 1991 had 35 affiliated institutions.[67]

Jewish women around the country have crafted new rituals and texts to express their sense of themselves as Jews and as women. They began in the early 1970s to publicly mark the birth of daughters with a formal ceremony, the *simhat bat*, which had never existed before. Jews who had received no Jewish education began to make up for that, and through congregations marked the completion of their course of study with an adult bat mitzvah. As Jewish women sought to find traditions for themselves, they manifested a deep identification with Judaism.[68]

Their actions made it possible for others to assert their right to participate. By the end of the twentieth century the issue of gay rights emerged as a public and pressing matter. In the 1980s separate gay congregations formed in San Francisco, New York, Washington, DC and elsewhere. Liberal rabbis and rabbinical bodies faced the question about the

---

[66] Leon Jick, ed., *The Teaching of Judaica in American Universities: The Proceedings of a Colloquium* (Waltham, MA: Association for Jewish Studies, 1970).

[67] *American Jewish Year Book* 91 (1991).

[68] Allegra Goodman, *Kaaterskill Falls* (New York: Dial, 1998): Rebecca Goldstein, *The Mind–Body Problem* (New York: Random House, 1983); Rebecca Goldstein, *Mazel* (New York: Penguin, 1995); Pearl Abraham, *Romance Reader* (New York: Riverhead, 1995); Nessa Rappaport, *Preparing for Sabbath* (New York: Morrow, 1981); Tova Mirvis, *The Ladies Auxiliary* (New York: W.W. Norton, 1999).

participation of homosexuals in congregations and the ordination of gays into the rabbinate. Should rabbis perform commitment ceremonies? Do gay couples constitute "families" for purposes of synagogue membership? Should gay candidates be admitted to the seminaries? Like the earlier feminist challenge, the decision by gay Jews to assert their right to be included within American Judaism provides a telling commentary on Jewish life in America. They had no desire to leave the Jewish community, but wanted to participate on their own terms. That they sought inclusion indicated that in an era in which so many Jews seemed not to care about Jewish life, so many others sought admission, but as they were.

In a society where individuals could be anything, or nothing, the fact that so many Jews sought some point of entry reflected the state of the community. Jews had a seemingly endless array of choices to pick from and being Jewish, being included within the Jewish people, moved them. They do not feel compelled to accept inherited institutions or practices. In a postmodern age, with its intense focus on personal choice, American Jews look for ways and places to function as Jews.

SELECT BIBLIOGRAPHY

Antler, Joyce, *The Journey Home: Jewish Women and the American Century.* New York: Free Press, 1997.

Ariel, Yaakov, *Evangelizing the Chosen People: Missions to the Jews in America, 1880–2000.* Chapel Hill: University of North Carolina Press, 2000.

Ashton, Diane, *Hanukkah In America: A History.* New York: New York University Press, 2013.

Cohen, Naomi, *Jews in Christian America: The Pursuit of Religious Equality.* New York: Oxford University Press, 1992.

Diner, Hasia, *The Jews of the United States, 1654 to the Present.* Berkeley: University of California Press, 2004.

    A Time for Gathering: The Second Migration, 1820–1880 (The Jewish People in America). Baltimore: Johns Hopkins University Press, 1992.

Faber, Eli, *A Time for Planting: The First Migration, 1654–1820.* The Jewish People in America Series. Baltimore: Johns Hopkins University Press, 1992.

Feingold, Henry, *A Time for Searching: Entering the Mainstream, 1920–1945,* The Jewish People in America Series. Baltimore: Johns Hopkins University Press, 1992.

Gerber, David, ed., *Anti-Semitism in American History.* Urbana: University of Illinois Press, 1986.

Goldman, Karla, *Beyond the Synagogue Gallery: Finding a Place for Women in American Judaism.* Cambridge: Harvard University Press, 2000.

Ivers, Gregg, *To Build a Wall: American Jews and the Separation of Church and State.* Charlottesville: University of Virginia Press, 1995.

Michels, Tony, *A Fire in Their Hearts: Yiddish Socialists in New York*. Cambridge: Harvard University Press, 2005.

Moore, Deborah Dash, *GI Jews: How World War II Changed a Generation*. Cambridge: Harvard University Press.

Prell, Riv-Ellen, *Fighting to Become American: Jews, Gender, and the Anxiety of Assimilation*. Boston: Beacon Press, 1999.

Raider, Mark, *The Emergence of American Zionism*. New York: New York University Press, 1998.

Sarna, Jonathan, *American Judaism: A History*. New Haven: Yale University Press, 2004.

Schultz, Kevin, *Tri-Faith America: How Catholics and Jews Held Postwar America to its Protestant Promise*. New York: Oxford University Press, 2011.

Schwartz, Shuly Rubin, *The Emergence of Jewish Scholarship in America: The Publication of the Jewish Encyclopedia*. Cincinnati: Hebrew University Press, 1991.

Slobin, Mark, *Chosen Voices: The Story of the American Cantorate*. Urbana: University of Illinois Press, 1989.

Sorin, Gerald, *A Time for Building: The Third Migration, 1880–1920*. The Jewish People in America Series. Baltimore: Johns Hopkins University Press, 1992.

CHAPTER 7

THE HISPANIC WORLD/LATIN AMERICA

JEFFREY LESSER AND RAANAN REIN

The social and political upheavals taking place in South America during the first decade of the twenty-first century have raised questions yet again about the future of Jewish communities in this region. In Venezuela, the radical populism of the late President Hugo Chavez led some Jews to make accusations of a surge in antisemitism that expanded on the already class-based uncertainty among many Jewish Venezuelans.[1] The economic crisis that hit Argentina at the beginning of the 2000s struck the middle and upper middle classes, not just the poor and working classes. Most Jews belonged to the former groups and this created a new phenomenon of Jewish poverty which in turn encouraged emigration to other parts of the Americas as well as to Israel and Europe.[2] Even so, Jews continue to be members of the dominant classes in almost all Latin American countries, holding significant spaces in the political, economic, educational, and cultural spheres. Why are so many Jewish Latin Americans in dominant positions, even as the region is often glossed as one of high antisemitism? This chapter traces Jewish immigration and social integration during the nineteenth and twentieth centuries into the area today called Latin America in order to show how one minority group was able to take advantage of the New World. Furthermore, we examine the historiographical trends that have led to an impression of Jewish life in Latin America often at odds with the experience of many Jews.

Although there is no continuity between the crypto-Jews of the colonial period (sixteenth to early nineteenth centuries) and the later waves of Jewish immigrants from Europe, the Balkans, and the Mediterranean basin, some colonial stereotypes about Jews and

---

[1] Luis Roniger, *Antisemitism, Real or Imagined?: Chávez, Iran, Israel, and the Jews* (Jerusalem: Hebrew University of Jerusalem, Vidal Sassoon International Center for the Study of Antisemitism, 2009).

[2] Natan Lerner, "Argentine Jewry in a Period of Economic Crisis." In *Contemporary Jewries: Convergence and Divergence*, ed. Eliezer Ben-Rafael, Yosef Gorny, and Yaacov Ro'i (Leiden and Boston: Brill, 2003), 335–340.

Judaism seem consistent over the centuries. This chapter begins with a brief section on the migration of Jews (both open and secret) during the period of Spanish and Portuguese domination, but focuses on the nineteenth- and twentieth-century entry, settlement, and institution building of Jews in the continent. Most of the attention will be given to three countries with large Jewish populations: Argentina, Brazil, and Mexico. The numbers of Jewish Latin Americans (we use this term to emphasize that Jews are citizens of the nations in which they live, not members of closed communities outside the national experience) are not, however, the only reason for this focus. Rather, these three paradigmatic cases highlight the Ashkenazi and Sephardic contribution to Jewish life in the Americas, different strategies of social integration, and the varied ways of maintaining ethnic identity. At the same time, the experience of smaller communities can shed additional light on these processes, as Leo Spitzer's research on Bolivia or Ruth Behar's work on Cuba have taught us.[3]

This chapter avoids the use of the concept of "Jewish Community." All too often scholarship gives a false impression of a cohesive and homogeneous Jewish population, ignoring the diverse, fragmented, and complex set of daily interactions among those who might broadly be defined by both self and other as Jewish Latin Americans. Thus, this essay seeks to shed light not just on Jewish institutions and affiliated Jews, but on the majority of Jews in Latin America for whom "being Jewish" is a personal ethnicity, not a statement of community belonging or religious faith. While we do not focus on antisemitism, we do suggest that the moments remembered as most antisemitic in various Latin American countries were often those in which various aspects of Jewish communal life continued and sometimes even flourished. Finally, in a world characterized by globalization and transnationalism, this chapter enlarges the territorial boundaries of "Latin America" to include Jewish Latin Americans who have relocated to various countries, including those who moved or "made aliyah" to Israel.[4]

---

[3] Leo Spitzer, *Hotel Bolivia: The Culture of Memory in a Refuge from Nazism* (New York: Hill and Wang, 2009); Ruth Behar, *An Island Called Home: Returning to Jewish Cuba* (New Jersey: Rutgers University Press, 2009); Allen Wells, *Tropical Zion: General Trujillo, FDR, and the Jews of Sosúa* (Durham and London: Duke University Press, 2009).

[4] See our edited volume: Jeffrey Lesser and Raanan Rein, eds, *Rethinking Jewish-Latin Americans* (Albuquerque: University of New Mexico Press, 2008).

CLANDESTINE PRACTICES AND OTHER
COLONIAL EXPERIENCES

Jews, converted Jews, and descendants of converted Jews (as well as Moors and heretics) were not allowed to settle in the colonial dependencies of the Spanish empire. Immigration was restricted to Christians of "pure blood." Laws, however, only tell us part of the story. In fact, a variety of Jewish public and secret rituals arrived in Latin America with the early European colonizers in the fifteenth and sixteenth centuries. The Inquisition had forced much Jewish practice underground, and many of those character-ized as "Jews" by Iberian political and religious leaders were actually the descendants of converted New Christians. Variously called *Judaizantes*, *Marranos*, *Conversos*, and New Christians, they went to Latin America in small numbers to escape economic, social, and religious persecution.

By the mid-sixteenth century, New Spain (today's Mexico and Central America) had a small population of Jewish descent. While many of them were surely sincere Catholics, some may have been crypto-Jews, while others maintained a syncretistic set of beliefs. An emblematic figure of presumed Jewish descent in colonial Mexico was Luis de Carvajal (1567–1596), tried twice by the Inquisition and finally burned alive at the stake as an unrepentant "Judaizer." Carvajal composed – out of his own will, not under Inquisitorial pressure – his memoirs detailing his observance of Jewish customs.[5] Another was Sor Juana Inés de la Cruz (1651–1695), Catholic author of lyric and mystical poetry, who is considered a major Baroque literary figure of Mexico.

There were several waves of persecutions against supposed Judaizers, both in Mexico and Peru. These actions were often motivated by politi-cal and economic, rather than religious, reasons. The climax of the Inquisition's persecutions was marked before the mid-seventeenth century. By the 1800s, there were hardly any crypto-Jews in the Spanish colonies and the vast majority of those of Jewish descent had assimilated.[6]

Most New Christians who came to settle in the New World were Portuguese or Jewish faithful who had first left Spain for Portugal and, once Portugal forced conversion of its Jews in 1497, then moved to the Americas. While there was an important sixteenth-century Jewish pres-ence in Brazil as a result of Portuguese colonial expansion, it would be

[5] On Carvajal and the Spanish Inquisition in Mexico, see Martin A. Cohen, *The Martyr: Luis de Carvajal, A Secret Jew in Sixteenth-Century Mexico* (Albuquerque: University of New Mexico Press, 2001); Anna Lanyon, *Fire & Song: The Story of Luis de Carvajal and the Mexican Inquisition* (Boston: Allen & Unwin, 2012).

[6] See Judith Laiken Elkin, *The Jews of Latin America* (New York and London: Holmes & Meier, 1998).

inappropriate to characterize it as a "community" in the contemporary academic sense of the word, since practice, when it occurred, was clandestine. The one exception came in 1630, when the Dutch invaded northern Brazil and allowed the open practice of Judaism. In 1654, following the expulsion of the Dutch by the Portuguese, some practicing Jews became crypto-Jews, others moved to the Netherlands, and still others migrated to the Americas, notably to the Dutch island of Curaçao, where a synagogue has been in continuous use since the mid-seventeenth century. The largest Jewish populations at that time were in Suriname and Brazil. The first Jews to settle openly in Latin America were therefore Sephardic.[7]

Much less is known about early Jewish communities in Latin America than the size of the historiography would suggest. While there is clear documentation on the Dutch colonies, a great deal of the discussion is based on contemporary discourses about the past rather than what would traditionally be defined as historical documentation. Even so, it is clear that there is virtually no link between the contemporary Jewish communities in Latin America in the nineteenth and twentieth centuries and the small numbers of individuals who practiced Judaism openly, or those who some scholars have labeled as Jews following Inquisition records.

THREE CASES: ARGENTINA, BRAZIL, MEXICO

ARGENTINA

Argentina has the largest number of Jews in Latin America, resulting from a great wave of European immigration that began during the last quarter of the nineteenth century and lasted for about fifty years.[8] Jews in Eastern Europe – especially in the Pale of Settlement – felt a growing pressure to seek a better future outside the continent. Physical harassment, social pressures, and economic plight all contributed to this scenario. While a few sought refuge in Palestine, most others looked across the Atlantic for a home in the Americas. Jewish organizations created a number of settlement plans following Theodor Herzl's description of the choice facing the Jewish masses in Eastern Europe as one between "Palestine or the Argentine." The agricultural settlements established in Argentina and Brazil (see below) seemed to offer a partial solution to the Jewish Question.

---

[7] Nathan Wachtel, *The Faith of Remembrance: Marrano Labyrinths* (Philadelphia: University of Pennsylvania Press, 2013).

[8] On Jewish demographics in Latin America, see Sergio DellaPergola, "Demographic Trends of Latin American Jewry." In *The Jewish Presence in Latin America*, ed. Judith L. Elkin and G. W. Merkx (Boston: Allen & Unwin, 1987), 85–133.

As Jews were looking for a safe haven outside Europe, Argentine author-ities adopted a policy to encourage European entry. The desire to increase the relatively small population and to improve – i.e. "whiten" – it by bring-ing European immigrants in order to ensure development and moderniza-tion were the main motivations behind the maxim coined in 1853 by the intellectual and politician Juan Bautista Alberdi, "*Gobernar es poblar*" (to govern is to populate). Indeed, from the 1870s until the economic reces-sion of the early 1930s, a huge wave of immigrants descended on Argentine shores.[9]

Rumors about the possibilities offered by Argentina, where one could live freely and prosper, spread among urban and rural Jews in Central and Eastern Europe. For most Jewish immigrants, Argentina proved to be a "promised land": by the end of the nineteenth century they had established communal institutions and Jewish schools that satisfied their social, eco-nomic, and cultural needs. The newcomers created a rich mosaic of social, cultural, political, and ideological life, which reflected a wide variety of faiths, identities, and social practices: communists and Zionists, Sephardi and Ashkenazi, Orthodox and secular, those who emphasized their Jewishness and others who preferred to stress their Argentine identity.[10]

Chronologically, the first Jewish immigrants began to arrive as early as the 1840s (unlike the case of Brazil, evidence of *conversos* during the colonial period is scant) and these "pioneers" included Moroccan Jews on the one hand and German Jews on the other. The first synagogue was established in 1862. An important milestone in Jewish immigration was recorded in 1881 when, following pogroms in Russia, the Argentine gov-ernment decided to send a special emissary to tsarist Russia to encourage Jews to immigrate. The first organized group of immigrants, consisting of 820 Russian Jews, arrived in August 1889 on board the ship *Wesser*. They were sent to establish Jewish agricultural colonies and some of its members indeed founded Moisesville, the by-now fabled agricultural settlement of the Jewish Colonization Association (JCA), today an important part of the Argentine national creation myth.

While mass Jewish immigration to Argentina was primarily Ashkenazi, Jews from Spanish Morocco were already arriving in the mid-nineteenth century. They were later joined by Sephardim from the declining Ottoman

---

[9] José C. Moya, "The Jewish Experience in Argentina in a Diasporic Comparative Perspective." In *The New Jewish Argentina: Facets of Jewish Experiences in the Southern Cone*, ed. Adriana Brodsky and Raanan Rein (Boston: Brill, 2013), 7–32.

[10] Haim Avni, *Argentina and the Jews: A History of Jewish Immigration*, trans. Gila Brand (Tuscaloosa, AL: University of Alabama Press, 1991).

Empire, especially from Aleppo and Damascus, who arrived alongside the waves of Jews from Eastern and Central Europe.[11]

The Argentine government's open immigration policy dramatically changed the demographic profile of the country, as became apparent in the 1914 census. Over twenty years, the country's population had almost doubled (to about 7.9 million) and more than a third of the inhabitants were foreign-born. In the capital city of Buenos Aires, this figure was around 50 percent. As for Jews, the rate of growth was much higher – between the years 1895 and 1919 the Jewish population increased from 6,000 to 125,000.

The original vision of a focused and expanding Jewish agricultural enterprise did not last long. While in the late nineteenth century most Jewish Argentines were concentrated in the JCA colonies, by the end of World War I the majority were urban dwellers, with Buenos Aires housing the largest Jewish population. With the exception of a temporary break during the Great War, when dwindling commercial ties with Europe contributed to economic recession and unemployment in Argentina, the flow of immigration continued. In contrast to the limitations imposed by the US and other countries, Argentina's liberal immigration policy remained almost unchanged, with minor revisions instituted in the mid-1920s. It was only the world economic recession in the wake of the Wall Street crash that brought immigration to a virtual halt. The ensuing political upheaval provoked the first successful military coup in Argentina's history (September 1930), in turn reinforcing nationalist, Catholic, and xenophobic social tendencies. Independent of immigration policy, Argentina did not always welcome ethnic minorities. Xenophobic attitudes constituted obstacles for non-Catholic immigrants, not just Jews, because of supposed difficulties in adjusting to Argentine society and culture. Furthermore, all newcomers – especially non-Catholics – were expected to abandon their customs in favor of the new culture that was emerging in Argentina. This became a source of permanent unease among Jewish Argentines.

During the 1930s the Jewish population grew to approximately a quarter of a million, but those Jews who had pinned their hopes on Argentina's position at the Evian Conference, convened by the League of Nations in July 1938 to discuss possible solutions to the problem of refugees from Germany and Austria, were disappointed. Argentina, like most other countries with the exception of the Dominican Republic under the dictator General Rafael Trujillo, was unwilling to open its gates to refugees. This same restrictive policy was maintained throughout World War II, although

---

[11] On Sephardim in Latin America, see Margalit Bejarano and Edna Aizenberg, eds, *Contemporary Sephardic Identity in the Americas: An Interdisciplinary Approach* (New York: Syracuse University Press, 2012).

between 1933 and 1945 around 40,000 Jews entered (legally or illegally) Argentina.

In the mid-1940s, following the defeat of fascism and the end of hostilities in Europe, immigration to Argentina resumed, albeit in smaller numbers than in the past. The populist president, Juan Perón, lifted most immigration restrictions in 1947, and during the next three years over 300,000 immigrants, primarily from Spain and Italy – the two "mother countries" of most Argentines – entered the country. As far as Jews were concerned, only 1,500 entered Argentina in the second half of the 1940s. More important, however, was the Peronist regime's decision to grant amnesty to all illegal residents, a measure which enabled some 10,000 Jews to obtain legal status.[12]

The 1950s witnessed the last wave of Jewish immigration to Argentina. These new arrivals were refugees from the communist repression in Hungary in 1956 or Jews who had escaped from the hostile policy adopted by the Nasser regime in Egypt. From that point onwards, the number of Jews in Argentina began to decline.

One of the most studied aspects of Jewish Latin American life has been antisemitism, and Argentina has often been a focus of that study.[13] While it is true that antisemitic manifestations have always accompanied the Jewish presence in Argentina, one must differentiate between the various types of antisemitism. Recent polls, for example, emphasize that Jews are hated no more than other ethnic or social groups, while many people consider multi-national corporations, the Catholic Church, banks, politicians, or the Army – and not Jews – as being "too powerful."

Government sponsored antisemitism has been rare in Argentina. It manifested itself in the limitations imposed on Jewish immigration during the 1930s and the 1940s (which were similar to those in other American republics), and was also noticeable during the years of the brutal military dictatorship that ruled the country between 1976 and 1983. According to many testimonies, Jews arrested by the military suffered more than non-Jews. However, community institutions continued with their normal activities, no antisemitic laws were ever instituted, and Argentine relations with the State of Israel were excellent.[14]

---

[12] Raanan Rein, *Argentina, Israel, and the Jews: Perón, the Eichmann Capture and After*, trans. Martha Grezenback (Bethesda, MD: University Press of Maryland, 2003).

[13] Haim Avni, "Antisemitism in Argentina: The Dimensions of Danger." In *Approaches to Antisemitism: Context and Curriculum*, ed. Michael Brown (New York: American Jewish Committee, 1994), 57–77.

[14] Daniel Goldman and Hernán Dobry, *Ser judío en los años setenta. testimonios del horror y la resistencia durante la última dictadura* (Buenos Aires: Siglo XXI, 2014).

The transition to democracy in the 1980s and 1990s witnessed the adoption of a more tolerant policy toward ethnic minorities and a growing awareness of the multi-cultural nature of Argentine society. This did not signal the complete disappearance of antisemitism or even of its occasional violent manifestations. In fact, the two bomb attacks on the Israeli Embassy and the Jewish community center in Buenos Aires – in 1992 and 1994, respectively – represented a different kind of danger for Jews in Argentina: transnational terror with local support. These bombings triggered grassroots mobilization and a continuing polemic among Argentine Jews as to their individual and collective identities, their place in Argentine society, and their relations with their imagined homeland, the State of Israel.

BRAZIL

It is an academic oddity that the literature on Brazilian Jewry tends to link Inquisition-era Jews (and secret Jews) from Iberia and twentieth-century Central and Eastern Jews even though the Brazilian census of 1872 recorded no Jewish inhabitants. It is also curious that the first *modern* Jewish *community* (we use this term in the traditional sense here) in Brazil, those 3,000 North African migrants who were attracted to the Amazon because of the rubber economy of the late nineteenth century, are all but forgotten.[15]

There are four reasons why this early and active Jewish community has been largely ignored by scholars, each linked to certain trends in the historiography. First, Sephardic Jewry is understudied in the scholarly literature. Second, the North African Jews who migrated to Brazil intermarried frequently, using non-halachic conversion techniques (see below), and much research focuses on Jews who fit a traditional (although not necessarily demographically firm) norm. Third, in Brazil Sephardic Jews were often called "Arabs" (*turcos*) and thus their appearance in the records often takes extra effort to discern. Finally, in this specific case, many Jews returned to Morocco after becoming Brazilian citizens and the documents on their transnational relationship with Brazil did not always make clear the families they had in Brazil, only their business interests.

As the nineteenth century progressed, hundreds of Moroccan Jewish families moved to Brazil, settling in both Rio de Janeiro and Belém do Para (a large city at the mouth of the Amazon). The Spanish–Moroccan War (1859–1860) and a profound sense of minority status were the main

---

[15] Jeffrey Lesser, *Welcoming the Undesirables: Brazil and the Jewish Question* (Berkeley: University of California Press, 1994).

catalysts; multilingualism – Arabic and Spanish were used for business, French and Hebrew learned at the Alliance Israélite Universelle (AIU) schools and Haquitia (Hispanic-Moroccan dialect) was spoken at home – gave them a transnational perspective. Indeed, a report from one of the AIU's directors noted that by the 1880s 95 percent of the boys completing an Alliance education migrated to South America.

By 1890 more than one thousand Maghrebi Jews had migrated to the Amazon, where the rubber economy was booming. Many Jews settled in small towns along the banks of the river where they traded urban products like clothes, medicine, and tobacco for rural products like fish, Brazil nuts, and rubber. Morocco's Jews also discovered they could easily obtain Brazilian naturalization certificates, which gave them a means of economic and social protection if they returned to Morocco. Indeed, many did return to Morocco, often creating two sets of families, one in Brazil based on marriage to indigenous women who were converted, according to oral tradition: the woman was brought into a room blindfolded and told that a spoonful of molten gold would be put in her mouth and that if she truly believed that the Jewish G-d was the one and only G-d, the gold would taste as sweet as honey.

While Moroccans formed Brazil's first modern Jewish community, it was the arrival from Eastern Europe that brought Jews to the mind of many Brazilian elites. Between 1904 and 1924 the Jewish Colonization Association formed two agricultural colonies on the frontier of Rio Grande do Sul, following the establishment of the Argentine JCA colonies discussed above. The Eastern European Jewish colonists who settled in Brazil never amounted to more than a few thousand people, yet they played two critical roles. First, the existence of the agricultural colonies challenged images of Jews as exclusively oriented toward finance and capital in urban areas. Furthermore, state and national elites perceived the residents of the colonies as having become Brazilian, challenging notions that Jews were a closed group.

The two farming colonies were the first step in the regular and organized migration of Jews to Brazil which picked up after World War I, as other countries in the Americas began to close their doors. Between 1918 and 1919 the number of arrivals to Brazil's ports almost doubled, and in 1920 almost doubled again, reaching 69,000. These post-war immigrants differed in many ways from the pre-war group. Although Portuguese, Italians, Spanish, Middle Eastern, and German immigrants continued to predominate, two new groups now entered in growing numbers: Japanese and Eastern Europeans.

Between 1924 and 1934 Eastern European immigration to Brazil increased almost ten times to over 93,000 persons. Jews made up about

45–50 percent of those immigrants and by the mid-1920s more than 10 percent of the Jews emigrating from Europe chose Brazil as their destination. By the early 1930s, the Jewish population of Brazil approached 60,000.[16] The Eastern European Jews who arrived in Brazil after World War I and the Russian Revolution settled primarily in the southern states of São Paulo, Rio Grande do Sul, and Rio de Janeiro and achieved a level of economic success matched only by a few other immigrant groups in Brazil, notably those from Asia and the Middle East.

The combination of economic success and cultural difference made Jews particular targets of nativists in the wake of the Depression. Immigrants had been expected to save Brazil's agricultural economy and Europeanize the culture at the same time. Jews seemed to do neither. In 1934 constitutional immigration quotas had been established and the growing Jewish immigrant population, a worsening economy, and rising nativism made the Jewish Question an important topic among intellectuals, state politicians from urban areas, and federal leaders. Beginning in 1935, Brazil began to deny visas to Jews, but the growing public discourse opposing Jewish immigration and the resulting prohibition neither stopped Jewish entry nor particularly changed its pattern. One of the most important reasons was that a philo-Semitic vision began to gain credence within the government. From this perspective, German, Italian, and Austrian Jewish refugees were increasingly seen as bringing skills and capital to Brazil. International pressure to accept refugees was matched by a change in perception among some of Brazil's most important immigration policy makers. By 1938 new rules regarding Jewish immigration re-opened Brazil's gates to such an extent that more Jews were to enter that year than in any of the ten years previously.

In the 1950s Jews again began to immigrate to Brazil in significant numbers, this time from the Middle East, especially following the Suez Crisis of 1956. By 1960 Jewish Brazilians numbered about 100,000 but, as is the case throughout the Americas, disputes about population size abound. Information collected for the 2000 Brazilian Census showed a Jewish population of 86,825, although Jewish organizations in Brazil place the number between 120,000 and 140,000. The most sizeable Jewish community is in São Paulo, Brazil's most populous city. Other significant Jewish communities are in Rio de Janeiro (25,000–30,000 Jews out of a population of 5.85 million), Porto Alegre, Rio Grande do Sul (10,000–12,000 Jews in a population of about 1.36 million), and in Belo Horizonte, Curitiba, Santos, and Recife (see Table 7.1).

[16] Maria Stella Ferreira Levy, "O papel da migração internacional na evolução da população brasileira (1872 a 1972)," *Revista de Saúde Pública* 8, sup. (1974): 49–90.

Table 7.1 *Total and Jewish Populations of Latin America, by country, 1960 and 2005.*

	1960		2005	
	Total Population	Jewish Population	Total Population	Jewish Population
Argentina	20,248,000	310,000*	37,900,000	185,000
Bahamas			300,000	300
Bolivia	3,311,000	4,000	8,800,000	500
Brazil	62,725,00	86,038*	179,100,000	96,700
Chile	7,298,000	30,000	16,000,000	20,800
Colombia	13,522,000	9,000	45,300,000	3,300
Curaçao	148,000	1,000	138,000	300*****
Costa Rica	1,072,000	1,500	4,200,000	2,500
Cuba	6,466,000	11,000	11,300,000	600
Dominican Republic	2,797,000	600	8,800,000	100
Ecuador	4,007,000	2,000	13,400,000	900
El Salvador	2,434,000	250	6,700,000	100
Guatemala	3,546,000	1,000	12,700,000	900
Honduras	1,282,000	150	6,700,000**	200**
Jamaica	1,630,000	2,200	2,600,000	300
Mexico	32,348,000	25,700	106,200,000	39,800
Netherlands Antilles			215,000	200
Nicaragua	1,578,000	200	5,570,000	60***
Panama	995,000	2,500	3,200,000	5,000
Paraguay	1,677,000	2,000	6,000,000	900
Peru	10,213,000	3,500	27,500,000	2,300
Puerto Rico			3,900,000	1,500
Suriname	223,000	1,000	400,000	200
Trinidad	789,000	400	1,305,000	10****
Uruguay	2,700,000	50,000	3,400,000	19,500
Venezuela	6,320,000	8,000	26,200,000	15,500
Virgin Islands			115,000	300
Total		552,038		397,770

American Jewish Year Book 61 (1960): 352–353.
American Jewish Year Book 105 (2005): 100.
* Revised numbers from: U. O. Schmelz and Sergio DellaPergola, "The Demography of Latin American Jewry," *American Jewish Year Book* 85 (1985): 51–102.
** Jewish Virtual Library www.jewishvirtuallibrary.org/jsource/vjw/Honduras.html.
*** United Jewish Committee, www.ujc.org/content_display.html?ArticleID=122735.
**** National Library and Information System Authority of Trinidad and Tobago www.nalis.gov.tt/Communities/COMMUNITIES_JEWSINTNT.html.
***** Jewish Virtual Library www.jewishvirtuallibrary.org/jsource/vjw/Curacao.html#Curacao.

Independent of the exact numbers, Jewish Brazilians today live in a multicultural nation that counts the largest populations of African and Japanese *descent* of any country in the world, as well as substantial populations of European and Middle Eastern descent. Multi-ethnicity does not hide the fact that Brazil is one of the most unequal countries (in terms of income distribution) in the world, and Jews, who as a group sit near the top of the income, educational, occupational, and residential pyramids, often find the line between class and ethnic tension hard to define. This lack of economic incentive may explain why Brazilian rates of "aliyah" are markedly lower than in Argentina, where they have always represented a minority as well (see Table 7.2).

Jews also find that Brazil's well-diffused myth of "racial democracy" (the false notion that the country is uniquely free of racism) is often a complication. While the myth allows dominant groups who are deemed white to dismiss race as a factor in their class positioning, the same myth makes fighting antisemitic actions difficult. For example, Brazil's constitution-based anti-racism laws often go unenforced although, in a case that made international headlines, the author of a series of Holocaust Denial books had his conviction upheld by the Brazilian Supreme Court.

MEXICO

Unlike Argentina and Brazil, Mexico never attracted large waves of immigrants in spite of an elite desire to remake the country in the image of a white Europe. Although the numbers of Jewish Mexicans are not large, their experiences are indicative of the diversity of Jewish Latin American life, notably because of the high percentage of Sephardim, a marked difference from the Ashkenazi majority in most countries of the Americas.[17]

A few Jewish adventurers and peddlers immigrated to Mexico soon after its independence from Spain (achieved after a long and bloody struggle in 1821). These newcomers were deprived of citizenship rights until 1843, when President Antonio López de Santa Anna repealed a law that limited nationality to Roman Catholics. Even so, public non-Catholic religious services continued to be outlawed. The fall of Santa Anna paved the way for the 1857 constitution, created by Mexican Liberals (those who believed in a strong centralized state, private property, wage labor, and an export based economy), which omitted any mention of Catholicism as a religion

---

[17] On the history of Ashkenazi in Mexico see Alicia Gojman de Backal, ed., *Generaciones judías en México: La Kehila Ashkenazi (1922–1992)* (Mexico City: Comunidad Ashkenazi, 1993). On the history of Sephardim in Mexico, see Liz Hamui de Halabe, ed., *Los judíos de Alepo en México* (Mexico City: Maguen David, 1989).

Table 7.2 *Latin American Immigration to Israel by Countries of Origin and Periods*

Period	Argentina	Brasil	Uruguay	Chile	Mexico	Colombia	Venezuela	C. America*	Paraguay	Total
1948–1951	904	304	66	48	48		–	17	–	1,387
1952–1960	2,888	763	425	401	168		–	43	42	4,730
1961–1964	5,537	637	726	322	125	126	109	18	194	7,794
1965–1971	6,164	1,964	1,118	1,468	611	289	188	111	16	11,929
1972–1979	13,158	1,763	2,199	1,180	861	552	245	104	73	20,135
1980–1989	10,582	1,763	2,014	1,040	993	475	180	8	62	17,117
1990–2000	9,911	2,161	827	604	986	598	378	140	28	15,633
2001–2004	10,014	793	1,158	299	218	275	201	341	47	13,346
Total	59,158	10,148	8,533	5,362	4,010	2,315	1,301	782	462	92,071

* Central America includes: Costa Rica, Guatemala, Cuba, Panama, Puerto Rico, El Salvador, Haiti.

Source: Luis Roniger and Deby Babis, "Latin American Israelis: The Collective Identity of an Invisible Community," in *Jewish Identities in an Era of Globalization and Multiculturalism*, ed. Eliezer Ben-Rafael, Yosef Gorny, Judit Liwerant and Raanan Rein (Leiden: Brill, forthcoming); Israel Central Bureau of Statistics, "Table 4.2: Immigrants by periods of immigration and last country of residence," *Statistical Abstract of Israel 2006*, No. 57, 238–239.

or as an institution. While the small numbers of Jews who settled in Mexico before the 1860s found it necessary to appear in public as Catholic, there is little doubt that political instability and limited economic opportunities were the main obstacles to immigration (Jewish and other).

Until World War II, Jews in Mexico did not have much of a presence for the majority of the population. The twisted memories of crypto-Judaism and the Catholic Church's teachings meant that, for most Mexicans, Jews were either Judas effigies burned during carnival or mythical evil spirits. Real Jews remained unnoticed, usually grouped with the rest of the immigrants from their country of origin: in the apex of immigration, Jews were not signaled as such, but rather as Poles, Russians, Arabs, or Turks. As part of an expansive "outsider" grouping, anti-Jewish sentiments were conflated with a broader governmental and popular xenophobia. While the Catholic Church supported periodicals with specific antisemitic messages, this rarely resulted in physical attacks against the Jewish population, at least until the late 1920s and the Great Depression.

Mexico's political and social culture, based on the myth of *mestizaje*, an ideology that idealized Mexicans as a new race with the best traits of their indigenous and Hispanic ancestors, left little room for pluralism. The state ignored and attacked the nation's indigenous population, the poorest and most vulnerable members of society. There was even less room for multiculturalism as immigrants were expected to adapt into a narrow definition of Mexicanness, that was racially mestizo, culturally and idiomatically Hispanic, and religiously Catholic. Mexican policies reflected this political ethos: while the government took certain measures to foster immigration, it also prohibited foreign individuals and corporations from owning land, a touchy subject after several invasions and territorial loses to France and the United States.

Superficial political and financial stability first came to Mexico during the long dictatorship of Porfirio Díaz (1876–1910) and this led Jews to settle in increasing numbers. The earliest arrivals were Alsatian Jews who had little interest in organizing traditional Jewish community life, often marrying Catholic women and integrating into economic and public life with little reference to their religion or ethnicity. Most notable among them was José Yves Limantour, Porfirio Diaz's Finance Secretary and head of the "*científicos*," Mexico's semi-progressive Liberal elite, for almost two decades. When financier Jacob Schiff and Baron Maurice de Hirsch studied the possibility of settling Russian Jews in Mexico, however, they came to the conclusion that the labor market was not conducive to such a project and that the rural areas lacked the basic infrastructure to sustain Jewish agricultural colonies. In later years Schiff and Hirsch even explored the possibility of establishing a Jewish homeland in Baja California. The

Mexican Revolution of 1910 and the subsequent decades of widespread political violence put an end to these initiatives, leaving a Jewish Mexican population of less than 10,000.

At the beginning of the twentieth century, most Jews in Mexico were Jews from Arab countries and/or Sephardim. The majority were poor peddlers living in rural areas, but the Mexican Revolution opened new opportunities for small merchants. As wealth increased, formal institutions representing Jews from Damascus, Aleppo, and other parts of the Ottoman Empire and the Balkans were created throughout Mexico. The 1920s, as Mexico began to stabilize politically, saw an increase in the number of Jewish immigrants, including significant numbers of Polish Jews who saw the country as a temporary stop on their way to the United States. As time passed, they remained in Mexico, and Jewish American organizations like B'nai B'rith opened offices in Mexico in order to extend a helping hand to these newcomers. Unable to find their way into Mexico's new export industries, many went into commerce, taking advantage of the lack of infrastructure, credit systems, and supply chains outside the big cities.

As in other Latin American countries, the economic depression of the 1930s contributed to a growing anti-foreign sentiment and xenophobia. Chinese and Jews were among the main targets of this agitation, led by the nationalist organization, Las Camisas Doradas (The Golden Shirts).[18] The use of Jews as scapegoats for economic problems was a late development in Mexico, especially when compared to the appearance of the phenomenon in Argentina, which dates back to the end of the nineteenth century. As in other Latin American countries, antisemitism encouraged community building and various Jewish associations were created.

Ashkenazi immigrants relied on the help of the already established Sephardic community that had built a synagogue in Mexico City in 1906 and had their own Jewish cemetery. As the number of Eastern European Jews increased, differences in ritual practice led them to create their own religious and burial institutions. In the mid-twentieth century, divisions within the Ashkenazi organized community created still more institutions. Bundists, Zionists, and communists each created their own schools, welfare organizations, and *landsmanschaftn*. Ashkenazi printing institutions, such as Yiddish newspapers and book editing, appeared only in the late 1920s, as there were no extant Yiddish lettering types in Mexico for the first quarter of the twentieth century. Despite efforts to promote Yiddish, the Mexican-born generations quickly adapted to Spanish. Spanish, English,

---

[18] On the Golden Shirts, see Alicia Gojman de Backal, *Camisas, escudos y desfiles militares* (México City: Fondo de Cultura Económica, 2000).

and Hebrew eventually became the languages of choice in the Jewish schools of Mexico.

During the World War II era, President Lázaro Cárdenas (1934–1940) was known for his willingness to open Mexico's doors to Spanish Republican exiles fleeing the dictatorship of General Francisco Franco. He was not as generous when it came to Jewish refugees from Nazism and fascism in Europe. This position was not unique among Latin American governments; neither was the fact that the number of Jews in Mexico still grew during the years of the Third Reich (1933–1945).[19]

In the post-World War II period, Jewish immigration to Latin America, including Mexico, dwindled, as there no longer were numerically significant Jewish populations in Eastern and Western Europe to serve as sources of immigration. Jews in the Soviet Union were not allowed to leave, the Jewish communities of the Arab countries and North Africa practically disappeared, and the United States and the newly established State of Israel became the destinations of choice for many Jews of the Diaspora.

Although divided and fragmented – on the basis of religious practices, language, cultural patterns, or political ideologies – the majority of Jewish Mexicans (nowadays estimated at over 40,000) are affiliated with institutions and belong to the higher-class strata of Mexican society. In this first regard, today's Mexico presents a very different case than that of Brazil or Argentina. The majority of the school-aged Jewish population attends one of the dozen and a half or so Jewish schools. Jewish Mexicans appear to be more spatially attached to Israel (as compared to others in the Americas) and tend to visit it more often than other Jews in Latin America. The marked increase in religiousness noticed among Jews all over the continent is even more pronounced in Mexico. Modern Mexico nuances still further the idea of a uniform "Jewish Latin America."

SOME NEW APPROACHES

Scholarly interest in Jews as a subject of Latin American studies has grown markedly in the last two decades, especially when compared to research on Latin Americans who trace their ancestry to the Middle East, Asia, or non-Jewish Eastern Europe. The historiography of the Jewish presence in Latin America, however, is still characterized by essentialist concepts and the overemphasis on Jewish particularity, which suggests that Jews are a minority unlike other minorities. Thus, comparative frameworks tend to be intra-ethnic (studying Jewish Argentines or Jewish Brazilians in

---

[19] Daniela Gleizer, *Unwelcome Exiles: Mexico and the Jewish Refugees from Nazism, 1933–1945* (Boston: Brill, 2013).

comparison with Jews in South Africa or Australia). Exceptionalism suggests that ethnicity is a non-national phenomenon and that ethnic group members are either separate from or victims of national culture.

This tendency is not exclusive to scholarship on Jews of course. Research on Latin Americans of Japanese, Chinese, and Lebanese descent, for example, usually presents the groups first and foremost in their Diasporic conditions. This kind of research presumes a dominance of transnational ethnicity over other components, such as national identity. Research on Jewish Latin Americans might focus on engagement in the national context in order to create comparison and contact zones with other ethnic minorities such as Latin Americans of Polish, Japanese, Chinese, Syrian, and Lebanese descent. It might be useful to eliminate the binary view of ethnic minorities as *either* Diasporic *or* national.

Research on ethnicity in Latin America often presumes that the children and grandchildren of immigrants feel a special relationship to their ancestors' place of birth or imagined homeland. Implicit in this assumption is the idea that ethnic minorities do not play a significant role in national identity formation. Studies of Jewish Latin Americans, for example, often assume that rank-and-file support of Zionist organizations has been first and foremost about the State of Israel. Yet recent research suggests that being Zionist in Latin America was not exclusively linked to the State of Israel. More often, it was one of the strategies espoused by Jews in order to become Latin Americans.[20] Like other immigrants, Jewish Latin Americans needed to have their *Madre Patria*. Just as Italian immigrants had Italy and Spanish immigrants had Spain, so Jews had their own imagined motherland, Zion, or Israel. This interpretation of Zionism was part of the effort to shape new identities and make a new home in Latin America, emphasizing the idea of a nation of origin rather than a political project to safeguard the future. Due to the conquest of the organized communities in Latin America by Zionist political parties in the early 1950s, the historiography (as is generally the case) has devoted little attention to non-Zionists, effectively erasing them from the national narratives of Jewish Latin experiences. Their experiences and efforts to integrate into Argentine, Mexican, or Peruvian society lay on the margins of the currently dominant or hegemonic narratives of Latin American Jewry.

Another common assumption in the historiography is that heritage makes one a member of an ethnic community. Jewish exogamy rates in Latin America, however, are often above 50 percent, and many individuals

[20] Raanan Rein and Mollie Lewis, "Cultural Zionism as a Contact Zone: Sephardic and Askenazi Jews Bridge the Gap on the Pages of the Argentine Newspaper *Israel*," in *Contemporary Sephardic Identity in the Americas*, ed. Bejarano and Aizenberg, 69–87.

do not see themselves (or wish to be seen) as members of a formally constituted ethnic or religious community. There are many studies of ethnic community leaders and institutions, but few about what might be termed "unaffiliated ethnics." Research also tends to ignore the 50 percent (or more in many places) of Jews who were or are not affiliated with Jewish institutions. The frequently used term "Jewish community" is misleading if it refers only to those affiliated with Jewish organizations, synagogues, social clubs, or youth movements. Documenting life stories and reclaiming the memories of unaffiliated Jews will provide important lessons on the nature of national and ethnic identity. Studies might be conducted of Jews married to non-Jews, individuals who express Jewish identity based on culture rather than on religion or ethnicity, and authors who do not explicitly express their Jewishness.

Much scholarship on Latin American ethnicity correctly notes that majority discourses are frequently racist. Yet there is often a gap between rhetoric and social practice. Indeed, racist manifestations have not prevented members of a number of Latin American ethnic groups (especially from Europe, the Middle East, and Asia) from entering the dominant political, cultural, economic, and social sectors. Yet scholars focusing on discourse tend to find victims, often suggesting that racism represents an absolutely hegemonic structure. Thus, ethnic identity formation appears based primarily on discrimination and exclusion. Scholars examining social status, on the other hand, have come to a different conclusion. They suggest that success among Asian, Middle Eastern, and Jewish Latin Americans places them in the 'white' category and thus as part of the dominant classes.[21] While antisemitism has been a favored topic for scholars of Jewish Latin America, there is often little social and cultural research on the ways in which Jews are embedded in prevailing national structures.

While studies on Jewish Latin Americans as members of the dominant classes are rare, the literature does focus on economic success, often giving the impression of homogeneous, unstratified immigrant-descended ethnic communities. Latin Americans of Asian and Middle Eastern descent seem to be uniformly situated in the middle class or higher and this image is even stronger with regard to Jewish Latin Americans. Many scholars

---

[21] On Brazil, see Sociedade Brasileira de Cultural Japonesa, *Uma epopéia moderna: 80 anos de imigração japonesa no Brasil* (São Paulo: Editora Hucitec, 1992); Bernardo Sorj, "Brazilian Non-Anti-Semite Sociability and Jewish Identity." In *Identities in an Era of Globalization and Multiculturalism: Latin America in the Jewish World*, ed. Judit Bokser Liwerant, Eliezer Ben-Rafael, Yosef Gorny, and Ranaan Rein (Boston: Brill, 2008), 151–171. On Argentina, see Eugene F. Sofer, *From Pale to Pampa: A Social History of the Jews of Buenos Aires* (New York: Holmes & Meier, 1982).

do not even consider research on the Jewish working class or the Jewish poor – possibly because these studies might shatter the myth, cherished by historians and Jewish Latin Americans alike, that celebrates the move from the Pale to the Pampa and the shift from working as peddlers to upper-middle-class status. While this was the case for many Jews, it was not a uniform story.

There are a number of other areas that have been under-researched in Latin American ethnic studies generally and in Jewish Latin American studies specifically. Notable among them is gender. Jewish women are virtually absent from the historiography on Latin America, although a number of recently published works will help to rectify the situation.[22] The same holds true for children and sexual minorities. Another issue relates to the presentation of homogenous ethnic communities, which means that Sephardic Jews have not been the subject of much research. Fewer in number, more traditional, and less enthusiastically Zionist, Sephardic Jews are not considered an important part of the Jewish Latin American story. Furthermore, scholars may have exaggerated their descriptions of the religious and cultural differences between Ashkenazi and Sephardic Jews in Latin America, as well as their alleged lack of interaction.

CONCLUSION

To make a single characterizing statement about contemporary Jewish Latin Americans would be an error. Intermarriage rates are high, but so is the growth of ultra-religious worship. Discourses of antisemitism remain critical to identity formation even though acts of violence are very rare, with the exception of the terrorist attacks against Jewish institutions in Argentina. Zionist movements are strong among affiliated Jews throughout Latin America, although "aliyah" rates are extremely low in Brazil and relatively high in Argentina and Mexico (see Table 7.2). Furthermore, the location of "Jewish Latin America" has expanded since 1960, to both Israel and North America, creating a Diaspora to the Diaspora.

There are currently around 100,000 Israeli citizens of Latin American origin. Their integration into Israeli society is considered a success story, since many have attained prominent positions in various fields. However, Latin American-Israelis have been an invisible community, preferring

---

[22] For a recent important contribution, see Sandra McGee Deutsch, *Crossing Borders, Claiming a Nation: A History of Argentine Jewish Women, 1880–1955* (Durham: Duke University Press, 2010).

individual mobility to communal assertiveness.[23] Two major factors help to explain this: First, there has never been a "wave" of immigration from Latin America to Israel, although there were peaks in the 1970s and 1980s, a time of military dictatorships in the Southern Cone (see Table 7.2). Second, the wide demographic distribution of Latin Americans throughout Israel has made community building particularly difficult.

The motivations for Latin Americans to immigrate to Israel have changed over the years. During the fifties, sixties, and seventies many moved for ideological reasons revolving around Zionism and Jewish identity, and a prime concern was for their children's future as Jews. During the brutal military dictatorships of the 1970s, many Jews moved to Israel in order to live under democratic regime or fled to save their lives. In recent years, economic upheavals and financial insecurity constituted the main motives for immigration to Israel. This has been particularly noticeable among Argentines, whose entry skyrocketed after the December 2001 economic crisis and who continue to be the largest single group of Israelis of Latin American descent.

The integration of Latin Americans into Israeli society was facilitated by similar social behaviors of informality and improvisation. In addition, Latin American music, novels, and films have been popular in Israel for decades. Interest in Latin American culture grew dramatically in recent years as a result of the increase in the number of Israeli youngsters traveling to South America and the new popularity of *telenovelas* (which are shown daily on various stations) among the Israeli public. Compared to many other newcomers to Israel, Latin Americans arrive with a stronger knowledge of Israel, Zionism, Judaism and the Hebrew language. Finally, there has been a dramatic increase in the number of Latin-Israeli internet sites that provide a space where Latin American identity can be asserted. These sites function simultaneously as an instrument of cohesion among Latin American-Israelis and as a means for their integration in Israel.

This essay argues that Jews are normative Latin Americans and that categories like "Argentine," "Brazilian," and "Mexican" are widely constructed and include members of numerous "minority" groups. We have looked critically at some of the traditional ideas about Jewish Latin American life and have asked if new approaches may generate new data and new conclusions. We suggest that Jews are not *in* Latin America but *of* Latin America.

---

[23] Luis Roniger and Deby Babis, "Latin American Israelis: The Collective Identity of an Invisible Community," in *Jewish Identities in an Era of Globalization and Multiculturalism*, eds. Eliezer Ben-Rafael, Yosef Gorny, Judit Liwerant, and Raanan Rein (Boston: Brill, 2008), 297–322. Donald L. Herman, *The Latin American Jewish Community of Israel* (New York: Praeger, 1984).

SELECT BIBLIOGRAPHY

GENERAL TITLES

Behar, Ruth. *An Island Called Home: Returning to Jewish Cuba*. New Jersey: Rutgers University Press, 2009.

Elkin, Judith Laiken. *The Jews of Latin America*. New York and London: Holmes & Meier, 1998.

Elkin, Judith Laiken and Gilbert W. Merkx, eds. *The Jewish Presence in Latin America*. Boston: Allen and Unwin, 1987.

Foster, David William, ed. *Latin American Jewish Cultural Production*. Nashville: Vanderbilt University Press, 2009.

Herman, Donald L. *The Latin American Jewish Community of Israel*. New York: Praeger, 1984.

Kalir, Barak. *Latino Migrants in the Jewish State: Undocumented Lives in Israel*. Bloomington: Indiana University Press, 2010.

Lesser, Jeffrey and Ignacio Klich, eds. *Arab and Jewish Immigrants in Latin America: Images and Realities*. London: Frank Cass, 1998.

Lesser, Jeffrey and Raanan Rein, eds. *Rethinking Jewish-Latin Americans*. Albuquerque: University of New Mexico Press, 2008.

Ruggiero, Kristin, ed. *The Jewish Diaspora in Latin America and the Caribbean: Fragments of Memory*. Brighton: Sussex Academic Press, 2005.

Sheinin, David and Lois Baer Barr, eds. *The Jewish Diaspora in Latin America*. New York: Garland Publishing, 1996.

Spitzer, Leo. *Hotel Bolivia: The Culture of Memory in a Refuge from Nazism*. New York: Hill and Wang, 2009.

Wells, Allen. *Tropical Zion: General Trujillo, FDR, and the Jews of Sosúa*. Durham: Duke University Press, 2009.

ARGENTINA

Avni, Haim. *Argentina and the Jews: A History of Jewish Immigration*. Translated by Gila Brand. Tuscaloosa: University of Alabama Press, 1991.

Brodsky, Adriana, and Raanan Rein, eds. *The New Jewish Argentina: Facets of Jewish Experiences in the Southern Cone*. Boston: Brill, 2013.

McGee Deutsch, Sandra. *Crossing Borders, Claiming a Nation: A History of Argentine Jewish Women, 1880–1995*. Durham: Duke University Press, 2010.

Rein, Raanan. *Argentina, Israel, and the Jews: Perón, the Eichmann Capture and After*. Translated by Martha Grezenback. Bethesda, MD: University Press of Maryland, 2003.

Sofer, Eugene F. *From Pale to Pampa: A Social History of the Jews of Buenos Aires*. New York & London: Holmes & Meier, 1982.

Weisbrot, Robert. *The Jews of Argentina: From the Inquisition to Perón*. Philadelphia: The Jewish Publication Society, 1979.

BRAZIL

Klein, Misha. Kosher. *Feijoada and Other Paradoxes of Jewish Life in São Paulo*. Gainesville: University Press of Florida, 2012.

Lesser, Jeffrey. *Welcoming the Undesirables: Brazil and the Jewish Question.* Berkeley: University of California Press, 1994.

Liebman, Seymour B. *New World Jewry, 1493–1825: Requiem for the Forgotten.* New York: KTAV Publishing House, Inc., 1982.

Spitzer, Leo. *Lives in Between: Assimilation and Marginality in Austria, Brazil, West Africa, 1780–1945.* Cambridge: Cambridge University Press, 1989.

Wiznitzer, Arnold. *Jews in Colonial Brazil.* New York: Columbia University Press, 1960.

MEXICO

Boxer Liwerant, Judit, ed. *Imágenes de un encuentro.* Mexico City: UNAM, 1992.

Cimet, Adina. *Ashkenazi Jews in Mexico: Ideologies in the Structuring of the Community.* New York: SUNY Press, 1997.

Gleizer, Daniela. *Unwelcome Exiles: Mexico and the Jewish Refugees from Nazism, 1933–1945.* Boston: Brill, 2014.

Gojman de Backal, Alicia, ed. *Generaciones judías en México: La Kehila Ashkenazi (1922–1992).* Mexico City: Comunidad Ashkenazi, 1993.

  Camisas, escudos y desfiles militares. Mexico City: Fondo de Cultura Económica, 2000.

Hamui de Halabe, Liz, ed. *Los judíos de Alepo en México.* Mexico City: Maguen David, 1989.

CHAPTER 8

COLONIAL AND POST-COLONIAL JEWRIES
The Middle East and North Africa

YARON TSUR

In its heyday European colonialism controlled vast areas of the globe, stretching from Far East Asia to the Atlantic Ocean. The variance in territories, in individual historical circumstances, colonial regimes etc., does not permit here a detailed examination of each stage and region that played a part in the Jewish colonial experience. Thus, I have chosen to concentrate on the Middle East and North Africa (MENA) where the majority of colonial Jewry resided, and to devote the bulk of the chapter to examining the initial and concluding stages of this experience.[1]

Another introductory qualification concerns the state of historiography. Asian and African Jewries were subject to Orientalist research which spawned their first modern historical narratives, tying the latter to colonial historiography, its stereotypes and perspectives. Later nationalist historiographies, Jewish and Arab, carried contradictory messages and marked a complex approach to existing colonial historiography. They accepted some of its attitudes and substance while rejecting others, but mainly they searched for new perspectives, in support of or attacking Zionism. In the last generation or so, Post-Colonial narratives have emerged, radically negating the historical products of the colonial period and often rejecting and/or ignoring the products of the Zionist historiography.

Coming from Israeli historiography which, at present, is rather divided between the camps, I developed my own vision. In the present chapter I commence with the French takeover of Algeria in 1830, which inaugurated Western policies towards colonial Jewries, and conclude in post-1948 Israel, where the massive encounter of European and non-European Jews engendered the most striking test-case for the impact of colonialism on internal Jewish relationships as well as for the role of Zionism in this affair.

---

[1] The author wishes to thank Dr. Noah Gerber for his careful reading of this chapter and his perceptive comments.

EUROPEAN MODELS AND COLONIAL
MUTATIONS – THE CASE OF ALGERIA

THE TRANSITION TO COLONIAL SECTORIAL SOCIETY

Algeria was the first territory conquered by France in what was to become the "French Maghreb." Algiers's Jews, like their Muslim neighbors, suffered during the actual conquest and were plagued by the moral and economic disintegration characteristic of such times of crisis. Nonetheless, for the Jewish minority the colonial conquest had immediate benefits, since the French did not regard themselves as committed to the former Muslim order with its hierarchical differences between Muslims and Jews. Though no decree was issued to this effect, the city's capitulation agreement reflected the values and concepts of post-revolutionary France and was interpreted as quasi-emancipation of the Jews in their relations with Muslims.[2] This became the typical introductory policy of the colonial power towards the Jewish minority in newly conquered territories.

The significance of equality among the natives, however, was diminished by a new phenomenon in Algeria's human landscape: settlers from France and other Christian newcomers, from Italy, Spain and elsewhere. The French contingent enjoyed privileges and a higher status from the beginning; the other Christian immigrants did not, but they felt entitled to, due to colonial hegemony and their European origins. In spite of French pretensions to spread the humanitarian and egalitarian values of Enlightenment and the French Revolution, Algerian colonial society, like any modern colonial society, was based on a European–Native dichotomy and maintained the pre-modern division, based on a person's origin, of two castes or estates: rulers (Europeans) and ruled (Natives).

Another line of continuity concerned the linguistic and cultural gaps between the estates, helping to symbolize and perpetuate the dichotomy and hierarchies that set rulers and ruled apart. In fact, in pre-colonial Algeria under the Turks, the cultural gap was chiefly symbolic, with Arabic in reality serving all echelons – both rulers and ruled. Under the French, however, and despite their "civilizing mission," the cultural rifts were very real, with real repercussions for the emerging social structure: all the local social networks dependent on oral and written communication naturally divided into what we would term "sectors": in the case of Algeria, into a

---

[2] For an updated discussion of pre-colonial Algerian Jewry and the immediate impact of French occupation see Joshua Schreier, *Arabs of the Jewish Faith: The Civilizing Mission in Colonial Algeria* (New Brunswick: Rutgers University Press, 2010), 10–19; Cf. the still useful piece of colonialist historiography, Claude Martin, *Les Israélites Algériens de 1830 à 1902* (Paris: Héraklès, 1936), 40–44.

French or (to borrow contemporary terminology) "European" sector and an Arab-Berber or "native" sector. The typical cultural capital of each sector determined the boundaries of economic mobility of its members: those belonging to the former had access to European markets in Algeria itself and beyond; those belonging to the latter were limited to local markets conducted in the country's Arabic or Berber dialects. However, unlike the legally defined estates, the socio-cultural "sectorial" division was not totally controlled by the colonial power and was dynamic. Some natives learned to benefit from the clash between "civilizing" pretensions and oppressive realities and used their access to European modern education to acquire access to French networks and markets as well. They constituted a kind of third sector, of people who could be active in both the native and the European networks and markets.

Such people who were at home in both cultural worlds could, of course, serve as the perfect mediators between Europeans and natives in the new colonial society. In fact, at the start of the conquest, a number of Jewish export–import merchants filled this function, continuing a role in which they had excelled in pre-colonial Algeria. But the close contact they maintained with local "disobedient" Muslim chiefs was viewed with suspicion by the French authorities, and once the French had consolidated their position in the country, the Jewish notables got the cold shoulder. Ultimately this Jewish elite shared the fate of other local elites and disappeared.[3]

IMPERIALISTIC MUTATION

What seemed to be a void left by the local Jewish leadership was filled by the Jews of France, demonstrating the revolutionary impact of the new world order on inter-communal relationships between distant Jewish communities. Up to the nineteenth century, every local Jewish community was fully autonomous in managing its own affairs; at most it followed the directives of a leadership seated in a large nearby city or in a regional capital. The interest now shown by Western powers in almost every remote spot on the globe threatened this age-old autonomous order. However, the shortening of time and space between continents was bi-directional, and distant events which, in previous generations, would not have affected Western Jewries, could now draw them into the arena. This change is clearly illustrated by the defining event in modern inter-community relations: the Damascus Affair (1840), in the course of which Syrian Jews were accused of ritual murder. The charge was supported by the local French consul, who was not dismissed by his government, thus not only placing

[3] Martin, *Les Israélites Algériens de 1830 à 1902*, 48–58.

the Damascus community in grave danger but also challenging French Jewry's sense of confidence in the true nature of their own emancipation. The French-Jewish leader, Adolphe Crémieux, turned to Jews from the other major Western power – Britain – and with his English counterpart, Moses Montefiore, set out on a journey to the East, where, taking advantage of Britain's rising power, they succeeded in settling the affair.[4]

The two lobbyists attempted to exploit their success to improve the status of the Jews of the East, and make an impact on the education of Jewish youth. They had in mind the process of modernization developed in Western Europe, a model based on legal equality, local acculturation, and social integration in all walks of life. Montefiore appealed to Istanbul with a request to instruct the young in the Turkish language, acting in the spirit of this preliminary model in which acculturation focused on the local majority language and culture. Crémieux, on the other hand, appealed to Egypt, envisioning a school network where the main language of instruction would not be local but the language of his own empire, France.[5] These two founding fathers of Western Jewish intervention in the fate of the Jews of the lands of Islam were naturally both opposed to the inferior legal status of the Jews, and, following their own model of emancipation, they pushed for equality with the Muslim majority. But as for the second component of the model, acculturation, Crémieux was in fact promoting an imperialistic mutation of the original model. He proposed that Jewish youth in eastern lands be educated in the spirit of the main high culture, not of the local milieu, but of a European power. Such changes in the model of acculturation would obviously affect integration, for full inclusion depends on cultural mingling, including literacy; Jewish youth would in fact be better equipped to connect with the economic and social extensions of that power than with the local institutions in their milieu.[6]

For the "other" non-European Jews, the Western Jewish leaders tended to invent models of modernization significantly different from their own.

[4] Jonathan Frankel, *The Damascus Affair: 'Ritual Murder', Politics, and the Jews in 1840* (Cambridge: Cambridge University Press, 1997).

[5] Ibid., 370–371; Aron Rodrigue, *French Jews, Turkish Jews: The Alliance Israélite Universelle and the Politics of Jewish Schooling in Turkey, 1860–1925* (Bloomington: Indiana University Press, 1990), 3–4; Yaron Tsur, *Yehudim bein Muslemim BeReshit Tekufat HaReformot* (Tel Aviv: Ha'Universiṭah HaPetuḥah, 2004), 220–227.

[6] For further discussion of the reformist models and their application in Islamic countries see Tsur, 228–240; Yaron Tsur, *Qehila Qeru'a: Yehudey Maroqo VeHaLe'umiyut, 1943–1954* (Tel Aviv: 'Am-'Oved, 2001); Cf. Daniel J. Schroeter and Joseph Chetrit, "Emancipation and Its Discontents: Jews at the Formative Period of Colonial Rule in Morocco," *Jewish Social Studies: History, Culture, Society* 13, no. 1 (2006): 170–206.

Likewise, they developed a typical discourse when speaking of them. Its first full expression is found in a common, familiar Jewish source, an early Haskalah book, *Massa ba-Arav*, Samuel Romanelli's Moroccan travelogue. Romanelli, an Italian Maskil, reached Morocco by chance, stayed there from 1787 to 1790, and left with mixed impressions. He admired the country's beauty and natural resources but disparaged its residents, believing that they were unable to take advantage of these resources and that only European conquest would improve the situation. This barefoot, enlightened intellectual had pretensions to being a mentor for the local Jewish population. Daniel Schroeter has classified his writing as orientalist in Said's sense of the term.[7] Indeed, consider the following passage and its extremely negative, sweeping attitude towards Morocco's Muslims: "deceit, oppression, licentiousness, greed, folly, jealousy, faithlessness and shamelessness – these are but a bare outline of the Arabs' ways. These characterize all their intentions and acts."[8] Romanelli looked down on Morocco's Jews as well, but his assessment of them was very different: "What about the Jews? Their intellects are muddied but their hearts are pure ... Though their foolishness is deplorable, the object of their hope is commendable.... their righteousness is turned toward their fellow men. Their homes are not full of wealth ... but they are happy with their lot. They are not overly clever, but neither are they very mischievous."[9]

In describing his fellow Jews, Romanelli expresses a sense of superiority mixed with both negative and positive assessments and feelings. While his basic sense of superiority remains intact, his negativism is mitigated by his sympathy for the "other" Jews; and while he refers to Muslims in classic orientalist and purely negative terms, meant to exclude the non-European object, he refers to Jews in what may be seen as "internal Orientalism," still expressing European superiority, but nevertheless leaving open the possibility of inclusion.

Traces of internal Orientalism amply fill the texts produced by French Jews, in which the writers try to draw Algeria's Jews closer to the European sector. In the spirit of the positive aspect of internal Orientalism, the Jews were depicted as the "good natives": amenable to learning and absorbing the culture of the conquerors, open to social contact with Christians, grateful and loyal, industrious and efficient – as opposed to the immutable Arabs, the "bad natives," who found it hard to learn and were closed to

---

[7] Daniel Schroeter, "Orientalism and the Jews of the Mediterranean," *Journal of Mediterranean Studies* 4, no. 2 (1994): 184–185.

[8] Samuel Romanelli, *Travail in an Arab Land*, trans. Yedida K. Stillman and Norman A. Stillman (Tuscaloosa: University of Alabama Press, 1989), 131.

[9] Ibid.

the influences of Western civilization, avoiding social contact with other religions, hating the Christian conquerors, lazy, etc.[10]

In parallel, in the spirit of the negative aspect of internal Orientalism, the French Jews condemned in the sharpest terms the contemporary cultural and moral state of the local Jews, especially targeting their leadership, religious and mundane alike. Like Romanelli before them, they too sought to replace the old leaders as mentors for their "ignorant" co-religionists.[11] Their views in this matter fell on receptive ears in government circles and led to the first turning point in Muslim–Jewish "native equality": adapting government norms vis-à-vis Jews in the mother country to the Jews in Algeria. The system of regional religious councils (consistoire) stripped of all autonomous function except in purely religious matters, and governed by a central consistory in the capital, was speedily imported to the new colony. This was followed by the importation of French rabbis to head the councils. Local rabbis were assigned subordinate functions.

The balance of power between the Jews of France and colonial Jews, the relations of dependency and rivalry, as well as solidarity, came to the fore in a series of arenas; among others, in that of documentation and research. There is no shortage of sources giving expression to the history and perspective of the French side. And historical works on the Algerian Jews, written by French Jews, often in apologetic tones, have for a long time been part and parcel of colonial historiography.[12] The material reflecting the perspective of the locals had to wait until decolonization, after 1962, in order to be studied, or even discovered. The first to examine this side were scholars who had been inspired by their Algerian Jewish ethnic identity[13] and/or by Zionism.[14] They were followed by others who were interested

[10] J. Altaras report (1842), in Simon Schwarzfuchs, *Les Juifs d'Algérie et la France, 1830–1855* (Jerusalem: Ben-Zvi Institute, 1981), 67–201.

[11] Ibid.

[12] Colette Zytnicky, *Les Juifs du Maghreb: Naissance d'une historiographie coloniale* (Paris: Presses de l'Université Paris-Sorbonne, 2011); idem, "The 'Oriental Jews' of the Maghreb: Reinventing the North African Jewish Past in the Colonial Era," in *Colonialism and the Jews*, ed. Ethan B. Katz, Lisa Moses Leff, and Maud S. Mandel (Bloomington: Indiana University Press, 2017), 29–53; Sarah Abrevaya Stein, *Saharan Jews and the Fate of French Algeria* (Chicago: University of Chicago Press, 2014).

[13] For instance: Joëlle Bahloul, *Le culte de la table dressée, rites et traditions de la table juive algérienne* (Paris: Editions A.M. Métailié, 1983); Richard Ayoun and Bernard Cohen, *Les Juifs d'Algérie: deux mille ans d'histoire* (Paris: Lattés, 1982).

[14] Yosef Chetrit, "Moderniyut Le'umit 'Ivrit mul Moderniyut Şorfatit: HaHaśkkalah Ha'Ivrit BiSefon-'Afriqah BaMe'ah HaTteša'-'Esreh," *MiQqedem UmiYyam* 3 (1990): 11–76; Michel Abitbol, *MiCrémieux LePétain: 'Anţišemiyut Be'Algeria HaQoloni'alit* (Jerusalem: Merkaz Zalman Šazar, 1993), 11–76; Yossef Charvit, *La France, l'élite*

in French colonial studies and/or inspired by post-colonial trends.[15] While Zionist historiography focused on the meager quantity of Hebrew manuscripts, rabbinical literature and Haskalah newspapers as its source material, others continued to base their investigations on the far richer reserve of French sources, extracting new voices from them. This re-vision resulted in the attribution of a much greater role to the local French administration and the westernized Jewish elite in the formation of French policy towards the native Jews. It also illuminated our understanding of the evolution of French colonial policy in general.

COLONIAL EMANCIPATION

The direct contact from 1830 between the Algerian territory and population and branches of the French government, army and economy greatly increased the demand for a role filled previously by a handful of people: cultural and economic mediation between foreigners and locals. What had been feasible in pre-colonial Algeria with the help of a few dozen merchant families now demanded hundreds of agents. French Jewry took advantage of this opening to fill the ranks of the mediators with Jews, especially from the younger generation. In the meantime there were amongst the Jewish youth some who had managed to convert large portions of their "native" habitus into a French one, thus managing to exit the native sector in favor of the third, mediating sector. One may term them "Westernized" and their sector "the Westernized sector," since they chose the culture of the dominating western empire as their high culture. But they did so without rejecting their original culture, thus distinguishing themselves as part of both the native and the European sectors; they exclusively enjoyed access to all three sectors while being able to mediate between the two extremes of the colonial order.

Crémieux and his colleagues believed, or at least argued, that the westernized were eager to complete the acquisition of their cultural qualification

rabbinique d'Algérie et la Terre Sainte au XIXe siècle: tradition et modernité (Paris: Champion, 2005).
[15] For instance Pierre Birnbaum, "French Jews and the 'Regeneration' of Algerian Jewry," in Jews and the State, ed. Ezra Mendelsohn. Studies in Contemporary Jewry 19 (New York: Oxford University Press, 2003), 88–103; Nathan Charles Godley, "Almost Finished Frenchmen: The Jews of Algeria and the Question of French National Identity, 1830–1902" (Ph.D. Diss., University of Iowa, 2006); Schreier, Arabs of the Jewish Faith. For a useful historiographical survey and critique, see Sophie Beth Roberts, "Jews, Citizenship and Antisemitism in French Colonial Algeria, 1870–1943" (Ph.D. diss. University of Toronto 2012), 1–42.

by identifying with the dominant Europeans and that they should strive to join them legally and politically, by attaining French citizenship. The first opportunity to acquire French citizenship took place some 35 years after the conquest, in 1865, when Napoleon III, in an unusual step, published a decree that gave natives in Algeria the right to full French citizenship on condition they express, in person, their agreement to fully abide by French laws. The decree was not aimed at the Jewish community, in particular, but there were expectations that it would attract many westernized, if not other, Jews. However, to the chagrin of the French-Jewish leadership, only slightly more than 150 of the country's 33,000 Jews chose at the time to accept the offer, which may be termed "individual emancipation by choice." Most of the Jews, presumably, were deterred by the obligations of citizenship on matters such as divorce or military service which were inconsistent with the traditional values of the Jewish faith. Divorce, for instance, was forbidden by French law; keeping kosher and celebrating religious holidays was virtually impossible during military service and so forth.

Crémieux – who worked behind the scenes all the way through – and his friends in the French government, drew the appropriate conclusions from this experience. The next time an opportunity presented itself to change the legal status of the Jews, in 1870, they saw to it that a decree would be issued that would change the Jews' status, collectively, from the top – an option that may be defined as "enforced emancipation" since it did not allow for individual choice.[16] Furthermore, "the Crémieux Edict," as it was known, created a new conception of possible emancipation in colonial territories alone: equality under the law, acculturation and integration, not into the local majority, but into the colonial estate of "Europeans." While the original French Jewish policy tended to create de facto equity with the Muslims, the new legal step marked a real revolution in the Jews' local status, by elevating them from the native estate to that of the rulers – that is, above the Muslims. The edict improved the Jews' legal status in relation with the settlers' non-French element as well, and in terms of French local politics, such as municipal elections, it made them the decisive factor in some places, notably Oran. In short, it was a shock to both the colonial and pre-colonial orders and world of values and, not surprisingly, led to anti-Jewish incidents and an especially radical antisemitic movement among the settlers.[17]

[16] See discussions and other interpretations of the 1865 decree and Crémieux Edict in the historical works cited above.

[17] Geneviève Dermenjian, *La crise anti-juive oranaise, 1895–1905: l'antisémitisme dans l'Algérie coloniale* (Paris: L'Harmattan, 1986).

For the Jews, however, the true test of the change was now in the dynamic arena of sectors, not of the legal estates. The new certificate of citizenship did not assure poor Jews automatic economic or social progress. However, it could certainly help, as the enactment of free primary education in the Second Republic showed (1882). It ensured elementary French education for all strata of the Jewish population. Most of Algeria's Jews were now on the path to westernization, with a staple diet of both French language and culture. The pre-colonial structure of the Jewish community – a broad Arabic speaking native sector and a narrow sector of multicultural mediators – was about to be overturned.

ALLIANCE ISRAÉLITE UNIVERSELLE

On their way to achieving their goal in Algeria, Crémieux and his colleagues wished to implement at least part of their vision in other areas as well. The means at their disposal was a Paris-based network of schools, founded and run by the Alliance Israélite Universelle (established in 1860) which was their own creation and the first international Jewish organization. Originally, Alliance had a political aim – the defense of Jewish rights – as well as a socio-economic one – philanthropic assistance to Jewish communities in crisis. However, its primary, enduring activity was in the field of education. It focused on realizing Crémieux's vision of 1840: spreading French elementary education among Jewish communities in the Muslim east, as well as to communities under Ottoman rule in the Balkans. In all these, a modernist revolution was to take place ultimately winning over the Jewish community to French culture.[18] We have termed the formula of modernization behind this approach "imperialist emancipation," which couched native equality within Western acculturation.

EXPANSION – A WAVE OF PROTECTORATES

The second stage of nineteenth-century colonial expansion, from the early 1880s to the eve of World War I, was conducted amidst endeavors to maintain a balance between the European powers. Colonialism expanded extensively but under the mantle of agreements, public or clandestine, and in an attempt to justify domination over new areas. A prime rationale claimed the inability of the incumbent rulers to meet their

---

[18] On the Alliance see André Kaspi, ed., *Histoire de l'Alliance Israélite Universelle: De 1860 à nos jours* (Paris: Armand Colin, 2010); Aron Rodrigue, *Jews and Muslims: Images of Sephardi and Eastern Jewries in Modern Times* (Seattle: University of Washington Press, 2003).

obligations – which obliged responsible parties – i.e., Europeans – to take the territories and their rulers under their wing. Native rulers were not ousted; they remained as nominal, "puppet" sovereigns, generally under a "protectorate" colonial regime. The nominal sovereignty of local rulers did not allow the European conquerors to annex colony lands and restricted them in other areas too, such as changing the legal status to which Jews had been subject for generations. Changes in the formal status of Jews had in fact often occurred before the colonial conquest: in the 50 years between the conquest of Algiers and that of Tunis, Muslim royal courts and modernist or "reformist" functionaries had made efforts to come to terms with the modernization processes characterizing European powers, which was perceived as the reason for their success.

PATTERNS OF EMANCIPATION

Among other things, local reformists envisioned the Western model of equality of religious minorities, and it was implemented in the Ottoman Empire and its provinces and vassal states in the 1850s and 1860s.[19] However, the pressure from above to exchange the old paradigm for the new modernist one in the lands of Islam encountered an obstacle uncommon in Europe. The demand for change was primarily external, emanating from European power representatives with whom a small circle of local reformists had chosen to associate; it did not rest on broad public support and at times was even perceived as yet another menace brought on by the foes of Islam, thus rendering it fragile and vulnerable. The European conquerors for their part had firmly launched their Jewish policy, as in Algeria, with real equality between the natives. The question now was whether, given the limitations of a protectorate regime, the new rulers would be interested in taking the further step of granting local Jews the "ultimate" prize in the process of colonial emancipation: European citizenship. In Egypt and Morocco the answer was a definite no;[20] in Tunisia, only after 30 years of colonial rule, a new, selective emancipation model was introduced to the whole native population and a certain part of the Jewish elite and middle class, not too large, requested and

[19] Rodrigue, *French Jews, Turkish Jews*, 28–35; Orit Bashkin, *New Babylonians: A History of Jews in Modern Iraq* (Stanford: Stanford University Press, 2012), 17; Yaron Harel, *Syrian Jewry in Transition, 1840–1880* (Oxford: Littman Library of Jewish Civilization, 2010), 97–111; Gudrun Krämer, *The Jews in Modern Egypt, 1914–1952* (Seattle: University of Washington Press, 1989), 30; Paul Sebag, *Histoire des Juifs de Tunisie* (Paris: L'Harmattan, 1991), 116–121.
[20] Krämer, *Jews in Modern Egypt*, 31–36; Daniel Schroeter, "From Dhimmis to Colonized Subjects: Moroccan Jews and the Sharifian and French Colonial State," in *Jews and the State*, 104–123.

received French citizenship.[21] In Libya, the local natives, Muslims as well as Jews, were granted a form of second-class Italian citizenship.[22]

Nowhere was there a return to the Algerian model of general colonial emancipation for the Jews, whether voluntary or forced. The French authorities had a neutral pretext for not repeating it: the legal status of the Protectorate territories. Beyond this however, the strong motivation, optimism and energy characteristic of the old integrationist French-Jewish leadership, was now exhausted and in short supply. Neither the British nor the Italian Jewish leadership manifested similar firmness. Only the Alliance, managed by a singularly capable technocrat, Jacques Bigart, continued to wield its power as an excellent tool for the times in the dual service of French imperialism and Jewish solidarity.[23]

LANGUAGE AND IDENTITY

Despite its noted fragility and lack of broad support, the potential change in the status of non-Muslims reflected the seeds of modernization in the pre-colonial Muslim world and the entry of its elites into the age of reforms inspired by the Enlightenment, and later by the world of nationalism. At the level of the Ottoman ruling class and social elites, a series of modernist movements was formed (*tanzimat*, Othmanism, the Young Turks), in which elite Jews could participate as long as they mastered the imperial language. Though few took this road, these movements left their mark on Ottoman Jewry. In the Arab provinces of the empire at the end of the nineteenth century, literary Arabic assumed its place as the focus of a revivalist literary and political movement – *al-Nahda* (the Renaissance). It inaugurated the entry of the Arabic-speaking elites into the Enlightenment zone of influence and at the same time prepared the ground for Arab nationalism. In the Mashreq (the Arab Middle East), *al-Nahda* had a considerable impact, penetrating some Jewish elite milieus. In Egypt, a Jewish militant of *al-Nahda*, James Yaacob Sanu'a, even found his way to the movement's Pantheon.[24]

---

[21] Sebag, *Histoire des Juifs de Tunisie*, 180–184.

[22] Eliyahu Lilo Arbiv, *HaStatus HaMišpati šel HaYehudim BeLuv* (Bat-Yam: Ha'Irgun Ha'Olami šel Yehudim Yoṣe'ey Luv, 1984), 5.

[23] On Bigart see Kaspi, *Alliance*, 92–94.

[24] On *al-Nahda* Jews see Lital Levy, "Historicizing the Concept of Arab Jews in the Mashriq," *Jewish Quarterly Review* 98, no. 4 (2008): 452–469. On Sanu'a specifically, see too Moshe Behar and Zvi Ben-Dor-Benite (eds), *Modern Middle Eastern Jewish Thought: Writings on Identity, Politics and Culture 1893–1958* (Hanover NH: Brandeis University Press, 2013), 10–29.

In the Maghreb (North Africa), partly Berber, partly subdued by the French, *al-Nahda* had in the meantime struck fewer roots and can be hardly traced amongst the Jews in this region.[25] Judging by literary and journalistic output, the liveliest community in the region was to be found in Tunis. The handful of Tunisian Jewish journalists and writers who, unlike their readership, did read literary Arabic, were no doubt aware of the *Nahda* and the moods among its followers. However, the movement influencing these Jewish intellectuals, according to their own writings, was not the Arabic *al-Nahda* but the Jewish Haskalah movement or, more precisely, its proto-nationalist Hebrew stream. As in Algeria, in Tunisia and Morocco the conquest brought with it an attempt by French Jewry to frenchify the new colonial community. The local leadership generally lined up with the demands of its new patron, French Jewry, but the rabbis and other intellectuals of the native sector, who manifested conservative attitudes or preferred to support the revival of the local Jewish languages – Judeo-Arabic and Hebrew (maskilim) – opposed full French acculturation and its tidings of secularization. Unlike the case of Algeria, at this stage these opponents did not necessarily suffer from total isolation or complete muteness. The Hebrew Haskalah press in Eastern Europe had opened its gates to them, and local printing expanded quickly with the advent of the French. Writing mainly in Judeo-Arabic but fluent in classical Arabic, some of the Jewish journalists and artists maintained close relations with their Muslim counterparts and, alongside support of early Jewish nationalism, they sometimes seemed to sympathize with Tunisian proto-nationalism. Likewise, the language of these maskilim was in fact composed of both Arabic and Hebrew, and in shifting between Judeo-Arabic and Hebrew they seemed to incarnate Hebrew and Arabic local modernisms in one and the same person.[26]

The general trend however tended to distinguish between Jews and Arabs, and the main Jewish public campaign before World War I was led

---

[25] Emily Benichou Gottreich, "Historicizing the Concept of Arab Jews in the Maghreb," *Jewish Quarterly Review* 98, no. 4 (2008): 433–451; Susan G. Miller, "Moise Nahon and the Invention of the Modern Maghrebi Jew," in *French Mediterraneans: Transnational and Imperial Histories*, eds., Patricia M. E. Lorcin and Todd Shepard (Lincoln: University of Nebraska Press, 2016), 293–319.

[26] On Haskalah and reformists in North Africa see Chetrit, "Moderniyut Le'umit 'Ivrit mul Moderniyut Şorfatit"; Yaron Tsur, "Haskala in a Sectional Colonial Society: Mahdia (Tunisia) 1885," in *Sephardi and Middle Eastern Jewries: History and Culture in the Modern Era*, ed. Harvey E. Goldberg (Bloomington: Indiana University Press, 1996), 146–167; Andre Levy, *Return to Casablanca: Jews, Muslims and an Israeli Anthropologist* (Chicago: University of Chicago Press, 2015), 32–60.

by a group of young westernized Jews demanding the transfer of the Jewish population from local Tunisian to French jurisdiction, aiming in fact at French citizenship. This time, it was not the French Jewish lobby that militated for colonial emancipation for North-African Jews, but a rising native Francophone elite. Likewise, it was not the European settlers who rose up against the Westernizers' initiative, but the Muslim pioneers of the Tunisian national movement.[27]

From Tunisia eastward, the French orientation encountered competition from a European rival, Italy. Italian Jewry had long maintained special ties with the MENA communities as Jews from Livorno (Leghorn) commonly settled in MENA's commercial centers and became a constant element of local Jewry.[28] When the Italian kingdom was established (1861), it spread its patronage over them and generously granted Italian citizenship to "Old" Italian Jews and new immigrants from Italy in Tunisia, Libya, and Egypt. Libya had become Italian territory (1911) and was the only country in North Africa with an exclusive Italian orientation dominating the westernization processes of the native sector.[29]

East of Libya, in Egypt, the English language of the colonial conquerors had not replaced the languages of other Western powers. In fact, the imperialist high culture dominating the local scene continued to be French.

The traditional Jewish community in Egypt had three components: the Arabized Jews living there for centuries (*Musta'arabim*), descendants of Ottoman government officials who considered themselves Sephardic in terms of ethnic background and, once again, a Livornese mercantile component. Both of the latter components had also been Arabized but to a limited extent, thus preserving something of their own unique identity. The more new immigrants the country drew, the more varied Egypt's Jewish mosaic became. Greek Jews arrived from the Balkans, Yiddish-speaking Ashkenazim from Eastern Europe, Ladino-speaking Sephardim from the large urban centers of the Ottoman Empire, and Jews speaking a variety of Arab dialects from the Arab-speaking regions of the Ottoman Empire as well as Morocco and Yemen.[30]

Even though British colonial settlement was not encouraged in Egypt, a European sector did emerge as a consequence of the large immigration from across the Mediterranean. This sector, as in Algeria, was joined by

---

[27] Sebag, *Histoire des Juifs de Tunisie*, 156–161.

[28] Lionel Lévy, *La nation juive portugaise: Livorne, Amsterdam, Tunis 1591–1951* (Paris: L'Harmattan, 1999).

[29] Renzo De Felice, *Jews in an Arab Land: Libya, 1835–1970*. Austin: University of Texas Press, 1985.

[30] Cf. Krämer, *Jews in Modern Egypt*, 8–67.

local Jews who had lost contact with the living culture of the Arab majority, including its Jewish element. But unlike in Algeria, Egypt's Jewish mosaic contained a core of intellectuals who displayed a conscious, active interest in cultivating facets of their Arab identity. Egypt became a center of the *Nahda* and the pioneer of nationalism in the Muslim world, with a clear participation by Jews. Due to the exceptional part immigration played in the demographic development of Egyptian Jewry, the country's *Musta'arabi* element was less dominant on the Jewish landscape than in the other countries under discussion. Though it had representatives in the higher classes, its presence was conspicuous in the poor, crowded Jewish neighborhoods. Even more so, alongside Rabbinic Jewry, Egypt also boasted a large Karaite community whose members were prominent amongst Jews writing in modern Arabic. Not many Egyptian Jews played an active part in the *Nahda*, but the movement's influence expanded, soon spreading from Egypt to other Arab-speaking areas.

Western empires created overseas cultural zones (*Kulturbereiche*) based on their national languages and maintained by their administrations, settlers, and westernized followers. The occupied natives themselves, in order to maintain their own language and nationalize, needed a modernist movement, either regional or supra-regional, as a catalyst. Thus, on the eve of the Great War two colonial cultural zones and two supra-regional cultural movements vied for hegemonic influence among the colonial Jewish communities on the northern shores of Africa, namely a French and an Italian cultural zone. The Hebrew Haskalah movement (in its late Jewish nationalist form) and the Arabic *al-Nahda* played a similar role but served the natives' movements of proto-nationalism. A fifth language, Judeo-Arabic, which was still the major language of the MENA communities, did not have – in contrast to Yiddish – an inter-communal movement behind it that would create a modernist cultural zone and unify its speakers. In the absence of such a movement, the Judeo-Arabic intellectuals associated themselves largely with the Jewish-Hebrew option, though not exclusively.

The linguistic scenario in 1914 manifested a clear hierarchy between the five languages. French, supported by thriving school systems, was on the rise everywhere. Italian was strong in Libya but restricted to a rather small milieu in Egypt and Tunisia. *Al-Nahda* influence was limited to the Mashreq, hardly making inroads into the Maghreb Jewish communities. The Jews' two traditional languages, Hebrew and Judeo-Arabic, were on the retreat. The use of Judeo-Arabic as the domestic language increasingly gave way to French and Italian, which then displaced also Hebrew as the linguistic axis of high culture. However, there was a decisive difference between Hebrew and Judeo-Arabic. Hebrew served no economic system in the region and could not, at this stage, assure the masses of a living, not even outside of these countries' borders. On the other hand, the language of the market and the street of the native sector had been and remained Arabic/Judeo-Arabic. While French and Italian were necessary for integration into the European economic sector, Arabic was needed for the native economic sector, which was also modernizing. These factors determined the downward fate of modern Hebrew at this stage. In most communities it did not hold its ground and was speedily marginalized. The pace of the demise of Judeo-Arabic was much slower, always corresponding to the Jewish native sector's dimension, but the absence of a Judeo-Arabic inter-communal movement was detrimental to the expansion and life of literary and journalistic creativity in that language. Even where it flourished for a while, as in Tunisia, it did not thrive for long.

THE INTERWAR PERIOD – THE ERA OF AUTONOMY

Until World War I, most of the Jews of Asia were beyond the reach of Western colonial regimes. The war changed the picture, as Britain and France emerged from the war ostensibly stronger and divided between them what was left of the Ottoman Empire in Asia, with the exception of Anatolia. In the international arena, however, the major player was the new kid on the block, the United States, whose president, Woodrow Wilson, introduced the concept of the self-determination of nations, i.e., the establishment of national states as a guiding principle for the League of Nations. Nationalism in this arena was awarded formal precedence over colonialism as expressed in the justification of the powers' control over new areas as temporary, for the purpose of training the local inhabitants for independence. The powers were given a mission, a "mandate," to rule in order to achieve this goal. Hereafter, these two world orders vied more vigorously for every territory with a generally looser colonialism in the new areas than in the colonies won before World War I.

Iraq was made up of former Ottoman provinces but soon after it was mandated to Britain; it transpired that while the British had conquered it in line with their long-term interests, they did not intend to rule it directly as a colony for long. They sought to place it in the hands of the Arab-national elite that had been their ally during the war, headed by Emir Feisal, and to grant it independence. The British Mandate lasted only about 10 years, during which time the foundation was laid for the national kingdom of Iraq. The Jews, like the other inhabitants, had to find their place in the new kingdom.

By the end of the Ottoman Empire, the transformations affecting Iraqi Jewry, when compared with other Muslim lands, already bore a unique character, marked by attention to local needs and limited dependence on

Western Jewish organizations. Baghdad was one of the rare communities that succeeded in forcing the Alliance to teach the local language seriously, thus providing its alumni with literary Arabic.[31] The same line now came to the fore in the formation of a central leadership of notables, backed by a rising milieu of intellectuals whose goal was to shepherd the flock towards swift, successful integration into the new, national Iraq. The ancient roots of Babylonian Jewry, traditionally perceived as the "duration of exile" and divine punishment, now became a positive tool of political symbolism, as their long residence in the country qualified the Jews as partners in the homeland. Their command of literary Arabic now made possible their integration into the different milieus which were engaged in constructing the national culture. Moreover, because Jewish youth had received a modern education earlier than Muslim youth, they helped fill the cadres necessary to initiate government administrations, such as railway and postal services. Finally, Ezekiel Sassoon, a Jewish notable, joined the government as Finance Minister. Broadly speaking, monarchist Iraq under the British Mandate was the first place to implement the Western Jewish model of emancipation, with no mutations.

In the 1930s, following independence in 1931, tensions increasingly flared between the Sunni Muslim majority and the religious minorities, particularly around the question of integration: every year government schools turned out Muslim graduates hungry for work, while numerous government jobs had already been taken by Christians and Jews. Muslims were driven to exclude the minorities from the "authentic" Iraqi nation. A small trickle of Jews began to emigrate to Palestine, but the great majority of Iraqi Jews were not overly perturbed by the tensions. Another obstacle to Muslim–Jewish relations, more serious in the long run, was the impact of the Zionist–Palestinian conflict. On the Zionist side were Jews, on the Palestinian side mainly Muslims, which made religious identity a potential powder keg in other places too. In Iraq, religious tensions were compounded by national tensions; as in all Arabic-speaking lands, two options of national identity developed, local (*wataniyya*) and pan-Arab (*kawmiyya*), and the latter clashed severely with the Zionist settlement enterprise in Palestine. Since Palestinian Arab identity was part of the pan-Arab identity, Iraqi Jews were expected to support the Palestinian cause. But while they were ready to identify with the idea of an Iraqi homeland, their identification with pan-Arabism and its siding with the Arabs in the Palestinian conflict could not be taken for granted. Certain key leadership figures and

---

[31] Riva Simon, "Haḥinuḵ BaQehilah HaYehudit BeBaghdad ʿAd Šenat 1914," *Peʿamim* 36 (1988): 52–63.

intellectuals did cross their Rubicon and identify with the Palestinians, but there are no signs that their position trickled down to broader strata of the Jewish population.[32]

Among the Jewish intellectuals supporting Iraqi nationalism and Arabism, some attempted to compromise and mediate between Arab and Zionist nationalisms. Joined by Jewish Arabic maskilim (i.e., Jewish intellectuals whose preferred modern language was literary Arabic, not modern Hebrew) from outside of Iraq, in Syria, Lebanon, the Sephardic community in Palestine, and Egypt, and being the second generation of Jewish *Nahda* followers in the Mashreq, they succeeded in creating a small intercommunal network of their own, a kind of embryonic Mashreq movement of Arab-Jews. They expressed themselves mainly through the press in such newspapers as *Al-Masbah* (The Lamp, Baghdad), *Al-'Aalam al Israeli* (The Jewish World, Beirut 1924–48), *Israail* (Israel, Cairo 1920–34) and *Al-Shams* (The Sun, Cairo 1934–48), giving voice to many maskilim in the Mashreq who chose acculturation and integration into the Muslim majority but refused to accept the negative definition of Zionism that was making increasing inroads among Muslim and Christian-Arab leaders and the masses. Though they themselves were well aware of the syndrome of internal Orientalism in their relations with the Zionist Yishuv and its institutions, that syndrome was far from the complete picture; the Yishuv was, in their eyes, the core of the rebirth of the Hebrew nation, another of the region's peoples who were gaining independence. They sought to mitigate the displacement of the Palestinians caused by the Jewish return and resolve it in peaceful ways, and they watched helplessly as relations between the sides deteriorated, their Jewish-Arab blueprint falling apart.[33]

The interwar period saw highly accelerated modernization of the Jews in the regions we have examined. In the colonial territories of the Maghreb there was a sharp increase in population, the primary indication that mass starvation had ended, and improved medical care was raising birth rates and lowering death rates. That was a major positive aspect of colonial conquest, but for the native sector it was outweighed by the destruction of traditional crafts and trades by industrialized production that brought about an economic regression spawning internal migration, urbanization, and slums. Poverty was the number one problem plaguing many Jewish

[32] Nissim Kazzaz, *HaYehudim Be'Iraq Bame'ah Ha'Esrim* (Jerusalem: Ben-Zvi Institute, 1991); Reuven Snir, *'Arviyut, Yahadut, Şiyyonut: Ma'avaq Zehuyot BiYşiratam šel Yehudey Iraq* (Jerusalem: Ben-Zvi Institute, 2005); Bashkin, *New Babylonians.*

[33] Guy Bracha, "'Al-'Aalam 'Al'Isra'ili': Meqomo Be'Olam Ha'Itonut HaYehudit 'al Reqa' HaTtemurot BaQehilot HaYehudiyot BeSuryah UviLevanon 1921–1948"(Ph.D. diss., Bar Ilan University, 2012).

communities, and in Casablanca, the biggest of them all, it grew to horrifying dimensions.[34]

The urban Jewish population increased sharply along with the general
population, but the Jewish population saw education opportunities multiply thanks to the Alliance or other European institutions. Every year saw
a new cohort of graduates, some of them westernized young people who,
even if stemming from poor families, could themselves embark on the road
to the middle class. In the French Maghreb they founded a network of
Alliance graduates and not being part of the establishment, they pressured
in this period for the modernization and democratization of community
institutions. In Tunisia and Morocco they also sought French citizenship.

In the interwar period, international Jewish interests focused on
European communities. Worldwide Jewish organizations had only a peripheral interest in the colonial communities, whether in the Maghreb or
the Mashreq. In terms of utilizing what may be denoted as the "era of
autonomy" in the relations of colonial communities with European Jews,
Moroccan Jewry may be said to have reached the apex. The main beneficiaries of this era, marked by, among other things, a let-up in the energy
and drive of the metropolitan Jewish leadership, were the colonial officials in the country. The founder of the Moroccan Protectorate, General
Lyautey, even tried to close the local branch of Alliance, and though he did
not succeed, he did mold the status and internal organization of Morocco's
Jews in accordance with his own tendencies, naturally implementing
"native emancipation," i.e., equity with the Muslims, though with a few
"dead spots."[35] His successors refused to implement in Morocco the type of
arrangements already instituted in the sister protectorate of Tunisia.

The new arrangements in the Moroccan Jews' communal organization
included modernization to a considerable extent but not democratization.
This left a convenient opening for the handful of Zionists in Morocco to
transform their stream into a protest movement and wage a struggle against
the local establishment, headed by a new appointee by the French, Yehya
Zagury, who represented the class of dignitaries. "My Zion is Morocco,"
wrote S. D. Lévy, the leader of the local Zionists in the early 1930s, depicting Zionism not as a movement of return, but as a Diaspora nationalism.
Himself a westernized notable and European in his legal status, he and
his local reformist colleagues used the ideas of national unity to campaign

[34] Mohammed Kenbib, *Juifs et musulmans au Maroc, 1859–1948* (Rabat: Faculté des Lettres
et des Sciences Humaines, 1994), 508–510; Yaron Tsur and Hagar Hillel, *Yehudey
Qazablanqah: 'Iyunim BeModernizaşyah šel Hanhagah Yehudit BiTtefuşah Qoloni'alit* (Tel
Aviv: Ha'Universiṭa HaPetuḥah, 1995), 165–203.
[35] Schroeter, *"From Dhimmis to Colonized Subjects."*

against the disintegration of Jewish society into colonial estates and sectors, drawing inspiration from Yishuv institutions and projects in trying to shape the community.[36]

It is not by chance that most of the examples of political activity in this period were taken from the Zionist camp, the most researched in the twentieth century. However, for the period discussed in this section there is little justification for it. Zionism had considerable influence in Tunisia in the 1930s, but elsewhere it had less and at times, as in Iraq, far less. In this period, community leaders were generally integrationists. But they were of various colors: in Morocco, Algeria, Tunisia, and Libya they were westernized, striving to integrate into the European sector, whether selectively or generally, as in Algeria. From Syria eastward, they were either westernized or Arabic maskilim who tried to integrate their flock into the Muslim majority according to the classic Western model. Egypt was a special case, and the separate Jewish sectors of society seemed to have different leaderships.

The leaders of the Jewish public in this period are known to us by name, but not much more. Indeed, Jewish colonial historiography emerges with blanks when it comes to the interwar period. Zionist historiography was not interested in integrationist leaders, nor were the national historiographies of each of these countries, as those leaders were Jews and therefore suspect as colonial collaborators or Zionists. In this, as in other cases, history was written by the victors.

ON THE EDGE OF A BLEEDING EUROPE – THE SECOND WORLD WAR

Due to the hegemony of the European powers, the entire world was caught up in a vortex of military conflicts which became a watershed for regions outside of Europe as well. But it is one thing to be in the eye of the storm and quite another to be on its periphery. For sure, in the colonial territories of Italy and Vichy France, which collaborated with the Nazis, the Jewish experience was rough. But distance from Europe helped: in North Africa there was no stage of extermination as in the metropole and even the earlier measures against the Jews were more moderate. Anti-Jewish legislation began in Mussolini's Libya and spread to the Maghreb of Vichy France. In large Jewish population centers, restrictions were imposed on education, occupations, residence, etc. But the legislation harmed mainly the colonial "upper" sectors, the European and the westernized, whose members relied on the educational institutions of the settlers, made a living in their

---

[36] Tsur and Hillel, *Yehudey Qazablanqah*, 137–145.

markets and lived in mixed neighborhoods. They had to part with all these for some time. Native Jews, the majority, were anyway far removed from European institutions and markets and the anti-Jewish legislation hardly affected them. Furthermore, Alliance schools continued to receive support from the colonial administration and to function.[37] In Algeria, where the Crémieux Decree was abolished, the Jewish leadership created an alternative education system from scratch.[38]

In one country, Tunisia, the capital's Jewish council became a *Judenrat* – obliged to follow orders damaging to the welfare of its flock. Libya saw the establishment of concentration camps where the entire Jewish population of Benghazi was sent, while specific labor camps for men were set up in both Libya and Tunisia.[39] These were camps slated for local Jews. Labor camps to which Jewish refugees from Europe were sent were established in Algeria and mostly in Morocco; in some of these, conditions were particularly harsh. Hundreds of Jewish residents of Libya were sent to concentration camps in Europe: these were citizens of countries at war with Italy and their presence there was for purposes of prisoner exchange.[40] In total, about a thousand people perished in all the camps from the severe conditions and Allied bombings. It was traumatic enough but nothing to compare with the destruction of European Jewry.

Attitudes among the local populations were also different. Attempts to enflame them against the Jews across North Africa met with some success among Arab nationalist militants but with little success amidst the masses.[41] Although anti-Jewish sentiments were manifested and small anti-Jewish incidents did occur, especially in Morocco, there was no general estrangement of Muslims vis-à-vis their Jewish neighbors, as often happened in Western Europe, and nowhere did they rise up and kill them as sometimes happened in Eastern Europe. Nor was it possible in North Africa to harness the railway system for transportation to Auschwitz as easily as in Europe. Then too, the war came to a close in the Maghreb in late 1942, early 1943 – just when the German means of mass murder were becoming fully operational.

North African Jews were able to differentiate between their own experience and the fate of their co-religionists across the Mediterranean. "When

---

[37] Kaspi, *Histoire de l'Alliance*, 319–322.

[38] Michel Abitbol, *Les Juifs d'Afrique du Nord sous Vichy* (Paris: Riveneuve, 2008), 98–102.

[39] De Felice, *Jews in an Arab Land*, 179–184; Irit Avramski-Bligh, *Pinqas HaQehilot: Luv Tunisyah* (Jerusalem: Yad Wašem, 1997), 14–16.

[40] Avramski-Bligh, *Pinqas HaQehilot*.

[41] Kenbib, *Juifs et musulmans au Maroc*, 584–585, 590–591, 595–621; Abitbol, *Vichy*, 2008, 52–56.

we heard what was happening to our brethren in Europe" – notes the first writer from Tunisia to sum up the local Labor Camps memoirs in his book – "we said it was better to keep quiet than talk."[42] Furthermore, basic sympathy for France continued, at bottom, to characterize all sectors of Jewish society and the small Libyan Jewish community was informed by a similar approach towards Italy, even after the war.

Real riots did not take place in the territories under the control of the Nazi collaborators but rather in Baghdad, ostensibly independent but actually under strong British influence and basic control. When the British toppled the regime of pro-Nazi officers to regain control of Iraq, a mob from Baghdad and its surroundings fell upon the Jewish quarter, murdering, wounding, raping, and pillaging. The number of dead reached 180.[43] In scope, it was an unprecedented occurrence in the history of Jewish–Muslim relations in the Iraqi capital. But the pattern was more familiar from the long-term history of Jewish experience in Muslim lands: a mob and tribesmen falling upon the city's Jews when the Jewish patron dies and before his heir accedes to the throne. This time, however, it seems that both Nazi propaganda and the conflict in Palestine served as accelerators.

Iraq's Jewish youth, in any case, made the connection between the Baghdad pogrom and Jewish persecution in Nazi Europe, and created an underground Zionist movement.[44] The extermination of the Jews in Europe fostered this trend also in other Jewish communities in the lands of Islam, as did the general tendency towards nationalism, boosted by the collapse of Italy, the fall of France, and Britain's need for help. But Zionism was not the only alternative. The weakness of the old colonial powers strengthened primarily local nationalism. In the Maghreb French protectorates, many communists, among whom Jews played a disproportionate part, now supported the nationalists and, as in Europe, the communists promoted integration into the local society. But the communists were generally detached from the common Jew, who still relied on the good counsel of community notables, whose traditional position had also changed. Some vocally supported Zionism while others spoke discreetly in local patriotic terms. A similar shift occurred among the young westernized Jews in both Morocco and Tunisia. While preferring integration into the society of their colony's mother country, they were now open to other

[42] Farağ Ḥay Gastin Guez, *Tadkarat AlKhaddama AlYahud Taḥat Jil Almania fi Tunes* (Tunis: private edition, [1946]), 12.

[43] Bashkin, *New Babylonians*, 100–140; Cf. Shmuel Moreh and Zvi Yehuda (eds), *Śin'at Yehudim UFera'ot BeIraq* ('Or Yehudah: Merkaz Mored̄t Yahadut Bavel, 1992).

[44] Esther Meir-Glitzenstein, *Zionism in an Arab Country: The Jews of Iraq in the 1940s* (London: Routledge, 2004), 63–191.

orientations as well. In fact, one could find among them a mix of multiple orientations, including identification with both the local liberation movement and Zionism at one and the same time.[45] The direction to be taken was still dependent on factors yet to be determined on the ground.

THE ERA OF NATIONALISM

Signs that turned out to be fateful for the status of the Jewish minority in the lands of Islam came from two different directions at the end of the war: Egypt and the Yishuv in Palestine. In Egypt, on the anniversary of the Balfour Declaration in 1945, a mob of anti-Zionist demonstrators, rallied by practically all the nationalist parties and associations, burst into the Jewish quarter in Cairo, torched the synagogue and destroyed other community institutions. Stores belonging to Jews were vandalized.[46] While in the 1920s, Egypt had been among the moderate Arab countries in its attitude to Zionism, the 1945 incident showed that Zionism had now been marked as the enemy of pan-Arabism, that Egyptian nationalists identified the local Jews with this enemy and did not hesitate to attack them.

As if to drive home Egypt's new role in setting the tone, two days after the riots in Cairo, widespread rioting broke out in neighboring Libya. It began in the capital of Tripoli and spread to Benghazi and inland, resulting in a serious refugee problem in this small community, which had barely recovered from its wartime ills.[47] In Libya as in Egypt, nationalist fervor ran high at the time and lay behind the blow dealt the Jewish population. Ideologically, the nationalisms of Libya and Egypt saw the Jews as generation-long residents and part of the local nation. Ostensibly, it was in their interest to promote Jewish sympathy and a sense of security, as well as loyalty and devotion towards the local nationalist movement. To be sure, in colonial times the Jews had not been oriented towards such identification nor sought it out on their own initiative, but World War II had created a window of opportunity for change in this area. The failure to distinguish between the mostly European Jews involved in the Palestinian conflict, and members of Jewish communities native to the lands of Islam, resulted in the identification of the latter with Zionism and their penalization as a result. This could only further sharpen the boundaries between the Jewish and Muslim components of the local people, distance the Jews from the nationalist camp, make their lives intolerable, and create a powerful "push" for them to emigrate.

[45] Tsur, *Qehilah Qeru'ah*, 186–236.
[46] Krämer, *Jews in Modern Egypt*, 162–163. The incidents extended to other localities as well.
[47] De Felice, *Jews in an Arab Land*, 191–210.

From the other side of the Arab–Zionist conflict, the Zionist Yishuv promoted a complementary "pull" factor, aimed at an imminent large migration. The mortal blow dealt by the Holocaust to Zionism's chief demographic reservoir led to a heightened interest in demographic sources formerly considered peripheral to the building up of the Zionist society in Palestine. The full significance of the turning point is revealed in David Ben-Gurion's diary. Ben-Gurion divided the world into five blocks, recorded the number of Jews in each and noted how many, in his estimate, could and should be brought to Palestine: "We should quickly bring all of bloc 5 [855,000 Jews from the Muslim world], most of bloc 4 [some 253,000 Jews of (central and western) Europe excluding Britain], all that is possible from bloc 3 [some 3 million Jews in Eastern Europe] and pioneers from bloc 2 [some 6 million Jews of the US, Britain and the other English-speaking countries, and the countries of Latin America]."[48]

From a minor, marginal status in pre-war immigration plans, the architect of the Jewish state went on to mark the Jews of the lands of Islam as a central demographic source for building the state that he expected to emerge imminently, and the only component of which in his assessment could be brought in its entirety. The other side of the coin of this population transfer implied that Jewish existence in Asia and Africa, outside of Palestine, would come to an end.

The change in status of Asian and African Jews in the eyes of Yishuv leaders was symptomatic of the same change in status as seen by the heads of other Jewish organizations and currents, western or international, such as the ultra-Orthodox, the American Joint (Jewish Distribution Committee), the World Jewish Congress, OSE, ORT, etc. They too, like the Zionist Organization, had just seen their original, primary target population liquidated.[49] Undeniably, in the early post-war years, most of their efforts were directed towards aiding the Jewish refugees in Europe's DP camps. But from the start it was clear that this work would be short-lived and temporary. At the very time that both the hearts and pockets of many American Jews were opening up for Jewish causes, against the background of the Holocaust, Jewish organizations faced an existential crisis, potentially prevented by the discovery of the Jews of the lands of Islam – "the forgotten million," as they were now denoted.

However, freedom of action for Jewish organizations was limited in independent Arab territories, formally freed of colonial rule, in contrast

---

[48] Ben Gurion's Diary, July 30, 1945, cited in Dvora Hacohen, *Toknit HaMilyon: Toknito šel David Ben Gurion Le'Aliyyah Hamonit BaŠanim 1942-1945* (Tel Aviv: Miśrad HaBiṭaḥon, 1994), 210, 217.
[49] Tsur, *Qehilah Qeru'ah*, 112–119, 152–155.

to areas still occupied. In this respect, there was a clear demarcation line between the Mashreq and the Maghreb. In the Mashreq, the formal government was in the hands of states committed to the policies of the Arab League, obliging the Zionist Organization, where it existed at all, to gradually go underground, while all other Jewish worldwide organizations ceased to function. The colonial Maghreb, on the other hand, opened up to brisk international Zionist and Jewish activity.

The difference between the two regions was highlighted in the fate of the Jews around the 1948 war. The Arab states that could and did enter into military confrontation with the Jewish state, were those that were independent: Egypt, Syria, Lebanon, Jordan, and Iraq. In all these countries, except for Jordan, there were Jews, and tensions naturally rose between the Muslim majority and the Jewish minority now identified with the direct national enemy. Various anti-Jewish incidents erupted, some accompanied by loss of life, Jews were arrested, and laws imposing restrictions were legislated. Governments were hard put to separate Zionist sympathizers from opponents and adopt a policy that would reinforce the sympathies of the loyal Jewish elements or, at least, like the communists, promote the idea of a nation and homeland common to Muslims, Christians, and Jews. The absence of a formidable player, international Jewish organizations with bases in the West where the model of classic integration prevailed, precluded the reinforcement and support of the local Jewish leadership who were so inclined. In the absence of assistance and support from either the regime or Jewish organizations, and against the background of the defeat of the Arab side in the 1948 war, the leadership weakened and disintegrated. On the other hand, the young local Zionists who went underground emerged as a vital new elite. They maintained ties with the Yishuv, drew strength from its victory, and continued to function in difficult conditions. This was true in Egypt, and in Iraq they succeeded in sweeping along most of the community members and in arranging an aerial transport of close to 70,000 people.[50]

Despite their deep-seated integration into Iraq's landscape and culture, more than 90 percent of its Jews immigrated *en masse* to Israel in less than a year. The speed with which Iraq's Jews had to leave the country, and the fact that they could be helped to move to one direction only, Israel, are the main factors explaining why Iraqi Jews reached the Jewish state en bloc, leaving behind only a few, mainly of the extremely well-off echelon. But perhaps the Iraqi Aliyah was influenced by the mono-sectorial structure of

[50] Meir-Glitzenstein, *Zionism*, 195–260; Bashkin, *New Babylonians*, 183–228; Moshe Gat, *The Jewish Exodus from Iraq 1948–1951* (London: Frank Cass, 1997); Cf. Abbas Shiblak, *The Lure of Zion: The Case of Iraqi Jews* (London: Al Saqi Books, 1986).

Babylonian Jewry as well. A deep cultural split did not divide communities and families, preparing their dispersion to different sides. Arabic was the axis of culture even for those who mastered or knew English and/or French.

In Egypt, despite a series of anti-Zionist and anti-Jewish measures and incidents, conditions did not develop that would encourage a general, immediate emigration of the Jewish population.[51] But the quite large emigration that did begin reflected the triple-sector structure of the local society as a whole, and of Jews in particular: Jews of the native sector generally turned towards Israel – among the westernized and Europeans quite a few turned to the same direction, but many more turned towards Europe and America. Hereafter, the correlation between sectorial identity and the preferred direction of emigration was to be the rule: natives would emigrate to the young Jewish state; the westernized would choose between Israel, Europe, and the US. In Egypt, many members of the European sector were Ashkenazi Jews who had come to the country via the Yishuv and many now returned to it. This trend was unique to Egypt; elsewhere, Jews of the European sector, like Christians of the same sector, emigrated to the European mother countries. The culturally fragmented structure of the Jewish community in Egypt engendered a quasi-fan-shaped emigration, resulting in an Egyptian–Jewish Diaspora ranging from Israel to the western coast of the US, with key slats in Europe (primarily France and Italy). This trend was to repeat itself in other sectorial communities.[52]

The plight of Syrian Jewry in 1948 also commenced with a violent outburst in Damascus after the riots of 1947 dealt a severe blow to the ancient Jewish community in Aleppo, but things then took a very different course from that in Iraq or Egypt. The Syrian authorities were the most consistent in efforts to prevent the country's Jews from joining the Jewish state. All Jewish emigration was banned and Jewish contacts with the outside world were closely monitored for decades.[53]

The 1948 war also saw violent anti-Jewish upsurges in some of the Maghreb countries. But because they were still under colonial rule, the course of events there differed considerably from that of the Mashreq. First, the colonial authorities did not declare all-out war against the

[51] Krämer, *Jews in Modern Egypt*, 211–219; Ruth Kimche, *Ṣiyonut BeṢel HaPiramidot: HaTenu'ah HaṢiyonit BeMiṣrayim 1918–1948* (Tel Aviv: 'Am-'Oved, 2009), 558–591.
[52] Joel Beinin, *The Dispersion of Egyptian Jewry* (Berkeley: University of California Press, 1998).
[53] Michael M. Laskier, "BeṢel HaSiksuk Ha'aravi-Yiśre'eli: Yaḥasey Muslemim-Yehudim BeSuryah BaŠanim 1948-1970," *Pe'amim* 66 (1996): 70-127.

Zionist organizations and their presence on Maghreb soil. In all Maghreb countries, from Libya to Morocco, Zionist activities continued, and when Israel won the war the reputation of the Zionists improved among French colonial officials, who regarded Arab nationalism as a foe. Israeli emissaries were granted much greater freedom, especially in Tunisia and Morocco with its large Jewish population. Secondly, France, as well as England, which ruled Libya after the war, could not object to the work of Western Jewish organizations in their territories, which allowed them wide scope in the region. The expanded Zionist activity and the massive inroads made by US Jewish organizations in the Maghreb marked the end of the monopoly of France and the Alliance over the path of modernization of the Jews of French Maghreb. Hereafter, it was to be influenced also by US Jewry and especially by Israel.

The attention of international Jewish welfare, health, and education organizations reached the Maghreb communities at just the right time. Cumulative economic crises – colonial industrialization, urbanization, the ravages of war, and subsequent shortages – all these brought a large portion of the population to the brink of poverty. All the countries of the Maghreb had witnessed internal migration in colonial times, which sometimes developed into an external labor migration. Thus economic forces supplying a major "push" to emigrate were already in place among the Jewish population, particularly the poor, when the Yishuv began to show an interest in encouraging immigration from the lands of Islam.[54] Hardship was not restricted to Jews; it affected the lower strata of the native sector as a whole. However, the special assistance Jews received from Western Jewish organizations distinguished them from their neighbors. Before the war, aid had been centered on elementary education alone; after the war it spread to other areas such as sanitation, health, vocational training, and, particularly, emigration.

In the period of large-scale emigration from all over the world to Israel (1948–51), the Maghreb share was not particularly significant. Numbering some 500,000 of the 850,000 Jews of Islam, only about 75,000 went to the Jewish state, versus close to 185,000 from the Arab Mashreq and another 48,000 or so from Turkey and Iran. And of the 75,000 from the Maghreb, almost 31,000 came from Libya, the smallest community of the countries in the region. In light of the blows the latter received during and after the war, and the predicted date for Libyan independence (1952), the aliyah (immigration) from Libya received priority. Nevertheless, it was conducted relatively freely and over time, its needs taking second place to those of the "rescue immigrations" from the Mashreq. The British colonial

[54] Meir-Glitzenstein, *Zionism*, 40–62.

environment, the presence of Zionist mechanisms and the possibility of Western Jewish organizations to extend a hand made this possible.[55] In similar fashion, it was possible to regulate immigration from the French Maghreb. Moreover, here, under the protection of the French who did not yet feel the political earthquake of impending nationalist movements under their feet, the impulse to emigrate was not general but restricted to certain groups, generally of the lower strata and\or the geographical periphery of the native sector, for whom the state of Israel was the "natural" and fascinating target for external emigration, and in fact the only relevant possibility at that stage. Other olim (immigrants) came from the ranks of the young who were moved by the image of Israel fighting for its life. They were mostly Moroccans from the westernized sector and the "seam" between it and the native sector. They came to enlist in the army but discovered, to their disappointment, that Moroccan Jews were the most spurned group of immigrants in the young state and after the battles were over, many returned to Morocco.[56]

ISRAEL'S "ETHNIC PROBLEM"

At the end of the first year of Israeli statehood, a new internal anxiety that had nested for some time among the veteran population from Europe, now erupted publicly. In the main, the question was what would happen if the Jewish state was inundated with immigrants from the lands of Islam, or rather: What would be the results of a drastic change in the internal demographic balance between European and non-European Jews? Would it harm the state's cultural character and endanger its achievements? Would it shake the political map and bring the "irresponsible" Zionist opposition to power? Arie Gelblum, the journalist who was the first to give an open, public expression to this anxiety, took an unequivocal stand on the issue and claimed that a wave of immigrants from the "African-Arab bloc" would undermine the Yishuv's success and its ability to confront its foes and called to exclude that block from aliyah projects.[57] Such proposals, however, ran counter to the dominant ethos of "ingathering the exiles"

---

[55] Michael M. Laskier, *Yiśra'el WeHa'aliyyah MiŞefon-'Afriqah: 1948–1970* (Be'er-Ševa': Ben-Gurion University, 2006), 155–185.

[56] Yaron Tsur, "The Brief Career of Prosper Cohen: A Sectorial Analysis of the North African Jewish Leadership in the Early Years of Israeli Statehood," in *Sephardic Jewry and Mizrahi Jews*, ed. Peter Y. Medding, *Studies in Contemporary Jewry* 22 (New York: Oxford University Press, 2008): 66–99.

[57] Yaron Tsur, "Carnival Fears – Moroccan Immigrants and the Ethnic Problem in the Young State of Israel." *The Journal of Israeli History* 18, no. 1 (1997): 73–103.

and the power of the melting pot. Among state leaders there were many, in particular Ben-Gurion, who opposed these anxieties and demanded faithfulness to the egalitarian ethos. But the anxiety nest erupted, incidentally exposing the self-evident: the Jewish settlers from Europe had not escaped the conventions of the colonial era and the typical hierarchy accompanying it. Internal Orientalism had made inroads into the Jewish national society as well. This led to one of the basic problems of the Jewish state, which would be known as "the ethnic problem": a latent, informal inequality between immigrants from Asia and Africa and from Europe in favor of the latter. Inequality was well known to the colonial Jew who, hoping to be rid of it, had left his homeland for the Jewish state expecting equality amongst Jews from every corner of the world. In colonial North Africa, the Jews' group of reference was the Muslims, the other natives; in Israel, for the Maghreb olim, it was the Ashkenazim, the other Jews. And while in colonial Morocco the European settlers' privileges did not generally bother the Jewish public, in ethno-nationalist Israel, Moroccan olim became extremely sensitive to acts of veiled discrimination against them in favor of European Jews.[58] The Moroccans were targeted for mixed and complex reasons, including the impressions they left in the army and elsewhere, but coming from the largest Jewish community in Asia and Africa they were especially fit to symbolize the new internal "menace," and were demonized.

The return to Morocco of many youngsters who had left it to join the IDF marked both the new outbreak of the ethnic problem but also the relative freedom that the Jews of French Maghreb still enjoyed in deciding their personal and collective fate. The early 1950s for them were years of progress. In part this was due to the short-lived general economic prosperity; in part it was due to the fact that the colonial officialdom was now embroiled in a struggle with the Moroccan nationalist movement and now made a last attempt to show that its policy benefited the natives. It accordingly approved of the plans of reform within the Jewish communities and encouraged the Alliance to penetrate ever further into Morocco. The presence of philanthropic Jewish organizations also had an impact. In addition, while most of the organizations acted under the influence of the new Jewish State in the international Jewish arena, they were not fully committed to Zionism and were able to offer alternatives. Thus, while the Mashreq Jewish communities dissolved and the leaderships that had supported local nationalism collapsed, in the French Maghreb new community institutions were built and an echelon of young leadership came up with a variety of orientations, including support for the local liberation

[58] Ibid.

movement. With every passing year, new cohorts graduated from the new and varied educational institutions, including universities in France and yeshivot in England and the US, and the graduates strengthened the ranks of the westernized and maskilim. Clearly, the development of the ethnic problem in Israel did not enhance its status in the eyes of the new Jewish elites in North Africa, and even the popular strata no longer rushed to the Jewish state. In Israel, the upper hand now belonged to those who opposed big, non-selective immigration from the lands of Islam, as long as there was no concrete danger to the lives of Jews in the Diaspora.

At the same time, however, various bodies in Israel – the Jewish Agency departments, youth movements and political parties – continued to make an effort to increase their presence among North African Jewry.[59] Israel, which was building its worldwide cultural network, rapidly developed its North African wing of activities by sending envoys whose role was to begin Israeli acculturation in Morocco, to teach Hebrew and the rest of the Israeli repertoire, in short, to cultivate Israeli norms of behavior on Moroccan soil. The Israeli local wing gained precious help when the Alliance decided to open its schools to progressive and systematic teaching of Hebrew. This language, which forty to fifty years previously had been summarily beaten in the "war of languages" waged within the Maghreb colonial communities, would eventually re-emerge triumphant – as vital as French had been earlier for integration in a developing economy. The ethnic problem affected the policy of aliyah, but the bottom line was that Israel, from her perspective, needed a larger Jewish population as well as working hands and was waiting for the right moment to move most of the Jews from North Africa to Israel.[60]

POST-COLONIAL EXPERIENCE AND IMMIGRATION

The time to empty the Maghreb communities seemed to arrive with the spread of the decolonization crisis of the French empire in North Africa, from the summer of 1954 onward. The expansion of the wave of terror dealt a particular blow to the Jews of Morocco, awakening anxiety among community members, and accompanied by a new economic crisis. This combination, found in smaller dimensions in Tunisia as well, for the first time engendered a strong impulse to emigrate, encompassing not only the poor of the native sector but also other strata in all the sectors. The impulse failed to become general and suppress the alternative trend towards integration, however, as the leadership of the nationalist movements tended

---

[59] Tsur, *Qehilah Qeru'ah*, 261–355.
[60] Ibid., 76–79, 93–99, 361–380.

to welcome Jews, promising them equality and brotherhood. The North African situation corresponded well with Israeli leadership's interests, as the dominant absorption personnel were not prepared to forego their control of the stream of newcomers, and continued to set immigration quotas from North Africa even in this time of emergency.[61] The wave of aliyah that accompanied the formal departure of the French from their protectorates in Morocco and Tunisia in 1956 was thus larger than those that preceded it, but far from all-encompassing.

Most of the Jews now found themselves, alongside their Muslim neighbors, no longer under a colonial regime, but in an independent nation-state. In the first post-colonial stage their future seemed rosy: a Jewish minister served in the government; the advocates of integration held the upper hand in the Jewish communities and in Morocco a special organization, Al-Wifaq, was set up to encourage Muslim–Jewish brotherhood. Aliyah to Israel slowed drastically and all Israeli activity was banned. The Mossad cast its net over Zionist activity, which was now underground and not very popular. For several years, the pattern of integration was attempted in practice: a number of westernized Jews took the place of the French in the government bureaucracy and civil service, and Jews joined the political activity of the different parties.[62]

However, in the early 1960s the Jews in each of the Maghreb countries found themselves in a fragile position. In Morocco the economic crisis worsened and the government drew closer to Egypt and the Arab League; in Tunisia, a military crisis between the authorities and France drew the Jews, France's protégés, into the fray; and in Algeria, the triumph of the liberation movement led the entire European population, including the Jews who had benefited from the Crémieux Decree, to leave the country en masse. At this time, 1961–64, all possible sources of aliyah from other places had been exhausted, and the Israeli authorities considered the time ripe for large-scale immigration from North Africa. The Mossad obtained the consent of the Moroccan regime to conduct the operation but it could obviously not compel anyone to immigrate to the Jewish state.[63] Most of

---

[61] Avi Picard, 'Olim BiMeśorah: Mediniyut Yiśra'el Kelapey 'Aliyyatam śel Yehudey Şefon-'Afriqah 1951-1956 (Be'er-Ševa': Ben-Gurion University, 2013), 172–352.

[62] Michael M. Laskier, North African Jewry in the Twentieth Century: The Jews of Morocco, Tunisia, and Algeria (New York: New York University Press, 1994), 186–217; Muhamad Hatami, AlJam'aat alYahudiya alMghrebiya walKhiyar als'ab bain Nida' alSahiuniya waRihan alMghreb almustaqil 1947–1961 (Ph.D. diss. University of Fez, 2007), 460–468.

[63] Yigal Bin Nun, "La négociation de l'évacuation en masse des Juifs du Maroc," in La fin du Judaïsme en terres d'Islam, ed. Shmuel Trigano (Paris: Denoël Médiations, 2009), 303–358.

the westernized and all members of the European sector set their sights on France and Canada. The same was true of Tunisia, where at this stage members of the westernized sector were the majority. For Israel, the attempt to bring Algeria's Jews to Israel was especially painful. Both Israel and France wanted to channel at least some of Algeria's Jews to Israel; but in vain.

France and Israel each absorbed a more or less equal proportion of emigrants, though the origins and average profile differed: the newcomers to France were mainly Algerian Jews, for the most part westernized and part of the European sector; the newcomers to Israel were mostly Moroccan Jews, from the native sector with a minority from those who were westernized. Many sources attest to this point, although contemporary observers and scholars alike tend to define the Moroccan olim in class terms, as "poor." I, on the other hand, prefer the sectorial terminology that puts an emphasis on the individual's cultural capital as a determinig factor in his choice during the period of crisis as well as the common split within the same family, between those who immigrated to Israel and those who headed to France or Canada.

The Algerians, who almost all went to France, settled in different regions of the country, mainly in the south and center, and quite a few in and around Paris. They were now joined by newcomers from Tunisia and a handful of westernized Jews from Morocco. Together they launched a new epoch in the history of the French Jewish community, the profile of which until then had been largely under Ashkenazi hegemony, and now opened up to intensive Sephardi influence.[64] While signs of internal Orientalism can be found in the history of absorption of new immigrants by Ashkenazi Jews in the French case as well, the sectorial profile of the immigrants and their need to integrate into French society as a whole, rather than merely into its Jewish wing, prevented the development of a French version of the ethnic problem, thus limiting it to the Jewish state.

THE LONGSTANDING "ETHNIC PROBLEM" IN ISRAEL

Between 1948 and1968 a total of about 700,000 Jews arrived in Israel from Asia and North Africa, realizing Ben-Gurion's 1945 projections of gathering 845,000 Jews from the lands of Islam. But Ben-Gurion probably did not realize the complex character of the social problem his vision was to create. Israeli

[64] On immigration to France see Jean-Jacques Deldyck, *Le Processus d'acculturation des Juifs d'Algérie* (Paris: Ciemi-L'Harmattan, 2000), 109–121; Maud S. Mandel, *Muslims and Jews in France: History of a Conflict* (Princeton: Princeton University Press, 2014). Ethan B. Katz, *The Burdens of Brotherhood: Jews and Muslims from North Africa to France* (Cambridge: Harvard University Press, 2015).

sociologists and anthropologists from various schools of thought – functionalists,[65] neo-Marxists,[66] pluralists,[67] post-colonialists, etc. – have explained
the ethnic problem according to their respective theories.[68] Pioneered by two
different perspectives, one which emphasized the Arabic character of the
Jews of Islam, and another which was open to all the Jewish cultures and
communities of origins in the Mediterranean basin, the post-colonial Arabic
orientation seems to be more attractive to scholars nowadays.[69]

Usually, each school of thought singled out a factor or cause for the
ethnic tensions: cultural gaps, class struggle, Orientalism, and so on. My
own view is that all these factors played a role in the ethnic problem's long
history, but none of them is solely responsible for its emergence, its multiple facets, its durability, and its occasional unpredictable eruptions. Its
complex character and blurred nature correspond with the contradicting
messages of solidarity and dichotomy characteristic of all the encounters
between European and non-European Jews in the age of colonialism and
nationalism. In other places, though, the confusion caused by the conflicting messages did not result in dramatic social clashes, since there was no
real social encounter; a sea, the Mediterranean, separated European and
non-European Jews. The native Jews met only with envoys of European
Jewry, generally embodying the philanthropic, benevolent aspect of internal Orientalism. The envoys did expect a modern cultural shift on the part
of their beneficiaries but they promised substantial economic relief and
individual progress in return.

The encounter within the national society was completely different. Here both parties met in large numbers on the eastern bank of the

---

[65] See S. N. Eisenstadt's key work: *The Absorption of Immigrants: A Comparative Study Based
Mainly on the Jewish Community in Palestine and the State of Israel* (London: Routledge
& Paul, 1954).

[66] Shlomo Swirski, *Israel, the Oriental Majority* (London: Zed, 1989).

[67] Sammy Smooha, *Israel: Pluralism and Conflict* (Berkeley: University of California, 1978).

[68] For further discussion of the different schools and their views see Sami Smooha, "Three
Approaches to the Sociology of Ethnic Relations," *Israel Jerusalem Quarterly* 40 (1986):
31–61; Uri Ram, *The Changing Agenda of Israeli Sociology: Theory, Ideology, and Identity*
(Albany: State University of New York, 1995); Yaron Tsur, "The Israeli Historiography
and the Ethnic Problem," in *Making Israel*, ed. Benny Morris (Ann Arbor: University of
Michigan Press, 2007), 231–277.

[69] Ella Shohat, "Sephardim in Israel: Zionism from the Standpoint of Its Jewish Victims,"
Social Text 19–20 (1988): 1–35; Ammiel Alcalay, *After Jews and Arabs: Remaking Levantine
Culture* (Minneapolis: University of Minnesota, 1993); Yehouda Shenhav, *The Arab
Jews: A Postcolonial Reading of Nationalism, Religion, and Ethnicity* (Stanford: Stanford
University Press, 2006); Lital Levy, *Poetic Trespass: Writing between Hebrew and Arabic in
Israel/Palestine* (Princeton: Princeton Universtiy Press, 2014).

Mediterranean, the natives coming *en masse* after the Europeans, and, to a large extent, through the latter's initiative and with their help. At the gates of Israel the newcomers received voluntary citizenship and were urged to undergo a process of Israeli Hebrew acculturation. The classic Western model of emancipation was formally applied to them, promising equal and harmonious integration into society. This was the official formula, though in fact the immigrants from Asia and Africa arrived at a society in the making, beset with struggles over political and cultural hegemony and place in its economy. The Ashkenazi socialist government saw itself, justifiably, as the benefactor in many ways of the immigrants from colonial communities, but it was responsible, at least partially, for the negative turn in the Arab–Jewish relationship that led to the new exodus. And it can be blamed for directing the immigrants to the geographic and occupational periphery, for taking advantage of their colonial status for *raisons d'état* and the comfort of the veteran Ashkenazi stratum. In sum, the "deal," as conceived by the Ashkenazi leadership of Israel, corresponded with the colonial world of stereotypes and practices and tended to allocate to the native populations a lower place in society.

But for Jews, Israel was founded sentimentally, morally, and officially on national, not colonial, grounds. And it is much easier to break through non-official glass ceilings of discrimination than to overcome discriminatory laws. Furthermore, the scale of internal Orientalism is wide, stretching from a positive extreme where the European embraces the native and sees no difference between him and himself, and a negative end where the European essentially denigrates the native and sees no affinities with him at all. Using the positive aspects of internal Orientalism and penetrating through glass ceilings, a few simple natives and many maskilim as well as westernized found their way to the middle or upper class of Israeli society. The bulk of the native Jews, however, did not; the mass of immigrants and their descendants fill, to this day, the ranks of the lower classes.

Against their background of similar Arabic cultural elements and common exclusion, the newcomers from the Maghreb and the Mashreq became one quasi-social block, generally denoted "Mizraḥim" (orientals). Even they, however, enjoyed power they had not possessed in their countries of origin. In 1977, using their electoral rights, they toppled the Ashkenazi-socialist government, realizing one of the nightmares of the veteran Ashkenazi establishment and determining the new face of the Israeli regime and leadership. Their weight in the Jewish state could no longer be ignored. The change in the balance of forces between the European and non-European sides, even if highly limited, launched a new era in the history of post-colonial Jewries, in a country where most of the descendants of the Afro-Asian Jewish communities now live.

SELECT BIBLIOGRAPHY

Abitbol, Michel. *Les Juifs d'Afrique du Nord sous Vichy.* Paris: Riveneuve, 2008.

MiCrémieux LePétain: 'Anṭišemiyut Be'Algeria HaQoloni'alit. Jerusalem: Merkaz Zalman Šazar, 1993.

ed. *Relations judéo-musulmans au Maroc: perceptions et réalités*: Paris: Editions Stavit, 1997.

Alcalay, Ammiel. *After Jews and Arabs: Remaking Levantine Culture.* Minneapolis: University of Minnesota, 1993.

Bashkin, Orit. *New Babylonians: A History of Jews in Modern Iraq.* Stanford: Stanford University Press, 2012.

Behar, Moshe and Zvi Ben-Dor Benite, eds. *Modern Middle Eastern Jewish Thought: Writings on Identity, Politics and Culture, 1893-1958.* Hanover, NH: Brandeis University Press, 2013.

Beinin, Joel. *The Dispersion of Egyptian Jewry.* Berkeley: University of California Press, 1998.

Boum, Aomar, Jessica Marglin, Khalid Ben-Srhir, and Mohammed Kenbib, eds. *Jews of Morocco and the Maghreb: History and Historiography,* Special Issue of *Hespéris-Tamuda* 51 (2016): Fasc. 2–3.

Chetrit, Yosef. "Moderniyut Le'umit 'Ivrit mul Moderniyut Ṣorfatit: HaHaśkkalah Ha'Ivrit BiṢefon-'Afriqah BaMe'ah HaTteša'-'Esreh." *MiQqedem UmiYyam* 3 (1990): 11–76.

Encyclopedia of Jews in the Islamic World. Executive editor, Norman A. Stillman. Leiden: Brill, 2011.

Fellous, Sonia. ed. *Juifs et musulmans en Tunisie: fraternité et déchirements.* Paris: A. Somogy, 2003.

Gerber, Noah S. *'Anu 'O Kitvey HaQodeš ŠeBeYadeynu? HaGiluy Ha'etnografi Šel Yahadut Teyman.* Jerusalem: Ben-Zvi Institute, 2013.

Goldberg, Harvey E., ed. *Sephardi and Middle Eastern Jewries: History and Culture in Modern Era.* Bloomington: Indiana University Press, 1996.

Gottreich, Emily Benichou and Daniel J. Schroeder, eds. *Jewish Culture and Society in North Africa.* Bloomington: Indiana University Press, 2011.

Harel, Yaron. *Syrian Jewry in Transition, 1840–1880.* Oxford: Littman Library of Jewish Civilization, 2010.

Hever, Ḥannan, Yehouda Shenhav, and Pninah Motzafi-Haller, eds. *Mizraḥim BeYiśra'el: 'Iyun Biqorti Meḥudaš,* Tel Aviv: HaQibuṣ HaMe'uḥad, 2002.

Katz, Ethan B. *The Burdens of Brotherhood: Jews and Muslims from North Africa to France.* Cambridge: Harvard Universtiy Press, 2015.

Katz, Ethan B., Lisa Moses Leff, and Maud S. Mandel, et al., eds. *Colonialism and the Jews.* Bloomington: Indiana University Press, 2017.

Kazzaz, Nissim. *HaYehudim Be'Iraq Bame'ah Ha'Eśrim.* Jerusalem: Ben-Zvi Institute, 1991.

Kenbib, Mohammed. *Juifs et musulmans au Maroc, 1859–1948.* Rabat: Faculté des Lettres et des Sciences Humaines, 1994.

Khazzoom, Aziza. "Tarbbut Ma'aravit, Tiyug 'Etni USegirut Ḥevratit: Hareqa' Le'I-HaŠivayon HaḤevrati BeYiśra'el." *Soṣyologyah Yiśre'elit* 1, no. 2 (1999): 385–428.

Kimche, Ruth. *Ṣiyonut BeṢel HaPiramidot: HaTenu'ah HaṢiyonit BeMiṣrayim 1918–1948.* Tel Aviv: 'Am-'Oved, 2009.

Krämer, Gudrun. *The Jews in Modern Egypt, 1914–1952*. Seattle: University of Washington Press, 1989.

Laskier, Michael M. *Yiśra'el WeHa'aliyyah Miṣefon-'Afriqah:1948-1970*, Be'er-Ševaʿ: Ben-Gurion University Press, 2006.

Levy, Andre. *Return to Casablanca: Jews, Muslims and an Israeli Anthropologist*. Chicago: University of Chicago Press, 2015.

Levy, Lital, *Poetic Trespass: Writing between Hebrew and Arabic in Israel/Palestine*. Princeton: Princeton University Press, 2014.

Lissak, Moshe (Moše Lissaq). *Ha'Aliyyah HaGedolah BiŠenot HaḤamišim: Kišlono šel Kur HaHituḵ*. Jerusalem: Mosad Bialik, 1999.

Martin, Claude. *Les Israélites Algériens de 1830 à 1902*. Paris: Héraklès, 1936.

Medding, Peter Y., ed. *Sephardic Jewry and Mizrahi Jews*. Studies in Contemporary Jewry 22. New York: Oxford University Press, 2008.

Meir-Glitzenstein, Esther. *Bein Baghdad LeRamat-Gan: Yoṣe'ey Iraq BeYiśra'el*. Jerusalem: Yad Ben-Zvi, 2009.

Miccoli, Dario. *Histories of the Jews of Egypt: An Imagined Bourgeoisie, 1880s–1950s*. London: Routledge, 2015.

Picard, Avi. *'Olim BiMeśorah: Mediniyut Yiśra'el Kelapey 'Aliyyatam šel Yehudey Ṣefon-'Afriqah 1951–1956*. Be'er-Ševaʿ: Ben-Gurion University Press, 2013.

Ram, Uri. *The Changing Agenda of Israeli Sociology: Theory, Ideology, and Identity*. Albany: State University of New York, 1995.

Raz-Krakotzkin, Amnon. "Orientalism, Mada'ey HaYahadut WeHaḤevrah HaYiśre'elit – Mispar He'arot." *Jama'a* 3, no. 2 (1998): 34–59.

Rodrigue, Aron. *French Jews, Turkish Jews: The Alliance Israélite Universelle and the Politics of Jewish Schooling in Turkey, 1860–1925*. Bloomington: Indiana University Press, 1990.

Saadoun, Haim, ed. *Qehillot Yiśra'el BaMmizraḥ BaMe'ot HaTteša'-'Esreh WeHa'Eśrim*. Jerusalem: Ben-Zvi Institute, 8 Vols, 2002–2013.

Schreier, Joshua. *Arabs of the Jewish Faith: The Civilizing Mission in Colonial Algeria*. New Brunswick: Rutgers University Press, 2010.

Schroeter, Daniel. "Orientalism and the Jews of the Mediterranean," *Journal of Mediterranean Studies* 4, no. 2 (1994): 183–196.

and Joseph Chetrit. "Emancipation and Its Discontents: Jews at the Formative Period of Colonial Rule in Morocco," *Jewish Social Studies: History, Culture, Society* 13, no. 1 (2006): 170–206.

Sebag, Paul. *Histoire des Juifs de Tunisie*. Paris: L'Harmattan, 1991.

Shenhav, Yehouda. *The Arab Jews: A Postcolonial Reading of Nationalism, Religion, and Ethnicity*. Stanford: Stanford University Press, 2006.

Shiblak, Abbas. *The Lure of Zion: The Case of Iraqi Jews*. London: Al Saqi Books, 1986.

Shohat, Ella. "Sephardim in Israel: Zionism from the Standpoint of Its Jewish Victims," *Social Text* 19–20 (1988): 1–35.

Smooha, Sammy. *Israel: Pluralism and Conflict*. Berkeley: University of California Press, 1978.

Śnir, Reuven. *'Arviyut, Yahadut, Ṣiyyonut: Ma'avaq Zehuyot BiYṣiratam šel Yehudey Iraq*. Jerusalem: Ben-Zvi Institute, 2005.

Stein, Sarah Abrevaya. *Saharan Jews and the Fate of French Algeria*. Chicago: University of Chicago Press, 2014.

Swirski, Shlomo, *Israel, the Oriental Majority*. London: Zed, 1989.

Trigano, Shmuel, ed. *La fin du Judaïsme en terres d'Islam*. Paris: Denoël Médiations, 2009.

Tsur, Yaron. "The Israeli Historiography and the Ethnic Problem." *Making Israel*. Edited by Benny Morris. Ann Arbor: University of Michigan Press, 2007, 231–277.

Qehila Qeru'a: Yehudey Maroqo VeHaLe'umiyut 1943–1954. Tel Aviv: 'Am-'Oved, 2001.

"Religious Internationalism in the Jewish Diaspora – Tunis at the Dawn of the Colonial Period." *Religious Internationals in the Modern World: Globalization and Faith Communities since 1750*. Edited by Abigail Green and Vincent Viaene. London: Palgrave MacMillan, 2012, 186–205.

and Hagar Hillel. *Yehudey Qazablanqah: 'Iyunim BeModernizasyah šel Hanhagah Yehudit BiTtefuṣah Qoloni'alit*. Tel Aviv: Ha'Universiṭa HaPetuḥah, 1995.

Zohar, Zvi. *Masoret UTemurah: Hitmodedut Hakmey Yiśra'el BeMiṣrayim UveSuryah 'im 'Etgarey HaModernizasyah*. Jerusalem: Ben-Zvi Institute, 2005 (1993).

Rabbinic Creativity in the Modern Middle East. London: Bloomsbury, 2013.

Zytnicky, Colette. *Les Juifs du Maghreb: Naissance d'une historiographie coloniale*. Paris: Presses de l'Université Paris-Sorbonne, 2011.

CHAPTER 9

ISRAEL

DEREK PENSLAR

INVENTING JEWISH NATIVENESS:
THE ZIONIST PROJECT

Zionism is a variety of Jewish nationalism. It claims that Jews constitute a nation whose survival, both physical and cultural, requires its return to the Jews' ancestral home in the land of Israel. Throughout most of its history, however, Zionism was far more than a nationalist movement: it was a revolutionary project to remake the Jews and their society. It was part of the great political convulsion that wracked the western world during the first half of the twentieth century. Despite the vast differences between them, social democracy, communism and fascism in Europe, anti-colonial nationalist movements in Asia and Africa, and Zionism all strove for a radical transformation of existing political realities, and they espoused utopian visions of social engineering. This was true primarily for Labor Zionism, which arose out of the European leftist tradition, but also characterized bourgeois varieties of Zionism and right-wing Revisionism.

All of the West's revolutionary political projects were pushed forward by a dialectic tension between views of humanity as a malleable mass, to be mobilized in the service of the collective, or as heroic individuals, masters of their fate, striving for ever greater levels of personal fulfilment. (In totalitarian movements, the former dominated; in liberal ones, the latter.) In Zionist thought, the former meant thinking of immigrants as "human material" (*homer enushi*) to be vocationally restructured, moved about the land, or hurled into battle as party or state needs dictated. The latter was embodied in the ideal type of the Hebrew laborer or tradesman who worked by day and by night revived his spirit through engagement with Hebrew culture.

In Zionism, as in the West's other revolutionary projects, religiosity was occluded but never eliminated; the godly was no less compelling for being conceived as attainable through human action. Conviction in the righteousness of one's cause and that its leaders read history correctly dwelled alongside fear that the project's internal and external enemies would overcome it – that the child of revolution would be stillborn. Zionism's audacity born of desperation bore the particular marks of centuries of persecution, culminating in the Holocaust, but a mixture of euphoria and existenial panic characterized all of the twentieth century's revolutionary movements.

In fact, not all of them survived. Fascism was destroyed by the world war that it brought upon itself. In the 1950s, Stalinism gradually gave way to more moderate forms of Soviet communism, but they were unsustainable and eventually collapsed. New Deal liberalism and European social democracy, however, laid the ground for the post-war welfare state, while in the Third World, anti-colonial movements achieved political independence, often in the form of socialist regimes. It was in this atmosphere of post-war possibility, in an era driven by a great transformative torque, that Zionism realized itself in the establishment of the state of Israel. The mass immigration of the 1950s preserved Zionism's social-revolutionary moment, and Israel's many wars fostered a sense of solidarity under crisis despite the country's yawning political, ethnic, and religious divides. Until the 1960s, Israel was still very much a country in khaki, a mobilized society, an heir to the states of interwar Europe. Thereafter Israel began to assume the characteristics of a Western social welfare state, but it retained some of its revolutionary élan until the 1980s. Israel rejected its secular, revolutionary heritage by simultaneously embracing Western neo-liberalism and religious fundamentalism, both of which were attached, albeit for radically different reasons, to the territories that Israel conquered in the 1967 war. By the 1990s, polarization within Israel between the forces of what Benjamin Barber famously termed "McWorld" and "Jihad" – economic and cultural globalization, on the one hand, and anti-republican theocracy, on the other – had put an end to the Zionist project as it had existed for over a century. Israel, a product of the nationalist, social-democratic and anti-colonial movements of the late nineteenth century, has belatedly become a creature of the new *fin de siècle*: an era of limitless individuation, radical religiosity, and intractable conflict.

The state of Israel is a product of not only the transformative movements of the twentieth century but also the specific circumstances of the modern Jewish Diaspora. Indeed, Israel may be described as the continuation of Diaspora Jewish civilization by other means. The Zionist project originated in the Jewish Diaspora and reflected myriad influences from the Jews' many homelands. The connections between the Diaspora and the Zionist project were at times linear and direct, but they could also be dialectical, a rejection of a Diaspora norm that triggered a new social practice, which was then shaped by waves of immigration and practical necessity into patterns similar to older Diaspora behaviors.

In most aspects, the Zionist project worked from a map of known practices and possibilities. There was one central component of the Zionist project for which Jews had no map, however, and that was rule over another
people. In Diaspora, individual Jews had on occasion exercised power over
individual Gentiles (e.g., as creditors or employers) but not since antiquity had Jews as a group ruled over another. To cite Kantian terminology,
Jews had wielded Macht (power) but not Herrschaft (domination), and
the levels of domination over the Palestinian Arabs increased exponentially
over time. During the interwar period, Orthodox-Zionist rabbis thought
through the permissibility within Jewish law for the establishment of a
Jewish commonwealth prior to the messianic era, but few conceived of
Jews as despoiling hundreds of thousands of Arabs and becoming lords
over those Arabs who remained within Israel's borders. After 1967, substantial numbers of Orthodox Jewish Israelis came to see settlement of
the newly conquered territories, especially the West Bank and eastern
Jerusalem, as religious commandments that took precedence over obedience to state law.

From the start, the Zionist project featured a constant tension
between continuity and rupture with the Jewish past; between its transnational structure and its goal to construct a national center concentrating much, most, or even all of world Jewry; and between the motley
linguistic environments of world Jewry and the Zionist goal of creating
a unifying Hebrew culture. The Israeli polity bore traces of Diaspora
Jewish politics, society, and economic life yet also struck out on its own.
Despite many similarities to nationalist movements of the twentieth
century, Zionism was unique in defining as its national home a place
with few nationals in it, to which hundreds of thousands of immigrants
had to be brought in order to create a viable Yishuv (pre-state community) of workers and farmers. The Yishuv had to create the pre-con-
ditions for its very existence, and this in a land that was nine-tenths
Arab in 1900 and still two-thirds Arab in 1948. Jewish immigrants to
Palestine, and even more so their children, quickly became indigenized
colonials, possessed of a culture that both bound them with and set
them apart from Diaspora Jewry.

Zionist nativeness was constructed with astonishing speed, over just a
few decades prior to 1948, and adopted no less quickly by the waves of
immigration that more than tripled the young state's population within
a decade. Until the 1980s, Israeli culture was stamped by the country's
hegemonic Ashkenazic elites and was thus more European than Middle
Eastern. In recent decades, however, Jews of Middle Eastern origin have
enjoyed increasing political power and influence over Israel's religious life
and popular culture. Israeli nativeness is an idiosyncratic and constantly

evolving melange of European, Jewish, and Middle Eastern sensibilities, but it is no less durable for its atypicality, or for its recent vintage.

Like the Zionist project, this essay is constructed along two axes, diachronic and synchronic. The former ties Zionism and the state of Israel with Jewish civilization, the latter with twentieth-century global history and with parallel developments in the twentieth-century Jewish Diaspora. In the brief space available here, I cannot aspire to provide a narrative history of the makings of modern Israel and its development since 1948. Rather, I apply our themes of continuity and rupture to selected moments in that history that illustrate the origins of Israeli nativeness and account for its survival even after the demise of its parent, Zionism itself.

BEFORE STATEHOOD

Despite massive changes over the past thirty years in the historiography of modern Jewry and the Zionist project, Zionism's origins remain stubbornly anchored in what Salo Baron famously called a lachrymose view of Jewish history. In this view, Jewish history is characterized primarily by collective suffering, mitigated by spiritual or cultural achievement.[1] To this day, textbooks present Zionism's origins in the miseries of Eastern European Jewry (poverty and pogroms), the insecurities of Western Jews (political antisemitism, epitomized by the Dreyfus Affair), and the musings of a handful of rabbis and Jewish intellectuals.[2] In fact, Zionism emerged out of a longstanding process, not only as a response to crisis. It was as much a product of modern colonialism as of Hebraic cultural revival, of the steamship,

---

[1] When Salo Baron coined the term, in 1928, his focus was the Jewish Middle Ages, which German-Jewish scholars associated with the *Wissenschaft des Judentums* had depicted in harshly negative terms, whereas Baron praised the period for the considerable liberties, security, and autonomy that Jews often enjoyed. Baron's view of Jewish modernity, however, was emphatically lachrymose, as he believed that the modern state robbed Jews of their previous liberties and traditional identities while granting them little of lasting benefit in return. In this sense, traditional Zionist historiography operated in a Baronian spirit, and more recent, positive accounts of modern diaspora Jewish life are influenced by a doctrine that David Engel has termed "neo-Baronianism." See David Engel, "Crisis and Lachrymosity: On Salo Baron, Neobaronianism, and the Study of Modern European Jewish History," *Jewish History* 20 (2006): 243–64.

[2] It is no coincidence that the first serious textbook on Zionist history in North America was Arthur Hertzberg's anthology *The Zionist Idea* (1958), followed shortly thereafter by Ben Halpern's *The Idea of the Jewish State* (1961), which admittedly included pioneering institutional and political analysis, but whose overarching framework remained the history of thought.

telegraph, and camera, which made Palestine visible and accessible, as of odes to Zion, of Christian restorationism as of antisemitism.

Over the century before the beginning of Zionist immigration in 1882, some 20,000 highly religious Jews immigrated to Palestine, dwarfing the 5,000 who made up its existing community. (In the 1880s, Palestinian Jewry became known as the Yishuv, a term that remained in force until Israel's creation in 1948.) Most of the pre-Zionist Yishuv consisted of Torah scholars who depended upon alms from Diaspora Jews. Some Western donors replaced the giving of alms with modern philanthropy, especially in the form of education aimed at training the Yishuv's youth for renumerative occupations. This was an early sign of Diaspora Jews' desire to transform the Yishuv according to its own self-image. In 1863, the Anglo-Jewish financier and philanthropist Moses Montefiore, who sponsored educational and economic reform within the Yishuv, wrote that "Palestine must belong to the Jews, and Jerusalem is designed to be the seat of a Jewish commonwealth."[3] A further step came in 1874, when a lead article in the world's most influential Jewish newpaper, the London-based *Jewish Chronicle*, considered the timing auspicious for a British protectorate over Palestine. While Montefiore enjoyed the support of Protestant restorationists in the pursuit of an ecumenical, imperial messianism, the rigidly ultra-Orthodox Hungarian rabbi Akiva Joseph Schlesinger was influenced by the romantic nationalism of the 1860s and 70s in his call for a Hebrew commonwealth populated by Jewish peasants and shepherds.[4]

In addition to imperialism and nationalism, international, non-governmental organizations were an important external influence on Zionism's origins. The Red Cross (founded 1863) and the Catholic Church's Peter's Pence network (founded 1871) were able to link people and send funds throughout the globe thanks to great leaps forward in transport and communications technology.[5] A cluster of Jewish NGOs, based in one country but tied to Jewish communities throughout the world, was established in North America and Western Europe between 1858 and 1871. These organizations combined political lobbying with philanthropy

[3] Cited in Michael Silber, "Alliance of the Hebrews, 1863–1875: The Diaspora Roots of an Ultra-Orthodox Proto-Zionist Utopia in Palestine," *The Journal of Israeli Hisotry* 27, no. 2 (2008): 119–147. On Montefiore's Palestinian activities, see Abigail Green's magisterial biography, *Montefiore: Jewish Liberator, Imperial Hero*. Cambridge, MA: Harvard University Press, 2010.
[4] Silber, "Alliance of the Hebrews."
[5] Abigail Green, "Rethinking Sir Moses Montefiore: Religion, Nationhood and International Philanthropy in the Nineteenth Century," *The American Historical Review* 110, no. 3 (2005): 631–658.

on behalf of oppressed Jewish communities, and they contributed heavily to the Yishuv. In their operating methods and division of labor, these Jewish NGOs adumbrated the quasi-governmental Zionist Organization, founded in 1897.

Although the philanthropic spirit of Jewish NGOs rarely condensed into an overt nationalism, their close bond with the Yishuv, defined through action not ideology, remained characteristic of the Western European and North American Jewish philanthropic elite until the 1940s. Such was the ethos of the non-Zionist component of the enlarged Jewish Agency for Palestine, established in 1929. On a more popular level, most members of the American Zionist Federation during the 1920s were women affiliated with Hadassah, the Women's Zionist Organization, which consistently subsumed ideology to practical philanthropic work in Palestine.[6] One did not have to be a confirmed Jewish nationalist to take pride in the Yishuv's growing towns and industry, its increasingly tanned and healthy residents, and, most of all, its agricultural settlements, where Jews were transformed from *luftmenschen* to laborers, and from scrawny peddlers to sturdy farmers. Since the time of the Enlightenment, Jews had called upon their brethren to abandon commerce for "productive" occupations in order to combat antisemitic accusations of parasitism, dishonesty, and physical weakness. This apologetic impulse was widespread in modern Jewish culture, and although it bore a deceptive resemblance to European agrarian romanticism, it possessed a unique internal dynamic.[7]

In contrast to Jews in the West, Eastern European Jewry produced a heartfelt Jewish nationalism anchored in Hebrew language and literature. However tied it was to the Jewish textual canon, the notion of a secular Hebrew culture assumed a massive break with Jewish tradition and an adoption of contemporary nationalist sensibilites. Similar was the case of the Zionist Organizations' Jewish National Fund, presented by its founder, the Russian-Jewish mathematician Hermann Shapira, as embodying ancient Jewish religious concepts of land as God's possession, available for temporary usufruct by the collective Jewish nation. In fact, the Fund reflected the spirit of contemporary Russian populism as well as modern developments in Western legal notions of the trust as administrator of inalienable property.[8]

---

[6] Michael Berkowitz, *Western Jewry and the Zionist Project, 1914–1933*. Cambridge, UK: Cambridge University Press, 1997.

[7] Derek J. Penslar, *Shylock's Children: Economics and Jewish Identity in Modern Europe*. Berkeley and Los Angeles: University of California Press, 2001.

[8] Compare Derek J. Penslar, *Zionism and Technocracy: The Engineering of Jewish Settlement in Palestine, 1870–1918*. Bloomington: Indiana University Press, 1991, 47–48, 53–55, with

In the late 1870s, there emerged from within the highly traditional Yishuv a handful of individuals whose Orthodoxy blended with European romanticism, humanitiarianism, and a concept of Jewish collective revival cut off from messianic goals – in short, a form of nationalism. In 1878, two agricultural settlements, Petah Tikva (near Jaffa) and Gei Uni (in the upper Galilee) were founded in this sprit. Three years later, Eliezer Ben-Yehuda moved from Russia to Palestine in order to create a modern Hebrew vernacular. Tellingly, he was strongly influenced by Russian cultural nationalism (Slavophilism) as well as his traditional Jewish religious education and the Hebrew journalism of the time. All of these forces preceded the crisis of 1881, as pogroms swept southern Russia, Zionist associations sprang up throughout Eastern Europe, and some 25,000 Jews left Europe for Palestine over the following decade.

Only a small fraction of them, or of the members of the next, larger wave of the years 1904–14, were nationalist idealists. Some were impoverished Jews attracted by cheaper fares to Palestine than to the New World, and many were traditional, Orthodox Jews untouched by nationalist ideology and committed to spending their days steeped in the study of sacred texts.[9] Among the more nationalistically minded immigrants, some attempted to farm, but most failed, and several of their colonies were rescued by Baron Edmond de Rothschild, whose cadre of French-trained agronomists preferred viticulture and orchard crops for export over the subsistence farming that had appealed to the settlers as living by the sweat of one's brow. Thus in the early 1900s, a chasm separated Zionist aspirations from the Yishuv's realities. While Zionist activists dreamed of a unifying Hebrew culture, most of the Yishuv spoke Yiddish, Russian, Ladino, Arabic, and French. Reactionary Orthodoxy was far more prevalent than an enlightened religiosity open to nationalist influences. The simple Jewish farmer "sitting under his fig tree and under his vine" was most often a colonial planter overseeing Arab laborers.

Nonetheless, the seeds of Zionist nativeness had been sown in those colonies. The planters' children were raised as Palestinian Jews, truly at home

Ritu Birla, *Stages of Capital: Law, Culture and Market Governance in Late Colonial India.* Durham, NC: Duke University Press, 2009, Chapter 2.

[9] Gur Alroey, "Journey to Early-Twentieth-Century Palestine as a Jewish Immigrant Experience," *Jewish Social Studies* 9, no. 2 (2003): 28–64; idem, *Imigrantim: ha-hagirah ha-yehudit le-eretz yisra'el be-reshit ha-me'ah ha-esrim.* Jerusalem: Yad Ben Zvi, 2004; Margalit Shilo, Ruth Kark, and Galit Hazan-Rokem, eds, *Ha-'ivriyot ha-hadashot: nashim ba-yishuv u-va-tsiyonut ba-re'I ha-migdar.* Jerusalem: Yad Ben Zvi, 2001; Margalit Shilo, *Princess or Prisoner? Jewish Women in Jerusalem, 1840–1914.* Hanover, NH: University Press of New England, 2005.

in the land with which their parents never felt entirely at ease. One of these children, Reuven Paikovitch, grew into a sturdy farmer and raised a family on the arid slopes of the eastern lower Galilee. In turn, his son Yigal, later known as Yigal Allon and one of the Yishuv's top military commanders, was the epitome of the new Zionist Yishuv's native sons.[10]

Meanwhile, in the Diaspora, Zionist politics represented both a continuation of traditional forms of intercession (*shtadlanut*) with Gentile authority and a new self-presentation as part of an international community pursuing collective interests in the name of universal norms. As Schlesinger wrote of the European states, "Just as they restored Greece ... so they have a great obligation to us. At the very least, we should be like Romania under Turkish rule."[11] Here we see the beginning of political Zionism's wedding of Jewish interests in Palestine with a Great Power protector, a process that would be accelerated vastly by Theodor Herzl and, following World War I, Chaim Weizmann. We also see a hedging of bets, a willingness to accept forms of autonomy short of statehood, which was expressed by a chorus of Zionist leaders and activists all the way up up to the early 1940s. Recent scholarship has analyzed the creative, flexible, and conciliatory thinking about Zionism's political aspirations that came in the interwar period from Diaspora-based intellectuals like Simon Rawidowitz, Mordecai Kaplan, and Hans Kohn. But similar ideas were also expressed by top Zionist leaders in Europe and the Yishuv. Weizmann and Chaim Arlosoroff were willing to compromise on Zionist demands for statehood and for a Jewish majority in Palestine.[12] Even the firebrand Revisionist Zionist leader Vladimir Jabotinsky endorsed a proposal in the late 1920s by the British politician Josiah Wedgwood that Palestine become a seventh dominion of the British Empire, incorporating British law and subservient to Britain in foreign affairs.

There were, in fact, key differences between old-style intercession by individual Jews and Zionist alliances with imperial power: first, the presence of a mass Zionist movement, claiming millions of adherents by the 1930s, to which its leaders were ultimately responsible; and second, the

---

[10] Anita Shapira, *Yigal Allon, Native Son*. Philadelphia: University of Pennsylvania Press, 2008.

[11] Cited in Silber, "Alliance of the Hebrews."

[12] Meir Hazan, *Metinut: ha-gishah ha-metunah be-Ha-Po'el Ha-Tsa'ir u-ve-Mapai, 1905–1945*. Tel Aviv: Am Oved, 2009, 189–191. For non-statist forms of Zionism in the Diaspora, see Dmitry Shumsky, "On Ethocentrism and Its Limits: Czecho-German Jewry in Fin-de-Siècle Prague and the Origins of Zionist Binationalism," *Jahrbuch des Simon-Dubnow-Instituts* 5 (2006): 173–188; and Noam Pianko, *Zionism and the Roads Not Taken: Rawidowicz, Kaplan, Kohn*. Bloomington: Indiana University Press, 2010.

justification for Zionist claims in history, right, and justice rather than the *shtadlan's* only form of power, money. (True, during World War I, while negotiating for a declaration of support for Zionist aims, Weizmann played to British fantasies about Jewish political power in the United States and Russia, but those fantasies proved short lived, and the Balfour Declaration long survived them.[13])

The pioneering "core" of the 1904–14 immigration wave was intensely political, inheriting the mantle of Jewish radical politics in Eastern Europe. (The year 1897 witnessed the founding of not only the Zionist Organization but also the Jewish Bund, for a time the largest social-democratic party in the Russian empire.) The youthful pioneers – many of them were adolescents – are often mistakenly called "socialists," but their Zionism was a mélange of Marxism, populism, Tolstoyan agrarianism, and anarchism. One of the two first Labor Zionist parties, the Workers of Zion (Po'alei Tsion) did pay lip service to Marxist doctrine, but even before World War I many of its members softened their views in the interest of nation building, which required co-operation, not conflict, with private capital and public Zionist funds.

During the interwar period, when the Yishuv grew in size from 50,000 to 450,000, Labor Zionism became hegemonic, and small parties merged into the politically moderate Eretz Israel Workers Party (Mapai). Mapai's leader, David Ben-Gurion, proclaimed the identity of interests of the laboring class and those of the Jewish nation, and he governed the largely autonomous Yishuv in coalition with middle class and religious parties. Historian Zeev Sternhell has caustically termed this ideology a form of "nationalist socialism," little more than a variety of European right-wing integral nationalism, which proclaimed the nation, not the working class, to be a victim of history and mobilized the masses in common cause against the nation's enemies, real or imagined.[14] But Ben-Gurion's inclusive approach had European parallels, in both Austria's "Red Vienna" and France under the Popular Front, not to mention the highly eclectic blend of socialism and nationalism found in anti-colonial movements throughout the globe.

It is often impossible to separate the pragmatic and ideological justifications for the actions of the Zionist labor movement and to determine if its sensibilities derived from prevalent Eastern European norms or a Jewish

[13] This theme has been picked up by many scholars, most recently Jonathan Schneer, *The Balfour Declaration: The Origins of the Arab-Israeli Conflict*. New York: Random House, 2010.

[14] Zeev Sternhell, *The Founding Myths of Israel. Nationalism, Socialism, and the Makings of the Jewish State*. Princeton, NJ: Princeton University Press, 1998.

cultural heritage. For example, in 1908 through 1910 small groups of Jewish laborers farmed land collectively, and over time these collectives, known first as *kvutzot* and later, in a much-expanded form, as *kibbutzim*, became a hallmark of Labor Zionism. According to sociologist Gershon Shafir, they formed collective settlements on publicly owned land in order to create a separate economy isolated from the capitalist labor market, which was dominated by cheap and docile Arab labor.[15] Yet at the *fin de siècle* Russian Jewish youth founded communal settlements in North America, where there was no thought of creating a separate national economy. Populist, anarchist, and other radical sentiments appear to have been exported by a swath of Russian Jewry to various lands. Moreover, Labor Zionists consistently invoked Judaic ideals of social justice, ideals that they expressed in a stilted yet vigorous Hebrew that could not be cut off from its ancient and religious origins, from what Gershom Scholem described with trepidation as its "apocalyptic thorn."[16]

The Zionist labor movement exuded a secularized religiosity, in which physical labor assumed the role of rabbinic commandments and fine points of socialist doctrine supplanted Torah study. It can be said that the European revolutionary left was in general a messianic movement, but that only begs the question why so many Jews were attracted to it, and it neglects the specific case of Zionist radicals, many of whom had been raised in highly observant and learned homes. The Zionist labor movement was thus quite different from Jabotinsky's Revisionism, whose ideology was stridently secular in its eschewal of social utopianism and of self-abnegating psychic transformation. There is nonetheless a vast difference between secularized religiosity and ritual observance. A powerful anti-clerical streak ran through Labor Zionism, so much so that until the mid-1930s Labor activists insisted on serving non-kosher food at public events. Labor's need for religious Zionist political support led it in 1935 to agree to the maintenance of Jewish dietary law and Sabbath rest in the public sphere, and this agreement was reiterated on the eve of the state's creation. But this was a wholly pragmatic affair, just as Israel's Herut party, the successors to the pre-state, right-wing Revisionists, turned away from anti-clericalism to a populist religiosity beginning in the 1950s, as it sought

---

[15] Gershon Shafir, *Land, Labour, and the Origins of the Israeli-Palestinian Conflict, 1882–1914*. Cambridge, UK: Cambridge University Press, 1988.

[16] Scholem to Rosenzweig, December 26, 1926, reproduced in Gilad Zuckerman, "Law, Religion and Identity in Israel," http://lethargicman.livejournal.com/251151.html; accessed December 13, 2010. See also Walter Grab and Julius Schoeps, *Juden in der Weimarer Republik*, Stuttgart: Burg Verlag, 1986, 148.

legitimacy and support from recent immigrants who respected religious traditions.[17]

Religious Zionists themselves were forced to separate their most ambitious goals from the needs of the moment. As Rabbi Isaac Herzog, Israel's first Ashkenazic chief rabbi, wrote in 1948, ideally the Jewish state would be a theocracy, and non-Jews would not be accorded equal rights, but the fledgling state's dependence upon the international community, and the constant scrutiny under which it would live, required that the state follow Western political and juridical norms. (Herzog did, however, continue to favor a monarchy over a republic.)[18] Despite the apparent chasm separating the religious Zionists, represented by the Mizrachi party, from the anti-Zionist, ultra-Orthodox Jews of Agudat Yisrael, leaders of the latter privately rejoiced in the United Nations' Partition Resolution of November 1947, seeing in it a sign of the beginning of redemption,[19] a concept reflected in the official prayer for the state of Israel, composed by, among others, the Mizrachi leader Rabbi Herzog. Two leaders from Agudat Yisrael signed Israel's declaration of independence, and the party was formally part of the government until 1952. (Even after Agudat Yisrael withdrew from the government, it remained zealous in promoting ultra-Orthodox interests in the Israeli parliament, in which its members served willingly as committee heads.) Both Mizrachi and the Agudah longed to see Torah reign supreme in the land of Israel, yet both were modern political movements that mobilized support via techniques such as rallies and the press. The main differences between them were that Mizrachi legitimized Western knowledge and practices and believed both that Jews must undergo a process of collective regeneration and that Eretz Israel was the only site on which that process could take place. Mizrachi thus considered a Jewish state, even a nominally secular one, legitimate and deserving of public recognition. The Agudah rejected all of these assumptions.

An essential component of the sea change that Zionists demanded of the Jewish people, and which the Agudah rejected, was the abandonment of passivity in the face of one's oppressors, and the valorization of military

[17] Nadav Shelef, *Evolving Nationalism: Homeland, Identity, and Religion in Israel, 1925–2005.* Ithaca, NY: Cornell University Press, 2010.

[18] Excerpts from Herzog's Hebrew writings on the halachic justification for a Jewish state have been reproduced in English translation in Eran Kaplan and Derek J. Penslar, eds, *The Origins of the State of Israel. A Documentary History.* Madison: University of Wisconsin Press, 2011.

[19] Menachem Friedman, "The Structural Foundation for Religio-Political Accommodation in Israel: Fallacy and Reality," in *Israel: The First Decade of Independence*, ed. S. Ilan Troen and Noah Lucas. Albany, New York: State University of New York Press, 1995, 51–82.

force. By 1948, Zionism had developed a militaristic ethos that, save for the ultra-Orthodox, encompassed the entire Yishuv.

This spirit is usually identified with Vladimir Jabotinsky, who was influenced by the aestheticized militarism of Italy's revolutonary tradition, from Giuseppi Garibaldi to Gabriele d'Annunzio. Accordingly, Jabotinsky demanded that Jews internalize and display *hadar*, which literally means "glory," but is best understood as something between the Renaissance concept of *virtù* and the modern Italian notion of *bella figura*. Jabotinsky also reflected darker influences from the *fin de siècle*, such as right-wing Polish nationalism, most notably the political pessimism of Roman Dmowski. Thus Jabotinsky's dire predictions of an imminent catastrophe befalling the Jews (though he did not envision attempted genocide), his blunt call that Jewish youth "learn how to shoot,"[20] his fondness for military dress, and his key role in organizing Jewish military forces, ranging from the 5,000-strong Jewish Legion that fought for Britain in World War I to the Haganah, the most important militia in the interwar Yishuv.

Yet Jabotinsky was hardly alone in championing military activism within the Zionist movement. Although there were pacifist strains within early Labor Zionism, far more prominent was a cult of physical strength, courage, and armed self-defense. Some of the youthful radical Zionists in Palestine on the eve of World War I had taken up arms during pogroms in Russia in the years surrounding the 1905 revolution. Members of the Yishuv's first militia, Hashomer (The Guard, 1909), adopted native Arab headgear as a sign of having overcome passive diasporic Jewish identities and assumed new ones rooted in indigeneity. This practice reflected the belief not only that Arabs were virile and courageous, but also that Arabs were the Jews' long-lost cousins, or even that the Arabs were direct descendants of ancient Hebrews who had never left the land of Israel.[21]

Despite claims to novelty, Zionist militance was deeply influenced by traditional Jewish sensibilities. First, Diaspora Jews had a long history

---

[20] "For the generation that grows before our eyes and who will be responsible, probably, for the greatest change in our history, the Aleph Bet has a very simple sound: young people learn how to shoot ... For one to be a true person, he must study 'culture' in general. To be Jewish, he must know the language and history of his people ... But if you will learn how to shoot, there might be hope. This is the language in which the historical reality of our generation and the next generation speaks to us." Vladimir Jabotinsky, "Al ha-ah – ha-aleph bet he-hadash," in *Ba-derech la-medinah*, Jerusalem: Eri Jabotinsky, 1953, 89–90.

[21] This subject has been thoughtfully treated in Jonathan Gribetz, *Defining Neighbors: Religion, Race, and the Early 'Zionist-Arab' Encounter*. Princeton: Princeton University Press, 2014.

of military service and of displaying valor in combat.[22] Zionist critiques of Jewish timidity reflected venerable antisemitic accusations of Jewish cowardice and draft-dodging as much as social reality. Second, Zionists continued to employ traditional tropes of martyrdom and sacrifice in their descriptions of Jews who died in confrontation with Arabs. Just as Christian writers drew on metaphors of medieval chivalry to interpret the death of millions of soldiers in World War I, so did Zionists depict Jews who fell in battle against Arabs as martyrs in the spirit of *kiddush ha-shem*, death as "sanctification of the name of God." In 1920, after eight Jews were killed by Arabs at Tel Hai, a settlement in the northern Galilee, Labor leader Berl Katznelson penned a memorial poem to the fallen in the form of the traditional Yizkor prayer for the dead. Twenty-one years later, as the Yishuv faced an imminent threat of a Nazi invasion from North Africa, Katznelson sponsored the publication of an anthology of texts documenting Jewish heroism over the millennia. In the introduction to the anthology, Katznelson walked a delicate line between presenting the Yishuv's situation as identical to the desperate state that characterized much of Diaspora Jewish life and as something categorically superior.[23] Similarly, reactions within the Yishuv to the mass slaughters of Jews in Europe ranged from traditional displays of public mourning to angry demands by kibbutz youth that they be sent in "ghetto-busting squads" behind enemy lines.[24]

The 1948 war maintained this ongoing tension in Zionist consciousness between victimhood and empowerment, the Jewish martyr and the Hebrew warrior. At the moment the state of Israel was born, its narrative swung between the tragic and the epic. Israel's sense of existential threat in 1948 had many sources: not only the Arab armies arrayed against her, but also the Jews' long history as an oppressed minority, the all-too-fresh scars of the Holocaust, and fear of British intervention (direct or indirect), which, ironically, created parallels to the anti-colonial struggles of Israel's Arab foes. Thus Israelis experienced and have remembered the war as one of the few against the many, or David against Goliath, very much in keeping with longstanding Jewish self-perceptions.

In fact, though, in December 1947 and again in May of 1948, spokesmen of the Haganah (which, after Israel's declaration of statehood, formed

---

[22] Derek J. Penslar, *Jews and the Military: A History*. Princeton: Princeton University Press, 2013.

[23] Katznelson's poem and introduction may be found in English translation in Kaplan and Penslar, *The Origins of the State of Israel*, 216–217.

[24] Dina Porat, *The Blue and the Yellow Stars of David: The Zionist Leadership and the Holocaust, 1939–1945*. Cambridge, MA: Harvard University Press, 1990; Uri Ben-Eliezer, *The Making of Israeli Militarism*. Bloomington: Indiana University Press, 1998.

the bulk of the Israel Defense Force) readily acknowleged the weakness and disarray of most of the Arab states' military forces, and they spoke confidently of victory. The United Nations' and United States' arms embargoes imposed in March and April made it difficult for Arab states to acquire armaments or munitions, but Israel obtained both through an international network that operated both legally and illicitly.[25] Most Palestinians did not take up arms against Israel, and many villages signed non-aggression pacts with the Haganah.[26] Israel experienced terrifying periods during the fighting, first against Palestinian guerillas during the winter of 1948 and then against the invading Arab armies in from mid-May to mid-June. In both cases, though, the Zionists gained military superiority, which resulted in the forced flight, or outright expulsion, of some 700,000 Palestinians and conquest of forty percent more territory than what was alloted to Israel by the United Nations.

Seen in this light, the 1948 war was the last of a series of violent population transfers that, over a period of some five years, remade the maps of Europe and Asia. During and after World War II, forced migrations transformed Eastern Europe from a multi-national patchwork to a series of ethnically homogenous regions and states. The making of modern India and Pakistan sent some twelve million people across borders as hundreds of thousands died. Israeli leaders were aware of these events and believed not only that their actions were justified but that they comprised but one component of a broader, and by the standards of the age, acceptable phenomenon.

Israelis perceived the war via Zionist optics, which magnified Jewish vulnerability and isolation but also focused on the new, heroic ideal-type of the native-born (or close to it) Israeli fighter. The native, the *sabra*, was alleged to be brave, even fearless, but also sensitive; simple and plain-spoken yet reflective and resourceful. He was simultaneously the antithesis

---

[25] Benny Morris's well-known work has scrupulously documented the balance of Isareli versus Arab armed forces in 1948. (See, most recently, *1948. A History of the First Arab–Israeli War*. New Haven: Yale University Press, 2008.) On Israeli access to armaments, and its ability to produce them, see Amitzur Ilan, *The Origin of the Arab–Israeli Arms Race: Arms, Embargo, Military Power and Decision in the 1948 Palestine War*. New York: New York University Press, 1996, 171–192. On diaspora, especially American, Jewish financial and military support for Israel in 1948, see Derek J. Penslar, "Rebels Without a Patron State: How Israel Financed the 1948 War," in *Purchasing Power: The Economics of Modern Jewish History*, ed. Rebecca Kobrin and Adam Teller. Philadelphia: University of Pennsylvania Press, 2015, 171–191.

[26] Ephraim Karsh, *Palestine Betrayed*. New Haven: Yale University Press, 2010. See also Hillel Cohen, *Army of Shadows: Palestinian Collaboration With Zionism, 1917–1948*. Berkeley: University of California Press, 2008.

and continuation of the disapora Jew, the native son to immigrant parents, the indigenized colonial on patrimonial soil. It was the task of his generation first to fight for the state's independence, and then to maintain it through what the founding father of the state, David Ben-Gurion, called "national missions." The newly born state sought to create something utterly new in Jewish history, yet at the same it bore the scars of the Holocaust and traces of a broader Jewish past.

STATEHOOD

The Israeli political system forged in 1949 was neither an individualist, Western democracy nor an authoritarian state. Procedurally, Israel was a parliamentary democracy, wherein the prime minister and the governing coalition controlled both the executive and legislative branches. Although interest-group politics are a fixture in any democracy, Israel was particularly fissured along ethnic, religious, economic, and ideological lines, and various communities (e.g., the kibbutz movements, urban workers, Orthodox Jews, Arabs) aggressively pursued collective interests via constant clashes within the country's political institutions. Israel quickly established an independent judiciary, yet like the pre-1948 Yishuv, the parliament (Knesset) was chosen by voting for parties and pre-set lists of candidates, not individuals, so there was no local representation. Aspiring politicos were co-opted into national machine politics, which drastically reduced opportunities for grass-roots activism. (Lively municipal politics certainly existed, but did not directly influence national policy.)

Also like the institutions of the Yishuv and the pre-1948 Jewish Agency, stable political rule was possible only in coalitions, most often between David Ben-Gurion's Mapai and smaller religious and middle-class parties. The religious parties exercised disproportionate influence on the government. In 1951, the National Religious Party (formerly Mizrachi) brought down the government over demands that Yemenite immigrant children be sent only to national-religious schools (as opposed to the "general" and "labor" educational streams).[27] Moreover, the secular government was obliged to grant rabbinical courts authority over marriage, divorce, burial, and the affirmation of an immigrant's Jewish identity. This last prerogative promoted a clash between the country's Law of Return (1950), which virtually guaranteed Israeli citizenship to anyone with at least one Jewish

---

[27] Zvi Zameret, *The Melting Pot in Israel. The Commission of Inquiry Concerning Education in the Immigrants During the Early Years of the State.* Albany, NY: State University of New York Press, 2002.

grandparent, and the rabbinate's insistence that a Jew could only be someone born to a Jewish mother, as per halachic norms.

Israel was hardly the only parliamentary state of the post-war era to blend religion with politics or to move from one coalition crisis to another. But it was unusual in that at the same time the government depended on small parties, while there was no effective opposition, no major competitor to Mapai that would force periodic power-switching as in many European countries. Minuscule Arab and Communist parties, ineffective liberals, the right-wing Herut party (successor to the Revisionists), and the left-socialist Mapam could not possibly mount an alternative to Mapai, which was brought down repeatedly during the 1950s but kept on forming governments. Cabinet ministries were doled out to coalition partners, who pursued their own interests, which often clashed with those of Mapai.

Another sign of Israel's compromised democracy was its failure to produce a comprehensive constitution, opting instead for a series of Basic Laws about specific institutions and principles. In 1949, Ben-Gurion and his ruling Mapai scuttled plans to compose a Western-style constitution, which would grant the judiciary the power to limit parliamentary authority. Moreover, a constitution, if truly based in the ideal of the equality of all citizens as enshrined in the state's declaration of independence, would have had to clarify the position of the state's Arab minority as well as the relationship between religion and state. Intriguingly, the right-wing Herut party, which was staunchly secular and, in a tradition going back to Jabotinsky, committed to guaranteeing individual rights to Arabs who were loyal to the state, championed the constitution. Similarly, in the early 1960s Herut opposed the continued subjection of most of Israel's Arabs to martial law, seeing it as an excess of state power and a denial of citizens' rights.

Israel in the 1950s was an imperfect democracy, but it also avoided the common, post-colonial practice of authoritarian, especially military, rule. The ruling authorities adhered generally to the rule of law and tolerated freedom of the press. (In one celebrated case in 1953, Ben-Gurion attempted to shut down a communist newspaper, only to be overruled by the courts.) Paradoxically, Israel never experienced a military coup although its society was steeped in militarism. Aside from the ultra-Orthodox, virtually all Israeli Jews performed compulsory military service. The army was the country's most revered institution, and its military and civilian functions were deeply intertwined. The army sent soldiers to found new settlements in border regions, and it played a powerful educational role for new immigrants. Throughout most of his thirteen years as prime minister (1948–53 and 1955–63), Ben-Gurion held the defense portfolio, thus blending defense and domestic policies. (Israel founded a civilian National Security

Council only in 1999.) Sociologist Uri Ben-Eliezer claims that the pervasiveness of the military and of military values in Israel, the army's prestige, and the intertwining of military and civilian affairs obviated the need for praetorian rule.[28] To use Gramscian language, in a society where the army was hegemonic, it did not need to display the brute force of a coup d'état.

To be sure, security concerns functioned like a forcefield that maintained cohesion among a highly fissiparous population. Not only did Israel avoid military rule, but it also suffered little of the internecine violence – political, religious, or ethnic – that has been common in the post-colonial world. Why, in 1948, did the Yishuv's sundry militias allow themselves to be forged into a single Israel Defense Force, despite the bitter acrimony that divided them? Why, when Herut leader Menachem Begin led an angry mob on the Knesset in 1952 to protest a reparations agreement with Germany, did Jerusalem not witness widespread rioting? Acts of extremist violence by Jews against other Jews surely occurred during the 1950s – e.g., in 1957 the Mapai functionary Rudolf Kastner was assassinated for his alleged collaboration with Nazi leaders in World War II. But for all the social discord and dysfunction that the young state experienced, a sense of collective fear, need, and fate, a sense forged by the Holocaust and maintained by Arab hostility, prevented the country from falling into outright civil war.

Solidarity among Israel's Jews was sorely tested by mass immigration that tripled the size of the country between 1948 and 1963. Half of the new immigrants came from Europe and half from the Middle East and North Africa. Veteran Israelis viewed the newcomers with a mixture of sympathy and derision – sympathy for their suffering at the hands of oppressors, derision for alleged psychic and cultural deficiencies. Even during the 1930s and World War II, Labor Zionist activists had debated the value of admitting into Palestine what they called "undesirable human material," undesirable for being bourgeois, or lacking strong bodies, fighting spirit, and a Zionist ethos.[29] After the war, new immigrants, and especially

---

[28] Consider the telling evaluation of Yishuv youth by Berl Katznelson in August 1934: "Their vocabulary of terms and concepts is military, whether relevant [to the matter at hand] or not. What is working inside of us is more than the idea, it is [the] terminology [of war]. The word 'war' drags along with it for us the idea of valour. And on the other hand the word 'agreement' is almost equated with cowardice; it awakens a feeling of unattractiveness." Cited in Hazan, *Metinut*, 15. See also Ben Eliezer, *The Making of Israeli Militarism*.

[29] On Zionist debates about selective versus open immigration, see Hava Eshkoli-Waman, *Ilem: Mapai le-nokhakh ha-Shoah, 1939–1942*. Jerusalem: Yad Ben Zvi, 1994; Yehiam Weitz, *Muda'ut ve-hoser 'onim: Mapai le-nokhah ha-Shoah, 1943–1945*. Jerusalem: Yad Ben Zvi, 1994; Aviva Halamish, *Be-merutz kaful neged ha-zeman: Mediniyut ha-'aliyah ha-tsiyonit bi-shenot ha-sheloshim*. Jerusalem: Yad Ben-Zvi, 2006.

Holocaust survivors, were called "human dust," a term reminiscent of the Russian "camp dust," used to describe those sent to the gulag. As Ben-Gurion wrote, "The diasporas that are being liquidated and are gathering in Israel do not yet constitute a people, but a motley crew and human dust, without language, without education, without roots, and without links to the tradition and vision of the nation."[30]

By the logic of this statement, Jews are not a people unless they are Israelis; nationalization demands indigenization. Nor do they have a language unless it is Hebrew. The tongues of the Diaspora – Yiddish, Ladino, Arabic, and more – were immediately to be given up, not to be lost or forgotten, but safely relegated to the realm of folklore, of the unrecoverable past. The government was only partially successful in its campaign against Yiddish, partly due to the sheer number of speakers of the language (who required, among other things, educational radio broadcasts in Yiddish), and partly because the ruling elite was itself Eastern European and could not help but respond warmly to the culture of their youth and extended families. (Levi Eshkol, prime minister between 1963 and 1969, prided himself on his command of Yiddish.) Arabic, however, the language of hundreds of thousands of immigrants from Yemen, Iraq, and the Maghreb, was considered as nothing else but the language of the enemy, and Arabic-speaking Jews were a source of considerable anxiety. Israeli educators saw the immigrants from the lands of Islam as hybrids whose Jewishness must be extracted from their Levantine qualities like diamonds encased in rock.[31]

The Zionist ethos of social engineering reached its pinnacle in the process of indigenization of the new immigrants. In 1950, a National Master Plan decreed that the country should be primarily urban and recommended establishing a network of small, self-contained cities ("development towns") complete with work sites and social services. The government also decided to set up in the country's periphery scores of new cooperative agricultural settlements (*moshavim*), where new immigrants could become

---

[30] Moshe Lissak, "Images of Immigrants: Stereotypes and Stigmata," in *David Ben-Gurion: Politics and Leadership in Israel*, ed. Ronald Zweig. London: Routledge, 2004, 236–349. On the mass immigration see Devora Hakohen, *Immigrants in Turmoil. Mass Immigration to Israel and its Repercussions in the 1950s and After*. Syracuse, NY: University of Syracuse Press, 2003.

[31] Derek J. Penslar, "Broadcast Orientalism: Representations of Mizrahi Jewry in Israeli Radio, 1948–1967," in *Orientalism and the Jews*, ed. Ivan Kalmar and Derek J. Penslar. Waltham, MA: Brandeis University Press, 2005, 182–200; Gil Eyal, *The Disenchantment of the Orient: Expertise in Arab Affairs and the Israeli State*. Stanford: Stanford University Press, 2006, Chapter 2.

sturdy tillers of the soil and establish a human bulwark against invasion from without.

None of these schemes, however, worked out as planned. The sheer number of immigrants almost bankrupted the country's fledgling economy. Transit camps – tent cities with primitive facilities – became sites of violent conflict between immigrants of different national origins. Black marketing flourished, immigrants fled the transit camps into the cities, and attempts by the government to restrict the immigrants' freedom of movement were often ineffective. The development towns quickly became shanty towns, and many of the moshavim collapsed. In the large cities, Jews of Middle Eastern origin were relegated to slums and quickly fell into a cycle of poverty.

Mass immigration and the enormous challenges of the transition from Yishuv to state profoundly transformed Zionism's social ethos. On the eve of statehood, the Yishuv was an enclave, barely a half million strong, ninety percent Ashkenazic, and dominated by the Zionist labor movement. It was sufffused with what was called "mobilized volunteerism" (*hitnadvut meguyeset*), an oxymoron that captured the spirit of autonomy and self-sacrifice that characterized the Yishuv's major institutions – the Histadrut trade union, the kibbutz movements, and the military. During the 1948 war, Ben-Gurion fused rival militias – the labor movement's Haganah, the right-wing Irgun, and far-right Lehi – into the Israel Defense Forces, and in early 1949, he dissolved the separate command structure of the Haganah's elite fighting force, the Palmah. Many in the Yishuv were bewildered and embittered by the weakening of intimate, autonomous associations at the hands of new institutions of state. Ben-Gurion now presented the state as the new locus of loyalty, and coined the term *mamlakhtiyut*, or statism, to describe this new ideal. The term "pioneering," which had previously been associated with agricultural settlement carried out by autonomous youth and kibbutz movements, now became the duty of all young citizens, and entailed a wide variety of what Ben-Gurion called "national tasks."[32] The Israeli state had trappings of authoritarianism. The Mapai-dominated government, for example, spied on rival parties during election campaigns,

---

[32] On the origins of *mamlakhtiyut* see the classic work of Mitchell Cohen, *Zion and State: Nation, Class and the Shaping of Modern Israel*. New York: Columbia University Press, 1992. Cohen's account has been supplemented by a good deal of recent Israeli literature, e.g., Avi Bareli, *Mapai be-reshit ha-atsma'ut 1948–1953*. Jerusalem: Yad Ben Zvi, 2007; Paula Kabalo, "Pioneering Discourse and the Shaping of an Israeli Citizen in the 1950s," *Jewish Social Studies* 15, no. 2 (2009): 82–110.

and during the years of economic rationing its functionaries were wont to burst into private homes to search for black-market contraband.[33]

But Israel was not the Soviet bloc, nor an Asian post-colonial dictatorship. Its founding leader fell from power not in a coup or purge but as a result of the mechanisms of a democratic regime and the popular will. In 1954, Israeli military intelligence botched an attempt to have Egyptian Jews plant bombs at British and American cultural institutions in order to give the appearance that Gamal Abdel Nasser's regime was unstable and thus prevent British withdrawal from the Suez Canal zone. In the ensuing scandal, Ben-Gurion became obsessed with protecting the good name of the army and so wished to fix the blame on one man alone, the defense minister, Pinchas Lavon. As Lavon gained allies among senior Mapai leaders like Eshkol and Golda Meir, Ben-Gurion's campaign grew increasingly desperate, and eventually both the Israeli press and his own party turned against him. Ben-Gurion resigned in 1963 and left Mapai altogether two years later.[34]

In general, post-colonial cultures of the 1950s and 60s valorized the collective, and Israel was no exception. Underpinning Israeli cultural collectivism was a remarkable level of economic equality; due to tight wage controls, professionals such as professors and physicians did not earn significantly more than skilled laborers.[35] But it also contained the seeds of rebellion. Activists within Mapai and across the political spectrum resented the party's hegemony. By the mid-1960s Israel had emerged fully from economic austerity and was beginning to enjoy affluence and, with it, increasing assertions of individuality. Professionals went on strike to demand higher wages. Mapai functionaries thundered impotently at what they called the "pursuit of luxury" by middle-class Israelis and the increasing popularity of private parties featuring boy–girl dancing as opposed to group folk-dancing.[36] Also in the mid 1960s, the first published works of the young Amos Oz and A. B. Yeshoshua delineated psychologically complex antiheros and underground men rather than stalwart pioneers.

[33] See the innovative monograph of Orit Rozin, *The Rise of the Individual in 1950s Israel.* Hanover, NH: University Press of New England, 2011.

[34] The best elucidation of the labyrinthine Lavon Affair is Shabtai Teveth, *Ben-Gurion's Spy. The Story of the Political Scandal That Shapes Modern Israel.* New York: Columbia University Press, 1996.

[35] Avi Bareli, "*Mamlakhtiyut*, Capitalism and Socialism During the 1950s in Israel," *The Journal of Israeli History* 26, no. 2 (2007): 201–227.

[36] Tom Segev, *1967: Israel, the War, and the Year that Transformed the Middle East.* New York: Metropolitan, 2007, Chapter 1.

At first glance, Israeli culture of the 1950s and 1960s appears to have broken radically with the Jewish past. Writers and poets distanced themselves from not only traditional Judaism but also the Diaspora, choosing to write about their local environment and phenomena with little precedent in Jewish life like the kibbutz or army. Biblical imagery was pervasive but harnessed to the cause of secular state-building. If one scratches beneath the surface, however, powerful religious currents emerge. Labor Zionist invocation of terms such as "redemption" and "prophetic vision" to describe the process of state-building, or calling the state of Israel "the Third Temple," suggest a desire to impute to Zionism a meta-political significance. Israeli Hebrew was replete with biblical and rabbinic words and phrases whose religious associations could not easily be discarded. Underneath secular Zionism's anti-clerical bluster was a dependence upon the rabbinic culture that many had hoped the Zionist project would supercede. Thus the state granted draft exemptions to yeshiva students, and it adopted the menorah, the candelabra of the ancient Hebrew tabernacle and temples, as the official symbol of the state. The Zionist Jacobins spoke the language of the *ancien régime*.

In turn, Orthodox Judaism was mobilized by Labor, which imbued it with the activist world view of pioneering and a militarized religious faith. At the time of Israel's temporary conquest of Sinai in 1956, the IDF's chief rabbi, Shlomo Goren, hailed "the combination of Bible and sword, of the cannon and Torah." "The machine gun and the spirit of Judaism," he wrote, "depend upon one another."[37] By the early 1960s, the youth movement of the National Religious Party had become considerably more militant than the party itself. Whereas the Yishuv's first Ashkenazic chief rabbi, Abraham Isaac Kook, had taught that the Jews would acquire Eretz Israel through the wars of Gentiles while themselves remaining at peace, Kook's son Zvi Yehuda began to argue as early as 1948 for the sacrality of Jewish armed force and saw Israel's wars as a necessary pre-condition for messianic redemption.[38] Israel's territorial conquests in 1967, especially of the old city of Jerusalem and the ancient Hebrew heartland of the West Bank, brought militance and territorial maximalism into the heart of Zionist Orthodoxy. Less than a year after the war, radical national-religious youth attempted to re-establish the Jewish community of Hebron, which had been partially

[37] Yona Hadari-Ramage, "War and Religiosity: The Sinai Campaign in Israeli Public Thought," in *Israel: The First Decade of Independence*, ed. S. Ilan Troen and Noah Lucas, 364.

[38] Elie Holzer, "Attitudes Towards the Use of Military Force in Ideological Currents of Religious Zionism," in *War and Peace in the Jewish Tradition*, ed. Lawrence Shiffman and Joel B. Wolowelsky. New York: Yeshiva University Press, 2007, 356–367.

destroyed, and its remnants evacuated, in 1929. Although this attempt failed, it did result in the founding of the settlement of Kiryat Arba on Hebron's outskirts, and in 1975 a knot of a hundred or so Jews won government support for permanent settlement in the heart of Hebron, a city of 40,000. The year before, national-religious youth, tired of their parents' moderation, had formed the Gush Emunim (bloc of the faithful), a pro-settlement and messianic movement that became a major force in Israeli politics.

For almost two millenia, the anchor of rabbinic Judaism had been what Heinrich Heine called the "portable homeland" of the Torah. Zionist Orthodoxy now identified itself fully, existentially, with territory. Even non-Zionist ultra-Orthodoxy was attracted to this new paradigm. From Israel's beginning, ultra-Orthodox Jews had accorded to the state a certain responsibility and respect for guaranteeing the sacrality of Jewish time (public observance of the Sabbath and holidays) and practice (granting the rabbinate control over matters of personal status such as marriage or burial). Now that the state had brought holy sites like the Western Wall, Rachel's Tomb near Bethlehem, and the Cave of the Patriarchs in Hebron under Jewish control, ultra-Orthodoxy came to include the custodianship of sacred Jewish space among its prime obligations. Although the Satmar Hasidim condemned the victory as the work of Satan, who wished to corrupt Jews with secular power, others, most notably the Lubavitcher Hasidim, began to interpret the war's outcome in outright messianic terms. Thus historic distinctions between Zionist Orthodoxy and non-Zionist ultra-Orthodoxy began to blur, as did those between Orthodoxy and the secular Zionist right, as both shared a commitment to territorial maximalism.[39] In 1977, when Menachem Begin's Likud party wrested control from Labor after thirty years of hegemony, the ultra-Orthodox Agudat Yisrael party entered the government coalition for the first time since 1952.

Although Begin's government vastly accelerated the pace of settlement expansion, the process began under the Labor governments of the period 1967–77, and most Israelis, regardless of political orientation or level of

---

[39] On the impact of the 1967 war on Israeli Orthodoxy, both Zionist and non-Zionist, see Aviezer Ravitzky, *Messianism, Zionism and Jewish Religious Radicalism*. Chicago: University of Chicago Press, 1996. On the settlement movement, see Gershom Gorenberg, *The Accidental Empire: Israel and the Birth of the Settlements, 1967–1977*. New York: Times Books, 2006; Idith Zertal and Akiva Eldar, *Lords of the Land: The War Over Israel's Settlements in the Occupied Territories, 1967–2007*. New York: Nation Books, 2007; Michael Feige, *Settling in the Hearts. Jewish Fundamentalism in the Occupied Territories*. Detroit: Wayne State University Press, 2009; and Gadi Taub, *The Settlers and the Struggle over the Meaning of Zionism*. New Haven: Yale University Press, 2010.

religious observance, favored retaining the territories. Much of the reasoning was based in security considerations, but for Labor's activist wing,
associated with the Ahdut Ha-Avodah political party and with the likes
of Yigal Allon and Yisrael Galilee, pioneering settlement was a cardinal
Zionist responsibility, and they had long championed expanding the state's
borders. Kibbutzniks in the Galilee were eager to found settlements in the
Golan, and the government established military outposts along the Jordan
Valley and in the Sinai Peninsula. The revolutionary élan of classic Labor
Zionism that had ossified during the transition from Yishuv to state now
was presented with an opportunity for revival.

The conquests of 1967 presented Israel with not only 25,000 square
miles of territory but also a million Arabs. This latter, unwelcome acquisition (Golda Meir spoke of Israel as wanting "the dowry without the bride")
further aggravated Israel's historic unease and uncertainty about how to
rule over its Arab minority. On this issue, unlike so many other aspects
of the Zionist project analyzed in this essay, there was no precedent in
Diaspora Jewish life or the post-biblical Jewish textual tradition. Decades
of violent antagonisms eviscerated earlier notions of Jewish–Arab consan-
guinity. Between 1948 and 1966, Israel's Arabs were considered a dangerous
national minority, and most were subject to martial law. Ironically, just
as the state dismantled the military administration and began to improve
the political status of Israel's Arabs, Israel occupied the West Bank and
Gaza and once more set up a military administration over a non-Jewish
population. The relationship between the Israeli state and the territories
became, on a small scale, that of a metropole and its colonies. The territories supplied inexpensive labor for Israeli industry (e.g., construction)
and menial service jobs, and the territories were, in turn, a captive market
for Israeli goods. Both Labor and Likud governments avoided annexing
the heavily populated West Bank and Gaza Strip. Formal incorporation
would have entailed granting citizenship to Arabs, thus endangering the
state's commitment, as expressed in its foundational declaration, both to
be a "Jewish state in the Land of Israel" and to ensure "complete equality
of social and political rights to all its inhabitants." Giving the occupation
the appearance of contingency (while cementing it ever deeper into the
bedrock of Israeli society and economy) made it possible to justify policy
entirely in terms of the needs of the moment as opposed to systematic
thinking about the state's obligations to a native population living under
military occupation.

Until the first Palestinian intifada of 1987, although Israel endured a
number of terrorist attacks, the occupation itself was not seriously challenged. The military ruthlessly suppressed unrest, and the security services
developed a network of informers and collaborators. Meanwhile, Israeli

military power was sufficient to hold Egypt at bay during a grueling war of attrition in the area of the Suez Canal (1967–70) and, in October of 1973, to hold off a Syrian-Egyptian full-scale attack and press forward with an audacious counter-attack. Israel invaded southern Lebanon in 1978 in order to stop Palestininian rocket fire upon Israel's northern towns, and in 1982 Israel launched a far more ambitious offensive, through which Defense Minister Ariel Sharon intended to rout the Palestine Liberation Organization from its Beirut headquarters and remake Lebanon into a Christian-dominated state at peace with Israel.

With each war, Israel wielded ever greater levels of force and firepower. In parallel, the two decades after 1967 brought Israel increasing prosperity, in part because of the territories, but largely due to rapid growth of an Israeli export market of textiles, medical devices, and military equipment. Yet the 1970s and 1980s brought a growing divergence between Israel's military and economic position, on the one hand, and, on the other, Israeli Jews' sense of collective control over their destiny. As the occupation of the Palestinian territories aroused increasing criticism of Israel from the international community, and Palestinian terrorism within Israel intensified, Israelis began to embrace traditional Jewish images of a "people that dwells alone," hated by Gentiles for no justified reasons, and faced with constant, existential threat. The more the Holocaust retreated in time, the larger it loomed in Israeli public life.

The Holocaust had been central to Israel's public culture since the state's founding, and the 1961 trial of Nazi war criminal Adolf Eichmann had moved Israelis to display greater empathy for the victims of the Nazi slaughter. But during the tenure of Menachem Begin, who had been personally scarred by the Holocaust and who remained haunted by it, the Shoah became a mandatory separate topic within Israel's Jewish history high school curriculum. In 1980, the Knesset officially integrated the Shoah into the 1953 state education law, and the Shoah became a separate category for the Israeli matriculation examinations in 1981. Begin himself justified Israel's invasion of Lebanon in 1982 with the claim that the only alternative to invasion was "Treblinka."

The Likud abandoned the Ben-Gurionist program of statist pioneering, just as Ben-Gurion had previously abandoned the Yishuv's paradigm of mobilized volunteerism. In an increasingly fissured country, memories of past genocide and anxiety over a future one served as a powerful, perhaps lone, unifying force. As we have seen, national-religious Jews increasingly privileged the land of Israel over the state of Israel. What's more, Mizraḥi Jews, whose political and cultural voice had been silenced under Labor hegemony, asserted themselves as a major source of support for the Likud (and, after 1984, as supporters of the ethno-religious political party, Shas).

Despite gradual social mobility, Mizraḥim remained among the most eco-nomically vulnerable Jews in the country, and so they favored populist economic policies. The Ashkenazic elite, on the other hand, engineered a massive shift from a social-democratic to a neo-liberal economic structure, beginning in the mid 1980s, when hyperinflation was tamed by privatizing state-owned industry and limiting the power of the trade unions. A sense of encirclement and of unremitting Arab hatred was apparently confirmed by the outbreak of the first Palestinian intifada in 1987 and by Iraqi missile attacks against central Israel during the 1991 Persian Gulf war. Israel was becoming a Western consumerist society but remained defined by its army, by the khaki of the soldier's uniform rather than the denim blue jeans of the civilian.[40]

Under Likud hegemony, Israel began to transform into a post-Zionist society. Classic Zionism's goals of collective regeneration – goals that had featured both leftist and rightist varieties – were slowly giving way to neo-liberal entrepreneurship, on the one hand, and meta-nationalist messian-ism, on the other. The former privileged the individual over the nation, and the latter the land over the state. Although Israel's character remained deeply Jewish in both its public culture and the private sensibility of the vast majority of its citizens, the state retreated from explicitly Zionist agen-das, except in the area of mass immigration, which it continued to organ-ize and welcome, as from Ethiopia and the former Soviet Union.

Ironically, the immigration during the 1990s of over one million Jews from the former Soviet Union testified to the ebbing of the Zionist project, as this was the first major immigration wave in the history of the Yishuv or Israel that was not pressured to slough off its diasporic language and culture and to become indigenized Hebrews. The "Russians," as they were known, proudly featured their own newspapers and political parties, and for many years Israeli television programs offered Russian subtitles.

The transition to a post-Zionist society during the 1990s was accelerated by three other, overlapping factors: the Labor party's return to power, the peace process with the Palestinians, and the rapid expansion of global invest-ment in Israeli business. Prime Minister Yitzhak Rabin was pragmatic, cold to the allure of the settlements, and, despite his well-earned reputation for hawkishness, eager to effect a sea-change in Israeli–Palestinian relations, as

[40] In *The Invention and Decline of Israeliness* (Berkeley and Los Angeles: University of California Press, 2001), Baruch Kimmerling writes of an ongoing "silent hegemony" of the state even as Israeli statist ideology has waned. On the replacement of a "republi-can" typology of Israeli citizenship with a liberal-individualist one, see Gershon Shafir and Yoav Peled, *Being Israeli: The Dynamics of Multiple Citizenship* (Cambridge, UK: Cambridge University Press, 2001).

embodied in the September 1993 signing of the Oslo accords. Diplomatic and economic normalization between Israel and many countries soon followed. Israel appeared to be on the verge of a brave new world in which it would be a fully accepted member of the international community, and not a quasi-pariah.

In this atmosphere, a cluster of intellectuals, mostly connected with Israel's universities, proclaimed themselves to be post-Zionists. The term "post-Zionism" was not new; Vladimir Jabotinsky's son Eri employed it in 1952, and a few Israeli intellectuals used it in the 1960s and 1970s. They meant the end of one era – that of the struggle for Jewish statehood and the ingathering of exiles – and the beginning of another, devoted to statecraft, the pursuit of national interests, and fostering the common good, economically and culturally. In its earlier form, "post-Zionism" looked upon the earlier Zionist era as a necessary precondition for the present, and it still assumed Jewish hegemony. In its new, 1990s manifestation post-Zionism criticized Zionism as a form of ethnic chauvinism and called for Israel to become a state of all its citizens in the spirit of Western liberal democracy.

In the decades that followed, post-Zionism continued to enjoy some currency among Israel's intellectual elites, but its justification shifted from hope for a new order rooted in Israeli–Palestinian peace to desperation over the failure of the Oslo peace process and the grim prospect of intractable and perpetual conflict. Throughout the 1990s, Jewish settlement in the occupied territories continued to expand, and both Jewish and Muslim radicals were determined to foil territorial compromise and national reconciliation. In 1995, Rabin was assassinated by a Jewish national-religious extremist. The following year, Islamicist suicide bombers wrought havoc on Israeli public buses. With the outbreak of a second intifadah in 2000, suicide bombings spread to cafes and public spaces throughout the country. In 2005, Israel withdrew its settlers and armed forces from the Gaza Strip, and in subsequent Palestine Authority elections the hegemonic Palestinian party Fatah was defeated by the radical Islamicist group Hamas, which took over Gaza. In the years that followed, Israel sustained frequent rocket atttacks from Gaza and from southern Lebanon (controlled by the Shiite Islamicist militia Hezbollah). It was also the brunt of threats of annihilation by the president of Iran, which appeared to be rapidly developing a nuclear bomb.

Fierce Israeli military actions preceded or responded to attacks from Gaza and Lebanon. Palestinians routinely attributed responsibility for military escalation entirely to Israel, and they, along with much of the international community, decried Israel's incursions into Gaza in December 2008/January 2009, November 2012, and July/August 2014. Most

Israeli Jews, however, were of the belief that the root of the conflict lay in neither the army's actions, nor in the ongoing settlement of Jews in the West Bank, but rather in Palestinian refusal to accept Israel as a Jewish state and insistence upon a right of return to Israel for the surviving Palestinian refugees from 1948 and their millions of descendants. Although in 2009 the Israeli prime minister cautiously accepted the principle of a negotiated two-state solution to the Israel–Palestine conflict, in practice separation from the Palestinians was implemented unilaterally through the construction of a barrier that in places extended deep into the West Bank and restricted Palestinian movement and access to their own lands. Only a small minority of Israeli Jews were enthusiastic supporters of the settlement enterprise in the West Bank, but most Israel Jews were unwilling to abandon support for hawkish or centrist parties based on this issue alone. A marked decline in suicide bombings in the center of the country caused people's concerns to shift more to economic issues, such as a skyrocketing cost of living and a widening income gap between the country's top decile of entrepreneurs and professionals, particularly in the flourishing high-technology sector, and the rest of the laboring population.

In the early twenty-first century, the clamor of the 1990s about post-Zionism as a fundamental rethinking of the nature of the Israeli state faded to a whisper. *Functionally*, however, Israel was very much a post-Zionist state in that it had lost its revolutionary élan, and no secular ideological force united and mobilized its society. The state remained profoundly Jewish, however – not only in its official symbols, language, and culture but also in its collective consciousness. Over previous generations, Israelis' sense of kinship with the Diaspora had faded, but paradoxically, Israelis increasingly displayed the sensibilities of Diaspora Jews, particularly regarding anxiety over their long-term security.

In addition to being a Jewish state, Israel was also a Western one in its democratic structure and protection of individual rights, including free speech and the expression of sexual orientation. Free speech, however, was threatened with erosion by legislation aimed at, among other targets, advocates of a boycott against goods manufactured in settlements, Arab communities or groups that observed Israel's Independence Day as the day of *al-naqba*, the Palestinian catastrophe, or dovish NGOs largely funded by foreign sources. Under the premiership of Benjamin Netanyahu, who as of 2016 was poised to surpass David Ben-Gurion's number of years at Israel's helm, the independence of the Israeli media became increasingly uncertain. Challenges to free speech had not, however, affected Israel's neo-liberal economic system and prosperity (Israel's gross domestic product per capita was slightly higher than that of Italy), and, most notably, its high-technology sector, which accounted for forty percent of the country's exports. Israel also featured among the greatest income disparities in the OECD between the top and bottom deciles, a function of the small size of the country's most productive economic sectors and the vast under-class of Arabs, ultra-Orthodox Jews and Mizraḥim. It was an increasingly diverse society, with hundreds of thousands of non-Jewish, foreign work-ers and, most recently, a growing population of refugees from Sudan and Eritrea. This diversity, on top of increasing numbers of Arabs amongst Israel's citizens (over twenty percent), placed pressures upon the country to become overtly multi-cultural, to transform itself from a Jewish state into what Bernard Avishai has called a Hebrew republic, united by democratic civic values and a Hebrew language that is more than an appendage to the Jewish cultural heritage.[41]

Israel's functional diversity received little legitimization from the coun-try's dominant nationalist and religious leadership, nor from the majority of Israel's Jewish citizens. In the second decade of the twenty-first century, Israeli Jewishness became increasingly ethnocentric. A new civics text-book for secondary schools emphasized Israel's Jewish character over its democratic obligations. African asylum seekers were targets of verbal and at times physical abuse. Tensions flared between Jewish and Palestinian citizens of Israel, and vigilante violence against Arabs in the West Bank became common. Almost half of Israeli Jews felt that ongoing Palestinian acts of terror justified removing Arabs from Israel proper.

The security environment alone did not necessarily account for these hardening views. The missile attacks and bus bombings of previous years had largely given way to random stabbings and car-rammings which, how-ever gruesome, did not cause large numbers of casualties. The occupation of the Palestinian territories, which was approaching its fiftieth anniver-sary, appeared to face no serious challenge from the international com-munity, and the collapse of Syria in the wake of the Arab Spring removed the last neighboring Arab state in a state of war with Israel. An impor-tant source of Israel's increasing ethnocentrism was an intensified public engagement with religion – the popular Hebrew neologism was *hadatah,* or "religionization."[42] It spoke to the general failure of classical Zionism to provide a viable system of beliefs and values in a world where secularism, liberalism, and democracy were in retreat. The resurgence of religiosity was a global phenomenon, yet specific parallels developed between Israel and the Arab Middle East, in particular regarding the concept of holy war. During the 2014 Gaza War, Col. Ofer Winter, commander of the IDF's

[41] Bernard Avishai, *The Hebrew Republic: How Secular Democracy and Global Enterprise Will Bring Israel Peace At Last.* New York: Houghton Mifflin Harcourt, 2008.
[42] Yoav Peled and Horit Peled are currently writing a book on this topic.

Givati Brigade, called for the IDF "to wipe out an enemy" who "curses and defames God."[43] At that time, some forty percent of the IDF's field commanders were Orthodox, and the military rabbinate played a growing role in soldiers' indoctrination.

Lines between anti-Zionist ultra-Orthodox and religious-Zionist Jews began to blur, and there was a slight but notable rise in the number of ultra-Orthodox males choosing to perform military service rather than seek an exemption in order to study in a yeshiva. Given that one in every four Israeli children entering kindergarten was ultra-Orthodox and the vast majority of other Israeli Jews were either Orthodox or somewhat observant, the religionization of Israeli society appeared likely to continue. Israel's transition from a statist-Zionist to an ethnoreligious polity was apparent in not only high politics but also popular culture, where religiously themed music became mainstream, and high-quality Israeli films and television programs, which had previously presented observant Jews in stereotypes, now took religiosity for granted as a component of normal life.[44]

Whether religious or secular, Israeli Jewishness, for all its myriad connections with the global Jewish past and present, retained unique features. Its vernacular language, Hebrew, was spoken fluently by few in the Jewish diaspora, and its high and popular culture were fully comprehensibile to fewer still. Israelis abroad formed distinct communities, tied loosely, if at all, to organized Jewish life. Israel's rhythms of life and forms of interpersonal interaction were less structured than in Western societies yet more intense than in other Middle Eastern lands. Israeli society was preternaturally energetic. Even by the standards of the United States, Israel's closest ally in sensibility as well as political interest, Israel was startlingly informal, anti-hierarchical, entrepreneurial, intellectually fecund, receptive to innovation, and prone to improvisation. These quintessentially Israeli qualities emerged from classical Zionism but were no longer dependent on a structuring ideology. Zionism as it had been known for a century passed from the stage of world history, but Israel had developed a post-Zionist dynamic of its own.

---

[43] www.haaretz.com/premium-1.628341 (November 25, 2014). Accessed November 7, 2016. Winter was subsequently promoted to Brigadier General and is currently the chief of operations for the Central Command, which is responsible military units in, among other places, the West Bank.

[44] See Yaron Peleg, *Directed By God: Jewishness in Contemporary Israeli Film and Television*. Austin: University of Texas Press, 2016.

SELECT BIBLIOGRAPHY

Almog, Oz. *The Sabra: The Creation of a New Jew.* Berkeley and Los Angeles: University of California Press, 2000.

Ben-Eliezer, Uri. *The Making of Israeli Militarism.* Bloomington: Indiana University Press, 1998.

Bernstein, Deborah, ed. *Pioneers and Homemakers: Jewish Women in Pre-State Israel.* Albany, NY: SUNY Press, 1992.

Cohen, Hillel. *Army of Shadows: Palestinian Collaboration with Zionism, 1917–1948.* Berkeley: University of California Press, 2008.

Cohen, Mitchell. *Zion and State: Nation, Class, and the Shaping of Modern Israel.* New York: Columbia University Press, 1992.

Gorenberg, Gershom. *The Accidental Empire. Israel and the Birth of the Settlements, 1967–77.* New York: Basic, 2006.

Harshav, Benjamin. *Language in Time of Revolution.* Berkeley and Los Angeles: University of California Press, 1993.

Helman, Anat. *Young Tel Aviv.* Waltham, MA: Brandeis University Press, 2011.

Horowitz, Dan and Moshe Lissak. *Origins of the Israeli Polity in Palestine.* Chicago: University of Chicago Press, 1978.

Kaplan, Eran and Derek Penslar, eds. *The Origins of the State of Israel 1882–1948: A Documentary History.* Madison: University of Wisconsin Press, 2011.

Kimmerling, Baruch, *The Invention and Decline of Israeliness.* Berkeley: University of California Press, 2001.

Lockman, Zachary. *Comrades and Enemies: Arab and Jewish Workers in Palestine, 1906–1948.* Berkeley: University of California Press, 1996.

Luz, Ehud. *Parallels Meet: Religion and Nationalism in the Early Zionist Movement, 1882–1904.* Philadelphia: Jewish Publication Society, 1993.

Morris, Benny. *The First Arab-Israeli War.* New Haven: Yale University Press, 2008.

Oren, Michael. *Six Days of War.* New York: Oxford University Press, 2002.

Peleg, Ilan and Dov Waxman. *Israel's Palestinians: The Conflict Within.* Cambridge, UK: Cambridge University Press, 2011.

Penslar, Derek J. *Israel in History. The Jewish State in Comparative Perspective.* London: Routledge, 2006.

Rivlin, Paul. *The Israeli Economy From the Foundation of the State Through the Twenty-First Century.* Cambridge, UK: Cambridge University Press, 2012.

Rogan, Eugene L. and Avi Shlaim, eds. *The War for Palestine: Rewriting the History of 1948.* Cambridge, UK: Cambridge University Press, 1988, 2001.

Rozin, Orit, *The Rise of the Individual in 1950s Israel.* Hanover, NH: University of New England Press, 2011.

Segev, Tom. *1949: The First Israelis.* New York: Free Press, 1985.

The Seventh Million. Israel and the Holocaust. New York: Hill & Wang, 1993.

One Palestine, Complete: Jews and Arabs under the British Mandate. New York: Metropolitan Books, 2000.

Shafir, Gershon. *Land, Labor and the Origins of the Israeli-Palestinian Conflict, 1882–1914.* Cambridge, UK: Cambridge University Press, 1988.

Shafir, Gershon and Yoav Peled. *Being Israeli: The Dynamics of Multiple Citizenship.* Cambridge, UK: Cambridge University Press, 2002.

Shapira, Anita. *Land and Power. The Zionist Resort to Force, 1881–1948.* New York: Oxford University Press, 1992.

Shimoni, Gideon. *The Zionist Ideology.* Waltham, MA: Brandeis University Press, 1998.

Shlaim, Avi and William Roger Louis, eds. *The 1967 Arab-Israeli War: Origins and Consequences.* Cambridge, UK: Cambridge University Press, 2012.

Stein, Kenneth. *The Land Question in Palestine, 1917–1939.* Chapel Hill: University of North Carolina Press, 1984.

Troen, S. Ilan. *Imagining Zion. Dreams, Designs and Realities in a Century of Zionist Settlement.* New Haven: Yale University Press, 2003.

Vital, David. *The Origins of Zionism.* Oxford: Clarendon Press, 1975; *Zionism: The Formative Years.* Oxford: Clarendon Press, 1982.

   Zionism: The Crucial Phase. Oxford: Clarendon Press, 1987.

Yablonka, Hannah. *State of Israel vs. Adolph Eichmann.* New York: New York University Press, 2004.

Zerubavel, Yael. *Recovered Roots: Collective Memory and the Making of Israeli National Tradition.* Chicago: University of Chicago Press, 1998.

PART II

EMANCIPATION: CHALLENGES AND CONSEQUENCES

CHAPTER 10

JEWS AND THE MODERN STATE

PIERRE BIRNBAUM

TRANSLATED BY SHAINA HAMMERMAN

In Jewish political tradition, it appears that the State does not represent a legitimate political body. Furthermore, the tradition seems to ignore crucial concepts of political theory, for Hebrew lacks the specific terms to evoke notions of citizenship, the public sphere, or civil society, which were elaborated upon in the Christian-European sector with the implementation of a separation between the public and the private. From this perspective, the process of making civil society autonomous vis-à-vis the State, its differentiation from institutionalized political power with regard to the Church, for example, belongs to a uniquely European story in which the Jews have no role. Jewish political tradition would remain shaped by the Covenant, which founded – ignoring citizenship as much as the notion of individualism – the "Community of Israel" (*Knesset Yisrael*). Instead, this tradition imagines a "civilized society" grounded in its own system of ethics that builds social ties.[1] It would largely ignore issues of society's secularization or the birth of a citizenship detached from identity. Likewise, Jewish political tradition would often stumble on the idea of liberal pluralism favorable to an extreme diversity of opinions and to the complete and legitimate presence of the Other, the very basis of the democratic process.

The question of Royalty is thus raised: if the Eternal is the king of Israel, what is the nature of this regime, which lacks specific political authority? When the Israelites implore Gideon to be their king, he answers them, "I will not rule over you myself, nor shall my son rule over you; the Lord alone shall rule over you" (Judges 8:23).[*] This absence of political authority, of a King or a dynasty, would not be without problems. For, "In those days there was no king in Israel; every man did as he pleased" (Judges 17:6). Suddenly, the elders neglect their own authority and demand of Samuel,

---

[*] Translator's note: All Bible quotations are taken from the JPS translation of the *TaNaKh* (Philadelphia: Jewish Publication Society, 1999).

[1] On these questions, see the opposing points of view of Suzanne Last Stone, Noam Zohar, and David Biale in Michael Walzer, ed., *Law, Politics and Morality in Judaism* (Princeton: Princeton University Press, 2006), 12–53.

"Therefore appoint a king for us, to govern us like all other nations ... We must have a king over us, that we may be like all the other nations: Let our king rule over us and go out at our head and fight our battles" (Samuel 8:5, 19–20). By abandoning the authority of their own elders, they thereby reclaim a monarchical regime as a means of political secularization. They form a dynasty that protects the people, anoint a king who takes on the functions of a judge, establish an authority grounded in itself to the great displeasure of the Eternal who can only observe, "it is not you that they have rejected; it is Me they have rejected as their king" (Samuel 8:7).

This questioning of the king's legitimacy as a moment of fostering political autonomy proved to be crucial, as it led to the institutionalization of the State. In exile, the royal question arose in a radically different context, at the hands of kings, emperors, and non-Jewish rulers. How can the legitimacy of a king be recognized if the Jews are to remain loyal to the King of kings? How far does submission to a foreign power extend in a situation of extreme political weakness, to the near exclusion of politics itself? Since Jeremiah's letter to the exiles from Babylon that encouraged them to recognize the king's legitimacy and to accept his "yoke," his protection, so as to "prosper," this politics of accommodation appeared as the price to pay against threats coming from below, from the people. It was enacted by the prophet Samuel according to the formula *dina-malkhuta dina*, the law of the land is the law – namely, the law of the king and not that of the people whom they always feared. This formula implies that the royal law is indeed the law to which Jews submit themselves as long as it presents itself in a universalist manner. It is by no means arbitrary or discriminatory, to the extent that it only concerns itself with civil or economic matters (*dinei mamonot*) and not with religious questions.

Such a distribution of rights and duties allows us to understand more easily why the Jews have always prayed for their kings. They follow the counsel of the prophet Jeremiah who wrote to the exiles in Babylon:

Thus spoke the Lord of Hosts, the God of Israel, to the whole community which I exiled from Jerusalem to Babylon: Build houses and live in them, plant gardens and eat their fruit ... seek the welfare of the city to which I have exiled you and pray to the Lord in its behalf (Jer. 29.4,7) ... I herewith deliver all these lands to My servant, King Nebuchadnezzar of Babylon ... give no heed to your prophets, augurs, dreamers, diviners, and sorcerers, who say to you, "Do not serve the king of Babylon." For they prophesy falsely to you ... "Put your necks under the yoke of the king of Babylon; serve him and his people and live!" (Jer. 27.6, 9–10, 12).

Exile thus demanded a strategy of complete submission to the king, his law, and his power, a necessary accommodation that must protect the Jews by establishing a vertical alliance with the State, a kind of secular covenant.

As Yosef Yerushalmi argues, it is preferable that the Jews, "remain in the hands of the kings of the Earth as they are servants of kings and not servants of servants."[2] In the modern period, it was Solomon ibn Verga who, in his *Shebet Yehudah*, had the greatest impact on this strategy of vertical alliance with the kings by deliberately closing his eyes to their hostile behavior toward Jews: in his eyes, despite evidence to the contrary, it was better to believe in a king's innocence and good will. For the king alone could save the Jews from popular antisemitic attacks – the fundamental hostility of the people at the origin of the pogroms – such as took place in Frankfurt in 1612. Of course, the King or Emperor's law was incapable of protecting the Jews during both the massacres at Lisbon in 1506 and the numerous pogroms that later erupted in the Russian Empire. The rise of absolutism nevertheless gave immense power to the State, which seemed to justify this alliance. The Jews' fear of the people remained overwhelming and their faith in the vertical alliance remained intact. Consent to foreign law before the law of the King of kings does not, however, go without saying. It is related to the birth of the modern state as an institution, which sometimes comes about in a context of intense centralization, undermining group autonomy. The *kahal*, the community that structured the lives of Jews in the Diaspora and which was supervised from below by "the virtuous men of the city," thereby lost a large part of its internal prerogatives. It abolished its own jurisprudence over the course of the process of emancipation, which liberated individuals from the weight of collective tradition. These States, even when they were immersed in Christian culture, claimed to be the representatives of the Enlightenment and to reject idolatry. Gradually becoming citizens, the Jews saw their destiny ruled more by common law than by halacha.

The scope of the law varied, however, depending upon the type of State. Jacob Katz's work espouses an evolutionary view of the State, resting primarily on the German model to analyze the passage from the ghetto to the State.[3] He presents this argument regardless of the fact that this State was largely controlled by the nobility, remained poorly institutionalized, and preserved its Christian nature, thereby denying Jews access to the public sphere. Contrary to Katz, it is important to address the question of the Jews and the State from a fundamentally comparative perspective.[4] This

---

[2] Yosef H. Yerushalmi, "Serviteurs des Rois et non serviteurs des serviteurs. Sur quelques aspects de l'histoire politique des Juifs," *Raisons politiques* 3, no. 7 (2002): 39. See Maurice Kriegel, "L'alliance royale, le mythe et le mythe du mythe," *Critique* (January–February 2000): 632–633.

[3] Jacob Katz, *Out of the Ghetto* (New York: Schocken Books, 1978).

[4] Pierre Birnbaum and Ira Katznelson, eds., *Paths of Emancipation: Jews, States, Citizenship* (Princeton: Princeton University Press, 1995).

approach alone will enable us to understand the reasons why common law became the norm for Jews in centralized France, whereas it impacted the Jews less in nineteenth-century Germany or the Russian and Austro-Hungarian empires in which particularly tight-knit, quasi-autonomous communities survived. These communities long preserved their specific laws and customs, just as we see today, paradoxically, within democratic societies such as Great Britain or the United States that are also fundamentally pluralistic. This approach alone poses the question of the Jewish relationship to the State in all its fullness: is the fate of the Jews more protected when a royal alliance works with the State? Or is the fate of Jews, on the other hand, fundamentally endangered when they have access to power rather than when they distance themselves from it, remaining nestled inside civil society?[5]

The intensity of their prayers to the king, the emperor, or even the State, illustrates the reality of the alliance that linked Jews to the State and which varied depending on the type of State. The example of France immediately comes to mind. It is there that we find the nation-state invented: it held a monopoly on lawful violence, was deeply centralized, rested on a powerful administration that it was able to maintain thanks to a considerable public treasury, put an end to Patrimonialism and limited political cronyism, had an autonomous civil service vis-à-vis the ruling classes, and imposed public order by preventing, through the use of force, any disturbances that threatened the majesty of the State. This manifestation of a nation-state stands out as an ideal ally for the Jews. Thus, in 1706, the Jews of Bordeaux prayed for Louis XIV:

Great God, Master of all that is visible and invisible, He who imprisons the Sea with his omnipotent word, He who seals the Abyss with his terrible Name … May He be the One who blesses, keeps, favors, helps, protects, saves, exalts, aggrandizes, and raises to the most luminous peak of happiness, Our Lord, King Louis XIV … May the sovereign King of kings protect him, defend him, and make him prosperous in peace, victories, trophies … and always ensure that his armies are victorious … O Eternal, God and Master, bend Your ears to our prayers by Your holy Name … Listen to our entreaty and blessed, magnified, and eternally raised be Your Name, Amen.[6]

---

[5] David Biale, *Power and Powerlessness in Jewish History: Jewish Tradition and the Myth of Passivity* (New York: Schocken Books, 1986). See also, Richard Cohen, "Jews and the State: The Historical Context," in *Jews and the State: Dangerous Alliances and the Perils of Privilege*, ed. Ezra Mendelsohn (Oxford: Oxford University Press, 2003), 3–16.

[6] Pierre Birnbaum, *Prier pour l'Etat* (Paris: Calmann-Lévy, 2005), 37. Prayers for the King may also be found in Ronald Schechter, *Obstinate Hebrews: Representations of Jews in France, 1715–1815* (Berkeley: University of California Press, 2003).

In 1744, the Jews of Metz likewise prayed to restore the health of Louis XV:

May You have compassion upon us, by sending a prompt, assured, and complete recovery to our very gracious King Louis XV, on his 248 parts as well as his membranes, his 365 veins as well as his muscles, for You are the very venerable healer as it is written in Psalm 103, verses 3, 4, and 5. You relieve every infirmity, You deliver the body from illness, You are crowned with grace and mercy ... Listen to our prayers, our sincere and abundant wailing, and grant our King Louis XV a long life, that his years accumulate one after another.[7]

In 1776, already envisioning Ernst Kantorowicz's beloved theory of the King's two bodies, the Jews of Paris exclaimed:

Please, O powerful God ... keep away every kind of illness and disease from the body of the King; his bones should be as a garden, reborn from the dew of Heaven. King of kings, by Your mercy, listen to the prayer of Your people who humbly persists in asking You to heal this Monarch.

These prayers are repeated in favor of each sovereign. Thus, when Louis XVI ascended to power, the Jews of Nancy sent out this prayer:

We cry out with all our might: Long live King Louis XVI ... in giving us this new king, the crown returns to its place on a beloved head and we recognize our duty to return to the path of righteousness and to merit Your high and mighty protection; let us bless him and cry aloud: Long live King Louis XVI.

It turns out that Louis XVI was the first in a project to reform the status of the Jews. He released them from a certain number of constraints under which they unjustly suffered. This action also quelled antisemitic hostilities that began in Alsace during the French Revolution, by justifying the love the Jews had for their absolutist ruler. The French Revolution at once abolished the monarchy and put an end to the royal alliance. From that point on, we find few prayers of this type: only Moshe Ensheim conceived of a prayer in the spirit of the Enlightenment that celebrated the end of the "despots" [*dominateurs*] and declared:

O Israel! For too long you have been persecuted by cruel intolerance ... Awaken to the ring of Liberty, the days of your happiness have arrived ... Let out a stream of thanksgiving, O my brothers; the sacred land on which we live has become our Homeland; the laws of the French Republic are also our laws; a holy alliance has placed us in the great family of free men.[8]

The French Revolution, deriving from the universalist Enlightenment, incessantly forced society to homogenize, challenged all forms of

---

[7] Birnbaum, *Prier*, 39.
[8] Birnbaum, *Prier*, 49.

particularism, and combatted the remnants of social and cultural plural-
ism by imposing a public sphere that was unfavorable to religion.[9] The
Revolution wanted particularistic groups to assimilate, whether they were
Britons, Occitans, or again, Jews. According to the words of Clermont
Tonnerre, "We must refuse everything to the Jews as a Nation, in the sense
of a corporate body, and accord everything to the Jews as individuals."
They disappeared as a nation only to be reborn as individuals. The Abbé
Grégoire, who fought for their emancipation, declared, "Let us bring them
closer to us, to our manners, let us open for them all the paths which
nurture talent and virtue, let us bind them to the State."[10] He did not
hesitate to invoke, "the guardianship of the state," in order to "blend"
the Jews into the "national masses," to "isolate" them in order to shatter
their communities. "Let us draw a plan," he said, "that encompasses every
detail and employ all our means."[11] It becomes clear that only the French
Strong State is able to implement such a centralized "plan."[*] The Jews of
Bordeaux, Avignon, or Paris welcomed such a unifying project, whereas
those from Metz wished, as citizens, to conserve their syndics,[**] preserving their communities. Their wishes would be ignored with the exception
of Mirabeau who declared: "every society is composed of smaller private
societies, each of which has its own distinctive principles ... When the
Christian or the circumcised – be it Jew or Muslim – diverge from one
another it is the great and noble job of the Government to ensure that
each of these divisions benefits the larger society."[12] Mirabeau, influenced
by Anglo-Saxon conceptions of pluralism, failed to implement this interpretation of emancipation.

As a zero sum game, the Jews were suddenly granted full citizenship on
September 27, 1791, and they benefited from all the rights that citizenship
confers: immediately, all across the land, they became voters and could
become elected officials. Common law imposed itself upon them in its
entirety; they were ordered to abandon their tribunals and their customs,

[9] Pierre Birnbaum, *The Idea of France* (New York: Hill and Wang, 2001).
[10] Abbé Grégoire, *Essai sur la régénération physique, morale et politique des Juifs* (Paris: Flammarion, 1989), 151.
[11] Abbé Grégoire, "Motion en faveur des Juifs," in *La Révolution française et l'émancipation des Juifs* 7 (Paris: EDHIS, 1968), 41.
[12] Mirabeau, "Sur Moses Mendelssohn, sur la Réforme Politique des Juifs" in *La Révolution française et l'émancipation des Juifs* 4, 84.
[*] Throughout the essay, the author uses the term *"Etat fort,"* translated here as "Strong State" to describe States which are centralized, strongly institutionalized, and differenti-ated (i.e., the separation of Church and State).
[**] Jews would likely refer to their syndics as *parnassim*, chairmen of the community.

to dissolve the legal forms that structured their community. On the other hand, they integrated into the nation-state and gained access to the offices of the State. *Dina de malkhuta dina* profoundly changed its meaning when the law became the law of the nation. From then on, it was no longer a question of submitting to the law of the Prince, thought to protect the people. Instead, they were forced to accept the protection of the nation, of the people they had feared since the dawn of time. Henceforth, prayers for the sovereign people were scarce. No one celebrated the virtues of Robespierre or Danton. The Jews extolled the ideals of the French Revolution, even though it put an end to the monarchy, which was once so revered.

In this manner, the Jews adhered to the spirit of the French Revolution that emancipated them, they committed themselves to the revolutionary State militias and behaved like devoted citizens, but they likewise later showed themselves, when Napoleon Bonaparte came to power, to be faithful servants of the new emperor. Chants, elegies, and hymns followed as proof of their love and endless devotion. They exceeded everyone else in their obsequiousness and submissiveness in celebrating the return of their traditional alliance with the State. In renouncing the achievements of the French Revolution, they recited the following prayer in the great synagogue on rue Sainte-Avoye:

So, O France, O my Homeland, ages ago you were drunk on the cup of bitterness: outside, the destructive terror spread its calamities; inside, terror reigned … a funeral shroud covered the altars.

Suddenly, Napoleon's star arises … He spreads justice and truth everywhere … from the gates of the orient to the setting sun, Napoleon's glory spreads; he commands with fairness, justice walks with him … the impious tremble at his side … O God! We raise our hands toward You, we fervently call upon You; That Your invincible arm protects him forever … that the rays of Your own glory shade his august head.[13]

At the same time, in Metz, sixty young girls dressed in white welcomed the Emperor by spreading flowers on his path while the Jews sang: "You cover us with your wings, you shall forever reign with justice and fairness … We bless you from the bottom of our hearts … We sing the praises of the Eternal! We praise Him with the lute and the harp! That He should multiply the precious days of the Emperor Napoleon." It would be impossible to list all their chants of joy and devotion. In a poem dedicated to the Emperor, they cry out again:

> But what do I see? O Zion, in solace you are reborn!
> Rise up, you are no longer captive and desolate!

[13] This prayer, along with those that follow, may be found in Pierre Birnbaum, *L'Aigle et la Synagogue: Napoléon, les Juifs et l'Etat* (Paris: Fayard, 2007), 208 and after. Prayers to the Emperor may also be found in Schechter, *Obstinate Hebrews*.

Come teach it to the land, to the empire of the seas
That Napoleon is the greatest of heroes.

This loyalty to the vertical alliance makes sense when we understand that Napoleon's reign was a time when the State was considerably
strengthened, it was the moment when its great administrations were
born – the prefectural body, the Grandes Ecoles – components of the State
that would further accentuate the strength it inherited from the absolutist regime. From then on, the law of the dreaded people became a distant memory and the Jews showed themselves to be reassured. However,
they were soon confronted by the violent antisemitic prejudices of the
Emperor. The influence of the Vicomte of Bonald and certain Catholic
reactionary members of his entourage unleashed his antisemitism. In
1806, he believed that the Jews "have replaced feudalism; they are a veritable flock of crows." In his eyes, "the evil that Jews do does not come
from individuals but from the very constitution of the people: they are
truly caterpillars, locusts who are ravaging France." In this sense, the
convening of the Sanhedrin quite simply aimed to put an end to collective Jewish identity by imposing specific, coercive measures that would
run counter to the universalism of the law. From that point on, they were
no longer considered citizens; they had first to prove, through the application of these unfair measures, including the "infamous decree," that
they were capable of becoming citizens. The Napoleonic moment in particular illustrates this expansion of State law. For example, in the domain
of marriage and divorce, the *get* (the religious Jewish bill of divorce) was
henceforth implemented according to the logic of the Civil Code, which
lent supremacy to court decisions.[14] Certain aspects of *dina de malkhuta
dina* were questioned for the first time by the Sanhedrin, which symbolized the nationalization [*l'étatisation*] of the Jews at the moment of
their entry into a particularly assimilationist modernity. Furthermore,
sensitive to the antisemitic prejudices of his entourage, the Emperor did
not hide his desire to abolish the "Orientalism" of the Jews, to reduce,
through the power of the State, their beliefs as well as their way of life by
destroying their specific sociality.

In this way, the stronger the State, the more it imposes its norms –
in the name of its universalist ideals or sometimes as a function of
the prejudices penetrating its institutions – on a nation of citizens
summoned to renounce their cultural identity. This is why, for many

[14] Charles Touati, "Le Grand Sanhédrin de 1807 et le droit rabbinique," in *Le Grand
Sanhédrin de Napoléon*, eds. Bernhard Blumenkranz and Albert Soboul (Paris:
Privat, 1979). See also Leo Landman, *Jewish Law in the Diaspora: Confrontation and
Accommodation* (New York: Schulsinger Bros., 1968).

commentators, the French model represents absolute evil because it pushes centralization to the extreme, reducing every form of cultural autonomy and increasingly driving religion into the private sphere, far away from the public sphere. From this perspective, the State, or rather, the citizen is marked by a kind of neutrality that excludes identity. Secularization – and soon, secularism itself [*la laïcité*] – incessantly emphasizes the exclusion of religion. Disappointed by such a policy, the Jews nevertheless continued to glorify the Emperor until the very end, to sing his praises, remaining ever faithful to the vertical alliance in spite of its limitations.

They remained faithful when the monarchy was restored, with the State upholding its dominant role. They revered the State once again even more fervently when it was embodied by a traditional monarch, for whom the vertical alliance again took on its full meaning. On January 21, 1815, they sent out the following prayer: "Yes, it was Louis XVI, it was his benevolent hands that laid the foundation stone on which the structure of our political regeneration is built ... This great prince, knowing that he is on earth as the first functionary of the King of kings, cast his paternal gaze over the scattered remnant of ancient Jacob." And they add, upon the death of Louis XVIII,

No, no, death has failed to stop for a single instant the reign of wisdom and gentleness. The fatal blow was barely struck when the reign was taken up once again by the illustrious brother of the prince whom we mourn, in the person of the august His Majesty Charles X, the beloved, the beneficent ... French Israelites! Beneath the shadow of a paternal government and under the aegis of just and protective laws, there are no excuses for those among us who stray from the path of honor ... we ask the King of kings that after the happiest of long lives, a Bourbon will always follow a Bourbon. This we request of the God of goodness, for the steadfast happiness of this beautiful France.

The vertical alliance thereby conserved its legitimacy with kings at the head of the Strong State and French Jews would adore in turn King Louis Philippe and Napoleon III. Thus, in August 1848, they composed the following supplication:

The raging winds proclaim the strength and power of God, the rumbling thunder announces His anger, the lightning shows His Majesty, and the surging waters proclaim His sublime acts ... People! Hail God. Praise the Eternal in your congregations. Louis Napoleon Bonaparte is the chosen elect in France where he resides, Heaven will support him in his ascent and his glory is everlasting for it is founded on justice and peace.[15]

---

[15] These two texts are cited in Birnbaum, *Prier*, 69 and 81.

Attached to the royal alliance, Jews in France were concerned about the consequences of democracy and therefore were unsure about the Revolution of 1848. Following the example of the eighteenth-century rabbi Ezekiel Landau, who passionately celebrated the merits of the Empress Maria Theresa of Austria, even though she was fiercely antisemitic, they often feared the reign of the sovereign people.[16] The birth of the French Third Republic, with its definitive installation of a parliamentary system controlled by the law of the people, unavoidably led to the weakening of these prayers, even though the Strong State remained. They continued to pray every Shabbat, of course, for the preservation of the French Republic. They celebrated the peace that protects governments, wishing for their leaders to receive divine guidance. However, with the disappearance of the royal alliance vis-à-vis the State, their adoration faded, especially during the Dreyfus Affair, which traumatized French Jewry. The State remained deaf to their concerns long before it finally defended them against the threat of pogroms, which, in 1848, became more and more likely. While the Affair concludes with the triumph of law and the captain's return to the army, a bitter taste remained for the Jews. Captain Dreyfus was the embodiment of these State Jews who, upon emerging from the Grandes Ecoles following a meritocratic recruitment, climbed to the very top of the State like so many other State Jews who became generals, prefects, deputies or ministers and even, briefly, head of the government.

France therefore embodies many aspects of this encounter between Jews and the modern State, differentiated and institutionalized. The stronger the State, the more it allowed Jews entry into its institutions. With the advent of this type of State, the Court Jews who formerly exercised a limited influence, such as the Pereires or the Foulds, saw themselves replaced by senior civil servants, numerous prefects, generals, judges in the Court of Cassation, and ministers whose legitimacy was such that they now acted on behalf of the State itself. This time, it was State Jews and not Court Jews who remained Ghetto Jews.[17] The influence of the latter is tied to the world of money. It is based on "the very personal relationship between the prince and the Court Jew, which rested on the complete trust of the

---

[16] Marc Saperstein, "Your Voice Like a Ram's Horn," *Themes and Texts in Traditional Jewish Preaching* (Cincinnati: Hebrew Union College Press, 1996). Saperstein emphasizes that, "any sovereign, no matter what the royal Policy toward the Jews, is preferable to the chaos. Not surprisingly, Landau is a royalist, not a democrat, in his political sympathies," 451. See also Landau's prayers for Emperor Joseph II in Marc Saperstein, *Jewish Preaching, 1200–1800* (New Haven: Yale University Press, 1992), 362.

[17] Pierre Birnbaum, *The Jews of the Republic* (Stanford: Stanford University Press, 1996).

prince and the complete loyalty and fidelity of the Court Jew."[18] In contrast, State Jews, coming from the bureaucratic meritocracy, exercised state power; they did not merely negotiate their influence in exchange for their financial services. Hannah Arendt failed to perceive this particularity of the French nation-state: her condemnation of French Jews' attitude during the Dreyfus Affair demonstrates that she did not take into account this specific bond that unites Jews to their State. She confused these State Jews with German Court Jews; she did not understand their loyalty, their profound attachment to this powerful, no longer Christian State, or the way they had distanced themselves from the world of money.[19] In reality, Court Jews do not have a true equivalent in France. The more the State is institutionalized and differentiated, the more the Jews reached the highest levels of meritocratic standards. Some of them came to embody the power of the State even if in their private lives they preserved their values and beliefs. We know that conversion is immensely less common in France precisely because state differentiation along with the establishment of a secular [laïc] public sphere enabled access to State offices without requiring conversion. In this sense, an interesting correlation emerges between the type of State and allegiance to a faith. If conversions are so numerous in Germany or Austria, it is because the public sphere remained closed to all Jews wishing to achieve full citizenship.

The triumph of the Strong State favored the Jews' rapid entry into the highest institutional levels. On the other hand, it also gave rise to a specific form of antisemitism that was a setback to the glory of the State. Political antisemitism, hatred of the "Jewish Republic," thus constitutes a new form of refusal of the Jewish presence that only appears in Strong State societies.[20] It is an unavoidable consequence within civil societies and even manages in certain circumstances to penetrate borders, undermining the supposed universalist function of the State. Thus, during the Dreyfus Affair, political antisemitism strangely manifested itself in official reports written by ministers themselves about the behavior of Jewish civil servants. Countless antisemitic expressions, until the time of Vichy, were scattered across the personnel files of State Jews.[21] In this respect, we find Vichy

[18] Selma Stern, *The Court Jew. A Contribution to the History of Absolutism in Europe* (New Brunswick: Transaction Books, 1985), 12. See Vivian Mann and Richard Cohen, *From Court Jews to the Rothschilds: Art, Patronage and Power, 1600–1800* (New York: Prestel Verlag, 1996).

[19] Hannah Arendt, *Origins of Totalitarianism* (New York: Schocken Books, 2004).

[20] Pierre Birnbaum, *Un mythe politique, "La République juive"* (Paris: Fayard, 1988), translated under the title *Antisemitism in France* (Oxford: Blackwell, 1992).

[21] Birnbaum, *The Jews of the Republic.*

before Vichy. When the State turned away from its mission, when it lost, during this period, its universalist calling, antisemitic prejudices increased and almost every civil servant of the State put himself entirely at the service of political antisemitism, thereby largely facilitating the politics of Nazi extermination.[22] In a stupefying paradox, the State – defeated by the war, having renounced its institutionalization and its differentiation – transformed itself, given its centralization, into an efficient ally of the Nazis. This time, help came from within society, from the anonymous Righteous Gentiles who saved the vast majority of French Jews who were being pursued by State police as well as its militias.[23]

Henceforth, French Jews distanced themselves somewhat from the State. To this day, with the restructuring of Europe undermining State privileges, with increasing globalization giving rise to an explosion of transnational exchanges, and with the long-term weakening of the State, French Jews follow the example of their non-Jewish compatriots: they seem to hesitate between their traditional strategies of vertical solidarity and the hope for a horizontal alliance by turning toward a society that rescued them.

If we apply this model of the State to other European societies or even to the United States, we can verify its potential by noting at the outset that in contemporary Western societies, Jews are no longer confronted with the same dilemmas. To this end, we hope to mention here some examples of societies from profoundly different types of States like Germany, Great Britain, and the United States, wherein Jews have been – for different reasons – long excluded from the State and were thus forced to remain within civil society.[24] Germany without a doubt represents the place *par excellence* where Court Jews managed – as a result of their financial resources – to exert real influence on those who held political power. These societies composed of multiple, powerful, autonomous States, barely distinguished

---

[22] Marc-Olivier Baruch, *Servir l'Etat français: l'administration en France de 1940 à 1944* (Paris: Fayard, 1997).

[23] Laurent Joly, *Vichy dans la "Solution finale"* (Paris: Grasset. 2006).

[24] It would be interesting to look at the example of independent Czechoslovakia in this pluralistic and powerful democratic logic. In the vein of S. Dubnow: "For the first time in European history ... the state made room for Jewish cultural and national self-expression without diminishing the value of emancipation." Hillel Kieval, *The Making of Czech Jewry. National Conflict and Jewish Society in Bohemia, 1870–1918* (Oxford: Oxford University Press, 1988), 191. In this manner, Czechoslovakia remains loyal to the spirit of the Habsburg State: "Habsburg Jewry never had the clarity of identity of Anglo-Saxon or French Jewry in the nineteenth and early twentieth century ... But in the sharing of a vast though amorphous cultural-political experience, it was as much there as the Habsburg state itself." William McCagg Jr, *A History of the Habsburg Jews, 1670–1918* (Bloomington: Indiana University Press, 1992), 223.

between the privileged classes and their Churches. The Junkers long wielded a decisive influence and the States remained profoundly marked by Christianity. If the Reich was a secularized State, we may consider de facto that Prussia was a Christian State. We may consequently understand the invention of the category of Court Jews as follows: from the eighteenth century to the beginning of the twentieth, from Abraham von Oppenheim to Gerson Bleichröder, they were known as figures whose importance was such that, until the Treaty of Versailles, they came to impose themselves on the political scene without necessarily belonging to the political or administrative worlds.[25] Even in Prussia, where we find a Strong State similar to France, endowed with a solid institutionalized bureaucracy, the Jews remained largely excluded, despite having obtained equal civil rights in 1812 and 1847. From then on, entry into the public sphere presupposed conversion, which contrary to the French example, affected them in large numbers.[26] In Prussia, despite new laws, no Jew was appointed to the State bureaucracy or the police. Between 1850 and 1858, no Jew was granted access to the Prussian Chamber of Deputies. Beginning in 1870, some Jews in Prussia became judges in the Duchy of Hesse, for example. But important positions such as president of the district or appeals courts were denied to Jews. They almost never became officers in the regular army to the extent that before 1918, there was not a single Jewish officer in the navy. More generally, Bismarck made it explicit that Jews must not enter into civil service. The same prejudices emerged in most of the States, although hostility toward Jews' entry into the administration was infinitely more acute in Prussia than in Bavaria, the two States where Jews mainly resided.

Higher education was slightly more open to them: in 1859 in Gottingen, Morris Abraham Stern became the first Jew appointed to the position of university professor in mathematics. Most Jews who entered the university taught almost exclusively scientific subjects; none were appointed a chair in German language or literature. In the same way, in nearly all the States, they were excluded from primary education, based on the principle of "Christian teachers for Christian pupils." Antisemitism was so widespread in the German States, particularly in Prussia and Bavaria, that Jews were

---

[25] Fritz Stern, *Gold and Iron. Bismarck, Bleichröder and the Building of the German Empire* (London: Allen and Unwin, 1977). On their equivalent in nineteenth-century Hungary, see the role of Court Bankers in William McCagg, Jr., *Jewish Nobles and Geniuses in Modern Hungary* (New York: Columbia University Press, 1972), chap. 3.

[26] There is considerable literature addressing this point. Recent examples include, Jonathan Hess, *Germans, Jews and the Claim of Modernity* (New Haven: Yale University Press, 2002) and Deborah Hertz, *How Jews Became Germans. The History of Conversion and Assimilation in Berlin* (New Haven: Yale University Press, 2007).

largely rejected by these Christian States.[27] The States appeared anxious to defend the Christian character of their public institutions. Furthermore, unlike in France, membership in the *Volk* – a notion long confused with the concept of shared origins – as opposed to membership in the citizenry, legitimated access to the public sphere. Consequently, again unlike France, as Peter Pulzer pointed out, in the German Empire from 1871 to 1918, "most branches of the public services, whether military or civil, [were] virtually barred to the unbaptized Jew."[28] Political positions within the Parliament were slightly more open to Jews, and between 1867 and 1878 sixteen non-converted Jews could be found in the Reichstag and thirty in the Landtage. Then, between 1881 and 1893, despite a surge in antisemitism and an insistent calling into question of liberalism, there were eleven Jews in the Reichstag and twelve in the Landtage. Finally, between 1893 and 1918, there were seventeen Jews in the Reichstag and forty-three in the Landtage.[29] Jews could no longer be found in the Prussian Landtage between 1886 and 1898. Before 1918, Morris Elstätter, in Baden, was the only non-converted Jew to enter the government of a German State.

German Jews also prayed beautifully for their Emperor, dedicating their prayers to him, writing poems glorifying him.[30] For all their reverence, it did not make them equal to others or grant them access to a State, which remained largely closed to them. Of course, the Emperor loved to surround himself with his "*Kaiserjuden.*" Jews such as Albert Balin, Max Warburg, or Walter Rathenau, heirs of the Court Jews, wielded a certain influence in the absence of State Jews in the French sense.

The war finally enabled Jews to access certain important politico-administrative functions, provoking an insurgence of antisemitism culminating later – after Balin's suicide in November 1918 – with the significant presence of Jews in the cabinet of revolutionary Berlin or with Kurt Eisner in Munich. Their notorious role in the political parties of Weimar

---

[27] See Ernest Hamburger, "Jews in Public Service Under the German Monarchy," *Leo Baeck Yearbook* 9 (1964): 223. See also Hamburger's remarkable study *Juden im öffentlichen Leben Deutschlands. Regierungsmitglieder, Beamten und Parlamentarier in der monarchischen Zeit, 1848-1918* (Tubingen: J.C.B. Mohr, 1968).

[28] Peter Pulzer, *Jews and the German State* (Oxford: Blackwell, 1992), 44, chaps. 2 and 3.

[29] See Ernest Hamburger, *Juden im öffentlichen Leben Deutschlands*, 252–253 and Jakob Toury, *Die politischen Orientierungen der Juden in Deutschland. Von Jena bis Weimar* (Tubingen: J.C.B Mohr, 1966), 351–354.

[30] At JTS in New York, a large number of Jewish prayers praising the German Emperor's glory may be found. For example, SHF 1869-1 p3 or (NS) PP 473. Upon the death of Emperor Wilhelm I in 1888, Moritz Levin delivered a sermon entitled, "A Messiah for our Times." Cited by Marc Saperstein, "Changes in the Modern Sermon," *The Encyclopedia of Judaism*, Vol. 5 (Leiden: Brill, 2004), 11n.

Germany – to such an extent that the SPD was renamed the *Judenpartei* – granted them access to important administrative functions at all levels of the State, including the judiciary. Rudolf Hilferding's appointment as Finance Minister or Walther Rathenau's role as Minister of Foreign Affairs, symbolized the Jews' rise to major political power. This fueled, as in France, a profound political antisemitism that rejected the Jews from a State that feared losing its Christian character. The antisemitism was marked by the sensational assassination of Rathenau in 1924, which represented "an assault on the new state as such."[31] In turn, the Weimar Republic was denounced as a "*Judenrepublik.*"[32]

Thus, the Jews' entry into the State provoked – in Germany just as in the Third and Fourth Republics of France – this same myth of a "Jewish Republic." The myth yet again brought about intense, collective, purely political antisemitic action that, even in the weaker German states, would lead to the mobilization of the Nazi party, which swept away this State on account of it being too weakly institutionalized. The Strong State of France, on the other hand, was able to resist the incredible antisemitic mobilization at the end of the nineteenth century. Hitler would have but one goal: to destroy the institutionalized Prussian State, this bureaucratic State that he hated all the more so when it became open to Jews. On behalf of a *Volk* whose profound identity would be negated by a State turned, as in France, toward universalism, Hitler was determined to destroy this State turned toward Reason and too favorable to Jews.[33] The vertical alliance with the State, in the specific context of the German path to modernity, provoked the most dramatic, radical consequences, going so far as to abolish a long Jewish history once rooted in civil society alone.

There were societies even more authoritarian than nineteenth-century Germany, where state differentiation never occurred and the aristocracy's fusion with the Church remained entirely intact. Jews in the Russian Empire, for example, prayed just as much for the health and magnificence of their Emperor regardless of how he persecuted them.[34] Despite their prayers, they remained excluded from the public sphere. Jewish life nevertheless persisted within civil society, in shtetls and yeshivot. Far from the State and, in general, far from every kind of assimilation, Jewish life

[31] Shulamit Volkov, *Germans, Jews and Antisemites* (Cambridge: Cambridge University Press, 2006), 293.

[32] Pulzer, *Jews and the German State*, 207 and after.

[33] Martin Broszat, *The Hitler State* (London: Longman, 1981). Pierre Birnbaum, *States and Collective Action: The European Experience* (Cambridge: Cambridge University Press, 1988), chap. 7.

[34] Michael Stanislawski, *Psalms for the Tsar* (New York: Yeshiva University Library, 1988).

flourished even though it regularly suffered the wrath of the antisemitic masses. The vertical alliance was not a pointless pursuit: it did not necessarily generate violent reactions threatening its existence. Only the birth of the Soviet Union, the emancipation of the Jews along with their presence in the State Party, provoked political antisemitism. Jews were faced with this antisemitism across the entire Soviet world, in the USSR as much as in Hungary or Poland.[35]

Paradoxically, the vertical alliance did not occur more often in Weak State Anglo-Saxon democracies. These pluralistic societies appeared favorable to legitimate Jewish life within civil society, but they were long dominated, from a cultural point a view, by a homogenous ruling class, an upper-class Protestant establishment that prevented state differentiation. The liberal path toward modernity prevailed in these Anglo-Saxon societies – where the market triumphed and capitalism inhibited the birth of the State – in the name of personal liberty that would be threatened by the Leviathan. Locke prevailed and with him the idea of democracy that was hostile to the Strong State in the French sense. Such a State was truly the bane of liberals who sought to protect political liberties while simultaneously protecting the law of the market. Jews, like their fellow citizens, following Ricardo, espoused the ideas of the market and economic liberalism. Their upward mobility unfolded via their involvement in civil society. Thus, Great Britain stands out as an example of a society from a State weakly institutionalized and differentiated, linked to the dominant class as much as to the Church. Similar to the Russian Empire, but for different reasons altogether, the Jews of Great Britain remained distant from political, social, and cultural power. There, they organized themselves collectively and maintained their traditions and their culture. They did so free from any intervention from the State which remained weak and respectful of cultural difference whether Scottish, working class, or Jewish. While French Jews entered into State power structures early on, abandoning all forms of collective auto-representation, British Jews – again, like the Scots – organized their own "parliament," the Board of Deputies, which maintained a dialogue with the central powers. Furthermore, the United Synagogue gathered all the different tendencies of British Jewry. There were so many functional, collective institutions in this pluralistic

[35] See, for example, Moshe Mishkinsky, "The Communist Party of Poland and the Jews," in *The Jews of Poland Between Two World Wars*, eds. Yisrael Gutman, Ezra Mendelsohn, Jehuda Reinharz and Chone Shmeruk (Hanover, NH: University Press of New England, 1989), 56–74; Victor Karady, "Les Juifs, la modernité et la tentation communiste: Esquisse d'une problématique d'histoire sociale," in *Le communisme et les élites en Europe centrale*, eds. Nicolas Bauquet and François Bacholier (Paris: PUF, 2006).

society that they counterbalanced the near eviction of Jews from the central powers.[36] British Jews prayed just as much as other Jews for the well-being of their King or Queen, but they never established an alliance with these rulers. In 1655, Manasseh ben Israel recited a "Prayer for the Head of the State,"

O most High God, to Thee I make my prayer, even to Thee, the God of our fathers ... Thou who by so many stupendous miracles didst bring Thy people out of Egypt ... graciously cause Thy holy influence to descend into the mind of the Prince (who for no private interest, or respect at all, but only out of commiseration for our affliction, hath inclined to protect and shelter us ...)[37]

They prayed with passion for the health and glory of their kings and queens, but the Jews remained excluded from avenues of politico-administrative power, even when Disraeli, a converted Jew, was appointed Prime Minister. Therefore, they had to wait until the beginning of the 1860s for some among them finally to gain access to the Parliament without having to take an oath to the Church.[38] At that time, Salomon, Saul Isaac, Lionel de Rothschild and his brothers, as well as Baron Henry of Worms entered into the House of Commons.[39] In general, very few Jews became MPs and even fewer became ministers; almost none of them entered into senior civil service, which remained a club reserved for the upper class of Eton or Oxford and Cambridge, elite scholarly institutions long shaped by Protestantism and from which the Jews remained largely excluded until the twentieth century. We must wait until the second half of the twentieth century in order to see a substantial number of Jews become politicians, in accordance with the logic of the Weak State, which followed the path of the market and not that of the State. Under the government of Margaret Thatcher, several Jews, also coming from the business world, were nominated to the Cabinet. In this way, the weakness of the State, at least comparatively, remains an indisputable fact, far from the temptation of the vertical alliance and the risk of rejection to which it sometimes leads.

[36] Eugene Black, *The Social Politics of Anglo-Jewry, 1880–1920* (Oxford: Blackwell, 1988), 38 and after. See also, Todd Endelman, *The Jews of Britain, 1656 to 2000* (Berkeley: University of California Press, 2002), 120 and after.

[37] Rev S. Singer, "The Earliest Jewish Prayers for the Sovereign," *Transactions (Jewish Historical Society of England)* 4 (1899): 105.

[38] M. C. N Salbstein, *The Emancipation of the Jews in Britain: The Question of the Admission of the Jews to Parliament, 1828–1860* (London: Littman Library, Associated University Press, 1982), chap. 12.

[39] Geoffrey Alderman, *The Jewish Community in British Politics* (Oxford: Clarendon Press, 1983), 25 and after. See also, from the same author, *Modern British Jewry* (Oxford: Clarendon Press, 1992), 62 and after.

The American example, in turn, demonstrates the importance of taking into account the variability of the State for Jewish history. There, the State also remained weakly institutionalized. Its bureaucracy long remained loosely structured, penetrated by partisan political cronyism. The State could not put the merit system into place where the spoil system reigned. Moreover, the Federated States preserved tremendous autonomy that also limited the strength of the federal State. Even if today certain authors challenge the notion that the American State was weak, from a comparative point of view, this fact is incontestable.[40] In place of the State, a WASP upper class from which Jews were rejected emerged over the course of centuries. From the very beginning, however, Jews knew how to find their place within this fundamentally pluralistic society without great difficulty. America was "home," inviting them to preserve their "hyphenated" personalities, cherished by thinkers like Mordecai Kaplan.[41] It was also American Jewry who collectively organized into a number of powerful, legitimate, and effective institutions or lobbies like the American Jewish Congress or the American Jewish Committee, networks of diverse and vibrant synagogues. They also integrated into civil society by entering into the liberal professions as much as the business world. On the other hand, their presence in politico-administrative service remained, until the mid-twentieth century, much more limited. When they prayed for the health of their rulers, they addressed less the State than the individuals they elected, whom they revered with greater moderation than the French or Germans did their rulers. Therefore, in August 1790, when the Jews of Newport welcomed President George Washington into their congregation, they declared:

Sir, permit the children of the stock of Abraham to approach you with the most cordial affection and esteem to your person and merit and to join with our fellow-citizens in welcoming you to Newport ... This so ample and extensive Federal Union whose base is philanthropy, mutual confidence and public virtue, we cannot but acknowledge to be the work of the Great God.[42]

---

[40] William Novack, "The Myth of the Weak American State," *American Historical Review* 113, no. 3 (2008): 752–772.

[41] Pierre Birnbaum, "The Missing Link: The State in Mordecai's Vision of Jewish History," *Jewish Social Studies* 12, no. 2 (2006): 64–72.

[42] Fritz Hirschfeld, *George Washington and the Jews* (Newark: University of Delaware Press, 2005), 35–36. See also, Jonathan Sarna, "Jewish Prayers for the U.S Government: A Study in the Liturgy of Politics and the Politics of Liturgy," in *Moral Problems of American Life: New Perspectives in Liturgical History*, eds. Karen Haltunen and Lewis Perry (Ithaca: Cornell University Press, 1998).

Almost entirely excluded up until the contemporary period from the State Department and a number of other central administrative offices in Washington, in the second half of the nineteenth century, just as many Jews were elected to the House of Representatives as the Senate. Many of them reached the level of state legislature as well: Jews were frequently elected in New York State as well as Michigan, Wisconsin, California, and even Alaska.[43] Others were elected mayors of large cities or governors, and a few Jews even became ambassadors, often to Turkey. Nearly excluded from the federal executive branch, they almost never reached the level of Cabinet: thus, from its beginnings until the Obama administration (2008–2016), we count only ten Jewish members of presidential Cabinets, most often as Secretaries of Education, Health, or Transportation. Oscar Salomon Strauss was named to the Cabinet by President Theodore Roosevelt in 1906. Later, Henry Morgenthau Jr., Lewis Strauss, Arthur Goldberg, Abraham Ribicoff, Wilbur Cohen, Henry Kissinger, James Schlesinger, Edward Levi and finally, Michael Blumenthal were appointed in turns to the Cabinet. This means that their presence at the top tiers of the State remained quite limited and appeared only in the second half of the twentieth century.[44]

Present in small numbers in congressional politics, especially in New York as well as at the local level, largely absent from the federal government, the Jews' access to power in this Weak State society materialized through judiciary power – the Supreme Court – a veritable substitute for the State. In the United States, the State acts less by its own devices and more by virtue of the federal courts, particularly the Supreme Court, that is to say the articulation of the law with respect to the Constitution.[45] Until the contemporary period and in accordance with their long history of praying for the State, of relying on it, American Jews showed themselves to have by far the most confidence in the virtues of the Supreme Court as a veritable substitute for the State. They were similarly confident in the

---

[43] Hugo Bieber, "Jews in Public Office," in *The Hebrew Impact on Western Civilization*, ed. Dagobert Runes (New York: Philosophical Library, 1951), 119. Also see the lists provided each year in the *American Jewish Year Book*.

[44] Stephen Isaac, *Jews and American Politics* (New York: Doubleday and Company, 1974), 60.

[45] Ira Katznelson and Ken Prewitt, "Constitution, Class and the Limits of Choice in US Foreign Policy," in *Capitalism and the State in US-Latin American Relations*, ed. R. Fagen (Stanford: Stanford University Press, 1979). See also, Stephen Skowroneck, *Building A New American State: The Expansion of National Administrative Capacities in Nineteenth-Century America* (Cambridge: Cambridge University Press, 1982); Reuel Schiller, "Saint George and the Dragon: Courts and the Development of the Administrative State in Twentieth-century America," *Journal of Policy History* 17, no. 1 (2005): 110–124.

virtues of the executive branch, whereas their confidence in the acts of Congress was far more limited.

In reality, access to the Court is part of a larger process of entry into the legal realm, whether as lawyers or judges. Does this royal road toward the upper classes, but also toward assimilation, almost always presuppose "a journey from Torah to Constitution"? Or, as Sanford Levinson notes, does it assume the fusion of the Torah and the Constitution as sacred texts of the Judeo-American legal tradition, which underline the biblical origins of the rule of American law?[46] In a Weak State society, the legal professions almost serve as a substitute for centralized political order: they oversee political tactics, regulate access to parties and lobbies, serve as a gateway to local and national elected office as well as the most prestigious positions in major companies. Like their fellow citizens, the Jews conceived of their upward social mobility in this privileged framework; legions became lawyers, attorneys, and especially judges at different levels of the states' judiciary organizations – from their appellate courts to their superior courts and finally to the United States Court of Appeals and the Supreme Court where eight Jews have sat between 1916 (Louis Brandeis) and 2010 (Elena Kagan). These numbers are all the more important today when three Jews sit together on the Supreme Court. Alone, they account for one third of the appointed judges, while Protestant judges coming from the WASP class have disappeared. In this way, in a Weak State society, these Supreme Court Jews may be understood as equivalent to the State Jews of France.

Appointed at successive steps of the progressive strengthening of the State – from the New Deal to Johnson's presidency to that of Barack Obama – can these few Jews be associated with the growth of the State? In particular, can they be associated with a State rejected by a society that fears its Christian nature being called into question by the institutionalization of a differentiated structure – as they were in France under the Third Republic or Germany during the Weimar Republic? A society that at the same time is not afraid of incessantly spreading secularization by attacking the presence of religion, prohibiting prayer or Bible study in public school? The Jews' sudden visibility is all the more striking when we consider that between 1964 and 2006 the number of Jewish Congressmen and women jumped from seventeen to forty-three, by far the most significant increase proportionally, even when compared to Catholics, who rose from 109 members to 155. These numbers are even more spectacular when we consider, to the contrary, the sharp decline in Episcopalians (from 68 to 37),

---

[46] Jerold Auerbach, *Rabbis and Lawyers: The Journey from Torah to Constitution* (Bloomington: Indiana University Press, 1990), XVII–XIX. Sanford Levinson, "Who is a Jew(ish) Justice)?," *Cardozo Law Review* 10 (1989): 2368.

Methodists (from 95 to 37), and Presbyterians (75 to 43).[47] Could a purely political antisemitism materialize, for example, from within the populist Tea Party movement or other extremist organizations, as a means to reject the Jewish presence within the political elite or the Supreme Court? Could it be that the variability of the State to which the Jews have long linked their fate, will yet again generate identical forms of rejection?[48] Could it be that the "encounter" between the Jews and the State, their access to power, revealed itself to be, for profoundly different reasons, as perilous in the Diaspora as in Israel?[49] Could it be that the Jewish State – for the first time in modernity possessing a monopoly on lawful violence, its very existence contested – is in some way, as in the Diaspora, the mythical "Jewish Republic"? In this respect, today, the increasing proximity of the Jews in the Diaspora and the Israeli nation-state to positions of State power, once again poses the risk of generating myths that may in turn spread political antisemitism.[50]

SELECT BIBLIOGRAPHY

Birnbaum, Pierre. *Les deux maisons. Essai sur la citoyenneté des Juifs en France et aux Etats Unis*. Paris: Gallimard. 2012.

Dubin, Lois. "Yosef Hayim Yerushalmi, The Royal Alliance, and Jewish Political Theory," *Jewish History* 28 (2014): 51–81.

Silber, Michael. "From Tolerated Aliens to Citizens-Soldiers. Jewish Military Service in the Era of Joseph II," in *Constructing Nationalities in East Central Europe*. Edited by Pieter Judson and Marsha Rozenblit, New York: Bergham, 2004.

Vital, David. "Power, Powerlessness and the Jews," *Commentary* 89 (1990), 23–28.

Volkov, Shulamit. *Walther Rathenau: Weimar's Fallen Statesman*. New Haven: Yale University Press, 2012.

[47] Cited in Henry Feingold, *Jewish Power in America: Myth and Reality* (New Brunswick: Transaction Books, 2008), 5.

[48] Office of Intelligence and Analysis. April 7, 2009, "Rightwing Extremism: Current Economic and Political Climate Fueling Resurgence in Radicalization and Recruitment," 4. In the same vein, see Chip Berlet, *Toxic to Democracy: Conspiracy Theories, Demonizing and Scapegoating* (Somerville, MA: Publication of Political Research Associates, 2009).

[49] Benjamin Ginsberg, *The Fatal Embrace: Jews and the State* (Chicago: University of Chicago Press, 1993).

[50] Ezra Mendelsohn, *On Modern Jewish Politics* (Oxford: Oxford University Press, 1993), 144.

CHAPTER II

ASSIMILATION AND ASSIMILATIONISM

TODD M. ENDELMAN

The term *assimilation*, when used in the narration and analysis of modern Jewish history, is problematic. In both historical writing and public debate, its use – without modification or interrogation – obscures as much as it clarifies the ways in which Jews responded to new circumstances in the nineteenth and twentieth centuries. Part of its problematic character arises from its elasticity and lack of clarity – its invocation to describe both a process of social and cultural transformation and an ideological program endorsing and promoting that process. In common parlance and in historical scholarship, the term *assimilation* is simultaneously descriptive – what happened – and prescriptive – what should happen – that is, what Jews should work to achieve. One way to circumvent this ambiguity is to turn to a derivative term, *assimilationism*, to distinguish the program from the process. Jews who envisioned closer Jewish involvement in Gentile society and created programs and institutions to make this happen are frequently described, for example, as *assimilationists* and their ideological stance as *assimilationist* (in contradistinction to their traditionalist and nationalist opponents – the Orthodox, Zionist, and Yiddishist camps).

Making a distinction between *assimilation* as process and *assimilationism* as project fails, however, to address the heart of the problem. The term *assimilation* itself has been so embedded in intra-communal debate and apologetic writing that its value as a neutral term of historical analysis has been compromised. It cannot be extricated from the historical and discursive circumstances in which it arose, and it is burdened with too much emotional and ideological baggage to serve as a useful conceptual tool. In the age of emancipation (1789–1871), the term carried a positive valence. Jewish spokesmen, optimistic about Judaism's future in the modern world, viewed *assimilation* as a praiseworthy, desirable, and necessary adjustment to new circumstances. But when emancipation was attacked and undermined toward the end of the century, it became a contested term. For the Zionist and Orthodox camps, who believed that Jews had surrendered too much of their distinctiveness when they embraced modernity, the term referred to a program that was, in their view, misbegotten and bankrupt. Meanwhile, their opponents continued to view it positively. No camp, however, bothered to clarify what exactly it meant when it referred to *assimilation*. Each party envisioned a different Jewish future, but their visions were vague and ill-defined, usually failing to specify the parameters of acceptable and unacceptable adjustment.[1]

To neutralize the ideological overtones and analytical imprecision of the term *assimilation*, I want to treat the changes to which it refers as three analytically distinct but connected processes: acculturation, integration, and secularization. Deferring for now a systematic exposition of their meaning and relationship to each other, I want to offer at this point concise, working definitions. Acculturation refers to the acquisition by Jews of the habits, values, and behaviors of the dominant non-Jewish group. Integration refers to the entry of Jews into non-Jewish social circles, institutions, and spheres of activity. Secularization refers to the rejection of Jewish religious beliefs (indeed, any religious beliefs) and the obligations and practices that flow from these beliefs. In each case, the term describes a process of transformation in which "tradition" wanes and even vanishes. Fueling these transformations in Jewish life were large-scale transformations in the structure, organization, and outlook of state and society more generally from the mid-seventeenth century to the mid-twentieth century – what historians term the demographic, industrial, democratic, and scientific revolutions. By placing the transformation of the Jews within the context of the modernization of Western societies in this way, I seek to emphasize that acculturation, integration, and secularization were not rooted in self-conscious ideological choices that Jews *qua* Jews made but were linked rather to broader forces of socio-economic change. These processes and their outcomes were not inevitable – few things in history are – but for most Jews they were unavoidable, even, as I will show, for those who continued to believe they were loyal to tradition.

ACCULTURATION

In early modern Europe, Ashkenazi Jews were set apart from their neighbors by a variety of markers. They spoke a Jewish language (Yiddish), wore distinctive dress, followed the Jewish calendar, studied only Jewish texts, observed dietary practices that hindered intimate socialization with Christians, worked in a narrow range of trades, and shunned the entertainments and recreations of their neighbors. However familiar they were with

[1] Todd M. Endelman, "Jewish Self-Identification and West European Categories of Belonging: From the Enlightenment to World War II," in *Religion or Ethnicity? Jewish Identities in Evolution*, ed. Zvi Gitelman (New Brunswick, NJ: Rutgers University Press, 2009), 108–111.

the customs of those around them, they chose not to imitate them, for nothing had occurred to disturb their confidence in the superiority and appropriateness of their way of life.

In Western and Central Europe, this began to change, even if in a slow piecemeal way, before any substantive shift in Jewish political status. In the German states, for example, Court Jews (*Hofjuden*) began to model their comportment, dress, and households along aristocratic lines. The wealth they accumulated in the service of the German princes (as mint masters, financial agents, tax farmers, military contractors, and suppliers of luxury goods) and their close contact with courtly circles encouraged them to adopt new ways of living. With fortunes whose size was hitherto unknown in Ashkenazi society, they built elegantly furnished palatial residences with costly gardens. They dressed according to the fashion of the time, replacing long, unadorned sober garments and skull-caps with silk and velvet frock coats, lace, and powdered wigs. Their beards shrank or vanished completely. They commissioned portraits of themselves and their wives and collected paintings, manuscripts, *objets d'art*, and books. Joseph Oppenheimer (1698/99–1738), widely known as Jud Süss, court factor to Duke Karl of Württemberg, owned over 4,000 engravings, in addition to collections of porcelain, paintings, and books. He and other *Hofjuden* rode in horse-drawn carriages, attended by liveried servants, and appeared in the streets with walking sticks, swords, and pistols.[2] While exempt from the most humiliating anti-Jewish measures by virtue of their privileged position, they were in no sense "emancipated"; they enjoyed privileges, bestowed on them by the princes they served, rather than rights guaranteed in law. Moreover, this kind of acculturation was no more than skin-deep. It was cosmetic and decorative, rather than a register of waning faith. The first generation or two of Court Jews remained firmly within the Jewish fold, marrying their children to the offspring of other Court Jews, defending Jewish interests, founding new communities, and generally observing traditional pieties. They were not integrated into the social fabric of Christian society, thought of themselves as Jews first and foremost, and remained aliens and outsiders.

---

[2] Richard I. Cohen and Vivian B. Mann, "Melding Worlds: Court Jews and the Arts of the Baroque," in *From Court Jews to the Rothschilds: Art, Patronage, and Power, 1600–1800*, eds. Vivian B. Mann and Richard I. Cohen (Munich: Prestel, 1996); Mordechai Breuer, "The Court Jews," in *German-Jewish History in Modern Times*, vol. 1, *Tradition and Enlightenment, 1600–1780*, ed. Michael A. Meyer (New York: Columbia University Press, 1996); Selma Stern, *The Court Jew: A Contribution to the History of the Period of Absolutism in Central Europe*, trans. Ralph Weiman (Philadelphia: Jewish Publication Society, 1950).

In the eighteenth century, this kind of cosmetic acculturation spread within the Ashkenazi world beyond the *Hofjuden* of Central Europe. As the pace of economic life quickened with the expansion of overseas commerce and financial markets, a Jewish *haute bourgeoisie* grew up in Europe's flourishing port cities – London, Amsterdam, Hamburg, and Trieste. Well-to-do urban Jews, whose fortunes owed more to the market than the patronage of princes, embraced ways of living that departed from earlier patterns. In London, for example, wealthy brokers and merchants purchased country homes, kept mistresses, assembled art collections, and entertained on a lavish scale. Their attire and their furnishings were *à la mode*. They provided their children with both a secular and religious education and found new ways to amuse themselves, visiting concert halls and theaters, taking the water at spas, and socializing in coffee houses and cafes.[3] Their attraction to what were initially Gentile pleasures was a function, in part, of their prosperity, but it also was a consequence of their settlement in bustling, expansive urban centers, where Jewish communal autonomy and rabbinic authority were weak or non-existent (as in the English case) and where social relations between Jews and Christians were freer. Behavior that was impossible in a market town or a village became possible in the metropolis. The growth of truly urban Jewish communities, of which there were few in Europe before the nineteenth century, encouraged individual autonomy and unconventional behavior. Significantly, these changes in Jewish behavior took place independently of the growth of the Haskalah, the first ideological movement that aimed to broaden the cultural and social horizons of Ashkenazi Jewry. The Haskalah took shape only in the second half of the eighteenth century (after acculturation was well under way) and was weaker in West European cities like London and Amsterdam than in Central European cities like Berlin, Vienna, and Frankfurt, where acculturation was less visible at this time.

In these port cities, acculturation was not confined to the very wealthy, although their behavior was more likely to attract public comment. Urban life also encouraged closer contact between poor Jews and Christians, who everywhere were the majority. In London and Amsterdam, especially, the Jewish lower classes selectively absorbed the habits of their immediate non-Jewish neighbors, among whom they lived on physically close terms in neighborhoods whose population was mixed rather than predominantly Jewish. Jews and Christians jostled each other in the streets, where much of the business of daily life was conducted, in taverns, at fairs, and in open spaces. In these circumstances, Jewish street traders acquired the language,

[3] Todd M. Endelman, *The Jews of Georgian England, 1714–1830: Tradition and Change in a Liberal Society*, 2nd ed. (Ann Arbor, MI: University of Michigan Press, 1999), chap. 4.

dress, and some habits of their neighbors. In London, for example, poor Jews accepted as normal the frequent recourse to physical violence that was common among their neighbors. Quarrels between Jews and Christians often ended in street brawls. Angry Jews settled disputes with other Jews with their fists – as in 1811, when a man whose Sabbath dish was cooking in a bakery oven physically attacked the baker when he refused to remove the seals that a rabbi had placed on the oven just before sundown to prevent customers from desecrating the Sabbath. The most conspicuous example of Jewish acculturation in London, among rich and poor, was a new-found enthusiasm for prizefighting, as spectators, sponsors, and participants. From the 1760s through the 1820s, at least thirty Jews distinguished themselves in the ring, including the greatest boxer of the period Daniel Mendoza (1763–1836), who was credited by early historians of the sport with introducing a more "scientific" style of boxing (one that emphasized finesse and agility, rather than brute strength).[4] Acculturation among the Jewish poor was, however, selective rather than wholesale. Drunkenness, for example, while not absent, was never widespread (whereas it was a plague among the poor more generally). While critics of the Jews often wrote about Jewish sharpers and toughs they almost never mentioned Jewish drunks.

Guidelines for understanding the process of Jewish acculturation elsewhere and later in the modern period emerge from this brief review of its earliest manifestations. First, acculturation was a selective process. Even Jews whose acculturation was so advanced that they appeared indistinguishable from non-Jews of the same socio-economic status continued to behave in ways that set them apart. For example, in late-imperial Germany, upper-middle-class urban Jews, while not distinctive in regard to externals like dress and language, preserved habits peculiar to their own group within the intimacy of domestic life. Their marital and fertility patterns (family size, age at marriage, infant mortality), levels of personal hygiene, anxiety about and support for their children's education, reading habits, and political loyalties set them apart from their non-Jewish peers. They may have thought that they had exchanged their Jewishness for Germanness, but in those intimate domains in which individuals express their hopes, fears, expectations, and anxieties, they remained distinctive.[5]

Second, the reference group for Jewish acculturation – the group whose customs, habits, tastes, and values were esteemed and borrowed – varied with the socio-economic status of the particular Jewish group and, in the

---

[4] Endelman, *The Jews of Georgian England*, chap. 6.
[5] Shulamit Volkov, *Antisemitismus als Kultureller Code: Zehn Essays* (Munich: Beck, 2000), chap. 7 and 10.

case of multi-national states like the Habsburg and Romanov empires, the political and cultural standing of the different non-Jewish peoples among whom they lived. In Georgian London, as we saw, poor Jews behaved, in some respects, like poor Christians, while Jewish brokers, overseas merchants, and loan-contractors patterned their behavior on that of the land-owning upper class. In the tsarist empire, acculturation took the form of borrowing bourgeois *German* or *Russian* cultural patterns, not those of the low-status, impoverished, powerless populations in the Pale of Settlement (Lithuanians, Belorussians, Ukrainians) who were the Jews' immediate neighbors.[6] In the Habsburg Empire, in the late eighteenth century and at least the first half of the nineteenth century, the reference group for middle-class Jews, whether in Prague, Budapest, or Lemberg, was the German-speaking imperial bureaucracy or professional upper-middle class. Only when nationalist movements began to challenge the hegemony of Vienna in the second half of the century did they begin to embrace Czech, Magyar, and Polish language and culture respectively. And even then, East Central European Jews never fully abandoned the attachment to German culture that they had acquired earlier.

Third, acculturation made little headway wherever it seemed unlikely to improve Jewish economic well-being or legal status. This explains, in part, why the great mass of Jews living in the Pale of Settlement and in Congress Poland, whose overriding concern was eking out a living, took little interest in transforming themselves into Russians or Poles even in cosmetic ways. In the long nineteenth century, at a time when acculturation was a hallmark of Jewish communities in Western and Central Europe and North America, few Jews (other than an elite of maskilim and russified industrialists, entrepreneurs, professionals, and intellectuals) saw any connection between acculturation and improved living conditions. In Central Europe, on the other hand, from at least the time of the French Revolution, the possibility of full emancipation and social acceptance always underwrote the acculturation process. While acculturation was linked as well to urbanization, mobility, and prosperity, Jews who desired to take part in social and cultural life outside their own community and who believed that such participation was in the realm of the possible were more likely to pursue acculturation than those who were unable to imagine a world that was fundamentally different from the one they knew. The pace of change in the Russian empire was too slow to inspire widespread optimism among the bulk of the Jewish population and, although there were increasing numbers of Jews who believed that Russia was evolving and that this required

---

[6] Zvi Gitelman, "Language and Ethnic Identity: Yiddish in the Soviet Union," unpublished paper.

the tsar's Jews to prove themselves worthy of inclusion in state and society, they were always a small minority. It also is clear that demography contributed to the absence of widespread acculturation in Eastern Europe. In regions where hundreds of thousands of Jews lived a distinctive existence, their way of life was, in their eyes, normative and natural rather than exceptional. Few could imagine embracing a way of living that was foreign to their family and friends.

Fourth, acculturation always outpaced integration and emancipation. The reason for this is clear: the pace and extent of acculturation were in the hands of Jews, not the state or Christian society. Emancipation became possible only when the state was fundamentally transformed, when *ancien régime* corporate distinctions among its subjects yielded, even in part, to notions of liberal individualism, parliamentarianism, meritocracy, and the free movement of persons and property. There was nothing that Jews themselves could do to effect transformations on this scale. Wherever they enjoyed the benefits of emancipation, it was the result of far-reaching political and social shifts. In France and the Netherlands, emancipation was tied to the French revolution and the wars of French conquest it inspired; in Britain, its North American colonies, and later the United States, to a burgeoning liberal consensus about the nature of state and society; in Germany, to unification and industrial expansion. Similarly, while Jews were able to prepare themselves for inclusion in voluntary institutions and social circles outside their community, their admittance and acceptance was beyond their control. Thus, in Germany, from the start of the nineteenth century until the Nazi takeover in 1933, acculturation always outstripped integration. At no time were Jews able to gain unrestricted access to non-Jewish social circles, to elite institutions, and to high-prestige occupations (such as the judiciary, the civil service, the professoriate, and the officer corps). Until the collapse of the Weimar Republic, most Jews continued to socialize in the intimacy of their homes only with other Jews.

Fifth, men and women often experienced acculturation differently. Because women rarely received a formal education in traditional Jewish communities and were not expected to devote themselves to the study of rabbinic texts, they were more likely than men, when the foundations of tradition began to shift, to be exposed to new literatures, fashions, and tastes, especially when their husbands were sufficiently wealthy to provide them with leisure time. In the late eighteenth and early nineteenth centuries, Jewish *salonières* in Berlin and Vienna were among the first in their communities to be exposed to German intellectual life. While their husbands remained enmeshed in business affairs, they were free to experiment with new ways of behaving and thinking. (Most of them eventually left the Jewish community, but that is another story.) In Russia, the wives and daughters of some traditional Jews were allowed to learn European languages – Polish, Russian, French, and German – and thus gained access to fashions and ideas that were foreign and forbidden to their husbands and brothers. In western Galicia, in the late nineteenth and early twentieth century, the daughters of Jewish tavern keepers, timber merchants, livestock dealers, and grain merchants were routinely enrolled in state-run, Polish-language schools. The education they received opened their eyes to ideas and fashions that later often alienated them from the yeshiva-educated husbands to whom their parents married them.[7]

In North America, Western Europe, and much of Central Europe, Jewish acculturation went forward largely unhindered by traditionalist opposition. In the early twentieth century, the sons of Eastern European immigrants in the United States learned to play baseball; their cousins in England and France, football – both sports that were unknown in the Pale of Settlement. In Germany, prosperous Orthodox Jews were no less accustomed than Reform Jews to listening to Bach and Beethoven. Both sent their children to elite secondary schools and then to university. Both avidly pursued *Kultur* and *Bildung*. From the mid-nineteenth century, German Orthodox men gave up the full beard for the goatee or were completely clean shaven. In urban Orthodox synagogues in Germany, the influence of the outward forms and aesthetic practices of mainstream Protestant society were felt: the service was "formalized to a high degree"; "every unnecessary noise and every unnecessary movement" were prohibited; and "overly ardent worship" was avoided.[8] In the West, in other words, religious observance and acculturation often went hand in hand, especially among middle-class Jews. In Eastern Europe, however, traditional resistance to changes in Jewish dress was widespread in the nineteenth century. Once acculturation became associated in the minds of traditionalists with religious laxity and even apostasy, a linkage that seemed clear to them from events in Western and Central Europe, they invested full beards and long, dark coats with unprecedented religious meaning and condemned those who dressed in *daytsmerish* (German) style. When the tsarist government, urged on by maskilim, introduced comprehensive measures between 1844

---

[7] Deborah Hertz, *Jewish High Society in Old Regime Berlin* (New Haven, CT: Yale University Press, 1988); Iris Parush, *Reading Jewish Women: Marginality and Modernization in Nineteenth-Century Eastern European Jewish Society*, trans. Saadya Sternberg (Hanover, NH: Brandeis University Press, 2004); Rachel Manekin, "The Lost Generation: Education and Female Conversion in *Fin-de-Siècle* Krakow," *Polin* 18 (2005): 189–219.

[8] Mordechai Breuer, *Modernity within Tradition: The Social History of Orthodox Jewry in Imperial Germany*, trans. Elizabeth Petuchowski (New York: Columbia University Press, 1992), 43.

and 1851 to force Jews to abandon traditional dress, the religious leadership, which saw the laws as a dire threat, worked unsuccessfully to annul
them. (The laws were not, in any case, well enforced.) However, when
young Eastern European immigrants began settling in North American
cities in the last decades of the century, few resisted the pull of popular
fashion. Only in the last decades of the twentieth century, with the expansion of strict Orthodoxy in the West, did resistance to acculturation again
materialize in Jewish society. In the sectarian world of *haredi* Orthodoxy in
Europe, North America, and Israel, viewing television, watching movies,
and using the internet, along with other diversions, were forbidden. Men
eschewed contemporary Western dress and let their beards grow freely.

One section of European Jewry – the Western Sephardim – largely
bypassed the acculturation process. The Sephardim in Italy, France, the
Netherlands, and Britain at the start of the modern period were the
descendants of *conversos*, or New Christians, who had lived at one time as
nominal Catholics in Spain, Portugal, and their overseas colonies. Having
lived or having ancestors who had lived as Catholics in Catholic societies, they were, in Yosef Yerushalmi's oft-cited words, "the first considerable
group of European Jews to have had their most extensive and direct personal experiences completely outside the organic Jewish community and
the spiritual universe of normative Jewish tradition."[9] In the early modern
period, when Europe's Ashkenazim lived in ways that visibly distinguished
them from the rest of the population, *conversos* and their descendants
were already comfortable with Western languages, literatures, dress, comportment, and the like. In the major centers of the Western Sephardi
Diaspora – Amsterdam, London, Bordeaux, Venice, Livorno, and their
colonial outposts in the New World – learning to live in the modern world
did not include the challenge of acculturation.

In those states where acculturated Jews saw the presence of masses
of unacculturated Jews as a threat to their own legal and social status –
because, in their view, they projected a dangerous image of all Jews as
unchanged and unchangeable – they took steps to accelerate the acculturation process. In Germany, Galicia, Congress Poland, and the Pale of
Settlement, they promoted Haskalah ideology, primarily by supporting
schools to provide the Jewish poor with a secular education and artisanal
and agricultural training programs to diversify their occupational base. In
the liberal states of the West – Britain, France, the Netherlands, and the
United States – where Jewish emancipation was not a long-festering issue,

---

[9] Yosef Haim Yerushalmi, *From Spanish Court to Italian Ghetto – Isaac Cardoso: A Study in
Seventeenth-Century Marranism and Jewish Apologetics* (New York: Columbia University
Press, 1971), 44.

ideological movements to promote acculturation were absent or inconsequential. Well-to-do Jews in these countries, whose citizenship was not contested, were under less pressure to demonstrate their civic worthiness. However, when several million Eastern European Jews settled in American, French, and British cities beginning in the late nineteenth century, their presence and their ostensible attachment to Old World ways led communal leaders, fearful of growing antisemitism, to fund programs to accelerate their Americanization, Gallicization, and Anglicization respectively. In retrospect, their fear about immigrant resistance to acculturation was unfounded. Eastern European Jews (with the possible exception of the elderly) and their children were eager to shed their status as newcomers fresh off the boat, however strong their attachment to religious observance. Measures by successive Israeli governments from 1948 on to transform new immigrants, especially those from North Africa and the Middle East, into Hebrew-speaking citizens with a modern, Western outlook should also been seen as projects to promote acculturation.

Until the last quarter of the twentieth century, historians characterized Haskalah projects, especially those in Germany, as barometers of modernization, as indices of the pace and strength of the transformation of a Jewish community. This interpretation, which privileges self-conscious, ideologically driven campaigns to transform Jewish life as the hallmarks of modernity, no longer enjoys universal assent. Some historians now argue that the Haskalah, both in Central and Eastern Europe, was a response to the strength of forces opposing the transformation of Jewish life, that it arose largely in those regions of Europe where acculturation and emancipation lagged and where a vanguard of already acculturated Jews, despairing at the slow pace of the transformation of the Jewish masses, believed they must hasten the process in order to demonstrate Jewish worthiness for incorporation into state and society. In Western Europe and North America, they observe, where changes in Jewish behavior and legal status were in advance of those in Central and Eastern Europe, the relative ease of the transformation process made Haskalah-like programs unnecessary. In this light, the existence of such programs in Central and Eastern Europe is more an index of the strength of opposition, both from within and without Jewish society, to its transformation than to its preeminence in pioneering modernization.[10] It also should be remembered that Haskalah programs touched the lives of a minority of Jews at any time. Most Jews who embraced new habits – wherever they lived – did so without the urging of ideologists and philanthropists.

[10] Todd M. Endelman, *Broadening Jewish History: Toward a Social History of Ordinary Jews* (Oxford: Littman Library of Jewish Civilization, 2010), chap. 3.

INTEGRATION

Acculturation was a prerequisite for integration. Jews whose comportment, dress, and language marked them as Jews were not candidates for acceptance into Gentile circles or institutions, nor, for that matter, did they aspire to or pursue admission. This was especially true in the case of Jews who continued to observe the mitzvot (commandments), since the dietary laws inhibited their ability to dine outside their own homes. That said, extensive acculturation was no guarantee of extensive integration. Integration was a function of the willingness of non-Jews to accept and befriend Jews, and such willingness fluctuated with the ebb and flow of anti-Jewish sentiments, whose strength, in most cases, was unconnected to how Jews behaved. Jews who had broken their ties to Judaism, whose manners and dress were refined and elegant, whose taste in literature, art, and home decoration was exquisite, and whose contributions to science, industry, and philanthropy were unmatched frequently met with rejection, especially in illiberal societies. Take the example of the industrialist and aesthete Walther Rathenau. During World War I, the German government recruited him to secure vital raw materials that the army had neglected to stockpile, but his upper-class colleagues in the War Ministry treated him as an interloper and a pariah. His friend Harry Kessler recalled, "One day his department was isolated by a wooden partition, which had grown up overnight, from those of the other old-established gentlemen in the War Office, as if it had been a cholera station."[11]

Jewish integration, like acculturation, was measured and piecemeal. In the early and mid-nineteenth-century Jewish men in Western and Central Europe and the United States began joining the learned societies, social clubs, and choral, sporting, and literary groups that were emerging and, in the second half of the century, increasingly took part in political movements. Bourgeois wives, however, were less likely to mix with Christians even in this limited way, since gender norms circumscribed their activities and confined them to the domestic sphere, where they associated with family and friends of similar background. Jewish men who attended university or performed military service were immersed for several years in structured non-Jewish institutions, but whether they forged close social ties with Christians at the time is another matter. Prestigious social institutions, especially city clubs where men dined, played cards, and discussed business and public affairs, tended to exclude Jews throughout the nineteenth and the first half of the twentieth century. (England was an

---

[11] Harry Kessler, *Walther Rathenau: His Life and Work*, trans. W. D. Robson-Scott and Lawrence Hyde (London: G. Howe, 1929), 181.

exception: in London and the provinces, wealthy or talented Jewish men were viewed as "clubable.") However, as the Jewish Question loomed ever larger in public discourse after 1870, some clubs and societies that had previously accepted Jewish members began to exclude them. In Germany, for example, *Burschenschaften* (nationalist fraternities) refused membership to Jews, while in the United States, elite city clubs closed their doors to new Jewish members, most prominently the Union League Club in New York, which in 1893 refused membership to Theodore Seligman, although his father was among the club's founders.[12]

Changes in Jewish occupational and employment patterns also contributed to fostering informal social contacts between Jews and Christians. At the start of the modern period, commerce in all its forms was the backbone of Jewish economic life everywhere. (It was somewhat less dominant in Eastern Europe, where artisans and craftsmen were more numerous than in Western and Central Europe.) Jews were self-employed or employed by other Jews. The suppliers, distributors, and customers with whom they traded were both Jews and Christians, but their relations with the latter were largely instrumental. In the modern period, Jewish involvement in commerce and manufacturing slowly decreased. The reasons for this were multiple. In some societies, romantic, anti-capitalist sentiment stigmatized buying and selling as "Jewish" and ambitious young men chose to make careers elsewhere – in the liberal professions, the academy, the civil service, and emerging occupations in the arts and popular culture. In some cases, economic forces dictated the switch, and in others the weakening of discrimination. As a result, Jewish occupations became more diverse everywhere, both in the East and the West, especially after World War I. Jews who chose to work in sectors of the economy that were historically not associated with Jews or who found employment (as clerks, secretaries, and salespeople) in large-scale enterprises to which industrialization and urbanization gave birth spent much of their day in the close company of Gentiles. Thus, grain brokers in *fin-de-siècle* Berlin and garment workers in interwar New York worked primarily in the company of other Jews, while scientists, journalists, military officers, and civil servants in Moscow and Paris in the twentieth century did not. The former continued to outnumber the latter (except in the Soviet Union, where free enterprise disappeared) until after World War II.

Enduring, informal, intimate social contact between Jews and non-Jews, however, was not common. Before the late twentieth century, most Jews remained enmeshed in extended family networks, while their

---

[12] John Higham, *Send These to Me: Jews and Other Immigrants in Urban America* (New York: Atheneum, 1975), 150, 152.

closest friends, like their spouses, were other Jews. However desiccated their attachment to religious tradition and however vigorous their participation in public forums, the people whom they invited to their homes (and who, in turn, reciprocated), with whom they relaxed when not at work, and to whom they married their children were Jews. That this was so in Poland or Russia or in immigrant neighborhoods in the West is not surprising. But it was also true among middle-class Jews in the German-speaking cities of Central Europe, a group whom historians often describe as *assimilated*. In recalling his upper-middle-class youth in late imperial Berlin, the fashion photographer Erwin Blumenfeld commented that his freethinking, atheist parents contentedly lived within "invisible walls," associating exclusively with other Jews, and "were probably not even aware of it themselves." Very rarely "a stray goy happened to find his way into our house," and when one did, "we had no idea how to behave." The situation was similar in Gershom Scholem's Berlin home. Despite his father's unswerving integrationist ideals, "no Christian ever set foot in our home," not even Christians who were members of organizations in which his father was active (with the one telling exception of a formal, fiftieth birthday visit).[13] Of course, there were exceptions to the rule: musicians, bohemians, radicals, writers, scientists, and intellectuals. But they were atypical individuals and their memoirs, letters, and biographies offer a misleading picture of the overall tenor of Jewish integration. In "an ordinary middle-class bourgeois home, neither rich nor poor" like the Scholem home, there was no social mixing between Jews and Gentiles.[14]

One sign of the absence of intimate social integration before the second half of the twentieth century was the low incidence of intermarriage (marriage between an unconverted Jew and an unconverted Christian). Intermarriage rates soar when social intimacy and secularization flourish, that is, when young Jews and Christians for whom religious tradition is no longer binding socialize freely. In most American and European Jewish communities, the rate of intermarriage was low before World War I and in many before World War II. For example, in Budapest,

---

[13] Erwin Blumenfeld, *Eye to I: The Autobiography of a Photographer*, trans. Mike Mitchell and Brian Murdoch (London: Thames and Hudson, 1999), 52; Gershom Scholem, "With Gershom Scholem: An Interview," in *On Jews and Judaism in Crisis: Selected Essays*, ed. Werner J. Dannhauser (New York; Schocken Books, 1976), 4–6.

[14] Gershom Scholem, "On the Social Psychology of the Jews in Germany, 1900–1933," in *Jews and Germans from 1860 to 1933: The Problematic Symbiosis*, ed. David Bronsen (Heidelberg: Winter, 1979), 18–19.

the number of Jews intermarrying relative to the total number of Jews marrying was 7 percent in the period 1896–1900, 17 percent in 1925, and 19 percent in 1932. In Vienna, the rate was 12 percent in 1926, 13 percent in 1929, 14 percent in 1932, and 10 percent in 1935. In Amsterdam, the rate was 6 percent at the turn of the century and 17 percent in the mid-1930s. In British and North American communities with large immigrant populations, intermarriage on the whole was inconsequential before the 1960s. Those who married out tended to come from families who had arrived in much earlier waves of immigration and whose acculturation was several generations old.[15] In Eastern Europe, where acculturation was less advanced, social intimacy was uncommon but not absent. However, on the rare occasions when it led to marriage, one partner, usually the Jew, was required to convert (in the absence of civil marriage). Only in the Soviet Union, where the state introduced revolutionary measures to create a new society, were Jews and Christians thrown together in circumstances in which intermarriage flourished. Here, and uniquely in the modern period, the government publicly championed inter-ethnic marriage – as a mark of socialist progress and harmony and of liberation from outmoded views. Thus, in 1936, in the Russian Soviet Federated Socialist Republic, 37 percent of Jewish women and 42 percent of Jewish men chose non-Jewish partners.[16]

While correct, describing American and European Jews in the modern period as more acculturated than integrated is insufficient. The breadth of the generalization masks other noteworthy patterns. First, in liberal societies, Jews who lived in smaller rather than larger communities were more likely to establish close social relations with non-Jews, often because there was no alternative if they wished to have a social life. The daughter of a rabbi who moved to Amsterdam in 1931 from Den Bosch in the southern Netherlands recalled that before moving it was necessary to have non-Jewish friends – "or else you'd be living in complete isolation" – but that after the move she associated only with Jews. It is no coincidence that the highest intermarriage rates in Europe before World War II (excluding the

---

[15] Arthur Ruppin, *The Jewish Fate and Future*, trans. E. W. Dickes (London: Macmillan, 1940); Emanuel Boekman, *Demografie van de Jooden in Nederland* (Amsterdam: M. Hertzberger, 1936), 59; Todd M. Endelman, *Radical Assimilation in English Jewish History, 1656–1945* (Bloomington, IN: University of Indiana Press, 1990), chap. 6; idem, *Leaving the Jewish Fold: Conversion and Radical Assimilation in Modern Jewish History.* (Princeton, NJ: Princeton University Press, 2015), chap. 5.

[16] Mordecai Altshuler, *Soviet Jewry on the Eve of the Holocaust: A Social and Demographic Profile* (Jerusalem: Ahva Press, 1998), 74, Table 4.2.

Soviet Union) were found in Denmark and Sweden, where the small size of the community, the length of Jewish settlement, and the weakness of widespread Jew-baiting made intensive intra-ethnic interaction and cohesion difficult to sustain.[17] Central European Jews who settled in rural and small-town America in the nineteenth century lived and worked in non-Jewish milieus and raised their children in isolation from Jewish society and institutions. Isaac Leeser, editor of *The Occident*, the first successful Jewish newspaper in the United States, frequently lamented the fate of the children: ignorant of Jewish learning and rites, they imbibed Christianity in school and at play with other children, and then, "having nothing Jewish within to restrain them," they married Christians and, even beforehand, started to attend church, since everyone they knew worshipped at one church or another.[18]

Second, as with acculturation, gender was a determinant of integration. In middle- and upper-middle-class families everywhere, men enjoyed greater freedom of movement outside the home than women and thus were more likely to mix socially with Christians. One consequence of this was that their intermarriage rate was usually higher than that of women. Significantly, when acculturated lower-class and lower-middle-class women began working outside the home in the second half of the nineteenth century – in workshops, offices, stores, and factories – their share of intermarriages rose, for they were more likely to meet and establish social ties with non-Jews than their better-off counterparts, whose social lives were circumscribed by gendered standards of propriety. In Breslau, for example, where the Jewish community included large numbers of newcomers of modest means from Posen and Silesia, young, unmarried women from the bottom half of the social scale went to work outside the home between leaving school and finding a husband. The parents of working daughters were unable to monitor their social life because they were financially independent, often living on their own, and because they (the parents) lacked the means to provide their daughters with a dowry, which would have enabled them to control their choice of marriage partner. Thus, in the two decades following the introduction of civil marriage throughout Germany (1874–1894), 60 percent of Jewish

---

[17] Philo Bregstein and Salvador Bloemgarten, eds., *Remembering Jewish Amsterdam*, trans. Wanda Boeke (New York: Holmes and Meier, 2004), 59; Ruppin, *Jewish Fate and Future*, 108; idem, *The Jews in the Modern World* (London: Macmillan 1934), 318–319.

[18] *The Occident*, 16 (January 1859): 468; 24 (September 1866): 242–247.

women marrying Christians in Breslau came from lower-class and lower-middle-class backgrounds.[19]

Third, integration, not surprisingly, went more smoothly in liberal societies, that is, societies in which merit and money trumped birth and in which corporatism yielded to individualism. In illiberal societies with inflexible status hierarchies – Germany, Hungary, Poland, and Russia before World War I, for example – acculturated, high-achieving, upwardly mobile Jews found their access to high-status occupations, associations, and circles blocked (unless they converted to Christianity, which was not always an effective strategy). In imperial Germany, with a few exceptions, otherwise qualified Jews were unable to make careers in the army officer corps, in the imperial civil service, in secondary state education, in the judiciary, and in the upper reaches of the academy. In Great Britain, Italy, and France, on the other hand, elite resistance to Jewish integration, while not absent, was weaker. In Britain, from the mid-nineteenth century on, Jewishness was not a stumbling block to serving in the cabinet, succeeding in the colonial civil service, riding with the county hunt, attending Eton or Harrow, or being elected to a gentleman's club. In France during the Third Republic, state employment was a popular choice for talented young men. Jewish graduates of the universities and *grandes écoles* rose into the highest administrative and judicial ranks, serving as prefects and subprefects and as members of the *Conseil d' État*, the *Cour de cassation*, and the *cours d'appels*. More than twenty Jews became generals during the Third Republic while hundreds became colonels and captains, including the unfortunate Alfred Dreyfus, whose initial rise and ultimate rehabilitation subvert the mistaken perception that *fin-de-siècle* antisemitism was worse in France than in Germany.[20] A German Dreyfus was unthinkable – not because Germany was more tolerant than France, but because it barred Jews from the officer corps altogether.

One exception to this generalization about the close correlation between Jewish integration, on the one hand, and economic and political modernization, on the other, was the United States from the late nineteenth century to the mid-twentieth century. There mass immigration in general (largely absent in Europe) and Jewish socio-economic mobility in particular aroused resentment and fear and promoted exclusionary trends. Quotas and bans restricted Jewish access to employment, education, housing, and

[19] Till van Rahden, *Jews and Other Germans: Civil Society, Religious Diversity, and Urban Politics in Breslau, 1860–1925*, trans. Marcus Brainard (Madison: University of Wisconsin Press, 2008), 101.

[20] Pierre Birnbaum, *Les Fous de la République: Histoire politique des Juifs d' État de Gambetta á Vichy* (Paris: Fayard, 1992), 93, 244, 251, 431, 488.

social facilities. In large cities, where most of America's Jews lived, choice apartment buildings, neighborhoods, private schools, and social clubs excluded Jews, even the most acculturated. The best private colleges and professional schools used quotas from the 1920s until the 1960s to lower the number of Jewish students, which had skyrocketed before World War I. In architecture, engineering, heavy industry, much of the academy, and corporate management Jews were largely absent. This began to change significantly in the 1960s, with one bastion of exclusivity after another opening its doors to Americans who were not white, male, and Protestant. The pace and extent of Jewish integration – social, occupational, educational, and residential – from then until the end of the century was historically unprecedented. One consequence of this was the explosion of intermarriage in the last two decades of the century. The second National Jewish Population Study in 1990 reported 52 percent of the Jews who married in the United States in the period 1985–1990 married non-Jews, a number that became pivotal to communal discourse about Jewish continuity at the turn of the century (even though some sociologists believed the figure was closer to 41 percent).[21]

SECULARIZATION

Histories of the transformation of the Jews in the modern period devote little attention to secularization *qua* secularization, as a dimension of change independent of acculturation and integration. I am not saying that they ignore or deny the decline of belief and observance since the eighteenth century (which would be difficult, in any case) but, rather, that they view this decline in an exclusively Jewish historical framework ("assimilation"), linking it to desires and needs that arose from the *Jewish* confrontation with modernity – specifically, the urge to erase or blur Jewish particularism (acculturation) and to hasten Jewish acceptance (integration). They imply that the decline in tradition was a Jewish response to a set of challenges that Jews faced as they struggled to find a place for themselves in the modern world. While it is undeniable that acculturated, upwardly mobile Jews intentionally discarded religious customs that marked them as "too Jewish," this is not the whole story. The decline of piety and the rise of laxity were European-wide phenomena, driven by forces that operated among Jews and Christians alike.

---

[21] Barry Kosmin and Sidney Goldstein, *Highlights of the CJF 1990 National Jewish Population Survey* (New York: Council of Jewish Federations, 1991); Steven M. Cohen, "Why Intermarriage May Not Threaten Jewish Continuity," *Moment* (December 31, 1994), 54.

Invoking the notion of secularization introduces a new complication, however. The concept has had a checkered career in the social sciences since the mid-twentieth century.[22] The primary reason is the confusion that emerged between the study of religious decline in specific historical contexts and the explanatory power of modernization theory as expounded primarily by sociologists and political scientists. The three most influential figures in European social theory – Karl Marx, Max Weber, and Émile Durkheim – bequeathed to mid-twentieth century sociologists of religion a master narrative of a one-way, long-term, universal trend toward secularization. After World War II, their narrative of the eclipse of religion blended with liberal modernization theory, which posited a teleological series of stages through which societies inevitably moved as they passed from "tradition" to "modernity." Beginning in the mid-1960s and continuing to the mid-1980s, sociologists and historians of religion, on the basis of empirical research on the persistence of religion and under the sway of their own faith commitments, mounted a scathing attack on the secularization paradigm.

In discrediting secularization theory, critics also brought into disrepute secularization as an analytical category (rather than as a master narrative). This led historians writing about waning religious beliefs to caution that they were not referring to a single, one-way process operating everywhere but were describing something that happened in a specific way in a specific setting, leaving open the possibility that in different historical circumstances the outcome could have been different. One result of this reevaluation was a turn toward thinking of varieties of secularization. In regard to Jewish modernization, at least three distinct kinds of secularization were at work. In ascending order of importance, they were intellectual secularization, political secularization, and nonreflective, behavioral secularization (discarding some or all of the mitzvot).

The first refers to the intellectual challenge to the theological foundations of Judaism with the aim of replacing them with a more naturalistic view of the world. Spinoza's repudiation of revealed religion and rabbinic law in seventeenth-century Amsterdam was one of the earliest examples and acquired legendary status for later generations of Jewish freethinkers. As a rule, whenever young Jews encountered secular science, history, and philosophy – whether in secular educational institutions (as in Central and

---

[22] Hugh MaLeod, *Secularisation in Western Europe, 1848–1914* (New York: Macmillan, 2000), 1–12; David Martin, *On Secularization: Toward a Revised General Theory* (Aldershot: Ashgate, 2005); Jeffrey Cox, "Master Narratives of Long-Term Religious Change," in *The Decline of Christendom in Western Europe, 1750–2000*, eds. Hugh McLeod and Werner Ustorf (Cambridge: Cambridge University Press, 2003), 201–217.

Western Europe) or less formally in study circles and from contact with enthusiasts and propagandists (as in Eastern Europe) – they were forced to reconcile the old with the new. Some found reconciliation impossible and thus embraced deism, pantheism, agnosticism, atheism, materialism, or some variation or combination thereof. While most Jews who experienced this kind of inner upheaval already were literate in a Western language, linguistic acculturation, let alone social integration, was not a prerequisite, for in Eastern Europe radical critiques and challenges to traditional think- ing circulated from the mid-nineteenth century on in Hebrew and then Yiddish. Intellectual secularization, however, was not a common, everyday experience. The few, not the many, abandoned tradition because modern critiques of revealed religion shook their faith. Reading Spinoza, Darwin, or Marx was never a pastime for everyday Jews even in periods of intense intellectual ferment. The weakening of religious tradition, on the other hand, was widespread, first in Western Europe, then in Central Europe, and finally in Eastern Europe, even before the Soviet regime campaigned to eradicate religion. As historians now widely acknowledge, immigrants from Eastern Europe to the United States between 1870 and 1914 were not the pious, scrupulously observant, deeply spiritual folk they were once thought to be. The milieu piety of the Pale of Settlement, Galicia, and Poland did not travel well and failed to cross the Atlantic intact.

Political secularization refers to the decline of religion in public life, especially the decline in the influence of religious authorities in spheres of activity outside ceremony and ritual. In the early modern period, even though Jews were a subject people, with neither sovereignty nor a state, the position of rabbinic Judaism was nonetheless similar to that of the various state churches. The political status of Jews was inseparable from their religious status. There was no Judaism outside the Judaism of the quasi-autonomous, state-recognized kehillah, to which all the Jews of a locale were subject (in theory if not always in practice). Informal ties, especially family ties, between the wealthy and the learned cemented this overlap between "church" (the rabbis) and "state" (the lay leadership). In the modern period, with emancipation dissolving Jewish corporate status, the reach of religion and the authority of its spokesmen shrank. More and more spheres of activity – including even marriage and divorce in the most liberal states – became subject to the authority of the state or were freed from any regulation at all (as often happened in economic life). While legal emancipation in Eastern Europe only came with the collapse of the tsarist regime in 1917, even there the state increasingly intervened in internal Jewish matters in the nineteenth century, taking steps to reform Jewish dress and education. The growth of state power, which western- ized lay elites tended to welcome, diminished the comprehensive religious framework of Jewish life, removing from communal control matters that previously enjoyed the imprimatur of the sacred. This, in tandem with other changes, slowly remade Judaism into a religion, like other religions – rather than a culture, a civilization, or a comprehensive way of life.

More powerful than either the ideological critique of tradition or the dissolution of communal autonomy were far-reaching shifts in material circumstances, shifts that affected Jews and Christians alike, weakening social arrangements that supported the authority of religion and the supernatural ideas that underpinned it, such as providence, revelation, and reward and punishment. Migration and urbanization, subjection to the competitive demands of capitalism, unhampered individualism, increasing material prosperity, burgeoning mass markets, decreasing random violence and destruction, and lengthening human mortality – all worked, in tandem and without notice, to bolster human confidence at the expense of divine power and to introduce novel distractions into the lives of everyday Jews.

Consider the case of urbanization. In the eighteenth century, most Jews in the West still lived in small, face-to-face communities in rural or semi-rural areas. They were subject to the informal discipline of communal conventions and norms and immune to – because distant from – the allures of urban life – amusements and entertainments like theaters, pleasure gardens, concert halls, coffee houses, brothels, taverns, gaming houses, fairs, public executions, and the like. Jewish newcomers to cities like London and Amsterdam in the eighteenth century and many more cities in the centuries that followed were not subject to communal discipline, either formal or informal. They found themselves living in crowded streets, squares, and courtyards, bursting with distractions and diversions. The reach of the synagogue and the rabbinate was reduced. The funding and building of voluntary institutions (synagogues and schools) did not keep pace with the growth of the population. In Amsterdam, for example, at the very start of the nineteenth century, only a fraction of Jewish children were enrolled in Jewish schools. In the two communal schools and the two orphan schools, there were fewer than 350 pupils in 1807. Another sixty private schools enrolled about 700 children in 1811. In all, a little more than one thousand children attended Jewish schools – at a time when the Jewish population was over 23,000. An additional several hundred attended the city's free schools for the poor.[23] The neglect of religious education in Amsterdam was a casualty of urbanization and, of course, the reorganization of Jewish life on a voluntary basis and owed little to critiques of revealed religion.

---

[23] Jozeph Michman, *The History of Dutch Jewry during the Emancipation Period, 1787–1815: Gothic Turrets on a Corinthian Building* (Amsterdam: Amsterdam University Press, 1995), 167f.

Embourgeoisement was also a potent solvent of traditional religious beliefs, even in Eastern Europe, where Jewish economic mobility was less common than in Western and Central Europe and North America. Writing in the 1940s, Salo Baron noted that with the shift to "the all-pervading force of money as the main instrument of production and political power … nearly all walks of human endeavor were permeated with a new spirit of materialism. This affected the Jew no less than his neighbors."[24] As a rule, Jewish families who achieved middle-class status – and especially those who rose into the *haute bourgeoisie* of finance and industry – became less observant (not necessarily non-observant) with the passage of every generation. There were exceptions to this rule, of course, but they were just that: cases whose exceptionality proved the rule. In the long run, over three or four generations, materially successful families slowly reduced their commitment to the observance of Judaism. They did not necessarily convert to Christianity, formally withdraw from the community, or quit synagogues and voluntary associations that their families historically supported. Rather, Judaism counted for less in their lives than in the lives of their ancestors; it was practiced with less fervor and attention to detail than earlier and as much from habit, social convention, and family tradition as from a sense of divine obligation.

The memoirs of Pauline Wengeroff offer vivid descriptions of the impact of increasing affluence on Jewish religious practice in tsarist Russia among families that remained within the traditional fold. Raised in a pious but not obscurantist home, she was disturbed to discover that her wealthy in-laws in Konotop in northern Ukraine, with whom she and her husband lived for four years after their wedding in 1849, marked the Sabbath with less rigor than her parents. Her father-in-law, who held the government concession for the manufacture of hard liquor, was the wealthiest person in town. He and his wife led "an elegant, well-to-do life." Because there were no other "distinguished Jewish families" in the town – most Jewish men there were grain merchants and tavern keepers – they entertained non-Jews (army officers, landowners, and their families) lavishly. In her in-laws' home, the Sabbath evening meal seemed to her "very prosaic." Her father-in-law talked business with his father. "The young people, my husband among them, often fell asleep out of boredom at the table, until my mother-in-law laughed and teased them awake in time for the blessing after the meal." No one gave a thought to singing the traditional Sabbath songs (*zemirot*). The laws of Sabbath rest "were observed as prescribed, but

---

[24] Salo W. Baron, "Modern Capitalism and Jewish Fate," in *History and Jewish Historians: Essays and Addresses* (Philadelphia: Jewish Publication Society, 1964), 54. This essay first appeared in *The Menorah Journal* 30 (1942): 116–138.

circumvented when necessary in a shrewd way." If a business letter arrived, for example, a Gentile (*shabbes goy*) would open it so that the family could read it.[25] Later Wengeroff witnessed the conversions of her grown children to Christianity – conversions that owed nothing to conviction and everything to convenience.

RADICAL ASSIMILATION

In both Europe and North America, in Jewish circles in which integration lagged behind acculturation, largely because of Gentile resistance, some Jews tried to overcome whatever obstacles remained by converting to Christianity.[26] Their conversions were, with few exceptions, pragmatic and strategic rather than spiritual and theological. They consciously pursued acculturation to its logical end, erasing completely what they thought still distinguished them (formal adherence to Judaism) from Christians. Their hope was that this unambiguous, full-fledged identification with the majority would secure their total integration. Because conversion represents an extreme form of acculturation deployed in the service of an extreme vision of integration, historians frequently refer to it and other strategies for breaking *completely* with Judaism and Jewishness as radical assimilation. Although baptized Jews often found their Jewish origins thrown in their faces and were unable to find the unambiguous acceptance they craved, especially after the rise of racial antisemitism, with its denial of the spiritual efficacy of baptism, conversion remained a strategy for a minority of deracinated Jews coping with exclusion and stigmatization through the 1950s. The number of Jews who chose this route in the modern period cannot be known with any precision. The best that can be said is that the order of magnitude was in the hundreds of thousands.

In addition to those Jews who tried to leave their Jewishness behind by becoming Christians, there were others who chose to rebrand themselves by claiming identities that transcended the usual dichotomous categories of Christian and Jew. These included Jews who identified themselves as internationalists, revolutionaries, socialists, and communists and who looked forward to radical upheaval to banish old-regime prejudices and the need for otherworldly religious consolation. Rosa Luxemburg voiced

---

[25] Pauline Wengeroff, *Rememberings: The World of a Russian-Jewish Woman in the Nineteenth Century*, trans. Henny Wenkart (College Park, MD: University of Maryland Press, 2000), 153, 156, 162.

[26] This is the central theme of Endelman, *Leaving the Jewish Fold*.

the outlook of revolutionary radical assimilation when she wrote sharply to a friend in regard to anti-Jewish violence during World War I:

What do you want with this particular suffering of the Jews? The poor victims on the rubber plantations in Putamayo, the Negroes in Africa with whose bodies the Europeans play a game of catch, are just as near to me ... Oh, this "sublime silence of eternity" in which so many screams have faded away unheard. It rings within me so strongly that I have no special corner in my heart reserved for the ghetto. I am at home wherever in the entire world there are clouds, birds, and human tears.[27]

(Her protest brings to mind Cynthia Ozick's shrewd observation that universalism is the ultimate Jewish particularism.) A few non-revolutionary Jewish universalists, including Ludwig Zamenhof, the creator of Esperanto, tried to establish new, humanistic religions that transcended both Christianity and Judaism. Only one was successful – Felix Adler, the son of a Reform rabbi in New York, whose Ethical Culture movement attracted tens of thousands of Jews in America's largest cities in the late nineteenth and early twentieth centuries.[28] Others detached themselves from the fate and future of the Jewish people by swearing loyalty to and finding redemption in science or aestheticism, universalist projects that offered, each in its own way, guidance and salvation.

While the cumulative impact of acculturation, integration, and secularization in the modern period was the weakening or dissolution of Jewish collective sentiments, this outcome was not foreordained. It is possible to imagine alternative outcomes. For example, in Central Europe, the flight from Jewishness was intimately linked to the intensity of exclusion and bias, becoming more or less pronounced as Jewish optimism about the success of emancipation waxed and waned. Had the political history of Germany been different in the long nineteenth century, the history of its Jews would have followed a different course as well, long before the rise of Nazism. Moreover, the history of these transformative processes was not as linear, untroubled, or monolithic as this short account suggests. Any historical balance sheet needs also to take notice of behaviors that do not conform to what was conventional and typical in the long term. Not only was the transformation of the Jews uneven and often fragmentary, often moving in faltering, even contradictory ways. It also elicited individual and collective responses that consciously aimed to change the direction in which Jewish history was apparently heading. Everywhere, beginning in the first half of the nineteenth century and

[27] Rosa Luxemburg to Mathilde Wurm, February 16, 1917, in *The Letters of Rosa Luxemburg*, new ed. Stephen Eric Bronner (Atlantic Highlands, NJ: Humanities Press, 1993), 7–8.
[28] Benny Kraut, *From Reform Judaism to Ethical Culture: The Religious Evolution of Felix Adler* (Cincinnati: Hebrew Union College Press, 1979).

continuing to the present, substantial numbers of Jews who were alarmed by the decline of ethnic and religious commitments responded by self-consciously and noisily embracing these commitments. Often they created movements to stem or reverse the dissolution they saw threatening the Jewish future; among them were modern Orthodoxy, ultra-Orthodoxy, Jewish Renewal, varieties of Jewish nationalism (including Zionism), and cultural revival movements, as in France and Germany in the decades before World War II and in the United States in the last third of the twentieth century. They did not succeed in stopping hundreds of thousands of Jews from severing their ties to the Jewish religion and the Jewish community and even from ceasing to think of themselves as Jewish. But they did offer a renewed sense of inclusion to those who identified with them, lending their lives a Jewishly-framed purpose and meaning. Jews who settled in the Land of Israel, both before and after the creation of the State of Israel in 1948, and Jews who embraced ultra-Orthodoxy (*baalei teshuvah, hozrim be-teshuvah*) and lived in communities of like-minded Jews in the second half of the twentieth century inoculated themselves, as well as their descendants, against the probability of deracination. Neither were likely candidates for total immersion in non-Jewish circles and full erasure of their sense of Jewish collective identity.

SELECT BIBLIOGRAPHY

Avrutin, Eugene M. *Jews and the Imperial State: Identification Politics in Tsarist Russia.* Ithaca: Cornell University Press, 2010.

Bering, Dietz. *The Stigma of Names: Antisemitism in German Daily Life, 1812–1933.* Trans. Neville Plaice. Ann Arbor, MI: University of Michigan Press, 1992.

Birnbaum, Pierre. *The Jews of the Republic: A Political History of State Jews in France from Gambetta to Vichy.* Trans. Jane Marie Todd. Stanford: Stanford University Press, 1996.

Cohen, Steven M. *American Assimilation or Jewish Revival?* Bloomington, IN: Indiana University Press, 1988.

Endelman, Todd M. *Broadening Jewish History: Towards a Social History of Ordinary Jews.* Oxford: Littman Library of Jewish Civilization, 2011.

Leaving the Jewish Fold: Conversion and Radical Assimilation in Modern Jewish History. Princeton, NJ: Princeton University Press, 2015.

Radical Assimilation in Anglo-Jewish History, 1656–1945. Bloomington, IN: Indiana University Press, 1990.

Feiner, Shmuel. *The Origins of Jewish Secularization in Eighteenth-Century Europe.* Trans. Chaya Naor. Philadelphia: University of Pennsylvania Press, 1992.

Gitelman, Zvi. *Jewish Identities in Postcommunist Russia and Ukraine: An Uncertain Ethnicity.* Cambridge: Cambridge University Press, 2012.

Goldscheider, Calvin and Alan S. Zuckerman. *The Transformation of the Jews.* Chicago: University of Chicago Press, 1984.

Hertz, Deborah. *How Jews Became Germans: The History of Conversion and Assimilation in Berlin.* New Haven, CT: Yale University Press, 2009.

Hyman, Paula E. *The Emancipation of the Jews of Alsace: Acculturation and Tradition in the Nineteenth Century.* New Haven, CT: Yale University Press, 1991.

Gender and Assimilation in Modern Jewish History: The Roles and Representations of Women. Seattle: University of Washington Press, 1995.

Kaplan, Marion A. *The Making of the Jewish Middle Class: Women, Family, and Identity in Imperial Germany.* New York: Oxford University Press, 1991.

Lowenstein, Steven M. *The Berlin Jewish Community: Enlightenment, Family, and Crisis, 1770–1830.* New York: Oxford University Press, 1994.

Mosse, Werner E. *The German Jewish Economic Élite, 1820–1935: A Socio-Cultural Profile.* Oxford: The Clarendon Press, 1989.

Naimark-Goldberg, Natalie. *Jewish Women in Enlightenment Berlin.* Oxford: Littman Library of Jewish Civilization, 2013.

Nathans, Benjamin. *Beyond the Pale: The Jewish Encounter with Late Imperial Russia.* Berkeley: University of California Press, 2002.

Piette, Christine. *Les Juifs de Paris (1808–1840): La Marche vers l'assimilation.* Quebec: Les Presses de l'Université de Laval, 1983.

Rozenblit, Marsha L. *The Jews of Vienna, 1867–1914: Assimilation and Identity.* Albany: State University of New York Press. 1983.

Van Rahden, Till. *Jews and Other Germans: Civil Society, Religious Diversity, and Urban Politics in Breslau, 1860–1925.* Trans. Marcus Brainard. Madison, WI: University of Wisconsin Press, 2008.

Volkov, Shulamit. *Germans, Jews, and Antisemites: Trials in Emancipation.* Cambridge: Cambridge University Press, 2006.

Weissbach, Lee Shai. *Jewish Life in Small-Town America: A History.* New Haven, CT: Yale University Press, 2005.

CHAPTER 12

LIBERAL JUDAISMS

CLAIRE E. SUFRIN

Initial efforts to liberalize Judaism in the modern period were closely tied to the civic emancipation of Jews in Western and Central Europe, a protracted process that unfolded through the eighteenth and nineteenth centuries. As with the emancipation of Jews, the rethinking of Jewish theology and Jewish practice characteristic of this time reflects the rise of the Enlightenment and its emphasis on the human capacity for reason and the rights of the individual. As Pierre Birnbaum and Ira Katznelson note, emancipation gave Jews access "to the profound shifts in ideas and conditions wrought by the Enlightenment and its liberal offspring: religious toleration, secularization, scientific thought, and the apotheosization of reason, individualism, the law of contract, and choice. ... Jews moved from the position of presociological and prepolitical persons to become sociological and political actors."[1] This shift in political and sociological standing had important consequences for the rituals, liturgy, and sacred spaces of Judaism and for the ideas of God and their implications taught by its rabbis and articulated by its thinkers more formally in theological texts.

The Enlightenment embrace of reason and rationality in the eighteenth century represented a challenge to religious traditions and institutions; no longer was revelation (i.e., Scripture) – or tradition more generally – to be seen as the authoritative source of truth. But there were always Christians and Jews who questioned whether rationalism was adequate. In many cases, such Jews were drawn to a liberalized understanding and practice of Judaism. What they found in liberal synagogues was a liturgy drawn from tradition but revised in light of a commitment to rationalism and a desire to express a religiosity in line with the mores of the time. The recitation of the liturgy was enhanced by the decorum of a reverent congregation of worshippers and by the performance of choral music. These ritual innovations mimicked the model set by worship services in local

---

[1] Pierre Birnbaum and Ira Katznelson, eds., *Paths of Emancipation: Jews, States, and Citizenship* (Princeton: Princeton University Press, 1995), 4.

Christian churches and signaled a purposeful departure from the loosely coordinated, even raucous, prayer found in a traditional minyan.

The impulse to reform Judaism – to liberalize it – reflected both the rational and romantic elements of the surrounding intellectual culture and values, as we see in the theology that arose alongside and in response to innovations in Jewish ritual practice. Rabbis and theologians justified the fact of on-the-ground religious reform amid shifting intellectual currents by redefining the history of Judaism and the very purpose of Jewish practice. No longer was ritual to be understood as a matter of fulfilling God's commandments; spiritual uplift and human holiness were now the primary goal and any ritual practices that failed to fulfill these aims could be discarded. Influenced by and also resisting the anti-Jewish implications of a strictly Hegelian philosophy of history, these theologians adapted historicist perspectives that sought to differentiate between an eternal Jewish teaching and its various temporal manifestations, that is, how it was expressed in different eras. On this basis, they argued that the widespread reform of Jewish practice was not only permissible but necessary both to preserve what they saw as the eternal Jewish teaching and to sustain Jews as full members of a modern society.

The process of adapting Jewish ritual and liturgy to the new possibilities and realities of modern life proceeded in fits and starts. Traditionalists protested that specific reforms of Jewish practice such as the introduction of organ music on the Sabbath violated rabbinic law, halacha; cynics saw these efforts at reform as little more than a series of concessions to the Christian public, whose suspicions of traditional Judaism spilled over from time to time into blatant antisemitism. In this line, Leora Batnitzky refers to the liberalization of Judaism in the modern period as "the invention of Jewish religion," arguing that modern Jewish thinkers re-conceptualized Judaism in terms borrowed from liberal Protestantism rather than native to the tradition's own understanding of itself. She writes that "prior to modernity ... Judaism was not a religion, and Jewishness was not a matter of culture or nationality. Rather, Judaism and Jewishness were all these at once."[2] In the pre-modern period, Jewish life was shaped largely by halacha and by its rabbinic interpreters, who held considerable power within the corporate Jewish communities of pre-modern Europe. As Jews gained rights as modern citizens through the process of emancipation, rabbis lost the power to monitor and enforce communal norms. The individual Jew was freed to determine how he would express his Jewishness.

[2] Leora Batnitzky, *How Judaism Became a Religion: An Introduction to Modern Jewish Thought* (Princeton: Princeton University Press, 2011), 2.

The decline of rabbinic authority thus entailed a loosening of communal norms and opened the door for ritual and theological innovation. At the same time, as Batnitzky emphasizes, it allowed for the redefinition of Jewishness as Judaism: a religion composed of beliefs and ritual practices and specifically not a nationality. Thus an individual could be Jewish while also being German. Or, as the founding document of the *Centralverein deutscher Staatsbürger jüdischen Glaubens* (Central Association of German Citizens of the Jewish Faith) asserted in March 1893,

We German citizens of Jewish faith stand firmly on the ground of German nationality. Our community with Jews of other countries is not different from the community of German Catholics and Protestants with the Catholics and Protestants of other countries. We happily fulfill our duties as citizens and keep to our constitutional rights.[3]

That this association was founded to combat a rise in antisemitism, however, suggests that the ground of German nationality was not as firm as Jews wanted it to be.

Batnitzky contends that by pursuing and eventually receiving citizenship with the overt understanding that German (or French or British, etc.) Jews would be Jewish just as German (or French or British, etc.) Protestants were Protestant, Jews transformed their Jewishness from an all-encompassing identity into Judaism, a set of beliefs and practices parallel to the beliefs and practices of Protestant Christianity. Her implication is that to understand Jewishness as Judaism and nothing else is to abandon Jewishness, for the beliefs and rituals of the Jews are tied inextricably with their identity as a people. I think, though, that Batnitzky's argument suggests that the modern reformers of Judaism approached their Jewishness from a purely utilitarian perspective, turning it into a currency that would allow them to buy their way into the larger society.

In what follows, I will present a more generous reading of the liberalization of Judaism in the nineteenth century, arguing that this process of reform reflected an earnest expression of commitment to Jewish practice and thus to Jewishness. The theologies that emerged alongside the liberalization of Jewish practice sought to define a modern Judaism in light of a commitment to liberal values of individualism and rationalism, but they also reflected a deep appreciation of the history of Judaism. I will argue further that it is the latter aspect of liberal Jewish theology that is more radical and ultimately more significant. What we see in the earliest liberal theologies is not an attempt to jettison the past so much as to argue that the past itself demanded change in the present. By the mid-nineteenth

---

[3] Cited in Birnbaum and Katznelson, *Paths of Emancipation*, 91–92.

century, secularism – the opting out of religious belief and practice and another consequence of Enlightenment – offered an alternative to Jews who were largely uninterested in their cultural or religious heritage yet did not want to convert to Christianity. Making Jewish ritual palatable to Jews who were turned off by Judaism because they found Orthodox practice foreign to their modern worldview was a crucial motivation for many of the reformers.

My account of liberal Judaism addresses three distinct spheres: the popular or lay experience of shifts into new modes of Jewish ritual practice; the development of new formal institutions to give structure, coherence, and stability to these new modes of Jewish practice; and the articulation of a theological underpinning for the movement and the emergence of thinkers to guide the movement intellectually and ideologically. In the first two sections of this essay, I examine the development of Reform Judaism in nineteenth-century Germany and twentieth-century America with attention to each of these perspectives. In the third section, I consider the legacy of the liberalizing impulse in twentieth-century Jewish thought. Throughout, my intention is to highlight central issues in the practice of liberal Judaism and the development of its theology.

THE LIBERALIZATION OF JEWISH PRACTICE AND THEOLOGY IN NINETEENTH-CENTURY GERMANY

Arnold Eisen defines modern Jewish practice as "the extremely varied sorts of behavior through which Jews over the last two centuries have (among other things) registered God's presence and absence, marked their own apartness and connection, celebrated their passages through the year and the years, fulfilled their communal duties, and remembered their distant or immediate ancestors."[4] In light of this definition, we might say that the liberalization of Judaism offered Jews the chance to express their Jewishness in a way that was in accord with their modernized worldview and to gain a spiritual sustenance that rang true with the Enlightenment values they had already adopted and that supported them as they pursued and attained civic emancipation.

Though efforts at reform were also undertaken in England, France, and elsewhere, I focus below on the reform movement in Germany. The German *Aufklärung* was far friendlier to religion than the French or British Enlightenments, and both liberal Judaism and liberal forms of Christianity flourished under its influence. As the nineteenth century unfolded, there

---

[4] Arnold Eisen, *Rethinking Modern Judaism: Ritual, Commandment, Community* (Chicago: University of Chicago Press, 1999), 79.

were more conservative periods when liberal Christianity was frowned upon and both Protestant and Catholic reform efforts were stymied; liberal Judaism was affected similarly. Nevertheless, the general trend in nineteenth-century Germany was toward the liberalization and reform of Jewish practice and theology.

Michael Meyer highlights changes made to Jewish practice and Jewish education in the Kingdom of Westphalia in the early nineteenth century as a starting point. Westphalia was composed of various territories conquered by Napoleon and then governed by his brother, who granted all subjects equality before the law, making Westphalia the first German state to emancipate its Jews. Religious reforms were largely instituted by a Jewish consistory of six deputies set up by the state to regulate Jewish life. These deputies took it upon themselves not only to ensure a uniform practice of Judaism across the state but also to update that practice to bring it in line with the changing times. The specific changes they proposed anticipated what would come to be the defining characteristics of liberal synagogue practice: Sabbath services were to include a sermon emphasizing moral reflection on the issues of the day and delivered by the rabbi, preferably in German; the synagogue service was to be orderly, with an emphasis on the cantor's role in chanting the liturgy rather than the active participation of the congregants; and limited changes were made to be made to the liturgy itself, mostly the elimination of medieval *piyutim*, "which breathed a spirit of oppression and suffering,"[5] having been written under the duress of anti-Jewish violence, a threat these moderns wanted to consider long past.

The structure of the Seesen Temple, which was completed in 1810, reflected these shifts in ritual practice: it included a raised platform for the delivery of sermons and an organ. As Meyer comments, "taken as a whole, the structure made a social statement: Jews worship as do Christians; they are their equals in religion as in civil life."[6] The Seesen Temple stood as a monument to the consistory's attempts to reform Jewish practice for an emancipated Jewish population; but within a few years the consistory disbanded in the face of communal resistance, financial difficulties, and the ultimate demise of the Kingdom of Westphalia in 1813.

Early efforts to change Jewish practice unfolded differently in Prussian Berlin and the free city of Hamburg. Together with the reformers of Westphalia, events in these cities in the 1810s and 1820s offer us a snapshot of the issues that liberal Jews would continue to face through the century. Berlin was home to about 3,500 Jews, whose attitudes toward Judaism

[5] Michael A. Meyer, *Response to Modernity: A History of the Reform Movement in Judaism* (Detroit: Wayne State University Press, 1995), 36.

[6] Ibid., 41.

varied from those who viewed their Jewishness as little more than a social hindrance to a traditionally minded observant community. Between these two poles were those who rejected conversion but maintained that Judaism needed to be updated and brought in line with modern values. Conflict among the Jews of Berlin was intensified by pressure from the conservative Prussian government that had replaced Napoleon and which tried to limit new developments in Jewish practice.

While practice in the central synagogue of Berlin continued in the traditional manner, those who wished to experiment with Jewish ritual and liturgy found the space to do so in private homes. Though Frederick William III shut down the earliest gatherings of this type, when the Berlin synagogue underwent renovations from 1817 to 1823, all Jewish worship had to be conducted in private homes and the monarch could no longer intervene to the same degree. Jacob Herz Beer hosted reform-minded worshippers in his home, where services included a boys' choir singing in German to the accompaniment of an organ and a sermon addressing the issues of the day and delivered in German. As in Westphalia, the prayerbook used in the Beer service eliminated medieval *piyutim*; it also altered or eliminated prayers calling for a messianic return to the Land of Israel, lest they call into question the loyalty of Jews to their adopted lands. Appeals made by Berlin traditionalists to Frederick William III – and, ironically, the monarch's preference that spiritually stymied Jews convert to Christianity rather than make their own religion more appealing – led the government to shut down the reformers' services in 1823.[7]

In Hamburg, unlike in Prussia, the government established after the defeat of Napoleon was largely uninterested in the Jewish community's internal affairs and did not jump to intervene on behalf of either the reform-minded or more traditionally oriented factions. The "New Israelite Temple Association in Hamburg," founded in 1817, called for "restoring dignity and meaning to Jewish worship and thus revising interest in the ancestral religion"; it aimed to do this through the introduction of an organ, a choir, and a sermon as well as the recitation of some prayers in German.[8] The Temple Association also undertook a comprehensive revision of the prayerbook, changing or eliminating prayers that referred to an ingathering of the exiles and the return of sacrificial worship in messianic times, lest they be taken as a statement of a collective "unrootedness" in the present. At its earliest peak, the Temple Association counted not quite 10 percent of the Jewish community as members; it drew many individuals and families who had not been at a synagogue service for many years

[7] Ibid., 52.
[8] Ibid., 54.

prior. Protests by Hamburg traditionalists opposed to the efforts of the Temple Association ultimately led to a compromise between the factions. When appointing a new community rabbi in 1821, Hamburg's Jews chose a rabbi who would institute limited reforms in the community's central synagogue while not interfering with the more radical reform of Jewish practice undertaken by members of the Temple Association, which continued to exist as an alternative.

These early cases highlight how efforts to make Judaism more attractive through the introduction of choral music and a greater emphasis on decorum – both adopted from the model of worship Jews would have known from Christian churches – as well as revisions of the traditional liturgy were shaped by the experience of German Jews within larger and ever-shifting political contexts. The reform of Jewish ritual was undertaken with an awareness that Jews were on display before a Gentile audience judging their collective suitability to be a part of broader society. But I do not wish to suggest that the liberal Judaism is an imitation of liberal Protestant Christianity. Rather, I agree with Eisen's argument that "decisions made by Jewish individuals, movements, and groups throughout the modern period to maintain, alter, or discard distinctive Jewish observances have ... ultimately represented decisions about the *marking of difference,* and thereby served to effect a greater or lesser degree of *separation from Gentile neighbors and fellow citizens.*"[9] That is to say, in re-presenting themselves as similar but not the same, liberal Jews took charge of their difference from the mainstream culture and turned it into a matter of degree rather than letting that culture define them as utterly different and apart. As we will see, theologians and rabbis defined Jewish difference as a commitment to ethical monotheism – belief in God as the source and guarantor of human morality – and viewed ritual as a means of inspiring Jews spiritually and cultivating the sense of purpose that this commitment demanded.

ARTICULATING A LIBERAL JEWISH THEOLOGY

In 1896, Solomon Schechter, who was soon to become the president of the Jewish Theological Seminary of America, noted that "Liberty was always given to the great teachers of every generation to make modifications and innovations in harmony with the spirit of existing institutions. ... The norm as well as the sanction of Judaism is the practice actually in vogue. Its consecration is the consecration of general use."[10] The standards of Jewish

---

[9] Eisen, *Rethinking,* 107.
[10] Solomon Schechter, "Historical Judaism," in *Tradition and Change: The Development of Conservative Judaism,* ed. Mordecai Waxman (New York: Burning Bush Press, 1958), 95.

practice and the norms of Jewish ritual, in other words, are set by everyday Jews living their lives as they see fit. The "great teachers" of each generation were those who followed the people and formally articulated – or justi- fied – the ritual and behavioral norms that were effectively already in place.

Schechter made his claim in the name of traditional Judaism, refuting those who feared that Higher Criticism of the biblical text endangered its future. Schechter claimed that the Torah text was never the sole guide for Jewish practice and thus that Judaism as a living tradition would not be threatened by attacks on the integrity of its scripture. Schechter himself had been raised in a traditional home in Romania before studying at the University of Cambridge, joining the faculty there, and eventually gain- ing renown for his work on the medieval documents found in the Cairo Geniza in 1896. He was rooted in tradition but deeply invested in historical study of Judaism.

In the essay cited above, Schechter points to the scholarship of Leopold Zunz (1794–1886), who was a founding member of the Verein für Kultur and Wissenschaft der Juden (Society for the Culture and Science of the Jews) in 1819. Zunz and his colleagues were dedicated to the pursuit of the evolution of understanding Judaism as a historical phenomenon. Though the society collapsed just a few years later, Zunz remained devoted to the *Wissenschaft des Judentums*, the Science of Judaism, the foundation of today's Jewish Studies, for the rest of his life. Describing his research, Zunz wrote that

Only by considering the literature of a nation as a gateway to a comprehensive knowledge of the course of its culture throughout the ages, by noting how at every moment the essence of the given and the supplementary, i.e., the inner and the external, array themselves; how fate, climate, customs, religion and chance seize one another in friendly or hostile spirit; how, finally, the present is the necessary result of all that preceded it – only thus will one tread with true reverence.[11]

Zunz did not view the Talmud as an oral Torah composed of content revealed by God to Moses on Mount Sinai and then passed down from generation to generation until finally recorded in writing, as the rabbis of the Talmud had themselves claimed. He did not presume that the Jewish culture and religion revealed through the study of rabbinic literature made an undeniable or unalterable claim upon the Jews of later times. Rather, what Zunz proposed to do is to historicize Judaism by studying its

---

[11] Leopold Zunz, "On Rabbinic Literature," in *The Jew in the Modern World: A Documentary History*, eds. Paul R. Mendes-Flohr and Jehuda Reinharz, 2nd edition (New York: Oxford University Press, 1995), 223.

literature as a human production influenced by the concerns and beliefs of the time and place in which it was written.

In claiming that Jewish practice at any given moment reflects the intellectual currents of the time, Zunz proposed to take a radically different attitude toward the history of Judaism. A traditional approach to Jewish practice looks to the past to determine what is permissible in the present. In contrast, Zunz's model pointed forward, as he intended that study of the past would reveal Judaism's course of evolution and thus inspire its re-expression in a new context. Zunz was aware that what he proposed broke sharply with traditional modes of study. His call for "true reverence," however, signals that he saw his approach as being more respectful of the rabbinic tradition than that of those liberals who might abandon it as hopelessly irrelevant or those traditionalists whose reverence prevented them from recognizing the dynamism of the tradition.

If Judaism has always been evolving, then it must continue to evolve, and Zunz was an active participant in the liberalization of Judaism. (Beyond his ideological commitment to the reform of Judaism, preaching in reform-minded synagogues provided him with a livelihood as he pursued his research outside of the structure of a university or research institute.) The ideas proposed by the Society for the Culture and Science of the Jews supplied an intellectual foundation for the theologians whose work provides us with a second piece in our understanding of the liberalization of Judaism. For illustration of this point, I turn to the work of Abraham Geiger (1810–1874), who like Zunz was both a historian and a rabbi. While Geiger's scholarship focused on early Christianity, his theological writings offer an important picture of the relationship between the historicization of Judaism and its liberalization in the nineteenth century.[12]

Geiger's most important contribution to the liberalization of Judaism in the modern period is in the theological principles he articulated in sermons and other writings, as he transformed the basic historicizing tendency of the *Wissenschaft des Judentums* into an attitude toward the Jewish past that empowered individual Jews to steer the course of Judaism in the present. In an 1838 sermon, Geiger admonished his audience to

be very mindful of the pure and genuine grain of wheat in your faith, of the pure fear of God, so that you will work in behalf of the welfare of mankind. The outer shell, the ritual forms, are but bearers of the spirit in which that spirit becomes visible and by which it may mature; but do not forget that they are of no further use to piety once they no longer bear that spirit within them. Times and circumstances change, and necessitate many modifications and new institutions which,

[12] Susannah Heschel, *Abraham Geiger and the Jewish Jesus* (Chicago: University of Chicago Press, 1998).

in keeping with contemporary circumstances, are needed to keep our religion alive.[13]

Using a stalk of wheat as a metaphor, Geiger portrayed Jewish ritual as existing solely to nurture and protect the precious core of Judaism as the outer husk protects the grain of wheat. At a certain point in the grain's development, the husk is no longer necessary and even blocks access to the nourishing potential of the grain. Geiger argued that ritual similarly threatens to outlast its purpose; the impulse to reform Jewish practice is an attempt to discard the dry husk that blocks the true teaching articulated in the Bible and nurtured through generations of Jewish history. Thus, he wrote, "do not complain when it seems to you that things are changing. The truth is that nothing has really changed. All that changes is the outer shell, only some outward forms undergo modification; the essence of things remains intact."[14]

In his writings, Geiger attempted to rethink Judaism in light of modern understandings of truth and the evolution of civilization, but he also insists that many of these understandings have deeply misconstrued Judaism. Within Geiger's writings, the philosophies of Hegel, Schleiermacher and others offer a new lens on Judaism while his accounts of Judaism offer a rejoinder to these philosophers' privileging of Christianity and their disparaging of Judaism or Jews.[15] As an example, we can consider how Geiger's 1838 sermon echoes themes central to Friedrich Schleiermacher's *On Religion* (1799). Written as a series of five speeches for philosophical friends who scoffed at religion, Schleiermacher's short book attempts to separate the individual's intuition of the divine from the metaphysical assertions of established religion. The former, he argued, is religion; every human being is capable of it. But the latter is also important, as the religious individual seeks the fellowship of others who are so inclined and seeks to ground his or her own religious experience in the teachings of a church. Though the church structure remains important, individual experience precedes its teaching. In this vein, Schleiermacher defined revelation as

Every original and new intuition of the universe … and yet all individuals must know best what is original and new for them. And if something of what was original in them is still new for you, and then their revelation is also one for you, and I advise you to ponder it well. What is inspiration? It is merely the religious name

---

[13] Abraham Geiger, *Abraham Geiger and Liberal Judaism: The Challenge of the Nineteenth Century*, ed. Max Wiener (Cincinnati: Hebrew Union College Press, 1981), 247–248.

[14] Ibid., 248.

[15] Ken Koltun-Fromm, *Abraham Geiger's Liberal Judaism: Personal Meaning and Religious Authority* (Bloomington: Indiana University Press, 2006), 2.

for freedom. Every free action that becomes a religious act, every restoration of a religious intuition, every expression of a religious feeling that really communicates itself so that the intuition of the universe is transferred to others, took place upon inspiration; for it was an action of the universe by the one on the others.[16]

Schleiermacher's emphasis on intuition and feeling marks him as a Romantic; his empowerment of the individual to determine his own course marks him as a liberal. He argued that human beings are universally capable of religious experiences, and organized religion exists for individuals to come together and share what they have sensed. But judging whether a religious teaching is a religious truth – what Schleiermacher described as an intuition of the universe – begins with the individual. The truth of any single teaching must be judged by the individual; the term revelation refers not to a divine disclosure captured in Scripture but to religiosity, a human capacity to sense the spiritual.

As the sermon quoted above illustrates, Geiger also distinguished between an eternal religious truth and the different trappings it takes. While for Schleiermacher religious experience intuits metaphysical truths, Geiger defined the central teaching of Judaism as a moral teaching, namely, that God demands and expects just action. He highlighted the biblical prophets' deriding of empty religious ritual as offensive to God in light of the inequality and injustice they observed in Israelite society.

Addressing himself more directly toward a Hegelian philosophy of history, in his book *Judaism and its History* Geiger described Judaism as "a grand, world-historic phenomenon," insisting that its importance is ongoing:

[Judaism] is not something that entered upon the world's stage for a certain time, and during that time exerted great influence, but as something finite, disappeared again and has become merely a subject for historical consideration. No, we may call it a world-historic phenomenon as an institution reaching back into that period whence historical knowledge began for the world, having not only existed for thousands of years and still existing, but because [it has] passed, as it were, as an immortal traveler through history, continuously accompanying history and co-operating with history from its very beginning to this day.[17]

Geiger intended his account of Jewish history to refute the Hegelian view that Judaism was an ancient phenomenon, which had made its contribution to human culture with the invention of monotheism and should have

---

[16] Friedrich Schleiermacher, *On Religion: Speeches to Its Cultured Despisers* (New York: Cambridge University Press, 1996), 49.
[17] Abraham Geiger, *Judaism and Its History: In Two Parts*, Brown Classics in Judaica (Lanham, MD: University Press of America, 1985), 13.

long since disappeared from the world's stage. As "an immortal traveler" among humanity, Geiger argued, Judaism is continually contributing to human culture through its understanding and expression of ethical monotheism, a morality rooted in God. As a reformer, Geiger believed that the shedding of archaic Jewish rituals was not only permissible but necessary for the preservation and continued promulgation of the Jewish teaching, and in this he hewed more closely to Hegel. Parallel to Hegel's account of *Geist* (Spirit), Geiger wrote that the Jewish truth itself demands expression; in a synagogue setting that expression should take a spiritually uplifting ritual form and be rid of rituals inherited from the past that no longer served that purpose. If we borrow Geiger's metaphor from his sermon, we might say that the Jewish truth was a grain of wheat demanding that it be stripped from the rabbinic chaff that had accumulated over centuries and now hid it from view.

But the relationship between theology and religious practice is not as simple as Geiger makes it out to be. Ken Koltun-Fromm points to a specific argument between Geiger and Zunz as an illustration of this point. In light of their shared interests in scholarship and in the reform of Jewish practice, Geiger and Zunz were for many years close colleagues. But their friendship was ultimately strained by Zunz's decision to observe the dietary laws of kashrut, which for Geiger exemplified an outmoded ritual law lacking in any meaningful spiritual content. While Geiger was willing to accept Zunz's kashrut if it was decision he had made for political reasons, namely, to support his role as a leader of the Jewish community, he could not accept that Zunz found the dietary laws to be in any sense compulsory.

Koltun-Fromm rightfully argues that this conflict reveals Geiger as more fully liberal than Zunz in their respective understandings of the relationship between the individual Jew and Jewish tradition:

> Geiger's religious idealism evokes the image of an eternal religious sensibility that continually seeks out more adequate ritual practices. Tracking the movement from an inner spiritual idea to an outer material world underwrites Geiger's reforming practice. ... In Zunz, Geiger has lost more than a liberal Jewish colleague. He confronts an enlightened scholar who acts from commitments hostile to Geiger's own.[18]

In his analysis of this episode, Koltun-Fromm highlights how Geiger's liberalism was influenced by the idealist philosophy that surrounded him. This example also illustrates a final piece of the intellectual milieu in which liberal Judaism developed, namely, the moral philosophy of Immanuel Kant.

---

[18] Koltun-Fromm, *Geiger's Liberal Judaism*, 78.

Like Hegel, Kant had little room in his philosophy for a living Judaism. As Eisen describes, Judaism's offense in Kant's eyes was threefold. The first problem was halacha, both for its emphasis on ritual and for its legalistic structure. The second problem was Judaism's promise of divine reward and punishment within this world (rather than solely after death). Finally, Kant suggested that Jewish claims to be God's chosen people might limit their ability to fit into a society that granted universal rights to all citizens.[19]

Kantian ethics is based in rational reflection, and rational religion, which inculcated its practitioners with moral sense so that they would be empowered to act ethically. Rational religion, which Kant found only in Christianity, was defined by belief in a moral Being and not by ritual. Promises of reward and punishment after death were acceptable only insofar as they might serve as a spur for the individual's development of moral autonomy. Halacha, in contrast, demanded obedience, not moral reflection, and it presumed an active divine providence. In contrast to Christianity, Kant viewed Judaism as a case of heteronomy, a law imposed upon the individual from outside that demanded blind obedience and left her moral sense undeveloped. As Eisen comments, "it was precisely the Jewish *religion* that Kant attacked – and he attacked it not in traditional Christian terms … but in the name and language of Enlightenment."[20] It was within this larger intellectual context that liberal Jewish theologians of the nineteenth century sought to redefine Judaism as a tradition that respected the autonomy of the individual and cultivated morality.

ORGANIZING

The reform of Judaism was made possible in part by the decline in rabbinic authority over Jewish communities concomitant with the processes of civic emancipation. But in the 1820s, the earliest reformers often found their efforts stymied by traditionalist factions among their fellow Jews and by state edicts issued by rulers interested in avoiding religious factionalism that might destabilize the society, as we saw above. Meyer points instead to the 1830s as the decade in which there was a growing sense of a reform *movement*, reflecting "a feeling of unity, direction, and quickened pace" among liberal rabbis and laity. Opposition from more traditional factions helped to define this movement, while internal disagreements slowed the pace of institutionalization.[21]

[19] Eisen, *Rethinking*, 28–29.
[20] Ibid., 29.
[21] Meyer, *Response to Modernity*, 108.

Liberal German rabbis gathered three times in the 1840s, at Brunswick (1844), Frankfurt (1845), and Breslau (1846). Participants discussed both philosophies of reform and specific questions such as whether prayer in German was permissible and/or preferable. While all agreed that the answer to the former question was "yes," it was the latter question – whether it was *preferable* to pray in German – that proved divisive. Zecharias Frankel famously left the Frankfurt Assembly over exactly this question, insisting that Hebrew was essential to Judaism and that Jews found spiritual and emotional meaning in Hebrew prayer even if fewer and fewer than ever understood it.

Frankel called his approach to reform "Positive Historical Judaism." It was *positive* because it asserted the inviolability of the written Torah as revelation from Sinai; it was *historical* because it was cognizant of Judaism changing over time and thus open to a limited updating of beliefs and practices in the present. Frankel understood the oral Torah not as revelation per se (as the Orthodox insisted) but as a human interpretation of written Torah developed in particular historical contexts. In practical terms, Frankel believed that changes to ritual had to resonate with *klal Yisrael*, with the laity as a whole. Thus, a group of rabbis had no authority to declare Hebrew out-of-date and impose prayer in German when the majority of Jews found praying in the language of their ancestors more meaningful than praying in their own vernacular and understanding the literal meaning of each word, as Frankel believed they did.

Though the Frankfurt rabbis were too liberal for Frankel, they were, on the whole, still moderates. There were a few who argued that the spirit of the times should be the most important determining factor in Jewish practice and that no aspect of the tradition was sacrosanct. But the majority sought to reject only the most offensive practices and also hoped both to reform and revive ritual customs with the potential to be spiritually uplifting and to introduce new practices. In Frankfurt, the rabbis also addressed a few doctrinal issues, messianism among them. As we saw above, the question of whether modern Jews believed in the coming of a messiah or a messianic return to the land of Israel and reestablishment of the ancient Jewish state was an issue for modern reformers of Jewish practice from the very beginning. What emerged from the rabbis' discussion was consensus around belief in a universal messianic redemption for all people and rejection of any specific hopes or prayers for return to Israel and reestablishment there of a Jewish state.

The rabbis in Frankfurt nevertheless affirmed that Jews had a special role to play in the world, that of a mission to bring religion – in the form of ethical monotheism – to all of humanity. This sense of mission would come to serve as a replacement for messianism; rather than sustaining hope in a divine redemption, the reformers' sense of a Jewish mission asserted human agency in shaping history and, ultimately, bringing all of humanity to a true morality. Redemption in these terms is decidedly universal rather than particular to the Jewish people. In universalizing messianism but stressing a sense of Jewish mission, the Frankfurt rabbis were also reasserting Jewish particularity. Their choice to embrace Jewish particularism, even if they avoided the language of chosenness, reflects the fact that by 1845 most German Jews enjoyed the rights and privileges of emancipation.

Meyer judges these rabbinical assemblies as having been something of a disappointment, noting that the rabbis who gathered together had no real claim to authority and that they themselves remained unsure of what they were setting out to do. They risked being seen as destructive, "more visibly lopping off leaves and branches than stimulating new growth." Most importantly, "the conference members had difficulty in deciding whether their assignment was simply to sanction changes and omissions already current or to influence the course reform would take. They were caught between conflicting desires not to offend traditionalists at home by supporting radical new proposals and their wish to play some role in shaping the Judaism of the future."[22] Even so, the conversations and decisions made at the three rabbinic assemblies attracted widespread support for the work of reform that had begun just a few decades earlier. Laypeople grew more interested in liberal Judaism, and the work of the German reformers began to spread across Europe and also to America.[23]

The first two stable and long-lasting institutions of liberal Judaism were both rabbinic seminaries. A synod in Leipzig in 1869 brought together liberal laypeople and rabbis from across Europe and from the United States to discuss issues of ritual practice, and it led to the establishment of a seminary, the Hochschule für die Wissenschaft des Judentums (The College of Jewish Studies) in Berlin, for the training of liberal rabbis. It was while teaching at this liberal seminary that the neo-Kantian philosopher Hermann Cohen turned his eye to Judaism and defended it as the most developed expression of ethical monotheism and thus, rational religion.[24] A decade after leaving the Frankfurt conference, Frankel served as the first president of the Jewish Theology Seminary in Breslau, where rabbinic

[22] Ibid., 141.
[23] On the relationship between German reformers and their counterparts in America, see Tobias Brinkmann, *Sundays at Sinai: A Jewish Congregation in Chicago* (Chicago: University of Chicago Press, 2012), 62–72; 76–78.
[24] Cohen's most extensive treatment of Judaism is his posthumous 1919 work *Religion of Reason out of the Sources of Judaism*. Hermann Cohen, *Religion of Reason Out of the Sources of Judaism*, trans. Simon Kaplan (New York: Frederick Ungar, 1972).

training was shaped by his positive-historical approach. Both seminaries were ultimately shut down by the Nazis.

LIBERAL JUDAISM IN AN AMERICAN KEY

Though its roots were European, liberal Judaism flourished most freely in the United States, where Jews have been present since the colonial period. The earliest American Jewish communities were largely lay-led, functioning without the presence of rabbis. More traditional rabbis, especially in Eastern Europe, considered it impossible to live a truly Jewish life in America; they themselves were extremely unlikely to immigrate, and they also discouraged their followers from doing so. As a result, the liberal rabbis who immigrated to the United States as part of a major wave of Jewish immigration from German states in the mid-nineteenth century found an opportunity to pursue their visions of a new and improved Jewish theology and practice. In America, they were relatively free of the disapproval of an established Jewish Orthodoxy or the interference of government authorities experienced by colleagues who remained in Europe.[25]

American laws of citizenship do not differentiate between Jew and non-Jew; no one could argue that Jewish practice needed to be adapted for the sake of civic emancipation. But the liberalization of Judaism in America was still viewed by many as a matter of keeping the tradition relevant in circumstances radically different from those encountered by Jews at any other point in their history. In the nineteenth century, American rabbis debated how best to attract American Jews to Jewish practice. Isaac Leeser's translation of the Hebrew Bible into English, done so that American Jews (women, especially) who did not read Hebrew would not have to rely on Protestant translations, was a modest attempt to accommodate Judaism to the American situation.[26] More liberal rabbis advocated the adaptation of the religion and its rituals so that American Jews would find it "more appealing and spiritually uplifting." The specific reforms they advocated included the same organ music and abbreviation of Sabbath worship

---

[25] Jonathan Sarna estimates that 150,000 Jews immigrated to America between 1820 and 1877. Though they came from around the globe – including 7,000 from Eastern Europe – the majority were from Bavaria, Western Prussia, and Posen. Jonathan Sarna, *American Judaism: A History* (New Haven: Yale University Press, 2004), 63–64.

[26] On the increased participation of women in nineteenth-century American synagogues and their corresponding desire for translated sacred texts, see Pamela S. Nadell, *Women Who Would Be Rabbis: A History of Women's Ordination 1889–1985* (Boston: Beacon Press, 1999), 8–10.

services that were common in Germany and thus appealed to many of the German Jewish immigrants arriving in this period.[27]

The lack of a firmly established American Jewish Orthodoxy also made it possible for liberal rabbis such as Isaac Mayer Wise to argue that American Jews could be organized into a single religious body to be guided by rabbis trained at a central rabbinical seminary. Over the course of his career, Wise, who arrived in the United States in 1846, inspired the Union of American Hebrew Congregations (UAHC, started by lay leaders in 1873), founded the Hebrew Union College (HUC, 1875) and the Central Conference of American Rabbis (CCAR, 1889), and published a prayerbook under the title *Minhag Amerika* (1857), the American custom. Jonathan Sarna describes Wise as "pragmatic, flexible, and politically savvy"; his approach to religious reform was not so much ideologically rigorous as it was practical (though he did firmly reject the traditional doctrine of bodily resurrection in the messianic era, an idea that also came under fire among German reformers).[28]

An 1862 editorial in Wise's journal *American Israelite* highlights how the differences between American and European political conditions shaped the liberalization of Judaism in each respective place. Like his fellow liberal rabbis in Europe, Wise described Jewishness as a religion. But he asserted that if American law were to conflict with his religious, that is, Jewish, convictions he would rebel against the state: "I and my conviction are identical, and I can not sacrifice it without renouncing my manhood, which no government has a right to demand."[29] For Wise, Jews were better Americans for being Jewish; their Judaism gave them a moral compass more sensitive and better tuned than that found in any government or legal system. Judaism's moral teaching, internalized and then realized in moral actions, provides Jews with their "manhood," their very selves. In contrast to the eternal Jewish teaching and the moral training it provides, citizenship is by its nature always temporary. Citizenship could be changed over the course of a life; one was either a man or not a man. Wise's essay reverberates with his own disappointment in emancipation and his own experience as an immigrant to America.

However much Wise might have hoped that the institutions he shaped would serve as unifying bodies, over the next decades the American Jewish community was reshaped by the arrival of immigrants from different

---

[27] Sarna, *American Judaism*, 83.

[28] Ibid., 96–98.

[29] Isaac Mayer Wise, "'First Americans, Then Israelites': An Editorial in the American Israelite," in *The Jew in the American World: a Source Book*, ed. Jacob R. Marcus (Detroit: Wayne State University Press, 1996), 206.

corners of the Jewish world. Though Orthodoxy continued to attract only a minority of Jews, the arrival of immigrants from Eastern European – first as a trickle and then in large waves between 1880 and 1920 – ensured that it did not disappear. As a definitive split between the Orthodox and reform movements emerged in the late nineteenth century and the two sides became more formally defined, HUC became the seminary for Reform rabbis; and CCAR the central professional organization of Reform rabbis. The UAHC became the organization of Reform synagogues, and changed its name to the Union for Reform Judaism (URJ) in 2003.[30]

The Pittsburgh Platform, composed by a group of rabbis convened by Wise's HUC successor Kaufmann Kohler in 1885, reflects the liberal Jewish theology of this era in eight succinct statements. It rejects rituals deemed archaic, such as the laws of kashrut and the priestly code of purity found in Leviticus; it also insists upon a modification of messianic ideals, including the rejection of any desire to return to the Land of Israel, to restore the ancient Kingdom of David, or to resume ritual sacrifices. The Platform affirms the evolution of Judaism in the past and the need for its continued evolution with an emphasis on the abiding moral content of the religion and the retention of "only such ceremonies as elevate and sanctify our lives." The Platform further describes Judaism as "a progressive religion, ever striving to be in accord with the postulates of reason."[31] In line with the theologies developed by the German reformers, the Platform's assertion that Judaism strives to be in accord with the principles of reason defines it as a religion according to the terms set by Kant; it claims both Christianity and Islam as "daughter religions," suggesting that there would be no religion of reason at all without Judaism. The Platform also describes Jews as charged with a mission to share the religion of reason; its writers are gratified to recognize "that the spirit of broad humanity of our age is our ally in the fulfillment of our mission ... and extend the hand of fellowship to all who cooperate with us in the establishment of the reign of truth and righteousness among men."[32] Unlike the German reformers who seemed eager to show their Christian neighbors that "we are just like you," the Platform sends a message to American Christians that "you are just like us," by highlighting both a shared history and a shared dedication to the

[30] Frankel's Positive-Historical Judaism also thrived on American soil in the form of the Jewish Theological Seminary of America and the Conservative Movement of Judaism that developed there. See Moshe Davis, *The Emergence of Conservative Judaism: The Historical School in 19th Century America* (Philadelphia: Jewish Publication Society, 1963).

[31] "Declaration of Principles" in *Platforms Adapted by the CCAR*, Central Conference of American Rabbis, accessed on July 24, 2013, www.ccarnet.org/rabbis-speak/platforms/.

[32] Ibid.

promotion of righteousness. That the Platform ends with a call to work against poverty reminds us, however, that the document was also born in the era of the Protestant Social Gospel in America.[33]

By succinctly and authoritatively summarizing a list of principles that would guide liberal Jewish congregations and individuals as they made their way as practitioners of Judaism and as citizens of the world, the Pittsburgh Platform achieved what the rabbinic conferences of the 1840s failed to do. It built on the concepts of progress, reform, and mission that had guided the movement's German forebears, but did so free from the pressures of an established Orthodoxy and government interference. The statements of the Pittsburgh Platform were also more liberal than any resolutions produced by the rabbinic assemblies in Brunswick, Frankfurt, and Breslau or by the Leipzig synod, particularly in their definitive rejection of the dietary laws and other customs associated with purity. The principles and practices of this era have come to be known as Classical Reform.

CRITIQUES OF LIBERAL JUDAISM IN THE TWENTIETH CENTURY AND TODAY

From its beginnings, liberal Judaism faced criticism from traditionalists who questioned its authenticity and defended the integrity of halacha. In the twentieth century, however, liberal Judaism's chief critics came from within. Below, I highlight three twentieth-century thinkers who critiqued the liberal ideologies developed by Geiger, Zunz, and others. I begin with the German Jewish thinker Franz Rosenzweig and his call for the return of a sense of commandedness as the essence of Judaism. I then skip forward to the post-war period in the United States, looking first at Eugene Borowitz's liberal covenantal theology and then at Rachel Adler's idea of a liberal halacha. I conclude with a few words about central tensions running through the history of liberal Judaism.

In his essay "The Builders" (1923), Rosenzweig argued that Jewish law is not halacha and that the relevance and necessity of Jewish law does not rest on the denial or defense of rabbinic Judaism. As he wrote, "the problem of the Law cannot be dispatched by merely affirming or denying the pseudo-historical theory of its origin, or the pseudo-juristic theory of its power to obligate."[34] For Rosenzweig, the immediate experience of God's love for humanity is the starting point of religion. Divine love of humanity commands human love of God in return; ritual is the Jewish people's

---

[33] Sarna, *American Judaism*, 151.

[34] Franz Rosenzweig, "The Builders: Concerning the Law," in *On Jewish Learning*, ed. Nahum N. Glatzer (New York: Schocken, 1989), 79–80.

answer to being commanded. Thus, for Rosenzweig, the validity of Jewish law is not the right question; he challenged *both* Orthodox and liberal Jews to restore a sense of commandedness, of being called to serve God. When fulfilled in response to a sense of commandedness, he argues, Jewish rituals express the essence of the Jewish people; they are not laws to be obeyed (as the Orthodox do) or baldly rejected (as liberals do).[35] As with God's love, rituals must be a lived experience, enacted and not analyzed: "What is doable and even what is not doable yet must be done nonetheless, cannot be known like knowledge, but can only be done. ... And the sphere of 'what can be done' extends far beyond the sphere of the duties assumed by orthodoxy."[36] In insisting that revelation is an ongoing experience that demands a response, Rosenzweig rejected the historicist platform of liberal Judaism.[37]

Over time, what was novel and new in the nineteenth century became outdated and irrelevant. At the same time, the rise of a postmodern era in philosophy (and its repercussions in Christian theology and other fields) signaled a serious questioning of the Enlightenment ideals that had undergirded the liberalization of Judaism. A general sense that modernity failed to live it up to its promises had particular resonance among Jews of all movements and perspectives in light of the six million European Jews murdered by the Nazis during the Holocaust. Particularly in the United States, the 1970s and 1980s saw the rise of Jewish theologians whose work focused on the implications of the Holocaust for understanding the relationship between the Jewish people and God. Could they affirm the biblical claim that God acts in human history? If so, why did God not act to stop the Nazis? If not, what had become of the biblical covenant between the Jewish people and God and the attendant claims of Jewish chosenness and/or mission?[38] At the same time, many found a measure of solace in the establishment of the State of Israel in 1948, whether they understood it as God's return to human history or viewed it as evidence that the Jewish

---

[35] On Rosenzweig's concepts of divine revelation, Judaism, and the Jewish people, see his magnum opus, the *Star of Redemption*, especially Parts II and III. Franz Rosenzweig, *The Star of Redemption*, trans. Barbara E. Galli (Madison: University of Wisconsin Press, 2005).

[36] Rosenzweig, "The Builders: Concerning the Law," 82.

[37] On anti-historicism in Jewish thought, see David N. Myers, *Resisting History: Historicism and Its Discontents in German-Jewish Thought* (Princeton: Princeton University Press, 2009).

[38] On post-Holocaust theology, see Zachary Braiterman, *(God) After Auschwitz* (Princeton: Princeton University Press, 1998); Michael L. Morgan, *Beyond Auschwitz: Post-Holocaust Jewish Thought in America* (New York: Oxford University Press, 2001).

people would now be able to take care of themselves and would no longer need to rely upon a God who had proven unreliable.[39]

In the second half of the twentieth century, the Holocaust and the establishment of the State of Israel replaced Emancipation and Enlightenment as the most significant events for Jewish theological reflection. In *Renewing the Covenant* (1996), Eugene Borowitz wrote that

> Once Jews could confront the Holocaust in its own satanic fullness and see it as the terrifying symbol of humankind's demonic energies, they identified Western culture as an ethical fraud. With modernist messianism discredited, we modern Jews, like many others in our civilization have had to rethink our most fundamental beliefs, particularly with regard to the age-old Jewish concern: How, really, must we live?[40]

Influenced by trends in postmodern thought, Borowitz sought to retrieve and renew concepts central to pre-modern Judaism but rejected by earlier reformers in the name of Enlightenment. This attempted retrieval, however, is balanced by Borowitz's affirmation that emancipation was, in sum, to the benefit of Jews and Jewish practice: two paragraphs after declaring "Western culture [to be] an ethical fraud," Borowitz wrote that "Jews overwhelmingly do not wish to return to the ghetto. We remain devoted to modernity's central benefit, equality, and to the democratic pluralism that has enabled us to live in human decency as rarely before in our history."[41]

Borowitz's critique of modernity represents a shift in liberal Jewish theology, and his attempt to retrieve a pre-modern concept of covenant that modern Judaism may have abandoned too quickly does give his theology a postmodern flavor. But Borowitz wanted to revive a concept of covenant that is specifically *biblical*, and in doing so he remains within Geiger's paradigm of embracing the Hebrew Bible and largely rejecting the conceptual and ritual traditions developed by the rabbis. Furthermore, Borowitz insisted that the individual Jew must remain empowered to decide for himself or herself how to act out the covenant. The authority of the individual

---

[39] The reform movement offered a tentative support of Zionism in the 1937 Columbus Platform. This support was restated in the 1976 San Francisco Platform and then again in 1997, in a special platform on Zionism. In these platforms, the movement's leaders affirm the desirability of a Jewish state but in various ways deny that the Jewish people should be defined as a nation. "The Guiding Principles of Reform Judaism," "Reform Judaism: A Centenary Perspective," "Reform Judaism and Zionism: A Centenary Platform," *Platforms Adapted by the CCAR*, Central Conference of American Rabbis, October 27, 2004, accessed on July 24, 2013, www.ccarnet.org/rabbis-speak/platforms/.

[40] Eugene B. Borowitz, *Renewing the Covenant: A Theology for the Postmodern Jew* (Philadelphia: Jewish Publication Society, 1996), 5.

[41] Ibid., 5–6.

is underscored by his writing that "God and the individual self are the two axes around which my faith pivots."[42] In discussing the idea of a human duty to God, he wrote that

caring non-halakhic Jews can be understood as fervently seeking to serve God as participants in the Jewish people's historic relationship with God and guided by its tradition, though convinced that Covenant-faithfulness today mandates their deviance from the past. ... Covenantal selfhood begins with the effort to base one's life on one's Jewish faith and then seek to give it expression in all one's ways.[43]

Thinking back to Geiger, we might say that for Borowitz, covenant is now the germ of Judaism, but rituals remain the chaff that threatens to choke it. The individual is the sole authority in evaluating and when necessary removing that chaff.

In *Engendering Judaism* (1998), Rachel Adler argued that the concept of covenant alone is not enough to bind a community together. She argued instead that liberal Jews must rejuvenate the concept of halacha by identifying and developing the practices that best reflect their communal values and then treat these practices as normative for the members of their community. While early reformers rejected halacha because they viewed it as an impediment preventing them from expressing their modern values, Adler argued that liberal Judaism has lost its progressive momentum and its practices are no longer in line with the values of its adherents; the careful articulation of a new halacha will serve to realign the two.

Adler presented a distinctively liberal understanding of halacha. Like generations of liberal Jews before her, she denied that halacha is rooted in revelation or that there is any sort of divine accountability for fulfilling it. However, for Adler, it is because halacha is a distinctly human system that restoring it has the potential to remake Judaism for the twenty-first century, and she stressed the role of halacha in drawing people together through their participation in interrelated and connected practices. As she wrote,

If we had a praxis rather than a grab bag of practices, we would experience making love, making *kiddush*, recycling paper used at our workplace, cooking a pot of soup for a person with AIDS, dancing at a wedding, and making medical treatment decisions for a dying loved one as integrated parts of the same project: the holy transformation of our everyday reality.[44]

---

[42] Ibid., 31.

[43] Ibid., 217.

[44] Rachel Adler, *Engendering Judaism: An Inclusive Theology and Ethics* (Boston: Beacon Press, 1999), 26.

Adler's list brought together practices that are clear examples of ritual (e.g., making *kiddush*) with practices that generally happen outside of ritual settings (e.g., recycling paper at work), purposefully presenting halacha as an all-encompassing way of living rather than something whose relevance is limited to sacred time and space. Her argument on behalf of halacha, much like the original reformers' rejection of halacha, attempted to open existing ritual practices to questioning. The purposeful construction of a new halacha requires asking: is this meaningful? Is it in line with our shared values? This in turn demands that the community articulate the values it holds central. Adler thus asserted that values evolve over time and that rituals must as well; she argued that the structure of halacha can enable this.

One of Adler's chief concerns in her theological work is to ensure that both men and women are active participants in the articulation of a liberal halacha. Her intention is that the formal structure of a halacha will overcome pervasive but informal limitations on women's participation in liberal Jewish communities. More broadly, the evolution of women's roles in Jewish practice and communal leadership offers a window onto the interplay between tradition and reform through the history of liberal Judaism. While the earliest reformers rejected practices such as *halitzah*, in which a childless widow is required to marry her dead husband's brother, they maintained the tradition of separate seating for men and women in the synagogues and continued to limit leadership roles to men. Speaking of liberal Judaism's foundations, Adler suggests that the early reformers eliminated the customs such as monthly immersion in a *mikvah* that once defined Jewish womanhood while also maintaining limits on women's participation in the public sphere. As she wrote, "deprived of the Orthodox practices that had distinguished them as women and of the education and leadership opportunities still reserved for men, women in liberal Judaism became even more invisible than they had been before."[45] It is worth noting that it was only in the 1970s, in the context of second wave feminism, that the Hebrew Union College began ordaining women as rabbis.[46]

---

[45] Ibid., 63.

[46] On the place of women in liberal American synagogues, see Karla Goldman, *Beyond the Synagogue Gallery: Finding a Place for Women in American Judaism* (Cambridge: Harvard University Press, 2009); Jonathan Sarna, "The Debate Over Mixed Seating in the American Synagogue," in *The American Synagogue: A Sanctuary Transformed*, ed. Jack Wertheimer (New York: Cambridge University Press, 1987), 363–394. On the ordination of women as rabbis, see Nadell, *Women Who Would Be Rabbis*. On Adler as a feminist theologian, see Claire Sufrin, "Telling Stories: The Legal Turn in Jewish Feminist Thought," in *Gender and Jewish History*, ed. Marion Kaplan and Deborah Dash Moore (Bloomington: Indiana University Press, 2010), 233–250.

Finding the proper relationship between ritual and belief was central to the earliest reformers who rejected rituals and liturgies that seemed to express beliefs that they did not hold. In some cases, these beliefs were incompatible with their modern values; in other cases, they had simply lost their relevance. Both Borowitz and Adler, even as they criticized the earlier reformers for having been too hasty in their pruning of Jewish traditions, continued to place values and beliefs first and rituals second.

We must also recognize that liberal Judaism emerged as Jews sought to be recognized as equal members of the general society. Its development was driven by a desire for rituals and liturgy that would allow modern Jews to express their Jewishness in a way that would not conflict with their embrace of Enlightenment ideals of freedom, individualism, and above all, the universal equality of all human beings. But how does a community determine its values and beliefs? How does an individual do so? Borowitz's mixture of praise for emancipation and criticism for the failures of Enlightenment reveals that the tension between the particularism inherent in the biblical concept of a covenant with God and the Enlightenment value of universal equality that opened the door for Jews to participate fully in the modern world remains alive. We might at this point ask whether Rosenzweig's critique also retains its force. In arguing that Judaism must be first and foremost a lived tradition, he put ritual first and belief second. It is important that the Orthodox who defend rabbinic halacha are no less guilty in Rosenzweig's eyes. What all of these moderns have done is to rob ritual and, by extension, God of power. Baldly rejecting modern individualism, Rosenzweig made duty a central piece of his theology; he also renewed a Jewish particularism positing an essential difference between Jewish and Christian modes of being. How might today's liberal Jews answer his claims?[47]

SELECT BIBLIOGRAPHY

Adler, Rachel. *Engendering Judaism: An Inclusive Theology and Ethics.* Boston: Beacon Press, 1999.

Batnitzky, Leora. *How Judaism Became a Religion: An Introduction to Modern Jewish Thought.* Princeton: Princeton University Press, 2011.

Birnbaum, Pierre and Ira Katznelson, eds. *Paths of Emancipation: Jews, States, and Citizenship.* Princeton: Princeton University Press, 1995.

---

[47] For one answer to this question, see Steven Kepnes, Peter Ochs, and Robert Gibbs, *Reasoning After Revelation: Dialogues in Postmodern Jewish Philosophy* (Boulder: Westview Press, 2000).

Borowitz, Eugene B. *Renewing the Covenant: A Theology for the Postmodern Jew*. Philadelphia: Jewish Publication Society, 1996.

Brinkmann, Tobias. *Sundays at Sinai: A Jewish Congregation in Chicago*. Chicago: University of Chicago Press, 2012.

Buber, Martin. *On Judaism*. New York: Schocken Books, 1996.

Cohen, Hermann. *Religion of Reason out of the Sources of Judaism*. Trans. Simon Kaplan. New York: Frederick Ungar, 1972.

Cohen, Steven M. and Arnold M. Eisen. *The Jew Within: Self, Family, and Community in America*. Bloomington: Indiana University Press, 2000.

Davis, Moshe. *The Emergence of Conservative Judaism: The Historical School in 19th Century America*. Philadelphia: Jewish Publication Society, 1963.

Eisen, Arnold. *Rethinking Modern Judaism: Ritual, Commandment, Community*. Chicago: University of Chicago Press, 1999.

Geiger, Abraham. *Abraham Geiger and Liberal Judaism: The Challenge of the Nineteenth Century*. Edited by Max Wiener. Cincinnati: Hebrew Union College Press, 1981.

Judaism and Its History: In Two Parts. Brown Classics in Judaica. Lanham, MD: University Press of America, 1985.

Goldman, Karla. *Beyond the Synagogue Gallery: Finding a Place for Women in American Judaism*. Cambridge: Harvard University Press, 2009.

Heilman, Samuel. *Sliding to the Right: The Contest for the Future of American Jewish Orthodoxy*. Berkeley: University of California Press, 2006.

Hess, Jonathan M. *Germans, Jews and the Claims of Modernity*. New Haven: Yale University Press, 2002.

Hirsch, S.R. *The Nineteen Letters*. Nanuet, NY: Feldheim Publishers, 1995.

Kaplan, Mordecai M. *Judaism as a Civilization: Toward a Reconstruction of American-Jewish Life*. Philadelphia: Jewish Publication Society, 2010.

Koltun-Fromm, Ken. *Abraham Geiger's Liberal Judaism: Personal Meaning and Religious Authority*. Bloomington: Indiana University Press, 2006.

Marcus, Jacob R, ed. *The Jew in the American World: A Source Book*. Detroit: Wayne State University Press, 1996.

Mendes-Flohr, Paul R. *Divided Passions: Jewish Intellectuals and the Experience of Modernity*. Detroit: Wayne State University Press, 1991.

Mendes-Flohr, Paul R. and Jehuda Reinharz, eds. *The Jew in the Modern World: A Documentary History*. 2nd edition. New York: Oxford University Press, 1995.

Meyer, Michael A. *The Origins of the Modern Jew: Jewish Identity and European Culture in Germany, 1749–1824*. Detroit: Wayne State University Press, 1979.

Response to Modernity: A History of the Reform Movement in Judaism. Detroit: Wayne State University Press, 1995.

Morgan, Michael L. *Dilemmas in Modern Jewish Thought: The Dialectics of Revelation and History*. Bloomington: Indiana University Press, 1992.

Myers, David N. *Resisting History: Historicism and Its Discontents in German-Jewish Thought*. Princeton: Princeton University Press, 2009.

Nadell, Pamela S. *Women Who Would Be Rabbis: A History of Women's Ordination 1889–1985*. Boston: Beacon Press, 1999.

Rosenzweig, Franz. "The Builders: Concerning the Law." In *On Jewish Learning*, edited by
    Nahum N. Glatzer, 72–92. New York: Schocken, 1989.

Sarna, Jonathan. *American Judaism: A History*. New Haven: Yale University Press, 2004.

Waxman, Mordecai, ed. *Tradition and Change: The Development of Conservative Judaism*.
    New York: Burning Bush Press, 1958.

CHAPTER 13

THE NEW JEWISH POLITICS

DAVID ENGEL

THE HISTORIOGRAPHICAL BACKGROUND

During the final third of the nineteenth century a relatively small number of Jewish intellectuals, most of them veterans of the Haskalah movement in the Russian and Austro-Hungarian Empires, began to urge their fellow Jews from all walks of life to engage in what was for virtually all of them a new sort of behavior: they called upon Jews to organize themselves into groups for the purpose of addressing collective demands to the rulers of the states in which they lived and to acquire the measure of political power needed to persuade the rulers to accede to them. Over the following decades, through the years of the Nazi Holocaust and beyond, increasing numbers of Jews in the two empires, as well as in their successor states and in the countries of large-scale Eastern European Jewish migration in Western Europe, North and South America, Palestine, and the southern hemisphere, answered those calls by forming and supporting an array of specifically Jewish ideological movements and political parties aimed at mobilizing the greatest possible number of Jews around their demands in the belief that mass mobilization would force the demands' acceptance.

Many of the Jews who led this mobilization effort ascribed to their calls and actions a twofold novelty. First, whereas in earlier times Jews had tended to entrust their relations with the state authorities to individual negotiators (*shtadlanim*), who acted on their own authority or at the behest of religiously sanctioned community elites, the exponents of mass political mobilization insisted that spokesmen for any Jewish community be empowered by the community's entire membership and represent its freely expressed will. Secondly, whereas Jews had traditionally sought to win the protection of state authorities through private pleading or by offering goods or services that the state needed and Jews could supply, advocates of mass politics saw the key to success in public enunciation of their demands combined with skillful organization and cultivation of support from non-Jewish elements. Many scholars who have studied the political engagements of Eastern European Jews in the late nineteenth and

363

twentieth centuries have taken these self-representations more or less at face value. In doing so they have made the phrase "modern Jewish politics" synonymous with that specifically Eastern European Jewish political activity: for them the story of "modern Jewish politics" is the story of the Jewish parties and movements - Zionist, socialist, Diaspora nationalist, and the various permutations of these diverse trends that emerged out of their interactions with one another – that crystallized in the final decades of Romanov and Habsburg hegemony and reached their apogee between the two world wars.

A rich literature describing those movements individually, often in considerable detail, first emerged during the 1920s and continues to grow. In contrast, sustained, systematic scholarly discussion of the character, origins, and trajectory of "modern Jewish politics" in general arguably dates only from 1981, when Jonathan Frankel published his monumental *Prophecy and Politics*, a 700-page exploration of "the political response to the crisis of Russian Jewry in the period 1881–1917."[1] That political response, Frankel claimed, extended well beyond the boundaries of the Russian Empire; it involved Jews throughout Europe and the Americas, mostly but not exclusively of Eastern European origin, in the creation of "one political subculture," whose "lingua franca was Yiddish; its economic base, the clothing industry and the sweat shop; its politics, the running dispute and constant interaction between socialist internationalism and Jewish nationalism; its organizational expression, the Yiddish press, the public meeting, the trade union, the ideologically committed party, and (where relevant) the armed self-defense unit."[2] Yet at the same time, he argued, that political subculture spoke only to that part of the Jewish world that had not experienced what he called the "liberal" pattern in modern Jewish life. Frankel posited a fundamental difference between the experience of Jews in Western and Central Europe, which had been molded by an evolutionary and ultimately successful campaign to obtain civic equality as individuals within the framework of the regimes under which they lived, and that of Jews of Eastern European origin, who, having seen their own quest for equality frustrated, sought revolutionary regime change in the name not only of liberty and equality but of self-determination for Jews as a group as well. Their "search for total solutions to problems that could be resolved only in part," he ventured, epitomized "the predicament of the Jewish people as it entered the twentieth century."[3] Hence he directed his spotlight toward

[1] Jonathan Frankel, *Prophecy and Politics: Socialism, Nationalism, and the Russian Jews, 1862–1917* (Cambridge: Cambridge University Press, 1981), 1.
[2] Ibid., 3.
[3] Ibid., 560.

what he called the "postliberal pattern in modern Jewish life."[4] "Modern Jewish politics" embodied for him a move "directly from a preliberal to a postliberal stage of development, from medieval community to projects for national revival, from a religious to a social and secular messianism."[5]

Frankel's magisterial synthesis aroused widespread discussion about several key issues he had raised. In 1993, Frankel's colleague from the Hebrew University of Jerusalem, Ezra Mendelsohn, observed that the movements about which Frankel had written had generated a "competition" among a broad range of groups "for hegemony on what was sometimes called the 'Jewish street'."[6] Those groups, he noted, included not only parties inspired by nationalist or socialist ideals but also organizations advocating religious orthodoxy or the amalgamation of Jews as individuals into the surrounding liberal or socialist society. Mendelsohn identified seven fundamental issues over which the various competitors divided: the definition of the Jewish collectivity, the language or languages in which Jewish life should be conducted, the place or places in which Jews should live, the episodes and periods in Jewish history that should be most highly valued, the elements in the non-Jewish world with whom Jews should seek alliances, the tactics to be employed in pursuit of Jewish collective aims, and the prognosis for Jewish life in the Diaspora. Any organization that ventured an opinion on these issues and that sought to draw Jews to its banner was, he suggested, a participant in "modern Jewish politics." Hence Mendelsohn posited a much wider scope for "modern Jewish politics" than had Frankel. Indeed, he included within the rubric even groups like the Jewish sections of the various Soviet Communist parties or of the American Socialist Party, which were parts of larger political formations, as well as "the so-called Jewish labor unions in the United States," like Sidney Hillman's Amalgamated Clothing Workers of America, which did not address Jews alone but whose largely Jewish membership displayed a keen interest in the modern Jewish political agenda and offered other Jews a distinct approach to its central problems.

Mendelsohn did not concern himself with "the early, formative period of modern Jewish politics, thereby avoiding the much-debated question as to when, exactly, it began."[7] Nevertheless, his work permitted the inference that for him the competition that animated "modern Jewish politics" had been born from the same catastrophic upheavals in Eastern Europe that

[4] Ibid., 1.
[5] Ibid., 2.
[6] Ezra Mendelsohn, *On Modern Jewish Politics* (New York: Oxford University Press, 1993), viii.
[7] Ibid.

Frankel had earlier identified as its crucible – the pogroms of 1881–82, the abortive Russian revolution of 1905–1907, the First World War, and the revolutions of February and October 1917. But by the time he published his survey, voices questioning that view had begun to be heard. In 1989 Eli Lederhendler had taken aim at the notion that revolutionary Jewish nationalist and socialist movements were best understood as spontaneous responses to the sudden traumatic ruptures that Frankel had emphasized. Noting that those movements constituted "an obvious break with Jewish tradition," which had never afforded popular will any "autonomous value or authority," Lederhendler wondered how they could arise "overnight in a community that presumably had no political institutions or political leaders." "Are purely external factors – such as government pressure, persecution, economic and social discrimination, and political alienation – sufficient," he asked, "to induce the creation of political movements if there are not some internal developmental factors at work in a society as well?"[8] Consequently, he looked for "the common elements of [those movements'] political activism, their definition of Russian Jewry as a political community, and their democratic and secularizing thrust" in the decades before 1881, the year of Frankel's "historical big bang."[9]

What Lederhendler called "internal factors" turned out to have been largely state-induced: the determination of those who ruled the bulk of Russo-Polish Jewry since the mid-eighteenth century – the authorities of the Polish-Lithuanian Commonwealth before the partitions of that country and successive Russian tsars thereafter – to govern Jews through the general instruments of state administration instead of allowing them the broad communal autonomy that had previously characterized their relations with the state had, he argued, "spawned new [Jewish] leadership groups ... stimulated the search for new forms of [political] activity, and ... facilitated the discovery of the 'people's will' as the foundation for a new type of political community."[10] At the center of his narrative stood a small group of maskilim – Jewish men possessing elements of a European education – who, he claimed, between 1830 and 1870 took over several crucial roles formerly the province of traditional elites, turning themselves in the process into the Russian government's principal advisers on Jewish affairs. In his view, this intermediary position presented them with the twofold task of intervening with the state on behalf of collective Jewish interests on

[8] Eli Lederhendler, *The Road to Modern Jewish Politics: Political Tradition and Political Reconstruction in the Jewish Community of Tsarist Russia* (New York: Oxford University Press, 1989), 3–4.

[9] Ibid., 5.

[10] Ibid., 155.

the one hand and instructing Jews concerning the state's expectations of them on the other. The latter, didactic mission was, he argued, a primary function of the Jewish press in the Russian Empire, which was largely a maskilic creation. The press, in turn, provided Eastern European Jewry with what Lederhendler termed a new "'public space' for conflict without coercion and for open-ended debate," becoming in the process the central arena in which the competition among Frankel's post-1881 movements.[11]

Lederhendler's work implicitly offered more than a mere chronological challenge to Frankel's notion of "modern Jewish politics"; it also subverted his argument that Russian Jewry had passed directly from a preliberal to a postliberal phase. As portrayed by Lederhendler, the maskilim who laid the foundation for "modern Jewish politics" resembled Western and Central European liberals quite closely: "their conviction [was] that both Jews and non-Jews must come to regard Russian Jewry as an integral part of Russian society."[12] Two subsequent works, by Christoph Gassenschmidt[13] and Benjamin Nathans,[14] made the challenge explicit. Nathans formulated it clearly: "Despite relatively unfavorable conditions, the historical trajectory of Russian Jewry was profoundly shaped by aspirations for civic emancipation and social integration. These aspirations separated what Frankel labels the 'medieval' and the 'postliberal' currents of Russian-Jewish life, and in fact competed simultaneously with both."[15] For him, "the politics of emancipation and integration" belonged most emphatically within the field of "modern Jewish politics" no less than did the politics of Jewish nationalism and socialism[16] Nathans recognized that such an incorporation was tenable only if "modern Jewish politics" was defined by something other than mass mobilization for acquisition of a share of state power. Accordingly, he adduced an alternative criterion for Jewish political modernity: modern Jewish politics differed from its pre-modern counterpart in its view of the state less as "the ultimate guarantor of the social and political order" than as an arena for ensuring the rule of law over arbitrary government.[17]

---

[11] Ibid., 133.

[12] Ibid., 110.

[13] Christoph Gassenschmidt, *Jewish Liberal Politics in Tsarist Russia, 1900–14: The Modernization of Russian Jewry* (New York: New York University Press, 1995).

[14] Benjamin Nathans, *Beyond the Pale: The Jewish Encounter with Late Imperial Russia* (Berkeley: University of California Press, 2002).

[15] Ibid., 10.

[16] Benjamin Nathans, "The Other Modern Jewish Politics: Integration and Modernity in Fin de Siècle Russia," in *The Emergence of Modern Jewish Politics: Bundism and Zionism in Eastern Europe*, ed. Zvi Gitelman (Pittsburgh: University of Pittsburgh Press, 2003), 21.

[17] Ibid., 22, 26.

But if such is the defining characteristic of modern Jewish politics, then the longstanding emphasis on Eastern Europe as its locus of origin and most exemplary development seems misplaced. Indeed, as Nathans recognized, the organizations that Russian Jewish liberals created in pursuit of their "judicial approach to advancing Jewish interests" had close parallels in Western and Central Europe.[18] Yet still the phrase "modern Jewish politics" continues to evoke primary association with the major ideological movements and parties that emerged in the Russian and Habsburg Empires toward the end of the nineteenth century.

What follows offers an alternative to this association. Beginning from consideration of the three terms that comprise the phrase, it suggests that a single fundamental political demand *vis-à-vis* the non-Jewish world and a fundamental strategic aim associated with it have long united a far broader range of Jewish groups than hitherto imagined, and it locates the origins of "modern Jewish politics" in the time and place where the demand was initially enunciated.

"MODERN JEWISH POLITICS": THE TERMS OF REFERENCE

Like most abstractions, "politics" is a protean term. In its earliest usage it denoted mainly intellectual activity – contemplation of the perfect society or the most efficacious manner of governance. From the seventeenth century, however, English speakers have increasingly placed its referents in the social realm, associating it with practical *acts* of governance, principally of bodies exercising executive functions or legislative prerogatives. That usage has also encompassed deliberate efforts to influence such acts, usually by acquiring a share of power within or over the bodies that initiate them.

"Politics" also carries widely varying connotations. Often the word has assumed derogatory overtones, especially when signifying pursuit of power. For nineteenth-century American journalist Ambrose Bierce it implied "a strife of interests masquerading as a contest of principles,"[19] while his contemporary Henry Adams, scion of one of the great political families of the United States, equated it with "the systematic organization of hatreds."[20] Others, in contrast – recalling, perhaps, the word's initial association with lofty ideals – have accorded it a morally positive valence, no matter what they have taken it to denote. Indian leader Mohandas Gandhi attributed his own efforts to influence acts of governance to his religiously rooted

---

[18] Ibid., 25, 24.
[19] Ambrose Bierce, *The Devil's Dictionary* (n.p. 2006), 191.
[20] Henry Adams, *The Education of Henry Adams* (Boston: Houghton Mifflin, 1918), 7.

identification with "the whole of mankind,"[21] while for twentieth-century philosopher Hannah Arendt, "politics rests upon the fact of human plurality ... [and] concerns itself with how *diverse* individuals might coexist" within a single community.[22]

Not surprisingly, the term's elasticity has been a source of much confusion, not least in discussions of the manner in which Jews have involved themselves collectively in politics during different eras in their past. Arendt, who spent a portion of her adult life in the employ of Jewish communal organizations, famously proclaimed in 1951 that "Jewish history offers the extraordinary spectacle of a people, unique in this respect, which began its history with a well-defined concept of history and an almost conscious resolution to achieve a well-circumscribed plan on earth and then, without giving up this concept, avoided all political action for two thousand years."[23] Her fellow Jewish intellectual of Central European origin, Hans Kohn, who likewise earned his living for several decades as a Jewish public servant, offered a similar assessment around the same time: "Judaism ... [has been] a unique phenomenon, strongly rooted in the spiritual instead of the political realm."[24] Each held that for most eras in Jewish history the phrase "Jewish politics" was meaningless; it suggested forms of thought or activity that simply did not exist. Yet for all their superficial similarities the two statements actually ascribed fundamentally different meanings to the word "politics" and embodied two radically divergent assessments of the Jews' historical (non)engagement with the political realm. Kohn associated that realm with the pursuit of particularistic self-interest, from which the universalist ideals of the Hebrew prophets – which Jews, he claimed, adopted as their governing ethos once the ancient Judean state disappeared – had (happily, to his mind) long protected them. Arendt, by contrast, understood politics as a vehicle for forging a sense of common humanity beyond individual and group differences in a manner that transcended particularistic self-interest. Hence for her, Jews' alleged avoidance of political action testified not to their prophetic universalist commitments but to precisely the opposite – pursuit of their own narrow group concerns without regard for the needs of the larger communities in which they lived. For that reason, she held, it was to be bemoaned and condemned.

---

[21] M. K. Gandhi, *Non-violence in Peace and War* (Ahmedabad: Navajivan, 1948), 1:170.

[22] Hannah Arendt, *Was ist Politik? Fragmente aus dem Nachlaß* (Munich: Piper, 2003), 9. Emphasis in source.

[23] Hannah Arendt, *The Origins of Totalitarianism* (New York: Harcourt, Brace and Co., 1951), 8.

[24] Hans Kohn, "Zion and the Jewish National Idea," in *Zionism Reconsidered*, ed. M. Selzer (London: Macmillan, 1970), 177.

True, many scholars have dissented from the assertion that over the centuries Jews have divorced themselves from politics, but they have done so more often than not by substituting their own particular understandings of the word for those of their interlocutors instead of engaging them on their own terms. As a result, they have often misrepresented the nature of their disagreement. For example, in an oft-cited essay historian Ismar Schorsch challenged all assertions of "the non-political view of Jewish history," especially Arendt's version, with the contention that "Jews have displayed over time an unusual ability to identify their collective interests, to assess the possibilities for action, to locate allies, to organize and deploy their resources, and to learn from their failures and mistakes."[25] Arendt, however, would doubtless have agreed that Jewish history was replete with such displays; her charge was rather that throughout their history Jews had misidentified their collective interests by refusing to associate them with actions that encouraged all groups to submerge their own immediate concerns and by disavowing the promotion of feelings of solidarity among them. On the empirical level, in other words, Arendt and Schorsch did not necessarily differ; their conflict lay rather in their antithetical evaluations of an active tradition whose existence both acknowledged.

That conflict, in turn, like the one between Arendt and Kohn, is itself a reflection of a debate Jews have conducted among themselves since, at the latest, the revolutionary era of the late eighteenth century – a debate over how collective Jewish interests ought to be formulated and pursued and how the physical security and material wellbeing of Jews throughout the world might be maximized. Virtually all of the many Jewish intellectuals, communal leaders, and social activists who have taken part in this debate have suggested that achieving such a goal demands that Jews strive to influence the manner in which the governing agencies of the states in which they live allocate the distribution of goods and resources among their subjects. The suggestions they have offered have varied widely. Some have indeed advised Jews to pursue an ostensibly "nonpolitical" path to that end, one that eschews any organized effort to obtain a measure of state power as Jews or even to appear publicly as a distinct interest group. Yet even those who have asserted this position with the greatest vigor (or who, like Kohn, have represented it as a traditional Jewish ideal) have done so in the context of a discussion of how Jews ought to interact with institutions of government – that is, with the object of virtually all thought or action considered "political" in ordinary speech. The phrase "Jewish politics" can thus reasonably encompass this assertion, together with activities to win

---

[25] Ismar Schorsch, *On the History of the Political Judgment of the Jew*, Leo Baeck Memorial Lecture 20 (New York 1976), 7, 9.

broad acceptance of it among Jews, just as it can comprehend contrary
assertions and activities by other participants in the ongoing give-and-take
over the question of how best to enhance Jews' security and prosperity.

To be sure, that question did not occur to Jews only under the impact of
modern revolution; Jews have confronted it over the course of many centuries. The terms in which they have debated it, however, changed fundamentally with the revolutionary suggestion that Jews might, under certain
conditions, possess a claim on available resources equal to that of other
subjects of the states under whose jurisdiction they lived. Before the late
eighteenth century Jews resided virtually everywhere under regimes that
denied any such claim to equality, insisting that the extent to which Jews
were permitted to benefit from government services or local economies be
strictly circumscribed and inferior (in theory, at least) to that enjoyed by
adherents of the majority religion. What is more, Jews themselves generally regarded their inferior status as altogether legitimate. Because, they
believed, God had banished them from their historic homeland as punishment for failure to uphold the divine covenant with Israel, they lik-
ened themselves to prisoners of war, labeling themselves mere "temporary
sojourners" (*ara'iyim*) among the "rightful inhabitants" (*dayorin*) of their
countries of residence and expecting those inhabitants to serve as rods of
divine chastisement until God Himself redeemed them in His own good
time.[26] The American and (even more emphatically) French Revolutions
dealt a powerful blow to that self-image. On September 28, 1791, the day
following a proclamation by the French National Assembly annulling all
restrictions that French law had hitherto imposed upon Jews and recognizing any Jew taking the standard oath of allegiance to the French state as a
full-fledged citizen, Alsatian Jewish manufacturer Berr Isaac Berr ventured
that the Assembly's act had transformed the Jews of France "of a sudden"
from "vile slaves, mere serfs, a species of men merely tolerated and suffered
in the empire, liable to heavy and arbitrary taxes," into "children of the
country, to bear its common charges, and share in its common rights."[27]
Over the course of the nineteenth century, steadily growing numbers of
Jews throughout the world came to believe that they both could and should
aspire to similar status in their own countries of residence. That change of
conviction, in turn, invited Jews who shared it to consider ways of maxi-
mizing the benefits and resources available to them, without imposing any
limits upon themselves or recognizing the legitimacy of limits imposed or

---

[26] Deut. Rabbah, 1:20.
[27] Berr Isaac Berr, "Letter of a Citizen to His Fellow Jews (1791)," in *The Jew in the Modern
World: A Documentary History*, eds. Paul Mendes-Flohr and Jehuda Reinharz, 2nd edition (New York: Oxford University Press, 1995), 119.

suggested by others. Such consideration signaled the advent of a peculiarly *modern* "Jewish politics."

ASSUMPTIONS AND QUESTIONS

The change of conviction that provided the basis for all modern Jewish politics (understood in this sense) had profound implications for the manner in which Jews comprehended the very nature of their collective being. The prospect that Jews might be included as equal citizens in their states of residence not only heralded a new era of solidarity between Jews and non-Jews sharing allegiance to a common political community; it also demanded that Jews cease to think of themselves in any way as banished captives of nations serving as instruments of divine discipline. Non-Jewish opponents of inclusion, who continued to resist the revolutionary settlement well after its advent, had long argued that that self-conception, along with the concomitant expectation of eventual messianic redemption and restored sovereignty, effectively barred Jews from developing feelings of patriotism and allegiance toward their countries of residence sufficient to justify granting them automatic claim upon the protection or resources of modern nation-states, let alone access to positions of political authority or sociocultural influence in them. Thus in 1806 Napoleon Bonaparte made it clear that the recently enfranchised Jews of France must not "consider the government under which [they] live as a power against which [they] should be on [their] guard." Only in this way, he explained, would they prove that Jews did not "seclude [themselves] from the rest of mankind" and could be counted as "faithful subjects, determined to conform in every thing to the laws and to the morality which ought to regulate the conduct of all Frenchmen."[28]

Jews who were prepared to accept this demand to modify longstanding attitudes toward the nature of their relationship with non-Jewish governing powers were convinced that citizenship in a modern nation-state (i.e., permanent inclusion within the political community that constituted the state, whose needs and interests the state existed to serve) promised far greater stability and security than had been possible under the earlier system of chartered corporate autonomy, in which the extent to which Jews enjoyed state protection was inscribed only in a finite contract negotiated between Jewish communities and territorial rulers without reference to the rights or privileges retained by any of the rulers' other subjects and depended entirely upon the rulers' ability and willingness to abide by its

---

[28] Count Molé, "Napoleon's Instructions to the Assembly of Jewish Notables (July 29, 1806)," in *The Jew in the Modern World*, 125.

terms. That belief was enunciated clearly in 1790 in a letter to US President George Washington by Moses Seixas, warden of the Jewish congregation in Newport, Rhode Island:

Deprived as we heretofore have been of the invaluable rights of free citizens, we now (with a deep sense of gratitude to the Almighty Disposer of all events) behold a government erected by the majesty of the people – a government which to big-otry gives no sanction, to persecution no assistance, but generously affording to all liberty of conscience and immunities of citizenship, deeming every one, of what-ever nation, tongue, or language, equal parts of the great governmental machine. This so ample and extensive federal union, whose basis is philanthropy, mutual confidence, and public virtue, we cannot but acknowledge to be the work of the Great God, who ruleth in the armies of heaven and among the inhabitants of the earth, doing whatsoever seemeth him good.[29]

Washington's response to Seixas's greeting could only have reinforced Jewish confidence in the linkage between civic equality and security:

The citizens of the United States of America have a right to applaud themselves for having given to mankind examples of an enlarged and liberal policy, a policy wor-thy of imitation. All possess alike liberty of conscience and immunities of citizen-ship. It is now no more that toleration is spoken of, as if it was by the indulgence of one class of people that another enjoyed the exercise of their inherent natural rights. For happily the government of the United States, which gives to bigotry no sanction, to persecution no assistance, requires only that they who live under its protection should demean themselves as good citizens, in giving it on all occasions their effectual support … May the children of the stock of Abraham who dwell in this land continue to merit and enjoy the good will of the other inhabitants, while every one shall sit in safety under his own vine and fig-tree, and there shall be none to make him afraid.[30]

Nonetheless the American president's message adumbrated both the limitations of the promise of security through citizenship and the intel-lectual reorientation the promise required. As Washington put it, though no doubt without intent, the achievement of the prophet Micah's vision of a peaceful end of days (here figured as physical security and material well-being for Jews in the here-and-now) depended henceforth upon the Jews' merit in the eyes not of God but of "the other [non-Jewish] inhabitants" of the countries that had emancipated them. An obvious implication of this secularization of the concept of redemption was that equal citizenship would now require Jews to interpret instances of insecurity more as the

[29] The Hebrew Congregation of Newport, Rhode Island, "Message of Welcome to George Washington (August 17, 1790)," in *The Jew in the Modern World*, 457–458.

[30] George Washington, "A Reply to the Hebrew Congregation of Newport (c. August 17, 1790)," in *The Jew in the Modern World*, 458–459.

result of their own failure to obtain non-Jews' good will than as divinely instigated trials or punishments for their religious lapses. The fundamental challenge for Jews who saw civic equality as an ideal thus became to discover the most effective way of gaining and retaining the widest possible non-Jewish approbation. This challenge has remained the central problem of modern Jewish politics ever since.

In his response to the 1791 act of the French National Assembly Berr Isaac Berr offered an early articulation of one possible strategy for meeting it. According to Berr, the potential benefits of equal citizenship would become actual to the extent that Jews endowed themselves with "the necessary qualifications to fulfill the duties" of active citizens, including fluent, unaccented command of the French language, mastery of "all moral and physical sciences," acquisition of "all the trades and mechanical occupations necessary to society," and abandonment of "that narrow spirit of corporation and congregation in all civil and political matters not immediately connected with our spiritual laws."[31] Such a supposition implied in the first instance a thoroughgoing reform of traditional Jewish educational patterns, with their almost exclusive concentration upon sacred texts. It also meant that Jews would need consciously to seek ways of earning a livelihood outside of the commercial fields in which they had been concentrated under the old regime. And it required that Jews organize themselves solely for the pursuit of such goals and for the exercise of their religious rites, not for the purpose of asserting any particular group interest within the French body politic. In fact, Berr argued, until Jews had made sufficient progress in the project of self-regeneration, it behooved them to maintain a low public profile:

The oath [of citizenship] once taken, let us exert ourselves to fulfill the duties within our reach, but let us avoid grasping at our rights; let us not rush headlong against the opinions of some of our fellow citizens who, rendered callous by prejudice, will reject the idea of Jews being fellow men, fellow creatures. Let it be sufficient for us, at present, to have acquired the invaluable right of assisting at all assemblies of French citizens; but let us not attend them, till we have acquired knowledge sufficient to make ourselves useful members; till we know how to discuss and defend the interests of the country; in short, till our most bitter enemies are convinced, and acknowledge the gross misconceptions they had entertained of us.[32]

Underlying this strategy was a firm confidence, typical of the European enlightenment, in the fundamental goodness, reasonableness, and

[31] Berr, "Letter," 119, 121.
[32] Ibid., 120.

corrigibility of human beings, Jews and non-Jews alike. Berr attributed the "gross misconceptions" that had led some non-Jews to oppose Jewish enfranchisement to a misreading of Jewish history. True, he confessed, the Jews of his day were on the whole far from possessing the qualities essential to good citizenship, but the reason for their shortcomings lay not in any essential feature of Judaism but in the disabilities that the old regime had misguidedly imposed upon them: because for centuries they had been compelled by the authorities in their places of residence "to abandon ... all sciences ... which tend to the improvement of the mind, in order to give [them]selves up entirely to commerce, to be enabled to gather as much money as would insure protection and satisfy the rapacity of [their] persecutors." But now, he averred (as had Seixas more obliquely a year earlier), God, though "finding that [Jews] were not yet worthy of seeing the accomplishment of His promises of a perfect and lasting redemption ... has not ... thought proper still to aggravate [their] sufferings." He had thus imbued Frenchmen with the gift of reason, which would allow them to free themselves from their former prejudices: "He has chosen the generous French nation ... to effect our regeneration, as, in other times, He had chosen Antiochus, Pompey, and others to humiliate and enslave us." For Berr, in other words, security for Jews under conditions of equal citizenship rested upon a foundation of divinely ordained mutual good faith between them and their neighbors, in which each party would earnestly and benevolently assist the other in eliminating the attitudes and behaviors on each side that had hitherto often militated against the Jews' physical safety. If Jews would only "make [themselves] useful to [their] fellow citizens," they would "deserve their [fellow citizens'] esteem and their friendship," and Jews and non-Jews alike would join together "in maintaining public tranquility, on which that of individuals depends."[33]

Berr's analysis was at first widely shared by Jews in countries where equal citizenship became (or seemed imminently likely to become) the preferred model for regulating their relations with the territorial authority and the surrounding society. Throughout the nineteenth century, however, Jews experienced incidents that seemed to contradict the assumptions of corrigibility and mutual good faith upon which the model was based. The 1819 "Hep! Hep!" riots in Bavaria and other parts of Central Europe, in which mobs looted Jewish homes and shops and demanded that Jews be expelled from several towns; the Damascus blood libel of 1840, in which French officials backed a charge that Jews had murdered a Christian monk for ritual purposes and supported the arrest and torture of local Jewish leaders; the 1858 Mortara case, in which a six-year-old Jewish boy from

[33] Ibid., 119.

Bologna who had been baptized as an infant by a Christian servant in his parents' household was kidnapped by papal guards and held forcibly in Rome despite worldwide protests; the crystallization of the so-called anti-semitic movement in the 1880s, first in Germany, then in other Western and Central European countries, with its call for the revocation of Jewish citizenship and the reimposition of restrictions upon Jewish access to state resources and positions of political, economic, social, and cultural influ-ence; the "Southern storms" in imperial Russia from 1881 to 1884, in which Jews in more than 250 cities, towns, and villages fell victim to a form of sometimes murderous mob violence later dubbed "pogroms"; the Dreyfus affair of the 1890s, in which a false charge of treason brought against a Jewish officer of the French general staff touched off anti-Jewish agita-tion and rioting throughout France and Algeria extending over a period of months – all of these episodes, and others, helped cumulatively to per-suade growing numbers of Jews that the old enlightenment faith in human goodness and reasonableness had been misplaced. These deviations from Berr's scenario came despite the steady progress of Western and Central European Jewry toward the ideals that Berr had predicted would guarantee their security. Hence more and more Jews became convinced that an irre-ducible residue of prejudice, irrationality, and ill will persisted within non-Jewish society throughout Europe – a residue that neither Berr's program of self-regeneration nor any other conceivable plan would ever banish alto-gether. As such doubts gradually permeated Jewish circles, new strategies for negotiating with the non-Jewish world were advanced.

SECURITY IN THE FACE OF ADVERSITY

Although these strategies unfolded along several fairly distinct lines, they nevertheless all inherited from the late eighteenth-century secularized notion of redemption the fundamental aim of cultivating the favor of as broad a segment of non-Jewish society as possible. That task fell largely to the new Jewish press in European vernaculars that blossomed dur-ing the first half of the nineteenth century. Between 1830 and 1850 more than seventy Jewish-owned newspapers and periodicals in the principal European languages, led by the *Allgemeine Zeitung des Judenthums* (pub-lished in Leipzig, then in Berlin, from 1837 to 1922), the *Archives Israélites de France* (Paris, 1840–1935) and the *Jewish Chronicle* (London, ongoing since 1841), took it upon themselves, as the *Allgemeine Zeitung* proclaimed in its inaugural edition, "to bring the truth [about Jews and Judaism] once again into the open" in order to dispel the "prejudice and antipathy" that were increasingly "confusing the issues" concerning the proper relationship between Jews and their socio-political environment.[34] During the second half of the century they were joined by the Polish-language *Izraelita* (Warsaw, 1866–1913) and the Russian *Voskhod* (St. Petersburg, 1881–1906), both of which advanced the position in their early years that security and prosperity would be guaranteed Jews only once their non-Jewish neighbors became convinced of their worthiness to participate as equals in their political community.

On the other hand, virtually all Jewish leaders who considered how best to implement the revolutionary promise of equality during the final two thirds of the nineteenth century and throughout the twentieth recognized that the favor of non-Jews would never be universal. As a result, all posited the additional necessity of rendering harmless the incurably malevolent elements among the Jews' neighbors. The divisions among them concerned how best to attain this latter goal.

In most of the countries of Western and Central Europe, as well as in the English-speaking regions of the Americas and the southern hemisphere, the dominant belief posited that the system of citizen-based constitutional nation-states that increasingly became the European norm as the nineteenth century progressed – states in which governments were supposed to be constituted not by dynastic rules but by the entire body of individuals subject to the state's jurisdiction in accordance with a set of basic laws to which both governors and governed were subject in equal measure – by itself offered Jews sufficient resources to thwart whatever threats their adversaries might mount. As citizens, this view held, Jews had recourse to instruments of state power – especially to the judicial and electoral systems – which could be employed in defense of their civil rights and status whenever these were under attack: Jews could press criminal charges or initiate civil actions against those who defamed them, discriminated against them, or harmed their persons or property, and they could withhold support from candidates for public office or from political parties that sought to restrict their participation in any aspects of their country's civic, economic, social, or cultural life. At the same time, advocates of this approach argued, Jews could utilize the public forum of liberal societies to enlighten non-Jews about the progress Jews had made toward self-regeneration and the manifold benefits non-Jews had derived from admitting Jews to citizenship status. Moreover, they could employ the same vehicle to remind the public of the impropriety, according to the liberal ethos, of disturbing individuals in matters of conscience, including the exercise of religion, and in this way strike out against conversionary pressures.

---

[34] "Was heißt das Judenthum? Die politische Richtung des Judenthums," *Allgemeine Zeitung des Judenthums* 1, no. 1 (May 2, 1837), 2.

Such a strategy required only a relatively slight modification in Berr's original blueprint for security in the age of citizenship; in fact, the adjustment lay more on the tactical than on the strategic level. Jews were now advised to refrain no longer from "grasping at [their] rights" or from "rush[ing] headlong against the opinions of ... fellow citizens who ... reject the idea of Jews being fellow men."[35] Instead they were to claim their rights as citizens unabashedly, to counter the opinions of their detractors in open forum, and to acknowledge the existence of a particular Jewish group interest to the extent that their rights or physical safety were threatened because of their identification as Jews. As a late nineteenth-century German proponent of the strategy put it, "It is surely time ... [for Jews] to assert themselves openly, with honor and courage, in private and public intercourse, in the press, in popular representative bodies, and before the throne, whenever [their] human rights are abused."[36] Simultaneously, however, they were to continue to strive to make themselves "useful citizens" in much the same way that that concept had been understood in the previous century; another German advocate insisted that the new assertiveness be coupled with the understanding that "we [Jews] require and demand as citizens no other protection than the duly constituted legal system" and that "we belong as Jews to no political party."[37] Perhaps because of the fundamentally tactical nature of this new direction, existing statewide Jewish organizations, such as the Board of Deputies of British Jews (founded in 1760) and the French network of Jewish consistories established under Napoleon beginning in 1808, were often able to incorporate self-defense and public education into the scope of their activities as representatives of Jewish religious communities. In other countries, where the existing Jewish organizational structure was fragmented along local or denominational lines, new statewide organizations, such as the Central Association of German Citizens of the Jewish Faith (*Centralverein deutscher Staatsbürger jüdischen Glaubens*, established 1893) and the American Jewish Committee (1906), assumed primary responsibility for fostering such undertakings.

From the second half of the nineteenth century, many of these statewide Jewish organizations also took on the task of defending the physical security of Jews in regions where citizenship had not yet been extended them, especially in the Russian and Ottoman Empires. They were joined in this venture by other organizations, such as the Board of Delegates of American

---

[35] Berr, "Letter," 120.

[36] F. Fischer, "Wehrt Euch!," quoted in Paul Rieger, *Ein Vierteljahrhundert im Kampf um das Recht und die Zukunft der deutschen Juden* (Berlin: Verlag des Centralvereins deutscher Staatsbürger jüdischen Glaubens, 1918), 16.

[37] [R. Löwenfeld], "Schutzjuden oder Staatsbürger," quoted in ibid., 14.

Israelites (established 1859), the Alliance Israélite Universelle (1860), and the Anglo-Jewish Association (1871), all of which were founded primarily with reference to the problems of Jews in those areas. The Jews who led these bodies endeavored to utilize the resources provided by their own status as citizens to generate public and diplomatic pressure upon foreign governments to reduce defamation, discrimination, and physical threats and to expand Jewish civic rights. They thought that they achieved a notable success at the Congress of Berlin in 1878, when the major European powers compelled three Ottoman successor states (Romania, Serbia, and Montenegro) to agree that "the difference of religious creeds and confessions shall not be alleged against any person as a ground for exclusion or incapacity in matters relating to the enjoyment of civil and political rights, admission to public employments, functions, and honors, or the exercise of the various professions and industries in any locality whatsoever."[38] Consistent breaches of this commitment in Romania over the next several decades convinced them, however, that in that country at least the residue of prejudice and ill will was of far greater proportions than in Western and Central Europe and that it extended into the highest reaches of the political structure. Fears that such a pattern was liable to be repeated in the new Ottoman, Russian, and Habsburg successor states in Eastern Europe and the Middle East that emerged from the First World War thus led some Jewish leaders to advocate a further modification of the initial citizenship model in order to guarantee security to Jews about to become nominal citizens of those countries.

That modification posited the necessity for Jews, or at least those living in the successor states, to obtain recourse to the new international institutions envisioned at the 1919 Paris peace conference, such as the League of Nations and the Permanent Court of International Justice, in case their physical security or rights as citizens were threatened. The leaders of organized British, French, and American Jewry, along with representatives of many Eastern European Jewish communities who formed a Committee of Jewish Delegations at the Peace Conference, strongly supported the so-called minorities treaties that were incorporated into the settlements by which fourteen states in Eastern Europe, the Balkans, and the Near East were admitted into the new international community. These treaties provided that all persons habitually resident in the territories of those states were to be acknowledged as citizens and that citizens of those states "who

---

[38] No. 518: Mr. Maynard to Mr. Evarts (Enclosure in no. 276: The Treaty of Berlin), United States Department of State, *Index to the Executive Documents of the House of Representatives for the Third Session of the Forty-Fifth Congress, 1878–79*, volume 1 (Washington, 1878–1879), 904.

belong to racial, religious, or linguistic minorities shall enjoy the same treatment and security in law and in fact" as citizens belonging to the majority.[39] More specifically, members of minority groups, including Jews, were to be permitted to use their own languages for official purposes; to manage their own religious, social, and educational institutions without state interference; and to receive state funding in proportion to their numbers for the education of their children in their own language. Together with the treaties, the major European powers discussed the establishment of international mechanisms for enforcing their provisions. Many Jewish spokesmen throughout the world hailed the minorities treaties publicly as "a really practical Charter of Liberties" that would empower the Jews of Eastern Europe just as citizenship had empowered their Western and Central European brethren and their co-religionists in the English-speaking world.[40] In private, though, many shared the sentiments of the American Louis Marshall, who had been a key advocate for the treaties at Paris:

If the League of Nations becomes an actuality I am confident that, in the course of time, the complete emancipation of the Jews will be brought about. Without the League of Nations, however, or an international tribunal of the character contemplated in the [League of Nations] Covenant, I fear that we shall only have obtained paper rights, although even the formulation and adoption of rights of so flimsy a nature as we would than have will be of considerable moral value.[41]

Underlying Marshall's assessment was a sense that Jews were likely to be most secure in a world in which the sovereignty of modern nation-states was limited through some sort of federal union. As Lucien Wolf, British Jewry's leading public spokesman, explained in 1920 (borrowing implicitly from James Madison), even in countries where Jews possessed citizenship rights they were liable to suffer from "domestic abuses of sovereign power;" but the adverse effects of such abuses could be mitigated once "the machinery of the League of Nations is ... speedily got into working order and its authority fortified in every possible way." Hence it behooved Jews to take "the widest and most active interest in the League of Nations," to prove themselves good and useful citizens not only of their countries of residence but of the new international order. At the same time, though,

---

[39] "The Treaty with Poland," in Jacob Robinson et al., eds, *Were the Minorities Treaties a Failure?* (New York: Institute of Jewish Affairs, 1943), 315.

[40] "Speech by L[ucien] W[olf] at a Meeting in Connection with the Minorities Treaties of 1919," June 8, 1920, YIVO Institute for Jewish Research Archives, New York, RG 348, Box 8, File 82.

[41] Marshall to Israel Zangwill, November 10, 1919, in Charles Reznikoff, ed., *Louis Marshall: Champion of Liberty* (Philadelphia: Jewish Publication Society, 1957), 677.

Wolf warned, Jews needed to continue "to pursue a policy of patience and conciliation and above all to avoid appealing to their treaty rights until as patriotic citizens they have made every possible effort to obtain redress from the laws and tribunals of their own countries." Only through such "punctilious loyalty," he believed, would Jews merit "the good will of [the treaties'] signatories ... to perform their stipulations and ... to enforce them should the disagreeable necessity for doing so arise."[42]

Other Jews, mostly from Eastern European countries, were inspired by the concept of federalism in another way. Their view led them to dissent more fundamentally than Wolf or Marshall from the earlier ideal of a system of sovereign citizen-based nation-states. For these Jews the minorities treaties had enshrined not only a mechanism for international checks upon state power but also the notion that states whose citizens belonged to several ethnic or religious groups should be organized less as unified nation-states than as federations of autonomous communities that did not need to be concentrated territorially. According to this view, only if Jews *as a group*, and not merely individual Jews, were recognized as having a claim on state resources and access to the centers of state decision-making power in proportion to their numerical share in the total population could they defend themselves successfully against the ineradicable residue of ill will toward them in each country. Those who held this view thus demanded that Jews be permitted to form separate corporate bodies and electoral curiae through which that claim could be made actual. The Galician Jewish political economist Max Rosenfeld, for one, argued that Jews "must still fear that [they] will come out poorly" in nation-states based upon equal individual franchise. In such a system the majority nation might often favor policies detrimental to the well-being of minorities, especially when, as in the case of Eastern European Jews, a minority's economic structure differed significantly from that of the majority. Hence minorities, and especially Jews, required a measure of countervailing political power: "The right of Jews to representation as a minority nation in the political community ... must be preserved; this representation has the possibility of succeeding [only] on the basis of proportional [group] voting."[43] Groups, not individuals, thus constituted the state.

The strategy of seeking to enhance Jewish security through this type of political arrangement owed much to the idea of nationalism that crystallized in Europe during the final third of the nineteenth century. This doctrine

---

[42] Speech by L[ucien] W[olf] at a Meeting in Connection with the Minorities Treaties of 1919.

[43] Max Rosenfeld, *Die polnische Judenfrage: Problem und Lösung* (Vienna: R. Löwit, 1918), 228.

located the source of political legitimacy not in a citizenry composed of equal individuals but in a nation – a particular sort of collectivity claiming some preexisting, extrapolitical common identity. Such a collectivity, nationalists asserted, possessed a natural right to form a state whose primary purpose was to serve its own collective needs and interests. Ideally nationalists envisioned a world in which anthropological and political boundaries would be congruent, in which each nation would reside in a compact mass on a single territory and operate its own state. However, the human geography of most of the globe – and particularly of Eastern Europe, where the bulk of the world's Jews lived – made the realization of this vision a practical impossibility, with the result that some groups who claimed national status found themselves incorporated into states created to serve another nation's needs. The concept of states as federations of autonomous communities represented an attempt to preserve at least a portion of the natural political rights of those nations who were not permitted to create states of their own, by guaranteeing that the states into which they were incorporated took their needs and interests into account along with those of the national majority. As a result, virtually all of the Jews who linked their security with the triumph of this political model simultaneously based their claim to autonomy and proportional political representation upon the contention that Jews constituted a nation. Only by persuading non-Jews of the fundamentally *national* character of Jewish group existence, they argued, could Jews gain sufficient approbation and good will from their neighbors to be granted the power necessary to withstand the attacks of their enemies.

The suggestion of defining Jews as a nation and of claiming the rights of nationality instead of citizenship was never universally accepted; in fact, the divide between proponents of citizenship and nationhood as the most effective models for obviating temporal adversity was a fundamental line of cleavage in the Jewish world throughout the twentieth century, even as during the second half of the century syntheses between the two were continually sought. The idea became especially controversial as increasing numbers of its proponents drew a new operative conclusion from it, one that led to a demand not for autonomy within existing states but for the creation of a single Jewish territorial nation-state in which the lion's share of the world's Jews would be concentrated. This demand became the watchword of the Zionist movement, organized formally by a Jewish playwright and journalist from Vienna, Theodor Herzl, in 1897. A year earlier Herzl had explained why he believed that physical security for Jews was possible only through such an arrangement:

The Jewish question persists wherever Jews live in appreciable numbers. Wherever it does not exist, it is brought in together with Jewish immigrants. We are naturally drawn into those places where we are not persecuted, and our appearance there gives rise to persecution. This is the case, and will inevitably be so, everywhere, even in highly civilized countries – see, for instance, France – so long as the Jewish question is not solved on the political level ... We have sincerely tried everywhere to merge with the national communities in which we live, seeking only to preserve the faith of our fathers. It is not permitted us. In vain are we loyal patriots, sometimes superloyal ... In our native lands where we have lived for centuries we are still decried as aliens, often by men whose ancestors had not yet come at a time when Jewish sighs had long been heard in the country. The majority decide who the "alien" is; this, and all else in the relations between peoples, is a matter of power.[44]

For Herzl, in other words, ill will toward Jews was not only ineradicable, it was bound to become more intense the more Jews prospered and multiplied in any particular location. Hence, according to his analysis, the citizenship model presented an internal contradiction: as Jews migrated to countries where the model was most fully developed and implemented (as they had been doing in increasing numbers for much of the second half of the nineteenth century), they would inevitably cause non-Jews in those countries to rethink the degree to which it served *their* needs and interests. The same result could be expected from the federal model, for even in states conceived as federations of autonomous nationalities, a large influx of Jews would necessarily change the proportion of state resources allocated to each community, thereby magnifying inter-communal tensions. Therefore, Herzl concluded, neither model held out much promise for long-term, universal Jewish security. Instead, he proposed not only that Jews claim recognition as a nation but that they assert a national claim to full territorial sovereignty "over a portion of the globe adequate to meet [their] rightful national requirements," equal to that of all other nations.[45] Only by creating their own nation-state, he argued, would Jews acquire the degree of political power necessary to attenuate the effects of ineradicable prejudice.

At the same time, Herzl suggested, creating a Jewish nation-state would enhance the Jews' merit in the eyes of their favorably disposed neighbors who had earlier underwritten the citizenship model. In his view, the irreducible residue of ill will toward Jews represented a threat not only to the Jews' physical well-being but also (and perhaps even more) to the vision of a reasonable, corrigible humanity that the citizenship model assumed and upon which the constitutional nation-states of Europe that

---

[44] Theodor Herzl, "The Jewish State," in *The Zionist Idea: A Historical Analysis and Reader*, ed. Arthur Hertzberg (Garden City, NY: Doubleday, 1959), 208–209.
[45] Ibid., 220.

had adopted it were based. Indeed, the execrators of Dreyfus in France and the anti-Semites in Germany directed their attacks not only against French or German Jews but against the French and German governments that had emancipated them; their recently increased prominence thus needed to trouble not only Jews but all supporters of a political system founded upon the idea of a free citizenry. Hence, Herzl reasoned, those supporters would profoundly appreciate the Jews' willingness to migrate *en masse* to a single territory over which they would hold sovereignty, for by leaving their current countries of residence they would effectively remove the wind from the sails of those for whom opposition to Jews served as the spearhead of opposition to the modern political order altogether. "The world needs the Jewish state," Herzl wrote; "therefore it will arise."[46]

In the end the Herzlian model of Jewish territorial sovereignty shared with the citizenship and federal models a faith that in one way or another Jews would eventually find physical security within the framework of some mixture of the concepts of citizenship and nationhood – concepts that represented the fundamental building blocks of the political order that evolved in Western and Central Europe during the century following the French revolution. Another strategy, which became increasingly popular during the first four decades of the twentieth century, mostly among Jews from Eastern Europe, denied that faith, positing instead the need for a fundamental restructuring of all political relations before Jews could be released from the ongoing threat of physical harm. This strategy adopted the basic premise of socialism that solidarity among individuals could not rest upon the basis of common citizenship or common nationality but only upon that of common class interest. Similarly, it postulated that the capitalist economic system as it had developed during the nineteenth century had seriously exacerbated class antagonisms. Jews had suffered grievously from this development, proponents of this view argued, because during the Middle Ages they had come to be identified as an economic class onto themselves; in this situation lay the roots of the irreducible residue of ill will that had bedeviled Jews throughout the nineteenth century. A young Polish-born Belgian Jewish socialist, Abram Leon, outlined this argument succinctly in 1941:

Capitalism has not only doomed the social function of the Jews; it has also doomed the Jews themselves ... It was capitalism, by virtue of the fact that it provided an economic basis for the national problem, which also created insoluble national

[46] Ibid., 206.

contradictions. Before the capitalist era, Slovaks, Czechs, Germans, French, lived in perfect understanding. Wars did not have a national character; they had interest only for the possessing classes. The policy of compulsory assimilation, of national persecution, was unknown to the Romans. Submission of barbarian peoples to Romanization or Hellenization was a peaceful process. Today, national-cultural and linguistic antagonisms are only manifestations of the economic antagonism created by capitalism.[47]

For those who accepted this analysis of the Jewish situation in the modern world, the operative conclusions were clear. Only an economic system that mitigated class antagonisms, a socialist one based upon workers' ownership of the means of production and planning on a worldwide scale, could neutralize ill will toward Jews. Jews thus needed to forge alliances with non-Jewish socialists and work actively for the overthrow of the capitalist system and the nation-state system that it had spawned. By doing so they would, in Leon's words, "make a far from unimportant contribution towards the building of a new world," thereby gaining the approbation of "the people of the factories and the fields," who would rule that new world and embrace them finally as their brothers.[48]

Throughout the first half of the twentieth century, advocates of the socialist strategy remained in lively competition with proponents of the citizenship, federal, and territorial models, who also competed intensely with one another. In countries in which Jews enjoyed the franchise and where the Jewish populations were sufficiently large to sustain multiple Jewish mass organizations, partisans of one or another approach even organized their own Jewish political parties to elect candidates to public office, not only in Jewish communities but in the local and central governments of the countries in which they lived. Those parties often represented themselves as institutions of broad ideological movements whose purpose was to win adherents for their own preferred security strategies. As a result, the parties and movements often assumed the role of Jewish cultural entrepreneurs, publishing newspapers and periodicals and sponsoring schools, libraries, and programs for youth and women, all aimed at propagating their unique understandings of how Jews might most effectively confront the adversity that all agreed was part and parcel of their current relations with their neighbors.

Another result of the ongoing rivalry among Jewish political parties and movements was the development of several synthetic models, combining elements of two or more of the basic strategic paradigms. Some

---

[47] Abram Leon, *The Jewish Question: A Marxist Interpretation* (New York: Pathfinder, 1970), 259, 266.

[48] Ibid., 262.

Jewish socialists, for example, imagined a future socialist world adminis-tered by federations of autonomous national proletariats strikingly similar in function to those envisioned by nonsocialist federalists. Such a vision, for example, became central to the program of the largest Jewish social-ist party, the Bund, during the decade following its 1897 establishment. By contrast, other socialists posited that a necessary prelude to creating a socialist society in which Jewish workers would not feel physically threat-ened was the removal of Jews to a territory of their own, where they would no longer constitute a class unto themselves but would man all the essen-tial positions in the economy at all levels of production. Most such Jewish socialists were absorbed into the ranks of the Zionist movement, and for four decades, from the 1930s through the 1970s, they effectively domi-nated it. For their part, some Zionists, including socialist Zionists, also showed affinity for federalism; they argued that while a Herzlian Jewish state represented the most desirable long-term situation, the Jewish masses of Eastern Europe would gain far more immediate benefit from guarantees of national autonomy in their countries of residence. In some Western and Central European countries, and especially in the United States, many Zionists sought ways to pursue the territorial and citizenship models simultaneously.

IN THE AFTERMATH OF THE HOLOCAUST

The second half of the twentieth century, however, witnessed a sharp decline in support for the federal and socialist strategies, with the result that the range of Jewish responses to the challenge of enhancing physical security was far more restricted than it had been for many decades. This development was mainly a result of the catastrophic losses of life sustained by the Jews of Eastern Europe, the principal devotees of those strategies, under the Nazi occupation – losses that effectively eliminated the pos-sibility that the surviving Jewries of Eastern and Central Europe might continue to play a significant role in worldwide Jewish political debates. Yet it also stemmed in no small measure from the lessons that leaders in world Jewry's two new principal centers of influence – the United States and the State of Israel – drew from the Second World War and the great geopolitical realignment that followed it. The war exposed severe weak-nesses in the existing mechanisms for curtailing domestic abuses of the sovereign prerogatives of nation-states – weaknesses that bore literally fatal consequences for large numbers of Jews. Hence it was not surprising that few Jews would be prepared any longer to place their faith in international guarantees of citizenship and group rights. At the same time, the system by which a number of more or less equally powerful European nation-states had dominated the world order since the mid-seventeenth century gave way to a world ruled by two superpowers, the Soviet Union and the United States, with all other peoples depending for their security upon the protection of one or the other. For Jews the choice of protector became automatic once the Soviet Union, for a variety of reasons, effectively declined to assume the role. That decision made it difficult for most Jews to associate their physical safety with the triumph of socialism.

Instead, since the early 1950s, Jews throughout the world have linked their physical safety largely with the strength of the United States. This fact, however, does not appear to signal the unqualified triumph of the citizenship strategy. On the contrary, through at least the late 1980s the Herzlian notion of a sovereign Jewish state as the prime guarantor of Jewish security gained much broader nominal acceptance, even among the majority of Jews who chose not to take up residence in the new State of Israel, while an alleged excessive affinity by American Jews for the citizenship model was widely believed to have prevented them from acting as effective advocates for the rescue of their brothers under the Nazi yoke. Thus organized American Jewry has actually taken on a role as champion of the interests of a foreign nation-state (Israel) in the US political arena, on the assumption that by doing so it will help Israel use its sovereign power to protect Jews wherever they are susceptible to harm. Ironically, though, such behavior tacitly acknowledges that Israel's ability to do so is heavily dependent upon US support.

Meanwhile, beginning in the final decade of the twentieth century, a growing number of Israeli Jews has questioned whether the State of Israel has been or can ever be a truly effective guarantor of Jewish security. They have noted that since its establishment Israel has been on a constant war footing, that violent clashes with its neighboring states (and with elements of the large non-Jewish population under its control) have cost many thousands of lives among the country's Jewish citizens (and others), and that offshoots of those clashes have at times endangered Jews living far from the eye of the storm. Some have argued that such a situation was the inevitable result of Herzl's call for Jews to claim sovereignty over a territory where they could constitute a majority only through massive immigration: the existing non-Jewish majority could not help but see in such immigration and such a claim to sovereignty a threat to its own collective interests, making violent opposition a foreseeable, perhaps even an inevitable outcome.

Thus, at the start of the twenty-first century the problem of reducing temporal adversity for Jews to a minimum continues to engage the imagination of Jewish leaders. It does so at a time of great uncertainty. Two of the four primary strategies for addressing the problem generated during the nineteenth and early twentieth centuries have all but been removed from public discussion, and seemingly serious imperfections in the other two have been exposed; yet no new strategies have yet been developed to take their place. The development of new strategies is made especially difficult, though, by the changing nature of the general political context in the wake of the dissolution of the bipolar international system precipitated by the collapse of the Soviet Union: the future structures through which Jews will negotiate with the non-Jewish world are in flux.

Such uncertainty has spiritual as well as temporal implications. The principal modern Jewish responses to the challenge of physical security in the age of citizenship and nationhood were rooted in a transfer of the traditional concept of exile and redemption from the divine to the human plane. Physical insecurity for Jews was understood not as part of God's cosmic plan but as a product of the manner in which Jews themselves operated in the political world; it could thus be significantly mitigated, or even eliminated altogether, it was believed, not through prayer, repentance, or any other form of divine service but through the adoption of a proper strategy of political behavior. Once the clay feet of those responses were uncovered, however, such confidence in the efficacy of any this-worldly strategy became vulnerable. The result has been a growing questioning of the preferability of modern over pre-modern Jewish understandings of the Jews' place in the world and of the political models forged in the post-revolutionary era.

SELECT BIBLIOGRAPHY

Arendt, Hannah. *The Origins of Totalitarianism*. New York: Harcourt, Brace and Co., 1951.
   Was ist Politik: Fragmente aus dem Nachlaß. Munich: Piper, 2003.
Bauer, Yehuda. *The Jewish Emergence from Powerlessness*. Toronto: University of Toronto Press, 1979.
Biale, David. *Power and Powerlessness in Jewish History*. New York: Schocken Books, 1986.
Fink, Carole. *Defending the Rights of Others: The Great Powers, the Jews, and International Minority Protection, 1878–1938*. Cambridge: Cambridge University Press, 2004.
Frankel, Jonathan. *Prophecy and Politics: Socialism, Nationalism, and the Russian Jews, 1862–1917*. Cambridge: Cambridge University Press, 1981.
Gassenschmidt, Christoph. *Jewish Liberal Politics in Tsarist Russia, 1900–14: The Modernization of Russian Jewry*. New York: New York University Press, 1995.
Gitelman, Zvi, ed. *The Emergence of Modern Jewish Politics: Bundism and Zionism in Eastern Europe*. Pittsburgh: University of Pittsburgh Press, 2003.
   The Quest for Utopia: Jewish Political Ideas and Institutions through the Ages. Armonk, NY: M. E. Sharpe, 1992.
Lederhendler, Eli. *The Road to Modern Jewish Politics: Political Tradition and Political Reconstruction in the Jewish Community of Tsarist Russia*. New York: Oxford University Press, 1989.

Mendelsohn, Ezra. *The Jews of East Central Europe between the World Wars*. Bloomington: Indiana University Press, 1983.

On Modern Jewish Politics. New York: Oxford University Press, 1993.

Nathans, Benjamin. *Beyond the Pale: The Jewish Encounter with Late Imperial Russia*. Berkeley: University of California Press, 2002.

Schorsch, Ismar. "On the History of the Political Judgment of the Jew" (Leo Baeck Memorial Lecture 20). New York: Leo Baeck Institute, 1976 (reprinted in idem, *From Text to Context: The Turn to History in Modern Judaism*. Hanover, NH: Brandeis University Press, 1994, 118–130.

CHAPTER 14

JEWS AND THE LEFT

JACK JACOBS

Jews played highly visible roles, over an extended period, in the leadership of leftist movements – including socialist, communist, and anarchist organizations – around the world. In the first half of the twentieth century, significant numbers of Jews were also evident in the rank-and-file of specific left-wing political parties. In addition to participating in general leftist movements, Jews in Eastern Europe created and fostered a number of distinctive Jewish socialist parties with tens of thousands of members. Why were so many Jews sympathetic to left-wing causes? Explanations revolving around the purported "racial qualities" of Jews, the impact of Jewish religious ideas, and the marginality of the Jewish population, have been expounded by prominent scholars. However, there is reason to question both of the first two of these explanations. At the present moment in time, left-wing ideas no longer hold the same degree of attraction for Jews as they did one hundred years ago. The relationship of Jews to the left was historically contingent, specific to political, historic, and economic conditions that prevailed between the late nineteenth and mid-twentieth centuries in Europe, and that impacted upon Jewish political opinion in the United States, Israel, and other countries that received large numbers of Jewish immigrants from Europe.

* * *

In a book which first appeared in 1911, the German sociologist Robert Michels noted "the abundance of Jews among the leaders of the socialist and revolutionary parties," and he attempted to illuminate this phenomenon by reference to "[s]pecific racial qualities" which "make the Jew a born leader of the masses, a born organizer and propagandist." Michels asserted that among these qualities were "sectarian fanaticism which, like an infection, can be communicated to the masses with astonishing frequency; next we have an invincible self-confidence (which in Jewish racial history is most characteristically displayed in the lives of the prophets) ... remarkable ambition, an irresistible need to figure in the limelight, and last but not least an almost unlimited power of adaptation."[1]

---

[1] Robert Michels, *Political Parties. A Sociological Study of the Oligarchical Tendencies of Modern Democracy*, trans. Eden and Cedar Paul (New York: The Free Press, 1962), 245.

He cites examples of "the quantitative and qualitative predominance of persons of Hebrew race" in leftist parties in Germany, Austria, the US, Holland, Italy, Hungary, Poland, and other lands, and adds that Jewish involvement with socialist parties is also linked to the "spirit of rebellion against the wrongs from which" Jewry suffers, that is, the Jewish response to continuing antisemitism.[2]

Some scholars interested in the relationship between Jews and the left have emphasized not supposed Jewish qualities but rather purported similarities between Jewish religious ideas and ideas supported by leftist writers. Dennis Fischman, for one, has argued that Marx "approaches the standpoint of the Jewish tradition ... In his stress on the indispensability of human action, Marx echoes the Jewish motifs of *partnership in Creation* and *dialogue*."[3] Michael Löwy, far more compellingly, has made creative use of Max Weber's notion of *Wahlverwandschaften*, has written of an elective affinity illuminating links between Jewish messianism and a revolutionary, libertarian, world view, and suggests that the views of such thinkers as Ernst Bloch, Walter Benjamin, Erich Fromm, Gustav Landauer, Leo Lowenthal, and Georg Lukács can all be clarified, to varying degrees, through reference to the affinity he describes.[4]

Yet another, alternative, explanation for the attraction of some (very prominent) Jews to leftist ideas revolves around Jewish marginality. Isaac Deutscher – himself a leftist of Jewish origin – claimed that Marx, Luxemburg, and Trotsky (among others) "dwelt on the borderlines of various civilizations, religions, and national cultures" and "were born and brought up on the borderlines of various epochs."[5] This, he proposed, "enabled them to rise in thought above their societies, above their nations, above their times and generations, and to strike out mentally into wide new horizons ..."

The notion that Jews are a race has long since been discredited by reputable social scientists (if not necessarily by all geneticists). The idea that Judaism per se is intrinsically progressive is not tenable. Jewish religious beliefs can and have led many to deeply conservative political positions. But Deutscher's explanation for the one-time link between Jews and the left, the fact that it is colored by his political sympathies notwithstanding,

---

[2] Michels, *Political Parties*, 246–248.

[3] Dennis Fischman, *Political Discourse in Exile. Karl Marx and the Jewish Question* (Amherst: The University of Massachusetts Press, 1991), 110–111.

[4] Michael Löwy, *Redemption and Utopia. Jewish Libertarian Thought in Central Europe. A Study in Elective Affinity* (Stanford: Stanford University Press, 1992).

[5] Isaac Deutscher, "The Non-Jewish Jew," in *The Non-Jewish Jew and Other Essays* (New York: Hill and Wang, 1968), 27.

has a great deal of merit. Jews were marginal when the left came into being and in the era during which it developed. Jewish marginality, and the political, economic, and sociological conditions which existed in the nineteenth and twentieth centuries and which led to marginality, does in fact clarify the political inclinations of any number of prominent Jewish leftists of earlier generations.

* * *

THE LEFT AND THE JEWS

The left arose out of the French Revolution, and was initially committed to that Revolution's ideals of liberty, equality, and fraternity. Indeed, the term leftist originally referred to those French political leaders who supported the Revolution. Specific French leftists in the National Assembly, none of whom were Jews, supported the emancipation of French Jewry. The positions endorsed by these founders of the French left led some Jews in France to ally themselves with the left. There are known to have been Jewish Jacobins, for example, in Saint-Esprit, near Bayonne.[6]

Left-wing movements later came into being in many other lands, and the left ultimately grew to encompass a range of views. In general, these movements tended to favor equal treatment of citizens, and opposed the legal disabilities which had been imposed upon Jews, in specific countries, in earlier times.

To be sure, individual, highly visible leaders of the left were not immune from anti-Jewish prejudices.[7] However, the left was generally open to the participation of individual Jews within its ranks in ways that the European right was often not, and many (though not all) late nineteenth-century leftists ultimately opposed the antisemitic political movements that came

---

[6] Zosa Szajkowski, *Jews and the French Revolutions of 1789, 1830 and 1848* (New York: Ktav, 1970), 822.

[7] The Russian anarchist Mikhail Bakunin, who was of aristocratic, non-Jewish, origin, and who was a foremost leader of the International Workingmen's Association (the First International), penned an essay in 1869 in which he proclaimed that "modern Jews ... considered as a nation ... are *par excellence* exploiters of others' labor, and have a natural horror and fear of the popular masses, whom, moreover, they despise, either openly or secretly. The habit of exploitation ... gives it an exclusive and baneful direction, entirely opposed to the interests as well as to the instincts of the proletariat." Edmund Silberner, "Two Studies on Modern Anti-Semitism," *Historia Judaica* XIV, no. 2 (1952): 96. Statements tinged with anti-Jewish sentiment can be found in the writings of any number of other socialists, anarchists, and communists. These leftists reflected negative attitudes towards Jews prevalent in the societies in which they lived.

into being in that era. It was by no means the case that outspoken opposition to political antisemitism and personal attitudes rooted in prejudice or stereotypes were mutually exclusive.[8] Nevertheless, it is significant that German Social Democracy, the world's strongest Marxist-influenced movement in the latter decades of the nineteenth century, was less antisemitic than many other major political parties in imperial Germany. It is worth noting that representatives of the Center Party advocated linking the number of Jewish judges in Bavaria to the proportion of Jews in the Bavarian population, that the National Liberals of Germany were not consistent defenders of equal rights for Jews, and that even the Progressives (to whom significant numbers of German Jews were attracted) were initially very cool to the notion of nominating Jewish candidates.[9]

Many Marxist-oriented parties operating at the end of the nineteenth and in the first decades of the following century had positions on the so-called "Jewish question" similar to that of German Social Democracy. The leading figures of the Marxist movement in France, Jules Guesde and Paul Lafargue, were opponents of political antisemitism, as were the leaders of the Russian Social Democratic Workers' Party. Edmund Silberner, among the first scholars to conduct sustained research on the attitudes of leftists towards Jews, once asserted that there is "an old anti-Semitic tradition within modern Socialism" and that this tradition sheds light on the views of quite a few socialist writers and parties.[10] However, the attitudes of leftists towards Jews were far more differentiated than Silberner's conclusions might lead one to believe. There are important, deplorable, examples of antisemitic leftists. Silberner to the contrary notwithstanding, on the other hand, there is no "tradition" of antisemitism on the left per se.

JEWS ON THE LEFT

The relative openness of the left made it possible for individuals of Jewish origin not only to become involved in leftist movements, but also, in some cases, to become leaders of such movements. Karl Marx and Ferdinand Lassalle, who were of Jewish descent, are manifestly among the most important mid-nineteenth-century leftists, and exemplify the highly visible roles played by individuals of Jewish origin in left-wing movements.

---

[8] For a recent discussion of this issue see Lars Fischer, *The Socialist Response to Antisemitism in Imperial Germany* (Cambridge: Cambridge University Press,) 2007.

[9] Marjorie Lamberti, *Jewish Activism in Imperial Germany: The Struggle for Civil Equality* (New Haven: Yale University Press, 1978), 25, 33, 34, 42.

[10] Edmund Silberner, "Anti-Semitism and Philo-Semitism in the Socialist International," *Judaism* II (1953), 122.

Marx knew little about Jews or Judaism. His father, Heinrich Marx, converted to the Lutheran faith in 1817, the year before Karl was born. Karl himself was converted to Lutheranism at the age of six. The school he attended as an adolescent, from 1830 to 1835, had been founded by Jesuits, and was attended primarily by Catholic students.

As a university student, however, Marx became friends with the Young Hegelian and Protestant theologian Bruno Bauer, and took a course taught by Bauer on Isaiah. It is not surprising, therefore, that Marx paid close attention to Bauer's work on the "Jewish question," and that he published responses to and critiques of Bauer's perspective.

Bauer had insisted that Jews, who did not have full civil rights in Prussia, would not be emancipated until they had renounced Judaism. Marx replied to Bauer, most famously in a piece entitled "On the Jewish Question," stressing that there was a distinction between political emancipation and human emancipation, and noted that Jews were entitled to the former even if they did *not* first abandon the Jewish religion. For Marx, the extent to which Jews had been granted equal political rights was a criterion by which to judge the modernity of a given state.

Marx never devoted sustained attention to the "Jewish question" after penning the discussions of Bauer's work noted above, though he referred to Jews in passing from time to time. In so doing, Marx sometimes made use of slurs and epithets (particularly in private letters to Friedrich Engels and other trusted confidants). These statements, and a review of Marx's writings, led Edmund Silberner to proclaim, in an article first published in 1949, that "If the pronouncements of Marx are not chosen at random, but are examined as a whole, and if … by anti-Semitism aversion to the Jews is meant, Marx not only can but *must* be regarded as an outspoken anti-Semite."[11]

Other academics have protested this label. Henry Pachter, for one, asserted in 1979 that "the term 'anti-Semitic' as we understand it today does not apply to the author of 'On the Jewish Question' and to his contemporary audience, which understood his meaning in the context of the Hegelian philosophy and its language … He is not preaching anti-Semitism but trying to defuse it."[12] But even if one rejects the label "anti-semitic" as inappropriate, and there is good reason to do so, it remains the case that Marx expressed personal antipathy towards individual Jews.[13]

---

[11] Edmund Silberner, "Was Marx an Anti-Semite?" *Historia Judaica* XI, part 1 (April 1949), 50.

[12] Henry Pachter, "Marx and the Jews," *Dissent* (Fall 1979), 452, 466.

[13] The most thorough study of Marx's attitude towards Jews is that of Julius Carlebach, *Karl Marx and the Radical Critique of Judaism* (London: Routledge & Kegan Paul, 1978), which contains an annotated guide to relevant works.

Lassalle, the founder and the first president of the General German Workers' Association, was, at the height of his career, one of the world's most prominent socialists, and was widely popular among German workers. He was born and raised in a Jewish family. Lassalle's mother was strictly Orthodox in her observance during Lassalle's youthful years. Lassalle never formally converted – though he became estranged from Judaism, particularly as he became acquainted with Hegelian and Young Hegelian thought.

However little Marx published on Jewish matters, Lassalle published even less. Indeed, there are no works by Lassalle meant for public consumption which focus directly on Jews, Judaism, or Jewry. But, as with Marx, so too with Lassalle, his private correspondence is revealing. In one letter he notes "I do not like Jews at all. I even detest them in general. I see in them nothing but the degenerate sons of a great, but long past epoch. As a result of centuries of servitude, these people have taken on the characteristics of slaves, and for this reason I am hostile to them."[14] At another point, he proclaimed: "There are above all two classes of people that I cannot stand, writers and Jews – and I, unfortunately, belong to both."[15] Thus, like Marx, Lassalle's attitude towards Jews was characterized by general lack of interest in Jewish affairs, and by personal antipathy (a matter quite distinct from advocacy of political antisemitism).

How might we explain this personal antipathy? Robert Wistrich relies on a psychological diagnosis – "self-hatred" – in explaining both Marx's attitude towards Jews and that of Lassalle.[16] As used by Wistrich, Jewish self-hatred refers to negative attitudes on the part of a person of Jewish origin towards Jews linked to "feelings of rejection" which "arise in the individual who cannot achieve full acceptance by virtue of his origin."[17] Though not out of the question in Lassalle's case, the diagnosis of Jewish self-hatred seems far-fetched in the case of Marx, who was not inclined to think of himself as Jewish.

Wistrich insinuates that Jewish self-hatred was evident not only in Marx and Lassalle but also in a number of other figures of Jewish origin active on the left, and writes in general terms about "the role which Jewish self-hatred played in activating latent prejudices in the socialist movement."[18]

[14] As translated in Robert Wistrich, *Revolutionary Jews from Marx to Trotsky* (London: Harrap, 1976), 56.

[15] Quoted in Edmund Silberner, *Sozialisten zur Judenfrage* (Berlin: Colloquium Verlag, 1962), 178.

[16] Wistrich, *Revolutionary Jews*, 36–37, 56. Cf. Sander L. Gilman, *Jewish Self-Hatred: Anti-Semitism and the Hidden Language of the Jews* (Baltimore: Johns Hopkins University Press, 1986), 188–208.

[17] Wistrich, *Revolutionary Jews*, 7.

[18] Wistrich, *Revolutionary Jews*, 6.

However, he does not provide compelling evidence in support of his contention, does not provide a list of those socialists who he believes were afflicted with Jewish self-hatred, and thus tars with an overly wide brush. To be sure, internalization of antisemitic hatred has affected any number of individuals of Jewish origin. On the other hand, as Wistrich was well aware, there is no reason at all to presume that self-hatred is (or was) more common among leftists than among conservatives.

Exceptionally prominent leftists of Jewish origin in the generations immediately following those of Lassalle and Marx include Eduard Bernstein and Rosa Luxemburg, Victor Adler, Otto Bauer, and Max Adler, Emma Goldman and Alexander Berkman, Pavel Axelrod, Julius Martov, Trotsky, and Leon Blum. Some may have exhibited traces of self-hatred. Others did not. They had rather different attitudes towards Jews and issues of interest to the Jewish community.[19] For example: Eduard Bernstein and Max Adler ultimately developed a sympathetic attitude towards Zionism; Rosa Luxemburg and Otto Bauer did not.

The list of world-renowned figures given above should not be taken as suggesting that most leftist leaders have been Jewish. August Bebel, Auguste Blanqui, Eugene V. Debs, Friedrich Engels, Charles Fourier, Antonio Gramsci, Jean Jaurès, Karl Kautsky, Peter Kropotkin, Wilhelm Liebknecht, Robert Owen, Georgii Plekhanov, Pierre-Joseph Proudhon, Karl Renner, and Henri de Saint-Simon were not Jewish, nor were many, many, other key figures of European, American, or other socialist, communist, or anarchist movements. Nevertheless, the presence of Jews and individuals of Jewish descent in the leadership of leftist movements was at one time considerable, and was regularly disproportionate to the percentage of Jews in the general populations of the countries in which these Jews were active.

Particularly in the first decades of the twentieth century, there were not only a remarkable number of Jews in the most prominent leadership

---

[19] I have discussed the attitudes of Bernstein, Luxemburg, Victor Adler and Otto Bauer to Jewish matters in Jack Jacobs, *On Socialists and "the Jewish Question" after Marx* (New York: New York University Press, 1992). Cf. Enzo Traverso, *The Marxists and the Jewish Question: The History of a Debate (1843–1943)*, translated Bernard Gibbons (Atlantic Highlands, NJ: Humanities Press, 1994), 58–91. On Emma Goldman, see Richard Drinnon, *Rebel in Paradise: A Biography of Emma Goldman* (Chicago: University of Chicago Press, 1961), 23–26. On Trotsky, see Joseph Nedava, *Trotsky and the Jews* (Philadelphia: The Jewish Publication Society, 1972). Wistrich discusses all of these leftist figures (except for Goldman), and also discusses relevant aspects of the life and ideas of Blum in Wistrich, *Revolutionary Jews*. Cf. Robert S. Wistrich, *Socialism and the Jews: The Dilemmas of Assimilation in Germany and Austria-Hungary* (Rutherford: Fairleigh Dickinson University Press, 1982).

positions of leftist parties, but also a disproportionately high number of Jews in (somewhat) lower-ranking positions within some of these parties, and in particular roles in party-related institutions. An analysis of the family backgrounds of those who participated in the Russian Social Democratic Workers' Party congress in 1907 reveals that 23 percent of the Menshevik delegates were Jewish, and that 11 percent of the Bolsheviks at this congress were Jews.[20] Robert Michels noted in 1911 that

Among the eighty-one socialist deputies sent to the [German] Reichstag in the penultimate general election, there were nine Jews, and this figure is an extremely high one when compared with the percentage of Jews among the population of Germany, and also with the total number of Jewish workers [in Germany] and with the number of Jewish members of the socialist party.[21]

Eighteen of the twenty-nine people's commissars in the government of the Hungarian Soviet Republic of 1919 were Jewish.[22] Eduard Bernstein suggested in 1921 that there were roughly 500 journalists employed by social democratic newspapers in Germany, and that it would not be unreasonable to estimate that 50 of those journalists were of Jewish descent.[23] By the end of 1923, roughly 20 percent of the membership of the Communist Party of Poland [KPP] was Jewish.[24] Official Communist sources (not inclined to exaggerate on this subject) estimated that 35 percent of the KPP membership was Jewish in 1930.[25] In 1949, it has been

[20] Robert J. Brym, *The Jewish Intelligentsia and Russian Marxism: A Sociological Study of Intellectual Radicalism And Ideological Divergence* (New York: Schocken Books, 1978). There was a smaller Jewish presence among the Bolsheviks than among the Mensheviks throughout the period preceding the Revolution of 1917. Moreover, the total number of Bolsheviks who were Jewish in the pre-Revolutionary period was rather small. A Communist Party census conducted in 1922 demonstrates that there were at that time merely 958 Jewish members in the party who had joined before 1917. The total membership of the Bolshevik group in January 1917 was 23,600. Zvi Y. Gitelman, *Jewish Nationality and Soviet Politics: The Jewish Sections of the CPSU, 1917–1930* (Princeton: Princeton University Press, 1972), 105–106.
[21] Michels, *Political Parties*, 246.
[22] Traverso, *The Marxists and the Jewish Question*, 33.
[23] Eduard Bernstein, "Di yidn un di daytshe sotsial-demokratie," *Tsukunft* XXVI (March 1921), 151.
[24] M. Mishkinsky, "The Communist Party of Poland and the Jews," in *The Jews of Poland Between Two World Wars*, ed. Yisrael Gutman, Ezra Mendelsohn, Jehuda Reinharz, and Chone Shmeruk (Hanover, NH: University Press of New England, 1989), 62.
[25] Celia S. Heller, *On the Edge of Destruction: Jews of Poland Between the Two World Wars* (New York: Columbia University Press, 1977), 254. There are no reliable statistics on the proportion of Jews active in Trotskyist movements. However, it appears to be the

alleged, approximately half of those in the American Communist Party were Jews.[26]

Though Jews were highly visible in the leftist movements of countries such as Hungary, Poland, and the US, at specific points in the twentieth century, this fact does not by any means imply that most Jews in these countries were affiliated with leftist parties. The total number of members of the KPP in 1930 was roughly 6,600.[27] To say that 35 percent of the members of the Party in that year were Jews is to suggest that 2,310 Jews were members of the KPP. A census conducted by the Polish government found that there were 3,113,933 individuals of the "Mosaic faith" in Poland in December 1931.[28] Thus, considerably less than 1 percent of the Polish Jewish population was enrolled in the KPP in the early 1930s.

On the other hand, there are all but certainly cases in which a plurality or even a majority of Jewish voters in a specific country has voted for a socialist or social democratic party in a particular election. Most Jewish voters in Germany in the first years of the Weimar Republic are likely to have cast their ballots for the German Democratic Party [DDP], which was left liberal and proudly bourgeois in orientation. However, there was, in all likelihood, an increase in support among German Jews for the Social Democratic Party [SPD] (which evolved over time from a Marxist into a reformist organization) during the course of the 1920s. One contemporary source suggests that in 1924, 42 percent of Jewish voters in Germany voted for the SPD, 40 percent for the DDP, and that 8 percent of the Jewish vote went to the Communist Party of Germany [KPD].[29] As

case that Jews played a disproportionate role in many of these movements. I have discussed Jews active in the Trotskyist movement in Poland in Jack Jacobs, "Communist Questions, Jewish Answers: Polish Jewish Dissident Communists of the Inter-War Era," in *Jewish Women in Eastern Europe*, ed. ChaeRan Freeze, Paula Hyman, and Antony Polonsky. Polin. Studies in Polish Jewry 18 (Oxford: Littman, 2005), 369–379.

[26] Gennady Estraikh, "Metamorphoses of *Morgn-frayhayt*," in *Yiddish and the Left*, ed. Gennady Estraikh and Mikhail Krutikov. Studies in Yiddish III (Oxford: Legenda, 2001), 145.

[27] Gabriele Simoncini, "Ethnic and Social Diversity in the Membership of the Communist Party of Poland: 1918–1938," *Nationalities Papers* XXII, Supplement 1 (1994): 59.

[28] Chone Shmeruk, "Hebrew-Yiddish-Polish: A Trilingual Jewish Culture," in *The Jews of Poland Between Two World Wars*, ed. Gutman, Mendelsohn, Reinharz and Shmeruk, 287.

[29] Ernst Hamburger and Peter Pulzer, "Jews as Voters in the Weimar Republic," *Leo Baeck Institute Year Book* XXX (1985), 48, citing a work published in 1928. A second source indicates that the DDP received 64 percent of Jewish votes before 1930, the SPD 28 percent, the KPD 4 percent, and that a fourth party, the German People's Party (DVP), which stood to the right of the DDP, received as many Jewish votes during that era as did the KPD. Arnold Paucker, "Jewish Defence Against Nazism in the Weimar Republic," *The Wiener Library Bulletin* XXVI, 1–2, new series 26–27 (1972): 26.

the strength of the Nazi party increased, and liberal parties like the DDP collapsed, it is quite probable that the proportion of German Jews voting for the SPD grew yet again. Arnold Paucker presents data suggesting that 62 percent of Jewish voters voted for the SPD after 1930, and that 8 percent voted for the KPD. Even if, as Paucker himself admits, the evidence that he provides may overstate German Jewish support for parties of the left, it is very likely that a majority of German Jewish voters did in fact support such parties in the Weimar Republic's last years.[30] But I hasten to add that many German Jews who voted in German elections in the early 1930s are likely to have supported the SPD not necessarily because they endorsed the general platforms of that party but because they believed that there were no viable alternatives open to them. In this and other cases Jewish support for the left was linked to existing historical and political circumstances.

THE JEWISH LEFT

THE JEWISH LEFT IN EUROPE

Jews created and became involved, during the nineteenth and twentieth centuries, not only in non-Jewish leftist movements, but also in explicitly Jewish leftist organizations. Urbanization, modernization, pauperization, proletarianization, and the decline of rabbinic authority all contributed to the sparking of left-wing sentiment among Eastern European Jews.[31] Unlike in Central and Western Europe, where many Jewish leftists were both acculturated and linguistically assimilated, and were therefore inclined to work within general leftist movements, Eastern European Jewish leftists (and certain Jewish radicals who left Eastern Europe to settle in other parts of the world) regularly felt that the needs of the local Jewish populations – including the fact that many Eastern European Jews were native-born Yiddish speakers and were not fluent in the languages of the non-Jews amongst whom they lived – made it necessary to create Jewish parties or organizations. Moreover, the socio-economic

[30] Though the proportion of German Jewish voters casting ballots for the KPD may not have changed in the early 1930s, the proportion of Jews playing leading roles in that party dropped precipitously. There were no Jews in the Central Committee of the KPD at the end of the Weimar period, and no Jews among the 89 KPD members elected to the Reichstag in November 1932. Hamburger and Pulzer, "Jews as Voters in the Weimar Republic," 46.

[31] Gerald Sorin, *The Prophetic Minority: American Jewish Immigrant Radicals, 1880–1920*, The Modern Jewish Experience (Bloomington: Indiana University Press, 1985), 18–27.

structures of the Jewish communities of Eastern Europe were sharply different from those of Jewish communities in Central or Western Europe. The proportion of Eastern European Jews who were middle class or wealthy was considerably lower than was, for example, the proportion of German Jewry that could be so characterized. The proportion made up of workers was much higher. This made Eastern European Jewry a more fertile recruitment ground for leftists than its counterparts in the German-speaking lands.[32]

The first explicitly Jewish socialist organization, the Hebrew Socialist Union, was established in London in 1876. However, it was not created by English Jews, but by Jews who had emigrated from the European mainland to England. The group's members were by no means self-haters. They identified themselves as Jews (presumably in an ethnic or national sense), though they rejected religion. The Hebrew Socialist Union condemned private property, argued that a universal upheaval was necessary, and advocated workers' control. It held public meetings, helped to establish a trade union for tailors, and caused a stir within Anglo Jewry, but it never had more than 40 active members and did not survive beyond the year in which it was created.[33] Though the Hebrew Socialist Union was inconsequential in size, it eventually provided inspiration to later Jewish socialists in Eastern Europe and elsewhere.

[32] Emanuel Scherer, "The Bund," in *Struggle for Tomorrow: Modern Political Ideologies of the Jewish People*, ed. Basil J. Vlavianos and Feliks Gross (New York: Arts, Incorporated, 1954), 137.

[33] William J. Fishman, *Jewish Radicals: From Czarist Shtetl to London Ghetto* (London: Harrap, 1976), 103–124. Russian Jewish radicals involved in political life in the 1880s did not emulate the example of the Hebrew Socialist Union. A relatively large number of radicals of Jewish origin became active in political affairs in the Russian Empire in the 1880s. There were only 67 Jews among those arrested in the Russian Empire for political offenses in the period 1873–1877. These Jews made up 6.5 percent of all those arrested on such charges. There were 579 Jews among the 4,307 individuals arrested on political charges in the years 1884–1890. Thus, close to 14 percent of those in this latter group were Jewish. See, E(lihu) Tcherikower (Tsherikover), "Revolutsionere un natsionale ideologies fun der rusish-yidisher inteligents," in *Geshikhte fun der yidisher arbeter-bavegung in di fareynikte shtatn*, vol. II, ed. E(lihu) Tcherikower (Tsherikover) (New York: Yidisher visnshaftlekher institut – YIVO, 1945), 195. Cf. Erich E. Haberer, *Jews and Revolution in Nineteenth-Century Russia* (Cambridge: Cambridge University Press, 1995). However, these individuals were involved with the Russian populist movement, and advocated that political activity be conducted primarily among Russian peasants. They made no attempt to found explicitly Jewish socialist groups. Indeed, most of the Russian radicals of Jewish origin of that era were ideological assimilationists, and were estranged from Jewish life.

In the period beginning with the 1870s and continuing through the 1880s and 1890s, there were sporadic attempts made by Jews living in the Russian Empire (some of whom were populists, and others of whom were Marxists) to organize radical circles among Russian Jewish artisans.[34] By the end of this period, participants in those efforts began to extend their activities in a variety of ways, including via the establishment of trade unions made up of Jewish workers and artisans, the organization of strikes conducted by these unions, and the creation of propaganda materials in Yiddish. This activity contributed to the creation of the General Jewish Workers' Bund, which was founded in Vilna in 1897.

Over time, the Bund became a relatively large party, operating in a broad swath of territory, despite the fact that it was an underground movement for almost all of the tsarist era.[35] It did not, initially, advocate on behalf of national rights for the Jews of the Russian Empire. The Bund, however, ultimately came to be characterized not only by a continuing commitment to Marxism, and by its anti-Zionism, but also by its advocacy of national cultural autonomy for the Jews of the Empire.[36] It played

---

[34] Ezra Mendelsohn, *Class Struggle in the Pale: The Formative Years of the Jewish Workers' Movement in Tsarist Russia* (Cambridge: Cambridge University Press, 1970), 30–31.

[35] Henry J. Tobias, *The Jewish Bund in Russia: From Its Origins to 1905* (Stanford: Stanford University Press, 1972).

[36] Scholars have offered a number of different explanations for how and why the Bund came to adopt a national program. The Bund leaders, Jonathan Frankel has argued, were navigating between Zionist critics on one flank, and Russian and Polish socialist critics on another, and charted a course in between the two. From Frankel's perspective, in other words, the Bund's ideological evolution in the years of the tsarist Empire can best be explained not by the need to respond to pressure from the rank-and-file (as Bundist historiography has sometimes suggested), or by sociological factors, but by a need to respond to the party's political opponents. "Bundist ideology turns out to have developed not inexorably as a superstructure reflecting the realities of the mass base but rather as a result of specific political contingencies." Jonathan Frankel, *Prophecy and Politics: Socialism, Nationalism and the Russian Jews, 1862–1917* (Cambridge: Cambridge University Press, 1981), 182. Yoav Peled has replied to Frankel by arguing, compellingly, that political factors alone cannot explain the ideological evolution of the party, and that Frankel devoted insufficient attention to underlying socio-historical processes. He notes that the experience of Russian Jewish workers in the labor market caused them to develop "ethno-class consciousness," and that the ideology which was adopted by the Bund was the political expression of this consciousness. "The evolution of Bundist ideology was neither a smooth process of adjustment to primordial reality [as Bundist historians have tended to argue] nor a search by a group of intellectuals for an ideological niche of their own [as Frankel suggests]. It was, rather, the continuous effort of a political party to strike the correct ideological balance between the various conflicting concerns of the constituency it was seeking to mobilize." Yoav Peled, *Class and Ethnicity in the Pale: The*

a key role in organizing the Russian Social Democratic Workers' Party, established armed self-defense groups to aid Jews threatened by pogromists, and was particularly visible in the period of the Revolution of 1905, during which it claimed to have 33,000 members.

A series of other Jewish socialist parties – the Zionist Socialist Workers' Party (often known as the SS, its Russian initials), which asserted that it had 27,000 members, and which advocated the territorial concentration of Jewry while not insisting that this concentration take place in Palestine, the Jewish Social Democratic Workers' Party Poalei-Zion, which believed that Jewish territorial concentration could and ought to be realized only in Palestine, and which purportedly had 16,000 adherents, and the Jewish Socialist Workers' Party (a.k.a. SERP, its initials in Russian), which boasted a membership of 13,000, many of whom were sympathetic to a social revolutionary rather than a Marxist understanding of socialism – came into being somewhat later than had the Bund, and competed with that party. These parties differed from one another, and from the Bund, in their conceptions of socialism, their attitudes towards territorialism and Zionism, and, more generally, in their proposed solutions to the problems confronting the Jews of the Russian Empire.[37]

The Jewish socialist parties which had been active in the Russian Empire did not survive the Bolshevik consolidation of power (because the Bolsheviks were ultimately unwilling to tolerate such parties, and pressured them to dissolve).[38] However, while the Bund was forced to stop operating in the USSR, it did quite well, in the 1930s, in Poland – the country in Europe with the largest Jewish population during that time, and the cultural heart of the Jewish Diaspora. An increase in the number of wage laborers in the Polish Jewish population (probably sparked

Political Economy of Jewish Workers' Nationalism in Late Imperial Russia (New York: St. Martin's Press, 1989), 131.

[37] Jews in Europe founded significant Jewish socialist parties not only in the Russian Empire but also in Austria-Hungary. The Jewish Social Democratic Party of Galicia, established in 1905, had a Bundist ideology, and attracted 4,500 members in the period immediately preceding the beginning of the First World War. Rick Kuhn, "Organizing Yiddish-Speaking Workers in pre-World War I Galicia: The Jewish Social Democratic Party," in *Yiddish Language & Culture: Then & Now*, ed. Leonard Jay Greenspoon. Studies in Jewish Civilization IX (Omaha, NE: Creighton University Press, 1998), 37–65. Labor Zionists in Austria-Hungary also organized a party of their own, the Jewish Socialist Workers' Party Poalei-Zion in Austria.

[38] Gitelman, *Jewish Nationality and Soviet Politics*, 151–230. Relatively large numbers of Jews flocked to the Russian Communist Party – which was perceived as a bulwark against antisemitism, and a source of employment – in the era of the Civil War and after the conclusion of that war.

by urbanization and economic modernization) led to the growth of trade unions linked to the Bund, which, in the 1930s, strengthened the Bund per se.[39] In addition, the Bund in Poland benefited to some degree from the creation of a constellation of Bundist-oriented movements focused on children, youth, physical education, and women.[40] Many of these Bundist-oriented movements acted as conveyor belts for the party, and thus help to explain how and why the Bund became the strongest Jewish political party in most major Polish cities with large Jewish populations in the period immediately preceding the beginning of World War II.

Labor Zionist parties never achieved political success in Poland comparable to that achieved by the Bund. The Left Poalei-Zion, a Marxist-Zionist party, had strength in some provincial towns, including Brest and Chelm, contributed to efforts to promote secular Yiddish culture in Poland in the interwar years, and had several impressive intellectuals – such as Emanuel Ringelblum and Raphael Mahler – in its ranks.[41] But the Left Poalei-Zion was squeezed, in interwar Poland, into a narrow political sliver between the Zionist movement, on the one hand, and the Bund and Communist movements on the other, and was unable to attract considerable numbers of Jewish workers or artisans in Poland's largest cities. The other left-Zionist parties in Poland – such as the Right Poalei-Zion, Hitahdut, and the Zionist-Socialist Party Zeire Zion – were generally more Zionist and less leftist than was the Left Poalei-Zion. As Ezra Mendelsohn has shown, they "had no parliamentary role and no real political responsibility."[42]

Most Jews active in or sympathetic to the Bund, the left-Zionists, or the non-Jewish leftist parties of Central Europe suffered the same fate as did the rest of the Jewish population during the Second World War. Almost all European Jewish leftists who remained in Nazi-occupied Europe during the War died or were murdered during the course of that conflict.[43]

[39] Gertrud Pickhan, *"Gegen den Strom": Der Allgemeine Jüdische Arbeiterbund "Bund" in Polen, 1918–1939*. Schriften des Simon-Dubnow Instituts Leipzig, vol. 1 (Stuttgart: Deutsche Verlags-Anstalt, 2001), 206.

[40] Jack Jacobs, *Bundist Counterculture in Interwar Poland* (Syracuse: Syracuse University Press, in cooperation with The YIVO Institute for Jewish Research, 2009).

[41] Samuel Kassow, "The Left Poalei Zion in Inter-War Poland," in *Yiddish and the Left*, ed. Estraikh and Krutikov, 109–128. Cf. Bine Garntsarska-Kadari, *Di linke poyle-tsien in poyln biz der tsveyter velt-milkhome* (Tel Aviv: Farlag i. l. peretz, 1995).

[42] Ezra Mendelsohn, *Zionism in Poland. The Formative Years, 1915–1926* (New Haven: Yale University Press, 1981), 172.

[43] A relatively small number of leaders of the Polish Bund escaped to the US or to other lands with the aid of the New York-based Jewish Labor Committee, as did a small number of leaders of the German and of the Austrian social democratic movements. On the fate of Bundists during the Second World War, see Daniel Blatman, *For Our*

The base of support for the Jewish left in Europe was all but completely eliminated.

There were attempts made to reorganize the Bund in Poland when the Second World War was over.[44] However, the Bund was no more able to exist in Communist-dominated Poland than it had been in the Communist-controlled USSR. The Bund in Poland was dismantled in 1948–1949.[45]

In sum, the explicitly Jewish left arose among Eastern European Jews at a specific point in the nineteenth century, in the context of urbanization, shifts in the class structure of the Jewish population, and a decrease in the strength of traditional Jewish religious authorities. The Bund – the most significant of the Jewish left parties – achieved successes both in tsarist Russia and in interwar Poland. Along with all other Jewish left parties in Europe, however, it was ultimately destroyed by world-historic forces far beyond its control. The Yiddish-speaking Jewish working class – which had been the Bund's core constituency – was virtually extirpated in Eastern Europe by the Nazis and by those who worked on behalf of the Nazis. Communist victories, first in Russia and, much later, in Poland and elsewhere, eliminated the political space within which the Bund (and the Eastern European Jewish left in general) had operated. In the wake of the Second World War, the Eastern European Jewish left per se could not and did not survive.

THE JEWISH LEFT IN THE USA

The founders of the Jewish left in the USA were generally similar to their counterparts in Eastern Europe, and the constituency within which American Jewish leftists conducted their work paralleled that in countries like Russia or Poland, to some extent. The very different political conditions

Freedom and Yours: The Jewish Labour Bund in Poland 1939–1949 (London: Vallentine Mitchell, 2003). On the aid and support provided by the Jewish Labor Committee to German and Austrian social democrats, some of whom were of Jewish origin, see Jack Jacobs, *Ein Freund in Not. Das Jüdische Arbeiterkomitee in New York und die Flüchtlinge aus den deutschsprachigen Ländern, 1933–1945* (Bonn: Forschungsinstitut der Friedrich-Ebert-Stiftung, 1993).

[44] David Engel, "The Bund after the Holocaust: Between Renewal and Self-Liquidation," in *Jewish Politics in Eastern Europe. The Bund at 100*, ed. Jack Jacobs (New York: New York University Press, 2001), 213–226; Natalia Aleksiun, "Where was there a Future for Polish Jewry? Bundist and Zionist Polemics in Post-World War II Poland," *Jewish Politics in Eastern Europe*, ed. Jacobs, 227–242.

[45] Blatman, *For Our Freedom and Yours*, 210–218; David Slucki, *The International Jewish Labor Bund after 1945: Toward a Global History* (New Brunswick, NJ: Rutgers University Press, 2012), 56–74.

in which American Jews lived eventually made it possible for the Jewish left to grow to an impressive size. Ultimately, however, the Jewish left in the USA also went into a sharp decline – though not for precisely the same reasons as had the Jewish left movements of Eastern Europe. In the USA, economic and social mobility over the course of the twentieth century diminished the proportional size of the Jewish working class. The relative openness of American society, which made assimilation possible, diminished the size of the Yiddish-speaking population. The American Jewish left, created in the nineteenth century, peaked in the twentieth century, and has dwindled in strength in the last few decades.

The pogroms of 1881, economic dislocation, and social changes within the world of Eastern European Jewry, all contributed to sparking massive waves of immigration by Jews from the Russian Empire to the United States. Approximately 750,000 Jews born in the Empire settled in the US in the period from 1881 to 1905.[46] The Jews who left Europe were often younger, more impressionable, and somewhat less committed to the practice of Jewish religious traditions than were those who remained behind.

Eastern European Jewish immigrants to the United States encountered extremely poor living and working conditions in neighborhoods such as New York's Lower East Side (to which a lion's share of the Eastern European Jewish immigrants of that era moved upon arrival in America). This wave of immigrants, heavily concentrated in certain industries, began to develop class consciousness, was influenced by radical intellectuals, engaged in a variety of forms of collective action, and evinced sympathy for socialist and radical ideas.[47] Entities that later became pillars of the American Jewish left – including the Workmen's Circle and the *Forverts* (Jewish Daily Forward) – were created by these immigrants during this period.

The Workmen's Circle [Arbeter Ring], first established on a local level in New York in 1892, snowballed in size after the beginning of the twentieth century. In an era when there was little in the way of government-provided social service in the US, the Workmen's Circle offered concrete mutual aid benefits to its members. It also emphasized education and provided recreational opportunities. Considerable attention was given, as the organization matured, to organizing lectures, choruses, and orchestras, to publishing, and, ultimately, to supplementary schools for children. The organization supported the work of trade unionists, including trade union organizing efforts undertaken in the garment industry, in particular; it supported the

[46] Hadassa Kosak, *Cultures of Opposition: Jewish Immigrant Workers, New York City, 1881–1905* (Albany: State University of New York Press, 2000).
[47] Tony Michels, *A Fire in Their Hearts: Yiddish Socialists in New York* (Cambridge, MA: Harvard University Press, 2005), 3–16.

American Socialist Party and also sent material support to Jewish socialists abroad, i.e., to Bundist institutions. Though the Workmen's Circle was broader in ideological range than was the Bund, and had a certain number of self-proclaimed anarchist members and members sympathetic to labor Zionism and other leftist currents, one-time Bundists tended to dominate the country-wide leadership of the organization for many decades following a secondary wave of post-1905 immigration. The most prominent leaders of the Workmen's Circle, like those of the Bund, were sympathetic to socialism, and identified themselves as Jewish, but were not themselves religiously observant. Over time, the leaders also came to be strong advocates of secular, Yiddish-language, culture. The organization was interested in defending the interests both of Jewish immigrants to America and of Jews who had remained in Eastern Europe. The order was open to non-Jews, but attracted few non-Jews into its ranks. It had 87,000 members at its peak in 1925, and also had sizeable material assets.

The *Forverts*, a Yiddish language daily newspaper founded in New York in 1897, was, at one time, another major bastion of Jewish leftists in the US. Though not a party organ, the newspaper was closely associated with the American Socialist Party in its early years. The *Forverts*, which was edited by Abraham Cahan during the period of its greatest strength, ultimately became not only the most powerful social democratic daily in the US, but also the largest daily newspaper published in Yiddish anywhere in the world. Around 1917, the *Forverts* reportedly had a circulation of over 200,000.[48]

The Workmen's Circle and the *Forverts* – which operated legally – were, in a number of respects, not directly comparable to European Jewish socialist parties like the Bund, or to the earliest Yiddish radical periodicals issued in Eastern Europe (which were often produced and distributed

---

[48] Melech Epstein, *Jewish Labor in U.S.A.* (New York: KTAV, 1969), vol. I, 323. The history and orientation of the *Forverts* are described by Epstein, *Jewish Labor in U.S.A.*, 318–334; Irving Howe, *World of Our Fathers* (New York: Harcourt Brace Jovanovich, 1976); Arthur Liebman, *Jews and the Left*, Contemporary Religious Movements (New York: John Wiley & Sons, 1979), 326–346; and Michels, *A Fire in Their Hearts*, 104ff. Jewish immigrants from Eastern Europe are known to have been involved with leftist causes not only in the USA, but also in Argentina, Canada, South Africa, and other countries. Philip Mendes, "The Rise and Fall of the Jewish/Left Alliance: An Historical and Political Analysis," *Australian Journal of Politics & History* XLV, 4 (December 1999), 492–493; Nancy L. Green, ed., *Jewish Workers in the Modern Diaspora* (Berkeley: University of California Press, 1998), 119–185. Regional variation notwithstanding, the history of Jewish involvement with the left in the first decades of the twentieth century seems to have been rather similar in virtually all the countries which attracted significant numbers of Jews from Eastern Europe during that era.

surreptitiously). Nevertheless, it ought to be noted that the Workmen's Circle was, at its moment of greatest strength, much larger than any European Jewish socialist organization of any kind, and that the *Forverts*, similarly, had a far greater reach than did its counterparts in other lands.

Jewish immigrants to the US from Eastern Europe played instrumental roles, in the twentieth century, not only in the Workmen's Circle and in the *Forverts* but also in the trade union movement. The most important trade unions with Jewish leadership were the International Ladies Garment Workers Union [ILGWU], which organized workers who made women's clothing and which was founded in 1900, and the Amalgamated Clothing Workers of America [the Amalgamated], which organized those who made men's clothing and which came into being in 1914. The cap makers union and the fur and leather workers union were also significant. None of these unions were explicitly or exclusively Jewish. But the early leaders of all four of these unions – including, most famously, David Dubinsky of the ILGWU and Sidney Hillman of the Amalgamated – were Jews, and so were significant portions of the memberships of these unions. In 1918, the ILGWU had 129,311 members. The Amalgamated is known to have had 177,000 members in 1920.

As was the case around the world, the Bolshevik Revolution led to deep divisions within the American Jewish left. Individuals sympathetic to the Bolshevik cause and living in the US ultimately helped to create (and/or controlled) a set of organizations and periodicals reflecting their perspective. The *Frayhayt* (founded in 1922, and later renamed the *Morgn-frayhayt*), a Yiddish daily newspaper published in New York, attracted readers who were further to the left than were those who read the *Forverts*.[49] Initially including among its leading figures individuals who were revolutionaries but not Communists, the newspaper was eventually dominated by Communists, and drew many of its earliest readers away from the *Forverts*. In the 1920s, the paid circulation of the *Frayhayt* reached 14,000.[50]

The International Workers Order, which was established in 1930, attracted Jews (and non-Jews) who were further to the left than were those in the Workmen's Circle. Jewish membership in the International Workers Order, which provided substantial material support to the *Morgn-frayhayt*,

---

[49] The founding and earliest years of the *Frayhayt* are described in Melech Epstein, *The Jews and Communism 1919–1941: The Story of Early Communist Victories and Ultimate Defeats in the Jewish Community, U.S.A.* (New York: Trade Union Sponsoring Committee, [1959]), 102–104, and Michels, *A Fire in Their Hearts*, 238–250.

[50] Epstein, *The Jews and Communism*, 138. Estraikh reports that the *Morgn-frayhayt* had a circulation of 21,000 in 1947. See Estraikh, "Metamorphoses of *Morgn-frayhayt*." 145.

reached 60,000 in 1947, at which time these Jews made up roughly one third of the total number of members of the Order.[51]

CONTEMPORARY JEWISH POLITICAL ATTITUDES

All of the components of the American Jewish left described above have declined precipitously in size and strength in recent generations. Linguistic acculturation contributed substantially to a long-term drop in the circulation of the *Forverts*. The Yiddish-language newspaper – which is now a weekly – currently has a paid circulation of less than 4,000.[52] The newspaper's editorial line is neither radical nor leftist.

The Workmen's Circle, which had done well when Jewish immigrants were densely concentrated in urban neighborhoods, was negatively affected by the geographic dispersion of the descendants of these immigrants (as well as by assimilation and other social changes).[53] Membership is now under 12,000, and continues to decline steadily.

Over the course of the twentieth century, the proportion of Jews in the garment industry unions went down very sharply as a result of Jewish social mobility. By the 1930s, it was already true that 11 percent of employed Jewish males in the US were in professional rather than working class positions. This figure rose to 15 percent shortly after WW II, to 20 percent in 1957, and to 30 percent in the 1970s.[54] Local 22 of the ILGWU, which at one time "was perhaps the largest single Jewish labor organization" in the US, had, at its height (in 1938) "nearly 28,000 members, of whom seventy-five percent were Jewish" and of whom a high proportion were female.[55] By 1950, Local 22 had only 12,500 members, of whom 30 percent were Jews. Similar trends were also evident by the middle of the twentieth century in other trade unions in which Jews had earlier been present in significant numbers, and have continued since that time. Only a negligible number of Jewish rank and file workers are currently employed in unionized positions in the American garment industry. More generally, a far smaller proportion of American Jews work in blue collar positions today than was true a century ago.

[51] Liebman, *Jews and the Left*, 311–315.
[52] The Forward Association, owner of the *Forverts*, has also published an English-language weekly, *Forward*, in recent years. This weekly does not have a leftist or radical editorial perspective.
[53] Liebman, *Jews and the Left*, 379.
[54] Liebman, *Jews and the Left*, 359.
[55] Epstein, *Jewish Labor in U.S.A.*, xii.

Many of the organizations and periodicals created (and/or maintained) by those American Jews who were sympathetic to the Bolshevik revolution – hurt not only by the factors mentioned above, but also by measures taken by government agencies against suspected Communists during the Cold War, and by a sharp drop in sympathy for communism within the American Jewish population in the wake of revelations about actions taken by the Stalinist regime in the USSR – are no longer extant.[56] The International Workers Order, which lost a series of court battles and which ultimately had its charter revoked at the request of an agency of the state of New York, was formally dissolved in 1954.[57] The *Morgn-frayhayt* ceased publishing in 1988.[58]

Arthur Liebman wrote, in a work published in 1979, that

The income, occupational, and geographical mobilities that Jews experienced in America in one or two generations were body blows to the maintenance of a sizeable, concentrated, and economically homogenous Jewish working class. Although limitations on where Jews might work or live continued (and continue), the opportunities were such that Jews as a people rather quickly moved from the working class to the middle class in America. This socioeconomic metamorphosis could not but be damaging to the Jews' commitment to socialism.[59]

The trends described by Liebman have continued over the course of the generation since the publication of his work, and they help to explain the continuing decline in ties between American Jews and the left. In recent years, leftist anti-Zionism and other factors have also contributed to further reductions of support for leftist causes within American Jewry. The number of contemporary American Jews who support socialist, communist, or anarchist movements is now rather small.

Though the USA is manifestly a vastly different country than was imperial Germany, contemporary American Jewry is more like early-twentieth-century German Jewry in it socio-economic structure and in its

---

[56] Exceptions to this generalization include Camp Kinderland, a summer camp for children currently based in Massachusetts, which, in an earlier era, had been close in spirit to the International Workers Order, and *Jewish Currents*, a periodical issued in New York and originally known as *Jewish Life*. On Camp Kinderland see Paul C. Mishler, *Raising Reds: The Young Pioneers, Radical Summer Camps, and Communist Political Culture in the United States* (New York: Columbia University Press, 1999), 89–94.

[57] Epstein, *The Jews and Communism*, 155; Liebman, *Jews and the Left*, 311.

[58] Estraikh, "Metamorphoses of *Morgn-frayhayt*," 144.

[59] Liebman, *Jews and the Left*, 592. Liebman also describes ways in which the "inadvertent strengthening of a sense of Jewish solidarity" by Jewish leftists in America ultimately undermined class consciousness and allegiance to the left. Liebman, *Jews and the Left*, 597.

political affiliations than like Russian Jewry of the tsarist era. Like the Jews of imperial Germany, a notable proportion of American Jewry is made up of individuals in high socio-economic status groups. Like the Jews of early twentieth-century Germany, contemporary American Jews are often sympathetic to liberal ideas. Indeed, American Jewry is more liberal than many other American ethnic groups on a broad range of issues. American Jewry is, however, not identified with the American political left, at this point in its history, but rather with powerful, mainstream, American political institutions.

Jews in other countries have likewise edged away from earlier sympathies for leftist ideas. The State of Israel had a string of Labor-dominated governments in its founding decades. In more recent elections, however, it has elected right-wing governments with nationalistic platforms. The decline of leftist ideas in Israel, and the rise of other perspectives, seems to be related to three different phenomena: 1. immigration patterns, 2. matters related to the conflict with the Palestinians and with other portions of the Arab World, and 3. changes in the class composition of Israeli society. Early waves of Jewish immigrants to Palestine (and, later, to the State of Israel) were made up, in part, of Eastern European Jews who had themselves been influenced by leftist ideas, of varying kinds. Socialist thinkers such as Nachman Syrkin and Berl Katznelson were widely admired by (some) Israelis of an earlier generation. Many kibbutzim (collective settlements), the Histadrut (the General Federation of Labor), and other institutions in Palestine were controlled, in an earlier era, by Labor Zionists. The political parties in which these institutions were influential regularly won major electoral victories. However, neither the large wave of Jews from North Africa (the Mizraḥim) which arrived in Israel beginning with the 1950s, nor the large wave of Jews from the USSR (and from the successor states of the USSR) which began to arrive in Israel roughly a generation after the Mizraḥim, were sympathetic either to socialism in general or to the Labor Party of Israel. Moreover, the descendants of Eastern European Jews who have immigrated to Israel in recent years from Western countries have often come from religiously Orthodox backgrounds, and have regularly advocated both conservative social values and conservative political views. Certain other segments of the Jewish population of Israel, including descendants of the Eastern European Jewish immigrants who had arrived in Palestine as idealistic leftists in earlier eras, became less sympathetic to leftist ideas than their ancestors had been as their class position altered. The descendants of Eastern European Jewish immigrants to Palestine currently living in Israel are regularly in very high socio-economic status groups, and are often sympathetic to business interests rather than to the interests of the working class. More generally, the Jewish population of Israel as presently constituted does not evince particular sympathy for the left.

Jews in France, home to the world's third largest Jewish community, were, in the recent past, sympathetic to Socialist Party candidates. Francois Mitterrand, the first Socialist elected to serve as President of the French Fifth Republic, apparently received a plurality of the votes of French Jews both in 1981 and in 1988. However, the Jewish population of France seems not to have given comparable support to Ségolène Royal, the Socialist candidate in France's Presidential election in 2007. Fears within the French Jewish population of rising antisemitism seem to have increased support for the "law-and-order" policies advocated by Nicolas Sarkozy (who is partially of Jewish origin), as did the perception among some French Jews that Sarkozy has taken pro-Israel positions. A large proportion of the Jews of France, it would appear, voted for Sarkozy (candidate of the right-wing Union for a Popular Movement) in 2007 rather than for Royal. Sarkozy also apparently received a plurality of Jewish votes in the Presidential election of 2012.

Current Jewish political opinion in the three largest Jewish communities (USA, Israel, and France), which, collectively, constitute the overwhelming bulk of world Jewry, corroborate the idea that the one-time ties between Jews and the left can best be explained by political, economic, and sociological conditions which came into existence in the nineteenth century, and which went out of existence in the twentieth, rather than by reference to Jewish religious ideas or other factors. The marginality of Jews in Central and Eastern Europe, the lack of opportunity for Jews in major institutions in tsarist Russia, poor living and working conditions not only in Eastern Europe but also in the USA, the explicit antisemitism of right-wing movements, and the relative openness of left-wing movements, all led some Jews in areas such as the Russian Empire and the USA to affiliate with the political left at a particular juncture in history. However, the dramatically altered conditions in which most Jews live in the twenty-first century have resulted in a very different Jewish political profile. The relationship of Jews to the left was a historically important phenomenon. This relationship, however, may well prove to have been of limited duration.

SELECT BIBLIOGRAPHY

Brym, Robert J. *The Jewish Intelligentsia and Russian Marxism: A Sociological Study of Intellectual Radicalism And Ideological Divergence*. New York: Schocken Books, 1978.

Carlebach, Julius. *Karl Marx and the Radical Critique of Judaism*. London, Henley and Boston: Routledge & Kegan Paul, 1978.

Deutscher, Isaac. *The Non-Jewish Jew and Other Essays*. New York: Hill and Wang, 1968.

Estraikh, Gennady. "Metamorpheses of *Morgn-frayhayt*." In *Yiddish and the Left*. Edited by Gennady Estraikh and Mikhail Krutikov. Studies in Yiddish III. Oxford: Legenda, 2001, pp. 144–166.

Fischer, Lars. *The Socialist Response to Antisemitism in Imperial Germany*. Cambridge: Cambridge University Press, 2007.

Fishman, William J. *Jewish Radicals: From Czarist Shtetl to London Ghetto*. New York: Pantheon Books, 1974.

Frankel, Jonathan. *Prophecy and Politics: Socialism, Nationalism and the Russian Jews, 1862–1917*. Cambridge: Cambridge University Press, 1981.

Gitelman, Zvi. *The Emergence of Modern Jewish Politics: Bundism and Zionism in Eastern Europe*. Pitt Series in Russian and East European Studies. Pittsburgh: University of Pittsburgh Press, 2003.

Jewish Nationality and Soviet Politics: The Jewish Sections of the CPSU, 1917–1930. Princeton: Princeton University Press, 1972.

Grab, Walter, ed. *Juden und jüdische Aspekte in der deutschen Arbeiterbewegung 1848–1918*. Jahrbuch des Instituts für Deutsche Geschichte, Beiheft 2. Tel Aviv: Universität Tel Aviv, Fakultät für Geisteswissenschaften, Forschungszentrum für Geschichte, Institut für Deutsche Geschichte, 1977.

Haberer, Erich E. *Jews and Revolution in Nineteenth-Century Russia*. Cambridge: Cambridge University Press, 1995.

Heid, Ludger and Arnold Paucker, eds. *Juden und deutsche Arbeiterbewegung bis 1933. Soziale Utopien und religiös-kulturelle Traditionen*. Schriftenreihe wissenschaftlicher Abhandlungen des Leo Baeck Instituts 49. Tübingen: J.C.B. Mohr (Paul Siebeck), 1992.

Jacobs, Jack. *Bundist Counterculture in Interwar Poland*. Syracuse, NY: Syracuse University Press, in cooperation with The YIVO Institute for Jewish Research, 2009.

ed. *Jewish Politics in Eastern Europe*. New York: New York University Press, in association with the Jewish Historical Institute, Warsaw, 2001.

On Socialists and "the Jewish Question" after Marx. New York: New York University Press, 1992.

Kessler, Mario. *On Anti-Semitism and Socialism: Selected Essays*. Berlin: trafo verlag, 2005.

Kosak, Hadassa. *Cultures of Opposition: Jewish Immigrant Workers, New York City, 1881–1905*. Albany: State University of New York Press, 2000.

Liebman, Arthur. *Jews and the Left*. Contemporary Religious Movements. New York: John Wiley & Sons, 1979.

Löwy, Michael. *Redemption and Utopia: Jewish Libertarian Thought in Central Europe. A Study in Elective Affinity*. Stanford: Stanford University Press, 1992.

Mendelsohn, Ezra. *Class Struggle in the Pale: The Formative Years of the Jewish Workers' Movement in Tsarist Russia*. Cambridge: Cambridge University Press, 1970.

ed. *Essential Papers on Jews and the Left*. New York and London: New York University Press, 1997.

Michels, Tony. *A Fire in Their Hearts: Yiddish Socialists in New York*. Cambridge, MA: Harvard University Press, 2005.

Peled, Yoav. *Class and Ethnicity in the Pale: The Political Economy of Jewish Workers' Nationalism in Late Imperial Russia*. New York: St. Martin's Press, 1989.

Pickhan, Gertrud. *"Gegen den Strom": Der Allgemeine Jüdische Arbeiterbund "Bund" in Polen, 1918–1939.* Schriften des Simon-Dubnow Instituts Leipzig, vol. 1. Stuttgart: Deutsche Verlags-Anstalt, 2001.

Silberner, Edmund. *Kommunisten zur Judenfrage. Zur Geschichte von Theorie und Praxis des Kommunismus.* Opladen: Westdeutscher Verlag, 1983.

   Sozialisten zur Judenfrage. Berlin: Colloquium Verlag, 1962.

Sorin, Gerald. *The Prophetic Minority: American Jewish Immigrant Radicals, 1880–1920.* The Modern Jewish Experience. Bloomington: Indiana University Press, 1985.

Tobias, Henry J. *The Jewish Bund in Russia: From Its Origins to 1905.* Stanford: Stanford University Press, 1972.

Traverso, Enzo. *The Marxists and the Jewish Question. The History of a Debate (1843–1943).* Translated by Bernard Gibbons. Atlantic Highlands, NJ: Humanities Press, 1994.

Wistrich, Robert. *Revolutionary Jews from Marx to Trotsky.* London: Harrap, 1976.

   Socialism and the Jews: The Dilemmas of Assimilation in Germany and Austria-Hungary. Rutherford: Fairleigh Dickinson University Press, 1982.

CHAPTER 15

JEWS AND COMMERCE

JONATHAN KARP

There is something schizophrenic about the place of Jews in modern economic life. On the one hand, Jews in some parts of Europe and the United States prospered with the development of capitalism. As a number of historians have suggested, liberal capitalism helped create freer institutions and policies that benefited Jewish life politically while also enabling many Jews to rise out of poverty. To an extent, Jews' familiarity with commercial practices in pre-modern Europe attuned them to the new market economies that were part and parcel of the industrial age. By the late nineteenth century, a new stratum of wealthy Jews had emerged in industry, commerce, and banking. As often as not, these Jews turned a portion of their attentions and resources to addressing the problems of severe and widespread poverty among their co-religionists, whether locally, regionally, nationally, or indeed globally. It would be difficult to overstate the contributions of this elite to the creation of new philanthropic and social welfare organizations and even to such political movements as Zionism. In twentieth-century America, especially in the period following World War II, prosperity if not affluence increasingly characterized a large segment of the Jewish population. Despite the rupture of the Holocaust, the post-war era saw the world Jewish population as a whole move increasingly into the middle classes of their respective lands – tendencies which had begun decades earlier.[1]

At the same time, attitudes to (and of) Jews were often highly critical of their presumed commercial bent. The modern period in Jewish history begins with demands for Jews' economic reform. These were not merely the relic of a moribund or nostalgic agrarian mentality but were embedded in the very fabric of modernity, in the idea of "productivization" as an expression of utilitarian values separable from commerce and exchange. The call for Jews' economic transformation accompanied and helped drive

---

[1] See Derek Penslar, *Shylock's Children: Economics and Jewish Identity in Modern Europe* (Berkeley: University of California Press, 2001), esp. 176–205.

processes of Jewish emancipation.[2] They persisted well into the twentieth century and provided ideological and rhetorical fuel for movements designed to reshape Jews not only economically but culturally and psychologically as well. Hostility to Jewish commerce is one of the central themes of the modern Jewish experience, affecting Jews in every geographical region and polity.

This chapter examines both features of modern Jewish economic life, sketching in broad outline the actual economic trends that transformed Jews' working life in the nineteenth and twentieth centuries, while also highlighting the ideological and programmatic demands for Jewish economic reform. The focus is wide but not kaleidoscopic. Far more emphasis will be given here to Jewish life in northern Europe, the United States, and modern Israel than to other regions; and more to the Ashkenazi cultural realm than to the Sephardi and Mizrahi ones. Many of the generalizations, however, if not the particulars, were characteristic of the broadest possible range of Jewish communities worldwide.

Economic history cannot be separated from demography, the study of population size and composition. This is true generally but even more so when considering the economic life of a minority group. A minority group characterized by distinctive religious and cultural features almost invariably occupies a specific position within the larger economy.[3] But how concentrated it is in singular activities and niches will depend partly on the size of the group. Small Jewish communities in medieval Rhineland Germany were often composed entirely of moneylenders (at least among the male population), whereas in eighteenth-century Poland, where Jews comprised perhaps 8 percent of the total population (but in many small and medium-sized towns might form as much as 30–60 percent), Jews were far more occupationally diversified. The reason is not hard to discern: when the Jewish population is large, a substantial segment will likely engage in activities that serve the Jewish "internal market," supplying not merely products of a ritual character but also basic handicrafts as well.

Jewish population figures at the start of the nineteenth century are merely estimates – or more likely "guestimates." It is reasonable to assume that of the approximately three million Jews worldwide at the end of the Napoleonic Wars, perhaps 400,000 lived in the combined territories of Britain, France, the Netherlands, and the multiple German states, by this time including (crucially, from a population standpoint), the former

---

[2] Jonathan Karp, *The Politics of Jewish Commerce: Economic Thought and Emancipation in Europe, 1638–1848* (New York: Cambridge University Press, 2012).

[3] Simon Kuznets, "Economic Structure of U.S. Jewry," in *Jewish Economies*, vol. 1, ed., Stephanie Lo and Glen Weyl (New Brunswick, NJ: Transaction, 2012), 5–11.

Polish territories of Poznań (acquired by Prussia in the first two partitions of Poland in 1772 and 1793 and formally annexed in 1848). The Habsburg dynasty after the 1815 Congress of Vienna (the Holy Roman Empire had ceased to exist after 1806) ruled over lands as far west as the future Belgium and as far east as the Balkans. It too acquired a substantial Jewish population – reaching perhaps 300,000 by swallowing up the bulk of Galicia during the Polish partitions (with another 100,000 in Hungary). By virtue of the same eighteenth-century partitions, the most numerous segment of Polish Jewry came under tsarist rule. Ironically, Russia, which for centuries had formally barred Jewish residence, now came to govern the largest Jewish population of any country, reaching perhaps 1.2 million after the Congress of Vienna ceded to it Congress Poland (the former Napoleonic Duchy of Warsaw). Back in the sixteenth century, the Ottoman Empire could lay claim to Jewish demographic preeminence; but by the start of the nineteenth century its portion had declined in both relative and absolute terms to approximately 280,000. That trend would accelerate dramatically of the course of the century, as Russian Jewry expanded approximately fivefold, while the Ottoman population grew far more slowly, or even declined as proportion of the general population.[4]

These regional, national, and imperial population estimates are of limited significance because they do not begin to capture population density in specific sites, not just major cities like Amsterdam, Vienna, Warsaw, Budapest, and Istanbul, but numerous small and medium-sized towns, especially in Eastern Europe. Nevertheless, in offering a brief survey of Jewish economic activity at the start of the modern era, generalizations by region will have to suffice. The historian Jonathan Israel has made one of the very few attempts to encapsulate global trends in Jewish economic life during the eighteenth century, which he views as a century broadly characterized by decline. Israel's path breaking books *European Jewry in the Age of Mercantilism* and *Diasporas within a Diaspora* depict the preceding century and a half as a veritable golden age of Jewish economic influence, replete with interlocking Jewish trade networks linking the Ottoman Mediterranean and Balkan spice and textile centers to merchants and bankers in northern Italy, Iberia, the European Atlantic seaboard, and even the Western Hemisphere. These latter merchants, traders, brokers,

---

[4] See Liebman Hersch, "Jewish Population Trends in Europe (prior to World War II)," in *The Jewish People, Past and Present* ed., Salo Baron and Mordecai Kaplan (New York: Jewish Encyclopedic Handbooks, 1948), vol. 2, 1–24; Calvin Goldscheider and Alan S. Zuckerman, *The Transformation of the Jews* (Chicago: University of Chicago Press, 1985); Paul Mendes-Flohr and Jehuda Reinharz, eds., *The Jew in the Modern World: A Documentary History*, 5th edition(New York: Oxford University Press, 2011), 879–891.

and financiers, in Israel's depiction, were comprised (often depending on the given locale) of either practicing Sephardi Jews (in Amsterdam and Hamburg) or of New Christians, who, for the most part, long retained business ties with their former co-religionists. At the same time, by the seventeenth century (with roots going back to earlier times), Polish Jews had come to play an important role in managing the large estates of the Polish nobility. While their role tended to focus on the local sale of commodities (especially liquor), Jews did enjoy a subsidiary place in the grain and timber trade that linked Poland commercially with Central, Western, and even southern Europe, regions that relied increasingly on Polish agricultural exports.[5]

According to Israel, the confluence of a number of factors led to a severe decline in European Jewry's economic fortunes by the era of the French Revolution. These included the commercial rise of Britain (where Jews were latecomers to the country's economic rise) at the expense of the Netherlands (where they had been integral), the relative decline of Central European Court Jews, and the related shift in mercantile policies of European states toward emphasizing domestic production and high tariffs.[6] While Israel's account may overstate the previous strengths of the interlinked Jewish economies of the "mercantile age," there can be no doubt that at the beginning of the modern period widespread Jewish poverty emerged as its distinguishing feature. At the end of the absolutist era, as state centralization gathered force, information gathering and policing increasingly called attention to the problem of Jewish itinerancy; the records of the semi-autonomous Jewish community (kehillah) confirm the phenomenon.[7] Jewish communities, overburdened by their native poor, were intolerant of the increasing numbers of the destitute seeking support. The Sephardic community of mid-eighteenth-century Amsterdam, its "embarrassment of riches" long depleted, was effectively bankrupted by its mounting burden of poor relief.[8] Amsterdam and Livorno became veritable clearing houses for experiments in outsourcing the Jewish poor to the

---

[5] Jonathan Israel, *European Jewry in the Age of Mercantilism* (Oxford: Oxford University Press, 1991); idem, *Diasporas within a Diaspora: Jews, Crypto-Jews and the World Maritime Empires (1540–1740)* (Leiden: Brill, 2002).

[6] Israel, *European Jewry*, 237–254.

[7] Zosa Szajkowski, *Jews and the French Revolutions of 1789, 1830 and 1848* (New York: Ktav, 1970).

[8] Tirtsah Levie Bernfeld, "Financing Poor Relief in the Spanish-Portuguese Jewish Community in Amsterdam in the Seventeenth and Eighteenth Centuries," in *Dutch Jewry: Its History and Secular Culture (1500–2000)*, ed. Jonathan Israel and Reiner Salverda (Leiden: Brill, 2002), 62–102.

Caribbean colonies. Yet, if Sephardic Jewry was in trouble, the situation of Ashkenazim appeared far worse. In part this was reputational. Eighteenth-century Poland was not called the poor man of Europe, but it was still a byword for national anarchy and decline. Naturally, the partitioning powers exploited and directly promoted this image. But even before the third and final partition of 1795, leading forces in the Polish Sejm sought to stem dissolution by staging a series of debates on reform. The "excessive" and "destructive" role of the Jews in the Polish economy came under repeated attack.[9]

In the middle of the seventeenth century, at the apogee of the Jewish activity in early modern overseas commerce, economic apologias penned by Jews and their advocates invariably stressed Jews' instrumentality in the international flow of goods and services. Writing in 1714, the Irish Deist and philosemitic pamphleteer John Toland explained that

Trade is by certain circumstances shar'd in such a manner, and parcell'd out among the inhabitants of the earth, that some, by way of eminence, may be call'd the Factors, some the Carriers, some the Miners, others the Manufactoers, and others yet the Store-keepers of the world. Thus the *Jews* may properly be said to be the Brokers of it, who, withersover they come, create business as well as manage it.[10]

Toland got some of his information and argumentation from earlier Jewish authors like the Venetian rabbi Simone Luzzatto (1638) and the Dutch Sephardi scholar Menasseh ben Israel (1654), both of whom similarly emphasized the utility of Jewish merchants in seeking out new avenues of trade, in linking commerce internationally through ties with co-religionists throughout the Diaspora and – crucially – in generating wealth for the host society without translating it into political power, which as a humbled and stateless nation they eschewed.[11] Naturally, neither called attention to the large numbers of Jewish poor, including at the time many Sephardim, a fact which has occasionally misled later scholars into overstating Jews' prosperity in this period. But by the late eighteenth century, the Jewish social problem was widely apparent. The new style of Jewish apologetics that emerged in the decade prior to the French Revolution, epitomized by the works of Christian Wilhelm von Dohm, Zalkind Hourwitz, and the Abbé Grégoire, readily acknowledged (in fact, probably exaggerated)

---

[9] Gershon Hundert, *Jews in Poland-Lithuania in the Eighteenth Century: A Genealogy of Modernity* (Berkeley: University of California Press, 2006), chap. 10.

[10] John Toland, *Reasons for Naturalizing the Jews in Great Britain and Ireland, On the same foot with all other Nations. Containing also, A Defence of the Jews against all Vulgar Prejudices in all Countries* (London, 1714), 14.

[11] Karp, *Politics of Jewish Commerce*, 12–66.

the extent of Jewish immiseration. Circumstances and sensibilities had shifted dramatically since the preceding century. Even though a scandal involving charges of Jewish criminality in the Venetian ghetto had actually occasioned Luzzatto's pamphlet, this was little noticed at the time. But by the 1780s Jewish itinerancy had become almost impossible to overlook. The pace of Jewish westward migration (and vagabondage) emanating from Poland had quickened. Stereotypically, many of these migrants were labeled "wandering beggar Jews" or "Jewish gypsies and criminals." Such impressions held sway for three or four decades in Central and Western Europe, but the fact that they faded by the mid-nineteenth century, when Jewish poverty and itinerancy were alleviated if not eliminated, suggests that these images were neither fabricated nor entirely prejudicial.[12]

The writings of Dohm, Grégoire, and others reflected Enlightenment sensibilities on Jewish commerce. Perhaps counter-intuitively in the age of Adam Smith, the merchant – and certainly the Jewish merchant – was no longer the hero he had been in the earlier mercantile and philo-Judaic literature. The Enlightenment placed a new emphasis on industriousness, productive labor, and especially the inventive mechanic and the improving farmer. At the same time, Enlightenment historicism stressed the malleability of human nature, its capacity for improvement when subjected to the shaping force of progressive institutions.[13] Jews were not by nature exploitative and deceptive, so went the argument, but rather as a result of millennia of mistreatment at the hands of misguided Christians. The Jews' confinement to commerce and moneylending, so argued Dohm and others, had habituated them to the vices that accompany constant immersion in one activity alone. The solution, they proclaimed, was to transform the Jewish occupational structure by opening up agriculture and crafts to this long-persecuted and marginalized group. Jews were emancipated in Revolutionary France precisely on the grounds that they must acculturate and cease to exhibit, outside of the private religious sphere, distinctive group loyalties and characters – not least of all in their economic life. The French *Régéneration* like the German *Verbesserung* (improvement) largely focused on the economic reform of the Jews.[14]

---

[12] Moses Shulvass, *From East to West* (Detroit: Wayne State University Press, 1971); Rudolf Glanz, *Geschichte des niederen jüdischen Volkes in Deutschland* (New York: n.p., 1968), 61–81.

[13] Jonathan Karp, "Can Economic History Date the Inception of Jewish Modernity?" in *The Economy in Jewish History*, ed. Gideon Reuveni and Sarah Wobick-Segev (New York: Berghan Books, 2011).

[14] Karp, *Politics of Jewish Commerce*, 135–169.

The assumption that Jews were capable of being reformed was some-times hedged by the insistence that they prove it first in order to win civic and political equality as a reward. While the French Constituent Assembly rejected this approach when it granted Jews' emancipation in 1790–91, Napoleon's implementation of it in 1806 set a precedent that was widely emulated by the German states after the 1815 Congress of Vienna (which accorded discretion on Jewish matters to the signatories). In the German lands making Jewish "productivization" a prerequisite for civic and polit-ical rights served as a pretext to delay emancipation indefinitely, but that does not mean no serious efforts at occupational transformation were attempted. On the contrary, in German lands during the first half of the nineteenth century, every significant Jewish community established voca-tional institutions to apprentice young Jews in skilled crafts (and to a lesser extent agricultural arts). In fact, these endeavors yielded some consider-able if temporary results.[15] Nevertheless, as Monika Richarz points out, the statistical evidence for a substantial rise in the percentages of Jewish arti-sans in *Vormärz* Germany (including Posen, where Jewish craftsmen were already plentiful) is probably inflated by the "wish fulfillment" agenda of the very same Jewish philanthropies that sponsored artisan education. And even the genuine gains proved short-lived.[16] During the second half of the nineteenth century, rapid German industrialization rendered Jewish voca-tional and artisanal education outmoded and counterproductive. Indeed, the remarkable expansion of the Jewish bourgeoisie after 1848 – or more important, the contraction in the percentage of Jewish poor (from about 50 percent in mid-century to around 15 percent in 1870) – took the air out of all efforts to transform the Jewish occupational structure, at least until the renewed large-scale migration of impoverished *Ostjuden* into Germany toward the end of the century.[17]

There were multiple sources of this economic rise. The Napoleonic Wars proved crucial in initiating a revival of Jewish economic fortunes that would only become apparent several decades later. While the meteoric ascent of the Rothschilds, who capitalized on credit and information markets dur-ing the latter phase of Wellington's campaigns against Napoleon, is an oft-told tale, far more significant were the countless cases of small-time Jewish

[15] Sucher B. Weinryb, *Der Kampf um die Berufsumschichtung. Ein Ausschnitt aus der Geschichte der Juden in Deutschland* (Berlin: Schocken, 1936).

[16] Monika Richarz, ed., *Jewish Life in Germany: Memoirs from Three Centuries* (Bloomington: University of Indiana Press, 1991), vol. 2, 130–131.

[17] Avraham Barkai, "German Jews at the Start of Industrialization," in *Revolution and Evolution: 1848 in German-Jewish History*, ed. Werner Mosse, Arnold Pauker, Reinhard Rürup, and Robert Weltsch (Tübingen: JCB Mohr, 1981), 123–145.

traders and peddlers who combed the land in search of supplies, clothing, textiles, saltpeter, and victuals, for the armies of the *Befreiungskriege*,
a process that laid the foundation for numerous Jewish businesses and
occasional later fortunes.[18] Prussian Jewry (outside of Posen, where restrictions remained severe) also benefited significantly from the emancipation decrees of 1812, even if the decrees were soon partly withdrawn. They
prompted a genuine expansion in the range of Jewish economic activity,
although restrictions on entry into the free professions and state bureaucracy ensured that business enterprise would remain the overriding focal
point. Another factor frequently cited is the effect of Jewish emigration
in siphoning off "excess" population and especially poor and dependent persons. While it is true that some communities were thereby partly
relieved of welfare obligations, most of the Jewish immigrants were young
males, who might have been expected to make productive contributions
in German Jewish economic life. Nevertheless, by the 1830s (the decade
when emigration to America got seriously underway), Jewish economic
fortunes were starting to show signs of serious vitality. There was a marked
decline in peripatetic commercial life (peddling, cattle trading, and the
like), replaced by the establishment of fixed shops. Railroad construction,
starting at the same time, opened up commercial markets as never before,
a process Jews adapted to quite well. Even after 1848, when Jews began a
gradual process of concentration in larger cities, the core of German Jewry
remained rooted in small and medium-sized towns. From the rural vantage
point, some began to utilize the putting-out system, based on work conducted in rural households for the manufacture of clothing and textiles.
Some Jews in the region of the Harz Mountains and other mining centers also became involved in businesses extracting precious metals. Since
German economic integration preceded political union by decades, the
drive to find capital for investment in new industries and endeavors gave
a new lease on life to the field of private bankers, one in which Jews had
traditionally exhibited strength. Not a handful and not dozens but literally hundreds of small Jewish banking firms emerged in this period, many
of them successful. It has been observed that a high percentage of Jewish
private banking families derived from southern and western Germany, precisely the region where small German states had led to a surfeit of *Hoffjuden*
and *Hoffaktoren*. Nevertheless, despite the undoubted importance of this
commercial, industrial, and financial *Grossburgertum* – particularly in its
crucial philanthropic support – the bulwark of mid-nineteenth-century
Jewish economic rise remained small businessmen engaged in a more

---

[18] Barkai, "German Jews."

modernized version of traditional Jewish activities: commercial, service, and brokerage enterprises.[19]

Crucial to any assessment of Jewish economy in nineteenth-century Europe is the complex relationship between demographic expansion, the start of industrial "take off," and the phenomenon of Jewish emigration, first from Central Europe and later from Poland and Russia. Scholarship has veered between extreme overemphasis on anti-Jewish persecution and discrimination as a motor of emigration, on the one hand, and a stress on purely demographic and economic factors, on the other. In fact, status and material circumstances are always intertwined. In the first half of the nineteenth century, around 100,000 Jews emigrated from the German-speaking lands, mostly to America. These constituted about 3 percent of the total contemporary emigration from these regions, thus about three times the percentage of Jews in the overall population. Jews responded to the same dynamics of "push and pull" that fueled the general exodus, only more so. The "push" factors included a higher growth rate (lower fertility more than compensated for by lower mortality), *expanded* means to fund transportation and resettlement abroad (spurred by a rise in the per capita income of Jews, which made it possible for young men to leave their homes and families, but also – crucially – supported the growth of local Jewish philanthropies which could help subsidize the emigration of the Jewish poor), and opportunities for marriage and settlement that were considerably more restricted for Jews than for the general population, which itself suffered from limited freedoms.

It is interesting that most of these emigrants (Jewish and non-Jewish) went to the United States, a country that in certain features bore a more than passing resemblance to the homeland. Like Germany, the United States was an agrarian society on the cusp of industrialization (a high proportion non-Jewish German immigrants became American farmers), and like Germany, it was characterized by small towns that could be readily serviced by peddlers, one of the most typical of German-Jewish occupations. But the differences also made the United States particularly attractive. In the first half of the century, America still retained a wide-open frontier, inviting to many with a thirst for opportunity. There were of course no special restrictions imposed on Jews: no quotas or *Matrikel* delimiting their marriage, procreative, and residency rights. Guild life (a perennial bane of Jewish commerce) on the European model was hardly known. While anti-commercial attitudes were certainly present, they paled in

[19] Arthur Prinz, *Juden im deutschen Wirtschaftsleben: soziale und wirtschaftliche Struktur im Wandel, 1850–1914* (Tübingen: JCB Mohr, 1984).

comparison what the immigrants had known back home.[20] For a Jewish population deeply rooted in commerce, America offered plentiful opportunities to earn a livelihood along accustomed lines. As one commentator has aptly noted of this "first wave" of German-speaking Jewish immigrants in America, "it was not so much a radically different life that they sought as an improved version of the old one."[21]

At the same time, it should be emphasized that at the very moment when circumstances, both politically and materially, were improving dramatically for German Jews, the pace of intense emigration resumed. The "second wave" of departures, from the end of the American Civil War to the early 1880s, admittedly differed somewhat from the preceding one. Now Jews were only marginally overrepresented in comparison with non-Jews from German lands. And whereas the geographical sources of the emigration had earlier been Southwestern Germany (Bavaria, Wurttemberg, Hesse), as well as Posen, the concentration was now more particularly from the eastern regions, Prussia, Silesia – especially Posen – as well as Alsace and Lorraine after it had been annexed in the wake of the Franco-Prussian War. The eastern German lands had been home to Jews who had benefited least from the recent growth in the German economy. Many became internal immigrants – and the 1860s and 1870s marks the real period of the intensive growth in the Jewish population of Berlin, with most Jews who came to settle in the Prussian capital having originated in Posen. Hence, the search for greater opportunity, and the existence by this time of established Jewish communities throughout the United States capable of facilitating the transition ("chain migration"), were the main factors driving this new wave.[22]

The Jewish population of the United States catapulted from 15,000 in 1840 to 150,000 on the eve of the Civil War. That conflict, in which (mostly immigrant) Jews participated on both sides and at all levels of military rank, proved an economic boon to them. Long involved in the sale of second hand clothes, and with ample European experience as military suppliers, American Jews were remarkably active in the business of providing uniforms to the Union army, if not always as primary government contractors then certainly as subcontractors in a wide-ranging network that harnessed the efforts of peddlers, wholesalers, and manufacturers, as well as sutlers stationed in the military camps. As often as not these endeavors

---

[20] Hasia Diner, *Roads Taken: The Great Jewish Migrations to the New World and the Peddlers who Forged the Way* (New Haven: Yale University Press, 2015), 51–83.

[21] Steven Mostov, quoted in Avraham Barkai, *Branching Out: German-Jewish Immigration to the United States, 1820–1914* (New York: Holmes and Meier, 1994), 22.

[22] See Barkai, *Branching Out*.

provided as the original basis for the emergence in the post-war decades of the elite of Jewish bankers and large-scale retailers in Chicago, Cincinnati, and, especially, New York, including such families as the Seligmans, Lehmans, and Guggenheims.[23] By 1880 American Jewry exceeded a quarter of a million souls, and while their broad economic success certainly began to provoke hostility, their relatively small numbers in the general population, along with their wide geographical dispersion, enabled them to blend fairly comfortably into the fabric of American commercial life.

Meanwhile, in the German lands, the Jewish population rose to about 1.3 percent by 1860 (its high point as a proportion of the general population), while in absolute terms the number of Jews in Germany peaked at about 600,000 by 1910.[24] Given that the latter figure includes sizable numbers of immigrants from Russia and other parts of Eastern Europe, these figures suggest a trend of severe decline in the demographic growth of "indigenous" German Jewry from the last third of the nineteenth century. Even earlier, as noted, Jews in Germany exhibited comparatively lower fertility rates, but these had been compensated for by significantly lower infant mortality rates in comparison with the general population. Now Jews were having fewer children (on average 2.8) while non-Jews were experiencing fewer deaths in the immediate years following childbirth. These trends reflect the broad processes industrialization and urbanization (and attendant improvements in the general standard of living). But the case of the Jews has usually been viewed by historians as reflecting patterns of urbanization and *embourgeoisement* earlier and faster than the population as a whole. Indeed, the mid-nineteenth century marks a clear turning point after which Jews were moving (and were at last permitted to move) within German territories to nearby (and sometimes more distant) cities in pursuit of greater economic opportunities for themselves and educational ones for their children. In keeping with this portrait, scholars like Arthur Prinz and Monika Richarz posit that in the crucial mid-century decades of Germany's industrial take off, Jews filled a major gap as the only group present that was able to supply investment capital (the proportion of Jewish owned or partially owned private banks in this period is remarkable) and exploit the new opportunities for supplying consumer goods to a population able to buy on a wider scale.[25] While Jews participated in heavy industry only to a limited degree (the financing of railroads, electronics,

[23] Adam Mendelsohn, *The Rag Race: How Jews Sewed their Way to Success in America and the British Empire* (New York: New York University Press, 2015), 201–203.

[24] Monika Richarz, "Demographic Developments," in *German-Jewish History in Modern Times*, Vol 3, ed. Michael A. Meyer (New York: Columbia University Press, 1997), 6–10.

[25] Prinz, *Juden im deutschen Wirtschaftsleben*, 38.

steel, and chemicals being partial exceptions), they played a powerfully disproportionate role in the promotion of consumer goods and services (transportation, real estate, dry goods and textiles, retail shops, publishing, mail order catalogues, and – toward the end of the century – department stores). This unique moment – for which Jews' long experience in finance, commerce and brokerage had well prepared them – allowed Jews to improve their circumstances more than at any prior time in history, but it also set them up as the perfect scapegoats when the Germany economy experienced its first truly modern depression in 1874. It was a facile matter to accuse Jews as a whole of weaving a magical web of speculation that entangled the entire country.[26]

Responding to this episode of anti-Jewish scapegoating, the (non-Jewish) Leipzig economic historian, Wilhelm Roscher, penned an influential essay that aimed to define the relationship between Jewish economic disutility and periodic outbreaks of antisemitism. Ostensibly writing about the Middle Ages, Roscher adduced a pattern whereby Jews are welcomed as commercial pioneers but discarded once "natives" advanced sufficiently to perform themselves the economic functions Jews had traditionally occupied. In reality, the essay reflected the actual situation in Germany when he wrote it in 1875, a period of broad advance in the activities and freedoms of Jews followed by a reaction against them, in which competition was masked by mythical and typological group character assassination. Nevertheless, Roscher's essay concluded on a hopeful note: unlike previous periods, the modern age, he believed, would be one of universal *embourgeoisement*; despite the recurrence of fierce antisemitism, a more fully capitalist economic life would create an expansive economy in which Jews and non-Jews alike could enjoy its fruits.[27]

In reality, Roscher was only half right: Jews continued to excel economically and professionally alongside non-Jewish Germans, but the general arc of prosperity did not gradually dissolve longstanding economic resentments against them. Given their rapid advance and ultimate victimization, it is tempting to view German Jewry as representative of modern Jewish economic history as a whole. But this would be highly misleading. It is in fact a story of extremes: a small population at the start of the modern period, one subject to severe occupational and residential restrictions, Jews in Germany won freedoms which tended especially to reinforce their commercial orientation at the very moment when a consumer revolution was

[26] Prinz, *Juden im deutschen Wirtschaftsleben*, 54.
[27] Wilhelm Roscher, "Die Stellung der Juden im Mittelalter, betrachtet vom Standpunkte der allgemeinen Handelspolitik," *Zeitschrift für gesamte Staatswissenschaft*, XXXI (1875), 503–523.

taking place. There may be some truth to the notion that the small size of the German Jewish population, which as noted declined after 1870 as a percentage of the overall population, limited internal class stratification and rendered them, as Monika Richarz has claimed, "a relatively homogenous minority with approximately two-thirds of its members belonging to the middle class."[28] Such a success story – even if exaggerated, as some recent historians suggest – was by no means typical of world Jewry as a whole in the period leading up to World War I.[29]

The eastern portions of Germany – Silesia, East Prussia, and Posen – as well as Austrian Galicia, had been part of pre-partition Poland, and the economic life of Jews there resembled, at least initially, that which prevailed in early nineteenth-century Russia, which now had the greatest concentration of Jews in the world. Leaving aside the Jews of Poland's crown cities, all of these regions had Jewish economies rooted in the efforts of the early modern Polish nobility to employ Jews to develop and manage the industrial and commercial enterprises on their estates. This was especially true in Poland's eastern regions (Lithuania, Belarus, and the Ukrainian territories of Volhynia and Podolia). Here there were few of the German burghers who had so crimped the activities of Jews in western Poland. Thus, with little competition, Jews dominated if not monopolized almost all aspects of the commercial life of eastern Poland, including wholesale commerce between regions or internationally and local retail trade, along with a sizeable portion of craftsmen. Whereas in late medieval Poland Jews engaged in moneylending and tax farming, the nobility encouraged Jews to lease their mills, tolls, fisheries, breweries, and other local enterprises. The ambition of the lord, and hence the function of the Jew, was to transform the estate into a commercial center, a *mestechko*. This became the principal basis for the eventual emergence of the shtetl.

The shtetls varied considerably in size but their typical features included a substantial Jewish population that entirely dominated the commerce of this market town, a regular commercial fair, and a tavern or inn – run by Jews – where alcohol was sold to local peasants and Jews, and where traveling merchants (usually Jewish) might find food and lodging. With the decline of the Polish grain exports, greater emphasis had been placed on alcohol production and sale (*propinacja*), which for many noble estate

---

[28] Richarz, "Occupational Distribution and Social Structure," in *German-Jewish History in Modern Times*, Vol 3., p. 65.

[29] Till van Rahden, *Jews and Other Germans: Civil Society, Religious Diversity, and Urban Politics in Breslau, 1860–1925*, trans. Marcus Brainard (Madison: University of Wisconsin Press, 2008), 21–63.

owners became the Jew's essential role and *raison d'etre*. By the time of the Polish partitions, the *propinacja* and the shtetl had become the twin pillars of Jewish economic life in much of Eastern Europe. While both reflected the reciprocal if hierarchical partnership of the Polish nobility and the Jews, both also survived the demise of the Polish noble commonwealth, and nowhere more than in Russia, which inherited the lion's share of Polish Jews. In Prussian Posen, the German authorities quickly curtailed Jewish merchants' access to eastern markets, a key factor driving the precipitous decline of Posen's Jewish population. Austrian Galicia, with approximately 200,000 Jews in 1800, was home to several large cities, including Kraków at the westernmost border, Lemberg (Lvov) toward the center of eastern Galicia, and Brody along the northeast Russian border. At the start of the period these cities, although boasting sizable Jewish populations, followed the early modern pattern of subjugation to the Christian guild regime. Over the course of the nineteenth century the Jewish proportion, both as percentages of the total population and in terms of commercial and artisanal activity, expanded dramatically. The vast rural territories of Galicia resembled those of Podolia and Volhynia, but with a far less dense Jewish presence. They were also considerably poorer. The "enlightened despotism" of the Habsburg regime superimposed on one of the most backward regions of Europe, and the eventual granting of full citizenship to Jews in 1867, along with severe discrimination and anti-Jewish economic agitation experienced later in the nineteenth century, made Galicia a study in contrasts.

Those parts of Poland absorbed into Russia (or, as in the Kingdom of Poland, ruled by Russia while maintaining a modicum of autonomy), contained a Jewish population amounting to close to one million at the start of the nineteenth century. Imperial policy was schizophrenic to say the least, cognizant of the vital role played by Jewish commerce and crafts in the vast region of the Pale, while also deeply suspicious of an alien population that had effectively served as the economic clients and agents of the Polish nobility, feared to be perpetually plotting insurrection. Catherine II made considerable strides (quite advanced for the time) to regularize the Jewish population by classifying them on the basis of residence, wealth, and economic function within the existing system of Russian urban estates. Fright inspired by the French Revolution put an end to Catherine's reformist tendencies, however, resulting in the imposition of protectionist policies designed as much to build a cultural as a commercial wall around the empire. "So she banned mirrors, gold decorations, toys, chess sets, wooden cabinets, chariots, leather and leather goods, fancy short boots, bone and silver combs, brushes, candies, and sugar toys – the articles we find regularly among the merchandise Jews brought to East Europe."[30] As Yohanan Petrovsky-Shtern explains, Catherine's attempts to restrict imports of all manner of commodities, superimposed on a system of borders fundamentally alien to Jews' traditional trading activities in this region, might have proved ruinous to Jewish fortunes had not the practitioners of this trade resorted to widespread smuggling, typically in cahoots with Catherine's own officials.[31]

While Catherine's protectionist policies were not aimed merely at Jews, they reflected a broader pattern in which imperial authority wound up criminalizing what had previously been normative Jewish commercial activity. The tendency is especially apparent in the government's efforts to reign in the Jewish liquor trade, particularly in the countryside. This trade had long proved controversial. The Four Year Sejm (1788–1792), a last-ditch effort by the Polish Commonwealth to forestall its own dissolution, had heard numerous speeches and petitions denouncing Jews for profiting from the inebriation of the peasantry. Yet even when such charges were leveled by enlightened Polish noblemen, the fact that it was the noble owners of private towns who insisted on entrusting alcohol sales to Jewish innkeepers, ensured that the calls for reform would go unheeded.[32] In contrast, the Russian state had a direct interest in undercutting its stubborn Polish rivals, in large part by separating them from their Jewish agents. At periodic intervals, 1804, 1812, the early 1820s, and more decisively 1844 and 1851, decrees were issued (in each case directed at the Jews of specific regions) to remove Jews *en masse* from the countryside or to impose such heavy taxes and restrictions as to all but eliminate Jewish involvement in the trade. Not only were most of the accompanying efforts at Jewish agricultural "productivization" ineffectual, but – as Glenn Dynner has demonstrated – they fell short of their aim of drastically reducing Jews' roles as rural innkeepers. Usually in cahoots with their noble patrons, Jews were able to evade the statutes by hiring Christians to front the taverns while they maintained control behind the scenes.[33] But, as with the periodic outbreaks of Jewish involvement in smuggling, the case of the liquor trade reveals a regime trapped between contradictory agendas. On the one hand, the tsarist bureaucracy exhibited an occasional awareness – even

[30] Yohanan Petrovsky-Shtern, *The Golden Age of the Shtetl: A New History of Jewish Life in East Europe* (Princeton: Princeton University Press, 2014), 59.

[31] Ibid.

[32] Hundert, *Jews in Poland-Lithuania in the Eighteenth Century*, 211–231.

[33] Glenn Dynner, *Yankel's Tavern: Jews, Liquor, and Life in the Kingdom of Poland* (New York: Oxford University Press, 2014).

appreciation – of the fact that Jews were the most vital commercial element in the Pale of Settlement. The liquor trade was perhaps the nucleus of a larger complex shtetl-based commercial activity that encompassed trade fairs, local manufacture and industry, regional and international trade. On the other, to the extent that tsarist officials acknowledged the necessity of commerce, they wished to control it themselves. Free trade was not only anarchic, it was wasteful; why not cut out the middlemen and allow the state to engross commercial activities and networks directly? This would not only increase state revenues but would help bring about the normalization (Russification) of the Jewish population whose near exclusive concentration in exchange appeared unnatural and anomalous. In the end, such efforts – however inconsistently applied or effectively defied by the ruses of peasants, nobles, Jews and venal officials – did contribute to the enervation of rural and shtetl economies in the Pale.

Equally important, though, was the progress of industrialization, which in Eastern Europe affected Jewish economic life very differently than in Germany. In Germany, Jews had constituted a minority conspicuous for its overrepresentation in commerce and banking activities, and in such professions as law, medicine, and journalism. In Eastern Europe the sizeable Jewish population, given its formidable place in the traditional commercial life of the region, might have been expected to play a far more decisive role in modernizing the region, but its contributions, though certainly of major proportions, were vitiated by a number of factors that came to define Jewish economic development in the nineteenth century. First and foremost, restrictions on the free movement of Jewish capital and labor meant that most of the population's energies would be expended in a limited geographic and urban sphere, excluding new areas of dynamic industrial development within Russia proper. Moreover, railroad construction in the Pale of Settlement, the prerequisite to the expansion of commercial markets, tended to bypass the traditional hubs of Jewish activity, such as Brody (within Galicia but bordering Russia) and Berditchev, diverting the international grain trade to New Russia and its entrepôt Odessa. The removal of industrial activity from the regions of Jewish concentration, in keeping with the discriminatory legislation discussed above, resulted in Jewish migration into the medium-sized cities of the Pale, where for the first time they became a major demographic presence. In such cities as Kovno, Dvinsk, and Gomel, Jews tended to find employment in urban workshops and sweatshops, rather than in the mechanized new factories which Jewish employees either deliberately avoided or from which they were consciously excluded. There were exceptions, of course. In Białystok and Lodz, Jews were instrumental as both entrepreneurs and industrial workers in high-volume textile production.[34] But on the whole only a fraction (10 percent?) of Jews became industrial proletarians in the more classical sense. In Belarus and Lithuania, as one historian has observed, the Jewish proletariat was "overwhelmingly a proletariat of artisans."[35]

It was from this Northwest region of the Pale that the largest percentage of Jewish migrants derived in the last decades of the nineteenth century. First and foremost these migrants left the large towns and cities of Belarus and Lithuania to seek work in southern (or New) Russia – or in Poland proper where, despite heavy competition, work in the textile manufacturing centers remained a powerful magnet.[36] The large-scale overseas emigration that took off in the early 1880s was sparked by the pogroms of those years and the discriminatory legislation that followed, but it certainly reflected more structural factors in Eastern European Jewish life: in particular, a fivefold population growth over the course of the nineteenth century (while the general population increased threefold) without any commensurate expansion of opportunity.[37] This exodus of close to two million souls between 1880 and 1914, 80 percent of whom went to the United States, was comprised more of semi-skilled artisanal workers (including many tailors) than of merchants, and often involved entire nuclear families rather than just young men, as was typical of such movements.[38] Yet even if anti-Jewish violence was more a catalyst than cause of the great migration, it is not wrong to view discrimination as a key factor in retarding the economic development of Eastern European Jewry as a whole. Jews remained overcrowded in a handful of cities and locked in futile competition with Russian, Polish, and Ukrainian industrial workers. Even outside of Russia, the development of producers' cooperatives in Galicia, Moravia and elsewhere, often with the express aim of combatting "parasitic Jewish commerce," threatened the livelihoods of Jewish traders and producers alike.

Throughout Eastern Europe industrialization had created the conditions for the emergence of modern middle-class strata within other national groups that had formerly been peasants or petty nobles. These nascent bourgeois groups had to contend with the reality of a sizable Jewish

---

[34] Yedida Sharona Kanfer, "Lodz: Industry, Religion, and Nationalism in Russian Poland, 1880–1914" (Ph.D. diss., Yale University, 2011).

[35] Ezra Mendelsohn, *Class Struggle in the Pale: The Formative Years of the Jewish Workers Movement in Tsarist Russia* (Cambridge: Cambridge University Press, 1970), 6

[36] Arcadius Kahan, *Essays in Jewish Social and Economic History*, ed. Roger Weiss (Chicago: University of Chicago Press, 1986), 33.

[37] Antony Polonsky, *The Jews in Poland and Russia, Vol. II: 1881–1914* (Oxford: Littman Library of Jewish Civilization, 2010), 170.

[38] Kahan, *Essays*, 33–34.

population that had long played the most vital role in the commerce and crafts of the region. Interventionist state policies tended to retard the rapid expansion of consumer markets along lines experienced in Western Europe, thus reinforcing fears of Jewish competition on the part of both the non-Jewish middle and working classes. Whereas Jews in Germany, a miniscule segment of the overall population, had managed to survive exclusion from state employment by taking full advantage of entrepreneurial and educational opportunities, the vastly larger Jewish population of Eastern Europe enjoyed few comparable outlets. True, a small but notable plutocracy had developed by the mid- to late nineteenth century, including a banking elite centered in Warsaw, financial brokers and grain exporters in Odessa, textile manufacturers in Volhynia, Lodz, and Czestichowa, and sugar moguls in Kiev and Crimea. St. Petersburg became the residence of the elite of Jewish bankers and railway financiers who championed a program of enlightened Russification.[39] Certainly, despite the numerous obstacles, the Jewish contribution to the Eastern European economy in the nineteenth century proved invaluable. But it proved as well to be unsustainable in the face of inimical circumstances. This is sufficiently clear not just from the retrospective vantage point of events during and after World War I. Rather, it is clear from the striking fact that in the two decades leading up the War, a period of widespread industrial growth, the Jewish poverty rate was only increasing.

The rapid growth of anti-capitalist ideologies, whether of a nationalist or assimilationist variety, among Jewish workers in the Pale can be understood against this backdrop. Emblematic if not necessarily typical in this regard were the influential theories of the Marxist-Zionist writer Ber Borochov, whose lifespan, 1881–1917, coincides with the period of severe crisis and upheaval of Russian Jewry just prior to the Russian Revolution. According to Borochov, because Jews lack a territory of their own, their class structure has become dangerously distorted. Excluded by indigenous working classes who view them as interlopers driving down the costs of labor, Jews lack access to the "primary" processes of production (agriculture, mining, and heavy industry) directly rooted in land and territory and are instead relegated to the "final levels," mere consumer goods and tradable commodities. Whereas a normal class structure resembles a pyramid marked by a large base of industrial workers and a small apex of bourgeois capitalists, the Jewish pyramid is inverted, containing only a minority of proletarians but top heavy with petty traders. The Jewish economy, Borochov concluded, was unnatural, exiled from nature, in short, a "Luft" economy. Only by acquiring a land of their own could "normal" development

[39] Polonsky, *The Jews in Poland and Russia, Vol. II,* 170–211.

occur (that is, healthy class struggle leading to revolutionary socialism). Whatever Borochov's prescriptions, what is important to note here is the essential resemblance, *mutatis mutandis*, to the century-old doctrines of Christian Wilhelm von Dohm and the Enlightenment. But whereas Jews had become so conspicuously bourgeois in late-imperial Germany that – at least until the Great Depression and the rise of Nazism – talk of occupational productivization generally abated there, in Eastern Europe it became woven into almost all proposed remedies for the economic problem afflicting the Jewish masses.[40]

Borochov believed that immigration to the United States would hardly solve the problem. Whatever initial advantages Jewish workers might enjoy in a new capitalist setting, he argued, would soon dissipate as the American "native" working class pushed them back again into the margins. And indeed, on the eve of World War I, it might not have been evident to many Jewish workers in the garment factories of New York's Lower East Side that their fate in the New World would be significantly better than the life they left behind in the crowded shops of Białystok and Grodno. Possessing more modest means than previous waves of Central European Jewish immigrants in America, these Jews could not afford to follow preceding patterns by moving to inland towns and cities in significant numbers. Rather, they remained largely trapped in the port cities – New York above all, but also Baltimore, Boston, and Philadelphia – where they landed.[41] Burdened with dependents, barely possessing enough to eke out a living for more than a few days or weeks after their arrival, their passage was mercifully eased by Jewish philanthropic organizations, such as the Russian Immigrant Relief Committee and HIAS (the Hebrew Sheltering and Immigrant Aid Society), that met them at their entry points and offered them assistance finding shelter and employment. Many of the Jews who helped fund these organizations stemmed from previous waves of Central European Jewish immigrants who had established themselves culturally and economically by the time of the Great Immigration from the East. But perhaps more important than the philanthropies were the German Jewish entrepreneurs who had established clothing businesses (more often than not small workshops rather than factories, particularly in New York) in the decades between the end of the Civil War and 1880s.[42] These entrepreneurs had initially hired Italian and Irish immigrants as workers. But

[40] Ber Borochov, *Nationalism and the Class Struggle* (New York: Poale Zion-Zeire Zion of America, 1937), 62–65.
[41] Henry Feingold, *Zion in America: The Jewish Experience from Colonial Times to the Present* (Mineola, NY: Dover, 2002), 123.
[42] Mendelsohn, *The Rag Race*, 205–206.

when the wave of Jewish immigrants hit, they tended to shift into the employment of their co-religionists. This favoritism toward co-religionists had not typically been the practice in Eastern Europe, where Jewish factory owners often avoided hiring Jewish workers. Yet the German Jews surely appreciated the fact that these destitute Jews were prepared to work for very modest wages while already possessing valuable experience and skills in garment production. These workers were used to the kind of small shops where they would now be employed. They were accustomed to a manufacturing processes that did not involve large-scale mass production techniques employed in modern factories but rather combined elements of the division of labor with the small artisanal shop and the putting-out system. Unlike big factories, these shops were sufficiently adaptive to be able to respond to subtle shifts in the market, a vital capacity at the very moment when readymade clothing was increasingly subject to rapid shifts in the fashion tastes of consumers.[43]

Ironically, the very same qualities that made the immigrants pliable, versatile, and attractive workers also made them potential competitors. It is important to emphasize that though they were severely impoverished, these immigrants were not products of generations of immiseration. Their "pauperization" had been fairly recent and had not typically denuded them of a desire to elevate themselves or deprived them of a capacity to realistically imagine and engage the pursuit of a better life. Many were *luftmenschen*, a percentage were lowly manual laborers. Yet there is no reason to assume that the managerial and brokerage skills many of them had lived by for so long simply vanished, despite the cruel tsarist policies to which they had been subjected. In this sense, they were actually not so far removed from the smaller waves of Central European Jews who had preceded them to America. These too had also derived mostly from rural commercial backgrounds. They too had faced substantial occupational limitations and been subjected to clumsy and overbearing efforts at social engineering (many even serving a period of apprenticeship in artisanal trades). Both populations had been displaced from traditional economic roles by the processes of early industrialization. Moreover, not a few of the Central European Jews who eventually become established in America actually derived from regions such as Posen, Galicia, and Hungary, which were strongly similar in economic and social organization to parts of Russia from which the

---

[43] Phyllis Dillon and Andrew Godley, "The Evolution of the Jewish Garment Industry, 1840–1920," in *Chosen Capital: The Jewish Encounter with American Capitalism*, ed. Rebecca Kobrin (New Brunswick, NJ: Rutgers University Press, 2012), 35–61.

new immigrants had themselves recently hailed.[44] Thus it is not surprising to find that in both cases a penchant for self-employment and small business orientation quickly emerged. As early as 1905, according to one contemporary report, over 20 percent of Russian Jewish men in New York had shifted from garment labor to some form of white-collar employment (usually sales clerks and office workers), however modest and precarious.[45] The percentages would rise still more dramatically through the 1920s and beyond. As far as Jewish small business was concerned, the neighborhoods encompassing and bordering Manhattan's Lower East Side were literally stacked with Jewish enterprises, not just clothing but furniture, textiles, dry goods, jewelry, watches, cigars, and food stands, but even arcades and entertainments, reflecting what Andrew Heinze has called "the commercial idealism of East European Jews."[46] Once the heavy hand of government oppression had been lifted, as occurred above all in America, dormant managerial, professional, academic, and entrepreneurial tendencies reasserted themselves in force.

Of course, that they did so under new conditions and in a decisively new setting is important. Historians are quite correct to emphasize the degree to which traditional European Jewries were now subject to drastic reorientation in lifestyle and mentality. Sabbath rest, for instance, stood little chance in a society as relentlessly materialistic as America in the early decades of the twentieth century (although there was ample precedent for this transition in the crowded cities of the late nineteenth-century Pale).[47] Still, America represented novelty not just in conveniences and commercial goods, but in the fields of popular culture and mass entertainment too. It is instructive in this regard that a preponderance of the Jewish entrepreneurs who came to dominate both the burgeoning film industry and the dynamic sheet-music publishing business were veterans of the garment industry.[48] In both cases too such pioneers derived almost equally from German and Eastern European backgrounds.[49] Despite real differences

[44] Hasia Diner, *A Time for Gathering: The Second Migration, 1820–1880* (Baltimore: Johns Hopkins University Press, 1992).

[45] Ibid., 219. See Thomas Kessner, *The Golden Door: Italian and Jewish Immigrant Mobility in New York City, 1880–1915* (New York: Oxford University Press, 1977), 88–89.

[46] Andrew Heinze, *Adapting to Abundance: Jewish Immigrants, Mass Consumption, and the Search for American Identity* (New York: Columbia University Press, 1990), 186–187, 192.

[47] Eli Lederhendler, *Jewish Immigrants and American Capitalism, 1880–1920: From Caste to Class* (Cambridge: Cambridge University Press, 2009), 61.

[48] Heinze, *Adapting to Abundance*, 203–218.

[49] Jonathan Karp, "Of Maestros and Minstrels: Jewish Composers between Negro Vernacular and European Art Music," in *The Art of Being Jewish in Modern Times*,

between earlier and later waves of Jewish immigrants to America, and the serious tensions that emerged between members of the two groups, they had far more in common than their religion.

Sephardic Jews (incidentally the first on North American soil) enjoyed a reputation – sometimes propagandistic – as formidable traders dating back to their Iberian roots. Though crucial in the reestablishment of a Jewish presence in the West, most Sephardim dwelt in the Ottoman Empire in the aftermath of the late fifteenth-century expulsions from Spain and Portugal. From the start, they had played an important role in the economic life of the empire. They were responsible for much of the manufacture and export of textiles, particularly woolens, from Salonika; they were prominent in commercial trade with Italy and Iberia, through familial connections with Jewish and New Christian merchants in Venice, Livorno, Barcelona, and Lisbon; and they occupied key positions as tax farmers and customs officials, including providing banking services as *sarrafs* to many Ottoman officials and critically to the janissaries, whose influence expanded throughout the seventeenth and early eighteenth centuries. But in a sense that was the rub. The Sephardim remained deeply entrenched in a moribund imperial system the reform of which, starting in the early nineteenth century, would have overall negative consequences for their economic fortunes. The elimination of the janissaries in 1826, tied in with the *tanzimat* reforms, proved severely damaging. More broadly, the increasing penetration of European trading companies in Ottoman trade had the effect of displacing existing commercial minorities, particularly Jews (numbering only about 250,000–350,000 in the mid-nineteenth century),[50] to a much greater degree than the far more populous Greeks and Armenians, who in fact possessed a more diversified occupational profile as well as a greater readiness to adapt to changing circumstances.

Without question, Jews remained important to the overseas trade of the empire, particular the émigrés from Livorno, the so-called Francos, who settled throughout the empire (especially in Aleppo, Izmir, and Salonika) and played an active role in overseas trade with North Africa and France. Nevertheless, in the nineteenth century Jews were rarely on the cutting edge, and in fact their communities became overburdened by poor relief and heavy taxation. While industrialization was piecemeal and halting, the introduction of train networks threatened Jews' ability to compete with

---

ed. Barbara Kirshenblatt-Gimblett and Jonathan Karp (Philadelphia: University of Pennsylvania Press, 2008), 57–77.

[50] On conflicting population estimates, see Julia Phillips Cohen, *Becoming Ottomans: Sephardi Jews and Imperial Citizenship in the Modern Period* (New York: Oxford University Press, 2014), 6, n. 18 and the sources cited there.

the influx of cheap manufactured goods from Western Europe. In a sense, what was occurring in the Ottoman lands in the nineteenth century paralleled the situation in Russia, with the disruption of customary ways of doing business that had served Jews adequately for centuries – except that, on the one hand, the weak Ottoman government was not nearly as hostile as the tsars to Jewish interests, while on the other, Ottoman Jewry failed to an even greater degree than Russian Jews to adapt to changing circumstances.

After the establishment in 1860 of the Alliance Israélite Universelle, its schools played an increasingly important role in the development of a westernized intelligentsia throughout the Ottoman and former Ottoman regions. The network of Alliance schools aimed at westernizing Ottoman Jewish youth, but the curriculum also typically offered vocational training. Nevertheless, the system's economic impact remained limited under the dire circumstances of imperial decline. While Jews played a substantial role in trade in many locales (dominating the textile trade, in Sarajevo, for instance, or an overwhelming proportion of the cereal export trade in Bulgaria), wealth tended to be concentrated in the hands of a few mercantile families, with the majority of Jews barely surviving through crafts, manual labor, and communal poor relief. The only true exception was Salonika, where Jews comprised about a third of the population but entirely dominated the city's commercial and financial enterprise. Here textile exports (wool, flannel, and cotton goods) continued to provide the bedrock, but these were supplemented by tobacco processing and even some heavy industry. A Jewish proletariat of not insignificant dimensions emerged in Salonika toward the end of the nineteenth century, suggesting the city's industrial expansion. Unfortunately, Salonika's shift to Greek rule in 1912 placed the local Jewish population under fresh strains, while hopes for continued economic revitalization were cruelly dashed by the outbreak of war and especially by the massive fire that engulfed the city in 1917.[51]

World War I momentarily disrupted Jewish commercial and financial exchange, which by this point had already become globalized.[52] The war required countries and communities to fall back on their own resources, and the Jewish communities of the Ottoman Mediterranean were economically isolated as never before. When the dust settled, three of the empires that had provided frameworks for Jewish transnational commerce,

[51] Esther Benbassa and Aron Rodrigue, *Sephardi Jewry: A History of the Judeo-Spanish Community, 14th–20th Centuries* (Berkeley: University of California Press, 2000), 36–49, 79–89.

[52] Sarah Abrevaya Stein, *Plumes: Ostrich Feathers, and a Lost World of Global Commerce* (New Haven: Yale University Press, 2008).

the Ottoman, the Habsburg, and the Romanov, had collapsed in defeat. In their wake (albeit gradually, in the case of the Mandate system imposed on former Ottoman territories), independent states based on principles of national self-determination came to employ economic policies designed to protect native industry through trade restrictions as well as to foster the development of an indigenous middle and commercial class. In practice, this often entailed efforts to curtail traditional Jewish commercial roles. Meanwhile, in Russia itself, the Bolshevik Revolution brought about dramatic changes in the traditional economic orientation of Russian Jewry, since Marxism–Leninism could have no truck with free enterprise; consequently, Jews were forced to adapt their livelihoods in fundamental ways.

The interwar period was one of deepening crisis for the Jews of East Central Europe, not just politically but economically as well. It is important to understand that this crisis was not unremitting, and there were moments of respite if not outright reversal of the general negative trends. Moreover, the Jewries of these regions – Hungary, Austria, Romania, Czechoslovakia, and Poland, among others – were diverse both internally and in relation to one another. For these reasons, no broad-brush treatment adequately captures the reality of their economic situation in the period between the two World Wars, although some patterns are indeed discernable. Most important is that while objective economic circumstances affected the Jewish economies in this period, above all the Great Depression, political and ideological developments tended to determine economic ones rather than the other way around. Antisemitism was in this sense more a cause than a result of the economic predicament in which Jews found themselves on the eve of World War II.

No place illustrates this point more vividly than interwar Hungary. While it is a truism to assert that Jews essentially constituted the bourgeoisie of Eastern Europe, in the case of Hungary it is actually true. As C. A. Macartney memorably put it, "The capitalist development of the new Hungary, in so far as it had been carried out by 'native' resources at all, had been almost entirely of their making, and the results of it were to an overwhelming extent in their hands."[53] In the late eighteenth century, Jews had already begun to displace other traditional merchant groups in the region, Balkan Greeks, Armenians, and Germans. As in much of Poland, Jews managed the estate enterprises of the Magyar nobility, its inns, mills, tolls, timber, and the like. Jews were the intermediaries between nobles and peasants (including in regions where Magyars were the ruling class

---

[53] C. A. Macartney, *A Short History of Hungary* (Chicago: Aldine, 1962), 191; this quotation also appears in Ezra Mendelsohn, *The Jews of East Central Europe between the Two Wars* (Bloomington: Indiana University Press, 1983), 92.

but not the popular majority). And Jews were essential to urban life in Hungary, modest though it was.[54] This dominance only intensified over the course of the nineteenth century, as the Jewish population grew exponentially through immigration (mostly from Austrian Galicia) and especially after 1867 when Jews throughout Austria-Hungary received full civil and political rights. Now Jews proved themselves indispensable as the most reliable (and dependent) allies in the Magyars' efforts to maintain control of a multi-national population of Germans, Croats, Romanians, and Slovaks. Their alliance with the Magyars authorized Jews to fulfill the essential commercial and financial functions of the region, developing industry, the mass production and export of grain, the development of a local system of railways and joint-stock banking, and at the non-elite level, the production of clothing, leather items, paper, furniture, and jewelry, among a host of other goods.[55] Although Hungarian Jewry was culturally distinctive (especially the magyarized majority), it operated economically as part of a common enterprise zone in the Habsburg lands, and thus benefited from extensive trading relationships and networks with Jewish businesses in Vienna and other parts of the empire.[56] As was the case with the Jewries of the former Russian and Ottoman empires, post-war imperial dissolution greatly curtailed traditional open trading relationships across nominally national borders.

Hungary's own borders were themselves greatly curtailed as a result of the Habsburg defeat in World War I. The Treaty of Trianon (1920) excised about 70 percent of the country's former territories and well over half its previous population (including close to half of its nineteenth-century Jewish population of 800,000).[57] In addition to the pervasive feeling of bitterness and victimization felt by the Magyar population, this radical transformation of the state brought two overt consequences for Jewish economic life there. First, it shifted Hungary's self-positioning as a grain exporting economy committed to foreign exchange into a highly protectionist economy focused on developing native industries. Second, it deprived Jewry of one key element of its former utility to the Magyar elite,

---

[54] Michael K. Silber, "A Jewish Minority in a Backward Economy," in Jews in the Hungarian Economy, 1760–1945: Studies Dedicated to Moshe Carmilly Weinberger on his Eightieth Birthday, ed. idem (Jerusalem: The Magnes Press, 1992), 3–23.

[55] Láslów Katus, "The Occupational Structure of Hungarian Jewry in the Eighteenth and Twentieth Centuries," in Jews in the Hungarian Economy, ed. Silber, 92–105.

[56] Yehuda Don, "Patterns of Jewish Economic Behavior in the Twentieth Century," in Jews in the Hungarian Economy, ed. Silber, 248.

[57] Mendelsohn, The Jews of East Central Europe, 85.

the political, since now there were far fewer non-Magyars to which they might provide a counterbalance with Jewish numbers.

In spite of both these factors, Jews continued to comprise the most substantial and crucial element of Hungary's bourgeoisie during the interwar period. They dominated banking and many professions in Budapest, Hungary's one truly major city; and they remained vital to Hungary's agri-businesses as well as its small-town commercial life (constituting over 50 percent of merchants in many of towns).[58] Yet economic utility on its own, without comparable political support, proved inadequate in the face of rising antisemitism, now no longer suppressed by the ruling elite. Ethnic nationalism found expression in economic prejudices and programs. Magyar chauvinists contrasted *shaffendes*, productive Christian capital, with *raffendes*, parasitical Jewish capital, a variation on a commonplace antisemitic motif.[59] In similar fashion, during the 1930s members of both the more moderate and the radical, quasi-fascist right, issued demands for the curtailment of Jewish economic and professional influence to afford opportunity and breathing room to the fledgling native Magyar middle class. That this tendency was mostly evident among students and professionals rather than entrepreneurs was not insignificant or entirely ignored by the political leadership. When two Jewish laws passed the Hungarian parliament in 1938, instituting progressively more draconian *numerus clausus* restrictions on the percentages of Jews permitted to own and work in businesses and professions linked to state contracts, the notoriously anti-Jewish former prime minister Gyula Gömbös denounced the legislation as leading inexorably to Hungary's economic self-destruction. In fact, the laws often went unenforced but nevertheless brought considerable damage to lower-level Jewish white-collar employees and countless small independent businesses – indeed, the backbone of Hungary's Jewish economy.[60]

Interwar Poland was a variation on the same story but with even far worse results prior to the start of World War II. As in much of Central and Eastern Europe the Jewish percentage of the general population in Poland had leveled off or even declined somewhat in the aftermath of World War I (dropping from 10.5 percent of the total population in 1921 to 9.8 percent a decade later).[61] This was due only partly to the horrendous destruction that decimated Jewish communities in the former Pale of Settlement during and immediately following the conflagration. Jews, who had urbanized

---

[58] Ibid., 101.
[59] Mária Kovács, "Interwar Antisemitism in the Professions: The Case of the Engineers," in *Jews in the Hungarian Economy*, ed. Silber, 238.
[60] Ibid. 243; Mendelsohn, *The Jews of East Central Europe*, 121–122.
[61] Mendelsohn, *The Jews of East Central Europe*, 23.

earlier and more intensively than any other group, were now having fewer children while non-Jews were beginning to move to cities in greater numbers and experiencing lower infant mortality rates. This was important because it signaled that to a significantly greater degree than in Hungary a "native" Polish middle class was beginning to emerge (particularly in the more industrialize region of Congress Poland). Contra Borochov, who believed that the decisive factor in Jewish social relations was the competition between national working classes, in reality what mattered more was competition – or perceived competition – between ethnic bourgeoisies. Jews' connection to the working classes was temporary and tenuous. From the perspective of the *longue durée*, they had formerly been middle class in a pre-modern sense and would again become middle class in a modern sense – despite their momentary sojourn among the proletariat.[62] Yet inter-ethnic and intra-bourgeois conflict was not inevitable. As Wilhelm Roscher understood, a modern capitalist economy, premised on continuous if not constant growth, could accommodate an expansive middle class. Unfortunately, both political and economic circumstances affecting Poland and the rest of the region did not allow time for modern capitalist societies to emerge. Consequently, Jews found themselves trapped in a scarcity economy beset by nationalist passions.

Poland was the most celebrated case of a country born anew in the aftermath of World War I, having been reconstituted as a fully independent state for the first time since the eighteenth-century partitions. As is well known, the new Polish state was burdened with the problem of aligning its aspirations to create a unitary nation-state with the reality that its expansive borders encompassed significant national minorities of Ukrainians, Germans, and Jews. While the dominant Poles favored territorial maximalism within an ethnically (or at least culturally) unitary state, the minorities – including the Jews – demanded a strong measure of autonomy. Although Poland signed the minorities provisions imposed by the Paris treaties, the resurrected state abided neither by their letter nor their spirit. There would be no state funding for an autonomous Jewish school system and no effort to support Jewish cultural autonomy in regions where Jews clustered in large numbers. At the same time, during the 1920s the Polish state did little to open up state bureaucracies and government employment (including in state schools) to Jews. Worse, the rightist Endek party led by the antisemitic Roman Dmosky clamored for the removal of Jews from economic sectors where they traditionally dominated – commerce and industry – through boycotts and the institution of *numerus clausus*. These efforts began even prior to the achievement of independence, but they gained

[62] Karp, "Can Economic History Date the Inception of Jewish Modernity?"

serious momentum only in the mid-1930s with the death of General Josef Pilsudski, who had led a coup d'etat in 1926 and charted a moderate course on the nationalities question.[63]

Meanwhile, international politics had already begun to affect Poland's (and its Jews') economic life in profound ways. Poland's leading industrial and commercial cities, Lodz, Warsaw, Białystok (the latter where Jews constituted an absolute majority), and Vilna suffered immeasurably from the loss of their traditional export markets once imperial Russia became the autarkic Soviet Union.[64] Likewise, Vilna, a demographic island of Poles and Jews, was now effectively cut off from its natural hinterlands in independent Lithuania and Soviet Belarus. Many of its larger factories could not adapt to the new market conditions or if they did were subsequently wiped out by the Great Depression.[65] Lodz, the great textile production center of the region, lost 70 percent of its export market with the closing of Soviet borders. Nevertheless, like Warsaw it remained home to some of Poland's leading Jewish capitalist firms, such as the Poznanski Cotton Textile Company and the Naum Eitingon Company. Jews retained control of 36 of the city's largest textile operations and remained a formidable industrial and commercial force there. Still, as in other large Polish cities the vast majority of businesses were one-man operations.[66] It has been estimated that there were approximately 225,000 such "dwarf workshops" owned by Jews in interwar Poland.[67] While Jews owned just short of 90 percent of the textile and clothing workshops in Białystok, only about 35 percent of these utilized mechanical machinery, the rest relying on outmoded hand production.[68]

In the countryside, where numerous shtetls somehow managed to survive the depredations of war and upheaval, Jews continued to ply their traditional role of providing peasants with consumer goods in exchange for their produce. But as in many regions of East Central Europe, this traditional role was being undercut by peasant cooperatives as well as the gradual migration of peasants to the cities. At the same time, the shetls were themselves slowly dissolving through a shift in the balance away from commerce and toward industry, as ties with American Jewish

---

[63] For general background, see Mendelsohn, *The Jews of East Central Europe*, 11–23 and more recently Antony Polonsky, *The Jews of Poland and Russia, vol. III, 1914–2008* (Oxford: Littman Library, 2012), 5–97.

[64] Polonsky, *The Jews of Poland and Russia, vol. III*, 103.

[65] Ibid., 113.

[66] Ibid., 106–108.

[67] Don, "Patterns of Jewish Economic Behavior," 268.

[68] Polonsky, *The Jews of Poland and Russia, vol. III*, 109.

philanthropic organizations were increasingly relied upon – especially in the wake of the Depression – to provide aid. The death of the old order was protracted but its signs were everywhere apparent.

The triumph of German National Socialism provided ballast to the indigenous Polish far right, and especially its antisemitic program. By 1937 the government itself (in the hands of the late Pilsudski's acolytes) came out strongly in favor of a policy of Polish "economic self-sufficiency," which in practice meant divesting Jews of all economic influence. This was to be achieved through a combination of pressuring Jews to emigrate *en masse*, organizing peasant cooperatives, laws preventing Jews from working on Sundays (when their shops were already closed on Saturdays), and the systematic boycott of Jewish businesses. While the government renounced anti-Jewish violence, it did little to combat the efforts of the far right to disrupt Jewish businesses through physical attacks on Jewish persons and property, including organized pogroms by the late 1930s. Between 1936 and 1938 these activities had a profound effect on Jewish small businesses, especially in the eastern parts of the country. They were somewhat less effective in industrial centers, underscoring the social and psychological shift Polish Jewry underwent during these years in its increasing identification with proletarian socialism. But unlike Hungary, where the bark of the boycott was somewhat worse than its bite, in Poland the overall effect was intolerable for the massive Jewish population (well above three million). Even before the September 1939 Nazi invasion, the centuries-long role of Jews as the commercial bulwark of the Polish life was coming to an end.

This was also the case for the Jews of the Soviet Union, although for very different reasons. The two and a half million Jews in Russia following the 1917 Revolution constituted the third largest Jewish community in the world (after Poland and the United States). The country included territories that lay at the heart of the tsarist Pale of Settlement: Belarus and Ukraine. The liberal February Revolution had already formally abolished this restricted region; indeed, as early as 1915 numbers of Jews from the Pale had fled the war zone into Russia's interior with the government's express permission.[69] The nearly continuous military conflict from 1914 to 1921 contributed to the Pale's further dissolution. In the aftermath, as the government set Russia on the path to socialism, its policies fundamentally transformed the long-established way of life for the Jews of this region.

Bolshevik policies sought to eliminate the private ownership of productive enterprises and the free-market exchange of commodities, to transform the population into a modern industrial proletariat and to collectivize

[69] Mordecai Altshuler, *Soviet Jewry on the Eve of the Holocaust: A Social and Demographic Profile* (Jerusalem: Ahva Press, 1998), 10.

agriculture. The traditional Jewish occupational profile – overwhelmingly commercial and artisanal – in no way fit these aims, and for this reason would require radical restructuring. Yet the Soviet government veered widely in its strategy and timeline for achieving its goals. While the Civil War still raged, the government's adoption of "war communism" imposed a command economy, while dispossessing "class enemies" that included many Jewish owners of large factories and large commercial enterprises. Even many among the vast majority of Jews lower down on the capitalist totem pole risked being labeled *lishentsy*, exploiters or former exploiters who did not engage in productive labor. The designation carried legal disabilities and a lasting stigma that made daily life harder but also prevented the pursuit of more ideologically acceptable work. Between 1923 and 1928, well after the period of war communism, 700,000 Jewish businesses (most of them small-scale operations) closed as a result of direct state intervention or the pressures of steep taxes and short supplies.[70]

A series of Soviet policies, only some of which were designed to address economic crisis in the former Pale's Jewish population, mitigated the hardships of these losses. First, the New Economic Policy (NEP), introduced by Lenin in March of 1921, gave some private enterprises temporary reprieve. Indeed, the policy succeeded in rescuing Russia's economy from collapse. Jews played an important role in its resuscitation. While constituting 1.8 percent of the population of the Soviet Union, at the mid-1920s height of NEP Jews were 20 percent of its private traders – 60 percent in Ukraine and 90 percent in Belarus where Jews were a much larger proportion of the urban population. In the major cities of the Russian Federation– Moscow, Leningrad, and Kharkov– Jews were heavily overrepresented among the wealthy entrepreneurs (33 percent in Moscow) and often a plurality of owners of drugstores, jewelry shops, furniture concerns, as well as fabrics, tobacco, dry goods, and the like. Under NEP, as Yuri Slezkine has written, "the new 'Soviet bourgeoisie' was Jewish to a very considerable extent."[71]

But even when Stalin's "Great Turn" overtook NEP, starting in 1928, and a version of war communism was reintroduced, this "Jewish bourgeoisie" managed to reconstitute itself on different grounds, now as a bureaucratic and professional stratum. The Civil War had decimated the tsarist technocracy (mostly through emigration), while economic centralization compounded demand for clerks, bookkeepers, accountants, coordinators, managers, supervisors, administrators, and technicians of all kinds. As a population of middlemen, Jews were ideally positioned to fill these gaps,

[70] Polonsky, *The Jews of Poland and Russia, vol. III*, 241–243.
[71] Yuri Slezkine, *The Jewish Century* (Princeton: Princeton University Press, 2004), 218.

although additional education and Russification would be required.[72] These qualifications young Jews pursued with alacrity, migrating in large numbers from the region of the former Pale to the major cities of the interior. Not just functional utility but political loyalty to the new regime predisposed them to the role of becoming "the backbone of the new Soviet bureaucracy," as Lenin himself had observed in 1924. True, only a small proportion of Jews (5 percent) became members of the Soviet elite, though their representation at the highest echelons during the late 1920s and 1930s was more than double that of the Soviet urban population as a whole. But lower down and spread out more broadly across the wide range of "white collar" occupations, it has been estimated that on the eve of World War II almost half of all Soviet Jews belonged to the Soviet equivalent of the middle class, a far larger proportion than for the Soviet urbanites as a whole, let alone the entire Soviet population.[73]

The Great Transformation of Soviet Jewry took place against a backdrop of mass famine, terror, and totalitarianism, which victimized thousands of Jews as well. Nevertheless, the ironic "embourgeoisement" of Soviet Jewry (their transformation into a disproportionately white-collar population of employees) was abetted by these tragic circumstances – and even by the Holocaust itself. The secret terms of the 1939 Molotov–Ribbentrop pact divided independent Poland between a German zone in the West and a Soviet zone in the East, the latter containing about 1.5 million Polish Jews. When Hitler launched Operation Barbarossa in June of 1941, those Jews able to flee, or those prioritized by the Soviet government for evacuation to the East, tended to be the young and better educated, those with technical training and professional orientation – including many whose experience of Sovietization occurred in the 21 months of the Russian occupation of eastern Poland prior to the Nazi invasion. The vast majority of Jews exterminated by the Nazis were the elderly, the children, the infirm, the religiously traditional, and the representatives of the old Jewish commercial and artisanal economy. Thus, in the aftermath of World War II, the occupational profile of Soviet Jewry was even more professional and middle class than on the eve of the Holocaust.[74]

Ironies likewise abound in the case of the Jewish community of interwar Palestine, the Yishuv. Although in 1924, when the British Mandate was established, Jews comprised less than one-fifth of the country's population, they had already established the basis of a Jewish majority society

---

[72] Altshuler, *Soviet Jewry on the Eve of the Holocaust*, 146.

[73] Altshuler, *Soviet Jewry on the Eve of the Holocaust*, 174.

[74] Ben-Cion Pinchuk, *Shtetl Jews under Soviet Rule: Eastern Poland on the Eve of the Holocaust* (Oxford: Basil Blackwell, 1990), 41–64.

and economy. This was accomplished through the Histadrut (General Federation of Labor, established in 1920) and the JNF (Jewish National Fund), which ensured that wherever possible labor and land would be predominantly or even exclusively Jewish. Thus, starting with the Yishuv and even more so with the 1948 establishment of a Jewish State, a new historical situation arose in which the "Jewish economy" no longer meant simply a Jewish niche within a far larger economic system but rather an economy in which Jews controlled and for the most part manned all the leading institutions.

The reality of course was rather more complicated. The Yishuv, no less than the Soviet Union, was committed to a fundamental restructuring of Jewish economic life. Given the strong agrarian socialist orientation of its leadership, the ideal was as much the Jewish citizen-farmer as the factory proletarian. In truth, the Yishuv's leading agricultural sector was not the kibbutz or moshav (collective farm), but rather the capitalistically run citrus industry that employed a high proportion of Arab labor.[75] At the same time, the Yishuv depended heavily on the importation of foreign capital – in most cases, capital raised through donations and investment from Western Jews. Imported capital amounted to about a third of the Net Domestic Product (NDP) of the Yishuv's Jewish economy, a remarkable proportion by any measure. These imports enabled the Yishuv to invest heavily in infrastructure, industry, and enterprise without resorting to foreign loans or high domestic taxation (while the British administration provided a broader framework of law, government, and infrastructure at low cost to Jewish and Arab inhabitants).[76]

Finally, the Yishuv imported its actual population on a massive scale. The Jewish population in Palestine grew from 84,000 in 1922 to 550,000 in 1945, a sixfold increase in 23 years! A society built on immigration to a degree unparalleled in modern history, the self-selecting character of the immigrants through the early 1920s, with their intense dedication to building a Jewish homeland, was complemented as well as contradicted by the business and middle-class orientation of the Fourth Aliyah (1924–29), largely from Poland, and the educated and professional character of the Fifth Aliyah, which included many refugees from Nazi Germany and Central Europe. By the middle of the 1930s about a quarter of Palestine's Jewish population could be characterized as white collar. Despite Zionism's commitment to collectivized agriculture, the bulk of the Yishuv's population

---

[75] Jacob Metzer, *The Divided Economy of Mandatory Palestine* (New York: Cambridge University Press, 1998), 146–156.

[76] Ibid., p. 106; Paul Rivlin, *The Israeli Economy from the Foundation of the State through the 21st Century* (New York: Cambridge University Press, 2011), 20–21.

was in fact urban and increasingly educated and middle class. These factors made the Yishuv a remarkable economic success. Like the Soviet Union, but unlike the rest of the globalized economy, Palestine experienced significant growth at very height of the Great Depression (the early 1930s), making it a more attractive destination for Jewish immigrants in this period than the United States, whose own immigration quotas (imposed in 1924) were not met during most years of the decade. With the outbreak of World War II, Palestine's agriculture sector expanded, despite the collapse of the international citrus market, now producing the great bulk of foodstuffs for domestic consumption (before the war a very large proportion had been imported) as well as becoming an engine and entrepôt for British military and industrial supplies.[77] Although the State of Israel would face enormous economic (not to mention military and political) challenges in its early years, the Yishuv had created a solid foundation for a truly Jewish national economy, albeit one that was more capitalist than socialist, and more middle class than proletarian.

CONCLUSION

In terms of its economic character, the Holocaust can be seen as a grotesque caricature of some of the main themes of this chapter. The Nazis exploited the image of the Jewish capitalist who lived parasitically off of the virtuous and honest labor of Aryan population. The ghettos that the Nazis created in many Eastern Europe cities, and the Jewish councils (*Judenräte*) they established to implement their policies there, were predicated on the cruel hoax that Jewish economic productivity would somehow function to stay the executioner's hand. The motto on the entry gates of the Auschwitz concentration camp, *Arbeit macht frei*, may have been the ultimate expression of this pretense.

True to their intentions, the Nazis effectively destroyed the economic dimension of the Jewish Problem along with much of the European Jewish population. The post-war period saw a dramatic diminution in the productization ideology that had hitherto been a key feature of modern Jewish politics. In the three largest surviving Jewish communities, the United States, the Soviet Union, and Israel, the project of remaking Jews as farmers, artisans, and industrial workers became essentially moot. In America it had always been at best a minor theme. There, despite the painful but momentary setbacks of the Great Depression, Jewish small business (both commercial and manufacturing) continued to predominate through

---

[77] Metzer, *The Divided Economy*, 166–169.

the wartime period.[78] But as early as the 1920s, white-collar occupations (including sales clerks, supervisors, and managers) and professions (especially dentists, physicians, lawyers, engineers, teachers, and accountants) were providing an alternative path to middle-class status. By helping to bring coordination and efficiency to this combative industry, even the Jewish labor unions of the garment trades showed themselves to be ultimately more committed to their members' upward mobility than their revolutionary sloganeering would suggest.[79] Through all these avenues, by the late 1940s Jews had become proportionately the most middle-class group in the country. And here as everywhere, education played the major role in this transformation.[80]

Although the post-war Soviet Union became increasingly hostile to Jewish identity and achievement, the gains of the interwar period were not altogether erased, and parallels with the paradigmatic American capitalist example of Jewish upward mobility are therefore not out of place. While post-war Soviet Jews excelled in the arts, engineering, and the sciences, it is suggestive of the vitality of repressed cultural carryovers that a class of Jewish entrepreneurs and "moguls" emerged phoenix-like from the ashes of the Bolshevik revolution in the aftermath of the 1989 fall of communism.[81] At the same time, something loosely analogous occurred in the State of Israel, where, following the advent of the Likud government under Menachem Begin in 1977, but especially during period of the 1990s, the country shed its (not entirely deserved) image as an economically egalitarian community to become the vaunted "start-up nation" of today, with the world's highest per capita ratio of new businesses, but within an economically polarized commercial society.[82]

In view of this post-World War II history, it is indeed hard to understand the profound ambivalence in which "Jewish commerce" had been

[78] Beth S. Wenger, *New York Jews and the Great Depression* (Syracuse, NY: Syracuse University Press, 1999); Henry Feingold, *A Time for Searching: Entering the Mainstream, 1920–1945* (Baltimore: Johns Hopkins University Press, 1992), 126–127.

[79] Salo W. Baron, *Steeled by Adversity: Essays and Addresses on American Jewish Life*, ed. Jeanette Meisel Baron (Philadelphia: Jewish Publication Society, 1971), 296–306.

[80] Carmel Chiswick, *Judaism in Transition: How Economic Choices Shape Religious Tradition* (Stanford, CA: Stanford University Press, 2014), 33, 69.

[81] Slezkine, *The Jewish Century*, 361–363.

[82] Dan Senor and Saul Singer, *Start-Up Nation: The Story of Israel's Economic Miracle* (New York: Hachette, 2009); Paul Krugman, "Israel's Gilded Age," *New York Times*, March 16, 2015. On contemporary Israel's impressive capacity to economically absorb extraordinarily large numbers of immigrants, see Sarit Cohen Goldner, Zvi Eckstein, and Yoram Weiss, *Immigration and Labor Market Mobility in Israel, 1990-2009* (Cambridge, MA: MIT Press, 2012).

regarded during the preceding century and half, by non-Jews as well as by many Jews themselves. That Jewish economic life has served as a barometer of attitudes to modern commerce and capitalism for over 200 years lends poignancy and significance to Jews' economic fate in the capitalist age.

SELECT BIBLIOGRAPHY

Altshuler, Mordecai. *Soviet Jewry on the Eve of the Holocaust: A Social and Demographic Profile*. Jerusalem: Ahva Press, 1998.

Barkai, Avraham. *Branching Out: German-Jewish Immigration to the United States, 1820–1914*. New York: Holmes and Meier, 1994.

Benbassa, Esther and Aron Rodrigue. *Sephardi Jewry: A History of the Judeo-Spanish Community, 14th–20th Centuries*. Berkeley: University of California Press, 2000.

Chiswick, Carmel. *Judaism in Transition: How Economic Choices Shape Religious Tradition*. Stanford, CA: Stanford University Press, 2014.

Diner, Hasia. *Roads Taken: The Great Jewish Migrations to the New World and the Peddlers who Forged the Way*. New Haven: Yale University Press, 2015.

Dynner, Glenn. *Yankel's Tavern: Jews, Liquor, and Life in the Kingdom of Poland*. New York: Oxford University Press, 2014.

Feingold, Henry. *Zion in America: The Jewish Experience from Colonial Times to the Present*. Mineola, NY: Dover, 2002.

Glanz, Rudolf. *Geschichte des niederen jüdischen Volkes in Deutschland*. New York: n.p., 1968.

Goldscheider, Calvin and Alan S. Zuckerman. *The Transformation of the Jews*. Chicago: University of Chicago Press, 1985.

Heinze, Andrew. *Adapting to Abundance: Jewish Immigrants, Mass Consumption, and the Search for American Identity*. New York: Columbia University Press, 1990.

Hundert, Gershon. *Jews in Poland-Lithuania in the Eighteenth Century: A Genealogy of Modernity*. Berkeley: University of California Press, 2006.

Israel, Jonathan. *Diasporas within a Diaspora: Jews, Crypto-Jews and the World Maritime Empires (1540–1740)*. Leiden: Brill, 2002.

European Jewry in the Age of Mercantilism. Oxford: Oxford University Press, 1991.

Kahan, Arcadius. *Essays in Jewish Social and Economic History*, edited by Roger Weiss. Chicago: University of Chicago Press, 1986.

Kanfer, Yedida Sharona. "Lodz: Industry, Religion, and Nationalism in Russian Poland, 1880–1914." Ph.D. diss., Yale University, 2011.

Karp, Jonathan. *The Politics of Jewish Commerce: Economic Thought and Emancipation in Europe, 1638–1848*. New York: Cambridge University Press, 2012.

Kobrin, Rebecca, ed. *Chosen Capital: The Jewish Encounter with American Capitalism*. New Brunswick, NJ: Rutgers University Press, 2012.

Kuznets, Simon. *Jewish Economies*, 2 vols., ed. Stephanie Lo and Glen Weyl. New Brunswick, NJ: Transaction, 2012.

Lederhendler, Eli. *Jewish Immigrants and American Capitalism, 1880–1920: From Caste to Class*. Cambridge: Cambridge University Press, 2009.

Levin, Mordecai. *Social and Economic Values: The Idea of Professional Modernization in the Ideology of the Haskalah Movement* (Hebrew). Jerusalem: Mosad Byalik, 1975.

Mendelsohn, Adam. *The Rag Race: How Jews Sewed their Way to Success in America and the British Empire*. New York: New York University Press, 2015.

Mendelsohn, Ezra. *The Jews of East Central Europe between the Two Wars*. Bloomington: Indiana University Press, 1983.

Metzer, Jacob. *The Divided Economy of Mandatory Palestine*. New York: Cambridge University Press, 1998.

Mosse, Werner. *The German-Jewish Economic Elite*. Oxford: Oxford University Press, 1989.

Arnold Pauker, Reinhard Rürup, and Robert Weltsch, eds. *Revolution and Evolution: 1848 in German-Jewish History*. Tübingen: JCB Mohr, 1981.

Penslar, Derek. *Shylock's Children: Economics and Jewish Identity in Modern Europe*. Berkeley: University of California Press, 2001.

Petrovsky-Shtern, Yohanan. *The Golden Age of the Shtetl: A New History of Jewish Life in East Europe*. Princeton: Princeton University Press, 2014.

Polonsky, Antony. *The Jews in Poland and Russia*, 3 vols. Oxford: Littman Library of Jewish Civilization, 2010–12.

Prinz, Arthur. *Juden im deutschen Wirtschaftsleben: soziale und wirtschaftliche Struktur im Wandel, 1850–1914*. Tübingen: JCB Mohr, 1984.

Richarz, Monika, ed. *Jewish Life in Germany: Memoirs from Three Centuries*, trans. Stella P. Rosenfeld and Sidney Rosenfeld. Bloomington: University of Indiana Press, 1991.

Rivlin, Paul. *The Israeli Economy from the Foundation of the State through the 21st Century*. New York: Cambridge University Press, 2011.

Silber, Michael. *Jews in the Hungarian Economy, 1760–1945: Studies Dedicated to Moshe Carmilly Weinberger on his Eightieth Birthday*. Jerusalem: The Magnes Press, 1992.

Slezkine, Yuri. *The Jewish Century*. Princeton: Princeton University Press, 2004.

Stein, Sarah Abrevaya. *Plumes: Ostrich Feathers, and a Lost World of Global Commerce*. New Haven: Yale University Press, 2008.

Van Rahden, Till. *Jews and Other Germans: Civil Society, Religious Diversity, and Urban Politics in Breslau, 1860–1925*, trans. Marcus Brainard. Madison: University of Wisconsin Press, 2008.

CHAPTER 16

JEWS AND SOCIAL CLASS

ELI LEDERHENDLER

The Jewish experience of modernity, in which there has been a range of outcomes along a continuum of integration, difference, and exclusion, can be effectively illuminated through the particular prism of social class, for "class" poses the question of social inclusivity and difference at a higher level of resolution than "modern society" writ large. At the same time, the particular Jewish experience of class requires us to rethink the universality of class categories.

The link between the economic and the political-social aspects of modernization is widely acknowledged. Mercantilism, the industrial and market revolutions, capitalism and imperialism are well known interpretive rubrics for the history of states, international relations, and social development. They are less often viewed as central to the historiography of the Jews in modern times, however, it being either assumed that Jews are in any case subsumed within large-scale epochal changes or else posited that Jewish history is driven by peculiar circumstances that cut across the main currents of social and political history.

In this essay, I will apply to Jewish modernity typologies that historians have used to analyze broad social and economic transformations. One such key typology is that of the free-market system as a harbinger of altered social relations, distinguishing the "modern" from the pre-modern. This abstract distinction is useful as a means of gathering disparate historical experiences together into readable patterns, but it cannot be applied uncritically. As varied as the world's experience of economic and political change has always been, we often over-generalize certain social situations. The societies that sought to implement the ideal of free-market exchange varied in the ways they abided by its ostensible terms of neutrality. Jews, like other racial and religious minorities, have been a significant aspect of that inconsistency, and the Jewish case therefore challenges the way we think about social class as a heuristic device. I shall present two ways in which scholarship can usefully mine the empirical experiences of Jewries around the globe for this purpose. One, in which Jewish marginality forces us to look more critically at free-market models, leads toward a more fragmentary theory of social class formation; and an alternative one, in which theories of Jewish exceptionalism are challenged, underscores the congruent patterns linking Jewish and non-Jewish social processes.

MODAL PATTERNS IN MODERNITY

To briefly summarize a generalized historical understanding, social relations in pre-modern times adhered to a prescribed authoritarian symmetry governing all ranks and estates. A mythic world picture, promoted by religious doctrine as a sacred order sanctioned by divine will, held that earthly affairs reflected the cosmic or heavenly order. Bonds of discipline and obedience reinforced these time-honored precepts, which extended to physical, spatial, and religious separateness according to a fixed hierarchy.

A central characteristic of the modern era has been the rearrangement of social relations according to a market or exchange model. The notion of a free exchange of labor, skills, knowledge, and wealth, and the unencumbered exploitation of new resources and opportunities began to take hold of the Western political imagination as early as the 1600s and was forged into a liberal economic philosophy in the 1700s. In the ideology representing that system, all individuals are theoretically free agents, voluntarily bringing various skills or assets and needs or desires to the marketplace. This worldview regards social interactions mainly as rationally motivated, not sacred or transcendental in purpose. In this it mirrors in social thought the operative principles of the scientific revolution, which aimed to explain observed phenomena as naturalistic (as opposed to supernatural) processes. Accordingly, the modern spirit tends to be this-worldly, and human endeavor in the modern era is limited no longer by force of custom but only by the variety of native capacities to be found at random in the natural and human realms.

Under the imprint of this perspective, modern governments began to promote markets and mobility. In the early phases of this transformation rulers regularized and centralized such vital functions as the administration and rule of law, taxation, issuance and standardization of currency, the guarantee of property and contracts and the promotion of secure and convenient road and water travel. In rationalizing social relations, and in creating the very notion of "state" as an impersonal vessel of governance, modernizing regimes set aside certain old privileges (thus reducing the authority as well as the economic influence wielded by the church and curbing the hereditary power of the aristocracy). They thus helped to create a national domain of law and commerce. In some cases, where the regime was slow to pursue these policies, liberal political and commercial interests began to demand the restriction of arbitrary royal authority and interference in the lives and enterprises of individuals.

Governments eventually followed through and expanded their own sphere by fostering a single, comprehensive citizenry, all of whose members were supposed to be subject to the same civic code of laws, accorded "natural" individual rights (piecemeal, according to class, religion, race, and gender), educated to communicate in a common national or imperial language, aided and supervised by standardized school systems and institutions of higher learning. A modern person might become detached from a given place, community, contractual obligation, or legal status and still exist as a person as far as the state is concerned: that is, a modern individual's status within society is portable rather than fixed. This fitted well with the need to facilitate the movement of population to prime sites of economic development (such as manufacturing and commercial centers as well as overseas colonies), to foster the wider acquisition and application of skills and to generate optimal opportunities for the creation of new wealth. Under these conditions, people of various qualities, personal backgrounds, mental habits, and perspectives on life were resettled into new patterns of acting. These patterns extended to the language spoken at home and abroad, the education of children, the pursuit of an occupation, the performance of public duties, the payment of taxes, the disposal of leisure time, and the readiness to travel and migrate.

In this modern political economy such "innate," seemingly fixed qualities as birthplace, religion, rank among the various social orders, and even national origin were made secondary. Eventually, they were replaced by a malleable concept of social class: a comparatively dynamic and considerably secularized modern construction that regulated social diversity. Not who one is, but what one does, how well one does it, and what one is able to acquire, are the basis for the gradation of modern individuals and families within society. As moderns we assume, for example, that education and training – acquired skills, not innate characteristics or inherited functions – afford an avenue for entering the marketplace with something of value to others, and therefore of great advantage to us.

The sequence of changes outlined above has applied as well to minority populations as to the mainstream of larger societies. Indeed, given our contemporary understanding of society as a multiple and varied set of interrelationships, nearly always constructed within a very heterogeneous population and exhibiting shifting internal boundaries, it would be difficult to place minorities neatly to one side while reserving "mainstream society" for others. "Society" consists of the whole, not just the parts, and members of minority groups are essential participants in the construction of society in one way or another. The market revolution implicates everyone, minority group members included, and that would automatically apply to the case of the Jews.

That having been said, the wide-ranging transformations alluded to above in schematic outline always and everywhere occurred in fits and starts rather than in neatly linear fashion, and sometimes in an atmosphere fraught with tension, conflict, apprehension, and suspicion. The development of a free market was not possible without facing the vexed questions of competition, trust, mutual rights and obligations, fair pricing, honesty and self-interest, easy credit or tight credit, enterprise and deal-making, access to professional employment, and the resentment of exploitation. Such divisive issues were sometimes contained and negotiated through the development of parties and interest groups; but since questions of moral equity were not easily separable from long-abiding attitudes toward religious, ethnic, or racial differences, it happened often enough that threatening or tainted images of the market economy were displaced onto an alien or marginal group (Jews, Gypsies, Greeks ...). Likewise, social classes, although relatively mobile and porous, tended to categorize, stereotype, and predetermine or restrict the options of individuals (men and women) and families. When combined, the effects of economic typing and ethno-religious or racial stigmas were difficult to ignore.

We therefore have to inquire: Was the impact of the market revolution so universal that smaller sub-populations were necessarily submerged within modern social classes? Or was the dissonance between the regnant ideology of social and class mobility and the particular destinies of social minorities a constant exception to rationalized social relations? How free was the market if ascriptive bonds and their associated limitations on individual endeavor continued to be upheld by state and society alike? Does this illiberal historical tendency in modern society create a problem for free-market ethical systems?

Or, yet again, ought we to revise the pristine market model itself by paying closer attention to omnipresent forces of division, conflict, and competition within classes? "Class as relationship has undermined class as a faction," declared historian William Reddy, arguing that no class operates on the stage of history as if its diverse members were really one united socio-political personality.[1] In a similar vein Peter Gay observed:

The slightest subdivisions in the middling ranks could generate social discrimination, nepotism, envy.... Economic self-interest, religious agendas, intellectual

---

[1] William M. Reddy, "The Concept of Class," in *Social Orders and Social Classes in Europe since 1500: Studies in Social Stratification*, ed. M. L. Bush (London and New York: Longman, 1992), 25.

convictions, social competition ... became political issues where bourgeois battled bourgeois.[2]

Bearing the socially intricate aspects of all economically based relations in mind, the variant histories of minorities and majorities could appear as interwoven aspects of the same experience. The Jewish case is an instance of differentiating factors within social classes, perhaps a particularly egregious one.

THE AMBIGUITIES OF JEWISH CLASS STATUS

The master narrative of modernity, if we may call it that, posits that sooner or later Jews along with others were able to enter the marketplace according to their personal aptitudes, needs, and assets and to attain a wider range of status positions vis-à-vis the secular realm. Participation qua individuals at various class levels differed from the Jews' situation under medieval conditions, in which Jews had constituted formal groupings – Jewries – founded and maintained as chartered legal bodies. Performing specialized functions as a source of revenue for the royal or manorial treasury or as suppliers of special goods and services, they were under the particular jurisdiction and legal protection of the crown or lord. As a peculiar "asset" of the ruler's domain, Jews were licensed to engage in certain pursuits and barred from others. Likewise, they were licensed (or required) to reside in certain towns and city districts but barred from others. Often the expansion of their numbers was regulated or limited by charter provisions and taxation per capita, and frequently the permission for their continued residence was revoked. Jews may have been internally differentiated according to their separate occupations and standards of living, but they were outwardly always a single corporate body – Jewry – and that status was their recognized part in the social-estate system. In pre-modern terms, "Jew" was a job description as well as a religious category.

Modernization of state and society meant that "Jewries" would be transformed into "Jews" and Jews' jobs would not be pre-defined by their Jewishness. Just as economic utility was served by transforming serfs into a free yeomanry or mobilized rural labor class, progressive social thought from the seventeenth to the nineteenth century saw economic merit in placing the Jews under the same market regime as everyone else, without special taxation or occupational prohibitions. Through the centralizing functions of governance which applied to the citizenry at large, the

---

[2] Peter Gay, *Schnitzler's Century: The Making of Middle-Class Culture 1815–1914* (New York: W. W. Norton, 2002), 4–5.

exclusive nexus between Jewry and the regime could be sundered. By the same token, a class-based parity between Jews and others of similar economic standing could be forged. From this point on, Jews' livelihoods, class identities, and political status could in principle be analogous to the rest of society.

This master narrative is necessary but insufficient in order to grasp the complexity of the matter of Jews and social class. Underneath that theme runs a different narrative thread, for in most if not all Diaspora settings modern Jews have been alert to the tensions between their aspirations to class (occupational, professional, educational, or income status) and their perceived role as a signifier of difference in society at large.

At times the tension or discrepancy has been shaped by a lag between prescriptive legal reforms and social realities. Thus, Catherine II of Russia ruled that Jews were to be enrolled among the ranks of the urban citizenry or merchant guilds, but in practice they were long denied the fruits of such civic integration. Similarly, in the 1780s Habsburg emperor Joseph II ordained that Jews educate their children in general state schools, but for decades this remained largely a dead letter due to resistance on the part of both Jewish and Christian society. Sometimes legislated change lagged behind social change – as when secularizing young Jews in nineteenth-century Russia attended universities in growing numbers and were permitted to study the law but not admitted to the bar. In still other instances, the state intervened to limit Jews' social and civic status by arbitrary action, as happened in 1808 to the Jews of Alsace under Napoleon. In imperial Germany the army officer corps remained barred to Jews (and other non-aristocrats) in military service, despite their being otherwise subject under the constitution to the same legal freedoms and obligations as their peers.

Though the ideology of the market tended over the long term to enlarge the scope of individual Jews' options, Jews often found it worthwhile or necessary to develop strategies of their own to deal with the discrepancies between the theory and practice of class integration. Conversion to the dominant faith to eliminate the problem of difference was one such response. Famous individual cases like Heinrich Heine's stand out in bold relief, but these represented a wider phenomenon, especially in Western and Central Europe.[3] Another somewhat irregular response is reflected in the incidences of Jewish criminality, indicative of alienation

---

[3] Some 100,000 conversions took place in the nineteenth century among Central and West European Jews, accounting for 8–11 percent of the Jewish population. In Eastern Europe, conversions were relatively rare (some 2–4 percent in the nineteenth century). See David Vital, *A People Apart: The Jews in Europe, 1789–1939* (Oxford: Oxford University Press, 1999), 124–125.

from the normative economic and legal system. Dickens's Fagin was a fictional device, of course, but criminality has factually dogged marginalized Jews for centuries, from Jewish highwaymen in eighteenth-century Germany to Jewish pimps and madams in turn-of-the-twentieth-century Buenos Aires.

Far more widespread and popular strategies have included the construction by Jews of parallel social institutions of their own alongside and in imitation of gentile ones. These would include working class institutions such as Jewish socialist parties and labor unions, middle-class organizations like fraternal and Masonic-type lodges (such as B'nai B'rith), and upper-class-based philanthropic societies and charitable funds.

Jews were often able to make exceptionalism work in their favor by capitalizing on internal family and inter-communal Jewish ties. Occupational, employment, educational, and even consumer networks long remained important features of social life among Jews as among other minority sub-populations. In some situations Jewish difference – even marginality – could be an asset, as we will note with reference to colonial-era Jews in the Middle East and Asia.

Some Jews inhabited their class-roles so comfortably that their ideas about Judaism took on a class-based hue, while their relations with Jews of a different social rank were framed accordingly: that is, defined by their dissonant interests. The dilemmas of making one's way in modern society led some Jews to observe the conventions of middle- or upper-class acquisitiveness and lifestyle, reflective of how they viewed society's expectations; others were more apt to embrace and even revel in their social marginality – these two patterns being, respectively, the "parvenus" and "pariahs" in Hannah Arendt's memorable reduction of this complex issue to a neat binary of archetypes.

The most representative response by far on the part of Jews who chafed at second-class status and social marginality was migration. The flow of Jewish migration, mainly westward, followed the trail of modern, urban economic development. Moving to a new social situation generally made it easier, in the long run, to revise one's status upward – or at least, that of one's children.

THE CASE FOR JEWISH MARGINALITY

PORT JEWS, *BETTELJUDEN*, AND BOXERS

In the period of the Reformation and incipient capitalism there were very few Jews living in Europe north of the Alps or west of Poland. The take-off point for the economic and social modernization of Europe (fifteenth–sixteenth centuries) was thus the low point for a Jewish presence throughout the western part of the continent, and this was reflected in the fragmentary state of their social and economic integration.

Jews had been banished from the late thirteenth to the late fifteenth centuries from England, France, Spain (the largest medieval Jewry), southern Italy, and many areas of the German-dominated parts of Central Europe. Muscovite Russia also barred Jews from entry. Jews were barely 0.6 percent of the European population in the seventeenth century: some 500,000 Jews out of 70–80 million Europeans (excluding Russia and Ottoman lands). An additional 500,000 Jews lived in Muslim lands. In north Italian cities and some of the Papal possessions, in some parts of Central Europe, in the Ottoman Empire, and in the Polish-Lithuanian Commonwealth, Jews inhabited a social space defined for them by the authorities – indeed, rulers in those regions often encouraged Jews to settle.

Around the mid-seventeenth century, former Iberian Jews, *conversos*, and crypto-Jews in France (Bordeaux, Bayonne), the Low Countries, London, Livorno, and Hamburg were the principal examples of successfully integrated Jewish commercial agents and traders. Typically, their "cover" as Portuguese traders enabled them to settle in areas where other Jews had long been absent. Typically, too, they arranged their affairs within extended family networks. These Jews of Sephardi (Iberian) background (who have been dubbed "port Jews") were the same populace that figured in the colonial enterprises of France, Holland, and England in the Western Hemisphere.

But the mid-seventeenth century saw the beginning of a prolonged influx to the West of poor Jews from East Central Europe and as far away as Lithuania and the Ukraine. As a result, a politically benign and economically inviting place like Amsterdam became not just an entrepôt for Sephardi Jewish merchants but also a funnel for Jewish poverty, especially among the immigrant Ashkenazim. Itinerant bands of Jews roamed throughout the German lands, France, Moravia, and Bohemia. Known pejoratively as "beggar Jews" (*Betteljuden*), they were often prevented from settling down in any one place.

For every Jewish individual who eventually obtained a permit to reside and take up an occupation (*Schutzbriefe*), many more had to manage by living illegally. Though tolerated at first in Prussia, for example, Polish Jewish refugees were considered "too many" by 1657 and were sent packing. In pre-revolutionary France, north Alsatian cities routinely barred Jewish residence. Jews were expelled from Habsburg Vienna in 1669–70 (under Leopold I). Seven decades later there were still only twelve tolerated Jewish families in the city: poor Jews were simply kept out. In 1744, Maria Theresa expelled Jews from Prague as well (though the order was rescinded). In general, the Habsburg crown sought to maintain firm controls over the expansion and occupations of its Jewish population.

Yet the influx of Jews with marginal means of subsistence continued over long decades, their numbers eventually reaching into many thousands. The Jewish population in the German lands stood at some 60,000 in the mid-eighteenth century; it more than tripled (to an estimated 200,000) by the end of the century. In Amsterdam the Jewish population doubled in just over thirty years, from 1748 to 1780. Eighteenth- and early nineteenth-century London was the scene of a newly emergent Anglo-Jewry composed to a large extent by lower-class Sephardi and Ashkenazi Jewish immigrants and their children, living alongside their non-Jewish class peers, and who were supported to an extent by the small Jewish commercial elite. Petty thievery and fencing of stolen goods were not unknown. In his study of London's lower-class Jewish milieu up to the 1850s, Todd Endelman pungently described it as a scene peopled by "pickpockets and pugilists" (the latter, because of the well-publicized instances of Jewish prizefighters). In France, the central Jewish communal authority (*Consistoire*) in Paris attempted to prohibit the local communities from lending care and support to wandering Jewish beggars. As late as the mid-nineteenth century, a significant share of Jewish poverty in Alsace was explained as hereditary poverty, rather than owing to immediate reversals of fortune such as illness or unemployment.[4]

The legacy of Jewish marginality could be seen in the disproportionate share of Jews in secondary trades such as used clothing, small-scale peddling and hawking of goods, pawnbroking, scrap or "junk"-dealing, tavern-keeping, and distilling. The Jewish artisan class at times found employment in lucrative luxury goods (watches, jewelry, gold- and silver-smithing) and was far more represented in the making or repair of such items, just as they also worked in the making or repair of shoes, apparel, cheap metalware, furniture, brushes, and the like. The role of Jews in the early development of factories was minimal (nor was the role of Jewish banking families notably crucial to large-scale industrialization in a later age).

Jewish marginality was also reflected in the persisting legacy of Jewish linguistic separatism. While many Jews were fully able to communicate, at least orally, in the language(s) of the surrounding population, they were still apt to communicate among themselves in their own tongue. The case of Yiddish is perhaps best known, having served for nearly a thousand years, until the Holocaust, as a Judeo-European lingua franca from the North Sea to the Black Sea. Other Jewish ethnic languages include Ladino

---

[4] Paula E. Hyman, *The Emancipation of the Jews of Alsace: Acculturation and Tradition in the Nineteenth Century* (New Haven: Yale University Press, 1991), 47.

(used among descendants of Iberian Jews in the Balkans, Turkey, and some other Mediterranean communities) and a handful of other languages and local dialects spoken and written among Jews in communities from Morocco to the Caucasus, Persia to Ethiopia.

As Derek Penslar has observed, early modern European discourse on Jews and social class was sharply bifurcated. On the one hand, the Jew as *homo economicus* was associated with the growth in trade, manufacturing and commerce, banking and enterprise; on the other hand, the Jew as alien migrant was also associated with vagrancy and viewed as a threat to stability and a healthy economy. That dualism pervaded public policy, in which some Jews were viewed as useful and even necessary, while others – perhaps the majority – were seen as a dangerous surplus population requiring special policing and special taxes as a deterrent to their permanent settlement. Tolerated or "certified" Jews were subjects of the realm who merited residence rights, occupational privileges and marriage permits; the Jewish underclass had to be restricted or excluded.

From one end of Europe to another, plans for civic reform regularly dealt with the question of Jewish economic utility and performance. In the seventeenth and early eighteenth centuries proposals were floated to colonize Ireland (problematic and Catholic and conveniently outside of England itself) with penurious but industrious Jews and foreign Protestant migrants. In French and German public affairs the Jews' "civic improvement" was a topic of particular interest in the mid- to late eighteenth century. In the Polish Commonwealth in the 1790s, on the verge of its dismemberment by the partitioning powers (Prussia, Austria, and Russia), an intense debate swept through parliament (the Sejm) and exploded in a vigorous pamphlet exchange over how to reform the Jews economically. Afterwards, the debate flourished under Russian rule and shaped Russia's Jewish policies for decades to come.

The discrepancy between the civil status of Jews who could be considered "beneficial" in society and economic life and those living on society's margins nourished a long-lasting tendency among Jews in Central and Western Europe to undertake a custodial responsibility for their less fortunate co-religionists, understanding rightly that the duality of Jewish social status was a barb in their own hides. By the same token, however, many of them were eager to distance themselves culturally from the unprivileged, so-called ghetto Jews. The sensitivity of upwardly mobile and "certified" Jews to the fragility of their social-status tended to make them hyper-sensitive to the stigmas attached to low-caste Jewish characteristics. This frequently found expression in their contempt for Yiddish or Yiddish-inflected speech. "Jewish" accents served for generations as a stock trait of the caricatured Jew of low origin and indeterminate social status.

The gap between the attainments of the few and the legally inferior or illegitimate status of the many eventually fueled a large and disproportionate Jewish migration from Central and Western Europe, lasting from the 1820s to the 1890s and beyond and accounting for a third of the Jewish population of the region (the equivalent of more than one person for every Jewish household). Much of that migrant stream went to the United States, a country that had no national church and, perhaps in consequence, espoused the free-market system as something akin to a national religion.

COLONIALS WEST AND EAST

The Europeans' conquest, settlement, and government of colonial possessions in Asia, Africa, and the Western Hemisphere formed part and parcel of their economic rise and dominance. Imperialism's basic violence is not at issue in this discussion (nor, for that matter, is the violence of the pre-imperial, native social order, before Western interference and conquests occurred). In the present discussion of social class in general, and that of Jews in particular, what is relevant is that Western imperial expansionism provided a new array of opportunities and choices for people of divergent backgrounds – mostly, but not limited to, emigrants of European origin. Frontier regions and far-flung outposts of empire were relatively permissive in terms of individual liberties and lifestyles, and, although colonial regimes often incorporated metropolitan norms of class privilege, religious, and social controls (to say nothing of their exploitative and racialist policies vis-à-vis "native" populations), colonial societies were also "rough" and heterogeneous.

Certain outposts of empire – most notably British America – were favored by special legislation, sometimes more liberal than social and legal institutions in the home country, which was designed to promote agricultural development and trade with the mother country under optimal conditions. Colonial settings promoted new wealth, militated against strict adherence to continuities of inherited privilege, and often enough became the seedbeds of republican or radical ideas that laid the foundations for new states.

As noted, the foundations for a Jewish presence in French, Dutch, and English colonial settlements in the New World were laid by the Sephardi Atlantic Diaspora. These trading families and the networks they established extended out from Europe to South America, the Caribbean islands and the North American mainland. Optimal conditions for Jewish colonial integration obtained in Dutch and British possessions. In particular, the religiously heterogeneous population in some colonies (Philadelphia, New York, Charleston, South Carolina, and Newport, Rhode Island, for example) mirrored a relatively open regime that held advantages for Jews. Here Jews participated in the local economy as well as in inland and transatlantic trade on an equal footing with others. Evidence of colonial Jews' involvement as individuals in civic affairs in the seventeenth and early eighteenth centuries indicates their social efficacy in earning a place among non-Jews of equivalent economic standing.

Equally, though, it indicates that the numerically minor Jewish representation in the colonies played little if any role in the way the social contract was promulgated. Unlike in France, Austria, or Poland, the "Jewish Question" never bulked large enough to stir much debate over the ways society ought to function.

The main and abiding distinction between British America and the European continent (including England itself) was the absence in America of a dual-status system dividing "tolerated" (authorized) Jewish inhabitants from other Jews. All were equally subject to the same civil regime, all equally entitled to move and reside at will. Jewish difference, in other words, was not in itself a factor in the spread or limitation of Jewish settlement in the colonies, nor was it a determinant of social and civic status (although in quite a few cases, elective political office was closed to non-Protestants). Clearly, this had something to do with the nature of living on the rim of European civilization, in contrast to its heartland. Where frontier conditions reigned, the maintenance of social institutions was dependent upon a much more explicit and inclusive social contract.

With American independence and the adoption of a federal Constitution, these trends were further enhanced. Jews by no means shared the occupational profile of the average American, who was most apt to be a farmer; but in towns and cities the prevalent practices and social discourse made it possible to retain denominational distinctions among fellow citizens while market relations, partnerships and even marital ties transcended sectarian lines.

By the 1820s, half a century before full citizenship would be granted to Jews of imperial Germany and the Habsburg Empire, the civic integration of Jews in American society on a par with other members of their social class was nearly a fait accompli. This owed much to the early and abiding influence of free-market ideas in the American colonies, well entrenched long before the Jews were a significant presence, and was not at all owing to social conditions specifically arranged with the Jews in mind. A few inveterate ethnic boosters might argue that Jews nonetheless played a constructive role in establishing a culture of social class in the United States.

Paradoxically, their peripheral status in a region that was itself peripheral made possible an entirely novel kind of class-defined civic participation.[5]

Popular images of the American continent as a wondrously wild and endless hinterland, sparsely populated by free-living ex-Europeans offered a chance to start from scratch, continued to frame European Jewish attitudes toward transatlantic immigration through the nineteenth century. In 1800 there were perhaps 3,000 Jews in North America; by 1880 their numbers reached a quarter of a million.

At the same time, it is generally agreed that as the Jewish population in America grew, Jews were disproportionately represented in some branches of the economy, particularly those that were less well developed and less "crowded." Ethnic difference, in that sense, did operate to create boundaries within classes, at times working to the advantage of a minority such as the Jews. As the economist and Nobel laureate Simon Kuznets observed:

> The range of industrial, occupational and status choices [available to] a minority ... is significantly narrower than the range open to a country's total population .... The minority is naturally directed to sectors with greater growth potentials .... [S]ince the immigrant minority tends to occupy the lower rungs of the economic ladder within these sectors, it has a greater opportunity to rise.[6]

Along with the major flow of immigrants already making their way to North America, a tributary of some significance took part in the colonization of agricultural land in Argentina. While Spanish colonial rule had been inhospitable to Jewish settlement, once the colonial regimes in Latin America were replaced with modern republics, some of these proffered plausible visions of unlimited social and economic betterment. The phenomenon of organized colonies of Jewish farmers (though not unknown in imperial Russia, and soon to become a regular fixture among the Jews of Ottoman Palestine) entered modern Jewish economic history mainly in Latin America. For nearly two generations, the European-bred Jewish farmers and *gauchos* offered a viable alternative in Argentina to the more traditional urban model.

---

[5] An indicator of the texture of Jewish class integration in nineteenth-century American society is the finding that Gentile women marrying Jewish men in the US were more likely than their European counterparts to convert to Judaism. "In what was a fluid societal setting, women in particular could raise their status by marrying a man from a higher status group .... Gentile women found Jewish men to meet their standards for social status and economic mobility." Dana Evan Kaplan, "Conversion to Judaism in America 1760–1897" (Ph.D. Diss., Tel Aviv University 1994), 103.

[6] Simon Kuznets, "Economic Structure and Life of the Jews," in *The Jews: Their History, Culture, and Religion*, ed. Louis Finkelstein (Philadelphia: Jewish Publication Society, 1966 [1949]), vol. 2, 1602–1603.

Apart from the role of empires in the extrusion of large populations to "new worlds" in the West, British and French imperialism also played a decisive role in altering social realities in the East, which had a direct impact on Jews living there. Empire builders drew upon the talents, resources, and connections of their local clients – minorities in their own native settings – such as Christians and Jews in Muslim lands. Thus, favored by imperial patronage, afforded new educational opportunities, subsidized and organized by Western missionary or philanthropic institutions, and offered protection under imperial aegis, their very marginality in terms of the larger social environment became a major advantage in their attainment of social betterment.

Some native-born minority protégés obtained European citizenships along with their acquisition of European languages and occupational connections. The most sweeping such instance was the 1870 decree that awarded French citizenship en bloc to most of the Jews of Algeria, a move advocated and presided over by Adolphe Crémieux, who was the French Minister of Justice as well as the vice-president of the Central Consistory of French Jewry.

Francophone culture was effectively spread throughout North African and Middle Eastern Jewish communities through the efforts of the French Jewish philanthropic organization, Alliance Israélite Universelle (AIU, founded 1860), which focused its main efforts on promoting and providing vocational and academic schooling for the children of urban Jewish families.[7] The Francophone project pursued among "Oriental" Jews by the AIU served the lower-middle-class Jews of the region as a means of side-stepping the second-class status that they (like the Christians) endured for centuries under Muslim regimes. As clients of empire, they were able to reap important benefits in quality of life terms and a heightened social capital. These developments formed the basis for a modern, bourgeois Jewish cosmopolitanism and multiculturalism that held sway for decades in such key urban centers as Algiers, Tunis, Damascus, and Beirut.

The work of the AIU and its institutions also created a new professional class of teachers, intellectuals and journalists which took its place alongside more traditional artisan and tradesman classes. It is important to note, as well, that the national French Jewish leadership, in sponsoring the AIU and its overseas programs, solidified its own standing vis-à-vis the upper

---

[7] Beginning in 1862 with a school in Tetuan, Morocco, the AIU educational network eventually stretched as far as Iran and by 1913 included some 180 schools attended by 43,700 pupils. See Esther Benbassa and Aron Rodrigue, *Sephardi Jewry: A History of the Judeo-Spanish Community, 14th–20th Centuries* (Berkeley: University of California Press, 1995), 83.

strata of French society as they exhibited full identification with the overall aims and expressions of French empire-building and nationalism.

The Anglo-Jewish leadership did likewise within the British Empire and with its wholehearted support, British colonial rule helped to create a modern Anglophone Jewish bourgeoisie in those areas. Burgeoning international trade in the imperialist age notably helped to spawn a far-flung Iraqi Jewish trading network emanating from Baghdad and maintaining enterprises in Bombay, Calcutta, Singapore, Shanghai and Hong Kong.[8]

Indirectly, the expansion of Europe and its involvement in North Africa and the Middle East also reinforced local trends of social, economic, and political innovation. Turkey, an independent empire in its own right, competed with European powers to retain power and influence in its own geographic sphere. Combined with Western pressures, these initiatives produced reform policies adopted from the 1830s through the 1870s, which included new guarantees of protected civil status for non-Muslims.

Ottoman Turkey, in its empire-building heyday up to the sixteenth century, had served as a base for a considerable network of urban Jewish communities. Petty tradesmen and artisans for the most part, Ottoman Jewry also came to harbor a significant Sephardi merchant class, particularly active in trade with Italian ports. In later times, the declining fortunes of the Ottoman Empire also saw the economic decline of this trading network. From the seventeenth century on, economic opportunity for Jews and other non-Muslims (chiefly Greeks and Armenians) was increasingly hitched to Dutch, English, and French activity in the region.

Imperial patronage was not an unmitigated blessing, however, especially when seen in retrospect. As colonial societies developed new political sensibilities, Jews were sometimes apt to be targets of militant post-colonialism. Nineteenth-century nationalist movements in Greece and the Balkans tended to undermine the relative social stability of Jewish communities formerly living under Ottoman rule. Jews in Corfu during the first half of the nineteenth century sought British protection as the only reasonable guarantee of their safety against local anti-Jewish

---

[8] Historian Jonathan Goldstein records the following piquant example: "Menasseh Meyer was British Singapore's supreme Jewish entrepreneur .... He was born in Baghdad in 1846, raised in Calcutta, and arrived in Singapore in 1873 to join his uncle's opium trading business, the largest in the port .... By 1900 he owned about three-quarters of the island [and] one contemporary described Meyer as 'the richest Jew in the Far East', exceeding even the [other Iraqi Jewish business magnates, the] Sassoons." See Goldstein, "Singapore, Manila and Harbin as Reference Points for Asian 'Port Jewish' Identity," in *Jews and Port Cities, 1590–1990: Commerce, Community and Cosmopolitanism*, David Cesarani and Gemma Romain (London and Portland, OR: Valentine Mitchell, 2006), 274.

sentiment. In the 1840s and 1860s in newly independent Serbia Jews were deprived of trading and landowning rights. They sought succor from Western powers and Western Jewish diplomacy, as did Jews in Romania suffering discrimination and violence in the 1870s. The "Jewish Question" as part of the "Eastern Question" culminated in demands insisted upon by the Western powers at the 1878 Congress of Berlin that Romania and Serbia provide constitutional guarantees for their Jewish citizens. Western patronage itself could reach a terminal point, however, as the Jews of Algeria learned to their dismay when the Vichy French regime revoked the seventy-year-old Crémieux Decree that had recognized and protected them in the past.

The dualism that dogged the fortunes of Jews in Europe, divided between naturalized and alien, "useful" and "parasitical" categories, in tandem with the ways that colonialism and migration to other parts of the world operated to neutralize Jewish disabilities (for many, if not for all), argue that in the Jews' case market-based class formation was not linear or always consistent with that of the general population.

The discourse of utility and rationality underlay some of the invidious policies that distinguished between different classes of Jews in certain European strongholds. In many instances, it appears that the rationalized, advantageous outcomes were strongly biased toward the lives of relatively few Jewish exemplars, while the realities of marginality and exceptionalism appear to color the lives of the many. The outstanding exception to this generalization is the United States.

THE CASE FOR A CLASS PARADIGM

MANUAL LABOR AND "GENTLEFOLK"

Jewries had internalized the sorts of social stratification that characterized all medieval and early modern societies, but, because there were no Jewish peasants or Jewish lords, all class distinctions within Jewish society could be reduced to a simpler division between manual laborers and "gentlefolk" (i.e., those who did not perform manual labor and sometimes employed others to do so). Manual labor did not simply refer to unskilled work (day laborers, draymen, and domestic servants); it extended as well to independent craftsmen and employed artisans. The majority of them were not well off enough to contribute to the communal tax rolls, and they were therefore barred from the decision-making local council and its executive board, the *kahal*. Gentlefolk included merchants, innkeepers, and small traders but also the learned men of the community (these tended to be linked through marriage ties). Sumptuary laws and sanctions imposed by the *kahal* sought to extend the division of social ranks into the sphere of consumption, so that the display of luxuries (clothing and finery) and out- lay of expenditures (food for festive occasions such as weddings) should reflect the pecking order, on the one hand, while keeping ostentation within bounds, on the other.

To some extent, this pre-modern social regimentation prefigured later class divisions within Jewish populations. But pre-modern distinc- tions rested to a large extent on the intermediary functions played by all Jewries, generating revenues for the crown or manorial lord while remaining strictly separate from peasant serfs, burgher communes, mer- chant and artisan guilds, and the gentry. That is: the stratified Jewish societies did not promote a class-based horizontal parity between Jews and others. At the heart of the pre-modern Jewish social order was the absolute dependence of every Jew on his or her *kahal*. The critical tran- sition to modernity would come when the feudal order was broken down: that is, when serfs became free rural labor; many among the landed gentry fell on increasingly hard times and had to manage their own estates; towns and cities were reorganized under state administra- tions; and the Jewish *kahal* was reduced from a complete civil juris- diction in its own right to a congregational apparatus for providing religious and social services.

Reddy asked about Prussian Junkers after 1807: "Are Junkers without serfs the 'same' class as Junkers with serfs?"[9] We may fruitfully ponder, then, whether Jews living in post-feudal societies were the same in terms of class status as Jews living in estate-ordered regimes, performing set roles as intermediaries between crown, gentry, and serfs, or between the gen- try and the urban poor? As modern class cultures crystallized, did Jewish master craftsmen, small householders, and small tradesmen re-emerge as a middle class, leaving the lowest orders to comprise a Jewish working class, the learned sector to give birth to a white-collar professional class, and the wealthy merchants to create an upper bourgeoisie? Were Jews who migrated Westward also migrating from a Jewish economic periphery into a more integrated role at the core of national economies?

To a large extent, these questions remain under-explored. Perhaps that is not surprising: the narrative of Jewish marginality works toward aggregat- ing Jews as a status category and the historiography of Jewish marginality deploys that strategy to achieve coherence. In studying Jews as instances of class diversification, however, historians have had to bring to bear far more generalizing concepts. "Jews," as such, are apt to become disaggregated in

[9] Reddy, "The Concept of Class," 17.

the process, leaving the historian of Jewish class relations with less, rather than more, Jewish specificity to work with.

Some broad trends appear suggestive, however, which may be outlined schematically:

(A) Modern conditions brought about a greater diversity in occupational and social ranks among Jews. Some Jews benefited from the expansion of white-collar employment opportunities; the greater availability of academic and vocational schooling; the opening to Jews and advancement of free professions and the arts and sciences; the opening of civil service positions to Jews in certain countries (France, for instance); the development of entrepreneurship in new industries, such as sugar refining and oil extraction and refining (in the Russian Empire's Baku area and in parts of Habsburg Galicia); and the emergence of small farming sectors within Jewish populations in the Austro-Hungarian Empire, North and South America, the Russian Empire (chiefly in Ukraine), and among Palestine Jewry – later Israel.

These occupational patterns differed somewhat from the old division between genteel and non-genteel occupations; consequently, social class became less dependent upon culturally embedded codes and more dependent upon individual assets and endowments. Former high-status occupations such as the rabbinate, for instance, gave way to higher-status secular professions (writers, teachers, journalists, engineers, physicians, lawyers), offering entrée to professional associations. Even the ranks of the rabbinate, it should be pointed out, showed signs of becoming an academicized profession in the West, while in Lithuania a kind of "mandarin" elite culture of Torah-learning could be observed at a select group of new yeshivot.

Mobility conduits also began to affect the traditionally low-status or menial labor sectors. Some shop assistants moved into office work. Numbers of successful artisans and craftsmen tended in time to become small-scale employers, sometimes progressing from subcontracting to independent manufacture, sales and product design. The famous instance here, above all, is the garment industry, in which upwardly mobile self-employed former workingmen formed a new stratum of Jewish society, aspiring to middle-class status.

(B) At the same time, an amalgam of petty tradespeople, wagoners, and draymen, low-level religious functionaries and craft workers – especially in Russia and Eastern Europe in the late nineteenth to early twentieth centuries – began to lose the traditional distinctions between manual and non-manual status as either they or their children formed a large, new Jewish lower class. Characteristic of this class were chronic seasonal unemployment; a high rate of employment of children and young women, representing the bottom of the wage scale; and a growth in female employment in domestic service.

The steep rate of natural increase among the Jewish population of Eastern Europe,[10] bringing the total number of Jews in Europe as a whole from about 0.5 million in the seventeenth century up to approximately ten million at the turn of the twentieth, combined with the declining fortunes of former petty tradespeople and their counterparts in the manual trades, created new migratory pressures. The relative freedom to leave provincial towns and resettle in cities within Central and Eastern Europe fed the creation of a new urban laboring class. Not yet an industrial working class in classic terms, Jewish working-class men, women, and children were far more likely than non-Jews to work in small shops and non-mechanized plants; they were very unlikely to be employed alongside non-Jews. Eventually they began to organize in strikes and embryonic labor unions, placing them within a European-wide labor and socialist movement, though retaining primarily Jewish occupational ties.

As the availability of migration routes further west expanded, particularly to the United States but also to England, France, South Africa, and Argentina (in addition to new migration to Palestine that picked up after the 1870s), younger age cohorts, totaling some 2.5 million up through the 1920s, left Eastern Europe in search of better conditions abroad. These immigrants, mainly working-age adults and younger families, found employment in small manufacture, the food, clothing, and building trades, and petty commerce. Because of their younger-than-average age distribution, their labor market participation was especially high. By the 1920s they had established the conditions for considerable upward mobility for their children via business, white-collar occupations, and the professions.

(C) Social status diversity notwithstanding, the great majority of Jews established class identities within Jewish employment networks, reflected in the retention of social barriers between Jews and non-Jews. Vertical ties within the Jewish sector, tying Jewish credit providers to Jewish entrepreneurs, and Jewish manufacturers to Jewish workers, competed powerfully with horizontal, non-sectarian class identities. The clustering of Jewish workers in Jewish-owned plants, for example, did lead some to espouse a class-antagonistic ideology that rendered traditional intra-communal bonds problematic, if not null and void; but the same conditions also

---

[10] Jewish population growth outpaced that of the general population in Romania, Habsburg Galicia (today southern Poland and Ukraine), and Russia until c. 1890, mainly due to a lower mortality rate among Jews, especially infant mortality.

eased the path for worker-entrepreneurs to work their way up within the ethnic enclave.

Thus, new Jewish middle classes and a Jewish haute bourgeoisie emerged in tandem with a Jewish working class. The various classes comprising Jewish societies made Jewish difference count in the public realm as in their private lives, though they did so in distinct ways. The haute bourgeoisie was active in high-profile communal projects such as erecting large and ornate new synagogues in high-rent districts, affecting a popular "oriental" or "Moorish" style of architecture, and filling these edifices with a class-appropriate piety of Jewish "high church" decorum. The workers who organized Jewish labor unions read a left-oriented Yiddish press for news, entertainment, and politics, and sponsored cooperative social, educational, recreational, and health services for their families. Middle-class Jews sponsored in-group outlets such as Jewish student fraternities, adult social clubs and political groupings, civic and intellectual associations, and an aesthetic culture of theater, art, music, and literary activity.

(D) Jewish class-conformity received expression in yet another sphere: that of the gendered division of middle-class consciousness. Modern market-based relations may be thought of as having two faces: one, a creative, innovative social creed dedicated to enhancing trust among strangers and to producing new goods and life-enhancing services; and the other, a capricious, exploitative pursuit of material values that is nearly always egoistic as a matter of principle. That duality was historically leveraged in Western bourgeois culture by invoking a distinction between men – tasked with becoming persons of substance – and women, tasked with the transubstantiation of matter into spirit. "The heroes of modern life exhibited prowess ... in the energetic but bloodless tournaments of commerce, industry, and politics .... [But] without the cult of womanliness, which was central to nineteenth-century bourgeois culture, the alibi for manly aggression remains incomplete."[11] It is in the domestic sphere that impersonal and amoral market calculations are subordinated to non-material values and given their moral justification as support for one's family.

As a general proposition, this has been confirmed as well for bourgeois Jewish families by feminist historians such as Paula Hyman and Marion Kaplan. Moreover, although we have had to abandon the archaic notion that middle-class Jewish women were economically passive, that does not

---

[11] Peter Gay, *The Bourgeois Experience, Victoria to Freud* (New York: W. W. Norton, 1993), vol. 3, 96.

materially diminish the significance of the domestic moral economy that middle-class Jewish families subscribed to along with their bourgeois peers. Women were meant to "bless" the household with those caring qualities held to be absent in the market and, thus, to provide a haven from its rigors, but also the necessary emotional and cultural reinforcement for their husbands and children to compete successfully outside the home. Women were the gatekeepers of taste and decency, fashion, aesthetic decorum, diversion, grace and desire, faith, piety and charitableness.

The framing of culture and spirit as matriarchal went against the grain of Jewish patriarchal codes, but Jews did adopt this new gendering pattern. As the trend toward a spiritualized femininity progressed, acculturating middle-class Jews (like their Christian peers) were disposed to assign core religious activities such as prayer and religious education more and more to women and children.

JEWISH ADAPTATIONS

By the early twentieth century, Jews might be observed around the world adapting to local economic developments and seeking to realign their social status with their non-Jewish peers. At the same time, Jews along with others faced huge challenges in modern economic relations and sought suitable ways to frame these issues and resolve them.

A large proportion of the world Jewish population at that time was weak in industrial skills and relatively poor in technological education and other higher-educational assets. Among mass concentrations of Jewish populace, such as the millions who lived in Eastern Europe, many if not most households were chronically overextended due to a relatively high number of non-working dependents per income producer. A substantial part of the several-million-strong stream of Jews heading toward new shores could be defined as political or economic refugees. The objective and perceived reality as summarized here drove the agendas of a plethora of organizations, social movements, a worldwide press and an engaged public.

Among the more interesting innovations in class relations that inspired the efforts and imaginations of large numbers of Jews, two that might be cited in particular are: industrial unionism in the United States and workers' and farmers' communes in Palestine. Jews neither "invented" these basic ideas nor did they grow out of previous Jewish historical experience. On the contrary, both represented adaptations to novel circumstances. And yet Jews were prominently identified with both of these historic innovations.

Industrial unionism emerged as a radical alternative to craft unions. The latter, which represented the mainstream of American labor organizations since the mid-nineteenth century, were based on a membership of skilled workers, divided by particular crafts. They tended to be socially conservative and sought primarily to defend and control professional standards, restrict the entry of new workingmen into the craft, and maintain the elevated pay scales that distinguished them from the large population of unskilled and semi-skilled workers located below them on the social ladder. The industrial unions, in contrast, grew out of labor opposition groups. They regarded all workers in a plant or branch of industry as belonging to one class, regardless of craft or skill, and organized strikes and wage agreements on a mass scale. During the era of mass migration, industrial unionism posed a critical challenge not just to the native American labor movement but also to the norms and practices of American free enterprise.

The two largest and most influential Jewish-led unions in the United States – the International Ladies Garment Workers' Union (ILGWU) and the Amalgamated Clothing Workers of America (ACWA) – were early pioneers and important advocates of industrial unionism. The Jewish role in both ACWA and the ILGWU was significant at the rank-and-file level as well as in the leadership echelon, given the large proportion of Jewish workers who were involved in the garment trades. Accordingly, many of both the unions' locals were Yiddish-speaking, at least in the early phases of the unions' history.[12]

What was equally significant, however, is that neither ACWA nor the ILGWU sought to maintain themselves as ethnic labor organizers. Rather, both of them successfully pursued a multi-ethnic (and interracial) mobilization strategy that placed class solidarity ahead of ethnic solidarity. Industrial unionism, with its appeal to those labor strata most regarded by other Americans as alien, racially stigmatized, radical, un-American, and "unorganizable," was also an avenue for the integration of Jewish with non-Jewish workers in a manner and on a scale unheard of in centers of Jewish labor activity in contemporary England, France, or Poland.

During the same period, a small but ongoing stream of Jewish immigrants – mainly from Eastern Europe (Romania, Poland, and Russia), Central Asia (Bukhara, Kurdistan) and the Middle East (Yemen) – augmented the

---

[12] It has long been supposed that Jewish immigrants became garment workers in the US because most of them were tailors from Russia, Romania, or Austria-Hungary; but many Jews in fact arrived without any particular skill and many others were required to adapt old skills they had plied in a handicrafts economy to the industrial conditions that prevailed in American manufacturing. Indeed, garment work, a major employer in American cities where Jewish immigrant families clustered, actually employed a greater proportion of Jewish immigrants' adolescent and adult children (none of whom were tailors or seamstresses to begin with) than it did among the adult immigrants themselves.

Jewish population already living in Ottoman Palestine. Debates over public policy and social ideology had raged in Jewish circles since the 1860s over how to "productivize" Palestinian Jewry and bring Western-style modernization to its health and education services. By the outbreak of World War I, the Palestine Jewish community (*yishuv*) numbered some 90,000 inhabitants (double its size in 1890), of which about 14 percent were living in rural communities.

Jewish land purchases and land use were coordinated through a group of public bodies established initially by Jews in Central and Eastern Europe (later expanded around the world) and directed locally by the Palestine Office of the World Zionist Organization. The establishment of a new (or renewed) Jewish society on such a footing as would benefit world Jewry at large – viewed, as noted, as requiring economic rehabilitation – required basic economic planning and policies. Given the economic weakness of the large reservoir of potential Jewish immigrants to Palestine, two interrelated goals were identified quite early: The sort of society envisioned for the future development of the *yishuv* had to include features of economic self-sufficiency, which could, of itself, become a powerfully motivating factor to attract Jews from the lower strata to immigrate and populate the community. To this end, it was necessary to avoid the creation of a planter-aristocracy that would dominate the top of the social pyramid while those at the widest part of the base were fated to depend on world Jewish largesse.

It may be argued that the social paradigm thus described vaguely recalled pre-modern patterns of Jewish social differentiation, insofar as pre-modern Jewries likewise possessed neither serfs nor lords. What is far more likely, as an immediate explanation of Jewish public policy in Palestine, is that social class engineering in the modern spirit took precedence over ethno-cultural legacies. The Jews involved in the Zionist project had benefited from over a century of progressive social and economic reform debates in the West, nearly everywhere demanding that paramount attention be paid to land reform and income redistribution. Coming late to the task of social engineering, Zionist leaders followed and adapted a path already well marked though (it must be admitted) scarcely, if at all, achieved in already functioning national economies. Indeed, the nationalization of Jewish land-ownership as a key public resource for the Zionist project was a precedent for other post-colonial societies later in the twentieth century.

More experiments in class relations and political economy were to follow. Chiefly in the years following 1905, a small but vocal cadre of young Jewish radicals and political refugees from imperial Russia brought with them a repertoire of egalitarian and communitarian principles. Their presence in the country, combined with the available public-owned lands, made it possible over the ensuing decade for several new communal models to emerge: mobile labor communes of worker "brigades" who undertook construction, road-clearing, and agricultural work; egalitarian farm communes (*kvutsot*) and collective farms (*kibbutzim*), as well as cooperative smallholder villages (moshavim). Rural communes had been a regular if marginal feature of sectarian and utopian collectives in Russia, Europe, and North America for decades. Jewish adaptations sought to reconcile the small-scale ideals of face-to-face egalitarian communitarian groups with the larger questions of class relations within a strategy of national welfare.

In the 1920s, the egalitarian model was expanded to the urban manufacturing sector, where the nascent Labor Federation (Histadrut) championed worker-managed cooperative enterprises as the progressive path toward combining modern industrial development with a worker-dominated society.

The cataclysmic events of the twentieth century – World War I, the Bolshevik Revolution in Russia, the Great Depression, World War II and the Holocaust, the establishment of the State of Israel – obviously altered the contours of Jewish lives around the world. It would require a great deal more detailed discussion to integrate these far-reaching changes into our analysis, but a few summary remarks are in order.

World War I and its aftermath brought new nation-states into being where previously empires had ruled, and this new political dispensation often had economic and social-class repercussions – not least, for the Jews. There are significant class-related aspects in the Jews' experience of Soviet rule. The rather sweeping *embourgeoisement* of America's Jews from the 1920s through the 1950s is a much-discussed topic in US social and ethnic studies.

Other topics whose mention is merited are the class-adjustments (usually downward) made by refugees, such as Jews who left Central Europe in the 1930s, Holocaust survivors in the early post-war years, Jewish refugees from Arab lands in Israel in the 1950s, and post-Soviet Jewish émigrés in the 1990s in Israel and the West. In the present limited context, however, an exhaustive catalogue of these and other class-inflected topics is neither possible nor required. My aim has been merely to juxtapose diverse trends across a span of places and times and in doing so to reveal some particular complexities as well as overall patterns.

As outlined above, the topic of Jews and social class has two possible routes of analysis: Jewish marginality and Jewish class formation and integration. Both have their particular uses for historians of modern Jewry and modern class relations. Both constructs are rooted not only in long-standing arguments over the definition and historical relevance of "class," but also in a binary distinction between pre-modern and modern conditions – and as such they are abstractions rather than "pure" empirical claims. In nearly all cases – not just the Jewish one – it would be imperative to point to the uneven, non-linear quality of social transitions such as the one entailed in the move toward market relations.

These disclaimers notwithstanding, it would accord well with the historical record to say that social class has been an increasingly salient factor in modern Jewish life. Contrasting the typical medieval situation of the Jews with typically modern ones, we might observe that although a modern Jew's Jewishness may still have been his or her calling card, it surely has ceased over time to be their "job description."

SELECT BIBLIOGRAPHY

Arendt, Hannah. *The Origins of Totalitarianism*. New York and London: Harcourt Brace Jovanovich, 1973 [1951].

Avni, Haim. *Mibitul ha`inkvizitsiah ve'ad hok hashvut: toledot hahagirah hayehudit le`argentinah*. Jerusalem: Magnes Press/Hebrew University, 1982.

Barkai, Avraham, *Branching Out: German-Jewish Immigration to the United States 1820–1914*. New York: Holmes and Meier, 1994.

Baron, Salo W. "Modern Capitalism and Jewish Fate," *The Menorah Journal* 30 (1942), republished in idem, *History and Jewish Historians: Essays and Addresses*. Philadelphia: Jewish Publication Society, 1964, pp. 43–64.

"Newer Approaches to Jewish Emancipation," *Diogenes* 8 (1960): 56–81.

A Social and Religious History of the Jews, vol. XII: Economic Catalyst. New York: Columbia University Press and Philadelphia: Jewish Publication Society, 1967.

Benayoun, Chantal, Alain Medam, and Pierre-Jacques Rojtman, eds. *Les juifs et l'économique, miroirs et mirages*. Toulouse: Presses Universitaires du Mirail, 1992.

Benbassa, Esther and Aron Rodrigue, *Sephardi Jewry: A History of the Judeo-Spanish Community, 14th–20th Centuries*. Berkeley: University of California Press, 1995.

Ben-Sasson, Menahem ed. *Dat vekhalkalah: yahasei gomlin*. Jerusalem: Mercaz Zalman Shazar, 1995.

Birnbaum, Pierre and Ira Katznelson, eds. *Paths of Emancipation: Jews, States and Citizenship*. Princeton: Princeton University Press, 1995.

Bush, Olga. "The Architecture of Jewish Identity: The Neo-Islamic Central Synagogue of New York," *Journal of the Society of Architectural Historians* 63, no. 2 (2004): 180–201.

Carlebach, Elisheva. *Divided Souls: Converts from Judaism in Early Modern German Lands, 1500–1750*. New Haven: Yale University Press, 2001.

Cesarani, David, ed. *Port Jews: Jewish Communities in Cosmopolitan Maritime Trading Centres, 1550–1950*. London: Frank Cass, 2002.

Cesarani, David and Gemma Romain, eds. *Jews and Port Cities, 1590–1990: Commerce, Community and Cosmopolitanism*. London and Portland, OR: Valentine Mitchell, 2006.

Diner, Hasia. *Roads Taken: The Great Jewish Migrations to the New World and the Peddlers Who Forged the Way*. New Haven: Yale University Press, 2015.

Endelman, Todd M. *The Jews of Georgian England 1714–1830. Tradition and Change in a Liberal Society.* Philadelphia: Jewish Publication Society, 1979.
— ed. *Jewish Apostasy in the Modern World.* New York and London: Holmes and Meier, 1987.
Fortune, Stephen A. *Merchants and Jews: The Struggle for British West Indian Commerce, 1650–1750.* Gainesville, FL: University of Florida Press, 1984.
Gay, Peter. *The Bourgeois Experience, Victoria to Freud.* New York: W. W. Norton, 1993.
— *Schnitzler's Century: The Making of Middle-Class Culture 1815–1914.* New York: W. W. Norton, 2002.
Gellner, Ernest. *Nations and Nationalism.* Oxford: Basil Blackwell, 1983.
Hyman, Paula E. *The Emancipation of the Jews of Alsace: Acculturation and Tradition in the Nineteenth Century.* New Haven: Yale University Press, 1991.
— *Gender and Assimilation in Modern Jewish History: The Roles and Representations of Jewish Women.* Seattle: University of Washington Press, 1995.
Israel, Jonathan. *Diasporas Within a Diaspora: Jews, Crypto-Jews and the World Maritime Empires (1540–1740).* Leiden: Brill, 2002.
— *European Jewry in the Age of Mercantilism, 1550–1750.* Oxford: Clarendon Press, 1985.
Kahan, Arcadius. *Essays in Jewish Social and Economic History.* Chicago: University of Chicago Press, 1986.
Kaplan, Dana Evan. "Conversion to Judaism in America 1760–1897," Ph.D. Diss., Tel Aviv University, 1994.
Kaplan, Marion A. *The Making of the Jewish Middle Class: Women, Family, and Identity in Imperial Germany.* New York: Oxford University Press, 1991.
Karp, Jonathan. *The Politics of Jewish Commerce. Economic Thought and Emancipation in Europe, 1638–1848.* New York: Cambridge University Press, 2008.
Klier, John Doyle. *Russia Gathers Her Jews: The Origins of the "Jewish Question" in Russia, 1772–1825.* Dekalb: Northern Illinois University Press, 1986.
Kobrin, Rebecca, ed. *Chosen Capital: The Jewish Encounter with American Capitalism.* New Brunswick: Rutgers University Press, 2012.
— and Adam Teller, eds. *Purchasing Power: The Economics of Modern Jewish History.* Philadelphia: University of Pennsylvania Press, 2015.
Kuznets, Simon. "Economic Structure and Life of the Jews," in *The Jews: Their History, Culture, and Religion,* ed. Louis Finkelstein. Philadelphia: Jewish Publication Society, 1966 [1949], vol. 2, pp. 1597–1666.
Lederhendler, Eli. *Jewish Immigrants and American Capitalism 1880–1920: From Caste to Class.* Cambridge: Cambridge University Press, 2009.
Lerner, L. Scott. "The Narrating Architecture of Emancipation," *Jewish Social Studies* 6, no. 3 (2000): 1–30.
MacCagg, Jr., William O. *A History of Habsburg Jews, 1670–1918.* Bloomington and Indianapolis: Indiana University Press, 1989.
Mekel, Sonja L. "'Salvation Comes from America': The United States in the *Allgemeine Zeitung des Judenthums,*" *American Jewish Archives Journal* 60, nos. 1–2 (2008): 1–23.
Mendelsohn, Adam D. *The Rag Race: How Jews Sewed Their Way to Success in America and the British Empire.* New York: New York University Press, 2015.
Mendelsohn, Ezra. *Class Struggle in the Pale.* Cambridge: Cambridge University Press, 1970.

Nadell, Pamela S. and Jonathan D. Sarna, eds. *Women and American Judaism: Historical Perspectives*. Hanover, NH: University Press of New England, 2001.

Penslar, Derek J. *Shylock's Children. Economics and Jewish Identity in Modern Europe*. Berkeley: University of California Press, 2001.

Pipes, Richard. "Catherine II and the Jews," *Soviet Jewish Affairs* 5 (1975): 3–20.

Raphaël, Freddy. *Judaisme et capitalisme*. Paris: Presses Universitaires de France, 1982.

Reddy, William M. "The Concept of Class," in *Social Orders and Social Classes in Europe since 1500: Studies in Social Stratification*, ed. M. L. Bush. London and New York: Longman, 1992, pp. 13–25.

Reuveni, Gideon. *Consumer Culture and the Making of Modern Jewish Identity*. New York: Cambridge University Press, forthcoming 2017.

and Nils Roemer, eds. *Longing, Belonging, and the Making of Jewish Consumer Culture*. Leiden: Brill, 2010.

and Sarah Wobick-Segev, eds. *The Economy in Jewish History: New Perspectives on the Interrelationship between Ethnicity and Economic Life*. New York: Berghahn Books, 2011.

Ruppin, Arthur. *Hasotsiologiah shel hayehudim*. Tel Aviv and Berlin: Shtiebl, 1932.

Schorsch, Ismar. "Emancipation and the Crisis of Religious Authority: The Emergence of the Modern Rabbinate," in *Revolution and Evolution: 1848 in German-Jewish History*, ed. Werner Mosse, Arnold Paucker, and Reinhard Rürup. Tübingen: Mohr, 1981.

Shulvass, Moses A. *From East to West. The Westward Migration of Jews from Eastern Europe During the Seventeenth and Eighteenth Centuries*. Detroit: Wayne State University Press, 1971.

Sonnenberg-Stern, Karina. *Emancipation and Poverty: The Ashkenazi Jews of Amsterdam, 1796–1850*. London: Macmillan, 2000.

Sorkin, David. "The Port Jew: Notes Towards a Social Type," *Journal of Jewish Studies* 50, no. 1 (1999): 87–97.

Stampfer, Shaul. *Hayeshivah halita`it behithavutah*. Jerusalem: Mercaz Shazar, 2005.

Stanislawski, Michael. *Tsar Nicholas I and the Jews*. Philadelphia: Jewish Publication Society, 1983.

Toch, Michael. "Aspects of Stratification of Early Modern German Jewry: Population History and Village Jews," in *Peasants and Jews in Medieval Germany*. Aldershot: Ashgate, 2003, pp. 77–89.

Vital, David. *A People Apart: The Jews in Europe, 1789–1939*. Oxford: Oxford University Press, 1999.

Wertheimer, Jack. *Unwelcome Strangers: East European Jews in Imperial Germany*. New York: Oxford University Press, 1987.

Zipperstein, Steven J. *The Jews of Odessa: A Cultural History 1794–1881*. Stanford: Stanford University Press, 1985.

CHAPTER 17

EDUCATION AND THE POLITICS OF JEWISH INTEGRATION

GARY B. COHEN

The sweeping social transformation experienced by Jews after the late eighteenth century included radical changes in educational patterns. Over the long nineteenth century, Jews in Europe, the Mediterranean, and the Atlantic world gradually adopted secular schooling and, where possible, attendance of general public schools. In many countries, Jewish enrollments grew rapidly in secular secondary and higher education after the 1840s and 1850s. In the process, Jews came to participate in the general expansion of primary education in Western societies and the growth of secondary and higher education and the white-collar and professional occupations which depend upon advanced education. Inseparable from the rapid increases in Jews' enrollments at all levels of public education were their growing numbers in white-collar employment, semi-professional pursuits, and the learned professions.

As this chapter will discuss, so strong was this development that by the early twentieth century Jews were significantly overrepresented among students in higher education, white-collar employment, and the professions relative to their share of the total population in most Western countries which had an appreciable Jewish presence. It is tempting to attribute this development in great part to the traditional Jewish respect for religious study, but a closer examination shows that the strong Jewish presence by 1900 in advanced secular education and educated and semi-educated occupations in many lands was not a simple, direct consequence of that tradition. In fact, Jews' overrepresentation in advanced education and educated pursuits can only be understood as a fundamentally modern phenomenon, part of the larger social and economic changes after the early nineteenth century, which produced a growing migration of Jews from traditional smaller communities to larger urban centers and new lands and the abandonment of many of their typical pre-modern occupations. All those changes, of which the growing presence of Jews in educated and semi-educated professions was only a salient aspect, transformed the terms of Jews' social and cultural interactions with non-Jews.

The changes in educational patterns contributed significantly to secularization and the erosion of many distinctive Jewish traditions. In fact, most of the statesmen and intellectuals who first advocated the integration of Jews into public educational systems during the late eighteenth and early nineteenth centuries intended to advance Jews' acculturation and eventual assimilation. Yet even though greater integration into non-Jewish society was a major purpose for offering Jews secular public education and new professional opportunities, the growing numbers who followed that path provoked vocal resentment in Central Europe by the last third of the nineteenth century and eventually called for new discriminatory measures and the restriction of opportunities for Jews in advanced education and the professions. Those sentiments soon found echoes in Western and Eastern Europe and North America.

The changes in Jews' educational patterns and the increasing number of those who entered white-collar employment and learned professions had many aspects that were specific to Jews, but these developments were integrally connected to larger processes of social and economic transformation that affected non-Jews as well. Economic development, technological advance, and the changing obligations of citizens in modern states all required high levels of general literacy and increases in primary, secondary, and higher education. Over the course of the nineteenth and twentieth centuries, the rising educational requirements of advancing industrial and commercial enterprises, the growing private service and professional sectors, and expanding government bureaucracy caused more and more youth after the 1880s and 1890s in many parts of Europe and North America to seek longer years of schooling, first among males, but increasingly among females as well. Industrialization and modern economic development caused a substantial growth in secondary and higher education and of popular demand for it across social classes even if the costs of advanced education and limited access to institutions created barriers for many. In many parts of Eastern Europe, North Africa, and the Middle East, however, where modern economic development proceeded more slowly, and Jewish traditions of religious studies remained strong, the demand among Jews for more secular education came at first as much or more from females than from males.

In all modern societies the state has treated the development of education as a matter of great political import, and since the late eighteenth century governments have played a powerful role in initiating and directing educational change. Proponents of enlightened absolutist reform in continental Europe committed their governments to expanding primary education in order to achieve general literacy, form a more useful and reliable citizenry, and assure adequate numbers of trained professionals. The American and French revolutions incorporated the goal of universal primary education into their egalitarian and democratic ideological frameworks. Continental European governments made efforts after the late eighteenth century to raise intellectual standards in secondary and higher education and make the curricula appropriate to contemporary needs, although they generally viewed advanced education as necessary only for elite groups who were to serve as government officials, clergy, physicians, lawyers, and educators.

Wherever Jews constituted a visible part of the population, enlightened reformers took up the questions of their education and relationship with the rest of society. Most who addressed this issue, in fact, considered Jews as fundamentally inferior and Jewish religious traditions as an impediment to progress, but the reformers argued for lifting many of the old legal restrictions in order to improve Jews' degraded conditions and make them more useful to the state and the larger society. Encouraging, indeed requiring, Jews to have more modern secular education was critical to achieving aims of the state and advancing broader social interests. The Habsburg emperor Joseph II summed up the purposes of the reforming statesmen with respect to ending the disabilities of Jews in his 1782 "Edict of Tolerance" for Lower Austria:

We have directed Our most preeminent attention to the end that all Our subjects without distinction of nationality and religion, once they have been admitted and tolerated in Our state, shall participate in common in public welfare, the increase of which is Our care, shall enjoy legal freedom and not find any obstacles in any honest ways of gaining their livelihood and increasing general industriousness.[1]

Characteristically, the "Edict of Tolerance" improved the legal rights of "officially tolerated" Jews but left in place most restrictions on where Jews might legally reside. As part of his reforms, the Habsburg emperor required Jews either to attend Christian primary schools or to establish their own; and he opened university studies to them.

European governments of the late eighteenth and early nineteenth centuries created dilemmas for both their Jewish subjects and themselves, however, when they pushed for modern secular education for Jews and their greater integration into society. Jews welcomed relief from the legal and economic disabilities, but most initially feared that government-mandated educational reform and greater social integration would erode

---

[1] Joseph II, "Edict of Tolerance" (January 2, 1782), in Paul Mendes-Flohr and Jehuda Reinharz, eds, *The Jew in the Modern World*, 2nd edition (New York: Oxford University Press, 1995), 36.

their religious traditions and were so intended. In their time Moses Mendelssohn (1729–1786) and other early voices of the Haskalah stood in the minority among Jewish thinkers and communal leaders in advocating the pursuit of both Jewish religious wisdom and secular learning. Jews also had to consider that through the early nineteenth century Christian clergy were responsible for providing much of general primary education in continental Europe and the British Isles and included Christian religious instruction and prayer as integral to schooling.

The Habsburg government was one of the pioneers in Europe in permitting Jews to attend the same primary and secondary schools as non-Jews and in admitting Jews to university faculties of law and medicine. Still, until the 1860s and later in some regions, the great majority of Jewish children in the Habsburg realm did not attend Catholic or secular public primary schools. For the separate Jewish primary schools, Habsburg regulations required a modern curriculum taught in the officially mandated vernacular language, i.e., German in much of the western territories. A number of German states reintroduced social and economic restrictions on Jews after the emancipatory measures of the Napoleonic era, but Baden in 1809, Bavaria in 1813, the Hessian states in 1817–23, Prussia in 1824, and Württemberg in 1825 enacted requirements for primary education for Jews, whether in separate Jewish schools or together with Christian pupils in general state schools. In many German states, as in the Habsburg Monarchy, the ability of Jews to study in universities was established as a principle during the first half of the nineteenth century, with medicine attracting the most Jewish students. While much primary education for Jews in the Habsburg Monarchy and the German states still took place in separate Jewish schools during the first third of the century, the inclusion of modern secular subjects in their curricula was well established by the 1830s and 1840s.[2]

With the partitions of Poland at the end of the eighteenth century, the government of tsarist Russia confronted the sudden addition to its population of a large mass of Jewish subjects. From the time of Tsar Alexander I to the reform era under Alexander II, the government worked to impose its administration and laws on the Jewish population and to break down

---

[2] Werner E. Mosse, "From 'Schutzjuden' to 'Deutsche Staatsbürger Jüdischen Glaubens': The Long and Bumpy Road of Jewish Emancipation in Germany," in *Paths of Emancipation: Jews, States, and Citizenship*, ed. Pierre Birnbaum and Ira Katznelson (Princeton: Princeton University Press, 1995), 78–79; David Sorkin, *The Transformation of German Jewry, 1780–1840* (Oxford: Oxford University Press, 1987), 124–130; and Simone Lässig, *Jüdische Wege ins Bürgertum. Kulturelles Kapital und sozialer Aufstieg im 19. Jahrhundert* (Göttingen: Vandenhoeck und Ruprecht, 2004), 113–183.

many of the divisions between Jews and non-Jews, while recognizing that the reality of religious differences required some treatment for Jews distinct from Russian Orthodox subjects, just like the Catholics and Lutherans in the western provinces. The tsarist government in its 1804 "Statute on the Jews" set out the principle that Jews might enroll in all primary schools, gymnasia, and universities and receive university degrees, but until the late nineteenth century the overwhelming majority of Jewish boys continued to attend *chederim* operated by their own local communities where they received basic instruction in Judaism and Hebrew.

The government of Tsar Nicholas I continued to restrict Jews' residence to the Pale of Settlement established under Catherine II but sought to break down many of the old legal and cultural divisions between Jews and their Christian neighbors. In 1827 the government revoked Jews' exemption as members of the merchant class from military conscription. In the 1830s and 1840s, it looked to a tacit alliance with maskilim such as Max Lilienthal to introduce modern secular subjects into Jewish education. The state authorities established in cities and towns of the Pale new state-sponsored separate primary, secondary, and rabbinical schools with strong secular elements in their curricula. The alien and secularizing character of these Crown Schools aroused hostility among the Jewish populace and rabbis, and they never attracted more than a few thousand students at any one time. The government finally gave up on the system of Crown Schools for Jews in 1873. By then, however, the larger processes of demographic, social, and economic change in the empire were causing slowly growing numbers of Jews to seek secular primary schooling and advanced education in the state gymnasia and universities to gain access to new professional pursuits.[3]

The Ottoman Empire preserved a tradition of separate schools for its Jewish subjects much longer than did any of the major states of Western or Eastern Europe. Under the *millet* system for non-Muslim subjects, the various religious communities had responsibility for the schooling of their members as part of each *millet's* autonomy. Western-inspired governmental reforms during the mid-nineteenth century aimed at centralizing and regularizing administration, ending corruption, and treating all subjects as equals. The push toward the principle of civil equality reached its pinnacle in the 1869 law on citizenship, which granted equal citizen's rights

[3] See John D. Klier, *Imperial Russia's Jewish Question, 1855–1981* (Cambridge: Cambridge University Press, 1995), 6–9, 222–244; Michael Stanislawski, "Russian Jewry, the Russian State, and the Dynamics of Jewish Emancipation," in *Paths of Emancipation*, ed. Birnbaum and Katznelson, 266–276; and idem, *Tsar Nicholas I and the Jews: The Transformation of Jewish Society in Russia, 1825–1855* (Philadelphia: Jewish Publication Society, 1983).

to all regardless of religion and established a direct relationship between the state administration and each citizen. Nonetheless, much of the legal system retained its religious foundations and distinctions. The Tanzimat decrees of 1839 did not address issues of education and allowed the semi-autonomous *millet* structures to continue. The *millet* authorities still operated separate systems of schools for their respective religious communities.[4] Some specialized institutions of higher education were open to students of all religions from the late eighteenth century, but the Ottoman state began only in the early 1860s to operate public secondary schools where students of different religions might study together. Through the last decades of the empire and into the early decades of the Turkish Republic, youth of different religions in the main still attended separate primary schools operated by their own religious communities; and much of secondary education also remained religiously segregated.

During the nineteenth and early twentieth centuries, reform initiatives in primary and secondary education for Jews in the Ottoman Empire and in much of North Africa as well came largely from within the Jewish population and were typically implemented in separate Jewish institutions. For Jews as well as Christians in these lands, adopting modern forms of education largely meant following Western European models. Some Jewish communities reformed existing local Jewish schools while others opened new ones on Western lines. More often during the mid and late nineteenth century, Jews in the Ottoman territories and North Africa who wanted modern schooling sent their children to new schools developed with foreign initiative or assistance, including many Catholic and Protestant missionary schools, but more frequently after the 1860s schools affiliated with the Alliance Israèlite Universelle (AIU), headquartered in France.[5]

The schools of the AIU followed French educational models and offered study of French and secular subjects. The AIU, however, typically negotiated the curriculum with local Jewish communities and offered religious instruction along with the secular subjects, particularly in lands like

---

[4] Aron Rodrigue, "From Millet to Minority: Turkish Jewry," in *Paths of Emancipation*, Birnbaum and Katznelson, 242–246; idem, *French Jews, Turkish Jews: The Alliance Israelite Universelle and the Politics of Jewish Schooling in Turkey, 1860–1925* (Bloomington: Indiana University Press, 1990), 25–46. See also Esther Benbassa and Aron Rodrigue, *The Jews of the Balkans: The Judeo-Spanish Community, 15th to 20th Centuries* (Oxford: Blackwell, 1995), 65–115.

[5] Norman A. Stillman, "Middle Eastern and North African Jewries Confront Modernity. Orientation, Disorientation, Reorientation," in *Sephardi and Middle Eastern Jewries: History and Culture in the Modern Era*, ed. Harvey E. Goldberg (Bloomington: Indiana University Press, 1996), 64.

Morocco, where traditional piety remained strong. By the first decades of the twentieth century, the primary and secondary schools of the AIU had achieved enormous reach and influence among Jews in the former Ottoman territories in the eastern Mediterranean, parts of the Balkans, and many parts of North Africa, despite rabbinical hostility in many places to modern secular studies. Few AIU schools developed in Algeria, which France only conquered in the 1830s and then integrated more thoroughly into metropolitan France. Algerian Jews, who were French citizens after 1870, sent their children to French public schools.

During the 1920s in republican Turkey, the AIU schools' connections with French Jewish circles and French education and their success in propagating the French language provoked strong government measures to cut the ties to France, impose greater local Turkish control and a state-mandated curriculum, and increase significantly the teaching of Turkish. Similar measures against AIU schools followed in other Muslim lands. Growing numbers of Jews in Turkey, Egypt, and Iraq attended state schools from the early twentieth century until the founding of the State of Israel and the mass emigration of Jews after the late 1940s. Elsewhere, Muslim opposition to having Jewish children taught in the same schools as Muslim children remained strong throughout the early and mid-twentieth century.[6]

France and the United States were the earliest among major Western countries to grant Jews general equality of rights as citizens and to open up far-reaching opportunities in public education. After heated debates during the first phase of the French revolution about the civic rights of Jews, all Jews in France gained full citizenship in the autumn of 1791. Leading Jewish figures in France, particularly among the Sephardic communities, welcomed equal rights as citizens and supported the adoption of French civic culture and, more gradually, the pursuit of secular learning. Napoleon Bonaparte's reimposition of some restrictions on occupations and movement briefly slowed the processes of acculturation, but the principle of complete equality for Jews was fully established under the July Monarchy after 1830. During the Napoleonic era, Jews slowly began to move from their traditional occupations into new commercial and artisanal pursuits, and some families in central and southern France began to send their children to local public primary schools. The great majority of French Jews, however, and certainly the more conservative Ashkenazim in

---

[6] Rachel Simon, "Education," in *The Jews of the Middle East and North Africa in Modern Times*, ed. Reeva S. Simon, Michael M. Laskier, and Sara Reguier (New York: Columbia University Press, 2003), 142–164.

Alsace, continued through the middle of the century to send their children to separate Jewish primary schools and to engage in the old occupations.

With encouragement from the Jewish consistories as well as the central government, many Jewish schools in France took major steps to modernize their curriculum after the end of the Napoleonic wars; and local Jewish communities founded a number of new schools. The Guizot law of 1833, which required universal primary education, also mandated local government support for the Jewish schools.[7] By the 1830s and 1840s *lycées* in various parts of France were accommodating Jewish students, and the number of Jewish students slowly began to grow in institutions of higher education.

With only around two thousand Jews in total in the thirteen American colonies in 1776, their status and rights were not a major concern for the founders of the United States. Nonetheless, various state governments guaranteed full freedom of worship and equal basic citizen's rights from early dates after independence. The federal constitution adopted in 1787 prohibited religious tests for public office, and the Bill of Rights added to the constitution in 1791 famously prohibited any federal legislation regarding an establishment of religion or infringing the free exercise of religion. Still, the American civic identity at the outset included a strong commitment to Protestant moral and religious values, and, as in Britain and Western Europe, many early oaths required for public office affirmed the Christian faith. It took decades for some of the American states to remove such language from their oaths.

Governmentally operated public schools in the United States were open to Jewish students, but until the second half of the nineteenth century their curricula commonly included Christian prayer and reading from the Christian Bible. In some parts of the country, this continued well into the twentieth century. During the early nineteenth century synagogues in the larger cities operated Jewish day schools as an alternative, and more Jewish day schools followed in the middle decades of the century, trying to keep up with the new waves of immigration from Central Europe. During the second half of the century, however, an increasing share of the Jewish children in the United States attended public primary schools; and at the end of the century, the great majority attended them rather than Jewish day

---

[7] See Paula E. Hyman, *The Jews of Modern France* (Berkeley: University of California Press, 1998), 30–70; and Pierre Birnbaum, "Between Social and Political Assimilation: Remarks on the History of Jews in France," in *Paths of Emancipation*, ed. Birnbaum and Katznelson, 94–127.

schools. By 1900 Jews counted among the strongest supporters of public nonsectarian education in America.[8]

A great expansion of public secondary and higher education characteristic of advanced industrial societies began in Europe and North America during the late nineteenth century and continued throughout the twentieth century. With that development came a remarkable increase in Jewish enrollments in secondary schools and universities and eventually also growth in the Jewish presence among the educators as well. The increasing representation of Jews in European and North American secondary and higher education resulted from the same forces of general economic development, urbanization, professionalization, and the expansion of public and private bureaucracy which fueled the general growth of advanced education. Secondary education was a requirement not only for entry into universities and other institutions of higher education but also increasingly for specialized vocational training and for various skilled occupations. Still, the increase in Jewish enrollments had some causes and dimensions specific to Jewish experience. That there were specifically Jewish features in this development was obvious in the disproportionately strong representation of Jews by 1900 in secondary schools and higher education relative to their share of the general population in many of these countries.

Growth in Jewish enrollments in secondary and higher education and Jews' resulting overrepresentation compared to their share of the population was particularly striking in Central Europe between the 1860s and 1920s. Here final emancipation of the Jewish population coincided with a period of strong economic development, rapid growth in the educational systems, and the opening of many new opportunities in educated professional and semi-professional activities which offered Jews alternatives to their previously limited commercial and artisanal pursuits. In many cases, population growth and the decline of Jews' old economic niches in petty trade and middleman functions provided a strong impetus not only to migrate to larger urban centers but also to move into educated and semi-educated pursuits that were expanding rapidly and offered good economic prospects.

The government in the Austrian half of the Habsburg Monarchy, which included Galicia (southern Poland) as well as the Alpine and Bohemian crown lands, repealed the last discriminatory laws against Jews and other religious minorities as part of economic and constitutional reforms between 1859 and 1867. So strong was Jewish demand for academic secondary education here that already by the end of the 1860s Jewish students (*not* counting

---

[8] Hasia R. Diner, *The Jews of the United States, 1654 to 2000* (Berkeley: University of California Press, 2004), 58–60, 142–147.

those born Jewish who were registered as without religion or who had converted) comprised some 10 percent of all students in the Austrian gymnasia and *Realschulen*, twice their percentage of the total population. By 1910 the Jewish share of the students had grown even further, reaching 15 percent; and Jews were studying in academic secondary schools at more than three and one-half times the rate of Catholics relative to their population. Jews accounted for more than one-third of all the Gymnasium students in the capital, Vienna. Gymnasium and university studies first became available to women in Central Europe around 1900, and the strong overrepresentation of Jews among women in secondary schools in 1900 demonstrated the support of many Jewish parents for greater educational opportunities for daughters as well as sons. Forty-one percent of the students in the nine women's gymnasia in Galicia in 1910 were Jewish.[9]

In Austrian higher education, the Jewish portion of the student enrollments rose from 9 percent of all those in Austrian universities and 12 percent of the technical college students in 1856–57 to nearly 18 percent of all university students and 14 percent of all technical college students in 1909–10. The rate of Jewish university and technical college enrollment relative to Austria's total Jewish population ran three to four times the rate for Catholics over the four decades before World War I. Due to the better economic opportunities for Jews in medicine than in law, government service, or teaching in secondary schools between the 1860s and the 1880s, the majority of Austria's Jewish university students in that period studied in medical faculties. During the early 1880s Jewish enrollment in the medical faculty of the Vienna University, perhaps the most respected in all Europe, reached a high point of 50 percent of the total. Only after the 1890s did the numbers in the law and philosophy faculties grow to exceed those in medicine, as job opportunities for Jews in law, teaching, and the sciences began to increase. In the Hungarian half of the Habsburg Monarchy, Jews were overrepresented among students in secondary and higher education at the beginning of the twentieth century to an even higher degree.[10]

---

[9] Österreichische Statistik, *Neue Folge* 7, no. 3 (1913): 68–71; Gary B. Cohen, *Education and Middle-Class Society in Imperial Austria, 1848–1918* (West Lafayette, IN: Purdue University Press, 1996), 75, 146–147. See also Harriet P. Freidenreich, *Female, Jewish, and Educated: The Lives of Central European University Women*. Bloomington: Indiana University Press, 2002.

[10] Cohen, *Education and Middle-Class Society*, 147–149, 152–154, 159–161, 276–279; Victor Karady, "Jewish Enrollment Patterns in Classical Secondary Education in Old Regime and Inter-War Hungary," *Studies in Contemporary Jewry* 1 (1984): 225–252; and idem, *The Jews of Europe in the Modern Era: A Socio-Historical Outline* (Budapest and New York: Central European University Press, 2004), 90–91.

In parts of Germany during the last decades before 1914, the overrepresentation of Jews among secondary school and university students relative to the Jewish share of the population was even greater than in imperial Austria. Around 5 percent of the Berlin population in the late 1880s and 1890s was Jewish, but in 1887 21 percent of all the male gymnasium students there were Jews. Nearly one-third of all the girls who enrolled in gymnasium education in Berlin in the same year were Jews. That Jews comprised 10 percent of all university students in Prussia in 1886–87 compared to only 1 percent of the Prussian population attracted considerable public attention. The rate of Jewish university enrollments relative to the total Jewish population increased further between the mid-1880s and 1911–12, although increases for other groups, particularly Catholics, resulted in Jews accounting for only 5.6 percent of the Prussian university enrollments by the latter date. In that year Jews studied in Prussian universities at some five times the rate of the Protestant majority relative to population.[11]

During the late nineteenth century, Jewish attendance of general state secondary schools and universities grew strongly in the tsarist empire as well, despite continuing limitations on where Jews might reside and what occupations they could practice. Legally, Jews could study in state gymnasia and universities in the 1830s and 1840s; but official hostility and occupational restrictions for Jews limited actual enrollments to miniscule numbers at any time. By the late 1850s and early 1860s, the lure of improving economic opportunities and the opening of some state employment to Jews persuaded increasing numbers to study in gymnasia and universities. In November 1861, Tsar Alexander II approved a new law permitting Jews with university degrees to enter the civil service and to reside where they found employment on the same terms as non-Jews, although much resistance persisted thereafter to employing Jews in official posts. An 1864 measure regularized the admission of Jews to gymnasia. The numbers of Jewish students enrolled in gymnasia and progymnasia throughout the empire grew from a little more than 1 percent of the total in 1853 to nearly 4 percent in 1865, nearly 10 percent in 1876, and nearly 11 percent in 1886. By the mid-1870s the rate of Jewish enrollment in Russian secondary schools compared to the Jewish school-aged population was three and one-half

[11] Peter G. J. Pulzer, *The Rise of Political Anti-Semitism in Germany and Austria*, rev. ed. (Cambridge, MA: Harvard University Press, 1988), 10–12; Konrad H. Jarausch, "The Social Transformation of the University: The Case of Prussia, 1865–1914," *Journal of Social History* 12 (1979): 619–620; and idem, *Students, Society, and Politics in Imperial Germany* (Princeton, NJ: Princeton University Press, 1982), 96–100. For nineteenth and twentieth century Germany, see also Monika Richarz, *Der Eintritt der Juden in die akademischen Berufe* (Tübingen: Mohr, 1974).

times the rate of enrollment for Russian Orthodox youth. In the universities Jews comprised 3 percent of all students in 1865, 5 percent in 1876, and more than 14 percent in 1886, with Jews accounting for as much as 40 percent of the law and medical students in a few universities by the end of Alexander II's reign in 1881.[12]

Russian institutions of higher education began to grant degrees to women already in the 1870s, and Jews had strong representation among the women students from the outset. By the 1880s their numbers ranged between 16 and 34 percent of the enrollments in the women's programs in Kiev, Moscow, and St. Petersburg, outnumbering the women students from the Catholic, Lutheran, and Muslim minorities combined.[13]

The rapid growth in the Jewish presence in Russian secondary and higher education and in some learned professions after the 1860s both within the Pale of Settlement and elsewhere in Russia provoked hostility in conservative Russian circles. The reactionary government of Tsar Alexander III (1881–1894) took steps to limit Jewish enrollments in secondary and higher education; restrictions followed on the admission of Jews to the legal profession and certain areas of government employment.[14] After the mid-1880s Russian Jews, both male and female, who were determined to pursue higher education and could not pierce the barriers of the quota system had little choice but to go to universities in Western and Central Europe, if they could find the means. Restrictions on Jewish enrollments in Russian higher education relaxed during the unrest of 1905, permitting a sharp increase in the numbers of Jewish students; but the government of Nicholas II soon reimposed stringent formal quotas.[15]

During the last decades of the nineteenth century and first decades of the twentieth, Jewish representation in secondary and higher education and in the educated and semi-educated professions grew in Western Europe and North America as well, subject to local and national levels of economic development and the constraints of institutional frameworks for advanced education and the professions. In France during the nineteenth century, as in many Western and Central European countries, Jews achieved upward social mobility largely by advancing within commercial pursuits rather than outside.[16] Still, the numbers of Jews in French secondary and

---

[12] Benjamin Nathans, *Beyond the Pale: The Jewish Encounter with Late Imperial Russia* (Berkeley: University of California Press, 2002), 217–220; and Stanislawski, "Russian Jewry, the Russian State, and the Dynamics of Emancipation," 274–275.

[13] Nathans, *Beyond the Pale*, 224–225.

[14] Stanislawski, "Russian Jewry, the Russian State, and the Dynamics of Emancipation," 276–278; and Nathans, *Beyond the Pale*, 257–282.

[15] Nathans, *Beyond the Pale*, 295–301.

[16] Hyman, *The Jews of Modern France*, 60.

higher education grew relative to their population during the last decades of the century and into the early twentieth century. In England, Oxford and Cambridge excluded Jews from undergraduate studies until the 1850s. University College, London, admitted Jews from its founding in 1828, but few Jews attended the older British universities before the late nineteenth century. Jews began to study in prestigious "public" schools such as Eton and Harrow from the 1860s onward, and after the 1890s the numbers of Jewish students began to grow significantly in University College, London, other regional civic universities, and ultimately Oxford and Cambridge.[17] The slow development of publicly supported secondary education and the limited numbers of universities in Britain until after World War I slowed the growth of enrollments overall, certainly for the offspring of low status, lower income groups, compared to the more rapid growth of institutions and general enrollments in Germany, the Habsburg Monarchy, and the United States during the last third of the nineteenth century.[18]

In the United States, the strong growth of Jewish enrollments in secondary and higher education around 1900 soon included the children of recent immigrants. The numbers of Jewish students grew large by the early 1920s even in elite institutions such as the Ivy League universities. Columbia University in New York City had the highest Jewish enrollment with some 40 percent of the student body by the 1920s.[19] Medical schools across the country saw strong growth in the numbers of Jewish students between the 1890s and 1920s. In 1935, despite quotas on Jewish enrollments in many medical schools, Jews comprised some 13 percent of all first-year medical students in the United States.[20] The novelty and strength of the growing numbers of Jewish students seeking advanced education for professional careers, where there had been few just a few decades before, provoked a backlash among professional groups, other elites, and college administrators, who soon began to impose formal quotas on Jewish enrollments, whether openly or covertly. That negative response in the United States echoed similar reactions in Britain to the growing Jewish presence in higher education and the professions and the reactions which had already begun in Central Europe back in the 1880s.

---

[17] Endelman, *The Jews of Britain*, 97–99.

[18] Fritz K. Ringer, *Education and Society in Modern Europe* (Bloomington: Indiana University Press, 1979), 206–231.

[19] Seymour Martin Lipset, "A Unique People in an Exceptional Country," *Society* 28, no. 1 (1990): 8.

[20] Manisha Juthani, "A Comparison of Asian-American and American Jewish Involvement in the Medical Profession," *Journal of the American Medical Association* 277, no. 9 (1997): 769.

Indeed, the rapid increase in Jewish enrollments in secondary and higher education and the growing Jewish presence in educated and semi-educated professions in many Western countries during the late nineteenth and early twentieth centuries provoked hostility in many quarters. Old religious and economically based prejudices against Jews persisted in many places, but much of the reaction to the advance of Jews among the educated represented part of a fundamentally new phenomenon: a backlash to the complex social, political, and economic changes of advancing urbanized, industrial society which were changing the residential, social, and occupational positions of Jews as a side-effect. Just when these changes began varied from one country or region to another, but in many places over just a few decades new Jewish populations arose where they had not lived before or had been minuscule before the nineteenth century. At the same time educated and semi-educated professions were expanding at a particularly rapid pace and taking in Jewish recruits. New white-collar occupations also emerged, while many pursuits of the pre-industrial agricultural and craft economies shrank or disappeared, including many petty commercial and middleman functions in which Jews had engaged.

The new or increased presence of Jews in many industrializing cities and the visible upward mobility of some made them an obvious target for the resentments of many non-Jews toward aspects of the broader transformation of society. When the pace of economic development temporarily slackened, demand weakened, and prices fell, such as after the stock market crash of 1873 and during the agricultural crisis of the 1880s and early 1890s, calls went up in many European countries and North America for the protection of small producers, restrictions on immigration, and tighter regulation of finance and industry. In Central Europe and later France as well, nationalists and some Christian social politicians demanded new discriminatory measures against Jews, who appeared to have benefited from liberal economic development and political reform.[21]

The new political antisemitism of the industrial age emerged among the Central European middle classes and lower middle classes after the late 1870s aligned with a populist nationalist ideology. The influential

---

[21] Raymond J. Sontag, *Germany and England: Background of Conflict, 1848-1894* (New York: Appleton-Century, 1938), p. 146; Hans Rosenberg, "Political and Social Consequences of the Great Depression of 1873-1896 in Central Europe," *Economic History Review* 13, no. 1/2 (1943): 63. See also Albert Lichtblau, *Antisemitismus und soziale Spannung in Berlin und Wien, 1867-1914* (Berlin: Metropol, 1994); Bruce F. Pauley, *From Prejudice to Persecution: A History of Austrian Anti-Semitism* (Chapel Hill: University of North Carolina Press, 1991); and Michael Wladika, *Hitlers Vätergeneration: Die Ursprünge des Nationalsozialismus in der k.u.k. Monarchie* (Vienna: Böhlau, 2005).

historian at the Berlin University, Heinrich von Treitschke, published his famous essays under the title "A Word about Our Jews" ("Ein Wort über unser Judenthum") in 1879–80. From 1880 students in many universities across Germany and Austria began to found antisemitic German national-ist associations, and many existing student fraternities, including both the corps and *Burschenschaften*, soon adopted rules to exclude Jews. Between the 1850s and 1880s Jews had been able to gain positions as assistants, *Dozenten*, and even professors in German and Austrian universities, although it was typically easier in medicine, the natural sciences, and law than in the humanities, and easier in Prussia, Baden, and Austria than elsewhere in the German states. The rise of political antisemitism after the early 1880s gradually made it more difficult for Jews to gain appointments in many German universities and the Vienna University, although it still remained possible. In German universities, Jews comprised some 13 per-cent of the faculty members in medicine and 17 percent in law for the whole period between 1864 and 1938. More than 16 percent of all the aca-demic personnel in Germany's universities during the 1870s whose religion is known were Jews, but only 5 percent in 1931.[22] With parlous economic conditions and even stronger antisemitic sentiments after World War I, career opportunities for Jews in German and Austrian universities tended to worsen. In 1919 the sociologist Max Weber warned his Jewish students to give up any hope for academic careers in Germany.[23]

The new political antisemitism in Germany and the Habsburg Monarchy after 1880 and in France after the Dreyfus Affair in the 1890s caused greater hostility to Jews than before in higher education and some professions. Nonetheless, with basic principles of civil equality fixed in law in those countries and in North America as well, it proved hard to impose explicit, formal restrictions on the admission of Jews to state schools and universities or on licensing them as professionals. Overall, Jews' enroll-ment in state-funded secondary schools and higher education remained strong relative to their population and tended to increase in most Western and Central European countries and North America up to the 1930s.

[22] Jarausch, *Students, Society, and Politics*, 264–270, 350–356; Konrad H. Jarausch, *Deutsche Studenten 1800-1970* (Frankfurt a.M.: Suhrkamp, 1984), 84–92; Cohen, *Education and Middle-Class Society*, 232–239; Fritz K. Ringer, "Academics in Germany: German and Jew – Some Preliminary Remarks," *Leo Baeck Institute Year Book* 36(1991): 211–212; and David L. Preston, "The German Jews in Secular Education, University Teaching, and Science: A Preliminary Inquiry," *Jewish Social Studies* 38, no. 2(1976): 106–110.

[23] Fritz Stern, "The German Professionals and their Jewish Colleagues: Comments on the papers of Konrad Jarausch, Geoffrey Cocks, and Fritz K. Ringer," *Leo Baeck Institute Year Book* 36(1991): 214.

Nonetheless, social discrimination, covert barriers, formal quotas in private educational institutions, and prohibitions on Jewish membership in student and professional societies increased in a number of locales.

In Britain, for example, the liberal legal framework for Jews after the middle of the nineteenth century, the rapid expansion of state-operated secondary schools after 1902, and the growth of university education after the 1880s opened the way for considerable expansion in Jewish enrollments, which benefited particularly the growing numbers of immigrants from Eastern Europe and their offspring. As in the United States during the same period, the rapid growth provoked hostile reactions in many British quarters after 1900 and even more after World War I. Discrimination against Jews increased through the 1930s in admissions to the elite English "public" schools and the most prestigious colleges and in some professions such as teaching. Jews who wished to become physicians and surgeons might be able to attend universities for their scientific preparation but encountered barriers in admission to the clinical training programs in some hospitals.[24] In the United States during the 1920s, Harvard, Yale, Princeton, Columbia, Barnard, Duke, Rutgers, Cornell, Johns Hopkins, Northwestern, Penn State, Ohio State, and the universities of Cincinnati, Illinois, Kansas, Minnesota, Texas, Virginia, and Washington, to name only some of the most prominent, all found ways to limit Jewish enrollments.[25] The Nazis' imposition of exclusionary policies against Jews in Germany after 1933 and in Austria after 1938 produced waves of Jewish refugees, including many professionals, which only heightened fears in British and North American professional circles of a glut of new Jewish recruits.

Nazi rule in Germany after January 1933 had a catastrophic impact on Jews' access to advanced education and professions there and after 1938 in the other European lands where Germany took control. Within a few months of coming to power in Germany, the Nazi authorities excluded Jews from all government employment, the judiciary, the legal profession, teaching in public institutions, and work in cultural and entertainment institutions. In stages thereafter the Nazi authorities prohibited Jews

---

[24] See Ringer, *Education and Society in Modern Europe*, 206–214; Endelman, *The Jews of Britain*, 98–99, 198–201; W. D. Rubinstein, *A History of the Jews in the English-Speaking World: Great Britain* (Basingstoke: Macmillan, 1996), 270–271; and *Pride versus Prejudice: Jewish Doctors and Lawyers in England, 1890–1990*, ed. John Cooper (Oxford: Littman Library of Jewish Civilization, 2003), 2–3, 49–67.

[25] Jonathan Sarna, *American Judaism: A History* (New Haven: Yale University Press, 2004), 219.

from studying alongside non-Jews in public education. In response Jewish groups took the initiative to organize separate schools for Jewish children. Soon Jewish organizations found themselves obliged to operate schools for Jewish children to meet continuing legal requirements for primary education, at least until the government ordered even those schools to close in summer 1942.

The strength of native antisemitic political forces in East Central Europe during the 1930s caused significant reversals of fortune for Jews there, too, in advanced education and the learned professions even before the arrival of Nazi military forces. Population growth, agricultural modernization, and advancing urbanization after the mid-nineteenth century gave rise to an ever larger non-Jewish wage-labor force and new middle and lower middle classes after the mid-nineteenth century. The latter increasingly saw Jews and other religious and national minorities such as Armenians, Greeks, and ethnic Germans as unwelcome competitors. Nascent "native" urban middle-class and lower-middle-class elements who wanted to displace Jews economically helped fuel antisemitic politics among Poles, Czechs, Slovaks, Magyars, and Romanians from the end of the nineteenth century up to World War II.[26]

Aware of the potential for discrimination against national and religious minorities in the newly independent states of East Central Europe, the victorious powers at the Paris Peace conference in 1919 insisted on treaties to protect minorities, including Jews. Having signed such a treaty, however, did not prevent Romania from enacting discriminatory measures against Jews in the 1920s, including special taxes and quotas on Jewish enrollments in the universities. Discriminatory measures followed in the 1930s against Jews in the learned professions. In Poland, nationalist political interests and the government invoked economic discrimination against Jews during the 1920s; only in the mid-1930s, though, did the state break through the protections required by Poland's minority treaty. Polish universities adopted informal quotas for Jewish students and required those enrolled to sit in separate sections of classrooms and lecture halls. In addition, various Polish professional associations took steps to exclude Jews from membership.

In Hungary in 1920, half of all lawyers and 60 percent of all medical doctors outside of government service were Jewish although Jews accounted for less than 6 percent of the total population.[27] After counterrevolutionary

---

[26] See Ezra Mendelsohn, *The Jews of East Central Europe between the World Wars* (Bloomington: Indiana University Press, 1983), passim; Karady, *Jews of Europe in the Modern Era*, 299–372; and Brian A. Porter, *When Nationalism Began to Hate: Imagining Modern Politics in Nineteenth Century Poland* (New York: Oxford University Press, 2000).

[27] Mendelsohn, *The Jews of East Central Europe*, 101.

forces put down the Communist government led by Béla Kun, they engaged in violent attacks on Jews and fierce antisemitc rhetoric; but that translated into few formal measures against Jews during the 1920s. The government enacted in 1922 a law to limit Jewish enrollments in universities to the Jewish share of the total population but did not enforce it. After May 1938, however, a series of new laws defined Jews in racial terms and set strict limits on their participation in professions and enrollment in advanced education.

Czechoslovakia guaranteed full equality of rights to its Jewish population up to autumn 1938, but after the Munich conference antisemitism became more public in both the Czech and Slovak territories. Soon after the break-up of the country in March 1939, Slovakia began to adopt sharply discriminatory laws against Jews.

Among the European countries with large Jewish populations during the 1920s and 1930s, it was only in the Soviet Union did Jews experience major advances in opportunities for advanced secular education and entry into learned professions compared to before World War I. With Yiddish initially recognized as their national language, the government opened secular public schools during the 1920s to teach Jews in Belorusssia and Ukraine in Yiddish. Hostile to anything connected with religious rituals or Zionism, the Soviet authorities opposed instruction in Hebrew. Quotas on Jewish enrollments in state secondary and higher education disappeared after the Bolshevik revolution, and the numbers of Jewish students grew rapidly. By 1927, more than 14 percent of all students in Soviet universities and other institutions of higher learning were Jews, compared to their 2 percent of the total population. By 1928 it is estimated that Jews comprised nearly one-quarter of all white-collar employees in the Soviet Union, and 10 percent of all employed Jews were in the educated professions or higher white-collar positions.

The Nazi invasion during World War II caused major losses to the Soviet Jewish population, and antisemitism became more open in official Soviet circles during the final years of the Stalin era. The Soviet authorities closed the Yiddish-language primary and secondary schools in the post-war era along with other Jewish cultural institutions. Few Jews were visible in high levels of the Communist party or the government after 1950, but in the early 1960s Jews still accounted for nearly 15 percent of all medical doctors and 10 percent of all lawyers in the Soviet Union.[28]

In the democratic states of the western world after World War II, Jews generally enjoyed equal opportunities with non-Jews in public education

---

[28] Benjamin Pinkus, *The Jews of the Soviet Union: The History of a National Minority* (Cambridge: Cambridge University Press, 1988), 96–97, 269–270.

and the learned professions. Any remaining discrimination in admissions to secondary schools and higher education and in university employment largely disappeared by the late 1950s or early 1960s, and Jews enjoyed strong representation in the learned professions wherever there were significant Jewish populations. Jews comprised less than 1 percent of the British population in the early 1970s but 3 percent of all university students, 4 percent of the doctors, and 9 percent of the lawyers.[29] In France, Jews achieved great prominence in academic and political life during the 1950s and 1960s. All over the western world, fresh memories of the Nazi horrors and heightened commitments to human rights and civil equality in national legal systems and the international legal order provided new support for equal opportunity in education and employment.

Before World War II Jewish settlers in Palestine under the British mandate began to create an elaborate network of vocational and academic education, which expanded even further in the State of Israel. Within a few decades, Israel developed an extraordinary number of institutions of higher learning for a country its size. Jewish immigrants from East Central Europe, North Africa, the Middle East, and Russia who settled after 1945 in Israel, Western Europe, North and South America, and Australia were able to take advantage of extensive educational opportunities open to them.

The disproportionate representation of Jews among students in secondary and higher education and many learned professions relative to Jews' share of the population was striking in many Western societies from the late nineteenth century through much of the twentieth century. Throughout, though, this development was historically conditioned and bounded. In general, the representation of particular social or cultural groups in advanced education and high status occupations tends to be self-perpetuating, so that once Jews established a strong representation, one could expect their presence to continue, other conditions being equal. On the other hand, even in societies where formal and informal discrimination against Jews in education and the professions largely disappeared after World War II, the strong overrepresentation of Jews was not a permanent phenomenon.

Since around 1980 there have been signs that the representation of Jews in certain parts of American higher education, for example, has peaked and may be declining, particularly in the natural sciences, engineering, and even medicine. While in 1935 Jews accounted for 13 percent of first-year medical students, in 1988 the Jewish share of all medical students in

---

[29] Howard M. Sachar, *The Course of Modern Jewish History*, new rev. ed. (New York: Vintage, 1990), 660.

the United States was only 9 percent.[30] In the meantime, other minority groups, particularly Asian Americans, rapidly increased their numbers in higher education as a way to achieve upward economic and social mobility in ways similar to Jews' behavior in the previous one hundred years. In 1995–96, for instance, Asian Americans accounted for only 2 percent of the American population, but 21 percent of all applicants to medical schools.[31] The parallels between the historic educational and occupational patterns of Jews and other minority groups in modern America may be a key, though, to understanding the underlying reasons for the strong push of Jews into advanced education and professional pursuits in the nineteenth and early twentieth centuries across Europe and North America.

The reasons for the disproportionate representation of Jews in advanced education and the professions in modern Western societies have been subject to much scholarly and popular debate.[32] Many observers point to Jewish traditions of the cultivation of learning, deriving from religious injunctions to study the Torah, the Talmud, and the associated rabbinical literature. Study of religious texts and respect for religious learning, it is argued, resulted in Jews having higher average literacy rates and a greater willingness to devote themselves to study in general than many Christians in medieval and early modern societies. These traditions presumably prepared Jews to pursue more eagerly advanced secular education and learned professions when they became more accessible during the nineteenth and early twentieth centuries.

The historical sociologist Victor Karady has summed up well the argument for the long-term importance of traditional Jewish culture in shaping the patterns of Jews' economic and occupational modernization: "The demands of Judaic religious practice played an especially important part in cultivating the socio-economic virtues, capabilities and attitudinal factors that were found across a broad spectrum of active Jewish men at the dawn of the modern age, and from at least three distinct viewpoints, namely, those of religious intellectualism, habitual discipline and self-control, and the sense of community."[33] Traditions of religious intellectualism, in this

[30] Juthani, "A Comparison of Asian-American and American Jewish Involvement," 768–769.

[31] Ibid., 769.

[32] See, for examples, Karady, *Jews of Europe in the Modern Era*, 88–113; Steven Beller, *Vienna and the Jews, 1867–1938: A Cultural History* (Cambridge: Cambridge University Press, 1989), 43–70; Marsha L. Rozenblit, *The Jews of Vienna: Assimilation and Identity* (Albany: State University of New York Press, 1983), 99–126; and Mariam K. Slater, "My Son the Doctor: Aspects of Mobility among American Jews," *American Sociological Review* 34, no. 3 (1969): 359–373.

[33] Karady, *Jews of Europe in the Modern Era*, 57.

view, gave Jews, or at least Jewish males, "cultural capital" in the form of experience, habits, and skills which provided great advantages for pursuing advanced education, educated professions such as medicine, law, journalism, and teaching, or other activities which required individual study and logical reasoning.

Traditions of religious study and respect for religious learning may well have had a positive impact on Jews' attitudes toward education in general and their interest in educated and semi-educated professions during the nineteenth and early twentieth centuries. One should be careful, though, not to posit a love of all learning and a commitment to study of all kinds as an essential part of an enduring Jewish culture, irrespective of changing historical conditions. Given the great strength of traditions among Jews of Europe and those Mediterranean before the nineteenth-century era of modernization, one cannot easily isolate those traditions as an encouraging factor and test their weight relative to the particular social and economic circumstances of the nineteenth and early twentieth centuries, which strongly favored Jews' pursuit of advanced secular education and entry into educated or semi-educated professions in an era of major social and economic transformation.

It is instructive in this connection to compare the historical experience of Jews with other groups in the same societies which prized religious learning and the study of sacred texts. Where Jewish minorities lived sided-by-side with historically disadvantaged Protestants in predominantly Catholic societies during the nineteenth century, such as in the Habsburg Monarchy, we might expect Bible-reading Protestants to have embraced modern advanced education at higher rates relative to their population than did Catholics. This was indeed the case in Austria, where in winter 1899–1900 Protestants studied in the universities at twice the rate relative to their total population as did Catholics; but still, at the same time Jews were enrolled at four times the rate of Catholics.[34]

Other historical circumstances, above and beyond the traditions of religious study, caused Jews to gain disproportionately strong representation in advanced modern secular education; and one can argue that the traditions of Jewish religious study had only an indirect effect in encouraging the pursuit of advanced secular education. Jews in the nineteenth and early twentieth centuries inherited traditions of respect for religious learning, but the strong and rapid increase in their pursuit of advanced secular education and their large-scale entry into educated and semi-educated professions were new phenomena generated in a new era of industrialization, urbanization, and legal emancipation for Jews, conditions utterly unlike

[34] Cohen, *Education and Middle-Class Society*, 148.

those experienced by their forebears in medieval and early modern societies. To a great extent, Jews' overrepresentation in modern advanced education and professions resulted from modern transformations in their social
relations, economic needs, and social aspirations which accompanied
emancipation, migration, and a general accommodation to new economic
relations in ever larger urban settings.

Valuable for understanding Jews' pursuit of advanced secular education
and their entry into educated and semi-educated secular occupations in
modern societies are arguments first formulated by the sociologist Mariam
Slater in a classic 1969 discussion of American Jewish experience.[35] Even
if one grants that the traditions of religious study had a positive general
influence on the pursuit of modern secular education, one must still ask
how the values favoring religious study translated into Jews' pursuing fundamentally different secular studies and practically oriented training for
professions. Moreover, continuities from traditional religious study cannot easily explain the disproportionately strong representation of Jewish
women in secondary schools, universities, and learned professions in many
European and North American countries during the first decades after
they began to admit women. Traditional Jewish religious study offered
only very limited basic instruction to women, and women had no role in
traditional ritual life outside the home.

Study in modern secular secondary schools and higher education differs fundamentally from typical Jewish religious studies of the preindus-
trial era. Jewish religious learning for the great majority of Jews in Central
and Eastern Europe and also for traditional Jews in North Africa and the
Middle East meant, above all, years of memorization of sacred texts for
boys in religious primary schools. Such studies did not encourage reading of secular texts in vernacular languages. Only a small number of male
students went on to the advanced study of Torah and Talmud, and only a
gifted few engaged in deeper analysis and creative debate over the meaning of the texts. Girls were generally excluded from formal study of the
Torah and Talmud until Orthodox Judaism began to make accommodations to the changed conditions of modern life and the growing need to
educate women, such as in the Beis Yaakov schools which began in Polish
territories in 1917.

Traditional Jewish religious learning was far removed from the
broad humanistic education of modern secular secondary schools and
fundamentally different from the worldly scientific and practically oriented advanced education needed for entry into a modern profession.
While traditional Jewish religious study at the lower levels involved little

---

[35] Slater, "My Son the Doctor," 359–373.

more than memorization of core biblical and liturgical texts, even at the higher levels it was still inherently other-worldly and non-practical. Many Orthodox defenders of traditional Jewish religious study during the nineteenth century were disdainful, if not openly hostile to modern scientific learning and advanced secular study. Only in the twentieth century did modern Orthodox Jewish groups begin to make secular studies integral to the curricula in their own schools. As recently as 1990 in the United States, though, the National Jewish Population Survey found that Orthodox Jewish religious observance and affiliation were only weakly correlated with advanced secular education and professional achievement, although high levels of participation in Jewish community life of various kinds did correlate strongly with advanced educational achievement.[36]

The realities of traditional religious study before the late nineteenth century offered few direct advantages and little encouragement for Jews to pursue advanced modern secular education and entry into educated and semi-educated secular professions. Moreover, one cannot assume that traditional religious studies at least helped give Jews higher overall literacy rates in majority vernacular languages than their non-Jewish neighbors before the major social transformations of the nineteenth century. As late as around 1900 many of the adult Jewish immigrants from Eastern Europe to North America were only minimally literate in any language other than Yiddish or Hebrew when they arrived; around one-quarter could not read the majority vernacular language of the lands from which they came.[37] During the late nineteenth century many Jews in the poorest and least developed Eastern European and Mediterranean lands had to rely on ill-developed state primary education or privately financed secular schools to gain any basic secular education. The high value placed by traditional Jews on Torah and Talmud studies for their sons created significant impediments for many to gaining any education in secular subjects and in majority vernacular languages until the pace of social change, migration, and secularization began to accelerate. Habits of women taking major responsibilities for business activities in traditional Eastern European Jewish household economies and prohibitions on formal study of the Torah and Talmud by women, in fact, gave them significant advantages in learning vernacular languages and pursuing secular education in those languages when educational opportunities began to expand for women.[38]

---

[36] Harriet and Moshe Hartman, "More Jewish, Less Jewish: Implications for Education and Labor Force Characteristics," *Sociology of Religion* 57, no.2 (1996): 175–193. See also Stephen Cohen, *American Modernity and Jewish Identity* (New York: Tavistock, 1983).

[37] Slater, "My Son the Doctor," 367.

[38] See Iris Parush, *Reading Jewish Women: Marginality and Modernization in Nineteenth-Century Eastern European Jewish Society*, trans. Saadya Sternberg (Waltham,

Additional evidence that traditional religious study did not give Jews special advantages or predispose them in a direct way to pursue modern advanced education and professional careers can be found in the behavior of the Sephardic and German-speaking Jews who predominated among the Jewish population of North America during the early and mid-nineteenth century. In the medieval and early modern periods, Jewish communities in the Iberian Peninsula and the German states contributed much to Jewish liturgy and religious scholarship. Nonetheless, their descendants in North America before the 1870s and 1880s engaged overwhelmingly not in learned professions but in commerce and manufacture, which offered them the greatest economic and social opportunities at the time they arrived. The German Jews' occupational and mobility patterns in the United States during the nineteenth century, in fact, much resembled those of contemporary Christian German immigrants.[39] Only after the second or third generation in North America did the professionalization of Sephardic and German Jews advance significantly.

While traditional religious study in itself gave Jews no special advantages nor a disposition to seek advanced secular education and entry into professions, the economic and social circumstances of the middle and late nineteenth century in Europe and the Atlantic world offered strong incentives to follow such a path. That development is best seen as the fruit of a complex economic, social, and cultural adaptation to a changing political and economic environment and the transfer of older occupational and social skills into new practical pursuits. As the legal emancipation of Jews spread from west to east in Europe after the French revolution, Jews gained opportunities to form closer social ties with non-Jewish society and to escape the old restricted array of low-status occupations. Legal emancipation opened up formerly closed occupations in craft production, commerce, and eventually public employment; and modern economic development created enormous new opportunities in industry, finance, advanced commerce, medical and legal practice, and new modes of white-collar employment. The development of modern commerce and industry in more thoroughly integrated regional, national, and international markets also caused the closing of many economic niches formerly occupied by Jews.[40]

Migration from smaller communities to larger cities or distant lands, seeking new occupations, and pursuing more advanced education were all

MA: Brandeis University Press, 2004), 38–96; and Shaul Stampfer, *Families, Rabbis, and Education: Traditional Jewish Society in Nineteenth-Century Eastern Europe* (Oxford: Littman Library of Jewish Civilization, 2010), 167–210.

[39] Slater, "My Son the Doctor," 364.
[40] See Chapter 15 in this volume.

aspects of Jews' adaptation to accelerating social and economic changes. With long traditions in petty commerce and some small-scale craft production, many Jews moved to larger communities initially to find new opportunities in small business and services, larger commerce, and some branches of skilled industrial labor. In much of Central Europe half or more of the working Jewish population still remained in commercial pursuits to the beginning of the twentieth century, despite the many social changes.

Jews' engagement in white-collar jobs and educated professions began to increase rapidly in Western and Central Europe after the middle of the nineteenth century as the growth of those occupations began to accelerate. The general expansion of white-collar employment in the private and public sectors and of educated professions in general encouraged the growth of secondary and higher education throughout Europe and the Atlantic world. White-collar employment and the professions rewarded people who were comfortable with city and town life and had traits of self-discipline, individualism, competitive instincts, rational calculation, and planful behavior.[41] These were traits which historical circumstances in Europe and the Mediterranean had encouraged among Jews, most of whom had lived in town society for centuries and had engaged in petty commerce, middleman functions, and low-status crafts. Advanced study in modern secondary schools and universities and work in white-collar jobs or the professions required and rewarded a secular, rational, competitive individualism which cannot be seen as a direct outgrowth of traditional Jewish religious study. Rather, the secular, rational individualism which European and North American Jews cultivated during the late nineteenth and early twentieth centuries built on the social and economic habits of competition and individual calculation developed in the petty commerce and trades of early modern cities and towns which Jews then adapted to new, transformed conditions.

For Jews and non-Jews alike, the great majority of those who have attended academic secondary schools and universities in Western societies since the middle of the nineteenth century have used that education to achieve higher social status, greater comfort and security and, many hoped, higher incomes than could be attained in manual labor, petty commerce, or many manufacturing pursuits. Into the early twentieth century, the great majority of all students who began academic secondary schools in Europe and North America did not actually complete

---

[41] Slater, "My Son the Doctor," 368–372; Karady, *Jews of Europe in the Modern Era*, 57–100 passim.

studies there and go on to university or technical colleges. From 1880 to the present, in both Europe and North America, far more of the Jews who studied in advanced secondary schools, colleges, and universities became white-collar employees in the private or public sectors than became physicians, lawyers, or professors. Only an exceptional minority of Jewish or non-Jewish students has turned to higher education primarily as a matter of intellectual curiosity and with the goal of becoming scholars or scientists.[42]

The experience of other minorities in Western societies over the last century and a half reinforces the conclusion that Jews' relative over-representation in advanced education and educated or semi-educated occupations has been an historically conditioned socio-economic and cultural phenomenon and that the values involved have not been unique to any one religious or national tradition. In Europe and the Atlantic world at a critical historical moment, when early modern social and economic relations were dissolving and modern capitalist urban industrial society developed into full flower, Jews were primed by their previous social and economic experience and by their new circumstances to enter in significant numbers into educated or semi-educated white-collar work and the professions. In North America in recent years, the strong overrepresentation in advanced education and in professions such as medicine and law that was so distinctive among Jews at the end of the nineteenth century and the beginning of the twentieth has begun to fade slowly while individuals of Chinese, Korean, Vietnamese, and East Indian origin, for example, are increasingly following the path taken earlier by Jews.[43] In various parts of the world, in fact, overseas Chinese, East Indians, and Armenians, for example, have long displayed educational and occupational patterns similar to those of Jews in Europe and North America. Wherever one finds appreciable concentrations of Jews today, they do continue to enroll in advanced education at high rates, but now with the continuing expansion and diversification of public and private white-collar employment and the service sector, both Jewish men and women enter a much wider range of educated occupations than at the end of the nineteenth century.

---

[42] Cohen, *Education and Middle-Class Society*, 222–227; Ringer, *Education and Society in Modern Europe*, 35–36, 102–104; Rozenblit, *Jews of Vienna*, 52–61, 108–125.

[43] Juthani, "A Comparison of Asian-American and American Jewish Involvement," 769.

SELECT BIBLIOGRAPHY

Beller, Steven. *Vienna and the Jews, 1867–1938: A Cultural History*. Cambridge: Cambridge University Press, 1989.

Benbassa, Esther, and Aron Rodrigue. *The Jews of the Balkans: The Judeo-Spanish Community, 15th to 20th Centuries*. Oxford: Blackwell, 1995.

Birnbaum, Pierre, and Ira Katznelson, eds. *Paths of Emancipation: Jews, States, and Citizenship*. Princeton: Princeton University Press, 1995.

Cohen, Gary B. *Education and Middle-Class Society in Imperial Austria, 1848–1918*. West Lafayette, IN: Purdue University Press, 1996.

Cooper, John, *Pride versus Prejudice: Jewish Doctors and Lawyers in England, 1890–1990*. Oxford: Littman Library of Jewish Civilization, 2003.

Endelman, Todd M. *The Jews of Britain, 1656 to 2000*. Berkeley: University of California Press, 2002.

Freidenreich, Harriet P. *Female, Jewish, and Educated: The Lives of Central European University Women*. Bloomington: Indiana University Press, 2002.

Hartman, Harriet, and Moshe Hartman. "More Jewish, Less Jewish: Implications for Education and Labor Force Characteristics." *Sociology of Religion* 57, no. 2 (1996): 175–193.

Hyman, Paula E. *The Jews of Modern France*. Berkeley: University of California Press, 1998.

Jarausch, Konrad H. *Deutsche Studenten 1800–1970*. Frankfurt a.M.: Suhrkamp, 1984.

    "Jewish Lawyers in Germany, 1848–1938." *Leo Baeck Institute Year Book* 36 (1991): 171–205.

    Students, Society, and Politics in Imperial Germany: The Rise of Academic Illiberalism. Princeton, NJ: Princeton University Press, 1982.

Juthani, Manisha. "A Comparison of Asian-American and American Jewish Involvement in the Medical Profession." *Journal of the American Medical Association* 277, no. 9 (March 5, 1997): 768–69.

Karady, Victor. "Jewish Enrollment Patterns in Classical Secondary Education in Old Regime and Inter-War Hungary." *Studies in Contemporary Jewry* 1 (1984): 225–252.

    The Jews of Europe in the Modern Era. A Socio-Historical Outline. Budapest and New York: Central European University Press, 2004.

Klier, John D. *Imperial Russia's Jewish Question, 1855–1981*. Cambridge: Cambridge University Press, 1995.

Lässig, Simone. *Jüdische Wege ins Bürgertum. Kulturelles Kapital und sozialer Aufstieg im 19. Jahrhundert*. Göttingen: Vandenhoeck und Ruprecht, 2004.

Nathans, Benjamin. *Beyond the Pale: The Jewish Encounter with Late Imperial Russia*. Berkeley: University of California Press, 2002.

Parush, Iris. *Reading Jewish Women. Marginality and Modernization in Nineteenth-Century Eastern European Jewish Society*, trans. Saadya Sternberg. Waltham, MA: Brandeis University Press, 2004.

Pinkus, Benjamin. *The Jews of the Soviet Union: The History of a National Minority*. Cambridge: Cambridge University Press, 1988.

Preston, David L. "The German Jews in Secular Education, University Teaching, and Science: A Preliminary Inquiry." *Jewish Social Studies* 38, no. 2 (1976): 99–116.

Pulzer, Peter G. J. *The Rise of Political Anti-Semitism in Germany and Austria*, rev. ed. Cambridge, MA: Harvard University Press, 1988.

Ringer, Fritz K. *Education and Society in Modern Europe*. Bloomington: Indiana University Press, 1979.

Rodrigue, Aron. *French Jews, Turkish Jews: The Alliance Israelite Universelle and the Politics of Jewish Schooling in Turkey, 1860–1925*. Bloomington: Indiana University Press, 1990.

Rozenblit, Marsha L. *The Jews of Vienna: Assimilation and Identity*. Albany: State University of New York Press, 1983.

Simon, Rachel. "Education." In *The Jews of the Middle East and North Africa in Modern Times*, edited by Reeva S. Simon, Michael M. Laskier, and Sara Reguier, 142–164. New York: Columbia University Press, 2003.

Slater, Mariam K. "My Son the Doctor: Aspects of Mobility among American Jews." *American Sociological Review* 34, no. 3 (1969): 359–373.

Sorkin, David. *The Transformation of German Jewry, 1780–1840*. Oxford: Oxford University Press, 1987.

Stampfer, Shaul. *Families, Rabbis, and Education: Traditional Jewish Society in Nineteenth-Century Eastern Europe*. Oxford: Littman Library of Jewish Civilization, 2010.

Stanislawski, Michael. *Tsar Nicholas and the Jews: The Transformation of Jewish Society in Russia, 1825–1855*. Philadelphia: Jewish Publication Society, 1983.

CHAPTER 18

PHILANTHROPY, DIPLOMACY, AND JEWISH INTERNATIONALISM

JONATHAN DEKEL-CHEN

Cross-border contacts between individuals and communities have been a nearly constant feature of Jewish life since the biblical-era exiles from the Holy Land. Actions meant to aid Jews in distress have often characterized these transnational contacts, occurring with greater frequency and increasing variety in the modern age. This essay offers a *longue durée* view of such transnational Jewish activism, starting with its pre-modern manifestations, leading eventually to the modernization of cross-border intercessions around the turn of the twentieth century, more or less in unison with the modernization of Jewish organizational life. In the main, this activism has been mobilized by relatively affluent communities in the West on behalf of less-fortunate Jews in the East. As shall be seen, interlocking threads of philanthropy, together with formal and informal acts of diplomacy, appeared throughout these decades wherever Jews lived and helped to create modern patterns of Jewish internationalism.

As a diasporic people often living in hostile political environments spread over immense space for nearly two millennia, Jews have had a unique perspective on transnational aid and intercession. Examples of such aid have been numerous, although it must be said from the outset that not all of these efforts yielded the desired outcomes or transpired without friction. Since the return from the Babylonian exile, Diaspora communities supported their brethren living in the Holy Land. Traditions of cross-border contacts and aid have endured as part of the modern Jewish religious ethos and group identity. Philanthropic aid across borders and the practice of transnational diplomacy merged in the Jewish world around the early modern period, sparked by rapid changes: the coming of absolutist states in Europe and improvements in the tools of communication. Starting no later than the eighteenth century, a sort of transnational "third sector" emerged as a central feature of Jewish life. The establishment of the State of Israel in 1948 did not diminish the value of transnational activity.

Research for this essay was supported by the Israel Science Foundation (grant no. 462/05).

PRE-MODERN ROOTS AND PATTERNS OF JEWISH PHILANTHROPY AND DIPLOMACY

Traditional practices of local charity preceded the development of transnational philanthropy. Compassion and aid for the poor and less fortunate members of the Jewish community were firmly rooted in the Hebrew Bible or Old Testament, where charity is commanded from all, made relatively simple at the time by the agrarian lifestyle. As Jewish society gravitated away from farming, the community assumed responsibility for charity, and in some cases, was required to do so by local rulers.[1] Deathbed declarations (*hekdesh*) and collections in synagogues were the primary funding sources for communal charities and religious institutions. From at least the Middle Ages, the practice of charity began to extend beyond political borders with Jewish communities from Istanbul to Amsterdam organizing to redeem captives in Europe and in the Ottoman Empire. These efforts took on semi-institutional characteristics by the mid-1600s when informal Jewish transnational networks mobilized to aid refugees.

Philanthropy developed during the modern age at an unsteady pace, driven mostly by outside events. European states – organized around the principles of absolutism and enlightenment – tended to weaken traditional structures but did not always deliver the kind of aid that Jewish communities still required. Consequently, the reorganization of existing charity and welfare networks (and the local fundraising that made them possible) became necessary. In France, voluntary organizations rose during the first half of the nineteenth century, funded mainly by contributions from the Rothschilds and other wealthy families infused with a sense of *noblesse oblige*. By the middle of the 1800s, similar charitable organizations arose in England, Germany, and the United States, with Russia following in the last decades of the century. These organizations gradually professionalized and expanded from the 1880s in response to the enormous demands of the mass westward migrations of Eastern European Jews.[2] In parallel, their focus shifted from charity to relief, then reconstruction and productivization. It is also probable that Jewish communal organizations in Eastern Europe, modeled after their philanthropic donors from the United States,

---

[1] For more on the early history, see Derek Penslar, "The Origins of Modern Jewish Philanthropy," in *Philanthropy in the World's Traditions*, ed. Warren F. Ilchman, Stanley N. Katz, and Edward L. Queen (Bloomington: Indiana University Press, 1998), 197–214.

[2] For more on this transition, see Mark Wischnitzer, *To Dwell in Safety: The Story of Jewish Migration since 1800* (Philadelphia: Jewish Publication Society, 1948), 3–66.

were a sort of model of organizational modernization for their non-Jewish counterparts during the first decades of the twentieth century.[3]

Jewish diplomacy also has biblical roots, reflected through intercessions with God, starting with Abraham's attempts to save the people of Sodom. Notwithstanding a prophetic tradition of negotiations with the Almighty on behalf of mankind, there was considerable hesitation in biblical tradition about the efficacy such attempts. Similar hesitation and uncertainty with "higher authorities" accompanied all pre-modern forms of Jewish intercession.[4] These doubts, however, did not deter Jewish leaders from attempts at intercession with the state or local rulers from the era of Roman rule in the Holy Land through the Middle Ages.

Beginning with the destruction of the Second Temple, Jewish communities were a religious and/or ethnic minority wherever they lived; at times welcomed by local authorities, at times repressed. Diasporic Jews could rarely rely on earthly rulers to act in their best interests. Therefore, responses to communal needs at home and abroad had to be initiated, if not entirely executed, by non-state actors within the Jewish community. This reality forced activists to craft an unofficial diplomacy, which could navigate sometimes treacherous domestic and international political waters. Because the creation of the state of Israel did not produce an ingathering of most of the world's Jews, this non-state politics infused Jews both before and after 1948.[5] Attempts at Jewish diplomacy faced a serious challenge: in general, no democratic mechanism has ever elected representatives for nationwide Jewish communities in the West. Jewish communities in the East also had no agreed-upon national leadership and periodically faced much greater perils. Hence, self-appointed leaders often took upon themselves the protection of Jewish interests in their own regions or countries, as well as those residing in foreign lands, with no clear license from a national constituency.

---

[3] Rebecca Kobrin, "Contested Contributions: Émigré Philanthropy, Jewish Communal Life and Polish–Jewish Relations in Interwar Bialystok, 1919–1929," *Gal-Ed* 20 (2006): 43–62; idem, "Empire of Charity: American Immigrant Jews in Poland, 1914–29," Lecture at the Workshop, Jewish Relief Organizations in pre-WW II Europe: A Comparative Perspective, New York University, April 2008; Boris Bogen, *Jewish Philanthropy: An Exposition of Principles and Methods of Jewish Social Service in the United States* (Montclair, NJ: Patterson Smith, 1969), 4.

[4] J. W. Bowker, "Intercession in the Qur'an and the Jewish Tradition," *Journal of Semitic Studies* 11 (1966): 69–82.

[5] David Biale pioneered a reevaluation of the popular conception of pre-1948 powerlessness as a feature of Jewish life. See David Biale, *Power and Powerlessness in Jewish History* (New York: Schocken, 1986).

508   THE MODERN WORLD, 1815-2000

Jewish philanthropy and non-state politics also coalesced around the biblical promise of redemption in the Land of Israel. For generations of religious Jewish donors, the idea of Israel as a future homeland was not just a vague aspiration, but rather an ongoing concern. For hundreds of years before the renewal of significant Jewish immigration to Palestine in the 1880s, networks of charitable distribution (*halukah*) in Europe and the Ottoman Empire funded the upkeep of the small Jewish communities in the Holy Land. Until the Balfour Declaration of 1917, however, there was no concrete basis for realization of a full-scale national redemption in one's lifetime.

Scholarly debate still exists about the very possibility of Jewish national diplomacy before Israel's independence in 1948. One interpretation insists that such diplomacy could not exist without Jewish national territory, or even a consensus among world Jewry about its leadership and collective interests.[6] This view seems affirmed by the fact that even the enlarged Jewish Agency (formed in 1929 to promote the development of the Land of Israel) quickly lost cohesion due to disagreements among its member organizations. The counter-argument interprets Jewish communal survival since the fall of the Second Temple as a series of vertical political alliances with higher authorities that resulted in charters and, consequently, the defense of Jewish rights. Moreover, before 1948, Jews were a polity (albeit without a national territory) because of a sense of shared fate that caused them to undertake a variety of actions for brethren across borders.[7] No matter the resolution of this debate, most of Israel's current welfare and educational agencies are descended from institutions established (and augmented to this day) with the help of philanthropic campaigns throughout the Jewish world begun during the decades *before* 1948.

Because the government of Israel has not spoken in the name of the Jewish people, the moment of its independence is debatable as a turning point in Jewish diplomacy or philanthropy. Rather, the skills and networks marshaled by individuals and groups committed to helping their

---

[6] For example, David Vital, "Diplomacy in the Jewish Interest," in *Jewish History: Essays in Honor of Chimen Abramsky*, ed. Ada Rapoport-Albert and Steven Zipperstein (London: Halban, 1988), 683. The general scholarly literature concurs that diaspora groups can function in the international arena. See Milton J. Esman, "Diasporas and International Relations," in *Modern Diasporas in International Politics*, ed. Gabriel Sheffer (New York: St. Martins, 1986), 341–345.

[7] Daniel J. Elazar, "The Jewish People as the Classic Diaspora: A Political Analysis," in *Modern Diasporas*, ed. Sheffer, 215, 217–218; Yosef Haim Yerushalmi, *"Servants of Kings and Not Servants of Servants": Some Aspects of the Political History of the Jews* (Atlanta: Emory University, 2005), 7, 13.

co-religionists gave Jewish non-state politics whatever power it possessed until 1948; this was not power derived from national wealth or military might. After 1948, Israel's sovereign policies (foreign and domestic) have at times enjoyed a consensus in the Jewish world, at other times less so.

JEWISH INTERNATIONALISM: CONTOURS AND LIMITS

The practice of transnational philanthropy and advocacy gradually fostered ties across class, ethnic, and denominational lines in the modern Ashkenazi world. The proliferation of cross-border and cross-class activism, accelerated with the coming of modernity, can be best described as internationalism. A sort of "peoplehood" (*umah* in Hebrew), internationalism is reflected and forged by widening circles of activism for one's co-religionists. Among Jews it is a community of opinion and action that emerged gradually from the mid-eighteenth century, mostly through philanthropy and non-state politics, both of which have been informed by a communal and religious conscious-ness. Given the friction within Jewish communities of the West throughout the modern period, transnational activism might be the *only* area in which internationalism developed.[8]

Many networks of Jewish internationalism have roots in the business world, not just in a sense of a shared fate. Extended family connections underpinned far-flung business interests throughout the Jewish world until the mid-nineteenth century much the same way that informal networks connected clergy and religious institutions. This paradigm shifted nearer to transnational activism in the mid-1800s, when wealthy Western European Jews began taking greater interest in the fate of their less fortunate co-religionists in the Ottoman and Russian Empires. Thereafter, traditional international business links assumed increasingly philanthropic directions. The transnational links that had brought wealth to many Western Jews strengthened philanthropic and unofficial diplomatic networks as the cen-tury progressed. These intercessors, perhaps best personified by the Houses of Rothschild, learned by trial and error to mobilize both philanthropic and political resources. They also had to strike a balance between philan-thropic goals and their business interests as bankers and merchants. For example, the Rothschilds' cancellation of loans to the Russian government in 1891, widely perceived as a response to the tsar's antisemitic policies,

---

[8] For more on religious internationalisms, including the Jewish example, see Abigail Green and Vincent Viaene, eds., *Religious Internationals in the Modern World: Globalization and Faith Communities since 1750* (Basingstoke, UK: Palgrave Macmillan, 2012).

resulted from both business and humanitarian considerations.[9] Even after the Rothschilds adopted more aggressive policies toward the Russian regime, they still offered credits to St. Petersburg. It should also be noted that not all Jewish bankers of the time worked in unison against Russia. In one case, the American-Jewish activist Jacob Schiff campaigned in 1904–05 to deny credit to Russia as a means of correcting its anti-Jewish policies while Jewish bankers in Europe lent money directly to them.

For lack of space, this essay cannot explore in detail those bodies appointed by their sovereigns to represent the interests of their local Jewish communities, like the *Consistoire Central* in France, the British Board of Deputies, or the Commissariat of Jewish Affairs (*Evkom*) in the Soviet Union. Nor shall we refer at length to developments within the Ottoman-controlled lands or attempts from abroad to intercede there, for example the efforts by American Jews to pressure their government on behalf of Moroccan Jewry in 1863.[10] It should be stated, however, that generations of Jews in the Ottoman lands had prominent formal and informal diplomatic roles in Europe, allowing them at times to intercede on behalf of impoverished or endangered Jews there.

TOWARD MODERNIZATION

Medieval and early modern charity between Jewish communities across borders remained relatively unchanged for generations, unlike modern transnational philanthropy which developed rapidly in three overlapping phases. The first phase can be described as *shtadlanut* (or intercession), as practiced by the Houses of Rothschild and other individuals from the 1870s until 1914. Intercessors provided charity, reconstructive programs, and political advocacy throughout the Jewish world. This type of philanthropy – based mainly on networks of wealthy families in the world of finance – survived the First World War but never regained its pre-war capacity. By 1915, the financial needs among the destitute Eastern European states far surpassed what the Jewish merchant bankers in the West could provide, thereby reducing the leverage that the latter could apply against anti-Jewish regimes. This change necessitated new tools for confronting illiberal regimes.

[9] Mattityahu Mintz, "Nesigat ha-Rotshildim me-milveh April 1891 le-Rusyah min ha-hebet ha-yehudi," *Tsion* 54 (1989): 401–435; Daniel Gutwein, *The Divided Elite: Economics, Politics and Anglo-Jewry, 1882–1917* (Leiden: Brill, 1992), 310–318, 323–325.
[10] Hasia R. Diner, *The Jews of the United States* (Berkeley: University of California Press, 2004), 177.

Organizational philanthropy emerged in the second phase, as practiced by the Jewish Colonization Association (JCA), the American Jewish Joint Distribution Committee (JDC) and others. These organizations intervened globally, like the *shtadlans*, but in a more systematized manner. The first such organization, the Alliance Israélite Universelle, formed in 1860. The Alliance, and the philanthropic organizations that splintered from it, mobilized action on behalf of Eastern European and Ottoman Jews starting in the 1870s. Organized and individual intercession coexisted until the First World War; thereafter, organizations eclipsed *shtadlans* as leaders in Jewish philanthropy. Many of the outstanding individuals, like Jacob Schiff, shifted their talents from old-world intercession to newer forms of philanthropy and advocacy through their involvement with groups like B'nai B'rith and the American Jewish Committee, even if they were not always comfortable with the democratized nature of these young organizations. The structure of transnational philanthropy changed in parallel to the migration of its "center" from Europe to the United States following the First World War; the Holocaust finalized this relocation.

The transatlantic shift changed transnational activism, but did not cause a "break" in its overall developmental trajectory. Before 1945, these efforts usually provided some sort of physical aid for endangered communities. Once the challenge of relief for Europe's displaced persons had passed in the early 1950s, however, transnational Jewish activism turned mostly to political advocacy, while the supra-national Claims Conference continued to dispense funds received from the German government for the relief of Holocaust survivors living around the globe. This shift in the "stuff" of philanthropy from relief to advocacy did not alter its meaning. Whatever the "deliverables," the fundamental aims and character of transnational intercession remained similar from at least the interwar period until the collapse of the Soviet Union, namely altruistic intervention on behalf of targeted Jewish communities abroad.

The third phase in the evolution featured "ground-up" mobilizations in the West. This began haltingly during the interwar period and proliferated during the 1960s. These campaigns have usually coalesced around humanitarian goals, and they reside in a grey area between philanthropy and advocacy. Mobilization for Soviet Jewry in the late 1960s greatly defined this phase but was not the first case of Western Jews organizing to aid Eastern European Jewry. A select group of "great" men – among them Schiff, Felix Warburg, Louis Marshall, and Alexander Kahn – formed the JDC in New York in 1914 expressly for this purpose. Unlike this antecedent, however, the Soviet Jewry movement of the 1960s featured sociological diversity, led by notable communal officials as well as people from the "grassroots"; some of the latter were described as "housewives who came out of nowhere" to help lead the movement.[11] The post-war movement also departed from its predecessors in terms of its "deliverables." If conditions on the ground in Eastern Europe had forced the JDC to concern itself with the delivery of soup kitchens, farm machinery and infirmaries, Soviet Jewry activists of the 1960s and 70s dealt mainly with advocacy.

INTERSECTIONS OF PHILANTHROPY WITH DIPLOMACY

Throughout the modern period, the peculiarities of Jewish life often caused overlaps between the practice of philanthropy and informal diplomacy. As noted above, the affluence of *shtadlanim* facilitated their rise as communal leaders, philanthropists, and informal diplomats. These roles intensified from the seventeenth into the eighteenth century, as the proliferation of absolutist states in Europe and a spiral of warfare between them forced Jewish communities on the continent to develop new *modi operandi* in response to crises at home and in distant lands. In parallel, the weakening of Ottoman Jewry forced a shift to Central Europe as the "headquarters" for funding these ransoms and the welfare of refugees.

Two cases from the early modern period are particularly illuminating. The international response to the expulsion of Prague's Jews in 1744 was a landmark in informal diplomacy. Here, the *shtadlanim* of Vienna and Prague attempted to mobilize their personal networks in Europe to intercede in Empress Maria Theresa's court.[12] As in many later intercessions, it is difficult to assess the exact impact. At the least, this mobilization set a precedent of demonstrative support for an embattled community. Moreover, no matter how one judges the "success" or "failure" of a specific intercession, the appearance of a concerted Jewish diplomatic effort affected the local rulers and elites, sometimes in unintended ways. In a separate case, the study of Jewish intercession in the Polish-Lithuanian Commonwealth (via the Council of Four Lands) illustrated a dilemma of informal diplomacy: a "successful" enlistment of support from non-Jewish authorities during a crisis can inadvertently allow an unwanted longer-term penetration of these state or church bodies into local Jewish autonomy.[13]

---

[11] Stuart Altshuler, *From Exodus to Freedom: A History of the Soviet Jewry Movement* (Lanham, MD: Rowman & Littlefield, 2005), 50. For the most recent assessment of the movement as a whole, see Gal Beckerman, *When They Come for Us We'll Be Gone: The Epic Struggle to Save Soviet Jewry* (New York: Houghton Mifflin, 2010).

[12] François Guesnet, "Textures of Intercession: Rescue Efforts for the Jews of Prague, 1744–1748," *Simon Dubnow Institute Yearbook* 4 (2005): 355–377.

[13] See, for example, Paweł Maciejko, "Baruch Yavan and the Frankist Movement: Intercession in an Age of Upheaval," *Simon Dubnow Institute Yearbook* 4 (2005): 333–354.

Problems occasionally sprouted alongside the successes of organized philanthropy in response to crises, starting with the earliest efforts for emigration and vocational training. Among these, the politics surrounding the Alliance revealed the fractiousness characteristic of the nineteenth-century Jewish world. In this case, nationalist tensions caused the Alliance to splinter into the Anglo-Jewish Association (1870), the Israelitische Allainz zu Wien (1873), and the Hilfsverein der deutschen Juden (1901).[14] Even within national communities, there was not always consensus about the goals of activism, particularly from the 1880s when they began to debate whether to resettle Jewish immigrants from Eastern Europe in their countries or elsewhere in the world.[15]

Moving from the phase of individual philanthropy into its more organized forms, the guiding ideal swung from charity toward productivization, as both a goal unto itself and an accelerator for emancipation.[16] The desire to promote the emancipation for the Jews of Eastern Europe and the Near East evolved into an important area of union between philanthropy and diplomacy before 1948. For example, the French Alliance and its German offshoot (Hilfsverein) promoted this cause in the "Orient"; they believed that making these Jews more "Western" would justify their equal treatment. Where education did not succeed in procuring emancipation, they tried to mobilize public opinion in the West to pressure Ottoman, Persian, and Russian authorities to correct injustices against Jews.[17]

Modern tools of communication extended the reach of the ideals and practice of transnational activism, but could produce unintended results. With the intensification of a cross-border consciousness, Jewish intercessors had to learn to balance their sense of solidarity with distant co-religionists against their national patriotism. Hence, *shtadlans* like the Rothschilds and Montagus warmed toward Zionism around the time of

[14] Lisa Moses Leff, *Sacred Bonds of Solidarity: The Rise of Jewish Internationalism in Nineteenth-Century France* (Stanford: Stanford University Press, 2006), 167.

[15] Eugene Black, *The Social Politics of Anglo-Jewry, 1880–1920* (New York: Blackwell, 1988), 98, 256–257, 263, 265; Gutwein, *Divided Elite*, 308–311, 322–323; Luisa Levi d'Ancona, "Philanthropy and Politics: Strategies of Jewish Bourgeois in Italy, France and England between the end of the nineteenth and the beginning of the 20th Centuries," *Traverse* 1 (2006): 86.

[16] Shmuel Almog, "Produktivizatsii, proletarizatsia, ve-avodah ivrit," in *Leumiut, tsiunut, antishemiut: massot vemeharim*, ed. idem (Jerusalem: Ha-sifriyah ha-tsiyonit, 1992), 139–168.

[17] Eli Bar-Chen, "Two Communities with a Sense of Mission: The Alliance Israélite Universelle and the Hilfsverein der deutschen Juden," in *Jewish Emancipation Reconsidered: The French and German Models*, eds. Michael Brenner, Vicki Caron, and Uri R. Kaufman (Tubingen: Mohr Siebeck, 2003), 111–117.

the First World War not just as an outgrowth of a national sentiment, but also from a belief that Jewish settlement in Palestine coincided with British imperial interests. Perhaps the actions of the Rothschilds in defense of the rights of Russian Jews best express this dilemma. The Paris and London houses interceded with the Russian regime in the late 1800s to restrain its anti-Jewish policies and periodic anti-Jewish violence. The decisions made by both houses did not just balance their loyalties to England and France against their "Jewishness."[18] As bankers, they also weighed the ramifications of their political advocacy with a client (Russia), at once a repressive autocracy and a site of significant business interests for the Rothschild family. Fiscal interests more often than not thereby played an important, if not equal, role in their decisions when engaging and disengaging St. Petersburg on Jewish issues before 1914. Somewhat later, American-Jewish philanthropists in the early 1920s had to find a way to support suffering Soviet Jews even if Washington had severed diplomatic relations with the new Bolshevik regime.

Balancing patriotism with concern for co-religionists abroad depends, in part, on the climate toward Jews or the foreign policy in one's own country in the West. Complicating this dilemma further, the delicate balance could be manipulated by anti-Semites and political forces in need of a unifying issue that could be fabricated by accusing Jews of "dual loyalties."[19] Perhaps in its most extreme expression, this dilemma influenced many Jewish activists before (and perhaps also after) 1948 to remain non-Zionist, for fear of being targets of suspicion among their countrymen; among those who adopted this orientation was Louis Marshall, a successor to Jacob Schiff as one of the most visible American-Jewish leaders of his time.[20]

Democratization triggered rapid proliferation of transnational activism from the second half of the nineteenth century. This was not just a transition from the leadership of "great" individuals to the "grassroots." Rather, it intersected with important events and trends in the Jewish world and beyond. Perhaps first in importance among these was the impact of the Zionist movement. Although "great" men eventually gravitated toward it, Zionism began as internationalist and democratic, featuring a Congress

---

[18] For example, Leff, *Sacred Bonds*, 4–11, 157–160.

[19] For example, see the clipping from the *Pall Mall Gazette*, May 4, 1891, "The Rothschilds and the Russian Jews," in The Rothschild Archive, London, Dept. II, series III, Box 108.

[20] Menachem Kaufman, *An Ambiguous Partnership: Non-Zionists and Zionists in America, 1939–1948* (Jerusalem: Magnes, 1991), 12, 24. For a recent reassessment of Marshall, see Matthew M. Silver, *Louis Marshall and the Rise of Jewish Ethnicity in America: A Biography* (Syracuse: Syracuse University Press, 2013).

populated with elected representatives from around the world and a fundraising apparatus (The Jewish National Fund) that challenged traditional sources of Jewish communal wealth and power. For the first time in the Jewish world, the unofficial diplomacy of the Zionist movement was not practiced (like traditional *shtadlanut*) by self-appointed representatives. Rather, it grew from a parliamentary-style electoral system.

Modernity brought challenges and opportunities to transnational aid. Pre-modern intercession across borders had mobilized mainly to ransom captives, whereas developments in early modern Europe demanded solutions for refugee crises. In order to propel Jewish communities toward modernity, philanthropies like the Alliance and the Organization for the Rehabilitation of Jews through Training (ORT) began in the late eighteenth century to prioritize education and vocational training to the purportedly "backward" Jewish communities in the East. Around the turn of the next century, these and other organizations (like JDC, JCA, and the Hebrew Immigrant Aid Society [HIAS]) increasingly emphasized resettlement as a solution for the "Jewish Question," at times in their home regions, at times in distant lands. Around the same period, women's philanthropic organizations (such as WIZO and Hadassah) also began to extend their reach beyond national borders. In all of these endeavors, the organizations operated from a world view in which the target communities would benefit both materially and politically through a process of modernization.

TYPES OF NON-STATE DIPLOMACY

The practice of Jewish non-state politics in the modern era included a range of activists and styles. The first type can loosely be described as diplomats or statesmen willing to intercede for Jewish interests while in service to their sovereign. One such individual was Gerson von Bleichröder, Chancellor Otto von Bismarck's economic wizard. This position, together with his deep connections in international finance, allowed Bleichröder to navigate the volatile, multi-polar European diplomatic arena while interceding for Eastern European Jews from the 1860s to the 1890s. Like most other such Jewish statesmen, his influence depended mostly on Bismarck's shifting worldview and status. Bleichröder's greatest achievement, embodied in the Berlin Treaty of 1878, included unprecedented protections for Romanian Jews; these were barely enforced, however, due to changes in world politics.[21]

---

[21] Gershom A. Knight, "The Rothschild–Bleichröder Axis in Action: An Anglo-German Cooperative, 1877–1878," *Leo Baeck Yearbook* 28 (1983): 43–57; Carole Fink, *Defending*

Sir Samuel Montagu was another informal diplomat for world Jewry while in the service of his state. As a Member of Parliament, he traveled to Russia in 1882 and 1886 at the request of a recently formed Anglo-Jewish advocacy group (The Mansion House Committee) to investigate the plight of that country's Jews. Montagu also visited other Jewish communities and negotiated on behalf of their emigration. Across the Atlantic a few decades later, Henry Morgenthau Jr. served as the United States Secretary of Treasury and authored what came to be known as the Morgenthau Plan, in 1944, which formulated the occupation regime in post-war Germany. While chairing a committee of the United Jewish Appeal in 1948, Morgenthau applied his formidable political, organizational, and financial skills to raise funds in the United States for the defense of Israel. His father, Henry Morgenthau Sr., had served as the American ambassador to Turkey during the First World War, was an American delegate to the negotiations for the post-war Minorities Treaty, and authored the controversial "Morgenthau Report" of 1919 on the violence and repression perpetrated against Jews in Poland. Other Jewish diplomats and political figures of this type included Leo Strauss, Herbert Samuel, Leon Blum, and Max Fisher.

A second type of Jewish diplomat acted informally on behalf of co-religionists abroad, without any appointment from the state although in some cases acting as representatives of national or supra-national Jewish organizations. Such individuals (both self-appointed and those chosen by organizations) represented what they perceived as Jewish transnational interests as a stateless, multi-national ethnic minority. These unofficial diplomats interacted with their home governments, foreign states and international institutions. The Houses of Rothschild usually stand out in this regard, but they were not alone. The first modern activists of this variety were Moses Montefiore and Adolphe Crémieux, who – during what became known as the "Damascus Affair" of 1840 – mobilized public opinion to apply pressure on their home governments and on the Ottoman Sultan to free a group of wrongly accused Jews. This campaign emboldened even state-sponsored Jewish bodies; the French *Consistoire* openly criticized official French policy on the matter.[22] The relatively successful campaign orchestrated by Montefiore and Crémieux – contrasted by the failed intercession against the Vatican during the Mortara Affair in 1856 – gave the founders of the Alliance in the 1860s a keen appreciation

the Rights of Others: The Great Powers, the Jews, and International Minority Protection, 1878–1938 (Cambridge: Cambridge University Press, 2004), 29–38.

[22] "Comment by Aron Rodrigue" in Bar-Chen "Two Communities," 125–127.

for the power of the press in the pursuit of philanthropic-diplomatic goals.[23]

Such lessons were not lost on a subsequent informal activist, Jacob Schiff. Like many intercessors, Schiff leveraged his considerable personal stature – in this case, in international banking – into substantial, but not unlimited, political influence. Through membership in government committees in the United States, Schiff gained access to officeholders who could be mobilized for intervention on Jewish issues. This position allowed him to clash openly with President Taft in 1911 over the abrogation of the 1832 commercial treaty with Russia as a means to pressure the latter on its Jewish policy; it also provided him entrée with European monarchs and helped him to convene an international conference on Jewish immigration in 1890. Later activists of this category included Louis Marshall, Felix Warburg, and Nahum Goldmann.

Zionist diplomacy before 1948 constitutes a separate, but interconnected, category of non-state politics. Many philanthropists and diplomats in the Diaspora had a role in this movement, even if they were not convinced of Zionism's potential to achieve sovereignty. The emotional surge surrounding the creation of Israel in 1948 caused many of these skeptics to change their position. Their mobilization took the form of lobbying governments in the West for the recognition and support of Israel's independence, as well as more concrete applications; among them, approximately 25 percent of the funds for the War of Independence were gathered abroad, primarily from American-Jewish businessmen who had not identified previously with Zionism.[24]

The Zionist movement, led by Theodor Herzl, was responsible at the turn of the twentieth century for the creation of a democratized institutional model for Jewish transnational activism. On the diplomatic front, Herzl negotiated with sultans and European ministers to gain charters for Jewish settlement in Palestine, Africa, and the Sinai Peninsula. Subsequent Zionist leaders, most prominently Chaim Weizmann, nurtured relationships with Ottoman and then British rulers, to strengthen Jewish settlement in Palestine. An offshoot of Zionism, the Jewish Territorial Organization negotiated with Europe's imperial powers for the resettlement of Eastern European Jews in colonial holdings in Africa and South America. This

[23] Jonathan Frankel, "Jewish Politics and the Press: The 'Reception' of the *Alliance Israélite Universelle* (1860)," in *Crisis, Revolution, and Russian Jews*, ed. Jonathan Frankel (Cambridge: Cambridge University Press, 2009), 36, 52–53.

[24] Derek Penslar, "Rebels Without a Patron State: How Israel Financed the 1948 War," in *Purchasing Power: The Economics of Modern Jewish History*, eds. Rebecca Kobrin and Adam Teller (Philadelphia: University of Pennsylvania Press, 2015), 171–191.

practice of non-state politics bore its most significant fruit with the Balfour Declaration, in 1917, which promised British support for a Jewish national homeland in Palestine. Although not all of the Jewish world, then or now, ascribed to Zionism, Herzl's model of elected representative leadership in the international arena (decades *before* the creation of the Jewish state) became the yardstick for all Jewish organizations, even if its world congress, executive committee and an independent fundraising apparatus did not achieve statehood in the short-term.

Jewish diplomacy and philanthropy did not change drastically after 1948. From the start of the modern era until 1917, *shtadlanim* and philanthropists tried to present a unified Jewish front to governments. Their campaigns often exhibited unity, owing in great part to the family and professional connections among many of the central activists. We know, however, that these "great" men were not elected representatives, nor did their actions necessarily reflect the desires of those they claimed to represent in the West. At the other pole, rifts among Jewish advocacy groups from the 1960s to the 1980s allowed governments in the West and the Soviet regime to deflect much of the force that could otherwise have been applied on behalf of Soviet Jewry. If unity ever really coalesced in the campaign, it probably occurred only during preparations for the mass rally in Washington DC on 6 December 1987.[25]

Competition between activists could, however, yield positive results in the long term by strengthening their campaigns. For example, during the interwar era, activists vied for funds, fueled by the JDC's huge investment in Eastern Europe. The flagship of this activity was the resettlement of hundreds of thousands of Jews from the former Pale of Settlement to agricultural colonies in Soviet Ukraine and Crimea.[26] According to the Zionist view, every dollar raised for activity in Eastern Europe, particularly in agricultural colonization, was a dollar wasted for reclaiming the Land of Israel. For a variety of reasons, the head of the JDC's fundraising campaign, David Brown, became a *bête noir* among American Zionists. In the mid-1920s, the recognized leader of the movement, Chaim Weizmann, expressed a mix of venom and respect, "People used to tell me wistfully that if we could only get for Zionism the whole-hearted support of Mr. David A. Brown, all our troubles would be over."[27] Over time, however, this competition strengthened all by forcing the JDC to pioneer and perfect fund-raising techniques.

---

[25] Henry Feingold. *"Silent No More": Saving the Jews of Russia: The American Jewish Effort, 1967–1989* (Syracuse: Syracuse University Press, 2007), 272–274, 310.

[26] For details, see Jonathan Dekel-Chen, *Farming the Red Land: Jewish Agricultural Colonization and Soviet Local Power* (New Haven: Yale, 2005).

[27] Chaim Weizmann, *Trial and Error: The Autobiography of Chaim Weizmann* (New York: Harpers, 1949), 311.

Although damaged at first by these improved methods for soliciting funds, Zionism benefited greatly when men like Brown gravitated toward it in the late 1930s. While both unity and fragmentation characterized Jewish diplomacy before and after 1948, the Jewish Diaspora has, for the most part, supported Zionism since the 1880s and, later, the State of Israel. The seeming unity of pro-Israel advocacy groups in Washington DC in the post-1948 era evidently prompted Senator William Fulbright to comment (with no small degree of frustration) that the "Israel lobby" could gather seventy votes in the Senate whenever it chose.

LANDMARK EVENTS IN INTERNATIONALISM

Eastern Europe was for many decades the most urgent arena for international mobilization. The case of Romanian Jewry embodies the success and failure of the first generations of sporadic efforts. Following earlier attempts by the chief rabbi of Turkey to intervene on behalf of Jewish land rights in Wallachia,[28] European Jews interceded at the Paris Peace Conference in 1856. Here, German and French *shtadlanim* advocated for the equal rights of Jews in the newly independent territories of Wallachia and Moldovia by publicizing their plight and through direct appeals to Napoleon III. In the first half of the 1870s, American and Hungarian Jews, among others, lobbied their governments to help Romanian Jewry, while the Alliance created a special international committee to deal with this growing crisis. Intercession on this issue reached its peak during 1878 in the negotiation of the Berlin Treaty, with von Bleichröder and the Alliance expending considerable energies to influence the major powers represented at the Congress. As mentioned above, these efforts did not yield enforceable civil rights for Romania's Jews. They did, however, powerfully insert the "Jewish Question" into international statecraft, with the unfortunate byproduct of affirming suspicions among anti-Semites about the supposed power of world Jewry.[29]

More systematic international action, paired with a radical new vision, surfaced during the response to a refugee crisis at the port city of Memel (today Klaipeda, Lithuania) in 1869–72, where famine in Eastern Europe brought together thousands of desperate Jews seeking relief. Following

---

[28] *Pinkas ha-kehilot: Romania*, vol. 1, ed. Theodore Lavi (Jerusalem: Yad Vashem, 1969), 32.

[29] N. M. Gelber, "The Intervention of German Jews at the Berlin Congress 1878," *Leo Baeck Institute Yearbook* 5 (1960): 221–247; Fink, *Defending the Rights*, 5–38; Leff, *Sacred Bonds*, 158–9; Michael K. Silber, "A Jewish Minority in a Backward Economy: An Introduction," in *Jews in the Hungarian Economy, 1760–1945*, ed. M. K. Silber (Jerusalem: The Magnes Press, 1992), 20–1.

calls for assistance from local committees in Memel and Konigsberg – both of which had been flooded by refugees – German, French, English, and American Jewries for the first time coordinated their efforts to solve an Eastern European humanitarian crisis. In so doing, they set vital precedents. First, they attempted to balance short-term relief for refugees with the need to correct the fundamental deficiencies of traditional Jewish society through vocational training programs. Second, the organizations determined that, unlike traditional charity, the scope of aid they delivered would no longer be measured solely by the degree of need among the people in the target group. Third, and most revolutionary, the organizations systematically resettled some of these refugees in the United States.

Although the tense political atmosphere prevailing in Western Europe during the 1870s hampered efforts to form an international body, Jewish philanthropy did exponentially increase throughout the continent at this time. Moreover, the lessons learned by transnational activists during the Memel crisis were brought to bear during the emergencies that followed the Russian pogroms of 1881–82. For their part, *shtadlanim* in the West (including the Rothschilds and Baron Maurice de Hirsch) launched public campaigns similar to those used in the Damascus and Memel crises. They also worked harder to forge alliances with other religious groups in the West to provide aid to Russia's Jews. The post-1881 campaigns departed from earlier efforts in their emphasis on resettlement projects inside and outside of Russia. By this time, philanthropists had concluded that – given the threats from antisemitic laws and renewed pogroms – masses of Russian Jews had to be moved from the Pale of Settlement. Baron de Hirsch's Jewish Colonization Association (JCA) pioneered these programs by creating a professional network of committees and offices throughout Eastern Europe with two interconnected goals: the productivization of Jews through agriculture, vocational training and cooperative loan societies, and the facilitation of their mass emigration to the "new" world. Henceforth, movement from repressive countries to the West or the Land of Israel became a centerpiece of Jewish internationalism.

Proper triage and absorption of these millions of emigrants triggered many developments. In North America alone, multiple organizations arose to deal with this challenge. Among the most noteworthy was the Russian Relief Committee, created in September 1881, reconstituted shortly thereafter as HIAS. American Jewry then went further toward systematic resettlement of immigrants from Eastern Europe with the creation of the Jewish Agricultural Society and the Industrial Removal Office. Directing masses of European refugees toward the Land of Israel became a major goal of transnational philanthropy and diplomacy only after the Holocaust. Beginning in 1948, organizations in the West (led by the JDC) also started to see the resettlement of Jews from Arab-speaking lands – and from the 1980s, Ethiopian Jews – to Israel as an important goal for world Jewry. Not all resettlement projects yielded the desired results. Among the relative "failures" can be counted Jacob Schiff's "Galveston Plan" (1903), which aimed to relocate immigrants from Eastern Europe to the southern and western United States and the JDC's frantic search for havens for Jews fleeing fascist Europe in places like the Dominican Republic and the Philippines on the eve of the Second World War.[30]

In parallel to the increasing focus on resettlement around the turn of the twentieth century, the mobilization of financial pressure against repressive regimes became an important feature of Jewish informal diplomacy. Starting with the expulsion of most Jews from Moscow in 1891, Jacob Schiff tried to limit the cash-hungry regime's access to credit in the West. This tactic reached its apex in his response to the increasingly deadly waves of pogroms that rocked Russia from 1903 to 1906; Schiff worked, together with the Rothschilds, to choke financing to the bankrupt Russian regime in the midst of its war with Japan in 1904–05. Their campaign failed for two reasons: Petersburg secured loans elsewhere and, perhaps no less important, governments and public opinion in the West wanted the tsar to defeat the growing "yellow peril" and to persevere over the growing forces of revolution in Russia.[31] Notwithstanding its failure in the short-term, this mobilization of financial pressure sparked an ongoing, and never fully resolved, debate among Jewish activists about wisdom of tactics for leveraging repressive regimes: was it more effective to pursue "quiet" diplomacy or more aggressive action? This debate was still evident decades later in the conduct of Hans J. Morgenthau, a prominent American-Jewish government official, intellectual, and activist. Until the early 1970s, he had advocated behind-the-scenes contacts with the Kremlin to ease the repression of Soviet Jews. By the middle of the decade, he waxed more combative, eventually becoming a vocal advocate of the Jackson–Vanik Amendment, a controversial Congressional act that tied American foreign trade policy to the Soviet Union's behavior toward its Jews and other minorities.[32]

Fractiousness often limited informal Jewish diplomacy. Surveying the outcome of the treaties signed following the First World War helps illuminate this problem. Delegates of the many Jewish philanthropic and

[30] The former is described in Marion A. Kaplan, *Dominican Haven: The Jewish Refugee Settlement in Sosúa, 1940–1945* (New York: Museum of Jewish Heritage, 2008).
[31] Diner, *The Jews of the United States*, 178–179; Naomi W. Cohen, *Jacob H. Schiff: a Study in American Jewish Leadership* (Hanover, NH: Brandeis University Press, 1999), 130–143.
[32] M. Benjamin Mollov, *Power and Transcendence: Hans J. Morgenthau and the Jewish Experience* (Lanham, MD: Lexington, 2002), 147–155.

advocacy organizations represented at the 1919 Paris Peace Conference disagreed about goals. Some – among them, the American Jewish Congress, the Alliance, and the Joint Foreign Affairs Committee of Anglo-Jewry – wanted the negotiations on Jewish issues to focus on civil rights in the new countries of Europe. Other delegations – the councils of Jewish communities in Eastern and Central Europe, the B'nai B'rith organization, and the Jewish community in Mandatory Palestine – tried to push the talks toward discussion of Jewish national rights. The resulting treaty – together with the associated Minorities Treaty negotiated by some of the great informal Jewish diplomats of the time, Lucien Wolf, Louis Marshall, and Henry Morgenthau, Sr. – did not, however, completely protect Jews from the growing antisemitic pressures in Eastern Europe. For the remainder of the interwar period, Jewish activists in the West attempted to intercede for Eastern European Jewry and other minorities through political lobbying, the press, and international law. Although only marginally successful at the time, the practices and personnel of this ongoing intercession formed the core of more fruitful campaigns after 1945.

Overall, straightforward transnational philanthropy accomplished more than diplomacy in Eastern Europe during the interwar period. Despite drawing resistance from Zionists, Western philanthropic organizations successfully engaged in the relief and reconstruction of Eastern European Jewry by the mid-1930s. These programs began in 1914 and gained momentum with the global post-war relief effort. The Western philanthropic organizations engaged in this work – the JDC, ORT and JCA – created a variety of educational, vocational, welfare, and agricultural resettlement programs that helped return these Jewish communities to normalcy after the devastation caused by the First World War, the Russian Civil War, and Soviet Russia's brief war against Poland. It is important to note that this relatively successful philanthropy was facilitated, in part, through the unofficial diplomacy practiced by some of its leaders.[33]

Undoubtedly the coming of fascism in Europe marked the darkest hours for transnational Jewish activism. Philanthropic organizations tried to intercede in the political arena and sought sites for refuge and the means to support European Jewry and, indeed, relatively small groups of European refugees were assisted in a variety of ways and places.[34] None of

---

[33] Jonathan Dekel-Chen, "An Unlikely Triangle: Philanthropists, Commissars, and American Statesmanship Meet in Soviet Crimea, 1922–37," *Diplomatic History* 27, no. 3 (July 2003): 353–376.

[34] For example, Henry L. Feingold, *Bearing Witness: How America and its Jews Responded to the Holocaust* (Syracuse: Syracuse University Press, 1995).

these efforts, however, rescued large numbers of Jews given the limits of unofficial diplomacy and the absence of a Jewish state as an available haven.

Supplying relief for survivors of the Holocaust and the establishment of Israel ignited enormous philanthropic and diplomatic campaigns. Massive mobilizations were launched in the West to assist displaced persons throughout Europe and to aid their relocation inside and outside of the continent. Before it was completed in the early 1950s, relief for Europe's Jewish DPs was made more difficult with the coming of the Cold War, wherein access to Jewish communities behind the spreading "Iron Curtain" proved increasingly difficult, particularly in the Soviet Union. Hence, while most survivors in Central and Western Europe benefited at least in some way from philanthropic or diplomatic intervention, the Jews of the Soviet Union lost almost all contact with these resources after 1945. Throughout the Diaspora, Israel's independence and security continued to be a primary concern and point of consensus into the early 1970s. As the decade progressed, however, the stabilization of Israeli infrastructure and security situation contributed to a more inward focus among many philanthropists and leaders, some of whom have preferred since then to address what they consider serious challenges at home, like Jewish education and demographic contraction.

Notwithstanding a tendency among domestic communities to look inwardly, Jewish transnational activism has in recent decades mobilized for Jewish communities abroad. The most striking case was the campaign for Soviet Jewry. The movement had parallel goals of ensuring the rights of Soviet Jews to practice their religion at home and allowing them unrestricted emigration to Israel or elsewhere. Action on this issue developed gradually from the mid-1950s, reached its height during the 1970s around the passage of the Jackson–Vanik Amendment in the United States Congress and the creation of the World Conferences on Soviet Jewry. The movement receded with the opening of the gates of the Soviet Union in the late 1980s. It departed from what had come before inasmuch as Soviet Jews did not face an existential threat and therefore did not require philanthropic relief in the conventional sense. Instead, the campaign in the West advocated for their basic civil rights and freedom of movement. It embodied Jewish internationalism, with branches sprouting throughout the West and Israel. The Soviet Jewry movement accelerated the democratizing process in Jewish organizational life, as dedicated "grassroots" advocacy groups like the Students Struggle for Soviet Jewry challenged the authority of what they considered the Jewish "establishment" represented by, among others, the American Jewish Congress. Relief and rescue for the Jewish community of Ethiopia constitutes another recent case of transnational activism. Narrower in overall scope than the campaign for Soviet

Jewry, the mobilization for Ethiopian Jewry embodied more classic elements of relief for a threatened community in the midst of a war zone, as well as intercession with governments to facilitate the nearly total resettlement of the community to Israel during the 1980s and 90s.

TRANSNATIONAL ACTIVISM THROUGH THE *LONGUE DURÉE*

Measuring the results of philanthropy and informal diplomacy is difficult, at best. For example, even if a specific attempt at intercession did not achieve its stated goals, short-term failures could lead to longer-term successes. In the "Mortara Affair" of 1856 in Bologna, for example, a collective sense of frustration engendered by an inability to convince the Vatican to return a kidnapped Jewish child to his parents led within four years to the establishment of the Alliance.[35] Efforts by American-Jewish leaders during the 1870s to convince President Ulysses S. Grant to intervene on behalf of Romanian Jewry was another such case. At face value, very little was gained: neither Grant's intervention nor the Berlin Treaty "rescued" Romania's Jews. This short-term failure did, nonetheless, inform subsequent intercessors. For example, during informal discussions with the Polish National Committee in 1918, Louis Marshall raised the failure of the Treaty of Berlin to protect Romanian Jewry as justification for his aggressive negotiating posture vis-à-vis the persecution of Polish Jews.[36]

Differentiating between "victory" and "defeat" is equally challenging when assessing the history of activism for Russian and Soviet Jewry. Before and during the First World War, Western Jewries created institutions meant entirely for international intercession. Nevertheless, they could not always translate this into significant results for Russian Jews, even at moments when the tsarist regime seemed vulnerable to outside pressures. These activists learned that mere goodwill from well-placed Russian officials, or pressure on their own administrations, did not guarantee concessions from the tsars on the "Jewish Question." With the benefit of hindsight, however, this short-term difficulty does not indicate total failure. Rather, these intercessors sparked public interest in the West about the fate of Russian Jewry that inspired activism up to the grassroots organizations like the Students Struggle for Soviet Jewry in the 1970s. In so doing, they promoted a sense of Jewish solidarity at home and in the target communities. Their activism catapulted the issue to the headlines in the Western body politic and press.

---

[35] David Kertzer, *The Kidnapping of Edgaro Mortara* (London: Picador, 1997).

[36] Louis Marshall, "Report of a Conversation between Messrs. Roman Dmowski and Louis Marshall, October 6, 1918," pamphlet (New York, 1918), especially p. 16.

This should not be taken for granted; the sufferings of Jews in faraway lands always "competed" with many other newsworthy items. Moreover, the precedents and expectations produced by Jewish activism during one crisis were inherited by activists and target communities in subsequent events. Hence, by the time of the Russian pogroms in 1881–82, there was already an expectation among the Russian-Jewish intelligentsia and masses that Western European Jewry would come to their aid.[37] Similar expectations eventually infiltrated into the Russian and Soviet administrations, thereby creating complex, reciprocal, transnational relationships.

Activism also played a role in the formation of social hierarchies. In many Western Jewish communities, the conduct of philanthropy and informal diplomacy at times allowed "native" elites to exert control over their home communities, particularly with the arrival of masses of immigrants. During the years following their arrival in the West, these "greenhorns" depended on the assistance and leadership of the older Jewish communal leaders, who for the most part also underwrote and headed the philanthropic organizations. Both domestic and transnational aid programs reinforced patron–client ties and behaviors between the givers and receivers of aid. Although power relationships shifted over time, their legacies remain in almost all Jewish communities today. That being said, transnational philanthropy also helped to empower the relatively powerless. For example, recent immigrants to the Americas from Białystok formed *landsmanschaften* and sent millions of dollars back to the "old country" during the interwar period. Whatever it accomplished for their beleaguered brothers in Poland, this effort helped the newcomers in New York and Buenos Aires to feel more like veteran Jewish citizens in their new countries.[38]

Mobilization for Jews abroad had many additional outcomes in the West, where it has given Jewish communities a sense of shared purpose since at least the 1840s. Campaigning for endangered communities abroad also periodically helped to jolt communities out of internal dissention or apathy. One such moment occurred at the end of the First World War, when Jewish communities in the West quickly mobilized for the relief of co-religionists in Eastern Europe, thereby compensating somewhat for the lingering discomfort of Jews fighting against Jews on the battlefields of Europe – even former comrades on the Left. Years later, the mobilizations for Israel's independence and aid to DPs in Europe helped simultaneously to relieve collective feelings of guilt and helplessness during the Holocaust and also to smooth the intense interwar friction between Zionists and

---

[37] Frankel, "The Crisis as a Factor in Modern Jewish Politics," 39.

[38] Rebecca Kobrin, *Jewish Białystok and Its Diaspora* (Bloomington: Indiana University Press, 2010), 131–75.

non-Zionists throughout the Diaspora. It must be remembered, however, that rarely more than an enthusiastic minority of Jews in the West participated directly in these mobilizations, notwithstanding the fact that such campaigns tended to characterize communal narratives.

Has modern Jewish international activism really emanated mainly from a sense of a shared past? Or should it be seen as a series of pragmatic attempts to deal with crises?[39] At times, there was indeed a unique kind of pioneering "Jewish" activism, like large-scale reconstruction projects abroad. At other times, however, Jewish philanthropy and diplomacy share much common ground with non-Jewish activism, like mobilizations to absorb immigrant communities and educational programs. Jewish activism has always been vulnerable to twists in the international arena. Even if successful at first glance, a philanthropic effort may not always be in the best interests of the target communities when judged in the longer term. A striking case of this kind of irony can be seen after the Holocaust. Some later observers believe that by helping to reintegrate Jewish survivors, evacuees, and war veterans back into their home countries in Eastern Europe (instead of assisting their emigration to the West or to Palestine) the World Jewish Congress and the JDC inadvertently condemned these survivors and their offspring to a type of imprisonment behind the "Iron Curtain."[40]

Intercession usually achieved the most when its goals matched the interests of one's home government. In the United States, Jewish leaders campaigned relatively effectively for action in Washington during the "Damascus Affair" because the government at that time sought to improve its foreign policy mettle. Consequently, this campaign not only rescued oppressed Jews in the East, but also helped American Jewry to establish an unofficial presence in international diplomacy.[41] On the other side of the coin, Schiff's "Galveston Plan" failed in great part due to general shifts in Washington's orientation toward immigration from Eastern Europe.

At the intersection between the past, present, and future of transnational activism, two challenges usually confront any practice of Jewish philanthropy and diplomacy. First, philanthropists must be aware that the provision of aid to Jews abroad can spark jealousy – with potentially fierce reactions – among that community's non-Jewish neighbors. Second, the

---

[39] Shmuel Sandler, "Is There a Jewish Foreign Policy?," *Jewish Journal of Sociology* 29, no. 2 (1987): 119–120.

[40] Kinga Frojimovics, "Different Interpretations of Reconstruction: The AJJDC and the World Jewish Congress in Hungary after the Holocaust," in *The Jews are Coming Back: The Return of the Jews to their Countries of Origin after WW II*, ed. David Bankier (New York: Berghahn Books, 2005), 279, 286, 292.

[41] Diner, *The Jews of the United States*, 175–176.

public profile of specifically Jewish diplomacy and transnational philanthropy risks providing fodder to those individuals and groups pre-disposed toward conspiracy theories about Jewish power.

SELECT BIBLIOGRAPHY

Bar-Chen, Eli. "Two Communities with a Sense of Mission: The Alliance Israélite Universelle and the Hilfsverein der deutschen Juden." In *Jewish Emancipation Reconsidered: The French and German Models*, edited by Michael Brenner, Vicki Caron, and Uri R. Kaufman, 111–121. Tubingen: Mohr Siebeck, 2003.

Biale, David. *Power and Powerlessness in Jewish History*. New York: Schocken, 1986.

Bogen, Boris D. *Jewish Philanthropy: An Exposition of Principles and Methods of Jewish Social Service in the United States*. Montclair, NJ: Patterson Smith, 1969.

Bowker, J.W. "Intercession in the Qur'an and the Jewish Tradition." *Journal of Semitic Studies* 11 (1966): 69–82.

Cohen, Naomi W. *Jacob H. Schiff: a Study in American Jewish Leadership*. Hanover, NH: Brandeis University Press, 1999.

D'Ancona, Luisa Levi. "Philanthropy and Politics: Strategies of Jewish Bourgeois in Italy, France and England between the end of the nineteenth and the beginning of the twentieth Centuries." *Traverse* 1 (2006): 83–100.

Dekel-Chen, Jonathan. "An Unlikely Triangle: Philanthropists, Commissars, and American Statesmanship Meet in Soviet Crimea, 1922–37." *Diplomatic History* 27, no. 3 (2003): 353–376.

Elazar, Daniel J. "The Jewish People as the Classic Diaspora: A Political Analysis." In *Modern Diasporas in International Politics*, edited by Gabriel Sheffer, 212–257. New York: St. Martins, 1986.

Esman, Milton J. "Diasporas and International Relations." In *Modern Diasporas in International Politics*, edited by Gabriel Sheffer, 333–349. New York: St. Martins, 1986.

Feingold, Henry. *"Silent No More": Saving the Jews of Russia. The American Jewish Effort, 1967–1989*. Syracuse: Syracuse University Press, 2007.

Bearing Witness: How America and its Jews Responded to the Holocaust. Syracuse: Syracuse University Press, 1995.

Ferguson, Niall. *The House of Rothschild*, 2 vols. New York: Penguin, 1998–99.

Fink, Carole. *Defending the Rights of Others: The Great Powers, the Jews, and International Minority Protection, 1878–1938*. Cambridge: Cambridge University Press, 2004.

Frankel, Jonathan. "The Crisis as a Factor in Modern Jewish Politics, 1840 and 1881–1882." In *Organizing Rescue: National Jewish Solidarity in the Modern Period*, edited by Selwyn Ilan Troen and Benjamin Pinkus, 33–49. London: Frank Cass, 1992.

Frisch, Ephraim. *An Historical Survey of Jewish Philanthropy*. New York: Macmillan, 1924.

Gelber, N.M. "The Intervention of German Jews at the Berlin Congress 1878." *Leo Baeck Institute Yearbook* 5 (1960): 221–247.

Guesnet, François. "Textures of Intercession: Rescue Efforts for the Jews of Prague, 1744–1748." *Simon Dubnow Institute Yearbook* 4 (2005): 355–377.

Gutwein, Daniel. *The Divided Elite: Economics, Politics and Anglo-Jewry, 1882–1917*. Leiden: Brill, 1992.

Knight, Gershom A. "The Rothschild–Bleichröder Axis in Action: An Anglo-German Cooperative, 1877–1878." *Leo Baeck Yearbook* 28 (1983): 43–57.

Kobrin, Rebecca. *Jewish Bialystok and Its Diaspora.* Bloomington: Indiana University Press, 2010.

Leff, Lisa Moses. *Sacred Bonds of Solidarity: The Rise of Jewish Internationalism in Nineteenth-Century France.* Stanford: Stanford University Press, 2006.

Maciejko, Paweł. "Baruch Yavan and the Frankist Movement: Intercession in an Age of Upheaval." *Simon Dubnow Institute Yearbook* 4 (2005): 333–354.

Mintz, Mattityahu. "Nesigat ha-Rotshildim me-milveh April 1891 le-Rusyah min ha-hebet ha-yehudi." *Tsion* 54 (1989): 401–435

Penslar, Derek. "The Origins of Modern Jewish Philanthropy." In *Philanthropy in the World's Traditions,* edited by Warren F. Ilchman, Stanley N. Katz, and Edward L. Queen, 197–214. Bloomington: Indiana University Press, 1998.

"Rebels Without a Patron State: How Israel Financed the 1948 War." In *Purchasing Power: The Economics of Modern Jewish History,* edited by Rebecca Kobrin and Adam Teller. Philadelphia: University of Pennsylvania Press, 2015.

Roberts, Priscilla. "Jewish Bankers, Russia, and the Soviet Union, 1900–1940: The Case of Kuhn, Loeb and Company." *American Jewish Archives Journal* 49, no. 1–2 (1997): 9–37

Sandler, Shmuel. "Is There a Jewish Foreign Policy?" *Jewish Journal of Sociology* 29, no. 2 (1987): 115–121.

Sheffer, Gabriel. *Diaspora Politics: At Home Abroad.* Cambridge: Cambridge University Press, 2003.

Vital, David. "Diplomacy in the Jewish Interest." In *Jewish History: Essays in Honor of Chimen Abramsky,* edited by Ada Rapoport-Albert and Steven Zipperstein, 683–695. London: Halban, 1988.

Yerushalmi, Yosef Haim. *"Servants of Kings and Not Servants of Servants": Some Aspects of the Political History of the Jews.* Atlanta: Emory University, 2005.

CHAPTER 19

JEWS AND MODERN EUROPEAN IMPERIALISM

ETHAN B. KATZ, LISA MOSES LEFF, AND MAUD S. MANDEL

Where are Jews in colonial history? Where is colonialism in Jewish history? Despite the recent outpouring of scholarly attention to modern colonialism, Jewish historians have been surprisingly reticent to explore these questions. Prior to the early 2000s, most historians of European Jewry sidestepped the issue or ignored it altogether. Like most of their colleagues in the wider field of European history, many specialists in Jewish history saw nation-states, rather than empires, as the framework within which the great changes that characterized modern Jewish life took place.[1] In addition, scholars of Jewish history were particularly resistant or late to come to many of the methodological developments that proved crucial to the so-called Imperial Turn. These included critiques of positivism and empiricism; attention to meta-narrative and the subjectivity of archival sources; and an emphasis on language, reflecting the influence of Foucauldian ideas about the nexus of knowledge and power.

Undoubtedly, the greatest elephant in the room has been Zionism. During the very period in which post-colonial studies emerged, debates raged over the place of colonialism in the history of Zionism and the State of Israel. This rendered colonialism a veritable minefield for Jewish studies scholars. From the vantage point of post-colonial studies, Jews and colonialism frequently became reduced to polemics over Zionism, flattening the issue rather than taking account of its nuances.

In fact, the modern Jewish experience connects to the history of colonialism by virtue of a number of its central components: mobility and exchange, Diaspora, internationalism, racial discrimination, and Zionism,

A version of this chapter was originally written as "Introduction: Engaging Jewish History and Colonial History," in *Colonialism and the Jews*, ed. Ethan B. Katz, Lisa Moses Leff, and Maud S. Mandel (Bloomington: Indiana University Press, 2017). Published here with permission of Indiana University Press.

[1] Frederick Cooper, "The Rise, Fall, and Rise of Colonial Studies, 1951–2001," in Cooper, *Colonialism in Question: Theory, Knowledge, History* (Berkeley: University of California Press, 2005), 33–55.

to name but a few. Little wonder that specialists of Jews in North Africa and the Middle East, by contrast with those of Europe, have always made colonialism part of the stories they told. And yet there too, little early work interrogated the distinctive roles Jews played in colonial societies, economies, and politics. Rather, scholars often simply celebrated the impact of European colonialism, by explicitly or implicitly depicting colonial rule as a harbinger of "progress" for non-European Jews, whether in the form of emancipation at European hands or Zionist migration to Palestine and then Israel. In this sense, earlier generations of scholars tended to work within the linear narrative of modernization that characterized the field of European Jewish history, in which colonized Jews became increasingly "modern" by virtue of their contact with Europeans. Such work typically saw colonialism's role in Jewish history and Jews' role in colonial history as a "gentler" one, that is, distinctively benevolent in the scheme of the broader history of European colonialism. Even when these historians revealed a colonial society far more complex than they recognized explicitly, they overlooked the ambiguities of colonial Jewish life.[2]

In failing to grapple with colonialism, Jewish historians disregarded essential dimensions of the modern Jewish experience. In European colonies from the British antipodes to French North Africa, Jewish economic, religious, and social life was transformed by the encounter with empire. Moreover, the effects of empire were as important in metropolitan Europe as they were in the colonies. Taking heed of Frederick Cooper and Ann Stoler's dictum that "Europe was made by its imperial projects, as much as colonial encounters were shaped by conflicts within Europe itself," a handful of historians have now started to explore the multifaceted ways in which European Jews engaged with empire.[3] Their studies reveal that Jewish modernization was not, in fact, simply an effect of the Jewish encounter with the nation-state, as was long assumed. Rather, the encounter with imperialism – its legal forms, its economic structures, and its cultural and intellectual underpinnings – shaped the contours of European Jewish modernization as well.

Examining the experience of Jews under modern European imperialism also yields new insights beyond Jewish history. In recent years, historians have focused on revealing and making sense of the contradictions at the heart of modern European empires. The imperial ventures

---

[2] We thank Sarah Abrevaya Stein for sharing with us her unpublished paper, "Jews and European Imperialism," from which we draw some of our insights on the literature.

[3] Ann Laura Stoler and Frederick Cooper, "Between Metropole and Colony: Rethinking a Research Agenda," in Stoler and Cooper, eds, *Tensions of Empire: Colonial Cultures in a Bourgeois World* (Berkeley: University of California Press, 1997), 1.

of nineteenth- and twentieth-century Britain, France, and Germany were highly inegalitarian, characterized by violent conquest, exploitation of resources, and subjugation of peoples. Yet they were frequently undertaken in the name of the universalist values of the Enlightenment, the French Revolution, and modern liberalism. These warrants cannot be dismissed as mere hypocrisy; rather, they reveal the formative contradictions that helped to shape modern European political cultures. Indeed, debates over imperialism were critical for shaping Europeans' understanding of the universal principles by which polities should be organized, such as popular sovereignty, the primacy of the nation-state, and the pursuit of the public good. Such debates were also sites for defining how far universalist principles should extend, and the criteria by which some groups would be included and others excluded (e.g., race, religion, gender, and wealth).[4] The fundamental contradictions at the heart of modern European imperialism – and Jews' frequent place in the crosshairs – have also animated much of the new scholarship on Jews and empire.

This chapter analyzes the emergence and implications of the burgeoning scholarship on Jews and modern European imperialism, which might productively be called a "Jewish Imperial Turn." We discuss the evolution of historians' understanding of the place of Jews in modern empires, outline the findings of recent scholarship, and assess the potential for bringing the fields of Jewish history and colonial history into direct conversation with one another.

We center our discussion on France and its empire. Some of the reasons for this focus are historical. As the seat of the French Revolutionary tradition and a vast global empire, France offers a particularly important instance of the paradoxes of inclusion and exclusion. Furthermore, in the nineteenth and twentieth centuries, France's Jewish population was as significant in its colonies as it was in the metropole. By the late 1940s, there were nearly half a million Jews total in French Morocco (250,000), Tunisia (100,000), and Algeria (140,000), a number that dwarfed not only mainland France's post-war Jewish population of a quarter million but also the pre-war peak of 330,000.[5] Moreover, Jews played an important

---

[4] Stoler and Cooper, "Between Metropole and Colony," 1–53; Cooper, "Introduction: Colonial Questions, Historical Trajectories," in his *Colonialism in Question*, 3–32, esp. 27.

[5] Figures for North Africa from Michael M. Laskier, "Between Vichy Antisemitism and German Harassment: The Jews of North Africa during the Early 1940s," *Modern Judaism* 11, no. 3 (1991): 343–369, here 366. For French Jews, pre-war figure from Renée Poznanski, *Jews in France during World War II*, trans. Nathan Bracher (Hanover, NH: University Press of New England, 1997), 1; postwar figure from Maud S. Mandel, *In the Aftermath of Genocide: Armenians and Jews in Twentieth-Century France* (Durham, NC: Duke University Press, 2003), 11.

role in shaping France's imperial history in both metropole and colony. There are historiographical reasons for this focus as well. In recent decades, scholarship in French and French imperial history has been dramatically reshaped by the Imperial Turn. Correspondingly, French Jewish historians have found the new directions particularly fruitful, and historians of French colonialism have begun to give greater attention to Jews.

We also consider developments beyond the Francophone sphere. Indeed, the history of Jews and empire requires a comparative approach. Such an approach can push scholars to consider how transnational and non-national factors, including not only imperialism but also the work of international organizations and trans-regional economic connections, shaped Jewish modernity. In turn, it permits us to reflect upon the ways in which Jews shaped those larger systems as well.

THE IMPERIAL TURN AS A CHALLENGE TO JEWISH HISTORY

The Imperial Turn has begun to transform our understanding of modern Jewish history in important ways. For too long, European Jewish historians remained wedded to a theory of Jewish modernization, first explicitly articulated by Salo Baron and later popularized by Hannah Arendt that depicted the nation-state as the key political formation that shaped modernization for Jews everywhere.[6] The enduring power of this perspective is clear in studies that trace the different "paths of emancipation" that Jews followed in various European nation-states. Indeed, in spite of the variety and complexity of Jewish experiences they have described, Jewish historians have nonetheless largely agreed that the assimilationist demands of liberal nation-states shaped the paths of Jews' transformation in the modern world, which led (albeit in different ways and following different timelines) from communal autonomy to increased political, socio-cultural, and economic integration.

Much of this scholarship has treated France as paradigmatic. For the revolutionaries who emancipated the Jews, Rousseauian logic dictated that there could be no legal distinctions among members of the nation. This meant that gaining political rights was predicated on the legal dissolution of Jews' semi-autonomous communal institutions and the minimizing of their social and cultural differences from other Frenchmen. In much early historiography, emancipation was thus depicted as leading to the full

[6] Salo Wittmayer Baron, "Ghetto and Emancipation," *Menorah Journal* 14, no. 6 (1928): 515–526; Hannah Arendt, *Origins of Totalitarianism* (New York: Harcourt, Brace & Jovanovich, 1951).

abandonment of a distinctive public Jewish identity in exchange for inclusion in the national community.[7] Subsequent scholarship challenged portrayals of modernization as leading toward the complete absorption of Jews into their wider national contexts, stressing instead the multiple "paths to, of, and from emancipation."[8] As they rejected a single story of assimilation, scholars sought greater nuance by employing notions of "acculturation," "integration," and the development of Jewish "subcultures."[9] Even this scholarship, however, rarely challenged the primacy of the nation-state in driving the social, cultural, political, and economic transformations of Jewish life in Europe.[10]

For the Jewish historians who saw the French model as normative, the experiences of Jews in the Habsburg and Russian empires represented, all too often, cases of delayed or even failed modernization.[11] But by the 1990s, the waning influence of modernization theory across the disciplines led

---

[7] Michael Marrus, *The Politics of Assimilation: The French Jewish Community at the Time of the Dreyfus Affair* (New York: Clarendon Press, 1971); Arthur Hertzberg, *The French Enlightenment and the Jews: the Origins of Modern Anti-Semitism* (New York: Columbia University Press, 1968); Shmuel Trigano, "From Individual to Collectivity: the Rebirth of the 'Jewish Nation' in France," in *The Jews of Modern France*, ed. Frances Malino and Bernard Wasserstein (Hanover, NH: Brandeis University Press, 1985), 245–281. For a more recent analysis, see Ronald Schechter, *Obstinate Hebrews: Representations of Jews in France, 1715–1815* (Berkeley: University of California Press, 2003).

[8] Pierre Birnbaum and Ira Katznelson, "Emancipation and the Liberal Offer," in *Paths of Emancipation: Jews, States, and Citizenship*, ed. Birnbaum and Katznelson (Princeton: Princeton University Press, 1995), 3–36, here 24.

[9] The literature on the complexities of Jewish acculturation in modern Europe is vast. Some important examples for the French case include Jay Berkovitz, *The Shaping of Jewish Identity in Nineteenth-century France* (Detroit: Wayne State University Press, 1989); idem, *Rites and Passages: the Beginnings of Jewish Culture in Modern France* (Philadelphia: University of Pennsylvania Press, 2004); and Paula Hyman, *The Emancipation of the Jews of Alsace: Acculturation and Tradition in the Nineteenth Century* (New Haven: Yale University Press, 1991).

[10] The primacy of the nation-state is particularly visible in several important comparative edited volumes in modern European Jewish history in the 1990s and early 2000s. See notably, Birnbaum and Katznelson, eds, *Paths of Emancipation*; Michael Brenner, Vicki Caron, and Uri R. Kaufmann, eds, *Jewish Emancipation Reconsidered: The French and German Models* (Tubingen: Mohr Siebeck, 2003); Jonathan Frankel and Steven J. Zipperstein, eds, *Assimilation and Community: The Jews of Nineteenth-Century Europe* (Cambridge: Cambridge University Press, 1992); and Frances Malino and David Sorkin, eds, *From East and West: Jews in a Changing Europe, 1750–1870* (New York: Basil Blackwell, 1990).

[11] Benjamin Nathans, *Beyond the Pale: The Jewish Encounter with Late Imperial Russia* (Berkeley: University of California Press, 2002), 370 and passim.

Jewish historians to reject the one-size-fits-all approach to the history of Jewish modernization as well, leading away from these stark conceptions.[12] Part of this change, still ongoing, has involved recognizing that in Eastern European Jewish history, change unfolded within the framework of empire rather than the liberal nation-state.[13] New studies have highlighted how the Habsburg and tsarist empires treated minorities in a different manner than nation-states. Indeed, both tended to cultivate rather than destroy diversity in order to rule more effectively, and these empires were predicated on the inequality rather than the equality of the governed.[14] Thinking of modernization as an imperial rather than national project has proven a productive framework for understanding Eastern Europe, where rights were granted to Jews by enlightened monarchs with a vested interest in ruling *through* the institutions of religious, ethnic, and national minorities rather than in dissolving them.[15] In this way, the notion that the nation-state represents the key political formation for understanding modern Jewish history has been substantially revised, and we now find ourselves in a moment where we have multiple models, a nation-state framework still treated as generally applicable in Western Europe, and an imperial framework that applies to Eastern Europe.

---

[12] Such diversity was already implicit in Jacob Katz, ed., *Toward Modernity: The European Jewish Model* (New Brunswick: Transaction Books, 1987) and was embraced more whole-heartedly in works like Birnbaum and Katznelson, eds, *Paths of Emancipation*; Brenner, Caron and Kaufmann, eds, *Jewish Emancipation Reconsidered*; Frankel and Zipperstein, eds, *Assimilation and Community*; and Malino and Sorkin, eds, *From East and West*. Of course, even as these works pointed away from the one-size-fits-all approach to Jewish modernization, they nonetheless still generally assumed a national, rather than imperial framework for its unfolding.

[13] Marsha Rozenblit, *Reconstructing a National Identity: The Jews of Habsburg Austria during World War I* (Oxford: Oxford University Press, 2004), for example, shows how Jews in the Austro-Hungarian empire were among the most fervently loyal to the imperial monarchy precisely because that form fostered a "comfortable tripartite identity" for them (p. 128) in ways that were only possible in an imperial, rather than a strictly national setting. Nathans also shows how important Russia's imperial framework was in shaping Jews' path to modernization in that setting, in *Beyond the Pale*, 367–381.

[14] See Frederick Cooper and Jane Burbank, *Empires in World History: Power and the Politics of Difference* (Princeton: Princeton University Press, 2010), esp. 347, where they discuss the modernization of Jews in the Habsburg empire in these terms.

[15] The same observation could fruitfully be extended to the *millet* system under the Ottoman Empire. See Esther Benbassa and Aron Rodrigue, *A History of the Judeo-Spanish Community, 14th–20th Centuries* (Berkeley: University of California Press, 2000) and Bruce Masters, *Christians and Jews in the Ottoman Arab World: The Roots of Sectarianism* (Cambridge: Cambridge University Press, 2004).

But these two models may be less different than we once thought. France too was an empire in the nineteenth and twentieth centuries. Yet as an overseas empire, it has generally been considered distinct from the multi-ethnic land-based empires because its colonies were far from the metropole and ruled with separate legal regimes. The presumed distance and separation between colonies and metropole long allowed French and French Jewish historians to imagine a republic based solely on the integrationist model of the modern nation-state. Yet Imperial Turn historiography has shown that even metropolitan France was, from the time of the Revolution, never simply a nation-state committed to the eradication of difference in the name of political equality. It was always also an empire, or, as Gary Wilder calls it, "an imperial nation-state."[16] As such, it was governed by two different logics that were in many ways at odds with one another, yet which nonetheless coexisted and even fed off each other in important ways. Works like Wilder's that examine France's republic and empire in a common frame have shown that modern France embraced not only universalism but also particularism; not only equality but also inequality, predicated on racial and religious difference; not only liberalism but also and no less fundamentally, illiberalism. Furthermore, both sets of tendencies appeared at once in metropole and colony.[17]

By recognizing that the very nation-state that emancipated the Jews was always *also* an empire, a handful of scholars have begun to explore the role that empire played in the history of the Jews of France and other colonial metropoles, such as Great Britain and Germany.[18] Such recognition

[16] Gary Wilder, *The French Imperial Nation-State: Negritude and Colonial Humanism between the Two World Wars* (Chicago: University of Chicago Press, 2005), 3.

[17] Ibid., 22; Alice L. Conklin, "Colonialism and Human Rights: A Contradiction in Terms? The Case of France and West Africa, 1895–1914," *The American Historical Review* 103, no. 2 (1998): 419–442; Lynn Hunt, ed., *The French Revolution and Human Rights: A Documentary History* (New York: Bedford St. Martins, 1996); Clifford Rosenberg, *Policing Paris: The Origins of Modern Immigration Control between the Wars* (Ithaca: Cornell University Press, 2006); and Todd Shepard, *The Invention of Decolonization: The Algerian War and the Remaking of France* (Ithaca, NY: Cornell University Press, 2006). For an examination of the impact of simultaneous liberal and illiberal tendencies on Jews across metropole and colony, see Michael Shurkin, "French Nation Building, Liberalism and the Jews of Alsace and Algeria, 1815–1870 (Ph.D. thesis, Yale University, 2000).

[18] Sarah Abrevaya Stein, "Dividing South from North: French Colonialism, Jews, and the Algerian Sahara," *The Journal of North African Studies* 17, no. 5 (2012): 773–792; idem, "Protected Persons? The Baghdadi Jewish Diaspora, the British State, and the Persistence of Empire," *American Historical Review* 116, no. 1 (2011): 80–108; David Feldman, "Jews and the British Empire, c. 1900," *History Workshop Journal* 63, no. 1 (2007): 70–89; Abigail Green, "The British Empire and the Jews: An Imperialism of Human Rights?" *Past & Present* 191, no. 1 (2011): 175–205; Christian S. Davis, *Colonialism, Anti-Semitism*

suggests that it is time to rethink the sharp contrast between Western Europe, where Jews lived in nation-states, and Eastern Europe, where they lived in empires. Extending this thinking to French Jewish history specifically and European Jewish history more generally creates new ways to understand how and why, throughout modern European history, two logics regarding the Jews developed simultaneously: on the one hand, a universalist, assimilating, and egalitarian rhetoric and, on the other, a logic of particularism, difference, and inequality.

As our frame of reference shifts, so too does our understanding of the key terms that shaped the paradigm of Jewish modernization. For example, scholars have long recognized a connection between the secular Enlightenment and the Jewish Haskalah, with recent work even going so far as to show a reciprocal relationship between them.[19] Moving to the larger framework of the imperial nation-state focuses our attention on the concept of the "civilizing mission," a term related to the Enlightenment notion of "regeneration." The work of Jay Berkovitz and Alyssa Sepinwall illuminates the importance of the latter concept for both wider French and internal Jewish debates about the process and meaning of emancipation.[20] Pushing beyond the boundaries of mainland France, Lisa Moses Leff, Joshua Schreier, and Michael Shurkin have emphasized how for French administrators and Jewish leaders alike, the question of regeneration was vital in assessing possibilities and implementing measures for Jews in French Algeria and the wider Francophone orbit.[21] In the process, they have revealed that the civilizing mission, although decidedly less egalitarian-minded than regeneration, was a concept every bit as central to European Jewish self-understanding, politics, and philanthropy in the era of imperialism.[22]

---

and Germans of Jewish Descent in Imperial Germany (Ann Arbor: University of Michigan Press, 2011).

[19] Schechter, *Obstinate Hebrews*; and Jonathan M. Hess, *Germans, Jews and the Claims of Modernity* (New Haven: Yale University Press, 2002).

[20] Berkovitz, *The Shaping of Jewish Identity*; and Alyssa Goldstein Sepinwall, *The Abbé Grégoire and the French Revolution: The Making of Modern Universalism* (Berkeley: University of California Press, 2005).

[21] Lisa Moses Leff, *Sacred Bonds of Solidarity: The Rise of Jewish Internationalism in Nineteenth Century France* (Stanford: Stanford University Press, 2006); Joshua Schreier, *Arabs of the Jewish Faith: The Civilizing Mission in Colonial Algeria* (New Brunswick: Rutgers University Press, 2010); Shurkin, "French Nation Building."

[22] On Jews and the civilizing mission, see also Aron Rodrigue, *French Jews, Turkish Jews: The Alliance Israélite Universelle and the Politics of Jewish Schooling in Turkey 1860–1925* (Bloomington: Indiana University Press, 1990).

A new imperial frame for Jewish history also highlights the multifaceted meanings of the concepts of the "Orient" and the "oriental." Sometimes the image of the "oriental" was one that European Jews as diverse as Benjamin Disraeli and Abraham Geiger proudly embraced to distinguish themselves from their non-Jewish neighbors. At other times, the Oriental was a trope European Jews disavowed and applied strictly to "Others" in order to bring themselves closer to gentiles in Europe. This was, for example, the case with the Russian Jewish ethnographer Nahum Slouschz's depiction of North African Jews, and in many French Jewish writings that distinguished Algerian Jews from their Muslim neighbors. For all its many-sided meanings, the term proved as central to Jewish modernization as to European discourse more broadly.[23]

Moreover, as Ivan Kalmar and Derek Penslar, Harvey Goldberg, and Colette Zytnicki have shown, the binaries that Edward Said made essential to analyzing the discourse of Orientalism do not work for understanding how the concept was employed by European Jews. This is because Jews positioned themselves on both sides of the dichotomy between "East" and "West" that Said regards as central to Orientalism.[24] Thus, studying the Jewish engagement with Orientalism not only helps to add nuance to our understanding of the transformation of Jewish self-identification, but also requires us to add complexity to the Saidian framework, or perhaps to reject it altogether.[25]

---

[23] Adam Kirsch, *Benjamin Disraeli*, Jewish Encounters (New York: Schocken, 2008). On the way that Geiger and certain other Jewish scholars of Islam in some cases used their scholarship to mark Jews as Oriental and at other times to "de-Orientalize" Jews, see Susannah Heschel, "German-Jewish Scholarship on Islam as a Tool of De-Orientalization," *New German Critique* 117 (Fall 2012): 91–117; idem, "The Rise of German Imperialism and the Jewish Engagement in Islamic Studies" in Katz, Leff, and Mandel, eds, *Colonialism and the Jews*, 54–80. On Slouschz's Orientalism, see Harvey E. Goldberg, "The Oriental and the Orientalist: The Meeting of Mordecai Ha-Cohen and Nahum Slouschz," *Jewish Culture and History* 7, no. 3 (2004): 1–30. For important initial work on Jews and Orientalism, see ibid; Ivan Davidson Kalmar and Derek Penslar, eds, *Orientalism and the Jews* (Waltham, MA: Brandeis University Press, 2005).

[24] Edward Said, *Orientalism* (New York: Vintage, 1979). Kalmar and Penslar, eds, *Orientalism and the Jews*; Goldberg, "The Oriental and the Orientalist"; Colette Zytnicki, "The 'Oriental Jews' of the Maghreb: The Colonial-Era Writing of North African Jewish History," in Katz, Leff, and Mandel, eds, *Colonialism and the Jews*, 29–53.

[25] Said's *Orientalism* inspired significant critiques from an early date; see Sadiq Jalal al-Azm, "Orientalism and Orientalism in Reverse," *Khamsin* 8 (1981): 5–26; Bernard Lewis, "The Question of Orientalism," *New York Review of Books*, June 24, 1982; and Emmanuel Sivan, "Edward Said and his Arab Reviewers," *Jerusalem Quarterly* 35 (Spring 1985): 11–23.

As we move to integrate the empire into the story of Jewish modernization, we find that we are forced to rethink not only the concepts and the political forms that structured it, but also the periodization within which modern European Jewish history unfolded and the processes that it entailed. With regard to emancipation in France, for example, a focus on empire points to Napoleonic expansion rather than the 1789 Revolution as the more crucial turning point for understanding the evolution of European Jewish modernity. The first post-Revolutionary empire offered Jews legal equality far beyond the bounds of France proper, while not necessarily erasing difference, which Napoleon and his agents often instrumentalized in the service of state power. Moreover, Napoleon's empire not only solidified Jews' rights as citizens, it established new institutions that guaranteed that Judaism as a religion would be publicly recognized.[26]

Attention to the impact of colonialism also raises new questions about the evolution of modern Jewish politics. Beginning in the nineteenth century and continuing well into the twentieth, the empire became a privileged site for working out the meaning and the contours of Jewish identity and Jewish politics. The social and economic practices adopted by metropolitan Jews as they modernized in various Western European countries also often originated in the colonies rather than the metropole. Exploring such phenomena forces us to rethink fundamentally the nature and geography of agency, power, and borders in the history of Jews across Europe.

* * *

The Imperial Turn has been equally thought-provoking for scholars working on the history of North African Jews. Earlier work tended to celebrate the relationship between North African Jews and the French state, seeing in imperialism an agent of progressive Jewish modernization or, as in the case of Eastern European Jewish history, conceptualizing the poorer, more traditional, and "oriental" Jews of colonial North Africa as "not yet" modernized. Recent scholarship, however, has begun to challenge those frameworks. Shaped by new perspectives on power relations in colonial territories, the agency of indigenous actors, and the intertwining of metropolitan-colonial historical developments, scholars have re-examined core assumptions regarding the North African Jewish past. As a result, linear narratives of Jewish progress have given way to far more nuanced assessments of the impact of European intervention on Jews, as scholars have re-conceptualized Muslim–Jewish relations so as to account for the

---

[26] Phyllis Cohen Albert, *The Modernization of French Jewry: Consistory and Community in the Nineteenth Century* (Hanover, NH: Brandeis University Press, 1977); Bart Wallet, "Napoleon's Legacy: National Government and Jewish Community in Western Europe," *Simon Dubnow Institute Yearbook* 6 (2007): 291–309.

impact of French colonial policies. With this work, historians have also begun to challenge the long-held assumption that Jews were subject to a "softer" form of colonialism.[27]

As Colette Zytnicki has detailed, the earliest attempts to write the history of Jews in North Africa were decisively marked by the colonial contexts in which they were produced. Written by local religious and cultural figures or others embedded within the colonial infrastructure, these works served both scholarly and ideological ends, presenting the history and ethnography of North Africa's Jewish population as a means for both supporting the colonial project and promoting the modernization and emancipation of the Jewish populations under study.[28]

The decolonization of North Africa brought a new critical lens to the study of local Jewish life. As Emily Benichou Gottreich and Daniel J. Schroeter have discussed, much of this initial work was carried out by Israeli scholars who used the tools of anthropology and historical ethnography to explain the rituals and practices of rural Maghrebi Jews to their European-born, urban co-nationals.[29] By the 1970s and 1980s, shifting intellectual and social trends in Israel saw a new generation of North African-born scholars challenge the Eurocentric focus of Israeli academic life with studies on the linguistic and literary heritages of Maghrebi Jews. This paved the way for historians like Michel Abitbol, Richard Ayoun, and Paul Sebag to craft new narratives that brought the colonial and even

---

[27] Stein, "Dividing South from North," 784.

[28] Colette Zytnicki, *Les Juifs du Maghreb: Naissance d'une historiographie coloniale* (Paris: Presse de l'Université Paris-Sorbonne, 2011).

[29] Emily Benichou Gottreich and Daniel J. Schroeter, "Rethinking Jewish Culture and Society in North Africa," in *Jewish Culture and Society in North Africa*, ed. Gottreich and Schroeter (Bloomington: Indiana University Press, 2011): 3–23. Early scholarship on rural North African Jews includes Shlomo Deshen, *The Mellah Society: Jewish Community Life in Sherifian Morocco* (Chicago: University of Chicago Press, 1989); Shlomo A. Deshen and Moshe Shokeid, *The Predicament of Homecoming: Cultural and Social Life of North African Immigrants in Israel* (Ithaca, NY: Cornell University Press, 1974); Harvey E. Goldberg, *Cave Dwellers and Citrus Growers: A Jewish Community in Libya and Israel* (Cambridge: Cambridge University Press, 1972); Mordekhai Ha-Cohen, *The Book of Mordechai: A Study of the Jews of Libya: Selections from the Haghid Mordekhai of Mordechai Hakohen: Based on the Complete Hebrew Text as Published by the Ben Zvi Institute Jerusalem*, ed. and trans. with introduction and commentaries by Harvey E. Goldberg (Philadelphia: Institute for the Study of Human Issues, 1980); Moshe Shokeid, *The Dual Heritage: Immigrants from the Atlas Mountains in an Israeli Village* (Manchester: Manchester University Press, 1971); Alex Weingrod, *Reluctant Pioneers: Village Development in Israel* (Ithaca, NY: Cornell University Press, 1966).

the post-colonial period under scholarly scrutiny for the first time.[30] In this work, scholars began to integrate the history of North African Jews into the broader story of Jewish modernity by examining the impact of such forces as westernization, antisemitism, and the Holocaust on Jewish life in the Maghreb.

These scholars of the 1970s and 1980s paid more attention to context and historical change than their predecessors, taking up the colonial and post-colonial periods as serious subjects of analysis. Yet many still accepted without challenge a relatively linear reading of Jewish modernity inherited from the wider field of Jewish history, rarely questioning French republican claims of Jewish betterment through the nation-state's assimilatory embrace. Other scholarship was shaped by a Zionist interpretive lens – of longstanding Jewish decline amidst Muslim persecution, leading to mass migration to Palestine or Israel.[31] Subsequent analysis by scholars such as Moshe Bar Asher, Yossef Charvit, Joseph Chetrit, and Yaron Tsur challenged the teleological perspectives in this earlier work by tracing the continuities rather than the ruptures in North African Jewish culture over time and problematizing binary views of tradition and modernity. Historical accounts such as these, however, have typically treated Jews in a vacuum rather than as part of the wider colonial landscape.[32]

[30] Michel Abitbol, *The Jews of North Africa during the Second World War* (Detroit: Wayne State University Press, 1989); idem, *Tujjar al-sultan: 'ilit kalkalit Yehudit be'Maroko* (Jerusalem: Institut Ben-Zvi, 1994); idem, *Le passé d'une discorde: Juifs et Arabes depuis le VIIe siècle* (Paris: Perrin, 1999); Richard Ayoun and Bernard Cohen, *Les Juifs d'Algérie: deux mille ans d'histoire* (Paris: Jean-Claude Lattès, 1982); and Paul Sebag, *Histoire des Juifs de Tunisie: des origines à nos jours* (Paris: L'Harmattan, 1991).

[31] Michael M. Laskier, *The Alliance Israélite Universelle and the Jewish Communities of Morocco, 1862–1962* (Albany: State University of New York Press, 1983); idem, *North African Jewry in the Twentieth Century: The Jews of Morocco, Tunisia, and Algeria* (New York: New York University Press, 1984); and Norman A. Stillman, *The Jews of Arab Lands: A History and Source Book* (Philadelphia: The Jewish Publication Society, 1979).

[32] See Joseph Chetrit's numerous articles on North African Jews in his journal *Miqqedem Umiyyam [mi-Kedem u-Miyam]*; Yaron Tsur, "L'époque coloniale et les rapports 'ethniques' au sein de la communauté juive en Tunisie," in *Mémoires juives d'Espagne et du Portugal*, ed. Esther Benbassa (Paris: Publisud, 1996), 197–206; idem, "Haskala in a Sectional Colonial Society: Mahdia (Tunisia) 1885," in *Sephardi and Middle Eastern Jewries: History and Culture in the Modern Era*, ed. Harvey E. Goldberg (Bloomington: Indiana University Press, 1996), 146–167; idem, "Jewish 'Sectional Societies' in France and Algeria on the Eve of the Colonial Encounter," *Journal of Mediterranean Studies* 4 (1994): 263–277; idem, "Yehadut Tunisya be-shilhe ha-tekufah ha-teromkolonialit," *Miqqedem umiyyam* 3 (1990): 77–113; Moshe Bar-Asher, *La composante hébraïque du judéo-arabe algérien: communautés de Tlemcen et Aïn-Témouchent* (Jerusalem: The Hebrew University Magnes Press, 1992); idem, *Masorot u-leshonot shel Yehude Tsefon-Afrikah* (Jerusalem: Mosad

Indeed, like their Europeanist colleagues, scholars of the North African Jewish past have been reluctant until recently to challenge the triumphalist narrative of European colonialism. Even as scholars have begun increasingly to emphasize colonial violence, inequities, and exploitation and thereby to undermine the simplistic links between European liberalism and a progressive modernity, rare still are works that provide a more complex picture of the deeply entangled relationships among the different social groups that comprised European colonial societies in North Africa and the Middle East. As Sarah Abrevaya Stein has noted, we still have much to learn about the processes by which Jews worked with, struggled against, supported, and benefited from the colonial order and the process of decolonization.[33]

In recent years, Stein and others have begun to address this lacuna by placing Jews and Muslims within a single analytic frame in order to re-conceptualize the strategies of colonial rule and the boundaries of communal identities. For instance, Emily Gottreich and Richard Parks have underscored how colonial authorities redrew traditional spatial divisions in colonial Marrakesh and Tunis, respectively, and in the process re-configured communal boundaries between Jews and Muslims.[34] Such scholarship compels us to re-think our understanding of antisemitism and

---

Bialik; Ashkelon: Ha-mikhlalah Ha-ezorit, 1999); Bar-Asher's articles in the journal *Massorot*; Yossef Charvit, *La France, l'élite rabbinique d'Algérie et la Terre Sainte au XIXe siècle: Tradition et modernité* (Paris: Champion, 2005); idem, *Elite rabbinique d'Algérie et modernisation, 1750–1914* (Jerusalem: Editions Gaï Yinassé, 1995).

[33] Stein, "Protected Persons," 84.

[34] Emily Gottreich, *The Mellah of Marrakesh: Jewish and Muslim Space in Morocco's Red City* (Bloomington: Indiana University Press, 2007); Richard Parks, "The Jewish Quarters of Interwar Paris and Tunis: Destruction, Creation, and French Urban Design," *Jewish Social Studies* 17, no. 1 (2010): 67–87. See also Joëlle Bahloul, *The Architecture of Memory: A Jewish-Muslim Household in Colonial Algeria, 1937–1962*, trans. Catherine du Peloux Ménagé (Cambridge: Cambridge University Press, 1996); Elizabeth Friedman, *Colonialism & After: An Algerian Jewish Community* (Boston: Bergin & Garvey, 1988); Claude Hagege and Bernard Zarca, "Les Juifs et la France en Tunisie: Les bénéfices d'une relation triangulaire," *Le Mouvement social* 197 (October–December 2001): 9–28; Schreier, *Arabs of the Jewish Faith*; Daniel J. Schroeter, "French Liberal Governance and the Emancipation of Algeria's Jews," *French Historical Studies* 33, no. 2 (2010): 259–280; Daniel Schroeter and Joseph Chetrit, "Emancipation and Its Discontents: Jews at the Formative Period of Colonial Rule in Morocco," *Jewish Social Studies* 13, no. 1 (2006): 170–206; Daniel J. Schroeter, *The Sultan's Jew: Morocco and the Sephardi World* (Stanford: Stanford University Press, 2002); and Benjamin Stora, *Les trois exils: Juifs d'Algérie* (Paris: Stock, 2006).

colonial racism in the region by unpacking the ways in which French colonial authorities used animosities against one group to govern the other.[35]

This new scholarship in Jewish history has increasingly been in conversation with work in wider French and French colonial history. In the latter fields, scholars have shown how porous metropolitan and colonial boundaries often were, highlighting in particular the ways pre- and post-colonial frameworks regarding religion, ethnicity, and race crossed the Mediterranean and informed developments on both of its shores.[36] In opening up new ways of thinking about colonial geography, these scholars have also re-conceptualized the historical rupture between the colonial and the post-colonial moment.

Still other scholars working in this field have focused on trans-regional intersections, demonstrating the way North African Jewish history was shaped by developments throughout the wider French empire and beyond.[37]

JEWS AT THE SEAMS OF COLONIAL HISTORY

If Jewish historians have done little to engage colonial studies, the absence of Jews from the wider field of colonial history has been equally stark. This

[35] See also Joshua Cole, "Constantine before the Riots of August 1934: Civil Status, Anti-Semitism, and the Politics of Assimilation in Interwar French Algeria," *The Journal of North African Studies* 17, no. 5 (2012): 839–861; and his "Antisémitisme et situation coloniale pendant l'entre-deux-guerres en Algérie: Les émeutes antijuives de Constantine," *Vingtième siècle* 108 (October–December 2010): 2–23.

[36] See Wilder, *The French Imperial Nation-State*; Rosenberg, *Policing Paris*; Shepard, *The Invention of Decolonization*; Naomi Davidson, *Only Muslim: Embodying Islam in Twentieth-Century France* (Ithaca, NY: Cornell University Press, 2012). Works that treat Jews in France that reflect an engagement with this wider scholarship include Ethan B. Katz, *The Burdens of Brotherhood: Jews and Muslims from North Africa to France* (Cambridge, MA: Harvard University Press, 2015); Leff, *Sacred Bonds of Solidarity*; idem, "The Impact of the Napoleonic Sanhedrin on French Colonial Policy in Algeria," *CCAR Journal* 54, no. 1 (2007): 35–54; and Maud S. Mandel, *Muslims and Jews in France: History of a Conflict* (Princeton: Princeton University Press, 2014).

[37] Ethan B. Katz, "Tracing the Shadow of Palestine: The Zionist-Arab Conflict and Jewish–Muslim Relations in France, 1914–1945," in *The Israeli–Palestinian Conflict in the Francophone World*, ed. Nathalie Debrauwere-Miller (New York: Routledge, 2010), 25–40; Maud S. Mandel, "Transnationalism and Its Discontents during the 1948 Arab-Israeli War," *Diaspora* 12, no. 3 (2003): 329–360; Joshua Schreier, "From Mediterranean Merchant to French Civilizer: Jacob Lasry and the Economy of Conquest in Early Colonial Algeria," *International Journal of Middle East Studies* 44 (2012): 631–649; Schroeter, *The Sultan's Jew*.

lacuna is, on the surface, difficult to explain. In the immediate post-World War II period and during decolonization, several analysts of the colonial situation made Jewish history critical to their narratives by drawing connections between antisemitism and the Holocaust on the one hand, and colonial racism and violence on the other. If Hannah Arendt saw the nation-state rather than the empire as the key framework for Jewish life in France, she also saw histories of antisemitic persecution and colonialism as inextricably linked in a common logic. Likewise, anti-colonial thinkers like Frantz Fanon, Aimé Césaire, and Jean-Paul Sartre, and early Holocaust memoirists such as Jean Améry and Primo Levi, thought about the colonial condition and the Jewish condition together.[38] Yet since the post-war interest in colonialism and antisemitism did not translate into a body of critical scholarship, the initial connections were not fully developed.[39]

When colonial history and post-colonial studies exploded in the 1980s and 1990s, Jews posed uncomfortable problems for many historical sources, theoretical frameworks, and political assumptions central to the field. These problems served to marginalize Jewish history within colonial history. Yet accounting for Jews refigures key questions in colonial history, particularly in the French empire. Since Jews so often fell in between many of the classificatory schemes used by colonial authorities, studying them at once advances and further complicates recent scholarship on interstitial groups under colonial rule. Moreover, Jews offer an exceptionally rich entry point for new efforts to write comparative and trans-regional accounts of empire, in particular with regard to histories of status, economy, and difference. In addition, Jewish history raises critical terminological issues for colonial history as a field.

The primary reasons for Jews' longstanding absence in colonial history are at once historical and historiographical. Jews' relatively small numbers and minority status in most imperial settings is surely a key factor. But the issues are not merely demographic. Colonial powers, anti-colonial nationalists, and, later, their historians and theorists relied heavily upon binaries to chart plans for the future and offer observations about the past and the

---

[38] Bryan Cheyette, *Diasporas of the Mind: Jewish and Postcolonial Writing and the Nightmare of History* (New Haven: Yale University Press, 2013); Michael Rothberg, *Multidirectional Memory: Remembering the Holocaust in the Age of Decolonization* (Stanford, CA: Stanford University Press, 2009).

[39] Cooper cites the trauma of the colonial wars and decolonization, post-colonial efforts to write indigenous histories of Africa and elsewhere from a distinctly non-colonial standpoint, and overriding narratives of progress as among the reasons that there was a lag of decades before the burst of scholarly interest in colonial history. Cooper, "The Rise, Fall, and Rise of Colonial Studies."

present. The place of Jews in colonial history does not fit neatly into such dichotomous frameworks. Very often, Jews were neither exactly masters nor victims of colonial exploitation. Instead, they often circulated between physical spaces of metropole and colony and enjoyed a status somewhere between equal citizens and oppressed subjects. Moreover, they could be both Orientalist and orientalized, and frequently knew the life of both the colonizer and the colonized.

During the colonial era, Jews never controlled nor collectively represented a metropolitan European power. At the same time, they were rarely situated on the bottom rung of colonial hierarchies. A few examples demonstrate just how widely their political status ranged. Abigail Green, Lisa Moses Leff, and Ethan Katz have illustrated how Jews such as Moses Montefiore, Adolphe Crémieux, and Léon Blum could become elite power brokers of empire in the French or British metropole.[40] Frances Malino has traced the complex positions of countless Europeanized indigenous female instructors in Jewish schools in North Africa.[41] Joseph Chetrit, Jessica Marglin, and Daniel Schroeter have shown the double vulnerability of Moroccan Jews under French rule, at the hands of both the French Resident-General and the Muslim Sultan.[42] Taking these questions further East, Israel Bartal has compellingly situated numerous Jews as simultaneous national agents and undesirables on Russian imperial frontiers.[43] Rarely, even in a single colonial territory, did all Jews' legal and social position fit a single category.

Because of their uncertain political status, Jews as a category have remained difficult to classify on several other lines as well. Ideologically, Jews often both sympathized with the discrimination faced by native colonial subjects and perceived a sense of possibility in the promise of European liberal citizenship. This was the case not only in overseas

[40] Abigail Green, "The British Empire and the Jews"; idem, *Moses Montefiore: Jewish Liberator, Imperial Hero* (Cambridge, MA: Harvard University Press, 2010); Leff, *Sacred Bonds of Solidarity*; Katz, "Crémieux's Children: Joseph Reinach, Léon Blum, and René Cassin as Jews of French Empire," in Katz, Leff, and Mandel, eds, *Colonialism and the Jews*, 129–165.

[41] Frances Malino, "Oriental, Feminist, Orientalist: The New Jewish Woman," in Katz, Leff, and Mandel, eds, *Colonialism and the Jews*, 101–115.

[42] Schroeter and Chetrit, "Emancipation and Its Discontents"; Schroeter, "Vichy in Morocco: The Residency, Mohammed V and his Indigenous Jewish Subjects," in Katz, Leff, and Mandel, eds, *Colonialism and the Jews*, 215–250; Jessica Marglin, *Across Legal Lines: Jews and Muslims in Modern Morocco* (New Haven: Yale University Press, 2016).

[43] Israel Bartal, "Jews in the Crosshairs of Empire: A Franco-Russian Comparison," in Katz, Leff, and Mandel, eds, *Colonialism and the Jews*, 116–126; idem, "Farming the Land on Three Continents: Bilu, Am Oylom, and Yefe-Nahar," *Jewish History* 21 (2007): 249–261.

empires like the French and British, but also in land-based empires like the Russian. Jews' economic position, meanwhile, was frequently that of an intermediary between metropolitan officials or businesses on the one hand and products, services, and menial laborers of the colonies on the other. Furthermore, many Jewish intellectuals perceived imperialism as a potential means of liberation in which Jews could play a critical role, while others saw it as a forcible oppressive occupation. Even culturally, particularly in French North Africa, Jews' simultaneous attachments to the clothing, food, language, music, and aesthetics of a native culture they shared with Muslims, and to French education and culture, defied dichotomous categories. Jews were thus particularly unsuited to what Cooper and Stoler have lamented as "the Manichaean dichotomies" that "had such sustaining power" for "contemporary actors [and] latter-day historians."[44] As Stoler has emphasized elsewhere, many of these dichotomies were deeply woven into the colonial archive itself.[45]

Meanwhile, Jews have posed thorny problems for post-colonial theory. As Bryan Cheyette has argued, post-colonial thinkers rejected discussing Jewish suffering and the Holocaust for a number of reasons. Many had an "anxiety of appropriation" with regard to Holocaust comparisons; that is, they feared that by making the Holocaust universal and the Jews metaphorical for all victims, other histories of suffering would be subsumed or ignored. Others cast aside histories of antisemitism and the Holocaust as part of "a dominant white 'Judeo-Christian' culture"; they likewise saw Jewish cosmopolitanism as rootless and unprincipled, in contrast to the transnational anti-colonial cosmopolitanism valorized in post-colonial studies.[46] Finally, due to the triumph of Zionism and the persistence of the Israeli–Palestinian conflict, these general patterns became inseparable from Middle East politics. Particularly under the formative influence of Said, many post-colonial scholars tended to assume a rapid and dramatic evolution of Jews from leading victims of Western persecution to Jews as violent, Western imperialist persecutors of Arabs and Muslims.[47]

---

[44] Cooper and Stoler, "Between Metropole and Colony," 8.

[45] Ann Laura Stoler, *Along the Archival Grain: Epistemic Anxieties and Colonial Common Sense* (Princeton: Princeton University Press, 2009).

[46] Cheyette, *Diasporas of the Mind*, 37–38.

[47] Said's *Orientalism* proved a fundamental text in the emergence and direction of postcolonial theory. Despite his acknowledgment of Jews as frequent victims of Orientalism, Said focused considerable attention elsewhere on Zionism as an example of Orientalism tied to Western colonialism. See "Zionism from the Standpoint of Its Victims," *Social Text* 1 (1978): 7–58. See Penslar and Kalmar, "Introduction: Orientalism and the Jews," in Penslar and Kalmar, eds, *Orientalism and the Jews*, xv. At the same time, as Said complained, many of his Jewish critics, rather than glean insight from the conceptual

New directions in the field of colonial history, however, make Jews' more complex, uncertain, and uneven relationship to colonialism of growing interest. Scholars have begun to appreciate the fluid, contested, and ever-shifting nature of colonial boundaries and categories, and how those "in-between" groups offer crucial insight about the tensions and contradictions within colonial society more broadly.[48] This has taken a number of forms. In her study of Dutch colonial archives, for example, Stoler focuses on the *Inlandsche kinderen*, which meant at various times those of mixed descent, Dutch born in the Indies, or impoverished whites. She argues that this group shows that supposedly fixed colonial categories, including those of "Europeans" and "natives," were actually unstable and ever-shifting, a fact of which colonial administrators themselves were well aware.[49] Yet what do trenchant new studies like this one tell us about European colonialism more broadly or in a comparative context? Here we would do well to ask: How similar or different from these "native whites" of the Dutch East Indies were the French-emancipated Jews of Algeria or their modernizing co-religionists in the schools of the Alliance Israélite Universelle in Morocco and Tunisia?

Recent scholarship on Jews of the Maghreb offers suggestive starting points. Even though Jews' ethnic status in this context appears on the surface less ambiguous than that of the *Inlandsche kinderen* in Dutch Java, Ethan Katz has found parallels between the reports examined by Stoler and those of French police in the 1950s on migrants from North Africa living in Paris. In these reports, Jews are present but in hiding. That is, the authors oscillate seamlessly between terms like "Algerians" and "Muslims" to describe people, cultural traits, neighborhoods, and cafes. Sometimes, administrators unwittingly lump Jewish individuals or establishments under such headings. At other times, they mention Jews in passing in a manner that makes them seem at once included within and exceptional to the report's general categories and observations.[50] In a similar vein, Sarah Abrevaya Stein's study of the Jews of the Algerian Sahara reveals

and empirical links between antisemitism and Orientalism, "have seen in the critique of Orientalism an opportunity for them to defend Zionism, support Israel and launch attacks on Palestinian nationalism." See "Orientalism Reconsidered," in *Orientalism: A Reader*, ed. Alexander Lyon Macfie (New York: New York University Press, 2001), 353. For an argument for the importance of Said's pro-Palestinian politics to *Orientalism* itself, see James Pasto, "Islam's 'Strange Secret Sharers': Orientalism, Judaism and the Jewish Question," *Comparative Studies in Society and History* 40, no. 3 (1998): 437–474, esp. 472.

[48] On this point, see Cooper and Stoler, "Between Metropole and Colony," 6.

[49] Stoler, *Along the Archival Grain*, 6.

[50] For further discussion on these lines, see Katz, *Burdens of Brotherhood*, Introduction and chap. 4. For related observations about Jews in the colonial archives, see Sarah Abrevaya

the contrast between French administrators' view of them as "indigenous" and the rest of Algerian Jewry as "French." Such work further illustrates the contingency in the colonial categories assigned to Jews even within a single territory. Likewise, Maud Mandel's depiction of the emergence of the "North African Jew" as a political and discursive category during the years of decolonization shows how colonial officials and international Jewish actors wrestled with Jews' uncertain place in the colonial order at a moment of great change.[51]

At the same time, certain North African Jews' place between binaries looks more ideological and less ethnic when we consider the formulation of one of the most insightful early observers of colonialism, the Tunisian Jewish writer and anti-colonialist Albert Memmi:

I know the colonizer from the inside almost as well as I know the colonized .... Like all other Tunisians I was treated as a second-class citizen, deprived of political rights, refused admission to most civil service departments, etc. But I was not a Muslim .... The Jewish population identified as much with the colonizers as with the colonized. They were undeniably 'natives,' as they were then called .... However, unlike the Muslims, they passionately endeavored to identify themselves with the French. To them the West was the paragon of all civilization, all culture.[52]

Such a characterization brings to mind the situation of the Egyptians in the Sudan studied by Eve Trout Powell, who were at once colonized by the British and themselves aspiring colonizers.[53] Memmi reminds us that, even absent the official license of their own colonial state, Jews in these territories resembled in certain respects what Powell calls "colonized colonizers." Indeed, the precise nature of Jews' interstitial positionality in many colonial empires could vary tremendously according not only to time and place but also authorial rendering.[54]

Stein, *Saharan Jews and the Fate of French Algeria* (Chicago: University of Chicago Press, 2014).

[51] Stein, *Saharan Jews*; Mandel, *Muslims and Jews in France*, 35–58.

[52] Albert Memmi, *The Colonizer and the Colonized*, trans. Howard Greenfeld with a new introduction by the author, preface by Jean-Paul Sartre (New York: Orion Press, 1965), xiii–xiv.

[53] Eve M. Trout Powell, *A Different Shade of Colonialism: Egypt, Great Britain, and the Mastery of the Sudan* (Berkeley: University of California Press, 2003).

[54] Stoler and Powell are hardly alone in recent efforts to focus on groups that defy simple classification in the colonial context. Among other examples are Engseng Ho, *The Graves of Tarim: Genealogy and Mobility across the Indian Ocean* (Berkeley: University of California Press, 2006); Linda Colley, "Going Native, Telling Tales: Captivity, Collaborations and Empire," *Past and Present* 168 (2000): 170–193; Shompa Lahiri, "Contested Relations: The East India Company and the Lascars in London," in *The Worlds of the East India Company*, ed. H.V. Bowen, Margarette Lincoln, and Nigel

Jewish historians have begun to contribute to a wider conversation about the uncertain, contradictory position of numerous groups long ignored in colonial historiography. Scholars of the French empire have started to attend to such issues, from Jews' complex position in webs of colonial and anti-colonial politics in the interwar Maghreb to their shifting position at the moment of decolonization.[55] Such histories begin to unravel the "us" versus "them" paradigm that long dominated colonial and post-colonial studies.

Yet as the above cases reveal, thinking across multiple colonial situations opens further possibilities, providing useful material for comparison. Stoler dubs the history of indigenous whites in the Dutch East Indies a "minor history" for the way that their in-betweenness is at once non-representative and deeply revealing. Along these lines, bringing Jews into the picture enables us to chart what we might call a "comparative minor history" of empires, through which historians utilize the periphery of the colonial experience to rethink the heart of imperial ideology and practice. In the process, we could better address the important question of how Jews' experiences of empire either tracked or diverged from those of non-Jews.

Because Jews lived in nearly all modern European empires in significant numbers in diverse roles, the comparative history of empires stands to gain a great deal from paying closer attention to them. The proposition is particularly timely, as scholars are more interested than ever in understanding the differences between land-based and overseas empires and between "multi-ethnic" empires and those grounded in racialized thinking.[56]

Looking at the case of Jews is especially fruitful in another realm of comparative imperial history: economic history. As recent work has shown, Jews have often acted as "middlemen": from the merchant Jacob Lasry in the early years of French colonization in Oran to the wealthy

Rigby (Woodbridge, UK: Boydell, 2002); Laura Tabili, "Outsiders in the Land of Their Birth: Exogamy, Citizenship, and Identity in War and Peace," *Journal of British History* 44, no. 4 (2005): 796–815.

[55] Cole, "Constantine before the Riots of August 1934"; idem, "Antisémitisme et situation coloniale pendant l'entre-deux-guerres"; Mary Dewhurst Lewis, *Divided Rule: Sovereignty and Empire in French Tunisia, 1881–1938* (Berkeley: University of California Press, 2013); Shepard, *The Invention of Decolonization*, chap. 6; Jonathan Wyrtzen, *Making Morocco: Colonial Intervention and the Politics of Identity* (Ithaca, NY: Cornell University Press, 2015).

[56] Cooper, "States, Empires, and Political Imagination," in his *Colonialism in Question*, 153–203; Ania Loomba, "Situating Colonial and Postcolonial Studies," in her *Colonialism/Postcolonialism* (New York: Routledge, 1998), 7–23.

British protectee Silas Aaron Hartoon in late nineteenth- and early twentieth-century Shanghai.[57] The ubiquity of this pattern lends itself to a comparison of structures of trade, exchange, labor, and exploitation not only between empires, but across multiple territories of a single empire. Furthermore, the networks that often linked Jews from one empire to the next are opening up perspectives in the trans-regional and borderlands history of empires and the interconnections across them.[58]

Finally, Jews offer crucial cases for comparison for colonial historians interested in the histories of difference, race-thinking, exclusion, and genocide. Most scholars agree that matters of difference, particularly racial difference, were critical to all modern empires, but they have only recently begun to emphasize the degree to which ideas and practices varied across historical periods and contexts.[59] Of late, scholars have turned to the highly sensitive questions that initially attracted students of colonialism and antisemitism to one another in the immediate post-war period. To better understand how race and other forms of difference operated in the French and British empires, some historians have begun to bring together the history of Jews with that of other subjects living under colonial rule, in particular Muslims of French North Africa.[60] Some have approached these

[57] Schreier, "From Mediterranean Merchant to French Civilizer"; Stein, "Protected Persons?"

[58] For further important efforts from a Jewish history perspective regarding Jews and economics in imperial contexts, see for example Rebecca Kobrin and Adam Teller, ed., *Purchasing Power: The Economics of Modern Jewish History* (Philadelphia: University of Pennsylvania Press, 2015); Schroeter, *The Sultan's Jew*; and Sarah Abrevaya Stein, *Plumes: Ostrich Feathers, Jews and a Lost World of Global Commerce* (New Haven: Yale University Press, 2008).

[59] Cooper, "Introduction," in his *Colonialism in Question*, esp. 23, 29; for a more sustained treatment, Stoler, *Along the Archival Grain*.

[60] For histories of colonialism and decolonization where Jews are incorporated for significant comparison or relations, see Shepard, *Invention of Decolonization*, chap. 6; Davidson, *Only Muslim*. For more sustained discussions of Jews along with other groups in the colonial and post-colonial context, see Cole, "Antisémitisme et situation coloniale"; Kimberly Arkin, *Rhinestones, Religion, and the Republic: Fashioning Jewishness in France* (Stanford: Stanford University Press, 2013); Mandel, *Muslims and Jews in France*; Aamir Mufti, *Enlightenment in the Colony: The Jewish Question and the Crisis of Postcolonial Culture* (Princeton: Princeton University Press, 2007); Katz, *Burdens of Brotherhood*; Gil Anidjar, *The Jew, the Arab: A History of the Enemy* (Stanford: Stanford University Press, 2003); Cheyette, *Diasporas of the Mind*; Rothberg, *Multidirectional Memory*; Schreier, *Arabs of the Jewish Faith*; David Feldman, "Jews and the British Empire, c. 1900."

questions through the lens of memory studies, examining how memories of colonial atrocities and the Holocaust informed one another.[61]

It is perhaps unsurprising that parallels and interconnections between the position of Jews and colonized native populations have been undertaken most directly in German history. These have revealed both tantalizing continuities and crucial differences between the ideas and actions of the German state toward the natives of colonial Africa under the Kaiserreich and Jews under the Nazis. Relocating Jews to the heart of the earlier story of German Orientalism and expanding colonial ambitions complicates the question even further. Susannah Heschel's work is exemplary of a related push from within Jewish studies to bring Jews together with other historically oppressed minorities in colonial contexts, examining sensitive topics such as the relationship between Jews and Orientalism or between racial ideologies in Europe and Zionist ideas about Arabs in Palestine.[62]

Indeed, for scholars of colonialism and post-colonialism, ultimately, Zionism cannot be ignored. The relationship of Zionism to colonial empires and colonialism has been historically complex and ever-shifting.[63]

[61] Cheyette, *Diasporas of the Mind*; Rothberg, *Multidirectional Memory*; Maxim Silverman, *Palimpsestic Memory: The Holocaust and Colonialism in French and Francophone Fiction and Film* (Oxford: Berghahn Books, 2013).

[62] See Susannah Heschel, "Revolt of the Colonized: Abraham Geiger's Wissenschaft des Judentums as a Challenge to Christian Hegemony in the Academy," *New German Critique* 77 (Spring–Summer 1999): 61–85; Davis, *Colonialism, Anti-Semitism*; Annegret Ehmann, "From Colonial Racism to Nazi Population Policy: The Role of the So-Called Mischlinge," in *The Holocaust and History: The Known, The Unknown, The Disputed, and The Reexamined*, ed. Michael Berenbaum and Abraham J. Peck (Bloomington: Indiana University Press, 1998), 115–133; Eric Ames, Marcia Klotz, and Lora Wildenthal, eds, *Germany's Colonial Pasts* (Lincoln: University of Nebraska Press, 2009); Hess, *Germans, Jews and the Claims of Modernity*; Isabel Hull, "'Final Solutions' In the Colonies: The Example of Wilhelmine Germany," in *The Specter of Genocide: Mass Murder in Historical Perspective*, ed. Robert Gellately and Ben Kiernan (Cambridge: Cambridge University Press, 2003), 141–161; Aziza Khazzoum, "The Great Chain of Orientalism: Jewish Identity, Stigma Management, and Ethnic Exclusion in Israel," *American Sociological Review* 68, no. 4 (2003): 481–510; Suzanne L. Marchand, *German Orientalism in the Age of Empire: Religion, Race and Scholarship* (Cambridge: Cambridge University Press, 2009); Pasto, "Islam's 'Strange Secret Sharers'"; Penslar and Kalmar, eds, *Orientalism and the Jews*; Achim Rohde, "Der innere Orient: Orientalismus, Antisemitismus und Geschlecht im Deutschland des 18. bis 20. Jahrhunderts," *Die Welt des Islams* 45, no. 2 (2005): 370–411.

[63] Efforts to discuss Zionism in comparison with other imperial contexts have only begun recently in earnest. Particularly thoughtful contributions include those in the volume of Caroline Elkins and Susan Pedersen, eds, *Settler Colonialism in the Twentieth Century: Projects, Practices, Legacies* (New York: Routledge, 2005); and the work of Lucy

Because Zionism emerged in an imperial context that cut across numerous metropolitan and colonial spaces, and took up colonial, anti-colonial, and post-colonial postures and alliances at various moments, studying it requires grappling with the full ambiguity of Jews' place in colonial history. In many ways, Zionism defies the binaries in which much of colonial history has been written, as well as the starkest assumptions of post-colonial studies. Derek Penslar has suggested that the colonial history of Zionism is best written in the type of comparative and trans-regional contexts that Jewish history demands of colonial history. Furthermore, the history of Zionism and, more broadly, Jews and empire could force a series of reckonings about the meaning of words like colonial and imperial; colonizer and colonized; and metropole and colony. Such discussions, however difficult, have the potential to advance the field substantially.[64]

THE STAKES OF MUTUAL ENGAGEMENT

For too long, the fields of colonial history and Jewish history paid little attention to one another, blinded by the prevailing narratives and paradigms in their respective fields. Systematic incorporation, they feared, could lead to major disruptions. Recently, some scholars have begun to rectify the situation, although substantial work remains to be done.

Bringing Jewish history together with the history of modern European imperialism has tremendous promise for both fields. In Jewish history writ large, the late twentieth and early twenty-first centuries have witnessed an extended rejection of grand narrative. This has taken the form most often of studies of Jews in individual nation-states or their leading Jewish centers. Despite the immense achievements of this scholarship, it has also bred reluctance among most Jewish historians to frame their studies in the kinds of comparative or transnational terms that assign causality to larger international forces, such as the rise, expansion, and decline of empires. "Thinking like an empire" about Jewish history, to borrow Frederick Cooper's evocative phrase, can enable the recovery of wider patterns of

Chester, e.g., "Boundary Commissions as Tools to Safeguard British Interests at the End of Empire," *Journal of Historical Geography* 34, no. 3 (2008): 494–515.

[64] See these four interlinked chapters in Katz, Leff, and Mandel in *Colonialism and the Jews*: Derek J. Penslar, "Is Zionism a Colonial Movement?"; Joshua Cole, "Derek Penslar's 'Algebra of Modernity': How Should We Understand the Relation between Zionism and Colonialism?"; Elizabeth F. Thompson, "Moving Zionism to Asia: Texts and Tactics of Colonial Settlement, 1917–1921"; and Derek Penslar, "What We Talk About When We Talk About Colonialism."

history that have too often become buried under the insularity of single-country studies.[65]

By the same token, colonial history needs Jewish history. The post-colonial critique that has had such a productive effect on both colonial and metropolitan histories has, at times, been harshly critical of modernity and the West in an undistinguishing manner. An equally misplaced nostalgia for empire has emerged from other, more conservative quarters of colonial history. The complex position of Jews within the cracks of colonial history, if taken seriously, forces reassessments that can move beyond stale debates about the demonic or benevolent character of colonialism and the modern West more broadly. Comparative history is one of the methodologies essential to this more nuanced approach; here, the long history of Jewish geographic diversity and trans-imperial connectedness offers an exceptional set of tools from which to build the field.

The importance of mutual engagement is hardly merely academic. Few questions animate current political debates about Jews more than the character of Zionism and the meaning of rising antisemitism. In each instance, conversations more often than not turn on absolutist assumptions about Jewish power or powerlessness, and about the place of Jews within or outside of liberal politics. The histories of Jews and colonialism presented here not only defy such polarized understandings, but they also offer essential context that can be fodder for suppler approaches in future discussions.

SELECT BIBLIOGRAPHY

Abitbol, Michel. *The Jews of North Africa During the Second World War*. Translated by Catherine Tahanyi Zentelis. Detroit: Wayne State University Press, 1989.
  Le passé d'une discorde: Juifs et Arabes depuis le VIIe siècle. Paris: Perrin, 1999.
  Tujjar al-sultan: 'ilit kalkalit Yehudit be'Maroko. Jerusalem: Institut Ben-Zvi, 1994.
Al-Azm, Sadiq Jalal. "Orientalism and Orientalism in Reverse." *Khasim* 8 (1981): 5–26.
Albert, Phyllis Cohen. *The Modernization of French Jewry: Consistory and Community in the Nineteenth Century*. Hanover, NH: Brandeis University Press, 1977.
Ames, Eric, Marcia Klotz, and Lora Wildenthal, eds. *Germany's Colonial Pasts*. Lincoln, NE: University of Nebraska Press, 2009.
Anidjar, Gil. *The Jew, the Arab: A History of the Enemy*. Stanford: Stanford University Press, 2003.
Arendt, Hannah. *Origins of Totalitarianism*. New York: Harcourt, Brace & Jovanovich, 1951.

---

[65] Cooper, "States, Empires, and Political Imagination;" Abigail Green, "Old Networks, New Connections: The Emergence of the Jewish International," in *Religious Internationals in the Modern World: Globalization and Faith Communities since 1750*, ed. Abigail Green and Vincent Viaene (Basingstoke: Palgrave Macmillan, 2012), 53–81.

Arkin, Kimberly. *Rhinestones, Religion, and the Republic: Fashioning Jewishness in France*. Stanford: Stanford University Press, 2013.

Ayoun, Richard and Bernard Cohen. *Les Juifs d'Algérie: deux mille ans d'histoire*. Paris: Jean-Claude Lattès, 1982.

Bahloul, Joëlle. *The Architecture of Memory: A Jewish–Muslim Household in Colonial Algeria, 1937–1962*. Translated by Catherine du Peloux Ménagé. Cambridge: Cambridge University Press, 1996.

Bar-Asher, Moshe. *La composante hébraïque du judéo-arabe algérien: communautés de Tlemcen et Aïn-Témouchent*. Jerusalem: The Hebrew University Magnes Press, 1992.

Masorot u-leshonot shel Yehude Tsefon-Afrikah. Jerusalem: Mosad Bialik; Ashkelon: Hamikhalalah Ha-ezorit, 1999.

Baron, Salo Wittmayer. "Ghetto and Emancipation." *Menorah Journal* 14, no. 6 (1928): 515–526.

Bartal, Israel. "Farming the Land on Three Continents: Bilu, Am Oylom, and Yefe-Nahar." *Jewish History* 21 (2007): 249–261.

Benbassa, Esther and Aron Rodrigue. *A History of the Judeo-Spanish Community, 14th–20th Centuries*. Berkeley: University of California Press, 2000.

Berkovitz, Jay. *Rites and Passages: The Beginnings of Jewish Culture in Modern France*. Philadelphia: University of Pennsylvania Press, 2004.

The Shaping of Jewish Identity in Nineteenth-century France. Detroit: Wayne State University Press, 1989.

Birnbaum, Pierre and Ira Katznelson, eds. *Paths of Emancipation: Jews, States, and Citizenship*. Princeton: Princeton University Press, 1995.

Brenner, Michael, Vicki Caron, and Uri R. Kaufmann, eds. *Jewish Emancipation Reconsidered: The French and German Models*. Tubingen: Mohr Siebeck, 2003.

Charvit, Yossef. *Elite rabbinique d'Algérie et modernization, 1750–1914*. Jerusalem: Editions Gaï Yinassé, 1995.

La France, l'élite rabbinique d'Algérie et la Terre Sainte au XIXe siècle: Tradition et modernité. Paris: Champion, 2005.

Chester, Lucy. "Boundary Commissions as Tools to Safeguard British Interests at the End of Empire." *Journal of Historical Geography* 34, no. 3 (2008): 494–515.

Cheyette, Brian. *Diasporas of the Mind: Jewish and Postcolonial Writing and the Nightmare of History*. New Haven: Yale University Press, 2013.

Cole, Joshua. "Antisémitisme et situation coloniale pendant l'entre-deux-guerres en Algérie: Les émeutes antijuives de Constantine." *Vingtième siècle* 108 (October–December 2010): 2–23.

"Constantine before the Riots of August 1934: Civil Status, Anti-Semitism, and the Politics of Assimilation in Interwar French Algeria." *The Journal of North African Studies* 17, no. 5 (2012): 839–861.

Colley, Linda. "Going Native, Telling Tales: Captivity, Collaborations and Empire." *Past and Present* 168 (2000): 170–193.

Conklin, Alice L. "Colonialism and Human Rights: A Contradiction in Terms? The Case of France and West Africa, 1895–1914," *The American Historical Review* 103, no. 2 (1998): 419–442.

Cooper, Frederick. *Colonialism in Question: Theory, Knowledge, History*. Berkeley: University of California Press, 2005.

and Jane Burbank, *Empires in World History: Power and the Politics of Difference.* Princeton: Princeton University Press, 2010.

and Ann L. Stoler, eds. *Tensions of Empire: Colonial Cultures in a Bourgeois World.* Berkeley: University of California Press, 1997.

Davidson, Naomi. *Only Muslim: Embodying Islam in Twentieth-Century France.* Ithaca, NY: Cornell University Press, 2012.

Davis, Christian S. *Colonialism, Anti-Semitism and Germans of Jewish Descent in Imperial Germany.* Ann Arbor: University of Michigan Press, 2011.

Deshen, Shlomo. *The Mellah Society: Jewish Community Life in Sherifian Morocco.* Chicago: University of Chicago Press, 1989.

and Moshe Shokeid. *The Predicament of Homecoming: Cultural and Social Life of North African Immigrants in Israel.* Ithaca, NY: Cornell University Press, 1974.

Ehmann, Annegret. "From Colonial Racism to Nazi Population Policy: The Role of the So-Called Mischlinge." In *The Holocaust and History.* Edited by Michael Berenbaum and Abraham J. Peck, 115–133. Bloomington: Indiana University Press, 1998.

Elkins, Caroline and Susan Pedersen, eds. *Settler Colonialism in the Twentieth Century: Projects, Practices, Legacies.* New York: Routledge, 2005.

Feldman, David. "Jews and the British Empire, c. 1900." *History Workshop Journal* 63, no. 1 (2007): 70–89.

Frankel, Jonathan and Steven J. Zipperstein, eds. *Assimilation and Community: The Jews of Nineteenth-Century Europe.* Cambridge: Cambridge University Press, 1992.

Friedman, Elizabeth. *Colonialism & After: An Algerian Jewish Community.* Boston: Bergin & Garvey, 1988.

Goldberg, Harvey E. *Cave Dwellers and Citrus Growers: A Jewish Community in Libya and Israel.* Cambridge: Cambridge University Press, 1972.

"The Oriental and the Orientalist: The Meeting of Mordecai Ha-Cohen and Nahum Slouschz." *Jewish Culture and History* 7, no. 3 (2004): 1–30.

ed. *Sephardi and Middle Eastern Jewries: History and Culture in the Modern Era.* Bloomington: Indiana University Press, 1996.

Gottreich, Emily. *The Mellah of Marrakesh: Jewish and Muslim Space in Morocco's Red City.* Bloomington: Indiana University Press, 2006.

and Daniel Schroeter, eds. *Jewish Culture and Society in North Africa.* Bloomington: Indiana University Press, 2011.

Green, Abigail. "The British Empire and the Jews: An Imperialism of Human Rights?" *Past & Present* 199 (2008): 175–205.

Moses Montefiore: Jewish Liberator, Imperial Hero. Cambridge, MA: Harvard University Press, 2010.

"Old Networks, New Connections: The Emergence of the Jewish International." In *Religious Internationals in the Modern World: Globalization and Faith Communities since 1750.* Edited by Abigail Green and Vincent Viaene, 53–81. Basingstoke: Palgrave Macmillan, 2012.

Ha-Cohen, Mordekhai. *The Book of Mordechai: A Study of the Jews of Libya: Selections from the Haghid Mordekhai of Mordecai Hakohen: Based on the Complete Hebrew Text as Published by the Ben Zvi Institute Jerusalem.* Edited and translated with introduction and commentaries by Harvey E. Goldberg. Philadelphia: Institute for the Study of Human Issues, 1980.

Hagege, Claude and Bernard Zarca, "Les Juifs et la France en Tunisie: Les bénéfices d'une relation triangulaire." *Le Mouvement social* 197 (October–December 2001): 9–28.

Hertzberg, Arthur. *The French Enlightenment and the Jews: the Origins of Modern Anti-Semitism*. New York: Columbia University Press, 1968.

Heschel, Susannah. "German-Jewish Scholarship on Islam as a Tool of De-Orientalization." *New German Critique* 117 (Fall 2012): 91–117.

"Revolt of the Colonized: Abraham Geiger's Wissenschaft des Judentums as a Challenge to Christian Hegemony in the Academy." *New German Critique* 77 (Spring–Summer 1999): 61–85.

Hess, Jonathan. *Germans, Jews, and the Claims of Modernity*. New Haven: Yale University Press, 2002.

Ho, Engseng. *The Graves of Tarim: Genealogy and Mobility across the Indian Ocean*. Berkeley: University of California Press, 2006.

Hull, Isabel. " 'Final Solutions' in the Colonies: The Example of Wilhelmine Germany." In *The Specter of Genocide: Mass Murder in Historical Perspective*. Edited by Robert Gellately and Ben Kiernan, 141–161. Cambridge: Cambridge University Press, 2003.

Hunt, Lynn, ed. *The French Revolution and Human Rights: A Documentary History*. New York: Bedford St. Martins, 1996.

Hyman, Paula. *The Emancipation of the Jews of Alsace: Acculturation and Tradition in the Nineteenth Century*. New Haven: Yale University Press, 1991.

Kalmar, Ivan Davidson and Derek Penslar, eds. *Orientalism and the Jews*. Waltham, MA: Brandeis University Press, 2005.

Katz, Ethan B. *The Burdens of Brotherhood: Jews and Muslims from North Africa to France*. Cambridge, MA: Harvard University Press, 2015.

"Tracing the Shadow of Palestine: The Zionist-Arab Conflict and Jewish–Muslim Relations in France, 1914–1945." In *The Israeli-Palestinian Conflict in the Francophone World*. Edited by Nathalie Debrauwere-Miller, 25–40. New York: Routledge, 2010.

Katz, Ethan B., Lisa Moses Leff, and Maud S. Mandel, eds. *Colonialism and the Jews*. Bloomington: Indiana University Press, 2017.

Katz, Jacob. ed. *Toward Modernity: The European Jewish Model*. New Brunswick: Transaction Books, 1987.

Khazzoum, Aziza. "The Great Chain of Orientalism: Jewish Identity, Stigma Management, and Ethnic Exclusion in Israel." *American Sociological Review* 68, no. 4 (2003): 481–510.

Kirsch, Adam. *Benjamin Disraeli*, Jewish Encounters. New York: Schocken, 2008.

Kobrin, Rebecca and Adam Teller, eds. *Purchasing Power: The Economics of Modern Jewish History*. Philadelphia: University of Pennsylvania Press, 2015.

Lahiri, Shompa. "Contested Relations: The East India Company and the Lascars in London." In *The Worlds of the East India Company*. Edited by H.V. Bowen, Margarette Lincoln, and Nigel Rigby. Woodbridge, UK: Boydell, 2002.

Laskier, Michael. *The Alliance Israélite Universelle and the Jewish Communities of Morocco: 1862–1962*. Albany: State University of New York Press, 1983.

"Between Vichy Antisemitism and German Harassment: The Jews of North Africa during the Early 1940s." *Modern Judaism* 11, no. 3 (1991): 343–369.

North African Jewry in the Twentieth Century: The Jews of Morocco, Tunisia, and Algeria. New York: New York University Press, 1984.

Leff, Lisa Moses. "The Impact of the Napoleonic Sanhedrin on French Colonial Policy in Algeria." *CCAR Journal* 54, no. 1 (2007): 35–54.

Sacred Bonds of Solidarity: The Rise of Jewish Internationalism in Nineteenth-Century France. Stanford: Stanford University Press, 2006.

Lewis, Bernard. "The Question of Orientalism." *The New York Review of Books* 29, no 11 (June 24, 1982): 49–56.

Lewis, Mary Dewhurst. *Divided Rule: Sovereignty and Empire in French Tunisia, 1881–1938.* Berkeley: University of California Press, 2013.

Loomba, Ania. *Colonialism/Postcolonialism.* New York: Routledge, 1998.

Macfie, Alexander Lyon. *Orientalism: A Reader.* New York: New York University Press, 2001.

Malino, Frances and David Sorkin, eds. *From East and West: Jews in a Changing Europe, 1750–1870.* New York: Basil Blackwell, 1990.

Malino, Frances and Bernard Wasserstein, eds. *The Jews of Modern France.* Hanover, NH: Brandeis University Press, 1985.

Mandel, Maud S. *In the Aftermath of Genocide: Armenians and Jews in Twentieth-Century France.* Durham, NC: Duke University Press, 2003.

Muslims and Jews in France: History of a Conflict. Princeton: Princeton University Press, 2014.

"Transnationalism and Its Discontents During the 1948 Arab-Israeli War." *Diaspora* 12, no. 3 (2003): 329–360.

Marchand, Suzanne L. *German Orientalism in the Age of Empire: Religion, Race and Scholarship.* Cambridge, UK: Cambridge University Press, 2009.

Marglin, Jessica. *Across Legal Lines: Jews and Muslims in Modern Morocco.* New Haven: Yale University Press, 2016.

Marrus, Michael. *The Politics of Assimilation: The French Jewish Community at the Time of the Dreyfus Affair.* New York: Clarendon Press, 1971.

Masters, Bruce. *Christians and Jews in the Ottoman Arab World: The Roots of Sectarianism.* Cambridge: Cambridge University Press, 2004.

Memmi, Albert. *The Colonizer and the Colonized.* Translated by Howard Greenfeld with a new introduction by the author. Preface by Jean-Paul Sartre. New York: Orion Press, 1965.

Mufti, Aamir. *Enlightenment in the Colony: The Jewish Question and the Crisis of Postcolonial Culture.* Princeton: Princeton University Press, 2007.

Nathans, Benjamin. *Beyond the Pale: The Jewish Encounter with Late Imperial Russia.* Berkeley: University of California Press, 2002.

Parks, Richard. "The Jewish Quarters of Interwar Paris and Tunis: Destruction, Creation, and French Urban Design." *Jewish Social Studies* n.s. 17, no. 1 (2010): 67–87.

Pasto, James. "Islam's 'Strange Secret Sharers': Orientalism, Judaism and the Jewish Question." *Comparative Studies in Society and History* 40, no. 3 (1998): 437–474.

Powell, Eve M. Trout. *A Different Shade of Colonialism: Egypt, Great Britain, and the Mastery of the Sudan.* Berkeley: University of California Press, 2003.

Poznanski, Renée. *Jews in France during World War II.* Translated by Nathan Bracher. Hanover, NH: University Press of New England, 1997.

Rodrigue, Aron. *French Jews, Turkish Jews: The Alliance Israélite Universelle and the Politics of Jewish Schooling in Turkey, 1860–1925.* Bloomington: Indiana University Press, 1990.

Rohde, Achim. "Der innere Orient: Orientalismus, Antisemitismus und Geschlecht im Deutschland des 18. bis 20. Jahrhunderts." *Die Welt des Islams* 45, no. 2 (2005): 370–411.

Roland, Joan G. *The Jewish Communities of India: Identity in a Colonial Era.* New Brunswick, NJ: Transaction, 1998.

Rosenberg, Clifford. *Policing Paris: The Origins of Modern Immigration Control between the Wars.* Ithaca: Cornell University Press, 2006.

Rothberg, Michael. *Multidirectional Memory: Remembering the Holocaust in the Age of Decolonization.* Stanford: Stanford University Press, 2009.

Rozenblit, Marsha. *Reconstructing a National Identity: The Jews of Habsburg Austria during World War I.* Oxford: Oxford University Press, 2004.

Said, Edward. "Zionism from the Standpoint of Its Victims." *Social Text* 1 (1978): 7–58.

Schechter, Ronald. *Obstinate Hebrews: Representations of Jews in France, 1715–1815.* Berkeley: University of California Press, 2003.

Schreier, Joshua. *Arabs of the Jewish Faith: The Civilizing Mission in Colonial Algeria.* New Brunswick: Rutgers University Press, 2010.

"From Mediterranean Merchant to French Civilizer: Jacob Lasry and the Economy of Conquest in Early Colonial Algeria." *International Journal of Middle East Studies* 44 (2012): 631–649.

Schroeter, Daniel J. "French Liberal Governance and the Emancipation of Algeria's Jews." *French Historical Studies* 33, no. 2 (2010): 259–280.

The Sultan's Jew: Morocco and the Sephardi World. Stanford: Stanford University Press, 2002.

and Joseph Chetrit, "Emancipation and Its Discontents: Jews at the Formative Period of Colonial Rule in Morocco." *Jewish Social Studies* 13, no. 1 (2006): 170–206.

Sebag, Paul. *Histoire des Juifs de Tunisie: des origines à nos jours.* Paris: L'Harmattan, 1991.

Sepinwall, Alyssa Goldstein. *The Abbé Grégoire and the French Revolution: The Making of Modern Universalism.* Berkeley: University of California Press, 2005.

Shepard, Todd. *The Invention of Decolonization: The Algerian War and the Remaking of France.* Ithaca: Cornell University Press, 2006.

Shokeid, Moshe. *The Dual Heritage: Immigrants from the Atlas Mountains in an Israeli Village.* Manchester: Manchester University Press, 1971.

Shurkin, Michael. "French Liberal Governance and the Emancipation of Algeria's Jews." *French Historical Studies* 33, no. 2 (2010): 259–280.

"French Nation Building, Liberalism and the Jews of Alsace and Algeria, 1815–1870." Ph.D. thesis, Yale University, 2000.

Silverman, Maxim. *Palimpsestic Memory: The Holocaust and Colonialism in French and Francophone Fiction and Film.* Oxford: Berghahn Books, 2013.

Sivan, Emmanuel. "Edward Said and his Arab Reviewers." *Jerusalem Quarterly* 35 (1985): 11–23.

Stein, Sarah Abrevaya, "Dividing South from North: French Colonialism, Jews, and the Algerian Sahara." *The Journal of North African Studies* 17, no. 5 (2012): 773–792.

"Jews and European Imperialism," unpublished paper.

Plumes: Ostrich Feathers, Jews, and a Lost History of Global Commerce. New Haven: Yale University Press, 2008.

"Protected Persons? The Baghdadi Jewish Diaspora, the British State, and the Persistence of Empire." *American Historical Review* 116, no. 1 (2011): 80–108.

Saharan Jews and the Fate of French Algeria. Chicago: University of Chicago Press, 2014.

Stillman, Norman A. *The Jews of Arab Lands: A History and Source Book*. Philadelphia: The Jewish Publication Society, 1979.

Stoler, Ann Laura. *Along the Archival Grain: Epistemic Anxieties and Colonial Common Sense*. Princeton: Princeton University Press, 2009.

Stora, Benjamin. *Les Trois exils: Juifs d'Algérie*. Paris: Stock, 2006.

Tabili, Laura. "Outsiders in the Land of Their Birth: Exogamy, Citizenship, and Identity in War and Peace." *Journal of British History* 44, no. 4 (2005): 796–815.

Tsur, Yaron. "L'Epoque coloniale et les rapports 'ethniques' au sein de la communauté juive en Tunisie." In *Mémoires juives d'Espagne et du Portugal*. Edited by Esther Benbassa, 197–206. Paris: Publisud, 1996.

———. "Haskala in a Sectional Colonial Society: Mahdia (Tunisia) 1885." In *Sephardi and Middle Eastern Jewries: History and Culture in the Modern Era*. Edited by Harvey E. Goldberg, 146–167. Bloomington: Indiana University Press, 1996.

———. "Jewish 'Sectional Societies' in France and Algeria on the Eve of the Colonial Encounter." *Journal of Mediterranean Studies* 4 (1994): 263–277.

———. "Yehadut Tunisya be-shilhe ha-tekufah ha-teromkolonialit." *Miqqedem umiyyam* 3 (1990): 77–113.

Wallet, Bart. "Napoleon's Legacy: National Government and Jewish Community in Western Europe." *Simon Dubnow Institute Yearbook* 6 (2007): 291–309.

Weingrod, Alex. *Reluctant Pioneers: Village Development in Israel*. Ithaca, NY: Cornell University Press, 1966.

Wilder, Gary. *The French Imperial Nation-State: Negritude and Colonial Humanism between the Two World Wars*. Chicago: University of Chicago Press, 2005.

Wyrtzen, Jonathan. *Making Morocco: Colonial Intervention and the Politics of Identity*. Ithaca, NY: Cornell University Press, 2015.

Zytnicki, Colette. *Les Juifs du Maghreb: Naissance d'une historiographie coloniale*. Paris: Presses de l'Université Paris-Sorbonne, 2011.

CHAPTER 20

ANTISEMITISM AND THE
JEWISH QUESTION

JONATHAN JUDAKEN

"Antisemitism" and "the Jewish Question" are Janus-faced sisters of modernity. The history of their entwinement reveals the inner workings of much of
modern cultural life, Jewish and not. The opening two sections of this chapter
historicize the constructs "the Jewish Question" and "antisemitism," tracing
the transformations in European and Jewish cultural life from the open-ended
discussions of the eighteenth century to the racialization and politicization of
anti-Jewish discourse toward the end of the nineteenth century, culminating
in the Holocaust, challenging the core ideas, values, and institutions that have
shaped modern Europe's self-definition. The third section provides a compendium of different accounts of antisemitism in modernity.

The chapter does not dwell upon the ongoing assault on Judaism by
Christians.[1] Anti-Judaism, treated in its various permutations in earlier
volumes of *The Cambridge History of Judaism*, persisted into modernity. This was evident in key episodes like the Damascus Affair (1840) and
the Mortara Affair (1858).[2] My focus instead is on what was new in the

I am deeply grateful for the input on this essay from Jeffrey Haus, Torbjorn Wandel, and
Robert Yelle.

[1] There are a number of writers who have examined the ongoing "teaching of contempt"
by Christian thinkers and the Christian churches beginning with Jules Isaac and Léon
Poliakov, but now including Rosemary Ruether, Roy Eckardt, Friedrich Heer, Franklin
Littell, Malcom Hay, John Gager, James Carroll, Robert Michael, Dora Bergen, and
Susannah Heschel.

[2] The Damascus Affair revolved around the charges of ritual murder and blood libel leveled against the Jewish community in Damascus, Syria, in 1840, ultimately becoming
an international cause célèbre when Jews from various countries publicly mobilized to
fight the anti-Jewish persecution. On the Damascus Affair, see Ronald Florence, *Blood
Libel: The Damascus Affair of 1840* (Madison: University of Wisconsin Press, 2004) and
Jonathan Frankel, *The Damascus Affair: "Ritual Murder," Politics, and the Jews in 1840*
(Cambridge: Cambridge University Press, 1997). The Mortara Affair involved the abduc-
tion of Edgardo Mortara by papal gendarmes so that he could be raised as a Catholic
as a result of his having been baptized by his teenage Catholic nursemaid in Bologna,
Italy, then a Papal State. Despite worldwide protests, Pope Pius IX refused to release the

expression of anti-Jewish antipathy. I emphasize how the deep-set typologies of Jews and Judaism elaborated over the course of Western civilization were recast in modern terminology and deployed in new institutions from the Enlightenment onwards. I consequently concentrate on how the category of race came to reshape anti-Jewish discourse, transforming blood libels and blood purity into a scientifically justified claim about the fixed nature of Jewish difference. This transformation dovetailed with how the mass politics of the late nineteenth century resulted in programmatic calls to confront the perceived threat posed by the rise of the Jews.[3] By the 1880s, a decade after Jewish emancipation was finalized across much of Europe, newly granted (Jewish) freedom(s) became the ultimate symbol of how modernity was overturning the natural order of things. The antisemitic clarion call promised restoration from the underside of the modern world in its myriad forms, just as Jews embraced and embodied these new possibilities.

"THE JEWISH QUESTION": HISTORICIZING A NEW CATCH PHRASE

Historian Jacob Toury has traced the catch phrase "the Jewish Question" to 1838 in Germany, first as *die Jüdische Frage*, then *Judenfrage*, and soon translated into other languages. Toury argues that, "The emerging 'Jewish Question,' was not the question of individual rights and of equality between private citizens, but rather the question of the corporate status of Jewry as a whole."[4] In this way it was similar to the "Irish Question," the "Social

---

boy. His case helped to spur the creation of the Alliance Israélite Universelle in 1860, the first Jewish rights and aid organization. See David I. Kertzer, *The Kidnapping of Edgardo Mortara* (New York: Vintage, 1998).

[3] Albert Lindemann in particular has stressed the "rise of the Jews" as the explanation of modern antisemitism. See *Esau's Tears: Modern Anti-Semitism and the Rise of the Jews* (Cambridge: Cambridge University Press, 1997). The problem with Lindemann's approach is that he consistently insists that Jews *really were* a demographic, economic, cultural, and political threat because they often refused to change what he characterizes as Jewish chauvinism and narrow separatism: "So long as most Jews retain an identity with a substantial connection to Jewish tradition, and so long as the rest of the world has some sense of that identity and its related history" then "the potential for new explosions of hatred will remain, sparked by 'bad times' – economic difficulties, wars, revolutions, natural disasters, or pandemic disease" (532). Lindemann conflates Jewish concentration in certain socio-economic sectors, principally in banking, medicine, law, and the press – Jewish *visibility* and *influence* – with real political and economic *power*.

[4] On "the Jewish Question" see, Jacob Toury, "'The Jewish Question': A Semantic Approach" *Leo Baeck Institute Year Book* 11 no. 1 (1966): 85–106, here 95.

Question," the "German Question" and the "Woman Question."⁵ The new construct corresponded to the new situation of mid-century Jews who were now integrating into every domain of modern life. The question for many non-Jews became how to distinguish the evermore-indistinguishable Jewish Other. Ultimately, the solution to that riddle took the form of so-called scientific racism or "antisemitism" per se, a term popularized by Wilhelm Marr in 1879. Thus, "the Jewish Question" as a slogan only took root between 1838 and 1879 when it established itself as "an anti-Jewish battle-cry."⁶

But if Toury insists upon understanding the new catch phrase as about the corporate status of Jewry as a whole, then the arguments that underpin this nineteenth-century category go back to a series of questions first articulated by Enlightenment thinkers and their Jewish counterparts, the *maskilim*, related to issues of rights and citizenship and modern ideas of freedom and emancipation. The terms of these discussions were new, in that they took place within a *secular* idiom. Enlightenment writers asked whether Jews as a group could be granted civil and political rights equal to Christian subjects and citizens; whether civic education would make them more like gentiles; and whether Jews could serve as loyal soldiers. Beneath this set of issues lay two central questions: did Jews constitute a distinctive people, race, or nation; and did an inherent dichotomy exist between Judaism and modernity? These questions stemmed from a broader Enlightenment debate about human nature, natural religion, natural rights, common humanity, tolerance, and "regeneration."⁷

English deists first articulated the terms of this discussion, most explicitly in John Toland's *Reasons for Naturalizing the Jews in Great Britain and Ireland* in 1714. Influenced by Baruch Spinoza and John Locke, Toland made his plea for religious tolerance on the basis of the notion of "Liberty of Conscience." He argued that Jews, like all people, were "a mixture of good and bad" and "that they are obedient, peaceable, useful, and advantageous as any; and even more so than many others." He insisted that if they were naturalized, their faults would be abated since they were a product of the conditions of their abject status.⁸ Toland's claims were but the

⁵ Albert Lindemann, "The Jewish Question," in *Antisemitism: A History*, ed. Albert S. Lindemann and Richard S. Levy (Oxford: Oxford University Press, 2010), 17.

⁶ Toury, "The Jewish Question," 92.

⁷ These connections are made by Jay Berkovitz, *The Shaping of Jewish Identity in Nineteenth-century France* (Detroit: Wayne State University Press, 1989), chap. 1. See also Paula E. Hyman, *The Jews of Modern France* (Berkeley: University of California Press, 1998), 18.

⁸ John Toland, *Reasons for Naturalizing the Jews in Great Britain and Ireland, On the same foot with all other Nations. Containing also, A Defence of the Jews against all Vulgar Prejudices in all Countries* (London, 1714), 6, 11.

first of a series of Enlightenment arguments for the civic equality of Jews.[9] This came to light in the disputes concerning the Bill of Naturalization in England in 1753, the so-called Jew Bill. In 1753, Parliament passed the Naturalization Act, enabling some foreign-born Jews to become citizens. Following passage of the law, however, there was an outburst of newspaper articles, songs, petitions, and visual materials, with a mob parading through the streets of London carrying signs that read, "No Jews, No Naturalization Bill, Old England and Christianity Forever!" Included amongst this flurry of pamphlets was one entitled *Reply to the famous Jew Question*.[10]

The debate on the "famous Jew Question" reached a high point in Berlin in 1781 with the publication of Prussian bureaucrat Christian Wilhelm von Dohm's *Über die bürgerliche Verbesserung der Juden* (*Concerning the Amelioration of the Civil Status of Jews*). Dohm's contentions encapsulated the ambivalence of the advocacy on behalf of Jews. On the one hand, Dohm claimed that "Asiatic" Jews "differ from others by beard, circumcision, and a special way ... of worshiping the Supreme Being"; on the other, that exposing them to Enlightenment ideas would alleviate their moral depravity.[11] Ameliorate the civil status of Jews and they would no longer be usurious, clannish, obstreperous, and malevolent. For his opponents, on the contrary, like biblical scholar and Orientalist, Johann David Michaelis, Jews had an innately "criminal" character and as such could never be reliable soldiers or loyal citizens.[12] Dohm's treatise was translated into French as *De la réforme politique des Juifs* in 1782, the same year that Hapsburg Emperor Joseph II's *Toleranzpatent* (Edict of Toleration) was issued, encouraging religious toleration, civic education, and opening up trades to Jews. In 1784 Louis XVI's *Lettres Patentes* would follow Joseph II's model.

Dohm's contentions, further advanced in 1787 by Honoré Gabriel Mirabeau in *Sur Moses Mendelssohn sur la réforme politique des Juifs*, clarified in the Royal Society of Metz's 1787 essay competition on the question, "Are there ways of making the Jews more useful and Happier in France?"

---

[9] The debate about Enlightened philosophes' views about Jews and Judaism continues to rage. The classic reference is Arthur Hertzberg, *The French Enlightenment and the Jews* (New York: Columbia University Press, 1968). See more recently, Adam Sutcliff, *Judaism and Enlightenment* (Cambridge: Cambridge University Press, 2003).

[10] Toury, "The Jewish Question," 85.

[11] Christian Wilhelm von Dohm, "Concerning the Amelioration of the Civil Status of the Jews" in *The Jew in the Modern World*, ed. Paul Mendes-Flohr and Jehuda Reinharz (New York and Oxford: Oxford University Press), 28, 30, 31.

[12] Michaelis in "Arguments Against Dohm," in *The Jew in the Modern World*, 42–43.

Bishop Henri Baptiste Abbé Grégoire's prize-winning response, *Essai sur la régénération physique, morale, et politique des Juifs*, demonstrated how transnational this conversation had become.[13] Grégoire disputed the facts on Jewish criminality presented by Michaelis, as well as his underlying contention that "man is born wicked." Jewish perversity stemmed instead from rabbinic Judaism, which could be overcome with a reformed education.[14] At the same time, Grégoire drew upon numerous eighteenth-century authorities, including the physiognomic studies of Johann Caspar Lavater, claiming that "the Jews in general had sallow complexions, hooked noses, hollow eyes, [and] prominent chins," which correlated with their deleterious moral character, and he adopted French naturalist Comte de Georges-Louis Buffon's assertions about how certain environments and "ill-chosen and ill-prepared food ... makes the human race soon degenerate," and applied this to Jews.[15] Summed up in the views of Grégoire, in different degrees Enlightenment thinkers agreed that it was Judaism that made Jews degenerate. But grant the Jews civic equality and transform social institutions and you will have solved the Jewish problem.

The debates in the National Assembly during the French Revolution made this discussion concrete. Jews in France were ultimately emancipated on the basis of the principles enunciated in the Declaration of the Rights of Man and Citizen on August 26, 1789. A month later, moderates like Mirabeau, Stanislas Clermont-Tonnerre, and Abbé Grégoire raised the issue of Jewish rights in the Assembly. The Assembly decreed "that the Jews are under the safeguard of the law and require of the king the protection that they need," thus effectively giving Jews *civil* rights.[16] After two more years of vehement debate, a decree of September 27, 1791 granted French Jews equal legal and *political* rights.

---

[13] Grégoire is often treated as the "icon of Jewish emancipation." See Alyssa Goldstein Sepinwall, "Strategic Friendships: Jewish Intellectuals, the Abbé Grégoire and the French Revolution" in *Renewing the Past, Reconfiguring Jewish Culture*, ed. Adam Sutcliffe and Ross Brann (Philadelphia: University of Pennsylvania, 2004), 2, and Sepinwall, *The Abbé Gregoire and the French Revolution: The Making of Modern Universalism* (Berkeley: University of California Press, 2005). See also Pierre Birnbaum, "A Jacobin Regenerator: Abbé Grégoire" in *Jewish Destinies: Citizenship, State, and Community in Modern France*, trans. Arthur Goldhammer (New York: Hill and Wang, 2000), 11–30.

[14] Abbé Grégoire, *Essai sur la regeneration physique, morale et politique des Juifs* (Metz, 1789), trans. as *An Essay on the Physical, Moral and Political Reformation of the Jews* (London, 1791), 134, 135, 136.

[15] Grégoire, *Essay*, 56 and 60.

[16] Cited in Gary Kates, "Jews into Frenchmen: Nationality and Representation in Revolutionary France," *Social Research* 56, no. 1 (1989): 213–232, 225.

The French Revolution consequently pushed the differing Jewish communities in France to the forefront as the first legally emancipated Jews in Europe, extending full citizenship to those who swore the civic oath that specifically renounced Jewish communal autonomy.[17] Jewish Emancipation had been passed despite vehement opposition and in two stages that reflected the duality of revolutionary attitudes caught between long-standing prejudices and Enlightenment principles.[18] The price of Jewish emancipation was cultural integration. Judaism and Jewishness were limited to the private sphere and national citizenship was deemed to conflict with communal affiliation. Clermont-Tonnerre's well-known statement in the Assembly encapsulated this state of affairs: Since "there cannot be one nation within another nation," "the Jews should be denied everything as a nation, but granted everything as individuals."[19]

As in so many other areas, Napoleon sought to reconcile Old Regime attitudes with Revolutionary ideals toward Jews. While he spread Jewish emancipation to Venice and Rome, the Kingdom of Westphalia, and as far east as the Grand Duchy of Warsaw, it was always within the defined limits of the new social contract, which linked citizenship with assimilation.[20] Final resolution on the matter eluded the Napoleonic regime. Responding to ongoing complaints about Jews in 1806, Napoleon convened an Assembly of 111 primarily non-rabbinical Jewish notables to distinguish between civil and Jewish law and to reinforce assimilation as the goal of emancipation. The Assembly codified the cleavage between ethnic and religious identity, with Jews subservient to the Napoleonic Code and French cultural norms, and rabbis serving thereafter as teachers and preachers, but not judges with an autonomous legal code that might conflict with Napoleon's. The Great Sanhedrin called for by Napoleon in 1807 was supposed to codify these decisions for the rest of European Jewry. In

[17] On the emancipation of the Jews of France, see Robert Badinter, *Libres et égaux...: L'émancipation des Juifs, 1789–1791* (Paris: Fayard, 1989). See also the essays by Shmuel Trigano, Stanley Hoffman, and David Landes under the title "Emancipation Reexamined" in Francis Malino and Bernard Wasserstein, eds, *The Jews in Modern France* (Hanover, NH: Brandeis University Press, 1985), 245–309.

[18] The Jews of southwestern and southeastern France were granted citizenship first, on January 28, 1790.

[19] "The French National Assembly: Debate on the Eligibility of Jews for Citizenship (December 23, 1789)" in *The Jew in the Modern World*, 114.

[20] Hyman acutely develops this argument in her chapter on "The Napoleonic Synthesis," in *The Jews of Modern France*. The classic study of Napoleonic attitudes to the Jews is Robert Anchel, *Napoléon et les Juifs* (Paris: Presses Universitaires de France, 1928). See also, Simon Schwarzfuchs, *Napoleon, the Jews and the Sanhedrin* (Boston: Routledge and Kegan Paul, 1979).

its short but active existence, the Grand Sanhedrin ratified the *quid pro quo* of emancipation: the state was secured in all civil and political matters including juridical, educational, taxation, and other administrative functions. Jewishness was limited to religious observance and private life.

As legally equal citizens, Jews were well positioned to ride the tide of modernization, impelled by industrialization and urbanization. French Jewry underwent rapid acculturation and geographical and social mobility with the last discriminatory legislation, the *more judaïco* court oath, abolished in 1846. They integrated into economic, political, and university institutions, leading to their progressive *embourgeoisement*. By the end of the nineteenth century, although a tiny minority of around 100,000, Jews were visible in every area of French life, especially after the advent of the Third Republic, to which they were zealously committed.[21]

Emancipation in Central Europe – specifically in Germany and Austria – unfolded more unevenly, caught between the reaction against Napoleonic era reforms and the struggles of liberals and socialists agitating for popular sovereignty and other Enlightenment values. After the defeat of Napoleon at Waterloo, the Congress of Vienna reinstated the subordinate status of Jews in June 1815. Hope for Jewish civic equality now lay in liberal and radical struggles for human equality, rights, and popular sovereignty.

Despite liberals' advocacy of emancipation, the conviction that Jews should *not* have political equality remained widely shared. In 1819, thousands of rioters expressed their opposition in a wave of pogroms known as the "Hep-Hep" riots. From Alsace to Bohemia, from Copenhagen and Hamburg to Riga and Kraków, the rallying cry for the rioters – *Hieroslyma est perdita*, or "Jerusalem is lost" – invoked the crusaders who had attacked Jews on their way to the Holy Land almost five hundred years earlier. The initial outbreaks of the "Hep-Hep" riots in Würtzburg on August 2, 1819 occurred just as the debate over Jewish emancipation in the Bavarian parliament was concluded, but before the results were made public. Within a few weeks, "Hep Hep" riots spilled across Germany and beyond.

Despite this resistance, the liberal agenda appealed strongly to Jews, since emancipation had yielded clear results for their Jewish brethren in France. Gabriel Riesser's activism serves as a case in point.[22] At a time when

---

[21] On the acculturation of Jews in the nineteenth-century, in addition to Berkovitz, Hyman, and Birnbaum, see Michael Graetz, *The Jews in Nineteenth-Century France*, trans. Jane Marie Todd (Stanford: Stanford University Press, 1996) and Phyllis Cohen Albert, *The Modernization of French Jewry: Consistory and Community in the Nineteenth Century* (Hanover, NH: University Press of New England for Brandeis University Press, 1977).

[22] For the example of Riesser as a Jewish activist, see Phyllis Goldstein, *A Convenient Hatred: The History of Antisemitism* (Brookline: Facing History and Ourselves, 2012), 179.

few Jews were allowed to study at a university, Riesser earned a doctoral degree in law from the University of Heidelberg. Although he graduated with highest honors, Riesser soon learned that no German would hire a Jewish lawyer or a Jew as a professor of law. He achieved notoriety in 1831 when he published an article demanding equal rights. Heinrich Paulus, a professor at the University of Heidelberg, vehemently opposed his petition, insisting that Jews were "Ausländer": foreigners, incapable of understanding the German soul.

The period 1820–1848, with those favoring emancipation pitted against those declaiming its impossibility, is nicely illustrated in the debate on the *Judenfrage* between the two young Hegelians, Bruno Bauer and Karl Marx. Their debate shows the transition in discussions of Jews and Judaism during the middle of the nineteenth century. In his 1843 *Die Judenfrage* (*The Jewish Question*), Bauer spoke as an opponent of Jewish emancipation. He lamented that while advocates of emancipation demanded that Christians give up their prejudices, they could not demand the same of Jews because the heart of Judaism was unchangeable and immutable. Following Hegel's line on Jews and Judaism, Bauer claimed that Jews are an unhistorical people possessing an "oriental nature" that limits human liberty and progress.[23] For Bauer, as for Hegel, Judaism and Christianity remained absolutely irreconcilable. In a starkly modern phrase, Bauer insisted, "The opposition is no longer religious, it is scientific." Jewish atavism, and their "perpetual segregation from others," meant that Jews could never be equal citizens.[24]

In his famous reply, *Zur Judenfrage* (*On the Jewish Question*), Marx argued *against* his one-time teacher and *for* the political emancipation of the Jewish community. In so doing, he clearly sided with the Prussian Jews in the central struggle that they faced. But the thrust of his argument, like Bauer's, stressed the distinction between political emancipation and human emancipation, and here it took a nasty turn. Flipping Bauer's Hegelianism on its head, Marx insisted that civic and political emancipation depended upon economic emancipation, which meant emancipation from commerce and "huckstering," which he identified with Jews. Judaism served as a synonym for financial and merchant capitalism, which Marx insisted objectified and alienated humans, transforming all human relationships into "exchange objects." "What is the profane basis of Judaism?," wrote Marx, "*Practical* need, *self-interest*. What is the worldly cult of the Jew? Huckstering. What is his worldly god? *Money*." Judaism as such had

---

[23] Leopold Davis, "The Hegelian Antisemitism of Bruno Bauer," *History of European Ideas* 25 (1999): 179–206.

[24] Bauer, in *The Jew in the Modern World*, 322–323.

thoroughly contaminated Christian society with "the practical Jewish spirit." Marx's equating Judaism with capitalism did not bode well: "The *social* emancipation of the Jew is the *emancipation of society from Judaism*," he wrote in his final line.[25]

While Marx's argument for Jewish emancipation differentiated his position from the French utopian socialists, he did echo their use of images of Jews and Judaism to critique capitalism. The utopian socialists had argued that industrialization and capitalism created a new aristocracy of money.[26] Their target was the July Monarchy (1830–1848), where under Louis Philippe, an emergent Orléanist elite dominated, including a number of Jewish families, especially the Rothschilds, who became the new symbol of everything that nascent socialism opposed. Charles Fourier (1772–1837) and Pierre-Joseph Proudhon (1809–1865) identified Jews with this new plutocracy of financial and merchant capitalism that like the aristocracy of the *ancien régime* were considered parasites on the body of the nation. One of Fourier's disciples, Alphonse de Toussenel (1803–1885), as the author of *Les Juifs, rois de l'époque* (The Jews, Kings of the Age, 1845), became the most influential socialist anti-Semite as a result of his impact on Edouard Drumont. Targeting the Rothschilds, he argued that Jews dominated France by controlling its financial markets. Idealizing rural France and ultramontane Catholicism, he saw monarchical authority allied with the Catholic Church as a bulwark against the Protestant and Jewish enemies of France.

Toussenel brought together socialist and conservative Christian anti-Jewish antipathy to emancipation and modernity. Seeing Jews as bent on the destruction of a traditional, aristocratic, hierarchical order, both Conservative Catholic and Protestant Christians often linked Jews to the

---

[25] Karl Marx, "On the Jewish Question" in *The Marx–Engels Reader*, second edition, ed. Robert C. Tucker (New York: W. W. Norton, 1978), 26–52, 48–49, 52. On Marxism and the Jewish Question, more generally, see Robert Wistrich, *Socialism and the Jews: The Dilemmas of Assimilation in Germany and Austria-Hungary* (Rutherford, NJ: Fairleigh Dickinson Press, 1982); Jack Jacobs, *On Socialists and "the Jewish Question" after Marx* (New York: New York University Press, 1992); and Enzo Traverso, *The Marxists and the Jewish Question: The History of a Debate, 1843–1943* (Atlantic Highlands, NJ: Humanities, 1994).

[26] The best overview on Socialism and "the Jewish Question" is still George Lichtheim, "Socialism and the Jews" *Dissent* (July–August 1968): 314–342. On the image of "the Jew" in the French utopian socialists see Jacob Katz, *From Prejudice to Destruction* (Cambridge: Harvard University Press, 1980),119–128; Robert F. Byrnes, *Antisemitism in Modern France: The Prologue to the Dreyfus Affair* (New York: H. Fertig, 1950), 114–125; Edmund Silberner, "Charles Fourier on the Jewish Question," *Jewish Social Studies* 8, no. 4 (1946): 245–266; J. Salwyn Schapiro, "Pierre Joseph Proudhon, Harbinger of Fascism," *American Historical Review* 50, no. 4 (1945): 714–737.

corrupting forces of modernity. Like socialists, they sought to purge society of the contagion they identified with Jewish banking, commerce, the stock market, industry, and the city.

After the revolutions of 1848, the forces of reaction were pitted against the struggles for expansion of suffrage and rights. As an icon of modernity, the Jews of Europe were caught in the crossfire. On the one hand, slowly across the continent and across the century, Jews were granted legal equality as part of a broader set of social reforms, first in France (1791), then in the Netherlands (1796), in Greece (1830), in the Ottoman Empire (1839), in the United Kingdom (1856), in Italy (1861), in the Habsburg Empire (1867), the North German Confederation (1869) and in the unified Reich (1871). On the other hand, in each debate "the Jewish Question" would repeatedly get addressed in the categories set by the Enlightenment and the French Revolution and the rejoinders to them. Since that reaction arose primarily in Central Europe, the emancipation of Jews there resulted from struggle rather than from governmental legislation of principles. As Jews were legally emancipated, however, the terms that defined "the Jewish Question" began to narrow, giving birth to a new construct, "antisemitism."

"ANTISEMITISM": THE MASS POLITICS OF SCIENTIFIC RACISM

The new legal status giving Jews equal rights spurred racial antisemitism. The terms of the discussion about Jews and Judaism now changed. Whereas for Enlightenment thinkers, the cause of Jewish depravity was religion, and the solution to the Jewish problem was assimilation, new racial arguments aimed at upending emancipation by maintaining that assimilation was impossible. "Antisemitism" as a new construct developed as the battle cry for a new form of modern mass politics. In this new era, the discourse of race replaced the earlier theological and then social distinctions between Christians and Jews with new scientific-sounding criteria based on blood and descent that could be easily welded onto an exclusionary nationalist, ethno-racial vision of "the people."

The language of race was secular, scientific, and positivist. The invention of "Semite" as a category suggested objectivity and science, making Jewish qualities fixed and unchanging, from which neither conversion nor assimilation was possible. The stock figure of 'the Jew' trotted out by the new mass press ostensibly made Jews identifiable in an era of social integration. Just as "the Jewish Question" emerged when Jews were beginning to integrate in vast numbers, the creation of the neologism "antisemitism" marked another step in the effort to exclude them: a more systematic and immutable racialization and its politicization among the masses.

German journalist Wilhelm Marr popularized the term "anti-Semite" in 1879, explicitly to replace religious anti-Judaism with a secular, scientific construct based on racial theory. Marr first used the term as the name of a short-lived political party, the Anti-semiten-Liga (Anti-Semite League), based on the success of his best-selling 1879 pamphlet, *Der Sieg des Judenthums über das Germanenthum* (The Victory of Jewry over Germandom).

Marr's own démarche is indicative of the changing direction of anti-Jewish discourse between 1848 and 1879. An itinerant journalist, political radical, and acolyte of the Young Hegelians in his early years, his first publishing successes came as a popularizer of Feuerbach's and Bauer's critiques of religion. Pinning all of his hopes on triumph in 1848, Marr emerged embittered from the collapse of the revolution. In 1859 he returned to his native Hamburg from America a white supremacist. In 1862 he published *Der Judenspiegel* (A Mirror to the Jews), which repeated ideas that could be found in Voltaire or the Young Hegelians. But Marr gave his indictment a pointedly racist rationale, alluding to "'tribal peculiarities' and 'an alien essence.'"[27]

The Victory of Jewry over Germandom was a more novel work than *A Mirror to the Jews* and struck a far deeper chord. In a few pages, Marr strung together a "historical-cultural" narrative covering the dispersion of the Jews by the Romans to Marr's present with a Jewish conspiracy at its core. This "Judaization" of European history, he told the reader, "corrupted society in all of its aspects." "This alien racial element," he insisted, "clashed too violently with the total character of Germandom." Germany was on her deathbed.[28]

A political program intended to revive Germany followed in his next pamphlet of 1879, *Elect No Jews!* (*Wählet keinen Juden!*), subtitled, *Der Weg zum Siege des Germanenthums über das Judenthum* or *The Way to Victory of Germandom over Judaism*, in which Marr cast himself as a "fighter against Jewish emancipation." Political equality for Jews allowed them to gain control of the state in order to guarantee the hegemony they had already established in the financial and cultural arena. In response, Marr made a bid for a

---

[27] Richard Levy, "Political Antisemitism in Germany and Austria" in *Antisemitism: A History*, ed. Lindemann and Levy, 127.

[28] Wilhelm Marr, *The Victory of Judaism over Germanism, Viewed from a Nonreligious Point of View*, trans. Gerhard Rohringer (Bern: Rudolph Costenoble, 1879), 6, 22, 23, 12. See also the selections translated in Richard Levy, *Antisemitism in the Modern World: An Anthology of Texts* (Lexington, MA: D.C. Heath and Company, 1991), 76–93.

new kind of political mobilization, institutionalized in parties, propaganda associations, and newspapers aimed at the purported Jewish power that came with emancipation. At the same time that Marr was publishing his *Antisemitische Hefte* (Antisemitic Pamphlets), he launched his newspaper *Deutsche Wacht* with the subtitle, *Monthly of the Anti-Jewish Association.*[29] A year later he was calling himself "the father of the anti-Jewish movement," and a decade further on "the patriarch of antisemitism."[30]

While Marr's Anti-semiten-Liga was, in fact, wholly ephemeral, the title for the association stuck. As Richard Levy explains, "over the next fifteen years, variants of *anti-Semitism*, *anti-Semite*, and *anti-Semitic*, made their way out of the German-speaking world into nearly every European language."[31] "Anti-Semite" now morphed into a *nom de guerre* that stood opposed to the dark side of modernity made possible by the French and Industrial Revolutions. Marr had given a name to a new vocabulary and a new set of strategies oriented toward mass mobilization. Against Jews as manipulators of money and controllers of levers of power, "antisemites" could now group in solidarity to defend the aristocrats, shopkeepers, artisans, low-level professionals, and minor bureaucrats left behind by the stock market crash of 1873 and the great depression of the late nineteenth century. A switch had thus taken place between the Enlightenment discourse that underpinned "the Jewish Question" and Marr's formulation of "antisemitism." Jews no longer represented atavism and backwardness; they were now also tagged as the vanguard of corrosive modernity.

A few months after Marr's coinage, Heinrich von Treitschke, distinguished professor of history at the University of Berlin, gave the word "Semitic" currency in his pamphlet *Ein Wort über unser Judenthum* ("A Word about Our Jews"). While not a straightforward racist like Marr, von Treitschke abetted in making antisemitism acceptable by declaring that "a cleft has always existed between Occidental and Semitic essences" and warning that Jews "will someday command Germany's stock exchanges and newspapers." His famous claim in "A Word About Our Jews" that "the Jews are our misfortune" became the masthead for a number of antisemitic news organs.[32]

But it fell to the popular Lutheran preacher and court chaplain, Adolf Stoecker, and his *Christian Social Party* to organize the first antisemitic

---

[29] Moshe Zimmerman, *Wilhelm Marr: The Patriarch of Antisemitism* (New York and Oxford: Oxford University Press, 1986), 90.

[30] Zimmerman, *Wilhelm Marr*, 88–89.

[31] Richard Levy, "Political Antisemitism in Germany and Austria," 123.

[32] Heinrich von Tretschke, "A Word About Our Jews" in Levy, *Antisemitism in the Modern World*, 73, 71.

movement that had a significant impact. In his speeches and writings, most famously in his 1879 "Our Demands on Modern Jewry," Stoecker put political antisemitism on the map. Like Marr and Treitschke, he warned about Jews that "finance, banking, and commerce are in their possession," and "the press is in their hands." As the chaplain to the imperial court, Stoecker gave antisemitism clout; as the founder of the Christian Social Party and the Berlin Movement, he was the first major leader of political antisemitism in Germany. Despite his Christian credentials, Stoecker also borrowed from the new racial discourse: "The Jews are and remain a people within a people, a state within a state, a tribe amid a foreign race," he fulminated.[33]

The first major campaign he mounted was the "Anti-Semite's Petition" (1880–1881), which garnered over 250,000 signatures and became the subject of debate in the Prussian Parliament. The petition called upon the Kaiser to implement four laws: (1) that "the immigration of alien Jews" be limited if not prevented; (2) "that the Jews be excluded from all positions of authority; that their employment in the judiciary – namely as autonomous judges – receive appropriate limitation"; (3) "that the Christian character of the primary school – even when attended by Jewish pupils – be strictly protected"; that only Christian teachers be allowed in these schools; and (4) "that a special census of the Jewish population be reinstituted."[34] These measures would have ended Jewish emancipation, which became the goal of the plethora of antisemitic parties that emerged in the 1880s after the creation of Stoecker's Christian Social Party.

While none of these now-forgotten political parties proved very successful (the antisemitic parties had their best showing in the Reichstag elections of 1893, electing 16 deputies out of 397), by the dawn of World War I antisemitic discourse had nonetheless become widely institutionalized in German political and cultural life.[35] Antisemitic discourse had spread into the Deutschnationale Volkspartei (DNVP), the Agrarian League (*Bund der Landwirte*), the Pan-Germanic League (*Alldeutscher Verband*), the White Collar Trade Union (*Deutschnationaler Handlungsgehilfenverband*), gymnastics clubs (like the *Akademischer Turnerbund*), student and youth groups, and lobbies and interest groups, and it was common in a variety of church groups.[36]

---

[33] Adolf Stoecker, "Our Demands on Modern Jewry," in Levy, *Antisemitism in the Modern World*, 65, 64.

[34] "Antisemites' Petition," in Levy, *Antisemitism in the Modern World*, 127.

[35] Peter Pulzer, "Third Thoughts on German and Austrian Antisemitism," *Journal of Modern Jewish Studies* 14, no. 2 (2005): 137–178, 143.

[36] George Mosse, *The Crisis of German Ideology: Intellectual Origins of the Third Reich* (New York: Schocken, 1981); Fritz Stern, *Politics of Cultural Despair: A Study in the Rise of*

Antisemitism across Central and Western Europe was winning wide circulation in part because of its scientific associations, but also precisely because of its elasticity as a concept. The appeals of antisemites also stuck because Jews were significantly overrepresented in the modern industrial economy. While less than 1 percent of Germany's population, and less than 5 percent of Austria-Hungary's, Jews had a disproportionately large role in the industrialization and modernization of Central Europe. With a long legacy, first as "Court Jews" and later as modern bankers, Jews were also key developers of railroads, important financiers of coalmining, and pioneers of sugar refinement, textile manufacturing, electrical machinery, transatlantic shipping, and department stores. Jews were overrepresented in the liberal professions, especially journalism, law, and medicine. And Jews were also in key positions that influenced the liberal, educated classes: as cultural creators, critics, impresarios, and managers of high culture. "Jews, as allies of modernity," writes historian Steven Beller, "thus became the targets of many of those in Central and Eastern Europe who suffered from the dislocations of economic modernization and the loss of moral and spiritual certitude that came with [it]." To many left behind by modernization, Jews had gone from despised pariahs to parvenus too quickly. The apparent success of Jews who went from iterant Talmudic scholars to journalists and critics and from peddlers and beggars to merchants and businessmen within a generation stung those who felt left behind or left out by the forces of modernity.[37]

The Dreyfus Affair in France (1894–1906) demonstrates the point. The Affair devolved into a *guerre franco-française* based on the false accusation of the Jewish Captain Alfred Dreyfus. Dreyfus was the grandson of a peddler and kosher butcher and the son of a prosperous textile manufacturer in the city of Mulhouse in Alsace. He moved to Paris after the Franco-Prussian War to continue his schooling, and eventually rose to a position as an adjutant to the French national staff. When a memorandum (the famous *bordereau*) was discovered in the wastebasket of the German embassy in Paris, it made clear that someone was selling military secrets to the Germans. The general staff quickly lit on Dreyfus, the only Jew in their midst at the time.

German Ideology (Berkeley: University of California Press, 1961); Peter Pulzer, *The Rise of Political Anti-Semitism in Germany and Austria* (New York: Wiley, 1966); Richard Levy, *The Downfall of the Anti-Semitic Political Parties in Germany* (New Haven: Yale, 1975); Uriel Tal, *Christians and Jews in Germany: Religion, Politics and Ideology in the Second Reich, 1870–1914* (Ithaca: Cornell, 1975); Shulamit Volkov, *The Rise of Popular Antimodernism in Germany: The Urban Master Artisans, 1873–1896* (Princeton: Princeton, 1978).
[37] Steven Beller, *Antisemitism: A Short History* (New York: Oxford University Press, 2007), 52, 36.

A military tribunal convicted him on trumped up evidence and sentenced him to military degradation and life in solitary exile on Devil's Island. Shipped off to die, Dreyfus was forgotten by most, except for a small group rallied by his brother. Following Emile Zola's intervention under the most famous headline in all of journalism – his "J'accuse" on January 13, 1898 – the Affair exploded onto the streets of Algeria, Lyon, Marseilles, Toulouse, and Rouen, with riots across France, splitting France into Dreyfusards and anti-Dreyfusards.[38] For the latter, Dreyfus was part of a syndicate of usurious "lords of finance and administration" (Drumont), a "hideous beast of treason" (Leon Daudet), a "Judas" reborn (Maurice Barrès).[39] By now, antisemitism had plainly become a political weapon, uniting the opponents of the modern, Republican state. While Dreyfus, in fact, was never found "not guilty," the case would come to a close when a civilian appeals court overturned his conviction in 1906.

While the anti-Dreyfusards failed in their immediate aims, the first place where political antisemitism actually came to power was in Vienna, where Jews made up nearly 10 percent of the population. Just as political antisemitism waned in Germany, but was reaching its boiling point in France, Karl Lueger was elected mayor of Vienna three times on an explicitly antisemitic platform before the Habsburg Emperor, Franz Joseph, allowed him to accede to the position in 1897, which he held until 1910. Lueger, the charismatic leader of the Catholic Christian Social Party, rose to power as a master of the new politics based on mobilizing along ethnic lines, common across the industrialized world, but particularly powerful in the ethnically divided Habsburg Empire.

Like Marr, Lueger followed the cultural shifts of his era in developing his political ideas. After studying law at the University of Vienna, Lueger won election to the municipal council as a liberal in 1875. Following the crash of 1873 and the lengthy economic crisis that followed, he slowly

[38] Michael Burns, *France and the Dreyfus Affair: A Documentary History* (New York: Bedford/St. Martin's, 1999), 107. The best histories of the Dreyfus Affair include Jean Denis Bredin, *The Affair: The Case of Alfred Dreyfus*, trans. by Jeffrey Mehlman (New York: George Braziller, 1986); Michael Burns, *Dreyfus: A Family Affair, 1789–1945* (New York: HarperCollins, 1991); Nancy Fitch, "Mass Culture, Mass Parliamentary Politics, and Modern Anti-Semitism: The Dreyfus Affair in Rural France," *American Historical Review* 97, no. 1(1992): 55–95; Norman Kleeblatt, ed. *The Dreyfus Affair: Art, Truth and Justice* (Berkeley: University of California Press, 1987); Michael Marrus, *The Politics of Assimilation: The French Jewish Community at the Time of the Dreyfus Afffair* (Oxford: Oxford University Press, 1980); and Stephen Wilson, *Ideology and Experience: Antisemitism in France at the Time of the Dreyfus Affair* (Rutherford, NJ: Fairleigh Dickinson University Press, 1982).
[39] Burns, *France and the Dreyfus Affair*, 7–8, 11, 52.

drifted rightward, rising to leadership of the Christian Social Party in 1890 after the death of its Austrian founder, Karl von Vogelsang. Under Lueger's leadership the Christian Socials became the first successful mass political party in Austria, with antisemitism a central plank of their ideology. Lueger mobilized the lower-middle classes in Austria by employing the same imagery Stoecker had in the "Anti-Semites' Petition." Denouncing Jewish influence in banking, industry, commerce, and the liberal professions, Lueger called for segregating the school system and banning the immigration of foreign Jews.[40]

It was, of course, in Lueger's Vienna that Hitler came of age, faulting his much-admired progenitor only for his lack of rigor when it came to racial antisemitism.[41] This was because Lueger famously once responded to the suggestion that he lacked conviction on the Jewish Question by retorting, "I decide who is a Jew." In having the power to decide who was a Jew, Lueger aggravated the fears of Austrians most directly affected by the influx of Jews from the eastern provinces of the Habsburg Empire: so-called *Ostjuden* made up 25 percent of Vienna's 175,000-strong Jewish community when Lueger took office.[42]

This vast immigration was in turn the result of Jews fleeing the Russian Empire. In 1897 when Lueger became mayor, there were 5.2 million Jews living in the Russian Empire, about 4.3 percent of the population, with nearly five million residing within the Pale of Settlement, making up fully 40 percent of world Jewry. For the first half-century after the creation of the Pale in 1772, no major legal changes affected Jewish existence. Under the general goal of modernizing the Russian Empire, however, Nicholas I transformed Jewish life in these areas. His first initiative was via the military. Jews were traditionally exempted from military service in exchange for a special head tax. In 1827, however, Nicholas

[40] Steven Beller, *Vienna and the Jews, 1867–1938: A Cultural History* (Cambridge: Cambridge University Press, 1989); John Boyer, *Political Radicalism in Late Imperial Vienna: The Origins of the Christian Social Movement, 1848–1897* (Chicago: Chicago University Press, 1981); John Boyer, *Culture and Political Crisis in Vienna: Christian Socialism in Power, 1897–1918* (Chicago: Chicago University Press, 1995); Bruce Pauley, *From Prejudice to Persecution: A History of Austrian Anti-Semitism* (Chapel Hill: University of North Carolina, 1992).

[41] Brigitte Hamann, *Hitler's Vienna: A Dictator's Apprenticeship* (New York: Oxford University Press, 1999).

[42] On the impact of the *Ostjuden* in German culture, see Steven Aschheim, *Brothers and Strangers: The East European Jew in German and German Jewish Consciousness, 1800–1923* (Madison: University of Wisconsin Press, 1983); Jack Wertheimer, *Unwelcome Strangers: East European Jews in Imperial Germany* (New York: Oxford University Press, 1987).

issued a decree creating a cantonist system, based on the demand that each Jewish community produce a quota of military recruits, who would serve for up to twenty-five years. In 1840, the government's approach conjoined creating loyal soldiers to educating Jews in special state schools – teaching secular subjects and the Russian language – all intended to foster Jewish integration. The effort to modernize the patently backward Russian Empire was given a boost when the "Tsar Liberator" Alexander II inherited the throne in 1855. The "Emancipating Tsar," manumitted more than fifty million Russian serfs, reformed the legal and administrative systems, and abolished the cantonist system. But his assassination on March 1, 1881 by the revolutionaries of the Narodnaia Volia (People's Will), including the Jewish comrade Gesia Gelfman, set off a wave of pogroms initiating a new phase of anti-Jewish persecution.

During Holy Week of 1881, a season always prone to anti-Jewish excesses, a pogrom broke out in Elisavetgrad, followed by more violent outbreaks in Kiev and Odessa. Over the next three years, pogroms would rage in 160 other cities and villages across the Russian empire. Mobs roamed the streets, attacked Jews, smashed into homes, and looted stores, often with the authorities looking on idly until it was too late. The pogroms were compounded by the passage of the Temporary Regulations of May 3, 1882, which prohibited Jews from living outside towns and shtetls within the Pale. The state also retreated from its reliance on education as a method of integration, imposing instead a *numerus clausus* on Jews: henceforward only 10 percent of Jews within the Pale of Settlement, 5 percent outside, and 3 percent in Moscow and St. Petersburg could attend secondary and higher education.

The pogroms beginning in 1881 were only the first of three waves (1881–84, 1903–06, 1918–20) that like a tsunami changed Jewish life in the Russian empire forever, cascading as they did with massive emigration. A second set of pogroms started in the city of Kishinev in 1903 at the instigation of P. A. Krushevan, the editor of a local newspaper and former government official. This time pogroms broke out in over 300 cities. From the end of the 1905–06 pogroms, as Heinz-Dietrich Löwe notes, "anti-Semitism developed a mass basis in the Union of the Russian People (URP) and other so-called Black Hundred Organizations."[43]

By far the most violent wave of pogroms, however, took place from 1918 to 1920, during the Civil War that followed the Bolshevik seizure of power. Every current opposed to the communist takeover engaged in pogroms: the White Armies under General Denikin, Wrangel, Kolchak, and others; the

---

[43] Heinz-Dietrich Löwe, "Antisemitism in Russia and the Soviet Union," in Lindemann and Levy, *Antisemitism*, 175.

anarchists under Nestor Makhno; and the Ukrainian national army commanded by Semion Petliura. The White armies identified Jews with disloyalty to the tsar and with Bolshevism itself. Once more the labels stuck, since Jews were overrepresented within Bolshevik and revolutionary ranks.

In December 1918, the momentary success of the communists in Bavaria and Hungary encouraged a widespread fear that the social upheaval of "Judeo-Bolshevism" would rage across Europe. Only a few years later, Hitler's message to a hobbled Germany offered national redemption by engaging in a crusade against this two-headed monster of modernity: Jewish Bolshevism. In *Mein Kampf*, which became the Bible of National Socialism after it was published in 1924, Hitler drew on a half century of antisemitic discourse in blaming Jews for the decadence that had infected modern social life. He decried "their unclean dress and their generally unheroic appearance ... in addition to their physical uncleanliness." Their tools were "the press, art, literature, and the theater." But their secret weapon was the Jewish theory of Marxism that proclaimed equality, which "contests the significance of nationality and race." "*By defending myself against the Jew,*" he concluded, "*I am fighting for the work of the Lord.*"[44] Hitler's harangues against Jews thus wound together motifs from Christian anti-Judaism with the medical discourse of degeneracy (Jews as abnormal, corrupt, and impure), wedded the integral nationalist arguments about Jews as foreigners (outsiders, strangers, aliens) with socialist accusations of Jewish materialism (bankers, financiers, parasites), and coupled the image of Jews as hyper-rational conspirators (unscrupulous, invisible, organized) with the danger of Revolution (subversion, disruption, chaos).

Combined with military models of organization (uniforms, torch-light parades, and hierarchy), National Socialism thus based its cohesion in the imaginary Jewish threat. As such, Saul Friedländer has termed the Nazi variety of Jew-hatred "redemptive anti-Semitism."[45] In using this formulation, Friedländer sought to bridge the major interpretations of Nazi antisemitism. While some scholars emphasize the centrality of science, social engineering, and a crisis of modernity for the rise of Nazism, others insist upon anti-Judaism as a root cause.[46] Friedländer suggests that religious anti-Judaism, secular and political antisemitism, and *völkisch* ideology were opposed neither in Nazi discourse nor in its institutions. Nazism

[44] Adolf Hitler, *Mein Kampf*, trans. Ralph Manheim (Cambridge, MA: Houghton Mifflin Company, 1943), 57, 65.

[45] Saul Friedländer, *Nazi Germany and the Jews: The Years of Persecution, 1933–1939* (New York: Harper Collins, 1997), chap. 3.

[46] Omer Bartov, ed., *The Holocaust: Origins, Implementation, Aftermath* (New York: Routledge, 2000), 79.

fused together the modern and the traditional into what Jeffrey Herf terms a "reactionary modernism" that was both rational and irrational, modern and anti-modern, bureaucratic and charismatic.[47] In short, the millenarian apocalypticism of the Nazis was key to their modern, managed, and bureaucratized genocidal antisemitism. The demonization of Jews – the notion that they were evil incarnate – made Nazi antisemitism different from Nazi racial views of Slavs or of the French masses: "If the Jew occupied Satan's place in Nazi eschatology," maintains Léon Poliakov, "then the non-German or 'sub-human,' lacking any sacred attribute was for the most part classified among the animals."[48] The sacred dimension of the Nazi assault on European Jewry differentiated the war against the Jews from Nazi genocide more generally, which targeted as many non-Jews as Jews, including Gypsies and the handicapped, who were likewise slated for extermination.

With Hitler's rise to the helm of the German state in 1933, the millenarianist and racialized antisemitism at the core of the Nazi creed became the basis of state policy. Nazism consequently transformed Germany into what historians Burleigh and Wippermann term, a "Racial State."[49] As such, Nazi antisemitism marks the final moment in our account of the categories "antisemitism" and "the Jewish Question," with the unfolding of what Hitler deemed *"die Endlösung der Judenfrage"* (the Final Solution of the Jewish Question).[50]

Nazi and SA documents used the phrase *"die Endlösung"* as early as 1931. A dispatch titled "The Jews in the Third Reich" outlined "a secret plan" for the stages of anti-Jewish restrictions: "removal of Jews from the courts, from the civil service, the professions; police surveillance, including residency and identity permits; confiscation of Jewish enterprises and property; detention and expulsion of 'unwanted' Jews; Nuremberg-type laws against intermarriage and sexual and social intercourse." "For the final solution of the Jewish Question [*die Endlösung*]" they "proposed to use the Jews in Germany for slave labor or for cultivation of the German swamps administered by a special SS division."[51] By January 1939, in his most

---

[47] Jeffrey Herf, *Reactionary Modernism: Technology, Culture and Politics in Weimar and the Third Reich* (Cambridge: Cambridge University Press, 1984).

[48] Léon Poliakov, *Harvest of Hate: The Nazi Program for the Destruction of the Jews of Europe* (New York: Holocaust Library, 1986), 263.

[49] Michael Burleigh and Wolfgang Wippermann, *The Racial State: Germany 1933–1945* (Cambridge: Cambridge University Press, 1991).

[50] François Furet, *Unanswered Questions: Nazi Germany and the Genocide of the Jews* (New York: Schocken Books, 1989), 182.

[51] Ron Rosenbaum, *Explaining Hitler: The Search for the Origins of His Evil* (New York: Random House, 1998), 42–43.

578 THE MODERN WORLD, 1815–2000

infamous declaration on the subject, Hitler bellowed to the Reichstag that, "If the international Jewish financiers in and outside Europe should succeed in plunging the nations once more into a world war, then the result will not be the Bolshevization of the earth, and thus the victory of Jewry, but the annihilation of the Jewish race in Europe!"

Raul Hilberg points out, however, that until 1941 Nazis followed a policy of exclusion and expulsion, not annihilation.[52] The conquest of the areas most populated by Jews in 1941 stimulated a change in that policy. Throughout the former Pale of Settlement, German soldiers – primarily the *Einsatzgruppen* roving in killing units behind military lines – mowed down more than one million Jews. Within six months, the opening lines of the minutes of the Wannsee Conference made clear that a new policy was to be implemented. The minutes begin by listing all those who participated "in the conference on the final solution [*Endlösung*] of the Jewish Question," which was being held because "the organizational, technical and material aspects of the final solution of the Jewish Question required prior joint consideration by all central agencies directly concerned with these problems in order to coordinate their subsequent course of action."[53] The horror of what transpired on the twisted road to Auschwitz – built by "redemptive antisemitism" and paved with indifference – is well enough known that I can conclude my narration simply by invoking it.

WHY THE JEWS?: POST-HOLOCAUST THEORIES

A number of accounts appearing shortly after the end of World War II offer a set of explanatory frameworks for understanding the mechanisms that drove antisemitism and the Jewish Question in the modern period. These include Hannah Arendt's interactionist approach, Jean-Paul Sartre's existentialist account, Talcott Parsons's sociological analysis, and the Frankfurt School's socio-psychoanalytic critical theory. Each provides a different vantage point for understanding antisemitism, modernity, and the Jewish Question.

Hannah Arendt's groundbreaking section on the history of antisemitism included in *The Origins of Totalitarianism* (1951) disparaged narratives of "eternal antisemitism," insisting that a wide chasm separated modern antisemitism from its earlier progenitors. "Antisemitism, a secular

---

[52] Raul Hilberg, *The Destruction of the European Jews* (Chicago: Quadrangle Books, 1961).

[53] "Minutes of the Wannsee Conference, January 20, 1942." Document NG-2586, Nuremberg Trial Record, *Das Drittes Reich und die Juden*, edited by Leon Poliakov and Josef Wulf. Reprinted in Simone Gigliotti and Berel Lang, *The Holocaust: A Reader* (Oxford: Blackwell, 2005), 243–251.

nineteenth-century ideology – which in name, though not in argument, was unknown before the 1870s – and religious Jew-hatred, inspired by the mutually hostile antagonism of two conflicting creeds, are obviously not the same," she argued.[54] Explanations based on narratives of eternal antisemitism answer the question "why the Jews?" with the question begging reply, "eternal hostility."[55] What explained modern antisemitism, for Arendt, was the role of the Jews in the development of modernity. "Modern antisemitism," she maintained, "must be seen in the more general framework of the development of the nation-state, and at the same time its source must be found in certain aspects of Jewish history and specifically Jewish functions during the last centuries."[56] Jews, seen as a nation without a state, simply did not belong in the Europe re-ordered by modern nation-states and the colonial world order.

Arendt offered this interactionist account of modern antisemitism partly as a response to her unfavorable assessment of Sartre's existentialism. "[E]ven a cursory knowledge of Jewish history," she wrote, "should be enough to dispel this latest myth ... that has become somewhat fashionable in intellectual circles after Sartre's 'existentialist' interpretation of *the* Jew as someone who is regarded and defined as a Jew by others."[57] Despite Arendt's dismissal, Sartre's *Réflexions sur la question juive* (*Anti-Semite and Jew*, 1946), has remained an influential examination of Jewish victimization and subjugation, explored as a dialectic between Self and Other. The book became a major contribution to post-war debates about antisemitism, Jewish identity, and the possibility of "Jewish emancipation" after the Holocaust.

The *Réflexions* is a phenomenological analysis of the Jewish Question and contains two major premises that structure Sartre's analysis. His first axiom is that the anti-Semite is a man of "*mauvaise foi*" (bad faith or self-deception), and that antisemitism is consequently a "fear of the human condition."[58] He insists (contra Arendt) that, to understand antisemitism, one cannot reduce it to economic, historical, or political analyses that do not reveal it as an existential choice. Rather, antisemitism must be understood as an inauthentic response to man's situation in the world and being-with-others. The antisemite fears the limits of the human condition

[54] Hannah Arendt, *The Origins of Totalitarianism* (San Diego and New York: Harcourt Brace Jovanovich, 1973 [1951]), xi.

[55] Arendt, *Origins of Totalitarianism*, 8.

[56] Arendt, *Origins of Totalitarianism*, 9.

[57] Arendt, *Origins of Totalitarianism*, xv.

[58] Jean-Paul Sartre, *Réflexions sur la question juive* (Paris: Gallimard: Collection Folio/Essais, 1954), 64.

(change, death, and a world shared with others who call into question one's essence and values). Denying their own freedom, antisemites legitimate their choices through the typology of the degenerate Jewish Other. As such, they avoid responsibility. They flee from it by focusing their passions on 'the Jew,' the free-floating symbol of decadence, decay, and degeneration that must be eliminated to redeem the modern world.

Sartre extends his analysis to the modern Jewish condition, calling upon Jews to assume the responsibility for their situations, which are defined in part by Sartre's second axiom: "The Jew is a man that other men consider a Jew."[59] Sartre here renders in existential terms the inescapability of Jewishness that constituted Nazi racial definitions. Every Jew must confront the possibility that the racial state, the individual antisemite, or even the banal or ordinary non-Jew may apprehend him as "the Jew." This possibility becomes a constitutive factor for Jewish self-consciousness.

Social scientists, for their part, took a different tack to explain antisemitism. Key figures included the psychologists Marie Jahoda, Bruno Bettelheim, Rudolph Loewenstein, Daniel Levinson, and Ernest Simmel, as well as the historians Eva Reichmann, Aurel Kolnai, Paul Massing, and Joshua Trachtenberg. Among these pioneers was the famed American sociologist of modernity Talcott Parsons. Parsons effort "The Sociology of Modern Anti-Semitism," was included in the large 1942 collection *Jews in a Gentile World: The Problem of Anti-Semitism*. Edited by Isacque Graeber and Steuart Henderson Britt, the volume was a groundbreaking interdisciplinary effort that brought together eighteen sociologists, anthropologists, psychologists, political scientists, economists, and historians to "examine the problems of anti-Semitism in a dispassionate, objective manner."[60]

Parsons's thesis is that "the most important source of virulent anti-Semitism is probably the projection on the Jew, as a symbol, of free-floating aggression, springing from insecurities and social disorganization,"[61] attendant upon the transformations of modernity. These include urbanization, industrialization, the developing complexity and instability of the economy, increasing heterogeneity and mobility of the population, shifts in consumption patterns, the "'debunking' of traditional values and ideas," the expansion of popular education and mass means of communication, which all result in the "large-scale incidence of anomie in Western society."[62]

---

[59] Sartre, *Reflexions*, 83–84.

[60] Isacque Graeber and Steuart Henderson Britt, *Jews in a Gentile World: The Problem of Anti-Semitism* (New York: The Macmillan Company, 1942), v.

[61] Parsons, "The Sociology of Modern Anti-Semitism," in *Jews in Gentile World*, 120.

[62] The itemization of the sociological processes of modernization listed here actually come from "Some Sociological Aspects of the Fascist Movement," where Parsons develops some of the points he makes in "The Sociology of Modern Anti-semitism" at greater

Borrowing the notion of anomie from Durkheim's study on *Suicide*, it is a state of rootlessness, disconnection, and social alienation. Parsons claims that anomie results in social and psychological insecurity, frustration, and resentment often expressed as aggression. The more heightened the anxiety, the more "free floating" the aggression. In these circumstances, people act out their frustration and insecurity on a symbolic object. In the case of modern Europe, this symbolic object was the Jew.

Members of the Frankfurt School offered a fourth set of theories of antisemitism. Their most ambitious effort was the *Studies in Prejudice* series, combining Weberian sociology, Marxism, and psychoanalysis, and involved multi-institutional efforts. The boldest undertaking of the *Studies in Prejudice* series was *The Authoritarian Personality*, a collaborative work led by Theodor Adorno.[63] The title linked it to the work of Erich Fromm in the Frankfurt School's first collective publication, *Studies on Authority and the Family* where the concept of the "authoritarian personality" was put forward as a link between psychological dispositions and political leanings. In his methodological chapter on "Types and Syndromes" Adorno warns that the assertion of an "authoritarian personality," risked essentializing the origins of antisemitism in a characterological type. Any doctrine of types, Adorno writes, could "tend towards pigeonholing and transform[ing] highly flexible traits into static, quasi-biological characteristics," just as fascist typologies tended to do.[64]

But Adorno justifies the drive to locate the etiology of the "authoritarian personality" and its correlate types – the anti-Semite, the facist, the xenophobe – since the social conditions of modernity were themselves typed. All social processes of modernity tended toward standardization and mass production, including the personality types of individuals. "Only by identifying stereotypical traits in modern humans, and not by denying their existence," Adorno therefore averred, "can the pernicious tendency towards all-pervasive classification and subsumption be challenged."[65] Social types were the products of social rubber stamps.

How these rubber stamps became constituted as socially produced phenomena forms the basis of Adorno's specific anthropology of antisemitism. His first principle for understanding antisemitism is to appreciate that the

---

length, focused less on antisemitism and more on fascism. See Talcott Parsons, *Talcott Parsons on National Socialism*, ed. Uta Gerhardt (New York: Aldine de Gruyter, 1993), 203–218.

[63] Theodor W. Adorno, Else Frenkel-Brunswik, Daniel J. Levinson, R. Nevitt Sandford, et al., *The Authoritarian Personality* (New York: Harper & Row, 1950).

[64] Adorno in *The Authoritarian Personality*, 744.

[65] Adorno in *The Authoritarian Personality*, 747.

582 THE MODERN WORLD, 1815–2000

object of prejudice – that is, "the Jews" – does *not* provoke the syndrome. Instead, he insists upon "the 'functional' character of anti-Semitism." The social functionality of the stereotype depends upon what Adorno terms, "stereotypy" and "ticket thinking": the social production of the stereotype, which is itself linked to psychological needs that are created by the "cold, alienated, and largely ununderstandable world" of modernity.[66]

The psychological motor of stereotypy is projection, whose key mechanism is the defamation of other groups as a way to code one's own status. Antisemitism consequently compensates for social alienation. But Adorno transcends Parsons's sociological analysis in arguing that antisemitism *personalizes* an explanation of the complicated contradictions that engender the social and psychological discomfort resulting from alienation. The ineloquence or confusion of social life can be unraveled in an instant through a set of stock images.

On a psychological level, too, Adorno suggests that antisemitism functions as a site for screening the internal contradictions of individuals – their inner conflicts between id and superego. Stereotypes are the externalization of these inner conflicts, which are themselves the internalization of the contradictions of global capitalism. As a result, many positive stereotypes are closely linked to their darker side. For example, the contention that Jews are solidly entrenched in family values has its double in the assertion of Jewish clannishness. This double set of values ascribed to the stereotyping of Jews fits Adorno's basic hypothesis: "the largely projective character of anti-Semitism."

Through the *Studies in Prejudice* series, Adorno and the Frankfurt School expanded the understanding of antisemitism to include not only a critique of capitalism and fascism, but of modernity more generally. The fullest fruit of these efforts was Adorno and Horkheimer's *Dialectic of Enlightenment*, published in 1947 with the concluding segment on the "The Elements of Anti-Semitism" added in 1949.[67] Here, they consider antisemitism within the development of Western civilization, rationality, and the administered society of modernity. As in *The Authoritarian Personality*, their foundational thesis is that antisemitism is a paranoid projection of fascism's own worldview.

Read together, the work of the Frankfurt School, Sartre, Arendt, and Parsons, offers a multi-causal explanation of "antisemitism" and "the Jewish Question" in modernity. Sartre helps us to understand the Self/Other dialectic of recognition. His point of view is intersubjective and

---

[66] Adorno in *The Authoritarian Personality*, 608.

[67] Max Horkheimer and Theodor Adorno, *Dialectic of Enlightenment*, trans. John Cumming (New York: Continuum, 2000), 168–208.

intrasubjective, exploring how the antisemite covers over the hole of emptiness in the Self by opposition to his image of the Jew as the degraded Other. Arendt refuses Sartre's existentialist analysis since it does not take account of the collective dimension of antisemitism. She analyzes the problem in terms of the interactions between the Jewish community and the shifting forms of states over the development of modernity. Talcott Parsons widens the lens one step further by offering a sociological account of the disenchantments that occasion modernity and how these result in a sense of anomie, which can be displaced onto the Jews as a symbolic target. The Frankfurt School's optic is one step wider still. In a fragmentary set of observations, they indicate how the same social processes that unpin the modern culture industry produce the stereotypes of Jews and Judaism. When internalized, these stereotypes help to personalize the social forces that the masses otherwise would lack the vocabulary to name. These modern discontents are certainly not past us, and coupled to the politics of the Arab–Israeli conflict, they help us to explain the spike in Judeophobia in our new millennium.[68]

SELECT BIBLIOGRAPHY

Adorno, Theodor, Else Frenkel-Brunswik, Daniel J. Levinson, and R. Nevitt Sandford. *The Authoritarian Personality*. New York: Harper & Row, 1950.

Albert, Phyllis Cohen. *The Modernization of French Jewry: Consistory and Community in the Nineteenth Century*. Hanover, NH: University Press of New England for Brandeis University Press, 1977.

Almog, Shmuel. *Nationalism and Antisemitism in Modern Europe 1815–1945*. Oxford: Pergamon, 1990.

Anchel, Robert. *Napoléon et les Juifs*. Paris: Presses Universitaires de France, 1928.

Arendt, Hannah. *The Origins of Totalitarianism*. San Diego: Harcourt Brace Jovanovich, 1973 (1951).

Aschheim, Steven. *Brothers and Strangers: The East European Jew in German and German Jewish Consciousness, 1800–1923*. Madison: University of Wisconsin Press, 1983.

Badinter, Robert. *Libres et égaux...: L'émancipation des Juifs, 1789–1791*. Paris: Fayard, 1989.

Bartov, Omer. "German Soldiers and the Holocaust: Historiography, Research, and Implications," in *The Holocaust: Origins, Implementation, Aftermath*, ed. Omer Bartov, 162–188. New York: Routledge, 2000.

Bein, Alex. "The Jewish Parasite: Notes on the Semantics of the Jewish Problem with Special Reference to Germany." *Leo Baeck Institute Year Book* 9 (1964): 3–40.

---

[68] For an overview of the discussions about the new Judeophobia, see Jonathan Judaken, "So What's New? Rethinking the 'New Antisemitism' in a Global Age," *Patterns of Prejudice* 42, no. 4–5 (2008): 531–560.

The Jewish Question: Biography of a World Problem. Trans. by Harry Zohn. London: Associated University Presses, 1990.

Beller, Steven. *Antisemitism: A Short History.* New York: Oxford University Press, 2007.

Vienna and the Jews, 1867-1938: A Cultural History. Cambridge: Cambridge University Press, 1989.

Berkovitz, Jay R. *Rites and Passages: The Beginnings of Modern Jewish Culture in France, 1650-1860.* Philadelphia: University of Pennsylvania Press 2004.

The Shaping of Jewish Identity in Nineteenth-century France. Detroit: Wayne State University Press, 1989.

Bernstein, Richard. *Hannah Arendt and the Jewish Question.* Cambridge, MA: MIT Press, 1996.

Birnbaum, Pierre. *L'Affaire Dreyfus: La République en peril.* Paris: Gallimard, 1994.

"A Jacobin Regenerator: Abbé Grégoire," in *Jewish Destinies: Citizenship, State, and Community in Modern France.* Trans. Arthur Goldhammer. New York: Hill and Wang, 2000.

Blumenkranz, Bernard and Albert Soboul, eds. *Les Juifs et la révolution française.* Toulouse: Privat, 1976.

Boyer, John. *Culture and Political Crisis in Vienna: Christian Socialism in Power, 1897-1918.* Chicago: Chicago University Press, 1995.

Political Radicalism in Late Imperial Vienna: The Origins of the Christian Social Movement, 1848-1897. Chicago: Chicago University Press, 1981.

Bredin, Jean Denis. *The Affair: The Case of Alfred Dreyfus.* Trans. by Jeffrey Mehlman. New York: George Braziller, 1986.

Browning, Christopher R. *Ordinary Men: Reserve Police Battalion 101 and the Final Solution in Poland.* New York: HarperPerennial, 1992.

Brustein, William. *Roots of Hate: Anti-Semitism in Europe before the Holocaust.* Cambridge: Cambridge University Press, 2003.

Burleigh, Michael and Wolfgang Wippermann. *The Racial State Germany 1933-1945.* Cambridge: Cambridge University Press, 1991.

Burns, Michael. *Dreyfus: A Family Affair, 1789-1945.* New York: HarperCollins, 1991.

France and the Dreyfus Affair: A Documentary History. New York: Bedford/St. Martin's, 1999.

Byrnes, Robert F. *Antisemitism in Modern France: The Prologue to the Dreyfus Affair.* New York: H. Fertig, 1950.

Carroll, James. *Constantine's Sword: The Church and the Jews, A History.* Boston: Mariner Books, 2002.

Cheyette, Bryan and Laura Marcus, eds. *Modernity, Culture, and 'the Jew'.* Cambridge: Polity Press, 1995.

Cohn, Norman. *Warrant for Genocide: The Myth of the Jewish World Conspiracy and the Protocols of the Elders of Zion.* Middlesex: Penguin Books, 1970.

Davis, Leopold. "The Hegelian Antisemitism of Bruno Bauer." *History of European Ideas* 25 (1999): 179–206.

Deák, István. *Essays on Hitler's Europe.* Lincoln: University of Nebraska Press, 2001.

Eckardt, A. Roy. *Christianity and the Children of Israel: A Theological Approach to the Jewish Question.* New York: King's Town Press, 1948.

Jews and Christians: The Contemporary Meeting. Bloomington: Indiana University Press, 1986.

Your People, My People: The Meeting of Jews and Christians. New York: Quadrangle, 1974.

Fitch, Nancy. "Mass Culture, Mass Parliamentary Politics, and Modern Anti-Semitism: The Dreyfus Affair in Rural France." *American Historical Review* 97, no. 1 (1992): 55–95.

Feuerwerker, David. *L'Emancipation des juifs en France: De l'Ancien Régime à la fin du Second Empire.* Paris: Albin Michel, 1976.

Florence, Ronald. *Blood Libel: The Damascus Affair of 1840.* Madison: University of Wisconsin Press, 2004.

Frankel, Jonathan. *The Damascus Affair: "Ritual Murder," Politics, and the Jews in 1840.* Cambridge, UK: Cambridge University Press, 1997.

Friedländer, Saul. *Nazi Germany and the Jews Volume I: The Years of Persecution, 1933-1939.* New York: HarperCollins, 1997.

Furet, François. *Unanswered Questions: Nazi Germany and the Genocide of the Jews.* New York: Schocken Books, 1989.

Gay, Peter. "Voltaire's Antisemitism," in *The Party of Humanity.* New York: Knopf, 1964.

Gigliotti Simone and Berel Lang, eds. "Minutes of the Wannsee Conference, January 20, 1942," in *The Holocaust: A Reader.* Oxford: Blackwell, 2005.

Goldhagen, Daniel Jonah. *Hitler's Willing Executioners: Ordinary Germans and the Holocaust.* New York: Vintage Books, 1997.

Goldstein, Phyllis. *A Convenient Hatred: The History of Antisemitism.* Brookline: Facing History and Ourselves, 2012.

Graeber, Isacque and Steuart Henderson Britt. *Jews in a Gentile World: The Problem of Anti-Semitism.* New York: The Macmillan Company, 1942.

Graetz, Michael. *The Jews in Nineteenth-Century France.* Trans. Jane Marie Todd. Stanford: Stanford University Press, 1996.

Grégoire, Abbé. *An Essay on the Physical, Moral and Political Reformation of the Jews.* London: J. Stock, 1791.

Hamann, Brigitte. *Hitler's Vienna: A Dictator's Apprenticeship.* New York: Oxford University Press, 1999.

Heer, Friedrich. *God's First Love: Christians and Jews over Two Thousand Years.* New York: Weybright and Talley, 1970.

Herf, Jeffrey. *Reactionary Modernism: Technology, Culture and Politics in Weimar and the Third Reich.* Cambridge: Cambridge University Press, 1984.

Hertzberg, Arthur. *The French Enlightenment and the Jews.* New York: Columbia University Press, 1968.

Heschel, Susannah. *Abraham Geiger and the Jewish Jesus.* Chicago: University of Chicago Press, 1998.

The Aryan Jesus: Christian Theologians and the Bible in Nazi Germany. Princeton: Princeton University Press, 2010.

Hilberg, Raul. *The Destruction of the European Jews.* Chicago: Quadrangle Books, 1961.

Hitler, Adolf. *Mein Kampf.* Trans. Ralph Manheim. Cambridge, MA: Houghton Mifflin Company, 1943.

Horkheimer, Max and Theodor Adorno. *Dialectic of Enlightenment.* Trans. John Cumming. New York: Continuum, 2000.

Hyman, Paula. *From Dreyfus to Vichy: The Remaking of French Jewry.* New York: Columbia University Press, 1979.

The Jews of Modern France. Berkeley: University of California Press, 1998.

Jacobs, Jack. *On Socialists and "the Jewish Question" after Marx.* New York: New York University Press, 1992.

Judaken, Jonathan. "So What's New? Rethinking the 'New Antisemitism' in a Global Age." *Patterns of Prejudice* 42, no. 4–5 (2008): 531–560.

Kates, Gary. "Jews into Frenchmen: Nationality and Representation in Revolutionary France." *Social Research* 56, no. 1 (1989): 213–232.

Katz, Jacob. *From Prejudice to Destruction.* Cambridge: Harvard University Press, 1980.

Kertzer, David I. *The Kidnapping of Edgardo Mortara.* New York: Vintage, 1998.

Kleeblatt, Norman, ed. *The Dreyfus Affair: Art, Truth and Justice.* Berkeley: University of California Press, 1987.

Kriegel, Annie. *Les Juifs et le monde moderne: Essai sur les logiques d'émancipation.* Paris: Éditions du Seuil, 1976.

Kritzman, Lawrence D., ed. *Auschwitz and After: Race, Culture, and 'the Jewish Question' in France.* London: Routledge, 1995.

Lang, Berel. "Genocide and Kant's Enlightenment," in *Act and Idea in the Nazi Genocide,* 169–190. Chicago: University of Chicago Press, 1990.

Levy, Richard. *The Downfall of the Anti-Semitic Political Parties in Germany.* New Haven: Yale, 1975.

Antisemitism in the Modern World: An Anthology of Texts. Lexington, MA: D.C. Heath and Company, 1991.

A Historical Encyclopedia of Prejudice and Persecution. Santa Barbara, CA: ABC-Clio, 2005.

Lichtheim, George. "Socialism and the Jews." *Dissent,* July–August (1968): 314–342.

Lindemann, Albert. *Esau's Tears: Modern Anti-Semitism and the Rise of the Jews.* Cambridge: Cambridge University Press, 1997.

and Richard S. Levy, eds. *Antisemitism: A History.* Oxford: Oxford University Press, 2010.

Littell, Franklin. *The Crucifixion of the Jews: The Failure of Christians to Understand the Jewish Experience.* Macon, GA: Mercer University Press, 2000.

Maccoby, Hyam. *Antisemitism and Modernity: Innovation and Continuity.* London: Routledge, 2006.

Mack, Michael. *German Idealism and the Jew: The Inner Anti-Semitism of Philosophy and German Jewish Responses.* Chicago: University of Chicago Press, 2003.

Malino, Francis and Bernard Wasserstein, eds. *The Jews in Modern France.* Hanover, NH: Brandeis University Press, 1985.

Marr, Wilhelm. *The Victory of Judaism over Germanism, Viewed from a Nonreligious Point of View.* Trans. Gerhard Rohringer. Bern: Rudolph Costenoble, 1879.

Marrus, Michael. *The Politics of Assimilation: The French Jewish Community at the Time of the Dreyfus Afffair.* Oxford: Oxford University Press, 1980.

Marx, Karl. "On the Jewish Question," in *The Marx-Engels Reader,* second edition. Ed. Robert C. Tucker, 26–52. New York: W. W. Norton, 1978.

Mendes-Flohr, Paul and Jehuda Reinharz, eds. *The Jew in the Modern World: A Documentary History*, second edition. Oxford: Oxford University Press, 1995.

Michael, Robert. *A History of Catholic Antisemitism: The Dark Side of the Church.* Basingstoke: Palgrave Macmillan, 2008.

　Holy Hatred: Christianity, Anti-Semitism, and the Holocaust. Basingstoke: Palgrave Macmillan, 2006.

Michelis, Cesare G. de. *The Non-Existent Manuscript: A Study of the Protocols of the Sages of Zion.* Trans. Richard Newhouse. Lincoln: University of Nebraska Press, 2004.

Mosse, George. *The Crisis of German Ideology: Intellectual Origins of the Third Reich.* New York: Schocken, 1981.

　Toward the Final Solution: A History of European Racism. Madison: University of Wisconsin Press, 1985.

Nochlin, Linda and Tamar Garb, eds. *The Jew in the Text: Modernity and the Construction of Identity.* London: Thames and Hudson, 1995.

Parsons, Talcott. "The Sociology of Modern Anti-Semitism," in *Jews in the Gentile World*, Isacque Graeber and Steuart Henderson Britt, eds. New York: The Macmillan Company, 1942.

　Talcott Parsons on National Socialism. Ed. Uta Gerhardt. New York: Aldine de Gruyter, 1993.

Pauley, Bruce. *From Prejudice to Persecution: A History of Austrian Anti-Semitism.* Chapel Hill: University of North Carolina, 1992.

Poliakov, Léon. *The Aryan Myth: A History of Racist and Nationalist Ideas in Europe.* New York: Basic Books, 1974.

　Harvest of Hate: The Nazi Program for the Destruction of the Jews of Europe. New York: Holocaust Library, 1986.

　The History of Antisemitism: Vol. 3: From Voltaire to Wagner. Trans. Miriam Kochan. London: Routledge & Kegan Paul, 1975.

　The History of Anti-Semitism, Volume 4: Suicidal Europe, 1870-1933. Philadelphia: University of Pennsylvania Press, 2003.

Pulzer, Peter. *The Rise of Political Anti-Semitism in Germany and Austria.* New York: Wiley, 1966.

　"Third Thoughts on German and Austrian Antisemitism." *Journal of Modern Jewish Studies* 14, no. 2 (2005): 137–178.

Rosenbaum, Ron. *Explaining Hitler: The Search for the Origins of His Evil.* New York: Random House, 1998.

Ruether, Rosemary Radford. *Faith and Fratricide: The Theological Roots of Anti-Semitism.* New York: Seabury, 1974.

Sartre, Jean-Paul. *Réflexions sur la question juive.* Paris: Gallimard, 1954.

Schapiro, J. Salwyn. "Pierre Joseph Proudhon, Harbinger of Fascism." *American Historical Review* 50, no. 4 (1945): 714–737.

Schechter, Ronald. *Obstinate Hebrews: Representations of Jews in France, 1715-1815.* Berkeley: University of California Press, 2003.

Schwarzfuchs, Simon. *Napoleon, the Jews and the Sanhedrin.* Boston: Routledge and Kegan Paul, 1979.

Sepinwall, Alyssa Goldstein. *The Abbé Gregoire and the French Revolution: The Making of Modern Universalism*. Berkeley: University of California Press, 2005.

"Strategic Friendships: Jewish Intellectuals, the abbé Grégoire and the French Revolution," in *Renewing the Past, Reconfiguring Jewish Culture*, eds. Adam Sutcliffe and Ross Brann, 189–212. Philadelphia: University of Pennsylvania, 2004.

Silberner, Edmund. "Charles Fourier on the Jewish Question." *Jewish Social Studies* 8, no. 4 (1946): 245–266.

Stern, Fritz. *Politics of Cultural Despair: A Study in the Rise of German Ideology*. Berkeley: University of California Press, 1961.

Sternhell, Zeev. *La Droite révolutionnaire, 1885-1914: Les Origines française du fascisme*. Paris: Seuil, 1978.

Sutcliffe, Adam. *Judaism and Enlightenment*. Cambridge: Cambridge University Press, 2003.

Tal, Uriel. *Christians and Jews in Germany: Religion, Politics and Ideology in the Second Reich, 1870-1914*. Ithaca: Cornell University Press, 1975.

Toland, John. *Reasons for Naturalizing the Jews in Great Britain and Ireland, On the same foot with all other Nations. Containing also, A Defence of the Jews against all Vulgar Prejudices in all Countries*. London: J. Roberts, 1714.

Toury, Jacob. "'The Jewish Question': A Semantic Approach." *Leo Baeck Institute Year Book* 11 no. 1 (1966): 85–106.

Traverso, Enzo. *The Marxists and the Jewish Question: The History of a Debate, 1843-1943*. Atlantic Highlands, NJ: Humanities, 1994.

Volkov, Shulamit. *The Rise of Popular Antimodernism in Germany: The Urban Master Artisans, 1873-1896*. Princeton: Princeton University Press, 1978.

Weeks, Theodore. *From Assimilation to Antisemitism: The "Jewish Question" in Poland, 1850-1914*. DeKalb: Northern Illinois University Press, 2006.

Wertheimer, Jack. *Unwelcome Strangers: East European Jews in Imperial Germany*. New York: Oxford University Press, 1987.

Wilson, Nelly. *Bernard Lazare: Antisemitism and the Problem of Jewish Identity in Late Nineteenth Century France*. Cambridge: Cambridge University Press, 1978.

Wilson, Stephen. *Ideology and Experience: Antisemitism in France at the Time of the Dreyfus Affair*. Rutherford, NJ: Fairleigh Dickinson Press, 1982.

Wistrich, Robert. *Socialism and the Jews: The Dilemmas of Assimilation in Germany and Austria-Hungary*. Rutherford, NJ: Fairleigh Dickinson Press, 1982.

Yovel, Yirmiyahu. *Dark Riddle: Hegel, Nietzsche, and the Jews*. University Park, PA: Pennsylvania State University Press, 1998.

Zimmerman, Moshe. *Wilhelm Marr: The Patriarch of Antisemitism*. New York: Oxford University Press, 1986.

CHAPTER 21

GENERATION, DEGENERATION, REGENERATION
Health, Disease, and the Jewish Body

TODD SAMUEL PRESNER

In 1781, Christian Wilhelm Dohm, a virtually unknown German archivist and councilor in Frederick the Great's department of foreign affairs, published an extraordinary treatise called *Ueber die bürgerliche Verbesserung der Juden* (On the Civic Improvement of the Jews).[1] The treatise represented Dohm's attempt to find both an explanation for and a way to fix what he, along with many of his contemporaries, perceived to be the "degeneration" of the Jewish people. He saw this degeneration exemplified by the purported fact that the vast majority of Jews throughout Western and Eastern Europe were ailing, itinerant hagglers, wed to rigidly archaic religious laws, who barely eked out a living on the edges of the modern, civilized world. Inverting traditional explanations for their condition, Dohm argued that the degeneracy of the Jews cannot be blamed on the Jews themselves but rather on the Christian rulers who refused to grant Jews civil rights and equality before the law. If these rights were granted to the Jews, they would become morally, spiritually, and physically regenerated.

Almost immediately after its publication, Dohm's book was widely read and debated, prompting responses from many of Germany's foremost intellectuals.[2] The following year it was translated into French and inspired several French treatises, most notably Abbé Grégoire's *Essai sur la régénération physique, morale et politique des Juifs* in 1788, a work that played a critical role in facilitating the emancipation of the French Jews shortly after the Revolution.[3] In Dohm's homeland of Prussia, Jewish emancipation

---

[1] Christian Wilhelm Dohm, *Ueber die bürgerliche Verbesserung der Juden*, 2 vols (Berlin: Friedrich Nicolai, 1781–83). All citations will be documented parenthetically as D, followed by the volume and page number.

[2] For the reception of Dohm's treatise and a thorough discussion of Dohm's biography, see Jonathan M. Hess, *Germans, Jews and the Claims of Modernity* (New Haven: Yale University Press, 2002); also David Sorkin, *The Transformation of German Jewry, 1780–1840* (Oxford: Oxford University Press, 1987), 23–30.

[3] Grégoire, *Essai sur la régénération physique, morale et politique des Juifs* (Paris: Editions d'histoire sociale, 1968). For a discussion of the genesis of the essay, see Alyssa Sepinwall's

came in 1812, and his treatise is often cited as a key turning point in the debate over Jewish civic equality.

Although Dohm, like Grégoire, accepted the contemporary antisemitic stereotypes of Jews as morally corrupt, spiritually bankrupt, and physically inferior (something for which Moses Mendelssohn would take him to task), the revolutionary significance of his argument was to be found in the fact that he shifted the discourse away from the belief that these "degenerate" traits naturally inhere within individuals or within the Jewish people as a whole and, instead, refocused attention on what he perceived to be the social, economic, and political causes and conditions for the disenfranchisement and subsequent corruption of the Jews. Dohm was particularly concerned about the Jews' investment in "trade" and "speculations" (D 1:143) and their apparent inability to become good citizens who served the state as disciplined soldiers, productive farmers, and conscientious artisans. This was not always the case, Dohm insisted, and argued that during the Roman Empire, "Jews earned confidence and commendations through their military service ... and that the many privileges and celebrated declarations by the Roman Senate represent the irrefutable proof of the bravery and loyalty that they demonstrated in war" (D 1:140). Only when Jews were declared "unfit" for military service in the fifth century, did the prejudice become grounded that the Jews were not able to fight as citizens on behalf of the state (D 1:141). "One and a half millennia later, it is natural," Dohm explains, that the Jews have "become unaccustomed to war" and that the "martial courage and strength of the body" (D 1:145) could not immediately return without the proper guidance, support, and training. Once the Jews are granted civic equality, Dohm proposes a program of regeneration that focuses on making them fit for military service, agriculture, and manufacturing. This approach, he believed, would stem the "degeneration" (*Ausartung*) and "corruption" (*Verderbtheit*) that has resulted directly from their "condemnation and persecution" (D 1:149). He is optimistic about the regenerative prospects of the Jewish people: "The necessary strength of body and the consistent diligence will reliably come back in a couple of generations" (D 2:259), thus enabling Jews to reenter the professions from which they were barred and restoring the Jewish people to their original strength and vitality.[4]

Shortly before the French Revolution, when Dohm published his treatise, the concept of "regeneration" had already come to designate moral,

very informative book, *The Abbé Grégoire and the French Revolution: The Makings of Modern Universalism* (Berkeley: University of California Press, 2005), 56–77.

[4] For an overview of the history of the "degenerate" Jewish body, see John Efron, *Medicine and the German Jews: A History* (New Haven: Yale University Press, 2001), 105–150.

spiritual, physical, and political rebirth. As Antoine de Baecque has demonstrated in a remarkable study of corporeal metaphors during the French Revolution, the concept of regeneration first referred to the impetus to return or restore a body to its original vitality.[5] Up until 1730, regeneration primarily referred to rebirth and resurrection within religious discourses and to the physiological processes of healing within medicinal discourses. But by the middle of the eighteenth century, it was explicitly linked with its antonym, "degeneration," and gained explanatory power as part of the Enlightenment ideology of progress and the concomitant belief in the perfectibility of the human race.[6] Not only could individual bodies be regenerated and perfected, but the larger social or political body could also be reborn, renewed, and revitalized. Regeneration thus gained a revolutionary corporeal meaning: it now signaled the possibility of political and social reform, in which degeneracy – in all its backward facing forms – could be permanently overcome. Strong, robust, and vital individuals would form a strong, robust, and vital body politic. For Dohm, Jewish degeneracy was not merely the prerequisite of their regeneration but also the proof of the Enlightenment idea of social and political progress. In fact, these arguments concerning the physical, moral, and spiritual regeneration of the Jews anticipate many of the ideas of Zionism, including its most important figure of regenerative self-refashioning: the "muscle Jew."[7]

But in order to understand the genesis of the muscle Jew, we must first look to the emergence of race science and Darwinism in the midnineteenth century, when the questions of "blood" and "race" took center stage in the debate over diagnosing national degeneration and imagining the possibility of regeneration.[8] In 1853–55, Arthur Comte de Gobineau published his treatise *Essay on the Inequality of the Human Races*, in which he argued that "racial vitality" was the key determinant of human history.

---

[5] Antoine de Baecque, *The Body Politic: Corporeal Metaphor in Revolutionary France, 1770–1800*, trans. Charlotte Mandell (Stanford: Stanford University Press, 1997), 131.

[6] Reinhart Koselleck, "'Progress' and 'Decline': An Appendix to the History of Two Concepts," *The Practice of Conceptual History: Timing History, Spacing Concepts*, trans. Todd Samuel Presner (Stanford: Stanford University Press, 2002), 218–235.

[7] The "muscle Jew" is a coinage by Max Nordau, first mentioned at the Second Zionist Congress in 1898. I will discuss the genesis and development of the concept below.

[8] The literature on this subject is enormous. For a comparative, interdisciplinary assessment of Darwinism, a key collection is David Kohn, ed., *The Darwinian Heritage* (Princeton: Princeton University Press, 1986). For an excellent overview of the German context for the rise of race science, see Paul Weindling, *Health, Race, and German Politics Between National Unification and Nazism, 1870–1945* (Cambridge: Cambridge University Press, 1989). See also the introduction to Daniel Pick, *Faces of Degeneration: A European Disorder, c. 1848 – c. 1918* (Cambridge: Cambridge University Press, 1989).

For Gobineau, degeneration is a problem of impure blood: "The word degenerate, when applied to people, means (as it ought to mean) that the people has no longer the same intrinsic value as it had before, because it has no longer the same blood in its veins, continual adulterations having gradually affected the quality of the blood."[9] Unlike Grégoire or Dohm, who viewed intermarriage and racial mixing as a desirable way for Jewish particularity to be overcome, Gobineau considered the intermixing of races to be dangerous because it would defile and thus weaken the vitality of a given nation:

So long as the blood and institutions of a nation keep to a sufficient degree the impress of the original race, the nation exists ... But if, like the Greeks, and the Romans of the later Empire, the people has been absolutely drained of its original blood, and the qualities conferred by the blood, then the day of its defeat will be the day of its death. It has used up the time that heaven granted at its birth, for it has completely changed its race, and with its race its nature. It is therefore degenerate.[10]

For Gobineau, degeneration was a problem of mixed blood and, hence, mixed races.

Although Gobineau's ideas were not initially well received in Europe, his argument for the supremacy of the "Aryan race" later became the basis of many ultra-right, nationalist ideologies. Karl Eugen Dühring, for example, one of the most influential proponents of racial antisemitism in Germany, applied many of Gobineau's ideas in his 1881 book, *Die Judenfrage als Racen-, Sitten-, and Culturfrage* (The Jewish Question as a Racial, Moral, and Cultural Question).[11] With the ascendancy of the Darwinian view of social evolution and human progress in the second half of the nineteenth century, the concern over racial degeneracy caused by modernization and industrialization took on new significance.[12] Here, a wide range of practices were instituted throughout Europe and the United States for

---

[9] Arthur de Gobineau, *The Inequality of the Human Races*, trans. Adrian Collins (New York: Howard Fertig, 1967), 25.

[10] Gobineau, *The Inequality of the Human Races*, 34–35.

[11] Karl Eugen Dühring, *Die Judenfrage als Racen-, Sitten-, and Culturfrage* (Karlsruhe: H. Reuther, 1881).

[12] Germany's foremost proponent of Darwinism was Ernst Haeckel who considered Darwin's selection principle to be the biological basis of social change. See Alfred Kelly, *The Descent of Darwin: The Popularization of Darwin in Germany, 1860–1914* (Chapel Hill: University of North Carolina Press, 1981); Daniel Gasman, *The Scientific Origins of National Socialism: Social Darwinism in Ernst Haeckel and the Monist League* (New York: Elsevier, 1971); and Richard Weikart, *From Darwin to Hitler: Evolutionary Ethics, Eugenics, and Racism in Germany* (New York: Palgrave, 2004).

"scientizing" cleanliness, professionalizing hygiene, administering public health, and monitoring social disorders.[13] The principles of Darwinism assumed a chief role in social and political affairs, and new fields such as psychiatry and criminology emerged to track deviations and stop their dangerous proliferation.[14]

By 1888, Friedrich Nietzsche emblematically summed up the anxieties of the late nineteenth century with the following words: "Nothing is better known today, at least nothing has been better studied, than the protean character of *degenerescence*."[15] Signs of degeneracy were detected and studied everywhere: The fast pace of modern life rendered the nerves of city dwellers weak;[16] the "natural" borders of races and classes had become porous, causing them to break down and merge together; the spread of venereal diseases and prostitution evidenced the loosening of codes for policing sexuality, while the eager embrace of the rhetoric of sickness and decadence in art and literature displaced traditional moral authorities.[17] But most of all, the birth of the discipline of race science and eugenics in the mid-1850s turned the regulation of degeneracy into an urgent social imperative, which, by the 1890s, had become indistinguishable from the enforcement of normative and prescriptive ideals of race and sexuality.[18]

[13] For a discussion of the German context, see Weindling, *Health, Race, and German Politics Between National Unification and Nazism*, chap. 1, "Social Darwinism," 11–59.

[14] See Pick, *Faces of Degeneration*; Robert A. Nye, *Crime, Madness, and Politics in Modern France: The Medical Concept of National Decline* (Princeton: Princeton University Press, 1984); Richard F. Wetzell, *Inventing the Criminal: A History of German Criminology, 1880–1945* (Chapel Hill: University of North Carolina Press, 2000).

[15] Friedrich Nietzsche, *The Case of Wagner*, trans. Walter Kaufmann (New York: Vintage, 1967), 5. For a discussion, see Gregory Moore, *Nietzsche, Biology, and Metaphor* (Cambridge: Cambridge University Press, 2002), 115.

[16] Joachim Radkau, *Das Zeitalter der Nervosität: Deutschland zwischen Bismarck und Hitler* (Munich: Hanser Verlag, 1998).

[17] Cultural and literary studies of degeneracy now comprise a genre in themselves. See, for example, Sander Gilman and J. Edward Chamberlin, eds, *Degeneration: The Dark Side of Progress* (New York: Columbia University Press, 1985); William Greenslade, *Degeneration, Culture, and the Novel, 1880–1940* (Cambridge: Cambridge University Press, 1994); Kelly Hurley, *The Gothic Body: Sexuality, Materialism and Degeneration in the Fin de Siècle* (Cambridge: Cambridge University Press, 1996); Charles Bernheimer, *Decadent Subjects* (Baltimore: Johns Hopkins University Press, 2002); and Barbara Spackman, *Decadent Genealogies: The Rhetoric of Sickness from Baudelaire to D'Annunzio* (Ithaca: Cornell University Press, 1989).

[18] For more on the relationship between "degenerescence" and sexuality, see Michel Foucault, *The History of Sexuality: An Introduction*, trans. Robert Hurley (New York: Vintage Books, 1990), esp. 118–119.

In his study of two late nineteenth-century paradigms for scientifically investigating human development, sexology, and psychoanalysis, Sander Gilman makes the important point that "no realm of human experience is as closely tied to the concept of degeneracy as that of sexuality."[19] Not only are degeneracy and sexuality "inseparable within nineteenth century thought" (72), but I hasten to add that the counter-concept of regeneration is inseparable from the regulative economies for policing sexuality that emerged in the same period. To the same extent that degeneration was a labile term for designating the pathology of the other through "sexual opprobrium" (89), regeneration was a similarly elastic term for consolidating and extending the power of the "normal" by way of sexual fitness and physical vitality. Both concepts are important insofar as they were simultaneously employed to designate and manage the pathology or health of individual bodies as well as that of the greater body politic, species, or population. As Michel Foucault argues, "Through the themes of health, progeny, race, the future of the species, the vitality of the social body, power spoke *of* sexuality and *to* sexuality."[20] Foucault uses the term "bio-power" to describe how these two poles – the disciplining of the individual body and the regulation of the population – came together through the deployment of sexuality as a form of state power.

The emphasis on an individual's physical health, strength, and sexuality thus became inextricably linked with national discourses on population politics, racial aesthetics, and eugenics.[21] This connection is recognizable throughout Western Europe and the United States at the end of the nineteenth and early twentieth centuries. As Robert Nye has shown in his study of the concept of national decline in *fin-de-siècle* France, the French "reacted favorably to a 'hygienic' physical culture that promised some hope of national regeneration" in light of the ever "deepening sense of anxiety about the biological (and therefore moral) health of the national stock."[22] Degeneracy was no longer considered to affect just the poor, inferior, or disenfranchised; rather it could strike any individual, class, or nation. With the anxiety over degeneration in almost every sphere of social and cultural

---

[19] Sander L. Gilman, "Sexology, Psychoanalysis, and Degeneration: From a Theory of Race to a Race to Theory," in *Degeneration: The Dark Side of Progress*, 72–96, here 72. Further citations from this essay are given parenthetically.

[20] Foucault, *The History of Sexuality*, 147.

[21] In addition to Foucault, see Mark B. Adams, ed., *The Wellborn Science: Eugenics in Germany, France, Brazil, and Russia* (Oxford: Oxford University Press, 1990); Michael Hau, *The Cult of Health and Beauty in Germany: A Social History, 1890–1930* (Chicago: University of Chicago Press, 2003).

[22] Robert Nye, *Crime, Madness, and Politics in Modern France*, 328.

life, the attack on disease, weakness, effeminacy, deviancy, and criminality also prompted a renewed attention to the possibilities of national regeneration, which were most often articulated in racialized terms.[23] Muscularity no longer simply signified fitness and strength but also racial exclusivity and even superiority. As one speaker at the American Physical Education Association maintained in 1910: "We need in America an aristocracy of blood ... the aristocracy of strength, of health and of efficiency."[24]

Altogether, this confluence of discourses in the European and American *fin de siècle* produced a racial foundation for thinking about the vitality of the body politic. As Foucault argued, the shift in emphasis moved from monitoring and correcting individual bodies to the monitoring and correcting of the strength and vigor of the population. Hence, the themes of progeny, racial fitness, the future of the species, birth and death rates, and other statistical indicators of social health took center stage.[25] Extensive statistical studies of national and non-national populations followed, all with the goal of determining the vitality of the population and the threats to its constitutive health.[26] In Germany, the Society for Racial Hygiene (Gesellschaft für Rassenhygiene), established by Alfred Ploetz in 1905, put forth a proactive plan for regenerating the German people as a whole, which included, among other things, the opposition to the two-child system (in order to foster larger families and, hence, more offspring), the means to support "the reproduction of the fit" while preventing "the reproduction of the inferior," the introduction of measures to fight disease (such as tuberculosis and syphilis) as well as social diseases (such as alcoholism), the protection of the population from "inferior immigrants," the preservation and increase of the peasant class, the institution of favorable hygienic conditions in urban and industrial areas, the elevation of the fitness and

---

[23] In addition to Nye's *Crime, Madness, and Politics in Modern France*, see Wetzell, *Inventing the Criminal.*

[24] W. W. Hastings, "Racial Hygiene and Vigor" (1910), quoted in James C. Whorton, *Crusaders for Fitness: The History of American Health Reformers* (Princeton: Princeton University Press, 1982), 294.

[25] Foucault, *The History of Sexuality*, 147–148. Also, see Nye's "Comparative Reflections on Great Britain and Germany," in *Crime, Madness, and Politics in Modern France*, 330–339.

[26] See, for example, the studies by Mitchell B. Hart, *Social Science and the Politics of Modern Jewish Identity* (Stanford: Stanford University Press, 2000); John Efron, *Defenders of the Race: Jewish Doctors and Race Science in Fin-de-Siècle Europe* (New Haven: Yale University Press, 1994), esp. chap. 6, "Zionism and Racial Anthropology," 166–174; Richard Soloway, "Counting the Degenerates: The Statistics of Race Deterioration in Edwardian England," *Journal of Contemporary History* 17 (January 1982): 137–164, and Robert A. Nye, "The Bio-medical Origins of Urban Sociology," *Journal of Contemporary History* 20 no.4 (1985): 659–675.

strength of the individual, and the expansion of the military capacity of the nation.[27] The very same year, the Bureau for Jewish Statistics began publishing the *Zeitschrift für Demographie und Statistik der Juden* (Journal of Jewish Demographics and Statistics), replete with comparative analyses of Jewish physical and racial characteristics, including statistics about the Jewish body (for example, its typical racial features, muscularity, mentality, and even average brain size) as well as statistics about the Jewish population such as marriage rates, criminality, suicide rates, education levels, lifespans, drug and alcohol use, health, and susceptibility to disease.[28]

It is no coincidence that Jews responded to these same fears over degeneration, applied them to their own situation, and built upon them to justify Jewish national regeneration. In a short article entitled "Degeneration – Regeneration" (1901) published in the first year of the Jewish cultural periodical, *Ost und West: Illustrierte Monatschrift für modernes Judentum* (East and West: Illustrated Monthly for Modern Judaism), an anonymous author posited that "all the adherents of the theory of degeneration underestimate the boundless regenerative capacity of human nature."[29] Not unlike Moses Hess, who had connected "the rebirth of Israel" with the struggle of other nations to redeem themselves on the stage of world history,[30] the optimistic author of "Degeneration – Regeneration" points out that world-historical nations have always had to emerge from turmoil and rebuild themselves from destruction: "After the Thirty Years War, Germany found itself in deep economic ruin, just as England did in the first half of the nineteenth century. The human material of both nations was demoralized, weakened, and corrupted" (DR 609). Yet each of these nations has become a world-historical power, variously reborn and regenerated. Today, although the Jews in Eastern and Western Europe are "psychically and physically hindered in realizing their strengths," they, too, will soon experience "a new upswing" due to "the elasticity of human nature itself and Jewish elasticity in particular as well as the wealth of slumbering strength and eager talents" (DR 611–612).

[27] Sheila Faith Weiss, "The Racial Hygiene Movement in Germany, 1904–1945" in *The Wellborn Science*, ed. Adams, 8–68, here 23–24.

[28] See Hart, *Social Science*; Efron, *Defenders of the Race*; also Mitchell B. Hart, *The Healthy Jew: The Symbiosis of Judaism and Modern Medicine* (Cambridge: Cambridge University Press, 2007).

[29] "Degeneration – Regeneration," *Ost und West: Illustrierte Monatschrift für modernes Judentum* (August 1901): 609–612, here 609. All further citations are documented parenthetically as DR, followed by the page number.

[30] Moses Hess, *Rom und Jerusalem: die letzte Nationalitätsfrage* (1862; Leipzig: M. W. Kaufmann, 1899), 94.

Later the same year, *Ost und West* featured an article on the burgeoning Jewish gymnastics movement in Europe written by Hermann Jalowicz, one of the strongest proponents of the regenerative powers of gymnastics. Jalowicz points out that "the corporeal degeneration of the Jewish nation" and the "degeneration process" itself can be effectively counteracted by physical exercise and the healthy benefits of light, air, and nutrition.[31] Modeled after the German gymnastics movement in the early nineteenth century, he cites the rapid growth of the "Jewish gymnastics movement" throughout Europe as a signal of the successful regeneration of the Jewish body: "The skills, muscular strength, and sinews of the gymnast are increased through training, while marching and formation exercises aim at cultivating a strict discipline (something that Jews need particularly). Gymnastics contributes to evoking a love of nature, to making the body more resilient in responding to stress and accustomed to small privations. The shared experiences strengthen and bring about a feeling of comradeship."[32] In the spirit of other advocates of body reform and racial hygiene, Jalowicz concludes by drawing a connection between the regeneration of the individual body and the reform of the race as a whole: "The Jewish gymnastics movement can fulfill its goal of elevating the race [*volkserziehlichen Zweck*]. It will contribute to the strengthening of the body, to the consolidation of the will, and the recovery of the Jewish people."[33]

More than a century after Dohm and Grégoire published their initial calls for the physical, moral, and spiritual improvement of the Jewish people, the discourses of regeneration, particularly the ideas of corporeal reform and racial hygiene, would be taken up by a host of Zionist thinkers such as Max Nordau, Theodor Herzl, Martin Buber, Hermann Jalowicz, Felix Theilhaber, Max Grunwald, Arthur Ruppin, Elias Auerbach, Alfred Nossig, and Davis Trietsch, each of whom variously contributed to the discourse of Jewish regeneration and the creation of "muscular Judaism."[34] As a program of national, spiritual, and physical regeneration, Zionism – particularly in its early twentieth century incarnations throughout Central Europe and into Palestine – can hardly be said to be unique or even original since virtually all of the "regenerative" movements across the political

---

[31] Hermann Jalowicz, "Die juedische Turnbewegung," *Ost und West* 1 no. 11 (November 1901): 855–858, here 856.

[32] Jalowicz, "Die juedische Turnbewegung," 858.

[33] Jalowicz, "Die juedische Turnbewegung," 858.

[34] I discuss these figures and the discourses of Jewish regeneration more fully in my book, *Muscular Judaism: The Jewish Body and the Politics of Regeneration* (New York: Routledge, 2007), and I draw on that discussion here.

spectrum posited the birth of a "new man"[35] and the revitalization of the nation as a way to combat degeneracy. Each of these thinkers reacted to the antisemitic stereotypes, many of which were solidified by the political disenfranchisement of the Jews, and variously internalized them in order to pursue a transnational, trans-generational project of rebirth, regeneration, and normalcy. The "muscle Jew" emerged as the emblem of the Jewish "*homo novus*," epitomizing the attempt to reinvigorate the individual Jewish body and the body politic through the varied discourses of bio-power, ranging from monitoring and improving racial characteristics, muscle composition, hygiene practices, and military fitness to fertility, birth rates, and life expectancies. In sum, the intellectual origins of both the muscle Jew and the modern Zionist idea of regeneration are to be found in the European *fin de siècle*.

FROM DEGENERATION TO "MUSCLE JEWS"

There is no book that more epitomized the *fin-de-siècle* anxieties over degeneracy than Max Nordau's *Entartung* (Degeneration).[36] Published in 1892, the book was an instant success, becoming one of the most hotly contested and ten best-selling books of the decade. Nordau posited a grandiose cultural critique of his "decaying" age, condemning virtually every contemporary artistic or literary movement as a proof of "degeneracy" (his unforgiving criticism jumps effortlessly from particular figures such as Manet and Tolstoy to the pre-Raphaelites, Symbolism, and "Ibsenism"). He argues that only the calm rationality and disciplined logic of scientific progress can save humanity from the woes of degeneration and its attendant horror of formlessness. When we speak of *fin de siècle*, he proclaims, we "ought to correctly say *fin-de-race*" (E I:5) since what is taking place is not simply the end of a century, but rather the breakdown of "kinds" and the degenerative end of races. To understand his point, we should dwell briefly on the etymology of "degeneration" or "*Entartung*." In German, the verb "*entarten*" ('to degenerate') means "*aus der Art schlagen*," approximately, 'not true to form or kind' (*Art*). It implies a process of withdrawal (*ent-arten*) or movement away from an ideal or, at least, normative type.

---

[35] Cf. George Mosse, *The Image of Man: The Creation of Modern Masculinity* (Oxford: Oxford University Press, 1996).

[36] Max Nordau, *Entartung* (Berlin: Duncker & Humblot, 1892–93). I will quote from the following edition: *Entartung* (Berlin: Carl Duncker, 1893). Further citations will be documented as E, followed by the volume number and the page number. For translations, I consulted the following English edition, but found it necessary to often use my own translations: *Degeneration* (New York: D. Appleton, 1895).

In English and French, the word "degenerate" (from the Latin *degeneratus*) also contains the idea of a debased movement away from a norm as well as the idea of a "natural" form, namely a "race" or genus. To be degenerate means "to deviate from one's race or kind." Moreover, the concept is intimately connected with sexuality, reproduction, and birth, since degeneration (like regeneration) is something that happens across generations to progeny, peoples, and races.

To explain his idea that degeneration represents the "fin-de-race," Nordau cites the seminal text of the French psychiatrist Bénédict-Augustin Morel, *Traité des dégénérescences physiques, intellectuelles et morales de l'espèce humaine et des Causes qui produisent ces Variétés maladives* (1857), the first articulation of degeneration as a hereditary, race-based problem:

Degeneration has to be spoken of as a pathological deviation from an original type [*Typus*]. This deviation, even if, at the outset, it was ever so slight, contains transmissible elements of such a nature that anyone bearing them becomes more and more incapable of fulfilling his tasks to humanity; moreover, intellectual progress [*geistige Fortschritt*], which is already inhibited in his own person, finds itself endangered in his descendants as well (E I:32).

Building on Morel's work, Nordau argues that degenerate organisms – as pathological deviations from the norm – produce offspring, which, to an even greater degree, suffer from debilitation and malformations. As examples of physical degeneracy, he names various deformities such as stunted growth, asymmetry of the face and cranium, protruding ears, squinted eyes, pointed or flat palates, syn- and polydactylia, all of which are meant to establish the power and value of the norm over the deviation.[37] These offspring, living among "us" today at the *fin de siècle*, represent the "end of race": Although Nordau is optimistic that they will "fortunately soon become sterile" (E I:32) and die out, the societal risk is that degenerates will be "imitated," rather than shunned, as if their deviations somehow represented new social norms. Here, we can detect the first expression of Nordau's social Darwinism, something that runs throughout the entire book and will, later, become an essential part of his conceptualization of the tasks of Zionism.

Nordau ends the book on a note of "therapeutic" optimism, directed at the "highest educated classes" (E II:545), who are not yet entirely seduced by the "ravings" of the degenerate artists: "The people will recover from their present fatigue. The weak, the degenerate will perish; the strong will

---

[37] The best study of the history of the terms "norm" and "pathology" within the context of medical-scientific discourses of the nineteenth century is George Canguilhem's *The Normal and the Pathological* (Cambridge: Zone Books, 1991).

adapt themselves to the achievements of civilization or will subordinate them to their own organic capacity. The aberrations in art have no future. They will disappear when civilized humanity has triumphed over its condition of exhaustion" (E II:544). In the end, only the "true moderns" (E II:562) – those who are best adapted to the demands of modern society through discipline, rationality, and clarity of vision – will survive. Nordau's apocalyptic fantasy ends with the degenerate "vermin" being crushed and beaten to death by the "true moderns." He writes: "whoever considers civilization to be a good that has value and deserves to be defended, must mercilessly crush the anti-social vermin [*Ungeziefer*] under his thumbs. ... We cry: 'Get out of our civilized society [*Gesittung*]! Rove far from us! ... There is no place among us for such lusting rapiers and if you dare return to us, we will pitilessly beat you to death with clubs' " (E II:556–57). The degenerate artists are no better than vermin and must be expelled or clubbed to death in order for Nordau and the ranks of the true moderns to found a new, regenerated society based on the mechanisms of social evolution. It is here that Nordau's own ideas for violent social exclusion evidence a decidedly uncomfortable resemblance to a whole host of racist ideologies obsessed with ridding society of its so-called "anti-social vermin."

In Nordau's wake, the concept of the "*Ungeziefer*" has consistently indicated the abject of society, the absolutely vile deviation from the norm. Franz Kafka famously thematized this in his short story *Die Verwandlung* (The Metamorphosis), in which Gregor Samsa wakes up to find himself transformed into an "*Ungeziefer*" and is ultimately killed by his family for the sake of preserving bourgeois society.[38] More ominously, the association of Jews with parasites and vermin was a persistent topos of Nazi propaganda, something that was given a direct visual association in the virulently antisemitic Nazi film *The Eternal Jew* (1940). Although I am not suggesting that the ideas expressed in Nordau's *Degeneration* led to the purifying ideology of National Socialism, it is worth remembering that Nordau's critique of degeneracy as well as the violence of his social Darwinism did have an afterlife in the fervid adoption of race science and eugenics in the service of state formation. Indeed, it is one of the ironies of history that Nordau has to be saddled with the responsibility for popularizing the very term "*Entartung*," a concept that was – in its violently normalizing corporeal dimensions – later elaborated and staged by the Nazis in their

---

[38] This is the famous first line of Kafka's story: "Als Gregor Samsa eines Morgens aus unruhigen Träumen erwachte, fand er sich in seinem Bett zu einem ungeheueren Ungeziefer verwandelt." *Die Verwandlung* (1915), in *Sämtliche Erzählungen*, ed. Paul Raabe (Frankfurt am Main: Fischer Verlag, 1995), 56.

infamous exhibition of 1937, "*Entartete Kunst*" (Degenerate Art), in a way that closely parallels Nordau's 1892 critique.

Although Nordau conceded a few years later that he was willing to accept the antisemitic stereotype of the weak Jew as a national-racial characteristic given the fact that some historical evidence exists that proves that Jews are "small" in stature and that present-day Jews are "on average somewhat smaller than Germans, Russians, Anglo-Saxons, and Scandinavians," he was convinced that Jews were not racially "degenerate" and that Jewish self-improvement was both possible and desirable.[39] Their small size and ostensible physical weakness – something that may, upon first sight, "appear to be degeneration" (*Entartungserscheinung*) – can easily be explained, Nordau says, by the fact that Jews have "necessarily lost their ability for physical fitness, having lived for a thousand years deprived of exercise in the ghetto" (JTZ 1902, no. 7:110). To regain it, all that is necessary is disciplined training. In this regard, Nordau is actually negating a fundamental tenet of antisemitism (that race is destiny and that seemingly inhering traits are immutable). At no point does Nordau situate Jews – whether assimilated, Western Jews, or Eastern European Jews – under the rubric of degeneracy that he developed in his 1892 book. If Jews have deviated from their race or kind, to invoke the conceptual history of the term "degeneration," then it is because the "original type" – namely, the heroic muscle Jew of the likes of Bar Kokhba and the Maccabees – has been temporarily "destroyed" through the violent, historical mechanisms of antisemitism. Far from replicating the racial grounds for explaining the pervasiveness and expected death of degenerates, Jews, Nordau maintains, represent a latent race of "Spartan" fighters who will not perish by the challenges that modernity presents.[40] Instead, through their discipline and adaptability – the two fundamental traits of the "true moderns" – the weak Jews will evolve back into muscle Jews, uniting, in turn, their scattered people and founding a new nation with all the scientific solidity, social order, and racial strength of the greatest European civil societies.[41]

[39] Nordau, "Was bedeutet das Turnen für uns Juden?" in *Die Jüdische Turnzeitung* (1902), no. 7:111. Further references to *Die Jüdische Turnzeitung* will be documented parenthetically as JTZ, followed by the volume, issue, and page number.
[40] Max Nordau, "Heloten und Spartaner" (1899), reprinted in *Max Nordau's Zionistische Schriften*, ed. Zionistische Aktionskomitee (Cologne: Jüdischer Verlag, 1909), 374–378.
[41] Nordau's critique of degeneracy and his racially inflected call for "true moderns" to step forth would be taken up in a surprisingly wide array of contexts beyond the Zionist Congresses. These ideas were imported almost immediately to England and the United States where they would be used to justify racialized ideologies. Perhaps most disturbingly, Nordau's racial theories – from *Degeneration* to his later works such as "The Degeneration of Classes and Peoples" (1912) and *Morals and the Evolution of Man*

THE MODERN WORLD, 1815–2000

In Nordau's conception, Zionism is not only a politic of Jewish regeneracy but also a social Darwinian imperative of nation building.

Indeed, other thinkers in this period, such as Martin Buber, did employ Nordau's original language to describe Jews, and also made use of organicist, proto-nationalist concepts such as soil, blood, and resurrection to explain the Zionist concept of Jewish regeneration.[42] In a programmatic essay entitled "Juedische Renaissance" that appeared in the first edition of *Ost und West*, Buber argued that Jews, like other nations coming into their own, were at the threshold of rebirth.[43] It was the Zionist movement, he argued, that – for the Jewish people – brought together the aesthetic universals with the specificity of national strength and tribal unity. Here, Buber is not hesitant to invoke the *völkisch* concepts of blood, race, and nation, concepts which Moses Hess had introduced decades earlier to justify the urgent modernity of the Jewish project of regeneration. As Mark Gelber provocatively and, I think, rightly indicates: "While it is true that the German words for race and blood, '*Rasse*' and '*Blut*,' are polysemic signifiers that, given specific contextualizations, may be free of racist or genetic connotations, these terms are employed by Buber and an entire segment of German Cultural Zionist writers precisely in their racialist sense."[44]

As such, Buber draws the conceptual antecedents of regeneration into clearer focus, while underscoring the specificity of the Zionist program: "[t]he Jewish people's participation in nationality has its own particular character: muscle flexing, looking up, and raising up. The word resurrection comes to mind" (JR 7). This corporeal concept of Jewish renaissance is neither a simple return nor a naive progression; rather, it is "a rebirth of the whole human being" (JR 8), "a new creation from ancient material" (JR 9), a national movement composed of "latent energies" (JR

(1922) – influenced racist thinkers such as Madison Grant and Lothrop Stoddard in the United States, providing a conceptual vocabulary for American eugenics and its European variants. See Johannes Hendrikus Burgers, "Max Nordau, Madison Grant, and Racialized Theories of Ideology," *Journal of the History of Ideas* 72 no. 1 (2011): 119–140.

[42] See George Mosse, "The Influence of the Volkish Idea on German Jewry," in *Germans and Jews: The Right, the Left and the Search for a 'Third Force' in Pre-Nazi Germany* (New York: Howard Fertig, 1970), 89–93. Also, see the discussions by David Biale, *Eros and the Jews: From Biblical Israel to Contemporary America* (New York: Basic Books, 1992), 188ff; and Mark H. Gelber, *Melancholy Pride: Nation, Race, and Gender in the German Literature of Cultural Zionism* (Tübingen: Max Niemeyer, 2000), 134ff.

[43] Martin Buber, "Juedische Renaissance," *Ost und West: Illustrierte Monatschrift für modernes Judentum* 1 (1901): 7–10. All further references to this article will be documented parenthetically as JR, followed by the page number.

[44] Gelber, *Melancholy Pride*, 134.

9) in which Jews, "feel themselves to be organic and strive for the harmonious unfolding of their powers" (JR 10). Zionism thus represented the harnessing of these newly resurrected energies, coupled with a drive toward physical health, racial strength, national unity, and aesthetic productivity. The Jewish consciousness of nationality would be strengthened by aesthetic education according to "the specific characteristics of our ethnic blood [*die spezifischen Eigenschaften eines Blutstammes*]" (JR 7). It was the Zionist movement, he argued, that – for the Jewish people – brought together the aesthetic universals with the specificity of national strength and tribal unity. For Buber, the emergence of Jewish national art was a key way that Zionism created and expressed the racial vitality of the body and body politic.[45]

But it would be Nordau and Herzl who most famously called forward a new "race" of Jews who, through their discipline and adaptation, would be capable of realizing the national goals of Zionism. Conceived as an antithetical counterpart to Herzl's description of *Mauschel* – the hapless Eastern European Jew of the ghetto[46] – the celebrated new genus was the "muscle Jew" (*Muskeljude*). Nordau first mentioned the "muscle Jew" in his opening speech at the Second Zionist Congress in 1898.[47] Although he did not start exploring the political and social implications of his initial call for a "muscular Judaism" (*Muskeljudentum*) until a couple of years later, he did, in this early speech, clearly allude to the necessity of creating a new type of Jew who is corporeally strong and morally fit as the very presupposition of realizing the national goals of Zionism. After providing an overview of the steadily deteriorating situation of Jews in Eastern and Western Europe, Nordau argues: "Zionism awakens Judaism to new life. ... It achieves this morally [*sittlich*] through the rejuvenation of the ideals of the Volk and corporeally [*körperlich*] through the physical rearing of one's offspring, in

[45] For a discussion of the race in cultural Zionism, see Gelber's chapter, "The Rhetoric of Race and Jewish-National Cultural Politics: From Birnbaum and Buber to Brieger's *René Richter*," in *Melancholy Pride*, 125–160. For more on Buber, see my chapter, "The Aesthetics of Regeneration" in *Muscular Judaism*, 65–105.

[46] Herzl writes that Mauschel, the Yiddish-speaking, Eastern European Jew, "is the curse of the Jews" because he lives parasitically off others as a haggler and crook. "Mauschel," in *Gesammelte zionistische Werke* (Tel Aviv: Hozaah Ivrith, 1934), 1:209–215, here 211.

[47] Max Nordau, speech delivered at the Second Zionist Congress (Basel, August 28–31, 1898) *Stenographisches Protokoll der Verhandlungen des II. Zionisten-Congresses* (Vienna: Verlag des Vereines 'Erez Israel,' 1898), 14–27. All further references to the *Stenographisches Protokoll* will be documented parenthetically as SP, followed by the conference number and page number. For a full discussion of Nordau and the history of muscular Judaism, see my book, *Muscular Judaism*.

order to create a lost muscular Judaism [*Muskeljudenthum*] once again"
(SP II:24).

A couple of years later, he fully articulated the concept in two articles
published in *Die Jüdische Turnzeitung*: "Muskeljudentum," (Muscular
Judaism) in June 1900 and "Was bedeutet das Turnen für uns Juden?"
(What does gymnastics mean for us Jews?) in July 1902. The same year,
Herzl even imagined the future Palestine to be populated by strong,
German-speaking muscle Jews in his colonial travel narrative, *Altneuland*
(Old-New Land).[48] Whereas earlier Enlightenment thinkers such as
Dohm and Grégoire called for cultural "*Bildung*" (education) and social
"*Verbesserung*" (improvement) to achieve Jewish assimilation within
European society, Nordau shifted attention to what he perceived to be "a
missing corporeal education" [*eine fehlende, körperliche Erziehung*] (JTZ
1902, no. 7:110). He urges Jews to become strong and muscular by participating in athletic associations and argues that exercise, specifically gymnastics, is of the utmost importance for the health of the Jewish race. It is
not coincidental that Jewish athletic and gymnastic associations began to
spring up simultaneously with the spread of Zionism throughout many
Central European cities. In fact, by 1903, just six years after the first Zionist
congress, *Die Jüdische Turnzeitung* boasted that there were already thirteen
"national-Jewish Gymnastics associations" and that "we should strive to
have every Zionist association develop a gymnastics division."[49]

In the opening statement of *Die Jüdische Turnzeitung* published in May
1900, the editors, Hermann Jalowicz, Richard Blum, and Max Zirker,
articulated the goals as follows:

What we want! Healthy minds live in healthy bodies! Although we never contested it, this old Latin word never found suitable observance by us Jews. It was
recognized in theory, but thought never became deed. The one-sided education of
the mind, which caused our nervousness and mental fatigue, is what we are fighting! We want to re-instill vigor in the limpid Jewish body, to make it fresh and
robust, agile and strong. We want to achieve this in a Jewish association, so that at
the same time we can strengthen our unity and raise our self-consciousness, two
things that have been dwindling. We want to show how old Jewish ideals, which
in our young people seem to have been almost entirely lost, can once again give
us an advantage and bring honor upon us. We want to stand up to anti-Semitism
with courage and energy (JTZ 1900, no. 1:1).

[48] Theodor Herzl, *Altneuland* (1902), in *Gesammelte Zionistische Werke*, vol. 5
(Tel Aviv: Hazaah Ivrith, 1935), 125–420. For a fuller discussion, see my *Mobile
Modernity: Germans, Jews, Trains* (New York: Columbia University Press, 2007), 179–204.
[49] "Diskussionen über die Frage der körperliche Hebung der Juden," *Die Jüdische
Turnzeitung* (January 1903), no. 1:3.

As the first journal dedicated specifically to the physical improvement of the Jewish body, the editors of *Die Jüdische Turnzeitung* articulated a clear program for corporeal regeneration that not only included the cultivation of Jewish strength but also entailed the fighting of antisemitism and the development of latent feelings of Jewish nationality.

A leitmotiv that ran throughout the journal was the "physical improvement" of the Eastern European Jew, often pejoratively characterized as the *Jammergeschlecht* (wretched race), with a hunched-over body, crooked posture, awkward gait, underdeveloped musculature, and nervous disposition. Pictures of strong Jewish gymnasts with upright postures, elegant movements, developed muscles, and assured confidence were not only meant to provide inspiration and reclaim an ancient, heroic ideal; the bodies they depicted were also hailed as the precondition of a successful project of nation building. A strict binary thus emerged on the pages of *Die Jüdische Turnzeitung*: On the one side was degeneracy, characterized by diasporic wandering, physical weakness, disease, mental nervousness, and particularity; on the other side was regeneracy, characterized by national groundedness, physical strength, health, mental agility, and universality.

Extending Nordau's critique of degeneration directly to Jews, Mandelstamm calls upon vitalist discourses, particularly the notions of energy and exhaustion popularized by psychologists and scientists such as Charcot, Bergson, and Freud during the *fin de siècle*, to critique the corporeal constitution of the Eastern Jew. He links the closed, unventilated, unhygienic spaces of the ghetto to the "exhaustion of the Jewish brain and that of the entire nervous system" and says that this explains "the significantly higher number of nervous diseases and mental disturbances" among Jews in comparison with other races (JTZ 1900, no. 6:66). The "pathological curvature" of the spinal cord studied, for example, by Charcot is not only used to explain nervousness and mental diseases but was now linked explicitly to the Jewish corporeal condition. Although Mandelstamm believed that a multi-faceted program of economic, social, and educational reform would ultimately be necessary to overcome degeneracy, it was precisely through "obligatory gymnastics" that the Jewish body could become upright and strong, such that, one day, even Eastern Jews could become "competent soldiers" and, at last, "devote themselves to the colonization of Palestine" (JTZ 1900, no. 7:77, 78). From the journal's very first year, then, corporeal regeneration was connected to nation building and the incipient Jewish colonial project.

In May of 1909, the publishers of the *Die Jüdische Turnzeitung* issued a commemorative volume called *Körperliche Renaissance der Juden* (The Physical Renaissance of the Jews), which celebrated the tenth anniversary of the founding of "Bar Kokhba," the Jewish Gymnastics Association in

Berlin.[50] Adorned with a lithograph of a young, muscular rendition of Bar Kokhba by the artist Hermann Struck, the volume consisted of twelve essays by various sports experts and medical doctors, who attested to the benefits of gymnastics, fitness, sports, farming, and military service for the regeneration of the Jewish people. In the foreword to the commemorative volume, Georg Arndt pointed out the tremendous successes enjoyed over the past decade in "training a race of upright and strong Jews" (KR 1). Although "the haunt of degeneration" still lurked, the motivating question – "How do we create a healthy Jewish race?" – had been successfully answered: through "ironclad self-rearing" in gymnastics associations, extensive involvement with sports, and military training, Jews would become "muscle Jews" (KR 1). In one of the programmatic articles in the volume, "Muscle Jews and Nervous Jews," M. Jastrowitz of the Berlin "Medical Council" (Sanitätsrat) tells the readership that "the desired results could be reached through fitness exercises, running, jumping, climbing, swimming, discus throwing, archery, and gymnastics" (KR 14). As another contributor confidently declared: "The Jews shall become muscle men instead of nervous men" [Muskelmenschen statt Nervenmenschen] (KR 12). Because of "the elasticity of our race" (something that Nordau and Dohm had also pointed out), "the bent over, cowardly [Ghetto Jew] with a small chest and shortness of breath, with stunted bone growth and withered muscles" would be reborn in a heroic fashion and, through the power of "modern Volkshygiene" (KR 16), bring about a new race of Jews with "healthy nerves and healthy muscles" (KR 13).[51]

While Foucault famously traced the origins of European bio-politics to the seventeenth and eighteenth centuries, a time in which the individual body began to be scientifically monitored and interventions were made on behalf of the population,[52] Jewish bio-politics did not begin in earnest until the very end of the nineteenth century with the creation of a discourse around muscular Judaism and the founding of the first Jewish gymnastics associations. According to Foucault, while "an anatomo-politics of

[50] Körperliche Renaissance der Juden: Festschrift anlässlich des IV. Turntages der Jüdischen Turnerschaft und der Feier des 10 jährigen Bestehens des Jüdischen Turnvereins Bar Kochba-Berlin (Berlin: Verlag der Jüdischen Turnzeitung, 1909). All further citations will be documented parenthetically as KR, followed by the page number.

[51] For a wide-ranging discussion of Jews and sport, see Michael Brenner and Gideon Reuveni, eds, Emancipation through Muscles: Jews and Sports in Europe (Lincoln: University of Nebraska Press, 2007).

[52] Foucault, The History of Sexuality. Also, see the discussion of bio-power in Foucault, Society Must be Defended: Lectures at the Collège de France, 1975–1976, trans. David Macey, ed. Mauro Bertani and Alessandro Fontana (New York: Picador, 2003), esp. 242ff.

the human body" focused on the disciplining, the optimization, and the usefulness of the individual body in order to assure its efficiency and docility, the regulation of the "species body" focused on the health and vitality of the race; and while the former is "individualizing," the latter is "massifying" because it "is directed not at man-as-body but at man-as-species."[53] With regard to Jews as a species, then, Nordau first called for the statistical analysis of the Jewish population at the fifth Zionist Congress, demanding answers to scores of questions including Jewish marriage and fertility rates, child-bearing statistics, demographic trends, mortality rates, life expectancies, patterns of diet and habituation, susceptibility to illness, contraceptive practices, and other statistical indicators of the population's vitality.[54] Building on this idea, Felix Theilhaber and other doctors who published in *Die Jüdische Turnzeitung* considered Zionism to be a form of "hygiene" for the Jewish people that would be necessary if the Jews were to produce progeny who would prosper as a colonial-national people. With respect to muscle Jews and Zionist gymnastics associations, Theilhaber affirms, "we have a true movement which is seriously interested in the corporeal well-being of the Volk" (JTZ 1911, no. 10:189). However, he insists that "the national [*völkisch*] health of the Jews" is nevertheless endangered by many things, ranging from mental and physical diseases to socio-economic conditions, sexually transmitted diseases, and even "the two-child system of modernity," that latter of which he considers to have "racially damaging [*rassenschädigende*] consequences" (JTZ 1911, no. 10:191).

Theilhaber, in effect, calls for a scientifically systematic approach to regenerating the Jewish race and its reproductive sexuality. In no uncertain terms, he labels this approach "Jewish eugenics" [*jüdische Eugenik*] (JTZ 1911, no. 10:190), the only thing that will forestall what he called, in the words of his eponymous book, "the destruction of the German Jews."[55] Theilhaber's statistical methodology for studying the so-called "destruction" of the German Jews was not only indebted to other, roughly contemporaneous studies of the Jewish population (such as those pioneered by Alfred Nossig, Elias Auerbach, and Arthur Ruppin), but also the broader, European context for developing sexual hygiene and racial medicine.[56] As

---

[53] Foucault, *Society Must be Defended*, 243.

[54] Max Nordau, Speech of December 27, 1901, in *Stenographisches Protokoll der Verhandlungen des V. Zionisten-Congresses* (Vienna: Verlag des Vereines 'Erez Israel,' 1901), 100. See the discussion by Hart, *Social Science and the Politics of Modern Jewish Identity*, 38.

[55] Felix Theilhaber, *Der Untergang der deutschen Juden: Eine volkswirtschaftliche Studie* (Munich: Ernst Reinhardt, 1911).

[56] Efron, *Defenders of the Race*, 148.

such, the Zionist politics of regeneration was infused by pan-European discourses of hygiene, fertility, reproduction, racial strength, eugenics, physical health, and mental fitness, all of which were part and parcel of nineteenth- and early twentieth-century ideas for scientifically managing populations and cultivating nationality.[57]

CONCLUDING REMARKS

The "muscle Jew" and "muscular Judaism" represent paradigms of regeneration that cannot be adequately understood apart from the condensation of multiple discourses concerning the corporeal politics of sexual reform, physical fitness, health, hygiene, and eugenics as well as the particularities of European and American nationalism, colonialism, and militarism. The muscle Jew initially emerged from Nordau's aesthetic reflections on degeneration and regeneration, but the ideal lived on in a wide range of cultural discourses that extended and justified the corporeal politics of early Zionism from the *fin de siècle* up through today. What is remarkable is that the strategies of social policing and regulation (eugenics, hygiene), bio-politics (sexual science, race science), and corporeal reform (sport, "body culture" movements, militarism) betray the extent to which Jews participated in, extended, and variously adopted these strategies of "bio-power" for reforming the Jewish body and conceiving of the regeneration of the Jewish nation-state. Jews – especially, but not exclusively, Zionist Jews – participated in the discourses of bio-power and actively formulated policies, programs, and strategies for creating a new, racially strong, physically fit, muscle Jew. Thus, it is no longer sufficient to see the Jewish body as simply "degenerate" and weak, and to posit the fascist body as its antithesis: "regenerate," strong, and masculine[58]; instead, the "muscle Jew" is the prototype of the hardened, strong, hygienic, and resolutely masculine warrior.

Indeed, most of the major studies on "degeneration" – particularly newer cultural and social histories such as those by Daniel Pick, Paul Weindling, and Kevin Repp – are quite sensitive about the risks of collapsing history into an inevitable procession toward Nazi racial policy and the rise of the racial state. Nevertheless, there are still many cultural studies of

---

[57] For more on the Jewish context, see Hart, *The Healthy Jew*; Efron, *Medicine and the German Jews*.

[58] See, for example, the classic studies of Klaus Theweleit, *Male Fantasies: 1. Women, Floods, Bodies, Histories* and *Male Fantasies: 2. Male Bodies: Psychoanalyzing the White Terror* (Minnesota: University of Minnesota Press, 1987–89). Also, Mosse, *The Image of Man*, particularly chap. 8 on "the new fascist man."

degeneracy that maintain an implicit teleology stretching from nineteenth-century conceptions of race and degeneracy to the Final Solution.[59] While Pick speculates that it may be "impossible ... to avoid teleology altogether in the reading of nineteenth-century degenerationism,"[60] the more problematic issue is the fact that Jews are given little agency in these histories of modernity. Instead, the rise of the purity and strength of the fascist male body is posited as the end-point of the dialectic of degeneration/regeneration, while the Jewish body is condemned to its perennial formlessness and passivity. Today, we must ask ourselves: What does it mean that Jewish militarism and its body ideals (aggressive, steeled, warrior-like) overlapped with other, more dangerous regenerative movements that also posited the birth of a "new man," including fascism? What does it mean – especially from our twenty-first century vantage point – that the "muscle Jew" and the "fascist body" draw, at least in part, from the same discursive well?[61] To be sure, these are profoundly complex and difficult questions, but answering them, I think, may paint a more thorough history of the genesis, dissemination, and influence of racial thought in the early twentieth century, one which zigzags between European antisemitism, the rise of Zionism, the transatlantic uptake of racial ideologies and world-views, and fascist implementations of these ideologies in the service of the eugenic state. There is much historiographic work still to be done in order to confront these zigzags with clarity and honesty, and, perhaps, more urgently, to confront the post-war incarnations of the politics of degeneracy and regeneration in contemporary racialized states.

[59] For examples of this kind of historiography, see George Mosse, *Toward the Final Solution: A History of European Racism* (London: J. M. Dent, 1979); Klaus Theweleit, *Male Fantasies*, 2 vols.; and Hal Foster, *Compulsive Beauty* (Cambridge: MIT Press, 1993). Although not focused on degeneracy per se, Richard Weikart's *From Darwin to Hitler: Evolutionary Ethics, Eugenics, and Racism in Germany* (New York: Palgrave, 2004) traces a similar development.

[60] Pick, *Faces of Degeneration*, 30.

[61] I am not the first to raise these questions. In fact, some four decades ago, George Mosse published an incendiary essay called "The Influence of the Volkish Idea on German Jewry," in which he sought to explain why certain Jewish intellectuals (both Zionist and assimilationist), just like certain fascist intellectuals, were attracted to *völkish* thought, including its ideals of rejuvenation, rootedness in nature, and the revitalization of the Volk. The essay is reprinted in *Germans and Jews: The Right, the Left and the Search for a 'Third Force' in Pre-Nazi Germany*, 77–115.

SELECT BIBLIOGRAPHY

Baecque, Antoine de. *The Body Politic: Corporeal Metaphor in Revolutionary France, 1770–1800*, trans. Charlotte Mandell. Stanford: Stanford University Press, 1997.

Brenner Michael and Gideon Reuveni, eds. *Emancipation through Muscles: Jews and Sports in Europe*. Lincoln: University of Nebraska Press, 2007.

Efron, John. *Defenders of the Race: Jewish Doctors and Race Science in Fin-de-Siècle Europe*. New Haven: Yale University Press, 1994.

Medicine and the German Jews: A History. New Haven: Yale University Press, 2001.

Foucault, Michel. *The History of Sexuality: An Introduction*, trans. Robert Hurley. New York: Vintage Books, 1990.

Gilman Sander and J. Edward Chamberlin, eds. *Degeneration: The Dark Side of Progress*. New York: Columbia University Press, 1985.

Hau, Michael. *The Cult of Health and Beauty in Germany: A Social History, 1890–1930*. Chicago: University of Chicago Press, 2003.

Hess, Jonathan M. *Germans, Jews and the Claims of Modernity*. New Haven: Yale University Press, 2002.

Kelly, Alfred. *The Descent of Darwin: The Popularization of Darwin in Germany, 1860–1914*. Chapel Hill: University of North Carolina Press, 1981.

Mosse, George. *The Image of Man: The Creation of Modern Masculinity*. Oxford: Oxford University Press, 1996.

"The Influence of the Volkish Idea on German Jewry," in *Germans and Jews: The Right, the Left and the Search for a 'Third Force' in Pre-Nazi Germany*. New York: Howard Fertig, 1970.

Nye, Robert A. *Crime, Madness, and Politics in Modern France: The Medical Concept of National Decline*. Princeton: Princeton University Press, 1984.

Pick, Daniel. *Faces of Degeneration: A European Disorder, c. 1848–c. 1918*. Cambridge: Cambridge University Press, 1989.

Presner, Todd. *Muscular Judaism: The Jewish Body and the Politics of Regeneration*. New York: Routledge, 2007.

Sorkin, David. *The Transformation of German Jewry, 1780–1840*. Oxford: Oxford University Press, 1987.

Theweleit, Klaus. *Male Fantasies: 1. Women, Floods, Bodies, Histories* and *Male Fantasies: 2. Male Bodies: Psychoanalyzing the White Terror*. Minnesota: University of Minnesota Press, 1987–89.

Weindling, Paul. *Health, Race, and German Politics Between National Unification and Nazism, 1870–1945*. Cambridge: Cambridge University Press, 1989.

Whorton, James C. *Crusaders for Fitness: The History of American Health Reformers*. Princeton: Princeton University Press, 1982.

CHAPTER 22

ZIONISM AND ITS CRITICS

ERAN KAPLAN

Unlike other national movements that battled an imperial power for inde-pendence or fought to unify smaller political entities into a nation-state, Zionism, the Jewish national movement that aimed to achieve Jewish polit-ical sovereignty, arose first and foremost as a much more abstract notion: a revolt against history. As David Ben-Gurion, Israel's first Prime Minister, phrased it: "All other revolts, both past and future, were uprisings against a *system*, against a political, social, or economic structure. Our revolution is directed not only against a system but against *destiny* ..."[1] Ben-Gurion, who was prone to grand statements, may have overstated Zionism's core revolutionary impetus – but he touched upon a theme that many Zionists embraced: that Zionism was first and foremost a revolt against the way Jewish history has evolved over the years according to theological and reli-gious values and the kind of ideas and mentalities that it created along the way.

Zionism, which emerged in Europe but envisioned a future state on a different continent, was an idea before it was an actual political movement. And as an idea, it was open to debates and struggles that were frequently charged with great emotional urgency yet did not require mobilizing armies or creating alternative social or political institutions. From its inception, the Zionist idea was exposed to criticism both from within and without the Jewish world that questioned its very legitimacy and viability. These debates have continued with undiminished ferocity until today when, arguably like no other national movement, Zionism (and the legitimacy of the very idea of a Jewish State) is openly questioned. In fact, several crit-ics have suggested in recent years that we are now living in a post-Zionist age in which Zionism has outlived its historical usefulness and can (or *should*) no longer define the contours of the Jewish experience in Israel or elsewhere. The aim of this chapter is to examine the history of the Zionist

---

[1] David Ben-Gurion, "The Imperatives of the Jewish Revolution," in *The Zionist Idea: A Historical Analysis and Reader*, ed. Arthur Hertzberg (Philadelphia: Jewish Publication Society, 1997), 607.

idea primarily from the point of view of its critics, to explore the changing dynamics of the "Zionist debates" and to try to assess what the critiques of Zionism reveal about the very nature, limits, and viability of the Jewish national idea. While the chapter alludes to a Zionist idea in the singular, there were in fact many varieties of Zionism: there were socialist Zionists, religious Zionists, Revisionist Zionists, and non-affiliated, General Zionists, only to mention some of the dominant factions within Zionism. But what all these movements had in common was a commitment to the notion of building a Jewish national home in the ancestral home of the Jewish people as the only viable way to solve the Jewish Question.

In this chapter it would be all but impossible to explore all the different schools and groups of Zionism's many critics. Instead this chapter will more narrowly focus on Zionism's critics, first in Europe, where the Zionist idea emerged, and then in Palestine and later Israel, where the Zionist idea materialized into a political entity, and where the debates became part of the political culture of the Zionist state. Of course, Zionism and the critique of Zionism play an important role in the cultural and social life of Jews and others outside of Israel. It is hard to understand American Judaism today without understanding Jewish American attitudes towards Israel. But these are ultimately dynamics that have to do with the evolution of American Jewish life as much as they have to do with the development of the Zionist idea itself, which is ultimately the focus our discussion here.

Zionism arose as a reaction to promises and failures of European modernity. In the aftermath of the French Revolution, Jews throughout the continent gradually became citizens of the lands in which they lived. They physically and spiritually began a long and complicated move from the segregated Jewish ghetto to the mainstream of European society. For centuries Jews were a religious minority that had to rely on special charters and privileges (always subject to expulsion) to reside in European cities or lands. In the pre-modern period, many Jews were shut off from the gentile world and relied on their own communal institutions and law. The modern state, with its universal aspirations, sought to break internal divisions and create a general citizenry that transcended (at least in theory) religious boundaries. This afforded a growing number of Jews the opportunity to assimilate, to rely on the state and its institutions (legal, educational, cultural). Jews became French, German, and British; and many Jews rejected traditional (Orthodox) Judaism. At the same time, historians and sociologists began to treat Judaism and Jewish history not strictly as a religious phenomenon, but as a community whose history and fate were determined by secular (economic, social, political) forces – not by some theological, messianic plan.

But the modern state was not a theoretical experiment in universalism and rationalism; it also relied on myths of national origin and organic cohesion. For centuries in Europe, Jews were the targets of hatred and persecution that were fueled and enhanced by religious incitement (they were the killers of the Lord). In the nineteenth century, more and more people began to view Jews as members of a foreign nation, as contaminating the social body or the race. By the latter decades of that century, this view came to be known as antisemitism, which became an integral part of European politics. Zionism addressed these very contradictions that modernity foisted on the Jewish people: it called for the creation of a modern, secular state for the Jews but outside the European political order that rejected the Jew as foreigner.

From a Zionist perspective, modern antisemitism was not some transhistorical, irrational force. Zionist ideologues from Theodor Herzl, the father of modern political Zionism, to the socialist Zionist Nachman Syrkin and others, argued that the modern hatred of the Jews could be explained by economic factors (different classes feared that Jews who now entered the general occupational market would threaten their economic interests) or national interests (hatred of the Jews as the stranger helped produce or maintain nationalist cohesion). So in order to solve the "Jewish problem" Jews had to upend the course of their history. They needed to exit the vicious cycle of persecution and exclusion; Jews, Zionists stipulated, had to control their historical destiny – and from a late nineteenth-century perspective, this meant they had to create an independent sovereign state. As Theodor Herzl put it in his 1896 pamphlet *The Jewish State*,

No one can deny the gravity of the situation of the Jews. Wherever they live in perceptible numbers, they are more or less persecuted. Their equality before the law, granted by statute, has become practically a dead letter ... Let the sovereignty be granted us over a portion of the globe large enough to satisfy the rightful requirements of a nation; the rest we shall manage for ourselves. The creation of a new State is neither ridiculous nor impossible. We have in our day witnessed the process in connection with nations which were not largely members of the middle class, but poorer, less educated, and consequently weaker than ourselves. The Governments of all countries scourged by Anti-Semitism will be keenly interested in assisting us to obtain the sovereignty we want.[2]

From the early Zionist perspective, though, the impediments that Jews faced in Europe were not only external; they faced challenges beyond antisemitism and its political implications. The way to achieve the lofty, if not outright fantastic, goal of creating a sovereign Jewish state was to first

---

[2] Theodor Herzl, *The Jewish State* (New York: Filiquarian, 2006), 17, 24.

create a new society that would reject the legacies of traditional, rabbinic Judaism, which placed Jewish scholarship and observance of Jewish law at the core of Jewish life. Or, as Max Nordau, Herzl's second in command in the Zionist Organization, argued, Jews had to embrace a new ethos of muscular Judaism: the Maccabees over the rabbis; Bar Kokhba, the leader of the last Jewish revolt against the Romans in Palestine, over Yohanan Ben Zakkai, the sage who escaped Jerusalem on the eve of the Temple's destruction in a coffin to establish his academy in Yavneh.[3]

This call for a (re)new(ed) Hebrew spirit as a way to redeem the Jewish people became the staple of Labor Zionism, the political movement that by the 1920s would emerge as the leading force in the Zionist movement. As A. D. Gordon, one of the early ideologues of Labor Zionism and a champion of Hebrew labor put it, "Our people can be brought to life only if each one of us re-creates himself through labor and life close to nature. This is how we can, in time, have good farmers, good laborers, good Jews, good human beings."[4] To Gordon, the new Zionist ethos was to be a negation of the exilic Jewish past. If in the Diaspora Jews were a persecuted minority that resided in unhealthy, urban ghettos removed from the land and manual labor, the new Jewish society that would pave the way to an independent Jewish state would have to liberate itself by taking hold of its own fate: "Every one of us is required to refashion himself so that the Galut Jew within him becomes a totally emancipated Jew ... so this, his Galut life, which has been fashioned by alien and extraneous influences, hampering his natural growth and self-realization, may give way to one that allows him to develop freely, to his fullest stature in all dimensions."[5] If the perceived ideal member of the Diasporic (Galut) Jewish community was the scholar, ensconced in his house of learning, the Zionist ideal type was the pioneer who returns to the land in order both to turn it into an independent state, but also to use the land as a means to liberate the Jew's body from millennia of external and self-imposed bondage.

Zionism, as it emerged as a political and ideological movement, then, was a thoroughly secular movement, even if some of the early champions of Zionist ideals were Orthodox rabbis. Zionism stipulated that the solutions to the problems that haunted European Jewry for centuries were to be sought immediately in *this world*. It should be of no surprise then that

[3] See Todd Samuel Presner, *Muscular Judaism: The Jewish Body and the Politics of Regeneration* (New York: Routledge, 2007), 55–56.

[4] A. D. Gordon, "Some Observations," in *The Making of Modern Zionism: The Intellectual Origins of the Jewish State*, ed. Shlomo Avineri (New York: Basic Books, 1981), 153.

[5] Ibid., 154.

Zionism's most vehement early opponents were Orthodox Jews and their spiritual and political leaders.

From a traditional Jewish perspective, which found its expression in legal rabbinical writings as well as Jewish mystical texts, the Jews were exiled from the Holy Land for their sins and internal divisions. Exile, then, was a condition brought about by divine forces and its end could only come through religious repentance and carried out through divine intervention. From this perspective Zionism was tantamount to *dehikat ha-ketz*, hastening the end of time: the Jewish people's contribution to the advent of the end of time should be conducting their lives according to Jewish law, not by reconstituting the Jewish commonwealth in the Holy Land by a secular movement. Rabbi Zadok Hacohen Rabinowitz, in an epistle with the unambiguous title, "The Zionists Are Not Our Saviors," argued,

Do we not know that the whole purpose of redemption is to improve our ways so that Israel may observe the Torah with all the restrictions that have been placed upon it by our sages, who should not, Heaven forbid, be men of power and influence among us. [Moreover] as the prophets foresaw our redemption, we will not require an army and strategies of war. From this we can see that [the aspirations of the Zionists] are opposed to the spirit of Judaism and the hope of redemption.[6]

Some rabbis, in their opposition to Zionism, relied on the Three Oaths, a Talmudic midrash, according to which Jews are sworn not to go up from the Exile to the Holy Land *en masse* and not to rebel against the nations of the world; at the same time, the nations of the world are sworn not to oppress the Jews extremely.[7] For many leaders of Haredi or ultra-Orthodox Judaism, then, Zionism was an apostasy, a public violation of Jewish law and tradition and a threat to the very continuity of Jewish life. In 1938, at the height of the Great Arab Revolt in Palestine, when the Zionist leaders of the Jewish community in Palestine tried to unify the entire community, the leaders of Neturei Karta (literally, the guardians of the city) the extreme anti-Zionist, ultra-Orthodox sect in Jerusalem, offered the following warning to observant Jews in Palestine:

A new ominous monster has arisen of late over our holy land. In light of the terrible situation and great calamity that the Jewish community in our holy land and in the Diaspora has been battling for several years [Zionism], the only option before us is to unify our nation's reserves and return to our original faith, seek ways to come back to our father in heaven, destroy the pagan altars, which are

---

[6] In Paul R. Mendes-Flohr and Jehuda Reinharz, eds, *The Jew in the Modern World: A Documentary History* (Oxford: Oxford University Press, 1995), 544.

[7] See Aviezer Ravitzky, *Messianism, Zionism, and Jewish Religious Radicalism* (Chicago: University of Chicago Press, 1996), 211–234.

the libertine schools that are based on heresy and apostasy (heaven forefend), to mend all the Jewish communities throughout the land according to Jewish family law, to abstain from forbidden foods and violating the Sabbath and holidays; for this is our true protection from all of our enemies and shall be our only salvation in this dire hour.[8]

By the late 1930s, the leaders of Neturei Karta were dismayed by the willingness of the leaders of Agudat Yisrael, the umbrella political party of Haredi Jews, to cooperate with the Zionist institutions in Palestine – the builders of pagan alters as they put it. This indicates that by that time the mainstream of Haredi Jewry, while rejecting the core of Zionist ideology, was willing to work politically with the Zionist movement, which represented the majority of Palestinian Jewry at that time. This cooperation would continue and strengthen until the present. (Although even now, the political representatives of Agudat Yisrael are allowed by their rabbinical leaders to serve only as vice ministers in the Israeli government, not as ministers – for that would entail full recognition of the Zionist project.)

As indicated before, even in the early days of the Zionist movement some Orthodox Jews supported Zionism. This group of more moderate (or modern) Orthodox Jews would create in the first decade of the twentieth century the national religious faction, Hamizrahi, within the Zionist movement. Until the 1960s, Hamizrahi and the majority of its leaders tended to have a minimalist ideological agenda: they focused their political efforts on insuring that the Zionist movement maintain certain traditional Jewish characteristics (kosher food would be served in its public institutions and that those institutions not operate on the Sabbath and Jewish holidays). An exception to this approach were the teachings and writings of Rabbi Abraham Yitzhak Kook, the first chief Ashkenazi Rabbi in mandatory Palestine, who maintained that Zionism, though secular, was a necessary step in the redemption of the Jewish people. To Kook, the Zionists, unconsciously, were carrying out the messianic plan for the Jewish people. According to Kook, "A Jew cannot be as devoted to his own ideas, sentiments, and imagination in the Diaspora as he can in Eretz Israel. Revelations of the Holy, of whatever degree, are relatively pure in Eretz Israel; outside it they are mixed with dross and much impurity."[9] And the Zionist (secular) liberation of the land was then critical in purifying the Jewish people from the impurity of exilic life. After the 1967 war and the Israeli conquest of the West Bank and Gaza, the young generation of

---

[8] The Neturei Karta Community of Haredi Jewry, "Public Announcement," in *The Origins of Israel 1882–1948: A Documentary History*, ed. Eran Kaplan and Derek Penslar (Madison: University of Wisconsin Press, 2011), 162.

[9] Rabbi A. I. Kook, "The Land of Israel," in Hertzberg, *The Zionist Idea*, 420.

national religious Jews, led by Kook's charismatic son, Zvi Yehudah Kook, would come to dominate the movement – they would make the messianic, pioneering aspects of Kook's teachings the dominant part of their ideological and political worldview, calling for the settlement of Jews in the occupied territories (which also happened to contain some important biblical sites) as a way to bring about the full redemption of the Jewish people in Zion. While secular Zionists then sought to return the Jews to history rather than to wait for the divine redemption of the Jewish people, Orthodox Jewry, either as critics or supporters of Zionism, ultimately judged Judaism through a messianic prism. And this debate over the very nature of Jewish history (and destiny) has defined the history of Jewish nationalism (and then the State of Israel) from its inception.

From the movement's early stages, Zionists were torn between their commitment to the particular fate and well-being of the Jewish people and an aspiration to formulate their solution to the Jewish problem according to universal values. Zionism was the national movement of the Jewish people, but the majority of mainstream Zionists sought to create a society and state imbued with universal and democratic principles. This dilemma was especially acute for socialist Zionists, the ideological camp that would come to dominate Zionist politics.

Labor Zionists had to reconcile their commitment to such notions as class struggle and universal equality (and their attendant internationalism) with the need to find an immediate (national) remedy to the Jewish problem. The early ideologues of Labor Zionism, of the Po'alei Zion (workers of Zion) party, were well aware of the inherent inconsistency between these seemingly opposing commitments. And their ideological solution was to claim that first and foremost the immediate Jewish problem had to be solved by creating an independent Jewish state, and only then should Zionists focus on creating a model society that would abolish all class distinctions. As Ber Borochov, the ideological "founding-father" of Labor Zionism put it, "Political territorial autonomy in Palestine is the ultimate aim of Zionism. For proletarian Zionists, this is also a step toward socialism."[10]

Po'alei Zion split in 1919, when some members decided to leave the party to form Po'alei Zion Left. Members of Po'alei Zion Left later established the anti-Zionist Palestinian Communist Party. These were not the first socialists to adopt an anti-Zionist stance; in fact, alongside Haredi Jews, Jewish Marxists were some of Zionism's most vociferous early critics. But whereas for religious Jews Zionism tended to be too universal – an imitation and importation of foreign customs and values – for Marxists it

---

[10] Ber Borochov, "Our Platform" in Hertzberg, *The Zionist Idea*, 366.

was too particular, too chauvinistic, placing the well-being of one nation over the universal struggle for equality.

Marxists decried Zionism's "chauvinism" and preferred an "internationalist" solution to the Jewish problem. However, many of them shared with Zionists the view that Jews in Europe were in dire straits and that the plight of the Jews could largely be attributed to modern capitalism and the volatility of world markets. But unlike Zionists, and especially Labor Zionists who maintained that any socialist or class-based remedy to the Jewish problem must be preceded by the creation of normal, national conditions for the Jewish collective, anti-Zionist Marxists argued that adopting this kind of bourgeois solution to the Jewish problem would only increase the danger for Jews both in Palestine and worldwide. When asked in 1934 if the rise of Nazism should change the way communists regarded the notion of a Jewish national home in Palestine, Leon Trotsky offered the following argument,

> Both the fascist state in Germany, as well as the Arabian-Jewish struggle, bring forth new and very clear verifications of the principle that the Jewish question cannot be solved within the framework of capitalism. I do not know whether Jewry will be built up again as a nation. However, there can be no doubt that the material conditions for the existence of Jewry as an independent nation could be brought about only by the proletarian revolution.[11]

From Trotsky's perspective, which in this case is indicative of the broader Marxist critique of Zionism, only an international revolution that would liberate all people would also solve the Jewish problem. Solving the Jewish problem independently of other problems (the Arab problem) would only create new conflicts rather than bring about peace and security.

A more systematic Marxist critique of Zionism was developed by Abraham Leon (born Abraham Wejnstock) in his 1940 book *The Jewish Question: A Marxist Interpretation*.[12] Leon was born in Poland to a Zionist family that immigrated to Palestine in the 1920s. After several years the family relocated to Belgium, where Leon joined Ha-Shomer ha-Tza'ir, a socialist Zionist youth movement, with a pronounced Marxist orientation. However, after the Nazi invasion of Belgium, Leon renounced Zionism and joined the communist underground (in 1944 he resurfaced to try and

[11] Leon Trosky, "On the Jewish Problem," in *Prophets Outcast: A Century of Dissident Jewish Writing about Zionism and Israel*, ed. Adam Shatz (New York: Nation Books, 2004), 102.

[12] The book was first published in French in 1946. An English edition was published four years later in Mexico City. The entire English version of the book is available online at www.marxists.de/religion/leon.

lead miners against the Nazis – he was arrested immediately and sent to Auschwitz where he perished at the age of twenty-six).

In his book, Leon offered a Marxist-inspired analysis of Jewish history that explained the marginalization and persecution of the Jews according to economic rather than religious or cultural factors. In the book, Leon dedicated a chapter to the Zionist question. Like the Zionists, he maintained that the Jewish problem only worsened in the modern period and called for an immediate solution (admittedly that was not difficult to argue in Nazi-occupied Belgium), but he rejected the Zionist political solution. To Leon, nationalism was a bourgeois solution. It was a solution that matched the economic and political realities of the late eighteenth century, but by the middle of the twentieth century, he argued, bourgeois capitalism was on the decline, and therefore adopting its remedy for the Jewish Question would mean adopting an outdated and therefore dangerous political plan. Modern antisemitism, according to Leon, was fueled by the decline of traditional capitalism – that was constricted by the borders of nation-states – and the rise of imperialism as a way for capitalism to exploit new markets and cheaper labor. It was then, when the nation-state exhausted its economic potential, that the lower classes began to repel the Jews, who were perceived as an economic threat to the organic nation. So as Leon put it, "Capitalist decay – basis for growth of Zionism – is also the cause of the impossibility of its realization."[13]

Zionism, then, is a product of imperialist expansion according to Leon (European Jews who were repelled from one continent and were forced to seek alternatives elsewhere), and therefore it was doomed to suffer from all the violent consequences of the imperial age: the clash of imperial, colonial interests and local ethnic clashes. According to Leon,

Today the whole world is colonized, industrialized and divided among the various imperialisms. Everywhere Jewish emigrants come into collision at one and the same time with the nationalisms of the 'natives' and with the ruling imperialism. In Palestine, Jewish nationalism collides with an increasingly aggressive nationalism. The development of Palestine by Jewish immigration tends to increase the intensity of this Arab nationalism ... To overcome Arab resistance the Jews need English imperialism ...[14]

Leon's preferred solution was a global revolution, and here the Jews, as the marginalized minority, already had an advantage: they existed outside the

[13] Abraham Leon, "The Jewish Question: A Marxist Interpretation" in *Prophets Outcast*, ed. Shatz, 111.

[14] Ibid., 113.

existing political and social order and therefore were ideally positioned to take a leading role in the anti-capitalist revolt.

Leon analyzed the position of the Jew as the eternal outsider strictly according to economic and material factors. Others, however, attached a moral dimension to that position of the Jew (the excluded and marginalized as a light unto the nations) and criticized Jewish nationalism as a betrayal of that moral legacy. Hannah Arendt, an early supporter of the Zionist idea and a champion of Jewish self-defense and militarism – became one of the more outspoken critics of Zionism and the policies of the young Jewish state. Arendt developed the idea of the Jew as a conscious pariah (which she took from Bernard Lazare), who eschews the temptation of statehood and political power, of ideology – which for Arendt inevitably lead to totalitarianism and terror. For Arendt, the role of the Jew, as a conscious pariah, was to remain outside the ranks, to become, consciously, an outcast; Jews, Arendt warned, should not accept the Gentile rules of society for fear that they would lose their uniqueness. They should reject the temptations of the nation-state, which would not only deprive Jews of their singular position, but also put them in real physical danger. According to Arendt, "The misfortune of the building of a Jewish National Home has been that it was accompanied by a Central European ideology of nationalism and tribal thinking among the Jews."[15] What Arendt hoped was that the Jews in Palestine/Israel would abandon their nationalist and tribalist inclinations and instead adopt a bi-national position. She wanted Jews to renounce the notion of an exclusivist Jewish society in Palestine and create mechanisms for full economic, social, and political co-operation with the Palestinian Arabs.

Arendt's plea for bi-nationalism was not new. In her writings she credited two movements in Palestine: Brith Shalom (the covenant of peace) in the 1920s and the Ihud (union) party of the 1940s – the movements were inspired and led by Judah Magnes, the co-founder and President of the Hebrew University in Jerusalem, as well as by other leading Hebrew University intellectuals such as Martin Buber, Gershom Scholem, and Hugo Bergmann –for introducing this idea into the Zionist public discussion. Ihud's platform from 1942 made the following claim: "Our basic tenet is that we cannot triumph over the catastrophe now engulfing the world, unless we reject the unbridled nationalistic idea for a vision of cooperation and unity between nations, as expressed by President Roosevelt's 'Four Freedoms.' The unchecked egotism of a single nation is bound to lead to wars and further devastation, if not to total annihilation." And the Ihud

---

[15] Hannah Arendt, "The Jew as Paraiah: Jewish Identity and Politics in the Modern Age," in *Prophets Outcast*, ed. Shatz, 85.

alternative to the exclusionist nationalist idea was: "a) Creating a political system based upon equal rights for both peoples; and b) Securing the
support of the expanding Yishuv and the entire Jewish people for a federative union of the Middle East that includes the Land of Israel, which will
guarantee the rights of all its member nations."[16] The members of Ihud
supported one of the basic Zionist claims: that there should be a territorial solution for the Jews of Europe in Palestine. But they claimed that this
solution needed to rely on universal, moral principles. They called for a
Jewish–Arab federation that would be integrated into the region. In the
struggle to locate Zionism between the universal and the particular, the
members of Brith Shalom and Ihud tried to remain within the broader
Zionist fold but to push Jewish nationalism away from what they perceived as bellicose tribalism towards a universal conception of the state as
a multi-ethnic and multi-cultural entity.

Another small group of Jewish intellectuals in Palestine also sought to
reform Jewish nationalism, though in the opposite direction from that
espoused by Magnes and his supporters: they wanted Jews in Palestine to
fully embrace their nativist identity and make Hebrew or Israeli nationalism the core of their ideological worldview: they came to be known as
the Canaanites. The New Hebrews (the Canaanites was a pejorative term
coined by the poet Avraham Shlonski which then became the common
name for the movement) were a small group of writers and intellectuals,
headed by the charismatic poet Yonatan Ratosh, that emerged in Palestine
in the 1940s and the early years of Israeli independence. Most of the
Canaanites came from the Revisionist movement and the pre-State paramilitary organizations affiliated with it: the Irgun and Lehi.

The Revisionists were a Zionist faction founded and led by Vladimir
Ze'ev Jabotinsky, a writer, editor, and one of the more original and controversial Zionist ideologues. Key to Revisionist ideology was the idea of
Jewish power and militarism. Unlike socialist Zionists (the Revisionists'
main ideological foes) who emphasized the role of labor and social institutions as a way to create an independent, self-sufficient Jewish society, the
Revisionists argued that strength, resolve, and military-like discipline were
the chief virtues that could lead Jews to negate millennia of oppression and
persecution; or as Jabotinsky phrased it,

For the generation that grows before our eyes and who will be responsible, probably, for the greatest change in our history, the Aleph Bet has a very simple
sound: young people learn how to shoot ... For one to be a true person, he must

---

[16] "Ihud Platform," in Yosef Gorny, *Mediniyut ve-Dimyon: Tokhniyot Federaliyot ba-*
Maḥashavah ha-Medinit ha-Tsiyonit 1917–1948 (Jerusalem: Yad Ben-Zvi and ha-Sifriyah
Ha-Tsivonit, 1993), 188–190.

study 'culture' in general. To be Jewish, he must know the language and history of his people... But if you will learn how to shoot, there might be hope. This is the language in which the historical reality of our generation and the next generation speaks to us.[17]

To the Revisionist leader and his followers, the creation of a self-sufficient society that works the land was not enough to negate the perceived passivity and haplessness of the Jewish experience in the Diaspora. To Jabotinsky and the Revisionist camp, it was the Jewish solider who represented the most radical and complete negation of the ghetto-dwelling Jew. To them, the Jews will become truly politically independent only when they develop an all-encompassing masculine, military ethos that would replace what they regarded as the effeminate meekness of traditional, Diaspora Judaism.

The Canaanites, who were inspired by Jabotinsky's nationalist worldview, sought to guide the negation of the Jewish past to its logical (from their perspective) conclusion: to renounce Judaism altogether as the defining quality of the new community in Palestine/Israel and adopt a radically new Hebrew identity. They were inspired by new archaeological and linguistic studies that described a pre-Jewish, or pre-monotheistic, Semitic sphere in which the ancient Hebrews, Phoenicians, Amorites, Edomites, Canaanites and other ethnic groups lived side by side using similar languages and worshiping a common pantheon of gods. Judaism, as a monotheistic religion, was to them a product of the Babylonian exile and therefore foreign to the national origins of the Hebrew nation in its ancestral homeland. If the Jews were to return to their homeland, they would have to shed their Jewish (exilic) identity, which was extra-territorial and international in nature, and embrace Hebrew (as a language as well as ethnicity) as their fundamental national characteristic. The Canaanites did not want the state to be defined by a religion – they feared that it would become a theocracy, and instead sought a secular republic. This would also entail, from a Canaanite perspective, severing the organic links between Palestinian Hebrews, residing in the authentic Hebrew region, and Diaspora Jews, and that would lead them ultimately to reject Zionism, which maintained that the movement represents all Jews everywhere. As one of the Canaanite movement's founding documents stated:

There is no Hebrew except a Hebrew who is the son of the Land of Ever, Land of the Hebrew, to the exclusion of all else. And whosoever is not a native of this land, the land of the Hebrews, cannot be a Hebrew, is not a Hebrew and never was a Hebrew. And whosoever comes from the Jewish Diaspora, from all its countries

---

[17] Ze'ev Jabotinsky, "The Fireplace" (On the New Aleph Bet) in *Ketavim: Ba-Derech La-Medinah* (Jerusalem, 1959), 89–90.

and for all its generations, from the beginning to the end of days, is a Jew and not a Hebrew.... And the Jew and the Hebrew can never be identical.[18]

The majority of the Canaanites combined their Hebrew nationalism and their earlier Revisionist leanings to develop a pronounced anti-Arab position in the Arab–Jewish conflict in Palestine. To them, the Arabs were an eastern Semitic people, who violently invaded the Hebrew sphere during the Islamic conquests in the seventh century CE. The Arabic language, they held, was foreign to the region– as was Islam. Instead, they envisioned an authentic Hebrew confederation that would include Palestinian Jews, the Druze, Maronites and Syriac-speaking Christians: some of the non-Muslim groups in the Western Semitic sphere (it is interesting to consider in this context that several decades later Palestinian Arab leaders would describe themselves as descendents of the original Canaanites, while describing the ancient Hebrews as invaders who forcefully, under Joshua, conquered the land).

Not all those who were part of the Canaanite orbit, however, adhered to an anti-Arab position – some of the more original critics of Zionism were influenced early on by Canaanite ideas, but they took the notion of Hebrew identity and arrived at drastically different positions. Hillel Kook (better known by his *nom-de-guerre* Peter Bergson) was a Zionist Revisionist activist who served as the Irgun's (the Revisionists' paramilitary organization in the pre-State era) representative in the United States during the Second World War. He made a name for himself during the war in a series of provocative newspaper ads and campaigns that called for the creation of a Jewish army to battle the Nazis and that challenged the American administration to save Jewish refugees in Europe (this was in stark contradiction to the position of the American Jewish leadership that sought to support the American administration in the overall war effort without singling out the Jewish perspective). By the end of the war, Kook changed his focus and began to lobby the American administration to support the Zionist cause – however, not for a Jewish state but for the creation of a Hebrew state (he established an "embassy" of the Hebrew State in Washington, DC). Influenced by Canaanite notions, Kook argued that the Jews living in the US or Great Britain were Americans or Britons: the future state in Palestine was to be the home of stateless (and therefore

---

[18] "The Opening Discourse: In Executive Session with the Agents of the Cells, First Meeting" in Gideon Shimony, *The Zionist Ideology* (Hanover, NH: Brandeis University Press, 1995), 319. For the most comprehensive analysis of the Canaanites' ideology see James S. Diamond, *Homeland or Holy Land?: The "Canaanite" Critique of Israel* (Bloomongton: Indiana University Press, 1986).

nation-less) Jews – the Jewish refugees all over Europe – and the Jews already residing in Mandatory Palestine.

In a letter to the Zionist leader Chaim Weizmann from 1945, Kook made the following assertions:

> The insistence of Jewish leaders to claim that there is a universal Jewish people, which allows every Jew to be a member of the American, Russian, Argentinean and even the German nation and at the same time to be a member of the "Jewish people," is utterly unrealistic and politically meaningless... Therefore we want the Land of Israel to be a free state and not a "Jewish State"... All that we are demanding... is to put an end to this scandalous condition where a great and ancient nation does not have a territorial homeland. To do that we must clearly understand that the Hebrew nation does not comprise all of the people in the world that are regularly referred to as Jews.[19]

To Kook, in true Canaanite (and Revisionist) manner, Judaism was by its very nature universal and extraterritorial; nationalism, on the other hand, is naturally linked to a specific territory and group of people. Therefore to Kook, Zionism, in order to truly become a national movement, had to shed its false universalism (the movement of all Jews everywhere) and seek new forms of universalism – to create a normal state (like all other states) for those Jews who lack any other form of nationality.

Kook returned to Israel from the US in 1948 and was elected to the first Knesset. According to Israel's Declaration of Independence the first Knesset was supposed to act as a constituent assembly – to draft a constitution for the new state; instead it served as a regular legislative body and Israel to this day does not have a constitution. Kook described this as Ben-Gurion's "putsch"; he believed that a constitution was necessary to define the nature and limits of Israeli nationalism and to sever the unnatural links between Israeli nationalism and Judaism. To Kook, Israel was a theocracy. It perpetuated the ethos of the ghetto – the notion of the eternally persecuted Jew against the entire gentile world. Instead, Kook wanted Israel to become a normal state that judges and treats its citizens as individuals that live under one sovereign ruler. (He sought, for example, to amend the Law of Return, which allowed any Jew to become an Israeli citizen, and instead sought to pass more universal naturalization legislation.) To Kook, this "ghetto siege-mentality" was the reason ultimately that Israel could not achieve peace with its Arab neighbors. As long as the Jewish state saw itself as caught in an existential struggle that involved trans-historical

---

[19] Hillel Kook to Chaim Weizmann, April 2, 1945. Jabotinsky Institute PA/137.

forces, Israel could not focus on achieving real peace and prosperity for its citizens.[20]

Kook argued that in May 1948, with the creation of Israel, the Jewish exile ended. Therefore, he claimed, Israel should not perceive itself as the guardian of all Jews everywhere – but rather as a country responsible for the well-being of everyone who resides in its territory regardless of their religion or ethnicity. And, he maintained, only with this kind of realization could Israel put behind it the kind of permanent emergency under which the state had operated since its inception and explore ways to resolve its conflicts with the Arabs within Israel (whom he claimed should be treated first and foremost as Israelis and only then as Muslims or Christians) and without.

Uri Avinery, who after 1967 became one of the leaders of the Israeli peace camp, made a similar ideological journey to that of Kook: he started in the revisionist Right influenced by Canaanite ideas. Avinery came to Palestine from Germany and he participated, as a member of the Irgun, in the war between Jews and Arabs, which broke out after the UN voted for the partition of Palestine into a Jewish and an Arab state on November 29, 1947. Avinery rose to prominence in the first two decades of Israeli independence as the publisher and editor of *Ha-Olam ha-Zeh* (This world). He used the publication to criticize what he perceived as the tyrannical tendencies of the Labor government under Ben-Gurion. Avinery, who would later become a leader of the Israeli Left, did not criticize Labor from the traditional leftist (socialist) position (in the early 1950s the biggest opposition party was Mapam, a Labor Zionist movement that adhered to a more socialist and pro-Soviet platform than that of Ben-Gurion's Mapai) but rather from a civic, liberal position that called for greater accountability, transparency, and individual expression.

In 1958, Avinery penned a *Hebrew Manifesto* that called on Israel to become a secular democracy and to align itself with other nations in the Third World fighting for national liberation. After the 1967 war, when Israel tripled its size and occupied the West Bank and Gaza Strip with their considerable Palestinian populations, Avinery championed the idea of federation between Israel and a new Arab-Palestinian republic. This, Avinery argued, would solve the problem of both the 1948 Palestinian refugees residing in the West Bank and Gaza as well as those who fled to other Arab countries. Moreover, in true Canaanite fashion, Avinery maintained that this Israeli–Palestinian federation should become part of a broader Semitic Union – a great confederacy of all the states in the region. To Avinery

[20] See Eran Kaplan, "A Rebel with a Cause: Hillel Kook, Begin and Jabotinsky's Ideological Legacy," *Israel Studies* 10, no. 3 (2005): 87–103.

the only reason for the belligerent relations between Jews and Arabs in the Middle East was the Palestinian problem: once this problem has been solved through a federative program, general peace in the region will prevail. Avinery, however, was keen to explain that his program is not some utopian socialist vision of a nation-less society. In fact, he argued, "I am a Hebrew nationalist, and I want to deal with Arab nationalists. I want to tell them: the last fifty years have shown that neither you nor we can achieve our national aspirations as long as we fight each other ... This is what the Semitic idea means – an ideal combining the two nationalisms, an ideal with which nationalists on both sides can identify."[21]

From Avinery's point of view, the overwhelming Israeli victory in 1967 proved that Israel no longer faced real existential threats and that it could transition from a revolutionary society into a normal state. To Avinery, the war proved that the state of emergency under which Israelis lived and which justified in the eyes of many the extreme power of the government (both in the economy but also by imposing military rule on Israel's Arab population) was no longer attainable. And to him, the Semitic Union could be an ideal vehicle to usher in this new chapter in Israeli history. Or as Avinery phrased it,

Joining a great Semitic confederacy would mean, for Israel, putting an end to the Zionist chapter in its history and starting a new one – the chapter of Israel as a state integrated in its region, playing a part in the region's struggle for progress and unity. For the Arabs it would mean recognition of a post-Zionist Israel as part of the region, a part which could and should not be abolished because, in its new form, it is a factor in the struggle for the common good.[22]

Zionism viewed itself as a revolutionary movement. Zionist ideologues from Herzl to Jabotinsky and Ben-Gurion held that only a radical change in the course of the lives of Jews could save them from the dangers of anti-semitism. To Avinery, this position may have been relevant before 1948, when European Jews faced immediate dangers, and to a lesser degree in the 1948–1967 period, when the viability of the Jewish State was still in question. But, Avinery claimed, the revolutionary ethos was no longer needed after the massive show of strength by the Israeli military. In fact, it only put Jews in Israel in greater danger than anywhere else in the world. To him, true nationalism entailed creating the most favorable conditions for individuals to attain peace and prosperity. Therefore, to realize the real goals of Zionism – to create a normal state for Jews – Israelis had to renounce Zionism (they had to treat it like a tool that they no longer need and they

[21] Uri Avinery, "Pax Semitica," in *Prophets Outcast*, ed. Shatz, 216.
[22] Ibid., 216–217.

can simply dispose of) and embrace a new post-Zionist condition – as members of a society that is fully integrated into its surroundings.

Uri Avinery assumed in 1967 that most Israelis would be able to shed their collective existential fears – to become post-Zionists– but he was a leading voice of a rather small group at that time. It would take a more substantial number of Israelis to reach the same position at least two decades later. After the 1967 war Israel experienced two seemingly opposite developments: on the one hand the Arab world rejected any offers to negotiate a peace treaty with Israel based on the formula brought up in UN Resolution 242 of land for peace. And indeed, in the years immediately following 1967, Israel was engaged in a prolonged war of attrition with Syria and Egypt and then in 1973 these two countries launched a surprise war against Israel on Yom Kippur. On the other hand, the victory and conquests of 1967 ushered in a new era of economic prosperity in Israel (a combination of vast new territories and cheap Palestinian labor) that gradually transformed Israel from a socialist, collectivist society into a free-market and more individualistic society. In this regard, Israel was indeed becoming post-Zionist from Avinery's perspective – but it would only be with the peace agreement with Egypt in 1979, the massive public outrage generated by the Israeli invasion of Lebanon in 1982, and the Palestinian Intifada, or uprising, in the late 1980s that broader swaths of the Israeli public – those that benefited from the economic boom and sought peace to advance their new prosperity – began to realize the post-Zionist ethos.

If, as we discussed earlier, Zionism from its inception was torn between universalistic aspirations and its commitment to a particular group, then in the post-Zionist condition, as the sociologist Erik Cohen has suggested, this duality began to unravel: some Israelis (wealthier, secular, and mostly Ashkenazi) sought to accentuate the universal elements of Israeli identity, seeking a more secular and democratic state – while others (religious, working-class Mizrahim Jews from Arab and Muslim countries) tended to cultivate their particular, tribal identities.[23] If for decades, in a collectivist Israel, the socialist Ashkenazim who founded and governed the country represented a universal type of an idealized new Jew, then with the

[23] Erik Cohen, "Israel as a Post-Zionist Society," *Israel Affairs* 1, no. 3 (1995): 203–214. See also Uri Ram, "Post-Zionist Studies of Israel: The First Decade," *Israel Studies Forum* 20, no. 2 (2005): 22–45; Daniel Gutwein, "Left and Right Post-Zionism and the Privatization of Israeli Collective Memory," in *Israeli Historical Revisionism From Left to Right*, ed. Anita Shapira and Derek Penslar (London: Frank Cass Publishers, 2003), 9–42; Ella Shohat, "Sephardim in Israel: Zionism from the Standpoint of Its Jewish Victims," *Social Text* 19/20 (1988): 1–35; Laurence J. Silberstein, *The Postzionism Debates: Knowledge and Power in Israeli Culture* (New York: Routledge, 1999), esp. 89–126.

dismantling of the collectivist ethos a variety of alternative Israeli identities entered the public space (or market) competing for power and control. For the new groups that vied for power, this process involved moving away from some of the old Zionist symbols and values and cultivating new forms of Israeliness. At the same time, parts of the old Israeli elite were reinventing themselves as part of a new globalized world order that no longer needed nationalist symbols (and state control over the markets); this was an elite ready to rid itself of its old myths of creation. It was in this social and cultural climate that a new or revisionist Israeli history and the post-Zionist critique emerged in the late 1980s and the 1990s.

The New Israeli Historians included among others Benny Morris, Ilan Pappe, and Avi Shlaim, and the focus of their studies that first appeared in the late 1980s was the 1948 war. While rather traditional in their methodological approach, these historians sought to upend the traditional view among Israelis (historians as well as the broader public) of their national myth of creation. Instead of the old narrative, which, they claimed, tended to portray Israel as a virtuous David caught in an all but unwinnable battle against a menacing Goliath, the Arab world, they argued that it was the Zionists who were the superior military force at the time; that the most significant outcome of the war was the creation of the Palestinian refugee problem as a direct result of Zionist policies; and that Israel did not seek peace with its neighbors after the war but rather sought to preserve its territorial achievements. Or as Ilan Pappe put it,

> It was a kind of David and Goliath mythology, the Jews being the David, the Arab armies being the Goliath, and again it must be a miracle if David wins against the Goliath. So this is the picture. What we found challenged most of this mythology. First of all, we found out that the Zionist leadership, the Israeli leadership, regardless of the peace plans of the United Nations, contemplated long before 1948 the dispossession of the Palestinians, the expulsion of the Palestinians. So it was not that as a result of the war that the Palestinians lost their homes. It was as a result of a Jewish, Zionist, Israeli – call it what you want – plan that Palestine was ethnically cleansed in 1948 of its original indigenous population.[24]

A confident society (both in its economic and military prowess), it seemed, could begin to openly and freely examine its past – and this is precisely what the New Historians tried to do. As Benny Morris rather pithily put it, "The old historians offered a simplistic and consciously pro-Israel

---

[24] Ilan Pappe, "The History of Israel Reconsidered," a talk at the NIHU Program Islamic Area Studies, University of Tokyo Unit, March 8, 2008. http://ilanpappe.com/?p=56.

interpretation of the past ... The new historians, by contrast, are able to be more impartial."[25]

In the 1990s, the New Historians were joined by a host of critical sociologists, philosophers, literary scholars, and other academics who drew on postmodern and post-colonial theories to debunk core Zionist beliefs and assertions. From this post-Zionist perspective, Zionism, from the very beginning, was not a national liberation movement (as most Zionists tended to portray their movement) that sought to provide refuge to a persecuted minority but rather a European colonial project that allowed Jews, who were denied entry into the modern European political project, to create in the orient a European enclave that at once exploited and excluded the native, colonized population.

From a post-Zionist perspective, Zionists sought to create in the mythical Jewish homeland the very society that they were denied in Europe and they imported all the evils of the modern world: nationalism, militarism, and corporate state mechanisms to the Middle East. From the post-Zionist point of view, Zionists manipulated antisemitism and European guilt, culminating with the Holocaust, to describe Jews as the eternal victims who deserve to dispossess others (Palestinian Arabs) of their native rights in order to create a state for themselves. Moreover, Israel treated Jewish immigrants from Arab and Muslim countries in a similar way, depriving them of their cultural identity and treating them as second-class citizens. As Ariella Azoulay and Adi Ophir, writing from a distinct post-Zionist position, put it,

We [Israel] are the encounter with the Orient that Europe always fantasized and feared ... Now we have an 'inner Orient' and an 'outer Orient' and the clear hierarchy of a master relationship between the 'White Jew' and his two 'Oriental Others' ... We are a laboratory for political and military experiments in various kinds of political messianisms that Europe had invented in the nineteenth century and since the end of the Second World War has worked so hard to forget. Many of those ugly nationalist and racist myths that Europe can no longer present in public...[26]

In a secure country that was engaged in a peace process that held the promise of bringing the Arab–Israeli conflict to a close, and in the era of globalization, when it seemed that international corporations and regional political union (the European Union) were the order of the day,

[25] Benny Morris, "The New Historiography: Israel Confronts Its Past," *Tikkun* 3, no. 6 (1988): 19–23; 99–102. For a critical account of the New Historians see Anita Shapira, "The Strategies of Historical Revisionism," in *Israeli Historical Revisionism*.

[26] Ariella Azoulay and Adi Ophir, "100 Years of Zionism, 50 Years of a Jewish State," *Tikkun* 13, no. 2 (1998): 68–71.

the nation-state may indeed have been viewed as a relic of a dangerous past. And the post-Zionist critique was the most distilled attack on this perceived anachronistic entity from a Jewish perspective.

And what was the post-Zionist alternative to the Jewish state, the culmination of the Zionist project? There is not a clear post-Zionist program, but here Azoulay and Ophir do provide some broad outlines: a weak state that would allow for open social and cultural relations for all those who reside west of the Jordan River. The state will have several official languages (Hebrew, Arabic, Russian, even English), it will have open borders, and universal naturalization laws would replace the Law of Return. In short, a version of the old Ihud bi-national platform or Avinery's Semitic Union set in the age of globalization and transnational corporations and organizations.

One theme that has dominated some segments of the post-Zionist worldview has been the notion of the wandering Jew as the negation of the Zionist New Hebrew. From a post-Zionist perspective, if the New Hebrew came to symbolize power and oppression (at the expense of Zionism's oriental "others") then the wandering Jew, the one who is not tied to a specific political – or any other rational, administrative – order, represents a moral alternative that eschews all the dangerous trappings of power and control.

The post-Zionist fascination with the wandering, exilic Jew is not new: thinkers from Lyotard to Derrida have cultivated an image of the wandering Jew as a signifier of radical otherness that escapes the limitations of systematic rationality. From a distinct post-Holocaust critique of enlightenment rationality and its projects of power and destruction, the ghetto Jew, the eternal target of European derision, emerged as a symbol that undermines the very core of the enlightenment idea and its political implications. To the post-Zionists, the State of Israel was a direct descendant of the (dark side) of the enlightenment project – and therefore the exilic, wandering Jew was the perfect negation of the Zionist idea. Post-Zionist thinkers did not necessarily advocate a full rejection of secularism in favor of an Orthodox Jewish way of life. Instead, they suggested that Jews in Israel should embrace a "diasporic" mentality: one that renounces power in favor of full acceptance of the other. Instead of proud strong Jews, they called for a new ethos that comes from a position of weakness and therefore can fully empathize with the plight of the very victims of the Zionist project. But, of course, one cannot ignore the fact that the ability to imagine such a radical transformation already assumes that Jews in Israel/Palestine have achieved such levels of security (and power) that they no longer need the state or other symbols of power to sustain them.

Using old Marxist concepts, this post-Zionist position is a version of the negation of the negation formula. If Zionism was a negation of Diaspora Judaism (and this was the core of Haredi opposition to Zionism), then post-Zionism is the negation of the negation, an elevation of certain aspects of Diaspora Judaism as a negation of the Zionist ethos. And in true dialectical fashion, this does not mean a return (physical or spiritual) to the Jewish ghetto of the past, but rather importing (real or imagined) aspects of the Jewish exilic condition and trying to integrate them into an existing Jewish state. In this regard, the history of the criticism of Zionism has come full circle. Zionism's first critics, Orthodox Jews, posited that only traditional Jewish life could save the Jewish people in the long run. Contemporary post-Zionists similarly argue that only by adopting the moral position of the detached, wandering Jew is there a future for the Jews living in Palestine (and elsewhere – because Israeli policies, from this perspective, jeopardize the well-being of Jews everywhere in the world). In this regard, the very particular condition of the Jew is used as a marker of a new kind of universality – which makes post-Zionism a direct heir of the Zionist project that too sought to resolve the tensions between the singular historical condition of the Jews and the desire for a universal solution to the Jewish problem. To put it differently, Zionism was a revolutionary movement that sought to radically alter the course of Jewish history; post-Zionism, in a Toquevillian manner, is decidedly anti-revolutionary. As such, it is both a critique of Zionism but also an affirmation of its revolutionary success.

SELECT BIBLIOGRAPHY

Avinery, Shlomo. *The Making of Modern Zionism: The Intellectual Origins of the Jewish State.* New York: Basic books, 1981.

Azoulay, Ariella and Ophir, Adi. "100 Years of Zionism, 50 Years of a Jewish State," *Tikkun* 13, no. 2 (1998): 68–71.

Diamant, Carol, ed. *Zionism: The Sequel.* New York: Hadassah, 1998.

Diamond, James S. *Homeland or Holy Land?: The "Canaanite" Critique of Israel.* Bloomington: Indiana University Press, 1986.

Ganz, Chaim. *A Just Zionism: On the Morality of the Jewish State.* New York: Oxford University Press, 2008.

Hermann, Tamar S. *The Israeli Peace Movement: A Shattered Dream.* New York: Cambridge University Press, 2009.

Kaplan, Eran and Penslar, Derek, eds. *The Origins of Israel, 1882–1948: A Documentary History.* Madison: University of Wisconsin Press, 2011.

Kushner, Tony and Solomon, Alisa, eds. *Wrestling with Zion: Progressive Jewish-American Responses to the Israeli-Palestinian Conflict.* New York: Grove Press, 2003.

Morris, Benny. "The New Historiography: Israel Confronts Its Past," *Tikkun* 3, no. 6 (1988): 19–23; 99–102.

One State, Two States. New Haven: Yale University Press, 2009.

Penslar, Derek. *Israel in History: The Jewish State in Comparative Perspective*. London: Routledge, 2007.

Presner, Todd Samuel. *Muscular Judaism: The Jewish Body and the Politics of Regeneration*. New York: Routledge, 2007.

Ram, Uri. "Post-Zionist Studies of Israel: The First Decade," *Israel Studies Forum* 20, no. 2 (2005): 22–45.

Ravitzky, Aviezer. *Messianism, Zionism, and Jewish Religious Radicalism*. Chicago: University of Chicago Press, 1996.

Shapira, Anita and Penslar, Derek, eds. *Israeli Historical Revisionism From Left to Right*. London: Frank Cass Publishers, 2003.

Shatz, Adam, ed. *Prophets Outcast: A Century of Dissident Jewish Writing about Zionism and Israel*. New York: Nation Books, 2004.

Shimoni, Gideon. *The Zionist Ideology*. Hanover, NH: Brandeis University Press, 1995.

Shohat, Ella. "Sephardim in Israel: Zionism from the Standpoint of Its Jewish Victims," *Social Text* 19/20 (1988): 1–35.

Silberstein, Laurence J. *The Postzionism Debates: Knowledge and Power in Israeli Culture*. New York: Routledge, 1999.

ed. *Postzionism: A Reader*. New Brunswick, NJ: Rutgers University Press, 2008.

Sprinzak, Ehud. *Brother against Brother: Violence and Extremism in Israeli Politics from Altalena to the Rabin Assassination*. New York: The Free Press, 1999.

CHAPTER 23

THE HOLOCAUST AND ITS AFTERMATH

SAMUEL KASSOW

INTRODUCTION

The Holocaust (*Shoah* in Hebrew, *Khurbn* in Yiddish) commonly refers to the Nazi implemented and Nazi inspired persecution of the Jews that claimed close to six million Jewish lives between 1939 and 1945. It destroyed the great centers of Yiddish-speaking Eastern European Jewry as well as the surviving strongholds of Ladino speaking Jewry in Greece and the Balkans. The disaster decimated Jewish communities in Central and Western Europe and even threatened to engulf the Jews of Tunisia. After the Holocaust, the centers of world Jewry shifted to Israel and to North America.

While a general historical term like "Holocaust" implies a discrete event with a clear beginning and end, the actual destruction of European Jewry was a complex process that involved many actors, many collaborators, and killing that ranged from bureaucratically planned deportations to spontaneous pogroms in hundreds of remote locales. Millions died in the death factories of the extermination camps but millions of others died by bullets in hastily dug pits or were beaten and tortured to death by neighbors whom they had known their entire lives (in towns like Jedwabne in Poland or in many Lithuanian townlets in the summer of 1941). In Romania and Croatia killers acted without any German supervision and often used methods that appalled even the SS. Nazi Germany took the lead in the Holocaust but other countries and individuals from other ethnic groups also joined the killing, albeit with varying degrees of enthusiasm and with differing motives that ran the gamut from hatred of Jews, crass opportunism, a desire to curry favor with the Germans, a determination to remove all minorities, and, of course, sheer greed. The looting of Jewish possessions ranged from valuable artworks and whole corporations to household goods and clothing that were sold to eager German consumers at bargain basement prices.

Study of the Holocaust has produced many scholarly controversies, including the decision-making process that led to the Final Solution; the

THE MODERN WORLD, 1815–2000

conduct of Jewish leadership under Nazi occupation; the scope and definition of Jewish resistance; and the actions of "bystanders" such as the Vatican or various Allied governments. Intense debates have also swirled around such issues as the attitudes of various European populations to the murder of the Jews and whether Jews in the free world and in the Yishuv in Palestine made a sufficient effort to help their beleaguered brethren.

Scholars have also debated to what degree the concept of "genocide" – a term invented by Raphael Lemkin in 1944 and codified by the UN Genocide Convention in 1948 – can apply to the Holocaust.[1] To what degree was the Holocaust unique or to what extent did it resemble other genocides? For Lemkin, genocide did not necessarily entail the physical murder of an entire people but could also include lesser measures meant to eradicate a group's cultural identity. Thus the Nazi murders of the Polish intelligentsia or Stalin's starvation war on the Ukrainian peasants in 1931–1933 could also qualify as genocide.

In her 1962 book *Eichmann in Jerusalem* Hannah Arendt criticized the State of Israel for charging Eichmann as a killer of Jews rather than as a perpetrator of genocide, which, she emphasized, was an entirely new crime. Produced by the multiple crises of modern politics, genocide, Arendt stressed, could well recur in new venues with a new cast of victims.[2] Other scholars such as Zygmunt Bauman also stressed the key role of modernity, and especially modern bureaucracy in executing the Holocaust.[3] Modernity, with its overarching narratives of total explanation and control and its dynamic bureaucracies facilitated projects of ethnic cleansing and terror aimed at producing homogeneity and obedience. The Holocaust was monstrous but hardly unique.

On the other hand, scholars such as Yehuda Bauer and Steven Katz have questioned the usefulness of defining the Holocaust mainly as a genocide or as a specific byproduct of modernity. It was, they argue, a singular event.[4] What made the Holocaust different was the absolutely central

---

[1] A useful introduction can be found in Alan Rosenbaum ed. *Is the Holocaust Unique?* (Boulder: Westview, 2009); also Yehuda Bauer, *Rethinking the Holocaust* (New Haven: Yale University Press, 2000).

[2] Hannah Arendt, *Eichmann in Jerusalem: A Report on the Banality of Evil* (New York: Viking, 1963).

[3] Zygmunt Bauman, *Modernity and the Holocaust* (Ithaca: Cornell University Press, 1989). In this regard the classic ground breaking study remains Raul Hilberg, *The Destruction of the European Jews*, revised and definitive edition (New York: Holmes and Meier, 1985). See also Mark Levene, "Why is the Twentieth Century the Century of Genocide?," *Journal of World History* 11, no. 2 (2000): 305–336.

[4] Steven T. Katz, *The Holocaust in Historical Context, Volume I: The Holocaust and Mass Death before the Modern Age* (New York, Oxford University Press, 1994).

role of antisemitism in a Nazi state which used its manifold resources to track down and murder every last Jew. Unlike previous persecutions, Jews could no longer save themselves through abandoning their faith. As Saul Friedländer pointed out, the Third Reich created a "redemptive anti-Semitism," whose quasi-religious mission was to save the world by killing the Jews: all of them.[5]

For Hitler, the Jews were not exactly sub-human but more precisely monstrous anti-humans possessed of an uncanny ability to worm their way into host civilizations and destroy them from within. In various venues, Hitler referred to Jews as vermin, viruses, parasites, and maggots. On July 22, 1941, he told a Croatian Marshal Kvaternik that

for even if just one state for whatever reason tolerates one Jewish family in it, then this will become the bacillus source for a new decomposition. If there were no more Jews in Europe, then the unity of the European states would no longer be destroyed. Where one will send the Jews, to Siberia or to Madagascar is all the same. (Hitler) will demand of every state (to get rid of their Jews).[6]

When Hitler said this to Kvaternik, the mass shooting of Jews in Soviet territories had already begun. Within two weeks of this meeting, the German killing squads would begin the murder of Jewish children.

For Hitler, history was about racial struggle, not the individual, or moral progress. If a race did not conquer land and resources it would go under. And the German race, Hitler believed, faced an existential crisis produced by two factors. First it entered the Great Game of conquest much too late, and when it did, it wrongly focused on overseas colonies rather than on the huge open spaces of Eastern Europe, where its true destiny lay. Second, the Jews had so infiltrated German life and institutions – through the press, banks, unions, newspapers, theaters – that they had almost destroyed the healthy racial instinct of the German nation. In 1918, they had, Hitler believed, stabbed Germany in the back when they fomented mutiny and revolution. Without the will to rise up and wrest the vast territories in the East, the Germans would go under. Hitler saw himself as the savior and redeemer who had appeared at the last possible moment.[7]

---

[5] Saul Friedländer, *Nazi Germany and the Jews: The Years of Persecution* (New York: Harper Collins, 1997).

[6] Quoted in Christopher Browning, *The Origins of the Final Solution: the Evolution of Nazi Jewish Policy, September 1939–March 1942* (Lincoln and Jerusalem: University of Nebraska Press and Yad Vashem, 2004).

[7] There is a vast literature on this subject. Some good starting points are Eberhard Jackel, *Hitler's Weltanschauung: A Blueprint for Power* (Middletown: Wesleyan University Press, 1972); Ian Kershaw, *Hitler, 1889–1936: Hubris* (New York: W. W. Norton, 1999); Ian Kershaw, *Hitler, 1936–1945: Nemesis* (New York, W. W. Norton, 2000).

While the Nazis did not decide to murder the Jews until sometime in the second half of 1941, the very nature of Hitler's antisemitism logically entailed from the very onset at least the fantasy of using radical means to solve a Jewish Question that was the world's greatest single problem. Traditional Christian antisemitism, in which the Jews were cursed for having killed Christ, certainly led to outbursts of violence against Jews. And in singling out the Jews as a despised other, Christianity contributed in no small way to prejudices that facilitated indifference to the Jews' plight or even collaboration in the Holocaust. But Christian antisemitism in no way implied killing as a solution to the Jewish problem. Jews could convert, or if they refused to do so, their very status as nomad pariahs would serve as welcome corroboration of the truth of Christian doctrine. But when Jews became the equivalent of malevolent and cunning vermin, then their "removal" demanded a final solution that went beyond emigration or even segregation.

Therefore the old debate between "intentionalists" and "functionalists" about whether the main impetus for the Holocaust came from Hitler's demonic hatred or from a more impersonal process of cumulative radicalization brought about by the pressure of war and bureaucratic zeal has been superseded by a new consensus that has recognized the interplay of ideology and circumstance, of center and periphery, and, above all, of the critical importance of antisemitism in the entire structure of the Third Reich.[8] Rudolph Hess, in a rare moment of lucidity, proclaimed that Nazism was "applied biology," and this determination to change the world through bold racial engineering captured the imagination of many ambitious officials and professionals eager, as Ian Kershaw noted, "to work towards the Führer," to anticipate Hitler's will. If race was the core value of the Third Reich, then antisemitism was its indispensable and ubiquitous source of energy. As Peter Longerich has pointed out, the Nazis had a much easier time defining race in negative terms than in positive terms. Exactly what was an Aryan? One German joke proclaimed that an ideal Aryan had to be as "blond as Hitler, as lean as Goering, as handsome as Himmler and as lithe as Goebbels." Given the scientific flimsiness of Nazi race theory, it became all the more critical to focus on the Jews as the antithesis of proper racial integrity. What mattered was to prove that one was not a Jew. Only then could one build a *Volksgemeinschaft* (a racial community) defined

---

[8] Insightful summaries and discussions of these controversies can be found in Dan Stone, *Histories of the Holocaust* (New York: Oxford University Press, 2010); Saul Friedländer, "The Extermination of the European Jews in Historiography: Fifty Years Later" in *The Holocaust: Origins, Implementation, Aftermath*, ed. Omer Bartov (London: Routledge, 2000), 79–91.

by exclusion, that was, as Peter Fritszche explained, "just us" (*unter uns*).[9] Thus cleansing German society of the Jewish taint became the vector that allowed Nazi racism to permeate ever-wider sectors of German society.

For a time many scholars who saw the Holocaust as "genocide" or who supported the "functionalist" approach tended to downplay the salience of antisemitism and Nazi ideology. Hannah Arendt saw Adolf Eichmann as a particularly dangerous product of the modern state, an example of the "banality of evil." Personally indifferent to Jews, not particularly anti-semitic, Eichmann, Arendt argued, facilitated mass murder because he was ambitious, aimed to please his superiors, and respected the law. This same tendency to minimize the importance of antisemitism surfaced in Christopher Browning's important study of a German police battalion, *Ordinary Men*. Browning examined the motives of middle-aged policemen from Hamburg who participated in the face-to face-shooting of Jews in Poland in July 1942. The major reason they participated in a direct murder that they could have easily avoided, Browning argued, was peer pressure, not antisemitism or Nazi indoctrination.

In every modern society, the complexity of life and the resulting bureaucratization and specialization attenuate the sense of personal responsibility of those implementing official policy. Within virtually every social collective, the peer group exerts enormous pressures on behavior and sets moral norms. If the men of Reserve Police Battalion 101 could become killers under such circumstances, what group of men cannot?[10]

While Browning entitled his book *Ordinary Men*, Daniel Goldhagen, who studied the actions of the same police battalion, entitled his book *Hitler's Willing Executioners: Ordinary Germans and the Holocaust*.[11] The difference in the titles was telling. Where Browning cast a wide net and speculated that any society might produce such killers, Goldhagen set his sights directly on the Germans and their culture, which was supposedly suffused with "eliminationist anti-Semitism." This centuries-old hatred of Jews made many ordinary Germans all too happy to take part in mass murder. While many scholars rejected much of Goldhagen's thesis, his book did encourage a shift in focus away from impersonal agents such as states and bureaucracies and towards the actual motivations of perpetrators. And

[9] Peter Fritzsche, *Life and Death in the Third Reich* (Cambridge: Belknap Press, Harvard, 2008).

[10] Christopher Browning, *Ordinary Men: Reserve Police Battalion 101 and the Final Solution in Poland* (New York: Harper Collins, 1992).

[11] Daniel Goldhagen, *Hitler's Willing Executioners: Ordinary Germans and the Holocaust* (New York: Knopf, 1996).

although Goldhagen's notion of a German culture marked by elimination-ist hatred of Jews got little support from historians, what did begin to receive more attention was the impact of Nazi propaganda and indoctrin-ation on the attitudes of ordinary Germans towards Jews. For example, Omer Bartov in his classic study of the Wehrmacht showed how the Third Reich effectively turned ordinary German soldiers into convinced haters of Jews and Slavs.[12]

To recognize the importance of antisemitism is not to deny the place of the Holocaust in a wider continuum of Nazi racial policy that aimed at a vast, utopian scheme of ethnic cleansing, forced migrations, and the opening up of enormous new vistas in Eastern Europe for domination by German settlers. Nazi plans included the mass murder of many categories of undesirables, including Germans who were feebleminded or mentally ill (the T4 program), many Sinti and Roma, Polish intellectuals, and other "surplus Slavs" who were not needed for forced labor.[13] Before the inva-sion of Russia, in June 1941, German planners casually assumed that as a result of massive German food shipments from the East to the Reich after victory, up to thirty million Soviet citizens would starve to death in the first year of German rule.[14] But within this racist Weltanschauung, it was radical antisemitism that provided cohesion and that served as a bridge to attract collaborationists from other nations. No matter how ruthlessly the Third Reich treated Russians or Poles, only the Jews were slated for total extermination.

II

Hitler led the assault on European Jewry, but he would have had fewer willing helpers had it not been for the effects of World War I and its after-math. Years of fighting coarsened sensibilities, brutalized entire societies, and cheapened the value of human life.[15] The war was followed, in Central and Eastern Europe, by armed conflict, massive violence, and political rad-icalization brought about by the Bolshevik Revolution and confrontation between anti and pro-communist forces.

[12] Omer Bartov, *Hitler's Army: Soldiers, Nazis and War in the Third Reich* (New York: Oxford University Press, 1991).

[13] Michael Burleigh and Wolfgang Wippermann, *Racial State: Germany 1933–1945* (New York: Cambridge University Press, 1991).

[14] A good discussion of this can be found in Adam Tooze, *Wages of Destruction: the Making and Breaking of the Nazi Economy* (New York: Viking, 2007).

[15] See for example Deborah Dwork and Robert Jan van Pelt, *The Holocaust: a History* (New York: Norton, 2002).

The 1914–1921 period saw an ominous escalation and transformation of antisemitism. During World War I the Russian military expelled hundreds of thousands of Jews from their homes and accused them of sabotage and treachery. In the Russian Civil War of 1918–1921, pogroms committed by various sides – mainly the forces of the Ukrainian Directory and the Volunteer Army – claimed up to 100,000 Jewish lives. What made these pogroms especially lethal was the targeted mass murder of Jews in order to combat Bolshevism. This theme of targeting the Jews in order to defend Russia (or Ukraine, or Poland) against the Bolsheviks not only increased the number of victims but intensified the sheer brutality of anti-Jewish violence, where the victims included women and children. Gratuitous torture was not uncommon. Many pogroms were carefully planned.

As Oleg Budnitskii has pointed out, in certain important respects, these pogroms of 1918–1919 can be seen as a prelude to the Holocaust.[16] In many towns the entire Jewish population was singled out for destruction. After the Bolsheviks won the civil war, émigrés from Russia spread the alarm about a Moscow-centered Jewish assault on Western civilization. In the immediate post war period, the notorious forgery, *The Protocols of the Elders of Zion*, enjoyed wide popularity, even in the United States, where Henry Ford serialized it in the *Dearborn Independent*. The *Protocols* disseminated the fear of a worldwide Jewish conspiracy, given credence by the rise of the new Soviet regime supposedly created by the Jews. This new wave of antisemitism fueled by anti-communism certainly played a role in the passing of the Johnson–Reid bill of 1924, which severely limited immigration into the United States, especially from Eastern and Southern Europe. Had Jews enjoyed the same opportunities for emigration in the 1930s and 1940s that they used after the pogroms of 1905 and 1906, then it is quite unlikely that the Holocaust would have taken the form it did.

The aftermath of World War I affected the status of Jews in other ways as well. In the new states that replaced the Russian and Habsburg empires, as well as in a truncated Hungary and an expanded Romania, resentment of Jews increased. Hungarian elites, who had needed Jews before World War I to spread Magyar culture in Slovakia and Transylvania, now saw them as hated, superfluous aliens. In Poland, the Baltic States, and Romania, Jews fell victim to a nasty zero-sum game, where Jews were seen as unwanted competitors for scarce resources in a period of economic depression. Thanks to the leadership of Tomáš Masaryk, political antisemitism was held in

---

[16] Oleg Budnitskii, *Russian Jews between the Reds and the Whites, 1917–1920* (Philadelphia: University of Pennsylvania Press, 2012).

check in interwar Czechoslovakia, but Slovak resentment of Prague's domination also had an anti-Jewish tinge.[17]

While post-war Germany did not see anti-Jewish violence on the scale of
the Russian Civil War, it did suffer a series of traumas that also intensified
antisemitism. When Germany surrendered, in November 1918, millions
of German troops were still on foreign soil while not one Allied soldier
stood on German soil. The legend that Germany did not lose the war on
the battlefield but was stabbed in the back by a Jewish-Bolshevik-Socialist
conspiracy became a staple of right-wing interwar German politics. The
stigma of defeat – exacerbated by large scale violence between Right and
Left as well as the perceived humiliation of Versailles – tarnished a Weimar
Republic that had to cope with the hyperinflation of 1923 and the onset
of a savage world Depression beginning in 1929. Germany's Jewish population once again became a conspicuous target. Jews, who made up less
than one percent of the population, took the blame for hyperinflation, for
depression, and for their "impudent" attempt to take over the professions
and major aspects of German cultural life, where they were numerous and
conspicuous.[18]

Were it not for the Great Depression, the Weimar Republic might have
gained legitimacy and stability. The rise of Nazism was far from inevitable.
In 1928, in the last elections before the onset of the Depression, Hitler and
the Nazis polled only 2.8 percent of the vote. But once a political crisis set
in, emergency rule replaced normal parliamentary government, and by
July 1932 the Nazis had become the largest single party in the Reichstag
with 230 seats. Indeed, the Nazis and Communists together polled more
than half the total vote. Nonetheless, by the end of 1932 Hitler was beginning to lose support. What saved him was a cabal of conservative opportunists who persuaded an elderly President Hindenburg to appoint him
Chancellor on January 30, 1933.

Hitler quickly bolstered his popularity, and built a "Hitler myth," to
borrow Ian Kershaw's term, that was quite distinct from mass support of
the Nazi party. He cleverly combined a yearning for revolutionary change
with a façade of legality and order. Hitler did not lead a "March on Berlin"
but consolidated his power in an apparently "legal way"; the assumption
of the Chancellorship, the Enabling Act of 1933, his assumption of the
role of Führer after the death of President Hindenburg in 1934, the clever
staging of plebiscites, all paved the way for growing acceptance of Hitler's

---

[17] Ezra Mendelsohn, *The Jews of East Central Europe between the Two World Wars*
(Bloomington: Indiana University Press, 1983).

[18] See for example Donald Niewyk, *The Jews in Weimar Germany* (Baton Rouge: Louisiana
State University Press, 1980).

legitimacy. Even his murder of SA cronies and political opponents on June 30, 1934, bolstered his image as a sane leader who wanted to protect the nation from instability and mayhem. One indication of his growing popularity was the overwhelming vote of the Saargebiet – an industrial area hardly known for Nazi leanings – to rejoin the Reich in 1935. When Hitler assumed the chancellorship in January 1933 some key power centers remained outside his control, especially the foreign office, the Presidency, and the Army. But by 1938 no one in Germany could challenge his rule and through his position as Führer, his word had the force of law. In the process his rule rested as much on his charisma and genuine popularity as it did on fear and terror. The progressive abrogation of the hated Versailles Treaty, the march into the Rhineland, the Anschluss with Austria, and economic recovery, ensured his standing with the German people.[19]

Hitler's racial antisemitism was hardly new, and its major contours had already emerged by the late nineteenth century. What made it so significant were the particular political skills of Hitler himself. There were hundreds of right-wing populist rabble rousers in the post-Versailles chaos of Central Europe, but what set Hitler apart was his sense of timing, an appreciation of the aesthetic dimensions of politics and leadership, honed by a fascination with Wagner and Nietzsche and a keen understanding of mass psychology. Hitler's hatred of Jews may have formed the core of his view of the world, but he understood that while many Germans shared various degrees of anti-semitism, they did not necessarily demand radical solutions of the Jewish Problem.

Pragmatism and caution thus tempered Hitler's first anti-Jewish initiatives. While elements in the Nazi movement, and especially the SA, demanded immediate boycott of Jewish shops and takeover of Jewish assets, Hitler understood that Germany was economically vulnerable and that his own grip on power was by no means solid. He authorized only a one-day boycott of Jewish stores on April 1, 1933 and called for the elimination of Jews from the civil service. But provisions that exempted war veterans at first tempered the impact of these measures and furthered hopes among German Jews that they might be able to wait the Nazis out until better times came.

The initial anti-Jewish legislation emphasized legal action rather than violence to tame the Jews' alleged outsize influence in German professional and cultural life (although plenty of violence in fact occurred before 1938). And these measures garnered fervent support from large sections of German elites. Universities, lawyers' guilds, and medical associations moved in to

---

[19] See Kershaw, *Hitler: Hubris*.

purge Jewish colleagues. Churches also gave qualified approval.[20] While the Catholic Church attacked Nazi racial ideology, many of its leaders agreed that Jews exercised a harmful influence on German culture and were all too prominent in European communism. The Vatican Concordat with Hitler in June 1933 paved the way for a modus vivendi between Hitler and the German Catholic church. Protestants were even more accommodating. The Evangelical Church staunchly supported the elimination of Jews from public life while some leading theologians elaborated the idea of an Aryan Jesus, untainted by Jewishness. Dissenting Protestants such as Martin Niemöller and Dietrich Bonhoeffer opposed the Nazis, but they too, at least in the early years of the Third Reich, also agreed on the alleged dangers posed by Jewish overrepresentation in German cultural life.[21]

A major milestone on the "twisted road to Auschwitz," to borrow Karl Schleunes's phrase, was the passage of the Nuremberg Laws in September 1935.[22] These Laws, along with subsequent commentaries, established the legal definition of a Jew, and thus prepared the bureaucratic and administrative foundation for the Final Solution – which at that point no one yet foresaw. Once the definition was in place, it paved the way for the torrent of restrictive legislation that followed, especially after 1938. A Jew was someone with three Jewish grandparents (even if they had converted to another faith) or someone with two Jewish grandparents who was married to a Jew or who was a member of a Jewish religious community. Those with two or one Jewish grandparent were classified as *Mischlinge* (half breeds) of the first or second degree. The Nuremberg Laws constituted the legal abrogation of Jewish Emancipation. German Jews were no longer citizens (*Staatsbürger*) but subjects of the State (*Staatsangehörige*). Marriages or sexual relations between Germans and Jews were forbidden.

Ironically, some German Jews greeted the Nuremberg Laws with relief. For those who still had their shops and small businesses, the laws made no mention of expropriation. Perhaps, they reasoned, the Nuremberg Laws

[20] Saul Friedländer, *Nazi Germany and the Jews: The Years of Persecution, 1933–1939* (New York: Harper Collins, 1997).

[21] Some useful studies are Susannah Heschel, *The Aryan Jesus: Christian Theologians and the Bible in Nazi Germany* (Princeton: Princeton University Press, 2008); Doris Bergen, *Twisted Cross: the German Christian Movement in the Third Reich* (Chapel Hill: University of North Carolina Press, 1996); Ernst Helmreich, *The German Churches under Hitler: Background, Struggle and Epilogue* (Detroit: Wayne State University Press, 1979); Gunter Lewy, *The Catholic Church and Nazi Germany* (New York: McGraw Hill, 1964); Richard Gutteridge, *Open Thy Mouth for the Dumb! The German Evangelical Church and the Jews, 1879–1950* (Oxford, Oxford University Press, 1976).

[22] Karl Schleunes, *The Twisted Road to Auschwitz: Nazi Policy toward German Jews, 1933–1939* (Urbana: University of Illinois Press, 1990).

would mark the worst of the Nazi anti-Jewish onslaught, the outlines of a modus vivendi that many Jews could accept. Many German Jews still managed to keep their economic footing. Zionists welcomed the fact that many previously assimilated Jews were showing a new appreciation of Jewish culture. Jews adapted to the new circumstances, with new initiatives in culture and education.

On the other hand, many Jews, especially young people, began to think of emigration. There were formidable obstacles, caused in large part by the economic depression. While the United States had a relatively high German quota, consuls had a great deal of leeway in rejecting applicants who might become a "public charge." Other countries had similar restrictions.[23]

The Nazis' priority in the 1930s was to force Jews to emigrate, even as the takeover of Austria and the dismemberment of Czechoslovakia brought greater numbers of Jews under Nazi rule. Between 1933 and the outbreak of the war in September 1939, 282,000 German Jews and 117,000 Austrian Jews had managed to leave. 95,000 went to the US, 60,000 to Palestine, 40,000 to Britain and 75,000 to Central and South America. 17,000 ended up in Shanghai, which did not require visas. During the 10 months between Kristallnacht in November 1938 and the outbreak of war in September 1939, restrictions on emigration loosened somewhat. President Roosevelt combined the German and Austrian quotas and ordered them filled, even as he refused to expend political capital on initiatives to admit Jews over established quota limits. At the same time, Britain agreed to admit unaccompanied children (the *Kindertransports*) as well as Jews who had prospects of emigrating to other countries. Between 1933 and 1936 Palestine also became a major destination of emigrants from Germany. This process was facilitated by the controversial Haavara agreement signed between the Jewish Agency and the Third Reich, which allowed emigrants to transfer some of their wealth to Palestine in the form of German products which, when sold, provided valuable indirect export earnings to the Reich. The emigration of German Jews to Palestine gave a major boost to the economy of the Yishuv at a critical time.

The vicious nationwide pogrom of November 9/10, 1938 – known as Kristallnacht (the Night of the Broken Glass) – removed what doubts Jews had about emigration. It also represented a fateful new escalation of Nazi persecution of the Jews.[24]

---

[23] David Wyman, *Paper Walls: America and the Refugee Crisis, 1938–1941* (New York: Pantheon Books, 1985); Deborah Dwork and Robert Jan van Pelt, *Flight from the Reich: Refugee Jews, 1933–1946* (New York: W. W. Norton, 2009).

[24] Alan E. Steinweis, *Kristallnacht, 1938* (Cambridge: Harvard University Press, 2009); Marion Kaplan, *Between Dignity and Despair: Jewish Life in Nazi Germany*

At 9:35 am Monday morning November 7, 1938, a young Jew named Herschel Grynszpan, distraught over the sudden and brutal deportation of his family and 17,000 other Polish Jews from Germany, walked into the German Embassy in Paris and shot Ernst vom Rath, a 29-year-old junior diplomat. Vom Rath died of his wounds on November 9 – a Nazi day of commemoration and the twentieth anniversary of the start of the German Revolution of 1918. A few hours after vom Rath died, Hitler allowed Josef Goebbels to authorize a massive assault on German Jewry. Before the violence abated late on the following day, squads of storm troopers helped by rampaging mobs had murdered 91 Jews, beaten hundreds more, and pillaged and smashed over 7,500 Jewish shops. Firemen stood by and watched as 267 synagogues went up in flames. They followed orders: let the synagogues burn and protect adjoining buildings. Police stations ignored frantic telephone calls from Jews calling for help as marauding thugs smashed their furniture, terrorized their wives and children, and assaulted them in their own homes.

The November pogrom of 1938 was a collective nightmare of thousands of humiliations and atrocities – such as a scene in the town of Elberstadt, described by Saul Friedländer, where an elderly Jewish woman was wantonly murdered in her apartment, or when sick Jews from a hospital were forced to walk across broken glass.[25] That same day, November 10, German police rounded up 30,000 male Jews and sent them to concentration camps.

Kristallnacht erupted about three years before Germany began the "Final Solution" of the Jewish Question. The horror unfolded in plain view, not in far-off Poland or Ukraine but in posh Berlin shopping streets and small town squares. While most Germans recoiled from the violence and the property damage, it was nonetheless true that the mobs that hounded and humiliated Jews included not just Storm Troopers but many ordinary citizens. And, especially in small towns, these mobs were jeering, beating, and humiliating neighbors, well-known shopkeepers and merchants, trusted physicians and dentists, former friends, people who had been a familiar part of the community. If at least some Germans could kill and beat their neighbors in 1938, then they had already crossed a moral line that, a few years later, made the unthinkable distinctly possible.

In the past, Hitler had been leery of pogroms. But by November 1938 Hitler had an urgent timetable. His armaments program had mortgaged the German economy to the hilt, and he had reached the point where he would have to accelerate his takeover of Eastern Europe – preferably

(New York: Oxford University Press, 1998); Deborah Dwork and Robert Jan van Pelt, *Flight from the Reich*.
[25] Friedländer, *Nazi Germany and the Jews: The Years of Persecution*.

through intimidation and diplomacy, but with violence and war as a real option. Would Britain and France continue their policy of appeasement or would they finally go to war?

Hitler was convinced that world Jewry – the Jewish "wirepullers" – was working behind the scenes to drag the British and French into a war with the Reich. If one goal of Kristallnacht was to force the Jews to get out, another was to send a warning to the Jews to stop working against Germany. On January 30, 1939, in a Reichstag speech, Hitler put the Jews on notice:

Today I want to be a prophet again. If international finance Jewry inside and outside Europe succeeds in pushing the nations into a world war, the result will not be the Bolshevization of the earth and with it the victory of Jewry, but the annihilation of the Jewish race in Europe.

On September 1, 1939, Hitler invaded Poland. Two days later France and Britain declared war on Germany. Germany quickly crushed Poland and in the spring of 1940 conquered Denmark, Norway, France, Belgium, and the Netherlands. Britain stubbornly refused to make a separate peace, and in late 1940 Hitler ordered his generals to plan for an invasion of the Soviet Union, Operation Barbarossa.

Some military historians have asserted that Hitler could have won the war had he crushed Britain in North Africa and the Middle East rather than invade the USSR. Going south certainly made sense from a military point of view. But what counted in 1941 was not rationality but ideology. Hitler's life-long dream was to secure *Lebensraum*, or living space, in the East, and to do that, he had to destroy the Soviet Union and its sponsor, Jewry.

When the war began in 1939 Germany's Jewish policy still focused on emigration, spearheaded by the SS and Adolf Eichmann's Central Office for Jewish Emigration. But the outbreak of war derailed emigration, just as Germany's conquests led to an enormous increase in the number of Jews under German control. After Germany partitioned Poland with the USSR, she acquired close to two million Polish Jews. By mid-1940, the conquests in the West had brought more than 500,000 additional Jews into the German orbit: 300,000 in France, 140,000 in the Netherlands, 65,000 in Belgium, 8,000 in Denmark, and 2,500 in Norway. The Nazis had more Jews than ever on their hands and they had no idea what to do with them.

In the two years between the invasion of Poland and the beginning of mass murder in June 1941, Nazi Jewish policy was a work in progress, determined by an interplay of ideology and circumstances.[26] Taking a cue

[26] Two of the best of many studies are Christopher Browning, *The Origins of the Final*

from Hitler, German elites agreed that there was a "Jewish Problem" that demanded a solution. Any solution had to rid not only Germany but all of Europe of the Jews. Through most of 1939 and 1940 the actual details were still hazy, and no real plan had emerged. But ambitious minions understood how important the Jewish Question was and how much Hitler and Himmler welcomed subordinates with initiative and creative suggestions.

In the meantime, in September 1939 Himmler reorganized the terror and surveillance apparatus by creating a new body, the RSHA (*Reichssicherheitshauptamt*) headed by Obergruppenführer Reinhard Heydrich. This body merged the SS security service (SD) and the Security Police (SiPO). When the Final Solution began in 1941, therefore, a bureaucratic engine was in place to push it forward. The RSHA would play a major role in the execution of the Final Solution; its department IVB4 dealt with Jewish affairs and was headed by Adolf Eichmann who reported to Heinrich Müller. As recent studies have shown, the ambitious and efficient officials of the RSHA belied Hannah Arendt's or Hans Mommsen's portrayal of bland, banal, disengaged pencil-pushers (*Schreibtischtäter*). Highly educated, ruthless, and self-styled idealists who were totally convinced of the Jewish menace, these RSHA officers were equally adept at sending memoranda, securing trains to Auschwitz, or personally supervising mass shootings in Russia.[27]

In 1939–1941 the Jewish Question sparked sharp competition between different German interest groups. Friction emerged everywhere over who would control expropriated Jewish property. The SS looked for places to dump Jews, first in the *Generalgouvernement* (GG; German designation for administered Polish territories that had not been annexed to the Reich), then in distant Madagascar. Hans Frank, the Governor of the GG, foiled the first plan while Winston Churchill's refusal to surrender rendered the Madagascar project moot.

As various Nazi leaders sparred and searched for a viable Jewish policy, German occupation authorities everywhere established Jewish leadership bodies that would bear responsibility for transmitting German orders and guaranteeing their fulfillment. In Poland this responsibility was vested in *Judenräte*, local councils of between 12 and 24 members. In occupied Western Europe, these Jewish councils functioned on a national level: the *Joodse Raad* in the Netherlands, the *Reichsvertretung* in Germany, the UGIF

Solution and Peter Longerich, *Holocaust: the Nazi Persecution and Murder of the Jews* (New York: Oxford University Press, 2010).

[27] Edward B. Westermann, "Killers" in *Oxford Handbook of Holocaust Studies*, ed. Peter Hayes and John Roth (Oxford: Oxford University Press, 2010), 142–145.

(*L'Union générale des Israélites de France*) in France. From the very beginning these councils would have a dual role: to transmit German orders and
to meet Jewish welfare needs.[28]

Beginning in 1939, the Germans began the ghettoization of Polish
Jewry, with the first ghetto established in Piotrków Trybunalski.[29] During
the course of 1940 and 1941 most but not all Polish Jews were herded into
ghettos. Unlike the order establishing the *Judenräte*, ghettoization did not
reflect a uniform policy but resulted from local initiatives and circumstances. Important advocates of ghettoization included the German public
health authorities in the GG, who warned of the danger of contagious
disease caused by Jews freely moving about. This stereotype of the filthy,
lice-ridden Jew became a staple of German propaganda posters during this
period and was a major theme of the notorious 1940 propaganda film,
Der Ewige Jude, which compared Jews to rats. The film was personally
approved by Hitler.[30] Such propaganda facilitated a sense of distance and
disgust that indirectly and directly facilitated acceptance of expropriation,
separation, and ultimately mass murder.

The establishment of ghettos led to many difficulties and to disagreements between various German bodies. The Lodz ghetto, established in
April 1940, was supposed to be a temporary holding pen until the Jews
were sent somewhere else, like Madagascar – but it lasted until August
1944. In Warsaw, the local *Judenrat* was able at first to use disagreements
between different German officials to postpone the establishment of a
ghetto until November 1940.[31] In some towns, ghettos were not established
until 1941, and there were a few places where there were no ghettos at
all. The regimes varied greatly. Most ghettos – like the Warsaw Ghetto
and the Lodz Ghetto – were closed, and Jews could not leave without a
special pass. Many ghettos, however, remained open or, at the very least,
very lightly guarded. As a consequence, while some ghettos suffered greatly
from hunger and disease, in others Jews were able to freely trade with

---

[28] Isaiah Trunk, *Judenrat: the Jewish Councils in Eastern Europe under Nazi Occupation* (New York: Macmillan, 1972).

[29] Dan Michman, *Emergence of Jewish Ghettos during the Holocaust* (Cambridge: Cambridge University Press, 2011).

[30] David Hull, *Film in the Third Reich: A Study of the German Cinema 1933–1945* (Berkeley: University of California Press, 1969); Richard Etlin, *Art, Culture and Media in the Third Reich* (Chicago: University of Chicago Press, 2002); Omer Bartov, *The Jew in Cinema: from the Golem to Don't Touch My Holocaust* (Bloomington: Indiana University Press, 2005).

[31] Christopher Browning, *Path to Genocide: Essays on the Launching of the Final Solution* (New York: Cambridge University Press, 1992).

the peasants for food. In the Warsaw Ghetto, close to 100,000 Jews succumbed to hunger and disease. But there were many ghettos where there was no starvation at all.[32]

It was one thing for local German authorities to herd Jews into ghettos and quite another to know what to do next. There were, for example, at one point close to 500,000 Jews in the Warsaw Ghetto, jammed into 2.6 square kilometers. 30 percent of the city's inhabitants were forced into less than 3 percent of its area. More than 100,000 refugees from smaller towns were jammed into overcrowded and squalid refugee centers – former schools and synagogues. How would these masses of Jews be fed? Official rations were only 300 calories a day! What about allocations of coal – without which there would be no heat and consequently no functioning indoor plumbing in buildings housing thousands of people? As Christopher Browning has pointed out, divisions quickly emerged within the German administration between "attritionists" and "productionists." Attritionists saw the closed ghettos as a convenient lever to force starving Jews to disgorge their supposed treasures of hidden valuables in exchange for food. And if they did starve to death, so what? "Productionists" had no great love for Jews but believed that the Reich would benefit from factories that would put the Jews to work and enable them to pay for their upkeep. Here and there productionists won temporary concessions, such as a plan to improve the food supply in the Warsaw Ghetto in the summer of 1941. But the invasion of Russia ruled out any meaningful increase in food deliveries. The very problems created by Nazi ghettoization – starvation and disease – now served as yet another argument for a more radical approach to the Jewish problem – murder. In July 1941 SS officer Rolf-Heinz Hoeppner, the head of the Central Resettlement Office in Posen wrote to Adolf Eichmann that:

This winter there is a danger that not all of the Jews can be fed anymore. One should weigh honestly, if the most humane solution might not be to finish off those of the Jews who are not fit for work by means of some quick acting device. At any rate that would be more pleasant than to let them starve to death.[33]

No ghettos were established outside of Eastern Europe, with the exception of Saloniki and the special case of Theresienstadt. Over time, however, the Germans and their helpers would organize hundreds of ghettos not only in Poland but also in the occupied Soviet Union and, in 1944, in Hungary. A few ghettos lasted for years – such as the ghettos in Kaunas or

[32] A good overview can be seen in Christopher Browning et al. *Ghettos, 1939–1945: New Research and Perspectives on Daily Life and Survival* (Washington: USMHM, 2005).
[33] Dwork and van Pelt, *Holocaust*, p. 277.

Lodz – while many others, especially the Hungarian ghettos, were holding pens where Jews were kept for a few weeks before being shipped off to Auschwitz.[34]

A fateful turning point in Nazi Jewish policy came with the decision to invade the Soviet Union. Unlike the wars in the West, this onslaught was planned as a race war without mercy. Its goal was to destroy the "Jewish-Bolshevik menace" once and for all. Hitler urged his generals to show no quarter and they needed little persuading. Historians no longer buy the old story of a "clean Wehrmacht."[35] In October 1941, Field Marshal Walther von Reichenau reminded his troops that the soldiers must appreciate "the severe but just retribution that must be meted out to the subhuman species of Jewry." Similar orders were issued by other German commanders such as Guderian, Manstein, and Hoeppner. The Wehrmacht joined the SS in a campaign of mass murder of Jews and other "sub-humans." The notion that all Jews were partisans or potential partisans eased whatever qualms some officers and soldiers might have had. Jews were not the only victims. Of the 5.7 million Soviet POWs captured by the Germans, most would die in captivity.

As part of the preparations for this war of annihilation, the SS set up four *Einsatzgruppen*: special killing units subordinated to the RSHA but attached to the major German Army Groups. Relations between the *Einsatzgruppen* and the military were excellent. Numbering 3,200 hand-picked men and commanded by SS "intellectuals" with advanced university degrees, the *Einsatzgruppen* prepared to destroy dangerous elements including communists and Jews. The four *Einsatzgruppen* on their own lacked the manpower to murder millions of Jews; the rapid buildup in 1941–42 of new cadres, such as the German Order Police and the mobilization of hundreds of thousands of Ukrainians, Balts, and others as auxiliary police and camp guards showed how quickly the killing of Jews became a top priority. The *Einsatzgruppen* set the pace but it was the sheer numbers of willing helpers that enabled the Germans to shoot, by 1944, close to two million Jews in the former Soviet territories, including eastern Poland.[36]

The first month of Operation Barbarossa – the invasion of the Soviet Union – saw the beginning of the mass murder of Jews. Many Jews were killed in pogroms unleashed by Polish, Ukrainian, and Lithuanian

[34] Guy Miron and Shlomit Shulhani, eds. *The Yad Vashem Encyclopedia of Ghettos during the Holocaust* (Jerusalem: Yad Vashem, 2009); *The United States Memorial Holocaust Museum of Camps and Ghettos* (Bloomington: Indiana University Press and USHMM, 2009).

[35] On this, Hannes Heer, "Killing Fields: The Wehrmacht and the Holocaust in Belarussia, 1941–1942," *Holocaust and Genocide Studies* 11, no. 1 (1997): 79–101.

[36] See Browning, *Origins* and Longerich, *Holocaust*.

neighbors. Many attackers were tempted by loot; in any case, they had convinced themselves that the Jews had to pay the price for their alleged collaboration with the Soviets. One notorious massacre occurred in the Polish town of Jedwabne in July 1941. Local Poles forced their Jewish neighbors into a barn and burned them alive.[37] Vicious killing sprees also occurred in Kaunas, Lwów, and other places.

The *Einsatzgruppen* and police battalions organized gruesome atrocities from the very first day of the invasion. In Białystok, Order Police Battalion 309 herded at least 700 Jews into a synagogue and set it on fire. In these very first weeks of Operation Barbarossa the *Einsatzgruppen* did not have clear orders to shoot Jewish women and children, but by August, they were routinely killing the entire Jewish population. The murder of Jewish children in Lithuania began on August 3, 1941. On September 15, 1941, 18,500 Jews were shot in Berdichev, while 33,771 were murdered in Kiev on September 29–30, 1941. By the end of 1941 the *Einsatzgruppen* had murdered about 750,000 Jews.

At some point between August 1941 and the end of that year, the Third Reich crossed the line from mass killings of Jews in the East towards the Final Solution, the plan to murder all the European Jews. Clearly the war against the Soviets provided important psychological impetus. Along with the mass killing of Jews, the struggle against Bolshevism created new rationales for murder that were embraced by the Wehrmacht, civil administrators, and economic officials. If one needed excuses, they were not hard to find. Jews were a security risk. And food was in short supply. The Wehrmacht had to live off the land and if that meant eliminating hundreds of thousands of Jews from the food chain so be it. To be sure, German administrators and officers often objected to the murder of skilled Jewish workers. A few ghettos – in Vilna, Kaunas, and Siaulai – therefore survived for a few years.[38] But the reprieve was temporary.

---

[37] Jan Gross, *Neighbors: The Destruction of the Jewish Community in Jedwabne Poland* (New York: Penguin, 2002). Jedwabne was far from an isolated occurrence. Bystanders could often turn into perpetrators. Recent research has shown that while many tens of thousands of Polish Jews sought to escape deportations to the death camps by fleeing and hiding, few survived, largely due to denunciations and killings carried out by Polish peasants and the Polish Blue Police. See Jan Grabowski, *Hunt for the Jews: Betrayal and Murder in German Occupied Poland* (Bloomington: Indiana University Press, 2013) and Barbara Engelking, *Such a Beautiful Sunny Day* (Jerusalem: Yad Vashem, 2017).

[38] Jurgen Mattaus, "Key Aspects of German Anti-Jewish Policy" in *United States Holocaust Memorial Museum. Center for Advanced Holocaust Studies. Lithuania and the Jews: The Holocaust Chapter. Symposium Presentations.* www.ushmm.org/research/center/publications/occasional/2005-07-03/paper.pdf; Yitzhak Arad, *Ghetto in Flames: the Struggle and Destruction of the Jews of Vilna in the Holocaust* (New York: Holocaust Library,

One clear sign that the Reich was planning the murder of all Jews was the October 1941 ban on all Jewish emigration from German-controlled areas. At the same time, the Nazis began to deport Jews from the Reich and the Protectorate to the East. Many of these deportees were immediately murdered when they arrived in Riga, Minsk, and Kaunas.[39] The Germans had now crossed another moral Rubicon. They were killing German Jews – including decorated World War I veterans – and not just *Ostjuden*, or Eastern European Jews.

In the first part of December 1941 the Soviet counteroffensive before Moscow signaled the definitive failure of the German Blitzkrieg. Still enraged by this setback, which coincided with the Japanese attack on Pearl Harbor, Hitler decided to burn all his bridges by declaring war on the United States on December 11, 1941. Now there was no more need to show any restraint on the Jewish Question. Now that Germany was fighting the US, the British Empire, and a resilient Soviet Union simultaneously, the die was cast. Fantasies of destroying the Jews could now be realized. The next day, December 12, Hitler called a meeting of high Nazi officials at the Reichchancellery in Berlin. According to an entry in Josef Goebbels's diary, Hitler was "to make a clean sweep of the Jewish Question." He had warned the Jews, Hitler declared, that if they started a world war, they would be destroyed and now they would have to pay the price. 160,000 Germans had already died at the front and the Jews bore the responsibility. There would be no mercy.[40]

On January 20, 1942, Reinhard Heydrich convened a conference at Wannsee to lay down basic principles for the Final Solution of the Jewish Problem.[41] The purpose of the conference was to establish SS authority, granted by Hitler, to carry through with the elimination of European Jewry and, in the process, to exact full cooperation from all other German agencies.

1982); Dina Porat, "The Holocaust in Lithuania: Some Unique Aspects," in *The Final Solution: Origins and Implementation* ed. David Cesarani (New York: Routledge, 1996), 159–174.

[39] Longerich, *Holocaust*, 297–300.

[40] An insightful discussion can be found in Ulrich Herbert, "Extermination Policy: New Answers and Questions about the History of the 'Holocaust' in German Historiography" in *National Socialist Extermination Policies: Contemporary German Perspectives and Controversies*, ed. Ulrich Herbert (New York: Berghahn Books, 2002), 1–52.

[41] One good treatment is Mark Roseman, *The Wannsee Conference and the Final Solution* (New York: Macmillan, 2003); also Christian Gerlach, "The Wannsee Conference, the Fate of German Jews and Hitler's Decision in Principle to Exterminate All European Jews" *Journal of Modern History* 70, no. 4 (1998): 759–812.

"After appropriate prior approval by the Führer," Heydrich told the invited guests, "emigration as a possible solution has been superseded by a policy of evacuating Jews to the East." The conference employed euphemisms, but there was no doubt that the subject was the murder of European Jewry. After all, one of the invited guests was Rudolph Lange, who had been busy killing Jews in Latvia, and another was Joseph Bouhler, from the *Generalgouvernement*, who pressed for making an "evacuation" of Polish Jews a top priority. The numbers were daunting. At the time of the Wannsee Conference, the Warsaw Ghetto alone contained almost as many Jews as the number in France, the Netherlands and Belgium combined.

Officials at the conference included representatives from many key groups, including the Interior Ministry, the Four Year Plan, the Foreign Office, the Party, the Gestapo, and the Reich Chancellery. There was a convivial atmosphere, lunch was served along with fine cognac. The only discord at the meeting involved objections from Interior Ministry representative Dr. Wilhelm Stuckart to including *Mischlinge* and Jews in mixed marriages in the murder program. The matter was deferred. Heydrich told the conference that that the SS was "gaining practical experience" in solving the Jewish Problem. What he meant was that plans were now underway to supplement shooting with gas chambers. Instead of the killers coming to the Jews, the Jews would now be sent to special death camps strategically located along key railway lines.

Implementation of the Final Solution demanded a coordinated bureaucratic effort to overcome myriad challenges: transportation, smooth operation of the death camps, negotiations with allies on the handover of Jews, allocation of confiscated property, legal complications about definition of Jewishness, the status of Jews in mixed marriages, decisions on deferring murder in order to use Jews for forced labor. Eichmann's skill in organizing Jewish emigration now found a new outlet – coordinating rounds-ups of Jews and transportation to the Death Camps in the East from Central and Western Europe. He and his efficient staff wangled trains from the Reichsbahn and negotiated acceptable fares. They secured third class excursion rates, with half fare for children under the age of twelve. Children under four traveled for free. Complementing Eichmann's efforts were German diplomats who tried to persuade various allied governments to release their Jews for deportation. One look at Eichmann's record in Hungary in the spring of 1944, where he efficiently and ruthlessly dispatched 437,000 Jews to Auschwitz in six weeks, certainly belies Arendt's caricature of a mediocre pencil-pusher.[42]

---

[42] David Cesarani, *Becoming Eichmann: Rethinking the Life, Crimes and Trial of a 'Desk Murderer'* (Cambridge: DaCapo Press, 2006).

While Eichmann concentrated on transportation, another group of experts had to organize the actual killing centers. One source of talent was the T4 project, the euthanasia program that had by the summer of 1941 gassed up to 100,000 Germans who were judged to be "unworthy of life."[43] T4 veterans like Christian Wirth, Franz Heckenholt, and Franz Stangl now moved to Poland, where they set up death camps at Treblinka, Sobibor, and Belzec. These camps used stationary carbon monoxide gas chambers. These were not labor camps. All Jews were immediately killed except for a very few who were selected to empty the gas chambers and do routine chores around the camp. Compared to the Einstazgruppen killings in the East, these death camps needed very little German manpower. 30 Germans and about 150 Ukrainian guards, for example, sufficed to run Treblinka.[44]

A major task of these camps was to implement Operation Reinhardt, the murder of most Polish Jews, which was mostly completed in 1942. Two Jews would survive Belzec, which murdered about 500,000. Treblinka killed up to 900,000; 67 would survive after an uprising by inmates in August 1943. 250,000 Jews died in Sobibor. That camp was shut down after an uprising in October 1943. About 30 Jews survived the end of the war. Administratively distinct from these camps was the killing center at Chelmno, set up in December 1941. Using mobile gas vans, its job was to kill Jews from the Warthegau and the Lodz ghetto.[45]

At the same time, Auschwitz was also emerging as a major extermination center. Unlike the Operation Reinhardt camps or Chelmno, Auschwitz was multi-purpose: a concentration camp for mostly political prisoners (mainly non-Jews), an important center of forced labor, and an extermination facility for Jews.[46] After some successful experiments on Soviet prisoners of war, camp commandant Rudolph Hoess introduced hydrogen cyanide as the gas of choice, which was much more efficient than carbon monoxide. Instead of depending on unpredictable diesel engines, which often broke down and needed smaller gas chambers, in Auschwitz an SS man could empty a tin of lethal crystals into a large room and kill 2,000 people within fifteen minutes. By early 1943 new complexes came on line

---

[43] A good general treatment can be found in Henry Friedlander, *The Origins of Nazi Genocide: from Euthanasia to the Final Solution* (Chapel Hill: University of North Carolina Press, 1995).

[44] On these camps see Yitzhak Arad, *Belzec, Treblinka, Sobibor: The Operation Reinhard Death Camps* (Bloomington: University of Indiana Press, 1987).

[45] Patrick Montague, *Chelmno and the Holocaust: A History of Hitler's First Death Camp* (Chapel Hill: University of North Carolina Press, 2012).

[46] Deborah Dwork and Robert Jan Van Pelt, *Auschwitz* (New York: W. W. Norton, 2002).

at Birkenau, which housed both gas chambers and crematoria. Auschwitz reached its peak as a death factory between May and October 1944 as it murdered Jews from Hungary, the Lodz Ghetto, Theresienstadt, Slovakia, and exhausted survivors of various German labor camps. To prepare for the mass influx of Hungarian Jews, Adolf Eichmann, who had an eye for detail, suggested moving the railroad tracks right into the camp, where the Jews could disembark only a few hundred yards from the gas chambers.

One question that nagged the SS and other German decision makers after the beginning of the Final Solution was how many Jews they should spare to perform forced labor. In theory all Jews were to be killed, regardless of their potential value as workers. The two million Polish Jews killed in Operation Reinhardt in 1942 included at least tens of thousands of skilled craftsmen, and most of the murdered Jews could have been used as unskilled labor. Another mass killing that defied rationality was Himmler's order to murder the 42,000 Jews who worked in SS Ostindustrie labor camps around Lublin. This mass killing, cynically named Operation Harvest festival, took place on November 3, 1943.[47]

But German policy in regard to Jewish labor was not consistent. In Lithuania and Belarus the Germans realized by late 1941 that if they killed all the Jews, they would have no skilled workers in that area at all, so a few ghettos survived until 1943 and, in Kaunas, until the summer of 1944.[48] (Yet, in April 1943, when the Germans were desperately short of labor, they still murdered 5,000 young, able-bodied Jews at Ponary, outside Vilna). The Lodz ghetto, with its large number of workshops, survived until August 1944.[49]

By 1944 the Germans were more likely to use able-bodied Jews for forced labor. Hitler himself approved the consignment of Hungarian Jews to work in armaments and airplane plants, even in the Reich itself. The hundreds of projects that employed Jewish slave labor included the Dora-Mittelbau that made rockets in underground tunnels, the Hasag munitions plants in Poland, and the I. G. Farben synthetic rubber complex at Auschwitz Monowitz. For the most part, little effort was made to prolong the life of Jewish slave laborers and the vast majority perished. German firms returned emaciated Jewish workers to the SS for shipment to the death camps. Jews fared much worse than non-Jewish foreign laborers.

---

[47] Arad, *Belzec, Treblinka, Sobibor*, 365-369.

[48] William Mishell, *Kaddish for Kovno: Life and Death in a Lithuanian Ghetto* (Chicago: Chicago Review Press, 1999); Avraham Tory, *Surviving the Holocaust: the Kovno Ghetto Diary* (Cambridge: Harvard University Press, 1991).

[49] A good overview can be found in Isaiah Trunk and Robert Shapiro, *Lodz Ghetto* (Bloomington: Indiana University Press, 2008).

Slaves at least represented an economic asset that had to be protected. In that regard, as Benjamin Ferencz pointed out, the Jews were "less than slaves."[50]

Jewish prospects for surviving the Final Solution depended largely on where they happened to live. Much depended on the degree of German control and whether or not the Reich had to negotiate with allies and satellites. Paradoxically, Jews were often better off – although not always– living under collaborationist governments than in areas whose governments continued the war against the Reich and where the Germans had a free hand. Germany, Poland, the Baltic States, and the occupied areas of the USSR, the Netherlands, the Protectorate of Bohemia and Moravia, Serbia, Greece, and Croatia saw the highest death rates. In Italy, however, the Germans could not touch the Jews until September 1943. 70 percent survived the war.[51] Bulgaria allowed the murder of the Jews of Thrace and Macedonia but at the last minute stepped in to protect its own Jews. Everywhere in southern Europe, Jews fared well in areas under Italian jurisdiction such as southeast France after November 1942, parts of Greece and Croatia, many Aegean Islands such as Corfu and Rhodes. But in September 1943 Germany moved into Italy, disarmed the Italian Army and murdered many of these Jews.

Some allied states were all too happy to get rid of their Jews. Slovakia, whose government was headed by a Catholic priest, Father Jozef Tiso, asked Germany in the spring of 1942 to deport Jews and even paid the Reich to do so. After a few months, when 58,000 Jews had already been shipped to Auschwitz, the deportations ceased, in part because of pressure from the papal nuncio, in part because some members of the government began to have qualms, and in part because of the determination of a group of Slovak Jewish leaders (The Working Group) to bribe Slovak officials and the SS. This Working Group, led by Rabbi Michael Dov Ber Weissmandel and an extraordinary woman named Gisi Fleischmann, also established contact with Hungarian Zionists and helped about 14,000 Jews flee to the relative safety of Hungary. But the killing of Slovak Jews resumed after the Slovak Uprising in late 1944.[52] In Croatia the Ustashe State, headed by

[50] Benjamin Ferencz and Telford Taylor, *Less than Slaves: Jewish Forced Labor and the Quest for Compensation* (Bloomington: Indiana University Press, 2002).

[51] Michele Sarfatti, *The Jews in Mussolini's Italy* (Madison: University of Wisconsin Press, 2006); Susan Zuccotti, *Italians and the Holocaust: Persecution, Rescue and Survival* (New York: Basic Books, 1987).

[52] On the destruction of Slovak Jewry see Livia Rotkirchen, "The Dual Role of the 'Jewish Center' in Slovakia" in *Patterns of Jewish Leadership in Nazi Europe, 1933–45*, ed. I. Gutman and C.Y. Haft (Jerusalem: Yad Vashem, 1979); Leni Yahil, *The Holocaust: the*

Ante Pavelic, took the lead and murdered most of its Jews – along with many Serbs – with minimal German help.

While only 15 percent of the Dutch Jews survived the war, 56 percent survived in neighboring Belgium. Explanations for the higher survival rate in Belgium underscored the importance of local context in understanding the dynamics of the Holocaust. The Belgian King stayed in the country, while the Dutch Queen Wilhelmina fled, along with the government but without the efficient Dutch Civil Service, which stayed behind. Its excellent record keeping made it easier for the Germans to round up Jews when the deportations began. While Belgium was under a German military administration that showed some concern for maintaining correct relations with the local population, the Netherlands was under the efficient rule of Reichskommissar Arthur Seyss-Inquart, a vicious anti-Semite who cooperated closely with the RSHA. Most Belgian Jews were refugees who had an ingrained suspicion of the authorities and who were quicker than the law-abiding Dutch Jews to evade arrest. Resistance organizations in Belgium were more effective at providing shelter.[53]

In France, which in 1940 was divided into an Occupied and an Unoccupied Zone, the Vichy government proved quite eager to pass anti-Jewish legislation. One key reason was that it wanted to keep Jewish wealth out of German hands and it was anxious to assert its authority in the Occupied zone as well. When the Final Solution began in 1942, the Vichy government agreed to deport non-French Jews and it was the French police that rounded up 14,000 Jews in Paris in July 1942 and handed over inmates of the internment camps to the Germans. But the roundups shocked many Frenchmen who had hitherto been ready to support Vichy's anti-Jewish measures. While the Church as a whole was passive, the Archbishop of Toulouse, Jules-Gérard Saliège, issued a sharp pastoral letter on August 30, 1942, denouncing the deportations.

The German occupation of all of France in November 1942 and the German defeat at Stalingrad hastened a marked shift in French attitudes. The French police were much less eager to round up native French Jews than it was to arrest foreign Jews. In a large country like France, the Germans lacked the manpower to do the job themselves. By the end of the war, 75,000 French Jews had perished, but 75 percent of French Jewry

Fate of European Jewry (New York and Oxford: Oxford University Press, 1987); Yehuda Bauer, *Jews for Sale* (New Haven: Yale University Press, 1994).

[53] See Jacob Presser, *Ashes in the Wind: The Destruction of Dutch Jewry* (London: Souvenir Press, 2010); Bob Moore, *Victims and Survivors: The Nazi Persecution of Jews in the Netherlands, 1940–1945* (London: Arnold, 1997); Dan Michman ed. *Belgium and the Holocaust* (Jerusalem: Yad Vashem, 1998).

survived. Helping the high survival rate was the growing willingness of Frenchmen to hide Jews, the decision of many French police and Vichy officials to build alibis for themselves after 1943, and the activities of such organizations as OSE, that played a major role in the saving of children through concealment and through smuggling them over the Swiss and Spanish borders. Le Chambon sur Lignon, one small French Protestant village, led by its pastor André Trocmé, hid hundreds of Jews.[54]

Romania, without doubt one of the most antisemitic countries in the world, also saw a high percentage of its Jewish population survive the war, certainly larger than Norway or the Netherlands where anti-semitism was much less prevalent. In 1941 Romania joined Germany in its war on the Soviet Union and the Romanian military eagerly carried through its own mass killings of Jews in Bessarabia, Bukovina, and the Ukraine – at times using methods that offended even the refined sensibili-ties of the SS. Romania also deported over 150,000 Jews from these regions to Transnistria, where 90,000 died under appalling conditions. In 1942 Marshal Antonescu promised Germany to deport all his Jews, including those in the Regat (pre-1914 Romania), but by 1943 he changed his mind. The disaster at Stalingrad certainly influenced Antonescu who now saw the Jewish Question as a way of asserting Romanian independence from Hitler and perhaps open lines of communication with the Allies. Not only were the Jews of the Regat spared deportation but Antonescu even allowed them to set up a committee to help the deportees in Transnistria.[55]

After 1939 Hungary also became a German ally and later joined in the attack on the Soviet Union. This pro-German policy won it back many territories lost after World War I: southern Slovakia, Carpatho Rus, and northern Transylvania. As a result, by 1941 over 700,000 Jews lived under Hungarian control. They suffered from antisemitic legislation and from the conscription of 50,000 able-bodied Jewish men into the notorious military labor service, where most perished. But Admiral Horthy and the Hungarian government resisted Hitler's direct demands for the deporta-tion of Hungarian Jewry, although in 1941 and 1942 the Hungarian army

---

[54] A classic study is Michael Marrus and Robert Paxton, *Vichy France and the Jews* (New York: Basic Books, 1981); also Bob Moore, *Survivors: Jewish Self Help and Rescue in Nazi-Occupied Western Europe* (Oxford: Oxford University Press: 2010); Renée Poznanski, *Jews in France during World War II* (Waltham, MA: Bradeis University Press, 2001); Deborah Dwork and Robert Jan van Pelt, *Flight from the Reich: Refugee Jews, 1933–1946* (New York: W. W. Norton, 2009); Susan Zuccotti, *The Holocaust, the French and the Jews* (New York: Basic Books, 1993).

[55] A good source is Jean Ancel, *History of the Holocaust in Romania* (Lincoln: University of Nebraska Press, 2012).

massacred some Jews on its own. Nonetheless, compared to other countries the Jews in Hungary were relatively safe.

Everything changed in March 1944. Angered by reports that Hungary was seeking negotiations with the Western Allies, Germany entered the country and Horthy now had to accept a new pro-Nazi government. Adolf Eichmann immediately enlisted the Hungarians in a massive assault on Hungarian Jewry. Eager to deport the Jews and take over their property, the new Hungarian government combed the country from east to west. Between May 15 and July 7, 1944, 434,000 Jews were sent to Auschwitz. Frightened by growing foreign pressure, Horthy suspended the deportations on July 7, greatly angering Eichmann who was just about to begin the killing of the Jews of Budapest. A change in regime renewed the danger to Budapest's 200,000 Jews in September 1944. 100,000 were killed in massacres and death marches by the Arrow Cross and by the Germans, but the intervention of the Swedes, the Swiss, the papal nuncio, and the US War Refugee Board saved many lives nonetheless.[56]

One bizarre aspect of the murder of Hungarian Jewry was Himmler's authorization of negotiations with Hungarian Zionist leaders led by Rezső Kasztner. Dealt a very weak hand, Kasztner tried to play for time, but his gambit was doomed to failure.[57] Denmark offered one of the most striking examples of rescue during the Holocaust. Most Danish Jews were saved in September 1943 because it was late in the war, there were relatively few Jews and Sweden was ready to receive them.[58]

In November 1944 Himmler ordered the dismantling of the Auschwitz gas chambers. With an eye on opening up talks with the Western Allies, he even used Jews as bargaining chips and hinted that he was willing to stop the killing altogether. Hitler, however, reacted furiously to any news that Jewish survivors had fallen into the hands of the advancing Allies. And some of Himmler's underlings, like Adolf Eichmann, did their sullen best to kill as many Jews as possible, right until the last minute.[59]

---

[56] A standard source is Randolph L. Braham, *The Politics of Genocide: The Holocaust in Hungary* (Detroit: Wayne State University Press, 2000); also Bauer, *Jews for Sale*.

[57] Kasztner did succeed in securing Eichmann's consent to a special train that took 1,700 Jews selected by Kasztner out of Hungary to eventual safety. His actions touched off a bitter controversy in Israel where Kasztner eventually settled and he was assassinated in 1957.

[58] One factor in Sweden's action was without doubt anger over the deportation of most of Norway's small Jewish population in November 1942, a joint operation carried out by the Germans and the collaborationist government under Vidkun Quisling.

[59] David Cesarani, *Becoming Eichmann*.

Indeed, one of the most lethal periods of the Holocaust occurred in the final few months before the collapse of the Reich, as conditions in the hundreds of labor camps deteriorated and as the Nazis began to herd hundreds of thousands of Jewish and non-Jewish prisoners in horrible death marches. Of the 714,000 prisoners registered in the Nazi concentration camp system in January 1945, between 200,000 and 250,000 would be dead by the time the war ended five months later. Some were gassed in newly built gas chambers in Ravensbruck, Dachau, or Stutthof. Others succumbed to starvation and disease as the Nazi camp system slowly disintegrated into chaos. In Klooga, Blechhammer, and many other camps, the Germans murdered Jewish prisoners at the very last moment, sometimes less than a day before the arrival of the Red Army. Most died in death marches associated with the evacuation of such key camp complexes as Auschwitz, Stutthof, Dachau, Mauthausen, and Dora-Mittelbau, but there were also many smaller marches of prisoners from the hundreds of sub-camps that had become such an important feature of the German war economy after 1942. Guards, lacking clear orders, shot any prisoners who could not keep up. As Daniel Blatman shows, German civilians, terrified of imminent vengeance, eagerly helped track down and kill fleeing prisoners.[60]

What kind of help did Jews get? Much depended on specific circumstances. In Poland, which had seen growing Polish–Jewish tensions before the war, the population detested the Germans and supported a far-flung underground state. But Jews were considered aliens, outside the sphere of Polish moral responsibility. Poles who risked the death penalty for hiding Jews had to worry about denunciations from their neighbors. In November 1942, when most Polish Jews were already dead, a group of Catholics, Socialists, and Polish liberals founded Zegota, an organization to help Jews. Officially attached to the Underground Polish State, Zegota provided forged papers, helped place children in Polish homes and convents and distributed some financial aid to Jews in hiding. All in all, between 10,000 and 15,000 Jews survived the war by hiding in Poland, in no small part due to the more than 6,700 Poles recognized by Yad Vashem as righteous among the nations.

In 1987, Jan Blonski's landmark article "A Poor Pole looks at the Ghetto" opened widespread discussion in Poland about Polish attitudes to Jews during the war. Blonski castigated his countrymen for indifference, but did not accuse them of actually killing Jews. Jan Gross, however, caused an even bigger controversy when his study *Neighbors* appeared in 2001. Here he actually documented how Poles killed their Jewish neighbors.[61]

---

[60] An excellent source on the death marches is Daniel Blatman, *The Death Marches: The Final Phase of Nazi Genocide* (Cambridge: Harvard University Press, 2011).

[61] In addition to *Neighbors*, good surveys in English of Polish Jewish relations during the War include Joanna Michlic, *Poland's Threatening Other: The Image of the Jew from 1880*

The attitude of the Allies and the Vatican has also produced a great deal of historical controversy. Most historians reject John Conway's thesis that Pope Pius XII was "Hitler's Pope," but they would be hard pressed to make the case that the Vatican made a valiant effort to help European Jewry. The Pope's priorities – determined by both theology and politics – were to protect the Church. He did not want to force German Catholics to have to choose between their country and their church. And compared to the prospect of a Soviet takeover of Eastern and Central Europe, he certainly saw Hitler as a lesser evil. It would be wrong to argue that the Catholic Church did nothing to save Jews. The intervention of the papal nuncio in Hungary in 1944 helped save many lives, and many individual priests and nuns sheltered Jews. It is not clear, however, how much the Pope himself directly inspired these decisions. And, as Susan Zuccotti points out, when the Germans arrested Italian Jews in October 1943 "under the very windows" of the Vatican and deported them to Auschwitz, the Pope did nothing. When Konrad Count Preysing, a German Catholic bishop, asked papal nuncio Cesare Orsenigo to persuade the Pope to speak out against the murder of the Jews, Orsenigo replied that "charity is well and good but the greatest charity is not to make problems for the Church."[62]

The stance of Franklin Delano Roosevelt has also come in for some controversy. David Wyman wrote a study of American policy tellingly entitled *The Abandonment of the Jews*. There is no doubt that for Roosevelt the Jews were not a major priority, but even if they had been, it is hard to see what the US could have done to stop the Holocaust in 1942 or 1943. It is also important to remember the tide in the U Boat War did not turn until March 1943, that the US did not achieve daytime air superiority over Germany until March 1944, and that there was no guarantee that the Normandy invasion would succeed. Preoccupied with the war, Roosevelt rationed his political capital quite carefully and he understood that

to the Present (Lincoln: University of Nebraska Press, 2006); Israel Gutman and Shmuel Krakowski, *Unequal Victims: Poles and Jews during World War II* (New York: Holocaust Library, 1986); Michael Steinlauf, *Bondage to the Dead: Poland and the Memory of the Holocaust* (Syracuse: Syracuse University Press, 1997). Still important is Emanuel Ringelblum's classic study written in 1943–1944: Emanuel Ringelblum, *Polish–Jewish Relations in the Second World War* (Evanston: Northwestern University Press, 1992). More recent studies include Grabowski, *Hunt for the Jews* and Engelking, *Such a Beautiful Sunny Day*.

[62] Saul Friedländer, *Nazi Germany and the Jews, 1939–1945: The Years of Extermination* (New York: Harper Perennial, 2008), 516. A good and critical study of the Vatican's role is Susan Zuccotti, *Under His Very Windows: The Vatican and the Holocaust in Italy* (New Haven: Yale, 2000). Also helpful is Michael Phayer, *Pius XII, the Holocaust and the Cold War* (Bloomington: Indiana University Press, 2008).

anti-refugee sentiment was one reason for the Republicans' strong showing in the November 1942 mid-term elections. However, when American
failure to help the Jews threatened to become a political liability in early
1944, Roosevelt finally responded. Bowing to pressure from his Treasury
Department, which presented evidence of systematic State Department
obstruction of rescue efforts, Roosevelt authorized the setting up of the
War Refugee Board in January 1944. The WRB, using mainly Jewish
money, did save Jewish lives in 1944 and 1945, especially in Hungary.[63]

III

Until relatively recently most scholarly research outside Israel focused on
the perpetrators, not on the Jewish victims. There were many reasons for
this. Few scholars outside Israel could read materials in Hebrew, Yiddish,
Russian, or Polish. Furthermore, scholars such as Raul Hilberg and others argued that actual documents and bureaucratic records were a more
trustworthy source than post-war testimonies by survivors, which were
naturally open to distortions of memory. Because the Germans and their
helpers left more documents than had the Jews, it was much easier for
scholars to study the decision-making process that led to the Holocaust.

This relative neglect of the study of Jewish society under the Nazis led
to generalizations based on flimsy evidence. For example, the pioneering
Holocaust scholar Raul Hilberg argued that during 2,000 years of Diaspora
existence, Jews had become conditioned to rely on compliance, negotiation,
and compromise rather than resistance. In a similar vein, Hannah Arendt
lambasted the policies of the Jewish Councils for fostering an insidious collaboration that made the job of the Germans easier. "If the Jewish people
had been unorganized and leaderless," Arendt wrote, "there would have
been chaos and plenty of misery, but the total number of victims would
hardly have been between four and a half and six million victims."[64]

Skewed perceptions were not just limited to analysts who lacked the
necessary languages. In Israel for many years after the Holocaust it was
common to draw a sharp distinction between the tiny number of Jewish
fighters – usually from Zionist youth movements – who rose up to defend
Jewish honor and the millions of Jews who marched passively to their
deaths, "like sheep to the slaughter." Such a dichotomy strengthened the
Zionist argument that the Diaspora experience led to moral paralysis.

[63] David Wyman, *The Abandonment of the Jews: America and the Holocaust*
(New York: Pantheon, 1984). For a defence of FDR's policy toward the Jews see Ariel
Hurwitz, *Jews without Power* (New Rochelle: Multi Educator, 2011).
[64] *Eichmann in Jerusalem*, 123.

Only a Jewish State could produce a proud, self-reliant Jew who would prevent such a disaster from happening again.[65]

In the early period of Holocaust research harsh appraisals of Jewish leadership under the Nazis were quite common.[66] Ber Mark, in communist Poland, lambasted the Jewish Councils as tools of the Jewish bourgeoisie who betrayed the Jewish masses and resisted Communist-led calls for armed resistance. Philip Friedman, one of the pioneers of serious Holocaust research and a survivor himself, offered an unsparing portrait of Jewish leaders such as Chaim Rumkowski of the Lodz ghetto, described as a power hungry, unscrupulous dictator who aped German ideas about discipline and leadership.[67] In his study of the Holocaust in the Netherlands, Jacob Presser, also a survivor, lambasted the leaders of the Joodse Raad, David Cohen and Abraham Ascher.

Nevertheless, one of the more significant developments of Holocaust research in recent decades has been a more nuanced appraisal of Jewish behavior under the Nazis, and especially the actions of the Jewish Councils. The 1972 publication of Isaiah Trunk's *Judenrat: the Jewish Councils in Eastern Europe under Nazi Occupation*, led the way, and this reappraisal of Jewish behavior has been a major focus of what Dan Michman has called the "Israel School" of Holocaust research. Led by Yehuda Bauer and Israel Gutman, this Israel school stressed Jewish collective identity and agency, even in the Holocaust. These historians also pointed out that conditions faced by Jews varied so widely that detailed local studies were a prerequisite to any meaningful generalizations about Jewish behavior.[68] Studies such as Gutman's history of the Warsaw Ghetto and Michal Ungar's monograph of the Lodz Ghetto used German and Polish sources but developed a conceptual framework that put Jewish sources and the Jewish experience front and center. These studies have been complemented by new research into the dilemmas faced by Jewish leadership in France, the Netherlands, Hungary, and other areas.

[65] See, for example, Tom Segev, *The Seventh Million: Israelis and the Holocaust* (New York: Hill and Wang, 1993).
[66] I. Gutman and C. Y. Haft eds. *Patterns of Jewish Leadership in Nazi Europe, 1933–45* (Jerusalem: Yad Vashem, 1979).
[67] Philip Friedman, "Pseudo Saviors in the Polish Ghettos: Mordechai Chaim Rumkowski of Lodz" in *Roads to Extinction: Essays on the Holocaust*, ed. Ada June Friedman (New York: Jewish Publication Society, 1980).
[68] Dan Michman, "Is there an Israel School of Holocaust Research?" in *Holocaust Historiography in Context: Emergence, Challenges, Polemics and Achievements*, ed. Dan Michman and David Bankier (Jerusalem: Yad Vashem, 2008).

Many scholars of Jewish leadership have recognized the important distinction between collaboration and cooperation.[69] Collaborators hoped for a Nazi victory and aligned their interests with Germany's. In that sense, hardly any Jewish leaders collaborated. But cooperation was another matter. From the very onset of the German occupation, Jews lost their livelihoods and needed economic assistance. In Eastern Europe, the Jewish Councils had to meet basic needs. Food supplies, however meager, had to be paid for. Refugees dumped into ghettos had to be housed. If an epidemic broke out, the Jewish council had to work with Jewish doctors to ensure that the outbreak remained secret from the Germans – who often used typhus as an excuse for mass murder. In order to forestall sudden raids for forced labor, it seemed preferable to provide the Germans with organized contingents of workers. If Jews were arrested by the Germans for various offenses, the Jewish Council was the body best able to collect gold and valuables in order to pay bribes and ransom.

Food, housing, and bribes all required income. The Jewish Councils needed to tax, and wartime conditions precluded such niceties as a graduated income tax or deductions. Many people had no income, and those who did – smugglers, illegal businessmen, etc. – were not going to declare it. Therefore, the Jewish Council had to grab money through a system of regressive taxation: levies on ration cards, burials, and apartments. Such a burden fell heavily on those who could least afford it and fueled resentment and anger against the *Judenräte*. In many ghettos, the Jewish Police became a particular target. Often policemen began their service with the best of intentions, and at the beginning of the war, their presence in ghettos elicited a certain measure of pride. But given the conditions of ghetto life, and in view of the fact that many policemen either received no salary at all or a very meager one, corruption and abuse became inevitable. In the Warsaw Ghetto in 1941, when the Germans demanded a certain number of Jews to be sent to labor camps, where they worked in dreadful conditions, the Jewish police took bribes to exempt the well-to-do. As Heinz Auerswald, the German-appointed commissar of the Warsaw Ghetto noted with satisfaction in 1941, the Jews hated the *Judenrat* more than they hated the Germans.[70]

Nevertheless, generalizations about the *Judenräte* are impossible to make. Each *Judenrat* had to operate in its own particular circumstances. Some *Judenrat* leaders, such as Elkhanon Elkes in the Kovno ghetto, enjoyed, for the most part, the respect and support of the Jewish community. It was

[69] This point was stressed by Trunk in *Judenrat*.

[70] Samuel Kassow, *Who Will Write Our History?* (Bloomington: University of Indiana Press, 2007), 94.

not uncommon for a *Judenrat* to be killed and replaced by individuals of lesser talent or even by criminals and opportunists. Everywhere, including those places where the *Judenrat* enjoyed relative respect, there was a natural tendency of its members to help their family and friends.

In judging Jewish behavior, and in particular the actions of the Jewish councils, it is vital to remember that since the Germans themselves did not decide to murder all the Jews until late in 1941, there is no reason to expect the Jewish leaders to assume the unthinkable. And after the Final Solution began, there were wide variations in how much Jews knew and more importantly, how they reacted to this knowledge.

It was one thing to hear that the Germans were planning to murder all the Jews and quite another to actually internalize such knowledge. When the Polish courier Jan Karski told Supreme Court justice Felix Frankfurter about the Final Solution in Washington in June 1943, Frankfurter replied that he didn't believe him. The Polish ambassador, who accompanied Karski, was offended that Frankfurter would question Karski's integrity. "Mr Ambassador," Frankfurter replied, "I am not saying that this young man is lying. I am saying that I do not believe him. There is a difference!"[71]

Rumors, reports, even eyewitness accounts met with incredulity and disbelief. It took some time before French, Dutch, and Belgian Jewish leaders actually understood that the "transports" to the East really meant death. As late as 1944, emissaries sent to provincial Hungarian towns to warn Hungarian Jews about the real meaning of Auschwitz were met with skepticism. Most Hungarian Jews who arrived on the ramp of Birkenau between May and July 1944 had no idea what was going to happen to them.[72]

And this was after at least two years of warnings. As early as 1941 British intelligence was intercepting radio decrypts of *Einsatzgruppen* massacres in Russia. In early 1942 an escapee from the Chelmno death camp arrived in the Warsaw Ghetto, and his report, as well as reports from escapees from Treblinka, was sent via the channels of the Polish Underground to London. In June 1942, the BBC broadcast a report that up to 700,000 Polish Jews had already been murdered.[73] In the summer of 1942 a prominent German industrialist, Eduard Schulte, warned Jewish contacts in Switzerland that Hitler intended to kill all the Jews of Europe. The World Jewish Congress representative in Geneva, Gerhart Riegner, passed the news to Rabbi Stephen Wise. The State Department confirmed the

---

[71] Walter Lacqueur, *The Terrible Secret: Suppression of the Truth about Hitler's Final Solution* (New York: Holt Paperbacks, 1998), 237.

[72] Bauer, *Rethinking the Holocaust*, 213–242.

[73] Kassow, *Who Will Write Our History?*, 298–299.

veracity of this report in November 1942.[74] Dozens of other reports followed, including first-hand evidence provided in April 1944 by Rudolph Vrba, an escapee from Auschwitz.[75] This information was passed to the Working Group in Slovakia and then on to Jewish leaders in Hungary and Switzerland.

In eastern Poland, the Baltic States, and Soviet Union, where Germans and their helpers shot Jews in mass executions, the Final Solution was no secret. But even so, what options did Jews have? In the tiny ghetto of Szarkowszczyzna near Vilna, on June 17 1942, the *Judenrat* set the ghetto on fire and told Jews to run through the cordon of killers who came to liquidate the ghetto. But within a few days most of the hapless and dazed survivors voluntarily entered the nearby Glebokie ghetto, even though by now they had no illusions about their eventual fate. Their options were limited. Only Soviet partisans offered Jews in this area even a slim hope of survival, and such a partisan movement was not yet in place. Neighbors were mostly hostile. In short, here was a *Judenrat* whose actions met Hannah Arendt's exacting standards. But it made absolutely no difference.[76]

In other ghettos, once the Final Solution began, Jewish leaders acted in different ways. Adam Czerniakow, the head of the Warsaw Ghetto *Judenrat*, had frantically asked various German officials about rumors concerning the imminent deportation of the Warsaw Jews. They cynically assured him that the Warsaw Ghetto was safe. On July 23, one day after the start of the deportations, Czerniakow decided to kill himself. In a note to his wife he wrote "they are asking me to participate in the murder of the children of my people. I have no other choice but to die."[77]

In the Lodz Ghetto Chaim Rumkowski made a different choice. When the Germans demanded the deportation of all Jews over the age of 65 and all children under the age of 10, Rumkowski complied. His desperate strategy was to buy time through work, and if that meant handing over children, so be it. On September 4, weeping and distraught, Rumkowski spoke to the ghetto: "Brothers and sisters, hand them over to me! Mothers and fathers! Give me your children!"[78] For a variety of complex reasons, Rumkowski did succeed in buying time. 70,000 Jews survived in the Lodz Ghetto until August 1944, when the Red Army was only 60 miles away.

---

[74] Lacqueur, *The Terrible Secret*.

[75] For Vrba's riveting account see Rudolph Vrba, *I Escaped from Auschwitz* (London: Robson, 2006).

[76] Personal conversations with Celia Kassow.

[77] Jacek Leociak and Barbara Engelking-Boni, *The Warsaw Ghetto: Guide to the Perished City* (New Haven: Yale University Press), 164.

[78] Trunk and Shapiro, *Lodz Ghetto*, 238–248.

And had Hitler been killed in the assassination plot of July 20, 1944, then it is highly likely that most of these Lodz Jews would have survived. And how, then, would historians – and fellow Jews – have judged Rumkowski?

Other *Judenrat* leaders also believed that their best strategy was to convince the Germans that Jewish labor made it worth their while to spare the ghetto. In Białystok, Ephraim Barash knew about the nearby Treblinka death camp and the deportations from Warsaw. But his own contacts with local German officials convinced him that the Nazis needed the productive potential of the Białystok ghetto. These German officials were probably sincere in their assurances to Barash, but the Jewish leader had no way of knowing that ultimately it was the SS, not they, who would decide the fate of the Jews. Furthermore, as Dan Diner pointed out, what seemed like a "rational" course of behavior to *Judenrat* leaders actually played into the Germans' hands. If the ghetto might survive through labor, then it was rational to buy time by sacrificing, if there was no alternative, the old, the sick, and even children.[79]

In Lwów *Judenrat* leader Joseph Parnas was shot for refusing to provide a list of candidates for "forced labor." Many other *Judenrat* leaders, including for example Adolf Weinberg, the chairman of the Dąbrowa *Judenrat*, met the same fate. The three top commanders of the Jewish police in the Kovno ghetto suffered excruciating torture but refused to reveal the hiding places of Jewish children. In the Warsaw Ghetto, on the other hand, the Jewish police rounded up most of the deportees in July and August 1942 – even as teachers and caregivers such as Janusz Korczak voluntarily accompanied their wards to their death. Generalizations are difficult.

How did the broader masses of the Jewish population react to the disaster that engulfed them? To what degree did they "resist"? Historians no longer regard the question of resistance solely according to the criterion of armed struggle. Especially in Israel, historians such as Yehuda Bauer have developed the concept of "amidah," which transcended a narrow focus on armed combat and encompassed a vast effort at self-help, education, and smuggling – anything to thwart Nazi schemes to starve, humiliate, and dehumanize Jews. Amidah, according to Bauer, was "any group action consciously taken in opposition to known or surmised laws, actions or intentions directed against the Jews by the Germans and their supporters." Bauer mentioned one example of such resistance. One Chanukah, prisoners in a Nazi camp lit pieces of cardboard and sang a Chanukah hymn. "None of the people who did this were religious," Bauer noted. "But on the threshold of death and in the hell of Auschwitz they demonstrated.

---

[79] Dan Diner, *Beyond the Conceivable: Studies on Germany, Nazism and the Holocaust* (Berkeley: University of California Press, 2006), 117–138

They asserted several principles. That contrary to Nazi lore they were human; that Jewish tradition, history and values had a meaning for them in the face of Auschwitz; and that they wanted to assert their humanity in a Jewish way."[80]

If 80 percent of the Jews in the Warsaw Ghetto managed to stay alive until July 1942, despite starvation rations and raging epidemics, that was due in no small part to stubborn resistance. Families struggled to survive, neighbors helped each other, massive smuggling brought food into the ghetto. Warsaw Jewry started more than one thousand house committees, which united in the *Aleynhilf*, or Self Help. Recent scholarship by Dalia Ofer, Marion Kaplan, and others has pointed out the critical role played by Jewish women in maintaining the integrity of the family and filling the vacuum left by men who had been arrested or killed.[81]

In all of Nazi-occupied Europe an important part of amidah was culture in all its forms: education, theater, the plastic arts. Underground seminars, cabarets, public poetry readings helped keep spirits up. When a theater began in the Vilna Ghetto in January 1942, many political figures reacted with shock and anger. One pamphlet angrily proclaimed that "one does not play theater in a cemetery." But the theater and cabaret quickly attracted the entire ghetto population, and former critics admitted that it fulfilled a vital psychological need.

After the war one Jewish literary critic, Shlomo Belis, lambasted exactly what many survivors of the Vilna Ghetto pointed to with pride – the intense cultural creativity of the ghetto. The Germans were happy, Belis scoffed, that poetry and theater lulled the Jews into an illusion of normalcy and fostered a welcome passivity. Instead of "culture," the Jews should have prepared to fight. But other survivors defended the importance of "cultural resistance." Mark Dvorzhetsky, a physician who worked in the Vilna Ghetto, pointed out that cultural activities countered despair and apathy.[82] Yitzhak Zuckerman, a leader of the Jewish Fighting Organization in the Warsaw Ghetto, recalled that when the ardent members of the Zionist youth movements first heard the news of the Final Solution, they bitterly regretted having spent so much time and energy in seminars and study groups when they should have been preparing to fight. But after the war, Zuckerman realized that it was the intense cultural activity that paved the

---

[80] Bauer, *Rethinking the Holocaust*, 126.
[81] Dalia Ofer and Lenore Weitzman eds, *Women in the Holocaust* (New Haven: Yale University Press, 1998).
[82] Samuel Kassow, "Vilna and Warsaw, Two Ghetto Diaries: Herman Kruk and Emanuel Ringelblum" in *Holocaust Chronicles: Individualizing the Holocaust through Diaries and other Contemporaneous Accounts*, ed. Robert Moses Shapiro (New York: Ktav, 1999).

way for the armed resistance. Young Jews who understood Jewish history and felt keen national pride were now ready to give their lives for the honor of their people.[83]

Another vital form of resistance was documentation and the organization of underground archives. The Jews knew that the Germans intended to write their history and determine how future generations would remember European Jewry. All over Europe, doomed Jews wrote diaries, collected documents, and left testimonies to ensure that posterity would see Jewish sources and not just German documents. There were archives in many ghettos. The largest such project was the *Oyneg Shabes* archive in the Warsaw Ghetto. Organized by Emanuel Ringelblum, a historian and a community organizer, the *Oyneg Shabes* included more than 60 collaborators. Only three would survive the war.[84]

Religious Jews and their rabbis faced new dilemmas. *Judenrat* leaders asked rabbis to rule on whether it was permissible to make up deportation lists for "forced labor." Maimonides had ruled that "If the gentiles say to them, 'give us one of you and we will kill him, or else we will kill all of you', they should all let themselves be killed rather than hand over one Jew." In Vilna, Lodz, Lwów, and elsewhere, rabbis vehemently objected to decisions to hand over the sick or weak in order to buy time and save lives. Such a course of action, rabbis ruled, was not saving Jewish lives (*hatzala*) but handing Jews over to be killed (*mesira*). When a group of rabbis in Lwów approached *Judenrat* head Henryk Lansberg to warn him against handing over Jews, Landsberg exploded: "You gentlemen appear to believe that we live in prewar times ... let me tell you, the times have changed completely. We are no longer a religious community but an instrument to carry out the orders of the Gestapo."[85]

As Esther Farbstein has pointed out, the Holocaust brought out tensions between a number of basic halachic, or Jewish legal, principles. *Pikuakh nefesh* enjoined the Jew to save his life, even at the cost of violating commandments. Thus, one could violate the Sabbath to save a life. But *sha't ha-shmad* – a time of false apostasy – had totally different implications. When gentiles were forcing Jews to renounce their religion, then a Jew should rigorously follow every commandment, even at the risk of death. Under what circumstances could he break Jewish dietary laws? Could a religious Jew acquire gentile documents and deny his Jewishness in order to save his

---

[83] See for example Yitzhak Zuckerman, *A Surplus of Memory: Chronicle of the Warsaw Ghetto Uprising* (Berkeley: University of California Press, 1993), 159.

[84] On the archive see Kassow, *Who Will Write Our History?*

[85] Esther Farbstein, *Hidden in Thunder: Perspectives on Faith, Halachah and Leadership during the Holocaust* (Jerusalem: Mossad Harav Kook), 173.

life? What about married women whose husbands were sent away? What was their religious status?

Rabbis sought to find meaning in the disaster. In the Warsaw Ghetto the Piaseczner rebbe, Kalonymous Shapiro, preached that God was suffering along with the Jewish people.[86] Rabbi Yissakhar Teichtal, the Head of the Pestany yeshiva in Slovakia, wrote in 1943 that the catastrophe showed how wrong he and other rabbis had been in opposing Zionism. God was telling the Jewish people that they had made a great mistake by staying in the Diaspora. If Jews survived they had to make every effort to help the secular Jews build up the Land of Israel.[87]

Another painful question, which lingered long after the Holocaust, concerned the decision of great religious leaders such as the Gerer rebbe, the Satmarer rebbe, and the Belzer rebbe to escape from Europe. Before the war they had told their followers to stay in Eastern Europe. Was this now abandonment? Or was the survival of Torah Sages a blessing, an instrument to hasten the reconstruction of Jewish life after the war?

Religious Jews grappled with the traditional concept of *Kiddush hashem* – a martyr's death to sanctify God's name. In past persecutions, Jews could save their lives through conversion. But since the Nazis now killed all Jews regardless of their religion, what sense did *Kiddush hashem* make now? Rabbi Shimon Huberband, who worked with Emanuel Ringelblum in the Warsaw Ghetto archive, wrote that in the past a Jew died for *Kiddush hashem* when he sacrificed his life rather than abandon his faith; or when he gave his life to save another Jew or a group of Jews; or when he died fighting to defend Jews. But in the conditions of the present catastrophe, Huberband stressed, Maimonides's dictate on *Kiddush hashem* had special significance. Maimonides had written that when a Jew was killed just because he was a Jew, regardless of whether he was religious, then that Jew had to be considered a martyr.[88]

A new concept arose to complement *Kiddush hashem*: *Kiddush hahayim* (sanctification of life). Since the German goal was to kill all Jews, Jews in turn had to make every effort to stay alive and survive.[89]

Armed resistance was also widespread, more so than has been commonly believed. In addition to the well-known uprising in the Warsaw

---

[86] David Roskies, *The Literature of Destruction: Jewish Responses to Catastrophe* (Philadelphia: Jewish Publication Society, 1988), 506–509.

[87] Steven Katz et al. eds, *Wrestling with God: Jewish Theological Responses during and after the Holocaust* (Oxford: Oxford University Press, 2007), 75–83.

[88] Kassow, *Who Will Write Our History?*, 168.

[89] Israel Gutman, *Resistance* (New York: Houghton Mifflin, 1994), 84.

Ghetto, Jews fought in many smaller ghettos. In several places *Judenräte* encouraged flight and burned ghettos themselves to sow confusion, facilitate escape and deny Jewish property to the Germans. There were uprisings in Sobibor, Treblinka, and in Crematorium Number Four in Auschwitz. Thousands of Jews fought in resistance groups in Western Europe and thousands more fought in partisan groups, almost entirely Soviet or pro-communist in Eastern Europe.

The first important step in the organization of Jewish armed resistance took place in the Vilna Ghetto on January 1, 1942. The Zionist youth leader and fiery poet Abba Kovner insisted that the killings in Lithuania were no isolated pogrom but the beginning of a Nazi plan to murder all the Jews of Europe. He wrote a proclamation calling on Jews "not to go like sheep to the slaughter." Couriers fanned out from Vilna to other ghettos to transmit news of the German killings and to call for armed struggle.[90]

The issue of armed resistance raised many complex questions. Killing a German meant exposing the entire Jewish population to savage collective reprisals. Even if ardent fighters raised in the intense atmosphere of Zionist youth movements were convinced that Jews were doomed anyway and should therefore die with honor, could they make that decision for other Jews? Where would they get weapons? The Polish or the French under-grounds could count on social support and their fighters also believed that today's fight would ensure a better post-war future. The Jewish fighters were isolated and they had no "tomorrow" to count on. Indeed, while it was more rational to fight in the forests, where their chances of survival were better, Jewish fighting groups often made the decision to stand and fight in the ghetto. At least their fight would be remembered as a Jewish struggle, rather than redound to the credit of non-Jewish partisan groups.

Most of the battles against the Germans were waged by young people who had already lost their parents and who had no children of their own. In one small town in eastern Poland nearby partisans asked a physician in the ghetto to join them in the forest. But he refused to leave his aged father and they died together. Was this behavior any less heroic?

It is significant that in many ways the Battle of the Warsaw Ghetto was unique. The fighters in Warsaw secured the ardent support of the remaining ghetto population, who refused to obey German calls to report for deportation and who instead built an elaborate network of underground bunkers. In Białystok and Vilna, however, the fighters were confronted by a hostile ghetto population. The Jews had already heard about the Uprising

---

[90] Arad, *Ghetto in Flames*, 221–262; Dina Porat, *Fall of a Sparrow: The Life and Times of Abba Kovner* (Palo Alto: Stanford University Press, 2010).

in the Warsaw Ghetto but when the decisive moment came, the fighters got no support.

In Vilna and in Białystok, there were still Jewish leaders – Gens and Barash – who offered the Jews hope: hope that the ghetto would keep working; hope that even if Jews were deported, it would be to labor camps. In Warsaw, on the other hand, there was a leadership vacuum which the fighters filled. The *Judenrat* had basically collapsed and the Jewish Fighting Organization had assassinated Jewish collaborators.

Although Jewish resistance had little military impact it played a major role in forging a narrative of pride and heroism that would be essential in the difficult task of rebuilding the Jewish people in the post-war period.

SELECT BIBLIOGRAPHY

Ancel, Jean. *History of the Holocaust in Romania*. Lincoln: University of Nebraska Press, 2012.

Arad, Yitzhak. *The Holocaust in the Soviet Union*. Lincoln: University of Nebraska Press, 2012.

Bankier, David and Michman, Dan. *Holocaust Historiography in Context: Emergence, Challenges, Polemics and Achievements*. Jerusalem: Yad Vashem, 2009.

Bartov, Omer. *Murder in Our Midst: the Holocaust, Industrial Killing and Representation*. New York: Oxford University Press. 1996.

Bauer, Yehuda. *Jews for Sale: Jewish–Nazi Negotiations, 1933–1945*. New Haven: Yale University Press, 1994.

Rethinking the Holocaust. New Haven: Yale University Press, 2002.

Bergen, Doris L. *War and Genocide: a Concise History of the Holocaust*. Boulder: Rowman and Littlefield, 2003.

Blatman, Daniel. *The Death Marches: The Final Phase of Nazi Genocide*. Translated by Chaya Galai. Cambridge: Harvard University Press, 2011.

Braham, Randolph L. *The Politics of Genocide: The Holocaust in Hungary*. Detroit: Wayne State University Press, 2000.

Breitman, Richard and Lichtman, Alan. *FDR and the Jews*. Cambridge: Belknap Press, 2014.

Browning, Christopher. *Ordinary Men: Reserve Police Battalion 101 and the Final Solution in Poland*. New York: Harper Collins, 1992.

Remembering Survival: Inside a Nazi Slave Labor Camp. New York: W. W. Norton, 2011.

Dawidowicz, Lucy. *A Holocaust Reader*. New York: Behrman House, 1976.

Dean, Martin. *Robbing the Jews: the Confiscation of Jewish Property during the Holocaust*. Cambridge: Cambridge University Press, 2001.

Dobroszycki, Lucjan, ed. *The Chronicle of the Lodz Ghetto*. New Haven: Yale University Press, 1987.

Engelking-Boni, Barbara and Jacek Leociak. *The Warsaw Ghetto: Guide to the Perished City*. New Haven: Yale University Press, 2009.

Friedländer, Saul. *Nazi Germany and the Jews: The Years of Persecution, 1933–1939*. New York: Harper and Row, 1998.

THE MODERN WORLD, 1815–2000

Nazi Germany and the Jews: The Years of Extermination, 1939–1945. New York: Harper and Row, 2008.

When Memory Comes. New York: Farrar Strauss and Giroux, 1979.

Gross, Jan. Neighbors: The Destruction of the Jewish Community in Jedwabne, Poland. Princeton: Princeton University Press, 2001.

Gutman, Israel. Jews of Warsaw, 1939–1943: Ghetto, Underground, Revolt. Bloomington: Indiana University Press, 1983.

Herf, Jeffrey. The Jewish Enemy: Nazi Propaganda during World War II and the Holocaust. Cambridge: Harvard University Press, 2006.

Hilberg, Raul. The Destruction of the European Jews. 3 volumes. New Haven: Yale University Press, 2003.

Hilberg Raul, Stanislaw Staron and Joseph Kermisz, eds. The Warsaw Diary of Adam Czerniakow: Prelude to Doom. Translated by Stanislaw Staron and the staff of Yad Vashem. New York: Stein and Day, 1979.

Kaplan, Marion. Between Dignity and Despair: Jewish Life in Nazi Germany. New York: Oxford University Press, 1999.

Kassow, Samuel. Who Will Write Our History: Emanuel Ringelblum and the Oyneg Shabes Archive. Bloomington: Indiana University Press, 2007.

Lang, Berel. Act and Idea in the Nazi Genocide. Syracuse: Syracuse University Press, 2003.

Langer, Lawrence. Art from the Ashes: A Holocaust Anthology. New York and Oxford: Oxford University Press, 1995.

Lanzmann, Claude. Shoah: An Oral History of the Holocaust, the Complete Text of the Film. New York: Pantheon, 1985.

Levi, Primo. Survival in Auschwitz. New York: Touchstone, 1995.

Longerich, Peter. Holocaust: The Nazi Persecution and Murder of the Jews. New York: Oxford University Press, 2012.

Marrus, Michael and Paxton, Stanley. Vichy France and the Jews. New York: Basic Books, 1981.

Michman, Dan. Holocaust Historiography: A Jewish Perspective. London: Valentine-Mitchell, 2003.

Moore, Bob. Victims and Survivors: The Nazi Persecution of Jews in the Netherlands 1940–1945. London: Arnold, 1995.

Ofer, Dalia and Lenore J. Weizman, eds. Women in the Holocaust. New Haven: Yale University Press, 1999.

Phayer, Michael. The Catholic Church and the Holocaust, 1930–1965. Bloomington: Indiana University Press, 2001.

Porat Dina. The Blue and Yellow Stars of David: the Zionist Leadership of Palestine and the Holocaust. Cambridge: Harvard University Press, 1990.

The Fall of a Sparrow: The Life and Times of Abba Kovner. Palo Alto: Stanford University Press, 2009.

Poznanski, Renée. Jews in France During World War II. Translated by Nathan Bracher. Waltham, MA: Brandeis University Press, 2001.

Presser, Jacques. *Ashes in the Wind: The Destruction of Dutch Jewry*. Translated by Arnold Pomerans. London: Souvenir Press, 2010.

Roskies, David. *Holocaust Literature: A History and Guide*. Waltham, MA: Brandeis University Press, 2013.

Sarfatti, Michele. *The Jews in Mussolini's Italy: from Equality to Persecution*. Madison: University of Wisconsin Press, 2006.

Spiegelman, Art. *Maus: A Survivor's Tale*. 2 volumes. New York: Pantheon, 1986.

Stone, Dan. *Histories of the Holocaust*. New York: Oxford University Press, 2010.

Teichman, Milton. *Truth and Lamentation: Stories and Poems on the Holocaust*. Champagne-Urbana: University of Illinois Press, 1993.

Trunk, Isaiah. *Judenrat: the Jewish Councils in Eastern Europe under Nazi Occupation*. New York: Macmillan, 1996.

Wyman, David and Charles Rosenzveig. *The World Reacts to the Holocaust*. Baltimore: Johns Hopkins University Press, 1996.

Zuccotti, Susan. *Under His Very Windows: the Vatican and the Holocaust in Italy*. New Haven: Yale University Press, 2002.

PART III

JEWISH CULTURES, NATIONAL AND TRANSNATIONAL

CHAPTER 24

JEWISH CULTURE: WHAT IS IT?
In Search of Jewish Culture

ZOHAR SHAVIT AND YAAKOV SHAVIT

In the consciousness of the nation, the term culture, in its comprehensive and human sense, has replaced the theological term Torah.

Haïm Nahman Bialik, 1925[1]

I

In 1899, the young Martin Buber read the first volume of Jacob Burckhardt's monumental *Griechische Kulturgeschichte*, which appeared in four volumes between 1898 and 1902. In a letter to a friend Buber wrote: "I ask myself when we shall have such a book, A History of Jewish Culture."[2] More than a century has passed since then, and we still have no comprehensive book on the history and nature of Jewish culture.

There are at least two explanations for this long-standing omission. The more general one is the difficulty of defining culture. In writing about it, authors have narrowed or broadened its scope to suit their own points of view, and their discussion of culture is frequently characterized by obfuscation, ambiguity, and elusiveness.[3] The more specific explanation is that Jewish culture is a dynamic phenomenon – with a variety of contents, forms, and styles – which has undergone many changes, and even upheavals, from its inception. Throughout Jewish history there have been particular Jewish cultures that were shaped, inter alia, by the influence of the host cultures in the varied geo-cultural environments in which Jews lived: for

[1] Haïm Nahman Bialik, "Liftichat haUniversitah haIvrit biYerushlayim" (On the Inauguration of the Hebrew University in Jerusalem), in *Divrei Sifrut*, 2nd ed, ed. Haïm Nahman Bialik. (Tel Aviv, 1965), 127–135 (Hebrew).
[2] In Paul Mendes-Flohr, "Hale'umiyut shebalev," in *In Memory of M. Buber on the Tenth Anniversary of his Death* (Jerusalem, 1987), 34 (the title represents the German title: *Nationalismus der Innerlichkeit*).
[3] See Alfred Louis Kroeber and Clyde Kluckhohn, *Culture: A Critical Review of Concept and Definitions* (New York: Kraus Reprint, 1953).

677

example, the Hellenistic Jewish culture or the Jewish culture in Spain in the Muslim period.[4]

In his introduction to *The Civilization of the Renaissance in Italy*, Burckhardt modestly described his work as "*Ein Versuch*" (an Essay).[5] What he probably meant to say, among other things, was that even such a comprehensive and detailed panorama of a particular culture could not include all its components and innumerable strata and, at the same time, also describe its complex dynamic. Burckhardt was writing about the history of Greek culture and of Renaissance culture in Italy, that is, "closed" cultures, which no longer exist and of which only the memory and heritage remain. In contrast, Jewish culture has not ceased to exist and is not only a heritage. Therefore, any attempt to describe its development and to paint a comprehensive panoramic picture of it is a much more difficult undertaking and certainly can be no more than an attempt.

The nineteenth century saw the emergence of an understanding of Judaism as a supra-temporal and unchanging entity, characterized by a singular essence. Consequently, Jewish culture was perceived as an embodiment of this essence, that is, as an all-inclusive system whose components manifest this essence. It was also seen as an entity which develops and renews itself without relying on external influences and without borrowing from them.

This essay does not attempt to discuss the essence of Judaism. Instead, it maintains that the view of Judaism that emerged in the nineteenth century, as an immanent entity rather than a set of beliefs and commandments, created an urgent need to anchor that entity in inherent traits, race, national psyche, and unique genius. This new view reflected the transition from a theocentric approach to an ethnocentric one, which constituted an important chapter in Jewish intellectual history in modern times. This ethnocentric view will serve as our point of departure; it is an understanding that the culture of a certain human group is a whole way of life – that group's intellectual, artistic, and material achievements – and that it is expressed and embodied in, inter alia, a value system, a symbolic system, a worldview, cultural codes and their practical translation into everyday life, creative products, organizations, and institutions.

---

[4] The literature on Jewish culture comprises hundreds, perhaps thousands, of essays, articles, and books which cover a variety of aspects and issues. Because of this literature's vast dimensions, we will refer to just a few of these works in the selected bibliography.

[5] Jacob Burckhardt, *The Civilization of the Renaissance in Italy*, trans. S. G. C. Middlemore (London: Penguin Books, 1990), 19. The original German edition bore the subtitle: *Ein Versuch*, and the English translation reads: "this work bears the title of an essay in the strictest sense of the word" – an attempt.

In the specific context of Jewish history, the discussion of the culture of Jews and of Jewish culture should deal with two preliminary questions:

First, are we talking about a single cultural unit whose components share a unifying platform, or are we talking about an assembly of distinct and separate cultures, which nevertheless have some shared elements?

Second, what is the "Jewish content" of Jewish culture? That is, what are the uniquely Jewish characteristics of the cultural components that are common to all the sub-cultures of the Jews?

These two questions have engaged Jewish thought and discourse over the past two centuries and they have received numerous, varied, and even diametrically opposed answers. The continuous historical existence of Jews for 3,000 years as a singular collective characterized as distinctive – both by itself and by others who describe its unique attributes – and the broad geo-cultural dispersal of Jews make it difficult to write a general and comprehensive history of Jewish culture as a unified and uniform culture. It is difficult, too, because we are dealing with three different historical spheres:

1. Jewish culture as a minority culture existing within hegemonic non-Jewish cultures, manifesting unique patterns and maintaining complex, stratified, and dynamic relations with the non-Jewish cultures.
2. The participation of individual Jews in non-Jewish cultures.
3. Jewish culture as a majority culture in a hegemonic and sovereign Jewish society.

II

Tarbut (the Hebrew word for culture) is a new concept in Jewish history. When it was first used, some Jews opposed it because traditionally it signified idolatry and apostasy. Consider, for example, *tarbut anashim chata'im* (a brood of sinful men), Num 32:14, or *tarbut ra'ah* (bad ways) bHag.15a. Therefore, the early Hebrew discourse on the topic used the Russian *kultura* or German *Kultur*. In 1902, Ahad Ha'am (Asher Ginsberg) described the opposition to the use of *tarbut* thus:

One has only to utter from the podium the terrible word *kultura* – perhaps the loftiest and most exalted word in the entire human linguistic treasury – to arouse tremendous excitement on all sides as if the great Day of Judgment had arrived.[6]

---

[6] Ahad Ha'am, "The Spiritual Revival," in *Selected Essays*, ed. and trans. Leon Simon (Philadelphia: The Jewish Publication Society, 1944), 253–307.

The opposition to the Hebrew word for culture stemmed not only from the traditional negative connotation of the word, or from resistance to the acceptance and internalization of certain non-Jewish cultural components, but mainly from the perception of culture as a total alternative to religion, an alternative that is the product of human creation.[7] However, it was difficult to oppose the acceptance of the term, and thus, from the end of the eighteenth century, and primarily during the nineteenth century, the great change that took place in Jewish life in Europe was marked by the growing use of the term. It signified a worldview, a value system, and daily practices and their concrete manifestations in daily life. In other words, culture now referred to a complex of specific manifestations of human endeavor. This complex was seen by more and more Jews as a comprehensive system, all-encompassing and sovereign, which should become an alternative to both religion and religious tradition. It seems safe to argue that the acceptance of the Hebrew term for "culture" in Jewish discourse can be seen as an expression of both acculturation and internal revolution. It ceased to signify apostasy, and instead became self-evident as a socio-historical phenomenon. This was expressed, for example, in the emergence of various other modern terms, such as Jewish religious culture, rabbinical culture, and traditional culture. Sometimes the term Judaism was used synonymously with the term culture, and "Jewish culture" came to mean that Judaism incorporated all the elements included in the newly accepted term culture.

The acceptance of the term culture and its widespread use in both scholarly and public discourses led the Hebrew author David Frischmann to write: "The word *kultura*, after all, [is] an indeterminate word which says nothing, or even worse than that, one that says too much. Whenever they cannot precisely designate some spiritual concept, they take the vague word *kultura* and sport it before us...."[8]

We contend that the term culture was adopted in Jewish polemics and literature to give new meaning to the term Judaism, or, in more radical cases, to provide a new definition of Judaism ("new Judaism") – a definition that would serve as a shared new platform for the affiliation and identity of Jews. According to this radical view, the Jews are not an ethnic group or a religious community but rather a *Kulturvolk*, a people with a culture, whose identity and uniqueness are expressed not only – nor

[7] On *Pulmus hakultura* (The Culture Debate) in early Zionism, see Ehud Luz, *Parallels Meet: Religion and Nationalism in the Early Zionist Movement (1882–1904)* (Tel Aviv: Am Oved, 1985), 187–213 (Hebrew).

[8] Quoted in Joseph Haïm Brenner, "Bachayim u-vasifrut" (In Life and in Literature) in *Kol kitvei J.H. Brenner* (Collected Writings), vol. ii (Tel Aviv: Magnes, 1961), 55–65 (Hebrew).

even mainly – through religious practices and religious creativity. At the same time, this view broadened and enriched the scope of Judaism, which now included a larger repertoire of cultural components. Even if these components had existed previously, they had not been considered inseparable, central, or crucial parts of Judaism, but rather marginal or neutral appendages to it. In contrast, according to the radical view, religion is but one of many cultural products and manifestations. Jewish culture was regarded as secular even though it drew on components from the religious tradition and secularized them. Part of the religious sector in modern times responded to this radical view by offering a new and broader understanding of Judaism, this time including a cultural repertoire that previously had not been defined as part of Jewish life and culture.

III

Jews always had a culture, but, as we have seen, they did not always use this term for it. That is because before modern times no distinction was made between religion and "non-religion," and because the term culture (like the term civilization), as distinct from religion, appeared only towards the middle of the eighteenth century. Without using the term culture, the Sages used to distinguish between Jewish culture and non-Jewish culture, not only in the religious sense but also in the human-existential sense, as can be learned from the words of R. Levi: "All Israel's actions are distinct from the corresponding actions of the nations of the world: this applies to their ploughing, their sowing, their reaping, their sheaves, their threshing, their granaries, their wineries – their shaving, and their counting" (Num. Rabbah 10:1 to Deut. Rabbah 7:7). Similarly, when a gentile said to R. Yohanan Ben Zakkai that gentiles and Jews have different holidays, and asked him: "Which is the day whereon we and you rejoice alike?" the response he received was, "It is the day when rain falls." In the same vein, the Sages warned: "Nor shall you follow their customs, the things engraved in their hearts, such as theatres and circuses and stadia" (Sifra, Acharei, 9:13, ed. Weiss, 86a).

At the same time, Jewish tradition sought to define permissible and non-permissible borrowing from other cultures. Despite the ideology and practice of isolationism, Jews were very much aware that no culture can be isolated, nor can influences and borrowings from other cultures be rejected totally. They understood that cultural influences are a necessary evil whose scope must be controlled. There were always broad and varied intercultural contacts between Jews and their surroundings, and a large repertoire of cultural items and cultural properties broke through from outside into

Jewish culture, broadening it, enriching it, and being internalized by it, sometimes by being "judaized" and undergoing a change in appearance.

Before modern times, the content and boundaries of Jewish culture were dictated by religion (the Torah and the halacha) and by practices that shaped traditions and customs. The halacha covered large parts of Jewish life: It determined the value system, the patterns of behavior, and the rules and codes of behavior in social and cultural contexts; it defined what was permitted and what was forbidden with regard to the consumption of cultural products; and to a great extent it determined the nature of those cultural products. The customs, in turn, determined and shaped rituals and obligatory rules of behavior in various parts of the Jewish life cycle. In addition to the halacha and *Minhag* (custom), there was the rich world of folklore, folk beliefs, and folk practices (folkways), and magic and witchcraft, some of which had a semi-halachic value.[9] In addition to all these, the culture of the Jews included the creation of literary and artistic works and philosophical and scientific treatises. The Jews had their own material culture whose components were only partly determined by halacha and *Minhag*. Halacha and custom included mainly restrictions and prohibitions that determined which cultural practices were to be regarded as an abandoning of tradition (*Darche Avot*, "the ways of the ancestors"), as "following in the footsteps of the gentiles," or as apostasy. They did not, however, set guidelines concerning the desired and permitted cultural products. The need to formulate such detailed guidelines developed only in modern times, for three reasons.

The first reason is that the notion of "culture" filled the void created by the "breaching of the fence," that is, the abandonment of the Jewish sphere (which was defined and enclosed by sets of commands and prohibitions and by communal scrutiny) and the departure for the world "outside the fence" (the non-Jewish sphere), a departure variously described as dissipation, acculturation, secularization, modernization, or westernization. Whatever name it was given, this departure shattered the old social frameworks and created a vacuum which was quickly filled by modern Jews' notion of "culture," consisting of elements, models, and repertoires which previously had not occupied a significant place in the Jewish sphere. The establishment of these new frameworks was usually the result of ideology, a program, and the activities of numerous cultural agents who collectively organized and even established Jewish endeavor. Moreover, the building of a new Jewish culture (or rather, Jewish cultures) was the most salient expression of the understanding that "Jewish culture" refers not only to life

[9] Israel M. Ta-Shma, *Early Franco-German Ritual and Custom* (Jerusalem: The Hebrew University, 1992), 13–105 (Hebrew).

in a secular sphere or to a moderate or radical change in the way of life but to an all-inclusive, singular Jewish system of culture.

The second reason is that the boundaries between Jewish and non-Jewish cultures had become blurred, and thus it was necessary to redefine the cultural boundary between what belonged to Judaism and was thus within it and what was outside it. Consequently, it was necessary to confirm the criteria for determining what was permitted or forbidden in adopting elements from the surrounding cultures. In modern times, the need to define cultural boundaries increased when many new cultural components – considered important and valuable by modern Western culture – were incorporated into the Jewish cultural system; these included, for example, literature, music, plastic arts, and science. These components entered Jewish culture with greater intensity than ever before and in unprecedented quantities, and their incorporation received legitimization and encouragement from circles that saw in them a sign of openness and an expression of cultural renewal and modernity. There was a great need to define the cultural boundaries because from that point on the cultural system was understood as a comprehensive whole that defined Jewish identity.

The third reason for the need to formulate guidelines is that Jews began to be active in cultural areas in which they had not been involved previously. This resulted in questions about the precise nature of the Jewish content or Jewish style of their work, and it became necessary to define the unique characteristics of that content and style. What is Jewish literature, what is Jewish art, what is Jewish music?

IV

The use of the term culture in the nineteenth century, which prompted these discussions and deliberations, appeared for the first time in the writings of the *Wissenschaft des Judentums* (science of Judaism) scholars in Germany, and was reflected in the name Verein für Kultur und Wissenschaft der Juden (The Society for Jewish Culture and Science), founded in Berlin in 1819. Its members strove to describe culture "in its fullest scope"; in their view, it included all types of written texts: literature, philosophy, and science. They were not trying to revive Jewish culture, but rather to assemble the corpus of past Jewish creation. In this, they, and the Haskalah movement before them, began a process, which grew more intense and comprehensive in later generations, of discovering and publishing all the assets of Jewish high culture. In doing so they were greatly influenced by their German intellectual environment. As is well known, before developing their national and political might, the Germans (especially the middle classes) based their national pride and self-esteem on achievements in science, literature, philosophy, and music – in short, on German *Kultur*.[10] The new ensemble of Jewish works was termed culture, and that created a need to find an organizing factor which would give this ensemble a "Jewish character," "Jewish originality," and a "Jewish identity." This need led to the adoption of a "holistic approach,"[11] that is, a view of all the manifestations of culture as rooted in a single principle.

The need to redefine the fundamentals of Jewish culture and to describe all its components led to scrutiny of the earlier culture in an attempt to find the constitutive principles of Jewish culture. In the nineteenth century this resulted in an upsurge of research into the history of culture, which sought to rediscover and portray all the manifestations of what would now be termed "Jewish culture." The aim of this intellectual activity was to prove that there had always been a wide-ranging and all-inclusive Jewish culture, that Jews were not isolated and cut off by their religious life, that they did not lack the mental capacity required for the creation of culture, and that therefore they were no less "cultured" than any other "cultured" people; perhaps they were even more so. This look to the past resulted from the growing rifts in the social and cultural barriers between Jewish and non-Jewish society in Western Europe, a process that began even before the nineteenth century as the contacts between them expanded. This process was facilitated by the secularization and modernization of European societies and by the emergence of the notion of cultural particularism and the view of national identity as rooted in the national culture. Thus, the history of Jewish culture became a cultural battleground and a vital and useful tool in the *Kulturkampf* between various factions in the Jewish community.

The search for the past served several objectives:

First, to counter the claim that "the Jews never worship the Graces,"[12] and to prove, instead, that they were endowed with the necessary abilities to participate in all aspects of cultural endeavor, thus ensuring their admission into non-Jewish society and leading to their integration into the culture of its elite;

Second, to supply internal legitimization (to the conservative Jewish community) for the expansion of the cultural field and the introduction of

---

[10] Norbert Elias, *The Germans: Power Struggles and the Development of Habitus in the Nineteenth and Twentieth Centuries*, trans. Eric Dunning and Stephen Mennell (New York: Columbia University Press, 1996), 323.

[11] E. H. Gombrich, *In Search of Cultural History* (Oxford: Clarendon Press, 1969), 29.

[12] Henri Baptiste Grégoire, *Essai sur la régénération physique et politique des Juifs* (Paris, 1789), chap. 25, p. 182.

cultural change, by arguing that similar past endeavors were granted legitimization and by describing those past endeavors;

Third, to prove that Jewish culture had enough internal vitality to generate a cultural revival that would include all the fundamentals and components which, by modern standards, turn an ethnic group or a religious community into a people (*Kulturvolk*).

V

The study of the nature of the "new Jewish culture" focused largely on the massive entry of Jews into non-Jewish culture, which led to the hyperbolic description of the nineteenth century as a "Jewish century." Thus, for example, the enthusiastic description of Kalman Schulmann, a maskil from Vilna, who in 1869 noted the fast pace and great intensity of Jews' involvement in every aspect of cultural activity in the nineteenth century:

Anyone who can see clearly will gaze with astonishment at the Jews' rapid ascent to the heights in modern times in all areas of wisdom and knowledge, in all arts and crafts. This they achieved in just a short while, whereas other peoples did not succeed in attaining such heights even over a period of many hundreds of years. For no sooner did the kings and counts of the land unloose their bonds, and favor them with civil rights and laws, than they opened their treasures and displayed precious qualities and fine talents that had lain dormant in their souls during dark years when they were persecuted by their foes, who gave them no respite until they devoured them.

Before many days had passed, there arose proudly from their midst great poets, wondrous rhetoricians, lauded authors in all realms, renowned mathematicians, and engineers, astronomers, chronologists, men well versed in religion and law and knowledgeable in all branches of the natural sciences, famous physicians, psalmists, musicians, diplomats, sculptors, visionaries. And there is no wisdom, art, or craftsmanship in which the Jews did not engage and become famous in the land for their prowess.[13]

Similarly, the historian Heinrich [Tzwi] Graetz wrote in 1883: "And now, dear friend, take a look at what the Jews have achieved in less than one century. They perform in all branches of science and literature and in some they are the leaders."[14]

In other words, it was not only a matter of the entry of Jews into a non-Jewish culture, but also of their growing and intense presence in it and

[13] Kalman Schulmann, *Divrei yemei olam*, iv (Vilna, 1867), 13–16.
[14] Heinrich [Tzwi] Graetz, "Correspondence of an English lady on Judaism and Semitism" letter eight (1883) in Heinrich Graetz, *The Structure of Jewish History and Other Essays*, ed. and trans. Ismar Schorsch (New York: Ktav, 1975), 220.

their increasing influence on it. The scholarly literature of the past one hundred and fifty years deals extensively with the question of the incorporation of Jews in various areas of cultural endeavor and their contribution, and it also attempts to explain the underlying incentive. Both scholarly literature and polemical texts tried to foster Jewish self-esteem by portraying the unprecedentedly intense participation of Jews in all these aspects of cultural life from the beginning of the nineteenth century as a central phenomenon of Jewish culture in the modern period. Some even argued that the "Jewish spirit" and its main assets (foremost among them the Hebrew Bible) were the "founding mother" of Western culture and of the modernization process that was leading humankind to the pinnacle of its achievement. Others went so far as to argue that the Jews were the initiators and fosterers of certain national cultures. The participation of Jews in the surrounding cultures and the great extent of their identification with them, to the point of giving up many earlier traits of Jewish culture, was seen by religious and nationalist Jews as assimilation. In anti-Jewish literature it was described as the Jews' gaining control over the surrounding culture and as a judaization of that culture. However, it was individual Jews who participated in non-Jewish culture, and the extent to which that participation can be considered part of Jewish culture is doubtful.

The great change that transpired in Jewish society in the nineteenth century and especially towards the end of that century was characterized by Jews leaving their religious and communal frameworks – controlled and directed by halacha, custom, and tradition – and entering the cultural world outside and integrating into it.

This led to the acceptance and absorption of non-Jews' value systems and behavioral patterns. The extent to which this occurred is evident from the reproaches against those Jews who had left: they were no longer classed as heretics or sceptics but were seen, instead, as dissipated, that is, as those who had abandoned the obligatory and accepted norms and behaviors in both private and public life and who had adopted a corrupt lifestyle and dissolute habits of cultural consumption. Later, what had been viewed as dissipation – such as shaving off a beard, sexual license, reading of non-Hebrew literature, attending the theater, or entering a tavern – was described as a sign of secularization. Entry into a non-Jewish culture was usually not the outcome of a change in the Jewish worldview, but rather the result of a lowering of some of the barriers that separated Jews from non-Jews and of the new opportunities which allowed large groups of Jews not only to consume cultural products but also to participate in their production. The nineteenth century was the century in which a passion for culture, in the sense of consumption of numerous cultural products, appeared at the same time as a surge of Jewish creation in many cultural fields.

In 1833, Michael Benedict Lessing published the following description of urban Jewish society in Prussia:

Let us look at the tremendous change in the language, dress, way of life, needs and entertainments, morals, and customs of the Jews! [...] Even their external appearance, [notice] how it has changed since then. Who would not have immediately identified a Jew by his clumsy eastern dress, by his wide and dark kapote, by his fur visor slung over his forehead, by the slippers, and by the beard that damages his face? Who would not have immediately identified the Jewish matron by her silver-embroidered cap, her severe visage with no adornment of hair? And how many Jews still look like that today, unless they are relics of the past or immigrants from Poland? With what strictness they then held on to the petty customs, and which Jew would have had the inner strength to open his shop on the Sabbath thirty years ago, or go about his business, write, or travel? [...] Was it indeed possible thirty years ago to see a Jew sit down with the Christian guests of a tavern or restaurant, speak freely with them, eat the same food as them, and consume the same drink as them? [...] Now nearly all the Christian schools in the towns admit the children of Jewish residents, especially in the upper grades [...] Only in a very few homes do old members of the household use the Jewish dialect, whereas the children – and yes – and mainly – the urban ones, speak, at home and in public, the same language as that of their Christian co-citizens [and] brethren [...] Apparently, there are still hundreds of thousands of people alive from the second half of the past century, and we call upon them to confirm whether, in their youth, they ever found a Jew at concerts, parties, balls, folk fests, [...] in cafés, and in the halls of the bourse, or saw them poring over daily newspapers, [...] or met them in the theatre, in music, and in art ... whether they ever found intellectual Jews in scientific circles and other circles who were not inferior to the rest of society in their social manners or knowledge.[15]

The portrayal of two diametrically opposed social and cultural realities – the traditional and conservative old one and the modern new one – apparently referred only to a small circle of Jews, probably bourgeois urban Jews in Western Europe. Lessing described the cultural portrait he painted not as German culture, but rather as modern culture, that is, the culture of the European bourgeoisie.

The appearance of this culture was partly the outcome of a social and cultural project of the Haskalah movement which, at the end of the eighteenth century, initiated a social reform that was meant not only to add knowledge and expand the Jewish textual world, but also to thoroughly reform Jewish society and culture. This reform aimed to change Jewish

---

[15] M. B. Lessing, *Die Juden und die öffentliche Meinung im preussischen Staate* (Altona: Hammerich, 1833), 129–132.

culture by replacing old norms with new ones, namely, with a new and different cultural repertoire, and by changing part of the *habitus* of individuals in the private sphere, that is, by introducing changes in the areas of both *Kultus* and *Kultur*. The maskilim (the members of the Haskalah movement) defined Haskalah as "true culture," "which is useful and necessary for every Jewish man."[16] Although the maskilim did not declare their goal as creating a new Jewish culture that was an integral whole, and although most of them were not secular, in practice they strove to build a comprehensive Jewish culture that would serve as a complement, or even as an alternative, to traditional Jewish culture, and which at the same time would establish new boundaries between the Jewish and the non-Jewish cultures. In other words, the Haskalah and other movements that succeeded it sought not only to set boundaries and restrictions on processes of acculturation in order to prevent the introduction of what they saw as the harmful components of non-Jewish culture, but also to propose an alternative to acculturation by filling the Jewish cultural system with cultural components that it lacked. Because the Haskalah movement tried to reconstruct Jewish culture by selectively combining old and new cultural components, it had to determine which components were lacking. Further, it had to decide which components, which had existed in the past and could be revived, were necessary, and which should be adopted from the surrounding cultures. In this sense, the Haskalah was the first to outline a cultural program. In practice, however, socio-cultural processes determined the pace, extent, and areas of acculturation.

VI

The culture of Western European Jewish society developed in modern times along two paths. The first was *integration into European culture*. This led to the belief that parts of the Jewish people in Western Europe were losing – or had already lost – their authentic shared culture, that the shared platform had disappeared, and that the Jewish people was splitting and dividing not only along religious or local lines, but also in accordance with the intensity of the processes of acculturation that it was undergoing. Jews were divided by their nationalities and became, for example, German Jews, Russian Jews, and American Jews. They were active in the surrounding culture and they adopted its value system and daily practices and lifestyle. Even if their cultural products had a distinctly "Jewish" character, they were not part of Jewish culture.

[16] Naphtali Herz Wessely, *Divre shalom veemet* (Words of Peace and Truth) (Warsaw, 1886), 5–6. Originally published Berlin, 1782.

The second path was the *construction or re-construction of Jewish culture* by expanding the areas and the number of cultural activities and by inventing traditions: The most prominent manifestation of this was the national-cultural revival called *Hat'chiya Ha-ivrit* (*The Hebrew Revival*). Autonomous Jewish cultural institutions were established, offering an equivalent to those of the surrounding cultures. Most prominent among them were institutes of Jewish education, public libraries, publishing houses, cultural clubs, theaters, newspapers, and periodicals. This process of filling up a distinct Jewish cultural system was intensive and multi-faceted, both in areas of "the great tradition" and of "the little tradition."[17] Here one can distinguish between those Jews who raised a barrier between themselves and the surrounding culture in an attempt to prevent its influence and those who lowered it. In general, relations with the surrounding cultures were characterized by a wide range of interactions, all of which involved absorbing and internalizing components of the modern pan-European culture. Such an alternative system existed in both Western and Eastern Europe, but it was much more typical of Eastern Europe with its 5 million Jews, and the areas of activity there were much more numerous than in Western Europe.

All Jewish subcultures absorbed and internalized new cultural components, including new areas of knowledge, such as the sciences. Jewish intellectuals, writers, artists, and scientists created a rich corpus of non-religious literature and offered the public the possibility of consuming various cultural products, such as theater, dance, and music. They established frameworks for modern education and participated in non-Jewish educational frameworks from kindergarten to university, created new patterns of leisure and entertainment, participated in sports, changed their external appearance and dress, took part in political activities, and so on. Jews who lived in these subcultures adopted, as we have said, a new *habitus*.[18] For some Jews, the autonomous cultural system acted as a subculture in the sense that they also participated – both as creators and consumers – in the hegemonic culture; thus they lived in a cultural reality that was split in two and they had a dual identity (*Zweiheit*). We will discuss the two cultural "realities" by briefly examining two components which played a major role in the creation of the new Jewish cultural reality: language and literature.

---

[17] Milton B. Singer, *When a Great Tradition Modernizes: An Anthropological Approach to Indian Civilization* (New York: Praeger, 1972), 3–10.

[18] Pierre Bourdieu, "The Habitus and the Space of Life-styles," in *Distinction: A Social Critique of the Judgement of Taste*, trans. Richard Nice (Cambridge, MA: Harvard University Press, 1984), 170–225.

The Hebrew language had always been a written language; in various contexts and periods it also served as a spoken language. Jews, however, had always lived in a state of linguistic diglossia, that is, in a state of a division of labor between the languages.[19] Especially from the nineteenth century, Jews were bilingual and often trilingual. Both the religious and the non-religious Jewish textual world, too, was bilingual or multilingual, and important works, such as, for example, Maimonides's *The Guide for the Perplexed* or Yehuda Halevi's *The Kuzari*, were written in "non-Jewish" languages (whereas languages such as Yiddish, Hebrew, and Ladino were used only by Jews).

From the end of the eighteenth century, and mainly during the nineteenth century, languages began to be considered both as giving expression to the inner life of a nation and as defining the unique worldview of an ethnic or national group. Language was also seen as having a central role in nation building and identity building. Various languages underwent standardization and became the unifying force of nations. But the status of the Hebrew language in Europe decreased as the command of the languages of the majority cultures – German, French, or Russian – became a necessary condition for civil integration, not to mention cultural and natural integration; to quote the learned Moritz Lazarus, who said, "*Die Sprache allein macht uns zu Deutschen*" – It is the language that makes us Germans.[20]

In Eastern Europe, Yiddish was the lingua franca of the large Jewish population. By the middle of the nineteenth century it was seen as an authentic national language and it developed as the language of high modern culture while continuing to function as the language of the folk. The revival of Hebrew as both a literary and spoken language in the Diaspora had a crucial role in creating "culture in Hebrew" and "Hebrew culture." Ideologues and agents of Hebrew culture saw it as the natural language of the Jews and as a necessary condition for national revival. Thus, it was necessary to expand Hebrew so it could function as a written language and as a language of communication in every aspect of life. Expanding the language, ensuring that all its levels and registers were filled, and disseminating it were the goals of the

---

[19] Charles A. Ferguson, "Diglossia," *Word* 15 (1959): 325–340; Itamar Even-Zohar, "The Nature and Functionalization of the Language of Literature under Diglossia," *Ha-Sifrut* 2, no. 2 (1970): 286–303 (Hebrew).

[20] Moritz Lazarus, *Was heißt national?* (Berlin, 1879), 29–30.

project of Hebrew language revival. Yiddish and Hebrew, the languages of Jews in Europe (though not in other places), attained high status in both the practical and the symbolic dimensions. Jews continued to live in a state of linguistic diglossia, but the Jewish languages began to play a major social and cultural role because of the symbolic value granted to them.

Jews wrote non-religious literature even before modern times, but only in modern times did this literature attain status as simultaneously expressing and creating the culture. In response to a description of Jewish literature as being poor and limited, various intellectuals argued that the Jews' creative imagination did enable them to produce all forms of literature (and art).

Jewish writers were now called upon to write Judeo-German literature (in German), or Judeo-Russian literature (in Russian), that would depict the Jewish world and the world outside it through Jewish eyes. "Jewish authors, start working," urged Moritz Goldstein,[21] who was referring to the writing of Jewish literature in German, not in the languages of the Jews. We will not address the question of what was "Jewish" about the literature written by Jews in non-Jewish languages, even when it was aimed mainly at a Jewish public, or what was "Jewish" in the literature written in Jewish languages addressing the Jewish public (except for the language in which it was written and occasionally its themes). In any case, as we have pointed out, in this context and in similar ones we are talking about individual writers and not a literary sub-system, and we are certainly not talking about a national literature.

In Eastern Europe there was a large circle of writers in Hebrew and Yiddish and a varied corpus of modern literature in the two languages that had played a significant role in reviving Jewish culture in general and Jewish national culture in particular. While Jewish literature in Jewish languages was growing and developing, a large and intensive project of translation from various languages into Yiddish and Hebrew developed simultaneously; the translated literature became an indispensable part of Yiddish culture and Hebrew culture.

VII

The Jewish culture created by the Jewish community (Yishuv) in Palestine-Eretz Israel starting in the 1880s was the product of a conscious and planned attempt to construct a different Jewish culture from that of the Diaspora, even if, to a great extent, it was a continuation of

---

[21] Moritz Goldstein, "Deutsch-jüdischer Parnass," *Kunstwart* 25 (1912): 281–294.

the Jewish cultural systems created in the Diaspora. Only in Palestine-Eretz Israel was it possible to try to construct a comprehensive Jewish culture based on an ideal and a program, which would be the hegemonic culture of the Jewish community and would give that community its uniqueness, identity, and unity. Only in Palestine-Eretz Israel could Jewish culture be self-sufficient, an autarchy "drawing on its own roots and nourished by its own strength," wrote Rachel Yanait Ben-Zvi in 1911,[22] adding, "A *free* [emphasis in the original] cultural autarchy like this would not be possible in the Diaspora." At the end of the Ottoman period, Palestine-Eretz Israel seemed a tabula rasa and thus the proper soil for planning an entirely new culture which would not need to answer to traditional Jewish culture or the surrounding culture. Jewish culture in a hegemonic society would be able to freely select the desired and required cultural components and implement mechanisms of cultural planning. Zionism, the Jewish national territorial movement, sought to create a modern Jewish society and polity that would ensure a high cultural standard and a cultural market that would meet all the needs of that society – in Hebrew. This was the rationale that underlay the initiation and implementation of a process of "filling the cultural system," both with regard to building cultural institutions and supervisory cultural mechanisms and to establishing cultural norms, a cultural repertoire, and a market of cultural products. Thus, in the context of Jewish culture in Palestine-Eretz Israel, from the end of the nineteenth century onward one can speak about both a "society creating culture" and a "culture creating a society."

The vision of Hebrew culture in the homeland – Palestine-Eretz Israel – required a cultural revolution in which a new Jewish cultural cosmos would be created, a set of values would be replaced, and Jewish creativity would burst forth to produce a free, total, and authentic Jewish culture. Yitzhak Tabenkin wrote:

All the elements of life and existence were re-examined. All the values and relations in life, the relation to man and to nature, to religion and to work, the relation to the child and the family, to Eretz Israel and the gentiles, everything was presented as problems to be discussed. For the first time an attempt was made to understand Jewish history, that there is Jewish-national poetry and Jewish folk poetry and Jewish performance of music.[23]

---

[22] See the series of articles by Rachel Yanait Ben-Zvi, "Lisheelat hakultura beEretz Israel" (To the Issue of Hakultura in Eretz Israel), *Haahdut* 15–24 (February–March 1911).

[23] Yitzhak Tabenkin, "Ha-mekorot" (The Sources), in *Sefer Ha-aliya Ha-shniya*, ed. Bracha Habas (Tel Aviv: Am Oved, 1947), 24.

And according to Nahman Sirkin:

To develop the spirit of the people, to improve its characteristics, to glorify and
to protect all the assets it had acquired in its historic life – assets such as language,
tradition, ethics, faith, and ways of life [...] The spirit of the people is the sum
of all its strengths, attributes, and content, and also of its ethics, tradition, faith,
feelings, opinions and morals, the concept of the good, the beautiful, the true –
which are culture.[24]

In practical terms, the creation of culture, or in the language of that
period, "a state of *Kultur*," necessitated the establishment of all the institutions and services that create culture and tell about culture. Thus, for
example, the program of Ze'ev Jabotinsky from 1910 declared: "It is necessary to create schools, night classes, kindergartens, playgrounds, Hebrew
theaters, textbooks, reading books, scientific books, dictionaries, scientific
terminology, maps to delineate the country, maps to portray nature, a university, a technical college, a polytechnic college – and there is no end to
the list."[25]

Changes in the private sphere were also discussed, as was the ecology
of the physical and aesthetic public space. But most important of all was
the uniqueness of Palestine-Eretz Israel. Only there could one create and
define *Tarbut Moledet* a "culture of the homeland," that is, create and
define all the components of a distinct national culture based on a linkage
to a particular territory, its history, its nature, and its landscape.

Building the new society and culture entailed the establishment of a
normative system. It also meant planning and realizing several cultural
projects in the various areas of the cultural system, including the establishment of an educational network and a curriculum and inventing
holidays, ceremonies, and the ingredients of popular culture. Rituals,
celebrations, and ceremonies were created and staged for the emerging
Jewish community; children's songs, tunes, and folk stories were written;
folk dances were invented as vital ingredients of the "folkway"; and non-
official culture consisting of popular literature and entertainment was
also created. Cultural institutions and a cultural repertoire that could
not exist even within the autonomous culture of a minority society in
the Diaspora could be created for the first time in Palestine-Eretz Israel
as part of the hegemonic society and even before Jewish society became
the majority society. Therefore, the cultural system that was established

---

[24] Nahman Sirkin, "Min ha-huza ha-ohela" (From the Outside into the Tent) in *Kitvei N.
Sirkin*, ed. Yehezkel Kaufman and Berl Kazenelson (Tel Aviv, 1939), I, 134–172 (Hebrew).
[25] Ze'ev Jabotinsky, "Avoda u-mazav ruah" (Work and Mood) *Hadashot mehaaretz*, October
27, 1919 (Hebrew).

in Palestine-Eretz Israel was the most extensive and comprehensive system the Jewish people ever had. Part of it was established by political and public bodies and part by private cultural entrepreneurs, and it was accepted by the majority of Jewish society.

This system consisted of a range of products of both high culture and folk and popular culture. Many of the components were a continuation of what had already appeared and developed in Europe, others resulted from a revival of Jewish traditional cultural assets that were adopted and adjusted to the needs of the new cultural system, and yet others were invented in Palestine-Eretz Israel. Because of all this, we contend that it is more accurate to describe this culture as a Jewish national-territorial culture than as a secular Jewish culture.

The new Jewish culture of the Jewish community in Palestine-Eretz Israel was often described by its ideologues and those who participated in its construction as Hebrew culture (and occasionally as "Eretz-Israeli culture"); the term Hebrew indicated the central and exclusive status granted in it to the Hebrew language as the distinctive expression of cultural revival and was meant to symbolize the fact that this culture was different from Jewish cultures in the Diaspora ("Diaspora culture"). The term Hebrew culture also signified that this was not an immigrants' culture but rather a national culture in a historical homeland, a culture that was being created according to models that established its ideals, ideology, and program. No less important was the fact that for the first time a Jewish culture emerged that was not the culture of a minority, and thus, even though it was filled to a very great extent with components imported from other cultures (especially Western culture), it was not a twofold culture.

Contemporary scholarship often tends to emphasize the deviations from the ideals and the ideology, to show that they were not always and fully realized, to point out that many of the components of the old culture were brought to Palestine-Eretz Israel by immigrants, and to argue that even in Palestine-Eretz Israel the culture was stratified and included subcultures. This critical perspective focuses on cultural realities that have been excluded or obliterated by the hegemonic narrative. Drawing attention to the much more complex and diverse cultural reality than the one portrayed by the ideological and propagandistic narrative is of course important. The notion of a single hegemonic culture with no subcultures is false in any discussion of culture. However, one must remember that the hegemonic, multi-layered system of Hebrew culture in Palestine-Eretz Israel was established in a very short period by a society that in 1948 numbered no more than 700,000 Jews, not all of whom shared the ideology of hebraization, and yet succeeded in creating a cultural reality that established a shared and unifying identity.

The culture of the Jews that was created and consolidated in Palestine-Eretz Israel consisted of several seemingly contradictory features, which in fact complemented each other:

- Modernization and secularization;
- Fostering of a homeland culture, that is, of romantic sentiments, symbols, and practices linked to the history, nature, and landscape of Palestine-Eretz Israel and manifested in such aspects as agricultural holidays, excursions, and interest in archaeology;
- Establishment of institutions and organizations that created culture and disseminated it;
- Appropriation of "foreign" values and cultural components, especially European ones, into the cultural system of the Jews;
- The existence of a parallel system of cultural import, which could not always be supervised and censored;
- The coexistence of partial subcultures, such as Orthodox culture or various ethnic cultures; and
- The existence of class subcultures, such as the workers' culture, bourgeois culture, urban culture, and rural culture.

VIII

The term Hebrew culture referred to the core of the cultural system of the modern Jewish community in Palestine-Eretz Israel, a community which created most of the cultural assets and symbols and forged its unity and identity. A description of this reality requires a separate analysis of each of its components. Thus, for example, one must discuss the debate over the nature of Hebrew literature as opposed to Jewish literature and to clarify what about it was Hebrew rather than Jewish.

The establishment of Israel in 1948 as a Jewish sovereign state created two cultural phenomena. On the one hand, the state had tools with which it could speed up the processes of modernization, fund cultural institutions and in some cases even supervise them, disseminate culture, and in the 1950s foster what is termed "the cult of the state." On the other hand, the profound changes in the demographic structure and the socio-cultural processes that characterized the newly established state enhanced the status of the cultures that had previously been considered secondary; they were now pushed from the margins towards the center, or into the center itself. Scholars offer differing evaluations of the melting pot policy of the 1950s and the degree of its success. To a great extent, the ideology of the melting pot was replaced by an ideology of multiculturalism. Yet the cultural reality of the Jewish community in Israel – Israeli culture – is the product of many components, including those that are a continuation of components from the Yishuv period, those that entered it as a result of the Americanization or globalization of the society and its culture, and those connected with traditional Judaism and the emergence of new orthodoxies.

IX

Studies of the development of the cultural reality of the Jews in the past 200 years – of the polemics with regard to culture and the culture wars – are an inseparable part of Jewish historiography; they give it expression and even shape it. The purpose of a history of Jewish culture and of the cultures of the Jews is to map the entirety of Jewish culture, all its expressions and strata, including both its organized and non-organized manifestations, its cultural products and their publics, the various cultural markets and their hierarchical relations, and the contacts between subcultures and the hegemonic culture. In all these respects, this dynamic, lively, multifaceted, rich, unifying, and divisive cultural map has neither peer nor precedent in the history of the Jewish people. Worldviews and ideologies will determine what is "Jewish" and what is "Judaism" in this map.

SELECT BIBLIOGRAPHY

Azaryahu, Maoz. *State Cults: Celebrating Independence and Commemorating the Fallen in Israel 1948–1956*. Beersheba: Ben-Gurion University of the Negev Press, 1995 (Hebrew).

Berkovitz, Jay R. *Rites and Passage: The Beginnings of Modern Jewish Culture in France, 1650–1860*. Philadelphia: University of Pennsylvania Press, 2004.

Berkowitz, Michael. "Mind, Muscle and Men: The Imagination of a Zionist Culture for the Jews in Central and Western Europe, 1897–1914." Ph.D. diss., University of Wisconsin, Madison, 1989.

Biale, David, ed. *Cultures of the Jews: A New History*. New York: Schocken Books, 2002.

Bourdieu, Pierre. "The Habitus and the Space of Life-styles," in *Distinction: A Social Critique of the Judgement of Taste*, 170–225. Translated by Richard Nice. Cambridge, MA: Harvard University Press, 1984.

Brenner, Michael. *The Renaissance of Jewish Culture in Weimar Germany*. New Haven: Yale University Press, 1996.

Cohen, Arthur Allen, and Paul R. Mendes-Flohr. *Contemporary Jewish Religious Thought: Original Essays On Critical Concepts, Movements, and Beliefs*. New York: Free Press, 1987.

Even-Zohar, Itamar. "The Emergence of a Native Hebrew Culture in Palestine 1882–1948," in *Essential Papers on Zionism*, ed. Jehuda Reinharz and Anita Shapira, 727–744. New York: New York University Press, 1996.

"Language Conflict and National Identity: A Mediterranean Perspective," in *Nationalism and Modernity*, ed. Joseph Alpher, 126–135. New York: Praeger; Haifa: Reuben Hecht Chair, 1986.

Feiner, Shmuel. *The Origins of Jewish Secularization in Eighteenth-century Europe*. Philadelphia: University of Pennsylvania Press, 2011.

Gelber, Mark H. "German-Jewish Literature and Culture and the Field of German-Jewish Studies," in *The Jewish Contribution to Civilization: Reassessing an Idea*, eds. Jeremy Cohen and Richard I. Cohen, 165–184. London: Littman Library of Jewish Civilization, 2008.

Harshav, Benjamin. *Language in Time of Revolution*. Berkeley: University of California Press, 1993.

The Polyphony of Jewish Culture. Stanford: Stanford University Press, 2007.

Kaplan, Marion A., ed. *Jewish Daily Life in Germany, 1618–1945*. New York: Oxford University Press, 2005.

Katz, Jacob. *Tradition and Crisis: Jewish Society at the End of the Middle Ages*. New York: New York University Press, 1993.

Kroeber, Alfred Louis. "Reality Culture and Value Culture," in *The Nature of Culture*, 152–166. Chicago: University of Chicago Press, 1952.

and Clyde Kluckhohn. *Culture – A Critical Review of Concept and Definitions*. New York: Kraus Reprint Co., 1953.

Levinson, Avraham. *The Hebrew Movement in the Diaspora*. Warsaw and London: The Executive of Brit Ivrit Olamit, 1935 (Hebrew).

Livneh-Freudenthal, Rachel. "The Verein für Kultur und Wissenschaft der Juden (1819–1824): Seeking a New Concept of Judaism." Ph.D. diss., Tel Aviv University, 1996.

Luz, Ehud. *Parallels Meet: Religion and Nationalism in the Early Zionist Movement (1882–1904)*. Tel Aviv: Am Oved, 1985 (Hebrew).

Pollack, Hermann. *Jewish Folkways in German Lands (1648–1806). Studies in Aspects of Daily Life*. Cambridge, MA: MIT Press, 1971.

Rosman, Murray Jay. *How Jewish Is Jewish History?* Oxford: Littman Library of Jewish Civilization, 2007.

Saposnik, Arieh Bruce. *Becoming Hebrew: The Creation of a Jewish National Culture in Ottoman Palestine*. New York: Oxford University Press, 2008.

Schweid, Eliezer. *The Idea of Modern Jewish Culture*. Boston: Academic Studies Press, 2008.

Shavit, Yaacov. "From Admission Ticket to Contribution: Remarks on the History of an Apologetic Argument," in *The Jewish Contribution to Civilization: Reassessing an Idea*, eds. Jeremy Cohen and Richard I. Cohen, 151–164. London: Littman Library of Jewish Civilization, 2008.

Athens in Jerusalem: Classical Antiquity and Hellenism in the Making of the Modern Secular Jew. London: Littman Library of Jewish Civilization, 1997 (1999 paperback).

"Supplying a Missing System – Between Official and Unofficial Popular Culture in the Hebrew Culture in Eretz-Israel," in *Studies in the History of Popular Culture*, ed. B. Z. Kedar, 327–345. Jerusalem: The Zalman Shazar Center for Jewish History, 1996 (Hebrew).

"The Yishuv between National Regeneration of Culture and Cultural Generation of the Nation," in *Jewish Nationalism and Politics*, eds. Jehuda Reinharz, Gideon Shimoni, and Yosef Salmon, 141–157. Jerusalem-Boston: The Zalman Shazar Center for Jewish History, 1996 (Hebrew).

and Shoshana Sitton. *Staging and Stagers in Modern Jewish Palestine: The Creation of Festive Lore in a New Culture, 1882–1948*. Detroit: Wayne State University Press, 2004.

Shavit, Zohar. "Children as Agents of the Hebrew Revolution," in *Dor Ledor* XXXVII: *Children as Avant-Garde: Childhood and Adolescence in Times of Crises and Social Change*, eds. Yael Darr, Tal Kogman, and Yehudit Shteiman, 15–38, 2010 (Hebrew).

ed. and main author. *The Construction of the Hebrew Culture in the Jewish Yishuv in Eretz Israel*. Jerusalem: The Israel Academy of Sciences and the Bialik Institute, 1998 (Hebrew).

"Fabriquer une culture nationale. Le rôle des traductions dans la constitution de la littérature hébraïque." *Actes de la Recherche en Sciences Sociales* 44 (September 2002): 21–32.

"The Habitus of the 'New Jew' of the Haskalah Movement." *Israel* 16 (2009): 11–38 (Hebrew).

"In Tel Aviv One Should Speak Hebrew. On the Partial Success of the Hebrew Revolution." *Panim* 45 (2008): 50–63 (Hebrew).

"Naissance d'une littérature de jeunesse et naissance d'un État." *La Revue des livres pour enfants* no. 239 (February 2008): 87–92.

Slezkine, Yuri. *The Jewish Century*. Princeton: Princeton University Press, 2004.

Ta-Shma, Israel M. *Early Franco-German Rituals and Custom*. Jerusalem: Magnes Press, The Hebrew University, 1992 (Hebrew).

Veidlinger, Jeffrey. *Jewish Public Culture in the Late Russian Empire*. Bloomington: Indiana University Press, 2009.

Volkov, Shulamit. *Germans, Jews, and Antisemites: Trials in Emancipation*. Cambridge: Cambridge University Press, 2006.

CHAPTER 25

SEPHARDIC AND MIZRAḤI LITERATURE

NANCY E. BERG

Sephardi and Mizraḥi cultures and traditions have often been seen as synonymous. Whereas there are significant commonalities, the two are distinct. This chapter will delineate the distinctions while also identifying points in common, discussing each separately except for where there is overlap.

THE SEPHARDIC SPHERE

LANGUAGE

Just as Sephardi is a term of some confusion and disagreement, so too is the name of the corresponding language. Sephardi (or Sephardic) refers to the Jews in the Iberian Peninsula, those expelled in 1492 and their descendants. It also refers to the style of prayer, customs, and traditions followed by these Jews. While the term Sephardi has also been used more broadly to include Jews from Arab and Islamic lands – that is, other than Ashkenazi – the term Mizraḥi (lit. Eastern) is considered a more accurate term (see below). And Sephardi, once needing the modification *Sephardi tahor* (lit. "pure Sephardi" i.e., from the Iberian Peninsula), has been – mostly – restored to its specific meaning.

Ladino, also known as Judezmo, Judeo-Spanish, (E)spaniolit, Muestra Spanyol, Djidyo, and variations thereof, was for many years the common tongue of Jews who could trace their ancestry to the Iberian communities. Some scholars reserve the term Ladino to refer more specifically to a word-for-word translation from Hebrew into Spanish.[1] As a calque of Hebrew it retains the syntax and some of the elements of the source language (Hebrew) rather than being a true translation. Over time Ladino has come to mean the family of dialects spoken by Sephardi Jews. What these dialects have in common is a base language of fifteenth-century Castilian;

---

[1] See for example, David Bunis, "The Language of the Sephardim: A Historical Overview" in *The Sephardi Legacy*, Vol II, ed. Haim Beinart (Jerusalem: Magnes Press, 1970).

some elements from other contemporary Spanish dialects (depending on the speaker's familial place of origin); many Hebrew and Aramaic words, some Spaniolized; old Spanish phonetics; and generous borrowings from local languages. Because the language developed in virtual isolation from the base language after the Expulsion it retains some forms and terms no longer extant in today's Spanish.

Over time the language developed into different variants or dialects, and shifted from using the Hebrew script[2] to being written in the Latin alphabet. The Hebrew script used in printed works was the Rashi script, halfway between print and cursive, that was used among Sephardi Jews at the time of the Expulsion, and became adopted as the typeface for Torah commentary. *Solitreo* was the cursive form of Hebrew used for handwritten Ladino among eastern Sephardim.

Local languages and geography contributed to the variance between the Eastern and Western forms of Judeo-Spanish. In the Ottoman Empire, Turkish influenced what was the primary language for the majority of Jews.[3] Similarly, so did Greek, Romanian, Bulgarian, and Serbo-Croatian, depending on country of residence. Romance languages other than Spanish also contributed to dialects in different degrees. French was especially fertile following the establishment of the Alliance Israel schools in Sephardic communities. In North Africa, the Arabic component – already present from the Arab conquest and the Andalusian era – was reinforced and augmented. In Morocco the dialect was known as *Haketiya*, and could be described as a cross between Judeo-Spanish and Judeo-Arabic. The Algerian version was called *Tetuani*. The Western dialects of Judeo-Spanish were generally much less influenced by European languages and hardly at all by Turkish.

Migration, modernization, and especially a flourishing press helped unify if not standardize the different subdialects. While currently an endangered language with fewer native speakers in each generation,[4] the idiom was for generations a unifying language of Jews in exile rivaling its better-known counterpart Yiddish.

---

[2] Using the Arabic script for Spanish text is known as *aljamiado*; the term is also used among scholars of Judeo-Spanish for the use of the Hebrew script.

[3] According to Walter Weiker 85 percent of Jews in the Ottoman Empire spoke Ladino at the turn of the twentieth century. See Walter Weiker, *Ottomans, Turks, and the Jewish Polity* (Lanham, MD: University Press of America, 1992).

[4] Tracy K. Harris, *Death of a Language: The History of Judeo-Spanish* (Newark: University of Delaware Press, 1994).

LITERATURE

Over the years a rich literary tradition developed, first in the religious domain. Ladino versions of sacred texts (literal translations), liturgical works, rabbinic commentary, and then quasi-folk literature: proverbs, folktales, and *coplas* – a popular genre of poetry – proliferated. Beginning from the study of religious sources and liturgical needs, the Ladino translations of the Hebrew Bible, of prayerbooks and the Passover Haggadah, expanded to include studies of laws, morals and ethics. *Me'am Lo'ez*, a comprehensive commentary on the Bible, is one of the great masterpieces in Ladino, rivaling any other such work. More than "mere" commentary, the popular work is a rich compendium of different approaches to the Hebrew Bible, Talmud, and Jewish life. Begun by Rabbi Ya'acob Meir Juli in the eighteenth century, *Me'am Lo'ez* was continued by a number of other scholars. Menahem Mitrani in Saloniki and Raphael Pontemoli in Smyrna completed the commentary in the nineteenth century. In addition to liturgical pieces, translations of important Jewish texts, and philosophical works, a modern secular literature developed through translations, adaptations and original works.

The nineteenth century saw a greater openness to the West and modernization in the wake of nationalist movements, the establishment of Alliance schools, and greater freedom. By the middle of the century there was a flourishing Ladino-language press with newspapers being published in all of the Sephardi population centers: *El Tyempo* in Constantinople, *La Esperanza* in Izmir, *La Epoka* in Thessaloniki (Salonika). The very titles of the periodicals point toward their modernizing objectives. In general, news, commentary, and *belles-lettres* filled the pages of these periodicals.[5]

Most were originally published in Hebrew letters (*aljamiado*), and only in the twentieth century was there a shift toward using the Roman alphabet. The Turkish Revolution (1908) led to even greater freedom, and newspapers flourished in Sephardic communities.

The Ladino-language newspapers gave writers opportunity to publish their works and to find readers. These included more traditional forms, as well as modern genres adopted from the West. Among the most traditional of these writings were the aforementioned *coplas* (or *complas*) – poetry in stanzas that frequently had refrains, and were often performed as song. They often fulfilled religious-related functions – that is, to celebrate holidays, the lives of patriarchs and famous rabbis, and religious

[5] Sarah Abrevaya Stein, *Making Jews Modern: The Yiddish and Ladino Press in the Russian and Ottoman Empires* (Bloomington: Indiana University Press, 2004).

accomplishments. These *coplas* also sang of events from history and other shared experiences.

Although generally considered folklore, these *coplas* demonstrated an erudition on the part of their composers that is not typical of the folk, and indeed, they often served didactic purposes. So, too, in a reversal of the folkloric tradition, these verses were first preserved in written form before being transmitted orally.[6] In the modern era, the writers of these *coplas* emerged from relative obscurity to lay claim to authorship. Ya'cob Yona (1847–1922) was among the most prolific of the modern-era copla composers, and one of the last.[7]

Other traditional genres include proverbs, stories, and ballads. Stories are divided into two categories: *consejas* and *cuentos*. *Consejas* are popular stories, such as those of the wise fool Djoha (al-Juha in Arabic, Nasraddin Hoca in Turkish, etc.) or based on biblical characters and tales. *Cuentos* generally rely on elements of fantasy and magic. Ballads were known as *canticas* (*cantigas*), lyric songs, and *romansas*, narratives or "true" ballads. Some of these works show clear Spanish origins from before the Expulsion; others were apparently composed in the Diaspora.

For the most part, Sephardic culture developed in isolation from Spanish Peninsular culture, but in great awareness of what was happening in other parts of the West, especially France. Ladino literature of the twentieth century continued the traditional forms, and adopted genres popular in the West as well. While some modern poetry in Ladino retained the traditional metric and rhyme schemes, others modified or eschewed these, even embracing free verse. The language became ever more Westernized.

Thus, the *romanso*, or novel, developed in light of Western literature. *El Chico Eliezer o el Muchacho Abandonado* (*The Kid Eliezer or the Abandoned Boy*, 1877) by Aharon de Yosef Hazan is thought to be the first Judeo-Spanish language novel.[8] The genre peaked in the first third of the twentieth century,[9] especially in Constantinople (Istanbul) and Salonika (Thessaloniki), but also in other areas where there were other Sephardic

---

[6] Paloma Díaz-Mas, *Sephardim: The Jews from Spain* (Chicago: University of Chicago Press, 1992), 110.

[7] Leonor Carracedo and Elena Romero, "Refranes publicados por Ya'acob Yona," *Sefarad* 41 (1981): 389–560; Paloma Díaz-Mas, *Sephardim*, 111–112.

[8] Ammiel Alcalay, "Intellectual Life," in *The Jews of the Middle East and North Africa in Modern Times*, ed. Reeva Spector Simon, Michael Menachem Laskier, and Sara Reguer (New York: Columbia University Press, 2003): 85–112. See also Aron Rodrigue, *A Guide to Ladino Materials in the Harvard College Library* (Cambridge: Harvard College Library, 1992), 68.

[9] David Altabe, "The Romanso 1900–1933," *Sephardic Scholar* 3 (1977–78): 96–106.

communities. Many of these novels were translations and adaptations of European works. Melodramatic plots tended to be favored, although they also drew from history – life in medieval Spain, tales from the Inquisition and the experience of Expulsion – as well as offering views of more contemporary life or plots that promoted Zionism.[10]

En turno de la torre Blanca (*Regarding the White Tower*, 1982) by Enrique Saporta Y Beja is purportedly the last novel written in Ladino. It is a fictional account of Jews in Salonika in the first part of the twentieth century, including a portrayal of the devastating fire of 1917. Rosa Nissán's family novel, *Novia que te vea* (*Like a Bride*, 1992) describes the life of a girl much like herself who grew up in a Sephardic family in Mexico in the 1960s. Although written mostly in Spanish, the language of the book includes a generous amount of Ladino, as does the movie version (1994).[11]

Sephardic writers not only adopted genres of the West, but also its languages. The proliferation of Alliance schools, combined with greater nationalizing sentiment and modernizing forces, led to linguistic assimilation, and the demise of Judeo-Spanish literature.[12] Jewish writers turned to the language of the larger communities in which they lived.

Yugoslavia was home to a number of Sephardi writers whose families had come to Belgrade, Sarajevo, and Dubrovnik from Spain via Italy and elsewhere. Only a few of these writers continued to write in Ladino in the twentieth century, albeit using the Latin alphabet. Laura Papo Bohoreta (1891, Sarajevo–1941 or 1942) was among the most prolific of Ladino writers in the twentieth century and popular among Jews for her vivid sketches of life among Sarajevo Jews, especially the poor and working class. "La Bohoreta" was also well known for her short stories on similar themes, and her efforts to preserve her community's culture and folklore. Others, including the novelists Isak Samokovlija (1889–1955) and Oskar Davico (1909–1989), wrote mainly in Serbo-Croatian. While the former wrote short stories about life in the Jewish community of Bosnia, the latter was acclaimed for his surrealism and his socialism. He wrote poetry and novels, experimenting with style but staying true to the revolution. Although most of his work was not specific to the Jewish community, in some he described the community in a lifelike fashion, including its less desirable elements.[13]

---

[10] Diaz-Mas, *Sephardim*, 102–150.

[11] Tabea Alexa Linhard, "'Ishica, ¿de quién sos tú?': Nostalgia for a Mother Tongue in Rosa Nissán's Novels" *Hispania* 92, no. 3 (2009): 456–464.

[12] Edouard Roditi, "The Slow Agony of Judeo-Spanish Literature," *World Literature Today* 60, no. 2 (1986): 244–246.

[13] Danilo Kis (1935–1989), a celebrated writer from the former Yugoslavia, is not actually Sephardic. His parents were a Hungarian Jew and a non-Jewish Montenegrin.

Clarisse Nicoidski née Abinoun (1938–1996), although born in Lyon, was from a Yugoslavian Sephardic family. She is perhaps better known for her novels in French than for her poetry in Judeo-Spanish. Her choice of language for her poetry is a deliberate response to the recognition of its endangered status.

Sephardic Jews who have become important writers of literature, although not necessarily identified as Sephardim, include Elias Canetti, Albert Cohen, and Edmond Jabes. Individually and together, they represent the exilic nature of twentieth-century Jewish reality. Albert Cohen (1895–1981), born in Corfu, Greece, became a French-language novelist and journalist, holder of a Turkish passport, and citizen of Switzerland. He was the founding editor of the *Revue Juive* (1925–), a Zionist literary journal. His first novel introduced the Solals, a Jewish family from the Greek islands (1930). The comic-satiric world of this family with colorful characters continued to unfold in two more volumes, the last of which, *Belle du Seigneur* (1968), received the French Academy's Grand Prix du roman. Cohen's characters were identified as Jewish, aware of their Jewishness, and living in a Jewish environment. He also wrote several works that are more directly autobiographical in nature, including the slim *Le livre de ma mere* (*The Book of My Mother*, 1954). Having fled France during the German occupation, he was in London when he heard that his mother had died in Marseille. He wrote the book in response to the news, commemorating both his mother and their complex relationship.

The 1981 Nobel laureate Elias Canetti (1905–1994), born in Bulgaria, was raised and educated in Vienna, Zurich, and Frankfurt. A native speaker of Ladino, he chose German – his fourth language – as his literary medium. He also chose to become a British citizen, and he lived in London until the last twenty years of his life when he lived mostly in Zurich. He is best known for his modernist novel *Die Blendung* (*Auto da Fé*, 1935), his interdisciplinary study of crowd behavior *Masse und Macht* (*Crowds and Power*, 1960), and his four-volume memoir (first published 1977–1987).

Edmond Jabes (1912–1991) left his native Egypt for Paris in the wake of the Suez Canal crisis. His family were Sephardi Jews who had settled in Italy before coming to Egypt. Jabes was associated with the surrealists, though not formally a member of their group. His work earned him the Grand Prix for poetry in 1987. Although not personally religious, his work is riddled with references to Kabbalah, Jewish mysticism.

Theater

While there has never been a professional Sephardi theater, the amateur plays growing out of the Purimspiel tradition (a comedic skit performed in honor of the Purim holiday) became a significant aspect of Sephardi culture in the larger Sephardic communities, and later migrated to North America with a segment of the population. Beginning with plays presented in schools for didactic purposes, and plays in the community to celebrate holidays (especially the aforementioned Purim and Hannukah), the corpus grew to include dramas that were specific to the Sephardic community's interests, such as those treating the history of Sephardim before, during, and after the Expulsion, local history, and contemporary social issues. The repertoire also included works of interest to Jews at large – biblical stories (Esther and Joseph were favorites), rabbinic figures, and key incidents of antisemitism (particularly the Dreyfus Affair). Classic dramas from Western culture, such as those of Molière, were also performed within the community.[14] The already-mentioned short story writer and folklorist Laura Papo Bohoreta was among the most productive of the playwrights, penning a series of dramas that portrayed the daily life of Jews in Bosnia.[15]

The Sephardis who immigrated to North America brought their culture and cultural outlets with them. While the formation of community was mostly expressed in the establishment of synagogues, burial societies, and other religious institutions, there was also Sephardi theater. Ladino language productions played to full houses on New York's Lower East Side from the early part of the twentieth century.[16] The repertoire was similar to that in the Balkans and elsewhere: historical, biblical, European classics (again Molière as well as Shakespeare) and social dramas. There was also an active Ladino-language community theater among the Sephardim of Seattle. Leon Behar (1900–1970), a Turkish immigrant, who was in turn a cobbler, electrician, and grocer, had also been an actor and director in Istanbul – experience he put to good use once he reached the United States. He was instrumental in producing plays centering on historical events (*Dreyfus*, *The Massacre of the Jews in Russia*), biblical stories (*Joseph and His Brothers*), and so forth. Theater served both entertainment and fundraising purposes through the interwar period. In 1994 David Altabe, scholar of Sephardi literature, founded The Ladino Players to preserve and restore Sephardi theater. For ten years it presented original Ladino-language plays to mixed audiences.[17]

---

[14] Elena Romero, "Literary Creation in the Spehardic Diaspora," *Moreshet Sepharad: The Sephardi Legacy*. Vol. II, ed. Haim Beinart (Jerusalem: Magnes Press, 1992), 438–460.

[15] Ana Cecilia Prenz Kopusar, "Dramaturgia de la cotidianidad en la obra de Laura Papo Bohoreta," *Verba Hispanica* XXII (2014): 151–161.

[16] See Aviva Ben-Ur, "Ladino (Judeo-Spanish) Theater in the United States," *Jewish Women: A Comprehensive Historical Encyclopedia*, March 1, 2009 https://jwa.org/ency-clopedia/article/ladino-judeo-spanish-theater-in-united-states.

[17] Marc D. Angel, "The Sephardic Theater of Seattle," *American Jewish Archives Journal* 25, no. 2 (1973): 156–160.

Revival

The Ladino Players are just one example of efforts to resurrect the language and culture of the Sephardim. Additional examples include New York's Judezmo Society which published *Adelantre*, Istanbul's *Salom* paper which continues to publish one page in Ladino, and other institutions such as Vidas Largas in Paris, the Turkish Cultural Center in Bat Yam, Sephardi synagogues, as well as the Sephardic Educational Center in Los Angeles.

The Argentine poet Juan Gelman (b. 1930, Buenos Aires), who is from an Ashkenazic Jewish family, adopted the Ladino language for one collection of his poetry *Dibaxu* (1994). While it has been argued that his purpose is to highlight and explore questions of ethnicity, identity construction, and exile,[18] rather than to recover or preserve the language culture, his collection does make a modern contribution to the continuity of Sephardic literary culture.

The Ladino Revival in Israel

The Ladino revival in Israel can be traced back to Yitzhak Navon's writing beginning in the late 1960s. Navon (b. 1921, Israel) came from a family that had lived in Jerusalem since the seventeenth century. A career politician, including a term as president, he wrote two musicals that are based in Sephardi folklore. The better known of these, *Bustan Sephardi* (*Sephardi Orchard*), was an immediate hit when it debuted in Jerusalem in 1970 and won the David's Harp prize for best play. The play introduced the language and culture of Ladino to a wide audience. In it, Navon wove stories and memories from his youth with legends, songs, and piyyutim. Revived in 1998, it played over one hundred performances at HaBima and remains a part of mainstream Israeli culture.

In 1996 the Knesset (Israeli Parliament) passed a law establishing the *Autoridad Nasionala del Ladino*, the National Authority of Ladino, to preserve the language and culture. Navon was its first board chair. It publishes *Aki Yerushalyim*, a magazine dedicated to the culture, a few times a year. There are other efforts as well: Radio Kol Yisrael (Voice of Israel) has established a Sefarad club and there is a Turkish Cultural Center in Bat Yam.

In addition to dedicated radio broadcasts and various events, several Israeli writers continue to write in Judeo-Spanish. Avner Peretz (b. 1942, Israel), also a scholar of the literature, and director of the Ma'ale Adumim Institute to Document Ladino Language and Culture, translates and writes poetry. Sara Benveniste Benrey (b. 1920, Izmir) was reportedly inspired by

---

[18] Monique Balbuena, *Sephardic Literary Identities in Diaspora* (Palo Alto: Stanford University Press, 2010).

Bustan Sefaradi to write in her native language of Judeo-Spanish and published her poetry (*poemas* and *kantes*), sketches and plays in one volume titled *Espertando el Djudeo Espanyol* (1996).[19]

Margalit Matityahu's (b. 1935, Israel) first four volumes of poetry were written in Hebrew, but after her mother's death she was inspired to visit the family's home in Salonika, and was inspired to write in Ladino. She wrote two volumes with each poem presented in Hebrew and in Ladino on facing pages (*Kurtiju Kemadu/ Hetzer Harukha*, 1988; *Algerika*, 1993) and has since published half a dozen monolingual Ladino collections and a single Hebrew-language collection. Her use of Ladino is a deliberate choice; aware that the readership for the language is dwindling she offers each poem in Hebrew. But she persists in using Ladino, joining the project to sustain the language.

Matityahu moved from mourning the loss of a once vibrant community in her first dual language volume, to recreating its vibrancy in the second. Since then her thematic range in Ladino has expanded to match that of her Hebrew poetry. Her bilingual poems are not strictly translations of each other, but rather two versions of the same poem. She works in both directions between the languages. Several of her Ladino language poems have been set to music, a tradition that was at least as strong in Ladino, as it has become in modern Hebrew.[20]

In her writing, and that of her colleagues, Ladino becomes the site of memory and nostalgia, not as much for Spain as in earlier Ladino literature, but for the diasporic communities established in its wake, and for the language itself. Even her short stories, written in Hebrew (*HaSafek, The Doubt*, 2010), belong to a diasporic sensibility, expressing a sense of alienation and a continued longing for the past and for home.

Literature in Spain

There is virtually no presence of Ladino in the Iberian Peninsula, but there is a small Jewish population. Perhaps the best-known Spanish Jewish writer is Leopoldo Azancot, first known as a literary critic. He has published at least ten novels to date, beginning with *La Novia Judia: Novela* (*The Jewish Bride: A Novel*) in 1977. The work won several prizes and was a finalist for the Ateneo Prize of Seville. Even before the prizes it was said that "La novia judía es la novela que más se esperó en el año pasado,"[21] and declared to

[19] Sara Benvensite Benrey, *Espertando el Djudeo Espanyol* (*Reviving Judeo-Spanish*). Privately published by Yossi Benveniste in Herzeliya, Israel, 1995.

[20] The independent record label Primary Music, based in Tel Aviv, has recorded several of Matityahu's poems set to music.

[21] "The Jewish Bride is the most anticipated novel of the year," Rosa Maria Pereda, "Entrevsita: Leopoldo Azancot, o la novela como misterio" *El Pais* (Madrid) July 15, 1977.

have "broke[n] new ground by defying all of the taboos that had existed under Franco's regime."[22]

Memoirs

In addition to the literary works discussed above, personal memoirs by Sephardic Jews proliferate. Albert Memmi's autobiographical novel *La Statue de sel* (*Pillar of Salt*, 1955) tells the story of his Tunisian childhood in the 1930s and 1940s. At times nostalgic, the work also portrays the predicament of the multicultural being: the author's alter ego can neither fully embrace nor fully reject the Jewish, French, Tunisian, Arabic, and African cultures that inform his upbringing.

Victor Perera, born and brought up in Guatemala, wrote about his childhood in *Rites: A Guatemalan Boyhood* (1986) and traced his ancestry in the memoir *The Cross and the Pear: A Sephardic Journey* (1995) against the history of Sephardim in general. In it he tells of the curse imposed by his great grandfather on the family for leaving Jerusalem. The book garnered him some critical acclaim, and a popular following, laying the groundwork for other memoirs to follow. Many of these are written in French or Spanish, some are published, and others are meant for family consumption.[23] They tend to recall the distant past – the expulsion from Spain – and the more recent past, preserving and documenting Sephardic communities in the territories of the former Ottoman Empire. Matilda Koen-Sarano (b. 1939) is one of the few to have published her memoirs in Judeo-Spanish, *Por el plazer de kontar Kuentos de mi vida* (*For the Pleasure of Telling Stories from My Life*, 2006).[24]

THE MIZRAḤI SPHERE

As mentioned above, Mizraḥi refers to those Jews who come from Arab and Islamic lands or whose families did. While the Hebrew term literally means Eastern (or Oriental), it includes the Maghrebi (lit. Western) Jews, the Jews of North Africa, some of whom hail from places geographically to the west of those who identify them as such. The term is generally

www.elpais.com/articulo/cultura/AZANCOT/_LEOPOLDO/Leopoldo/Azancot/ novela/misterio/elpepicul/19770715elpepicul_1/Tes.

[22] Dennis Klein, "Leopoldo Azancot" *Dictionary of the Literature of the Iberian Peninsula*, ed. German Bleiberg (Westport, CT: Greenwood Press, 1993), Vol. 1, 142.

[23] Gloria Sananes Stein, *Marguerite: Journey of a Sephardic Woman* (Morgantown, PA: Masthof, 1997).

[24] Matilda Koen-Sarano, *Por el plazer de kontar Kuentos de mi vida* (*For the Pleasure of Telling Stories from my Life*) (Jerusalem: Kana, 1986).

used to make the distinction from Ashkenazim, although it also separates Mizraḥim from Sephardim. To add to the confusion, many of the
Maghrebi Jews are from Sephardi families. In addition to waves of Jewish
immigration from ancient times – at least dating back to the Romans (the
first century of the common era), if not the Phoenicians (nine to ten centuries earlier) – to Berber converts, and to those who migrated from elsewhere in the Ottoman Empire, the Jewish population of North Africa
has also included refugees from the Inquisition and Expulsion and their
descendants.[25]

The best-known Mizraḥi culture is that of the Arab Jews. The history
of the Jews among the Arabs dates to the beginnings of Iraqi Jewry during the Babylonian exile (586 BCE) or perhaps even to the time of King
Solomon as per some legends of the Yemenites. With the establishment
and spread of Islam Jews found themselves accorded the special status of
dhimmi,[26] a status that at times accorded them protection from certain
restrictions. Different aspects of the *dhimmi* law were enforced to different
degrees depending on the tolerance of the ruler, the times, and the local
community.

While there are almost as many Jewish languages as there are languages
that hosted Jewish communities, few had as much literary output as that in
Ladino, Judeo-Arabic, and even Judeo-Persian. Similar to the Sephardim's
Ladino and the Ashkenazim's Yiddish, the Arab Jews created their own
variants of the local languages: Judeo-Arabic. Beginning as far back as the
pre-Islamic period (before the eighth century), Jewish communities in the
Arab world adopted languages of the larger community (*al-fusha* or classical Arabic and *al-`ammiya*, or colloquial). With the addition of Hebrew
and Aramaic vocabulary items, roots, and orthography, they created their
own ethnolect. Around the same time that Ladino was developing in relative isolation from Peninsular Spanish in the wake of the Expulsion, Jewish
communities became less integrated in the Arab lands, and their dialects
developed with less association with Arabic. The dialects of Judeo-Arabic,
also known as *illuga dyalna* (our language), *il`arabiyya dyalna* (our Arabic),
or *al-Yahudiyya* (Jewish) often include elements from other Arab dialects
not present in the area, illustrating the phenomenon of "displaced dia-
lectalism." The language is almost always written in Hebrew letters. The
Judeo-Arabic counterpart of Ladino calque is known as *sharh*: literal translations of sacred and liturgical Hebrew texts. Like Ladino, Judeo-Arabic is

[25] In the twentieth century Jews also immigrated to North African countries from Europe,
but they generally continued to identify as Ashkenazim and not as Mizrachim.
[26] Non-Muslim subject of state ruled by Islamic law (sharia).

also in decline, mostly because of the mass emigration from Arab lands in the last century.[27]

Other Jewish languages, such as Judeo-Persian, have met with a similar fate. This dialect of (middle) Persian written in Hebrew script created a significant corpus of texts,[28] before falling into decline during the modern period. In the twentieth century Persian script replaced the Hebrew, and newspapers were published in Judeo-Persian for the Jewish community. However, by the middle of the twentieth century there was very little demand for Judeo-Persian, as most Iranian Jews were comfortable in Persian.[29]

In the middle of the nineteenth century, the founding of a Hebrew press in several cities in North Africa led to a proliferation of Judeo-Arabic publications. In addition to a fairly active and often changing journal scene, well over a thousand bound volumes were published. Most literature written in Judeo-Arabic has been written on Jewish topics. Many were sacred texts and their explication, and include *piyyutim* (liturgical poetry), sermons, translations of the books of the Bible and other classic Jewish sources, and works on halacha (religious law). Quasi-liturgical works such as stories about the Jewish holidays and Hasidic tales were also composed and published in Judeo-Arabic. There were also secular texts, ranging from a book on the Tunisian constitution, to medical texts, translations of Western novels (Defoe, Dumas, etc.), and some original *belles-lettres*.[30]

Farther to the east, communities of Iraqi Jews, whether in Iraq or displaced in India and elsewhere, published periodicals in Judeo-Arabic. Otherwise, most literary production in the dialect was religious poetry, and mostly ceased by the mid-twentieth century. In each of the Judeo-Arabic

---

[27] For more about Judeo-Arabic see for example, Benjamin Hary, "Judeo-Arabic in Its Sociolinguistic Setting," *Israel Oriental Studies* 15 (1995): 129–155; Jacob Mansour, *The Jewish Baghdadi Dialect, Studies and Texts in the Judaeo-Arabic Dialect of Baghdad* (Or-Yehuda: The Babylonian Jewry Heritage Center, 1991); Joshua Blau, *The Emergence and Linguistic Background of Judaeo-Arabic* (Jerusalem: Ben-Zvi Institute, 1981).

[28] For an excellent anthology of translated texts see Vera B. Moreen, *In Queen Esther's Garden: An Anthology of Judeo-Persian Literature* (New Haven: Yale University Press, 2000).

[29] There is a less-well-documented literature of Persian Jews in the modern period, after the peak of creative work in Judeo-Persian. In the contemporary period, a handful of women – including Gina Nahai, Roya Hakakian, and Farideh Goldin – have written novels and memoirs that recreate life for Persian Jewry in the twentieth century.

[30] Yosef Tobi, "The Flowering of Judeo-Arabic Literature in North Africa, 1850–1950," in *Sephardi and Middle Eastern Jewries: History and Culture in the Modern Era*, ed. Harvey Goldberg (Bloomington: Indiana University Press), 213–225. He writes of his own efforts to collect volumes of Judeo-Arabic, and the dominance of Tunisia in publishing.

speaking communities there was a rich oral tradition, some of which has been recorded by folklorists mainly working in Israel with immigrants.

Not all literary production by Arab Jews was in their own dialect, however, and there is a substantial contribution to modern Arabic literature on the part of Jewish writers. In Egypt, among the best known of these is Murad Farag (1867–1955), a Karaite (non-rabbinic) Jew, trained as an attorney and the author of twenty-five books. These include a translation of the first Hebrew novel *Ahavat Tziyon* (*Love of Zion*, 1853), volumes of biblical stories, and works of philosophy, law, philology, and poetry.[31]

The prolific playwright Ya'qub Sanu'a (1839–1912), also known as Sheikh James Sanua Abu Naddara, was a Sephardi Jew from an Italian family, who was born and grew up in Egypt. His more-than-thirty plays were farces, comedies, and romantic dramas. They were a mixture of the traditional shadow plays and adaptations of Western classics, especially Molière. He was critical of the religious authority – especially the allowing of polygamy and the practice of marrying off young girls to older men – and of the government. The theater in which one of his plays was being performed was closed by the khedive (viceroy) in 1872, and a few short years later he was expelled for the satirical journal he edited. He continued to publish his paper in France, and was noted for being the first to include cartoons (with bilingual captions) and to use colloquial Egyptian Arabic.[32] Preceding him, Abraham Daninos (1798–1872), an Algerian Jew, was the author of the first known Arabic play in print, *Nuzhat al-Mushtdq wa-ghussat at- Ushshdq*.[33]

Journals such as *Adziri* in Algeria and *Al-`Alam Al-Israelite* in Lebanon, founded and edited by Esther Azhari Moyal (1873–1948),[34] offered venues for the writings – political, literary, scholarly, etc. – of Arab Jews in their respective communities. The most prolific of these communities was that of the Iraqi Jews. The oldest continuous Jewish community, they traced their deep roots back to the first Jewish exile in 586 BCE. In the last century the Iraqi Jewish community was well integrated into the larger society.

---

[31] See also Leon Nemoy, "A Modern Karaite Poet: Mourad Farag," *The Jewish Quarterly Review* 70, no. 4 (1980): 195–209.

[32] Shmuel Moreh, "Ya'qub Sanu': His Religious Identity and Work in Theater and Journalism," in *The Jews of Egypt: A Mediterranean Society*, ed. Shimon Shamir (Boulder: Westview, 1987), 111–129.

[33] Merzac Bagtache, "Abraham Daninos, La première pièce théâtrale arabe est née à Alger," *El Watan*, December 12, 2005, www.djazairess.com/fr/elwatan/33348, accessed February 5, 2011; Clement Huarte, *A History of Arabic Literature* (New York: D. Appleton and Company, 1903), 430.

[34] Beth Baron, *The Women's Awakening in Egypt: Culture, Society, and Press* (New Haven: Yale University Press, 1994), 20–21.

The largest single ethnic group in the capital, Baghdad, Jews were at the forefront of the forces of modernization, secularization and urbanization, and an integral sector of the city.

Jews were also among the most significant figures in the Iraqi literary renaissance of the 1930s and 1940s, as poets, short story writers, editors and publishers. In Iraq the Jewish journals *Al-Misbah* (*The Lamp*, 1924–29) and *al-Hasid* (*The Harvest*, 1929–37) were important venues for writers of Iraq, Jews and non-Jews alike. The first short story published in Iraq was written by a Jew, Murad Mikhail (1906–1986). Anwar Shaul (1904–1984), Yaakov Bilbul (1920–2003), and Shalom Darwish (1912–1997) were pioneers in the genre, and played a prominent role in the development of modern Iraqi literature. Shaul was famous for his poetic ode to the Arabic language. He was especially effective in encouraging other writers, most prominently as editor of the *al-Hasid*. The Dangoor Press,[35] founded by the man who became chief rabbi, was "reputedly the world's largest printer of books in Arabic."[36]

In general, the Jews were instrumental in the Iraqi literary renaissance. Many continued to write after the mass exodus 1948–1951, whether in a new country or, as in the case of Anwar Shaul and Meir Basri, in Iraq, although in each case they faced a diminished audience.

Before the first waves of Zionist immigration to the land of Israel beginning at the end of the nineteenth century (the New Yishuv), many of the Jews who lived in the land (the Old Yishuv) were Sephardic by legacy, but also Mizraḥi by geography. They were often from families that migrated from other areas of the Ottoman Empire such as Izmir, or Constantinople (Istanbul) where they lived after the expulsion from Spain. Even while the European-centered Haskalah (Jewish Enlightenment) movement gave rise to a modern literature in the revived language of Hebrew, there were also Sephardim and Mizraḥim claiming the language for their own literary production. Three of the most famous were Yitzhak Shami, Yehuda Burla, and Yaakov Hurgin. Shami (1889–1949) was born in Hebron to a Syrian Jewish family. Despite his meager output, his writing gives voice to both the Arabs in Palestine and to the Sephardim, to stories of vengeance and loyalty, disappointment and abandonment. Major life cycle events dominate his writing that depicts the worlds from within. In his piece "Av Ubanotav" ("A Father and his Daughters") the reader is privy to the inner

---

[35] Shmuel Moreh, "Naim Dangoor Honored By UK Queen with OBE Order," *Nehardea*, no. 16, Spring 2008; the press was founded by Hakham Bashi Ezra Reuben Dangoor (Chief Rabbi 1923–27), and expanded by son Eliahou Dangoor, Naim's father.

[36] Joel Millman, "Iraq's Forgotten Exiles Seek Redress," *The Guardian*. www.rense.com/general38/own.htm.

thoughts of the father as he reluctantly begins to understand how his wife and daughters have turned from him while he was away gathering their dowries.

The family of the Jerusalemite Burla (1886–1969) came from Izmir. He is best known for his stories of Sephardic Jews living in Old Jerusalem. And Hurgin (1898, Jaffa–1990, Tel Aviv), although perhaps best known as an author of children's literature, wrote about the Old Sephardi Yishuv, as well as their Ashkenazi, Armenian, Turkish, and Arab neighbors.

Writers who have continued their legacy include Dan Benaya Seri (b. 1935) and A. B. Yehoshua (b. 1936). Seri writes almost exclusively about the life of the Sephardi Jewish community in Jerusalem.[37] His stories have an almost folkloric quality, although they work towards an unrelenting destruction of the myths constructed by folklore. The language of his narratives is richly textured, weaving in simple structures with archaic terms from rabbinic sources and elsewhere. The characters are held captive by superstitions. His first novel *Ugiyot hamelah shel savta Sultana* (*Grandma Sultana's Salty Biscuits*, 1980) is infused with the aroma of home baking. It introduces us to a world in which ignorance – especially sexual ignorance – leads inevitably to tragedy. His novella "Elef nishotav shel Simantov" ("The Thousand Wives of Simantov"), set in the Bukharan quarter of Jerusalem, continues developing some of these ideas. The eponymous *Mishael* (1993) is partially ostracized when he begins to show signs of pregnancy, following the death of his wife. Despite his foray into the grotesque, Seri's characters are not without warmth and charm.[38]

Seri's sixth and latest book, *Adam Shav el Beito* (*A Man Returns Home*, 2009) is the first he has labeled as autobiography. In it, he plumbs his memory to recreate the poor Yemenite neighborhood of his childhood on the edges of the wealthier Bukharan quarter. While all of his writings up until now have been based on the same time and place, these stories are more directly memories from his own life. He writes of his father's death at the hands of an Arab sniper, concretizing the reason he allegedly began to write in the first place.[39] Even with the intrusion of harsh reality, Seri's memories are softened with a measure of nostalgia, and the care he lavishes on their recording.

---

[37] See, for example, Gershon Shaked, "Towards the Nineteen Nineties: A Generation Without Dreams," in *Modern Hebrew Fiction*, ed. Emily Budick, trans. Yael Lotan (Bloomington: Indiana University Press, 2000), chap. 12.

[38] Dan-Benaya Seri, *Ugioyt HaMelah Shel Savta* (Tel Aviv: Neumonn Tcherikover, 1980); "Elef nishotav shel Simantov," in *Tziporei Tzel* (*Birds of the Shade*) (Jerusalem: Keter, 1987); *Mishael* (Jerusalem: Keter, 1993).

[39] Dan Benaya Seri, *Adam Shav el Beito* (Jerusalem: Keter, 2009).

A. B. Yehoshua, one of the most prominent Israeli writers, is a fifth generation Jerusalemite on his father's side (and Moroccan-Sephardi on his mother's). Yet it was not until his fourth novel (after publishing several volumes of short stories, two plays, and two collections of essays), *Mr. Mani* (1990), that readers began to take note of his ethnic identity. Although less willing to be identified as a Sephardi writer, an ethnic label he considered reductive, Yehoshua included Sephardi characters from his first writings: Arditi in "Masa ha'erev shel yatir" ("The Evening Train in Yatir," 1962); Veducha Ermozo and Gabriel Arditi in *HaMeahev* (*The Lover*, 1977); Rafael Calderon in *Gerushim Meucharim* (*A Late Divorce*, 1982), the title character Molcho (1991).[40] While the first, Arditi, is not specifically identified as Sephardi – indeed little is known about him and the story is dislocated in time and place – the name itself is traced back to fifteenth-century Aragon.[41]

The novel *Mr. Mani* continues to be considered by many to be Yehoshua's masterpiece. A family saga in reverse, it indirectly tells the story of the Sephardi Mani family. He traces the family from Jerusalem, Constantinople, Crete, and Salonika. While calling into question the term *sephardi tahor* (pure Sephardi) it rewrites Jewish and Israeli history to include the Sephardi story or stories.

In addition to the well-established Sephardic Jewish communities, there were mass immigrations of Jews from Arab and Islamic lands to Israel. The best-known wave followed in the wake of the establishment of the state and the ensuing War of Independence. The majority of the Jewish populations from Iraq (120,000), Libya (30,000), and Yemen (50,000) joined immigrants from places such as Bulgaria, Romania, Poland, and from displaced persons camps in Germany, Austria, and Italy. The decades that followed saw the shift of Jewish communities from North African countries and Iran to Israel (and elsewhere). Many Israelis today are immigrants from those countries and their descendants.

The first generation of immigrant writers eventually found their way to print. The literature they wrote was initially categorized as "ethnic,"[42] and

---

[40] A. B. Yehoshua, *Mar Mani* (*Mr. Mani*) (Tel Aviv: Hakibbutz Hameuchad/ Siman Kriah, 1990); "Masa HaErev" in *Mot HaZaken* (*The Death of the Old Man*) (Tel Aviv: Hakibbutz Hameuchad, 1962); *HaMeahev* (*The Lover*) (Jerusalem: Schocken, 1977); *Gerushim Meucharim* (*A Late Divorce*) (Tel Aviv: Hakibbutz Hameuchad/ Siman Kriah, 1982); *Molcho* (Tel Aviv and Jerusalem: Hakibbutz Hameuchad/ Siman Kriah, Keter, 1987).

[41] Dan Rottenberg, *Finding our Fathers: A Guidebook to Jewish Geneaology* (New York: Random House, 1977), 159.

[42] Here – and elsewhere – ethnic means non-Ashkenazi.

dismissed as marginal or as a curiosity. Only later was their literature and that of the next generation embraced and celebrated, even while still being considered a curiosity to some extent. Recently the literature of this generation has gained full inclusion in the literary landscape, retrospectively refiguring literary history and aesthetics.

Already active in Baghdad's literary scene prior to their emigration, Iraqi Jewish writers were overrepresented among these transplants. They had discussions in the 1950s regarding the question of language choice, and eventually most adopted Hebrew. Samir Naqqash (1938–2004) is the most prominent of those who continued to write in Arabic throughout his lifetime. Despite having moved to Israel at the relatively young age of twelve, Naqqash wrote his novels, short stories, and novellas in Arabic, and even used the Jewish Baghdadi dialect in some of his works, beginning with his third volume *Ana wa Haulai wal-Fisam* (*I, Them and the Vagaries*, 1978).[43] In much of his writing he recreates the world of his childhood: the Jewish Iraq of the 1940s. His writings were influenced by both contemporary Western philosophy (Sartre, Bergson), and modern Arabic literature (Edward al-Kharrat, Naguib Mahfouz). His worldview was existentialist, his writing dense and multilayered. These stories preserve the language, times, and folklore of his past, one that he shared with over 100,000 Israeli immigrants. Itshaq Bar Moshe (1927–2003) was another writer who wrote only in Arabic, and whose quartet of memoirs – *Khuruj min al-Iraq* (*Exodus from Iraq*, 1975) *Bayt fi Baghdad* (*A House in Baghdad*, 1983), *Ayyam al-Iraq* (*Days in Iraq*, 1988), *Yawmayn fi Haziran* (*Two Days in June*, 2004) – are perhaps the most detailed record of life in Baghdad and Israel.[44]

Eli Amir (b. 1937, Baghdad) was approximately the same age as Naqqash upon his arrival from Iraq to Israel. His semi-autobiographical first novel, *Tarnegol Kapparot* (*Fowl of Atonement*, 1984) tells the story of a boy who is placed on a kibbutz with other young immigrants, and finds himself torn between his new friends and his family. His family lives under difficult conditions in the transit camp, and are concerned about the boy's acculturation at the cost of their traditions.[45] The novel continues the

[43] Samir Naqash, *Ana wa Haulai wal-Fisam* (*I, Them and the Vagaries*) (Tel Aviv: Jamaʿiyat Tashjiʿ al-Abḥāth wa-al-Funūn, 1978).

[44] Yitzhaq Bar-Moshe, *Khuruj min al-Iraq* (*Exodus from Iraq*) (Jerusalem: Council of Sephardi Community, 1975); *Bayt fi Baghdad* (*A House in Baghdad*) (Jerusalem: Association of Jewish Academics from Iraq, 1983), *Ayyam al-Iraq* (*Days in Iraq*) (Shefaram: Al-Mashreq, 1988), *Yawmayn fi Haziran* (*Two Days in June*) (Jerusalem: Association of Jewish Academics from Iraq, 2004).

[45] Eli Amir, *Tarnegol Kaparot* (Tel Aviv: Am Oved, 1983).

tradition of *sifrut hama'abarah* (transit camp literature) – works written by the immigrants themselves about their experiences. Earlier novels in this category include Shimon Ballas's (b. 1930) *HaMa'abarah* (*The Transit Camp*, 1964) and Sami Michael's (b. 1926) *Shavim Veshavim Yoter* (*More and More Equal*, 1974).[46] The former tells of the residents of a transit camp adopting some of the values and strategies of the host country in order to better their living conditions. The latter tells of a young man who manages to escape the transit camp only to face continued prejudice and challenges. For many of its readers it was the first expression of what they themselves felt, or their first glimpse into the world of the other.

Amir's literary career continued with the publication of a novel recreating life in Jewish Baghdad, *Mafriach HaYonim* (*Farewell Baghdad* (literally, *The Pigeon Keeper*), 1992) on the eve of departure; *Ahavat Shaul* (*Saul's Love*, 1998), a love story between a Sephardi man from a Jerusalem family and an Ashkenazi Holocaust survivor; and *Yasmin* (2005), in which the author's alter ego – an Iraqi Jewish immigrant working in the Israeli government – falls in love with a young Palestinian Christian widow.[47]

Shimon Ballas's transit camp novel was the first of the genre in Hebrew literature. He had initially hoped to continue to write in Arabic, but reluctantly came to the realization that it was necessary for him to write in the language of the land in which he resides. After writing a number of novels investigating the experience of the outsider – whether an Iraqi immigrant left behind in the fighting of the Six Day War (*Hitbaharut, Clarification*, 1972), an Egyptian Jewish communist in exile (*Horef Aharon, Last Winter*, 1984), an Iraqi Jewish convert to Islam (*Vehu Aher, And He Is Different*, 1991), a Muslim housekeeper left behind in Baghdad by her Jewish family during the mass immigration ("Iya" in *Otot Stav, Signs of Autumn*, 1992) or others – he returned to the story of the characters from his first novel in the trilogy *Tel Aviv Mizrach* (*Tel Aviv East*, 2003).[48]

Sami Michael used the form of the transit camp novel to be one of the first to address the ethnic question through fiction, pitting the Ashkenazim against the Mizraḥim (labeled here as Sephardim).[49] Like Amir and Ballas,

[46] Shimon Ballas, *HaMa'abarah* (Tel Aviv: Am Oved, 1964); Sami Michael, *Shavim VeShavim Yoter* (Tel Aviv: Boostan, 1974).

[47] Eli Amir, *Mafriach HaYonim* (*Farewell, Baghdad*) (Tel Aviv: Am Oved, 1992); *Ahavat Shaul* (*Saul's Love*) (Tel Aviv: Am Oved, 1998); *Yasmin* (*Jasmine*) (Tel Aviv: Am Oved, 2005).

[48] Shimon Ballas, *Hitbaharut* (Clarification) (Tel Aviv: Sifriyat Poalim, 1972); *Horef Aharon* (*Last Winter*) (Jerusalem: Keter, 1988); *Vehu Aher* (*And He Is Different*) (Or Yehuda: Zmora Bitan, 1991; translated as *Outcast*, San Francisco: City Lights, 2007); "Iya," in *Otot Stav* (*Signs of Autumn*) (Or Yehuda: Zmora Bitan, 1992); *Tel Aviv Mizrach* (*Tel Aviv East*) (Bnei Braq: HaKibbutz HaMeuchad, 2003).

[49] Holocaust survivors are exempt from the binarism because of their suffering.

he returned to Iraq in some of his later works, both in his writing with books for young adults (*Sufah Ben Ha-Dekalim, Storm among the Palms*, 1975) and *Ahavah Bein Ha-Dekalim* (*Love among the Palms*, 1990) and for older adults: *Hofen Shel Arafel* (*A Handful of Fog*, 1979), *Victoria* (1993), and *Aida* (2008).⁵⁰ Although all of his works draw from his own life, *Victoria* was especially personal, it being a portrait of his mother as a young girl growing up in a crowded courtyard in the Jewish quarter of Baghdad. It was both a popular and critical success, signaling a major change in the acceptance of so-called ethnic literature.

Michael also wrote a roman à clef about the Communist Party in Haifa, a mixed community of Jews and Arabs, in *Hasut* (*Refuge*, 1979); explored an unlikely but tender romance between a Christian Arab woman and her Russian immigrant neighbor in *Hazozrah BeVadi* (*A Trumpet in the Wadi*, 1987); portrayed the hydrology service and "little Israel" of the fifties (*Mayim Noshkim LeMayim*, Water Kissing Water, 2001); penned a response to Ghassan Kanafani's Arabic novella "Return to Haifa" (*Yonim BeTrafalgar, Pigeons in Trafalgar Square*, 2005); and returned to Iraq in *Aida* (2008).⁵¹ Overall his writing shows great interest in the relationships that reach across ethnic divisions, harkening back to the lively multiculturalism of the Baghdad he experienced in his youth.

The multicultural dynamic was not limited to Baghdad, but was also found in other cosmopolitan centers of the Middle East, and thus in the writing of their scribes such as the short story writer and novelist Amnon Shamosh (b. 1929 Aleppo, Syria) and novelist and playwright Yitzhak Gormezano-Goren (b. 1941 Alexandria, Egypt). Shamosh's family saga *Michel Ezra Safra U-Banav* (*Michel Ezra Safra and His Sons*, 1978)⁵² was one of the first works to bring the world of Sephardi and Mizraḥi Jews to Ashkenazi-dominated mainstream culture. The story of the larger-than-life patriarch was adapted for the first televised Israeli miniseries. Business and family are intertwined as the family first leaves Aleppo for Israel, and then disperses as branches leave for South America and elsewhere. Similar to other works

---

⁵⁰ Sami Michael, *Sufah Ben Ha-Dekalim* (*Storm among the Palms*) (Tel Aviv: Am Oved, 1975); *Ahavah Bein Ha-Dekalim* (*Love among the Palms*) (Jerusalem: Domino, 1990); *Hofen Shel Arafel* (*A Handful of Fog*) (Tel Aviv: Am Oved, 1979); *Victoria* (Tel Aviv: Am Oved, 1993); *Aida* (Or Yehuda: Zmora Bitan, 2008).

⁵¹ Sami Michael, *Hasut* (*Refuge*) (Tel Aviv: Am Oved, 1977); *Hazozrah BeVadi* (*A Trumpet in the Wadi*) (Tel Aviv: Am Oved, 1987); *Mayim Noshkim LeMayim* (*Water Kissing Water*) (Tel Aviv: Am Oved, 2001); *Yonim BeTrafalgar* (*Pigeons in Trafalgar Square*) (Or Yehuda: Zmora Bitan, 2005).

⁵² Amnon Shamosh, *Michel Ezra Safra U-Banav* (*Michel Ezra Safra and His Sons*) (Tel Aviv: Massada, 1978).

that reconstruct a world now lost, the novel describes an integrated heterogeneous environment (Michel Ezra Safra is respected by Jews, Muslims, and
Christians alike) and its unraveling: the beginning of the end of a once thriving Jewish community and persecutions that suggest that the Ashkenazim
were not the only victims of antisemitism.

Once in Israel the proud Aleppan Jews discover a new form of discrimination. One of them cannot find entrepreneurial success until he
changes his last name to the very Ashkenazi-sounding Schrieber; his business doubles overnight. The idea that one must speak the language of the
Ashkenazim, Yiddish, is expressed in this story and others as well.[53]

Not only do the newcomers have to contend with the prominence of the
Ashkenazim, but also with their prevailing expression of Zionism. Instead
of the spiritual longings of the traditional Sephardi and Mizraḥi liturgy,
the forms of Zionism that led to the establishment of the State of Israel
with their emphases on secularism, communalism, and socialism, were
alien to most Sephardi and Mizraḥi communities. In Shamosh's novel – as
in Amir's *Tarnegol Kapparot* a few years later – these alien principles are
represented by the kibbutz, a place where one of Michel's sons ends up, to
everyone else's surprise and even consternation.

Gormezano-Goren's reconstructions of Alexandria seem to share a similar air of nostalgia, but at the same time they hold up class relations, sexual
repression, and hypocrisy for scrutiny and criticism. His first novel, *Kayitz
Alexondroni* (*Alexandrian Summer*, 1978) recreates the world of a cosmopolitan Jewish family during the reign of King Faruk. Although they identify more with Europeans than with their Egyptian neighbors, their world
is colored by the Arab city in which they live.[54] *Blanche*, of 1986, uses the
conventions of a telenovela to tell the story of the title character whose life
brings her from Corfu to Alexandria then Cairo and Beersheva where she
makes a home with her husband Rafael Vital.[55] The narrative delights in
the irony of the urban Egyptian Jews ending up in the desert.

Other works of his include *Miklat BeBavli* (*A Shelter in Bavli*, 1998) and
Ba-Derech La-Itztadyon: Roman Al Alber Gormezano Ve-Al Bno (*The Path
to the Stadium*, 2003).[56] The former is based on a true incident in which

[53] Nancy E. Berg, "Sephardi Writing: From the Margins to the Mainstream," in *The Boom
in Contemporary Israeli Fiction*, ed. Alan Mintz (Lebanon, NH: Brandeis, 1997), 123.

[54] Yitzhak Gormezano, *Kayitz Alexandroni* (*Alexandrian Summer*) (Tel Aviv: Am Oved,
1978).

[55] Gormezano, *Blanche* (Tel Aviv: Am Oved, 1986).

[56] Yitzhak Gormezano-Goren, *Miklat BeBavli* (*A Shelter in Bavli*) (Tel Aviv: Bimat Kedem,
1998); *Ba-Derech La-Itztadyon: Roman Al Alber Gormezano Ve-Al Bno* (*The Path to the
Stadium*) (Tel Aviv: Bimat Kedem, 2003).

a man was tragically killed by police resisting the destruction order of an illegal addition to his home. The author consciously chose to inhabit his book with a wide variety of Mizrahi characters, especially focusing on those in the middle class, and in the university setting.[57] In the latter work Gormezano returns to the autobiographical mode, this time writing about his father and his father's life.

The next generation of Mizrahi writers were born in Israel, or came to Israel at the beginning of their lives, before they had a chance to create lasting detailed memories of "there." The parents of Orly Castel-Bloom (b. 1960, Tel Aviv) came from Egypt, but she is not primarily thought of as a Mizrahi writer. She is best known for her innovations in style and content. Her writing has been characterized as spare, yet lush with extended metaphors, and details that accumulate. The language mimics the street idiom, seemingly mere transcription, but closer analysis reveals a very carefully crafted medium. The world she creates is woven from unconnected and unrelated bits in unlikely juxtaposition, a comic absurdity that represents contemporary urban reality. The tone is emotionally flat, and short of coherence. Between her short stories and novels she has only a few characters who are unambiguously Mizrahi: the woman on the park bench whose Egyptian ethnicity connects her to an Arab bag lady ("Ummi fi Shughl") and the Kurdish Kati Hallahmi who becomes the face of poverty in Israel (*Human Parts*).[58]

Others of the generation are more readily identified by their ethnicity. Albert Suissa, Ronit Matalon, and Dorit Rabinyan offer three very different approaches to the "ethnic" novel. Although Suissa was born in Casablanca in 1959 he was brought to Israel just a few years later with his family, and it is the impoverished neighborhood in Jerusalem that inhabits all but his very earliest memories and his writing. His book, *Akud* (*Bound*, 1990), is one of the most significant narratives of failed immigration.[59] Either a trilogy of novellas or a novel in three parts, it describes this noisy, crowded neighborhood and the nearly hopeless lives of its denizens. The protagonist fails completely to assimilate into Israeli culture, fails to thrive in the slums in which he lives, fails to transform or even escape them. He and the other main characters are all on the threshold of adolescence. The root of the title is the same as that used in the biblical story of the binding of Isaac, and the ideas of sacrifice and substitution reverberate throughout the narrative.

---

[57] "Tel Aviv and Alexandria: An Interview with Yitzhak Gormezano-Goren," in *Keys to the Garden: New Israeli Writing*, ed. Ammiel Alcalay (San Francisco: City Lights, 1996), 162–167.

[58] Orly Castel-Bloom, *Halakim Enoshiyim* (*Human Parts*) (Or Yehuda: Kinneret, 2002).

[59] Albert Suissa, *Akud* (*Bound*) (Tel Aviv: Hakibbutz Hameuchad/Siman Kriah, 1990).

Reviewers and scholars have most frequently noted the harshness of the story and the language of the narrative, a mixture of different registers and dialects. The language of the narrative is an inventive mix of Judeo-Berber, North African French, biblical phrasings, rabbinic morphology, and contemporary street slang. The depiction of the children's cruelty easily rivals *Lord of the Flies*, but the source of this cruelty is, unlike in Golding's novel, the frustration of failed absorption. The reasons for each immigrant's failure are different, but in the aggregate they show Israeli society to be less welcoming of the newcomer, and less welcoming of diversity, than the Zionist dream would suggest.

While Suissa's characters remain outside of the Zionist dream, Matalon's (b. 1959, Israel) seem to remain nearly untouched by it. Her first novel, *Zeh im haPanim Eleynu* (*The One Facing Us*, 1995) has been celebrated as another breakthrough in so-called ethnic literature.[60] Matalon explores the saga of an Egyptian Jewish family through the eyes of a defiant teen who is sent to stay with her uncle in Cameroon. The raw ingredients of her novel include a series of photographs, the author's own family story, an essay from Jacqueline Kahanoff[61] – "A Childhood in Egypt" – and the larger story of Egyptian Jewry. The photographs serve as a catalyst for Esther and for the narrative. Through the photographs included in the novel (as well as some that are missing), letters, and what her grandmother and others have told her, the protagonist Esther recalls the stories of her family, including the pro-Arab father, the Zionist idealist uncle, and another uncle whose capitalism brings him to Africa, and whose cynicism allows him to thrive there. They are at once individual to the extreme, and representative of a larger group of pan-Mediterranean or Levantines. While Matalon draws on her own life and her own family for elements of the story, the story she tells is that of Egyptian Jewry in general. In Egypt they identify much more strongly with European culture than with Arab or African, and once they leave home, they are nostalgic for Egypt. But just the specific Euro-Levantine Egypt they experienced.

The novel counters the Zionist narrative, but not – as in the works by Michael, Amir, Gormezano-Goren, etc. – by critiquing Israel's inability to absorb its immigrants and to treat all fairly, but by placing most of the story and the narrative outside of Israel and outside of Zionism. Egypt is home; Israel, like New York, Paris, and Cameroon, is the Diaspora. As long as they can no longer live as they used to in Egypt, it does not matter

---

[60] Ronit Matalon, *Zeh Im HaPanim Eleynu* (*The One Facing Us*) (Tel Aviv: Am Oved, 1995).

[61] For more on the writer see Deborah Starr and Sasson Somekh, eds. *Mongrels or Marvels: The Levantine Writings of Jacqueline Shohet Kahanoff*, Stanford Studies in Jewish History and Culture (Palo Alto: Stanford University Press, 2011).

so much where they are, and thus the family ends up scattered to at least three of the four corners.

The very same year as Matalon's novel debut, Dorit Rabinyan (b. 1972, Kfar Saba, Israel) published her first novel. *Simtat Ha-Shkediyot BeOmrijan* (*The Alley of the Almond Trees in Omerijan*, 1995)[62] was also based on the stories the author heard from her mother, aunts, and grandmother, but it is written in a very different style. She has knit these stories together to depict a very colorful Persian Jewish family and neighborhood in the last century. The novel tells the stories of two cousins, each on their own quest for a husband: Flora, pregnant and abandoned, leaves home to track down her disreputable husband, and Nazie, too young to marry legally, eagerly seeks an exception so as to marry her intended. The characters are ruled by superstitions and folk beliefs; they often laugh at each other's expense, inviting the reader to join in. The book seems to embrace a neo-orientalist attitude to Jews from the East, but in doing so, co-opts it.[63]

This was a strategy also employed by a number of the poets who came from similar backgrounds. The ethnic culture loses its flavor when brought to Israel. Erez Biton (b. 1942, Oran, Algeria to a Moroccan family; aliyah in 1948) writes of Zohara Alfassi, the legendary singer from Morocco, who is now a pathetic character, relegated to a life of poverty and anonymity. Others write of the difficulties of adapting to the new culture, of finding their way and of finding acceptance. Although born in Baghdad (1951), Ronny Someck immigrated to Israel two years later, so that he identified with the second generation, the children of Iraqi immigrants, more than with the immigrants themselves. "My mother dreams in Arabic/I dream in Hebrew." With his use of slang and references to pop culture he has developed a distinct voice that straddles the mainstream and the Mizrahi.

Among other topics, Amira Hess (b. 1943, Baghdad) writes memories of her first eight years in Iraq: "At the time of Hoshana Rabba prayers in Baghdad/ the time when we were praying in my grandmother's courtyard,/ the courtyard filled with the voices of Hebrew prayer;"[64] of the first days after arrival in Israel in the transit camp, and about the Holocaust. A number of Mizrahi and Sephardi writers have addressed the Holocaust;[65] Hess

---

[62] Dorit Rabinyan, *Simtat Ha-Shkediyot BeOmrijan* (*The Alley of the Almond Trees in Omerijan*) (Tel Aviv: Am Oved, 1995). Translated into English as *Persian Brides*, 1998.

[63] It has been compared to Avi Shmuelian's novel *Hamaniyot Mukaf Yareach* (Moonstruck Sunflowers) (Jerusalem: Keter, 1992).

[64] Amira Hess, *HaBulimiya shel HaNeshamah* (*Bulimia of the Soul*) (Tel Aviv: Helikon, 2007), 13.

[65] See for example, Yochai Oppenheimer, "The Holocaust: A Mizrachi Perspective," *Hebrew Studies* 51 (2010): 303–328.

is especially passionate about the topic: "When I was born a Jewish soul/ entered my body full of ashes/from Europe to Baghdad."[66]

Sami Chetrit (b. 1960, Morocco) expresses a pan-Mizrahi sentiment in his poetry. He writes not only of the Moroccans in Israel, but those from Azerbaijan ("Yosef Giyugashvili dies twice"), from Yemen ("we're dark kids/ a little Arab/we're dark kids/a little Hebrew"), and elsewhere. In his poetry he also remembers his first babysitter back in Morocco, a Muslim, with affection, and his attempts at assimilation ("On the way to `Ayn Harod/I lost my trilled resh"). He has also written a novel *Ein HaBuba* (*A Doll's Eye*, 2007) and the monograph *HaMa'avak HaMizrahi B'Yisrael 1948–2003* (*The Mizrahi Struggle in Israel*, 1948–2003, 2004).[67]

Unlike his counterparts discussed above, Shimon Adaf was born in Israel (in 1972). The town in which he grew up, Sderot, began as a transit camp for immigrants from Iran (Kurdish and Persian Jews). By the 1960s the vast majority of residents were immigrants from Morocco, like Adaf's parents. Sderot becomes a topic, almost a character in his writing: "It took me twenty years to love/this hole in the middle of nowhere," and an emblem for the experience of the immigrant, and the child of immigrants. Morocco for him is part of the mysterious background of his parents: "It's hard to believe he once crossed the sea and once saw snow/in the cramped houses of Morocco/ at the end of the forties/ the cradle of time."[68] Adaf also writes novels peopled by characters who have Moroccan parents, grew up in a town that sounds a great deal like Sderot, and pen songs for rock bands, much like himself. Although he began publishing earlier than most, he belongs to the generation of writers of the new millennium. Writers such as Dudu Busi, Mois Benarroch, Yosi Avni-Levy, Sami Berdugo, Yosi Sucary, and Almog Behar are among those contributing to the flourishing of Mizrahi writers in the new century.[69]

---

[66] Hess, *HaBulimiya shel HaNeshamah*, 23. See Almog Behar, "HaDma`ot, katav haBra'ille shel HaNeshamah" ("The Tears, Wrote the Braille of the Soul") *HaAretz*, March 30, 2007.

[67] Sami Chetrit, *Ein HaBuba* (*A Doll's Eye*) (Tel Aviv: Xargol- Am Oved, 2007) and *HaMa'avak HaMizrachi B'Yisrael* (*The Mizrahi Struggle in Israel*) (Tel Aviv: Am Oved, 2004). See also Frederick Brenner, *Diaspora* (New York: HarperCollins, 2003).

[68] From "Shir Eres" ("Lullaby"), translated by Gabriel Levin, www.poetryinternationalweb. net/pi/site/poem/item/3479/auto/0/LULLABY; originally published in Shimon Adaf, *Ha-Monolog Shel Icarus* (Icarus' Monologue) (Jerusalem: Gvanim, 1997).

[69] See for example Dudu Busi, *Pere Atzil* (*Nobel Savage*) (Jerusalem: Keter, 2003); Mois Benarroch, *Keys to Tetuan* (Tel Aviv: Bimat Kedem Lesifrut, 2000); Yossi Avni-Levy, *Doda Farhuma Lo Haita Zona* (*Auntie Farhuma Wasn't a Whore After All*) (Tel Aviv: Am Oved, 2002); Sami Berdugo, *Yetomim* (*Orphans*) (Tel Aviv: Hakibbutz Hameuchad/

THE MEMOIR

The memoir has become a very popular genre in general, and for Jews from Arab and Islamic lands in particular. In Israel it seems that a greater acceptance of heterogeneity, a greater interest in the personal and individual, a softening of the grip of the collective, and a felicity of timing has contributed to waves of memoirs. Some of course are more literary than others. The increase in memoirs suggests a growing interest in "ethnic" literature, celebration of the personal narrative, and embrace of the immediate past.

The memoir offers the Mizraḥi Jew a way to return home when it is no longer physically or politically possible. Among the most prominent subgenres are the intellectual's memoir, the food memoir, and the memoir of the second generation. The books recreate vibrant Jewish communities on the eve of their annihilation. The narratives are governed by movement from, something by the leitmotif of leaving, the almost ubiquitous scene of departure at the climax. They depict the communities at the point of their unraveling, the process of home becoming inhospitable. While some take pains to establish the lack of inevitability in the decision to leave at the time, departure is a foregone conclusion, echoed in the very titles: *Adieu Babylone*, *The Last Jews in Baghdad*, *Exit from Iraq*, and *Out of Egypt*.[70]

The memoirs weave narratives from the textures of life from back then, whether illness, poverty, and suffering, or lives of privilege and abundance. Taken together they show the range of experiences, living conditions, and social status, presenting a world that was engaging and vibrant.

Some of these memoirs aspire to respond to stories from the Holocaust, showing how Jews suffered at the hands of the Arab majorities. Itzhak Bar Moshe's posthumously published *Yawmein B'Khazeiran* (*Two Days in June*) and Shmuel Moreh's memoirs, serialized in the popular Arabic news website, Elaph, offer graphic descriptions of the Farhud, the 1941 Baghdadi disturbances that left scores of Jews dead and many more injured. Both writers describe the changes in Iraqi society wrought by political upheavals, external factors, economic distress, and their impact on the Jewish community next to personal slurs and affronts.

Others focus on the lively cultural scene and the interconnectedness of the Jews with their Arab neighbors, Muslims and Christians alike.

Siman Kriah, 2006); Yosi Sucary, *Emilia U-Melach Ha-Aretz: Vidui* (*Emilia and the King of the Land: Confession*) (Tel Aviv: Babel, 2002); Almog Behar, *Ana Min al-Yahoud* (*I Am One of the Jews*) (Tel Aviv: Babel, 2008).

70 Naim Kattan, *Adieu Babylone* (*Farewell, Babylon*). trans. Sheila Fischman (New York: Taplinger, 1980); Nissim Rejwan, *The Last Jews in Baghdad* (Austin: University of Texas Press, 2004); Yitzhaq Bar Moshe, *Khuruj min al-`Irak* (*Exit from Iraq*) (Jerusalem: Association for Academics from Iraq, 1975); Andre Aciman, *Out of Egypt* (New York: Riverhead Trade, 1996).

Sasson Somekh, Nissim Rejwan, and Shimon Ballas all write of intellectual exchanges and literary encounters in Baghdadi cafes. They credit these encounters with giving them the intellectual education that continues to serve them.

In each case there is an insistence on putting events in context. Writers such as Claudia Roden, Colette Rossant, and Rivka Goldman penned their memories intertwined with recipes, developing the language of food as a path to the past.[71] While the balance between recipe and narrative, and the connection between the two vary widely, in each case ethnic cuisine takes a central role. The recipes arise from, contribute to, and assuage a gastronomic nostalgia, offering the reader a chance to reclaim or discover these foods redolent with the past. They may serve as a memory trigger for those from similar backgrounds, but even more so, they serve as a legacy for the next generation, for the children of exile.

The second generation has begun to generate a literature of its own. Often homage to a parent (or grandparent), the works also explore the relationship someone has to a home never known, and share curious parallels with the Sephardi literature of generations following the Expulsion. Violette Shamash's daughter and son-in-law edited, augmented, and published her *Memories of Eden: A Journey through Jewish Baghdad* (2008),[72] which tells of a near idyllic childhood lived among Jews and Arabs in harmony until events such as the Farhud brought it to a close. Lucette Lagnado's *The Man in the Sharkskin Suit: My Family's Exodus from Old Cairo to the New World* is both a tribute to her father and a record of the demise of Cairene Jewry (2007).[73] Jack Marshall's exploration of the insular community of displaced Syrian Jews in New York, Marina Benjamin's *Last Days in Babylon: The History of a Family, the Story of a Nation*, and Ariel Sabar's *My Father's Paradise: A Son's Search for His Jewish Past in Kurdish Iraq* all begin with a rejection of their respective parents' past in the Arab world, and move to recover and understand their backgrounds.[74] They

---

[71] Claudia Roden. *A Book of Middle Eastern Food* (New York: Penguin, 1984); Colette Rossant, *Memories of a Lost Egypt: A Memoir with Recipes* (New York: Clarkson Potter, 1999; Rivka Goldma, *Mama Nazima's Jewish-Iraqi Cuisine*. New York: Hippocrene Books, 2006.

[72] Surrey: Forum Books, 2008.

[73] New York: Ecco, 2007.

[74] Jack Marshall, *From Baghdad to Brooklyn* (Minneapolis: Coffee House Press, 2005); Marina Benjamin, *Last Days in Babylon: The History of a Family, the Story of a Nation* (New York: Free Press, 2006; Ariel Sabar, *My Father's Paradise: A Son's Search for His Jewish Past in Kurdish Iraq* (New York: Algonquin Books, 2008).

conclude with appropriating their parents' memories and stances toward the past.

While the worlds of Sephardi and Mizraḥi Jews began as separate universes on very different time tables they share experiences of multicultural heterogeneity and exile which allows them to come together and occasionally overlap in the Arab world, the Americas, and Israel. The worlds of both have changed radically in the modern period, their ancestral homes are gone – whether centuries ago, or just in the last generation – and their traditional languages and ethnolects are dying. Yet their literatures and legacies are incredibly alive. Their rich contributions to contemporary and future Jewish culture are indisputably worthy of remembering, reading, and recording.

SELECT BIBLIOGRAPHY

Aciman, Andre. *Out of Egypt*. New York: Riverhead, 1996.

Angel, Marc D. "The Sephardic Theater of Seattle," *American Jewish Archives Journal* 25, no. 2 (1973): 156–160.

  Sephardi Voices: 1492–1992. New York: The Women's Zionist Organization of America, 1991.

Balbuena, Monique. *Sephardic Literary Identities in Diaspora*. Palo Alto: Stanford University Press, 2010.

Ballas, Shimon, *Outcast*. Translated by Ammiel Alcalay and Oz Shelach. San Francisco: City Lights, 2005.

Beckwith, Stacy. *Charting Memory: Recalling Medieval Spain*. New York: Garland, 2000.

Beinart, Haim, ed. *Moreshet Sepharad: The Sephardi Legacy*. Vol. II. Jerusalem: Magnes Press, 1992.

Benbassa, Esther and Aron Rodrigue, *Sephardi Jewry: A History of the Judeo-Spanish Community, 14th–20th Centuries*. Berkeley: University of California Press, 2000.

Benjamin, Marina, *Last Days in Babylon: The History of a Family, the Story of a Nation*. New York: Free Press, 2006.

Berg, Nancy E. *Exile from Exile: Israeli Writers from Iraq*. Albany: SUNY, 1996.

Díaz-Mas, Paloma. *The Sephardim: The Jews from Spain*. Chicago: University of Chicago Press, 1992.

Harris, Tracy K. *Death of a Language: The History of Judeo-Spanish*. Newark: University of Delaware Press, 1994.

Kattan, Naim. *Adieu Babylone (Farewell, Babylon)*. Translated by Sheila Fischman. New York: Taplinger, 1980.

Koen-Sarano, Matilda. *Por el plazer de kontar Kuentos de mi vida*. Jerusalem: Kana, 1986.

Lagnado, Lucette. *The Man in the Sharkskin Suit: My Family's Exodus from Old Cairo to the New World*. New York: Ecco, 2007.

Lehmann, Matthias B. *Ladino Rabbinic Literature and Ottoman Sephardic Culture*. Bloomington: Indiana University Press, 2005.

Michael, Sami. *Victoria*. Translated by Dalya Bilu. New York: MacMillan, 1995.

Moreen, Vera B. *In Queen Esther's Garden: An Anthology of Judeo-Persian Literature*. New Haven: Yale University Press, 2000.

Perera, Victor. *The Cross and the Pear Tree: A Sephardic Journey*. New York: Alfred A. Knopf, 1995.

Rejwan, Nissim. *The Last Jews in Baghdad*. Austin: University of Texas, 2004.

Roden, Claudia. *A Book of Middle Eastern Food*. New York: Penguin, 1984.

Roditi, Edouard, "The Slow Agony of Judeo-Spanish Literature," *World Literature Today* 60, no. 2 (1986): 244–246.

Rossant, Colette. *Memories of a Lost Egypt: A Memoir with Recipes*. New York: Clarkson Potter, 1999.

Roth, Norman. "What Constitutes Sephardic Literature?" in Yedida K. Stillman and Norman A. Stillman, eds. *From Iberia to Diaspora: Studies in Sephardic History and Culture*. Leiden: Brill, 1999.

Sabar, Ariel. *My Father's Paradise: A Son's Search for His Jewish Past in Kurdish Iraq*. New York: Algonquin Books, 2008.

Schorsch, Jonathan, "Disappearing Origins: Sephardic Autobiography Today," *Prooftexts* 27 (2007): 82–150.

Shaked, Gershon, *Modern Hebrew Fiction*. Translated by Emily Budick. Bloomington: Indiana University Press, 2000.

Shimony, Batya. *Al Saf HaGeulah*. Beersheva & Or Yehudah: Heksherim & Dvir, 2008.

Simon, Reeva Spector, Michael Menachem Laskier, and Sara Reguer, eds. *The Jews of the Middle East and North Africa in Modern Times*. New York: Columbia University Press, 2003.

Stein, Sarah Abrevaya, *Making Jews Modern: The Yiddish and Ladino Press in the Russian and Ottoman Empires*. Bloomington: Indiana University Press, 2004.

Yehoshua, A. B. *Mar Mani*. Tel Aviv: Hakibbutz Hameuchad/ Siman Kriah, 1990.

CHAPTER 26

ANGLOPHONE LITERATURE

AXEL STÄHLER

The conceptualization of an Anglophone Jewish Diaspora is a recent development in Jewish studies, which suggests a transnational and transcultural coherence specific to Anglophone Jewry. While the agency of literature in the widest sense in the formation of the Anglophone Diaspora since the end of the first half of the nineteenth century has recently been acknowledged,[1] a corresponding comprehensive conceptualization of Anglophone Jewish literature has not yet been sufficiently engaged in.[2] The implications are nevertheless significant, for the latter, if not taken simply to refer to literature written by Jews in the English language, in turn suggests that the literary creativity of Jewish writers in the Anglophone Diaspora is the product of its socio-cultural coherence and that it sustains its perpetuation while continually contributing to and being shaped by its ongoing transformation. The Anglophone Jewish Diaspora and Anglophone Jewish literature are then inextricably linked, and the conceptualization of the latter must therefore be considered crucial to that of the former and vice versa.

Perhaps most significantly, the conceptualization of an Anglophone Jewish literature indicates that traditional perceptions of Jewish cultural creativity may need to be revised. The current preeminence of narratives of hyphenated Jewish literatures in English, such as Jewish-American or British-Jewish, may have to be rethought. Moreover, the remapping of what may then appear to be the permeable boundaries of 'national' Jewish cultural production may equally entail shifting notions of center and

---

[1] See, e.g., Arthur Kiron, "An Atlantic Jewish Republic of Letters?," *Jewish History* 20 (2006): 171–211; Adam Mendelsohn, "Tongue Ties: The Emergence of the Anglophone Jewish Diaspora in the Mid-Nineteenth Century," *American Jewish History* 93, no. 2 (2007): 177–209; and Jonathan D. Sarna, "Port Jews in the Atlantic: Further Thoughts," *Jewish History* 20 (2006): 213–219.

[2] An attempt to encompass the linguistic dimension of the Anglophone Jewish literature, but without specifically exploring the historical dimension, was Axel Stähler, ed., *Anglophone Jewish Literature* (Abingdon, 2007); see also more recently *The Edinburgh Companion to Modern Jewish Fiction*, ed. David Brauner and Axel Stähler (Edinburgh, 2015).

periphery. Ultimately, writers previously considered marginal, or simply less known, may gain in recognition while the position of others, iconic in their various national contexts, may need to be reassessed in the more comprehensive historical and socio-cultural framework suggested by the larger Anglophone context, as may notions of distinct coherent traditions.

It would certainly be misguided to disavow entirely the particularity of specific traditions originating in specific cultural contexts and circum-scribed, once again, by the proliferating use of hyphenations. However, to disregard the manifold historical and cultural affinities between polit-ical entities in the Anglophone world must be considered no less inju-dicious. David Brauner, for instance, in what was the first comparative study of American and British Jewish fiction, published in 2001, has noticed various "thematic connections" resulting from "a shared transat-lantic sensibility"[3] and has "found that the border between British- and American-Jewish fiction is becoming increasingly difficult to locate."[4] In fact, he concludes that in response to "international cross-fertilization" and "the ever increasing proximity of British and American culture," but also "because of an insistent transnational (and to some extent transhistorical) sense of Jewishness, it is possible to speak in general terms of British- *and* American-Jewish fiction."[5] It has, moreover, been argued by the historian William D. Rubinstein that, despite "considerable differences in both the Jewish communities of each of the English-speaking countries and, still more, in the national histories and institutions of each country," the simi-larities are "more significant still."[6] He suggested, in particular, that the ties between Jewry and English as a vernacular increased "both the importance of English-speaking Jewry *per se* and the centrality of English to Jewish communications, as with the communications among all other groups."[7]

Rubinstein concluded (in 1996) that "the implications of this linguistic transformation remain only partly explored, if at all."[8] A decade later, this was echoed by Jonathan D. Sarna. In response to Arthur Kiron's attempt to connect to the paradigm of the Port Jew the development of what he called an "Atlantic Jewish republic of letters" as "a self-conscious cultural pro-ject constituted by a network of opinion makers, information providers,

---

[3] David Brauner, *Post-War Jewish Fiction: Ambivalence, Self-Explanation and Transatlantic Connections* (Basingstoke and New York, 2001), xi.

[4] Brauner, *Post-War Jewish Fiction*, 186.

[5] Brauner, *Post-War Jewish Fiction*, 186–187; emphasis in the original.

[6] William D. Rubinstein, *A History of the Jews in the English-Speaking World: Great Britain* (London, 1996), 7.

[7] Rubinstein, *History*, 21.

[8] Rubinstein, *History*, 5.

authors, and translators, who exploited the agency of print both for positive and apologetic purposes,"[9] Sarna proposed that "English-speaking Jews
created what may one day be seen as modern Jewry's wealthiest and most
vibrant Diaspora subculture."[10] He argued that this was "something new
and quite different," of much wider significance and far greater impact,

> the creation of a distinctive English-language Jewish diaspora that ultimately came
> to embrace Great Britain, the United States, Canada, Australia, New Zealand,
> South Africa, and the English-speaking communities of the Caribbean. The emer-
> gence of this trans-national diaspora, characterized more by language and culture
> than by commerce and trade, is one of the most important, and least recognized
> features of the 19th century. The circulation of books, periodicals, ideas and Jewish
> migrants (particularly religious leaders) around this diaspora, and its subsequent
> emergence as the largest and most culturally creative Jewish diaspora in the world
> cries out for greater historical analysis.[11]

Sarna's suggestions were further developed by Adam Mendelsohn who
identified the Anglophone Jewish Diaspora as "a radical transformation
in modern Jewish history" because it "knitted the Jewish communities
of English-speaking countries into a new cultural, religious, and social
sphere."[12] Elaborating on Sarna's criticism of Kiron, Mendelsohn argued
that the 1840s

> heralded a radical new departure from preexisting patterns. The period of the
> Port Jew had passed. In its place emerged a nascent Anglophone diaspora, a cul-
> tural and social sphere whose tentacular grasp stretched across the expanding
> British Empire and deep into the American frontier. Although distant from the
> traditional trade routes of the Atlantic world, Jews who moved to the flourishing
> British imperial outposts in Canada, Australia, and South Africa participated in
> this novel cultural domain.[13]

Thus, it was only towards the end of the first half of the nineteenth century that the formation of the Anglophone Jewish Diaspora, arising in
dialogue with the previously existing interconnections of mostly Sephardic
Jews around the Atlantic rim, gathered momentum and was eventually
augmented with the further reaches of the Pacific and the antipodean

---

[9] Kiron, "An Atlantic Jewish Republic," 171–211; 175–176. On the Port Jew see Lois Dubin,
"Introduction: Port Jews in the Atlantic World," *Jewish History* 20 (2006): 117–127; 117.
For a critical view, see C. S. Monaco, "Port Jews or a People of the Diaspora? A Critique
of the Port Jew Concept," *Jewish Social Studies* n.s. 15, no. 2 (2009): 137–166; 159.

[10] Sarna, "Port Jews," 217.

[11] Sarna, "Port Jews," 217.

[12] Mendelsohn, "Tongue Ties," 178.

[13] Mendelsohn, "Tongue Ties," 181–182.

world. Its demographics changed rapidly and radically with the increasing mass migration of Jews, in particular from Eastern Europe, to English-speaking countries. Paralleling, and taking advantage of, the expansion and consolidation of the British Empire and of the continuous advance of the 'frontier' in America, the Anglophone Jewish Diaspora took shape in the wake of improving communication pathways. Technical progress, most importantly the development of the railway and the steamship, the industrialization of printing, and the telegraph, not only facilitated wide-ranging geographical dispersal, but also the creation of numerous inter-secting communication networks and a cultural cohesion that bridged frequently formidable distances.[14]

Nevertheless, cohesion was constantly challenged by the continuing influx into the Anglophone Jewish Diaspora and differing degrees of assimilation. Waves of immigration, following pogroms in Eastern Europe and, in the twentieth century, the Shoah, impacted crucially on the development of the Anglophone Diaspora and arguably changed its character. Ultimately, the sys-tematic destruction of many Eastern European communities shifted cultural predominance towards the Anglophone sphere. By the end of the Second World War, the Anglo-Jewish community was the largest in Europe outside the Soviet Union. But in global terms, it was the American Jewish commu-nity which emerged as the most numerous, influential, and internally diverse, even though the establishment of the State of Israel in 1948 – rewarding Zionist efforts of re-establishing a Jewish 'center' and cementing the rebirth of Hebrew as a 'modern' language – initiated the polarization of English and Hebrew (or Ivrit) as the most prominent Jewish languages.

It is crucial, however, to bear in mind that the Jewish Diaspora in the English-speaking countries was never a monolithic one, nor was it homoge-neously Anglophone. Alongside the languages spoken in the old countries, Jewish immigrants frequently brought with them Yiddish and Hebrew. Literary creativity in the Anglophone Diaspora by no means completely excluded these languages. In America they persist to the present day; in the other countries of the Anglophone Diaspora they may have all but van-ished in the meantime, but with the notable exception of Britain and, to some extent, America and the Caribbean, the origins of Jewish writing can mostly be traced to immigrants whose first literary language was Yiddish.

Besides, as suggested by Hana Wirth-Nesher, there remains for many Jewish writers in the Diaspora a residual bilingualism or even bicultural-ism informed by the latent presence of Hebrew and Yiddish.[15] Although

---

[14] See also Kiron, "An Atlantic Jewish Republic" and Mendelsohn, "Tongue Ties."
[15] Hana Wirth-Nesher, *Call It English: The Language of Jewish American Literature* (Princeton, NJ, 2006), 5.

Wirth-Nesher focuses in her analysis on the American Jewish experience, the phenomenon as such can surely be observed in all Jewish writing. In a curious inversion, it is evident even in Israel where, as Karen Alkalay-Gut has shown, Anglophone Jewish writers are in the position of a "double diaspora,"[16] and where, as argued by Karen Grumberg, the use of English in modern Hebrew fiction is revealed to challenge the success of Hebrew as a language of national homogenization as it has been promoted in accordance with the anti-colonial ambitions of the Zionist project.[17]

Moreover, the countries designated as English-speaking were never exclusively Anglophone. Certainly, they are no longer so. This, in fact, is a significant characteristic of the Anglophone Diaspora which can be traced to the colonial origins of its geographical expansion and the subsequent development of multicultural societies. With the exception of Britain, all the countries in which the Anglophone Jewish Diaspora thrived most successfully were settlement colonies and, later, countries of immigration, now including Britain. While indigenous languages appear to have held little attraction – unsurprisingly, because they were the languages of the subaltern[18] – in most of these countries, and depending on their social and geographical situation, Jewish immigrants were faced with a choice between competing European languages which also implied and entailed cultural affiliations. Besides English, French is spoken in Canada,[19] Afrikaans in South Africa,[20] French and Spanish in the Caribbean, and, more recently, the latter also in the United States, where French and, even more importantly, German were also of historical significance to the Jewish Diaspora. It was only England, and perhaps Australia and New Zealand, where such a choice did not have to be made, and where, in fact, it was not possible.

The significance of such a choice should be obvious. As Sophia Lehmann observes, diasporic communities are faced with the struggle of "articulating a cultural identity in which history and home reside in language,

---

[16] Karen Alkalay-Gut, "Double Diaspora: English Writers in Israel," *Judaism* 51 (2002): 457–468; 458.

[17] Karen Grumberg, "Ricki Lake in Tel Aviv: The Alternative of Orly Castel-Bloom's Hebrew-English," in *Anglophone Jewish Literature*, ed. Axel Stähler (Abingdon, 2007), 234–248.

[18] Intriguingly, writers of Jewish heritage such as Kate Bosse-Griffiths and Judith Maro in Wales and David Marcus in Ireland became active in the Welsh and Irish language movements, respectively, and contributed also to Welsh and Irish literature.

[19] There are a number of significant Canadian Jewish Francophone writers such as Monique Bosco, Naim Kattan, Victor Teboul, and Régine Robin, all of whom immigrated after the Second World War.

[20] Jewish authors to write in Afrikaans were, among others, Jan Lion Cachet, Sarah Goldblatt, and J. M. Friedenthal.

rather than nation, and in which language itself must be recreated so as to bespeak the specificity of cultural experience."[21] More succinctly, because of the alleged centrality of language to Jewish culture, "creating a mother tongue which incorporates both history and contemporary culture and experience is tantamount to creating a home within the Diaspora."[22]

English as a diasporic language accordingly appears to encompass the past and the present and to envisage, at least tacitly, also the future of Jewish communities in the Anglophone Diaspora. It is thus a tool of identity formation, community building, and the creation of culture in this linguistically defined space. Yet, significantly, it is also a shared language and an archive of the memory and culture of several 'others'. As a shared language, it not only admits into Jewish cultural creativity the experiences and patterns of cultural engagement of others, but makes Jewish history, contemporary culture, and experience in turn accessible to those others.[23] English is a vehicle, and, indeed, a process, of "border-crossings" between the particular and the universal.[24]

Cynthia Ozick must have felt this potential of English when, in 1970, she made her notorious proposal to create a New Yiddish. More specifically, the American Jewish writer ascribed to the appropriated and transformed language the potential of facilitating Jewish reconstruction after the Shoah.[25] Although she hastened to add that this was not "to deny culture-making to the Land of Israel,"[26] Ozick looked to the Anglophone Diaspora, and more specifically to America, for the creation of a centrally Jewish literature:

We can give ourselves over entirely to Gentile culture and be lost to history, becoming a vestige nation without a literature; or we can do what we have never before dared to do in a Diaspora language: make it our own, our own necessary instrument, understanding ourselves in it while being understood by everyone who cares to listen or read.[27]

Controversially, the writer maintained that "there are no major works of Jewish imaginative genius written in any Gentile language, sprung out of any Gentile culture."[28] Indeed, she polemically insisted on the liberating

[21] Sophia Lehmann, "In Search of a Mother Tongue: Locating Home in Diaspora," *Melus* 23 (1998): 101–119; 101.

[22] Lehmann, "In Search of a Mother Tongue," 115.

[23] See also Cynthia Ozick, "Toward a New Yiddish," in *Art & Ardor. Essays* (New York, 1983), 151–177; 177.

[24] Lehmann, "In Search of a Mother Tongue," 106, 111–112.

[25] Ozick, "Toward a New Yiddish," 173.

[26] Ozick, "Toward a New Yiddish," 173.

[27] Ozick, "Toward a New Yiddish," 177.

[28] Ozick, "Toward a New Yiddish," 167–168.

potential of her proposal: "From being envious apes we can become masters of our own civilization – and let those who want to call this 're-ghettoization,' or similar pejoratives, look to their own destiny."[29] Echoing bygone antisemitic claims of the lack of Jewish creative genius and evoking early Zionist essentialism,[30] Ozick's search for an "authentic" and previously abandoned or suppressed voice that would serve to return the Jewish people to history also invites comparison with the colonial/postcolonial paradigm.

Significantly, Ozick's proposal was determined by an essentialist nostalgia which imbued both the old and the "new" Yiddish with the exclusivity of being creators of a coherent cultural system which neither could have ever had. At the same time, her suggestion was predicated on a conscious and concerted effort of turning English into a specifically Jewish language analogous to one that had developed over centuries of cultural contact. This was historically not viable and, predictably, the writer's suggestion elicited much controversy.[31] By the time she included her essay in her collection *Art & Ardor*, in 1983, Ozick conceded that she no longer held "that the project of fashioning a Diaspora literary culture, in the broadest *belles-lettres* sense, can be answered by any theory of an indispensable language – i.e., the Judaization of a single language used by large populations of Jews."[32]

English nevertheless had become a major tool of Jewish cultural creativity, and long before Ozick voiced her proposal. The creative potential attributed by Lehmann to the diasporic language and the cultural productivity of bilingualism suggested by Wirth-Nesher may go some way toward explaining why Anglophone Jewish literature – perhaps as a result also of the rise of what is now referred to as the new English literatures and an ever-expanding global market for literature in English – has never before been as creative and as varied. In fact, in the larger context of overall Jewish cultural creativity it may even be considered, to some extent, to be hegemonic. At the same time it may be said to be the ever-changing product of the hybridity which Homi Bhabha described as the effect of the colonial and postcolonial confrontation and whose recognition entails "an important change of perspective" in that it challenges any essentialism.[33] Indeed, in a "post-essentialist" age it seems necessary to recognize in their

[29] Ozick, "Toward a New Yiddish," 177.
[30] See Axel Stähler, "Introduction: Jewish Literature(s) in English: Anglophone Jewish Writing and the 'Loquation' of Culture," in *Anglophone Jewish Literature*, 3–32; 4–8.
[31] See, e.g., Ruth R. Wisse, "American Jewish Writing, Act II," *Commentary* 61 (1976): 40–45.
[32] Ozick, "Toward a New Yiddish," 152.
[33] Homi K. Bhabha, *The Location of Culture* (London, 1994), 112.

very hybridity the dynamic aesthetic, social, and political potential of all literatures which emerge from the cultural contact zones of immigration or colonial engagement – including Anglophone Jewish literature.

Another and perhaps even more pervasive form of essentialism makes itself felt with the Americanization of Jewish cultural creativity in public discourse. Its American component tends to dominate the perception of Jewish literary production in English[34] and correlates with the increasing, though also increasingly contested, global dominance of American popular culture. In the past, the Jewish presence in America has frequently been associated, at least implicitly, with the Diaspora.[35] Moreover, the popular assumption has often been that American Jewish creativity is entirely defined by its Anglophone component, thus ignoring or denying Jewish bilingualism and biculturalism, whether residual or active. This is due, at least partly, to the high visibility, nationally and internationally, of writers such as Saul Bellow (born in Canada but raised in the United States), Philip Roth, Bernard Malamud, Joseph Heller, Grace Paley, and Cynthia Ozick – as well as, more recently, Michael Chabon, Jonathan Safran Foer, Nicole Krauss, and Nathan Englander.

Nevertheless, the Israel–Diaspora dichotomy and, even more specifically, the Israel–America dichotomy as paradigmatic of the former have since been challenged with reference to "the emergence of a trans-national Jewish culture."[36] To be sure, globalization and the development, once again, of new communication structures – among them cheap and easy worldwide travel, satellite-TV and, perhaps even more drastically, the worldwide web – must be considered as giving the Anglophone Jewish Diaspora and its cultural creativity new momentum and new shape. The internet in particular is a highly productive vehicle of cultural change, not least because its virtual space transcends conventional boundaries and promotes linguistic change from which new internet literacies develop.[37] It has even been suggested that English, one of the most pervasive languages on the worldwide web and invested with "a charismatic power," may conceivably "be approaching an irrevocable split" into various new languages,

---

[34] Bryan Cheyette, "Diasporas of the Mind: British-Jewish Writing Beyond Multiculturalism," in *Diaspora and Multiculturalism: Common Traditions and New Developments*, ed. Monika Fludernik (Amsterdam and New York, 2003), 45–82; 52.

[35] See Carole Gerson, "Some Patterns of Exile in Jewish Writing of the Commonwealth," *Ariel* 13 (1982): 103–114; 104.

[36] Jerome A. Chanes, "Beyond Marginality," *Judaism* 48 (1999): 387–390; 387–388.

[37] See Mark Warschauer, "Language, Identity, and the Internet," in *Race in Cyberspace*, ed. Beth E. Kolko, Lisa Nakamura, and Gilbert B. Rodman (New York and London, 2000), 151–170; 152.

similar to the Romance languages developing from the old European *lingua franca* of Latin.[38] In this case, Cynthia Ozick's controversial notion of a New Yiddish may not seem so eccentric after all.[39]

At the same time, the internet brings with it a deluge of (hyper-)textual material. It not only disseminates literary texts of all periods in various stages of their genesis, frequently fragmented or reshuffled in ever-changing and often arbitrary contexts, it is also a means of circumventing publishing strictures and has spawned new genres which are specific to the medium and frequently interactive – digital poetry, zines, blogs, and tweets, etc. The internet has also, no less significantly, engendered new reading (and viewing) practices which are adapted to the plethora of possibilities offered by the new medium, but also to its limitations. Ultimately, the hypertext raises new challenges to and renegotiates notions of authorship, text, and readership as well as the construction of identities and of transnational and transcultural literatures.[40] In the long term, the internet will redraw, in all likelihood, the map of transnational and transcultural exchange and creativity.

Many of these changes do not, yet, have a wider impact on the literary scene and its institutions, nor on its academic appreciation. It may be indicative of the transformative and frequently empowering potential inherent in the worldwide web, however, that many Anglophone Jewish writers in Israel, marginalized in their own country because of the choice of their linguistic affiliation, have also turned to the internet.[41] By doing so, they have found a way of asserting and developing their literary productivity in English and of becoming contributors to the creation and development of an Anglophone Jewish internet community while still maintaining their national and geographical affiliation with Israel. The internet offers these writers a means of subverting the "double diaspora" which Alakaly-Gut has described as their lot.

Their case in many ways constitutes an anomaly which paradoxically may nevertheless be considered paradigmatic of some aspects of the

---

[38] Mark Abley, *The Prodigal Tongue: Dispatches from the Future of English* (New York, 2008), 23.

[39] For the increasing use of languages other than English on the internet, see Warschauer, "Language, Identity, and the Internet," 156.

[40] For a discussion of the implications of the internet on constructions of identity and group affiliation, see *Race in Cyberspace*. The question of an alternative "internet nationalism" is also significant in this context; see Joe Lockard, "Babel Machines and Electronic Universalism," in *Race in Cyberspace*, 171–189; 180–183.

[41] Karen Alkalay-Gut, "The Anglo-Israeli Writer: Double Identities in Troubled Times," in *Anglophone Jewish Literature*, 195–208; 200.

Anglophone Jewish Diaspora. The diasporic origins of most Jewish writers in English in Israel – hailing from the United States, Britain, Canada, South Africa, and Australia and New Zealand– resembles almost a miniature cross-section of the Anglophone Jewish Diaspora. The very tenacity with which these writers adhere to the diasporic language even in the Land of Israel suggests a specific force of cohesion which ties them both to the cultural contexts of the Anglophone Diaspora and to one another. Their literary creativity may therefore perhaps also be considered as a miniature version of the sustained transnational and transcultural intertwinings of Anglophone Jewish literature in the global context.[42]

The emergence and development of Anglophone Jewish literature across the early Anglophone Jewish Diaspora was neither entirely random nor predominantly dictated by external pressure. At least in part, it was driven by the vision of individuals who deliberately pursued with varying degrees of success the cultural cohesion of Jewish communities across the English-speaking world with the objective of creating an enlightened Jewish public sphere.[43] But although the actual publication and reproduction process was not limited to the imperial center, at least initially the works of secular literature disseminated across the Anglophone Jewish Diaspora mostly originated in England: the writings of Grace Aguilar were particularly popular, but the works of the Moss sisters (later Celia Levetus and Marion Hartog) were also widely read.[44]

In contrast to Central European countries, the Anglo-Jewish community as a whole had not been sufficiently substantial to engage in processes of modernization and the creation of communal structures before the 1830s. Then, however, literature and journalism proved crucially instrumental to developing a distinct Anglo-Jewish subculture. Jewish women, traditionally barred from gaining and displaying learning, assumed a voice of their own in the emerging debates on the removal of civil and municipal disabilities in England predominantly through the vehicle of fiction and promoted their own empowerment within the larger context of Jewish emancipation and religious reform. This led to an anomaly which was

---

[42] For a more detailed exposition, see Alkalay-Gut, "Double Diaspora" and "The Anglo-Israeli writer"; and Axel Stähler, "From the Belly of the Fish: Jewish Writers in English in Israel: Transcultural Perspectives," in *Transcultural English Studies: Theories, Fictions, Realities*, ed. Frank Schulze-Engler and Sissy Helff (Amsterdam and New York, 2009), 151–167. For the first comprehensive survey of Anglophone writing in Israel, see Nadežda Rumjanceva, *Roots in the Air: Construction of Identity in Anglophone Israeli Literature* (Göttingen, 2015).

[43] See Kiron, "An Atlantic Jewish Republic."

[44] See Kiron, "An Atlantic Jewish Republic," 177 and Mendelsohn, "Tongue Ties," 192.

unique to the emergence of Anglo-Jewish secular literature in that it was initially shaped decisively by female writers.[45] Although they did not limit themselves to fiction,[46] their most significant contribution to Anglophone Jewish literature is nevertheless in fictional narrative. Intriguingly, as Michael Galchinsky emphasizes, among other Jewish traditions, these women writers "drew on the ancient literary forms of the Aggadah, creative retellings of biblical narratives with contemporary relevance"[47] – just as Ozick was to envisage for her liturgical literature in the New Yiddish.[48] But they were also the first Jewish writers in England to write novels, a literary form, as Galchinsky observes, "through which many concerns about the place of the Other in society were circulated."[49]

The early Anglo-Jewish writers explored Jewish themes but, frequently reworking prevalent English cultural images of Jewishness, construed in their apologetic fiction a largely private religious Jewish identity which was often outwardly mirrored by a fully assimilable public persona. Transmission of these patterns of engagement soon made them available in other contexts across the Anglophone Diaspora. In the event, the popularity of the early Anglo-Jewish women writers was short-lived. They had, as Galchinsky suggests, "produced an indigenous literature that played a significant role in the invention and maintenance of an Anglo-Jewish subculture"[50] and indeed, far beyond England, in the Anglophone Diaspora. However, with successive waves of mass migrations following the assassination of Tsar Alexander II in 1881, the demographics of Jewish communities across the Anglophone Diaspora changed dramatically, as did the contexts of their literary creativity. In response to different stimuli, a diversification set in, which acknowledged and facilitated the particular, but was still based, as the case might be, on the acquisition and shared use of English, and on negotiations of identity which now, however, prominently encompassed the immigrant experience and the challenges it engendered.

In England, the pressure to present Jewish difference in terms of its assimilability increased. Nevertheless, there also arose critical and self-critical voices.[51] Amy Levy and Julia Frankau (writing as Frank Danby) questioned

---

[45] Michael Galchinsky, *The Origin of the Modern Jewish Woman Writer: Romance and Reform in Victorian England* (Detroit, 1996), 15.

[46] See Galchinsky, *Origin*, 17.

[47] Galchinsky, *Origin*, 33.

[48] Ozick, "Toward a New Yiddish," 173.

[49] Galchinsky, *Origin*, 33.

[50] Galchinsky, *Origin*, 19.

[51] Subsequent paragraphs on British Jewish literature are based on Axel Stähler, "Jewish Fiction," in *The Encyclopedia of Twentieth-Century British and Irish Fiction*, ed. Brian W. Shaffer (Oxford and New York, 2011), 198–202.

the assumptions of an English national culture as well as the complacent self-image of British Jewry. At the same time, the evolving "ghetto" of the impoverished Jewish East End in London found literary attention, first sympathetically and apologetically in the fiction of Benjamin Farjeon and Israel Zangwill, but then, in the interwar years, increasingly critically. Writers like Simon Blumenfeld and William Goldman reacted with their autobiographical works against the bourgeois trends in the previous generation, but concentrated on class difference rather than ethnicity.

In the 1920s and 1930s emerged a Jewish literature in English also from the periphery in Britain. Louis Golding, addressing British antisemitism with an assimilationist bias, wrote about the fictitious community of Doomington. This was a rendering of his native Manchester and the second center of Jewish culture in the country. In Wales, Lily Tobias associated in her fiction an ardent Zionism with nascent Welsh national aspirations. Dating back to the eighteenth century, the Welsh Jewish community had expanded considerably with the immigration waves of the late nineteenth century.[52] The best-known Jewish writers in English to emerge from Wales are perhaps Bernice Rubens and Maurice Edelman. In Scotland, notable Jewish writers have been few. Muriel Spark (born Muriel Sarah Camberg) was of Jewish extraction but the engagement with Jewish concerns in her fiction is mostly oblique and the writer converted to Catholicism in 1954, a decision reflected in her 1965 novel *The Mandelbaum Gate*, which focuses searchingly on the identity crisis of a "Gentile Jewess, neither one thing nor another."[53] J. David Simons more recently turned in his historical novels to the Jewish immigrant experience in early twentieth-century Scotland.

After the Second World War, the Holocaust, and the foundation of the state of Israel, the productivity of British Jewish writers burgeoned. The 1950s, when writers like Ronald Harwood, Dan Jacobson, David Marcus, and Mordecai Richler gravitated towards London from the far-flung corners of the Anglophone Diaspora, have been credited with producing a "new wave" of Jewish writing in Britain.[54] Crucially, this was a time of

---

[52] Grahame Davies, "Welsh and Jewish: Responses to Wales by Jewish Writers," in *Culture and the State*, ed. James Gifford and Gabrielle Zezulka-Mailloux, vol. 3: *Nationalisms* (Edmonton, 2004), 211–223; 211.

[53] Muriel Spark, *The Mandelbaum Gate* (London, 1965), 48. For a perceptive analysis of the novel in relation also to Spark's other works, see Bryan Cheyette, *Diasporas of the Mind: Jewish and Postcolonial Writing and the Nightmare of History* (New Haven and London, 2013), esp. 142–148.

[54] Alexander Baron, "A 'New Wave'," *Jewish Quarterly* 7 (1960): 42. See also Efraim Sicher, *Beyond Marginality: Anglo-Jewish Literature after the Holocaust* (Albany, 1985), 20.

rapid and sweeping cultural change which affected all of Britain and which saw the emergence and gradual rise of a plurality of ethnic voices.

Particular to the success of British Jewish writers in this period was that the context of their literary production was determined by the new discovery not only of their ethnicity but their working-class roots and their social commitment. These authors did not, however, develop distinctive group characteristics and, as a rule, they had to rely very much on recognition beyond the relatively small British Jewish community toward which they were highly ambivalent and whose perceived complacency and hypocrisy was frequently challenged by writers such as Brian Glanville, Frederic Raphael, and Bernard Kops. Nevertheless, many British Jewish authors also engaged with Jewish concerns in a less controversial way and showed themselves to be more committed to the notion of a communal Jewish identity in Britain. Among them, Chaim Bermant, Gerda Charles, William Goldman, and Chaim Raphael are perhaps the most notable.

The wide-ranging destruction of European Jewry in the Holocaust received a literary response rather late, often indirectly, and mostly by émigré writers with a personal connection, such as George Steiner, Thomas Wiseman, Gabriel Josipovici, and Eva Figes. The immediate concerns the Holocaust provoked were mostly about a Yiddish culture which seemed to have been irretrievably lost. Yet, while in America *Yiddishkayt* proved to be tenacious, in Britain Yiddish never achieved literary prominence. And although the East End poet Avram Stencl and some others, such as Itzig Manger, staunchly continued to write in Yiddish there is not, as there was in the Jewish American context, a marked multilingual dimension to British Jewish writing.

While remaining linguistically committed to England, for many British Jewish writers turning to non-English territories in their fiction – especially to the Diaspora and, less frequently, to Israel – became a way of sidestepping the hegemony of English, or even British, constructions of the past that excluded Jewishness. This phenomenon, designated by Bryan Cheyette as "extraterritoriality,"[55] has been described as the defining characteristic of much of British Jewish writing in the latter half of the twentieth century, investing it with a critical potential which challenges rigid conceptions of history and established constructions of the past as well as essentialist conceptions of identity, of which the work of Ruth Fainlight and Elaine Feinstein, Simon Louvish, and Clive Sinclair provides examples.

---

[55] Bryan Cheyette, "Englishness and Extraterritoriality: British-Jewish Writing and Diaspora Culture," *Literary Strategies: Jewish Texts and Contexts*, ed. Ezra Mendelsohn. Studies in Contemporary Jewry 12 (New York, 1996), 21–39; 21.

The oppressiveness of a fixed Englishness which, in contrast to America, neither permitted nor admitted the shaping influence of ethnic minorities in Britain, has also been used to explain the success of Jewish émigré writers like Figes, Josipovici, Steiner, Arthur Koestler, Ruth Prawer Jhabvala, and Dan Jacobson; precisely because they were not bound and bounded by the historical fixity of the dominant culture and its unremitting pressure of assimilation.[56] However, in contemporary British Jewish writing the "extraterritoriality" which still informs the more recent voices of Elena Lappin, Jonathan Treitel, and Jonathan Wilson, has been superseded by a succinct feeling of place connected to specific locations in Britain whose particularities are confidently explored in correlation with questions of belonging and alienation. Contemporary British Jewish writers such as Naomi Alderman, David Baddiel, Lana Citron, Jeremy Gavron, Zoe Heller, Anna Maxted, Charlotte Mendelson, William Sutcliffe, Adam Thirlwell, Lisa Appignanesi, Rachel Castell Farhi, Jenny Diski, and Tamar Yellin, many of them of a younger generation, explore critically the creative tension offered by different forms of identification in twenty-first-century Britain.[57] Howard Jacobson's recent success with his Man Booker Prize winning novel *The Finkler Question* (2010) confirms this trend and demonstrates what may still turn out to be short-lived mainstream recognition of Jewish writing in Britain.

In the (former) British Empire – in Ireland, Canada, South Africa, New Zealand and Australia – Jewish writing in English was also largely a product of the mass migrations of the late nineteenth and early twentieth centuries which affected America and the imperial center itself. However, a recognizable contribution of their own to the Anglophone Jewish literature disseminated since the 1840s across the Anglophone Diaspora emerged in these countries only in the first half of the twentieth century. Here too, the immigrant experience informed much of the early literary production but later gave way to concerns more specific to these countries and to the Jewish experience of the twentieth century.

There is not a very large body of Irish Jewish literature. This corresponds to the relatively small number of Jews in Ireland, not because, as Mr Deasy maintains in Joyce's *Ulysses*, Ireland had "never let them in,"[58] but rather

---

[56] Bryan Cheyette, "Introduction," in *Contemporary Jewish Writing in Britain and Ireland: An Anthology*, ed. Bryan Cheyette (London, 1998), xiii–lxxi; xliii–liii.

[57] For a recent study of contemporary British Jewish writing, see Ruth Gilbert, *Writing Jewish: Contemporary British-Jewish Literature* (Basingstoke and New York, 2013); see also the special issue of *European Judaism* 47 (2014): *Writing Jews in Contemporary Britain*, ed. Axel Stähler and Sue Vice.

[58] James Joyce, *Ulysses*, ed. Hans Walter Gabler (London, 1986), 30.

because the country's economic situation was precarious and did not attract immigration. It was only at the beginning of the twentieth century that a larger group of Jewish emigrants from Lithuania settled in the country. In 1954, David Marcus – at the time also, like so many others, drawn to the imperial center in London – emerged as a writer with his first novel *To Next Year in Jerusalem* in which he draws the explicit analogy between the anti-colonial struggle in Ireland and in Mandate Palestine. More recently, the Israeli Irish writer Ronit Lentin has established herself as a critical voice in the post-Zionist debate. A social activist and committed feminist, the Irish Jewish journalist and writer June Levine published her novel *A Season of Weddings* in 1992. While said to have a strong sense of Jewish tradition,[59] Levine's literary output does not reflect to any significant degree on her Jewishness but is eclipsed by her interest in feminist issues. This interest originated in a period of her life when, as a young mother, she lived in involuntary isolation in rural Canada from which she eventually "fled back to Dublin."[60]

In general, however, the Jewish experience in Canada has been a very different one. Although habitually overshadowed by its big neighbor to the South,[61] Canada sustains a vibrant Jewish community. Montreal, in particular, asserted itself as an early center of Jewish culture. Attempts to establish a Yiddish press date to the late 1880s and in the early twentieth century Yiddish journalism and literature flourished. It was only in the years preceding the Second World War that a Jewish literature in English emerged of which A. M. Klein was the most prominent exponent. Among later Montreal writers, Leonard Cohen and Mordecai Richler are probably the best known. Nobel Prize winner Saul Bellow was born in Quebec but as a child moved to the United States where he was to achieve lasting recognition. Toronto, Winnipeg, and the prairies have produced significant contributions to Anglophone Jewish literature in Canada since the Second World War with the work of Miriam Waddington, Adele Wiseman, and Norman Ravvin. Post-war Canadian Jewish literature in English has, moreover, been enriched by refugees and survivors of the Holocaust, like Henry Kreisel. It has thrived on the interplay with the polyglot culture in Montreal in the recent work of writers such as Robert Majzels and Régine Robin. Formal and stylistic innovations have been explored by writers like Lilian Nattel and Aryeh Lev Stollman, who frequently engage in a dialogue

---

[59] Mary Kenny, "My Extraordinary, Contradictory, Beautiful Friend June Levine," *Irish Independent* (October 18, 2008), www.independent.ie/national-news/my-extraordinary-contradictory-beautiful-friend-june-levine-1502916.html (accessed October 15, 2012).

[60] Kenny, "June Levine."

[61] Gerson, "Some Patterns," 198.

with Jewish traditions. The experience of the Holocaust has been confronted, for instance, in the fiction of J. J. Steinfeld and, with international success, Anne Michaels.

Much of Canadian Jewish literature is characterized by the frequently critical engagement with its own emerging tradition, in particular the works of A. M. Klein; but it also seeks to position itself in response to specifically Canadian and Canadian Jewish concerns, such as Jewish marginalization or the separatist and nationalist tendencies in Quebec which have occasioned the decline of Montreal as a center of Anglophone Jewish writing in the country.

In contrast to Canada, in the South African context, Jewish immigrants were initially positioned as non-whites in the dominant racial discourse.[62] The first Anglophone Jewish writer of note in the country was Sarah Gertrude Millin. Her earlier fiction, novels like *God's Stepchildren* (1924) and *The Coming of the Lord* (1928), frequently engages with the racial dynamics in her homeland and challenges racial boundaries with the concept of a common humanity. It has, however, been suggested that Millin, like the Nobel Prize winner Nadine Gordimer, succeeded through her writing in English "in obscuring her Jewishness and in securely locating herself within the dominant European group."[63] Both writers are at least latently engaged in negotiating their misgivings about Jewishness in the conflict between white and black. But unlike Millin, who later issued an "unashamed defense of apartheid and white supremacy,"[64] Gordimer unequivocally promotes equality in her writings. Doubts about Jewish assimilability resulted, however, not only in attempts to claim whiteness and white supremacy, but also in the formation of allegiances with the oppressed in the anti-apartheid struggle and the exploration of the black perspective by writers such as Lewis Sowden, Gerald Gordon, Harry Bloom, Henry John May (born Herzl J. Schlosberg), and J. Grenfell Williams.

The specific context of South Africa and its impact on identity, memory, and conceptions of race are crucial to any understanding of Jewish cultural creativity in this country. As Claudia Bathsheba Braude asserts:

Methodologies that seek to demonstrate essential continuities among all Jews worldwide have functioned in the South African context to conceal the influences of apartheid ideology and social organization and have thereby promoted the apartheid illusion that South African Jews, Judaism, culture, and identity

---

[62] Claudia Bathsheba Braude, "Introduction," in *Contemporary Jewish Writing in South Africa: An Anthology*, ed. Claudia Bathsheba Braude (Cape Town, 2001), ix–lxxvi; xviii.

[63] Braude, "Introduction," xxx.

[64] Braude, "Introduction," xlvi.

were a "separate," "group" affair, distinct from other equally discrete "groups" and "communities."[65]

The same is true, of course, also for other cultural and political contexts in the Anglophone Diaspora, even though the force fields of these influences may be less visible (if perhaps only from a historical distance) and the demands for negotiating a position between them less obvious. The impact in America of the civil rights movement on Jewish literature is another historical precedent,[66] as is the much less tangible challenge posed to constructions of Jewish identity and cultural creativity by the subtle hegemony of American pop culture which appears to be integral to processes of negation and redefinition.[67]

The recent transformation, in 1994, of South Africa after decades of racial discrimination into a fully democratic state confronted white South Africans with the choice of leaving the country or of staying and collaborating in its reconstruction. In view of the difficulties posed by the reconciliation process, it would have been unlikely to expect post-apartheid Jewish writing to focus on the parochial concerns of an aging and diminishing Jewish community.[68] Jewish authors like Damon Galgut, who first began to write in the period leading up to the transformation of the country, consequently consciously elected to work on South African and secular subjects and thus implicitly to efface their Jewishness from their literary production.[69] Other Jewish writers, exiled for their political activities, like Joe Slovo, Ronnie Kasrils, and Albie Sachs, chose to return to South Africa; their mostly autobiographical work, neither denying nor emphasizing the Jewish particular, also serves the larger purpose of reconciliation.

The case is different for South African writers in the wider Anglophone Diaspora. Dan Jacobson, for instance, although he continued to engage with South African Jewish concerns after his emigration in 1954, has felt "no obligation to explore a post-liberation South African identity."[70] Indeed, Margaret Lenta poses the question "of whether Jewishness, in the sense which it might have had in the early decades of the twentieth century, is ceasing to matter in the postcolonial state" and suggests in partial answer "that Jews are now free to live where and how they like, and that

---

[65] Braude, "Introduction," xi.

[66] See, e.g., Emily Miller Budick, *Blacks and Jews in Literary Conversation* (Cambridge, 1998).

[67] See Victoria Aarons, *What Happened to Abraham? Reinventing the Covenant in American Jewish Fiction* (Newark, 2005), 121.

[68] Margaret Lenta, "Jewish Writers and Postcolonial Choices in South Africa," in *Anglophone Jewish Literature*, 161–173; 163.

[69] Lenta, "Jewish Writers," 171.

[70] Lenta, "Jewish Writers," 163.

most are secular and remote in time and interests from the ancestors for whom their identity as Jews was primary."[71]

Freedom of movement and linguistic affinity are crucial characteristics of the Anglophone Jewish Diaspora. During the apartheid period many Jews left South Africa and emigrated to the United States, to Israel, the United Kingdom, and Canada and, about 40 percent of all emigrants, to Australia.[72] Among the latter was the writer Rose Zwi whose biography may be considered paradigmatic of Jewish mobility into and across the modern Anglophone Diaspora: born in Mexico to Lithuanian parents in 1928, she went to South Africa as a girl and in 1949 left the country for Israel where she lived for three years, only to return via London to South Africa; in 1988 she emigrated to Australia.

The pattern of immigration to Australia differed from that to other Anglophone countries. Prior to the gold rush of 1851 and the mass migrations of the late nineteenth century, which reached the antipodes only as a trickle, Jews from England arrived in small numbers from the end of the eighteenth century as both convicts and free settlers.[73] It was not until the 1930s that Jewish emigration from Europe to Australia began to emulate migration patterns to other parts of the world. Eventually, the Second World War once again transformed the pattern of Jewish immigration into Australia and New Zealand with the, if limited, influx of enemy alien internees, exiles, and survivors of the Holocaust.[74]

Although a small minority, Jews have nevertheless contributed significantly to cultural creativity in Australia. As early as 1949, as pointed out by Elisa Morera de la Vall,[75] the Australian Jewish writer Judah Waten confidently identified Jewish writing as a distinct component of Australian literature: "It is a fact that, of all the groups of people from non-British countries residing in Australia, only the Jewish people have even the beginnings of a literature about themselves that has become a part of the general literature of the country."[76] Following an initial focus on the immigrant

---

[71] Lenta, "Jewish Writers," 172–173.

[72] Of all emigrants, an estimated 40 percent chose as their destination Australia, 20 percent the United States, 15 percent Israel, and 10 percent each the United Kingdom and Canada, see Mark Avrum Ehrlich, *Encyclopedia of the Jewish Diaspora: Origins, Experiences, and Culture* (Santa Barbara, CA, 2009), II, 500.

[73] Ehrlich, *Encyclopedia*, II, 522–523.

[74] Ehrlich, *Encyclopedia*, II, 523.

[75] Elisa Morera de la Vall, "Jewish Literature in Australia," in *Anglophone Jewish Literature*, 174–185; 176.

[76] Judah Waten, "Contemporary Jewish Literature in Australia," *Australian Jewish Historical Society Journal* 3 (1949): 92–96; 96.

experience, as explored in the work of writers like Nathan Spielvogel and Waten, more recently a younger generation of writers such as Diane Armstrong, Mark Baker, Peter Kohn, Arnold Zable, and Elliot Perlman, many of them descendants of Holocaust survivors, engage in their writing with the Shoah and its aftermath.

American Jewish literature is nowadays without doubt the most visible segment of Anglophone Jewish writing and, possibly, of Jewish cultural production worldwide. The rise of English as a Jewish literary language in this country owes much to the efforts of Isaac Leeser. In 1845, Leeser not only produced the first translation of the Hebrew Bible into English to be published in America but also established the American Jewish Publication Society (AJPS). Two years earlier, he had already started the periodical *The Occident and American Jewish Advocate*, whose readership was not limited to Jews and attracted subscribers far beyond the United States – in Canada, the West Indies, Venezuela, and England.[77] While both the publications of the AJPS and Leeser's periodical initially drew heavily on Anglo-Jewish writing, they also fostered the beginnings of an American Jewish literature in English. Next to Leeser, the most prominent advocate of Anglophone Jewish literature in mid-nineteenth-century America was perhaps Isaac Mayer Wise. Frequently publishing under the programmatic pseudonym of "The American Jewish Novelist," Wise was a prolific author in whose writings, as Michael P. Kramer notes, "American history and Jewish history coalesce."[78] Wise was to set a trend that remained dominant until America too experienced the impact of the mass migrations beginning in and following the 1880s.

One of the consequences of the mass migrations of the late nineteenth and early twentieth centuries was the rise of Yiddish in America. It was promoted, for instance, by Abraham Cahan, who was born in Lithuania. After his emigration to America Cahan worked for *Di Arbayter Tsaytung* (*Workman's Paper*) and *Forverts* (*Forward*); but he also published fiction in English that reflected the immigrant experience of which his novel, *The Rise of David Levinsky* (1917), is an important example. Anzia Yezierska, Mary Antin, Elias Tobenkin, and Ezra Brudno were also immigrant writers. Their conscious decision to write in the newly acquired language, which ran counter to the undiminished currency of Yiddish at least into the late 1920s,[79] is indicative of the importance they attached to Jewish

[77] Kiron, "An Atlantic Jewish Republic," 180.
[78] Michael P. Kramer, "Beginnings and Ends: The Origins of Jewish American Literary History," in *The Cambridge Companion to Jewish American Literature*, ed. Hana Wirth-Nesher and Michael P. Kramer (Cambridge, 2003), 12–30; 25.
[79] Pascal Fischer, "Voices of Identity: Language in Jewish-American Literature," in *Anglophone Jewish Literature*, 211–223; 213.

integration into American culture. With their works, campaigning for the acceptance of Jewish immigrants in America, they sought not only to reflect on the immigrant experience, but to intervene in current debates on immigration restrictions and assimilation.[80] An indicator of the transnational dimension of Anglophone Jewish writing in this period is the Anglo-Jewish writer Israel Zangwill's concern not only with the East End, for instance in *Children of the Ghetto* (1892), but also with the Lower East Side, in *The Melting Pot* (1905).

America frequently appears in the texts of the immigrant writers as another promised land which offers the American Dream – it is *di goldene medina*, "the Golden Land." To the post-war generation, this promise and the processes of assimilation lost some of their luster. These writers – such as Saul Bellow, Bernard Malamud, and Philip Roth – often engage in more or less direct criticism of the American Dream and, laboring also in the shadow of the Holocaust, express the unease of alienation and estrangement while foregrounding questions of identity.

The experience of the younger generation of Jewish American writers is different. Writers such as Michael Chabon, Dara Horn, Nathan Englander, Shalom Auslander, Steve Stern, Jonathan Safran Foer, and Nicole Krauss frequently explore the present through a (re)imagining of the past; immigration is no longer an issue for them, and they address assimilation from a different perspective: none of them has any quarrel with their Jewishness, their work is affirmative and explores the many manifestations of Jewishness in relation to an Americanness which, in their experience, is not challenged by their Jewishness. A potent symbol of this is the *New American Haggadah* (2012), translated and annotated in a collaborative project by Jonathan Safran Foer and Nathan Englander. Indeed, in contemporary Jewish American writing there is a new sense of the almost aggressively affirmative which embraces Jewishness and Americanness and from this position sometimes ventures into direct, occasionally acerbic and vitriolic, criticism of current political and cultural issues and which also does not shy away from breaking the odd taboo, such as in Shalom Auslander's funny and iconoclastic *Hope. A Tragedy* (2012) or Michael Chabon's alternative history of a Jewish state in Alaska in *The Yiddish Policemen's Union* (2007).

Mention should also be made of America's "Russian" Jewish writers, such as Gary Shteyngart, Lara Vapnyar, and David Bezmozgis, whose

---

[80] Gert Buelens, "The New Man and the Mediator: (Non-)Remembrance in Jewish-American Immigrant Narrative," in *Memory, Narrative, and Identity: New Essays in Ethnic American Literatures*, ed. Amritjit Singh, Joseph T. Skerrett, Jr. and Robert E. Hogan (Boston, 1994), 89–113; 89.

work offers an alternative perspective on recent immigrant experience. Nor should one forget those writers who frequently explore the more unfamiliar experience of their Sephardi (oriental Jewish) background, such as Ruth Knafo Setton, Rosaly Roffman, Herbert Hadad, and Jordan Elgrably. The spectrum of Jewish writing in America has also progressively expanded with a number of female writers, such as Allegra Goodman, Rebecca Goldstein, Tova Mirvis, and Israeli-born Pearl Abraham, who explore the tension between Orthodox Judaism and the modern world. This is a trend which is manifest also in Naomi Alderman's writing in Britain and in the work of American-born Israeli writer Naomi Ragen.

Curiously, like in Britain, the Holocaust was initially conspicuously absent from Jewish post-war writing in America.[81] It is only since the 1970s that the Shoah has increasingly become a pervasive theme in American Jewish literature.[82] Approaches to the Holocaust by authors such as Art Spiegelman and Thane Rosenbaum have not only demonstrated formal originality but have also advanced challenging reflections on the cataclysmic event. The frequently provocative work of Leslie Epstein, Cynthia Ozick, Marcie Hershman, and Melvin Jules Bukiet has also explored new approaches to the Shoah. More recent American Jewish Holocaust writing, by authors like Joseph Skibell and Jonathan Safran Foer, encompasses the traumatic effect of the Shoah also on second and third generation survivors. Their focus is frequently on the transmission of trauma and on strategies to address the legacy of the past.

Oddly, Jewish writers in America were initially similarly reluctant to engage with Zionism and with Israel.[83] It has been argued that one reason for this reticence was that, to begin with, as has been mentioned, many writers focused on the immigrant experience in the United States which had been stylized as another promised land.[84] Mary Antin's aptly named autobiographical novel *The Promised Land* (1912) is only one example of this process of substitution. Indeed, Emily Miller Budick suggests that from the perspective of national self-definition, Jewish immigration in the United States was no less important than the foundation of the State of

[81] See Brauner, *Post-War Jewish Fiction*, 9.

[82] See Brauner, *Post-War Jewish Fiction*, 113–153.

[83] See Harold U. Ribalow, "Zion in Contemporary Fiction," in *Mid-Century: An Anthology of Jewish Life and Culture in Our Time*, ed. Harold U. Ribalow (New York, 1955), 570–591; 570 and Alvin H. Rosenfeld, "Promised Land(s): Zion, America, and American Jewish Writers," *Jewish Social Studies* 3 (1997): 111–131; 112.

[84] See, e.g., Rosenfeld, "Promised Land(s)," 112–116 and Emily Miller Budick, "Introduction," in *Ideology and Jewish Identity in Israeli and American Literature*, ed. Emily Miller Budick (Albany, 2001), 1–22; 13–16.

Israel in 1948, even though she acknowledges that the latter occasioned a "major shift in Jewish reality" which impacted significantly on the creation of a Jewish literature.[85]

However, it was only after the Second World War and more specifically the Shoah, that a recognizable literary engagement with the Land and later with the precarious existence of the State of Israel emerged. Initially, into the 1970s, these texts participated mostly in a discourse of political legitimization. Prominent examples are Meyer Levin's *My Father's House* (1947), Leon Uris's worldwide bestseller *Exodus* (1958), Chaim Potok's *The Chosen* (1967), and Mark Helprin's *Refiner's Fire* (1977).

Religiously motivated, rather than politically, and quite exceptional in this, was the Canadian Jewish writer A. M. Klein's novel *The Second Scroll* (1951). An ardent Zionist, who had vehemently argued in favor of the establishment of a Jewish state in Palestine, Klein interpreted the foundation of the State of Israel as the redemptive fulfilment of a Jewish eschatology. Understood after the cataclysm of the Shoah by the author as analogous to the Haggadah or as an exegesis, or even a continuation of, the Pentateuch, his novel is a striking articulation of this eschatology.[86]

Following the consolidation of the state and its successful repulsion of external enemies, literary negotiations of Jewish identities between Israel and the Diaspora proliferated. The Six Day War of 1967 was a decisive event which, as in Britain and elsewhere in the Anglophone Diaspora, engendered in many American Jews a feeling of solidarity with Israel,[87] although in many leftist intellectuals it produced rather "a more visible, more reasoned resistance to Zionism."[88] However, in the wake of the Lebanese War of 1982 the parameters for literary engagement with Jewish national sovereignty changed dramatically. Coinciding with an increasing interest in Israel, a change of perspective emerged which prioritized the critical engagement with the moral integrity of the Jewish State and the contrastive negotiation of Diaspora-Jewish and Israeli-Jewish identities.[89]

---

[85] Budick, "Introduction," 13.

[86] See Roger Hyman, *Aught from Naught: A. M. Klein's The Second Scroll* (Victoria, BC, 1999) and Axel Stähler, "The Black Forest, the Unspeakable Nefas, and the Mountains of Galilee: Germany and Zionism in the Works of A. M. Klein," in *Refractions of Germany in Canadian Culture and Literature*, ed. Heinz Antor, Sylvia Brown, John Considine, Klaus Stierstorfer (New York and Berlin, 2003), 171–193.

[87] Andrew Furman, *Israel through the Jewish-American Imagination: A Survey of Jewish-American Literature on Israel, 1928–1995* (Albany, 1997), 1–2, 6–7.

[88] Emily Miller Budick, "The African and Israeli 'Other' in the Construction of Jewish American Identity," in *Ideology and Jewish Identity*, 197–212; 210.

[89] Furman, *Israel*, 7–11.

Philip Roth, Anne Roiphe, and Tova Reich[90] have confronted these issues; nor do writers of younger generations, such as Pearl Abraham, Allegra Goodman, Carol Magun and Melvin Jules Bukiet, shy away from the confrontation with the Jewish "other" in Israel.

A similar process can be observed in other production contexts of the Anglophone Jewish Diaspora. In British Jewish fiction, too, a serious literary engagement with the Jewish state surfaced surprisingly late. Earlier attempts – by Brian Glanville, Gerda Charles, or Frederic Raphael and Chaim Bermant – were of little impact. In 1963, Alexander Baron voiced what were obviously not only his own sentiments when he maintained that he was deeply interested in Israel but that it had not entered into his imaginative world.[91]

It is only in more recent British Jewish writing, once again especially in response to the First Lebanese War and the subsequent deterioration of the situation in the Middle East, that a proper and often highly critical engagement with Israel, or Palestine, emerges which, in turn, is frequently tied to reflections on Jewish life in England. Clive Sinclair, for instance, addresses the issue of British antisemitism in his *Blood Libels* (1985), while lashing out at the same time at Israeli transgressions. Less conflictually, but no less poignantly, Jonathan Wilson in *The Hiding Room* (1995) and Bernice Rubens in *I, Dreyfus* (1999) also engage with British antisemitism and Israel. Linda Grant, in *When I Lived in Modern Times* (2000), which is highly ambivalent towards Zionist self-fashioning and Israeli political expediency, construes a Jewish claim to post-coloniality by overtly suggesting that British Jews have been subject to an internal colonization. In Jacobson's *The Finkler Question*, finally, British Jewish ambivalence toward Israel is explored extensively and controversially.[92]

However, writers like David Marcus and Israeli-born Ronit Lentin in Ireland,[93] or the Australian Jewish writers Maria Lewitt and Lilian Barnea also contributed to the literary debate,[94] which gained in significance and urgency in the wake of the so-called post-Zionism debates and the Israeli

[90] See, e.g., Roth's *The Counterlife* (1986) and *Operation Shylock* (1993), Roiphe's *Lovingkindness* (1987), Reich's *Master of the Return* (1988) and *The Jewish War* (1995).
[91] Alexander Baron, "On Being English and Jewish," *Jewish Quarterly* 10 (1963): 6–10; 10.
[92] See, e.g., Axel Stähler, "Anti-Semitism and Israel in British Jewish Fiction: Perspectives on Clive Sinclair's *Blood Libels* (1985) and Howard Jacobson's *The Finkler Question* (2010)," *Jewish Culture and History* 14 (2013): 112–125.
[93] See Catherine Hezser, "Postcolonialism and the Irish-Jewish Experience: the Novels of David Marcus and Ronit Lentin," in *Anglophone Jewish Literature*, 143–160.
[94] See, e.g., Barnea's *Reported Missing* (1979), Lewitt's "All the Storms and Sun-sets" (1980) and Lentin's *Songs on the Death of Children* (1996).

"new" historiography which subjected geographical and ideological definitions of Jewish identity to alternative, pluralistic and conflictual patterns of
interpretation.[95] The confrontation with Israel frequently proved to be unsettling because it challenged the moral integrity of Jewish identities in the
Anglophone Diaspora in view of the potential complicity in, or at least the
shared responsibility for, its controversial policies. Jews in the Diaspora were
also faced at least implicitly with the choice of following the call of the *kibbutz galuiot* (the ingathering of the exiles) in response to initial Zionist claims
to the exclusive Jewish authenticity of Israeli identity.[96] Yet the Diaspora, and
in particular perhaps the Anglophone Jewish Diaspora, continues, as A. M.
Klein phrased it in 1953, to be "exemplar, model, inspiration."[97]

Anglophone Jewish literature has been inextricably tied to the emergence and the development of the Anglophone Jewish Diaspora since
the mid-nineteenth century. In a dynamic process of cultural creativity,
it emerged in response to the challenges and opportunities originating in
modernity and its effect on both the Anglophone world and the specifically Jewish experience. It developed as a transnational and increasingly
transcultural phenomenon which contributed crucially to the formation
of a public Jewish sphere. Initially, the dissemination of mostly the incipient Anglo-Jewish literature was enlisted to support and sustain deliberate
individual initiatives to realize the potential of the English language. The
objective was the creation of an enlightened Jewish sphere encompassing
the Anglophone countries in an atmosphere of emancipation and reform.

Within changing social, political, and cultural environments across the
Anglophone Diaspora, and decisively influenced by the mass migrations
of the late nineteenth and early twentieth centuries and the impact of the
Shoah, Anglophone Jewish literature soon diversified and was informed by
cultural change in its various production contexts as well as by their cultural
specificity. Certainly, Jewish culture is neither monolithic nor homogeneous and the cohesive forces of transnational and transcultural convergence
in the Anglophone Diaspora and an (imaginary) collective experience are
countered by the centrifugal forces of different national environments and

[95] For the post-Zionism debates, see Laurence J. Silberstein, *The Post-Zionism Debates: Knowledge and Power in Israeli Culture* (New York, 1999); for the new Israeli historiogra-phy, see the seminal text by Benny Morris, "The New Historiography: Israel Confronts its Past," *Tikkun* 3, no. 6 (1988): 19–23, 99–103.

[96] See Budick, "Introduction," 17. This was poignantly dealt with in Philip Roth's *Operation Shylock* (1993).

[97] A. M. Klein, "In Praise of the Diaspora (An Undelivered Memorial Address)," in *Beyond Sambation: Selected Essays and Editorials, 1928–1955*, ed. M. W. Steinberg (Toronto, 1982), 463–477; 477.

individual experiences. Nevertheless, across the Anglophone Diaspora there emerged pervasive themes and concerns, such as the immigrant experience, questions of alienation and identity, tensions between the religious and the secular, the Holocaust, and Israel. Based on linguistic and cultural affiliation and both internal and external dialogue, a Jewish literature in English emerged and flourished which, as an agent of identity formation and historical self-reflection, appears to be a decisive element in the process of creating cultural cohesion in the Anglophone Jewish Diaspora.

To predict with any degree of reliability the changes that the Anglophone Jewish Diaspora and Anglophone Jewish literature will experience within the framework of the larger context of global cultural change would seem not only hopeless but presumptuous. There can, however, be no doubt that the Anglophone Jewish Diaspora is in constant flux and needs to be constantly re-conceptualized. Both the Anglophone Jewish Diaspora and Anglophone Jewish literature continue to be intensely and interactively "in progress."

SELECT BIBLIOGRAPHY

Literature

Antin, Mary. *The Promised Land* (Boston and New York: Houghton Mifflin Company, 1912).

Auslander, Shalom. *Hope. A Tragedy* (New York: Riverhead Books, 2012).

Barnea, Lilian. *Reported Missing* (London: HarperCollins, 1979).

Cahan, Abraham. *The Rise of David Levinsky* (New York: Harper and Brothers, 1917).

Chabon, Michael. *The Yiddish Policemen's Union* (New York: HarperCollins, 2007)

Grant, Linda. *When I Lived in Modern Times* (London: Granta Books, 2000).

Helprin, Mark. *Refiner's Fire* (New York: Hamish Hamilton Ltd., 1977).

Jacobson, Howard. *The Finkler Question* (London: Bloomsbury, 2010).

Klein, A. M. *The Second Scroll* (New York: Knopf, 1951).

Lentin, Ronit. *Songs on the Death of Children* (Dublin: Poolbeg Pr. Ltd., 1996).

Levin, Meyer. *My Father's House* (New York: The Viking Press, 1947).

Levine, June. *A Season of Weddings* (Dublin: New Island Books, 1992).

Lewitt, Maria. "All the Storms and Sun-sets" (1980), in *Jewish Writing from Down Under: Australia and New Zealand*, ed. Roberta Kalechofsky (Marblehead, MA: Micah Publications, 1984), 276–285.

Marcus, David. *To Next Year in Jerusalem* (London: St. Martin's Press, 1954).

Millin, Sarah Gertrude. *God's Stepchildren* (London: Grosset and Dunlap, 1924).

The Coming of the Lord (London: Horace Liveright, 1928).

New American Haggadah, ed. Jonathan Safran Foer, trans. Shalom Auslander (New York: Little, Brown and Company, 2012).

Potok, Chaim. *The Chosen* (New York: Simon and Schuster, 1967).

Reich, Tova. *Master of the Return* (New York: Harcourt, 1988).

The Jewish War (New York: Pantheon Books, 1995).

Roiphe, Anne. *Lovingkindness* (New York: Summit Books, 1987).

Roth, Philip. *Operation Shylock: A Confession* (New York: Simon and Schuster, 1993).
The Counterlife (New York: Farrar, Straus and Giroux, 1986).
Rubens, Bernice. *I, Dreyfus* (London: Little, Brown, 1999).
Sinclair, Clive. *Blood Libels* (London: Allison and Busby, 1985).
Spark, Muriel. *The Mandelbaum Gate* (London: Knopf, 1965).
Uris, Leon. *Exodus* (New York: Doubleday and Co., 1958).
Wilson, Jonathan. *The Hiding Room* (New York: Viking, 1995).
Zangwill, Israel. *Children of the Ghetto: A Study of a Peculiar People* (London: Macmillan, 1892).
The Melting Pot (1905; New York: Macmillan, 1909).

WORKS CITED

Aarons, Victoria. *What Happened to Abraham? Reinventing the Covenant in American Jewish Fiction* (Newark: University of Delaware Press, 2005).
Abley, Mark. *The Prodigal Tongue: Dispatches from the Future of English* (New York: Houghton Mifflin Harcourt, 2008).
Alkalay-Gut, Karen. "The Anglo-Israeli Writer: Double Identities in Troubled Times," in *Anglophone Jewish Literature*, ed. Axel Stähler (Abingdon: Routledge, 2007), 195–208.
"Double Diaspora: English Writers in Israel," *Judaism* 51 (2002): 457–468.
Baron, Alexander. "A 'New Wave'," *Jewish Quarterly* 7 (1960): 42.
"On Being English and Jewish," *Jewish Quarterly* 10 (1963): 6–10.
Bhabha, Homi K. *The Location of Culture* (London: Routledge, 1994).
Braude, Claudia Bathsheba. "Introduction," in *Contemporary Jewish Writing in South Africa: An Anthology*, ed. Claudia Bathsheba Braude (Lincoln, NE: University of Nebraska Press, 2001), ix–lxxvi.
Brauner, David. *Post-War Jewish Fiction: Ambivalence, Self-Explanation and Transatlantic Connections* (Basingstoke and New York: Palgrave Macmillan, 2001).
Brauner, David and Axel Stähler, eds. *The Edinburgh Companion to Modern Jewish Fiction* (Edinburgh: Edinburgh University Press, 2015).
Budick, Emily Miller. "The African and Israeli 'Other' in the Construction of Jewish American Identity," in *Ideology and Jewish Identity*, ed. Emily Miller Budick (Albany: State University of New York Press, 2001), 197–212.
Blacks and Jews in Literary Conversation (Cambridge: Cambridge University Press, 1998).
"Introduction," in *Ideology and Jewish Identity in Israeli and American Literature*, ed. Emily Miller Budick (Albany: State University of New York Press, 2001), 1–22.
Buelens, Gert. "The New Man and the Mediator: (Non-)Remembrance in Jewish-American Immigrant Narrative," in *Memory, Narrative, and Identity: New Essays in Ethnic American Literatures*, ed. Amritjit Singh, Joseph T. Skerrett, Jr. and Robert E. Hogan (Boston: Northeastern University Press, 1994), 89–113.
Chanes, Jerome A. "Beyond Marginality," *Judaism* 48 (1999): 387–390.
Cheyette, Bryan. "Diasporas of the Mind: British-Jewish Writing Beyond Multiculturalism," in *Diaspora and Multiculturalism: Common Traditions and New Developments*, ed. Monika Fludernik (Amsterdam and New York: Rodopi, 2003), 45–82.
Diasporas of the Mind: Jewish and Postcolonial Writing and the Nightmare of History (New Haven and London: Yale University Press, 2013).
"Englishness and Extraterritoriality: British-Jewish Writing and Diaspora Culture," *Literary Strategies: Jewish Texts and Contexts*, ed. Ezra Mendelsohn. Studies in Contemporary Jewry 12 (New York: Oxford University Press, 1996), 21–39.

"Introduction," in *Contemporary Jewish Writing in Britain and Ireland: An Anthology*, ed. Bryan Cheyette (Lincoln, NE: University of Nebraska Press, 1998), xiii–lxxi.

Davies, Grahame. "Welsh and Jewish: Responses to Wales by Jewish Writers," in *Culture and the State*, ed. James Gifford and Gabrielle Zezulka-Mailloux, vol. 3: *Nationalisms* (Edmonton: University of Alberta Press, 2004), 211–223.

Dubin, Lois. "Introduction: Port Jews in the Atlantic world," *Jewish History* 20 (2006): 117–127.

Ehrlich, Mark Avrum. *Encyclopedia of the Jewish Diaspora: Origins, Experiences, and Culture* (Santa Barbara, CA: ABC-Clio, 2009).

Fischer, Pascal. "Voices of Identity: Language in Jewish-American Literature," in *Anglophone Jewish Literature*, ed. Axel Stähler (Abingdon: Routledge, 2007), 211–223.

Furman, Andrew. *Israel through the Jewish-American Imagination: A Survey of Jewish-American Literature on Israel, 1928–1995* (Albany: State University of New York Press, 1997).

Galchinsky, Michael. *The Origin of the Modern Jewish Woman Writer: Romance and Reform in Victorian England* (Detroit: Wayne State University Press, 1996).

Gerson, Carole. "Some Patterns of Exile in Jewish Writing of the Commonwealth," *Ariel* 13 (1982): 103–114.

Gilbert, Ruth. *Writing Jewish: Contemporary British-Jewish Literature* (Basingstoke and New York: Palgrave, 2013).

Grumberg, Karen. "Ricki Lake in Tel Aviv: The Alternative of Orly Castel-Bloom's Hebrew-English," in *Anglophone Jewish Literature*, ed. Axel Stähler (Abingdon: Routledge, 2007), 234–248.

Hezser, Catherine. "Postcolonialism and the Irish-Jewish Experience: The Novels of David Marcus and Ronit Lentin," in *Anglophone Jewish Literature*, ed. Axel Stähler (Abingdon: Routledge, 2007), 143–160.

Hyman, Roger. *Aught from Naught: A. M. Klein's* The Second Scroll (Victoria, BC: English Literary Studies, 1999).

Joyce, James. *Ulysses*, ed. Hans Walter Gabler (London: Vintage, 1986).

Kenny, Mary. "My Extraordinary, Contradictory, Beautiful Friend June Levine," *Irish Independent* (October 18, 2008), www.independent.ie/national-news/my-extraordinary-contradictory-beautiful-friend-june-levine-1502916.html (accessed October 15, 2012).

Kiron, Arthur. "An Atlantic Jewish Republic of Letters?," *Jewish History* 20 (2006): 171–211.

Klein, A. M. "In Praise of the Diaspora (An Undelivered Memorial Address)," in *Beyond Sambation: Selected Essays and Editorials, 1928–1955*, ed. M. W. Steinberg (Toronto: University of Toronto Press, 1982), 463–477.

Kramer, Michael P. "Beginnings and Ends: The Origins of Jewish American Literary History," in *The Cambridge Companion to Jewish American Literature*, ed. Hana Wirth-Nesher and Michael P. Kramer (Cambridge: Cambridge University Press, 2003), 12–30.

Lehmann, Sophia. "In Search of a Mother Tongue: Locating Home in Diaspora," *Melus* 23 (1998): 101–119.

Lenta, Margaret. "Jewish Writers and Postcolonial Choices in South Africa," in *Anglophone Jewish Literature*, ed. Axel Stähler (Abingdon: Routledge, 2007), 161–173.

Lockard, Joe. "Babel Machines and Electronic Universalism," in *Race in Cyberspace*, ed. Beth E. Kolko, Lisa Nakamura, and Gilbert B. Rodman (New York and London: Routledge, 2000), 171–189.

Mendelsohn, Adam. "Tongue Ties: The Emergence of the Anglophone Jewish Diaspora in the Mid-Nineteenth Century," *American Jewish History* 93, no. 2 (2007): 177–209.

Monaco, C. S. "Port Jews or a People of the Diaspora? A Critique of the Port Jew Concept," *Jewish Social Studies* n.s. 15, no. 2 (2009): 137–166.

Morera de la Vall, Elisa. "Jewish Literature in Australia," in *Anglophone Jewish Literature*, ed. Axel Stähler (Abingdon: Routledge, 2007), 174–185.

Morris, Benny. "The New Historiography: Israel Confronts its Past," *Tikkun* 3, no. 6 (1988): 19–23, 99–103.

Ozick, Cynthia. "Toward a New Yiddish," in *Art & Ardor. Essays* (New York: Knopf, 1983), 151–177.

Ribalow, Harold U. "Zion in Contemporary Fiction," in *Mid-Century: An Anthology of Jewish Life and Culture in Our Time*, ed. Harold U. Ribalow (New York: Beechhurst Press, 1955), 570–591.

Rosenfeld, Alvin H. "Promised Land(s): Zion, America, and American Jewish Writers," *Jewish Social Studies* 3 (1997): 111–131.

Rubinstein, William D. *A History of the Jews in the English-Speaking World: Great Britain* (London: Palgrave Macmillan, 1996).

Sarna, Jonathan D. "Port Jews in the Atlantic: Further Thoughts," *Jewish History* 20 (2006): 213–219.

Sicher, Efraim. *Beyond Marginality: Anglo-Jewish Literature after the Holocaust* (Albany: State University of New York Press, 1985).

Silberstein, Laurence J. *The Post-Zionism Debates: Knowledge and Power in Israeli Culture* (New York: Routledge, 1999).

Stähler, Axel, ed., *Anglophone Jewish Literature* (Abingdon: Routledge, 2007).

"Anti-Semitism and Israel in British Jewish Fiction: Perspectives on Clive Sinclair's *Blood Libels* (1985) and Howard Jacobson's *The Finkler Question* (2010)," *Jewish Culture and History* 14 (2013): 112–125.

"The Black Forest, the Unspeakable Nefas, and the Mountains of Galilee: Germany and Zionism in the Works of A. M. Klein," in *Refractions of Germany in Canadian Culture and Literature*, ed. Heinz Antor et al. (New York and Berlin: De Gruyter, 2003), 171–193.

"From the Belly of the Fish: Jewish Writers in English in Israel: Transcultural Perspectives," in *Transcultural English Studies: Theories, Fictions, Realities*, ed. Frank Schulze-Engler and Sissy Helff (Amsterdam and New York: Rodopi, 2009), 151–167.

"Introduction: Jewish Literature(s) in English: Anglophone Jewish Writing and the 'Loquation' of Culture," in *Anglophone Jewish Literature*, ed. Axel Stähler (Abingdon: Routledge, 2007), 3–32.

"Jewish Fiction," in *The Encyclopedia of Twentieth-Century Fiction*, ed. Brian W. Shaffer (Oxford and New York: Wiley-Blackwell, 2011), 198–202.

Stähler, Axel and Sue Vice, eds. *Writing Jews and Jewishness in Contemporary Britain*. Special issue of *European Judaism* 47 (2014).

Warschauer, Mark. "Language, Identity, and the Internet," in *Race in Cyberspace*, ed. Beth E. Kolko, Lisa Nakamura, and Gilbert B. Rodman (New York and London: Routledge, 2000), 151–170.

Waten, Judah. "Contemporary Jewish Literature in Australia," *Australian Jewish Historical Society Journal* 3 (1949): 92–96.

Wirth-Nesher, Hana. *Call It English: The Language of Jewish American Literature* (Princeton, NJ: Princeton University Press, 2006).

Wisse, Ruth R. "American Jewish Writing, Act II," *Commentary* 61 (1976): 40–45.

CHAPTER 27

HEBREW LITERATURE

SHACHAR PINSKER

MODERN HEBREW LITERATURE

In recent decades, Hebrew literature has been written and read almost exclusively in the State of Israel. However, the question of whether Israeli literature is continuous with the literature produced in Hebrew in the Jewish Diaspora since the second half of the eighteenth century is a complex one. It makes little sense to recount the history of modern Hebrew literature as if it were a "normal" national literature that developed in a monolingual environment and in one territory. Rather, modern Hebrew literature has been part of a multilingual Jewish literary system, what the scholar Dan Miron has called "the modern Jewish literary complex." Literature in Hebrew was produced and read wherever Jews lived in the modern world – mainly in Europe, the United States, and the Middle East.

When did modern Hebrew literature begin? Is there any clear point of departure? What distinguishes modern ("new") from "old" Hebrew literature? These questions ring familiar from the debates about the advent of Jewish modernity, but there are also unique elements that have to do with the status of Hebrew in Jewish culture, and with the fact that literature in Hebrew had been written since antiquity. It flourished especially in the Iberian Peninsula (Islamic and Christian) and throughout the Mediterranean during the Middle Ages, as well as in Italy and Holland in the sixteenth and seventeenth century, before the dawn of Jewish modernity.

When pondering these issues, it is important to note that the very term "modern Hebrew literature" (*sifrut 'ivrit ḥadasha*) was created in the 1860s and 1870s, with the appearance of the first works of Hebrew literary criticism by several Eastern European maskilim. It is not a coincidence that the term was conceived at the same time that the Hebrew word *sifrut* (and *sifrutenu* – "our literature") – designating *belles-lettres* rather than *ecriture* (writing in general) – had been used for the first time. The vexed question of secularization has also been a source of confusion in defining and recounting the history of modern Hebrew literature. It has been claimed frequently that what separates "old" Hebrew literature and the modern one is that the former is "religious" while the latter is "secular." But this is a simplification that does not account for the complexity of the literary texts, their authors, and readers, as well as the historical-social contexts in the different places in which they were produced.

Some scholars identified the point of departure of modern Hebrew literature with the writing of Rabbi Moshe Hayim Luzzatto (Ramhal), who lived in Italy and wrote Hebrew poems and plays such as the allegorical drama *La-Yesharim Tehillah* (Glory to the Righteous, 1743), alongside important works of *musar* (Jewish ethics) and Kabbalah. Other scholars maintained that modern Hebrew literature began only in the 1880s, with the advent of proto-Zionist Jewish nationalism in Eastern Europe, and the appearance of "masters" like S. Y. Abramovitsh and H. N. Bialik. However, the more adequate point of departure is the 1780s, with the Haskalah in Prussia, when a group of Jewish intellectuals like Naphtali Hertz Wessely, Isaac Abraham Euchel, and Mendel Bresslau – all of them influenced by the work of Moses Mendelssohn – published a Hebrew literary periodical by the name *Ha-me'asef* (The Gatherer) in 1784. It was the wish to establish a literary arena that conveyed a sense of doing something unprecedented. They regarded the public that they confronted as potentially new because it lived in "new time," namely the period after the *Toleranzedikt* (Edict of Tolerance) issued by the Habsburg emperor Joseph II in 1781. For the Prussian maskilim, the edict signaled a momentous change that made it incumbent upon Jews to prove their willingness to integrate into the cultural, social, and economic life of their surroundings. This change called for an involvement in a new institution, which had to be a literary-cultural one. Hebrew literature was to become a self-appointed custodian of the national welfare, by promoting the ideas of humanism throughout European Jewry, by encouraging rationalist thinking (that goes hand in hand with religious beliefs) and a broader educational system, and by developing new sensibilities through emotive literary writing based on European models.

Almost all these ideas were circulating before the middle of the eighteenth century, both in Sephardi and Ashkenazi Jewish communities, but the fundamental innovation of the maskilim was to posit literature as a guiding institution that would replace the rabbinical establishment in everything that did not pertain to the domain of halacha (religious law). This was the beginning of the concept of Hebrew literature functioning as "the watchman unto the House of Israel" – the title of Yitzhak Ereter's book of satires based on Ezekiel 3:17 – indicating the notion that writers amounted to modern-day prophets or seers. The writers were supposed to tackle this momentous task by engaging the Jewish public in a dialogue, and this dialogue, according to the maskilim, had to be conducted in Hebrew.

The choice of writing Hebrew (rather than German or Yiddish, which were also used by the maskilim but with great ambivalence) was practical, but even more so was motivated by aesthetic and ideological reasons. On the practical side, the intended audience of the early maskilim in Prussia (and to some degree also during the nineteenth century in the Austrian and Russian empires), was composed almost exclusively of traditional male Jews from the new middle-class, or those who aspired to be middle-class. These men used Yiddish for daily communication and were familiar with the Hebrew of the Bible, Mishnah and the liturgy, but by and large did not read literature in German (or Russian and Polish). On the more significant aesthetic and ideological side, the maskilim believed that Hebrew is intrinsically "poetic" and sublime. The emphasis on the Bible, which dominated the themes and styles of Hebrew literature for many years to come, was based on the presumed aesthetic perfection of the scripture and its sanctity, its high cultural prestige in the non-Jewish world, as well as the new maskilic understanding of Bible as the only vestige of genuine Jewish national literature. This assumption presented the maskilim with a major challenge, namely the need to breathe new life into biblical Hebrew, removing it from the synagogue and house of study and using it as a national asset by writing in the modern, European genres and forms of literature.

In the early Haskalah in Prussia, the main genres of Hebrew literature were the neoclassical didactic epic poetry and the allegorical drama. A good example of the former is the cycle of poems, *Shirei Tiferet* (Poems of Splendor, 1788), by Naphtali Herz Wessely, which was dedicated to the life and deeds of Moses. A good example of the latter is *Melukhat Shaul* (Saul's Kingdom, 1794) by Yosef Ha'efrati, in which Saul is presented as a tragic king who refuses to comply with God's demand to annihilate the defeated enemy, Amalek.

The importance of the Hebrew literature of the Haskalah in Prussia was its pioneering spirit, innovative work, and the reorientation of Hebrew literature, but it declined rapidly. *Ha-me'asef*, inaugurated as a monthly in 1784, turned into an annual in the 1790s, and by 1797 it had only 120 subscribers. The decline had to do both with the fact that the wealthy merchants who supported the authors and their literary project lost interest, as well as with the rapid acculturation of many young Jews (often the children of maskilim) who drifted away both from Jewish tradition and from Hebrew literature.

Nevertheless, the ideas of the Haskalah and the essential role assigned to Hebrew literature did not disappear at the end of the eighteenth century.

Throughout the nineteenth century, Hebrew literature of the Haskalah moved, together with the movement itself, from Prussia to the Habsburg Empire (Vienna, Prague, and especially the eastern Galician cities of Lemberg –now L'viv – and Brody). A generation or two later, the most important centers had moved still further eastward and southward to the Russian Empire. Hebrew literature, influenced by the ideas and works of Haskalah, was produced in Sephardi communities as well, not only in Italy, but also, from the second half of the nineteenth century, in the Arab countries of the Middle East and North Africa.

With the final demise of *Ha-me'asef*, a new Hebrew journal had been launched in Vienna, *Bikkurei Ha-'Ittim* (1820–1831), to be followed in the next generation by *Kerem Ḥemed* (1833–1856). The Hebrew literature written by the writers of the so-called Galician Haskalah was clearly influenced by the work done in Prussia and Vienna, but the genres they created, as well as the very nature of their literary works, shifted significantly due to the Eastern European contexts in which they had written. Side by side with the continuous presence of neo-classical poetry, we see the appearance and proliferation of satirical and parodic prose fiction, which was mostly directed against the Hasidic movement and its growing popularity. The most prominent example of this work is Yosef Perl's *Magale Temirin* (The Revealer of Secrets, 1819), written originally in Hebrew, and followed by a Yiddish version. This fictional book pretends to record the "authentic" correspondence of various Hasidim who discuss their livelihoods, current events, and the deeds of their masters. The plot centers on a convoluted attempt by the Hasidim to lay their hands on a German book (the non-fictional book written by Perl himself) that denounces them to the authorities. Another important cycle of satirical works is *Ha-tsofe le-beyt Israel* (The Watchman of the House of Israel, 1822–1851) by Yitzḥak Erter. One of the most vivid stories of the cycle, *Gilgul nefesh* (Transmigration of the Soul, 1845), describes the successive "reincarnations" of a soul, when each of its nineteen embodiments (among them, a cantor, a kabbalist, a grave-digger, and a Hasidic master) represents a different dimension of the dark panorama of contemporary traditional Jewish life.

During the 1840s and 1850s, Hebrew literature was gradually shifting to the Russian Empire. The first center of Hebrew maskilic literature was in Lithuania, as reflected in the publication of the journal *Pirḥe Tsafon* (Flowers of the North, Vilna, 1841), which was followed by other journals and newspapers in the Russian Empire. The most respected poet of this period was the conservative Avraham Dov Lebensohn (Adam ha-Kohen). His poems and dramas showed a preference for the neoclassical, harmonizing literary forms removed from concrete reality and tending toward a more generalized observation, a commitment to the exaltation of the Hebrew language with strict adherence to the usage of biblical Hebrew.

At the same time, new genres such as the autobiography, the novel and the *poema* (long narrative poem), began to appear in Hebrew in the Russian empire. These new kinds of writing, as well as the appearance of new forms of literary criticism (influenced by Russian models) gradually brought a major transformation in Hebrew literature. In 1844, the Lithuanian maskil M. A. Guenzburg published in the literary journal *Devir* chapters of a groundbreaking autobiography entitled *Aviezer* (the unfinished book was published in 1864). Influenced by the autobiographies of Jean-Jacques Rousseau and Salomon Maimon, Guenzburg's work described not only the shortcomings of the Jewish educational system but also his own childhood and adolescent years in a remarkably candid way, exposing his physical and psychological world. The unfinished book had a momentous influence not only on Hebrew autobiographies written later, by Mosheh Leib Lilienblum and Peretz Smolenskin, but also on the development of Hebrew prose in general.

Even more revolutionary was the appearance of Avraham Mapu's novel *Ahavat Tsiyon* (The Love of Zion, 1853) in Vilna. It was the first true Hebrew novel. The model for Mapu's novel was in fact not the contemporary realistic novel of Europe, but the narrative of romance, adventure, and intrigue of the early modern period. The virtuous language of Mapu's novel, the descriptions of ancient Palestine in biblical time, and especially the convoluted plot about young lovers, enchanted readers and marked a significant turning point in Hebrew prose. After *Ahavat Tsion*, Mapu wrote another historical novel, *Ashmat Shomron* (The Guilt of Samaria), set in biblical times, and also *'Ayit Tsavua* (The Hypocrite, 1857–1869), a novel that depicts contemporary Jewish society in Lithuania from a maskilic point of view; all these demonstrated that it is possible to present a broad mimetic representation of life even in pseudo-biblical Hebrew.

The presence of Mapu's novels as well as other original and translated novels (*The Mysteries of Paris*, by Eugène Sue was translated into Hebrew by Kalman Shulman in 1857 and was a true "best-seller" in Hebrew) brought more Hebrew readers than the meager numbers of the Haskalah in Prussia or Galicia. It also served as a catalyst for an extended debate about the place of the novel in Hebrew literature – a polemic that eventually determined the centrality of the genre as a "mirror of reality." Thus, in the 1860s and 1870s, the focus of Hebrew literature shifted from poetry to narrative fiction with the appearance of maskilic novels and short stories by Mapu, the early works of S. Y. Abramovitsh, Peretz Smolenskin, and Re'uven Asher Braudes.

The shift towards narrative may also explain the changes in Hebrew poetry in this period, especially the appearance of the genre of the *poema* – the long narrative poem prevalent in Russian, German, and English poetry of the eighteenth and nineteenth century. The first Hebrew *poemas* were written by Adam ha-Kohen's son, the talented poet Mikha Yosef Lebensohn (Mikhal), who created some of the best lyrical Hebrew poems in this period before dying at a young age from tuberculosis. However, it was Lebensohn's younger friend, Yehuda Leib Gordon (*Yalag*), who became, beginning in the mid-1860s, the master of the Hebrew *poema* and the most dominant Hebrew poet of the second half of the nineteenth century in Europe.

Gordon first made a name for himself in historical *poemas* like *Bein shinei arayot* (Between the Lion's Teeth, 1868), dedicated to the war between the Judean rebels and Rome around the destruction of the Second Temple, and *Bi-Metsulot Yam* (In the Depths of the Sea), which retells episodes from the exodus of the Jews from Spain. However, the real interest of Gordon's writings did not lie in ancient or medieval history but in the legacy of Jewish history in contemporary life, as both poems dealt with the theme of national *ḥurban* (destruction or catastrophe), and with the meaning of Jewish heroism and martyrdom. Gordon's deep involvement with the here and now is most evident with the seminal narrative poems *Hakitsah 'ami* (Awake My People, 1863) and *Kotso shel yud* (The Tip of the Yud, 1875). The former called on Jews to abandon their isolation from Russian and European culture and partake of the great civilization around them while remaining committed to Jewish traditions. The latter is dedicated to the role of women in Jewish society and asks: "Hebrew woman, who knows your life?"

This period also witnessed the development and proliferation of the Hebrew press, with the arrival of the first Hebrew weekly, *Ha-Magid* (founded in 1856 and published outside the Russian Empire because of problems with censorship), followed by other Hebrew weeklies such as *Ha-Melits* (Odessa, 1860), *Ha-Karmel* (Vilna, 1860), and *Ha-Tsefirah* (Warsaw, 1862). Together with periodicals like Peretz Smolenskin's *Ha-Shaḥar* (1868–1884) and Avraham Ber Gottlober's *Ha-Boker or* (1876–1886), this Hebrew press served as a source of news and information (for readers whose main reading language was Hebrew), a lively platform for works of poetry and prose, and the rise of the Hebrew feuilleton, as well as a new breed of Hebrew literary criticism. A group of critics such as Avraham U. Kovner and Avraham Y. Paperna, who were influenced by contemporary Russian literary criticism, brought a new sense of maturity and sophistication to Hebrew letters by pointing to both its shortcomings and positive developments.

While most activities of the Hebrew Haskalah in the nineteenth century took place in Eastern Europe, Jews in communities throughout the Middle East and North Africa played active roles in both the Haskalah and the Arabic *Naḥda* ("awakening" or "renaissance") during the second half of the nineteenth century through the first decades of the twentieth century. It is important, though, to keep in mind that works in Hebrew (and standard Arabic) form a small portion of modern Middle Eastern Jewish literary production, while writing in Judeo-Arabic literature was much more widespread. With the educational and social reforms of the late nineteenth century Ottoman Empire, growing numbers of Jews in the Middle East began to take advantage of the new educational opportunities proffered by the Alliance Israélite Universelle, Christian missionary schools, new state schools and other modern Jewish schools.

This process exposed Jewish communities to similar dilemmas of modernity of the Haskalah in Europe and the "cultural awakening" in the Arab world. For example, in 1863, a Baghdadi maskil named Barukh Moshe Mizrahi had established the first modern printing press in Baghdad, which he used to print a Hebrew newspaper, *Ha-Dover*. Published intermittently through 1871, *Ha-Dover* was in direct dialogue (and competition) with Hebrew newspapers from both Europe and the East. In such journals and newspapers, modernizing rabbis (*rabbanim maskilim*) presented the "enlightened" face of their communities, declaring that they desired Haskalah, but on their own terms, not necessarily those promoted by those in Europe. They strongly promoted educational reforms in the community, such as the teaching of foreign languages and crafts; they sought to weed out superstition and to restore religion to its "true" principles. In 1885, a Baghdad-born Jew named Sliman Menahem Mani published a polemic narrative, a short story called *Emek ha-Shedim*, in Eliezer Ben-Yehuda's newspaper *Ha-Tsevi*. This is one of the few examples of Hebrew fiction by an Arab Jew in the nineteenth century, but examples of modern Hebrew poetry abound.

In North Africa, the winds of modernization swept through Jewish communities both before and during the colonial period, with its strong French cultural influence. Since the 1860s, North African Jews contributed to Haskalah's newspapers and journals published in Europe. In the 1880s and 1890s, publishing houses and journals in Hebrew and Judeo-Arabic were founded in Algeria and Tunisia, edited and produced by writers who were in direct dialogue with the Haskalah. Shalom Flaḥ (1855–1936), in Tunisia, wrote Hebrew textbooks as well as Hebrew books of literary-historical narrative *Ẓedek ve-Shalom* (Peace and Justice). David Elkayam (1851–1940), in Mogador (Morocco), wrote countless poems in the tradition of the *piyyut* (liturgical poetry), as well as articles in Hebrew journals in Europe. In his book of poetry, *Shirei Dodim*, he used the venerated genre of the *piyyut* to introduce ideas of the Haskalah as well as to recount events in his life in a manner that was influenced by the writers of the Haskalah. Mordekhai Ha-Cohen (1856–1920), in Tripoli (Libya), produced Hebrew narratives like *Higid Mordekhai* (Thus Said Mordekhai).

Meanwhile, in Eastern Europe, the late nineteenth century inaugurated a series of changes. Zionist Hebrew literary historiography presented the waves of anti-Jewish violence of 1881–82 (following the assassination of Alexander II) as the watershed moment in the development of this literature, but in recent years this view has been questioned and challenged. We now realize that it was not necessarily the pogroms that brought dramatic literary changes. The notion of "national repentance" – a total change of heart of the maskilim who had been "converted" after 1881 to Zionism – has been exaggerated, and the effects of this process on literary history have been overly dramatized. As much as the changes had to do with the gradual demise of the Haskalah movement and the rise of modern Jewish nationalism, they were at the same time a result of the maturation of internal literary, aesthetic, and ideological processes that had taken place since the 1860s.

In the realm of Hebrew prose fiction, the most significant developments were created by S. Y. Abramovitsh, who began his literary career in the early 1860s as part of the Hebrew maskilic center in Lithuania, but within a few years made the crucial decision to switch to Yiddish. Twenty years of writing fiction in Yiddish had established him as the founder of modern Yiddish literature, using the pen-name and persona of *Mendele Moykher Sforim* (Mendele the Book-Seller). In 1886, after making Odessa his permanent home, Abramovitsh returned to writing in Hebrew. He published a series of dazzling original Hebrew short stories based on events of the 1880s in Eastern and Central Europe. In the 1890s, he prepared Hebrew renditions of his major Yiddish novels that stunned readers. Through these stories and self-translated novels, Abramovitsh established his highly influential style (known as *nusakh*), integrating biblical and talmudic language with the later strata of Hebrew literary language, thus breaking the Haskalah's fixation on the Bible, and the exclusive reliance on biblical Hebrew. The Hebrew *nusakh* style, which owes much to the stylized Yiddish idiomatic language that Abramovitsh developed, became a rich and versatile instrument for literary depiction (and critique) of contemporary Jewish reality, and as a resonator for endless intertextual play.

Hebrew fiction cultivated another form of tentative realism initiated by Ben-Avigdor (the pen-name of Avraham Leib Shalkovich) in Warsaw. In 1891, he began to publish a series with the name *Sifre Agorah* (Penny Novels) written by himself and other Hebrew writers. This was the first time that a publisher of literature tried to take advantage of the growth of the Hebrew reading public (from a few thousand in the period of the Haskalah to hundreds of thousands in the 1890s). These works presented the experiences of Jews in naturalistic detail, using straightforward, unadorned language (which nevertheless was influenced by Abramovitsh's *nusakh*). Here we see the first attempts at cultivating individualistic characters, most strikingly in the work of Yesha'yahu Bershadsky, author of the novel *Be-'en matarah* (Without a Goal, 1899).

The final years of the nineteenth century also saw a trend toward romanticism or neo-romanticism in Hebrew fiction, which relied on stylized poetic, picturesque motifs. This mode employed the style of, and often based itself on, legends and myths, including tales from Hasidic sources. The most prominent representatives of the trend were Y. L. Peretz, David Frishman, Mordekhai Ze'ev Feierberg, and Mikha Yosef Berdichevsky.

In the realm of Hebrew poetry, the 1880s marked the appearance of poets associated with the *Hovevey Zion* (Lovers of Zion) movement in Eastern Europe. Motifs of yearning for Jewish national revival in Palestine are mixed with sentimentality and the rudiments of lyrical romantic poetry. The formal shift away from the poets of the Haskalah period is evident in rhythmic schemes as poetic works abandoned the syllabic meters of the Haskalah for the richer possibilities of tonal-syllabic meter. The 1880s constituted a transitional period in Hebrew poetry, until two great poets, Ḥayim Nahman Bialik and Shaul Tchernichovsky, appeared on the horizon in the early 1890s (both of them made Odessa, which became a major center for Hebrew literature at the time, their home at that time).

Bialik began his career writing in a manner similar to the so-called Ḥibat Zion poetry, but soon he was able to convey a more credible lyrical speaker who is also an allegorical representative of "the people." A few years after, at the turn of the twentieth century, Bialik was assigned the role of a "national poet" (like Alexander Pushkin in Russia), which was ascribed both to the poet's exceptionally deep identification with the national psyche and to the sheer dynamism of his lyrical talent. Bialik's most powerful poems, written in the first years of the twentieth century, are not necessarily those that deal with collective "national" themes, but those that create a perfect unity of a personal music with the projection of a unique, idiosyncratic sense of being. Meter, rhythm, rhyme, inflection of syntax, and accentuation of statement formed an entity that directly reflected the interior space of an individualized poetic speaker. They combine the romantic quest for childhood, nature, and erotic love with motifs (sometimes very dark ones) from the contemporary poetic trends of symbolism and decadence.

Bialik's stylistic and linguistic achievements were considerable and redefined poetic Hebrew for many years to come. The power of his language also derives, to a great extent, from the complex intertextual play with Jewish textual traditions. Bialik perfected the short lyric poem, based on a series of concentrated experiential moments, into a figurative, musical, and rhythmic whole. He also introduced the long, lyrical *poema* that replaced (to a large extent) the historical and rhetorical narrative poems of the Haskalah. Paradoxically, it was Bialik's resolve to watch over the boundaries of his personal identity and purge the vestiges of collectivity that allowed him to write the more memorable and significant of his public "prophetic" poems like *Be-'ir Ha-harega* (In the City of Slaughter, 1903, written in the wake of the Kishinev pogrom), a poem which shocked readers with the power of its condemnation of the behavior of Jewish victims.

Shaul Tchernichovsky's considerable poetic talent was overshadowed by that of Bialik's, but he was the great romantic poet in Hebrew and the one to truly open Hebrew poetry to world poetry. Tchernichovsky's poetry expressed a universal humanism, a direct connection with nature, and uninhibited eroticism. He created in European poetic forms that had been previously neglected in Hebrew: the idyll, the ballad, and the sonnet. Tchernichovsky accorded to translation work considerable energy and he translated into Hebrew works by Homer, Lermontov, Heine, Longfellow, and many others. He was considered as (and cultivated an image of) an "alien" in Hebrew-Jewish culture, but there are strong connections in his poetry to the traditional Jewish background in which he grew up. That background is revealed clearly in his idylls "Brit milah" (Circumcision) and *Ḥatunatah shel Elkah* (Elka's Wedding), which are filled with details from Ukrainian Jewish life, and also in his autobiographical long poems.

Highly important at the turn of the twentieth century was Ahad Ha'am (Asher Ginsubrg), the father of "cultural Zionism." Ahad Ha'am was a strong opponent of the growth of Yiddish literature and culture, and claimed that Hebrew is the only language that could culturally tie Jews all over the world. This is why the creation of modern Hebrew literature was so important for Ahad Ha'am, in spite of the fact that he did not have a high regard for most of the literature that was produced in this language. His role as a critic and the editor of the monthly *Ha-shiloaḥ* was as crucial as his influential, lucid style of Hebrew essays, which set new standards for non-fictional Hebrew prose. Ahad Ha'am's dominance (together with Bialik, Abramovitsh, and other members of the so-called Odessa Sages circle) was challenged by the critic, editor, writer and translator David Frishman, who worked in Warsaw and St. Petersburg, and most vehemently by M. Y. Berdichevsky, who called for a Nietzschean "transvaluation of values" and challenged Ahad Ha'am's conservatism, and what he saw as his limited understanding of Hebrew literature.

Berdichevsky became a guiding figure during the first years of the twentieth century, when a new generation of writers in Europe produced astonishing modernist experiments in Hebrew, mainly in works of narrative fiction and gradually also in poetry. This was the first time that Hebrew literature was in accord with (sometimes even anticipating) literary developments in Europe and America and achieved unprecedented artistic maturity and sophistication. Yosef Ḥayim Brenner, Uri Nissan Gnessin, Gershon Shofman, S. Y. Agnon, David Fogel, Dvora Baron (the first woman writer who became part of the Hebrew canon), L. A. Arieli-Orlof, and Yaakov Shteinberg were all born in small Jewish communities in the Pale of Settlement. They received traditional educations, but were also exposed from early age to modern literature and culture in Hebrew, Yiddish, Russian, German, and sometimes other languages as well. Unlike the writers of the previous generation (the writers of the Haskalah and even Bialik and Berdichevsky), the process of "loss of faith" was not as traumatic, but the anguished search for meaning and for religiosity in a secular world is very prominent in their writing. Most of them moved from small towns to cities in Eastern and Central Europe and were exposed to the overwhelming new pace of urban life and they gave expression to this experience in their writings, which hovered between realism, expressionistic intensity, symbolism, decadence and lyrical impressionism. Their writing, which was extremely varied in spite of common themes and styles, was mainly in the form of the short story and the novella, which led to decline of the novel, especially the large-scale social-realistic novel. In their fiction they explored the inner world of individual characters (often based on autobiographical experience), sexual identity, homoeroticism, and eros as a dark and disruptive force.

Bialik and Tchernichovsky continued to dominate Hebrew poetry in Europe at the beginning of the twentieth century, but there was a new group of young poets such as Yaakov Fichman, Zalman Shneour, Yaakov Shteinberg, and David Shimonovitz (Shimoni), who refined the achievements of the two great poets (especially Bialik), but brought new experiential worlds into their poetry.

Until the mid-1920s, the most innovative literature in Hebrew was produced in various cities of Europe, where there were scattered but very active enclaves of Hebrew literary activity. The first and second Zionist waves of migration to Palestine (aliyot) made Jaffa (and later the new city of Tel Aviv, established in 1909) a small center, with a handful of important writers, journals, and publishing houses. Much of the literature that was written there (by writers like Sh. Ben-Zion, Moshe Smilansky, and

Yosef Luidor) was full of high-flown nationalist rhetoric about creating "A New Hebrew Man" in Palestine, mixed with orientalist depictions of the native Arab and Bedouin populations whom the *halutsim* (pioneers) tried to emulate. Brenner, who remained a thoroughly European writer after his immigration (about which he was highly ambivalent), heavily criticized this literature. Perhaps the most interesting Hebrew texts in Palestine during the first two decades of the twentieth century were written by women like Dvora Baron, Nehama Pohatchevsky, Hemda Ben Yehuda and others who transposed Zionism into the realm of "women's issues," weaving it with women's gendered traumas, their projects of liberation and equality, and their fraught relations with work, writing, and love.

Towards the end of the 1920s, in the aftermath of the First World War, the Russian Revolution and Civil War, the Balfour Declaration and the growth of the Yishuv (the Jewish community in Palestine), Europe and its various enclaves ceased to be the chief arena for Hebrew literature. Writers from different generations and of various poetic styles like Bialik, S. Y. Agnon (who lived in Germany for twelve years until 1924), Uri Zvi Greenberg, Yitzhak Lamdan, Avigdor Ha-meiri (Foyershtein), Eliezer Shteinman, Avraham Shlonsky, Ya'acov Horovitz, Hayim Hazaz, and Lea Goldberg arrived in Palestine in the 1920s and 1930s, from cities like Berlin, Vienna, Warsaw, Odessa, Moscow, and Paris. There were many other Hebrew writers (Shaul Tchernichovsky and Natan Alterman among them), who traveled back and forth between Europe and Palestine throughout the 1920s and eventually settled in Palestine. Within a decade, a full-fledged Hebrew literary center had emerged in the Yishuv, including a fairly large readership, publishing houses, journals with relatively stable and continuous publication (like *Moznayim*, 1933–1947; *Ktuvim*, 1926–1931; *Turim*, 1933–1938; *Gilyonot*, 1933–1954), daily Hebrew newspapers with literary supplements, and several literary groups that competed against each other.

Hebrew literature also flourished in North America during the early decades of the twentieth century, with writers who emigrated from Europe. In 1927, Daniel Persky counted no less than 110 active writers of poetry, prose, criticism, scholarship, essays, and journalism, who published their work in Hebrew journals, newspapers, and books, most of them edited and produced in the United States. Although they never reached the mass readership that the Yiddish press attracted and always were an elite (even aristocratic) minority group, their numbers and their literary and cultural activity were impressive.

The 1920s also saw a rebirth of modern Hebrew writing in Baghdad, partly influenced by contacts between the community and the Yishuv and by the dispatching of modern Hebrew teachers to Iraq. The Hebrew cultural option was epitomized by a short-lived bilingual Hebrew and Judeo-Arabic cultural journal, *Yeshurun*, produced by an association called *Agudat 'Ivrit Sifrutit* (Baghdad Hebrew Literary Society). The group apparently had several hundred members at its peak. In 1920–1921, it produced five issues of the journal. Around the same time, we see Arab Jews in Palestine like Yitzḥak Shami, whose family came from Damascus, who portray in Hebrew – in novellas like *Nikmat Ha-avot* (The Vengeance of the Fathers, 1927) – the life of Arabs and Jews in a way very different from the European immigrants and their mixture of romantic Orientalism, fear and ignorance.

The poets who immigrated to Palestine in the 1920s and 1930s – Avraham Shlonsky, U. Z. Greenberg (who made a name for himself as a Yiddish and Hebrew modernist in Warsaw and Berlin before he immigrated), Natan Alterman, and others, challenged the relatively stable poetic system of Bialik and his followers in the name of revolutionary modernism ("the wild poem"), influenced by futurism, expressionism, acmeism, and neo-symbolism. In the period between the 1920s and the 1940s the different modernist poetic trends gradually became dominant, and existed side by side with the more minor-key poetry of David Fogel in Vienna and Paris and the women poets Rachel Bluvstein, Esther Rabb, and Elisheva in Palestine. By 1938 – the date of the publication of Alterman's book *Kokhavim ba-ḥutz* (Stars Outside) – the urban neo-symbolism of the *moderna* was indisputably the prevailing and most influential trend in Hebrew poetry. Politically, Shlonsky and the poets of the so-called *moderna* group (together with Alterman and Goldberg) were both products and shapers of Labor Zionism. Greenberg and his poetry, on the other hand, became associated, from the 1930s onward, with the Revisionist movement of Vladimir (Ze'ev) Jabotinsky. All of this new poetry in Palestine was written with the Sephardic accentuation system, which became the norm for spoken Hebrew in the schools and communities of the Yishuv, and this was the basis for the new rhythmic organization of Hebrew poetry, which was written until then in the Ashkenazi system.

The Hebrew poets in America – figures like Abraham Regelson and Shimon Halkin who were active in Hebrew and Jewish education – strove not for a total revolution but for continuity of the Bialik and Tchernichovsky poetic system, accompanied by renewal, principally through the assimilation of the positive influence of the English and American poetic traditions. Most of what they wrote was lyrical poetry, but they also described the American urban landscape of New York and other great cities and the open American vistas from New England to California. Some of the Hebrew writers produced great *poemas* and cycles of poems about Native Americans and African-Americans, in which they attempted to decipher the United States – and the place of Jewish culture within it – through engagement with its "others."

In the realm of Hebrew prose, the interwar period produced many new writers, especially in the Yishuv, but one writer – S. Y. Agnon – became the undisputed master. Agnon managed to develop the innovations of the Hebrew modernists in Europe, at the same time that he produced some of the best realist novels and short-stories in Hebrew. In short stories like the cycle *Sefer Ha-ma'asim* (The Book of Deeds) and novels such as *Ore'aḥ nata la-lun* (A Guest for the Night) and *Tmol Shilshom* (Only Yesterday), Agnon examined the tension between the two fictional foci of his world: Shibush – modeled after Buczacz, his hometown in eastern Galicia – and Tel Aviv and Jerusalem of the Yishuv. The richly allusive nature of Agnon's Hebrew writing and his highly ironic employment of unreliable narrators and the slogans of Zionism barely mask his view of the traumatic nature of modernity. Agnon's works expose how the Zionist project was continually haunted by what it sought to reject.

Apart from Agnon, a number of writers like Aharon Revuni, A. A. Kavak, Dov Kimhi, and Ḥayim Hazaz created realist fiction in the manner of the nineteenth-century novel, depicting life in the Yishuv. Hazaz's fiction focuses on the stormy period of the Russian Revolution as a prototype for his later novels and novellas that dealt with events in Jewish history as well as the diverse Jewish communities in Palestine. A number of important poets in Europe, Palestine, and America (David Fogel, Lea Goldberg, Shimon Halkin, Elisheva Bikhovsky) created in the 1930s and 1940s some of the best works of modernist Hebrew fiction that did not deal with the turbulence and struggles of the Yishuv but rather with the inner life of individuals in the urban centers of Vienna, Berlin, Moscow, and New York City.

Around the time of the establishment of the State of Israel in 1948, a new generation of Hebrew writers and poets ("The 1948 generation") burst onto the literary and cultural scene and began to create Hebrew literature that was very different from what had come before. It is important to note that Israeli literature has been (and still is) written not only in Hebrew, but also in Arabic, Yiddish, German, Russian, and other languages, both by the Jewish majority and the Arab minority. Nevertheless, it is figures like Ḥayim Guri, S. Yizhar, Moshe Shamir, Ḥanokh Bartov, and many others who were the first native-born children of the immigrants (mostly from Eastern Europe), who defined the new parameters of what is considered canonical Israeli literature. Hebrew was the mother-tongue of these writers and they grew up with an education of the dominant Labor Zionist movement, rather than the traditional Jewish and cosmopolitan upbringing of most Hebrew writers who created in Europe, America and the Middle

East before the establishment of the State. This was the first time that Hebrew did not function as part of a complex multilingual system, but as the exclusive language of communication, and it affected the style and literary language in many ways.

The writers of 1948 wrote stories, novels, poems and plays about the Zionist collective and about the struggle to establish the State and to win the 1948 War ("War of Independence"). Their literary style was mostly naturalist (with influences from the school of Soviet "socialist realism") and constructed the figure of the Israeli-Jewish native (nicknamed "sabra") as an organic product of the physical and social landscape of the Yishuv, especially the dominant labor-Zionist youth movements, agricultural schools, Kibbutzim and the military units (like the Palmaḥ) that later became the core of the Israel Defense Force. The war itself was a defining moment in the biography of the writers (almost all of them men) and numerous works were written about the soldiers, especially the fallen soldiers who became the heroic model of the society in the new State. The fallen soldiers were portrayed as "the living-dead" both by writers of the Yishuv like Natan Alterman in his famous poem *Magash ha-kesef* (The Silver Platter, 1947) and by sabra poets like Guri.

Side by side with this dominant group of writers, there were also others who did not share their experience and point of view. In reality, the native-born "sabras" were a small minority of the population of the young State of Israel that more than doubled in the 1950s with mass migration of Jewish refugees – Holocaust survivors from Europe and Jews from Arab states who suddenly found themselves in the midst of the Arab–Israeli conflict. In the face of this mass migration there was a pronounced fear by the elites about the fledgling Israeli culture and a strong push for monoligualism and rejection of everything that was deemed "exilic." Nevertheless, the fact that Hebrew became the national language of Israel did not prevent writers from writing in their native languages: Arabic (Samir Naqash), Yiddish (Avrom Sutzkever), Polish (Ada Fink), and German (Ludwig Strauss) among others. Moreover, some writers who began their careers writing in these languages gradually moved to Hebrew or wrote in two languages side by side, as the case of the Yiddish writer Yosl Birshteyn (who was part of the Yiddish literary group *Yung Yisroel*) or the Iraqi writer Shimon Ballas (who wrote Arabic and moved to Hebrew) clearly show.

On the other hand, there was another small but influential group of writers and intellectuals known as the Canaanites who tried to create "native" Israeli culture based on Hebrew and disconnected from the Jewish past, Jewish Diaspora and Jewishness altogether. Writers such as Yonatan Ratosh, Binyamin Tamuz and Aharon Amir wrote about and called for a merging of the "Semitic populations" of the Middle East (Arabs and "Hebrews"), based on local, pre-Jewish cultures.

Gradually, during the 1950s, a neo-modernist poetic movement arose. It had begun rather modestly with the group and journal *Likrat* ("Towards" 1952–54) and developed into what became known as The Statehood Generation of Hebrew poetry (*dor ha-medina*) with figures such as Natan Zach, Moshe Dor, Aryeh Sivan, Yehuda Amichai, and Binyamin Harushvsky (who was also active in modernist Yiddish poetry at the time). They fought against the *moderna* group of Shlonsky and Alterman, and the 1948 generation poets. Natan Zach's 1955 book of poetry *Shirim Shonim* (Various/Different Poems) puts a secular, individualistic, cosmopolitan subject at the center of poems that were written in free verse, "prosaic" language and a major toning down of metaphorical overload. Zach, Amichai, and others like David Avidan and Dan Pagis moved away from the Eastern European influence of symbolism, expressionism, and socialist-realism, and from the collectivist "we" to the poetic "I."

These new parameters of the "Statehood Generation" poetry suddenly made a number of highly individual poets who belonged to the generation of Alterman and Shlonsky – figures like Gabriel Preil in New York and Avot Yeshurun (Yehiel Perlmutter) in Tel Aviv – more relevant and popular in Israel. Yeshurun's avant-garde poetry broke the flow of literary Hebrew and brought a heady mixture of Yiddish, Polish, and Arabic into the poetic idiom that was able to depict effectively the traumas of immigration and the Holocaust as well as those of the indigenous Arab population in 1948 (the *Nakba*). Preil, the last major Hebrew writer in America, and the only one who was read and appreciated in Israel, wrote imagistic free-verse poetry about an urban poetic subject in New York City. Priel was influenced not only by Anglo-American poetry but also by the "introspectivist" movement of Yiddish poetry (Yankev Glatshteyn and A. L. Leyeles), in which he participated as a bilingual poet.

In the realm of prose-fiction, during late 1950s and 1960s a new generation of authors emerged, known also as "Statehood Generation" or "New Wave" (Gershon Shaked's designation). It included the new voices of Amos Oz, A. B. Yehoshua, Amalia Kahana-Carmon, and Yehoshua Kenaz who focused, at least initially, on the short story rather than on novels. They rejected the naturalistic modes of the 1948 writers and were influenced by older writers such as Agnon, as well as by European and American writers such as Kafka and Faulkner. Their works, which were a mixture of realism and symbolist lyricism, exposed collective and national issues, generational struggles reflected in Oedipal narratives, and a partial merging of the limits between self and others, Israelis and their enemies.

Amos Oz wrote his first collection of stories (1966) around the inner life of characters in the kibbutz, especially with the younger generation who rebel against their fathers, often with tragic results. For example, at the end of the story *Derekh haruaḥ* (The Way of the Wind), the young paratrooper protagonist hangs from a high-tension wire in his parachute, his head down and his feet up in the air. In A. B. Yehoshua's *Facing the Forests* (1963), the story's main protagonist, an Israeli student who is assigned to guard a national forest, escapes from the city with the aim of achieving a breakthrough and making some discovery in his doctoral dissertation on the Crusades. A discovery does take place, but not in the research, but rather the remnants of an Arab village (probably destroyed in the 1948 war) are revealed, first by a mute Arab, and then after the forest which covered them goes up in flames. Here, as elsewhere in the fiction of this period, the Arab appears as a demonic, haunting figure, capturing the fantasies and deep fears of the young Israeli-Jewish characters.

Aharon Appelfeld belongs to the same generation, but his life experience and his writings are far removed from the writers of the "Statehood Generation." Born in 1932 in the city of Czernowitz, he survived World War II and arrived in Palestine in 1946 as a refugee, learning Hebrew with a good deal of effort and struggling with the unfamiliar language and environment. Appelfeld began writing poetry and essays in the 1950s when he was a student (of Yiddish literature), but came out of relative obscurity with his first collection of stories, *Ashan* (Smoke, 1962). Virtually all of Appelfeld's stories (and later novellas and novels) deal with the Holocaust, but without recounting the horrors of the War. Instead his impressionistic writing focuses on the everlasting influence of the Holocaust on the survivors after the War in Europe or in Israel, or on Jewish life in Europe before, during and after World War II. Appelfeld lives and writes in the State of Israel, but his writings, which insist on exploring the Jewish predicament and religiosity, seem to belong more comfortably with multilingual Jewish writing around the world.

Amalia Kahana-Carmon was the first Israeli woman writer to be part of the emerging canon of the "Statehood Generation." She published her first collection of stories, *Bi-kefifah aḥat* (Under One Roof), in 1966. Unlike her male contemporaries, Kahana-Carmon has written about the inner lives of female characters, exploring realms of desire and fantasy. The language of her stories is highly stylized and lyrical with an intertextual echo-chamber that goes back to the Bible and Mishnah as well as to nineteenth and early twentieth century European writers from Europe.

If Kahana-Carmon was the only woman to enter the canon of Israeli fiction, Dahlia Ravikovitch accomplished a similar achievement in her poetry. Ravikovitch's first book of poems, *Ahavat tapuaḥ ha-zahav* (The

Love of an Orange) published in 1959, created a literary sensation. While these poems expressed an utterly contemporary sensibility, it was their rare diction and archaic cadences, distilled from the most ancient layers of biblical Hebrew, that made readers in Israel and around the world marvel. The Jewish American critic Irving Howe wrote that although her poems often deal with "extreme states of personal life: desolation, loss, estrangement, breakdown," she is "a poet of wit, severe and costly," and her "language bristles with sharpness."

In the 1960s and early 1970s, we see for the first time Mizraḥi writers, part of a mass migration from Arab countries to Israel during the 1950s, entering the Israeli literary scene. Writers such as Shimon Ballas and Sami Michael from Iraq began writing in their native Arabic, but switched to Hebrew and published novels – *Hama'abara* (The Transit Camp, 1966), *Shavim ve-Shavim Yoter* (Equal and More Equal, 1974) – on the life of immigrants and the cultural and economic gaps between them and the Ashkenazi sabras. These writers brought new Hebrew idioms, styles and themes that were in direct dialogue with Arabic language, literature, and culture.

At the same time, we find immigrant writers such as Yosl Birshteyn, who began writing in Yiddish, switching gradually into bilingual Hebrew-Yiddish writing. During the 1960s, Birshteyn, together with the playwright Nissim Aloni, translated his short stories into Hebrew, and they were published in a collection *Nesia'to ha-rishona shel Rolider* (Rolider's First Journey, 1970). These stories, and subsequent novels which Birshteyn wrote in Hebrew and Yiddish, represent the Jewish story of immigration and disintegration in the twentieth century, and of the precarious Israeli present as suspended between irrecoverable loss and utopian redemption. Similar themes were explored by the Israeli writer Ya'akov Shabtai, who was born and raised in Labor-Zionist Tel Aviv. Shabtai published his short story collection *Ha-dod Peretz Mamri* (Uncle Peretz Takes Off, 1972) and his masterpiece novel *Zikhron Dvarim* (Past Continuous, 1977), written in a sweeping stream-of-consciousness style, which became one of the most influential Israeli novels. In spite of the fact that almost all of his fiction is set in Tel Aviv, the urban setting is radically transformed in the context of the extended family of immigrants and refugees. This focus enables the literary representation of what has been exiled from the Zionist discourse: the Diaspora Jewish immigrants who were kept hidden behind the sabra's broad back.

Birshteyn's and Shabtai's transition from the short story to the novel was not unusual. In the 1970s, Yehoshua, Oz, Kenaz, Kahana-Carmon, Appelfeld, and others who excelled in short stories published novels. The general euphoria of the 1967 War (Six Days War) and the occupation of large parts of territories, which was followed by the trauma of the 1973 War (Yom Kippur War) left Israeli writers with many political and existential questions and dilemmas. We see in this period some literary attempts to deal with a more complex Israeli reality, and at the same time utopian and dystopian novels that imagine a different future and at the same time look back to the Jewish past for answers.

In poetry, the poets of the Statehood Generation such as Zach, Amichai, Avidan, and Ravikovitz continued to dominate and found more subtle and sophisticated ways to integrate the universal and existential individualism with the unique Israeli experience. Yehuda Amichai in particular gradually emerged as a kind of national Israeli poet, capturing the many moods of Israel in a colloquial voice with an extraordinary mixture of wit and compassion. These poets were joined by a younger generation of poets, mostly working and living in Tel Aviv: Meir Wieseltier, Yona Wallach, Yair Hurvitz, and others centered around the literary journals *Aḥshav* and *Siman Kri'ah*. These writers attempted to make Israeli poetry more concrete and at the same time open to more diverse experiences and poetic styles. Yona Wallach brought a new spirit of linguistic and stylistic experimentation with an unprecedented focus on female sexuality together with religiosity (Jewish and non-Jewish), mixing high registers with street talk, rock and roll with Jungian psychology, manifest sexuality with provocative feminism.

In Jerusalem, Dan Pagis began his poetic career in a way that appears to be similar to those of Zach and Amicahi, but in his book *Gilgul* (Transmigration, 1970) he gave a concise and powerful expression to his experience as a Holocaust survivor and to moral and existential questions of human life, authority, responsibility, power, and memory.

Two political events in this period shook Israel and also shattered the façade of a relatively stable political, cultural, and literary hegemony: In 1977 the hegemonic Labor party lost power to the right-wing Likud, and in 1982 Israel invaded Lebanon, which caused a long and controversial war. These events, as well as the growing polarization in Israeli society around the continuing occupation of the territories captured by Israel since 1967, brought political poetry and protest poetry to the fore. Poets such as Yeshurun, Zach, and Ravikovitz as well as Yitzḥak Laor and Aharon Shabtai confronted the political without giving up the lyrical, highly personal nature of their poetry. At the same time, Mizraḥi poets such as Erez Biton (who started publishing in the late 1960s), Roni Somek, Eli Bachar, and Peretz-Dror Banai expressed in their writing the ethnic experience, the trauma of migration, and the estrangement from mainstream Israel. At the same time, they highlighted Arab-Jewish traditions of religious and secular poetry from North Africa and the Levant that were hardly present in Israeli literature until then.

Hebrew fiction experienced an unprecedented boom in the 1980s, which went hand in hand with the expansion and the fragmentation of the canon. The literature that was previously at the margins – works written by Mizrahi writers, women, Holocaust survivors (and their children), and Arabs – became numerous and much more visible and influential. This period also saw the rise of genres of popular literature such as detective and romance novels in Hebrew (these had existed before, mainly through translations). While women writers such as Yehudit Hendel, Amalia Kahana-Carmon, and Rachel Eytan had, since the 1950s, published their work with varying degrees of critical and popular success, it was only in the 1980s that writing by women truly flourished. Writers like Shulamit Hareven, Shulamit Lapid, Ruth Almog, Savion Liebrecht, Batya Gur, Hannah Bat-Shahar, and Orly Castel-Bloom have written in a range of styles and on a variety of themes.

Mizrahi writing also moved from the margins to the center. Established writers like Michael and Ballas were joined by other writers from Arab countries or Israeli-born writers from Mizrahi families like Eli Amir (Iraq), Itzhak Gormenzo-Goren and Ronit Matalon (Egypt), Albert Swissa (Morroco), Amnon Shamosh (Syria), Dan Bnaya Seri (Yemen), and others. These writers questioned the assumption that "Israeliness" is synonymous with an Ashkenazi-Sabra hegemony. Even A. B. Yehoshua, who was highly identified with the literature of the "Statehood Generation," explored Mizrahi characters and themes in his novels *Molcho* (Five Seasons, 1987) and *Mr. Mani* (1991), an inverted family saga that begins with the Israel of the 1980s and reaches back to eighteenth century Mizrahi and Arab-Jewish culture.

In some sense, Yehoshua's *Mr. Mani* was a response to the publication of Anton Shammas's novel *Arabeskot* (Arabesques, 1986), a major event in Israeli literature and culture. Although it was not the first literary text written in Hebrew by an Israeli-Palestinian writer, it was the first to catch the attention of the reading public. With rich and allusive language, pulsating lyricism, subtle humor and irony, and no less subtle subversion of Israeli cultural and political codes, *Arabeskot* was received with near universal acclaim. The novel, as well as Shammas's essays and journalistic Hebrew writing and translation, tested the underlying Jewish ethnocentrism of Israeli (and Hebrew) literature and the underlying assumption that it is synonymous with Jewishness. Shammas's writing also presented a utopian horizon in which Hebrew can be a shared Israeli language of Jews and Palestinian Arabs. Although Shammas's novel is still considered a singular achievement, other Israeli-Palestinian writers such as Sayed Kashua continue to explore the complex Palestinian, Israeli, and Arab identities in Hebrew.

Another crucial development in Israeli fiction since the 1980s is the writing of the "second generation" of the Holocaust. Increasing numbers of Israeli writers are exploring the effects of the Holocaust – on their own life and on Israeli society in general – in spite of the fact that they did not experience it. Perhaps the most prominent example of this is David Grossman's masterpiece *Ayen 'erekh Ahava* (See Under Love, 1986), a wildly inventive novel of historical reimagination in four parts that begins with Momik, an Israeli child growing up in the 1950s in the shadow of the Holocaust, ends with a fantastical set of encyclopedia entries detailing the adventures of children's book heroes raising a child in the Warsaw zoo, and in between rescues the Polish writer Bruno Schulz from death by turning him into a salmon. The fact that Grossman himself is *not* a son of Holocaust survivors is a testimony to the pervasive impact of the Holocaust on Israeli society and culture.

The boom in Israeli fiction went hand in hand with a decline in the status of poetry in Israeli culture. Excellent poetry continued to be written by both established and new poets, but the audience for poetry, as well as its cultural status was on the wane. Perhaps the most interesting development in Israeli poetry in the 1990s was the rise of what became known in Hebrew as *shira emunit*, poetry of religiosity. Poets such as Admiel Kosman, Rivka Miriam, Yondav Kaplun, and Miron Izakson – some of them affiliated with the Israeli Orthodox community and others not – questioned the assumption of the underlying secularity of Israeli and Hebrew poetry and brought to the surface questions of secularism and religiosity that existed in Hebrew writing since the advent of modernity.

In the last decades, Israeli literature has undergone further processes of diversification and decentralization. It is impossible to identify a stable or agreed-upon canon or thematic center. Side by side with so-called thin literature of writers such as Orly Castel-Bloom and Etgar Keret – whose stories, children's books, and graphic novels have been extremely popular in Israel and (in translation) around the world – we find writers who explore the richness of the Hebrew language and its endless intertextual echo-chamber. Likewise, we find a tension between focusing on the here and now of Israeli reality (including a substantial amount of "regional literature," especially literature that takes place in Tel Aviv) and an ever more complex examination of the Jewish past, as well as the global postmodern society. Many established and new writers have created autobiographical novels, which has become one of the most prominent genres in contemporary Israel. There are also signs of renewed popularity of poetry, with a vibrant community of poets writing in journals and books, reading their works in poetry festivals and other public events to a growing and enthusiastic audience.

It also seems that in the first decades of the twenty-first century more Hebrew literature is written and read all over the world and not just in Israel. However, most of it is created not by Diaspora Jews (although there are a handful of American and European writers of Hebrew), but by a growing community of Israelis residing outside the State of Israel. In 2014, the winner of the Sapir Prize for Hebrew literature, awarded in Israel, was given to Reuven Namdar for his novel *Ha-bayit asher neḥrav* (The Ruined House). The entire Hebrew novel takes place in New York City. As of 2016, at least one new Hebrew journal, *Mikan Veʾeylakh* (From Here and Further), which defines itself as an "intellectual and literary platform for contemporary diasporic Hebrew," is being edited and published in Paris and Berlin, the cradle of modern Hebrew literature in the last decades of the eighteenth century.

SELECT BIBLIOGRAPHY

Alcalay, Ammiel, ed. *Keys to the Garden: New Israeli Writing.* San Francisco: City Lights, 1996.

Alter, Robert. *The Invention of Hebrew Prose: Modern Fiction and the Language of Realism.* Seattle: University of Washington Press, 1988.

——— ed. *Modern Hebrew Literature.* New York: Behrman House, 1975.

Band, Arnold J. "The Beginnings of Modern Hebrew Literature: Perspectives on Modernity." *AJS Review* 13, nos. 1–2 (1988): 1–26.

Bar-Yosef, Hamutal. *Maʾgaim shel dekadens.* Beʾer Shevaʿ: Hotsaʾat ha-Sefarim shel Universitat Ben-Guryon Ba-Negev, 1997.

Berg, Nancy. *Exile from Exile: Israeli Writers from Iraq.* Albany, NY: SUNY Press, 1996.

Burnshaw, Stanley, T. Carmi, Susan Glassman et al., eds. *The Modern Hebrew Poem Itself.* Second Edition. Detroit: Wayne State University Press, 2003.

Ezrahi, Sidra. *Booking Passage: Exile and Homecoming in the Modern Jewish Imagination.* Berkeley: University of California Press, 2000.

Feldman, Yael S. *No Room of Their Own: Gender and Nation in Israeli Women's Fiction.* New York: Columbia University Press, 1999.

Gluzman, Michael. *Ha-guf ha-tsiyoni: leʾumiyut, migdar u-miniyut ba-sifrut ha-ivrit Ha-Ḥadashah.* Tel Aviv: Hakibutz Hameuhad, 2007.

Halkin, Simon. *Modern Hebrew Literature: From the Enlightenment to the Birth of the State of Israel: Trends and Values.* New York: Schocken Books, 1970.

Harshav, Benjamin. *Language in Time of Revolution.* Berkeley: University of California Press, 1993.

Hever, Hannan. *Sifrut she-ikhtevet mi-kan: kitsur ha-sifrut ha-yiśreʾelit.* Tel Aviv: Yediʿot aḥaronot, 1999.

Hirschfeld, Ariel. "Locus and Language: Hebrew Culture in Israel, 1890–1990," in *Cultures of the Jews: A New History,* vol. 3, ed. David Biale. New York: Schocken, 2002.

Holtzman, Avner. *Ahavot tsiyon: panim ba-sifrut ha-'ivrit ha-hadashah.* Yerushalayim: Carmel, 2006.

Kaufman, Shirley, Galit Hasan-Rokem, and Tamar S. Hess, eds. *The Defiant Muse: Hebrew Feminist Poems from Antiquity to the Present.* New York: Feminist Press at CUNY, 1999.

Kronfeld, Chana. *On the Margins of Modernism: Decentering Literary Dynamics.* Berkeley: University of California Press, 1996.

Kurzweil, Baruch. *Sifrutenu ha-hadashah: hemshekh o mahpekhah?* Jerusalem: Shocken, 1959.

Levy, Lital. "Reorienting Hebrew Literary History: The View from the East." *Prooftexts* 29, no. 2 (2009): 127–172.

Milner, Iris. *Ḳir'e 'avar: Biyografyah, Zehut Ve-Zikaron Be-Siporet Ha-Dor Ha-Sheni.* Tel Aviv: 'Am 'oved, 2003.

Mintz, Alan, ed. *The Boom in Israeli Literature.* Hanover, NH: University Press of New England, 1997.

———. *Sanctuary in the Wilderness: A Critical Introduction to American Hebrew Poetry.* Palo Alto: Stanford University Press, 2011.

Miron, Dan. *Ben hazon le-emet: nitsane ha-roman ha-'ivri veha-yidi ba-me'ah ha-tesha'-'eśreh.* Jerusalem: Mosad Bialik, 1979.

———. *From Continuity to Contiguity: Toward a New Jewish Literary Thinking.* Stanford: Stanford University Press, 2010.

———. *The Prophetic Mode in Modern Hebrew Poetry.* New Milford, CT: Toby Press, 2010.

Pelli, Moshe. *Haskalah and Beyond: The Reception of the Hebrew Enlightenment and the Emergence of Haskalah Judaism.* Lanham, MD: University Press of America, 2010.

Pinsker, Shachar. *Literary Passports: The Making of Modernist Hebrew Fiction in Europe.* Stanford: Stanford University Press, 2011.

Sadan, Dov. *'Al sifrutenu: masat mavo.* Jerusalem: Mass Publishing, 1949.

Shaked, Gershon. *Ha-siporet ha-'ivrit, 1880–1980.* 5 volumes. Jerusalem: Keter, 1977–1998.

Shavit, Uzi. *Ba-'alot ha-shahar: shirat ha-haskalah, mifgash 'im ha-moderniyut.* Tel Aviv: Hakibutz Hameuhad, 1996.

CHAPTER 28

YIDDISH LITERATURE

MIKHAIL KRUTIKOV

Between the mid-nineteenth and mid-twentieth centuries the world's largest and most active Jewish population, the Ashkenazim of Eastern Europe, created a new modern culture in their own vernacular. Yiddish culture rapidly developed during the second half of the nineteenth century as a product of the complex modernization process, which combined universalist aspirations rooted in the ideals of the Enlightenment, the rise of nationalist ideologies, and political mobilization of the masses for socialist causes. The defining feature of Yiddish culture was the use of a vernacular that was identified, by both Jews and non-Jews, as a (or, as some argued, *the*) "Jewish" language. As the most authentic and effective vehicle for expressing Jewish concerns, hopes, fears, and ideas, Yiddish was contrasted by its champions to the "archaic" and "religious" Hebrew on the one hand, and the "assimilationist" co-territorial languages such as German, Russian, and Polish, on the other. From its origins in the Middle Ages, Yiddish has served two different, but complementary, functions: as a language of Jewish internal discourse and as a bridge to the outside world. Written in Hebrew characters and saturated with idioms that stemmed from the Hebrew Bible, the Talmud and other rabbinic sources, it was fully accessible only to those who were firmly anchored in the traditional Jewish way of life of Eastern Europe. But as a Germanic language, it was open to outside influences and could be easily attuned to modern ideas and sensitivities.

Until the mid-nineteenth century, Yiddish was the Ashkenazic vernacular widely used across Europe, from Amsterdam to Shklov and from Hamburg to Kraków. Yiddish books were historically published in such cities as Venice, Basel, Amsterdam, and Prague and distributed across Europe. From the seventeenth century on Yiddish became increasingly identified with Polish Jewry, which comprised, by the eighteenth century, more than half of the world's Jewish population. After the partitions of Poland in 1772–1795, the largest group of Yiddish speakers lived in the Russian empire, in the territories which today are part of Poland, Ukraine, Belarus, Lithuania, Latvia, and Moldova; the second largest group resided in the Austrian province of Galicia – today divided between Ukraine and Poland; Yiddish was also spoken in parts of today's Romania, Czech Republic, and Slovakia. Various dialects of Yiddish were used in many communities, predominantly rural, in Germany, France (Alsace and Lorraine), and Switzerland, but the rapid acculturation of Jews in those countries during the nineteenth century preempted the creation of what would become known as modern Yiddish culture.

Contrary to nation-states, such as France and Germany, authorities in the multi-cultural Habsburg and Romanov empires did not try to impose one national language on all their subjects. Yiddish was unique among the "national minority" languages, such as Belorussian, Ukrainian, or Lithuanian, because it was never spoken by a majority in any given territory, although in some towns with predominantly Jewish populations, such as Berdichev in Ukraine, it was widely used by Jews and non-Jews alike. With the rapid growth of Jewish emigration starting in the late nineteenth century, Yiddish was exported overseas. In some of the nation-states which emerged in 1918–1920 after the collapse of the imperial order in Central and Eastern Europe, Yiddish was reluctantly accorded official recognition as a minority language, but, with the exception of the Soviet Union until 1948, Yiddish culture received no support from the state. Yet despite its low status and the general poverty of its speakers, Yiddish literature boasted, during its peak period between the two World Wars, thousands of book editions, hundreds of periodicals, dozens of clubs and associations, and millions of readers. Yiddish literature was highly diverse in its ideological and religious outlook, its political loyalties, and aesthetic preferences. Nevertheless, one can justifiably regard it as a worldwide transnational cultural phenomenon, a kind of "virtual territory," to quote the American critic Borekh Ryvkin, stretching from the Birobidzhan taiga in the Russian Far East to the Argentine pampas and the South African bush, with major centers in Moscow, Kiev, Minsk, Warsaw, Vilnius, Lodz, Berlin, Paris, London, New York, Chicago, Montreal, Tel Aviv, Mexico City, Buenos Aires, and Melbourne.

THE HASKALAH BEGINNINGS

Built on three foundations – traditional Judaism, Eastern European Jewish folk culture, and European (in the first place, Russian and German, but also English and French) literary traditions – modern Yiddish literature was born at the turn of the nineteenth century under the impact of the Haskalah, the Jewish Enlightenment movement. It was the third component, the European cultural orientation, that differentiated modern Yiddish literature from its predecessor, which is often called, perhaps somewhat anachronistically, "old" Yiddish literature. Initially, education and propaganda of new ideas using European genres and styles among the masses were the chief reasons for and the justification of writing in the "jargon" (as Yiddish was referred to, often pejoratively, until the early twentieth century). The historian Simon Dubnov remembered the Odessa circle of major Yiddish and Hebrew writers of the late nineteenth century: "It was the general rule – Yiddish was written for the ordinary folk, whose language it was, but among themselves the intellectuals spoke the language of the country, Russian. Nobody in our circle thought of speaking Hebrew."[1] However, this widely held view has been challenged recently by the concept of "two discrete beginnings," which initiated, correspondingly, the "highbrow" maskilic and the "lowbrow" mass literature, each one with its own aesthetics and audience.[2] Although it is not always easy to draw a clear line between these two branches, the "highbrow" literature used more sophisticated literary devices, borrowed both from European culture and rabbinic tradition, whereas the "lowbrow" branch drew its expressive potential from folklore and popular religious books in Yiddish, as well as from European and Russian mass fiction.

The earliest examples of the "highbrow" modern Yiddish literature, such as the comedies *Laykhtzin un fremelay* (Lack of Seriousness and Hypocrisy, 1796) and *Reb Henekh, oder vos tut men dermit* (Reb Henekh, or, What Can Be Done with It?, 1792) by the Prussian maskilim and disciples of Moses Mendelssohn, Aaron Halle Wolfssohn (1754–1835) and Isaac Eichel (1756–1804), or the Yiddish version of the Hebrew novel *Megale temirin* (Revealer of Secrets, 1819) by the Galician maskil Joseph Perl (1773–1839), circulated in manuscripts among like-minded maskilim and remained unpublished until the twentieth century. They show clear orientation towards the European models of comedy and satire, whereas the folkloric elements signify the "backwardness" of Polish Jews as the object of ridicule. Many maskilim in Galicia and Ukraine regarded Yiddish as the language of their main enemy, Hasidism, and used it primarily in satire, parody, and comedy, the most popular genres of the new Yiddish literature in the first half of the nineteenth century. Yiddish thus served both as the linguistic vehicle and an object of mockery. This ambivalent attitude to the language made it suitable for use in dialogue and monologue, especially by characters who were objects of satire, but created problems when in the "high" register, in particular as the authoritative narrative voice in the novel. This

---

[1] Quoted in Joseph Leftwich, ed., *The Way We Think: A Collection of Essays from the Yiddish*, vol. 2 (South Brunswick, NJ: Thomas Yoseloff, 1969), 526.

[2] Alyssa Quint, "'Yiddish Literature for the Masses'?: A Reconsideration of Who Read What in Jewish Eastern Europe," *AJS Review* 29 (2005): 61–89.

challenge was successfully addressed by Shloyme Etinger (1803–1856) and Yisroel Aksenfeld (1787–1866). Etinger created in his comedy *Serkele* (1861) the first complex, albeit still negative, character in Yiddish literature – a nouveau-riche woman who is prepared to commit a crime out of love for her daughter. Inspired by a variety of sources, such as Molière and the popular playwrights of his time, August von Kotzebue in German and Alexander Fredro in Polish, Etinger shifted the focus of his satire from ideological to moral issues, offering a critical comment on the process of Jewish *embourgeoisement* in Galicia. The Soviet scholar Meir Wiener associated Etinger with the beginning of the "Polish" line in new Yiddish literature, more urban and bourgeois in its outlook and less radical in its critique of Hasidism.[3]

The "Ukrainian," or "Russian" line was initiated, according to Wiener, by Aksenfeld, a prolific novelist and playwright, most of whose work has been lost. Using the form of the picaresque novel and inspired by such diverse writers as the French novelist Giles Blas and the Ukrainian-Russian author Vasilii Narezhny, Aksenfeld created a whole fictional universe, modeled after his native Podolia, the historic Polish–Ottoman borderland and the cradle of Hasidism. This ingenious construction of an imaginary "Yiddishland" had a long life in Yiddish literature. Aksenfeld's generic shtetl, whose name Loyhoyopolye (No-such-ville) signified the precariousness of Jewish existence in Eastern Europe and became the prototype of various literary images of the shtetl as the archetypical Jewish space. But Aksenfeld's artistic imagination was not confined by the shtetl, and he took his characters – as we can see in his only surviving novel, *Dos shterntikhl* (The Headband, 1861) – as far as Breslau (today Wrocław in Poland), then in Prussia, exposing them to the ways and ideas of the Haskalah. Having served as a military supplier to the Russian army during the Napoleonic war of 1812–14, Aksenfeld developed a positive attitude to the Russian empire, which is evident in his representation of the Russian military in his works. But he was critical of the communal oligarchy and Hasidic tsaddikim (spiritual leaders) for their corruption and backwardness. The protagonist of *Dos shterntikhl* breaks with the oppressive regime of the shtetl, seizes the opportunity to see the world in the service of the Russian army, and returns to the shtetl to expose the machinations of the tsaddik and marry his sweetheart. The play *Der ershter yidisher rekrut* (The First Jewish Conscript, after 1828) presents a sad story of a poor folk poet who loses his verbal battle against the communal leadership and is sent off to military service, losing his freedom and his beloved. Apart from its great

[3] Meir Wiener, "Tsu der oysgabe," *Y. Aksenfelds verk*, vol. 1 (Kharkov: Literatur un kunst, 1931), viii.

value as a source of historical anthropology of the shtetl, this play touches upon many issues – such as the fate of a creative personality in a traditional society, social and moral justice, freedom of love – that would become central for future generations of Yiddish writers.

The first professional and best-selling Yiddish writer was Ayzik Meyer Dik (1807/14?–1893), who composed numerous didactic stories that were issued as chapbooks by the major Vilna publisher Romm, and were aimed at a mass readership. These stories combined gripping plots with rich ethnographic background, and extolled simple moral values. Dik criticized outlived customs such as underage marriages and men spending their time studying instead of supporting their families. His most productive period coincided with the reign of Tsar Alexander II (1856–1881), who liberalized public life and allowed a Jewish press in Russian, Hebrew, and Yiddish.

THE CLASSICAL TRIAD: MENDELE, SHOLEM ALEICHEM, PERETZ

Kol mevaser (Voice of Messenger), launched in 1862 by the energetic editor and shrewd businessman Alexander Zederbaum (1816–1893) as the Yiddish supplement to the Odessa Hebrew journal *Hamelits*, became the tribune for a new cohort of Yiddish writers. The most famous among them was Sholem Yankev Abramovitsh (1835–1917), by that time a young but already well-known Hebrew publicist. Dissatisfied with the limited expressive potential of Hebrew when it came to the depiction of real life, he invented the character of the itinerant book peddler Mendele Moykher Sforim, who became both his Yiddish literary persona and a hero of his fictions. The early novellas of the Mendele series, *Dos kleyne mentshele* (The Little Man, 1864), *Vintshfingerl* (The Magic Ring, 1865) and *Fishke der krumer* (Fishke the Lame, 1869), were written in the Volhynian Yiddish vernacular and carried a clear didactic message couched in an adventurous narrative. Building on Aksenfeld's legacy and more radical in his critique of the traditional Jewish community than Dik, Abramovitsh situated his works in and around the fictive town of Glupsk (Fooltown), based on Berdichev, the bustling commercial center of Volhynia where he himself resided during 1858–68. Using Mendele as a mediator between the maskilic writer and his intended mass readership, Abramovitsh was able to create a sophisticated artistic narrative style, resembling the French and the English novel of the late eighteenth and early nineteenth centuries.

Abramovitsh's Yiddish style matured in the 1870s, when the motifs of ambivalence and doubt regarding the feasibility of the Haskalah program became more pronounced in his fiction. The novel *Di klyatshe* (The Mare, 1873), written simultaneously in Yiddish and Hebrew versions, anticipates elements of modernist and even postmodernist writing, and remains one of the most sophisticated works of Jewish literature until today. Introduced to the reader as an edited and improved manuscript by Mendele the publisher, it is a confession of a young shtetl intellectual Yisrolik committed to the ideals of the Haskalah but unable, due to external social and internal psychological reasons, to carry them out. Having failed the graduation exams for the Russian gymnasium, he sinks into a mental abyss, turning into a medium for transmitting fears and anxieties about the general state of humanity and the particular situation of Jews in Europe. Written in a highly elaborate allegorical style which draws on the Bible, midrash, and the European tradition of the grotesque and satiric, the novel reflects on the inherent irrationality of human behavior in politics, culture, and daily life, anticipating the tragic turns that awakening nationalist ideologies will take in the future.

Yisrolik shares some psychological features with Binyomin, the hero of the last novel from the Mendele cycle (*Masoes Binyomin hashlishi*, Travels of Benjamin the Third, 1878). The familiar shtetl turf serves Abramovitsh as a launching pad for a satire cast as a story of an adventurous journey in search of the mythical Ten Tribes of Israel who would bring about redemption to Russian Jews. Set in the last years of Nicholas's I reign, the novel reflects on the sad state of Jewish communal life and its inability to adjust to modern conditions. But the main character, modeled after Don Quixote, however ridiculous in his medieval backwardness and naiveté, is nevertheless one of the most human and sympathetic in his idealism and determination. *Di klyatshe* and *Masoes Binyomin hashlishi* are recognized as Abramovitsh's finest achievements, but they also mark the aesthetic and intellectual limitations of his concept of Yiddish literature based on the fictive construct of Mendele as the mediator between the intellectual author and his folk audience. At the turn of the 1880s, Abramovitsh experienced a severe personal crisis, which was exacerbated by the outburst of antisemitic violence of 1881–82. In Odessa, where he moved in 1881 from the provincial town of Zhitomir to assume the directorship of a modern-style Jewish school, he found himself among the new intellectual elite engaged in forging new ideologies of Zionism and Diaspora nationalism. Abramovitsh spent the rest of his writing career – nearly forty years – revising and polishing his earlier works, translating them from Yiddish into Hebrew and updating them according to new ways of thinking and new literary standards, and also writing his memoirs. His Yiddish style, initially based on the spoken dialect of Volhynia, now sounded coarse and uncultivated, and was replaced by a more universal version of literary Yiddish with fewer slavicisms and less local color.

Two other important writers of that last generation of the Russian Haskalah, Yitskhok Yoyel Linetsky (1839–1915) and Avrom Goldfaden (1840–1908), also started their literary careers in *Kol mevaser*. Famous and popular in their day, today they look less accomplished intellectually and aesthetically than Abramovitsh. Linetsky's major work is a hilarious satire *Dos poylishe yingl* (The Polish Boy, 1867), a burlesque pseudo-autobiography filled with sharp criticism of Hasidic customs, which was reprinted about thirty times. Linetsky introduced a naive childish narrative persona as an instrument of social and moral critique, which would have many reincarnations in Yiddish literature, from Sholem Aleichem to Itsik Manger. Goldfaden began as a poet in Yiddish and Hebrew but became famous for his transformation of Yiddish theater, turning it from the medium of maskilic propaganda and social critique into entertainment with song and music. He was particularly popular in the southern provinces of the Russian empire and in Romania, where Jews had been actively involved in the local musical culture that became known as klezmer.

The next important stage in the institutional development of Yiddish literature was the creation of literary almanacs and anthologies, modeled on the Russian "thick" journal devoted to literature and social issues with sections dedicated to prose, poetry, essays, memoirs, literary criticism, and opinion pieces. The most ambitious project of this kind, *Yidishe folks-bibliotek* (Jewish Folk Library), was launched by the young Kiev writer Solomon Rabinovitsh (1859–1916) who took as his pen-name the traditional Yiddish greeting "sholem aleichem" (literally – "peace upon you"). His goal was to bring under one cover the best of "serious" Yiddish writing in different genres which would form a canon of the emerging Yiddish literature. Part of this task was to exclude those authors who did not fit the editor's criteria of genuine "folk literature," most notably Shomer (pseudonym of Nokhem Meyer Shaykevitch, 1849?–1905), arguably the most commercially successful author of what Sholem Aleichem dismissed as "*shund*" – "trash." Sholem Aleichem's own contribution to this volume was the novel *Stempenyu* (1888), which was intended to serve as a model of a new "Jewish novel," educational and entertaining romance addressed to the younger shtetl readership. Although this enterprise collapsed after the second volume, when Sholem Aleichem lost his fortune and had to flee Kiev, it left a lasting formative impact on Yiddish literature. Apart from introducing strict aesthetic and moral criteria, Sholem Aleichem invented the paradigm of "classical triad," which in his version included Abramovitsh as the grandfather and Linetski and Goldfaden as founding fathers. By the early twentieth century the two latter authors gave way to Sholem Aleichem and Y. L. Peretz.

Unlike Abramovitsh's Mendele, whose influence Sholem Aleichem gladly acknowledged but also politely dismissed by bestowing upon him the venerable title of the "grandfather of Yiddish literature," Sholem Aleichem's narrative persona was not an active character but a passive mediator between the crowd of shtetl Jews eager to tell their stories and an urbane and sophisticated readership. His most memorable characters are the hyperactive entrepreneur Menakhem-Mendl, who is perpetually engaged in business enterprises which inevitably end up in failure, and the patriarchal raconteur Tevye, who is equally unfortunate in his attempts to control his daughters' fate but takes his failures with resignation bolstered by quotations from the staple Jewish sources in his own subversive interpretation. Despite the difference in temperament, both are equally incapable of comprehending and responding to the challenges of modernity as the source of their misery. To amplify the effect of the characters' immediate presence, Sholem Aleichem employed the genres of monologue (for Tevye) and letters (for Menakhem-Mendel), publishing these works in series over the course of more than fifteen years.

Although Menachem-Mendl and Tevye traced their literary genealogy to Binyomin and Mendele, they belonged to a different age, when the combined forces of capitalist development and increasing political antisemitism were quickly destroying the traditional fabric of shtetl life, turning it into a dream. The new synthetic image of the shtetl, which combined irony and nostalgia, was developed in the cycle of stories about Kasrilevke, an imaginary shtetl modeled on Voronkov in Ukraine, where Sholem Aleichem spent his childhood. By creating this generic shtetl with a mocking name carrying biblical connotations (Kasri-el means "God is my crown"), Sholem Aleichem gestured towards the tradition of Aksenfeld and Mendele. But his Kasrilevke, although rich in ethnographic detail, was less real than their Loyhoyopolye or Tuneyadevke – thus indicating that the shtetl was no longer the real center of Jewish life. The existential precariousness of the shtetl was made even clearer in Sholem Aleichem's two later masterpieces, *Di ayznban-geshikhtes* (The Railway Stories, 1902–09) and *Motl, Peysi dem khazns* (Motl, the Cantor's Son, 1907–14) both of which reflect on the theme of the decline of the shtetl in the wake of the failed 1905 revolution and ensuing pogroms. While the former cycle of monologues, told in the third-class coaches of the trains crisscrossing the Pale, emphasizes the fragmentation of Jewish life, the latter tackles the new theme of the mass emigration of Russian Jews to America. The mask of Sholem Aleichem as a ubiquitous listener, capable of translating the diverse voices of simple Ukrainian Jews into a smooth and elegant Yiddish prose, lends itself easily to different, sometimes opposing interpretations. While the Marxist critics, such as Meir Wiener and Max Erik, praised his ability to capture in great detail the decline of the Jewish petty bourgeoisie under the pressure of advancing capitalism, others, such as the Polish critic Y. Y. Trunk, valued him for the creation of supra-historical, archetypal characters which embodied the core qualities of the Jewish collective psyche; this view has been elaborated upon by such contemporary interpreters of Sholem Aleichem as Dan Miron, Ruth Wisse, and David Roskies.

Today the figure of Sholem Aleichem overshadows two other writers of his age, who also had a substantial impact on the formation of modern Yiddish literature. Yankev Dinezon (1856?–1919) made his name in literature with the bestselling melodramatic adventure romance *Ha-ne'ehavim veha-ne'imim, oder der shvartser yungermantshik* (The Beloved and the Pleasant, or the Black Young Man, 1877), and later produced several sentimental novellas about orphans (Sholem Aleichem once jokingly called him "the father of all orphans in Yiddish literature"), which appealed especially to a female readership. Mordkhe Spektor (1858–1925) was an accurate if not very imaginative chronicler of Jewish life of his age, responding to major social developments, such as agricultural colonization (*Der yidisher muzhik*, The Jewish Peasant, 1883) and pogroms, as well as faithfully recording the vicissitudes of shtetl life. He was one of the first authors to give voice to young Jewish women, turning them into a medium of his moderate social critique. Spektor edited a serialized almanac of Yiddish literature, *Der hoyzfraynd* (The House Friend, 1888–1896), which proved more stable than Sholem Aleichem's endeavor and played a major role in creating a mass readership for Yiddish literature.

The third member of the classical triad, Yitskhok Leybush Peretz (1852–1915), made his Yiddish debut in Sholem Aleichem's *Yidishe folksbibliotek* with the poem "Monish," a playful and ironic ballad about a young Talmudic prodigy seduced by a beautiful young woman sent by the devil. To Peretz's dismay, the poem was substantially edited by Sholem Aleichem to fit his notion of *folksliteratur*. In a letter to Sholem Aleichem, Peretz explained the fundamental difference between their visions of Yiddish literature: whereas Sholem Aleichem sought to provide ethical and aesthetical guidance to simple Jews who "speak jargon in jargon-land," Peretz was writing primarily for his own pleasure, having in mind an audience with a "higher level" of culture, familiar with other literatures in "living tongues" (Yiddish apparently did not belong to that category).[4] Peretz regarded Sholem Aleichem as a humorist, "our Mark Twain," rather than a serious writer interested in the problems faced by modern Jews.

Born in the historic Polish town of Zamosc on the western border of the Russian empire and educated in the rigorous spirit of Talmudic Judaism,

[4] Nachman Meisel, ed., *Briv and redes fun Y. L. Peretz* (New York: YKUF, 1944), 139.

Peretz had little personal exposure to Hasidism and the shtetl way of life. Much of his thinking about life and literature came from Polish, German, and French books which he read unsystematically in his youth. His first major Yiddish work, *Bilder fun a provints-rayze in tomashover poviat um 1890 yor* (Impressions of a Journey through the Tomaszów Region in 1890; 1891), was an impressionistic reportage about the shtetlekh of Eastern Poland, which he visited as a data collector for a statistical expedition. Peretz depicted the miserable condition of the shtetl as a compassionate outsider, always aware of the deep cultural and social divide between himself (not to mention his readers) as an educated middle-class urban Jew and the impoverished, "backward" shtetl population. Unlike Mendele and Sholem Aleichem, Peretz did not try to invent an "authentic" mediating narrative voice that would help him bridge that gap. In his later Yiddish works Peretz became increasingly fascinated and, indeed, enchanted by Hasidic folklore, but his narrative persona remained quintessentially modern. Breaking with the maskilic tradition of satire, he represented Hasidism in neo-romantic style, focusing on its spiritual and psychological aspects rather than on social reality. Although initially sympathetic to socialist ideals, Peretz became increasingly skeptical of the tactics of the growing Jewish socialist movement, which he perceived as a threat to Jewish unity. In his plays, most famously *Di goldene keyt* (The Golden Chain, 1903) and *Bay nakht afn altn mark* (A Night in the Old Marketplace, 1907), which paved the way for the avant-garde Yiddish theater, he invented a new symbolist language for the stage representation of metaphysical conflicts between time and eternity, death and life, destruction and redemption.

Unlike the peripatetic Sholem Aleichem, who spent much of his life in Western Europe and America, Peretz spent his entire Yiddish career in Warsaw. His home became the place of pilgrimage for aspiring young talents who came to seek his blessing, while his charismatic personality and innovative style had a major influence on the new generation of Yiddish writers, whose formative years coincided with the period of the failed Russian revolution of 1905. The wave of pogroms, which started in Kishinev during the Easter of 1903 and peaked in the autumn of 1905, radicalized Jewish youth and sent a new wave of mass emigration overseas; Peretz was deeply troubled by both developments. Most of the young Yiddish writers shared socialist ideals, and their active engagement in politics went hand in hand with the growing interest in contemporary Russian and European culture, which radicalized, both ideologically and aesthetically, Yiddish literature. Political parties and movements, from Russian and Polish Social-Democrats to Zionists, turned to Yiddish as a language for the propaganda of their ideas among the growing Yiddish-speaking working class.

YIDDISH MEETS MODERNITY

Yiddish literature also became increasingly prominent in the emergent Jewish public sphere. *Der yud* (The Jew, 1899–1903), a Kraków-based Zionist semi-weekly paper with a broad cultural agenda, introduced a new generation of writers to the Yiddish readership. It was purchased by the first daily newspaper, *Der fraynd*, which began to appear in St. Petersburg in 1903 and moved to Warsaw in 1908, the largest Jewish city and the major center of Yiddish cultural life in Europe. The Czernowitz conference of 1908, a gathering of cultural activists and writers, which declared Yiddish a Jewish national language (along with Hebrew) and set up an agenda for a future construction of Yiddish culture, was instrumental symbolically in the public recognition of the growing status of Yiddish.

The major figure in the younger generation of Yiddish writers who debuted in *Der yud* and *Der fraynd* was Sholem Asch (1880–1957). His prose "poema" *A shtetl* (1904) presented a highly idealized and romanticized vision of the shtetl as a harmonious ensemble, in which each social group plays its own "melody"; this work was warmly received by some Russian critics who contrasted Asch's "authentic" voice to the "flat" and "characterless" style of Russian Jewish writers. The play *Got fun nekome* (God of Vengeance, 1907) tackled such "scandalous" issues as Jewish prostitution, brothel keeping, and lesbian love, and became an instantaneous success on the Russian and German stage. In his first novel *Meri* (1907), Asch critically portrayed the assimilated Russian-Jewish bourgeoisie and intelligentsia of St. Petersburg, which reflected his love/hate relationship with Russian culture. On the eve of World War I he moved to the US and soon became the most popular and versatile American Yiddish novelist. His themes ranged from the massacre of Jews in seventeenth-century Ukraine (*Af kidesh hashem*) to the life of Jewish immigrants in New York (*Uncle Moses*). By using a variety of styles, from neo-romanticism to sentimentalism and critical realism, Asch appealed to different audiences, but always remained in touch with popular concerns of the day. Never afraid of taboo themes, he showed interest in and sympathy for Christianity, and continued to write about sexuality.

On the opposite end of the post-1905 literary spectrum was another Polish writer, Itshe-Meir Vaysenberg (1881–1938). In his meticulously crafted naturalist novella, "A shtetl," which some critics perceived as a critical response to Asch's idealized image, Vaysenberg presented an anatomy of social conflicts that tore apart the already frayed fabric of the shtetl society. He portrayed shtetl Jews as primitives driven by elemental instincts and unable to adjust to the changing world around them. The moral and economical decline of the shtetl was exacerbated by the impact of the revolutionary propaganda that came from Warsaw. Contrary to both Asch and Vaysenberg, the Ukrainian David Bergelson (1884–1952) positioned himself as an elitist writer who preferred perfection to popularity. In meticulously crafted impressionist prose, Bergelson chronicled the slow decline of the upper crust of the shtetl society, exposing, through the minute details of everyday life and nuances of mood and behavior, the depressive and empty character of the shtetl existence. Mirl, the heroine of his first novel *Nokh alemen* (The End of Everything, 1913), was the first modern young woman to become the main character of a Yiddish novel. Unlike his predecessors, who used conventional techniques of first- and third-person narration, Bergelson blurred the borders between the narrative voice and the characters' inner monologues, creating a continuous narrative stream that anticipates the stream-of-consciousness technique of Virginia Woolf and James Joyce. Influenced by Turgenev, Chekhov, and Knut Hamsun, Bergelson artistically recreated the situation of young men and women who were born and raised in the shtetl and dreamt of a new life in the world of big cities, but remained forever stuck in-between. In his pre-revolutionary novellas and second novel, *Der opgang* (Descent, 1918), he dealt with the same themes of alienation, depression, and eventual self-destruction of sensible and educated young men and women in the stifling atmosphere of the shtetl.

On the eve of World War I Bergelson gained recognition as the most accomplished Yiddish stylist; his Kiev associates were a small circle of young writers and poets, among them the enigmatic symbolist Pinkhes Kahanovitsh (1884–1950), known under the pen-name Der Nister (The Hidden One, an allusion to the concept of a hidden tsaddik), the author of mystical tales suffused with kabbalistic imagery and sublimated eroticism, as well as the symbolist poets Osher Shvartsman (1890–1919) and Dovid Hofshteyn (1889–1952), who later became known as the Kiev Group. They positioned themselves as the aesthetic and social opposition to the dominant trends in Hebrew and Yiddish culture, which they criticized for its nationalist and bourgeois outlook.

YIDDISH COMES TO AMERICA

"Yiddish literature in America has its own history, its own genesis; it is neither a continuation of the old Yiddish literature in Russia, nor has its development been affected by the newest Russian Yiddish literature," proclaimed Leon Kobrin (1872–1946), one of the most prolific American Yiddish authors, in 1910[5] (this view, however, was vehemently contested by

[5] Leon Kobrin, *Gezamlte shriftn* (New York: Hebrew Publishing Company, 1910), i.

European writers and critics). Yiddish culture made an energetic start in America in the late 1880s, and by the beginning of the twentieth century it already had a flourishing network of newspapers, publishing houses, theaters, and political and cultural institutions with its center on the Lower East Side of Manhattan. Immigrant intellectuals, many of whom were former maskilim, quickly realized the commercial potential of Yiddish literature in the city with a rapidly growing immigrant population, and began to churn out numerous novels which soon became popular on both sides of the Atlantic. The American poets of the first generation – Dovid Edelshtat (1866–1892), Joseph Bovshover (1873–1915), Morris Rosenfeld (1862–1923), and Morris Vinchevsky (1856–1932) – responded to the inhuman working and living conditions of the immigrant Jewish workers by creating new "proletarian" poetry, taking as their model German and Russian revolutionary poetry. By the beginning of the twentieth century, American Jewish immigration had its own chroniclers who portrayed the daily experience of Eastern European newcomers in numerous newspaper sketches, plays, and novels, written in the tradition of nineteenth-century European realism.

Unhappy about the state of Yiddish literature in America, which in their view was subordinated to commercial or ideological interests, a group of younger writers in New York came up with an aesthetic program that emphasized the artistic aspect of literature. All but one of them came from Russia, where they became acquainted with new modernist trends such as symbolism and impressionism as well as with revolutionary ideas. The moving force behind the Di Yunge group was Dovid Ignatov (1886–1954), a prose writer who embraced America as a country that would rejuvenate the Jews as an ancient people by bringing them close to the eternal biblical foundation of their spirituality. Drawing from Russian symbolism, as well as from his own Hasidic legacy, Ignatov set out to forge a new Yiddish symbolic idiom that would be adequate to the vast scope of America. His characters were young men and women trying to square the circle between Jewish spirituality, socialist idealism, and American modernity. The trilogy *Oyf vayte vegn* (On Far-Away Ways, 1932), a Yiddish version of the "great American novel," covers the most dynamic period in American Jewish history between the early 1880s and 1917. Set against the broad background of the Eastern European Jewish immigrant society, it follows the transformations of the charismatic protagonist Berman from a Russian revolutionary to an American labor organizer, to a religious preacher trying to return Jews back to their spiritual roots but defeated by the forces of American capitalism. A writer with a rich but sometimes bizarre imagination, Ignatov is remembered today mostly for his role as the organizer and publisher of Di Yunge, while his ambitious novels are largely forgotten even by literary scholars.

Another major novelist to emerge from the Di Yunge circle was Joseph Opatoshu (1886–1954). His first major work, the short novel *Fun nyu-yorker geto*, was a naturalist study set in an ethnically mixed area of the Bronx, which conveyed its tense atmosphere by using the coarse American Yiddish vernacular, mixed with English and Italian. In *Roman fun a ferd-ganef* (Romance of a Horse Thief, 1912), Opatoshu followed the criminal career of a young man engaged in smuggling horses across the Russian–German border during the Russo-Japanese war. Opatoshu soon abandoned this naturalism in favor of a more complex psychological realism. In the novel *Hebrew* (1920) he explored the anxieties of young bohemian intellectuals who make their living as Hebrew school teachers, and are frustrated by the inadequacy of Jewish education in America and depressed by their own low social status. The third and the most ambitious novel of Opatoshu's New York cycle, *Arum grend-strit* (Around Grand Street, 1929; published also under the title, *Di tentserin*, The Female Dancer), depicts the fortunes of a group of Polish Jewish immigrants in New York and New Jersey before World War I. The novel came out in two editions, in Kharkov and Vilna, but was never published in book form in the US – a fact that points to the remarkably transnational character of Yiddish literature at that time. While Ignatov was primarily interested in spirituality and ideas, Opatoshu was fascinated by human instincts, conflicts, and material interests. Both authors examined the transformation of familiar old-world Jewish characters in America, and both come up with a dark prognosis regarding the sustainability of *yidishkayt* in either religious or national form. Opatoshu's life-long interest in Jewish history resulted in the trilogy *In poylishe velder* (In Polish Woods, 1921), *1863* (1926) and *Aleyn* (Alone, 1919), which traces the story of two generations of a Polish Jewish family from the Polish uprising against Russian rule of 1863–64 to the early twentieth century, as well as in the novella *A tog in Regensburg* (A Day in Regensburg, 1933), set in one of the greatest medieval German Jewish communities on the eve of the expulsion of 1519. In his last novel, *Der letster oyfshtand* (The Last Revolt, 1955), Opatoshu examined ideological, religious, social, and cultural tensions in Jewish society in Roman Palestine in the second century CE on the eve of the Bar Kokhba rebellion.

Although a few other writers associated with Di Yunge produced fine works of prose which explored the vicissitudes of acculturation (Morris Haimowitz) or the experience of Jewish farmers and frontiersmen (Isaac Raboy), the group came to be associated with the creation of modernist poetry with a distinct American flavor. At a time when Yiddish poetry in Europe lagged behind prose in terms of originality, the American poets

Mani Leib, M. L. Halpern, H. Leyvick, A. Leyeles, Zishe Landoy, and others invented a fluid and rich poetical language. Influenced by Russian symbolism and acmeism, those poets sought perfection of form, harmony between sound, melody, and imagery. They were aesthetic aristocrats, even though most of them came from humble shtetl backgrounds and supported themselves in America by manual labor. But Di Yunge was not a group bound by a shared program, and its members soon went in different directions. Perhaps the most impressive achievement of that moment in Yiddish literary history was the collection *In New York* (1919) by Moishe Leib Halpern (1886–1932). Born in the Austrian province of Galicia, Halpern spent a few years in Vienna before immigrating to America, and his poetic style was closer to German Expressionism than to Russian symbolism. Arranged according to the hours of the day, *In New York* opens with short fragments which present a dark picture of the American urban "soulscape" as it is experienced by the disturbed clown Moishe Leib, the poetic persona of the author. The personal nightmare of dislocation and alienation grows out of control in the later parts, culminating in the apocalyptic final part *A Night* (written as a separate poem in 1916), in which the vision of the destruction of Jewish life in Europe merges with the narrator's own erasure from life. By breaking with the poetics of Di Yunge, with its balance and harmony, and introducing his own, coarse and subversive, voice, Halpern became the single most influential American Yiddish poet. In contrast to the mercurial and depressive Halpern, H. Leyvick (1888–1962), perhaps the most celebrated American Yiddish poet during his lifetime, cultivated a lofty prophetic persona, addressing big issues in a way that combined modernist sensitivity to poetic form with a strong moralist stand. His revolutionary youth in Russia and imprisonment in Siberia, followed by his escape, partly on foot, across Russia to America, provided him with a rich reservoir of imagery and metaphors from which to draw. Leyvick's major achievement from that period was the dramatic poem *Golem*, a neo-romantic rendition of one of the most popular legends of Jewish folklore, which resonated with the tragic spirit of the revolutionary age. Written under the influence of Peretz, this poem was a popular choice for stage adaptations by avant-garde Yiddish and Hebrew theater companies around the world. Although not a member of any group, Anna Margolin (Rosa Lebensboim, 1887–1952) engaged in daring poetic experimentations casting her lyric persona in a variety of images, from a handsome boy to Mary, the mother of Jesus. Always exquisite in form, her poems create an imaginary world filled with anxiety, loneliness, and longing for love.

Halpern was a source of inspiration for proletarian poets engaged in class struggle as well as for a new group, *In zikh*, which brought Yiddish poetry closer to Anglo-American modernism, with its free forms and rhythms and emphasis on the freedom of individual expression. The *Inzikhistn* rejected the "over-refinement" of poetic diction by Di Yunge in favor of immediacy and individuality. The new group, formed around the "small" literary journal designed after an American rather than Russian model of literary periodical, included poets of a different poetic temperament and outlook.

Two major *inzikhist* poets, Yankev Glatshteyn (1896–1971) and A. Leyeles (Aaron Glantz, 1889–1966), were less keen on grand themes and ideas. More at home in American culture, they sought to register the nuances of confused experiences, focusing on the tension between an often-suppressed Eastern European past and the present situation amidst the labyrinth of the biggest American metropolis. Instead of using language as a means of engaging with reality, they tried to reach to the depth of their own psyche and reproduce its voice through kaleidoscope sounds and images, sometimes even before they took the shape of words.

America opened new opportunities for women writers who by the early twentieth century came to occupy a significant place in Yiddish letters. Newspaper editors of different ideological persuasions welcomed women as contributors of short topical fiction which attracted female readers. This fiction was modern in themes and concerns but not modernist in form and style. As a rule, Yiddish women writers had received a secular education in Europe and were well read in world literature. In their Yiddish works they often used stylistic devices and plot constructions from contemporary European literature, but rarely ventured into modernist experimentation given their dependence on the taste of their editors and readers. This trend is exemplified by Kadia Molodowsky (1884–1975), who made her name as a modernist Yiddish poet in Poland and immigrated to the US where she worked as a teacher and wrote numerous sketches for the Yiddish daily *Der tog*. A keen and sympathetic observer, Molodowsky was attentive to the social dynamics of New York Jews as they made it into the middle class and consequently moved from dense ethnic enclaves to mixed neighborhoods. She favored energetic heroines who asserted their independence against the still powerful conventions of the *landsmanshaft* (hometown society) culture.

DILEMMAS OF THE INTERWAR PERIOD

A breakthrough in Yiddish poetry occurred in Eastern Europe in the wake of World War I. Until then its tone was largely elegiac and melancholic, rhymes and meters conventional, and themes confined to bewailing the miserable condition of Jews and the longing for the lost patriarchal idyll of the shtetl. Now it had to find a new language to respond to the unprecedented violence and destruction that befell Eastern European Jewry. The most innovative were the poets of the Kiev group who, partly inspired by Di Yunge, sought to emancipate the poetic individual from the obligation to serve as a spokesman for the national or religious community. They placed emphasis on individual emotion and imagination, but did not break from Jewish religious traditions completely, drawing their vocabulary and imagery from such sources as Kabbalah, Hasidism, and folklore. Other sources of inspiration came from Russian literature, such as Pushkin for Hofshteyn and Mayakovsky for Perets Markish (1895–1952). They embraced the messianic ideal of the revolution as redemption, but not the Bolshevik concept of the dictatorship of the proletariat, which by the early 1920s drove many of them into temporary emigration to Central Europe. Most of them moved to Berlin, where Jewish modernism in Yiddish and Hebrew came in close contact with contemporary German and Russian cultures. The brief period of 1921–25, when Berlin served as home to such diverse figures as the Yiddish writers Bergelson, Der Nister, Moishe Kulbak, the Hebrew poets Bialik, Zalman Schneour, Shaul Tchernikhovsky, and the artists Marc Chagall, El Lissitzky, and Boris Aronson, was the last time in Jewish cultural history that Yiddish and Hebrew literary spheres creatively interacted. By the late 1920s, Yiddish became identified with Ashkenazi Jewish life in the Diaspora, whereas Hebrew came to serve the cultural needs of the Zionist project in Palestine.

The newly reconstituted Polish state incorporated a number of Jewish centers which previously belonged to the Russian or Austro-Hungarian empires, such as Vilnius, Warsaw, Lodz, Białystok and Lwów (formerly Lemberg). After three years of terrifying war experience in the Balkans, Uri Tsevi Grinberg (1896–1981) emerged as the major Yiddish expressionist voice, not dissimilar to Halpern's, in his apocalyptic meditations on the fate of European Christian civilization and Jews: *Mefisto* (1921) and *In malkhes fun tseylem* (In the Kingdom of Cross, 1923). Having miraculously escaped death at the hands of Polish legionnaires in his native Lwów, he moved to Warsaw and formed, together with Markish, Melekh Ravich, and Israel Joshua Singer, a radical literary group known as Di Khalyastre (The Gang). They rejected traditional bourgeois ideas of beauty and propriety, often in a provocative and scandalous way. Grinberg's expressionist Yiddish period came to an end in Berlin in 1923, when he switched to Hebrew and moved to Tel Aviv. In his angry farewell manifesto he accused Europe of mistreating its Jews and ignoring their culture, and predicted a new catastrophe. In his analysis of the Jewish situation in Europe, Grinberg rhetorically considered – but then dismissed in favor of Zionism – communism as an option for the Jews of Europe.

The Soviet option was most clearly articulated in Bergelson's essay "Three Centers" (1926) as the most promising one for the future of the Jewish people and Yiddish literature. The return of Kvitko, Markish, Hofshteyn, Der Nister, and Bergelson, as well as the immigration to the Soviet Union of the poet Moyshe Kulbak and the scholars Max Erik and Meir Wiener during 1925–1934 brought new creative and intellectual energy to Soviet Yiddish culture. The state sponsorship of Yiddish as one of the officially recognized minority languages offered writers, scholars, artists, and actors a stable income and respectable social status in exchange for their loyalty to the communist ideology and aesthetics. The first significant prose work of Soviet Yiddish prose was a short novel, *Khadoshim un teg* (Months and Days, 1926), by the Ukrainian author Itsik Kipnis (1896–1974), who was introduced to Yiddish literature by Hofshteyn. Narrated by a tanner's apprentice, it is a romantic love story set against the background of the gruesome pogrom experience in a shtetl during the civil war written in a style that alternates between sophistication and naiveté. Drawing on Sholem Aleichem's children stories, Kipnis contrasts the idyllic joys of youthful love to the fear and horror of violence and murder. Although conforming to the official history – the bandits are chased away by a Red Army unit, which the narrator joins in the end – the book was nevertheless criticized for its vague ideology.

The period of relative freedom of expression, when modernist styles different from the officially promoted "proletarian realism" were still tolerated, came to an end by 1929. That "year of great break," as it became known in Soviet history, still saw several remarkable publications, such as the collection *Figurn oyfn rand* (Figures on the Fringe) by Shmuel Godiner (1892?–1942), which portrayed assorted characters who were pushed to the social margins by the consolidation of Soviet society, ranging from a Chabad Hasid selling cigarettes on the streets of Moscow to a heroic Red Army commander sentenced to death for embezzling state money, and the short novel *Ele Falik's untergang*, a tragic story of a young man in pre-war Kraków written in the style of Viennese psychological modernism by Meir Wiener (1893–1941), a brilliant student of Hebrew mystical literature who emigrated from Vienna to the Soviet Union attracted by the new opportunities in Marxist Yiddish scholarship. The most remarkable piece that captured the uncanny atmosphere of the time was the novella "Unter a ployt" (Under a Fence), the last symbolist work by Der Nister. This parable tells a story of a scholar who betrayed his vocation to become a circus performer under the control of a sadistic dominatrix Lily (Lilith). Using enigmatic symbolist language and a deliberately confusing style, it portrays, in a series of nightmarish visions, the process of disintegration of a creative personality under the pressure of a hostile environment. Even uncannier than the story itself was the critical campaign against its author, which in an eerie way replayed Der Nister's dark fantasy in real life. No longer able to publish his symbolist works, he was nevertheless allowed to earn his living by translations and journalism; at the same time he began working on a realist novel in the tradition of the European family saga.

A similar trajectory from experimental modernism to more traditional realism can be traced through the works of Moyshe Kulbak (1896–1935). His short novels *Moshiekh ben Efraim* (Messiah, the Son of Ephraim, 1924) and *Montog* (Monday, 1926) and poetry of the early 1920s, were a complex blend of expressionism, primitivism, and symbolism, and they earned him a great fame among young readers. Dissatisfied by the political and social conditions in Poland, he moved to Soviet Minsk in 1928, where he wrote his major novel *Zelmenyaner* (1931–1935), a mock epic story of an extended Jewish family's adjustment to Soviet city life. Kulbak's irony, sharp eye for detail, and ability to create memorable characters by mixing old and new idioms, make this novel the most accomplished portrayal of Soviet Jewish life of the interwar period. The last Yiddish writer to return to the Soviet Union was Bergelson, who was forced out of Berlin by the Nazis in 1933. A superb stylist and keen psychologist, he explored the precarious condition of uprooted fellow émigrés in Berlin, while eagerly looking for new characters in revolutionary Russia. The novel *Midas hadin* (A Stern Judgment, 1927) became a daring experiment at writing a new revolutionary novel. By choosing a Gentile Red Army commander as the messianic revolutionary hero and portraying most of the Jewish characters as active or passive enemies of the revolution, Bergelson made a radical gesture toward Soviet ideology, although his narrative technique remained largely modernist and his metaphoric language rooted in Jewish mystical symbolism. In his next and last major work, the autobiographical novel *Baym Dniepr* (At the Dnieper, 1932–40), Bergelson set out to settle accounts with his personal past as part of the disappeared world of the pre-revolutionary shtetl.

By the end of the 1920s, prose regained its dominant position in Yiddish literature worldwide. Its main market was Poland, which had a developed network of publishers, press, and educational and cultural institutions, many of which were also affiliated with political parties and movements. Young writers took up naturalism, inaugurated by Vaysenberg and Opatoshu, as a style most suitable for the representation of the disastrous effects of the war. The most accomplished examples of this style are the two novels by Oyzer Varshavski (1898–1944), *Shmugliars* (Smugglers, 1920) and *Shnitsayt* (Harvest Time, 1926), which chronicle the German occupation of Poland in 1915–18 and the ensuing decomposition of the traditional shtetl. Varshavski created the effect of immediate presence by shifting the narrative perspective between different voices, using fragmented dialectical speech, which enabled him to convey an increasing sense of fear, confusion and disorientation. In a similarly gloomy mood, but in a style that mixes high-brow expressionism with sensationalist "shund," Yisroel Rabon (1900–1941) portrayed in *Di gas* (The Street, 1928) the alienation of a nameless Jewish soldier who returned from the Polish–Soviet war only to find himself homeless and jobless in a hostile and alien city (modeled after Rabon's native Lodz). The naturalist trend found its further development in the shtetl novels of Mikhoel Burshtin (1897–1945), Shimon Horonchik (1889–1939), and Leyb Rashkin (1903?–1939), whereas the expressionist line was developed by Isaac Bashevis and Aron Tseytlin, who employed mystical imagery and allegory to respond critically to the modern situation of Jews in Poland and elsewhere. Alter-Sholem Kacyzne (1885–1941), today known for his photographic images of Polish Jewish life, which appeared on the pages of the illustrated supplement to the *Forverts*, was also a prominent playwright, journalist, and writer, who considered himself a follower of Peretz. His major work, the monumental novel *Shtarke un shvakhe* (The Strong and The Weak, 1929–1930), presents a kaleidoscopic panorama of different Jewish milieus in Poland around the time of World War I.

In the international arena Yiddish literature was personified by Sholem Asch, who achieved worldwide fame with his trilogy, *Three Cities*, about the Russian revolution (1927–33). A key to this success was the adoption of the Tolstoyan model of the epic novel that combined panoramic description of cataclysmic historic events with memorable personal character lines. The trilogy's protagonist, Zachary Mirkin, the alienated son of a Russian Jewish industrialist, was modeled after Pierre Besuhoff from *War and Peace*. He drifted through time and space, observing but not actively participating in the events that changed the world. The first novel, *Petersburg*, took the reader to the privileged Jewish bourgeoisie of the pre-revolutionary Russian capital. This egoistic, deracinated, and decadent milieu was contrasted with the more "authentic" and genial Warsaw Jewry portrayed in the second novel, *Warsaw*. The third novel, *Moscow*, which depicted the revolutionary events of 1917, was least convincing – perhaps due to the fact that Asch was familiar neither with the events nor with the location. The trilogy was the first Yiddish book to get a full front-page review in the *New York Times*; it also earned Asch a medal from the Polish government, which he accepted despite the protests from many corners of the Yiddish world, and which made him persona non grata in the USSR. The next novel, written according to the same recipe, *Baym opgrunt* (At the Abyss, in English translation: The War Goes On, 1936), was set in Berlin during the hyperinflation of 1923 and explored the roots of Nazism; it received a lukewarm reception.

A much greater success was the novel *Thilim-yid* (The Sayer of Psalms; in English translation: Salvation, 1934), which some scholars today consider Asch's most important "canonical" work. Essentially a largely extended version of "A Shtetl," the novel celebrates the traditional Jewish spirituality embodied in the main character, a simple devout Jew. Asch created a sympathetic character of a simple "saint" that would appeal to both a Jewish and Christian popular sense of spirituality, a gesture that can be seen as a response to the rise of antisemitism and Nazism in Central Europe. His next ambitious project, the "Christological" trilogy, caused the biggest controversy in modern Yiddish culture. The first novel, *Der man fun Natseres* (The Nazarene, 1938) which told the story of Jesus from a Jewish point of view, was a great success among liberal Protestant and Catholic audiences, but was harshly rejected by many Yiddish critics, who accused Asch of betraying his people and preaching Christianity. This was certainly not his intention. *The Nazarene* was Asch's artistic response to the crisis of European humanism: by reclaiming Jesus as a Jewish tsaddik, Asch wanted to remind readers of the common spiritual foundation of the Judeo-Christian civilization. Although not published in the original Yiddish until 1942, *The Nazarene* was one of Asch's stylistically most accomplished and original works. The Christological trilogy (two other parts, *Mary* and *The Apostle*, appeared only in English) was followed by two novels on biblical themes: *Moses* and *The Prophet* (about the age of Isaiah). Asch's last great novel was *East River* (1946), a large-scale portrayal of New York Jewish life in the first half of the twentieth century. The reader meets here reincarnations of major character types from Asch's previous works, which brings together the American and European lines of his creative imagination.

During the 1930s and early 1940s, Asch's two major competitors were his fellow staff writers for the New York Yiddish daily, *Forverts*, Zalman Shneour (1886–1959) and Israel Joshua Singer (1893–1944). Shneour entered literature in the 1920s as a Hebrew poet of great promise; by the late 1920s Yiddish prose became his main genre, but he remained a bilingual writer during his entire literary career. His most popular work was a series of tales about the people of his native Shklov, a witty mixture of sentimental memories and cunning observations. Published in Yiddish (*Shklover yidn*, Jews of Shklov, 1929 and *Feter Zhome*, Uncle Zhome, 1930) and Hebrew versions, these sweet and humorous vignettes from the old shtetl life responded to the nostalgic mood of both Jewish readerships. In his epic novel *Noekh Pandre* (1938–1939), also set in Shklov, Shneour turned from the middle-class shtetl milieu to the simple folk by choosing as his protagonist a physically strong and emotionally dynamic wagon driver. A subtler stylist and sharper observer than Asch, Shneour was particularly successful in recreating the poetically evocative landscapes of his native Polesye, in conveying psychological nuances, and in inventing lively dialogue. His ironic, rich, and idiomatic Yiddish does not lend itself to translation as easily as the more straightforward language of Asch, which was probably one of the reasons why Schneour never became popular outside the Yiddish and Hebrew linguistic spheres. In his other saga, *Keyser un rebe* (Emperor and Rebbe, 1944–1952), a historical chronicle of late eighteenth- to early nineteenth-century Russia, he traced the vicissitudes of the group of Shklov merchants who became Russia's "first modern Jews." Shneour took his reader to the aristocratic salons of the favorites of Empress Catherine, to the secluded study of the Gaon of Vilna, and to the bedrooms of Hasidic rebbes. *Di meshumedeste* (The Apostate Woman, 1948), a novel about a Jewish girl who falls in love with a Russian peasant boy and eventually converts to Christianity in order to marry him (a motif made prominent by Sholem Aleichem in *Tevye the Dairyman*), can be seen as a skeptical response to Asch's promotion of Christian–Jewish symbiosis.

Less prolific than Asch and Shneour, I. J. Singer focused on the exploration of Polish Jewry under the pressure of modernity. *Di brider Ashkenazi* (The Brothers Ashkenazi, 1936), his foremost achievement, tells the story of a business family against the broad social background of the Lódz textile industry before the Russian revolution. In contrast to Asch's optimistic humanism and Zalman Shneour's bitter-sweet nostalgia, Singer's vision of humanity in general and Jews in particular was dark and pessimistic. In his social Darwinian deterministic scheme, Jews were ill-fitted for survival in the modern world due to some inherent flaws of their character. The theme of degeneration is prominent in his last novel, *Di mishpokhe Karnovski* (The Family Carnovsky, 1943) which traces the fortunes and misfortunes of a Jewish family on its way from Poland to Berlin and further to New York. This somber vision of the contemporary situation had a strong influence on I. J. Singer's younger brother, Isaac Bashevis Singer (1904–1991), whose first novel, *Der sotn in Goray* (Satan in Goray, 1935) was a dark fantasy about the destructive effects of the Sabbatean messianic movement on the Polish shtetl in the seventeenth century, which can also be read as a veiled critique of the Jewish infatuation with communism. His second major novel, *Di familye Mushkat* (The Family Moskat, 1950) was both a tribute to his late brother, who died in 1943, and one of the first literary memorials to the world of Polish Jewry that perished in the Holocaust. In his memoirs of childhood, published over many years in installments in the *Forverts*, he recreated the atmosphere of Jewish Warsaw through the prism of numerous cases resolved by this father in his private rabbinic court. By the 1960s, Bashevis emerged as the most popular Yiddish writer in English translation thanks to his ability to capture the imagination of a wider American audience with his tales from the world that was forever lost. Critical of any attempts by other writers to transplant Yiddish culture onto American soil, he nonetheless created memorable images of Jewish immigrants' struggles with the ghosts of their past in the wake of the Holocaust, such as Herman Broder in the novel *Sonim, di geshikhte fun a libe* (Enemies: A Love Story, 1966).

Although Jewish immigration to the United States dramatically decreased in the 1920s due to political restrictions, the cultural exchange between the Old and the New Worlds continued until the outbreak of World War II. Eastern Europe was much closer to Yiddish-speaking Jews than to other Americans, and its presence can be strongly felt even in the works of writers who began their Yiddish literary career in America, such as Lamed Shapiro (1878–1948), Borekh Glazman (1893–1945), Sh. (Isaiah) Miller (1895–1958), and Yankev Glatshteyn. Yet their relationships with their "old home" were far from simple. One of most accomplished stylists in American Yiddish literature, Shapiro began his literary career as a follower of Peretz and Bergelson and achieved early fame with his hyperbolic horror-filled pogrom stories, which he later regarded as a burden from which he tried to liberate himself. His later works, such as the collection *New-yorkish* (1931) and the unfinished novel *Der amerikaner shed* (American Devil) addressed a set of immigrant concerns such as alienation, anxiety, political radicalization, and the moral price of commercial success in a capitalist society. In contrast to the pogrom stories, the depictions of American life are minimalist in style, employing the cinematic devices of montage and close-up to create specific effects of the urban atmosphere of New York City. Glazman, who was close to the Kiev group in his youth, had little contact with Yiddish during his first ten years in America, where he immigrated in 1911. Having graduated from the Ohio State University, he went back to Yiddish and produced a series of remarkable prose works, dealing with a wide range of topics, from sexual abuse of African-American women by Jewish men in the American South to Soviet agricultural colonies in Ukraine, which he visited during his long sojourn in Eastern Europe during the late 1920s. Collected editions of Glazman, Opatoshu and other American Yiddish writers were published in Poland and distributed all over the world.

Like most American Yiddish writers, Glatshteyn also visited Eastern Europe and recorded his impressions in a travelogue. The fictionalized two-part account of his "midlife journey" to his native Lublin in 1934 (*Ven Yash is geforn*, 1937; *Ven Yash is gekumen*, 1940; English translation: Glatstein Chronicles, 2010) is regarded by some critics as the most accomplished work of modern Yiddish prose. Written in the highly sophisticated but also lyrical style cultivated by the *Inzikhistn*, the narration constantly shifts between personal memories and external impressions, conveying the emotional and intellectual intensity of the author's encounter with Europe at a critical historical moment. In 1938 Glateshteyn responded to the surge of antisemitism in Europe by renouncing his modernist cosmopolitanism and proclaiming his return to the "humpbacked Jewish life" in the programmatic poem "Good Night, World."[6]

AFTER THE HOLOCAUST

The Holocaust not only eradicated the majority of Yiddish readers and writers, but also had a profound psychological effect on the remaining ones. This trauma was compounded by Stalin's purges during 1948–1953, aimed specifically at Soviet Yiddish culture. The most remarkable author to emerge from this catastrophic condition was the poet Avrom Sutzkever (1913–2010). A member of the modernist Yung Vilne group in his twenties, he survived the Holocaust in the Vilna ghetto and among partisans in Lithuanian forests, from where he was airlifted to Moscow in 1944. Moving to Tel Aviv after the war, he became the editor of the most important post-war Yiddish journal, named after Peretz's play *Di goldene keyt* (1949–1995). In his poetry he continued the pre-war tradition of high modernism, writing in a unique metaphorical blend of prophetic biblical diction, intimate lyricism, and intellectual agility. Sutzkever's thematic diapason ranged from the dark visions of destruction to tender love poetry, and from metaphysical reflection to capturing fleeting momentary impressions. Another important writer to emerge from the fertile soil of pre-war Vilna was Chaim Grade (1910–1982), who turned from poetry to prose with the purpose of commemorating the lost world of traditional Lithuanian Jewry. In the Soviet Union, the Yiddish cultural magazine *Sovetish heymland* (Soviet Homeland, 1961–1991) served as the only legal outlet for Jewish cultural creativity. Attempting to build on the legacy of the Kiev Group, it gradually fell into decline, due to the death or emigration of its leading authors, and the shrinking of its audience caused by the closure of Yiddish schools during the era of Stalin's rule.

The nearly two hundred years of modern Yiddish literature produced a culture which remains in many respects unique. Radically reformist during its early stages, it gradually came to embrace different strands of Jewishness and absorbed a wide range of aesthetic and ideological impulses from outside, and became increasingly conservative and introverted after the Holocaust. Since Yiddish literature does not fit the common notion

---

[6] Benjamin and Barbara Harshav, *American Yiddish Poetry: A Bilingual Anthology* (Berkeley: University of California Press, 1986), 305.

of national literature, its originality and creativity have been largely overlooked by the general public.

SELECT BIBLIOGRAPHY

Dauber, Jeremy, *The Worlds of Sholem Aleichem* (New York: Schocken, 2013).

Estraikh, Gennady, *In Harness: Yiddish Writers' Romance with Communism* (Syracuse,
NY: Syracuse University Press, 2005).

Estraikh, Gennady, Kerstin Hoge, and Mikhail Krutikov, eds, *Uncovering the Hidden: The
Works and Life of Der Nister* (Oxford: Legenda, 2014).

Estraikh, Gennady and Joseph Sherman, eds, *David Bergelson: From Modernism to Socialist
Realism* (Oxford: Legenda, 2007).

Frieden, Kenneth, *Classic Yiddish Fiction: Abramovitsch, Sholem Aleichem, and Peretz*
(Albany: State University of New York Press, 1995).

Garrett, Leah, *Journeys beyond the Pale: Yiddish Travel Writing in the Modern World*
(Madison: University of Wisconsin Press, 2003).

Hadda, Janet, *Passionate Women, Passive Men: Suicide in Yiddish Literature* (Albany: State
University of New York Press, 1988).

Harshav, Benjamin, *The Meaning of Yiddish* (Berkeley: University of California Press, 1990).

Koller, Sabine, Estraikh, Gennady, and Krutikov, Mikhail, *Joseph Opatoshu: A Yiddish
Writer between Europe and America* (Oxford: Legenda, 2013).

Kronfeld, Chana, *On the Margins of Modernism: Decentering Literary Dynamics*
(Berkeley: University of California Press, 1996).

Krutikov, Mikhail, *From Kabbalah to Class Struggle: Expressionism, Marxism, and Yiddish
Literature in the Life and Work of Meir Wiener* (Stanford: Stanford University
Press, 2011).

Yiddish Fiction and the Crisis of Modernity (Stanford: Stanford University Press, 2001).

Leksikon fun der nayer yidisher literatur, 8 vols (New York: Alveltlekher yidisher kultur-
kongres, 1956–1981).

Liptsin, Sol, *A History of Yiddish Literature* (Middle Village, NY: Jonathan David, 1985).

Miron, Dan, *The Image of the Shtetl and Other Studies of Modern Jewish Literary Imagination*
(Syracuse, NY: Syracuse University Press, 2000).

Traveler Disguised: The Rise of Modern Yiddish Fiction in the Nineteenth Century, second
edition (Syracuse, NY: Syracuse University Press, 1996).

Moseley, Marcus, *Being for Myself Alone: Origins of Jewish Autobiography* (Stanford: Stanford
University Press, 2006).

Norich, Anita, *Discovering Exile: Yiddish and Jewish American Culture during the Holocaust*
(Stanford: Stanford University Press, 2007).

The Homeless Imagination in the Fiction of Israel Joshua Singer (Bloomington: Indiana
University Press, 1991).

Roskies, David, *Against the Apocalypse: Responses to Catastrophe in Modern Jewish Culture*
(Cambridge, MA: Harvard University Press, 1984).

A Bridge of Longing: The Lost Art of Yiddish Storytelling (Cambridge, MA: Harvard
University Press, 1995)

Schwarz, Jan, *Imagining Lives: Autobiographical Fiction of Yiddish Writers* (Madison: University of Wisconsin Press, 2005).

Sherman, Joseph, Gennady Estraikh, Jordan Finkin and David Shneer, eds. *A Captive of the Dawn: The Life and Work of Peretz Markish* (Oxford, Legenda, 2011).

Stahl, Nanette, ed. *Sholem Asch Reconsidered* (New Haven, CT: Beinecke Rare Book and Manuscript Library, 2004).

Wiener, Leo, *The History of Yiddish Literature in the Nineteenth Century* (New York: Hermon Press, 1972).

Wisse, Ruth, *I. L. Peretz and the Making of Modern Jewish Culture* (Seattle: University of Washington Press, 1991).

A Little Love in Big Manhattan (Cambridge, MA: Harvard University Press, 1988).

Wolitz, Seth, ed. *The Hidden Isaac Bashevis Singer* (Austin: University of Texas Press, 2001).

YIVO Encyclopedia of Jews in Eastern Europe, 2 vols., ed. Gershon Hundert (New Haven: Yale University Press, 2008).

CHAPTER 29

JEWISH STUDIES
History, Memory, Scholarship

DAVID N. MYERS

Among the conceptual and terminological touchstones of the founding generation of *Wissenschaft des Judentums*, one scarcely encounters the notion of
"memory," either as a repository of transmitted recollections that anchors
group identity or as an analytical category worthy of study. Nor, surprisingly,
does the term "history," in the sense of a discrete disciplinary orientation to
guide scholars, abound. Far more ubiquitous in the writings of the founding
generation was the term *Wissenschaft*, with its perceived curative powers.

The formulation of "history and memory" that has been such a routine
part of scholarly discourse in recent decades is a much later, twentieth-
century invention. Its emergence required, it would seem, a clear sense of
the unbridgeable distance to a past that can be conjured up imaginatively
but not relived. This distance was a product of the "rupture of equilibrium"
of which Pierre Nora speaks in his introduction to *Les lieux de mémoire*: "An
increasingly rapid slippage of the present into a historical past that is gone
for good, a general perception that anything and everything may disappear
… The remnants of experience still lived in the warmth of tradition, in the
silence of custom, in the repetition of the ancestral, have been displaced
under the pressure of a fundamental historical sensibility."[1]

In the first decades of the nineteenth century, the members of the Verein
für Kultur und Wissenschaft der Juden, in Berlin, still dwelt in proximity to "the warmth of tradition." Two of the key founders, Leopold Zunz
(1794–1886) and Isaac Marcus Jost (1793–1866) were raised in traditionally
observant homes "but slightly touched by the rays of Enlightenment." And
yet, they were educated together in a new-style school informed by the
ideals of the Haskalah, whose headmaster aimed to show students how "to
appear better and more respected among the nations than heretofore."[2]

---

[1] Pierre Nora's introduction to the multi-volume *Les lieux de mémoire*, which appeared
between 1984 and 1992, has been translated as "Between Memory and History: Les lieux
de mémoire," *Representations* 26 (Spring 1989), 7.
[2] Quoted in Michael A. Meyer, *The Origins of the Modern Jew: Jewish Identity and European
Culture in Germany, 1794–1824* (Detroit: Wayne State Press, 1967), 146, 148.

The logical path toward respectability for them was university study, where they were introduced to the latest methods of the German academy. They set out to apply these methods to the sources of the Jewish tradition to which they had been amply exposed as children. In so doing, they came to articulate and memorialize the growing distance they felt from the world of their forebears. Indeed, they set in motion a process of distanciation that transformed living memory into a more mediated form of analysis, collection, and commemoration.

Pierre Nora's words are again worth recalling in this context. Commemoration, particularly in the form of *lieux de mémoire*, "occurs at the same time that an immense and intimate fund of memory disappears, surviving only as a reconstituted object beneath the gaze of critical history." Such objects are "the ultimate embodiments of a memorial consciousness that has barely survived in a historical age that calls out for memory because it has abandoned it." The impulse to preserve, though not reconstitute, a once vibrant memory prompts the creation of archives, anniversaries, and celebrations – preservative agents and symbols of what once lived.[3]

It is this very impulse that guided Zunz in his well-known manifesto from 1818, "Etwas über die rabbinische Literatur." The young Zunz set out a sweeping agenda for modern Jewish studies, calling for the systematic collection and examination of a vast trove of post-biblical (or, as he called it, "neo-Hebraic") literature. Writing at a point of growing distance from the past, when his fellow German Jews were increasingly unfamiliar with the textual pillars of classical Judaism, Zunz declared that "science [*Wissenschaft*] steps in demanding an account of what has already been sealed away." The antiquarian function that Zunz imagined for the emerging *Wissenschaft des Judentums* was a telling reflection, we might say, of the transition from memory to history, at least in Nora's terms.

And yet, that function was not the entirety of Zunz's mission, nor of his comrades in the fledgling *Wissenschaft des Judentums*. In fact, the annals of modern Jewish scholarship reveal the persistent presence of two animating functions or impulses: what we might term, with a trace of exaggeration, the taxidermic, on one hand, and the instrumental, on the other.[4] Zunz and other founding members of the Verein held out the hope that elevating their enterprise to the rank of other *Wissenschaften* – indeed, the very ones they studied in university – would have a salutary effect not only on Jewish scholarship, but on Jews as well, specifically, by hastening or

---

[3] Ibid., 12.

[4] Michael Meyer has identified this phenomenon in "Two Persistent Tensions in Wissenschaft des Judentums," *Modern Judaism* 24, no. 2 (2004): 105–119.

facilitating their path to full emancipation. A generation later, the most popular Jewish historian in Germany, Heinrich Graetz (1817–1891), utilized his multi-volume *Geschichte der Juden* to carve out a more particularist sense of collective identity for the Jews. Graetz was no longer content with the emancipatory model of his predecessors, and instead agitated for a richer, more self-conscious, and distinctive sense of Jewish identity rooted in the past. It was in part because of his audacious renunciation of the deferential path of an earlier generation that he earned the enmity of both Jews and non-Jews in Germany, perhaps most famously, the Christian historian Heinrich von Treitschke.

Like Zunz and Graetz, later Jewish scholars in the twentieth century continued to navigate between the poles of critical distance from and empathic identification with the past. They frequently pledged fealty to the norms of objectivity first articulated by the early *Wissenschaft* scholars, while at the same time seeking to stoke the embers of the past to ignite a vibrant memory in the minds of Jews. Especially energetic in advancing this latter impulse were those operating under the ideological aegis of nationalism. The renowned Russian-Jewish historian, Simon Dubnow (1860–1941), crafted a narrative of the past that comported fully with his own Jewish nationalist agenda. Thus, he regarded Jewish history as marked by a series of evolving cultural centers, one after another, up to his own day. The present center in Dubnow's time was the large concentration of Jews in Eastern Europe. It was this center that deserved recognition as the cultural capital of the Jewish nation – and that stood at the heart of his Diaspora nationalist vision.

Other nationalist historians shared the ambition of mobilizing the past to frame an active historical memory for the Jewish collective, but on different ideological grounds. Most prominently, Zionist scholars placed "Zion," the ancestral land of Israel, as the axis around which all of Jewish history revolved. For an historian such as Ben-Zion Dinur (1884–1973), historical description and political prescription converged at the point at which the age-old aspiration of Jews to return to Zion began to be realized. Even with his fervent and unabashed embrace of Zionism, Dinur clung firmly to the ideal of objectivity that received new attention and approbation among his colleagues at the Hebrew University in Jerusalem.

It would seem as if history and memory, at some level and in some sense, had been melded together anew in this generation of Jewish nationalist historians, reversing the trend of distanciation that the founders of *Wissenschaft des Judentums* set in motion more than a century earlier. Yet this seeming conjunction was short-lived. In the latter half of the twentieth century, the gap between the project of critical history and the possibility of recreating a rich and nurturing memory seemed to widen even further.

It was at that point, at the brink of the chasm, that scholars became conscious about and gave voice to the distinct properties of "history and memory." The mission of this chapter is to chart the evolution and growth of that discourse in the field of Jewish studies. In particular, it will focus on the impact of the American scholar, Yosef Hayim Yerushalmi (1932–2009), whose 1982 book, *Zakhor*, introduced a new vocabulary and consciousness about history and memory into Jewish studies.

Arguably the most significant book in the field of Jewish studies over the past fifty years, Yerushalmi's *Zakhor* posited a stark distinction between the rich fabric of pre-modern collective memory, comprised of strands of ritual, liturgy, and commemorative literature, and the dispassionate labors of the modern historian. If "Jews were the fathers of meaning in history" in biblical and medieval times, they surrendered that patrimony by the nineteenth century, a development that Yerushalmi analyzed with a mix of melancholy, empathy, and deep insight.[5] Indeed, history in its modern guise had become, in Yerushalmi's memorable phrase, the "faith of fallen Jews," at once a symptom of the unraveling of the fabric of traditional memory and a sharp and unsentimental critique of traditional Judaism.[6]

The dolorous tenor of Yerushalmi's reflections in the fourth chapter of *Zakhor* on the modern practice of history, and particularly of Jewish history, would seem to be rooted in an oft-quoted line attributed to Moritz Steinschneider (1816–1907) that is perhaps the boldest articulation of the taxidermic function of Jewish scholarship mentioned earlier. According to a younger colleague Gotthold Weil, the great German-Jewish bibliographer believed that the goal of Jewish scholarship was to "give Judaism a decent burial."[7] Whether Steinschneider articulated or even harbored such a desire to entomb is not at all clear (although Gershom Scholem, the towering twentieth-century scholar, certainly argued that he did in

---

[5] Yosef Hayim Yerushalmi, *Zakhor: Jewish History and Jewish Memory* (Seattle: University of Washington, 1982), 8. A number of recent works have appeared that shed additional light on Yerushalmi and his oeuvre. See Sylvie Anne Goldberg, *Transmettre l'histoire juive: Entretiens avec Sylvie Anne Goldberg* (Paris: Albin Michel, 2012), as well as the conference volume edited by Goldberg, *L'histoire et la mémoire de l'histoire: Hommage à Yosef Hayim Yerushalmi* (Paris: Albin Michel, 2012). See also the recent collection of Yerushalmi's writings, *The Faith of Fallen Jews: Yosef Hayim Yerushalmi and the Writing of Jewish History*, ed. David N. Myers and Alexander Kaye (Hanover, NH: Brandeis University Press, 2014).

[6] Yerushalmi, *Zakhor*, 86.

[7] Weil made this oft-quoted assertion in an obituary in the *Jüdische Rundschau* 6 (February 8, 1907), 54. For an extended gloss on the comment, see Charles Manekin's appreciative tribute, "Steinschneider's Indecent Burial," http://seforim.blogspot.com/2007/08/charles-h-manekin-moritz.html.

his famous 1944 essay "Mi-tokh hirhurim ʿal Hokhmat Yisraʾel"). For his part, Yerushalmi came to believe that Steinschneider and his fellow standard-bearers of *Wissenschaft des Judentums* were products of a *Zeitgeist* and possessed of a set of surgical tools that mandated dissection rather than construction of a holistic collective memory. As a product of the same modern mindset, and possessed of a similar set of critical tools, Yerushalmi could not disavow his own historicist calling. But he observed that the broader Jewish world drew no consolation from the historicist turn. On the contrary, it – and it would seem, he – yearned for "a new metahistorical myth" for which fiction rather than historiography "provides at least a temporary modern surrogate."[8]

The yearning for such a myth, and for the very strands of collective memory that Yerushalmi so probingly analyzed, gained urgency in the half-century after the Holocaust. In the wake of the catastrophe, the historian, like the owl of Minerva, stepped in to sift through the shattered remnants of Jewish life, community, ideology, and memory in Europe. Dissatisfied with the historian's status as mere sifter – and, I would argue, mindful of the hulking if unnamed presence of the Shoah – Yerushalmi did not merely reflect on the relationship between history and memory in *Zakhor*. Surprisingly, he imagined a tighter bond between history and memory.[9] He did so fully cognizant of the long martyrological tradition in Jewish history, and particularly of the role of past tragedies as foundations of Jewish collective memory. Ironically, the Holocaust – the greatest of Jewish tragedies – marked not only the culmination of that tradition, but also its disruption. Just as Auschwitz shattered the tools of historical measurement, in the famous image of Jean-François Lyotard, so too the repositories and purveyors of Jewish collective memory were completely uprooted.[10] Indeed, the Shoah brought a conclusive end to the crowded marketplace of competing ideologies that engaged so many Jewish intellectuals in the first decades of the twentieth century – and served as the font of inspiration for Jewish historians who saw a close link between

[8] Yerushalmi, *Zakhor*, 98.
[9] Professor Yerushalmi did not agree with the assessment that his interest in memory reflected a post-Holocaust sensibility or context, as he made clear in response to a paper I delivered at a conference in Germany in July 2000. See my "Selbstreflexion im modernene Erinnerungsdiskurs" and Yerushalmi's response, "Jüdische Historiographie und Postmodernismus: Eine abweichende Meinung," in *Jüdische Geschichtsschreibung heute: Themen, Positionen, Kontroversen*, ed. Michael Brenner and David N. Myers (Munich: C. H. Beck, 2002), 55–74, 75–94.
[10] Jean-François Lyotard, *The Differend: Phrases in Dispute*, trans. Georges Van Den Abbeele (Minneapolis: University of Minnesota Press, 1988), 57–58.

their labors as students of the past and the future of the Jewish collective (e.g., the Eastern Europeans Simon Dubnow, Meir Balaban, Emanuel Ringelblum, and Ignacy [Yitzhak] Schipper).[11]

We shall revisit the Jewish martyrological tradition at the end of this essay. For now, we return to our reading of Yosef Yerushalmi and his efforts to escape the fate of fallen Jews, a reading that cuts against the grain of the standard account of *Zakhor*. "The burden of building a bridge to his people," he wrote, "remains with the historian." The challenge ahead was to maintain a connection not only to one's group but to the guiding issues that concerned and preoccupied them in the present. Concomitantly, Yerushalmi maintained that it was imperative to overcome the "calamitous" divide between literature and history and marshal the healing narrative powers of the former to the latter. In advancing such suggestions, he was drawn to the prospect of summoning his formidable talents to reverse the erosion of memory by delineating a more serviceable form of historical labor.[12]

This facet of Yerushalmi's position is often forgotten in light of his better-known assessment in *Zakhor* that "modern Jewish historiography can never substitute for Jewish memory."[13] Nonetheless, it is interesting to trace his efforts to overcome the very professional inhibitions with which he was raised by seeking a tighter bond between history and memory. It is especially noteworthy in light of his well-known "debate" with the one scholar of Jewish history who can be deemed his peer in terms of erudition and profundity: Amos Funkenstein (1937–1995). The great Israeli-born historian wrote an essay in the first issue of the Tel Aviv-based journal *History and Memory* in 1989 that was a response to Yerushalmi's *Zakhor* and an important statement on the subject in its own right. In the course of this essay, Funkenstein endeavors to undo Yerushalmi's stark juxtaposition between history and memory. Concurring with Yerushalmi that "historiography hardly existed at all in the sphere of traditional Judaism," he nonetheless argued that "a well-developed historical consciousness existed elsewhere." It was part and parcel of the long tradition of rabbinic Judaism that offered up "a continuous and chronological record of innovations in halakha." Funkenstein went on to argue that this kind of historical

---

[11] In addition to these notable historians who died during the Holocaust, Raphael Mahler has identified seventeen other Jewish historical researchers from Warsaw alone who were killed during the Nazi reign of terror. See Mahler, "Der krayz 'yunge historiker' in Varsha" in idem, *Historiker un vegvayzer* (Tel Aviv: Yisro'el-Bukh, 1967), 309–315. I thank Mark Smith for calling my attention to this article.

[12] Yerushalmi, *Zakhor*, 100.

[13] Yerushalmi, *Zakhor*, 101.

consciousness contradicted neither collective memory nor modern historicism. All three, he affirmed, "express the same 'collective mentality.' "[14] And indeed, this convergence was present in the very historians whom Yerushalmi saw as detached from the once-vibrant current of collective memory. Funkenstein, for his part, asserted that the modern "nation-state replaced the sacred liturgical memory with secular liturgical memory," and concomitantly, that the modern historian had become a "priest of culture."[15] In other words, there was a "functional reoccupation," to borrow Hans Blumenberg's term, of the pre-moderns' work of fostering collective memory by moderns.[16]

Whereas Funkenstein imagined nineteenth-century historians as "priests of culture" who served at the altar of collective memory, Yerushalmi depicted his nineteenth-century forbears as priests delivering last rites to "fallen Jews." It would seem as if the distance between the two outstanding Jewish historians of the late twentieth century – and particularly the ways in which they understood the relationship between history and memory – could not be stretched further. And yet, Yerushalmi's own yearning for the historian to act as "a bridge to his people," expressed late in *Zakhor*, collapses the gap between the two categories, all the more surprising given his general pessimism about the eviscerating effects of modern historicism. This yearning was not a mere episodic sentiment. More than a decade before the appearance of *Zakhor*, in a little-known address in 1970, he insisted to his audience of graduating Jewish educators at Hebrew College in Brookline that "we must consciously carry a Jewish past within us" as a way to "build a Jewish future."[17] Over time, he became less confident of the historian's ability to advance this goal and more introspective about his own professional calling, but he never surrendered the aspiration for a

---

[14] Amos Funkenstein, "Collective Memory and Historical Consciousness," *History and Memory* 1 (Spring–Summer 1989): 17, 18, 19.

[15] Ibid., 21. Funkenstein makes a similar point, emphasizing that it was in the nineteenth century that the historian served as "the high priest of culture" in "Toldot Yisra'el ben ha-hohim: ha-historyah le-mul ditsiplinot aherot," *Zion* 60 (1995): 336.

[16] Of course, we should not oversimplify Blumenberg's "functional reoccupation" by suggesting that he imagined a simple and undifferentiated replication by moderns of earlier structures of thought. It is that position he ascribed to Karl Löwith in *Meaning in History*, maintaining in contrast that there were both strong continuities and discontinuities between modern and pre-modern epochs. See the discussion by David Ingram, "Blumenberg and the Grounds of Philosophical Historiography," *History and Theory* 29, no. 1 (1990): 1–15.

[17] Yosef Hayim Yerushalmi, "A Jewish Historian in the 'Age of Aquarius'," Commencement Address, Hebrew College, Brookline, MA, June 1970, reprinted in *The Faith of Fallen Jews*, ed. Myers and Kaye.

more meaning-laden historical project of which the Hebrew Bible was the first major exemplar.

That said, it would be a reach to argue that Yerushalmi's main legacy to the field of Jewish studies was as a "physician of memory" (a term he borrowed from Eugen Rosenstock-Huessy).[18] Rather, it was as the blazer of a number of entwined research paths that have been popular and consequential in the field, two of which will be discussed here. One of the most relevant for our purposes was the study of the content, function, and impact of Jewish historiography. Yerushalmi's growing preoccupation with the history and philosophy of history, culminating in *Zakhor*, did not take rise in isolation. Rather, the 1970s and 1980s were a period of intense new inquiry in the American academy into the semiological and literary properties of the historiographical text. Hayden White's provocative and influential *Metahistory* (1973) consciously blurred distinctions long held sacred by historians – between history and the philosophy of history, history and literature, and, most daringly, fact and fiction.[19] In the process, it induced a new sophistication into the analysis of the process of historiographical production. At the same time, the engagement by North American scholars with a select but diverse array of European thinkers, including Derrida, Gadamer, and Foucault, generated new interest in the hermeneutics and discursive practices of history – to the point that observers spoke of a "linguistic turn" in the field.[20] Yerushalmi barely acknowledged the impact of these developments in *Zakhor*.[21] But he read widely and was keenly aware of important trends in the field. And, in fact, his meditations in *Zakhor* contributed to an important moment of new scholarly scrutiny of the practice of history and the function of the historian.

The second and closely related scholarly trend that Yerushalmi set in motion in the field of Jewish studies was the study of the formation and adaptation of collective memory. Here too he did not operate in a vacuum. Around the time of the appearance of *Zakhor*, Pierre Nora, as we have already noted, was opening new horizons of research into collective memory through the multi-volume *Les lieux de mémoire*. Similar to Yerushalmi, Nora posited a widening chasm between "real memory – social and

---

[18] Ibid., 59, and Yerushalmi, *Zakhor*, 93.

[19] Hayden White, *Metahistory: The Historical Imagination in Nineteenth-Century Europe* (Baltimore: Johns Hopkins University Press, 1973).

[20] See, for example, John E. Toews, "Intellectual History after the Linguistic Turn: The Autonomy of Meaning and the Irreducibility of Experience," *The American Historical Review* 92, no. 4 (1987): 879–907.

[21] Perhaps the sole exception is the footnote devoted to Hayden White in Yerushalmi, *Zakhor*, 142, n. 14.

unviolated, exemplified in but also retained as the secret of so-called primitive or archaic societies – and history, which is how our hopelessly forgetful modern societies, propelled by change, organize the past."[22] In articulating this divide, and especially in their shared understanding of the category of collective memory, both Nora and Yerushalmi drew on the landmark book of the earlier French sociologist, Maurice Halbwachs (1877–1945), *La mémoire collective* (1950).

Consistent with the first current, Yerushalmi did not take conscious note of Nora or other French scholars working in this area until after the publication of *Zakhor*, when he began to make frequent visits to France for extended periods and befriended leading intellectuals there.[23] The effect of this encounter – and the resulting convergence of interests acknowledged more readily by younger scholars – served to erode the boundaries that often separated an insular Jewish studies from broader historical and literary studies, and thereby generated added cachet to the burgeoning field of Jewish memory studies. What follows in the next section is a survey of the entwined scholarly lineages that Yerushalmi's pioneering work inspired. In surveying this field, we will also see the traces of Yerushalmi's great peer, Amos Funkenstein, especially as reflected in the work of students of his who opened new pathways of research at the juncture of history and memory.

HISTORY AND MEMORY AS ENTWINED
PATHWAYS OF RESEARCH

Yerushalmi and Funkenstein were not, it should be said, the first Jewish historians of the twentieth century to focus attention on the professional and textual practices of their discipline. Yerushalmi's own teacher, Salo W. Baron (1895–1989), published a collection of essays with an historiographical focus in 1964 entitled *History and Jewish Historians*. Baron opened this volume with the statement that "a history of history is an

---

[22] Nora, "Between Memory and History," 8.

[23] Of course, it was not only scholars in France who were immersed in the study of collective memory. It is important to note the contributions of German scholars, impelled in no small part by their society's freighted relationship to the Nazi past. Of particular note are the interlacing projects of Jan Assmann and Aleida Assmann; the former has developed a key distinction between cultural and communicative memory in *Das kulturelle Gedächtnis: Schrift, Erinnerung und politische Identität in frühen Hochkulturen* (1992), whereas the latter has undertaken important theoretical work on group memory formation in a series of books and articles from *Arbeit am nationalen Gedächtnis. Eine kurze Geschichte der deutschen Bildungsidee* (1993).

excellent mirror of the changing attitudes of human societies." He went on to point out that "a comprehensive history of Jewish historiography" was a long-standing desideratum in the field, especially since the last study of any significance to be published was Steinschneider's bibliographic survey from 1905, *Geschichtsliteratur der Juden*.[24] Baron was also quite forward in acknowledging the utilitarian function of historical research. In the first issue of *Jewish Social Studies*, in 1939, he envisaged history as "an applied social science, which is of practical significance to statesmen, men of affairs, and the intelligent public at large."[25]

Following Baron, a number of prominent scholars began to devote substantial labors to the study of Jewish historiography. Among them were two American scholars, Ismar Schorsch and Michael A. Meyer, both experts in German-Jewish history. Meyer commenced a career-long interest in the subject in 1967 with his book, *The Origin of the Modern Jew*, whose final chapter discussed the emergence of the *Wissenschaft des Judentums* movement through the lens of one of its founding figures, Leopold Zunz.[26] Some years later, in the mid-1970s, Ismar Schorsh began to write a series of article-length studies that explored the intersection of history, faith, and denominational struggle in the early *Wissenschaft* generations. In exploring this juncture – and later in his position as Chancellor of the Jewish Theological Seminary – Schorsch sought to understand how and when history was mobilized to the task of Jewish religious and communal fortification. He brought together this body of work over two decades in 1994 in a collection whose subtitle bore the revealing title "The Turn to History in Modern Judaism."[27]

The theme of the turn to history – or more accurately, the return to history – figured prominently in a major study devoted to the leading Jewish studies scholar of the twentieth century: David Biale's *Gershom Scholem: Kabbalah and Counter-History* (1979). Biale wrote the dissertation on which the book was based at UCLA under Amos Funkenstein,

[24] Salo W. Baron, *History and Jewish Historians* (Philadelphia: Jewish Publication Society, 1964), xiii. See also Baron's chapter, "Moritz Steinschneider's Contribution to Jewish Historiography," in ibid., 276–321.

[25] See Salo W. Baron, "Emphases in Jewish History," *Jewish Social Studies* 1 (1939): 15.

[26] Meyer, *The Origins of the Modern Jew*. Schorsch has recently published a full-length biography of Zunz. Ismar Schorsch, *Leopold Zunz: Creativity in Adversity* (Philadelphia: University of Pennsylvania Press, 2016).

[27] Ismar Schorsch, *From Text to Context: The Turn to History in Modern Judaism* (Hanover, NH: Brandeis University Press, 1994).

who provided inspiration for the concept of "counter-history" that figured so centrally in his treatment of Scholem.[28]

Three years later, Yosef Yerushalmi published *Zakhor*, and in its wake the pace of research into Jewish historiography hastened significantly.[29] The book was a touchstone – and in some cases, a polemical foil – for many of the authors who contributed to the special issue of the prominent journal *History and Theory* in 1989 devoted to Jewish historiography. Edited by the British-Israeli scholar Ada Rapoport-Albert, the issue featured essays on Jewish historiography ranging from antiquity through the modern age, and accorded a new degree of recognition and respectability to the study of Jewish historical writing.[30]

In this new age of visibility, Jewish historiography attracted a generation of younger researchers the world over. In France, Perrine Simon-Nahum widened the lens of inquiry into modern Jewish historiography beyond its largely German focus in her 1991 study on French Jewish scholarship, *La cité investie: La "science du judaïsme" français et la République*.[31] In the same period, the Israeli historian Shmuel Feiner undertook a study of the embrace of history by advocates of the Jewish Enlightenment movement, the maskilim. Published in 1995 as *Haskalah ve-historyah* (Haskalah and History), this volume challenged a key claim of Yerushalmi's, that the shift from the late eighteenth-century maskilim to the early nineteenth-century practitioners of *Wissenschaft des Judentums* represented "a drastic leap into a new kind of thinking."[32]

In the same year, I published a revised version of my Columbia dissertation (1991) on the transfer of European Jewish scholars and scholarship to Palestine. This book, *Re-inventing the Jewish Past: European Jewish Intellectuals and the Zionist Return to History*, explored the interplay between Zionist ideology and the writing of history within the institutional

---

[28] David Biale, *Gershom Scholem: Kabbalah and Counter-History* (Cambridge, MA: Harvard University Press, 1979). On his idiosyncratic use of "counter-history," see also Biale's essay in the special issue of *Jewish Social Studies* devoted to the memory of Amos Funkenstein, "Counter-History and Jewish Polemics against Christianity: The *Sefer toldot Yeshu* and the *Sefer zerubavel*," *Jewish Social Studies* 6 (Autumn 1999): 131.

[29] Notice should be given to a book of wide scope, though lesser renown, that appeared five years before Yerushalmi's, Lionel Kochan, *The Jew and His History* (London: Macmillan, 1977).

[30] See *History and Theory* 27, no. 4 (1988): "Essays in Jewish Historiography."

[31] Perrine Simon-Nahum, *La cité investie: La "science du judaïsme" français et la République* (Paris: Cerf, 1991).

[32] Yerushalmi, *Zakhor*, 93. See Shmuel Feiner, *Haskalah ve-historyah: toldoteha shel hakarat-'avar Yehudit modernit* (Jerusalem: Merkaz Shazar, 1995), translated into English as *Haskalah and History* (Oxford: Littman Library, 2002).

framework of the Hebrew University. It was directly inspired by the work of Yosef Yerushalmi, who supervised the dissertation; at the same time, it sought to demonstrate the large gray area that marked off the space between the mythic poles of history and memory, as laid out in *Zakhor*. Simultaneously, Amnon Raz-Krakotzkin was completing a dissertation in Israel that examined from a critical historical and political angle the relationship between Zionism and history: "The Nationalist Representation of Exile, Zionist Historiography, and Medieval Jewry" (1996). Written under the direction of Amos Funkenstein at Tel Aviv University, this dissertation introduced Raz-Krakotzkin's well-known claim that Zionism had internalized the early modern Protestant rejection of exile (as fall from grace) in the name of a triumphant and triumphalist return to homeland–and history.[33] In both cases, Raz-Krakotzkin and I depicted an historiographical enterprise frequently motivated by and mobilized to the cause of Zionism – in particular, to a narrative of the Jewish past that placed Zion as the primary axis of historical development.

When noting the interest of scholars in the interplay between Zionism and history, it must be recalled that the Zionist movement, in it various strains and as a whole, sought to re-imagine the contours of Jewish history – and promoted the growth of institutions in which that work of scholarly re-imagination could flourish. The institutions that subsequently took rise in Israel contain within them the largest concentration of Jewish studies scholars in the world, as well as the largest concentration of scholars devoted to the study of Zionism. What fostered the intense new focus not only on Zionist history, but on Zionist historiography, was a pair of factors: first, a new interest in the historiographical text as open to and worthy of careful scrutiny in its own right. This impulse was an indirect effect of the postmodern outlook, with its attention to textual and hermeneutic nuance and skeptical stance toward master-narratives and claims of objectivity. Although often wary of postmodernism's alleged nihilism, historians found it hard to escape some of the intellectual byproducts of the postmodern moment. They trained a critical gaze on the guiding principles of their forbears, pointing out the ideological dispositions that undergirded their work. This perspective served to leaven a novel interest in Zionist historiography as a subject on its own.

A second factor in the growth of this sub-field was the challenge to historiographical convention posed by a group of Israeli (or former Israeli) scholars of Zionism and the Middle East (e.g., Benny Morris, Ilan Pappé,

---

[33] Amnon Raz-Krakotzkin, "Yitsuga ha-le'umi shel ha-galut: ha-histoyografyah ha-Tsiyonit ve-yehude yeme ha-benayim" (Ph.D. diss., Tel Aviv University, 1996). See also his essay, "Galut mi-tokh ribonut," *Te'oryah u-vikoret* 4 (1993): 23–55 and 5 (1994): 113–132.

Tom Segev, Avi Shlaim) who came to be known in the late 1980s and early 1990s as the "New Historians." Their work took direct aim at a number of foundation myths undergirding the creation of the State of Israel, including claims about British opposition to Zionism and preference for the Arab side, the logistical and quantitative disadvantage of the Jewish side in the 1948 War, and, most provocatively, the voluntary nature of Palestinian Arab flight in the war. The jolt that the "New Historians" delivered to established assumptions and norms emboldened scholars, directly and indirectly, to approach their predecessors with a new-found independence of mind. This meant a willingness to upend the reverential portrait of the historiographical establishment, symbolized by the founding generation of historians in Jerusalem (Raz-Krakotzkin). Not surprisingly, this project of historical revisionism prompted a reaction that pushed back against the perceived irreverence of revisionists by affirming foundational principles, including the ideal of objective or nonpartisan scholarship. This latter tendency can be seen in the defense of the principles of historiographical integrity offered by scholars of Zionism such as Shabtai Tevet, Anita Shapira, Efraim Karsh, and Yoav Gelber.[34] One of the most interesting and detailed responses by an historian came from one of the oldest, Jacob Katz, the dean of Israeli scholars of Jewish history in the last quarter of the twentieth century. In his own rejoinder to the New Historians, Katz introduced a sense of the history of methodological and theoretical criticism of historicism absent in others. At the same time, he ended up affirming that if historians adhered to the same "methodological rules of the profession" and relied on a shared body of sources, there would inevitably be considerable overlap in their descriptive work.[35]

This statement points to the emerging boundary line between reverential and critical, as well as continuous and disjunctive, visions of the past – indeed, between an old guard and a new group of firebrands. But in the course of this scholarly and political contest, which was often quite heated,

[34] See, for example, the well-known response of veteran journalist and biographer, Tevet, to the work of the New Historians, and particularly, Benny Morris, in Shabtai Tevet, "Charging Israel with *Original Sin*," *Commentary* 88, no. 3 (1989): 24–33. See also Anita Shapira, "Politics and Collective Memory: The Debate over the 'New Historians'," *History and Memory* 7, no. 1 (1995): 9–40; Efraim Karsh, "Benny Morris and the Reign of Terror," *Middle East Quarterly* VI, no. 1 (1999): 15–28; and Yoav Gelber, "The Disease of Post-Zionism," http://zioncon.blogspot.com/2007/07/yoav-gelber-disease-of-post-zionism.html (accessed October 17, 2011).

[35] See Katz's chapter "Historyah ve-historyonim, hadashim ke-yeshanim," in *'Et laḥakor ve-'et le-hitbonen: masah historit 'al darko shel Bet Yisra'el me-'az tse'ato me-artso ve-'ad shuvo aleha* (Jerusalem: Shazar Center, 1998–99), 21.

the field of Jewish historiography became an accepted and legitimate domain of research in Israel. In addition to Raz-Krakotzkin's provocative work, the Haifa scholar Jacob Barnay shifted his attention from the history of Palestine to the place of Palestine in Jewish historiography in a 1995 book, *Historyografyah u-le'umiyut* (Historiography and Nationalism).[36] New dissertations were now devoted to the historiographical past, including two studies in 2000 of Ben-Zion Dinur, a key architect of Zionist historical consciousness, by Arielle Rein and Daniel Marom. Several years later, Yizhak Conforti sought to address, in a dissertation later published as a book, the broader role of Zionist historiography in shaping a new national memory.[37]

To be sure, these were not the first Israeli scholars to address the history of Jewish historiography. A lineage commencing with Dinur and including Shmuel Ettinger, Shmuel Almog, Yisrael Kolatt, and the contemporary Yisrael Bartal evinced an active interest in the subject. But the topic, it is fair to say, became far more common and legitimate in its own right in the Israeli academy in the last two decades. On the face of it, we might be tempted to see the rising interest in historiography – and the accompanying critical perspective on previous generations – as connected to the fracturing of a once-coherent collective memory in Israel, a process sometimes thought to have commenced after the unpopular Lebanon War of 1982. But such a claim presumes both a unified collective memory hitherto – in the face of often bitter internal Jewish divisions within Israel and the Yishuv – and, more to the point, a deep ontological divide between history and memory. In fact, historiography was yoked to the Zionist movement from its early decades, serving as an indispensable tool in framing a new Jewish collective memory. There was, then, a closeness, even inextricability, to the categories of history and memory that has been noticed and scrutinized with new vigor by recent scholarship.

Meanwhile, the interest in Jewish historiography developed in parallel fashion in the other major centers of scholarship in North America and Europe. Following on the labors of Yerushalmi, Michael Meyer, and Ismar Schorsch, Susannah Heschel undertook to study a major figure of *Wissenschaft des Judentums*, Abraham Geiger. Her 1998 book portrayed

---

[36] Jacob Barnay, *Historyografyah u-le'umiyut: megamot be-ḥeker Erets-Yisra'el ve-yishuvah ha-Yehudi, 634–1881* (Jerusalem: Magnes Press 1995).

[37] See Arielle Rein, "Ha-historyon be-vinui umah: tsemihata shel Ben-Zion Dinur u-mif'alo ba-Yishuv" (Ph.D. diss., Hebrew University, 2000), and Daniel Marom, "The Thought and Practice of Ben Zion Dinur as Educator" (Ph.D. diss., Hebrew University, 2000). See also Yitzhak Conforti, *Zeman `avar: ha-historyografyah ha-Tsiyonit ve-`itsuv ha-zikaron ha-le'umi* (Jerusalem: Yad Ben-Zvi 2006).

Geiger, the Reform rabbi and scholar, as a self-possessed and assertive scholar, aggressive in resisting the anti-Jewish impulses of Protestant historical and biblical scholarship. In her view, Geiger's project was "a rebellious effort, a contestation of the prevailing viewpoint established by the Christian eye." More generally, she portrayed *Wissenschaft des Judentums* not as defensive and apologetic, but as intent on "reversing the gaze" and casting a critical eye on the history of Christianity. Its adepts, and Geiger chief among them, conformed more to Funkenstein's model of "priests of culture" than to Yerushalmi's "fallen Jews." They were possessed of their own agency and powers of criticism as Jews – so much so that Heschel, in a fit of admiring enthusiasm, declared them post-colonialists *avant la lettre*.[38]

This approach challenged a long-standing image rooted in Zionist historiography and most famously associated with Gershom Scholem's previously mentioned essay from 1944, "Mi-tokh hirhurim ʿal Hokhmat Yisraʾel" (Reflections of Jewish Scholarship). In that famous polemic, Scholem argued that *Wissenschaft des Judentums*, as a project, manifested a disconcerting degree of subservience to German Christian hosts. Joining Heschel in proposing a corrective to Scholem was Nils Roemer, a student of Yerushalmi who followed in his mentor's trail in exploring the history of modern Jewish scholarship. Roemer wrote a dissertation at Columbia that was published in 2005 as *Jewish Scholarship and Culture in 19th-Century Germany: Between History and Faith*. He aimed to demonstrate that German-Jewish scholars readily assumed responsibility for combating the rising currents of antisemitism in late nineteenth-century Germany. At the same time, these scholars, many of whom were alumni of the new rabbinical seminaries that took rise in Germany in the latter half of the century, came to see their labors as a key tool in augmenting the religious knowledge of the broader Jewish public in Germany.[39] In illuminating these dual functions, Roemer sought to depict a Jewish historiography decidedly in the service of the broader German-Jewish public. Further work in this direction has been undertaken recently in Germany and the United States by Jeffrey Blutinger, Anthony Kauders, Markus Pyka, and Gideon Reuveni.[40]

[38] Susannah Heschel, *Abraham Geiger and the Jewish Jesus* (Chicago: University of Chicago, 1998), 2–3.

[39] Nils Roemer, *Jewish Scholarship and Culture in 19th-Century Germany: Between History and Faith* (Madison: University of Wisconsin Press, 2005), 126.

[40] See, for example, the two studies on Heinrich Graetz: Jeffrey Blutinger, "Writing for the Masses: Heinrich Graetz, the Popularization of Jewish History, and the Reception of National Judaism," Ph.D. diss. University of California, Los Angeles, 2003; and Markus Pyka, *Jüdische Identität bei Heinrich Graetz* (Göttingen: Vandenhoeck & Ruprecht, 2009). For a recent source collection of Jewish historiographical writings, see *Jüdische Geschichte*

If this scholarship has called into question and rendered more complex the earlier historiographical assumption of a unidirectional assimilatory agenda for German Jews, the case is less clear in France. Along with the book by Simon-Nahum, Aron Rodrigue has written a number of articles that attempt to steer away from the Germanocentric orientation of the study of modern Jewish historiography. Rodrigue's work traces the outlines of a different tradition in France, where powerful universalist and emancipatory impulses animated the writings of scholars such as Léon Halévy, Théodore Reinach, Salomon Reinach, and James Darmesteter. Their narratives of the past describe – and between the lines, prescribe – a sweeping current that propelled Jews from an early state of superstition to a new and glorious age of civilization, in France of course.[41]

Rodrigue's focus on France expands our range of knowledge about Western European Jewish historical scholarship.[42] And yet, the historiographical turn post-*Zakhor* has hardly been confined to Western or Central Europe. The largest concentration of world Jewry prior to the Second World War in Eastern Europe generated a wealth of historical scholarship – in Yiddish, Polish, and Russian – that has drawn increased attention in recent decades. Among those who have contributed to this new attention are Natalia Aleksiun, Brian Horowitz, Joshua Karlip, Samuel Kassow, Viktor Kelner, Jess Olson, Barry Trachtenberg, Kalman Weiser, and Steven Zipperstein.[43] The body of work produced by these scholars

lesen. Texte der jüdischen Geschichtsschreibung im 19. und 20. Jahrhundert, ed. Michael Brenner, Anthony Kauders, Gideon Reuveni, Nils Roemer (Munich: Beck Verlag, 2003).

[41] See Aron Rodrigue, "Léon Halévy and Modern French Jewish Historiography," in *Jewish History and Jewish Memory: Essays in Honor of Yosef Hayim Yerushalmi*, ed. Elisheva Carlebach, John M. Efron, and David N. Myers (Hanover, NH: University Press of New England, 1998), 413–437; and "Totems, Taboos, and Jews: Salomon Reinach and the Politics of Scholarship in Fin-de-Siècle France," *Jewish Social Studies* 10 (2004), 1–19.

[42] In similar fashion, Todd Endelman (who, like Rodrigue, was a Yerushalmi student) has proposed to enlarge the Jewish historiographical map in two regards: first, he has endeavored over the course of three decades to introduce England as a venue of significance in the narrative rendering of modern Jewish history; and second, his research is a call to overcome the privileging of intellectual and cultural elites in favor of the quotidian experience of "average" Jews. See most recently Todd M. Endelman, *Broadening Jewish History: Towards a Social History of Ordinary Jews* (Oxford: Littman Library, 2011).

[43] See, for example, Natalia Aleksiun, "Ammunition in the Struggle for National Rights: Jewish Historians in Poland between the Two World Wars" (Ph.D. diss., New York University, 2010); Joshua M. Karlip, *The Tragedy of a Generation: The Rise and Fall of Jewish Nationalism in Eastern Europe* (Cambridge, MA: Harvard University Press, 2013); Samuel Kassow, *Who will Write our History? Emanuel Ringelblum, the Warsaw Ghetto, and the Oyneg Shabes Archive* (Bloomington: Indiana University Press, 2007);

reveals the extent to which historiography was mobilized by a variety of modern, often secular, ideological movements – chiefly nationalist – intent on imagining and building a new Jewish future.

In parallel to this current, a growing cohort of researchers, including David Assaf, Israel Bartal, Benjamin Brown, Adam Ferziger, Haim Gerter, Nahum Karlinsky, Jacob J. Schacter, and Michael Silber, has excavated a large body of "Orthodox historiography" – that is, history written by Orthodox Jews – in Europe, Israel, and North America. By its very nature, this body of writing revealed the extent to which its authors owed fealty to two masters: the goal of chronicling important historical events, and the goal of demonstrating God's hand, or that of a charismatic rebbe, in the Jews' march through history. Ada Rapoport-Albert has referred to this tradition as "hagiography with footnotes," in recognition of its unapologetic traversing of the boundary between scholarship and advocacy, or in the terms of our discussion, history and memory.[44]

If the past thirty years have witnessed a significantly increased focus on the historiographical text as a source of prime value to the historian, we have not seen a large number of synthetic works that tie together the various historiographical centers, generations, and schools into a larger whole. A few exceptions are worth noting. The Israeli scholar Reuven Michael offered a simple, though comprehensive, bio-biographical description of Jewish historiography from the Renaissance through the twentieth century in 1993.[45] More recently, Michael Brenner has written a history of

---

Viktor E. Kelner, *Simon Dubnow: Eine Biografie* (Göttingen: Vandenhoeck & Ruprecht, 2010); Jess Olson, *Nathan Birnbaum and Modernity: Architect of Zionism, Yiddishism, and Orthodoxy* (Stanford: Stanford University Press, 2013); Barry C. Trachtenberg, *The Revolutionary Roots of Modern Yiddish, 1903–1917* (Syracuse: Syracuse University Press, 2008); Kalman Weiser, *Jewish People, Yiddish Nation: Noah Prylucki and the Folkists in Poland* (Toronto: University of Toronto Press, 2011); and Steven Zipperstein, *Imagining Russian Jewry: Memory, History, Identity* (Seattle: University of Washington Press, 1999).

[44] Among other important contributions, see Ada Rapoport-Albert, "Hagiography with Footnotes: Edifying Tales and the Writing of History in Hasidism," *History and Theory* 27, no. 4 (1988): 119–159; Israel Bartal, "True Knowledge and Wisdom: On Orthodox Historiography," in *Reshaping the Past: Jewish History and the Historians*, ed. Jonathan Frankel, Studies in Contemporary Jewry 10 (Oxford: Oxford University Press, 1994); Adam Ferziger, *Exclusion and Hierarchy: Orthodoxy, Nonobservance, and the Emergence of Modern Jewish Identity* (Philadelphia: University of Pennsylvania, 2005); Haim Gerter, "Reshitah shel ketivah historit ortodoksit be-Mizraḥ 'Eropah: Ha'arakhah meḥudeshet," *Tsiyon* 67 (2002): 292–336; Nahum Karlinsky, "The Dawn of Hasidic-Haredi Historiography," *Modern Judaism* 27, no. 1 (2007): 20–46; and Jacob J. Schacter, "Facing the Truths of History," *Torah u-Madda Journal* 8 (1998–1999): 200–273.

[45] Reuven Michael, *Ha-Ketivah ha-historit ha-Yehudit: meha-Renesans 'ad ha-'et ha-ḥadashah* (Jerusalem: Mosad Bialik, 1993).

modern Jewish historiography, *Prophets of the Past*, that combines chronology, geography, and biography, while organizing each chapter of the book around a different "master narrative."[46]

Similar to a good number of those mentioned above, Brenner was a student of Yosef Yerushalmi, who began to refine his interest in historiography while studying at Columbia. It is not only the preponderance of Yerushalmi students that is interesting (alongside a noticeable number of students of Amos Funkenstein). Nor is it that these students draw on their teacher's interest in historiography. It is rather that their work frequently blurs the bright line of demarcation between history and memory made famous in *Zakhor*. Yerushalmi's legacy, then, is not one of uncritical imitation by his students, but of opening up a wide, relatively uncharted terrain that has been traversed in both predictable and unpredictable ways by succeeding generations.

Within that terrain of research, it is not always easy to separate the history from memory. The two frequently overlap insofar as acts commemorating the past rely, of necessity, on a measure of historical knowledge and even labor. And yet it may be helpful, if only to reveal the richness of the recent scholarly discourse on history and memory, to isolate a number of works that explore Jewish memory in a more dedicated fashion. One of the most important markers of memory is time, and it is to the intersection of the two that Sylvie Anne Goldberg, a French disciple (though not formal student) of Yerushalmi, devotes a major study. Her wide-ranging *Le Clepsydre: Essai sur la pluralité des temps dans le judäisme* (2000) takes up the challenge of analyzing the different modes, regimes, and registers of time operative in the lives of Jews over the course of centuries. At the heart of her inquiry is the desire to observe how Jews "navigate between historical consciousness and the play of memory, between sacred temporality, their own, and profane temporality, that of the nations." Between those two poles exists, as Goldberg suggests in the subtitle, "a plurality of times" through which Jews make sense of the near and distant past.

Meanwhile, the American scholar Elisheva Carlebach, who was a student of Yerushalmi, addresses the relationship between time and memory in her recent *Palaces of Time: Jewish Calendar and Culture in Early Modern Europe* (2011). Carlebach places at the center of her study the early modern Jewish calendar, which emerges as a tool of negotiating different temporal regimes, cultural worlds, and social habits. As an illuminating "mirror of

---

[46] Michael Brenner, *Prophets of the Past: Interpreters of Jewish History* (Princeton: Princeton University Press, 2010).

experience," the calendar also served to chronicle and preserve pathways of Jewish memory.[47]

Whereas both Goldberg and, to a lesser extent, Carlebach treat the formation of memory over the entire span of Jewish history, an especially noticeable body of scholarship has been devoted to the nineteenth and twentieth centuries. This is not surprising for a variety of reasons. First, the past two hundred years witnessed what Pierre Nora called "the acceleration of history" according to which events, and knowledge about them, proceeded at a dramatically escalated pace. The constant barrage of new information about both past and present rendered far more difficult the safeguarding of cherished memories. One result, Nora astutely observed, was that "(w)e speak so much of memory because there is so little of it left."[48]

As we recall from the beginning of this chapter, the yearning for memory in modern times prompted, as a compensatory mechanism, a new commitment to commemoration. That commemorative work, similar to the calendar, served as a mirror reflecting on a specific group, era, and set of concerns. One of the most interesting and counter-intuitive sites of memory that Jews fashioned in modern times revolved around the figure of the great seventeenth-century philosopher, Baruch Spinoza (1632–1677). Jews of different historical contexts have manifested a keen fascination – even a sense of identification – with Spinoza, who was excommunicated from the Amsterdam Jewish community in 1656. The combination of Spinoza's Iberian background and religious iconoclasm pointed toward a condition that has been called "Marranism," a sense of being caught between new and old worlds, as well as between competing religious and social authorities. And that condition spoke to the predicament of European Jews after Spinoza, especially in nineteenth and twentieth-century Germany, who studied, fictionalized, and devoted commemorative days in honor of their fallen hero.

Jonathan Skolnik and David Wertheim have explored the interest of German Jews in Spinoza, while Daniel Schwartz has cast a wider net in tracing this fascination in different centers and genres of modern Jewish culture. In a related vein, the Israeli philosopher Yirmiyahu Yovel has written a number of books that cast Spinoza as the preeminent "Marrano of reason" – and as such, as the first modern, and secular, Jew.[49]

---

[47] See Sylvie Anne Goldberg, *Le Clepsydre: Essai sur la pluralité des temps dans le judaïsme* (Paris: Albin Michel, 2000), 317, and Elisheva Carlebach, *Palaces of Time: Jewish Calendar and Culture in Early Modern Europe* (Cambridge, MA: Harvard, 2011).

[48] Nora, "Between Memory and History," 7.

[49] See, for example, Jonathan Skolnik, "Writing Jewish History between Gutzkow and Goethe: Auerbach's Spinoza and the Birth of Modern Jewish Historical Fiction,"

The existence of Jewish memory cultures in modern times has animated studies of distinct national and regional variants. In *Mémoire juive et nationalité allemande* (2000), Jacques Ehrenfreund adopted a "sociocultural historical" approach focused on the dissemination and popularization of historical knowledge among Jews in late nineteenth and early twentieth-century Germany – that is, in the generations that followed the rise of the more elitist *Wissenschaft des Judentums*. Ehrenfreund chronicled the rise of learned societies, historical commissions, museums, and commemorative days, all of which were symptoms of a number of defining impulses for German Jews: first, the impulse to grasp onto a rapidly vanishing memory of the past through historical reconstruction; second, the desire to create a canon of heroes and iconic images suitable to the demands of German Jews in this period; and third, the need to assert with certainty the antiquity of and accompanying justification for Jewish settlement on German soil.[50]

Some years before Ehrenfreund, Joëlle Bahloul undertook to study the formation of memory in a different setting through a different pair of methodological lenses. Relying on her training as an anthropologist, Bahloul employed ethnographic tools to reconstruct a family home – her grandmother's – in Sétif, Algeria. More accurately, she used those tools to reconstruct the overlapping and divergent lines of memory of that home, as articulated by relatives of hers who once inhabited it. Her textured study yielded an "architecture of memory" that captured the loss, longing, and estrangement of its one-time residents, who had long ago migrated from Algeria to France.[51]

It almost goes without saying that the study of loss, longing, and estrangement has been most pronounced in Jewish studies and related fields around the subject of the Holocaust. For the Holocaust left behind a massive crater of historical destruction, but also a rich trail of evidence and the many voices of survivors. The gap between the enormity of destruction and the abundance of evidence yields a decided air of incomprehensibility.

Prooftexts 19 (May 1999): 101–125; David Wertheim, *Salvation through Spinoza: A Study of Jewish Culture in Weimar Germany* (Leiden: Brill, 2011); Daniel Schwartz, *From Heretic to Hero: Spinoza in the Modern Jewish Imagination* (Princeton: Princeton University Press, 2011); and Yirmiyahu Yovel, *Spinoza and Other Heretics: The Marrano of Reason* (Princeton: Princeton University Press, 1992) and *The Other Within: The Marranos: Split Identity and Emerging Modernity* (Princeton: Princeton University Press, 2009).

[50] Jacques Ehrenfreund, *Mémoire juive et nationalité allemande: Les juifs berlinois à la Belle Époque* (Paris: Presses universitaires de France, 2000).

[51] Joëlle Bahloul, *The Architecture of Memory: A Jewish-Muslim Household in Colonial Algeria, 1937–1962* (Cambridge: Cambridge University Press, 1996).

At the same time, both fuel among survivors, their descendants, and others an intense longing for a lost past that yields a rich and complicated web of memories.

Among scholars who have studied history and memory in the Holocaust, the figure of Saul Friedländer stands out. Friedländer's exceptional career has woven together a pair of interlocking pursuits, each of which alone would have amounted to a significant achievement: first, recording, with a vast command of the evidentiary field, the history of the Nazi genocidal campaign; and second, marshalling his considerable theoretical sophistication to address the challenges of representing and narrating the Shoah in light of claims of its incommensurability. These two tasks reach their culmination in Friedländer's *magnum opus*, the two-volume historical account published over the course of a decade: *Nazi Germany and the Jews: The Years of Persecution, 1933–1939* (1997) and *Nazi Germany and the Jews: The Years of Extermination, 1939–1945* (2007).

To these works, and to the two tasks mentioned above, Friedländer adds another major contribution: profound reflection on the relationship between history and memory. He has thought and written about the relationship at some length in his scholarly works. In *Memory, History, and the Extermination of the Jews of Europe* (1993), he argued that between the poles of collective memory and "dispassionate" historical inquiry rests a middle ground where the informed observer might profitably stand. This blended perspective is especially intriguing and potentially beneficial for the generation of scholars of which he is part. In the introduction to *Nazi Germany and the Jews*, he wrote: "For my generation, to partake at one and the same time in the memory and the present perceptions of this past may create an unsettling dissonance; it may, however, also nurture insights that would otherwise be inaccessible."[52]

The distinct properties of the historian as participant-observer are on full display in Friedländer. He, after all, was a victim of Nazism's ravages, having been displaced from his native Prague as a child and surviving only by being disguised as a Catholic boy in France. And he saw fit to give voice to his own memories. Thus, in addition to his scholarly work, Friedländer published a moving and powerful autobiographical account, *When Memory Comes* (1979), in which he retells his own physical and spiritual journey from Prague to Jerusalem via Vichy France.

[52] See Saul Friedländer, *Memory, History, and the Extermination of the Jews of Europe* (Bloomington: Indiana University Press, 1993), vii and *Nazi Germany and the Jews: The Years of Persecution* (New York: Harper Collins, 1997), 5. See also the incisive review essay by James E. Young, "Between History and Memory: The Uncanny Voices of Historian and Survivor," *History & Memory* 9 (Fall 1997): 47–58.

Beyond his own work, Friedländer has encouraged research on the inter-section of history and memory in several ways. He was a founding editor of the journal *History & Memory*, established in 1989, in which a number of key articles devoted to Holocaust history and memory appear alongside articles on a wide range of other topics (including the important rejoinder to Yerushalmi by Friedländer's close friend, Amos Funkenstein in the first number). And he has directly trained and indirectly inspired dozens of leading scholars of the Holocaust in North America, Europe, and Israel, including Gulie Neeman Arad, Omer Bartov, Phillippe Burrin, Alon Confino, Dominick LaCapra, and James E. Young, as well as his UCLA students Wulf Kansteiner, Gavriel Rosenfeld, and Alexandra Garbarini.

Friedländer's impact has been vast in the field of Holocaust studies, but hardly solitary. The field generates hundreds of new scholarly publications a year, and has attracted to it historians of the highest distinction and achievement including his contemporary and fellow Prague native, Yehuda Bauer. Recently, in pondering the state of this robust field, the New York University scholar David Engel has posed a provocative question: why has Holocaust studies grown outside of, rather than within – or at least adjacent to – Jewish studies? His 2010 book *Historians of the Jews and the Holocaust* seeks to answer this question. He identifies a set of conscious and subconscious factors in the workings of Jewish studies scholars that led them to engage in "sequestering the Holocaust and removing it from the mainstream of Jewish history."[53] Thus, he argues for example, that the leg-acy of Salo Baron's renowned admonition against the "lachrymose theory" of Jewish history hovers over Jewish studies, encouraging its practitioners to avoid the most exceptional and lugubrious of events in favor of the more routine lived experience of the Jews. Engel's evidence in arguing for the neglect of Holocaust studies is not altogether persuasive. But his plain-tive tone in making this claim brings us back to a number of central issues with which this chapter began and has been preoccupied: the relationship between history and memory, and the function of the modern Jewish his-torian. At the end of his book, Engel, who was himself a student of Amos Funkenstein, returns to Yosef Yerushalmi's *Zakhor*, alternately rereading, correcting, and affirming several key arguments in the book. Engel believes that what he sees as the unwillingness of Jewish studies scholars to engage more directly with the Holocaust necessarily consigns them to irrelevance. Moreover, it amounts to an abdication of their mission as guardians of memory and servants of their community. To highlight this point, Engel recalls Yerushalmi's charge: "The burden of building a bridge to his people

---

[53] David Engel, *Historians of the Jews and the Holocaust* (Stanford: Stanford University Press, 2010), 23.

remains with the historian." Far more directly than Yerushalmi, Engel yearns for a broader fulfillment of that calling, especially by integrating the ultimate lachrymose event, the Holocaust, into the broader narrative of Jewish history. At the same time, and in evocation of Yerushalmi's more doleful side, he expresses skepticism that the historian will be able to rise to the challenge.[54]

ON MARTYROLOGY AND HISTORIOGRAPHY: A CODA

By way of conclusion to this essay, I'd like to recall and, ultimately, call into question a number of standard assumptions made about Jewish history and memory. It has been oft-remarked that post-biblical Jews manifested little interest in history before the modern age, except in the wake of per-secution or crisis. While the first part of that assertion depends to a great extent on how one defines history, the second part seems more straight-forward and sustainable, at least from the Middle Ages on. Commencing with the late eleventh-century Crusades, Jews responded to crisis and per-secution in dual and entwined fashion, by chronicling and memorializing the past. They continued to do so throughout early modern times. But did they continue to do so in modern times, including in the wake of the greatest of all persecutions?

Before answering that question directly, it is worth noting that the Holocaust induced an interesting moment of self-reflection on the Jewish practice of recording and memorializing the past. Yosef Yerushalmi's *Zakhor*, on my reading, belongs to that period of self-reflection. His prob-ing and introspective insights into the historian's function – and the com-plex, interlacing relationship between history and memory – took root in a post-War vacuum of faith and comprehension. The "golden age" of Jewish ideology had passed, or more accurately, was violently uprooted; in its place came a considerable degree of intellectual skepticism and lack of certitude that would metamorphose over time into a philosophical and methodological stance known as postmodernism.

In his own nostalgic moments, Yosef Yerushalmi understood and, in part, lamented that an abundance of historical research in his time was not the magic remedy. Jews still sought out and required "a new, metahistori-cal myth," for which fiction was a far likelier source than history.[55] In the more distant past, that mythic power was provided by a mix of chronicling and memorializing without the attendant expectation of objectivity and accuracy that accompanies the modern historian.

[54] Ibid., 227–229.
[55] Yerushalmi, *Zakhor*, 98.

Yerushalmi's reflections on the momentous transitions in the relationship between history and memory call to mind a brief text written forty years earlier, in the dark days of the Second World War; it serves as a prescient adumbration of the later *Zakhor* in a number of important regards. In June 1941, the Russian-Jewish historian, Elias Tcherikower (1881–1943), delivered a lecture at YIVO in New York entitled "Jewish Martyrology and Jewish Historiography." Tcherikower opened his address with a very Yerushalmian line: "The Jews are a people of the richest history in the world, but of a very scant recording of that history." Given both the duration and eventfulness of the Jewish past, and given the fact that "the Jews have a classical historical monument – the Bible," it was surprising that the post-biblical age yielded so little by the way of historiography.[56] Tcherikower went on to discuss a number of the same points that anchored Yerushalmi's analysis, especially in the second and third chapters of *Zakhor*. Thus, on Tcherikower's reading:

- The Talmud was largely uninterested in "mere events, history for history's sake, chronologies" (11);
- "Historical-mindedness" was often suppressed in the name of "religious dogmatism," though it did not die out among the Jews (11);
- The "dark days of the crusades" yielded a new phenomenon in Diaspora history, "Jewish chronicles" (14);
- The persecutions of the Middle Ages also prompted a kind of ritual-liturgical historiography in the form of *selihot* (penitential prayers);
- A more significant wave of Jewish historical writing arose in the late Renaissance in the work of Capsali, Usque, Yosef Ha-Kohen, and Azariah di Rossi (18);
- While this body of work often challenged existing rabbinic norms, it was manifestly not "purely scientific historiography";
- The "modern scientific study of history" came about later, in the nineteenth century, and sought to unmoor itself from the strong martyrological impulse of previous Jewish historical writing.

What is striking about this essay is not only the overlap with Yerushalmi's analysis, but rather the tersely articulated, though undeniable, yearning in both authors. Both trace the modes in which pre-modern Jews sought to record and render meaning to their past. Both regarded the modern

---

[56] Elias Tcherikower, "Jewish Martyrology and Jewish Historiography," *Yiddish Annual of Jewish Social Science* 1 (1946): 9–10. The English version is based on "Yidishe martirologe un yidishe historiografiye," *YIVO Bleter* 17 (1941): 97–112. On this article, see Joshua M. Karlip, "Between Martyrology and Historiography: Elias Tcherikower and the Making of a Pogrom Historian," *East European Jewish Affairs* 38 (2008): 257–280.

historiographical enterprise as a break from those modes, yielding at once more data but less meaning. Just as Yerushalmi cast that enterprise as the sacrament of "fallen Jews," Tcherikower acknowledged that "our modern scientific study of history ... is no longer instigated by surrounding catastrophes." He immediately added that "without the old historical primitives we should never fully understand the Jewish past and the innermost experiences of the people, and would soon lose our historical bearings."[57] These "historical primitives" – alluding to the recollection of past persecutions – could not be left behind altogether if modern Jewish historical scholarship were to play a vibrant and relevant role. A deeply engaged and effecting collective memory, on this view, was an essential leaven for historiography.

We began this essay by noting the presence of competing impulses, antiquarian and utilitarian, from the inception of modern Jewish scholarship in Germany in the early nineteenth century. Though not alone in this task, Elias Tcherikower and Yosef Yerushalmi sought to overcome, each in his own idiom and circumstances, the divide between these impulses by doing what they knew how to do best: tracing the history of the relationship between history and memory. Possessed of varying degrees of intentionality and self-awareness, each harbored the hope to nudge historians beyond their narrow disciplinary comfort zone. Whereas Tcherikower's meditations have been largely forgotten, Yerushalmi deserves significant credit for inspiring a generation of scholars to investigate more intensively Jewish history and memory, and particularly, the terrain shared by them. Moreover, he maintained throughout his career the desire to explore and even inhabit that terrain himself, notwithstanding the sober diagnosis of the modern Jewish historian he delivered in *Zakhor*.

This is, admittedly, a strong reading of Yerushalmi, one that militates against the received view of *Zakhor*. Whether or not one agrees that he maintained such a desire to bridge the gap between history and memory, it is clear that Yerushalmi did not see historical scholarship in his day as filling that role. But his assessment of other laborers in the field may have been too sweeping. After all, it is hard to ignore the cumulative weight of the historical work devoted to the Shoah that has been produced over the past half-century. It has carved out a broad ridge of memory in American and American Jewish cultures, prompting us to reconsider Yerushalmi's judgment that the event's "image is being shaped, not at the historian's anvil, but at the novelist's crucible."[58]

[57] Tcherikower, "Jewish Martyrology and Jewish Historiography," 23.
[58] Yerushalmi, *Zakhor*, 98.

Indeed, as one surveys the landscape, it appears that the tasks of chronicling and memorializing – those distinctive medieval Jewish pathways to history – have not, in fact, been abandoned altogether. Scholars, many of whom are animated by a sense of moral obligation to give voice to the victims of the Holocaust, have generated an ever-expanding mass of historical research that carefully charts the horrors of Nazi rule down to the last minute. Furthermore, it is scholars, many of them motivated by a sense of obligation as Jews, who have played key roles in conceiving, advocating for, and providing historical content to museums and memorials dedicated to the preservation of Holocaust memory.

To be sure, this set of labors is not equivalent to the medieval chronicle or penitential prayer in genre or even intent. But it does suggest to us a pair of concluding suppositions: first, that the modern historian has not been quite so disengaged from the living currents of memory (or at least, from the more mediated realm of commemoration) as we might have believed; and second, that the binary opposition between history and memory yields, upon close scrutiny, to a far more complicated, enmeshed, and mutually reinforcing relationship.

SELECT BIBLIOGRAPHY

Barnay, Jacob. *Historyografyah u-le'umiyut: megamot be-ḥeker Erets-Yisra'el ve-yishuvah ha-Yehudi, 634–1881.* Jerusalem: Magnes Press 1995.

Baron, Salo W. *History and Jewish Historians.* Philadelphia: Jewish Publication Society, 1964.

Brenner, Michael. *Prophets of the Past: Interpreters of Jewish History.* Princeton: Princeton University Press, 2010.

Ehrenfreund, Jacques. *Mémoire juive et nationalité allemande: Les juifs berlinois à la Belle Époque.* Paris: Presses universitaires de France, 2000.

Engel, David. *Historians of the Jews and the Holocaust.* Stanford: Stanford University Press, 2010.

Feiner, Shmuel. *Haskalah and History: The Emergence of Modern Historical Consciousness.* Oxford: Littman Library, 2002.

Friedländer, Saul. *Memory, History, and the Extermination of the Jews of Europe.* Bloomington: Indiana University Press, 1993.

Nazi Germany and the Jews: The Years of Persecution. New York: Harper and Row, 1997.

Funkenstein, Amos. "Collective Memory and Historical Consciousness." *History and Memory* 1 (Spring–Summer 1989): 5–26.

Goldberg, Sylvie Anne. *Le Clepsydre: Essai sur la pluralité des temps dans le judaïsme.* Paris: Albin Michel, 2000.

ed. *L'histoire et la mémoire de l'histoire: Hommage à Yosef Hayim Yerushalmi.* Paris: Albin Michel, 2012.

Transmettre l'histoire juive: Entretiens avec Sylvie Anne Goldberg. Paris: Albin Michel, 2012.

Heschel, Susannah. *Abraham Geiger and the Jewish Jesus*. Chicago: University of Chicago, 1998.

Meyer, Michael A. *The Origins of the Modern Jew: Jewish Identity and European Culture in Germany, 1749–1824*. Detroit: Wayne State University Press, 1967.

Myers, David N. "Recalling *Zakhor*: A Quarter Century's Perspective." *Jewish Quarterly Review* 97 (2007): 487–490.

——— *Re-inventing the Jewish Past: European Jewish Intellectuals and the Zionist Return to History*. New York: Oxford University Press, 1995.

——— "Remembering 'Zakhor': A Super-commentary." *History and Memory* 4 (1992): 129–148.

——— "Selbstreflexion im modernene Erinnerungsdiskurs." In *Jüdische Geschichtsschreibung heute: Themen, Positionen, Kontroversen*, ed. Michael Brenner and David N. Myers, 55–74. Munich: C. H. Beck, 2002.

——— and Alexander Kaye, eds. *The Faith of Fallen Jews: Yosef Hayim Yerushalmi and the Writing of Jewish History*. Hanover, NH: Brandeis University Press, 2014.

Nora, Pierre. "Between Memory and History: *Les lieux de mémoire*." *Representations* 26 (Spring 1989): 7–24.

Raz-Krakotzkin, Amnon. "Jewish Memory between Exile and History." *Jewish Quarterly Review* 97 (Fall 2007): 530–543.

——— "Yitsuga ha-le'umi shel ha-galut: ha-histoyografyah ha-Tsiyonit ve-yehude yeme ha-benayim." Ph.D. diss., Tel Aviv University, 1996.

Roemer, Nils. *Jewish Scholarship and Culture in 19th-Century Germany: Between History and Faith*. Madison: University of Wisconsin Press, 2005.

Schorsch, Ismar. *From Text to Context: The Turn to History in Modern Judaism*. Hanover, NH: Brandeis University Press, 1994.

——— *Leopold Zunz: Creativity in Adversity*. Philadelphia: University of Pennsylvania Press, 2016.

Simon-Nahum, Perrine. *La cité investie: La "science du judaïsme" français et la République*. Paris: Cerf, 1991.

Tcherikower, Elias. "Jewish Martyrology and Jewish Historiography." *Yiddish Annual of Jewish Social Science* 1 (1946): 9–23.

White, Hayden. *Metahistory: The Historical Imagination in Nineteenth-Century Europe*. Baltimore: Johns Hopkins University Press, 1973.

Yerushalmi, Yosef H. "A Jewish Historian in the 'Age of Aquarius.'" Commencement Address, Hebrew College, Brookline, MA, June 1970. Reprinted in Myers and Kaye, *The Faith of Fallen Jews*, 49–59.

——— "Jüdische Historiographie und Postmodernismus: Eine abweichende Meinung." In *Jüdische Geschichtsschreibung heute: Themen, Positionen, Kontroversen*, ed. Michael Brenner and David N. Myers, 75–94. Munich: C. H. Beck, 2002.

——— *Zakhor: Jewish History and Jewish Memory*. Seattle: University of Washington, 1982.

CHAPTER 30

JEWS AND MATERIAL CULTURE

LEORA AUSLANDER

A first encounter with the concept, "Jewish material culture," may provoke puzzlement. What, the reader may ask, is "material culture"? And, what would make it "Jewish"?[1] The broadest usable definition of material culture is: things produced by human beings.[2] It is the very nature of human perception and psychology that renders material culture important as an object of research. Not all thoughts, memories, or emotion are expressed linguistically rather than through other media whether material, visual, or musical; if scholars limit our investigations to linguistic sources our understanding will be impoverished.[3] The two boundaries that scholarly production of the last generation has shown to be particularly fraught are those between the material and the linguistic and the material and the visual. In defending the salience of the former, the curator Susan Pearce has argued, "perceptions about colour, shape and decoration are not part of our linguistic inheritance, but part of our material tradition in the strict sense."[4] And, as the archaeologist Roland Fletcher cogently stated: "… it is clear that non-verbal signaling may possess its own internal formal coherence and is not reducible to the 'structures' of verbal meaning."[5] People,

---

[1] My thinking on Jewish material culture was greatly improved by conversations during my stay at the Jean and Samuel Frankel Center for Judaic Studies at the University of Michigan in 2009. My profound thanks to Deborah Dash Moore for making my visit possible and to her and my fellow fellows for productive discussion. I would also like to thank Rachel Neis and Tara Zahra for their careful readings and perceptive comments and Ilana Miller for research assistance for the final version of this chapter.

[2] For a more thorough elaboration of the general argument see Leora Auslander, "Beyond Words." *American Historical Review* 110, no. 4 (2005): 1015–1045 and Leora Auslander, "AHR Conversation: Historians and the Study of Material Culture." *American Historical Review* 114, no. 5 (2009): 1354–1404.

[3] Daniel Miller, *Material Culture and Mass Consumption* (Oxford: Blackwell, 1987).

[4] Susan M. Pearce, *Museums, Objects, and Collections: A Cultural Study* (Washington: Smithsonian Institution Press, 1992), 23.

[5] Fletcher in Ian Hodder, *The Meaning of Things: Material Culture and Symbolic Expression* (Boston: Unwin Hyman, 1989), 35.

in other words, use both things and words to communicate, to remember, and to express themselves, but both the *what* and the *how* of words and things are different. A primary reason to study material culture, then, is to gain access to the extra-linguistic range of human meaning-making and communication.[6]

Things, in their three-dimensionality, touchability, and mortality mirror human embodiedness. Things, like bodies, are accessible not only to our eyes but also our fingers and our skin. Time and use mark them, as they mark the human body. Our bodies sometimes quite literally inscribe themselves on things; the permanent folds left in a jacket-sleeve (called "memories" in British English) or the marks of the carpenter's chisel on a doorframe come to mind. Like human bodies, things have a finite life-span, a specific moment of coming into existence and of ceasing to exist. Those endings are sometimes natural and peaceful, a result of age and use, but often also a result of accidental or intentional violence. Destroying a valued possession can be a means of attacking its owner. It is that close relation to the human body that gives material culture its particular meaning- and memory-bearing capacities. Psychoanalysts, psychologists, poets, and philosophers have written reams on the importance of things throughout the lifespan.[7] From a baby's transitional object, used to make parental absence tolerable, through wedding rings, to the small possessions carried by refugees when they leave home, to the cherished mementos of a beloved dead spouse, people, across time and space, have put objects to work for them.[8] That work is different than, and complementary to, the work done by language. This work of fostering memory, making meaning, constituting relationships, and expressing feelings is one kind of labor done by concrete things. People also use objects, of course, for much more pragmatic purposes.

In the domain of the pragmatic (which always overlaps with the symbolic) people have made things with which to acquire, prepare, cook, serve, and eat food. They have constructed shelters and furniture to lie and sit upon within them. They have crafted clothing to keep themselves warm or cool, or to protect the skin or the feet. They have built means of transportation and the tools needed to make all of these things. Some

---

[6] It should be noted, however, that this is a highly contested position; some theorists argue that there is no extra-linguistic domain. See Auslander, "AHR Conversation" for references.

[7] Gaston Bachelard, *The Poetics of Space*, trans. Maria Joias (Boston: Beacon Press, 1964); Henri Bergson, *Matière et mémoire: essai sur la relation du corps à l'ésprit* (Paris: Alcan, 1896); Donald Woods Winnicott, *Collected Papers: Through Paediatrics to Psycho-analysis* (New York: Basic Books, 1958).

[8] Yolande Tisseron-Papetti, *La Passion des étoffes chez un neuro-pyschiatre* (Paris: Solin, 1990).

anthropologists argue, in fact, that it is tool-making, not language, that separates human beings from other species. One may debate the productivity of attempting to establish the priority of language and tool-making, but the reality of the specificity of the material in relation to the linguistic, and therefore the importance of its study, has been clearly established.

The boundary between the visual and the material has been less debated than that between the linguistic and the material, in part because it is often assumed to matter less. The basic differentiation between the visual and the material is that between two dimensions and three. That is, even if the attribute of two-dimensionality cannot be taken too literally – paintings are three-dimensional and one could argue that images on a computer screen do not fit into the conventional system of dimensionality at all – two dimensional objects are primarily encountered and perceived with the eyes and not with the other senses. Scholars working on the senses have demonstrated both the historical and cultural specificity of their mobilization and the consistent differentiation among them.[9] In some societies and some periods, the training of the eye is given precedence over that of the skin, the ears, the nose, or the mouth; in others it is another sense that is dominant or greater stress is put on their complementarity. A concept that puts emphasis on studying the material, the touchable, is crucial to our understanding these differential and complementary roles of these senses.

A reader might still object that however persuasive all of this may be in general, it seems to have either little relevance for Jews, or, if it does have relevance, then there would seem to be no obvious reason to believe that Jews have a particular relation to material culture. Some would even argue that the combination of the second biblical commandment and the textual focus of Judaism have rendered Jews especially indifferent to both visual and material culture. There is, however, a very substantial literature demonstrating that Jews, despite the prohibition on graven images, have, since antiquity, been intensely engaged in producing and consuming images and objects.[10] And, while the centrality of texts, their recitation and

[9] Constance Classen, *Worlds of Sense: Exploring the Senses in History and Across Cultures* (London: Routledge, 1993); Fiona Candin, *Art, Museums, and Touch* (Manchester: Manchester University Press, 2010); Alain Corbin, *The Foul and the Fragrant: Odor and the French Social Imagination* (Cambridge, MA: Harvard University Press, 1988); Jonathan Crary, *Techniques of the Observer: On Vision and Modernity in the Nineteenth Century* (Cambridge, MA: MIT Press, 1990); Veit Erlmann, *Reason and Resonance: A History of Modern Aurality* (Boston: Zone Books, 2010).

[10] For visual culture, see Richard I. Cohen, *Jewish Icons: Art and Society in Modern Europe* (Berkeley: University of California Press, 1998); Vivian B. Mann, *Jewish Texts on the Visual Arts* (Cambridge: Cambridge University Press, 2008); Kalman P. Bland, *The Artless*

study, has remained unquestioned, Jewish studies scholars, particularly in the last forty years, have turned their attention to the Jewish body and discovered its salience for understanding Jewish culture. This literature, in large part motivated or inspired by feminist and queer engagement with Judaism, on the place of the body in Jewish thought, ritual, and experience is clearly crucial to the study of material culture, even if that is not its explicit focus.[11]

Analysis of Jewish material culture *per se* has been slower to appear, but excellent work has been done on Jews as producers of material culture and Jewish use of objects.[12] This very varied research reflects the particularities of how Jews have used things, how that use differs in each time and place, and transformations in the field of Jewish studies. There is a well-established literature, much of it by curators, on the objects used in the performance of religious ritual, whether at the synagogue or at home: Torah scrolls, their ornaments, and the cabinets that hold and protect them; mezuzot; ketubot; Kiddush cups; tallisim; and teffilin; but also challah covers, spice and etrog boxes, and candlesticks.[13] Choices made concerning

Jew: Medieval and Modern Affirmations and Denials of the Visual (Princeton: Princeton University Press, 2000); Maya Balakirsky Katz, *The Visual Culture of Chabad* (Cambridge: Cambridge University Press, 2010). For material culture see below.

[11] Daniel Boyarin, *Carnal Israel: Reading Sex in Talmudic Culture* (Berkeley: University of California Press, 1993); Daniel Boyarin, *Unheroic Conduct: The Rise of Heterosexuality and the Invention of the Jewish Man* (Berkeley: University of California Press, 1997); Melvin Konner, *The Jewish Body* (New York: Schocken, 2009); Elliot R. Wolfson, "The Body in the Text: A Kabbalistic Theory of Embodiment," *The Jewish Quarterly Review* 95, no. 3 (2005): 479–500; Howard Eilberg-Schwartz, *People of the Body: Jews and Judaism from an Embodied Perspective* (Albany, NY: SUNY Press, 1992); Lawrence A. Hoffman, *Beyond the Text: A Holistic Approach to Liturgy* (Bloomington: Indiana University Press, 1989); Maria Diemling and Giuseppe Veltri, eds., *The Jewish Body: Corporeality, Society and Identity in the Renaissance and Early Modern Period* (Leiden: Brill, 2009); Deborah A. Green, *The Aroma of Righteousness: Scent and Seduction in Rabbinic Life and Literature* (State College: Pennsylvania State University Press, 2011).

[12] One of the very few works that articulates the problematic as that of "material culture" is Ken Koltun-Fromm, *Material Culture and Jewish Thought in America* (Bloomington: Indiana University Press, 2010).

[13] Barbara Kirshenblatt-Gimblett, *Fabric of Jewish Life: Textiles from the Jewish Museum Collection* (New York: Jewish Museum, 1977); Stephen Bailey, *Kashrut, Tefillin, Tzitzit* (Northvale, NJ: Jason Aronson, 2000); Vivian B. Mann, "Spirituality and Jewish Ceremonial Art," *Artibus et Historiae* 24, no. 48 (2003): 172–183; Vivian B. Mann, *Art and Ceremony in Jewish Life: Essays in the History of Jewish Art* (London: Pindar Press, 2005); Alice M. Greenwald, "The Masonic Mizrah and Lamp: Jewish Ritual Art as a Reflection of Cultural Assimilation," *Jewish Art* 10 (1984): 87–101; Claudia Nahson, *Ketubbot: Marriage Contracts from the Jewish Museum* (San Francisco: Pomegranate,

the aesthetic presentation of sacred texts have also long been the object of study. Historians of the book have analyzed the myriad forms taken by the Passover Haggadah, for example.[14] Anthropologists and historians have studied the material culture associated with religiously mandated sartorial practices, particularly forms of head-covering and modest clothing.[15]

The role of Jews in the making and circulation of material culture not linked to religious ritual or practice has also attracted considerable scholarly attention.[16] Some of this work has focused on the distorting effects of discrimination; Jews were often excluded from some artisanal trades and forced to congregate heavily in others.[17] This history of discrimination has also been traced in the domain of consumption; historians have shown how Jews have been, on the one hand, refused access to certain goods by means of sumptuary law or, on the other, marked by the obligation to purchase

1998); Jeremy Stolow, "Holy Pleather: Materializing Authority in Contemporary Orthodox Jewish Publishing," *Material Religion* 3, no. 3 (2007): 324–335. See also notes to the literatures on each object below.

[14] Katrin Kogman-Appel, *Jewish Book Art between Islam and Christianity: The Decoration of Hebrew Bibles in Medieval Spain*, trans. Judith Davidson (Leiden: Brill, 2004); Bezalel Narkiss, *Illuminated Hebrew Manuscripts* (New York: Alpine Fine Arts Collection, 1983); Michael Epstein, *The Medieval Haggadah: Art, Narrative, and Religious Imagination* (New Haven: Yale University Press, 2011).

[15] Jenna Weissman Joselit, *New York's Jewish Jews: The Orthodox Community in the Interwar Years* (Bloomington: Indiana University Press, 1990); Barbara Kirschenblatt-Gimblett and Jeffrey Shandler, eds., Special Issue of *Material Religion* 3, no. 3 (2007): "Material Cultures of American Jewry."

[16] Sarah Abrevaya Stein, *Plumes: Ostrich Feathers, Jews, and a Lost World of Global Commerce* (New Haven: Yale University Press, 2008); Nancy L. Green, *Ready-To-Wear and Ready-To-Work: A Century of Immigrants in Paris and New York* (Durham: Duke University Press, 1997); Gabriel M. Goldstein and Elizabeth E. Greenbert, eds., *A Perfect Fit: The Garment Industry and American Jewry, 1800–1900* (Lubbock: Texas Tech University Press for the Yeshiva University Press, 2013); Roberta S. Kremer, *Broken Threads: The Destruction of the Jewish Fashion Industry in Germany and Austria* (Oxford: Berg, 2007).

[17] Mark Wischnitzer, *A History of Jewish Crafts and Guilds* (New York: J. David, 1965); Steven A. Epstein, *Wage and Labor Guilds in Medieval Europe* (Chapel Hill: University of North Carolina Press, 1991); Angela Groppi, "Jews, Women, Soldiers and Neophytes: the Practice of Trades under Exclusions and Privileges from the Seventeenth to the Early Nineteenth Century," in *Guilds, Markets, and Work Regulations in Italy, 16th–19th centuries*, ed. Alberto Guenzi, Paola Massa, and Fausto Piola Caselli (Aldershot: Ashgate, 1998); Jacek Sobczak, "The Chronology and Distribution of Jewish Craft Guilds in Old Poland, 1613–1795," and Maurycy Horn, "Jews and Trade at the End of the Sixteenth Century and in the First Half of the Seventeenth," both in *The Jews in Old Poland, 1000–1795*, ed. Antony Polonsky, Jakub Basista, and Andrzej Link-Lenczowski (London: I.B. Tauris, 1993).

particular clothing or other goods.[18] Research on Jewish consumers has probed deeper, showing how Jews have voluntarily used objects as identity markers, to communicate – whether consciously or unconsciously – who they are to others.[19] On a parallel track, other scholars claim that objects are essential to the making of the self; they are an externalization of an individual's psychic "furniture," enabling self-recognition.[20] When investigating diasporic Jews, this scholarship on the production, distribution, and consumption of goods, focuses on Jews as members of a minority, often immigrant, culture.[21] It productively borrows from, and speaks to, parallel research on other such groups.

This chapter reflects both the Jewish experience of material culture and recent scholarship in the field. It argues, first, for the existence throughout history of a particular relation to the senses, and therefore to material culture, in Jewish religious practice. The essay then moves to an analysis

---

[18] Felix Singermann, *Über Juden-Abzeichen: Ein Beitrag zur sozialen Geschichte des Judentums* (Berlin: L. Lamm, 1915); Gerbern S. Oegema, *The History of the Shield of David: The Birth of a Symbol* (Frankfurt am Main: P. Lang, 1996).

[19] Edna Nahshon, ed., *Jews and Shoes* (Oxford: Berg, 2008); Nils H. Roemer and Gideon Reuveni, eds., *Longing, Belonging, and the Making of Jewish Consumer Culture* (Leiden: Brill, 2010); Julia Phillips Cohen, "Oriental by Design: Ottoman Jews, Imperial Style and the Performance of Heritage," *American Historical Review* 119, no. 2 (2014): 364–398; Esther Juhasz, "The Material Culture of Sephardic Jews in the Western Ottoman Empire (19th and 20th Centuries)," in *The Jews of the Ottoman Empire*, ed. Avigdor Levy (Princeton: Darwin Press, 1994), 575–583; and Leonard J. Greenspoon, ed., *Fashioning Jews: Clothing, Culture and Commerce*, Studies in Jewish Civilization, 24 (West Lafayette, IN: Purdue University Press, 2013).

[20] Simon J. Bronner, ed., *Jews at Home: The Domestication of Identity* (Oxford: Littman Library of Jewish Civilization, 2010); Gideon S. Golany, *Babylonian Jewish Neighborhood and Home Design* (Lewiston: Edwin Mellen Press, 1999); Juliet Steyn, *The Jew: Assumptions of Identity* (London: Cassell, 1999); Jenna Weissman Joselit, *The Wonders of America: Reinventing Jewish Culture 1880–1950* (New York: Hill and Wang, 1994); Eric Silverman, *A Cultural History of Jewish Dress* (New York: Bloomsbury Academic, 2013).

[21] Jenna Weissman Joselit, *A Perfect Fit: Clothes, Character and the Promise of America* (New York: Metropolitan Books, 2001); Barbara A. Schreier, *Becoming American Women: Clothing and the Jewish Immigrant Experience, 1880–1920* (Chicago: Chicago Historical Society, 1994); Joseph Buckman, *Immigrants and the Class Struggle: The Jewish Immigrant in Leeds, 1880–1914* (Manchester: Manchester University Press, 1983); Andrew R. Heinze, *Adapting to Abundance: Jewish Immigrants, Mass Consumption, and the Search for American Identity* (New York: Columbia University Press, 1990); Jenna Weissman Joselit and Susan L. Braunstein, *Getting Comfortable in New York: The American Jewish Home, 1880–1950* (New York: The Jewish Museum, 1990); Deborah Dash Moore, *At Home in America: Second Generation New York Jews* (New York: Columbia University Press, 1981).

of how Jews have used material culture to feel at home as minority communities within larger populations. The third section demonstrates the importance of material culture in the Zionist movement in Europe as well as in Palestine, while the fourth addresses the consequences of the Shoah for Jewish material culture; the conclusion discusses recent developments. Contrary to both the notion that Jews are too preoccupied with words to be interested in things and that insofar as they are engaged with objects that engagement is no different than that of any other group, I argue that the nature of Judaism itself, the centuries lived as often highly mobile diasporic minorities, the realities of discrimination and marginalization, and the Shoah, have created a specifically Jewish relationship to material culture.

EMBODIMENT, MATERIALITY, AND RELIGIOUS EXPERIENCE

The conceptualization of the human perceptual apparatus encoded by Aristotle as one of five senses – sight, hearing, smell, taste and touch – entered into the Jewish literature along with other elements of Greco-Arabic philosophy. There is, however, an important difference. While for Aristotle there was a clear hierarchy among the senses, with sight having pride of place, that is not true for Judaism. Although some scholars argue that sight and hearing are both considered nobler in Judaism than taste, touch, and smell, others have made the counter-argument that there is something close to parity among the five. There is, in any case, consensus that sight is not prioritized and that all of the senses are engaged in spiritual practice.

A key text for thinking through this Jewish relation to the senses is the French philosopher Catherine Chalier's, 1995 *Sagesse des sens: Le regard et l'écoute dans la tradition hébraïque.*[22] *Sagesse des sens* makes a powerful argument, based in part on the work of the philosopher Michel Emmanuel Lévinas, for both the particular importance of hearing in that tradition, but also, and this is more important for us here, *for a division of labor among the senses.*[23]

Chalier argues that the particular relation to the senses found in Hebrew texts is reinforced and transmitted through everyday religious practice and the ways in which those practices engage the body. In daily prayers, for

[22] Catherine Chalier, *La sagesse des sens: Le regard et l'écoute dans la tradition hébraïque* (Paris: Albin Michel, 1995).

[23] Judah M. Cohen takes the argument for a Jewish relation to hearing in a different direction. See "The Jewish Sound of Things," *Material Religion* 3, no. 3 (2007): 336–353.

example, not only is the Shema, which starts "Hear O Israel" – thereby emphasizing hearing – recited but leather boxes containing liturgical texts are strapped onto the forehead and upper arm (the teffilin) and the body is wrapped in a prayer shawl (tallit) made of particular fibers. When one doesn't understand an argument or a text, one does not say that one cannot *see* the point but rather that one cannot *hear* it. In prayer one stands and moves the body, or the body moves, in particular ways. The Sabbath is both welcomed in and ushered out, on a weekly basis, with all of the senses, and its twenty-four hours are filled with embodied requirements and prohibitions.[24] This pattern of sensory, bodily, engagement is to be seen throughout the Jewish year at each of the many festivals and holidays. And, one important variant of Judaism, Hasidism, further encourages bodily engagement through the chanting of wordless tunes (niggunim) and dancing (and sometimes alcohol) to reach a transcendent state. In sum, sight and the study that sight facilitates is indeed centrally important to Judaism, and the book – the Torah – has a unique place in Jewish religious life. But sight is far from the only sense taken seriously and study far from the only spiritual activity. It is not, furthermore, the synagogue that is central to these practices, but rather the home and everyday life beyond the home. In fact, most of the laws that govern the lives of the observant concern bodily practices outside the walls of the synagogue. There has always, therefore, been a particularly intimate blending, a complementarity, albeit not an equal one, of the public and the domestic, the institutional and the familial, and the masculine and the feminine in Judaism.

Indicative of the importance of the senses to Jewish religious practice is the presence of a very substantial array of objects and ceremonial art for embodied ritual for both the synagogue and the home. Kiddush cups, special challah knives, and woven, embroidered covers, spice boxes, and candlesticks, to name only a few – were owned by many if not most households, reminding members of those rituals at other moments of the week and year. From their first appearance in the twelfth century, objects dedicated exclusively to ritual use multiplied throughout the Diaspora.[25] As the objects became more common debate arose around them, some rabbis arguing that they were important because beauty was a means of honoring God, others claiming that they were inherently distracting. On the positive side, for example, the fourteenth-century philosopher Profiat Duran wrote, "… the places for study should be desirable, the study halls beautifully built so that people's love and desire for study will increase.

---

[24] Jennifer Cousineau, "Rabbinic Urbanism in London: Rituals and Material Culture of the Sabbath," *Jewish Social Studies* 11, no. 3 (2005): 36–57.
[25] Mann, "Spirituality and Jewish Ceremonial Art."

Memory will also improve since contemplation and study occur amidst beautifully developed forms and beautiful drawings, with the result that the soul will expand and be encouraged to strengthen the powers ..."[26] Even those who interpreted the second commandment most strictly, however, accepted the centrality of embodied ritual to Jewish spirituality.

The objects used in Jewish religious practice fall into two main categories: 1) those that carry the quality of holiness and, 2) those that are essential to the performance of a ritual.[27] Holy objects include Torah scrolls themselves and any object in direct contact with them, tefillin, and mezuzot. It is the sacred texts these objects contain that render them holy. That holiness is considered an active force powerful enough to permeate two layers of material. Thus, not only is the Torah scroll holy, but its mantle is holy and the ark which contains it.[28] A sign of their importance, and of the importance of their embodiedness, is that when these objects are worn or damaged beyond repair and can no longer be used they are ideally to be buried in a Jewish cemetery, often near someone noted for his holiness or learning.

In all three cases – the Torah scrolls, and the tefillin and mezuzot texts – there are very precise rules governing the material upon which the text is written – often parchment – the ink used, and the qualifications of the scribe. The texts, for example, must be perfectly written, in the proper order.[29]

The Torah scroll – containing the five books of Moses – is, of course, the essential object, if one can put it that way. Unlike Christian Bibles, the text itself is never decorated or illustrated, but the scrolls are very often not just provided protection, but beautified. There has, furthermore, been the convention in many communities of "dressing" the Torah, providing it with a cover, finials, and a breast-plate. Thus, the Torah is not only the words it contains but the object itself – an object to be carefully made, cared for, revered, touched, smelled, kissed, paraded, and even danced with.

While Torah scrolls are generally kept in the synagogue, the two other key textual objects – tefillin and mezuzot – are simultaneously domestic and public.[30] Tefillin are two small perfectly square black boxes, each

---

[26] Cited in Mann, "Spirituality and Jewish Ceremonial Art," p. 182.

[27] Virginia Greene, "'Accessories of Holiness': Defining Jewish Sacred Objects," *Journal of the American Institute for Conservation* 31 no. 1 (1992): 21–39.

[28] Greene, "'Accessories of Holiness'," p. 34.

[29] Emmanuel Tov, *Scribal Practices and Approaches Reflected in the Texts found in the Judean Desert* (Leiden: Brill, 2004).

[30] For a guide to the use of tefillin and mezuzot see Rabbi Zeev Rothschild, *The World of Tefillin and Mezuzos* (Lakewood, NJ: STAM Gemilas Chessed Fund Publications, 1987).

containing the same four biblical texts.[31] Traditionally all adult men (although this, like many other gendered rituals, is now also practiced by women in some communities) are required to lay tefillin every morning, excepting only the Sabbath and most other holidays. Wrapping the straps is a somewhat involved process; teaching someone how to do so is often understood to be part of an overall spiritual education. Once learnt, the process of laying tefillin serves, like a number of other rituals, as a moment of transition of body and soul from secular to sacred concerns, and back again. Tying them properly takes time, concentration, and effort, which altogether comprise an embodied spiritual exercise.

Laying tefillin is intended to remind Jews of the need for cooperation among the three essential components of human behavior: intellect, emotion, and action: elements often understood to be at war with each other. Knowledge of what is right is not, for example, necessarily accompanied by a desire to act righteously. Judaism attempts to address this particular human frailty through an embodied daily ritual, engaging the senses of touch and hearing. One box of tefillin is placed on the forehead, in contact with the mind, the other on the upper arm, as close to the heart as possible, but twined around the arm which is the source of action. The three are, furthermore, connected, since the straps of the head tefillin, which is also intended to connect the intellect to God's will, lie loose and thus touch the heart to allow the wisdom to touch the source of passion, in turn connected to the arm that can turn good thoughts into good deeds. Implicit in the form and the ritual of the laying of tefillin is the conviction that people need to be reminded, very concretely and physically, of these connections. The practice is thought to facilitate the mastering of passion, to reinforce the courage or will to live according to one's good intentions, and the ability to avoid fascinating but perhaps empty or dangerous intellectual puzzles.

One can see another instantiation of this conception that religious practice requires a melding of gesture, object, thought, and text in the mezuza.[32] The mezuza is another small container holding two biblical passages (from

---

[31] For details on the materiality and use of tefillin see Shmuel Rubenstein, *The Tefillin Manual: An Illustrated Analysis of the Component Parts of the Tefillin* (New York: S. Rubenstein, 1962) and Rabbi Moshe Shlomo Emanuel, *Tefillin: The Inside Story* (Southfield, MI: Targum Press, 1995). For interpretation see Stephen Bailey, *Kashruth, Tefillin, Tzitzit: Studies in the Purpose and Meaning of Symbolic Mitzvot Inspired by the Commentaries of Rabbi Samson Raphael Hirsch* (Northvale, NJ: Jason Aronson, 2000).

[32] Rothschild, *The World of Tefillin and Mezuzos*; Eva-Maria Jansson, *The Message of a Mitsvah: The Mezuzah in Rabbinic Literature* (Lund: Novapress, 1999).

Deuteronomy). It is posted on the right side of every doorpost into, or within, a Jewish home, or public place. As one passes the threshold, one kisses one's fingers and with them touches the mezuza in order to express both love of God and awareness of God's presence.

The above two examples indicate how sight and touch work in cooperation, although quite differently. Jewish law does not specify the form a mezuza must take, and that freedom has inspired generations of makers and users of mezuzot. Since their everyday, constant, physical presence is a reminder of God and God's laws, they are often very beautifully crafted in God's honor. They can, however, also be playful, to attract a child's gaze. Jewish tradition understands their physical presence, contacted through the kissed hand, to be as important as their visual appearance.

The precise physical form of the tefillin, by contrast, is mandated. They are functional objects, generally hidden away when not in use. They must be touched, worn in fact, on the appropriate parts of the body to do their work. In both cases it is crucial that the texts be present, written in correct form, although not necessarily visible. They are not intended, therefore, to be read. Their embodied presence is what matters.

The tzitzit provide a different kind of example of a Jewish object intended to provide a bodily, sensory reminder of one's spiritual obligations.[33] In modern practice, tzitzit are fringes worn under one's shirt but hanging outside one's trousers. Tzitzit in some ways combine the omnipresence of the mezuza with the embodiment of the tefillin. The tzitzit are worn constantly against the body so that one does not forget the commandments. This notion of a daily bodily reminder is carried further of course through kashrut, that is, the laws that mandate what food is edible, and rules governing its preparation and consumption.[34] Clothing and ritual bathing prescriptions likewise keep Judaism physically as well as textually ever-present.

---

[33] For a detailed discussion of tzitzit see Rabbi Hertzel Hillel Yitzhak, *Tzel Heharim: The Comprehensive Halachic Guide to the Ritual Four-Cornered Garment According to the Sephardic Tradition* (Chicago: Tzel Heharim, 2006).

[34] Sue Fishkoff, *Kosher Nation* (New York: Schocken Books, 2010); Joëlle Bahloul, *Le culte de la table dressée: Rites et traditions de la table juive algérienne* (Paris: Editions A.-M. Metailie, 1983); Jordan D. Rosenblum, *Food and Identity in Early Rabbinic Judaism* (Cambridge: Cambridge University Press, 2010); David Charles Kraemer, *Jewish Eating and Identity through the Ages* (New York: Routledge, 2007); Claudine Fabre-Vassas, *The Singular Beast: Jews, Christians and the Pig*, trans. Carol Volk (New York: Columbia University Press, 1997); Robin Judd, *Contested Rituals: Circumcision, Kosher Butchering, and Jewish Political Life in Germany, 1843–1933* (Ithaca: Cornell University Press, 2007).

Sabbath ritual provides further evidence of the importance of the senses and objects that stir those senses in Jewish ritual, while also underscoring the importance of home and food in Jewish life. The Sabbath, celebrated in Judaism from sunset on Friday until sunset on Saturday, is governed by thirty-nine prohibitions, and a less precise number of encouragements and requirements. These are inspired by the fourth commandment that mandates that the Sabbath be kept holy. The positive mandates generally engage the senses. They include feeling the heat and seeing the glow of lit candles, tasting blessed wine and bread (and eating well), enjoying the sensation of a clean body and fresh clothes (and, if one is married, having sex with one's spouse), singing music, and at the holy day's end, smelling sweet smells in the Havdallah ceremony as well as repeating, in altered form, many of the embodied rituals from Friday night. These ceremonies are intended to both honor the Sabbath itself and to facilitate transitions from secular to holy and back to secular time.

Various objects were gradually developed to enact these rituals and although they do not have the status of the Torah scrolls (and the objects used to beautify or protect the Torah scrolls), mezuzot, or the tefillin, they, too, have come to play an important role in reminding Jews of their beliefs.[35] Starting in the twelfth century, but developing in the fifteenth, Jewish households and communities commissioned elaborate ritual objects for use in both the synagogue and at home, including Kiddush cups, candlesticks, challah and matzah covers, spice boxes, etrog containers, seder plates, and hannukiot. Jewish artisans and artists have, at times, understood crafting such objects as part of their spiritual and religious practice.[36]

Challah and its meanings within Jewish traditions provide a helpful starting point.[37] The first definition of "challah" is that it was the portion (thought of as the head or "rosh" in Hebrew) of unbaked dough set aside for the priests, for the Kohanim, in biblical times (Leviticus 24:5–7; Numbers 15:17–21 and Ezekiel 44:30). This was not a symbolic offering, but rather constituted an essential part of the priests' food supply. (The dough was baked and the resulting bread displayed in the Temple before it was consumed.) After the destruction of the Second Temple in 70 CE, this gesture was

---

[35] For example Vanessa L. Ochs, "What Makes a Jewish Home Jewish?", *Cross Currents* 49, no. 4 (Winter 1999–2000): 491–510.

[36] See for example, for the contemporary period, Tobi Kahn's work. Emily Bilsky, ed., *Objects of the Spirit: Ritual and the Art of Tobi Kahn* (New York: Avoda/Hudson Hills, 2004); Chava Weissler, "'Art *is* Spirituality!': Practice, Play, and Experiential Learning in the Jewish Renewal Movement," *Material Religion* 3, no. 2 (2007): 354–378.

[37] Frede Reider, *The Hallah Book: Recipes, History and Traditions* (Hoboken, NJ: KATV, 1987).

remembered through a symbolic offering of bread dough and through a ritualized consumption of bread in the home. The dining table upon which the bread is beautifully presented replaced the temple altar upon which the bread offerings to the priests were displayed.

Separating the symbolic portion of dough, blessing it, and then destroying it in commemoration of the Temple became one of the three key rituals performed by women. The others are blessing the Sabbath candles and maintaining family purity through following the laws of sexual abstention and ritual bathing around the period of menstruation. Although the original meaning of challah as a portion to be given the priests remains, its everyday signification became the braided loaf eaten by Ashkenazi Jews on the Sabbath (from around the fifteenth century) as well as major holidays.

Although also eaten on annual holidays, it is with the weekly return of the Sabbath that the bread is most powerfully associated. The Sabbath, for all observant Jews, is truly a day set aside in the week, a day of sacred rather than secular time and preoccupations. The gateway into that other space is understood to be both intellectual and emotional, engaging the mind and the body. Study has played a crucial role in the observance of the Sabbath, but, especially for women, embodied practices have been as central. It is not surprising then, that each of the three meals of the Sabbath – Friday night, Saturday breakfast and midday – traditionally start with blessing and tasting two challahs. (The doubledness is understood to commemorate the doubled portion manna that fell from the sky on the Sabbath and holidays during the Exodus in Egypt.) A common interpretation for the braids is that they look like arms intertwined, symbolizing love. Some say that the three strands of the braid symbolize truth, peace, and justice, but there are many other interpretations. For example, the twelve humps formed from two small or one large braided bread recall the miracle of the 12 loaves for the 12 tribes of Israel. It is a rich bread, both sweetened and containing a substantial number of eggs and carefully crafted into shape.

Challahs are generally covered, often with beautifully crafted cloths, until the moment of the blessing. Some argue that this is because the Sabbath is often compared in Jewish tradition and liturgy to a bride; in the wedding ceremony the bride is only unveiled after the blessings have been recited. In parallel, the challah, symbolizing the bride, is only revealed when "she" is about to be blessed.

Candlesticks represent another key element of diasporic Judaism's domestic ritual. The Sabbath conventionally starts with the woman of the household lighting two candles eighteen minutes before sunset on Friday. The duality in this case represents the two commandments to remember and keep the Sabbath. This mitzvah, or commandment, postdates biblical times and, one could argue, is therefore particularly emblematic of

Judaism as practiced in the Diaspora. The forms of Sabbath candlesticks have been as diverse as the communities in which Jews have found themselves across time.

The body is mobilized not only in these acts of consumption and of touch, but also in appearance. Conceptions of modesty and purity led to the elaboration of ritual bathing practices for women as well as clothing restrictions, and a convention for married women to cover their hair, either with a piece of fabric or a wig. Women's hair – when and if it can be revealed – has long been and continues to be a fraught topic for Jews as for many other groups.[38] Some commentators have argued that the sight of a woman's hair would incite men's sexual desire and should therefore be avoided. Others claim that the key point is not desire as such, but *whose* desire.[39] Beauty and eroticism are fine, but only to be seen and experienced by one's husband. And from a man's point of view, the appreciation of beauty and pleasure of erotic attraction must be limited to one's wife. Although both the Bible and the rabbinic literature are either vague or inconclusive on whether hair was to be covered at all, to say nothing of why, from the Middle Ages until the modern period, the norm was for married Jewish women to cover their hair. The seriousness of the issue was signaled by the fact that in the Talmud, non-compliance was considered grounds for divorce without financial support.

The range of form of head-covering has been vast. As early as the sixteenth century, Jewish women in France started wearing wigs as an alternative to fabric coverings. In Central Europe of the same period, the practice of shaving women's heads upon marriage gained widespread currency. Both were highly controversial practices. Up to and including the present, then, what one does with one's hair is a question for virtually all Orthodox women, although the wearing of wigs (whether or not one shaves one's head underneath) remains a common strategy.

In short, Judaism is anything but a disembodied religion for both women and men, and one can persuasively argue that Judaism envisaged

[38] For the discussion of head-covering see Leila Leah Bronner, "From Veil to Wig: Jewish Women's Hair Covering," *Judaism* 42, no. 4 (1993): 465–477; Lynne Schreiber, ed., *Hide and Seek: Jewish Women and Hair Covering* (Jerusalem: Urim Publications, 2003); Barbara Goldman Carrel, "Hasidic Women's Head-Coverings," in *Religion, Dress and the Body*, ed. Linda B. Arthur (Oxford: Berg, 1999) 163–179; Orit Yafeh, "The Time in the Body: Cultural Construction of Femininity in Ultraorthodox Kindergartens for Girls,"*Ethos* 35, no. 5 (2007): 516–533; Yitshak Ya'acov Fuchs, *Halichos Bas Yisrael: A Woman's Guide to Jewish Observance*, vol. 1 (Jerusalem: Feldheim, 1985).

[39] See Bronner, "From Veil to Wig," fn. 7 and passim.

an intense, daily, engagement of all five of the senses in specific ways. Those rituals, taken collectively, required a particularly acute distinction among the senses and their integration. That is, hearing, touching, seeing, feeling, and tasting were all complementary, each powerful in their ritual purpose, and each distinct. Those who live an observant life are aware of the bodily discipline and joy this life imposes. Jewish religious practice produced a Jewish relation to the senses, different from that produced in Catholicism, Protestantism, or Islam. The question of what happens to that distinct relation when practice becomes monthly, or even annual, rather than quotidian is too complex to be properly addressed here, but I would like to suggest that a bodily hexis, and an associated material culture, connected to that practice was (and is) transmitted trans-generationally, producing a continuity in a distinctive Jewish sensorium.[40] That distinctiveness was underscored by another, very different one: that of living in Diaspora, as minorities, and often as persecuted minorities.

DIASPORIC AND MINORITY CULTURE

Jewish relation to things has been formed not only by Judaism's particular embodiment and use of material culture but also by Jews' social experience, marked by paradox. Jewish life has been characterized by considerable mobility (both involuntary and voluntary) and long term, centenary, residence. Many Jews have lived as small, minority, populations, but they have often been, again both involuntarily and voluntarily, majoritarian within neighborhoods, cities, or even regions. Thus, Jews were a very small minority in the Austro-Hungarian Empire, but a very substantial presence, numerically and culturally, in Vienna and Budapest. Jewish families have often found themselves dispersed across the globe, cosmopolitan whether they so chose or not, sharing a sense of "Jewishness" but not necessarily a language in which to converse. The degree of interaction between Jews and the cultures in which they live has also varied greatly, but there has never been a hermetic seal. All Jewish cultures, including material cultures, are syncretic in form.

In pre-modern Europe, some of the syncretism came from the exclusion of Jews from certain artisanal trades and their concentration in others. By the twelfth century, Jews in much of Europe and Britain were barred, for example, from working in silver and gold.[41] They were therefore

---

[40] This argument will be fully developed in my book-in-progress, *The Everyday of Citizenship: Jewish Parisians and Berliners in the 20th century.*

[41] Robert Ian Moore, *The Formation of a Persecuting Society: Authority and Deviance in Western Europe*, 2nd edition (Malden: Blackwell, 2007), 81.

dependent upon Christian goldsmiths and silversmiths for the production of the whole range of ritual objects crafted from metal, including
not only Kiddush cups, candlesticks, menorahs, and Havdallah boxes, but
also the adornments of the Torah itself. Those artisans necessarily brought
their own aesthetic to the ritual objects they were commissioned to make,
generating new forms that melded the Christian and the Jewish. Parallel
exclusions in Muslim-dominant lands produced a similar effect. Jewish ritual material culture was therefore relatively homogeneous with respect to
the kinds of objects produced but their form varied considerably. Sabbath
candlesticks, for example, made wherever Jews came to live, are always
recognizable but even the materials from which they are made, their size,
and their style were shaped by the context in which they were crafted.
This syncretism in material culture both created ties among Jews across the
Diaspora and emblematized Jewish integration in their varied homelands.

While European Jews' exclusion from certain trades for much of the
medieval and early modern periods made them dependent on Christian
and Muslim artisans for some of their material culture, their very high
concentration in other key trades – tailoring, shoemaking, furs, cabinet-
making, bookbinding – gave them an opportunity, particularly from the
nineteenth century, to shape the aesthetics of both dress and domestic
interiors. Those possibilities were reinforced by the strong presence of Jews
in distribution, and eventually, advertising and publishing industries. In
Germany, for example, Jews owned most of the early department stores;
through their commissions and purchases of finished goods, they had a
strong influence on the style and form of the goods on the market.[42] Mass
distribution also required innovative display and advertising strategies,
both of which influenced consumers' perceptions of the place and importance of material culture in their everyday lives. Jews were active, then,
at all moments in the cycle of design, production, distribution, and consumption of clothing, shoes, books, and furniture. By the late nineteenth
century, they were also present, if not as numerous, in the domains of
tableware and household textiles. The relation to material culture developed within Jewish ritual life in combination with both the necessary
coming to terms with syncretism and hyper-specialization in certain trades
occasioned by the Diaspora, shaped the use Jews made of things, both as
producers and consumers.

The massive migration westward of Eastern European Jews from the
last third of the nineteenth century through the interwar period provides

[42] Green, *Ready to Wear*; Stein, *Plumes*; Roemer and Reuveni, *Longing and Belonging*; Paul
Lerner, *The Consuming Temple: Jews, Department Stores, and the Consumer Revolution in
Germany, 1880–1940* (Ithaca: Cornell University Press, 2015).

a vivid example of the effects of population movement on Jewish material culture. These emigrants were of every social class and religious proclivity, but the majority were poor and observant. As they thought about
departure, they reflected on what they would no longer smell, touch, see,
taste, and hear and what they could bring with them to remind them
of home. Most brought something with them from their old lives into
the new, but given the difficulties of travel and limitations on shipping,
most often very little. One of the most frequently carried objects, along
with Sabbath candlesticks and Kiddush cups, was the family's samovar,
used to heat the water with which to make tea. The choice of the samovar is surprising both because its size and weight made it very burden-
some, but also because it was so strongly associated with Russia, the home
the migrants felt forced to flee. But I would like to suggest that it was
samovars' very ambiguity that made them attractive to those going into
exile. Once arrived in their new homelands, samovars, unlike kiddish cups,
united religious and secular migrants; they all drank tea. Samovars also
enabled those who had once been like, but who emigration had rendered
alien, to feel at home with each other. When Jews who found themselves
scattered across the Southern Africa, the Caribbean, and North and South
America had the opportunity to visit, the landscape, food, and language
spoken on the streets might all be strange, but the samovar was constant.
Samovars provided a bodily connection (through the tea drinking ritual)
among them and with the land they had left.[43] And even when migrants
could not travel, they did read, and they rediscovered the samovar on the
pages of a global diasporic literature. Finally, the samovar also allowed emigrants whose memories of the Russian Empire were most often very bitter
to remain connected to the dominant culture in which they had grown up.
The Ashkenazi Diaspora might express nostalgia for the Jewish community
of the old country; they could not say that they missed the Russia that had
abused them. Thus, while the samovar is, in some ways, a typical migrant
object, the Jewish exiles' appropriation of a Russian object as their own, its
play with and against ritual objects, and its deployment to unite a highly
differentiated emigrant group is distinctive, if not unique. But it was not
only those objects that accompanied Jewish migrants on their voyages that
influenced the material cultures of their new communities, but the taste,
skill, and knowledge they carried in their heads.

[43] Eduardo Stilman, *El samovar de plata* (Buenos Aires: Ediciones de la Flor, 1993) and the
discussion in Edna Aizenberg, "How a Samovar Helped me Theorize Latin American
Jewish Writing," *Shofar* 19, no. 1 (2001): 33–40; Sophie Guralnik, *El Samovar* (Santiago:
Ergo Sum, 1984).

848 THE MODERN WORLD, 1815–2000

The celebrated "Jewish Renaissance" of Berlin and Moscow in the 1920s was shaped by the encounters and sometimes collisions between the Jewish practice and aesthetic forms brought by newcomers and those already in place in those cities. The crucial catalysts for these productive interactions were massive westward migration, contact between German-Jewish soldiers and Eastern European Jews during the First World War, post-war disillusionment in the face of continued German antisemitism, and disenchantment with Reform Judaism.[44] The result was a reinvigoration of Jewish scholarship, of the Yiddish theater and press, a religious revival, but also the development of explicitly modern forms of Jewish book art and other design practices.[45] Part of a generation born around the turn of the century, then, whose parents had moved away from active religious practice and conscious participation in the Jewish community, reacted against what they perceived to be the aridness of their parents' choices and found in the Renaissance a more dynamic and satisfying life, and not coincidentally, a life that melded the old and the new. A life in which the revival of Yiddish theater would take, for example, the form of Sh. An-sky's *Dybbuk*, a thoroughly modernist play, and in the design of ritual objects and synagogues, the influence of *Jugendstil*.[46]

It is important to emphasize the term "Renaissance" here, for this was a definitively modern movement, striving to revive but also transform Judaism, not as had been done in the nineteenth century, by making it look, feel, and function more like Christianity, but rather by finding its form of renewal within itself, and building on those coming from afar. Thus geographic mobility, even if often incited by persecution and economic hardship, was often the source of extraordinary creativity in shaping Jewish material life. Close parallels may be found among other groups, as can be witnessed in the Harlem and Haitian Renaissances of the same period. A similar parallelism between Diasporic Jewish and non-Jewish innovation in material culture may be seen in the nationalist movements,

---

[44] Jack Wertheimer, *Unwelcome Strangers: Eastern European Jews in Imperial Germany* (New York: Oxford University Press, 1987); Steven E. Aschheim, *Brothers and Strangers* (Madison: University of Wisconsin Press, 1982).

[45] On the Jewish Renaissance see Michael Brenner, *The Renaissance of Jewish Culture in Weimar Germany* (New Haven: Yale University Press, 1996); Inka Bertz, *"Eine neue Kunst für ein altes Volk": Die jüdische Renaissance in Berlin 1900 bis 1924*. Museumpädagogischer Dienst Berlin, Ausstellungsmagazin No. 28 (Berlin: Berlin Museum, 1991); Andreas Herzog, ed., *Ost und West: jüdische Publizistik 1901–1928* (Leipzig: Reclam, 1996).

[46] Gabriella Safran and Steven J. Zipperstein, eds, *The Worlds of S. An-sky: A Russian Jewish Intellectual at the Turn of the Century* (Stanford: Stanford University Press, 2006).

including Zionism, at the *fin de siècle*.[47] An obsession with training the body (through gymnastics), the eyes (through art education), and the hands (through *Handwerk*) was common to all Central European nationalist movements in this period, but the forms specific to Zionism were given a Jewish inflection.

ZIONISM

It is well known that Zionist thinkers and leaders as different as Theodor Herzl, Achad Ha'am, Max Nordau, Franz Rosenzweig, and Martin Buber were convinced, each in his own way, of the need for an aestheticized embodiment of the wished-for-nation.[48] In order for a new nation to come into existence, Jewish bodies required recreation. And in order for the Jews to unify as a nation they needed a new, shared aesthetic. Like traditional Jewish ritual, the new aesthetic had to engage all the senses, the hands as well as the eyes. This thinking was most eloquently expressed by Martin Buber who argued that art of all kinds, not just the visual arts, was needed to "fashion a national soul for Jewry."[49] And, although Herzl originally thought that a Jewish style should follow, not precede, the establishment of a Jewish state, he was rapidly convinced of the utility of such a style in facilitating the creation of a state.

Thus, less than a decade after the first Zionist Congress in Basel (1897) the Bezalel Academy of Arts and Design was founded in Jerusalem. It is difficult to exaggerate the importance of this institution. By 1910 it had

[47] Michelle Facos and Sharon L. Hirsh, eds., *Art, Culture and National Identity in Fin-de-Siècle Europe* (Cambridge: Cambridge University Press, 2003); Celia Applegate and Pamela Potter, eds., *Music and German National Identity* (Chicago: University of Chicago Press, 2002); Rudy Koshar, *Germany's Transient Pasts: Preservation and National Memory in the Twentieth Century* (Chapel Hill: University of North Carolina Press, 1998); Annie E. Coombes, *Reinventing Africa: Museums, Material Culture, and Popular Imagination in Late Victorian and Edwardian England* (New Haven: Yale University Press, 1994).
[48] See, for example: Ahad Ha-'am, "Imitation and Assimilation," in *Selected Essays by Ahad Ha'am*, trans. and ed. Leon Simon (Philadelphia: Jewish Publication Society, 1936); Martin Buber, *On Judaism* (New York: Schocken, 1967); Max Nordau *Von Kunst und Künstlern* (Leipzig: B. Elischer, no date) and Nordau, "Der Zionismus der Westlichen Juden," in *Max Nordaus Zionistische Schriften* (Cologne and Leipzig, 1909); Michael Berkowitz, "Art in Zionist Popular Culture and Jewish National Self-Consciousness, 1897–1914," in *Art and Its Uses*, ed. Ezra Mendelsohn, Studies in Contemporary Jewry 6 (New York: Oxford University Press, 1991), 17–42; Michael Stanislawski, *Zionism and the Fin de Siècle: Cosmpolitanism and Nationalism from Nordau to Jabotinsky* (Berkeley: University of California Press, 2001).
[49] Cited in Berkowitz, *Art in Zionist Popular Culture*, p. 19.

become, according to the art historian Margaret Olin, the largest employer in Jerusalem; in 1914 it had 450 enrolled students, and a museum collection, and it had mounted substantial traveling exhibitions. It was arguably one of the central Zionist institutions in early Palestine.[50]

The school was named Bezalel after the biblical figure anointed by God to craft the ark of the tabernacle. This figure was to provide inspiration in finding a truly "Hebrew" mode of life. In the words of the institution's founder, Boris Schatz:

The great idea is not to copy Arab or European models, but to derive new inspiration from Hebrew ideals, from the flora and fauna of the land, to create an art nouveau, with a Hebrew background, to utilize incidents of Palestinian life – old and new – to mould the Hebrew alphabet into artistic forms for decorative purposes, in short, to create a Palestinian renaissance.[51]

Schatz even spoke of Bezalel as the foundation for the Third Temple. The vision was lofty, and although the institution was a secular, nationalist one, the name itself evoked Jewish religious practice and tradition.

Bezalel's workshops produced a variety of goods, ranging from graphic design to carpets and metal work. They produced Jewish ceremonial objects, but also secular items to furnish Jewish homes: portraits of Herzl, thousands of postcards, pictures, and picture books to be diffused globally. Part of the mission was to raise money to support the cause, but no less important was the idea of creating a new aesthetic form.[52] Even more emphatically, as Laurence Jay Silberstein and Sarah Chinksi have argued, Schatz thought that the objects created in the new Hebrew spirit would instill in those who made, used, and dwelled among them a strong identification with the past and present as conceived within Zionist discourse.[53] The Hebrew artifacts were seen as having the power to shape the structure of feelings of those who connected to them.[54] These artistic objects were

[50] Margaret Olin, *The Nation without Art: Examining Modern Discourses on Jewish Art* (Lincoln: University of Nebraska, 2001) and Arieh Bruce Saposnik, "'…Will Issue Forth from Zion'?: The Emergence of a Jewish National Culture in Palestine and the Dynamics of Yishuv-Diaspora Relations," *Jewish Social Studies* 10, no. 1 (2003): 151–184.

[51] Quoted in Olin, *The Nation without Art*, p. 48.

[52] Richard I. Cohen, "Self-Image Through Objects: Toward a Social History of Jewish Art Collecting and Jewish Museums," in *The Uses of Tradition: Jewish Continuity in the Modern Era*, ed. Jack Wertheimer (New York: Jewish Theological Seminary, 1992), 203–242.

[53] Laurence J. Silberstein, *The Postzionism Debates: Knowledge and Power in Israeli Culture* (New York: Routledge, 1999), 189–200.

[54] Nurit Shilo Cohen, "The 'Hebrew Style' of Bezalel, 1906–1929," *The Journal of Decorative and Propaganda Arts* 20 (1994): 141–163.

not, then, only expressions of identity, but also functioned to construct that identity by positioning those who viewed and used them.[55]

Some archaeologists have made a very different kind of use of material culture to Zionist ends. Instead of seeking to create a new Jewish aesthetic, they have hoped to demonstrate the continual presence of Jews in Palestine from biblical days, thereby legitimating the Jewish claim to the territory.[56] This project has been controversial on many grounds. The first is simply that both the ambiguity of much archaeological data and the syncretic nature of culture in the period make it very difficult to know when an object is evidence of a "Jewish" presence. A further critique has been that even if one were able to prove that there had always been Jews on the territory claimed by Israel, that does not, in any immediate way, justify a Jewish state in the present. Both the efforts to create a specifically national aesthetic and to legitimate territorial claims through archaeology became even more important after the human and material destruction of the Shoah.

THE SHOAH

The first steps taken by the National Socialists charged with the excision of Jews and Judaism from Europe was the expropriation of property. That expropriation was remarkably thorough, aided and abetted by an efficient bureaucracy and erstwhile neighbors throughout occupied Europe. One of the motivations for the theft was simply material: the dwellings, businesses, art collections, libraries, musical instruments, and capital owned by Jews were to be appropriated for the use of the Reich and its Aryan citizenry. The other motivation, however, was directly linked to the extermination project. National Socialist ideologues understood that a key step in making murder acceptable was the gradual marginalization and exclusion of the victims from society. Part of that process was the denial of access to public space, including parks, restaurants, and schools. Part of that process was the isolation of Jews through their re-ghettoization. Part of that process was the imposition of Israel and Sara as obligatory middle names for all Jews. Part of the process was visually marking Jews with the yellow star. And, part of the process was the gradual theft of the things that Jews had

---

[55] I should note that there were (and are) many critiques of the Bezalel project, and it foundered in 1929, to reopen in new form in the 1930s.

[56] Yael Zerubavel, *Recovered Roots: Collective Memory and the Making of Israeli National Tradition* (Chicago: University of Chicago Press, 1995); Nadia Abu El-Haj, *Facts on the Ground: Archaeological Practice and Territorial Self-Fashioning in Israeli Society* (Chicago: University of Chicago Press, 2001).

acquired to furnish their lives, to mark important events, provide sensual pleasure, and serve as memory cues.[57]

Some of the victims of this process, furthermore, were fully aware of its implications. In France, for example, during the third year of the Occupation, Isaac Schneersohn created the Center for Contemporary Jewish Documentation (*Centre de Documentation Juive Contemporaine*). The primary goal was to document the seizure of Jewish goods to support post-war restitution and reparations claims, but he also saw this documentation process as restorative for those who had been victims of persecution. It would enable them to reclaim their past, revive their memories, and renew their sense of belonging, once the rule of law was re-established. Not all efforts were collective. The most common reaction, of course, was to try to protect one's things, particularly those of high emotional or financial value. In the early years, some, generally wealthy, families were able to ship the contents of their European home to wherever they were seeking refuge. This turned out to be a not-unmitigated good. When refugees were able to move their entire dwelling, the testimonies of their children and grandchildren are often haunted by the effects of growing up in a home lifted whole from another time and place. Even those who were able or chose to bring little, however, often imposed an unintentional burden on their children. Too much was invested in those objects; they were, and are, too significant and yet mute.

The Shoah has also, of course, posed a daunting pedagogic challenge. How does one, particularly as the Third Reich retreats further and further into the past, effectively communicate its horror to subsequent generations? Certain strategies, notably presentations by survivors to youth groups and others, inevitably become unavailable over time. Although the material culture of the Shoah, too, is mortal, much of it has a longer lifespan than that of humans. The existence of clothing, letters, musical instruments, furniture, buildings, and sites may be artificially prolonged; some concentration and death camps are carefully maintained and the efforts of nature to reclaim the place resisted.[58] Museums regularly acquire, preserve,

[57] Johannes Ludwig, *Boykott, Enteignung, Mord: die "Entjüdung" der deutschen Wirtschaft* (Hamburg: Facta, 1989); Annette Wieviorka and Floriane Azoulay, *Le pillage des appartements et son indemnisation* (Paris: Documentation Française, 2000); Caroline Piketty, *Je cherche les traces de ma mère: Chroniques des archives* (Paris: Autremont, 2005).

[58] Jennifer Hansen-Glucklich, *Holocaust Memory Reframed: Museums and the Challenges of Representation* (New Brunswick: Rutgers University Press, 2014); Ulrike Dittrich and Sigrid Jacobeit, eds., *K-Z Souvenirs: Errinerungsobjekte der Alltagskultur im Gedenken an die nationalsozialistischen Verbrechen* (Potsdam: Brandenburgische Gedenkstätten/ Mahn- und Gedenkstätte Ravensbrück, 2005); Oren Baruch Stier, *Commited to Memory: Cultural Mediations of the Holocaust* (Amherst: University of Massachusetts

and display the possessions – shoes, eyeglasses, or dolls – of the victims of the Shoah to communicate the everyday horror. The conflicts between the relatives of the erstwhile owners of these objects and the museums currently holding them are not as well-known as those between art museums and the works of fine art of dubious provenance they hold, but they are just as bitter. Heirs argue that possessing the worthless object, perhaps a suitcase, that was once touched by their father, grandmother, or cousin would lessen their grief.[59] Museums argue that they have an obligation to posterity to retain these goods, that they provide irrefutable proof of the reality of the Shoah; this, they insist, is a more important task than easing an individual family's sorrow. The violence of these conflicts is indicative of the objects' significance.[60] While many cultures seek to preserve a link to their pasts by carefully preserving some physical, tangible traces, the attempted annihilation of European Jewry and their cultures, has inevitably and profoundly shaped Jewish relations to material culture.

Very conscious of the gap left in German life by the destruction of Jewish life and culture, a small but culturally significant group of German gentiles has sought to give Judaism new life in Germany.[61] Starting in the late 1970s, these young Germans set about learning Hebrew and Yiddish, listening to Jewish music, familiarizing themselves with the taste of "German-Jewish" food, and acquiring Jewish objects. Some would also convert to Judaism, but the acquisition of Jewish culture, including material culture, was not limited to those who chose to become Jews. Trips to Israel (common among this group) and flea markets and antique stores in which the ritual objects orphaned by the Shoah were ubiquitous, provided ample sources of Judaica. Given the rather small number of Jews in both East and West Germany through the 1980s and into the 1990s, it is probable that the majority of homes that read to a newcomer as Jewish – on the

Press, 2003), chap. 5; Bozena Shallcross, *The Holocaust Object in Polish and Polish-Jewish Culture* (Bloomington: Indiana University Press, 2011).

[59] For elaborations of these arguments see Leora Auslander "Coming Home? Jews in Postwar Paris," *Journal of Contemporary History* 40, no. 2 (2005): 237–259; Leora Auslander, "Archiving a Life: Post-Shoah Paradoxes of Memory Legacies," in *Unsettling Histories*, ed. Alf Lüdtke and Sebastien Jobs (Frankfurt: Campus Verlag, 2010), 127–146.

[60] Oren Baruch Stier, "Torah and Taboo: Containing Jewish Relics and Jewish Identity at the United States Holocaust Memorial Museum," *Numen: International Review for the Study of Religions* 57, no. 3/4 (2010): 505–536.

[61] Jonathan Karp and Adam Sutcliffe, eds., *Philosemitism in History* (New York: Cambridge University Press, 2011), Part V; Frank Stern, *The Whitewashing of the Yellow Star: Antisemitism and Philosemitism in Postwar Germany*, trans. William Templer (New York: Pergamon, 1992).

basis of the objects, music, books, and art displayed – were not, in fact, inhabited by Jews. This appears to be, at first glance, the domestic branch of the museumification of Jewish life in Central and Eastern Europe in this period. A closer analysis, however, reveals a more nuanced picture, one that would be an important area of further research. These objects are not, after all, in a museum, but rather part of the fabric of daily life. Open questions include: What happens to a material culture when it passes from those who use it, in some senses unthinkingly, to those for whom it is a project? What happens to everyday domestic religious objects when they remain in the quotidian, home, environment, but no longer bear religious meaning?

CONCLUSION: THE CONTEMPORARY WORLD

The salience of objects to Jews, like to all other groups, only increased in the age of intensified consumerism that has characterized the last half-century. Modifications in religious practice have provided the occasion for the development of new objects; as more women choose to wear tallit and kippot, feminine versions have appeared, whether hand-crafted by artisans who see their labor as part of their spiritual practice, or machine-made, produced by entrepreneurs who see a market niche.[62] Ultra-Orthodox interpretations of kashrut have also provided the occasion for a heavy investment in material culture of a particular kind; it is now possible to have a dual kitchen (one for milk and one for meat) within one, doubling one's appliance purchases. The upsurge in Jewish, along with all other, forms of tourism, too, has intensified investment in things. The souvenir business, whether providing visitors to Israel with memorabilia or those who make their way to the formerly thriving Jewish communities of Central and Eastern Europe with keepsakes, has altered the contents of Jewish homes.[63]

---

[62] Vanessa Ochs, *Inventing Jewish Ritual* (Philadelphia: Jewish Publication Society, 2007); Leonard J. Greenspoon, *Rites of Passage: How Today's Jews Celebrate, Commemorate, and Commiserate* (West Lafayette, IN: Purdue University Press, 2010). See some of the contributions to Marion A. Kaplan and Deborah Dash Moore, eds., *Gender and Jewish History* (Bloomington: Indiana University Press, 2011) and Riv-Ellen Prell, *Women Remaking American Judaism* (Detroit: Wayne State University, 2007).

[63] Barbara Kirshenblatt-Gimblett, *Destination Culture: Tourism, Museums, and Heritage* (Berkeley: University of California Press, 1998); Jeffrey Shandler, *Adventures in Yiddishland: Postvernacular Language and Culture* (Berkeley: University of California Press, 2006); Jeffrey Shandler and Beth S. Wenger, eds, *Encounters with the 'Holy Land': Place, Past and Future in American Jewish Culture* (Hanover, NH: University Press of New England, 1997); Shelley Shenhav-Keller, "The Jewish Pilgrim and the Purchase of a Souvenir in Israel," in *International Tourism: Identity and Change*, ed. Marie-Francoise

Finally, the perpetually changing nature of diasporic communities and their relations to Israel, to the cultures within which they live, and to Jews elsewhere in the world also produces new forms of material culture and new relations to it. One particularly interesting phenomenon has been "chalala." Chalala is a clothing style invented in the 1980s by affluent French-Jewish teenagers of North African descent. Characterized by expensive, form-fitting, branded, unisex clothing, shoes and sunglasses, chalala wearers are also identifiable by their visible Jewish emblems including very large Stars of David, memorabilia of the Israeli army including military kippot and IDF dog tags. According to anthropologist Kimberly Arkin, the point of this style is both to enable young Arabo-Jews to recognize each other on the street and to ensure that others do not confuse them with those of North African Muslim parentage.[64] Thus, the clothing is both very expensive, and thereby beyond the reach of most Muslim youth in France, and choice of brands and boutiques very selective. Young French Arabo-Jews choose clothing marketed in France by US-based rather than French-based companies, believing that their non-Jewish contemporaries are purchasing Adidas and Lacoste. Finally, emblems that are shared with Muslims from the same region (like the five-fingered hand or hamsa), as well as those thought to be unidentifiable outside the Jewish community (like the chai, the Hebrew word for life) are avoided. Through these strategies they hope to enlarge their own endogamous social worlds as well as avoid the discrimination that they know Arabo-Muslim youth experience in contemporary French society.

This is a distinctive stylistic form, born of the particular history of migration from North Africa to France starting in the mid-1950s. In Algeria, Morocco, and Tunisia, although violent antisemitism was far from unknown and Jews suffered from legal discrimination, everyday life was generally both intimate and peaceful. Those of Jewish and Muslim origin shared neighborhoods (and often buildings), clothing and linguistic practices, musical forms, and foodways.[65] The physical intimacy was reproduced in metropolitan France, sometimes voluntarily, sometimes as a result of the French state's housing policies. This proximity and cultural likeness became much more complicated following the independence of those three states and the creation of the state of Israel. The Algerian war

Lanfant, John B. Allcock and Edward M. Bruner (London: Sage Publication, 1995): 143–158.

[64] Kimberly Arkin, "Rhinestone Aesthetics and Religious Essence: Looking Jewish in Paris," *American Ethnologist* 36, no. 4 (2009): 772–734.

[65] Joëlle Bahloul, *La maison de mémoire: Éthnologie d'une demeure judéo-arabe en Algérie (1937–1961)* (Paris: Métailié, 1992).

also left a legacy of great bitterness and mistrust among all parties, but particularly between non-Jewish North African migrants and the "host" society, a bitterness that translated into discrimination in education, housing, and employment. It is not surprising then, that Jews of North African origin, who had already experienced privilege under colonial rule, found it desirable to sharply differentiate themselves from those who read as Muslim in the French context.

As in the past, the future of Jewish material culture lies in the particular place that things occupy in Jewish life, a particularity born simultaneously of Jewish religious practice, the dynamism of the Diaspora in conjunction with the centrality of Israel for many non-Israeli Jews, transnational Jewish networks, and the syncretism that life as a minority brings with it.

SELECT BIBLIOGRAPHY

Arkin, Kimberly. "Rhinestone Aesthetics and Religious Essence: Looking Jewish in Paris," *American Ethnologist* 36, no. 4 (2009): 772–734.

Auslander, Leora. "Coming Home? Jews in Postwar Paris," *Journal of Contemporary History* 40, no. 2 (2005): 237–259.

Berkowitz, Michael. "Art in Zionist Popular Culture and Jewish National Self-Consciousness, 1897–1914." *Art and Its Uses: The Visual Image and Modern Jewish Society*, ed. Ezra Mendelsohn, 17–42. Studies in Contemporary Jewry 6. New York: Oxford University Press, 1991.

Bronner, Simon J. ed. *Jews at Home: The Domestication of Identity*. Oxford: Littman Library of Jewish Civilization, 2010.

Buckman, Joseph. *Immigrants and the Class Struggle: The Jewish Immigrant in Leeds, 1880–1914*. Manchester: Manchester University Press, 1983.

Cohen, Julia Phillips. "Oriental by Design: Ottoman Jews, Imperial Style, and the Performance of Heritage," *American Historical Review* 119, no. 2 (2014): 364–398.

El-Haj, Nadia Abu. *Facts on the Ground: Archaeological Practice and Territorial Self-Fashioning in Israeli Society*. Chicago: University of Chicago Press, 2001.

Golany, Gideon S. *Babylonian Jewish Neighborhood and Home Design*. Lewiston: Edwin Mellen Press, 1999.

Greene, Virginia. "'Accessories of Holiness': Defining Jewish Sacred Objects," *Journal of the American Institute for Conservation* 31 no. 1 (1992): 21–39.

Greenspoon, Leonard J. ed. *Fashioning Jews: Clothing, Culture and Commerce*, Studies in Jewish Civilization, 24. West Lafayette, IN: Purdue University Press, 2013.

Hansen-Glucklich, Jennifer. *Holocaust Memory Reframed: Museums and the Challenges of Representation*. New Brunswick: Rutgers University Press, 2014.

Heinze, Andrew R. *Adapting to Abundance: Jewish Immigrants, Mass Consumption, and the Search for American Identity*. New York: Columbia University Press, 1990.

Joselit, Jenna Weissman. *A Perfect Fit: Clothes, Character and the Promise of America*. New York: Metropolitan Books, 2001.

The Wonders of America: Reinventing Jewish Culture 1880–1950. New York: Hill and Wang, 1994.

Katz, Maya Balakirsky. *The Visual Culture of Chabad.* Cambridge: Cambridge University Press, 2010.

Kirshenblatt-Gimblett, Barbara. *Fabric of Jewish Life: Textiles from the Jewish Museum Collection.* New York: Jewish Museum, 1977.

and Jeffrey Shandler, eds. *Special Issue: Material Cultures of American Jewry. Material Religion* 3, no. 3 (2007).

Koltun-Fromm, Kenneth. *Material Culture and Jewish Thought in America.* Bloomington: Indiana University Press, 2010.

Kremer, Roberta S. *Broken Threads: The Destruction of the Jewish Fashion Industry in Germany and Austria.* Oxford: Berg, 2007.

Lerner, Paul. *The Consuming Temple: Jews, Department Stores, and the Consumer Revolution in Germany, 1880–1940.* Ithaca: Cornell University Press, 2015.

Mann, Vivian B. *Art and Ceremony in Jewish Life: Essays in the History of Jewish Art.* London: Pindar Press, 2005.

Moore, Deborah Dash, *At Home in America: Second Generation New York Jews.* New York: Columbia University Press, 1981.

Nahshon, Edna. ed. *Jews and Shoes.* Oxford: Berg, 2008.

Ochs, Vanessa L. *Inventing Jewish Ritual.* Philadelphia: Jewish Publication Society, 2007.

"What Makes a Jewish Home Jewish?" *Cross Currents* 49 (Winter 1999–2000): 491–510.

Roemer, Nils H. and Gideon Reuveni, eds. *Longing, Belonging, and the Making of Jewish Consumer Culture.* Leiden: Brill, 2010.

Schreiber, Lynne, ed. *Hide and Seek: Jewish Women and Hair Covering.* Jerusalem: Urim Publications, 2003.

Shallcross, Bozena. *The Holocaust Object in Polish and Polish-Jewish Culture.* Bloomington: Indiana University Press, 2011.

Shandler, Jeffrey. *Adventures in Yiddishland: Postvernacular Language and Culture.* Berkeley: University of California Press, 2006.

Silverman, Eric. *A Cultural History of Jewish Dress.* New York: Bloomsbury Academic, 2013.

Stein, Sarah Abrevaya. *Plumes: Ostrich Feathers, Jews, and a Lost World of Global Commerce.* New Haven: Yale University Press, 2008.

Steyn, Juliet. *The Jew: Assumptions of Identity.* London: Cassell, 1999.

Wischnitzer, Mark. *A History of Jewish Crafts and Guilds.* New York: J. David, 1965.

CHAPTER 31

JEWS AND POPULAR CULTURE IN THE TWENTIETH CENTURY
North America

ANDREA MOST

THEATRICAL LIBERALISM: SECULAR JUDAISM AND POPULAR ENTERTAINMENT IN AMERICA

On Armistice Day, November 11, 1938, Kate Smith introduced a new song, "God Bless America," on her CBS radio program, recorded live at the New York World's Fair. The song was instantly popular. Ms. Smith continued to sing it on every one of her radio broadcasts for the next year; she recorded it for RCA in 1939; the lyrics were introduced into the Congressional Record, and it has long been considered an alternate national anthem.[1] The song remains central to American popular culture today, and it experienced a renewed burst of popularity after September 11, 2001, when Congressmen, Broadway performers, baseball players, and stock traders all sang the song as a way of asserting their patriotism.[2] "God Bless America" was originally written for the musical revue *Yip, Yip, Yaphank,* by Irving Berlin, a Russian-Jewish immigrant to America at the turn of the twentieth century, the son of a cantor, and one of the most successful writers of popular theater music in American history. The complete lyrics to the song are as follows:

> While the storm clouds gather
> Far across the sea,
> Let us swear allegiance
> To a land that's free;
> Let us all be grateful
> For a land so fair,
> As we raise our voices
> In a solemn prayer.

---

[1] See "God Bless America," in *Performing Arts Encyclopedia,* Library of Congress, http://lcweb2.loc.gov/diglib/ihas/loc.natlib.ihas.200000007/default.html.

[2] Richard Corliss, "That Old Christmas Feeling: Irving America," *Time,* December 24, 2001, http://content.time.com/time/arts/article/0,8599,189846,00.html.

God bless America,
Land that I love,
Stand beside her and guide her
Through the night with a light from above.
From the mountains, to the prairies,
To the oceans white with foam,
God bless America,
My home sweet home.[3]

Berlin's choice to become a secular American song-writer rather than a cantor like his father has long been the stuff of American immigrant legend.[4] Indeed, "God Bless America" helped to solidify a paradigmatic narrative of Americanization in which a religious Jew becomes a secular American. But what about those bits about "solemn prayer" and God blessing America? How can one connect a song that is, in a sense, also a prayer, to a Jewish writer who insisted on a secular identity? What exactly does *secular* mean in the context of Berlin's hallowed song? In addressing these questions, this chapter explores subtle Jewish influences that infused American popular entertainment in the twentieth century. To be sure, the notion of a Jewish influence can be elusive and confounding, but these influences were nonetheless real. This chapter excavates the roots and forms of this distinctive version of secular Jewish expression, detailing its formative influences on popular American theater and film of the twentieth century.

As we can see in the popularity of "God Bless America" (and its composer), American entertainment has, over the twentieth century, formed a central part of established national culture. Songs, plays, and movies often expressed the core values of this culture, through stories which rarely focus directly on God and blessings, but rather on the theater itself. In works of American popular culture created by individuals of Jewish background, however, the distance between God and the theater is far shorter than one might assume. American Jews created a popular theatrical realm that is commonly understood as secular yet on closer examination reveals itself to be far more Jewish than the

---

[3] "God Bless America" by Irving Berlin; © Copyright 1938, 1939 by Irving Berlin; © Copyright Renewed 1965, 1966 by Irving Berlin; © Copyright Assigned the Trustees of the God Bless America Fund; International Copyright Secured. All Rights Reserved. Reprinted by Permission.

[4] See Michael Freedland, *A Salute to Irving Berlin* (London: WH Allen, 1986), Laurence Bergreen, *As Thousands Cheer* (New York: Viking, 1990), especially pages 12 and 410, and Philip Furia, *Irving Berlin* (New York: Schirmer Books, 1998), 11. Max I. Dimont, *The Jews in America: The Roots, History and Destiny of American Jews* (New York: Simon and Schuster, 1978), Howard M. Sachar, *A History of the Jews in America* (New York: Random House, 1992), 353–373, and Irving Howe, *World of Our Fathers* (New York: Schocken Books, 1976) all offer examples of the rags-to-riches legends of Jewish popular entertainers.

word *secular* would indicate. In this world of popular entertainment, Judaic
values about freedom, performance, action, and communal obligation exist
in productive tension with Protestant liberal ideals. Grounding the history of
American popular culture in the multiple religious traditions that informed
the worldviews of its practitioners allows us to understand more clearly why
Jews were and are so deeply involved in American popular entertainment,
how Jews successfully acculturated to America in the twentieth century, and
how American liberalism developed and changed in response to the arrival of
millions of immigrants from many different religious backgrounds.

It is by now a well-known fact that, throughout the twentieth century,
American Jews were deeply involved in the creation of American popular
culture. Never much more than 3 percent of the population, Jews were nonetheless instrumental in the development of the major industries and forms
of entertainment that provided mass culture to a majority of Americans
through much of the twentieth century: Broadway, Hollywood, the television and radio industries, stand-up comedy, comics and cartoons, and the
popular music industry have all been deeply influenced by the activity of
Jews.[5] Popular scholarly explanations for the persistent relationship between
Jews and popular entertainment in America generally argue that the Jews who
created Broadway musicals, Hollywood films, superhero comics, or Tin Pan
Alley songs were, above all, interested in leaving behind their (or their parents' or grandparents') immigrant roots and traditional religious observance
and assimilating into mainstream American society, and that the theater
and other forms of popular entertainment offered a clear escape route.[6]

[5] See Paul Buhle, ed., *Jews and American Popular Culture* (Westport, CT: Praeger, 2006).

[6] The first books to appear on Jews and entertainment in America tended to offer a celebration of the contributions of Jews to American culture or an anxious commentary
on the so-called power of Jews to dictate the direction of American mass culture. See
Lester D. Friedman, *The Jewish Image in American Film* (Secaucus, NJ: Citadel Press,
1987), Patricia D. Erens, *The Jew in American Cinema* (Bloomington: Indiana University
Press, 1984), the articles in Sarah Blacher Cohen, ed. *From Hester Street to Hollywood*
(Bloomington: Indiana University Press, 1983). The next generation of scholars and
journalists built on these early studies, focusing on why Jews were drawn to particu-
lar art and media forms, how these forms aided in acculturation, and why Jews were
able to create culture that spoke so successfully to the American public. My own book,
Making Americans: Jews and the Broadway Musical (Cambridge, MA: Harvard University
Press, 2004), falls into this category. See also Jeffrey Melnick, *A Right to Sing the
Blues: African Americans, Jews, and American Popular Song* (Cambridge, MA: Harvard
University Press, 1999), Michael Rogin, *Blackface, White Noise: Jewish Immigrants in the
Hollywood Melting Pot* (Berkeley: University of California Press, 1996), Neal Gabler, *An
Empire of Their Own: How the Jews Invented Hollywood* (New York: Doubleday, 1989),
Buhle, ed. *Jews and American Popular Culture*, Stephen Whitfield, *In Search of American*

Popular entertainment offered a way for Jews to acculturate by creating a fantasy version of America that was tolerant of outsiders like themselves. But this fantasy – and the analyses that explicate it – posit the existence of a secular space outside of and untouched by religious ritual and values. This American secular space operates as a kind of level playing field on which ethnic groups encounter one another and reshape that field to accommodate various forms of difference.[7] This model of a neutral public sphere fails to take into account the deep-seated religious underpinnings of this form of secularism, the multiple ways in which religious communities express values and beliefs, and the unexpected venues in which those expressions appear.

The terms *religious* and *secular* share a distinct history firmly rooted in the Protestant Reformation and Enlightenment. In his foundational essay, "Religion, Religions, Religious," Jonathan Z. Smith tracks the use of the term "religion" by explorers and scholars beginning in the sixteenth century, and of the development of the study of "world religions," arguing that the category of religion is "a category imposed from the outside on some aspect of native culture."[8] Tomoko Masuzawa builds on Smith's argument, showing how the notion of religion as a particular aspect of social life, rather than the organizing principle of a civilization, is a uniquely Protestant and modern idea, and the idea of "world religions" is closely linked to the rise of a particular nationalist and imperialist ideology.[9] Robert J. Baird pushes this further, arguing that "world religions" have long been understood in terms of their resemblance to or difference from Protestantism. Pointing to David Hume's eighteenth-century tract, *The Natural History of Religion*, Baird argues that Hume and other Protestant Enlightenment thinkers grouped together those aspects of a culture's social life that, like Protestantism, emphasized

---

Jewish Culture (Hanover, NH: Brandeis University Press, 1999), Henry Bial, *Acting Jewish: Negotiating Ethnicity on the American Stage and Screen* (Ann Arbor: University of Michigan Press, 2005), Donald Weber, *Haunted in the New World: Jewish American Culture From Cahan to the Goldbergs* (Bloomington: Indiana University Press, 2005), J. Hoberman and Jeffery Shandler, *Entertaining America: Jews, Movies, and Broadcasting* (Princeton: Princeton University Press, 2003), Vincent Brooks, *You Should See Yourself: Jewish Identity in Post-Modern American Culture* (New Brunswick: Rutgers University Press, 2006).

[7] Courtney Bender and Pamela Klassen, Introduction to *After Pluralism* (New York: Columbia University Press, 2011).

[8] Jonathan Z. Smith, "Religion, Religions, Religious," in *Critical Terms for Religious Studies*, ed. Mark C. Taylor (Chicago: University of Chicago Press, 1998), 269. See also Talal Asad, *Genealogies of Religion* (Baltimore: Johns Hopkins University Press, 1993).

[9] Tomoko Masuzawa, *The Invention of World Religions, or, How European Universalism Was Preserved in the Language of Pluralism and Diversity* (Chicago: University of Chicago Press, 2005).

private, individual confessions of faith and called them "religion."[10] Hume was, of course, preceded by John Locke, whose "Letter on Toleration" of 1689 virtually invented the idea of the private sphere by defining religion as an inward matter of faith. Janet Jakobsen and Ann Pellegrini have argued that this new classification system not only created a set of practices called "religions," but also created pressure on non-Protestant groups to reinvent themselves *as* religions in order to achieve rights, freedoms, or social powers.[11] If certain private, individual acts are labeled as religion, then the rest of the culture becomes secular. American secularism therefore is built on a Protestant-derived model that divides aspects of culture into public and private spheres and relegates religion to the private sphere.

How does Judaism, which has never neatly conformed to this public–private model, fit into this picture? Contemporary religion scholar, Laura Levitt, has argued that many Jewish communities in Western and Central Europe, which up until emancipation were "self-governing corporate bod[ies]," were transformed in the nineteenth century into collections of voluntary individual adherents to a particular faith.[12] In other words, in order to achieve civil rights, liberalizing Jews redefined themselves as members of a religion, Judaism, which much more closely resembled Protestantism. As Levitt and other scholars have explained, many Jews of Central European descent gladly embraced a new identity in America that defined them as members of a particular faith, with all the religious and political freedoms granted to such faith groups; the Reform movement modelled many of its practices on mainline American Protestant behaviors. A number of Jewish thinkers in early twentieth-century America were self-consciously critical of Jewish movements modelled along Protestant lines. Rabbi Israel Friedlaender, an important figure in the early days of the Conservative movement, wrote in 1919:

It was a fatal mistake of the period of emancipation, a mistake which is the real source of all the subsequent disasters in modern Jewish life, that, in order to facilitate the fight for political equality, Judaism was put forward not as a culture, as the full expression of the inner life of the Jewish people, but as a creed, as the summary of a few abstract articles of faith, similar in character to the religion of the surrounding nations.[13]

[10] Robert J. Baird, "Late Secularism," *Social Text* 18, no. 3 (2000): 128.

[11] Janet R. Jakobsen with Ann Pellegrini, "World Secularisms at the Millenium: Introduction," *Social Text* 18, no. 3 (2000): 8.

[12] Laura Levitt, "Impossible Assimilations, American Liberalism, and Jewish Difference: Revisiting Jewish Secularism," *American Quarterly* 59, no. 3 (2007): 811–812.

[13] Israel Friedlaender, *Past and Present* (Cincinnati: Ark Publishing, 1919), 267. Quoted in Mordecai Kaplan, *Judaism as a Civilization* (New York: MacMillan, 1934), vii.

Mordecai Kaplan, the founder of the Reconstructionist movement in Judaism, likewise argued in his 1934 manifesto, *Judaism as a Civilization*, that Judaism can survive in the face of science and skepticism only if it re-embraces the concept of Jewishness as a complete way of life, not simply a matter of private faith. Levitt demonstrates how Eastern European Jewish immigrants to America developed not only new religious movements in response to this transformation of Judaism but also a variety of Jewish secularisms.[14] She argues that many Eastern European Jewish immigrants turned to secular Yiddish culture – theater, literature, politics, and art – as a means of achieving the rights and religious freedoms promised by American law while resisting self-definition as a faith group. Some secular Jews likewise turned to Zionism and the Hebrew language for similar reasons. And of course, some American Jews retained their traditional practices and resisted secularization altogether, while others severed all ties to the Jewish community, intermarried with Christians, and fully assimilated into the mainstream culture.

In Jewish-created popular culture in the non-Jewish public sphere – the Hollywood films, Broadway plays, and popular novels written by secular American Jews – we find yet another distinctively Jewish response to the pressures of Protestant-style secularization. These secular Jews can be understood not simply as Jews who have given up religion, but as Jews struggling to inhabit a public space shaped by a liberal Protestant conception of faith as an aspect of private life. The quality of this American and English-language version of Jewish secularization is more elusive than its Yiddish counterpart not only because it is embedded directly within Protestant secular culture, but also because it is designed expressly to appeal to members of that culture. At the same time, this form of Jewish secular culture has turned out to be extremely resilient, perhaps because it is so indigenously American. Although these writers and artists come from a wide variety of Jewish backgrounds, they are united by a liberal Jewish perspective that insists on the potential compatibility of Judaism with American liberalism. Rather than creating alternative secular spaces

---

[14] Levitt, "Impossible Assimilations," 828. Other scholars of Jewish secularization such as Naomi Seidman and David Biale argue that Eastern European Jews resisted (or at least were ambivalent about) a secularization that so circumscribed religious identity, and they point to aspects of Eastern European Jewish literary and political culture – Hebraic, Zionist, Yiddish, Socialist – as sites of this resistance. Naomi Seidman, "Secularization and Sexuality: Theorizing the Erotic Transformation of Ashkenaz," a pre-circulated paper for a session on "Secularization and Sexuality" at the annual meeting of the Association for Jewish Studies, December 17, 2007 and David Biale, *Not in the Heavens* (Princeton: Princeton University Press, 2011).

in which to inhabit a Jewish cosmos, therefore, these artists worked within the existing Protestant secular culture and found ways to reshape it to better reflect their own values, practices, and larger worldview. They wanted to be Americans, so they created works of American popular culture that not only would allow them to participate in that culture but would allow them to do so on their own terms.

Put simply, Judaism has always existed beyond organized religious practice, and in the early and mid-twentieth century, aspects of Jewish culture and thought continued to shape the worldview of so-called assimilated or secular Jews, albeit in ways that were not as obviously religious or Jewish as the observance of holidays or the maintenance of dietary laws. This elusive American Jewish secular culture is therefore not necessarily best represented by overtly religious or ethnic representations on stage and screen; more subtle affinities between Judaism, liberalism, and the theater are often more revealing. The films, plays, and novels discussed here offer complex visions of imagined communities, individual desire, communal responsibility, and sacred space that emerged from the encounter of Judaic and Protestant worldviews that characterized the twentieth-century American Jewish experience. Furthermore, the Jewish worldview that permeates much of American theatrical culture of the twentieth century reached far beyond the Jews who created it. Its enormous popularity demonstrates the power of these ideas for many Americans, and shows how religious communities intersected and transformed themselves within a pluralistic national context.[15]

First and second generation American Jewish writers and directors negotiated positions for themselves within and alongside multiple strains of Protestant American liberalism by reimagining key aspects of traditional Jewish culture in theatrical forms.[16] In the process, they created a new form of secular Judaism, expressed in a syncretic and enormously successful popular culture that tapped into the inherent theatricality of American

---

[15] This chapter focuses specifically on the American-Jewish case, and the particular relationship between Jewish-created popular culture and Judaism. But equally fascinating narratives could be told about the Catholic secularism of Irish American drama and the relationship between the Black Baptist church, African cultures, and the development of jazz, ragtime, and tap dancing. In addition, I am not arguing for an exclusive claim to theatricality on the part of these Jewish writers and directors; rather, I highlight the affinity between theatricality and certain aspects of Judaism as at least a partial explanation of the Jewish attraction to and success in American popular entertainment. These Judaically inflected ideas are by no means the exclusive property of Jews and many were later adopted by those with no particular connection to traditional Jewish life.

[16] For a discussion of this Protestant multiplicity, see Jeffrey Stout, *Democracy and Tradition* (Princeton: Princeton University Press, 2004).

democracy and spoke (and continues to speak) to a broad American public, a form of Judaism I call theatrical liberalism.[17] The liberalism to which I refer here is classical liberalism – the set of ideas about individual freedom, capitalism, and representative government which informed the founding of American democracy in the eighteenth century – as distinct from the use of the term liberal to mean politically left-wing, or a member of the American Democratic Party. This more recent definition of the word "liberal," however, does have an important historical relationship to the development of theatrical liberalism. Indeed, at the same time that theatrical liberalism became synonymous with certain forms of American popular culture between the two world wars (including, as we shall see, musical comedies, backstage dramas and musicals, screwball comedies, and others), American Jews emerged as a consistently liberal voting bloc, and the epithet "New York Jewish liberal" came to express both a particular political position and a particular kind of popular culture. Classical liberalism, however, refers to a complete system of political, economic, and metaphysical concerns about the nature of the self and community.

Jewish writers and directors of popular culture wrestled with the challenges of constructing a modern liberal Jewish self and imagining a society in which such selves could reach their fullest potential. They probed the boundaries of both Judaism and liberalism to figure out what liberty might mean for a Jew: how free were individual Jews to fashion their own selfhood while remaining within the parameters of an ethical and spiritual tradition that placed limits on individual freedom? Their works raised questions about whether Jewish men and women were equally free to fashion selves and explored the ways in which the particular structure of Jewish families and communities shaped possibilities for self-fashioning. Engaging with ideas drawn from Protestant liberalism, Judaism, and acting theory, these writers and directors wondered about the source of the self, which is, after all, the basis for a doctrine of natural rights. Is it a gift from God, a product of race, or history? Or is it defined by one's actions in the world? Similarly, their works questioned whether identity is private or public, unified or multiple, shifting or stable. Making use of theatrical metaphors, they vigorously debated the role of a liberal individual in relation to his or her community. In a world that privileged individual rights over the obligations that form the core of Jewish practice, what would keep liberal Jews bound to one another, if anything? Is liberal individualism morally defensible in Jewish terms?

[17] On the theatricality of American democratic forms, see Alan Ackerman, *The Portable Theatre* (Baltimore: Johns Hopkins University Press, 1999) and Philip Fisher, *Still the New World* (Cambridge, MA: Harvard University Press, 2000).

Hundreds of American plays and films written and directed by Jews in the twentieth century found common ground in their shared responses to these questions. Four key features distinguish works of theatrical liberalism from other works of American popular culture. First, these works reconstruct the theater as a sacred space, a venue for religious expression and the performance of acts of devotion, thereby turning theatricality into a respectable cultural mode. All of the works discussed here are, to a greater or lesser extent, about the theater and the performance of identity. Most are explicitly meta-theatrical, and many are part of a genre which gained in popularity in the early twentieth century – the backstage musical (or backstage play) – which combines the conventions of romantic comedy with the drama of putting on a show and offers the ideal structure in which to consider questions of individual choice, self-fashioning, and communal obligation. Second, in celebrating theatricality, these plays and films privilege a particularly Jewish attitude toward action and acting in the world, stressing the external over the internal, public over private. Third, these works strenuously resist essentialized identity categories, promoting a particular kind of individual freedom based on self-fashioning. Theatrical liberalism guaranteed secular Jews the freedom to perform the self, a freedom cherished by a people so often denied the right to self-definition, whether by Christian dogma or racial science. And, fourth, theatrical liberalism expressed the idea that individual freedom is circumscribed by a set of incontrovertible obligations to the theatrical community. In these plays and movies, there is a palpable tension between the liberal rhetoric of rights and the Judaic rhetoric of obligation (mitzvot) and the moral weight of these stories turns on the fulfilling of theatrical obligations, even at the expense of individual rights. And while these shows embrace the commercial demands of the free market – indeed their success is most often judged on the basis of their popularity – when theatrical obligations come into conflict with the logic of the marketplace, the obligations take priority. "The show must go on" was the new dogma of the theatrical liberal.[18]

For the purposes of this argument, I focus on writers with a clear connection to Judaism, through their own education, contact with the Jewish *habitus* and belief systems of parents or grandparents, or through otherwise

---

[18] My ideas about self-fashioning, and the relationship between theatricality and modernity more generally, are deeply influenced by the work of scholars of the early modern period such as Stephen Greenblatt, *Renaissance Self-Fashioning* (Chicago: University of Chicago Press, 1980). I address the fascinating ways in which Jewish self-fashioning builds on this early modern notion of the self in the larger work from which this chapter is taken, *Theatrical Liberalism: Jews and Popular Entertainment in America* (New York: New York University Press, 2013).

living in close enough proximity to a traditional Jewish community to have absorbed clear messages about what constitutes Jewish values and practices.[19] These writers and artists emerged from many different types of Jewish communities. A majority of those who achieved success in the first few decades of the twentieth century were second-generation descendants of Central European Jews (such as Edna Ferber, George S. Kaufman, Jerome Kern, Oscar Hammerstein, Richard Rodgers, Lorenz Hart). By the 1920s, 1930s, and 1940s, many American-born Jews of Eastern European descent (such as Irving Berlin, Arthur Miller, Leonard Bernstein, Jerome Robbins), as well as a number of assimilated German-Jews (Ernst Lubitsch, Kurt Weill), had entered the sphere of American popular culture as well. But the evidence for Jewish sensibility lies more directly in the texts than in the biographies of the writers. In the texts, the distinctions one would expect of Jews from different geographical and class backgrounds break down in favor of a remarkably coherent set of distinctively American-Jewish cultural ideas. As these cultural ideas became part of the popular culture, they took on a life of their own.

In the early twentieth century, with the explosion of mass culture, the arrival of millions of immigrants on American shores, and the entrance of Jews into popular culture in America, the image of the theater went through a remarkable transformation from a space of dubious morality to one of sacred ritual. One of the most Jewish, and most successful, musical theater works of the 1920s, *The Jazz Singer*, by Samson Raphaelson, made into the first "talking picture," starring Al Jolson, in 1927, explicitly depicts the theater as the place where religion goes in secular America.[20] In this play and film, Jakie Rabinowitz becomes the American Jack Robin by performing on the vaudeville stage. This causes a rift between him and his immigrant father, an Orthodox cantor on the Lower East Side. Jack tries to convince his father that his choice to be a jazz singer is not so different

[19] For a definition of "habitus," see Pierre Bourdieu, *Distinction: A Social Critique of the Judgement of Taste* (Cambridge, MA: Harvard University Press, 1984), chap. 3.

[20] *The Jazz Singer* was produced on Broadway by Sam H. Harris and had a very successful run of 303 performances with George Jessel as star. It appeared as a film a year later, directed by Alan Crosland, and featuring the vaudeville star Al Jolson. Warner Brothers chose this story to introduce their new synchronized sound technology, and its success is partially attributable to this. The film has been the subject of scholarly interest because of its use of blackface and the connections it draws between blacks and Jews. While that is not the subject of my analysis here, I have written about it elsewhere. See Most, *Making Americans*, 32–39. On this issue, see also Michael Rogin *Blackface, White Noise* (Berkeley: University of California Press, 1996); Matthew Frye Jacobson, *Whiteness of a Different Color* (Cambridge, MA: Harvard University Press, 1998); W. T. Lhamon, *Raising Cain* (Cambridge, MA: Harvard University Press, 1998).

from being a cantor, but to no avail. When asked to replace his father in the synagogue instead of performing on Broadway, Jack argues that the stage is a religion too: "Show business is different from anything else," he says, "The finest actors keep right on working, even if there's a death in the family. The show must go on ... It's like a religion."[21] Although Jack does grant his father's wish, it is his ultimate conversion to the stage that is most typical of plays and movies of the time. There is a distinctly religious quality to such secular narratives; writers describe theater as an all-consuming passion, a tradition, heritage, and way of life to which its adherents owe undying allegiance. There are countless rituals and myths that shape this religion, and a complex value system that determines the morality of those who operate within it. But Jack argues for the theater itself as a new object of devotion. That theme of devotion appears repeatedly in the works that comprise theatrical liberalism.

This quasi-religious conception of the theater was a radical idea in early twentieth-century America. Indeed, anti-theatricality in Western culture can be traced all the way back to Plato, who was famously hostile to impersonation, and the idea has shown remarkable resilience in two millennia of European culture. The Catholic church for many centuries tolerated theatrical spectacle, but only that which emerged from religious activity. With the rise of Protestantism, religiously based anti-theatrical movements gained momentum in many parts of Western Europe. Various Puritan pamphleteers labeled actors hypocrites, considered the creation of an alternate world on the stage tantamount to idolatry (competing with God for the gift of creation), fulminated against cross-dressing on the stage, and generally accused the theater of encouraging lewd and lascivious behavior. Sincerity was considered the mandate of every good Christian, and the stage was seen as a sinful impediment to that goal.[22] Lingering Puritanical influence led to highly ambivalent reactions to theatrical activity in the newly formed American republic. A bias against actors continued even when other prejudices against the theater began to soften. In nineteenth-century America, while high-society theater audiences often enjoyed stage spectacles, they rarely consented to admit professional performers into their ranks. An overview of popular plays and melodramas of the period reveals a persistent sense that performing on the stage is sinful and vulgar, and that those who practice the theatrical arts are neither respectable nor trustworthy. Jews were often implicated in this anti-theatricality; Jewish

---

[21] Samson Raphaelson, *The Jazz Singer* (New York: Brentano's, 1925), 96. All further page references will be given in the text.

[22] See Jonas Barish, *The Antitheatrical Prejudice* (Berkeley: University of California Press, 1981) for a useful history of this phenomenon.

homelessness was conflated with theatricality in the works of numerous European and American novelists of the nineteenth and early twentieth centuries, and both were viewed with suspicion by many nineteenth-century dramatists as well. One example among many of the popular anti-theatrical melodramas of the late nineteenth century that makes use of unfavorable depictions of Jews to make its point is *Trilby*, adapted by American playwright Paul M. Potter from George Du Maurier's novel of the same name. This play centers on the actions of the evil Svengali, a Jewish maestro who snatches a young innocent French girl from her fiancé and forces her, through the powers of hypnosis, to perform as a singer on the stage.[23]

Early modern traditional Jewish communities were also suspicious of the theater. Aside from Purim, when role-playing, pageantry, costumes, and general hilarity were mandated by Jewish law, theatrical activity was constrained by a number of factors: biblical prohibitions against cross-dressing, rabbinic prohibitions against a woman singing (or, by extension, performing) in public, and the general resistance to any form of intellectual or artistic pursuit that fell outside of the study of Torah. At the same time, traditional European Jewish communities, with a few exceptions, did not subscribe to Puritanical notions about sincerity and constancy. While lying is certainly not sanctioned in traditional Jewish life, certain allowances are made for acting that leads to righteous behavior or the furthering of God's will – think of the biblical Jacob pretending to be Esau, for example. Furthermore, because of the particular historical circumstances Jews faced, it was understood that one might have to "pretend to be what one was not" in order to survive in a hostile world.

In both Europe and America, the emergence of Jewish culture *from* this traditional religious context was nearly always accompanied by significant Jewish production of secular theater, and, in particular, plays that explored the ambivalence Jews felt about the shifting identity boundaries characteristic of modern life. Indeed, the duality of identity which characterized Jewish modernity – to be a Jew in your tent and a man in the street, as J. L. Gordon expressed it – can itself be understood as a kind of role-playing theatrical endeavor.[24] The theatricality of Jewish modernity reached an apotheosis in early twentieth-century America. With the entrance *en masse* of first and second generation Jewish writers, directors, and producers into

---

[23] The play premiered in New York in 1895, and was revived on Broadway in 1905, 1915, and 1921.

[24] Judah Leib Gordon, "For Whom do I Toil?" reprinted in *The Jew in the Modern World: A Documentary History*, ed. Paul Mendes-Flohr and Jehuda Reinharz (New York: Oxford University Press, 1980), 315.

the world of American entertainment, the theater underwent a radical shift. Theatrical life was transformed from the "wicked stage" to the most celebrated, most American, and most desirable way to live. An enormously successful new form – the backstage musical – emerged to articulate this ethos, and plays about actors, or about putting on a show, became a popular and long-lasting feature of American culture.

A scene at the end of *The Jazz Singer* explicitly shows how religion is connected with theatricality in early twentieth century popular culture. Torn between replacing his father at services on the eve of Yom Kippur and performing opening night in his first Broadway show, Jakie finally decides to honor his father and return to the Lower East Side. He passionately chants the Kol Nidre service as his father dies. The ghost of the cantor father taps him gently on the shoulder as Jakie sings, conferring his blessing upon him, and then slowly fades away. At the same time, his producer and girlfriend listen through a window. The girlfriend directly compares his chanting to his stage performances, with an inter-title that reads "a jazz singer – singing to his God." As Jakie sings the final climactic note of Kol Nidre, the film cuts immediately to an inter-title that reads, "the season passes – and time heals – and the show goes on," and then immediately afterward to Jolson's famous star turn as Jack Robin in blackface singing "Mammy." "The show goes on" is an ambiguous inter-title here. Which show does it allude to? Is the synagogue service "going on" in Jakie's plaintive mammy-songs? Or vice versa? As the film ends, with a shot of Jakie's beaming mother in the front row of the audience, it becomes clear that in America, the best possible answer is *both*.

The second feature of theatrical liberalism, the privileging of external action over internal motivation, likewise offers an ingenious Judaic approach to secular popular culture. In the opening scene of the 1934 Ben Hecht/ Charles Milholland film *Twentieth Century*, the star director Oscar Jaffe (John Barrymore) teaches a lingerie model, Lily Garland (Carole Lombard), to act. The process is slow, methodical, and painful. First, she must learn to enter a room with the proper bearing and composure. She must speak with the right accent and tone. Then she must walk across the stage in the correct manner, and stop in a particular place before speaking her next line. Lily has difficulty remembering when and where to walk and to speak, and so Jaffe demands chalk, and begins to draw lines on the stage indicating exactly where she should be at each moment in the play. Towards the end of the scene, a shot from above reveals a stage completely covered by white chalk lines. Lily must also learn how to scream in agony when her character learns that her lover is dead. She cannot do it. Finally, Jaffe helps her along by sticking a pin into her backside at the appropriate moment. It works, Lily screams convincingly, and is soon on her way to becoming a Broadway star. This method of building character involves no discussion of the actor's own internal psychological motivations. The acting philosophy of *Twentieth Century*, and of countless similar representations of acting from this time period, is simple and straightforward: walk here, say this, a little louder, now walk there, look behind you, sit down, moan softly. Do it over and over again until you feel it, understand it, and can convey it to those sitting in the very back row of the balcony.[25]

Glancing through a prayerbook in my synagogue one Shabbat morning, I found a set of pencilled-in notes, a reminder a congregant, or perhaps a nervous bar mitzvah boy had jotted down, indicating how one should recite the set of prayers that conclude the morning Shabbat service. A paraphrase of the instructions: "Rise. Take three steps forward, then three back. Bow slightly. Sing altogether. Say this part to yourself. Mumble aloud. Repeat. Rise up on toes three times. Bend knees and bow slightly. Say this part only between Sukkot and Passover. Step backwards and forwards, sway to the right, the left and bow forwards. Sit down." Similarly detailed instructions can be found in the Passover Haggadah: "Distribute pieces of the bottom matzah. Take a piece of matzah and break it into two pieces. Add the bitter herbs, dip it into the charoset, and eat it while reclining to the left." How do you light candles on Hanukkah? Put the candles into the menorah from right to left, and light them from left to right, using not a match, but a separate candle, called a shamash. There are two blessings to say each night, and an additional blessing to say on the first night. This kind of detailed instruction about how to act Jewishly is not limited to rituals related to praying in synagogue and observing holidays. One can find explicit, detailed instructions for daily behaviors of all sorts. How does a Jew wash his or her hands before eating? Use a cup, not the faucet. Pour water on each hand three times, alternating hands each time. Then say the blessing, while drying your hands. If you are washing as part of the Friday evening Shabbat dinner, bless the wine first, then wash, then bless and cut the bread. No one should speak until the bread is blessed, but humming is permitted.

For the director, Oscar Jaffe, acting in the theater demands, above all, close and careful attention to the details of everyday behavior. So does Judaism. Jaffe knows that if Lily practices enough, and does so with the proper spirit and attitude, eventually she will be a great actor. For Abraham Joshua Heschel, one of the most important American Jewish theologians of the last century, practicing is also key: "A good person is not he who

---

[25] This acting theory was the hallmark of David Belasco, the most important American Jewish director of the turn of the twentieth century and the historical figure upon which the character of Oscar Jaffe is based.

does the right thing, but he who is in the habit of doing the right thing."[26] Heschel argued for the importance of *acting* Jewishly, even if one doesn't understand exactly why or doesn't feel spiritually moved to do so. "Judaism insists upon the deed and hopes for the intention," Heschel writes. (403) From doing will eventually come understanding: "It is the act that teaches us the meaning of the act." (404) Acting on the stage and acting Jewishly clearly have many affinities, and this common ground provided a space for secularizing Jews to maintain a familiar stance toward everyday behavior while simultaneously dispensing with the overtly religious rituals that formed obstacles to acculturation to the American way of life. Theatrical liberalism privileged a Judaic notion of the self, an external and public version of a self, the acting self.

Americans have long wrestled with questions about where the "truth" of a self lies, and while action in the world has often been seen as a sign of good internal character, for most Protestants, *internal*, private faith is the driving force that animates action (rather than the other way around); faith, and the kinds of character traits that allow for and support Christian faith, determine one's chances of salvation and move one to act morally in the world. This Protestant divide between action in the world and private faith deeply influenced early liberal thinkers and helped to shape American attitudes about the separation of church and state. Freedom of religion is actually *freedom of conscience*, the freedom to believe whatever you would like. For those whose religion focuses on deeds and actions in the world, this definition of religious freedom can be challenging. Until the modern period, to be a Jew did not primarily require profession of a particular set of beliefs, but to act Jewishly in everything one did, from the foods one ate, to the clothes one wore, to the ways in which one interacted with other members of the community, to the role one took in caring for one's house, crops, livestock, or the earth itself.

Thousands of Jewish immigrants arrived on America's shores with this kind of direct, lived experience of a traditional society deeply concerned with the ethical and spiritual implications of everyday behavior. Accustomed to a culture which asserted the primacy of ritual and deed over declarations of faith, these immigrants confronted in early twentieth-century America the oppositional force (and seductive energy) of a liberal political and social model that granted them freedom of belief and freedom of speech, but not necessarily the cultural freedom to *act* in accordance with those beliefs. For the most part, no civil law in America circumscribed the practice of Jewish rituals like kashrut, Sabbath observance, or

---

[26] Abraham Joshua Heschel, *God in Search of Man* (New York: Farrar, Straus, and Giroux, 1955), 345. All further references will be cited in the text.

the covering of heads. But an apparently secular but deeply Protestant cultural and social worldview shaped all of the contours of modern American life, from the calendar, to the proper place and time for religious practice, to the forms and content of public education, to attitudes toward social life, eating, fashion, relations between the sexes and between parents and children. This transparent overlay of Christian social practice in America made it almost impossible for Jews to become fully accepted Americans without giving up outward signs of religious difference. Yet while most American Jewish writers and thinkers of this generation departed from Orthodox Jewish practice, even the most assimilated of them resisted a worldview that privileged intention over action. Rather, Jewish writers and performers shaped a new kind of American public sphere, one which relocated the Jewish spiritual obligation to *act* in the world from an Old World religious context to a legitimately *American* arena, the world of popular entertainment.

Just as Heschel insists that "we do not have faith because of deeds; we may attain faith through sacred deeds," the plays and films of theatrical liberalism argue for the power of acting to shape belief and feeling. In Rodgers and Hammerstein's 1951 musical *The King and I*, for example, the female lead Anna teaches her son to banish fear by whistling. In "Whistle a Happy Tune," the external performance of bravery actually effects an internal change from fear to confidence:

> I whistle a happy tune,
> And every single time
> The happiness in the tune
> Convinces me that I'm
> Not afraid!

The King and I, and many other plays and films, stress the power of "make believe" to change reality, a phrase which itself indicates that acting creates faith, not the other way around. Anna continues:

> Make believe you're brave
> And the trip may take you far.
> You may be as brave
> As you make believe you are![27]

Theatrical liberalism represented for Jewish writers not only a spiritual calling, but also a means by which to model a self, to integrate into

---

[27] Richard Rodgers and Oscar Hammerstein, *The King and I* in *Six Plays By Rodgers and Hammerstein* (New York: Random House, 1955), 373. See my analysis of this musical in *Making Americans*, 183–196.

American society, and to gain the freedoms inherent in social and economic mobility. Traditional Jews defined themselves as a displaced nation, as God's chosen people, carrying out a sacred task until the arrival of the messiah and the long-awaited return to Jerusalem. But in the nineteenth and early twentieth century, Jews began to leave traditional communities and enter the public sphere of European and American culture, where they adopted the dress, habits, and citizenship of mainstream Christian society. Jewish identity, both national and religious, was destabilized by this change. The question of "who is a Jew" became a pressing one both for modernizing Jews and for the Christian societies into which they were integrating. Multiple possibilities for communal self-definition arose: Zionist, socialist, Yiddish secularist, cultural humanist, assimilationist, and many others. Anxious about the increasing difficulty of distinguishing between Jews and non-Jews, liberal Christian societies and governments looked for ways both to assimilate Jews and, at the same time, to articulate markers of Jewish difference. By the late nineteenth century, European and American Jews were being regarded less and less as a nation unto themselves. Jewish national identity conflicted with the project to incorporate Jews as citizens of the United States and other liberal democracies. Instead, Jews were more and more commonly seen as a race (by Jews as well as non-Jews).

Racial science became popular in America and Europe in the mid- to late nineteenth century. This so-called science created a hierarchy of peoples (with "white" Anglo-Saxons at the top and "black" Negroes at the bottom). It offered security to those at the "top" of the race-defined ladder, especially those who were anxious about the instability of identity in liberal cosmopolitan society. The rhetoric of race played a major role in the response to Jewish immigrants in America around the turn of the century. Jews were seen as a distinct race which was situated somewhere in the middle of the racial hierarchy, not "white," but also not quite "black." Jewish physical, psychological, and intellectual features were assumed to be racially determined. In a nation divided by race, racial status played a major role in the distribution of rights and privileges, and race was a central feature of discussions over immigration and citizenship policy. Many Jews at first embraced racial self-definition as a mode of self-identification that asserted belonging while demanding little in the way of communal or religious obligation.[28] But with the rise of nativist immigration policies and

---

[28] See Matthew Frye Jacobson, *Whiteness of a Different Color: European Immigrants and the Alchemy of Race* (Cambridge, MA: Harvard University Press, 1998), Karen Brodkin, *How Jews Became White Folks and What That Says About Race in America* (Newark: Rutgers University Press, 1999), and Eric L. Goldstein, *The Price of Whiteness: Jews, Race and American Identity* (Princeton: Princeton University Press, 2007).

American antisemitism in the 1920s and 1930s it quickly became clear that "off-white" racial designations (or indeed any labels imposed by outsiders) were dangerous for Jews, as these could prevent Jews from achieving full civil rights in America. And with the rise of Nazism in the early 1930s, it became even clearer that a race-based identity was a trap to be escaped at all costs.

Theatricality emerged as a way for Jews to escape this race-based identity. American Jewish writers and artists argued forcefully against the snare of racial self-definition by writing or producing works which argued for the theater as a space of free self-transformation. The third feature of theatrical liberalism is the right to self-fashion, to determine one's own identity. In the works of theatrical liberalism, decisions about inclusion and advancement are based on the merit of a particular performance and not on the possession of an essential, consistent, racially defined self. Furthermore, one can advance in the world, or escape oppression, by changing one's role. Indeed, many Jewish-created popular performance styles ended up celebrating changeability itself. Ethnic comedians of vaudeville, for example, who could adopt a character with the change of a hat, a nose, a feather, or colored face paint, were a central feature of high-class Broadway revues of the 1920s and 1930s such as the *Ziegfeld Follies*. In a flash, Jewish vaudeville star Eddie Cantor transformed himself from Jewish hypochondriac to Greek cook, to black errand boy, to Indian chief and back again in the play and film *Whoopee* (1928). Jewish comedienne Fannie Brice was likewise well-known for her ability to do "imitations," a skill that became a set piece in Jewish stand-up comedy for decades to come. Early Jewish animators like the Fleischer Brothers (who created Betty Boop and Popeye) and the artists working on Looney Tunes cartoons at Warner Brothers made changeability the centerpiece of their new medium. Betty Boop and Bugs Bunny regularly change shape, size, character, gender, costume, and performance style in order to outwit pursuers or seduce lovers. Similarly, superheroes like Superman and Batman, invented by Jewish comic book artists in the 1930s, based their success on their ability to change identity, thereby eluding and ultimately triumphing over their enemies.

The Larry Gelbart, Burt Shevelove, and Stephen Sondheim musical *A Funny Thing Happened on the Way to the Forum* (1962) offers an excellent example of the centrality of self-invention to theatrical liberalism. The play tells the story of a Roman slave named Pseudolus who wants to secure his freedom. He schemes to marry off his young master, Hero, to the girl of his dreams, Philia, and thereby buy his (Pseudolus's) ticket to freedom. Early in the show, Pseudolus dreams about achieving his freedom in a duet with Hero entitled simply "Free." The song consists of a series of questions

posed by Pseudolus to Hero about the many roles he could perform if he
were free:

PSEUDOLUS: Can you see me as a Roman with my head unbowed?
  Sing it good and loud!
HERO: Free!
PSEUDOLUS: Like a Roman having rights and like a Roman proud?
  Can you see me?
HERO: I can see you.
PSEUDOLUS: Can you see me, a reformer fighting graft and vice?
  Sing it soft and nice!
HERO: Free!
PSEUDOLUS: Why, I'll be so conscientious that I may vote twice!
  Can you see me?
  Can you see me?[29]

How does Pseudolus imagine freedom? He asks, over and over again, "Can
you see me?" As the song develops, the roles Pseudolus will play when he
is "free" pile up: poet, artist, lover, patriarch, citizen, man. For Pseudolus,
freedom *is* performance; to be free is to have the right *to be seen as*, to
play, whatever role he desires. This tendency toward performance is already
indicated in his name, which literally means "lying one" or "false one." At
the same time, the song indicates the ways in which Pseudolus, the undisputed star of the show, is *already* a performer and therefore already free.
Pseudolus, the (Jewish) slave, directs Hero, the (Roman) master, throughout the play, telling him how to dress, how to behave, where to look, where
to go, how to *act*. In this song about Pseudolus's freedom, it is Pseudolus
who tells Hero how to perform the word "free": "sing it good and loud,"
"sing it soft and nice." Pseudolus is an expert not only on the freedom of
performance but on the performance of "free:"

PSEUDOLUS: When a Pseudolus can move, the universe shakes,
  But I'll never move until I'm free.
  Such a little word, but oh, the difference it makes!
  I'll be Pseudolus, the founder of a family,
  I'll be Pseudolus, the pillar of society,
  I'll be Pseudolus the man, if I can only be –
HERO: Free!
PSEUDOLUS: Sing it!

[29] *A Funny Thing Happened on the Way to the Forum*. Music and lyrics by Stephen Sondheim;
  Book by Burt Shevelove and Larry Gelbart (New York: Dodd, Mead and Company,
  1985), 31–32. FREE (from "A Funny Thing Happened on the Way to the Forum"). Words
  and Music by STEPHEN SONDHEIM. Copyright © 1962 (Renewed) BURTHEN
  MUSIC CO., INC. All Rights Administered by CHAPPELL & CO., INC. All Rights
  Reserved. Used By Permission of ALFRED MUSIC.

HERO: Free!
PSEUDOLUS: Spell it!
HERO: F-r- double –
PSEUDOLUS: No, the long way!
HERO: F-r-e-e!
PSEUDOLUS AND HERO: Free!

Hero, a fine upstanding Roman citizen, does not know how to spell "free" such that it will coordinate with the syncopated beat of the music and give the duet the necessary climactic finish. Pseudolus must direct him. In teaching Hero to perform the word "free," and thereby to grant Pseudolus his freedom, Pseudolus is tutoring Hero (and the audience) in a particular worldview that equates theatrical performance with the right to choose one's own identity.

By insisting on *actor* as the most liberating of all identities, theatrical liberalism created a secular, universal rhetoric that protected Jews' newly acquired and deeply treasured civil rights. At the same time, this kind of rights-based freedom – the individual right to self-fashion – is deeply rooted in Enlightenment liberalism and liberal Protestantism and differs in important ways from Jewish values. Throughout these works of theatrical liberalism, the language of rights – the right to be oneself, to self-fashion, to take advantage of opportunities and advance to fame and fortune free of interference – is in tension with another legal rhetoric, emerging from a different legal culture, the system of obligation or mitzvot. In the genre-defining Warner Brothers film *Golddiggers of 1933*, directed by Mervyn LeRoy, the plot turns on a climactic moment when a show may not be able to go on. Barney, the producer, is stuck without a leading man and is trying to convince Brad – investor, songwriter, and love interest in the film – to take his place. Brad, who has hidden the fact that he comes from a deeply anti-theatrical Boston Brahmin family, is resistant to appearing on stage because he doesn't want his older brother to discover that he has been involved in the theater. The girls in the company, however, think he won't perform because he is hiding from the police:

BARNEY (FORCEFULLY): You've got to go on in his place!
BRAD: (POSITIVELY): I can't do that, Barney. [All cluster around Brad]
BARNEY: What do you mean you can't? The curtain is ready to go up. There's a show going on. Your songs are in it, your girl is in it, your money is in it – you've got to go out and do it.
BRAD: (Shaking his head) There's a reason why –
BARNEY: There is *no* reason – There can't *be* any reason (Brad shrugs.)[30]

---

[30] *Gold Diggers of 1933*, edited and with an introduction by Arthur Hove. Madison: University of Wisconsin Press, 1980, p. 94. With some small additions to the dialogue taken from the film itself.

Trixie, the straight-talking showgirl, steps in to give Barney a hand, backed up by Polly, another performer and Brad's girlfriend:

TRIXIE: Listen, I don't care even if you have to go to jail after the performance. You ought to forget about yourself and do it anyway. Do you know what this means – if the show doesn't go on? It means that all those girls in this show – all those poor kids who threw up jobs – and who'll never get other jobs in these times – all those kids been living on nothing – starving themselves these five weeks we've been rehearsing – hoping for this show to go on – and be a success – They're depending on you! You can't let them down – you can't – if you do – God knows what will happen to those girls – They'll have to do things I wouldn't want on *my* conscience. And it'll be on *yours*–You can go out and sing Gordon's part and put this show over – and if you don't – I don't care what the reason is – [Brad looks at Trixie, then at Polly, wavering in his decision.]
POLLY: (catching his arm) She's right, Brad, *I* don't care what the reason is.

Finally, Brad is won over:

BRAD (THOUGHTFULLY): I hadn't thought about it that way. (He pauses. All look at him hopefully. With sudden decision.) Yes, of course, I'll do it! [There is a general gasp of delight][31]

Brad has every *right* to refuse to go on the stage. But the language by which he is convinced is not that of rights, but of obligation. Barney could have given Brad a fiery speech about his right to live up to his potential, to be his own person, to resist the anti-theatrical prejudice of his brother that keeps him from doing what he loves. Instead, he insists that Brad is *obliged* to take on the role. Trixie goes on to argue that the entire company is depending upon him and if he doesn't perform, everyone will suffer. But what obliges him? Why is it incumbent upon Brad to save the show? Theatre is fundamentally a collective practice, and the ultimate source of authority in the theater is the collective itself. In other words, without a number of participants each fulfilling a set of prescribed obligations – producer, director, actors, designers, technicians, house staff, and audience – the show cannot proceed and the entire theatrical system would cease to function. In the unwritten, but universally acknowledged, laws of theatrical liberalism, all members of the company are obligated to do what they can to make sure that the show goes on.

This is the fourth element of theatrical liberalism: obligation. The freedom to shape the self in these plays and movies is embedded within and circumscribed by a set of communitarian obligations that closely resemble mitzvot. In twentieth-century America, while the individual freedom to perform (and, if one is very talented and lucky, to become a star) is central

---

[31] *Gold Diggers of 1933*, p. 95.

to the ethos of theatrical liberalism, this freedom is only possible within a system of obligations imposed by the covenant of The Theatre, and shared by each member of a theatrical community. When someone in a 1930s play or movie insists to his or her co-star that "the show must go on," the conversation is over. There is no alternative.

As legal theorist Robert M. Cover makes clear in his work in comparative jurisprudence, the liberal rhetoric of rights and the Jewish rhetoric of obligations are based in two different collective myths: the individualist myth of the social contract and the corporate myth of Sinai.[32]

Social movements in the United States organize around civil rights, while in Judaism, the kinds of entitlements that rights legislation protects have little meaning without an accompanying obligation. In other words, US law determines what protections an individual is entitled to. Jewish law determines who is obligated to act in particular situations and what they are obligated to do. Cover illustrates how both systems have devices in place to address injustice, but, depending on the situation, he argues that one system might be more effective than the other in addressing these problems. For example, in the struggle over women's roles in Judaism, feminists tend to argue for women's *right* to lead prayer. But for traditional Jews, this argument from rights is unpersuasive. They argue that women are not obliged under the law to do these things and so the only persuasive way to change the system would be to re-interpret the obligation to include women (a difficult, but not impossible task). On the other hand, while American law may guarantee children the "right" to an education, he notes that this right is hard to enforce unless we know to whom it is addressed. How to turn the right to education into reality? Of course, American government makes this happen through a complicated system of taxation and legislation, but when failures in education occur, no particular person or group is held responsible. Jewish law, on the other hand, never discusses the rights of the child; rather, it addresses the specific obligations of parents, teachers, communities, and homeowners to provide education. It is no accident that nearly universal (male) schooling amongst Jews has been a reality for at least two millennia.

The notion of "doing a mitzvah" is an extraordinarily resilient one amongst Jews, even Jews who are, in all other respects, resolutely secular. Theatrical liberalism created a cultural form within which Jews could balance these competing notions of *obligation* and *rights*. To be a performer is to assert one's right to self-fashion; to perform as well as one can is a

---

[32] Robert M. Cover, "Obligation: A Jewish Jurisprudence of the Social Order," in *Law, Politics, and Morality in Judaism*, ed. Michael Walzer (Princeton: Princeton University Press, 2004).

means of fulfilling one's obligation to the theatrical community. Cover ends his article with an attempt to synthesize the two legal systems, arguing that believing in the moral value of certain rights is only part of the project of correcting injustice; one is also obligated to make every effort to realize those rights. The theater offered a similar synthesis to secular Jews, albeit a synthesis that required belief not in a transcendent God who issued commandments, but in a community of believers and a set of theatrical traditions.

In 1946, Irving Berlin penned a rousing anthem to theatrical liberalism which combines all of its salient features in a powerful conversion narrative. Introduced in the musical *Annie Get Your Gun*, "There's No Business Like Show Business" is sung by a couple of theater producers aiming to convert the backwoods Annie Oakley into the world, and worldview, of the theater. They describe the many roles available: "The cowboys, the wrestlers, the tumblers, the clowns, the roustabouts who move the show at dawn." They note that this is a world which is actively self-fashioned: "the costumes, the scenery, the makeup, the props," a world in which external acting takes precedence over internal truths: "There's no people like show people / They smile when they are low." And even in a *business* (show business), the obligation to the theater trumps concerns about profit: "Even with a turkey that you know will fold / You may be stranded out in the cold / Still you wouldn't change it for a sack of gold / Let's go on with the show."[33] In refusing to exchange one's commitment to the stage for a "sack of gold," Berlin's devotees of "show business" revise the Protestant work ethic in a manner typical of theatrical liberalism. To stick with a show, even when it does not generate a profit, does not make rational sense in the world of business. But theatrical liberalism is not a rational worldview, it is a spiritual and moral one. Individual plays may run forever or fold overnight, but the theater itself is not up for sale. To trade the theater for a sack of gold would be to place oneself outside of the theatrical liberal system altogether. In turning the "wicked stage" into a site for American virtue, theatrical liberalism transformed assimilationist American ideology from an either/or choice between religious Judaism and secular liberalism into a remarkable synthesis of the two, a new American ethos for the twentieth century.

As powerful as it was, and remains, theatrical liberalism has not always been consistently espoused by Jewish writers and performers of popular culture throughout the twentieth century. While the basic values of

---

[33] Irving Berlin, *Annie Get Your Gun* (New York: Irving Berlin Music Corporation, 1949), 22–25. © Copyright 1946 by Irving Berlin. © Copyright Renewed. International Copyright Secured. All Rights Reserved. Reprinted by Permission.

theatrical liberalism characterize a majority of the works of popular culture created by American Jews, the allure of its ideology waxed and waned over the century in response to historical circumstances which made Jews more or less inclined to embrace a worldview which emphasized performance as a means of establishing identity and community. In the wake of the Great Depression, World War II, the Holocaust, and the post-war Red Scare, for example, many artists began to raise questions about the ability of theatrical liberalism to deliver on its promises of individual freedom, personal agency, and communal acceptance. Numerous plays and films from the immediate post-war period question whether or not we actually have the freedom to fashion our own selves, at times violently rejecting an earlier generation's investment in self-fashioning as naive and misguided. Some, like the modernist musical *Pal Joey* by Richard Rodgers and Lorenz Hart, which opened in 1940 and was revived in 1952, retained a theatrical worldview, but used the backstage musical form to critique rather than celebrate that worldview. The play's central character Joey, a corrupt hoofer and ladies' man, his lover Vera, and the nightclub world in which they operate reveals theatricality as a morally and spiritually empty mode, a vehicle for a selfish individualism devoid of communal connection, much less obligation. Other plays questioned the location of truth itself and turned to a new acting style – method acting – to reverse theatrical liberalism's emphasis on external action. One of the most popular plays of the post-war period, Arthur Miller's *Death of a Salesman* (1949), suggests that external action is a kind of illusion, and the authentic core of the self is found not in what one does, but in who one *really is*. A character obsessed with performance and illusion, Willy Loman's commitment to imaginative self-transformation is no longer seen as an asset. He is instead revealed to be hopelessly deluded and at times dangerously psychotic. Other musicals of the 1950s such as Leonard Bernstein, Stephen Sondheim, Arthur Laurents, and Jerome Robbins's *West Side Story* (1957) and Sondheim, Laurents and Jule Styne's *Gypsy* (1959) likewise test the values of theatrical liberalism by critiquing its most identifiable generic features: romantic comedy and backstage drama. They attempt to rewrite the genre of the backstage musical to reflect deep disillusionment with the very ideals that genre was invented to express.

This ambivalence towards theatrical liberalism in the early Cold War era shifted in response to the ethnic revival of the 1960s and the heroic representations emerging from and about the new State of Israel. These decades featured simultaneous celebration of and skepticism about "authentic" ethnic identities, and Jewish intellectuals were at the forefront of this discussion: most notably Erving Goffman, whose *Presentation of Self in Everyday Life* introduced the "dramaturgical" notion of the performed self into scholarly literature, as well as Lionel Trilling, in *Sincerity and Authenticity* (1972), and Cynthia Ozick in "Towards a New Yiddish" (1970). Jews began to emerge onto the popular culture landscape *as Jews* in the 1960s, but what exactly it meant to be an *authentic* Jew was the subject of great debate. *Fiddler on the Roof* (1964) featured openly Jewish characters who were, despite their European identities, already becoming liberals, if not theatrical liberals. Tevye's daughters' desires to "follow their hearts" in romantic love – and his willingness to enable those choices – indicates a willing, if wary, embrace of liberal values, privileging a society which bases major life choices on individual internal motivation rather than traditional and communally sanctioned external action. Theatrical liberalism gains equally ambivalent treatment in another musical of the same year, *Funny Girl* (1964). The central character, the historical Fannie Brice, is represented as a natural comedienne who achieves stardom not via self-fashioning, but through "being herself." By insisting on celebrating her authentic Jewish identity in the face of assimilationist pressures, Brice – as represented in *Funny Girl* – became one of the most successful performers on the Broadway stage of the 1920s and 30s. Indeed, it is when she tries to "act" in order to save her gambler husband from humiliation that she destroys her own personal life. Other works of Jewish American popular culture from the 1960s and 70s remained far more committed to theatricality, self-fashioning and external action and often overtly lampooned the naiveté of the embrace of authenticity which characterized so many works of the ethnic revival. Alan Jay Lerner and Frederick Loewe's *My Fair Lady* (1964), for example, celebrated the power of theatricality for socio-economic mobility while subtly questioning the ethics of rampant self-fashioning. Mel Brooks and Gene Wilder's *Young Frankenstein* (1974) took a different approach to the ethics of the (literal) fashioning of selves, using parody to critique the cult of Jewish ethnic authenticity and turning to cinematic and theatrical models from the 1920s and 30s to re-animate the values of theatrical liberalism for a new era.

The popularity of multiculturalism and identity politics in the 1980s and 1990s was accompanied by a renewed burst of interest in theatricality – now re-configured as performativity – amongst Jewish academics such as Judith Butler, Marjorie Garber, and Eve Kosofsky-Sedgwick. The performance of Jewish identity likewise became a key theme in works of popular culture of the 1980s and early 1990s and was, more often than not, discussed in theatrical terms. In the best-selling 1986 novel *The Counterlife*, Philip Roth's character Nathan Zuckerman, after a lengthy search for the "truth" of Jewish identity, determines that the heart of Jewishness is performance: "I am a theater, and nothing but a theater," Nathan concludes. Woody Allen's pseudo-documentary *Zelig* (1983) likewise investigates the performance of Jewish identity via Leonard Zelig, who gains notoriety in the 1920s and 30s by being *too* theatrical – he is a chameleon who unwittingly adopts the appearance, gesture and accent of whomever he encounters. An ultimate assimilationist, Zelig is finally "cured" when he develops a stable interior self through love with a gentile woman, his doctor. Tony Kushner's Pulitzer-prize winning play *Angels in America* likewise investigates the moral status of theatrical liberalism by setting the naively "authentic" and morally compromised Louis against the radically self-fashioned and equally morally problematic Roy Cohn.

Replaced for more than fifty years in the popular culture by the secular Judaic values of theatrical liberalism, explicitly Judaic texts, rituals, and ideas began to slowly re-emerge into the popular public sphere at the end of the twentieth century in the work of performers and writers such as graphic novelists Ben Katchor (*The Jew of New York*) and J.T. Waldman (*Megillat Esther*), Mandy Patinkin's translation of songs from American popular culture "back" into Yiddish on *Mameloshen* as well as the overtly religious work of popular musicians such as Matisyahu (*Shake off the Dust. Arise*), Joshua Nelson (*Kosher Gospel*) and Josh Dolgin (*Hip Hop Haggadah*). Novelists such as Jonathan Safran Foer (*Everything is Illuminated*), Michael Chabon (*The Yiddish Policeman's Union*), and Myla Goldberg (*Bee Season*), comedians such as Jon Stewart and Sarah Silverman, films such as *A Serious Man*, *Kissing Jessica Stein*, and *The Hebrew Hammer*, a veritable explosion of Jewish film festivals across America and around the world, and performance artists such as Amichai Lau-Lavie (*The Rebbetzin Hadassah Gross* and *Storahtelling*) draw on Jewish history, religious practices, ethics, and comic and literary traditions to build a deliberately Judaic American popular culture for the twenty-first century. These Jewish artists have rediscovered the Judaic roots of many American popular culture forms and proceeded to use these forms to make art which is simultaneously secular, religious, Jewish, and American.

SELECT BIBLIOGRAPHY

Bender, Courtney and Pamela Klassen, eds. *After Pluralism*. New York: Columbia University Press, 2011.

Bial, Henry. *Acting Jewish: Negotiating Ethnicity on the American Stage and Screen*. Ann Arbor: University of Michigan Press, 2005.

Biale, David. *Not in the Heavens*. Princeton: Princeton University Press, 2011.

Brodkin, Karen. *How Jews Became White Folks and What That Says About Race in America*. Newark: Rutgers University Press, 1999.

Brooks, Vincent. *You Should See Yourself: Jewish Identity in Post-Modern American Culture*. New Brunswick: Rutgers University Press, 2006.

Buhle, Paul, ed. *Jews and American Popular Culture*. Westport, CT: Praeger, 2006.

Cohen, Sarah Blacher, ed. *From Hester Street to Hollywood*. Bloomington: Indiana University Press, 1983.

Cover, Robert M. "Obligation: A Jewish Jurisprudence of the Social Order," in *Law, Politics, and Morality in Judaism*, ed. Michael Walzer. Princeton: Princeton University Press, 2004.

Erens, Patricia D. *The Jew in American Cinema*. Bloomington: Indiana University Press, 1984.

Friedman, Lester D. *The Jewish Image in American Film*. Secaucus, NJ: Citadel Press, 1987.

Gabler, Neal. *An Empire of Their Own: How the Jews Invented Hollywood*. New York: Doubleday, 1989.

Goldstein, Eric L. *The Price of Whiteness: Jews, Race and American Identity*. Princeton: Princeton University Press, 2007.

Heschel, Abraham Joshua. *God in Search of Man*. New York: Farrar, Straus, and Giroux, 1955.

Hoberman, J. and Jeffrey Shandler, *Entertaining America: Jews, Movies, and Broadcasting*. Princeton: Princeton University Press, 2003.

Jacobson, Matthew Frye, *Whiteness of a Different Color*. Cambridge, MA: Harvard University Press, 1998.

Levitt, Laura. "Impossible Assimilations, American Liberalism, and Jewish Difference: Revisiting Jewish Secularism." *American Quarterly* 59, no. 3 (2007): 807–822.

Lhamon, W.T. *Raising Cain*. Cambridge, MA: Harvard University Press, 1998.

Melnick, Jeffrey. *A Right to Sing the Blues: African Americans, Jews, and American Popular Song*. Cambridge, MA: Harvard University Press, 1999.

Most, Andrea. *Making Americans: Jews and the Broadway Musical*. Cambridge, MA: Harvard University Press, 2004.

Theatrical Liberalism: Jews and Popular Entertainment in America. New York: New York University Press, 2013.

Rogin, Michael. *Blackface, White Noise: Jewish Immigrants in the Hollywood Melting Pot*. Berkeley: University of California Press, 1996.

Weber, Donald, *Haunted in the New World: Jewish American Culture From Cahan to the Goldbergs*. Bloomington: Indiana University Press, 2005.

Whitfield, Stephen. *In Search of American Jewish Culture*. Hanover, NH: Brandeis University Press, 1999.

CHAPTER 32

JEWS AND POPULAR CULTURE IN THE TWENTIETH CENTURY
Israel and the Middle East

AMY HOROWITZ AND GALEET DARDASHTI

ENDURANCE AND ERASURE: JEWISH CONTRIBUTIONS TO TWENTIETH-CENTURY POPULAR CULTURE IN THE MIDDLE EAST AND NORTH AFRICA

Twentieth-century Middle Eastern and North African Jews have made enduring contributions to popular culture in the Middle East and modern Israel. These men and women embraced national consciousness as Iraqis, Egyptians, and Moroccans, among others, while maintaining a complicated and often ambivalent affinity with European Zionism. From the late 1800s until 1948, Jews achieved recognition in music, film, theater, journalism, and literature throughout the region. As colonial regimes transformed into post-colonial Middle Eastern and North African states in the twentieth century, popular culture provided powerful identity symbols. Jewish artists played a central role in popular culture, despite – and sometimes because of – their minority status. Islamic prohibition against mixed-gender performance and Jewish competence in European languages (often a result of class) may have factored into Jewish success in these fields.

Yet as the collision between Arab and Jewish nationalisms intensified in the mid-twentieth century, hundreds of thousands of Jews immigrated to Israel (with financial assistance from Zionist organizations), while many of those with financial means, immigrated elsewhere. While some immigrants were religious, others held an historical attachment to a celestial Zion embedded in their imagination as a spiritual longing, and did not share the Zionist commitment to Palestine as a physical destination. Once in Israel, immigrants from the Middle East and North Africa experienced

We are very grateful to our colleagues Ari Ariel and Bryan Roby and to the editors Mitchell Hart and Tony Michels for their very helpful and thoughtful suggestions on drafts of this article. Much of Dardashti's research for this article occurred in conjunction with a generous Taub Postdoctoral Fellowship at the Taub Center for Israel Studies at New York University from 2012 to 2013.

a double erasure, from the historical record in their former homelands and from the emerging cultural industry in Israel.

In this essay, we explore the interconnected poles of erasure and endurance of Jewish artists, producers, publishers, and audiences in their former homelands and in Israel. Focusing primarily on Arab-speaking societies, we ask: how have Jews purposefully contributed to mainstream popular culture in the first half of the twentieth century and how have their children and grandchildren artistically re-imagined such engagement in Israel and globally by reconnecting with their Arab identities? By mainstream, we refer to Jewish contributions to popular culture within the Muslim communities in which they lived. We do, however, include Jewish newspapers, because these attracted a mainstream readership among Muslims and Christians. Throughout our individual fieldwork over the past decades, Muslims, Christians, and Jews, whether from Lebanon, Morocco, Afghanistan, Libya, Egypt, or Palestine, expressed nostalgia for the days when they were creatively engaged in developing artistic networks together.

The ever-shifting and selective nature of memory is always at play at the permeable borders of popular culture. We suggest that popular culture is a location in which we can understand erasure and endurance not as fixed oppositional binaries but rather as fraught dialectical processes that faced Jews as a minority in the Middle East and North Africa and as a marginalized majority in Israel after the 1950s. Yael Zerubavel's notion of commemorative density (1995), that is, the privileging or neglect of a particular historical period within collective memory, helps to posthumously reposition Middle Eastern Jews both within the national narratives of their former homelands and in Israel.

While Zerubavel discusses this seepage in myth and legend, it is equally relevant to the stories, songs, journalistic writing, and theater that form the basis of our inquiry. Zerubavel's commemorative density offers a cautionary tale about selective memory. A partial recounting of merely the exclusion of Jewish artists reinforces the narrative of conflict, while a narrative highlighting only the inclusion of Jewish artists promotes romanticization of the "way things were." We aim to represent the multiple and conflicting realities that coexisted.

NATIONALISM

Popular culture played a crucial role in forging national identity in the emerging Middle Eastern states of the early twentieth century. Governments sought to unite their diverse populations by creating nationalistic discourses that valorized religious pluralism. Thus Iraqi King Faysal declared to Iraqi Jews, in 1921, that "in the vocabulary of patriotism, there is no such thing as Jew, Muslim, or Christian. There is simply one thing called Iraqi" (Snir 2006: 382). In the early 1920s, Iraq initiated a national education campaign to promote Arabic language and patriotism. Jews responded with a plethora of literary Arabic writing directed toward the general Iraqi population.[1]

Emphasizing shared national culture rather than religious difference, a popular Arabic slogan heard throughout the Arab world was "Religion is for God, but the nation is for the people" (Starr 2011; Snir 2006). In certain discourses of Arab nationalism, some Jews perceived an opportunity to transcend their minority status. As Lital Levy has argued, it was in the "melting pot" mentality of this historical context that a small group of politically astute intellectual Jews first began to employ the term "Arab Jew," as a political maneuver in order to discursively align and situate their Jewish identities within the modern Arab collective (2008). In Egypt and Iraq – two of the major centers of Arab nationalism – popular culture was a crucial facet of the nationalist zeitgeist of the early 1900s, and Jews were eager to participate. Both through their artistic collaborations with non-Jews and by producing popular culture that emphasized the shared experiences of Jews and Arabs, Jewish artists living in the Arab world in the aftermath of the Ottoman Empire, underscored the fact that they were no different from their co-nationals. Jews throughout the region encountered modernity not as a moment of liberation from a ghettoized existence but rather as engaged citizens.

JOURNALISM

Jews living in the Arab world in the late nineteenth through the midtwentieth centuries published newspapers and journals that enjoyed both Jewish and non-Jewish readership. These publications appeared in various modalities (dailies, weeklies, monthlies), formats and genres (news, current events, satire, literary features), and languages (Arabic, French, Turkish, Judeo-Arabic, Italian, Yiddish, and Hebrew). In some cases, a paper published several editions, each in a different language, spoken by the local readership.

Jews also participated in the mainstream press in the Islamic world, as reporters and editors. For example, the Jewish Tunisian socialist Albert Cattan published *Tunis-Socialiste*, a newspaper that appealed to Muslim, Christian, and Jewish Tunisian socialists (Saadoun 2005). In Egypt, the prolific Karaite[2] author Murad Farag was known beyond the Jewish

---

[1] See Chapter 25 in this volume, which addresses literature.

[2] Beinin (1998) implies that Karaites were more integrated into Egyptian "Arab" culture than other Jews, so perhaps this represents Jewish integration from an exceptional group.

community; he wrote for two major Egyptian papers – al-Jarīda and al-Mu'ayyad – prior to World War I. One of the only Jewish Egyptian writers who wrote in Arabic, he actively supported Jewish–Muslim collaboration (Somekh 1989).

As early as the nineteenth century, Egyptian Jews developed a thriving communal press while also actively participating in the mainstream press. The satirical Egyptian magazine Abou Naddara was first published in 1877 by Jewish journalist and writer/intellectual Ya'qūb Ṣanu'. He was exiled in 1878, in part due to the paper's critical political position toward the government. However, Ṣanu' continued publishing in France and copies of the paper were smuggled into Egypt where they circulated widely.[3]

The Jewish press in Egypt, like the population it served, was quite diverse, with publications in Yiddish, Ladino, Italian, Judeo-Arabic, French, and Hebrew. In addition, a full one-third of the Jewish-owned papers in Egypt, some thirty publications, aimed to reach a broad Egyptian readership (Yerushalmi 2008: 124).

The newspaper Israel's founder and editor Albert Museri was an Italian-Egyptian Jew who enjoyed the immunities granted a foreign national, including relative freedom from censorship. Although technically a "Jewish" publication, the paper's multi-lingual editions (French, English, as well as Judeo-Arabic) resulted in an elite Egyptian and international readership: it was distributed in fourteen locations in Europe, North Africa, and the Middle East. The French edition remained in publication from 1920 to 1939. The paper maintained a non-partisan stance (Hillel 2004: 53–54). Each edition, nonetheless, had an agenda; Judeo-Arabic-language contributors sought to straddle the boundaries of Arab-Jewish local identity while French contributors pursued the Europeanization of Egyptian readers. A competing paper, L'Aurore, originally from Istanbul, was relaunched in Egypt in 1924 and was popular among the large Greek and Turkish expatriate Jewish communities (Yerushalmi 2008: 119–121).

Al-Shams emerged as an offshoot of Israel, founded by editor Sa'd Malki when the Judeo-Arabic edition of Israel was closed by the Egyptian government. Al-Shams reflected Malki's affiliation with a movement of young Jews who combined Jewish nationalism with Arab nationalism, a dual commitment that led them to the study of Arabic and Hebrew. The newspaper went so far as to encourage readers to contribute monetarily to Egypt's war effort in the late 1930s. Its popular cinema section was edited by 'Abd al'Aziz Ahmad, a non-Jewish Egyptian journalist (Yerushalmi 2008: 122). Al-Shams's readership of some 1,500–2,200 included Muslims and Copts,

---

[3] See below for Ṣanu''s contribution to Arabic theater.

and the paper was distributed at governmental offices (Nahmias 2013: 128–141).

Many Jewish businesses had reservations about the paper's simultaneous support for both Jewish and Arab nationalism and refused to purchase advertising space, but external criticism ultimately led to the paper's demise. With the establishment of the state of Israel the paper came under increasing attack. It was castigated in an article in *al-Aharam* in 1948, and the Egyptian censor closed it later that year (Yerushalmi 2008).

The Jewish press in Egypt was a site in which conflicting cultural and political trends coexisted in tense proximity for seven decades, from the late nineteenth century through the mid-twentieth century (Ayalon 1988). These political tensions are evident in the case of Albert Mizrahi, Jewish publisher of the mainstream daily paper *al-Ṣarāḥa* ("Sincerity"). *Al-Ṣarāḥa* was the first paper to publish the declaration of the Free Officers Movement a few days after the 1952 revolution. The government closed it in 1954, not because Mizrahi was Jewish but because the paper was closely affiliated with the *Wafd* party. The demise of *Al-Ṣarāḥa* ended the rich chapter of Jewish journalism in Egypt (Yerushalmi 2008: 122).[4]

THEATER AND FILM

Following the modern Arabic renaissance (al-Nahḍa) Arabic drama became an important focal point for the Egyptian national movement in the late nineteenth and early twentieth centuries and Jews made their mark early as pioneers acting (on stage and in film), writing, directing, and investing. The innovators of modern Arabic drama looked to European drama as a source for both the form and content for a new theatrical popular art form in Arabic. Many view the Egyptian Jew Yaʿqub Ṣanuʿ (1839–1912) as the founder of the Egyptian national theater in 1870. Many argue that he established the theater in order to encourage political action among the Egyptian populace.

By 1872, Ṣanuʿ had written and produced at least thirty-two plays, and had translated many others from European languages. His two primary innovations for modern Arabic theater were the use of native Egyptian dialect and political satire. Now, for the first time, the uneducated and illiterate – who did not speak Fusha (classical literary Arabic) – could experience

---

[4] There were two exceptions, as Joel Beinin notes: "E. J. Blattner continued to publish and edit the annual *Le Mondain égyptien: L'Annuaire de l'élite d'Egypte* (The Egyptian Who's Who) through the 1950s. The Weinstein stationery and printing firm continued to operate in Cairo under Jewish ownership as of the mid-1990s" (Beinin, 1998).

the same theatrical productions as high-society Egyptians. His plays poked fun at issues of love and marriage, criticized polygamy, and satirized the ways in which middle- and upper-class Egyptians attempted to adopt European customs. Ultimately, the implicitly subversive content of his plays toward the regime – a regime which had previously supported him – resulted in a royal decree that closed his theater in 1872 – two years after it had been founded. His innovations, however, determined the future of Arab theater and even cinema (Gendzier 1961; Shafik 2007).[5] Although Ṣanu' is buried in a Jewish cemetery, numerous rumors of his conversion to Islam circulate to this day.

During the interwar period, known as the "golden age" of Arabic Theater, the art spread throughout the region. Several Jewish women launched successful careers. As the first non-European woman to appear in Algerian theater, the celebrated Marie Soussan is remembered as a trailblazer for Algerian theater who paved the way for other women to enter the art form in the early 1930s. Previously, men had appeared in drag to perform women's roles. Soussan was a successful variety-show performer during the interwar period who also recorded more than twenty 78 rpm records. At some point in her career, however, Soussan – like several other noted female artists from the Arab world – converted to Islam (Miliani 2011: 180–181).

Another North African Jewish actress of note was the bold Ḥabība Messika (1899–1930), Tunisia's most celebrated actor throughout the 1920s. Born into a family of Jewish musicians in Tunisia, she began her career as a wedding singer before establishing herself as a serious actress by the time she was twenty. She performed several roles for al-Shahāma, one of the two most important theaters of this period, including a starring role in the play Ṣalāḥ al-Dīn, an Arab nationalist drama that demonstrated the superiority of the Muslim world over Christian Europe. The theater also staged many European plays performed in Arabic, and Messika performed the role of Desdemona in Shakespeare's Othello. She also performed in French during al-Shahāma's European tours and received rave reviews. Some sources even claim that Messika played the role of Romeo in a Tunisian version of Romeo and Juliet opposite the actress Rachida Lotfi; the two allegedly shared a kiss on stage in the 1920s and caused a riot.[6]

---

[5] Moshe Behar and Zvi Ben-Dor Benite's important book, *Modern Middle Eastern Jewish Thought: Writings on Identity, Politics, and Culture, 1893–1958* (Waltham, MA: Brandeis University Press, 2013), came out just as we put final touches on this chapter. It provides English translations of several of Ṣanu's important works.

[6] Our colleague, Bryan Roby, has heard several references to this version of Romeo and Juliet during his time in Tunisia.

She is perhaps most widely known in her day for provocatively singing what later became the Tunisian national anthem in the film *Patrie: Les Martyrs de la Liberté* (Homeland: The Martyrs of Freedom); in the film she sings defiantly draped in the Tunisian flag and is then led off the stage by French authorities for her subversive behavior – singing in Arabic as opposed to French.[7] Such a subversive role for a young Jewish actress of this period is certainly noteworthy. In 1930, at the height of her career, Messika was murdered by a former lover at the age of thirty-one (Tobi 2014).

From its inception, the Arab film industry based in Egypt predicated its success upon artists who had already achieved stardom in theater and music. This enabled the film industry to attract audiences throughout the Arab world. The film industry was therefore reliant upon the Arab music industry in order to remain profitable. Some of the primary musical stars of the early years who went on to become film stars included Abd al-Wahab, Umm Kulthum, Farid al-Atrash, Asmahan, and the Jewish Layla Murad (Shafik 2007).

Jewish involvement in Arabic cinema began with Tunisian Albert Samama Chikly, who first brought film to North Africa in 1922. Many view his daughter, Haydée Chikly, who starred in both of his films, as the first Arab actress. Egypt was the center of the young film industry of the 1920s and 1930s and Jews as well as other minority groups were important to these initial efforts. Viewed as a pioneer of Egyptian cinema, the Egyptian Jew Togo Mizrahi became the most prolific director and producer of his day. Born in 1901, he earned a certificate in commerce in Alexandria and completed a Ph.D. in France. During his studies abroad, he developed an interest in film and returned to Egypt in 1928 to apply his artistic interests and business training to the fledgling Alexandrian film industry; he shot his first film, *Cocaine*, in 1930. Soon thereafter, he established the second most successful studio and production company of the period, releasing thirty-six films between 1931 and 1946 – Mizrahi directed thirty-three of those and occasionally played acting roles as well. Mizrahi was known widely for the farce genre, and was also instrumental in making the musical, the melodrama, and films combining the latter genres, into fixtures of Egyptian cinema.

Most notable among Mizrahi's later works were his films featuring the popular Jewish-born Egyptian singer Layla Murad. As the daughter of the famed musician, Zaki Murad, Layla had important connections

---

[7] For the video clip see www.youtube.com/watch?v=wi63nzHbmu0, accessed September 18, 2014.

in the Cairo artistic scene, which contributed to her highly successful career. At the young age of fourteen she had already recorded a song composed for her by the renowned Karaite Jewish singer and composer Daud Husni, who had helped herald in the new Arabic music era, and soon thereafter she began acting under the tutelage of Togo Mizrahi. Although Murad's notoriety as a singer in the 1930s preceded her work in film, it was the sudden advent and popularity of Egyptian film that jettisoned her to stardom. As the story goes, Abd al-Wahab – the most prominent male musician of the period – heard her perform at an event hosted by her father and chose her to play his love interest in the musical film *Yaḥyā al-Ḥubb* (Long Live Love) in 1938 (Seroussi 2010; Robins 2010).

Over the next six years (1939–1945), Murad starred in five musical dramas produced and directed by Togo Mizrahi. As a testament to her fame and commercial viability, the film's promoters incorporated her name into many of the films' titles: *Laylā bint al-rīf* (Layla the Girl from the Country, 1941), *Laylā* (1942), *Laylā fi 'l Ẓalām* (Layla in the Shadows, 1944), and *Laylā bint al-fuqarā'* (Layla, Daughter of the Poor, 1946). The last of these, in particular, was a media sensation, since Murad's off-screen relationship with its actor/director/producer Anwar Wajdi had titillated the public since 1945; the film's final scene featured the couple's actual wedding ceremony. Murad's fame, her Jewish faith, and her tumultuous marriage with Wajdi made her the target of unsavory gossip in the Egyptian media; news about Murad's conversion to Islam featured prominently in the tabloids. Wajdi and Murad appeared in six more films together before their divorce in the early 1950s (Seroussi 2010; Bizawe 2009, Beinin 1998).

Why was Jewish women's involvement in theater and music disproportionately high? This subject deserves further study. Nevertheless, it is clear that while under the rule of some conservative Islamic authorities the female voice was particularly problematic, and the veiling of women was necessary for many of the religious-abiding, such restrictions no longer applied to non-Muslim women in the Middle East as they "Westernized" earlier. This, perhaps, offers some explanation for Jewish women's pervasiveness in popular culture.

Other Jewish Egyptians achieved success in the early years of the film industry – almost all of them converting to Islam. One example is Murad's brother, Munir, who initially achieved success in the music industry and soon achieved greater notoriety as an actor in three films; he too converted to Islam. Negma Ibrahim became a star performing the role of "female gangster" in the films *Raya wa-Sakina* (Raya and Sakina) in 1953, and *Ga alūnī Mujrimān* (I Have Been Made a Murderer) in 1955.

She is said to have converted to Islam when she married the playwright Abbas Yunis. Another convert was Egyptian actress Raqya Ibrahim, who starred in several films, including *Ruṣāṣa fi-'l Qalb* (A Bullet in the Heart) in 1944 and *Bint Zawat* (The Daughter of the Nobles) in 1942 (Robins 2010). While several of the above sources mention conversion to Islam among Jews in the music, theater, and film industries, there is a lack of explanation as to why this occurred. Perhaps the absence of commentary underscores the self-evident benefits of conversion for Jews in popular culture. Despite the national rhetoric of religious pluralism, Jewish artists likely believed that their identity stood as an impediment to full commercial success.

Egyptian films, particularly those made during the 1930s and through the late 1940s, were ripe with discourses of coexistence, both in terms of theme and diversity of the characters acting together on screen. Such films emphasized the diverse Egyptian population comprised of Muslims and Copts, as well as large Jewish and Greek populations. Togo Mizrahi began his work in farcical film with a five-part series starring the Jewish comedian Shalom between 1933 and 1937 (Robins 2010; Starr 2011; Shafik 2007). Mizrahi took special pains to fashion his films utilizing the national unity concept of this period, thereby placing the Jewish character of Shalom as thoroughly Egyptian.

In the film series, Shalom was a simple, naive, yet uncannily fortunate Egyptian citizen. As Shafik notes, Shalom's loyalty to Egypt "is expressed in his clothes – *gallabiya* and jacket – and in his loyal and generous behavior, but also in his profession: in *Shalom, the Sportsman* he sells the indispensable Egyptian national dish, *ful*, and is a fanatical supporter of the Alexandria soccer team." (Shafik 2007: 28). Establishing Shalom's character as "typical" Egyptian was key to this series.

Some critics have pointed to the egalitarian treatment of Jewish and Muslim characters in these films as a reflection of the acceptance of Jews and other minorities as Egyptian citizens during this period (Robins 2010). Shafik's view, however, is that rather than representing a realistic idyllic moment, Mizrahi's series starring Shalom, produced in the 1930s, represents "early signs of unrest that require the reassuring image of peaceful coexistence." In this interpretation, Mizrahi's farcical coexistence films attempted to address an increasingly nationalist environment characterized by intolerance toward Jews. The first anti-Zionist demonstrations occurred in Egypt in 1938, one year after the release of two of Mizrahi's films starring Shalom. A few years later attacks against the Egyptian Jewish community began (Shafik 2007). Such a reading of these films, then, renders them utopian discourses of coexistence envisioned by an Egyptian-Jewish filmmaker who saw the "writing on the wall," so to speak.

JEWISH MUSIC IN THE ARAB WORLD 1900–1950

Amnon Shiloah[8] outlines a family tree for Jewish performers in the Middle East during the twentieth century, and Edwin Seroussi (2010) provides future generations of researchers a rich field of inquiry including the names, dates, and locations of hundreds of Jewish musicians, producers, and institutions. Future scholars will draw upon these sources in thoroughly analyzing these individual musicians, a project outside of the scope of this brief chapter.

North African and Middle Eastern Jewish musicians in the twentieth century – a century punctuated at midpoint by Israel's establishment – were active in a wide range of mainstream and Jewish community music networks. Jewish musicians throughout the region enjoyed an integrated, albeit minority, status, sharing language, food, music, jokes, dress, and even intimate relations with their Muslim and Christian neighbors. However, the fabric of community for Jews in the Arab world was already beginning to fray in the early part of the century, as the Zionist movement intensified alongside a growing ambivalence and resistance to European colonialism and the ascent of the nascent Arab national cause. For those musicians who relocated to Israel after 1948, minority status was reproduced as inferior status; their music as well as their cultural and even religious customs were deemed too "Arabi" by the Euro-Israeli powerbrokers. Zohra el-Fassia (1905–1994), for example, was born near Fez, Morocco, and by the time she emigrated from Casablanca to Israel in 1962 she was a star throughout the Middle East and France – especially beloved for her renditions of traditional Moroccan genres such as Malhoun; in Israel she never found an audience.

The music industry was vibrant, and new technologies were constantly emerging in the early twentieth century – glass cylinders, gramophones, radio, television, and film were followed in the second half of the century by cassettes, super-eights, CDs, DVDs, and the Internet. Jewish entrepreneurs were deeply engaged in the music industry; for example, Albert Mizrahi's thriving Cairo publishing house maintained a contract with state radio to print the programs for Umm Kulthum's monthly concerts in the 1950s (Beinin 1998: 83). The Tunisian Jewish percussionist Elie Touitou (1932–1794) owned the prestigious Dounia Records in Paris and released

[8] Erik Cohen and Amnon Shiloah, "Major Trends of Change in Jewish Oriental Ethnic Music in Israel," *Popular Music* 5 (1985): 199–223; Amnon Shiloah, "Eastern Sources in Israeli Music," *Ariel* 88 (1992): 4–19; idem, *Jewish Musical Traditions* (Detroit: Wayne State University Press, 1992); idem, *The Dimension of Music in Islamic and Jewish Culture* (Aldershot: Ashgate, 1993); idem, *Music in the World of Islam: A Socio-cultural Study* (Aldershot: Scolar, 1995, republished in 2007 with many new citations).

recordings by Jewish and Muslim musicians including Farid al-Atrash (Seroussi 2010).

As Edwin Seroussi and Amnon Shiloah have both noted, Middle Eastern and North African musics comprise dozens of local and regional music traditions that transgress and subvert the boundaries of the local, national, and regional. For Jewish musicians in the twentieth century this porousness possesses political overtones, as artists contended with dueling nationalities that impacted their music, their careers, and ultimately their sense of home itself.

The tripartite tale of Jewish musicians in the Arab world moves from engaged participation to double rejection, first in their former homelands, as Zionist and Arab national movements butted heads, and, then, for those who immigrated to Israel, by Eurocentric policies and attitudes there. Many scholarly studies, however, assign causality to one movement rather than highlighting the dynamic incompatibility of the two movements as the root of the trauma.

LATE 1940s AND 1950s – THE BEGINNING OF THE END

In the 1940s, the careers of Jewish artists unfolded against the dynamics between colonialism, Zionism, and Arab nationalism – political forces that changed the playing ground decades before Israel was established; political discord trumped cultural affiliation, and Jews relocated to Israel, Europe, and North and South America. Many Jews in the Middle East who had achieved success in the popular culture realm in the 1920s and 30s witnessed a shift in their social status by the mid-1940s. With the end of World War II and the ghastly legacy of the Holocaust, the Zionist movement understandably took on a new urgency, and this had an impact on the Arab nationalist movement's increasingly anti-colonial stance. The Jewish population in Palestine had already increased during the 1920s and 30s, however those numbers expanded with the arrival (often clandestinely) of concentration camp survivors. As the numbers of Jews in Palestine expanded so did the animosity between the Jewish and Arab national movements, ultimately leading to war in 1947.

Though previously integrated in Arab societies, the loyalty of many Jews in the Arab world became suspect. One root of the tension was a reaction against colonialism – particularly in Egypt – where Europe was no longer in vogue. The fact that many Jews had European dual-citizenship strengthened the perception of Jews as outsiders, linked to the colonialist powers Arab nationalists aligned themselves against. This situation coupled with anti-Zionist discourse spilled over into anti-Jewish sentiment. Although at the height of prominence just years before, in 1946, amidst rumors of Zionist loyalties, Togo Mizrahi abruptly terminated his film career as director and producer and emigrated from Egypt to Italy, never to return. While many Jews in the arts had converted to Islam in order to achieve the highest possible stature in their fields, even they were not immune from challenges to their national loyalty. Several newspapers in the early 1950s accused Layla Murad of donating large sums of money to the recently established Israeli state. These rumors circulated throughout the Arab world despite her protests and publicly stating "I am an Egyptian Muslim." Some countries continued boycotting her music on the radio even after the Egyptian government formally cleared her of all charges (Robins 2010; Beinin 1998).

In Iraq, a series of riots known as the "Farhud" broke out in 1941 Baghdad, during which approximately 200 Jews were murdered and up to 2,000 injured. Many Jews viewed this as an isolated instance of anti-semitism, and in 1947 there were still 118,000 Jews in Iraq. Once Israel achieved statehood in 1948, however, many Iraqi Jews were fired from their jobs, and emigration to Israel was declared illegal. An Iraqi law passed in 1950 allowed Jews to emigrate on condition of relinquishing their Iraqi citizenship, and by 1951 107,603 Jews – many, quite financially successful – had renounced their Iraqi citizenship (Saadoun 2002: 38).[9]

The Iraqi National Orchestra lost the bulk of its musicians when Jews – who comprised the largest portion of its instrumentalists – immigrated to Israel. A large number of these Iraqis never harbored Zionist senti-ments – many defined themselves as communist and areligious. After the Iraqi government enacted a series of legal restrictions and property con-fiscations upon its Jews, however, most left. Legendary masters of Iraqi music, the Jewish brothers Saleh and Daoud Al-Kuwaity – who composed and performed with some of the most celebrated Arab singers and musi-cians, including Salima Mourad, Umm Kulthum, and Muhammad Abed-el Wahab – immigrated to Israel in 1950. The Al-Kuwaity musical legacy slowly faded in Iraq, and in 1972, Saddam Hussein officially ordered the Iraqi Broadcasting Authority to erase the names of the Al-Kuwaity broth-ers from every official publication and from the curricula of the academy of music. From that point on in Iraq, their compositions were labeled "of folk origin" (Dardashti 2008; Schweitzer 2006).

The Iraqi literary scene similarly became inhospitable to Jews during this period. In Sasson Somekh's 2007 autobiography, *Baghdad Yesterday: The Making of an Arab Jew*, he relates many anecdotes of the way in which Jewish writers who had previously thrived in Iraq found themselves no

---

[9] Shenhav (2006) asserts that the Israeli government played a role in hastening the emigra-tion of Jewish Iraqis to Israel by setting off bombs between 1950 and 1951.

longer welcome in Iraqi literary circles with the birth of the state of Israel. In 1950 he submitted a love poem entitled "Victorious" to an Iraqi literary magazine:

> Good God! Has my heart been so humiliated
> That even your victorious smile
> Rekindles the fire of love within it?

Though Somekh composed his poem in a traditional Arabic form in terms of its strong Romantic bent and its meter and rhyme, he recounts that the editors rejected the poem, not because of its quality but because they believed he was speaking about the victory of the Jewish state, rather than his unrequited love. He immigrated to Israel in 1951 in light of the difficult political climate (Somekh 2007).

Though Jews had participated in the nascent Arab cinema movement as producers, directors, and actors in its first decades, there were few Jews left in the field (or in the Arab world) by the 1950s; this significantly influenced the representation of Jews in Arab film. As Robins notes, this decade marked a decided shift to the depiction of Jews "either negatively, as foreigners, or, most commonly, both. Jewish characters that had previously been vaguely foreign were soon assigned a nationality – Israeli – and thus became total outsiders, essentially 'de-Arabized'" (Robins 2010). With the Jewish population no longer present in the region, Egyptian film moved away from the pluralistic messages of previous years, reflecting shifts toward pan-Arab nationalism that would endure into the next millennium.

JEWISH MASS MIGRATION TO ISRAEL IN THE 1950s

With the founding of Israel, some 300,000 Middle Eastern and North African Jews sought refuge from the increasingly anti-Israeli sentiments in their former homelands. Jewish artists who immigrated to Israel from across the Middle East shared cultural affinities, in music and other art forms, across their previously distinct national lines; they also shared the experience of being estranged within their new homeland by marginalization and rejection. These dual experiences fostered the creation of a new community of communities – a pan-ethnic group that became known as Mizrahim.

Mizrahim – Middle Eastern and North African Jews – traded minority status as Jews in the Arab world for second-class citizenship in Israel. Although Muslim and Christian audiences did not forget the Jewish artists whom they had admired, the legacies of these men and women, or at least their Jewish identity, now remained largely absent from mainstream national discourses in the Arab world. At the same time, these artists were excluded from mainstream culture once in Israel due to the Arabness of their culture. The immigrant absorption policies, while intended to promote equality and integration, were also designed to prevent the "Levantization" of the state, because the Arab cultural practices of incoming Middle Eastern and North African Jews (as well as local Palestinian traditions) might dominate the European orientation of the pre-state Jewish population.

In practice, Ashkenazim could maintain their European identities (short of the Yiddish language and shtetl manners). Yiddish and other markers of an Eastern European Jewish past may have been greeted with disdain, but the intolerance resembled the patronizing of an elder family member's antiquated ways. On the other hand, North African and Middle Eastern Jews were asked to suppress their culture while at the same time providing local flavor, in the form of food, dress, and music, thereby creating an indigenous link for a Middle Eastern nation conceived by European architects.

The cultural "architects" of the new nation fought the intrusion of Arab music, manner, and mentality in the practices of both local Palestinian residents and incoming Middle Eastern and North African Jews. Nonetheless, Jewish culture that had evolved for hundreds of years in Arab lands survived in diminished and less visible forms. The lack of opportunities for becoming proficient in Arabic language, music, and philosophy created cultural poverty without erasing the culture itself.

The Israeli ethnic problem is rooted in the establishment's attitudes toward new Middle Eastern and North African immigrants who, under the Law of Return, should have been accorded all the rights and privileges of citizens without discrimination. In Israel, North African and Middle Eastern communities had less access to free transportation, choice housing, and other incentives used to attract potential Western immigrants with professional skills and capital. Discriminatory practices prevailed in many realms of society and the next generation was channeled into inferior positions that reproduced the initial social inequality.

MIZRAḤI IMMIGRANTS IN POPULAR CULTURE: ISRAEL'S EARLY YEARS

Once Jews immigrated to Israel from the Middle East and North Africa, in the 1950s–60s, they continued, despite representing over half of the Jewish Israeli population, to live as a disenfranchised community of communities. Fraught relationships with Israeli powerbrokers were evident in the mainstream Israeli press – largely a European-Israeli industry, which, aside from coverage of the Black Panther movement, was all but void of Mizraḥi discourse; even the term Mizraḥi was absent until the 1990s (Madmoni-Gerber 2009). While they were active both in mainstream and Jewish community presses in their former homelands, very few Mizraḥi Jews became journalists in the mainstream press, whose Eurocentric agendas marginalized their non-Western roots. Moreover, coverage of their music consisted largely of sensationalistic gossip column items rather than serious discussion of their emergent soundtrack.

It took decades for Mizraḥim to develop their own communal newsletters and to become journalists in the local and then the mainstream press. Local newspapers in Israel, as small businesses, attracted disenfranchised communities including Mizraḥi Jews, giving voice to those not heard in the mainstream media (Caspi 1986). The first local papers appeared in Eilat and Ashdod, part of Israel's social and economic "periphery." By the 1990s, the local Tel Aviv newspaper *Ha'Ir* gave column space to Mizraḥi issues. By 1998, a backlash was evident; for example, perceiving a Mizraḥi cultural takeover in Israel, *Ha'Ir* ran a series entitled "The Ashkenazis from the Bunker" (Gerber 2009: 65) reflecting European-Israeli aversion to Mizraḥi infiltration of mainstream culture.

With the increasing resistance on the part of Arab countries to the founding of a Jewish state in Palestine, many successful Jewish Iraqi writers had little choice but to immigrate to other countries. In Iraq, they had been part of the Arabic literary renaissance of the 1930s and 40s, writing primarily about love, male–female relations, and the meaning of life. For those who immigrated to Israel, the shock of the negative reception that they experienced affected the themes in their literary work. Two primary streams of Arabic literature soon emerged: one based in the Israeli establishment and supported in part by the Histadrut, the other associated with the Communist Party and that addressed the urgent political and social circumstances of Mizraḥim and Palestinian Israelis (Snir and Einbinder 1991).

The Histadrut encouraged the publication of "positive" Arabic literature by offering literary competitions with financial incentives and sponsoring the Arab Book Fund. It is no coincidence that this literature maintained traditional Arab literary themes (love, relationships, philosophy) while avoiding political critique of the Israeli government. The political situation was only addressed through literature that expressed yearnings for peace (Snir and Einbinder 1991).

The communist strand of Arabic literature represented by Iraqi immigrants such as Sami Michael, Shimon Ballas, Sasson Somekh and David Semah expressed a political and anti-establishment struggle; most did not identify with the Zionist movement. In Israel, they continued their communist alliances and their writings criticized the establishment for the disgraceful manner of absorption of new immigrants (primarily the Mizraḥim), the socio-economic divide between Ashkenazim and Mizraḥim, and the treatment of Palestinian Israelis.

During the early 1950s, Palestinian Israeli intellectuals briefly joined forces with Jewish Iraqi immigrant writers. While the majority of Palestinian intellectuals had no choice but to flee the newly established State in 1948, those who remained in Israel included communists from the Haifa region and younger poets from the Nazareth area. Sami Michael joined the staff of the Israeli Communist Party's (MAKI) monthly literary journal, *Al-Jaddid*, in 1952, which was edited by Palestinian Israelis Emil Habiby and Jabra Nicola (Somekh 1999).[10]

While still in their twenties, Semah and Somekh founded the "Club of the Friends of Arabic Literature in Israel," which later became the "Hebrew-Arabic Literary Club." The club helped to bring the Arabic reading public in Israel relevant news, literature, and Arab political topics. As Snir and Einbinder document, David Semah's poem "Sawfa Ya'du" (He Shall Return) was one of the first poems to address the massacre of almost fifty men, women, and children at Kafr Qasim on October 29, 1956. An excerpt of his poem reads:

> The day of the final struggle is near
> The storm already blows
> Over the world, raging and sweeping
> Striking oppression and oppressors
> (Snir and Einbinder 1991: 169)

The joint venture between Jewish Iraqi immigrants and Palestinians was short-lived and ended in the late 1950s. By the 1960s as Stalinist war crimes became public and the Communist Party in Israel grew more radical and anti-establishment, many Jews became disenchanted with communism and abandoned the party. Concurrently, the interest in Arabic literature among Jewish immigrants had significantly waned by the 1960s and the Israeli government withdrew its already limited support of Arab literature. With no Arabic literary infrastructure in place (writing clubs, pubs, or writers associations) or mechanisms for publishing, there was no means for those writing in Arabic to support themselves. Some writers successfully switched to Hebrew while others abandoned writing entirely (Snir and Einbinder 1991; Chapter 25 in this volume).

[10] See Sami Michael's "The Newly Arrived Men of Letters" from *Al-Jadid* in *Modern Middle Eastern Jewish Thought: Writings on Identity, Politics, and Culture, 1893–1958*, ed. Moshe Behar and Zvi Ben-Dor Benite (Waltham: Brandeis University Press, 2013).

In spite of the marginalization of Arab culture in Israel at the time, several prominent Iraqi immigrant musicians did attain professional positions in the Israel Broadcasting Authority (IBA) Arabic Orchestra soon after arriving in Israel. This Orchestra was established in 1948 by the IBA's "Voice of Israel (Kol Israel) in Arabic" Radio Station. Its Arabic language programming was primarily intended as public diplomacy toward Israel's Arab neighbors across the borders. Its secondary target was its Palestinian population. The Arabic-speaking Mizraḥim within Israel were its last priority. Composed of Iraqi musicians and – after 1957 – some Egyptian musicians, the IBA's Arabic Orchestra served a valuable political function for the state by attracting its listeners to the propaganda programming that followed its high-quality Arabic musical interludes. Only those musicians who could perform the more mainstream urban Arabic music from Egypt and Lebanon that had become popular throughout the Arab world gained steady employment in the Orchestra.

Those musicians whose musical mastery did not serve an expedient national goal, however, found it quite difficult to pursue their music professionally in Israel. A case in point is the history of Younes Dardashti – grandfather of the co-author – nationally renowned master singer of Persian classical music in Iran. In spite of some of the antisemitism he experienced early in his career, in the early 1950s Dardashti began performing at Iran's most coveted concert halls, such as Talare Farhang, and at the Royal Palace for Mohammad Reza Shah Pahlavi, and he garnered a prime-time weekly radio performance with the Iranian National Radio Orchestra. As Iran had only one radio station at the time, this position brought Dardashti instant national fame. He maintained this weekly radio spot for the next fifteen years, until moving to Israel in 1967.

When Dardashti and his wife immigrated to Rishon le-Ziyon, Israel, he found no forum for his music. He did perform on Israeli television and radio once or twice on programs featuring new immigrants, but very seldom performed concerts in Israel. Instead, he traveled back to Iran a few times a year to give performances up until the Islamic Revolution in 1979, after which he could never again return. He supported himself mostly through various jobs in Israel, such as gardening, and earned a small income giving short performances at Iranian weddings. Many musicians like Younes Dardashti, who specialized in localized musical forms (e.g., Persian, Iraqi, Moroccan) were marginalized, finding few opportunities for performance in Israel.

In 1976, Moroccan-Israeli poet Erez Bitton testified to the cultural shock experienced by many non-European Jewish musicians with his poem about Moroccan singer Zohra El-Fassia. This poem excerpt juxtaposes

her renown in Morocco with her relative obscurity once she resettled in
Ashkelon, Israel:

> Zohra El Fassia
> Singer at Muhammad the Fifth's court in Rabat, Morocco
> They say when she sang
> Soldiers fought with knives
> To clear a path through the crowd
> To reach the hem of her skirt
> To kiss the tips of her toes
> To leave her a piece of silver as a sign of thanks
>
> Zohra El Fassia
>
> Now you can find her
> In Ashkelon
> Antiquities
> By the welfare office the smell
> Of leftover sardine cans on a wobbly three-legged table
> The stunning royal carpets stained on the Jewish Agency cot
> Spending hours in a bathrobe
> In front of the mirror

The representation of Mizraḥim in early Israeli pop culture begins primarily with the highly successful Israeli film genre during the 1960s and 70s
known as the Bourekas films. Bourekas, a popular and inexpensive Middle
Eastern pastry associated with the Mizraḥi working-class, came to denote
a comic or melodramatic film that featured stereotypical and unbecoming
Mizraḥi characters. The most notorious character from this genre is the eponymous *Sallah Shabbati* (a role performed by Haim Topol, a well-known actor
of Ashkenazi background) from the 1964 film made by Ephraim Kishon, an
Ashkenazi filmmaker. The Mizraḥi, like Sallah, is often represented as lazy,
irrational, male-chauvinistic, patriarchal, sexist, oversexed, and manipulative.
As in most of these films, the primitiveness of the Mizraḥi immigrant and his
difficulty in understanding Israeli culture is spoofed. But this film, like most
Bourekas films, ends happily with the child of the "backward" Mizraḥi immigrant marrying an Ashkenazi, suggesting the resolution of ethnic tensions
through ethnic "intermarriage," via an enlightened acculturation.

Of course, such "happy endings" did not reflect the harsh reality for
most Mizraḥim during this period. But perhaps the success of these films
(even among Mizraḥi moviegoers) can be partially attributed to their ability to utilize humor and melodrama to sidestep a genuine engagement
with social problems. The Bourekas films were the most financially – and
perhaps the only – successful films in Israel in the 1970s despite the high

ethnic tensions of that decade and their predominantly negative portrayal of Mizraḥim.

THE EMERGENCE OF A
MIZRAḤI POLITICAL STRUGGLE

The 1967 Six Day War and the 1973 Yom Kippur War altered the balance of power within Israel in profound ways and became flashpoints for increased visibility of the ethnic struggles. After the Yom Kippur War, the mainstream European power grip was shaken by an anti-Labor Party outcry issuing from Israel's underclass, now consolidated into a pan-ethnic Mizraḥi coalition. Since the Mizraḥi vote was vital to the Likud victory in 1977, it seemed that society was headed on a new course in which Mizraḥi voices would be reconfigured in the mainstream equation. The Wadi Salib riots of 1959 were initiated by Moroccan residents, one of whom was shot by police while resisting arrest. The shooting and subsequent arrest unleashed pent-up frustrations and culminated in a series of demonstrations, stone throwing, and car burnings, as well as thirty-two arrests.

In the early 1970s, Mizraḥi youth in the neighborhoods rose to challenge what were by then widely called "the mistakes of the 50s." Mizraḥi social and cultural movements sprouted. The Black Panthers, born in a Moroccan Jerusalem neighborhood of Musrara, gave voice to issues of inequality in housing, economics, and education. The "East For Peace" (Mizraḥ la-shalom) organization claimed that only Mizraḥim would succeed in making peace with the Arabs since they had hundreds of years of shared history together in the Middle East. Ammiel Alcalay suggests that for Mizraḥi Jews the new proximity to Arab territories that resulted from Israeli occupation after the 1967 war triggered illicit recollections, what Ella Shohat has called "taboo memories" of ancestral homelands, emotions that had been sealed from consciousness or at best expressed in the privacy of community events, as Mizraḥi Israelis assumed a new national identity at war with their past.

While a number of Mizraḥi Jews, for example Yemini singers Aharon Amram and Shlomo Dahyani, maintained a sonic continuity with their past by continuing to perform "ethnic music" in their own communities, by the 1970s Mizraḥim began employing popular culture to connect to their Middle Eastern roots in order to appeal to the broader Israeli public sphere. Drummer/composer Shlomo Bar formed a band called *ha-Bererah hativ'it* (The Natural Choice) in the late 1970s and claimed, through the pointed texts of poets such as the Moroccan-Israeli Erez Bitton, that Mizraḥi communities experienced exploitation within Israeli society and that Israel would succeed only if it recognized that it was part of the Middle

East and not an extension of Europe. In the same period, Moroccan film-maker Haim Shiran journeyed back to his hometown of Meknes to show Israeli society the richness of Jewish life in North Africa and to reclaim the historic roots of holiday traditions such as the *Mimouna,* which then took on a pan-ethnic scope in Israel (Horowitz 1989: 92).

MEDITERRANEAN ISRAELI MUSIC: MUSIKA YAM TIKHONIT YISRAELIT OR MIZRAḤI MUSIC[11]

While some communities that had existed in pre-state Palestine main-tained communal frameworks adapted by integrating new national con-cepts into pre-existing communal structures, recent North African and Middle Eastern immigrants in the *maʿabarot* (transit camps) experienced profound culture shock. Lacking their former communal structures, Middle Eastern and North African immigrants came to form a pan-ethnic or Mizraḥi subclass. Distinct localized traditions that had been maintained in the homes and neighborhoods began to merge and take priority over the Euro-centered Israeli culture that had failed to integrate its North African and Middle Eastern communities. For example, the predominant music transmitted in Israel at that time, in schools, at official occasions, on the radio, as well as throughout the *maʿabarot,* was *Shirei Eretz Yisrael* (Songs of the Land of Israel), a repertoire created by European Jews consisting largely of Eastern European melodies and Hebrew lyrics unfamiliar to Jews from Yemen, Morocco, Syria, and elsewhere.

In the neighborhoods that grew from the original *maʿabarot, Shirei Eretz Yisrael* shared space with Mediterranean, North African, and Middle Eastern musics and developed new shapes through intensive interaction. Neighborhood singers sang the *Shirei Eretz Yisrael* that they learned at school along with Arabic songs and Hebrew liturgy that they learned at home and in the synagogue. As Yemenite, Mediterranean Israeli musician Haim Moshe explains: "My voice I got from God, it's my inheritance from God. My knowledge of music came from the synagogue, family gatherings on holidays and festivals, and from Yemenite prayers. The whole family got together around the table and sang Sabbath songs, folksongs, lots of songs that we don't hear on the radio" (Moshe in Horowitz, 2010).

---

[11] Creators of this music genre, notably Avihu Medina, take issue with the designation Mizraḥi music, claiming that they blend Arabic, Persian, Turkish, Spanish, French, English, and American aesthetics. They contend that the Mizraḥi designation is largely a Euro-Israeli device to marginalize their soundtracks from the mainstream discourse (Horowitz 2010).

With the development of Kol Yisrael (the Israeli national radio broad-casting network founded in 1948), the local recording industry, and national television, the gap between Mizraḥi neighborhood traditions and national folk, popular, and art musics intensified. Like the *Mimouna* that had been a specific Moroccan Passover festival, many formerly specific traditions were transforming into Mizraḥi pan-ethnic celebrations in the 1970s and 1980s. Mizraḥi-ness itself was becoming a construct formed out of these new cultural intimacies.

Neighborhood weddings especially were sites for merging cultural traditions in which Syrians and Iraqis, Egyptians and Libyans intermar-ried, new relationships were forged, and musicians learned each other's styles and repertories. Inter-ethnic weddings constituted an actual merg-ing of otherwise discrete groups into a pan-ethnic culture, not only for the couple but for the guests in attendance. Most of the wedding sing-ers were, like Haim Moshe, Yemenites; they learned diverse repertoires in order to perform for different ethnic groups. Mirroring the polyglot culture of the neighborhoods, they learned Greek, Turkish, and Kurdish tunes and embedded them within rock 'n' roll, light Mediterranean and Spanish popular music such as Samba, and Italian San Remo rearrange-ments. They sang Eastern European Jewish tunes like "Hanaleh hit-balbelah" (Hanale Got Confused) but with Yemenite vocalization and a Mediterranean twist.

Despite increased media coverage and sporadic nightclub appearances, however, the music – which came to be known most commonly as *musika Mizraḥit* (Mizraḥi music) – remained a neighborhood phenomenon that did not really threaten the status quo. With the rise of Yemenite singer Zohar Argov, however, and his cassette *Elinor* (a Greek song reupholstered with Hebrew lyrics) this emerging neighborhood music came to the atten-tion of unreceptive European Israeli audiences. This homegrown cassette, produced by "The Reuveni Brothers," a neighborhood cassette company in Shkunat HaTikva, soon became so successful that it outsold LPs recorded in professional studios by mainstream celebrities. Alternative producers of homemade cassettes that had previously been available only at live neighborhood performances now sidestepped the state-controlled radio programs and other mainstream music industry channels. The dominant players in the Eurocentric music business rejected their raw combination of Middle Eastern and Mediterranean influences with Western pop music and regarded the proliferation of these cassettes as a form of aesthetic pollution. The cassette production was part of a larger concern about the increasing visibility and audibility of the emerging Mizraḥi culture.

MIZRAḤI PRIDE

Beginning in the early 1990s Israelis witnessed crucial changes in their access to media. In addition to the one Israeli national TV channel operating since 1968, in 1993 the commercial Channel Two began broadcasting. By 1994, with the cable television infrastructure in place, Israelis had the option of choosing between forty television channels in more than a dozen languages. Non-government regulated commercial radio stations were also introduced in the early 1990s. With the shift to commercial media, *musika mizraḥit* (Mizrahi music) infiltrated new radio and television stations now influenced more by ratings than the tastes of government officials. The mainstream success of *musika mizraḥit* by the late 1990s with acts such as Sarit Hadad and Eyal Golan not only made the sounds of Arab music begin to sound less foreign to Israelis but also emboldened Mizrahi and Palestinian Israeli musicians interested in bringing more traditional Middle Eastern music to the fore.

After decades of systemic discrimination in Israel, second- and third-generation Mizraḥim revived and reinvented their cultural heritages that had been absent from or misrepresented by the mainstream culture industry. Through film, music, television and literature, Mizraḥi pride often took a retrospective glance that reflected their Arab, Persian, and Turkish roots. These works served as a corrective to the dim portrayal of Jewish life in Muslim societies.

While there were several Mizraḥi-produced films in the 1970s, notably by Moshe Mizrahi and Haim Shiran, it was not until the 1990s that Mizraḥi-themed and produced films appeared in greater numbers. This blossoming followed Ella Shohat's searing critique of representations of Mizraḥim in Israeli film (Shohat 1989) and Yaron London's attack on her on national television (Horowitz 2010). Antagonism toward Shohat's work intensified as she was a forerunner of a growing global cadre of Mizraḥi Jews who embraced the term "Arab Jew" and who considered themselves, along with Palestinians, victims of Zionist policies.

After significant antipathy between Mizraḥim and Palestinians in previous decades, such Mizraḥi identification with Palestinians beginning in the late 1980s reflected a "New Levantine discourse." Mizraḥi filmmakers, poets, and academics created works reflecting new conceptions of the "Arab" identity they shared with Palestinians. Haim Buzaglio's film *Fictitious Marriage* (1988), for example, challenge fixed notions of Israeli identity; when Eldi, an Arab-Jew, is mistaken for a Palestinian worker in Tel Aviv he adopts that identity, which takes him to Gaza. Similarly, in Mizraḥit poet and activist Tikva Levi's poem "Purim Sequence" she listens to the Palestinian band Sabrin and expresses anxiety that she might be mistaken for a Palestinian.

Yair Dalal emerged onto the ethnic music scene in the mid-1990s. He was a leader in clearly articulating that his Iraqi-Jewish identity was part of a cultural heritage shared by Israel's Palestinians. While Dalal certainly did his share of East–West musical fusions in the 1990s, it was the East meets East concept of shared culture between Jew and Palestinian that made his image so appealing, particularly to audiences abroad (Dardashti 2009). In 1994 Dalal, still relatively unknown in Israel, performed in Oslo to mark the one-year anniversary of the Oslo Peace Accords and the ceremony during which Israeli and Palestinian leaders jointly received the Nobel Peace Prize. Dalal invited a Palestinian and Israeli children's choir and a Norwegian children's choir to perform on his composition "Zaman es-Salaam" ("Time of Peace") in Oslo.

After the assassination of Prime Minister Rabin and the Second Intifada, Mizrahi filmmakers and musicians turned inward, primarily reflecting upon their specific ethnic heritages. Mizrahi filmmakers created works that deliberately referenced the Bourekas genre, while underscoring the fraught issues of identity politics that the Eurocentric films of the 60s and 70s had elided. Films such as *Turn Left at the End of the World* (2004), *Lovesick on Nana Street* (1995), and *James' Journey to Jerusalem* (2003), for example, challenged essentialist depictions of Israeli identity and the triumphant melting pot characteristic of Bourekas films. Such films are transgressive, post- or neo-Bourekas films with "a depiction of a society marred by ethnic divisions" (Shemer 2011: 131).

Mizrahi filmmakers also created documentary and "mock" documentary genres. Early Mizrahi characters in Israeli media were portrayed as "primitives" despite the fact that many came from urban backgrounds. Such films contrasted images of Jewish misery in North Africa and the Middle East with the blissful faces of new immigrants arriving in Israel (Shohat 1988). One trend in Mizrahi documentary and mockumentary cinema of the 80s, 90s, and 2000s is for filmmakers to refute this narrative by commemorating their characters' rich Arab culture in their former homelands. These films epitomize this second and third generation's anxiety that, with the aging of the immigrant generation, their own rich cultural histories will be lost.

The 2003 film *Charlie Baghdad* (Baghdad Bandstand), for example, highlights the lives of six Iraqi musicians – in Iraq and later in Israel after their immigration. The film starkly contrasts the worlds the musicians inhabited. One segment features *qanun* player Avraham Salman, who reminisces: "In Baghdad, I'm telling you, musicians lived like kings. Musicians had a good life over there. We used to, but not anymore." On the other hand, several musicians depicted in the film objected to the filmmaker's omission of the successful careers many of them maintained performing for the Iraqi community in Israel, performing on the radio with the Arab Orchestra and performing abroad for the remainder of their lives (Dardashti 2008). Romanticization of former lives, therefore, often replaced the absence or stereotypes in the public sphere that had characterized previous Israeli (mis)representations of Jewish culture in the Middle East.

FINAL THOUGHTS

The last decade has witnessed interesting shifts in Mizraḥi popular cultural expression and representation. Such changes are particularly noteworthy in the realm of mainstream Israeli music where many successful Mizraḥi musicians are drawing upon their historical legacies in new ways. Some of Israel's most noted secular rock singers have discovered traditional Middle Eastern sacred songs (*piyutim*), and many are performing their own renditions for large crowds of adoring fans; several of their recordings of these songs have soared to the top of Israeli pop charts.[12] Secular Israeli rock musician Berry Sakharof, for example, released a 2009 CD that included his creative renditions of the poetry of Ibn Gvirol – a medieval Jewish poet influenced by the Arabic culture in which he lived.

Other recent artists re-claim the secular music their families sang in the Muslim world as their own. In 2009 the popular Israeli rock artist Dudu Tassa released *Dudu Tassa and the Kuwaitis* featuring his rock-infused interpretations of songs written by his grandfather and great-uncle, the al-Kuwaiti brothers of Iraq. Consequently, that same year, the Tel Aviv municipality named a new street *Rechov Ha'achim al-Kuwaiti* (al-Kuwaiti Brothers Street) posthumously honoring the two musicians after sixty years of "collective amnesia" (Zerubavel 1995: 8) in both Israel and Iraq. Tassa provides a musically sophisticated third-generation commemoration and reclamation of his rich Arab musical genealogy. Zehava Ben, a well-known singer in the realm of Mizraḥi pop music, was one of the first to sing classical Arab songs in the nineties, but it is primarily in the past several years that more mainstream artists such as Tassa and the pop music diva Rita (who released a Persian album in 2011) have made a significant mainstream

---

[12] See Galeet Dardashti, "Patronage and Expediency: The Deployment of Middle Eastern Music in Israel," Ph.D. diss., University of Texas at Austin, 2009; and Galeet Dardashti, "The Piyut Craze: Popularization of Mizrahi Religious Songs in the Israeli Public Sphere," *Journal of Synagogue Music* 32, no. 1 (2007): 142–163.

impact through such retrospective projects. Not only has Rita's Persian album received rave reviews in Israel but it has become an underground favorite in Iran.

Narratives of erasure and endurance are messy in Israel and in the former homelands of Mizraḥi Jews. Egyptian state radio continues to observe the anniversary of the death of Daud Husni, the renowned Jewish Karaite composer (Beinin 1998). Despite Saddam Hussein's efforts to expunge the Al-Kuwaity legacy, the song "Wallāh, ʿajbanī jamalak" (Oh My God, I Loved Your Beauty), arranged and performed by the Al-Kuwaity brothers, is still a favorite of radio stations in the Persian Gulf. Habiba Messika's version of the Tunisian national anthem still airs on the country's airwaves today.

Similarly, while Layla Murad's Jewish roots (despite her conversion to Islam) were detrimental in the context of mid-twentieth-century Arab nationalism, cherished memories of her legacy live on in the Arab world. While rumors of Murad's support for Zionist causes re-emerged after her death in 1995, the Egyptian government released a Layla Murad commemorative stamp in 1999. More recently, a 2009 prime-time television series on the rags to riches story of Murad's life entitled, "Ana Albi Dalili" (My Heart Is My Guide)[13] aired throughout the Arab world every night during Ramadan. The series portrays Murad and other Jews as remaining loyal to Egypt while many less admirable Jews turned to Zionism. Though the goal of the series was to demonstrate that it was the Zionists that ruined the idyllic relationship between Egyptian Jews, Muslims, and Christians, representing Jews as an important part of Arab history in prime time is no small development (Bizawe 2009).

As we have demonstrated, constructing a retrospective account relies heavily on the memories of elderly practitioners whose backward glance is necessarily tinged with either romantic or dismissive agendas (or both) that are further re-imagined by their children and grandchildren. Even "hard" evidence such as newspaper articles, photographs, films, posters, and conference proceedings are open to multiple interpretations. Which stories are privileged and which receive short shrift is often idiosyncratic, and this returns us to Zerubavel's notion of commemorative density (or in some cases thinness), which can be deployed here to explore political and commercial motivation. The stories of and about Jewish artists and entrepreneurs in the Middle East, North Africa, and Israel in the twentieth and dawn of the twenty-first centuries are crucial. Given the paucity of reliable data, however, one must be cautious of tales laden with landmines

---

[13] The series was named after a very famous Murad film and song.

that embellish the sensational and minimize or omit the complexities and contradictions of Jewish life within the Muslim world and in contemporary Israel.

SELECT BIBLIOGRAPHY

Ayalon, Ami. "The Jewish Press in Egypt," (Hebrew). *Kesher* (Tel Aviv), no. 4 (November 1988): 85–95.

Behar, Moshe and Zvi Ben-Dor Benite, eds. *Modern Middle Eastern Jewish Thought: Writings on Identity, Politics, and Culture, 1893–1958*. Waltham: Brandeis University Press, 2013.

Beinin, Joel. *The Dispersion of Egyptian Jewry: Politics, and the Formation of a Modern Diaspora*. Berkeley: University of California Press, 1998.

Biale, David. *Cultures of the Jews, Volume I: Mediterranean Origins*. Jerusalem: Schocken Books, 2006.

Bizawe, Eyal Sagui. "The Return of Cinderella." *Haaretz*, October 1, 2009.

Caspi, Dan. *Media Decentralization: The Case of Israel's Local Newspapers*. New Brunswick: Transaction Books, 1986.

Cohen, Erik and Amnon Shiloah, "Major Trends of Change in Jewish Oriental Ethnic Music in Israel," *Popular Music* 5 (1985): 199–223.

Dardashti, Galeet. "The Buena Vista Baghdad club: negotiating the local, national, and global representations of Jewish Iraqi musicians in Israel." In *Jewish Topographies; Visions of Space, Traditions of Place*. Edited by Julia Brauch, Anna Lipphardt and Alexandra Nocke, 309–26. Aldershot: Ashgate, 2008.

———. " 'Sing us a *Mawwal*': the Politics of Culture-Brokering Palestinian-Israelis in Israel." *Min-Ad: Israel Studies in Musicology Online* 7, no. 2 (2008–2009): 30 pp.

Gendzier, Irene. "James Sanua and Egyptian Nationalism." *Middle East Journal* 15, no. 1 (1961): 16–28.

Hillel, Hagar. *"Yisrael" in Cairo: A Zionist Newspaper in Nationalist Egypt, 1920–1939* (Hebrew). Tel Aviv: Am Oved, 2004.

Horowitz, Amy. "The Irresolvable Geographies of Mediterranean Israeli Music." In *Israeli Identities: From Orient to Occident*. Edited by David Tal. New York: Routledge, 2013, 105–117.

———. *Mediterranean Israeli Music and the Politics of the Aesthetic*, Raphael Patai series in Jewish Folklore and Anthropology. Detroit: Wayne State University Press, 2010.

———. "Resetting Ethnic Margins, Sephardic Renaissance through Film." *Jusur* 5 (1989): 91–104.

Levy, Lital. "Historicizing the Concept of Arab Jews in the *Mashriq*." *Jewish Quarterly Review* 98, no. 4 (2008): 452–469.

Madmoni-Gerber, Shoshana. *Israeli Media and the Framing of Internal Conflict: The Yemenite Babies Affair*. New York: Palgrave Macmillan, 2009.

Miliani, Hadj. "Crosscurrents: Trajectories of Algerian Jewish Artists and Men of Culture since the End of the Nineteenth Century." In *Jewish Culture and Society in North Africa*. Edited by Emily Benichou Gottreich and Daniel J. Schroeter. Bloomington: Indiana University Press, 2011, 77–190.

Nahmias, Victor. "'Al-shams' – 'Iton Yehudi be-Mitzrayim, 1934–1948." *Peamim* 16 (2013): 128–141.

Robins, Walker. "Cinema, Arabic, Jews in." *Encyclopedia of Jews in the Islamic World*. Edited by Norman A. Stillman. Brill Online, 2010. Online at http://referenceworks.brillonline.com/entries/encyclopedia-of-jews-in-the-islamic-world/cinema-arabic-jews-in-SIM_000349.

Saadoun, Haim. "Demography." In *Kehilot Yisrael ba-Mizrah ba-Meot ha-Tesha Esre ve-ha-Esrim: Irak*. Edited by Saadoun Haim, 31–38. Jerusalem: Ministry of Education, Ben Zvi Institute, 2002.

——— ed., "The Press" in *Tunisia* (Hebrew), Kehilot Yisrael ba-mizrah be-meot ha-tesha' 'esreh ve-ha-'esrim. Jerusalem: Yad Ben Zvi and Israeli Ministry of Education, 2005, 41–158.

Schweitzer, Erez. "From the King's Palace to a 'Ghetto' of Oriental Music." *Haaretz*, June 5, 2006.

Seroussi, Edwin. "Music." *Encyclopedia of Jews in the Islamic World*. Edited by Norman A. Stillman. Brill Online, 2010. Online at http://referenceworks.brillonline.com/entries/encyclopedia-of-jews-in-the-islamic-world/music-COM_0016170.

Shafik, Viola. *Arab Cinema: History and Cultural Identity*. Cairo: The American University in Cairo Press, 2007.

Shemer, Yaron. "Trajectories of Mizrahi Cinema." In *Israeli Cinema: Identities in Motion*. Edited by Miri Talmon and Yaron Peleg. Austin: University of Texas Press, 2011, 120–133.

Shenhav, Yehuda. *The Arab Jews: A Postcolonial Reading of Nationalism, Religion and Ethnicity*. Stanford: Stanford University Press, 2006.

Shiloah, Amnon. *The Dimension of Music in Islamic and Jewish Culture*. Aldershot: Ashgate, 1993.

——— "Eastern Sources in Israeli Music," *Ariel* 88 (1992): 4–19.

——— *Jewish Musical Traditions*. Detroit: Wayne State University Press, 1992.

——— *Music in the World of Islam: A Socio-cultural Study*. Aldershot: Scolar, 1995.

Shohat, Ella. *Israeli Cinema East/West and the Politics of Representation*. Austin: University of Texas Press, 1989.

——— "Sephardim in Israel: Zionism from the Standpoint of Its Jewish Victims." *Social Text* 19/20 (Autumn 1988): 1–35.

Snir, Reuven. "'Religion is for God, the Fatherland is for Everyone': Arab-Jewish Writers in Modern Iraq and the Clash of Narratives after Their Immigration to Israel." *Journal of the American Oriental Society* 126, no. 3 (2006): 379–399.

Snir, Reuven and Susan Einbinder. "'We Were Like Those Who Dream': Iraqi-Jewish Writers in Israel in the 1950s." *Prooftexts* 11, no. 2 (1991): 153–173.

Somekh, Sasson. "Lost Voices: Jewish Authors in Modern Arabic Literature." In *Jews Among Arabs: Contact and Boundaries*. Edited by Mark R. Cohen and Abraham L. Udovitch, 9–20. Princeton: Darwin Press, 1989.

——— *Baghdad Yesterday: The Making of an Arab Jew*. Jerusalem: Ibis Editions, 2007.

Somekh, Sasson and Moshe Tlamin. "'Reconciling Two Great Loves': the First Jewish–Arab Literary Encounter in Israel." *Israel Studies* 4, no. 1 (1999): 1–21.

Starr, Deborah. "Masquerade and the Performance of National Imaginaries: Levantine Ethics, Aesthetics, and Identities in Egyptian Cinema." *Journal of Levantine Studies* 1, no. 2 (2011): 31–57.

Tobi, Yosef. "Messika, Ḥabiba." *Encyclopedia of Jews in the Islamic World*. Edited by Norman A. Stillman. Brill Online, 2010. Online at http://referenceworks.brillonline.com/entries/encyclopedia-of-jews-in-the-islamic-world/messika-h-abiba-SIM_0015200.

Yerushalmi, Ovadia, "The Jewish Press" (Hebrew). In *Egypt* (Hebrew), Kehilot Yisrael ba-mizrah be-meot ha-tesha' 'esreh ve-ha-'esrim. Edited by Nahem Ilan, 115–130. Jerusalem: Yad Ben Zvi and Israeli Ministry of Education, 2008.

Zerubavel, Yael. *Recovered Roots: Collective Memory and the Making of Israeli National Tradition*. Chicago: University of Chicago Press, 1995.

PART IV

JEWS IN THE MODERN WORLD

CHAPTER 33

THE DYNAMICS OF MODERNITY
Shifts in Demography and Geography

TOBIAS BRINKMANN

Migration, often over long distances, has been a defining characteristic of the modern Jewish experience, as has Jewish life in the city. Modern Jewish history is inextricably linked with Jewish movement to and community building in "global cities," which encapsulate modernization and have driven globalization processes, ranging from ancient Rome to medieval Baghdad, seventeenth-century Amsterdam, and twentieth-century New York. After 1800, Central and Eastern European Jews were drawn in particular to new and rapidly expanding cities such as Odessa or Chicago. Here everybody was a newcomer and Jews could redefine themselves in ways not possible in traditional communities on the social margins of rural societies. Jewish and other migrants flourished in the inclusive and innovative milieus cities offered. It was hardly a coincidence that some of the most influential Jewish scientists, artists, writers, and entrepreneurs were migrants, in cities ranging from *fin-de-siècle* Vienna, to Berlin and Paris in the 1920s, and New York in the 1940s. Before 1914 most Jews exercised a remarkable agency over the decision to move to a specific place. After 1914, however, many European Jews were deprived of agency and frequently forced to move. Jewish city migrants of the twentieth century were as innovative and influential as their nineteenth-century antecedents, but many were displaced, separated from their families, and caught in a state best described as permanent transit.

Shifting centers and migrations, voluntary and forced, have long shaped the history of the Jewish Diaspora. Yet the twentieth century witnessed movements that were unprecedented in kind and scale. At the end of the nineteenth century more than half of the world Jewish population lived dispersed across Eastern Europe; smaller communities existed across the Middle East, the Maghreb, in Central and Western Europe, in the United States, and in the Americas. After 1880 the Jewish mass migration from Eastern Europe rapidly transformed many smaller centers of the Diaspora around the globe. Within less than three decades after 1890 the "*goldene medine*," America, emerged as a major center of Jewish life. The

"Great War" interrupted the migration. Hundreds of thousands of Eastern European Jews were displaced, many by force. After the collapse of the Russian, Austro-Hungarian, and Ottoman Empires in 1918, large numbers of Jews were stranded almost literally on the margins of European societies, as unwanted minorities or as displaced persons. For most the traditional overseas destinations, the United States in particular, were beyond reach due to travel and immigration restrictions introduced in the aftermath of the war. Long before the Nazis implemented the "Final Solution" in 1941, many Jews had been exposed, rejected and isolated as unwelcome refugees and minorities across Central and Eastern Europe. In just four years, the Eastern European communities largely perished. Smaller Jewish centers in Central, Western, and Southern Europe were also almost completely destroyed.

The founding of Israel in 1948 constituted the fourth radical shift, after the Jewish mass migration from Eastern Europe, mass displacement during and after World War I, and the Holocaust and its aftermath. As Israel's neighbors attacked the new state after the declaration of independence, Jews in most Middle Eastern states and the Maghreb became unwanted minorities; many were expelled almost immediately. Within a few years, Jewish communities across the region – some, notably in Egypt, Yemen, and Syria, older than 2,000 years – dissolved. In addition to Middle Eastern Jews, survivors and refugees from war-torn Europe moved to the new Jewish state, completely changing the dynamic of the Diaspora. The most recent movement began in the 1970s and accelerated after the collapse of the Soviet Union in 1991. Well over a million Jews left the Soviet Union and its successor states – for Israel, the United States, and Germany. The post-Soviet Jewish migration has reduced the last remaining major center of Jewish life in Eastern Europe after the Holocaust to secondary status. Today only few traces betray the existence of once famous Jewish communities such as Baghdad and Vilna. At the end of the twentieth century, most Jews lived in two centers, both products of movements that largely occurred after 1900: the United States of America and Israel. This chapter will discuss the background and implications of these major shifts.

EXCEPTIONAL OR TYPICAL? JEWISH MIGRATIONS AND THE SCHOLARSHIP

At first glance, the history of Jewish migrations after 1800 is one of the best-researched subjects in modern Jewish history. The literature on Jewish immigrants in New York City alone is substantial. Dozens of studies deal with Jewish immigration to important cities such as London, Paris, or Odessa, and to countries such as Britain, France, Germany, Argentina,

South Africa, and, of course, Israel. Recent works even shine light on the integration of Jews from the former Soviet Union in Israel and Germany after 1991.[1] And yet, the best overviews of Jewish migration history in the modern era date from the late 1940s. Some of the most insightful texts on the subject were published in the same period – during and in the immediate aftermath of the Holocaust. The founding of Israel drew the attention of scholars away from the wider implications of the Jewish refugee problem and permanent displacement. Instead of reconstructing the history of major movements and tracing the impact at different destinations, or discussing the wider impact of Jewish migrations around the world, in the last fifty years the scholarship has tended to focus on Jewish *im*migration. Surprisingly little is known about the causes of the mass migration and the context of out-migration in Eastern Europe before 1914, about links between migrants who settled at different destinations, and even less about the actual process of migration. More important, Jews who failed to reach their intended destination, who were displaced or expelled, especially between 1914 and 1948, have received relatively little attention because they never really arrived anywhere.

Two of the most substantial academic texts on Jewish migration processes in the modern era were published during the 1940s under the auspices of the American Jewish Committee.[2] Both authors, like several other scholars mentioned in this essay, were very much part of the story they wrote about, although they dealt very differently with it in their works. For

---

[1] On Jewish immigration see for instance Moses Rischin, *The Promised City: New York's Jews 1870–1914* (Cambridge: Harvard University Press, 1962); Irving Howe, *Immigrant Jews of New York, 1881 to Present* (New York: Schocken, 1976); Nancy Green, *Ready-to-Wear and Ready-to-Work: A Century of Industry and Immigrants in the Women's Garment Trade in Paris and New York* (Durham: Duke University Press, 1997); Annie Polland and Daniel Soyer, *Emerging Metropolis: New York Jews in the Age of Immigration, 1840–1920* (New York: New York University Press, 2012); Steven J. Zipperstein, *The Jews of Odessa: A Cultural History, 1794–1881* (Stanford: Stanford University Press, 1986); Lloyd Gartner, *The Jewish Immigrant in England, 1870–1914* (London: Allen & Unwin, 1960); Eli Lederhendler, *Jewish Immigrants and American Capitalism, 1880–1920* (Cambridge: Cambridge University Press, 2009); Víctor A. Mirelman, *Jewish Buenos Aires, 1890–1930: In Search of an Identity* (Detroit: Wayne State University Press, 1990); Jeffrey Lesser, "The Immigration and Integration of Polish Jews in Brazil, 1924–1934," *The Americas* 51 (1994): 173–191; Nelly Elias, *Coming Home: Media and Returning Diaspora in Israel and Germany* (Albany: SUNY Press, 2008).

[2] Mark Wischnitzer, *To Dwell in Safety: The Story of Jewish Migration since 1800* (Philadelphia: Jewish Publication Society, 1948); Eugene M. Kulischer, *Jewish Migrations: Past Experiences and Post-War Prospects* (New York: American Jewish Committee, 1943).

one, Jewish migration after (and implicitly before) 1800 was an exceptional story; for the other, Jewish migrations were very much part of and did not diverge from the general movement, not even during the 1940s.

Mark Wischnitzer (1882–1955) and Eugene Martin Kulischer (1881–1956) were both Jewish émigrés from the Russian Empire. Wischnitzer, who had graduated with a Ph.D. in history from Berlin's Friedrich Wilhelms University in 1906, directed the Russian edition of the Jewish Encyclopedia and taught at the Oriental Institute in St. Petersburg before World War I. Kulischer was a legal scholar before leaving Russia. He obtained his Ph.D. at St. Petersburg University. From 1916 to 1917 he worked as advisor for the Russian ministry of Commerce and Industry and taught at the universities of Petrograd and Kiev. Like so many others who left Russia after the rise of the Bolsheviks, Wischnitzer and Kulischer settled in Berlin in the early 1920s. Both had been academics before their emigration; in Berlin, however, their paths diverged. In 1921 Wischnitzer became chief manager of the leading German Jewish philanthropic organization, the Hilfsverein der deutschen Juden. From the early 1920s to the late 1930s he was occupied on an almost daily basis with the travails of Jewish refugees, first from Eastern Europe and then, after 1933, from Germany itself. Wischnitzer soon emerged as one of the key players in the world of transnational Jewish philanthropic organizations. After helping countless people into exile he himself emigrated, with his wife, art historian Rachel Wischnitzer, via Paris and the Dominican Republic to the United States in the late 1930s. After arriving in New York in 1941, Wischnitzer worked for the Joint Distribution Committee and began teaching Jewish history at Yeshiva University. After a twenty-year hiatus he returned to academic publishing in 1941, devoting his attention almost exclusively to a single subject: Jewish migration history.

Kulischer managed to continue his academic career in the early 1920s as an adjunct professor at the Institute for International Law at Berlin's Friedrich Wilhelms University. In 1932 he and his younger brother and collaborator, Alexander, published the first major account of global migrations in the first and second millennia. This accomplished work is still regarded as a classic in the field of migration studies and demography. While keenly aware of the importance of Jewish migration as a subject, Kulischer considered migration as the norm rather than the exception in the history of mankind. Therefore he (and his brother) devoted only limited space to Jewish migrations. In 1934, Kulischer lost his teaching position and he left Nazi Germany a short time later. In Paris, he was affiliated with the French Ministry of Education. After the German occupation in 1940 he fled across the demarcation line into the unoccupied zone of France and reached the United States in 1941. During the attempt to reach the South of France,

Vichy officials arrested his brother Alexander. He was not heard of again. In New York and later Washington, Eugene Kulischer held a number of positions. He was an advisor for the International Labor Office, and for government agencies, especially the Office of Strategic Services. In 1949 he found a permanent post at the Library of Congress.[3]

Wischnitzer and Kulischer approached the same subject – Jewish migrations – from different vantage points. This was related less to their own migrations as Jews and more to their different professional backgrounds and careers. Wischnitzer experienced the dramatic changes affecting migrants after 1918 primarily in a Jewish context and up close. His publications grew out of his experiences as manager of a refugee organization. For him it was more important to tell the story than to explain it, especially since, in his opinion, the cause for Jewish migrations in the modern period was obvious. Kulischer, on the other hand, was searching for an in-depth explanation for human migrations as such. As a generalist, he was intrigued by the distinctive experience of Jewish migrants and refugees but judged it strictly within the broader context.

In his extensive and pioneering account *To Dwell in Safety* (1948), written under the impact of the Holocaust, Wischnitzer highlighted the specific experience of Jewish migrants: "The recent world conflict has displaced, uprooted, and scattered millions of human beings. No single group has suffered heavier blows in this respect than the Jews of Europe." He deplored the fact that many "Jewish survivors of the Holocaust" remained homeless. The book was completed on May 14, 1948, the day Israel declared its independence. This news reached Wischnitzer at the last minute, and he added a single hopeful paragraph to an otherwise pessimistic introduction. *To Dwell in Safety* focuses almost exclusively on the Jewish experience and has no overarching thesis other than highlighting the impact of anti-Jewish persecution and violence on processes of Jewish migration after 1800. Nevertheless, it is a well-researched and reliable account of Jewish migrations that is still widely used. Interestingly, Kulischer reviewed the book for *Jewish Social Studies*, commending Wischnitzer for presenting the first comprehensive overview on the topic and basing his study largely on primary sources. However, Kulischer could not refrain from criticizing Wischnitzer's focus on "factors specific for the Jewish population" and his

---

[3] W. Parker Mauldin, "Obituary of Eugene M. Kulischer," *American Sociological Review* 21 (1956): 504; A. J. Jaffe, "Notes on the Population Theory of Eugene M. Kulischer," *The Milbank Memorial Fund Quarterly* 40 (1962): 187–206; Alexander and Eugen Kulischer, *Kriegs- und Wanderzüge: Weltgeschichte als Völkerbewegung* (Berlin: De Gruyter, 1932); Necrology (Wischnitzer), in *American Jewish Year Book* 58 (1957): 477; Mark Wischnitzer, *Visas to Freedom: A History of HIAS* (Cleveland: The World Publishing Co., 1955), 12–13.

neglect of "those general factors which make the Jewish migration part of the European migration."[4]

Kulischer's 1943 short text, *Jewish Migrations*, remains one the few works he ever published in a Jewish context – and on a specific Jewish subject. He rejected the thesis of the "everlasting Jewish wanderings" as a specific Jewish experience because it seemed to confirm the stereotype of the "Wandering Jew." For Kulischer, the Jewish experience was typical rather than exceptional because "the story of the whole of mankind is a history of migrations." In 1943, of course, Kulischer could not know the full extent of the Holocaust, but he pointed to the "deliberate and cold-blooded process of extermination of the Jews" and the murdering of "millions of Jews ... by the Germans."[5] Nevertheless, the final statement of *Jewish Migrations* is characteristic of his later publications, notably his magisterial study *Europe on the Move* (1948) and departs clearly from Wischnitzer and other contemporary Jewish historians. Kulischer wrote: "The question of post-war migration is especially vital for the Jewish people. We must remember, however, that it is not an exclusively Jewish Question, and should therefore not be treated as such."[6] *Europe on the Move* covered the complex history of mass displacement in Europe between 1918 and 1948; it remains unsurpassed as a comprehensive treatment of population movements in Interwar Europe.[7] As in the 1932 volume, Kulischer argued that voluntary migrations during peacetime and war-related migrations were closely related. He called for a liberal but regulated system of mass migration to avoid military conflicts that, in his view, were driven by demographic pressure and exacerbated by migration restrictions.

Yet, in this detailed study, Kulischer devoted little attention to Jewish migrations. In the introduction he mentioned his own flight from Nazism and the tragic death of his brother, but not their Jewish background. About the Holocaust he wrote only these two sentences: "Up to the end of the war more than 5,000,000 Jews were deported to extermination camps in Poland and elsewhere. Almost all perished."[8] Why did Kulischer pass over this important topic? The Holocaust and the history of mass displacement of Jews in the aftermaths of World War I and II were hardly footnotes in

---

[4] Wischnitzer, *To Dwell in Safety*, ix (Wischnitzer's choice of the term "Holocaust" is noteworthy); Eugene M. Kulischer, "Review of Wischnitzer, *To Dwell in Safety*," in *Jewish Social Studies* 12 (1950): 281–283.

[5] Kulischer, *Jewish Migrations*, 7, 37, 42.

[6] Ibid., 49.

[7] Eugene M. Kulischer, *Europe on the Move: War and Population Changes, 1917–47* (New York: Columbia University Press, 1948).

[8] Ibid., 264.

the history of twentieth-century European migrations. Unlike Wischnitzer, who wrote primarily for a Jewish audience and worked for Jewish organizations and institutions, Kulischer aimed at a much broader academic public. In the four countries where he had worked as advisor and academic – pre- and post-Revolutionary Russia, Weimar and Nazi Germany, France, and the United States – Jewish academics faced varying degrees of open and informal discrimination. Tellingly, Kulischer never landed a position commensurate with his standing as a pioneering scholar. If he wanted to be taken seriously in academic circles where informal antisemitism was rife, even after the Holocaust, Kulischer felt he had to play down his own background and the experience of Jewish migrants. Since he really looked at the *longue durée* of human migrations (voluntary and forced) he did not want to give undue notice to Jewish migrations and possibly reconfirm existing stereotypes. Hannah Arendt, in sharp contrast, based her path-breaking study, *The Origins of Totalitarianism*, published in 1951, explicitly on the experience of Jews in the modern period. Although she was younger than Kulischer, she – a stateless émigré, a Jew, and a woman – struggled for years to find an adequate academic position in the United States.

The more recent scholarship on Jewish migrations after 1800 has not managed to bridge these two very different approaches – one highlighting the Jews as a "people apart" who faced persecution on an almost constant basis, the other judging Jewish history from without, stressing the impact of general over specific factors.[9] Although few authors have followed Wischnitzer and analyzed Jewish migration *processes* beyond borders, his exclusivist focus is still characteristic of many works on Jewish immigration, admittedly in varying shades. The long shadow of the nation-state paradigm in modern Jewish history has contributed to this rather one-sided perspective because it obscures cross-border movement.[10] Kulischer's approach has shaped general migration studies in the social sciences and political science, much less in history, and hardly in modern Jewish history. Apart from a few important exceptions, notably, Joseph B. Schechtman's, *European Population Transfers*, Hannah Arendt's *The Origins of Totalitarianism*, *The Unwanted* by Michael Marrus, and Peter Gatrell's *A Whole Empire Walking* – books that discuss the history of refugees in

[9] Representative works for these mutually opposing positions are: David Vital, *A People Apart: The Jews in Europe 1789–1939* (Oxford: Oxford University Press, 1999) and Gabriel Sheffer, *Diaspora Politics: At Home Abroad* (Cambridge: Cambridge University Press, 2003).

[10] Two notable exceptions are Ewa Morawska, *Insecure Prosperity: Small-Town Jews in Industrial America, 1890–1940* (Princeton: Princeton University Press, 1996) and Green, *Ready-to-Wear and Ready-to-Work*.

twentieth-century Europe extensively and draw on Kulischer – the history of Jewish migrations is subsumed, even marginalized, in studies on general migration history.[11] Ironically, *if* Jewish migrations are mentioned in general studies, authors tend to subscribe to a lachrymose interpretation. In his otherwise informative overview of Global Diasporas and Migrations, Thomas Sowell begins the chapter on the Jews: "The tragic history of the Jews as a people wandering the world through centuries of persecution ...." The essay not only echoes the stereotype of the "Wandering Jew," but Sowell plays down the agency of Jews as migrants. Likewise, the author of a recently published ambitious survey of global migrations in the second millennium emphasizes the impact of violence and persecution on Jewish migrations in the last thousand years.[12] Kulischer would have emphatically disagreed with these positions, even though his personal migration *was* shaped tragically by persecution *because* he was Jewish.

Were Jewish migrations in the twentieth century exceptional or typical? The answer depends very much on the perspective, the author's agenda, and the intended audience. This chapter will try to steer a middle course between these divergent approaches represented by Wischnitzer and Kulischer. The twentieth century is often described as the century of refugees. The history of Jewish migrations, especially between 1914 and 1948, powerfully illustrates the precariousness and dangers refugees faced, as both Wischnitzer and Kulischer stress in their otherwise very different works. In hindsight, as I will argue, the specific experiences of Jews on the move during the first half of the twentieth century, even though hardly uniform but neither exceptional, can help to better address the predicament of permanently displaced and marginalized groups in the late twentieth and twenty-first centuries. Like many Jews in the period between World War I and the founding of the state of Israel, modern refugees frequently have very limited agency over their fate and lack sufficient protection.

---

[11] Joseph B. Schechtman, *European Population Transfers, 1939–1945* (New York: Oxford University Press, 1946); Hannah Arendt, *The Origins of Totalitarianism* (New York: Harcourt, 1951); Michael R. Marrus, *The Unwanted – European Refugees in the Twentieth Century* (Oxford: Oxford University Press, 1985); Peter Gatrell, *A Whole Empire Walking: Refugees in Russia during World War I* (Bloomington: Indiana University Press, 1999).

[12] Thomas Sowell, *Migrations and Cultures: A World View* (New York: Basic Books, 1996), 234–308, here 234; Dirk Hoerder, *Cultures in Contact: World Migrations in the Second Millennium* (Durham: Duke University Press, 2002), 95, esp. 341.

CAUGHT BETWEEN BORDERS:
THE TRAVAILS OF STATELESSNESS

On November 7, 1938 Herschel Grynszpan walked into the German Embassy in Paris and fatally shot diplomat Ernst vom Rath. The Nazi leadership used this incident as a fait accompli for the notorious Kristallnacht pogrom on November 9 and 10.[13] The most likely cause for Grynszpan's desperate act has been almost completely overshadowed by the events that followed in its wake. Ten days earlier, on October 27 and 28, the Nazi authorities rounded up circa 17,000 Polish Jews across Germany (and Austria) and deported them to the Polish border. Among this group were Herschel's parents and his sister. Like most other deportees the Grynszpans had lived in Germany for years. Herschel, in fact, had been born in Hanover in 1921. The deportation did not go as "smoothly" as the Nazi leaders had perhaps envisioned it. Polish guards at various crossings along the border refused to admit the deportees, even though they were citizens of Poland, turning them back to the German checkpoints. At one border post, German officials forced Jews into the river, which marked the border; on the other side, their Polish counterparts drove them back in. In at least one instance, at the Zbaszyn (Bentschen) crossing, border guards on both sides threatened Jewish deportees with guns. At Zbaszyn large groups of people were stranded for many hours in no man's land, in chilly and wet weather, without access to food or support. Grynszpan knew his parents and sister had been taken from their home in Hanover, and he feared the worst. Eventually, the Polish authorities relented, admitting most of the women, men, and children – only to lock up thousands in a makeshift camp near the border. The Zbaszyn camp on the main rail line between Berlin and Warsaw housed up to 8,000 Jews under unspeakable conditions for almost two years. Only a few Jews were allowed to return to Germany. No government volunteered to offer them asylum.[14]

---

[13] Grynszpan may have been inspired by the 1926 assassination of the notorious Ukrainian nationalist Simon Petlura by the Jewish anarchist Scholem Schwarzbard in Paris. See David Engel, "Being Lawful in a Lawless World: The Trial of Scholem Schwarzbard and the Defense of East European Jews," *Simon Dubnow Institute Yearbook* 5 (2006): 83–97.

[14] Jerzy Tomaszewski, *Auftakt zur Vernichtung: Die Vertreibung polnischer Juden aus Deutschland im Jahre 1938* (Osnabrück: fibre, 2002), 136–144, 178–202; Trude Maurer, "Abschiebung und Attentat: Die Ausweisung der polnischen Juden und der Vorwand für die 'Kristallnacht,'" in *Der Judenpogrom: Von der 'Reichskristallnacht' zum Völkermord*, ed. Walter H. Pehle (Frankfurt am Main: Fischer, 1988), 52–73; until the 2005 immigration law German citizenship was not conferred by birth in Germany but primarily through proof of "German" descent.

Brutally expelled by the country where many of them had been born, rejected by the country whose citizens they were, Polish Jews from Germany found themselves literally dumped in a no man's land, rendered de facto stateless, with nowhere to go – and no one willing to help. Their absurd affliction points to a much larger problem – the unclear status and the vulnerability of stateless refugees during the interwar period and beyond. The British liberal politician John Hope Simpson defined the refugee in 1939 as the "unwanted inhabitant of the world, unwanted in the country of his origin, unwanted in any other country." Only a few months before the expulsion of the Polish Jews, in June 1938, the United States convened an international meeting on the refugee problem at the French resort of Evian. While the brutal Nazi expulsion campaign against Austrian Jews in the wake of the March 1938 Anschluss had shocked the world, not one of the thirty-two countries participating at the conference was willing to accommodate more than a few Jewish refugees. The failure of Evian seemed to confirm the worst allegations of the Nazi propaganda machine: no country wanted "the" Jews.[15]

In *The Origins of Totalitarianism*, Hannah Arendt linked the rise of the refugee problem to the collapse of the large multi-ethnic empires in Eastern Europe in 1918. The territorial nation-states, which replaced the empires, literally fenced out many members of unwanted minorities, ranging from ethnic and religious groups to political opponents. Jews, by no means the only group affected by this transition, stood out, as Arendt stressed, compared with other transterritorial Diaspora groups like ethnic Germans from the Russian Empire or Greek Orthodox Christians from the Ottoman Empire. After the empires ceased to exist, the former Jewish subjects could not move (or be "transferred") to an obvious territorial homeland. At the Paris peace conferences the successor states of the empires such as Poland only grudgingly accepted Jews, Germans, and other groups as minorities. Yet instead of providing minorities with autonomy rights as they had promised in Paris, governments in Romania, Hungary, and Poland gradually deprived their Jewish citizens of rights. Indeed, Arendt depicted members of minorities as "cousins" of stateless DP's. The latter, however, were even worse off because they were de jure stateless. They were frequently denied citizenship and access by the successor states when they wanted to return to their actual homes. Turkey and the Soviet Union took

---

[15] John Hope Simpson, *The Refugee Question* (London: Oxford University Press, 1939), 3; Solomon Adler-Rudel, "The Evian Conference on the Refugee Question," *Leo Baeck Institute Year Book* 13 (1968): 235–276; only the Dominican Republic offered asylum to Jewish refugees in 1938. See Allen Wells, *Tropical Zion: General Trujillo, FDR, and the Jews of Sosúa* (Durham: Duke University Press, 2009).

an even more blatant step in the early 1920s by revoking the citizenship of Armenian refugees and Russian exiles respectively, creating a precedent for similar actions by Nazi Germany, falangist Spain, and fascist Italy during the 1930s. Already on July 14, 1933, the Nazis stripped prominent political émigrés and several hundred Jews from Eastern Europe who had been naturalized during the 1920s of their German citizenship. But, as we shall see, that was just the beginning of a policy that would play a crucial role in the Final Solution.[16]

In the aftermath of World War I it was not clear where the hundreds of thousands of permanently displaced Jews and millions of other stateless people could actually go. The sheer scale of statelessness and mass displacement was without precedent. After the United States and other important immigration countries closed their gates during and soon after the war, partly in anticipation of the European refugee wave, many refugees but also migrants who could not reach their intended destination were stranded in permanent transit. While the League of Nations took some steps to alleviate the situation of permanently displaced persons, no solution had been reached by the late 1930s when the Nazis brutally forced tens of thousands of German and foreign Jews to leave Germany. In an only-recently published 1940 manuscript, Arendt depicted the "conundrum" of the Jews as a transterritorial people succinctly, describing them, in a play on the well-known Zionist saying, as "a people without land in search of a land without people." After 1918 such a "land" of course did not exist, except, as Arendt sarcastically remarked, on the moon.[17]

Stateless people found themselves in a legal no man's land outside the territorial nation-state system. They were not only deprived of cross-border mobility, lacking the necessary "papers"; in the early 1920s and late 1930s some states with large populations of stranded stateless people also restricted their internal mobility. According to Arendt, by the late 1930s the "internment camp" constituted "the only practical substitute for a nonexistent homeland." It is noteworthy that none other than Kulischer coined the term "Displaced Persons" in a 1943 study prepared for the International Labor Office.[18] Like Kulischer and Wischnitzer, Arendt experienced the travails of displacement and statelessness up close. Having fled from Berlin

---

[16] Arendt, *The Origins of Totalitarianism*, 267–269, quote: 268; Marc Vishniak, *The Legal Status of Stateless Persons* (New York: American Jewish Committee, 1945), 24–33.

[17] Hannah Arendt, "The Minority Question," in *Hannah Arendt – The Jewish Writings*, ed. Jerome Kohn and Ron H. Feldman (New York: Schocken, 2007), 125–132, here 130.

[18] Eugene M. Kulischer, *The Displacement of Population in Europe* (Montreal: International Labour Office, 1943); idem, "Displaced Persons in the Modern World," *Annals of the American Academy of Political and Social Science* 262 (1949): 166–177.

to Prague in 1933, she lost her German citizenship like many other anti-Nazi émigrés. She joined, as she put it in the 1940 manuscript, "the great masses of people who have no right of residence or consular protection of any sort – modern pariahs." She wrote these lines as she was waiting for a US visa in Marseilles. Only weeks before, she had escaped from the notorious Gurs internment camp in the unoccupied zone of France. Against considerable odds the stateless Arendt secured a visa and reached New York in May 1941.[19]

In *The Origins of Totalitarianism,* Arendt hinted at one significant but dubious advantage of statelessness. People who became stateless or whose citizenship could not be established could not be easily expelled because no country was obliged to accept them. A curious example was none other than Adolf Hitler. In 1925, he formally renounced his Austrian citizenship to avoid being deported from Germany after serving his prison sentence for his involvement in the failed 1923 "Beer Hall Putsch." For his candidacy in the 1932 presidential election Hitler secured German citizenship after members of the Nazi party joined a coalition government in the small state of Brunswick. And here lies the explanation for the decision to expel Polish Jews from Germany in late October 1938.[20]

Long before 1933 Poland had raised various obstacles for its Jewish citizens who wanted to return from Germany, or were indeed expelled. But the Nazi regime was alarmed when in October 1938 Warsaw announced most Jews with Polish citizenship living in Germany would lose their citizenship if they did not return to Poland permanently and immediately, by November 1 – a deadline so tight that only a small minority could realistically meet it. Returning voluntarily to Poland, even from Nazi Germany, was not an option for many Polish Jews. After the death of the longtime ruler Jósef Piłsudski in 1935, the authoritarian regime in Warsaw stepped up the pressure on its Jewish minority (and on other national minorities), pursuing a discriminatory policy similar to Nazi Germany's. The initial refusal of the Polish authorities to accept the Jewish deportees – before the deadline had actually passed – and the decision to place them in internment camps near the border, illustrates that for the Polish government Polish Jews were already unwanted strangers, even though they still had Polish passports. After late 1938 many German (and Austrian) Jewish refugees too became "de facto stateless" (Arendt). In October 1938, following negotiations between the German Foreign Office and Swiss officials, the

[19] Jerome Kohn, "A Jewish Life, 1906–1975," in *Hannah Arendt – The Jewish Writings,* ix–xxxii. Arendt, "The Minority Question," 128.

[20] Arendt, *The Origins of Totalitarianism,* 269–289, quote: 284; Ian Kershaw, *Hitler, 1889–1936: Hubris* (New York: W. W. Norton, 2000), 238.

passports of German Jews were stamped with a "J." This actually made it harder for the Nazi authorities to force German Jews into exile. Yet it was adopted in the interest of "Aryans" who could move with much less hassle across borders as welcome guests, unlike now easily recognizable (and most unwelcome) Jewish refugees.[21]

Avoiding deportation was, however, a dubious advantage for stateless persons, if they were living in a country ruled by a ruthless regime. Governments cannot deport stateless persons to another sovereign country without its prior permission. But this gives a state enormous leverage over stateless persons (and their property), since no other state is responsible for them. When the Nazis invaded neighboring countries such as France, the Netherlands, and Poland, stateless refugees could be easily identified – for instance through police registries, as in France. Some Jewish refugees had already been placed in internment camps such as Westerbork in the Netherlands, and Gurs and Les Milles in France. It is noteworthy that of the more than 75,000 Jews deported from France to German extermination and concentration camps between 1942 and 1944, 90 percent were rounded up by the French police. More than two thirds of these deportees were foreign-born Jews who overwhelmingly had moved to France during the 1920s and 1930s. Suffice to say, all over Europe Jews who had been stateless since the early 1920s perished in disproportionate numbers in the Holocaust.[22]

Admittedly, it would be too shortsighted to reduce the story of Jewish migration during the twentieth century to the three decades between 1914 and 1948 marked by permanent displacement, statelessness, and eventually genocide. However, a closer look at the period of relatively open borders in the early years of the twentieth century reveals that some of the obstacles Jewish migrants encountered after 1914 can be traced to the pre-war years. And even after the defeat of the Nazi regime, as Wischnitzer emphasized in *To Dwell in Safety*, many Jewish survivors could not move to a destination of their choice. Overwhelmingly stateless, they were forced to live in DP-camps for years. The first Jewish immigrants to Israel were mostly European DP's and refugees but also Jews expelled from countries in the Middle East and the Maghreb in and soon after 1948. Ironically, the wars in which Israel had to defend its right to exist produced a new refugee problem among the Palestinian population that remains very much at the center of the Middle East conflict. Does the experience of twentieth-century Jewish migrations,

[21] Saul Friedländer, *Nazi Germany and the Jews: The Years of Persecution, 1933–1939* (New York: Harper Collins, 1997), 266–268.

[22] Clifford Rosenberg, *Policing Paris: The Origins of Modern Immigration Control Between the Wars* (Ithaca: Cornell University Press, 2006), xiii.

voluntary and forced, offer answers to the challenge of how to overcome the travails of permanent displaced refugees who still live uneasily outside of the territorial system of states? I will return to this question.

THE JEWISH MASS MIGRATION FROM EASTERN EUROPE 1860–1914

Until 1914 Jewish migrants faced relatively few hurdles in and beyond Europe. They could and indeed did migrate in large numbers to many countries around the globe, in particular to the United States. Even a superficial glance at the numbers illustrates the far-reaching repercussions of this movement. During the middle decades of the nineteenth century, in the early stages of the migration, more than two thirds of the world Jewish population lived dispersed in several regions across the Russian and Austro-Hungarian Empires, and in Southeastern Europe, most in small towns. In 1870, the strongly growing Jewish population in the Russian and Austro-Hungarian Empires comprised about four million. Germany, the largest Jewish community outside of Eastern Europe, was home to about 400,000 Jews; the Jewish communities in Western Europe, around the Mediterranean, the Middle East, and the United States were significantly smaller. Within little less than twenty-five years, between 1890 and 1914, more than two million Jews left Eastern Europe. The overwhelming majority settled in the United States, smaller groups went to Britain, France, Argentina, Canada, Germany, and even to far-flung destinations like Manchuria and South Africa. The return migration was relatively low, but not negligible.[23]

The Jewish movement out of Eastern Europe was not just a global movement, it was closely related to two other transformations, internal Jewish migration within the Russian and Austro-Hungarian Empires, and a process the Jewish sociologist Arthur Ruppin depicted as Jewish "metropolization." Before 1800 many European Jews lived in midsized towns and, due to settlement restrictions, in the countryside; only few were permitted to settle in cities. As the population increased and restrictions were lifted in Central and Western Europe soon after the French Revolution, economic opportunities drew Jews, like their Christian neighbors, to newly forming industrial and commercial centers. In Europe and beyond, Jewish urbanization rates were far higher than for other groups. More important, in the

---

[23] Arthur Ruppin, *Soziologie der Juden* (Berlin: Jüdischer Verlag, 1930), Vol. 1, 67–86 (these numbers are based on estimates); Jonathan Sarna, "The Myth of No Return: The History of Jewish Return Migration to Eastern Europe 1881–1914," *American Jewish History* 71 (1981): 256–268.

last third of the nineteenth century the fastest growing and largest urban Jewish communities were located in a handful of Europe's and America's biggest cities: in Berlin, Warsaw, Lodz, Odessa, Vienna, Budapest, London, Philadelphia, Chicago, and especially New York. The Jewish migration from Eastern Europe drove the Jewish "metropolization." In Eastern Europe and especially beyond, new immigrants soon outnumbered longer-settled Jewish populations. Especially in the United States and Britain they completely reinvented Jewish life within a few years. In cities that only flourished after 1870, such as Lodz – the Polish "Manchester" – or the South African gold mining hub Johannesburg, Jewish immigrants established entirely new communities.[24]

Internal Jewish migration in Eastern Europe was extensive. In the Austro-Hungarian Empire, Jews from the economically deprived province of Galicia flocked especially to Vienna; Budapest attracted even more Jews from regions across the Hungarian part of the monarchy. In the Russian Empire large numbers left the Pale of Settlement for the Polish provinces, providing enterprises and labor for the rapidly industrializing cities of Lodz and Warsaw. The Jewish urbanization rates were remarkably high for members of a relatively small group: In 1914, the 170,000 Jews living in Lodz made up over a third of the city's population. In Białystok, Jews comprised 75 percent (!) of the population of 63,000 in 1897. Another important center was the Black Sea port Odessa. Restrictions prevented larger groups of Jews from settling in Kiev and in the imperial cities Moscow and St. Petersburg before 1917. Only Warsaw and Budapest attracted similarly high numbers as the American cities Chicago and Philadelphia before 1914. New York, the "Megashtetl on the Hudson," of course was already in a league of its own. Around 1910 its Jewish population surpassed the one-million threshold.[25]

An important exception to this trend among the major destination countries was Germany. Restrictions and repeated expulsions drove many Jewish and other Eastern European migrants out. Nevertheless, the majority of Berlin's new Jewish inhabitants were internal migrants from "Hinterberlin" – the eastern provinces Prussia had annexed from Poland in the late eighteenth century. *Ostjuden* (eastern Jews) from the province of Posen and neighboring regions encountered much

---

[24] Ruppin, *Soziologie der Juden*, 67–88.

[25] Rebecca Kobrin, *Jewish Białystok and Its Diaspora* (Bloomington: Indiana University Press, 2010), 19–20; Moses Rischin, "The Megashtetl/Cosmopolis: New York History Comes of Age," in *People of the City: Jews and the Urban Challenge*, ed. Jonathan Frankel, Studies in Contemporary Jewry 9 (Oxford: Oxford University Press, 1999), 171–178, here 171.

Table 33.1 *Jewish Population in Millions, 1881 to 1991 (based on estimates).*

	1880	1910	1939	1948	1991
Eastern Europe	7	9	8	2.6	1.1
United States	0.25	3.3	4.8	5	6
Palestine/Israel	0.05	0.08	0.5	0.6	4
South America	0.03	0.1	0.5	0.5	0.3
Greater New York	0.6	1	2	2	2
World Jewish Population	10	15	17	11.5	12.8

Source: *American Jewish Year Book* 20 (1918/19): 339–352; 44 (1942/43): 422–430; Ruppin, *Soziologie der Juden*, 67–88; *New York Times* January 27, 1912.

discrimination by antisemites and established Jews. In 1910, a mere 16 percent of the Jewish population in Berlin had been born abroad.[26] The reverse was true in the United States. In 1910, more than 90 percent of a significantly larger Jewish population was made up of immigrants (overwhelmingly from Eastern Europe) and their American-born children.

Tables 33.1 and 33.2 illustrate the impact of the Jewish mass migration in the period between 1881 and 1910 – and of the Holocaust and the founding of Israel. Apart from boosting the metropolization, the mass migration established the United States as the second most important center of the Jewish Diaspora within just three decades. Between 1880 and 1910, the American Jewish population increased from circa 250,000 to well over three million.

The pogroms directed against Jews in the Russian Empire after 1881 are still widely regarded as the main cause behind the mass migration, especially in the popular literature. Admittedly, in many contemporary accounts the Jewish migrants were depicted as "refugees." Accordingly, in *To Dwell in Safety* Wischnitzer did not distinguish between earlier refugees and the post-1914 refugees. In his view, the pogroms were the prime cause for the Jewish mass migration. And yet, in contrast to the following period, the pre-1914 Jewish migration was actually a "normal" rather

---

[26] Gabriel E. Alexander, "Die jüdische Bevölkerung Berlins in den ersten Jahrzehnten des 20. Jahrhunderts: Demographische und wirtschaftliche Entwicklungen," in *Jüdische Geschichte in Berlin: Essays und Studien*, ed. Reinhard Rürup (Berlin: Hentrich, 1995), 117–148, here 142; Jack Wertheimer, *Unwelcome Strangers. East European Jews in Imperial Germany* (New York: Oxford University Press, 1987).

Table 33.2 *Jewish Population of Metropolitan Area in Millions (1881 to 1991), percent of general population (based on estimates).*

	1880	1910	1925	1948	1991
New York City	0.06[1]	1	1.75	2	2
Chicago	B	0.2	0.3	0.3	0.25
Philadelphia	0.05	0.2	0.3	0.25	0.25
Vienna	0.07	0.18	0.2	B	B
Budapest	0.07	0.3	0.2	0.1	B
Berlin	0.05	0.14	0.17	B	B
London	0.03	0.15	0.2	0.23	0.3
Paris	B	0.06	0.14	0.13	0.2
Lodz	B	0.1	0.2[2]	B	B
Warsaw	0.1	0.3	0.3	B	B
Moscow	B	0.01	0.1	0.2	0.2
St. Petersburg, Petrograd/ Leningrad	B	0.01	0.1	0.2	0.1
Tel Aviv/Jaffa	B	B	B	0.25	2

Legend: B= Below 25,000; n/a= no data available; [1]includes Brooklyn; [2]1929.
Source: *American Jewish Year Book* 20 (1918/19): 339–352; 51 (1950): 245–250; 100 (2000): 242–258, 484–495; Ruppin, *Soziologie der Juden*, 67–88.

than an exceptional movement. Already in 1943, Kulischer, a recognized authority on internal migrations and social history within Russia before 1914, dismissed the pogroms as cause for the migration, pointing to economic factors and the strong migrations of other Eastern Europeans.[27] More detailed research on the 1881 pogroms has confirmed this thesis. The Jewish mass migration was distinctive, due to the specific economic profile of Jews in Eastern Europe, but it cannot be separated from the wider socio-economic context. Strong population growth, the displacement of Jews from traditional roles in rural and proto-industrial economies, uneven economic development, and the lack of opportunities were the main driving factors of the migration. The sudden rise of the Jewish *and* non-Jewish migration from the Russian Empire in the early 1880s can be traced to the expansion of the railroad which brought America

[27] Wischnitzer, *To Dwell in Safety*, 37–140; Kulischer, *Jewish Migrations*, 25.

literally within reach. The exponential growth of the Jewish migration in the early 1890s and 1900s followed the boom and bust cycles of the American economy. And Jews, like most other migrants, moved in networks: as more Jews settled across the Atlantic, they helped close relatives, friends, and potential employees to make the journey, and these, in turn, pulled over more people when the conditions and outlook appeared promising.[28]

Although the journey to America was relatively uncomplicated before 1914, Jewish and other migrants from Eastern Europe encountered obstacles early on. The Eastern European migrations were part of a global pattern of rising mobility. As markets for labor and goods were integrating, and the transportation infrastructure improved, more people decided to move over long distances to improve their living standard and respond to the growing demand for cheap labor. Eastern and Southern Europeans, and East Asians were heading in rising numbers to North and South America, while South Asians were moving across the British Empire. In the receiving countries temporary labor migrants and immigrants from distant countries were at once welcomed as a source of cheap labor and perceived as culturally and racially threatening. The US Congress began to pass restrictive immigration legislation already during the 1880s, excluding "paupers," migrants with contagious illnesses, prostitutes, convicts, and in 1882, Chinese immigrants. American officials began to check arrivals more closely as they stepped off the boat, sending back suspicious immigrants to European and Asian ports. The opening of Ellis Island in 1892 and immigration stations at other ports, and increasing controls along the US–Canadian border and the stationing of US immigration inspectors at Canadian ports highlight the gradual turn to a more restrictive regime. But while the number of migrants rejected at Ellis Island remained relatively low before 1914, many migrants never even reached Ellis Island.[29]

Jews (and non-Jews) from Russia in particular were already traversing a legal gray zone long before 1914, because the overwhelming majority

---

[28] Simon Kuznets, "Immigration of Russian Jews to the United States: Background and Structure," *Perspectives in American History* 9 (1975): 35–124; John D. Klier and Shlomo Lambroza, eds, *Pogroms: Anti-Jewish Violence in Modern Russian History* (Cambridge: Cambridge University Press, 1992); Ewa Morawska, "Polish-Jewish Relations in America 1880–1940: Old Elements, New Configurations," *Polin* 19 (2007): 71–86.

[29] Aristide R. Zolberg, "The Great Wall Against China: Responses to the First Immigration Crisis, 1885–1925," in *Migration, Migration History, History*, ed. Leo Lucassen and Jan Lucassen (Berne: Peter Lang, 1997), 291–315; Tobias Brinkmann, "Traveling with

could only leave Russia and even the Habsburg monarchy illegally. Many migrants were young men evading the draft and thus forfeiting diplomatic protection during the journey. Admittedly, the majority made the crossing without much hassle. But thousands were caught up in the net of restrictions and turned back by employees of the steamship lines and state officials in the transit countries because they *supposedly* would face rejection at Ellis Island. Transnationally linked Jewish philanthropic organizations provided some cover, by guarding the transit routes, supporting destitute migrants, and publicizing abuse. In a revealing 1905 report, the Hilfsverein, the leading German Jewish aid organization, deplored the fact that Jewish migrants, especially from Russia, were de facto stateless because they enjoyed no "*Untertanenschutz*" (protection enjoyed by legal subjects of a state). Therefore, not just the Hilfsverein but "world Jewry," as represented by Jewish aid organizations, had "to do what otherwise would be the task of the state."[30] Jewish organizations were aiming to protect the migrants against arbitrary decisions as they crossed the extralegal space of transit. The Hilfsverein suggestion to provide de facto stateless Jewish transmigrants with a quasi-citizenship during the journey is remarkable because it would have given migrants a universally recognized status, not tied to a specific territory and state – as long as they were in transit and not affiliated with a country. This idea remained, indeed still remains, a lofty vision.[31]

FORCED MIGRATIONS AND CLOSED BORDERS

Most likely the year 1914 would have witnessed a new record high in the number of Jewish immigrants to the United States; but this did not come to pass. The declaration of war in early August 1914, and the early Russian advance into eastern Prussia closed down the transcontinental transit route almost overnight. Between 1914 and the early 1920s millions of Eastern Europeans, among them hundreds of thousands of Jews, were displaced,

---

Ballin: The Impact of American Immigration Policies on Jewish Transmigration within Central Europe, 1880–1914," *International Review of Social History* 53 (2008): 459–484; see the essays in *Points of Passage: Jewish Transmigrants from Eastern Europe in Scandinavia, Germany, and Britain 1880–1914*, ed. Tobias Brinkmann (New York: Berghahn Books, 2013).

[30] Hans Rogger, "Tsarist Policy on Jewish Emigration," *Soviet Jewish Affairs* 3 (1973): 26–36; *4. Geschäftsbericht (1905) des Hilfsvereins der deutschen Juden* (Berlin: Hilfsverein, 1906), 79.

[31] Seyla Benhabib, *The Rights of Others: Aliens, Residents and Citizens* (Cambridge: Cambridge University Press, 2004), esp. 71–128.

often by brutal force. In 1915/16 the Russian military authorities uprooted tens of thousands of Jews and ethnic Germans as potential "collaborators." They were taken from their homes in the western provinces of Russia and transported to the eastern hinterlands, often without any provisions. A few hundred made their way through Siberia to Vladivostok and Yokohama. In 1917/18 the New York based Hebrew Immigrant Aid Society (HIAS) successfully evacuated many dozens of completely destitute Russian Jewish refugees from Japan, after lobbying with the United States immigration authorities. The large majority, however, remained stranded in the Russian interior beyond the reach of Jewish aid organizations.[32]

Along the eastern border of the Austro-Hungarian Empire intense fighting affected regions with a high number of Jewish residents. Thousands of Galician Jews fled to Vienna, and to a lesser extent to Prague and Budapest, overwhelming Jewish communities in these cities. Many of the deportees and refugees lost everything they owned and lived for years in primitive makeshift camps. Often they were displaced again soon after the war officially ended in 1918. From the Baltic Sea to the Mediterranean various nationalists, troops of new and older nation-states such as Poland, Turkey, and Greece, Bolshevists, German, British, American, and French troops, and paramilitaries fought over the spoils of the collapsing empires into the early 1920s in a series of extremely violent conflicts. In terms of violence and destruction these conflicts overshadowed the four years before 1918. At least 50,000 Jews were killed in Poland and Ukraine alone in 1918/19.[33]

Just when the pressure for many Eastern Europeans to leave was greater than ever, the United States Congress closed the gates to most Eastern and Southern Europeans and Asians. This was of course hardly a coincidence. Fears of a communist takeover and of destitute refugee masses from Eastern Europe provided the strong anti-immigration movement with the decisive momentum; antisemitism and racism heavily influenced the design of the law. After 1921 prospective immigrants had to apply for an immigrant visa at the US embassy or consulate in their home country. Often they had to wait many months for a visa or a negative decision, which they usually could not appeal. After 1918 most countries required immigrants and transmigrants to carry valid passports and apply for visas. This requirement explains why stateless people were literally deprived of

---

[32] Gatrell, *A Whole Empire Walking*, 15–32; Hebrew Immigrant Aid Society, *Ninth Annual Report 1917* (New York: HIAS, 1918), 6–8.

[33] Marrus, *The Unwanted*, 52–80; David Rechter, *The Jews of Vienna and the First World War* (Oxford: Littman, 2001); Marsha L. Rozenblit, *Reconstructing a National Identity: The Jews of Habsburg Austria during World War I* (Oxford: Oxford University Press, 2001).

the ability to cross borders.[34] Since the United States restricted access fully only in 1925, more than 200,000 Jews managed to get in legally between 1921 and 1924; more than 150,000 went to other destinations, especially Canada, Argentina, and Palestine in the same period. The Third Aliyah ("going up" in Hebrew, a biblical term for the return of exiles to the land of Israel) brought circa 35,000 mostly Eastern European Jews to Palestine between 1919 and 1923. The Fourth Aliyah saw a strong increase, but this was already a consequence of the restrictive American policy: circa 70,000 Jews moved to Palestine between 1924 and 1929. However, challenging economic conditions forced many to leave Palestine during the second half of the 1920s. Another important option was the Soviet Union. Those Jews in particular who had been displaced within Russia during the war moved to the Soviet cities after the internal mobility restrictions had been lifted in 1917.[35]

By the mid-1920s the outlook was bleak. The Soviet Union made emigration difficult years before formally banning its citizens from moving abroad in 1929. Like other groups, Jews, especially in the Ukraine, were affected by Stalin's brutal resettlement policies that began at the end of the decade. A newsletter published by the Hilfsverein under the auspices of Wischnitzer illustrates the diminishing options. Some Latin American countries were relatively open, especially Brazil and Mexico, but beyond reach for many Jews in Eastern Europe who lacked the means and the necessary papers for the journey.[36]

The travails of Jewish refugees and migrants after 1914 were certainly not exceptional. Many other people around the world, not least in Eastern Europe, were also displaced by force, and hit hard by the shift to migration

[34] Daniel Tichenor, *Dividing Lines. The Politics of Immigration Control in America* (Princeton, Princeton University Press, 2002), 142–146; John Higham, *Strangers in the Land: Patterns of American Nativism, 1860–1925* (New York: Athenaeum, 1977), 277–286; John Torpey, "The Great War and the Birth of the Modern Passport System," in *Documenting Individual Identity: The Development of State Practices in the Modern World*, ed. John Torpey and Jane Caplan (Princeton: Princeton University Press, 2001), 235–255.

[35] Mark Wischnitzer, "Die Tätigkeit des Hilfsvereins in den Nachkriegsjahren mit besonderer Berücksichtigung der Auswandererfürsorge," in *Festschrift Anlässlich des 25 Jährigen Bestehens des Hilfsvereins der deutschen Juden* (Berlin: Marx, 1926), 47–59; *Jahresbericht für 1928* (Berlin: Hilfsverein der Deutschen Juden, 1929), 30; Gabriele Freitag, *Nächstes Jahr in Moskau! Die Zuwanderung von Juden in die sowjetische Metropole 1917–1932* (Göttingen: V&R, 2004); Ruppin, *Soziologie der Juden*, 147.

[36] Kate Brown, *A Biography of No Place: From Ethnic Borderland to Soviet Heartland* (Cambridge: Harvard University Press, 2004), 90–91; *Korrespondenzblatt des Centralbüros für jüdische Auswanderungsangelegenheiten des Hilfsvereins der deutschen Juden* (Berlin), March/April 1927.

restrictions after the war. Yet Jews in Eastern Europe were affected harder than most of their non-Jewish neighbors because territorially defined nation-states deprived transterritorial groups almost literally of the legitimate place and space they had occupied in the multi-ethnic empires. Apart from discriminatory minority policies in various Eastern European successor states, the most visible predicament of the Jewish migrant experience after 1918 was statelessness and thus the lack of papers. Pre-1914 imperial borders had been relatively permeable; post-1918 national borders in Eastern Europe were contested and fortified. The post-1918 period witnessed the rise of "Paper Walls" around the world – borders defined by restrictive and constantly changing access regulations, the obligation to carry state-issued identity papers, and the requirement to apply for entry permissions before departure. Paper walls were (and are) remote borders. Before and especially after 1933 many Jews did not even come close to real borders, because they were defeated by paper walls.

"Of course: The papers! Half a Jewish life is wasted by the useless struggle against the 'papers.'" This desperate call opens the section on Berlin in a 1927 essay *Juden auf Wanderschaft* ("Wandering Jews") by the Galician-born Jewish journalist and writer Joseph Roth. The short text is a unique document of the precarious topography of Jewish migrations after 1918. Traditional destinations like America and Britain were out of reach. In the Soviet Union, *Ostjuden* (Eastern Jews) could stay – if they managed to get in. For the anti-Zionist author Palestine constituted a dead end. Berlin was the place of passage – a gloomy waiting room between East and West: "No *Ostjude* goes voluntarily to Berlin. Who from all over the world comes to Berlin voluntarily?" Jewish life in post-war Europe, as Roth described it, was characterized by the experience of uprootedness, transition, and marginality. *Juden auf Wanderschaft* captured a specific epistemology of Jewish migration from Eastern Europe: "Many return. More move on. The *Ostjuden* have no home anywhere, but graves on every cemetery."[37]

The Great Depression brought even tighter restrictions on cross-border mobility, especially in the United States. President Hoover instructed all consular officers to reject all visa applicants who *might* not be able to sustain themselves after immigration. In 1930 and 1931 alone, more than 100,000 visa applications were turned down that otherwise would have

---

[37] Joseph Roth, *Juden auf Wanderschaft* (Berlin: Die Schmiede, 1927), 65–68, 14 (my own translation); Anne-Christin Saß, *Berliner Luftmenschen: Osteuropäisch-jüdische Migranten in der Weimarer Republik* (Göttingen: Wallstein, 2012).

been processed.[38] After 1933 the situation worsened considerably as German Jews joined the groups of displaced refugees across Europe, at the height of the Depression. Only very belatedly, on the eve of World War II, did the United States ease access somewhat. The 50,000 Jews who immigrated in 1939 constituted more than half (!) of the general immigration to the United States in that year. This remarkable and deeply troubling number (for a relatively small group) illustrates the scale of the Jewish refugee problem, and more importantly, the specific challenges Jewish refugees and migrants faced after 1914. Thanks to the restrictive quotas it was almost impossible for de jure stateless Jews and for Jews with passports of Eastern European states to obtain an immigrant visa for the United States. Only one larger group managed to escape after the German invasion of Poland in September 1939. 300,000 Polish Jews fled into the Soviet-occupied eastern half of Poland. In 1940 most were deported to Siberia, and in 1941 to Central Asia. Facing antisemitic discrimination and violence in Poland upon their return in 1945 most moved to DP-camps in the American zone of Germany. For the 1930s and 1940s in particular, Wischnitzer's argument for interpreting Jewish migrations as an exceptional story cannot be easily dismissed.

When all other possibilities had been exhausted, the Chinese port city Shanghai became the last safe haven for Jewish refugees from Nazi persecution. Already during the 1920s hundreds of Jews from the former Russian Empire had settled the city. Like the League of Nations mandate Danzig (Gdańsk), Shanghai was an obvious destination for stateless refugees because the international settlement in Shanghai did not belong to any state. Until 1941 more than 10,000 mostly German and Austrian Jews joined the circa 5,000 Jews from the former Russian Empire, often after complicated travels. The German attack against the Soviet Union in June 1941 closed the land route to Shanghai. When the Japanese took full control of the international settlement after the attack on Pearl Harbor in December 1941, all stateless Jewish refugees were forced into a ghetto. Although the conditions were challenging, the Japanese treated the refugees relatively fairly.[39]

Statelessness had affected Jews and members of other transterritorial Diaspora groups such as Armenians and Roma disproportionally after 1918. In the 1940s statelessness emerged as the administrative precursor to systematic genocide. In October 1941, when mobile killing units had

---

[38] Roger Daniels and Otis L. Graham, *Debating American Immigration, 1882–Present* (New York: Rowman & Littlefield, 2001), 25.

[39] *American Jewish Year Book* 42 (1940/41): 618; Marcia Reynders Ristaino, *Port of Last Resort: The Diaspora Communities of Shanghai* (Stanford: Stanford University Press, 2001).

already murdered large numbers of Jews in the western part of the Soviet Union, SS leader Heinrich Himmler officially banned Jewish emigration from Nazi occupied Europe. According to a November 1941 decree, all German Jews who were living outside of Germany or would move (or be deported) to foreign countries, including the areas occupied by German troops after September 1, 1939, were stripped of or would lose their citizenship and property. Thus, all German Jewish deportees were legally deprived of the (rather limited) protection they still enjoyed as German citizens. As Poland, Hungary, and Romania had gradually rendered their Jewish populations stateless in the late 1930s, Vichy France and Italy began to revoke the naturalization of Jews who had immigrated during the 1920s. At some point after 1938, the Nazi planners of the Final Solution recognized the advantage of placing Jews into an extralegal sphere before murdering them. Stateless Jews could be quite legally expropriated, deported to collection centers and ghettos, and eventually murdered. In addition to administratively stripping people of their legal personhood and property before actually killing them, the highly sophisticated organization and unprecedented logistical management of forced migration was another distinctive aspect of the Holocaust. Large numbers of Jewish victims were transported over long distances to the killing sites and extermination camps, usually according to a carefully kept train schedule, some from distant communities in Norway, the Aegean Sea, Tunisia, and even the British Channel Islands.[40]

In the immediate aftermath of the Holocaust, the United States briefly was the sole major center of the Jewish Diaspora – in numerical terms. Most of the 2.6 million Jews remaining in Eastern Europe just after the German defeat lived under Soviet rule. They had escaped persecution or lived in areas never occupied by the German army. Ironically, some of these surviving Jews had been deported as "bourgeois elements" to Stalin's Gulag from Soviet occupied parts of Poland and Lithuania shortly before the German invasion in late June 1941. Israel – home to circa 600,000 Jews in May 1948 – experienced strong immigration in its early years. However, its population only reached two million, surpassing the Jewish community of Greater New York, in the 1960s. From 1950 to 1990 the Soviet Jewish population decreased significantly from two million to about one million. Jewish emigration from the Soviet Union began in the 1970s, especially to Israel and to a lesser extent to the United States. The movement gained

[40] Arendt, *The Origins of Totalitarianism*, 280; Vishniak, *The Legal Status of Stateless Persons*, 24–33; Patrick Weil, *How to be French: Nationality in the Making since 1789* (Durham: Duke University Press, 2008), 107–124; Saul Friedländer, *Nazi Germany and the Jews: The Years of Extermination, 1939–1945* (New York: Harper Collins, 2007), 261–329.

a new momentum in the wake of the dissolution of the Soviet Union in 1991. In 2007, the Jewish population of the successor states of the Soviet Union had dropped to circa 350,000.[41]

CONCLUSION

Were Jewish migrations in the modern era exceptional or typical? Kulischer's claim for assessing Jewish migrations, voluntary and forced, strictly as part of broader movements is indeed compelling. The gradual reinterpretation of the Jewish mass migration from Eastern Europe between 1880 and 1914, as a movement driven by social and economic transformation rather than "the" pogroms, confirms Kulischer's approach. Yet the period between the collapse of the multi-ethnic empires at the end of World War I and the founding of the Jewish state constitutes an exceptional phase in the history of Jewish migration, even if viewed from an overarching perspective, and even in a century marked by mass flight and displacement around the globe. The experience of displaced Jews during the 1920s and especially during the 1930s and 1940s proved the inability of the international system to sufficiently address the plight of refugees. The absurd case of the Polish Jewish expellees, stranded in the no man's land between Nazi Germany and Poland in late October 1938, symbolically illustrates how unwanted refugees and minorities were deprived of a legitimate place and the most basic human rights.

Mass migration and even displacement have long been an integral part of Jewish history and general history. During the twentieth century, Jews were not the only group affected by forced migration and statelessness, not even genocide. But the impact of the dramatic upheavals and transformations the Jewish Diaspora underwent, especially between 1914 and 1948, reached far and beyond the history of an actually small and widely dispersed group. The experience of Jewish migrants during the twentieth century serves as a paradigm to better understand the far-reaching repercussions of the transition from a system of relatively free migration around the globe before 1914 to a system characterized by restrictions imposed by territorial nation-states on cross-border movement, officially recognized "population transfers," and permanent displacement of large numbers of people. The Holocaust illustrates the threat for people who have been (dis-)placed permanently outside of the territorial nation-state system, lacking sufficient legal protection and representation.

[41] William W. Mishell, *Kaddish for Kovno: Life and Death in a Lithuanian Ghetto, 1941–1945* (Chicago: Chicago Review Press, 1988), 9–10; *American Jewish Year Book* 51 (1950): 247; *American Jewish Year Book* 93 (1993): 427; *American Jewish Year Book* 107 (2007): 563.

How can unwanted refugees be better protected? Hannah Arendt was thinking along similar lines in 1940 as the Hilfsverein in 1905. If members of a group, whether they belong to a minority or have been displaced, cannot establish or move to their "own" state, or to a state where they are not treated as an unwanted minority, they require some form of internationally recognized status that provides the same protection as the citizenship of a territorially defined state. Arendt's concept of a "commonwealth of European nations with a parliament of its own" bears a strong resemblance not to the European Union as it emerged during the 1950s but to the system of transterritorially defined group rights in the multi-ethnic empires. Arendt proposed to decouple nations and territorialism. National groups rather than territorial states would have formed her European commonwealth. It remained a utopia. The establishment of a territorial Jewish state solved the predicament of a displaced "people without land" and without citizenship in a post-imperial world defined by territorial statehood. Yet, as a territorial nation-state and a successor state of the British Empire, the Jewish state encountered the same challenges as the nation-states that succeeded the multi-ethnic empires in Eastern Europe twenty years earlier. Since the founding of Israel, non-Jewish Israelis have constituted a minority with an unclear status. Large numbers of Palestinians remain displaced (and overwhelmingly stateless) in refugee camps across the Middle East. Thus in hindsight, the founding of Israel confirmed the norm rather than the exception.[42]

SELECT BIBLIOGRAPHY

Arendt, Hannah. *The Origins of Totalitarianism*. New York: Harcourt, 1951.

Brinkmann, Tobias, ed. *Points of Passage: Jewish Transmigrants from Eastern Europe in Scandinavia, Germany, and Britain, 1880–1914*. New York: Berghahn Books, 2013.

Elias, Nelly. *Coming Home: Media and Returning Diaspora in Israel and Germany*. Albany: SUNY Press, 2008.

Freitag, Gabriele. *Nächstes Jahr in Moskau! Die Zuwanderung von Juden in die sowjetische Metropole 1917–1932*. Göttingen: V&R, 2004.

Gartner, Lloyd, *The Jewish Immigrant in England, 1870–1914*. London: Allen & Unwin, 1960.

Gatrell, Peter. *A Whole Empire Walking: Refugees in Russia during World War I*. Bloomington: Indiana University Press, 1999.

Green, Nancy. *Ready-to-Wear and Ready-to-Work: A Century of Industry and Immigrants in the Women's Garment Trade in Paris and New York*. Durham: Duke University Press, 1997.

Howe, Irving. *Immigrant Jews of New York, 1881 to Present*. New York: Schocken, 1976.

---

[42] Hannah Arendt, "The Minority Question," 130.

Kohn, Jerome and Ron H. Feldman eds. *Hannah Arendt – The Jewish Writings*. New York: Schocken, 2007.

Kulischer, Eugene M. *Europe on the Move: War and Population Changes, 1917–47*. New York: Columbia University Press, 1948.

 Jewish Migrations: Past Experiences and Post-War Prospects. New York: American Jewish Committee, 1943.

Kuznets, Simon. "Immigration of Russian Jews to the United States: Background and Structure," *Perspectives in American History* 9 (1975): 35–124.

Lederhendler, Eli. *Jewish Immigrants and American Capitalism, 1880–1920*. Cambridge: Cambridge University Press, 2009.

Marrus, Michael R. *The Unwanted – European Refugees in the Twentieth Century*. Oxford: Oxford University Press, 1985.

Mirelman, Víctor A. *Jewish Buenos Aires, 1890–1930: In Search of an Identity*. Detroit: Wayne State University Press, 1990.

Polland, Annie and Daniel Soyer, *Emerging Metropolis: New York Jews in the Age of Immigration, 1840–1920*. New York: New York University Press, 2012.

Rechter, David. *The Jews of Vienna and the First World War*. London: Littman, 2001.

Ristaino, Marcia Reynders. *Port of Last Resort: The Diaspora Communities of Shanghai*. Stanford: Stanford University Press, 2001.

Rischin, Moses. *The Promised City: New York's Jews, 1870–1914*. Cambridge: Harvard University Press, 1962.

Roth, Joseph. *Juden auf Wanderschaft*. Berlin: Die Schmiede, 1927.

Ruppin, Arthur. *Soziologie der Juden*. Berlin: Jüdischer Verlag, 1930.

Schechtman, Joseph B. *European Population Transfers, 1939–1945*. New York: Oxford University Press, 1946.

Wells, Allen. *Tropical Zion: General Trujillo, FDR, and the Jews of Sosúa*. Durham: Duke University Press, 2009.

Wertheimer, Jack. *Unwelcome Strangers. East European Jews in Imperial Germany*. New York: Oxford University Press, 1987.

Wischnitzer, Mark. *To Dwell in Safety: The Story of Jewish Migration since 1800*. Philadelphia: Jewish Publication Society, 1948.

 Visas to Freedom: A History of HIAS. Cleveland/New York: The World Publishing Co., 1955.

CHAPTER 34

IN SEARCH OF AUTHENTICITY

Issues of Identity and Belonging in the Twentieth Century

JONATHAN BOYARIN

INTRODUCTION: AUTHENTICITY AS A HUMAN PROBLEM

The choice to begin an essay about the problem of Jewish authenticity with an emphasis on authenticity as a *human* problem is not merely dictated by a concern for establishing at the outset a measure of objectivity. Such a concern, motivated by the desire to avoid a narrow focus on what might or might not turn out to be uniquely or distinctively Jewish, might well be legitimate in itself. For in conventional terms, the "human" is always a broader category of which what is "Jewish" is always a subset. However, the search for authenticity in recent experience, when carried out by individuals or groups conventionally designated for at least some purposes as "Jewish," is not best represented as a Jewish experience *contained within* a human experience. On the contrary, how to be *both* authentically Jewish and authentically human – or whether one must ultimately choose between the primary claims of a particularly Jewish authenticity and those of a generally human authenticity – has itself been one of the key themes of the search for authenticity in modern Jewish history. Perhaps it is more useful – terrifying and repulsive as the notion may be to us, since we are so well aware of the murderous legacy of the treatment of Jews as less or other than human – to think of Jewishness and humanity for the purposes of this essay as forms in a Venn diagram which coincide, to a greater or lesser degree, but never coincide fully, and neither of which is contained within the other.

Posing the question of authenticity as a human question also suggests that it is an existential problem for every member of the species or for each human group. It seems, however, that the problem of authenticity is not in fact universal in human culture. The very least that may be said is that the salience of authenticity varies from period to period, from group to group. Rather, like so many other of our analytical categories, it appears to have at least some significant particular Protestant and modern determinants ("To thine own self be true" taken already by Shakespeare, following the character of Polonius, as both self-evident and hence fatuous).

One initial distinction that seems inevitable separates the possibilities and modalities of *individual* (or personal) authenticity from those of *collective* (or group) authenticity. But this distinction itself may upon reflection seem more authentically "modern" than authentically "Jewish." To be sure, "individuals" as separate persons, with their own realms of moral choice and partially consequent fate, were present in lifeworlds long before the era of Western modernity. Nevertheless, the notion of a fundamental distinction between the individual and the group – and the correlated notion of a basic tension between fidelity to oneself and genuine participation in the group to which one adheres – is, again, closely bound with distinctively Protestant notions of self-making. Thus, the sort of quest represented by a question such as "How can I be 'me' and also be truly Jewish" has a particularly contemporary character. To paraphrase Walter Benjamin, it too often seems that Jewishness has lost its aura of authenticity; and where Benjamin strove to find hope in the loss of aura (Benjamin 2002), most commonly that apparent loss is the occasion for mourning.

Some scholars describe that contemporary situation as postmodern. We need not engage the relation between modernity and postmodernity, or even question too closely the wisdom of deeming a moment in chronological history as "postmodern," to see the value of formulations such as the following. It is part of one of the most sustained analyses of Jewish authenticity to have appeared until now, notable not least because in its very title it acknowledges that there are "Varieties of Authenticity in Contemporary Jewish Identity:"

In a postmodern world, Jewish identity is authentic – true to its own nature – only when it assumes the instability of its own nature … [O]ne can be a Jew only by realizing that one cannot *be* a Jew in an essentialistic sense … Part of authentic Jewish identity is to assume the role of an identity problematizer (Charmé 2000: 149).

The value of this formulation is its forthright acknowledgment that self-reflexive identities are not ipso facto inauthentic, and that indeed, reflexivity may itself be a deeply ingrained aspect of traditional strategies of identity formation. As a general rule, personal responsibility (and hence the exercise of reflexivity) in the expression of strongly grounded collective identities is to be encouraged and might ultimately prove indispensable to collective human survival. That value is weakened, however, to the extent that this author creates a new category of exclusive, "true," or authentic Jewish authenticity, denying in effect (and indeed explicitly) the true Jewishness of those who do not reflexively explore the construction of their own identities. The consequent danger is that individual Jews – especially academics and other intellectuals, operating in secular contexts if not necessarily non-religious in their personal practice – are set up as the standard-bearers of Jewish authenticity in this "postmodern" world. The majority of other Jews – the less or only traditionally learned, religious women, all members of communities who don't agonize over their own Jewishness too much but tend instead to "just do it"– seem to be excluded from this circle.

Identity and authenticity are closely linked in Stuart Charmé's discussion. Indeed, although the present chapter focuses on the question of authenticity, it is often difficult to separate that notion from the perhaps more commonly discussed concept of "identity" (again, at both the group and individual level). "Identity," derived from the Latin *idem*, same, implies a measure of both integrity (something that is well-bounded) and consistency (something that remains intact over time). "Authenticity" is related to the adjective "authentic," derived from the Greek *authentes*, "one acting on one's own authority." In our everyday usage, authenticity is perhaps best glossed as "real being," but this Greek etymology emphasizes the aspect of self-authorizing action or being and hence reinforces the association between personal or group authenticity and achieved identity.

This discussion of the search for authenticity thus may be enriched by critical discourses interrogating identity, many of which have been developed in the context of feminist and post-colonial theories. Perhaps the most powerful strand in those discourses stresses that identities are "constructed," not "natural." Simone de Beauvoir's famous assertion that "one is not born a woman" remains striking no matter how many times we read it, inasmuch as our everyday lifeworld still assumes a powerful and almost unbreakable linkage between sex and gender. One may likewise assert that "one is not born a Jew." It is perhaps a less dramatic formulation, yet it effectively points to the contingency of the notion, still common to folk discourse as well as traditional Jewish legal standards, that birth to a Jewish mother necessarily and sufficiently determines Jewishness.

Other useful tools for thinking about the search for authenticity in terms of contingent selfhood and constructed identities have been developed by scholars identified (sometimes by others, sometimes by themselves) as Jewish, though it often remains an open and vexing question whether their Jewishness informs their engagement with other identity formations and how. Thus, for example, Stephen Greenblatt's exploration of *Renaissance Self-Fashioning* (1980) is emblematic of a turn in cultural and literary history toward understanding that, even in epochs less characterized by obsession with autonomy and personal fulfillment, groups and individuals shaped their own identities in contingent ways that could

not have been foreseen, often ways they themselves only partially comprehended. Accordingly, what might be called a similar concern with "Jewish
self-fashioning" has become part of the agenda of Jewish cultural studies
(whether oriented toward current or historical formations of Jewishness).
Aside from their inherent intellectual vitality, the practical present interest
of such studies is not hard to discern: they reassure scholarly Jews today
that, even in the distant past, rhetorics of naturalized Jewish continuity
often masked profound ruptures and losses, and thus, in short, ours are
not the first generations to have been faced with the task of inventing "how
to be authentically Jewish."

From the ranks of feminist theory comes this key lesson: asserting that
personal and group selves and their identities are "constructed" does not
mean they are not real or, in our terms here, inauthentic. In a series of
key works the philosopher Judith Butler developed notions of iteration
(repetitions of actions, statements, gestures and the like, *not* obsessively or
mechanically but with the cumulative effect of normalizing and stabiliz-
ing identity) and of performance (not in opposition to "natural" behavior
and not necessarily as a sign of dissociation, but in an expanded sphere
of social interaction that negotiates standardized role expectations) that
help constitute a more dynamic notion of authentically inhabiting a given
identity such as Jewishness (Butler 1990, 1993). While some of Butler's
own recent writings make more evident her explicit concerns and associations with Jewishness, these and similar ideas within what is sometimes
called today "performance theory" have been productively applied to the
way Jewishness is also iterated in more conventional performance venues, such as the theater and television (Bial 2005). As Henry Bial points
out, such performances are not merely enactments of Jewishness; for many
Americans, including American Jews, they are likely to serve as models for
how viewers may "act Jewish" in turn.

To be sure, it's not at all clear whether (for example) viewers of Larry
David's series *Curb Your Enthusiasm* in US communities who do not themselves have a strong, distinctive and visible Jewish collective worry about
whether the very explicit, generally unapologetic, and often quite unflat-
tering Jewishness they see "performed" on its episodes is authentic or not.
Some of those viewers are self-identified or identified by others as Jewish,
and hence learning to be Jewish from television; others may merely be
gaining a picture of "what Jews are like."

The authenticity of what is performed does seem to be less salient
in the context of watching *Curb Your Enthusiasm* than it is, for example, with respect to the variety of Eastern European Hasidism promoted
to Jews around the world by today's Chabad/Lubavitch missionaries
(Fishkoff 2003). If that is indeed the case, we are reminded that desire

for authenticity, powerful as it may be in certain historical moments and cultural contexts, is itself a contingent and variable aspect of personal and collective self-fashioning. Yet a recent scholarly volume titled *Inauthentic: The Anxiety over Culture and Identity* (Cheng 2004) takes American Jewish culture as the paradigm case for the problem of authenticity. The cover of that book depicts a Hannukah menorah, all nine candles blazing, set into bases made out of mah-jong tiles. Moreover, the title word "Inauthentic" is set in a mock-Chinese font identified by the author as "Wonton." The book's author, Vincent J. Cheng, refers to himself as a "Chinese boy" and "native Chinese speaker" now married to a Jewish woman. Yet more than his personal identity informs the choice of Chinese and Jewish idioms as his paradigms for the problem of authentic identity in the contemporary United States. Both Chinese Americans and Jewish Americans face particular dilemmas, held up as members of "model minorities" (and thus rewarded for "really being" authentic members of that group) and pressed to conform to the model by becoming more American (whatever that might continue to mean). Model minority status, that is, places Asian Americans and Jews in the double-bind of being neither authentically this nor that. For at least some Asian Americans, the dilemma has been further compounded by the presence of the Jewish model, as they are taught the works of Philip Roth and wonder why their experience, too, is not represented as authentic and canonical American literature (Ling 1987).

Cheng, in *Inauthentic*, adopts a highly skeptical attitude toward the desire for authenticity. He suggests it is illusory, perhaps neurotic, asserting that "with the globalization of our own postmodern era … cultures all grow increasingly to resemble, not distinct and separate uniquenesses, but predictable simulacra of millennial inauthenticity" (Cheng 2004: 5). But to suppose that one may so confidently identify the "inauthentic" necessarily entails that one would recognize the authentic if it were still available. Moreover, if all that globalized culture can produce is indeed "predictable simulacra," why *wouldn't* people yearn for something more authentic, and why should such a yearning be seen as pathological? But Cheng's point is well taken – at least insofar as he reminds us that whatever is found in the search for authenticity is not, just because it is found, in itself authentic. Let me be clear, then: My intent here is not to determine some expressions, productions, or performances of Jewishness in the twentieth century and beyond as authentic, others inauthentic. An exploratory essay such as this one *must* adopt an agnostic stance toward whether there are "authentic" Jewishnesses, let alone what they might be.

More urgently, it is vital to acknowledge at the beginning the highly contingent nature of the themes and examples articulated here. Historians, especially in summary or encyclopedic works, hold both their own and their fellows' work to the standard of a reasonable approximation of the broad outlines of what happened and usually some notion of why. It might well be possible to produce such a history of the search for Jewish authenticity in the modern period, and there would be a number of plausible starting points for such an account.

One could, for example, begin with accounts of what was called at the time, and indeed is still remembered, as the "Jewish Enlightenment" (Feiner 2004), in its movement from Germany in the eighteenth century toward the "less progressive" mass of Yiddish-speaking Jews in the Eastern empires later in the century, and assert that for the first time, Jews were faced with the challenge of determining how to make themselves; how to make themselves *authentically* would then be born as a corollary challenge. But the Jewish Enlightenment was most certainly *not* the first time a Jewish community had to reconstitute itself, and in that process decide what it would be. This was, to cite just one example, the task of those "Hebrews of the Portuguese Nation" who, in Miriam Bodian's words, had to "rejudaize" themselves in seventeenth-century Amsterdam (Bodian 1997, 96).

One could also quite plausibly posit that Jewish authenticity was effectively "lost" (and thus a search had to be launched in order to refind it) in the revolutionary French National Assembly, when the Count of Clermont-Tonnerre declared (famously and, to be sure, quite fatefully), "The Jews should be denied everything as a nation, but granted everything as individuals" (quoted in Mendes-Flohr and Reinharz 2011: 124). Speaking in opposition, the Bishop of Nancy rhetorically asked, "must one admit into the family a tribe that is a stranger to oneself?" (ibid.). Surely the Bishop missed the Count's point: at that moment the categorical distinction between individual Jews and their collective loyalties was starkly posed; those proposed for admission to the "family" were no longer to be tribals. Yet to stress the French Revolution overmuch as a watershed risks, once again, naturalizing Jewish identity prior to that moment – which means assuming precisely that before 1789 the problem of Jewish authenticity had either never appeared or had only been a trivial one. Such an assumption seems premature at best.

Whether or not a synoptic history of discourse on Jewish authenticity is possible, even for the modern period, such a history is not the task undertaken here. Rather, this chapter seeks to clarify why the question of authenticity has been so compelling in recent Jewish experience, and some ways it is possible to study the topic without falling once again into the debate about what is and is not authentically Jewish. Moments, figures and artifacts discussed below have been chosen because they seem ready examples to assist in such clarification. If there is a bias toward recent decades, toward middle-brow and popular culture, and toward Jewish culture in the

United States, that is not because these are the culmination of any grand historical trajectory, but because they may require less exposition before the workings of the search for authenticity can be detected in them. The examples certainly are not and could not possibly be exhaustive, nor are they the same set of examples another writer would choose.

The remainder of this essay comprises four sections. The next section, "What Is Jewish?" is intended to shift the discussion of Jewish identity a bit from the putative Jewishness of persons, and to point out some of the ways that Jewishness pertains to *things* such as food and books (which then may well become the subject of discourse in terms of their "authentic Jewishness"), and also back to the ways Jewish "real being" is inscribed, as it were, upon human bodies through processes such as circumcision. "What Shall Jews Be?" explores various dimensions of Jewishness rhetorically (and problematically) structured as one of *becoming what one already is.* "Can a Jew Be Anything Else?" engages variations on the proposition that persons denominated "Jews" can, in fact, only be authentic when embracing the identity associated with that name. In the concluding section, I reflect briefly on some of the Jew I do.

WHAT IS JEWISH?

Addressing the question of Jewish authenticity to persons – asking, that is, who is authentically Jewish – is, to be sure, a highly charged, rich and troubled question. In certain quite consequential contexts of modern Jewish history, it has been an overtly political one, perhaps nowhere more so than in the Jewish state of Israel since 1948. This section focuses more, however, on material, linguistic, and other cultural markers of Jewishness, and thus it seems more fruitful to ask *what* is Jewish, rather than who. Rather than offering any general criteria for identifying authentically Jewish items, we will take up in turn a number of such markers as exempla of the contest for authenticity.

A first observation is that "authentic" Jewish culture is not necessarily opposed to commercialism. Indeed, and as many have noted, authenticity often becomes a selling point. When it does so, it is often billed (as Dr. Brown's sodas once were) as a "cure for nostalgia." Not for nothing did those soda cans reproduce images of the Brooklyn Bridge, or the iconography of the old seltzer bottles that were once delivered door to door in neighborhoods such as New York's Lower East Side. Indeed, food seems to be an especially receptive field of culture for the association of nourishment, nostalgia, and authenticity. Thus, not so many years ago an entire wall of the Noah's Bagels shop in Albany, California (next to Berkeley) was taken up with a mural of Brooklyn, comprising iconography that ranged from a generic old rabbi to a portrait of Jackie Robinson. That mural effectively reinforced the notion of Noah's Bagels as "being real," suggesting that to bite into one was to transport oneself back to the old country of Brooklyn. More broadly, items of food that Jews shared with their non-Jewish neighbors in pre-migration homelands have, through the alchemy of ethnic nostalgia, become authentically Jewish in the United States. The most spicy example is pastrami.

Debates about authenticity frequently appear in the context of interrupted and "revived" traditions, such as the so-called klezmer revival of the late twentieth century. Even the *name* is new; in Jewish Eastern Europe, there were musicians known as *klezmorim* (singular *klezmer*), but the music they played was in various styles, none of which was designated "klezmer music" per se. Nevertheless, the new name in this case was readily adapted as referring to something that "really is." The authenticity trouble that surrounds the klezmer revival centers instead on choices its performers and advocates must repeatedly make between fidelity to older forms, styles, and arrangements on one hand, and fidelity to the improvisational, multicultural, and crowd-pleasing tendencies that frequently led the earlier performers themselves to borrow, combine, and forge constantly new musical constellations. Happily, for the most part the musicians have come to accept the different forms of authenticity represented by reproduction of older performances and by the generation of new syntheses from a recognizably "klezmer" base.

In the case of other interrupted forms, "religious" criteria and concepts may raise doubts about the authenticity of Jewish tradition. Audiences and tour groups are thus sometimes astonished to see Lower East Side synagogues that are still adorned by murals depicting the twelve signs of the zodiac, known in Yiddish or Ashkenazi Hebrew as *mazoles*. Such depictions go back at least as far as late antique Levantine synagogues, and the tradition had its exemplars in medieval and early modern Europe. Yet somehow it seems to contradict the very notion of Judaism as an ethical monotheism, free from any contamination with notions of astral determinism. In its time – the heyday of late hippie culture in California – the East Bay's "Aquarian Minyan" seemed a strikingly inauthentic attempt to create a space where Jews as Jews could be fully hip, but here it seems are at least some resources for that formation to claim as properly Jewish not only its "minyan" but its "Aquarian" identity as well.

That supposed rock of Jewish identity, the book, can also serve as a contested icon of authenticity, perhaps especially when it appears in translation into a new language that is not traditionally marked as Jewish. For example, the Babylonian Talmud, in the recent edition published by the ArtScroll Mesorah Foundation and known, after a major benefactor, as the Schottenstein Edition, uses the form of the original language edition referred to therein as "the classic Vilna edition" to ground and mitigate the actual radicalism of what it calls its own "annotated, interpretive elucidation, as an aid to Talmud study."[1] Because the "elucidation," presented on pages facing the "Vilna edition" reproductions, takes up much more space than the traditional commentaries it both summarizes and effectively replaces, each column of Hebrew-alphabet Talmudic text requires several pages of elucidation. The publishers of this edition spared no expense, reproducing each "Vilna" page as many times – often five or six – to make sure that the "elucidation" would never appear on its own, without the authenticating anchor of the "classic edition."

To be sure, the human body itself, perhaps most notably that of the newborn infant, is also a material site of contestation about which calls for authenticity, coming from which quarters, are to be heeded. From the perspective of the search for universal human authenticity, when this search is understood as somehow in tension with the particularism of authentic Jewishness, the recent wave of opposition to male circumcision is thus sometimes cast as a refusal to mar a "perfect" infant (J. Boyarin 1996). If new human males are "supposed to" possess a foreskin, then mutilation of a child's genitalia might be understood as making that child less than fully, authentically human. More obviously, for much of Jewish history it is precisely circumcision that has been the inalterable mark of Jewishness, a fact inseparable from the observation that for just as long the term "Jew" has, by default and without further qualification, been taken to refer to a male. Is it in fact the case (as it seems at first consideration) that the "authentic Jewishness" of Jewish women has been less of a theme through even the recent centuries? That seems to be far too broad a conclusion to suggest without further consideration. On the other hand, it seems clear enough that, despite the remarkable prominence of Jewish women in the so-called second wave of feminism (especially in the United States), it has not been easy to find the rhetorical space for simultaneous affirmations of Jewishness and feminism. (Heschel 1983, Antler 2010)

WHAT SHALL JEWS BE?

Notions of authentic Jewishness – who has it, how and where it may have once been possessed, how it was lost (or is in danger of being lost) and how it might be preserved or regained – are intimately related to what Jews are perceived to have been, especially at nodal moments in the past. Recent

---

[1] This text appears on the double title page of each of the 73 volumes, e.g., Tractate Berachos, 1997.

Jewish experience hardly lacks for notions of some time or place when Jews were what they really are; some especially poignant examples come from the cultural history of German Jews in the modern period (Biemann 2009, Brenner 1996).

To be sure, there are also places that are especially charged with the aura of authentic Jewishness. Jerusalem and the Land of Israel are, of course, exemplary in this regard, but they are only in a category of their own from the perspectives of theology and political science. Pilgrimages to Jewish sites of memory (see Nora 1984) may be viewed as trips to the well of Jewishness for those who seek to refresh and revive their identities. These pilgrimages may be made in space, through temporary physical removals to an ancestral old country; both Moroccan Jews and their descendants, and Polish Jews and their descendants, have in recent decades ritualized visits to the old country, often with the primary purpose of rendering homage and drawing blessing at the gravesites of their saints (Kugelmass 1993, Levy 1997). In pilgrimages, authenticity can also be sought through a form of reliving, a temporary "becoming" of the ancestors who experienced critical moments in Jewish history "at that time, at that place." This strategy of seeking and finding fragments of real being can be found, for example, at the ancient Israelite city of Beit Govrin, where tourists have the chance to crawl through narrow underground tunnels designed to allow the city's inhabitants to sneak in and out during a Roman siege (Langfur 1992). But it also characterizes the "March of the Living," in which large contingents of Israeli and Diaspora groups annually come together to visit the most infamous Nazi death camp of Auschwitz (Feldman 2008).

Historiographic and ethnographic reconstructions provide another avenue to authenticity, complementing and sometimes taking the place of any possibility of physical pilgrimage. The very notion of "the world of the shtetl – " the subtitle of Mark Zborowski and Elizabeth Hertzog's 1953 volume *Life Is With People* – encapsulates the formation of a crystallized image of this social form as some fundamental ground, a place and time when Jews were truly themselves, when they possessed the resources for full expression of selfhood and had no substantial motivations to try to be anything less or anything else. Notably, *Life Is With People* is precisely not about any shtetl in particular; indeed, partly for that reason and partly because it works so strenuously to excise the effects of modernization, secularization, urbanization, and migration from its purview, the book has come to be regarded as somehow an inauthentic representation by later scholars of Jewish Eastern Europe.

Nevertheless, the warm response that book received, and the astonishing success of *Fiddler on the Roof* which drew closely on its sensibility, are significant cultural phenomena quite apart from these scholarly evaluations. Book and play both evoked the notion of a cultural world where, instead of the constant tension between the desire for authentic Jewishness and the desire for authentic humanity, "Jew" and "person" are synonymous – or more precisely, where there were a multitude of contexts in which *yid* could mean anyone within earshot, where *mentsh* would most probably indicate a Jew. The world of the shtetl was understood, that is, to have been inhabited by Jewish masses in late-nineteenth- and early twentieth-century Eastern Europe, and for anyone but perhaps an elite, critical intellectual, the experience of the masses was deemed ipso facto authentic. Indeed, the *greater and more general (the less minoritized) the mass, the more authentic was their identity deemed to be.* Hence it is hardly a surprise that Shlomo-Zanvl Rappoport (Sh. An-sky) joined the Socialist Revolutionaries and aimed his attention at the Russian peasant masses before turning his attention to Yiddish culture (Safran 2010). Nor is it to be wondered that Russian-speaking, middle-class Bundist cadre first learned, and then promoted the use of Yiddish rather than Russian among the Jewish working classes – sometimes at cross-purposes to their working-class students who desperately sought to learn Russian (Mendelsohn 1970).

Orthodox Judaism might plausibly be taken as the most authentic form of contemporary Jewish expression according to the criterion of fidelity to ancestral practice, and sometimes it is indeed granted, even by non-Orthodox Jews, the status of the most "real Jewish being" (see Rubel 2010). But, of course, as has become clearer to scholars of modern Jewish history in recent decades but was no secret at the time, the identity of a formation known as Orthodox Judaism arose not as some unchanging conservatism, but precisely in reaction to nineteenth-century movements for reform (Cohen 2002). The supreme irony here (at least, for those who expect that intellectual leadership will be guided by an overarching search for logical consistency) is the radical new formulation of the Hatam Sofer, intended to provide a bulwark for the preservation of current (and not perennial) practice at his time: "Innovation is forbidden according to the Torah."

Not all discourses centered on or closely touching the search for Jewish authenticity assume that this is something that can be achieved; some pose, at least implicitly, the question whether it is possible to "really be" a Jew. Much of the history of Jewishness in recent times has been cast as a story of the attempt to hold onto an authenticity which modernity threatens (and which is thus implicitly understood to be inherently outmoded). Yet much Jewish religious and social thought in the same period incorporates heightened reflection on the grounds of identity itself. The agon of authenticity, when expressed by Jewish thinkers, did not so much reflect a particular Jewish dilemma as the extent to which Jews (including "traditionalist" or "Orthodox" ones) were part and parcel of European modernity. That a radical Polish Hasidic leader who broke with the penchant for courtly grandeur and wonder-working into which tsaddikism had evolved by the early nineteenth century was known simply as "the Jew of Przysucha" was not merely a mark of his humility. It may have been that as well. It is said that he obtained the nickname for his habit, when asked where his Torah insights came from, of responding "a Jew told me," rather than claiming them as original. But, given the centrality of introspection, concern for proper motives in the fulfillment of mitzvot and the struggle to overcome self-delusion in the thought of the Jew and his followers, it is clear that in his case being called a "Jew" was an honorific as well. For that paragon of his generation, the status of Jew was achieved, and certainly not merely ascribed.

If Hasidim, both those like the Jew of Przyucha who lived many generations ago and those who live in flourishing and growing communities in the twenty-first century, have become paradigmatic authentic Jews, it is at least in part because *becoming so* is central to their own religious discipline. And as suggested above, the search for authenticity (of experience and memory, not only of personal identity) is a theme in modern culture that extends well beyond the bounds of the Jewish collective. For Jews as well as their non-Jewish neighbors, fellow-citizens, colleagues, and antagonists, the technologically expanded scope of historical trauma has fueled this authenticity trouble. Notably, the struggle to comprehend the failure of European liberalism to create a democracy sufficiently robust to prevent the horrors inflicted by the Nazis and their fascist allies included Sartre's *Anti-Semite and Jew*. Sartre's analysis famously includes a portrait of the Jew who mistakenly expects or demands to be accepted into liberal civic society solely on the basis of his abstract humanity; in Sartre's view, such an expectation in the end only fuels the anti-Semite's conviction that the Jew is not quite real, certainly not a real Frenchman (or Englishman or German), and cannot be trusted. Just a couple of decades later, a young French Jewish intellectual named Alain Finkielkraut launched his own career with *Le Juif imaginaire* (1983; published in English in 1994). The book was a kind of riposte to Sartre, but more directly aimed at those of his own generation, the "generation of '68," who according to Finkielkraut had falsely and illegitimately claimed the mantle of their suffering Eastern European ancestors. You are not really Jews, or at least not really *those* authentic Jews, Finkielkraut insisted, and once you acknowledge that we can begin to figure out who we really are.

CAN A JEW BE ANYTHING ELSE?

If at certain moments of European and Anglo-Atlantic modernity Jews are taken as untrustworthy, unsolid, anything but real, it seems that in late twentieth-century, multi-ethnic United States culture Jews have also often stood as the very touchstone of down-to-earth, genealogical authenticity (Freedman 2008). That role of Jewish "realness" is both explored and undercut in a key, and famous, scene from Woody Allen's "Annie Hall." To be sure, when Woody Allen's fictional WASP Midwesterner character Annie Hall says to Alvy Singer, the New Yorker played by Allen himself, "You're what Grannie Hall would call 'a real Jew,'" the film makes clear that in Grannie's eyes that's no compliment. Nevertheless it is an appellation that Alvy Singer assumes as his own, almost despite himself. At dinner with the Halls, Grannie looks at Allen's character and he is momentarily transformed precisely into that "real Jew," represented by a red-haired Hasid in full regalia. *That fictional Grannie Hall would not have known what such a "real Jew" looks like*, but both Woody Allen and his character Alvy do, and they take the opportunity offered by the magic of film literally to model, to try on for a moment, such Jewish authenticity for display to the audience as well. Moreover, while nothing in the film suggests that the character of Alvy maintains any distinctive practices relating to strictures of Judaism, in the same dinner scene he is nevertheless shown straining to encompass a "Gentile" diet, as he forces himself to compliment the meal: "Great ham!" Again, the audience is expected to recognize a residual distaste for ham, that paradigmatic non-kosher food, as part and parcel of Alvy Singer's "real Jewishness" despite himself. This might, indeed, be one way to assay a summary characterization of the figure of the modern Jewish anti-hero of literature and film, a figure through which burns satirical and sharp ethnographic commentary on the dilemma of the simultaneous demands for universally human and ethnically particular authenticity. This anti-hero cannot become really himself (and such representations are almost inevitably of male figures) as long as he is limited by his Jewishness; nor can he escape the Jewishness of his real self. Here as elsewhere in his work, Woody Allen plays out (whether he knows the phrase or not) the theme of what is called *dos pintele yid*, the little core or essence, the jot of ineradicable Jewishness understood to be a fact of birth.

If a Jew can never stop being a Jew – or even if, in a somewhat more moderate formulation, some fundamental part of one's true being is denied when Jewishness is not socially expressed – then by definition, "assimilation" to a majoritarian or otherwise more powerful "non-Jewish culture" is an inauthentic act. And indeed, to the extent that, for many centuries, and by both Jews and non-Jews, Jewishness has ultimately been defined as a genealogical condition, the general consensus has probably been that a Jew can indeed never stop being a Jew.

Yet the picture changes somewhat if we adopt Butler's language and view Jewishness not as an essence but as a performance (without any connotations of inauthenticity necessarily attached to that designation). If Jewishness is understood not as an invariant component of the distinctive being of some (always a small minority) members of *homo sapiens*, but rather as the covering concept for a range of behaviors, idioms, associations, rhetorics and the like, it might make sense to ask not only "what is Jewish?" but also "when is a Jew?" From the common perspective, in which Jewishness is "really" an invariant component of personhood, someone who moves in society without Jewish associations attached to her person is said to be "passing," that is, suppressing her Jewishness in an inauthentic way. Jewish "passing" (in this respect, quite closely analogous to the passing behavior attributed to "African-Americans" or "homosexuals") is usually regarded as a distinctive feature of modernity, on the assumption that in some vaguely specified traditional culture which, whenever it putatively existed, preceded and contrasted sharply with modernity. But we know that Western modernity is hardly the first time and place where Jewishness has not been consistently salient in public situations. Thus, Judah al-Harizi, "writing early in the thirteenth century somewhere in the Arabic-speaking Middle East," described a confrontation he and his friends had one day with an astrologer by the city gate:

I suggested to my friends that we test his powers by agreeing on a question among ourselves: When will the Jews be restored from their exile, and when will the Jewish kingdom be restored? When our turn came, we offered him a good fee if he could tell both the question and the answer. The astrologer ... turned a furious face on us and exclaimed: "[Y]ou are neither Muslims nor Christians, but members of a despised and lowly people! Could you be Jews?" (quoted in Scheindlin 2002: 314).

As Raymond Scheindlin accurately notes in conveying this rich story, one of the reasons the story is remarkable from our perspective is that the Jewishness of al-Harizi and his friends was not immediately obvious in this pre-modern, multi-religious world. It is hard nevertheless not to read a measure of Jewish pride, and indeed of youthful braggadocio, in the young friends' decision to raise the stakes by demanding that the astrologer guess their question, and by structuring their question so that a successful guess would in fact reveal their Jewishness. To be sure, the point is not that al-Harizi and his friends would likely have conceived Jewishness as a matter of performance, nor even less that they would have thought of themselves as sometimes Jewish, sometimes not. Yet the anecdote stands as a worthwhile reminder that exercising the choice whether or not to express Jewishness in a given context is neither one that Jews have first had to confront since emancipation, nor inevitably a sign of inauthenticity.

That reminder is particularly pertinent to the recent scholarly exchanges concerning Jews and the "whiteness" question in the United States (see Brodkin 1998, Goldstein 2006). The primary lesson of this scholarship is that, in the course of Jews' absorption into a society already defined by a sharp dichotomy between white and black "races," the ultimate placement of Jews in that racialized scheme was hardly a foregone conclusion. More complex, and more controversial, is the suggestion (most famously made by the political scientist Michael Rogin, 1996) that Jewish performers achieved whiteness by the adoption of blackface – thus, as it were, at once borrowing or stealing the aura of authenticity from African Americans, and making a strong assertion of their own whiteness by demonstrating the need to artificially blacken themselves in order to "perform" blackness. Such critical scholarship certainly helps dispel notions of a golden age of Black–Jewish understanding sometime earlier in the twentieth century, based on the mutual sympathies of two peoples whose common experiences of shared oppression gave them special means of conveying to each other their genuine humanity. It should not, however, entirely overshadow another impression from the past which still seems valid – that it was often precisely in the expressions and experiences of subaltern groups such as African Americans and Native Americans that Jewish immigrants and their descendants (in this respect like many other Euro-Americans) sought the wellsprings of authentic America.

Surely, even Al Jolson's character in *The Jazz Singer*, Rogin's key text for the exploration of Jewishness being safely made American through and, so to speak, on top of Blackness, by no means hides his Jewishness. The camera reminds us that it is precisely to his Jewish mother, sitting adoringly in the audience, that he sings "Mammy," not to some generic mother associated with the flag and apple pie. Whether Jewishness is regarded as ultimately escapable or not, a certain strand in American discourse regards Jewishness itself, in its open expression and especially on its own turf, as one of several touchstones for real being in America. An expression of this in early twentieth-century Progressive writing was Hutchins Hapgood's *Spirit of the Ghetto*, which begins with a quantitative assertion about the amount of "life" in the Jewish immigrant quarter of New York: "No part of New York has a more intense and varied life than the colony of Russian and Galician Jews who live on the east side and who form the largest Jewish city in the world" (Hapgood 1902: 9). Notably, although the assertion of Jewish liveliness is a standard trope for the period, and although Hapgood also refers to the racial characteristics of the Jews, these are by no means immutable in his account. He describes the passage of the immigrant boy to Americanization as he goes to school and "achieves a growing comprehension and sympathy with the independent, free, rather skeptical spirit of the American boy; he rapidly imbibes ideas about social equality and contempt for authority, and tends to prefer Sherlock Holmes to Abraham as a hero" (Hapgood 1902: 24). Far from true identity being frozen or fixed here, Hapgood's account encompasses both the possibility of enhanced "traditional" liveliness and genuine mutability in changed situations.

Almost a century later, Jewishness appears on display in television's *Seinfeld*, transported from the Lower East Side to the Upper West Side. In one of the early episodes of the show, Jerry Seinfeld (playing "Jerry") and Jason Alexander (playing George Costanza) pitch to network executives a "show about nothing." We are given to understand that this is an apt characterization of *Seinfeld* itself. It's just these people, living their lives, some but not all "Jewish" lives, only some of whose moments are distinctively marked by that Jewishness. *Seinfeld*'s producer, Larry David, went on to make the series *Curb Your Enthusiasm*, where the Jewish themes are much more central and much more explicitly subject to Larry David's particular brand of satire. But to the question "Is *Seinfeld* a Jewish Series?" (Stratton 2000), perhaps one good answer is that its Jewishness is tied to the theme of its being "about nothing." If Jewishness is one of the manifestations of real being in contemporary America, then a refusal of the style of allegory, in which "*this* is [always] a story about *that*" (Clifford 1986) and the message is always deferred, might be taken as a mark of Jewishness that supersedes, for example, the ambiguous ethnicity of George's last name.

The theme of Jewish being as real, material, unmediated, or non-allegorical is closely related to the traditional Christian trope of Jewish "carnality," a charge addressed at once to supposed Jewish obsessions with the physical, and to the alleged Jewish penchant for literal reading – both linked closely to the struggle between nascent rabbinic Judaism and the early Church over the "fleshly" versus "spiritual" inheritances of the divine promise to Abraham and his children (D. Boyarin 1993). Although logically inconsistent, it is far more than a mere historical irony that traditional anti-Jewish rhetoric came to see this Jewish carnality as an inherited characteristic, something Jews could not escape if they wanted to. This process, by which the supposed "carnality" of Jewish particularism was itself somatized into a pseudo-biological fact, might be identified as a promising starting point for understanding the relationship between "traditional" anti-Judaism and racial antisemitism. In the early decades of the twentieth century, it was in any case hardly uncommon for Jewish apologists to proclaim their authentic Jewishness in terms of inheritance – not cultural inheritance, not inheritance of ancestral witness (passed down orally from generation to generation) to the revelation at Sinai, but because of some quantum of "memory" inherited as if genetically. Thus a theory of race memory fundamentally underlies Freud's late work *Moses and Monotheism*:

[T]here exists an inheritance of memory – traces of what our forefathers experienced, quite independently of direct communication and of the influence of education by example. When I speak of an old tradition still alive in a people, of the formation of a national character, it is such an inherited tradition, and not one carried on by word of mouth, that I have in mind (quoted in Rubinstein 2010).[2]

If Freud, like the pioneering cultural anthropologist Franz Boas and so many other foundational Central European Jewish intellectuals, was a "secular Jewish heir to the German Enlightenment" (Rubinstein 2010: 3), both he and Boas struggled as well with a different German intellectual tradition, the notion of authentic national culture and identity articulated and passed down from such earlier, non-Jewish Germanophone intellectuals as Herder and the von Humboldt brothers. It is this Romantic tradition, and not the heritage of Enlightenment, that led Freud to assert that he was "in his essential nature a Jew" (ibid.) Indeed, perhaps one useful distinction we might make between "modern" and "postmodern" approaches to the question of authenticity is to remember modernity as an ethos where it was still possible for a secular intellectual – indeed the very paradigm of the self-analytical ego – to write in a wholly unironical way about what he was in his essence, about his own authentic Jewish being.

But the context of that utterance by Freud – a preface to the Hebrew-language edition of *Totem and Taboo* – is significant as well. The effort to revive the Hebrew language and make it adequate to modern daily life, culture, and thought were key intellectual tasks of the Jewish nationalist project known as Zionism. To be sure, the turn toward Hebrew was fueled by dreams of restoration, even in modern form, of the independent biblical Jewish kingdoms. It was also driven by the rejection of what Zionists understood to be all of the pathological aspects of Diaspora Jewish expression. These ranged from the Yiddish language (denigrated as a bastard *zhargon* of illegitimate descent, neither a properly Jewish language nor the proper form of any modern European language) to the supposedly "abnormal" family structure of Eastern European Jewry (Diamond 1957). However, in the Zionist search for Jewish authenticity, not all that was old nor all that was of the Diaspora was rejected. Yemenite Hebrew, for

---

[2] Rubinstein's study *Members of the Tribe: Native America in the Jewish Imagination* is another recent study that might be glossed as an account of the search for American authenticity on the part of American Jews. The question of Freud, race, and Jewishness is analyzed in Eliza Slavet's recent *Racial Fever: Freud and the Jewish Question* (2009).

example, was treasured as having preserved the ancient forms more closely than any other living tradition of Hebrew pronunciation. Indeed the Yemenites become, for certain purposes in Zionist culture, the successfully authentic ancestors that the "shtetl Jews" (who were the actual ancestors of the Zionist pioneers) failed to be. Nor was the Zionist search for authentic models of Jewishness in the present restricted to those designated as Jews now; famously, members of the Second Aliyah looked to contemporary Bedouins as the living exemplars of patriarchal Israelite forms of being.

Zionism is not now and never was a monoform movement. Yet a common theme running through the many stripes of Zionist ideology and identity formation is the notion that – whether on racial, religious, historical or any other conceivable grounds – in the end Jews cannot be anything else but Jews, and that Jews can most truly be themselves by themselves. Nor is this Zionist conviction to be found only among those who call themselves Jews; it can also be a "non-Jewish" view of Jewish authenticity, as articulated for example in George Eliot's classic 1876 novel *Daniel Deronda* (Mufti 2007).

Yet the call to Jewish authenticity in post-emancipation discourse is by no means limited to Zionism, nor has the heritage of the romantic and collectivist strand in European thinking about nation and identity only taken the form of the Zionist call for separation, ingathering and territorially based national independence. Much more generally, Jewish loyalty (one form of authenticity) has been repeatedly understood as in agonistic tension with loyalty to oneself, even as the perquisites of communal identification have retained a good deal of informal vitality. That collective loyalty has been and continues to be identified in various manifestations, such as retaining the use of Jewish languages and other forms of communal expression, passing on consciousness of Jewishness to one's children, maintaining the discipline of Jewish endogamy, or simply refusing the formal rituals that mark exit from "the Jewish faith." Persisting in these forms of "authentic" Jewish expression as a response to the call of authenticity is presumed to accompany sacrifice of short-term, material or social interest, and actions taken by Jewish individuals in pursuit of those worldly interests seem inherently to call for some kind of apologetic. Heinrich Heine famously rationalized his baptism as his "entry ticket into European society." The quip was certainly a nod to his Jewish brethren, suggesting that in his heart Heine remained one of them, and a good deal of his literary production was to reinforce that implicit claim still to belong. In the retrospective of twentieth-century European history, it may seem of course that such an entry ticket was only valid for a time. Yet if we resist that retrospective, what appears most remarkable is that so overtly *inauthentic* (we would more commonly say in this context, "insincere") a conversion could have been socially effective. One might, that is, profitably examine the search for convention in modern Jewish history, and not merely the search for authenticity.

Yet as we have seen, at least one strand in thinking about Jewish authenticity insists that conventionality, a Jewishness that is taken for granted, unreflective, or essentialized, is precisely inauthentic. Taken a bit further, this may lead to the suggestion that authentic "Jewishness" ultimately has nothing to do with either genealogy or whether or not one happens to be self-identified or identified by others as a "Jew." That, at least, is the thrust of a provocative text by the French philosopher Jean-François Lyotard (1990). Lyotard argued that the politics of the German Martin Heidegger should be debated not in terms of Heidegger's relation to upper-case Jews (that is, to a defined set of people with a particular culture and history) but to all of the 'jews,' that is, all of those categorically abjected by normative European society. This formulation would seem precisely to obviate the possibility of a particularist Jewish authenticity (and hence be antithetical to Jewish identification), and indeed it veers closely toward the ancient Pauline strategy of denying Israel in the flesh in favor of the (potentially) universal Israel in the spirit. On the other hand, the strategy of generalizing Jewishness (jewishness?) beyond tribal boundaries is not merely an imposition from "outside" the boundaries of majuscule Jewishness, but has sometimes been adopted by those born, raised, vilified, and threatened as Jews in the name of their own upper-case Jewishness. Such, for example, was the thrust of the Trotsykist Isaac Deutscher's famous post-war essay "The Non-Jewish Jew" (1968).

Concomitant with the discourses about first, whether it is possible to surrender Jewishness, second, whether it is possible to "really be" a Jew, and third, whether the truest "jews" are all the wretched of the earth (whether Jewish or not), is another that should be touched on at least briefly here. The question this fourth discourse centers on is whether it is possible to "become Jewish." Are converts regarded, by their families or their adopted Jewish communities, as "truly" Jewish? Curiously, this is one area where traditional rabbinic strictures insisting that the convert must never be reminded of that status and always spoken of as Jewish, suggest a greater degree of personal identity choice than do those folkways that persist in demarcating converts as somehow other (less or more!) than fully and solely Jewish. In a further remarkable development, some converts have no interest in that status being suppressed. They do not wish to "pass" as genealogically Jewish; it is their particular trajectory that marks their own variety of Jewish authenticity. This is perhaps best indicated by a naming practice that is, as far as I know, novel and that would otherwise seem trivial. As is well known, converts conventionally take a Hebrew name and then add the designation "son of/daughter of Sarah" or "son of/ daughter of Abraham," as contextually appropriate. Since there are Jewish parents named Sarah and Abraham, the status of a convert is not necessarily indicated by this nomenclature. But at least once I have heard such an individual called to the Torah (in a modern Orthodox, rather than a liberal congregation) as "x, son of Abraham Our Father." This clearly marks the convert as such, and even more, it boldly asserts an unmediated descent (according to the promise or according to the flesh, it becomes impossible to say) from the "father" of all Jews.

CONCLUSION: (SOME OF) THE JEW I DO

The reflections above are those of an anthropologist trained in the Boasian tradition, with all its internal contradictions, the most salient of which here is the combination of a profound respect for cultural difference combined with a deep skepticism in the face of essentialist claims, especially since the line separating "my culture" from "my race" cannot always be drawn as neatly as that tradition would like (Michaels 1995). The anthropological mode of self-making does not, perhaps, force one to decide once and for all whether one's identity is natural or constructed, authentically grounded or haphazardly patched together – but it does force one to acknowledge that each of these characterizations is pertinent to the question of identity, to greater and lesser degrees, varying from time to time and from situation to situation. At a more general level, and in an attempt to produce some specificity while evading rank or arbitrary essentialism, Jewishness may be defined "polythetically," as a fluctuating combination of some set of elements taken as central, such as Torah, God, and peoplehood (Satlow 2006). Yet such efforts are almost always betrayed by a lingering normatizing impulse, such as the exclusion from the definition of contemporary Jewishness of so-called Messianic Jews. The alternative most ready to hand, a performance or discourse-based notion of Jewish authenticity, yields the intellectual benefit of opening our vision beyond the limits set by our preconceived notions, formed as we formed our bonds with our parents, teachers, and colleagues (see Aviv and Shneer 2005). Pushed to the limit, however, the notion that "Jewish is as Jewish does" risks making Jewishness an empty concept. Or at least it risks making Jewishness absolutely whatever anyone wants it be; it must be added, however, that why anyone wants to be Jewish, or wants certain things to be identified as Jewish, remains a rich and fruitful question.

Let the last word belong to another name. If, as Rachel Rubinstein has recently documented, cross-identification of American Jewish immigrants with native Americans has been one of the laboratories in which these immigrants tried to work through the problem of remaining authentically Jewish while becoming real Americans, the vanishing point of authentic Jewishness – as a goal and as a problem–may well be hinted at by Franz Kafka's "wish to be a red Indian" (1971: 390):

If one were only an Indian, instantly alert, and on a racing horse, leaning against the wind, kept on quivering jerkily over the quivering ground, until one shed one's spurs, for there needed no spurs, threw away the reins, for there needed no reins, and hardly saw that the land before one was smoothly shorn heath when horse's neck and head would be already gone.

Then, at last, the spurs to fulfill an authentic identity would no longer be needed, for one would be that Indian without thinking about being an Indian; one would not need to be reined in from the temptation to be anything else, inauthentically, for one would always be too totally taken up with racing straight ahead, together with the horse; and nothing more would need to be said.

But, as it happens, one is not born an Indian.

SELECT BIBLIOGRAPHY

Antler, Joyce 2010. "We Were Ready to Turn the World Upside Down: Radical Feminism and Jewish Women." In *A Jewish Feminine Mystique? Jewish Women in Postwar America*. Edited by Hasia R. Diner, Shira Kohn, and Rachel Kranson, 210-233. New Brunswick, NJ: Rutgers University Press, 2010.

Aviv, Caryn and David Shneer 2005. *New Jews: The End of the Jewish Diaspora*. New York: New York University Press.

Baumann, Zygmunt 1988. "Exit Visas and Entry Tickets: Paradoxes of Jewish Assimilation," *Telos* 77: 45–77.

Benjamin, Walter 2002. *The Arcades Project*. Translated by Howard Eiland and Kevin McLaughlin. Cambridge: Harvard University Press.

Bial, Henry 2005. *Acting Jewish: Negotiating Ethnicity on the American Stage and Screen*. Ann Arbor: The University of Michigan Press.

Biemann, Asher 2009. *Inventing New Beginnings: On the Idea of Renaissance in Modern Judaism*. Stanford: Stanford University Press.

Bodian, Miriam 1997. *Hebrews of the Portuguese Nation: Conversos and Community in Early Modern Amsterdam*. Bloomington: Indiana University Press.

Boyarin, Daniel 1993. *Carnal Israel: Reading Sex in Talmudic Culture*. Berkeley: University of California Press.

Boyarin, Jonathan 1996. *Thinking in Jewish*. Chicago: Chicago University Press.

Brenner, Michael 1996. *The Renaissance of Jewish Culture in Weimar Germany*. New Haven: Yale University Press.

Brodkin, Karen 1998. *How Jews Became White Folks and What that Says about Race in America*. New Brunswick, NJ: Rutgers University Press.

Butler, Judith 1993. *Gender Trouble: Feminism and the Subversion of Identity*. New York: Routledge.

———. 1990. *Bodies That Matter: On the Discursive Limits of "Sex."* New York: Routledge.

Charmé, Stuart 2000. "Varieties of Authenticity in Contemporary Jewish Identity." *Jewish Social Studies* 6, no. 2: 133–155.

Cheng, Vincent J. 2004. *Inauthentic: The Anxiety over Culture and Identity*. New Brunswick, NJ: Rutgers University Press.

Clifford, James 1986. "On Ethnographic Allegory." In *Writing Culture: The Poetics and Politics of Ethnography*. Edited by James Clifford and George Marcus, 98-121. Berkeley: University of California Press.

Cohen, Richard I. 2002. "Urban Visibility and Biblical Visions: Jewish Culture in Western and Central Europe in the Modern Age." In *Cultures of the Jews: A New History*. Edited by David Biale, 731–796. New York: Schocken Books.

Deutscher, Isaac 1968. *The Non-Jewish Jew and Other Essays*. New York: Hill and Wang.

Diamond, Stanley 1957. "Kibbutz and Shtetl: The History of an Idea." *Social Problems* 5, no. 2: 71–99.

Feiner, Shmuel 2004. *The Jewish Enlightenment*. Philadelphia: University of Pennsylvania Press.

Feldman, Jackie 2008. *Above the Death Pits, Beneath the Flag: Youth Voyages to Poland and the Performance of the Israeli National Identity*. New York: Berghahn Books.

Finkielkraut, Alain 1994. *The Imaginary Jew*. Lincoln: The University of Nebraska Press.

Fishkoff, Sue 2003. *The Rebbe's Army: Inside the World of Chabad-Lubavitch*. New York: Schocken Books.

Freedman, Jonathan 2008. *Klezmer America: Jewishness, Ethnicity, Modernity*. New York: Columbia University Press.

Goldstein, Eric 2006. *The Price of Whiteness: Jews, Race, and American Identity*. Princeton: Princeton University Press.

Hapgood, Hutchins. *The Spirit of the Ghetto; Studies of the Jewish Quarter in New York*. New York: Funk & Wagnalls, 1902.

Heschel, Susannah, ed. *On Being a Jewish Feminist*. New York: Schocken Books, 1983.

Kafka, Franz. *The Complete Stories*. New York: Schocken Books, 1971.

Kugelmass, Jack 1993. "The Rites of the Tribe: The Meaning of Poland for American Jewish Tourists." *YIVO Annual* 21: 395–453.

Langfur, Stephen. *Confession from a Jericho Jail*. New York: Grove Weidenfeld, 1992.

Levy, André 1997. "To Morocco and Back: Tourism and Pilgrimage among Moroccan-Born Israelis." In *Grasping Land: Space and Place in Contemporary Israeli Discourse and Experience*. Edited by Eyal Ben-Ari and Yoram Bilu, 25–46. Albany, NY: State University of New York Press.

Ling, Amy. "I'm Here: An Asian American Woman's Response." *New Literary History* 19, no. 1, Feminist Directions (1987): 151–160.

Lyotard, Jean-François 1990. *Heidegger and "the jews."* Minneapolis, MN: University of Minnesota Press.

Mendelsohn, Ezra 1970. *Class Struggle in the Pale: The Formative Years of the Jewish Workers' Movement in Tsarist Russia*. Cambridge: Cambridge University Press.

Mendes-Flohr, Paul and Jehuda Reinharz 2011. *The Jew in the Modern World: A Documentary History*, third edition. New York: Oxford University Press.

Michaels, Walter Benn 1995. *Our America: Nativism, Modernism, and Pluralism* Durham: Duke University Press, 1995.

Mufti, Aamir 2007. *Enlightenment in the Colony: The Jewish Question and the Crisis of Postcolonial Culture*. Princeton: Princeton University Press.

Nora, Pierre 1984. *Les lieux de mémoire*. Paris: Gallimard.

Rogin, Michael 1996 *Blackface, White Noise: Jewish Immigrants in the Hollywood Melting Pot*. Berkeley: University of California Press.

Rubel, Nora 2010. *Doubting the Devout: The Ultra-Orthodox in the Jewish American Imagination*. New York: Columbia University Press.

Rubenstein, Rachel 2010. *Members of the Tribe: Native America in the Jewish Imagination*. Detroit: Wayne State University Press.

Safran, Gabriella 2010. *Wandering Soul: The Dybbuk's Creator, S. An-Sky*. Cambridge: Belknap Press of Harvard University Press.

Sartre, Jean-Paul 1965. *Anti-Semite and Jew*. New York: Schocken Books.

Satlow, Michael 2006. *Creating Judaism: History, Tradition, Practice*. New York: Columbia University Press.

Scheindlin, Raymond P. 2002. "Merchants and Intellectuals, Rabbis and Poets: Judeo-Arabic Culture in the Golden Age of Islam." In *Cultures of the Jews: A New History*, ed. David Biale, 313–386. New York: Schocken Books.

Slavet, Eliza. *Racial Fever: Freud and the Jewish Question*. New York: Fordham University Press, 2009.

Stratton, Jon 2000. *Coming Out Jewish*. New York: Routledge.

CHAPTER 35

GENDER AND THE RE-MAKING OF MODERN JEWRY

NAOMI SEIDMAN

The recent contributions of feminist history and gender studies are evident in every area and period of Jewish studies from biblical studies to contemporary popular culture, but perhaps nowhere more so than in modern Jewish history. For researchers interested in sources that record women's experience, the modern period offers an abundance of material, something less true for earlier periods; it is the very mark of modernity that women's voices begin to be heard. Just as importantly, modernity can be productively conceived as the arena for Jewish gender transformations, in which traditional sexual, marital, and gender ideals and practices gave way to radically new models. Modernity is also the matrix for the emergence of feminism, including the second-wave American feminism in which Jewish women played a prominent role, and which forms the immediate background to the academic feminism that has transformed Jewish Studies. Feminist and gender approaches to Jewish modernity have not only contributed new insights into the range of modern Jewish experience, they have also transformed the field, changing the ways that such central concepts as emancipation, assimilation, modernization, and modernity itself are understood. It is now abundantly clear that even those aspects of Jewish modernization that may seem tangential to the question of Jewish gender – urbanization, secularization, immigration, acculturation, new religious movements, nationalism – were experienced differently by Jewish women and men, and contributed to new formations of sex and gender. The transformation of Jewish gender in modernity should thus be understood as a product of both ideological shifts and historical contingencies, involving new norms and models of gender and sexuality as well as historical forces that shaped the lives of men and women in different ways.

The first gender readings of modern Jewish history emerged from the double context of feminist activism and women's history; landmarks include such influential works as Marion Kaplan's *The Making of the Jewish Middle Class* (1991) and Paula Hyman's *Gender and Assimilation in Modern Jewish History* (1995).[1] Building on the work of Kaplan, Hyman argued that

---

[1] Marion Kaplan, *The Making of the Jewish Middle Class: Women, Family, and Identity in*

"such fine historians as Michael Meyer and Jacob Katz" had misread the phenomenon of assimilation by ignoring the "persistence of Jewish ritual and of the expression of religiosity among Jewish women in assimilated families."[2] Such misreadings emerged from their narrow focus either on male experience or on the unrepresentative case of the "salon Jewesses" of late eighteenth-century Germany; in Meyer and Katz, this small group of women, with their intermarriages and conversions, stands in for "the vulnerability of Jewish women to the blandishments of secular Western culture."[3] Hyman argues that, more typically, "middle-class gender norms of behavior eroded traditional patterns of Jewish practice among men while facilitating a measure of Jewish ritual observance among women."[4] German Jewish women of the imperial era were thus, as Kaplan sees it, both "powerful agents of class formation and acculturation" and "determined upholders of tradition."[5] These two apparently contradictory functions – of acculturation and of conserving tradition – were in fact intricately connected. German Jewish women conserved religious traditions not because – as the reigning discourse had it – as women they were "naturally spiritual," but by virtue of their very acculturation to German bourgeois ideologies that linked spirituality with femininity and the domestic sphere. Acculturation and traditionalism, in Kaplan's analysis of the German-Jewish bourgeoisie and Hyman's reading of "the paradoxes of assimilation," are not in mutual contradiction but rather mutually implicated, when one takes not male but female experience as the representative model.

Hyman's insight about the paradoxical nature of assimilation in contributing to Jewish women's religious practice, as the chapters in her book on Eastern European and American immigrant cultural formations demonstrate, does not illuminate the full range of Jewish women's responses to modernity. In Eastern Europe, Hyman points out, *embourgeoisement* was not a cultural or – more to the point – economic option for the urbanizing and proletarianizing masses, even if German-Jewish cultural models held sway for the westernizing merchant class and for the maskilic (Jewish Enlightenment) avant-garde, which looked westward to Berlin for literary and social inspiration. Jewish Eastern Europe did not generally

---

Imperial Germany (Oxford: Oxford University Press, 1991); Paula Hyman, *Gender and Assimilation in Modern Jewish History* (Seattle: University of Washington Press, 1995).

[2] Hyman, *Gender and Assimilation*, 21.

[3] Hyman, *Gender and Assimilation*, 21. Hyman cites Michael A. Meyer, *The Origins of the Modern Jew* (Detroit: Wayne State University Press, 1967), 85–114, and Jacob Katz, *Out of the Ghetto* (Cambridge: Harvard University Press, 1973), 56, 120.

[4] Hyman, *Gender and Assimilation*, 25.

[5] Kaplan, *The Making of the Jewish Middle Class*, 11.

have the luxury of producing "angels in the house," or a discourse which saw women "as the linchpin of cultural transmission, as they were in the West."[6] Rather, a submerged continuity between traditional and modernizing cultural patterns shaped gender roles in the post-traditional period. Speaking of the concerted attempts in the late nineteenth and early twentieth century of Jewish girls and women to acquire a secular education, Hyman writes: "Trained by the gender division of traditional Jewish society to take the initiative, at least economically; respected for their abilities to manage; aware of the value attached to Jewish learning, from which they were largely excluded – Jewish girls often hungered for education and dedicated themselves to acquire it."[7] Thus, while conditions in Central Europe conspired to domesticate women, conditions in Eastern Europe worked rather to produce publicly active and often politically radicalized women, both in Eastern Europe and in its American Diaspora. Exploring Eastern European modernization from the perspective of new patterns of women's readership, Iris Parush details the ways that the exclusion of women from Jewish learning worked to speed their modernization, as an effect of what Parush terms "the benefit of marginality." As Parush writes,

The very inferiority of women within the gender hierarchy [of traditional Eastern European Jewish society] granted them a considerable degree of freedom. With nineteenth-century European Jewish society undergoing processes of secularization and modernization, the exclusion of women from Torah study and from the public religious sphere, and the redirection of them to "inferior" forms of study and reading, turned out to be a source of advantage and of empowerment.[8]

Eastern European Jewish women, in Parush's view, were well positioned to function as the very engine of Jewish secularization and modernization, a role they fulfilled less by the transformation or reversal of traditional gender roles than by the mobilization and dialectical redirection of traditional patterns for newly secular purposes.

As this brief summary has no doubt signaled, the study of Jewish gender, from its beginnings in feminist scholarship and activism of the 1970s and 1980s and until the present, has taken women as a central focus – justifiably, given the neglect of women that preceded and impelled this field of study. But important research has been done, as well, in sexuality studies, with such works as David Biale's *Eros and the Jews* (1992) focusing on

---

[6] Hyman, *Gender and Assimilation*, 92.

[7] Hyman, *Gender and Assimilation*, 75.

[8] Iris Parush, *Reading Jewish Women: Marginality and Modernization in Nineteenth-Century Eastern European Jewish Society*, trans. Saadiya Sternberg (Waltham, MA: Brandeis University Press, 2004), 63.

the role changing sexual patterns played alongside evolving gender models in the modernizing projects of the Jewish Enlightenment. This expanded focus has often bolstered feminist insights. Thus, in a chapter on "Eros and Enlightenment" (originally published in 1986), Biale argues against the assumption that the Eastern European Haskalah (Jewish Enlightenment) lobbied to reform the practice of early, arranged marriage because they favored individual choice, women's equality, or erotic freedom. In Biale's view, the maskilim, or Enlightenment reformers, wished not so much to liberate Jewish sexuality from traditional constraints as to subject it to a new set of bourgeois proprieties; in emulating European models, Biale writes, the Enlighteners attempted to replace the "coarse" and mercenary approach of traditional Ashkenazic culture to sexual matters with a bourgeois respectability:

While the maskilim directed their polemics against a specifically Jewish system of marriage and family, their goal was the same as that of other nineteenth-century advocates of domesticity – upholding such values as privacy and chastity. Their solution to what they saw as the promiscuity and sexual dysfunction of traditional Jewish society was the imposition of bourgeois constraints upon desire.[9]

The argument put forward by Biale, Kaplan, Hyman, and others that the modernization of sex and gender had little to do with sexual or women's liberation, but rather involved the Europeanization and *embourgeoisement* of traditional Jews, received more radical formulation under the growing influence in the 1990s of post-colonialism and queer studies. In post-colonial perspective, the dense intersections between gender and Jewish modernization reveal themselves within the project of "internal European colonialism," in which European "civilizing" impulses were directed not only at the colonized outside of Europe (including Jewish non-Europeans) but also – indeed from the very outset – at "backward" Jews inside Europe. Daniel Boyarin's 1997 *Unheroic Conduct*, in investigating the stigmatization of traditional Jewish gender and sexual practices in encounters with European bourgeois perspectives and patterns, argues that "For some three hundred years now Jews have been the target of the civilizing mission in Europe." Such a mission, in Jewish as in other targets of the colonial gaze, justifies itself by "the imputed barbarity of the treatment of women within the culture under attack." Boyarin continues:

The civilizing mission, and its Jewish agents among 'the Enlighteners,' considered the fact that Jewish women behaved in ways interpreted as masculine by European bourgeois society to be simply monstrous. Modern Jewish culture, liberal and

---

[9] David Biale, *Eros and the Jews: From Biblical Israel to Contemporary America* (New York: Basic, 1992), 161.

bourgeois in its aspiration and its preferred patterns of gendered life, has been the result of this civilizing mission. As Paula Hyman has recently demonstrated, the very Jewish religiosity of the modern bourgeois Jewish family is an assimilating mimicry of Protestant middle-class piety, not least in its portrayal of proper womanhood. The richness of Jewish life and difference has been largely lost, and the gains for Jewish women were largely illusory.[10]

From this vantage point, Jewish modernization, Europeanization, and *embourgeoisement* involved the encounter between asymmetrical gender orders and sexual systems: on the one hand, the traditional Ashkenazic structure, with roots in rabbinic-Talmudic culture and continuing embodiment among the masses of Eastern Europe; this system comprised a variety of Jewish formations, including some in which women were the primary or sole breadwinners and may well have been, as Hyman puts it, "respected for their abilities to manage," and an approach to kinship and marriage that focused on forging family alliances rather than granting young people erotic choice. On the other hand stood the bourgeois European sexual system, with roots in Greco-Roman, Christian, and heroic-chivalric cultural formations and a division of labor which put men in the public productive sphere and limited women to domestic activity; this system functioned through a powerful ideology of proper masculinity, femininity, and sublime ideals of romance, courtship, and marriage. Jewish modernity, in this view, was propelled by the aspiration of modernizing Jews to move from the first sex-gender system to the second, as a crucial part of the larger project of integration into non-Jewish society. The cost to Jewish women of this participation, as Biale and Boyarin point out, is clearest in terms of women's economic activities: while the traditional model took for granted women's economic influence (whether primary or shared), the bourgeois model confined women to the home and deprived them of the economic activity that traditional society had seen as an important part of women's role in the family. But the cost to men was also significant: the adoption of Western and Protestant-inspired models of religious behavior led to the "feminization of the synagogue" and the ceding of Jewish religious and spiritual authority to women, while shifting the burden of economic life to Jewish men, who were expected to support their wives by earning a "productive" living within a public realm shaped by anti-Jewish attitudes. Hyman describes the price paid by Jewish men as resulting in "profound ambivalence about this transfer of responsibility within Jewish families, the enhancement of Jewish women's status of guardians of Jewishness, and

---

[10] Daniel Boyarin, *Unheroic Conduct: The Rise of Heterosexuality and the Invention of the Jewish Man* (Berkeley: University of California, 1997), xvii–xviii. Boyarin cites Hyman, *Gender and Assimilation*, 26–27.

the further conflation of Jewishness and femaleness."[11] Jewish modernization not only took a separate toll on Jewish women and men, it also drove
a wedge into the relations between the sexes. As Riv-Ellen Prell argues
in her analysis of American Jewish gender relations, "gender has served
to symbolize Jews' relationship to nation, family, and work because both
Americanization and mobility place specific yet different demands on men
and women."[12] The demands of Americanization and mobility, felt separately by Jewish men and women, gave rise to, among other effects, the
stereotyping of Jewish women as devouring mothers and materialist wives.

While a wide range of scholars share the view of "modern Jewish culture" as a product of the widespread transformation from the traditional
to the bourgeois model of gender and marriage, it is crucial to the story
that some of them also insist that the Jewish romance with the West – and
Westernized romantic ideals – was notoriously unreciprocated, especially
in Europe. In the judgment of the dominant European culture into which
Jews were (imperfectly) integrating – a perspective thoroughly and pain-
fully internalized by aspiring Jewish citizens of Europe – Jewish men were
unmanly cowards and effete hysterics, while Jewish women were coarse
and unfeminine. Jewish sexual and gender modernization was thus not
a success but rather an ambivalent and incomplete project: the persistent
phenomenon of Jewish "queerness" is a symptom of Jewish modernity as
cultural mismatch, category crisis, incomplete integration and colonial
mimicry. It is no coincidence, as Sander Gilman and others have noted,
that the "invention of homosexuality" coincided with the entry of Jews
into the Central European bourgeoisie, an entry productive of and complicated by the sexual stigmatization of Jewish men.[13] Psychoanalysis, in
a variety of related readings, is a primary effect of this stigma, while also
providing tools for its diagnosis and "cure," but it was not the only one.
Among the other significant reverberations of this socio-sexual crisis was
Zionism, as both the collective internalization of Jewish sexual stigma

---

[11] Hyman, *Gender and Assimilation*, 154.

[12] Riv-Ellen Prell, *Fighting to Become Americans: Assimilation and the Trouble between Jewish
Women and Jewish Men* (Boston: Beacon Press, 1999), 4

[13] See Sander Gilman, particularly in *The Jew's Body* (New York: Routledge Press, 1991) and
Freud, Race, and Gender (Princeton: Princeton University Press, 1993); Ann Pellegrini,
Performance Anxieties: Staging Psychoanalysis, Staging Race (New York: Routledge,
1996); Boyarin, *Unheroic Conduct*, and Jay Geller, *On Freud's Jewish Body: Mitigating
Circumstances* (New York, Fordham University, 2007) and such earlier essays on the
subject as "'Glance at the Nose': Freud's Inscription of Jewish Difference," *American
Imago* 49, no. 4 (1992): 427–444 and "(G)nos(e)ology: The Cultural Construction of
the Other," in *People of the Body: Jewish and Judaism from an Embodied Perspective*, ed.
Howard Eilberg-Schwartz (Albany: SUNY Press, 1992), 243–82.

and treatment for the wounds of modern Jewish masculinity. Both of these fields of study, psychoanalysis and Zionism, have been enormously enriched by their framing as responses to modernization as a sexual and gender crisis for European Jews.[14] The Europeanization of Jewish sex and gender, then, was as culturally productive in its misfires and in the Jewish dialectical responses to these misfires as it was in its "successes."

The insights of post-colonialism, first put to use to illuminate the Jewish modernizing experience within the borders of Europe, have been mobilized as well to conceptualize the relationship between European Jewish modernization and the expansion of the European Jewish cultural orbit of influence outside Europe. Aron Rodrigue has amply demonstrated that the Alliance Israélite Universelle, founded in Paris in 1860 with the aim, according to its statutes, of working "throughout the world for the emancipation and moral progress of the Jews," followed the pattern Boyarin describes, encouraging the "moral progress" of the Jewish communities it served by educating Jewish women to adopt Western bourgeois roles and stigmatizing traditional Jewish gender roles as barbaric and backward.[15] The "internal European colonialism" of the Jews, first enacted within the borders of Europe, soon took the familiar form of "the civilizing mission" of European colonialism proper, with European Jews aiming to "civilize" the Jews in the Ottoman Empire and elsewhere in the East. Such a project not only singled out the "backwardness" of traditional Jewish women, it was often explicitly directed toward women. As Sarah Abrevaya Stein has shown, women readers of the Ladino press played an important part in spreading French customs of dress and behavior in the Sephardi Ottoman world:

Women were regarded as the critical target for acquiring and transmitting this knowledge, and it was to women that a great number of the articles in the Ladino instructional press were directed. This fact reiterates a hypothesis advanced by other scholars of modern Sephardi culture: that is, that in the Southeastern European context, it was Jewish women rather than men who were responsible for promoting cultural change. This was quite a different model from that of Western and Central Europe, where Jewish women were often the guardians of tradition.[16]

[14] On psychoanalysis, see Gilman, *Freud, Race, and Gender*; on Zionism, Michael Gluzman, *Haguf hatsiyoni: le'umiyut, migdar, uminiut besifrut ha'avrit hahadashah* (Tel Aviv: Hakibbutz hameuchad, 1997).

[15] Aron Rodrigue, *Jews and Muslims: Images of Sephardi and Eastern Jewries in Modern Times* (Seattle: University of Washington Press, 2003), 7.

[16] Sarah Abrevaya Stein, *Making Jews Modern: The Yiddish and Ladino Press in the Russian and Ottoman Empires* (Bloomington: Indiana University Press, 2003), 127.

Rodrigue has similarly demonstrated that Jewish women were both rich targets of reformist critiques of Jewish "backwardness" and prime engines for the "forward-looking" project of westernization. In some cases, women also served as the conservators of tradition, the pattern Kaplan and Hyman find among German Jewry – although whether this, too, could be considered as much an effect of westernization as resistance to modernization remains an open question:

> By the end of the nineteenth century, many Jewish women in Eastern lands began to receive instruction in Western schools, which constituted the only type of formal education to which they were exposed [unlike boys, who traditionally received a religious education]. As a result, the place of gender in the transmission of tradition in these societies became an increasingly ambiguous one. There were many counterparts in the Muslim world of women who, like their sisters in Central Europe, maintained tradition and folk culture in the home. However, as in many instances in Eastern Europe, Sephardi and Eastern Jewish women sometimes also became vectors of the most radical forms of westernization, bringing the latter into the home and influencing the next generation.[17]

Resisting the post-colonialist narrative that tends to view westernization as a culturally alien imposition resulting in a net loss for Jewish women, Rodrigue draws attention to the attractions modernization held for women in particular:

> Westernization appeared to many women as even more positive than it did to the men. Within the constraints of deeply patriarchal societies, it worked to improve their status within the home and within the larger society by creating a new value system which offered a new, bourgeois sensibility that could be aspired to even by the poorer classes. Though the new Western model still fixed women in profoundly unequal gender roles, for the educated Jewish women in Muslim lands these roles were preferable to the traditional female domain left behind.[18]

The notion that modernization appealed to women by freeing them from "the constraints of deeply patriarchal societies" is not a new one. Shmuel Feiner has shown that, although the Haskalah in its initial Berlin setting displayed no real interest in the plight of women, in the second half of the nineteenth century, "the women question" was an important part of the Russian maskilic agenda: moderate maskilim argued for the importance of educating Jewish girls and women; these maskilim, as is clear from their writings, were motivated less by respect for women's intellects than by their fears that women with no Jewish education posed a threat to the Jewish family; reading maskilic excoriations of the "False Enlightenment,"

---

[17] Rodrigue, *Jews and Muslims*, 81.
[18] Rodrigue, *Jews and Muslims*, 81.

which generally applied to women's "superficial" assimilation, Feiner demonstrates that the break of Jewish women from traditional roles was the
occasion for maskilic anxiety and opprobrium about women's behavior,
on the one hand, and Jewish apologetics, on the other. "The moderate
maskilim," writes Feiner, "strived to prove from rabbinic sources that
Judaism respected and valued women, and granted them rights. The ideal
Jewish family, then, was in their view the traditional one – which guarded
the sanctity of married life, kept men and women from alien impulses, and
was faithful to the couple and the honor of women."[19] But such domes-
ticating and anxious views of women's freedom were only part of the
story of Jewish modernization; more radical maskilim – including a few
women among them – increasingly demanded women's economic and sexual equality and independence, influenced by similar sentiments among
Russian radicals. Modernization, in this nineteenth-century debate, often
pitted the needs of the community and Jewish survival against the rights
of the individual, and the individual woman. Echoes of the anxiety audi-
ble in the maskilic writings on "the women's question" can be heard, for
instance, in Katz's discussion of the "salon Jewesses" as "vulnerable" to "the
blandishments of secular Western culture." This implicit judgment of the
weak national sentiments of Jewish women is stylistically countered, a little
later, in Deborah Hertz's argument that intermarriage and conversion were
attractive options for Central European Jewish women otherwise limited
in their life choices.[20] Nevertheless, Hertz also gives powerful voice to this
tension in her research between feminist sympathy for the converts and
her disappointment with them. Candidly describing her disgust, in particular, with Rahel Varnhagen's "craven social climbing," Hertz acknowledges that she continues to wonder whether Rahel's behavior "was truly
necessary to achieve even a minimal fulfillment as a brainy and ambitious
Jewish woman." In a passage that recalls Boyarin's calibration of the price
of modernization, Hertz continues:

More and more I contrasted her to the business wife Glückel of Hameln, who had
lived only a century before. Because Glückel was so serene, so confident, so industrious, so communitarian, and so beloved, I increasingly see her as an alternative
role model for contemporary women. Much was lost for Jewish women between
Glückel's life and Rahel's life, to be weighed against what was gained.[21]

---

[19] Shmuel Feiner, "Ha'isha hayehudiya hamodernit: Mikre mivkhan beyakhasei hahaskalah
vehamoderna," in *Eros erusin ve-isurim: miniyut u-mishpaḥah ba-hisṭoryah*, ed. Israel
Bartal and Isaiah Gafni (Jerusalem: Zalman Shazar Institute, 1998), 278–279.

[20] Deborah Hertz, *How Jews Became Germans: The History of Conversion and Assimilation in
Berlin* (New Haven: Yale University Press, 2007).

[21] Hertz, *How Jews Became Germans*, 219.

The historical trajectory from Glückel to Rahel embodies, for Hertz, not only the transformation of Jewish gender roles, but also the different demands of "a passionate ethnic identity" and personal fulfillment. Here, as elsewhere, the changing boundaries of the Jewish collective are intricately connected to changing expectations of Jewish women's existential options. More generally, research on Jewish secularization, intermarriage, or conversion exposes the extent that the charged intersection between Jewish collectivity and Jewish sexuality continues to trouble modern Jews and the study of Jewish modernity.

The "master narrative" of Jewish modernization as the Europeanization of Jewish sexual practices and gender roles, laid out by Kaplan, Biale, Hyman, Boyarin, Hertz, and Parush among many others, has amply demonstrated its flexibility and power, for Europe and far beyond the European arena for which it was first mobilized. Nevertheless, even this broad survey has begun to show some of its remaining ambiguities. The sharpest fault line in these narratives of modernization as gender transformation is the one that distinguishes between modernization as the loss of women's economic power and the narrative that views modernization as the break with oppressive patriarchal structures. These ambiguities are certainly at least partially related to the different formations and cultural contexts for modernization: the economic autonomy of women in Europe had no obvious parallels in North African Jewry, which generally relegated women to domestic spaces; the calculus of modernization as relative gain or loss in women's mobility surely must be computed differently in these cases. But context does not entirely account for the remaining rifts in the field – in which the same cultural phenomena are understood in radically divergent ways. Are such maskilic works as, for instance, Yehuda Leib Gordon's 1875 epic poem "The Tip of the Yod" – which protests the rabbinic legalism that keeps a woman chained to the husband who abandoned her – to be read as proto-feminist screeds against tradition or rather as attempts to charge Jewish tradition with barbarity against women, the better to impose bourgeois notions of gender and romance?[22] The poem allows for both of these readings, with its attention to the patriarchal asymmetries built into Jewish marriage law, on the one hand, and its sentimental evocations of the female protagonist's spirituality and the narrator's apparent distaste for her economic activities. But even with close reading there may be no "neutral" way of understanding Gordon's "feminism," or the embrace of secular gender roles Rodrigue records on the part of some Jewish women in the Islamic world: hewing closely to the consciousness of these women themselves

---

[22] For the poem, its English translation, and commentary, see Stanley Nash, "*Kotso shel Yod*," *CCAR Journal: A Reform Jewish Quarterly* 53, no. 3 (Summer 2006), 1–82.

might yield the interpretation that Rodrigue arrives at, that modernization "liberated" Jewish women from traditional Jewish restraints; from the
post-colonial perspective, this perception could be read as a kind of false
consciousness engendered by the colonial project, an inability to recognize
and value traditional Jewish sexual systems in the overpowering light of
modern alternatives masquerading as liberatory. This tension dogs even
the most straightforward scholarly assertions: in ChaeRan Freeze's claim
that Russian maskilim like Gordon "sought to heighten public consciousness of Jewish women's issues and the need for fundamental changes to
improve the woman's role and status in the family, workplace, and religious
sphere,"[23] are we to read the word "improve" as a paraphrase of what these
maskilim (perhaps mistakenly) believed, or as evidence of Freeze's (or our)
sense of what constitutes improvement in the lives of women?

   At stake in these questions is the still unclear nature of Jewish patriarchy, and its descriptive power for either traditionalizing or modern Jewish
formations. The difficulty is compounded by a number of factors beyond
the usual one, in the post-Foucauldian academy, of tracing the contradictory, paradoxical, and multi-directional trajectories of power in the public
and private spheres: in traditional Judaism, women were excluded from
religious authority and Jewish learning – values of supreme importance
within the traditional sphere – while in some formations still wielding
influence or exerting some form of overt or covert power in the economic and domestic realms – values of apparently lesser importance in
the traditional hierarchy than in post-traditional systems. The workings of
patriarchal power may be obscured, as well, by the particular character of
traditional Jewish gender norms, in which, as Boyarin points out, "Jewish
men do not (normatively) maintain power through physical violence."
Nevertheless, he continues, it is important "to interrogate the ways that
hierarchy and power imbalance were and are maintained within traditional
Jewish culture without the exercise of violence or, precisely, with the participation of men who are *not* violent."[24]

   The task of understanding a patriarchy that works otherwise than
through open physical domination is no less complicated for the modern period. Among the difficulties of theorizing modern Jewish patriarchal
formations is that different scholarly approaches gauge Jewish patriarchy
according to different metrics: On the one hand, the stereotype of the
"feminized Jewish male" that Boyarin and others see as agitating the Jewish
modernization project (particularly in psychoanalysis and Zionism) takes

---

[23] ChaeRan Y. Freeze, *Jewish Marriage and Divorce in Imperial Russia* (Hanover,
NH: Brandeis University Press, 2002), 191.

[24] Boyarin, *Unheroic Conduct*, 166.

its distinctive character from what might be called "comparative masculinity," in which Jewish men are seen, and see themselves, in relation to their non-Jewish counterparts; it is this perspective that shapes the queer studies and post-colonial approaches to Jewish modernity. On the other hand, the problem of Jewish men and masculinity must also be understood in relation to Jewish women and femininity; this is the approach at the center of such analyses of the relationships between Jewish men and women as those of Hyman and Prell. What is no doubt required is an attempt to think through the intersection of Jewish male effeminacy and Jewish patriarchal privilege, Jewish "queerness" and Jewish heteronormativity, the disruptions of modernity and the persistence of traditional responses to these disruptions. One such attempt is Bluma Goldstein's analysis of the phenomenon of wife-abandonment, a ubiquitous feature of Jewish urbanization, immigration, radicalism, and proletarianization, and already featured in one of the pioneering texts of the Jewish Enlightenment, which narrates Solomon Maimon's journey from the "darkness" of his native Eastern Europe to Enlightenment Berlin. As Maimon's marriage and its complicated dissolution attest, a disempowered Jewish male, as Maimon certainly was in the difficulty of his entry into Berlin society, nevertheless retains a number of masculine privileges vis-à-vis women, including that encoded in the halachic system that "chains" a woman (the Hebrew term for a grass widow is *agunah*, a chained woman) most powerfully in the absence of her husband, testimony to a symbolic order that functions best when it works independently, as it were, of its agents. As Goldstein argues, a certain submerged continuity connects traditional and modern Jewish masculinity:

Both the esoteric religious scholar of the pre-Enlightenment tradition and the modern capitalist or erotic adventurer ... shared at least one salient characteristic: their sense that they owned the male privilege of freedom to carry on their activities without interference. Indeed, this idealized or sovereign identity, whose masculine entitlement excluded all those feminized spaces usually inhabited by women and children, provided a critical nexus between the cultural discourse of the luftmentsch of Jewish tradition and that of the modern European adventurer.[25]

Maimon's dysfunctional marriage, at the threshold of Jewish modernity, thus demonstrates the impossibility of precisely distinguishing between modern and traditional formations, of measuring the weight of the various factors that contributed to the marital situation: the mismatch between traditional and modern spouse; the blindness to women's rights of much Enlightenment thought; the rage of the "feminized Jewish male" in reaction

---

[25] Bluma Goldstein, *Enforced Marginality: Jewish Narratives on Abandoned Wives* (Berkeley: University of California Press, 2007), 52.

to new models of masculinity; the patriarchal asymmetries of Jewish marriage law; the new mobility of modernizing Europe; and the traditional female capacities that enabled the philosopher's wife to successfully chase her husband down.

Despite the prevalence of abandonment documented by Goldstein, we should not necessarily assume that marital dissolution is a symptom, most primarily, of modernization. The connections between desertion, divorce, and modernity, as ChaeRan Freeze has shown of imperial Russia, are complex: "Contrary to the ubiquitous tendency in modern Europe for divorce rates to skyrocket, Jews experienced a decline from extraordinary high rates in the first half of the nineteenth century to a much lower frequency later in the second half."[26] Among the multiple circumstances that contributed to this decline was a sharp rise in marital age, suggesting that modernity had the effect – in some cases – of easing strains native to early marriage; but other factors included a particularly dysfunctional state-sanctioned rabbinate, with little coercive power. As Freeze notes, "a declining divorce rate does not … mean increasing stability in the family,"[27] and bigamy and desertion became more attractive options for men than divorce.

If the relative claims or even character of traditional versus modern Jewish gender orders are hard to judge, that may be because such calibration involves more than the usual work of substantiating and qualifying historical claims or expanding the field of inquiry to previously neglected areas. It also inevitably draws on the presuppositions of a researcher implicated in the work of describing and necessarily evaluating competing gender systems, adjudicating between systems marked as "Jewish" but (arguably) patriarchal, and (arguably) liberatory but also (apparently) non-Jewish, Western, and assimilationist. If it is a truism that the "neutrality" and "objectivity" of the historian can no longer be sustained, the self-reflexive nature of modern and postmodern studies of Jewish sex and gender amply demonstrates the mutual implications of critical methodologies and ideological assumptions, the "location" of the historian and the "object" of her study. Jewish modernity is not only the subject of scholarly inquiry, it is also the very matrix from which the methods of feminist historiography, queer studies, and post-colonialism were born. Indeed, the centrality of Jewish women in second-wave feminism in the United States – the immediate background to the emergence of feminist Jewish studies – suggests that the distinctive patterns of Jewish gender, especially the Eastern European Jewish women's activism traced by Hyman and others, inform not only Jewish modernity, but also the feminist approaches with which it

---

[26] Freeze, *Jewish Marriage and Divorce*, 281.
[27] Freeze, *Jewish Marriage and Divorce*, 284.

is studied. Feminism and gender studies are thus both an especially powerful lens for analyzing modern Jewish history and itself an important and
still-unresolved dimension of the modern Jewish historical narrative – does
modern Jewish feminism emerge from traditional Jewish gender formations, in opposition to those of the West, or does it rather represent a
primary critique of Judaism? Given this self-reflexivity, it may be no surprise that the gender analysis of modern Jewish history has been a site of
complex and unresolved political-cultural tensions that no contemporary
historian can evade.

Alongside these ideological tensions, the master narrative of modernization as the Europeanization of Jewish sex and gender faces a different set of
challenges. As for other narratives of Jewish modernity, the issues of periodization and characterization remain unresolved: when does the modern
era begin, or should we rather speak of waves of modernization, overlapping, contingent in their effects, divergent in different regions? Marion
Kaplan has suggested that "Historical 'turning points' were not necessarily the same for women as for men, because popular historical periodization is derived from political history, an arena from which women have
been excluded."[28] The gender study of Jewish culture, then, will require
the discovery of new "turning points" unexplored in more normative history: Kaplan suggests both political markers focusing on women's political
rights and changes "in health care, in household and office technology,
in the availability of birth control, and in attitudes toward sexuality and
childbearing."[29]

Attempts at calculating the periodization of Jewish modernity in relation to pivotal moments in women's history and sexual patterns inevitably
raise the related issue of what constitutes the modernity of these changes.
With gender as a primary consideration, we might tentatively begin by
positing that modernity, in this sense, begins with challenges to the traditional gender system, whether these occur in the context of secularization, integration, and assimilation, or whether they emerge from other,
perhaps internal or religious, contexts. But what represents such a challenge, before the forthright feminist declarations of the radical maskilim
charted in Feiner's study, is not always easy to ascertain: The emergence of
women's writing represents one such possible development, although the
memoirs of Glückel of Hameln (written between 1690 and 1719), to take
an obvious example, seem to describe a fully traditional world and Glückel
makes no claim for the novelty of the genre in which she is working.
Whether the text can be read for early glimmers of secularization remains

---

[28] Kaplan, *The Making of the Jewish Middle Class*, 15.
[29] Kaplan, *The Making of the Jewish Middle Class*, 15.

an open question: While Chava Turniansky stresses Glückel's absolute religious faith – which is not without complaints against God or creative self-expression – Feiner discovers in Glückel not only her perspective on the new rage for French fashions and piano-playing, but also a telling moment of anti-clericalism in Glückel's own rage at discovering that her son's teacher was a charlatan; he links this critique of religious authority with the first strains of modernization in early modern Germany.[30]

The growing attention to early modernity might also reshape the master narrative of the beginnings of Jewish modernity, with consequent shifts in the understanding of the shift from traditional to post-traditional gender orders and sexual practices. Shmuel Feiner's most recent work substantially backdates "the origins of secularization," finding traces of opposition to Jewish traditional practices generations earlier, and spread out over a wider region, than Katz, Kaplan, and Hyman had discovered them. More radically, his work puts in question the link between secularization and westernization and *embourgeoisement*, once the literary production of the bourgeois elite ceases to be the primary source for understanding the modernization of Jewish gender. Feiner's descriptions of challenges to traditional sexual patterns in the first half of the eighteenth century, not only in Central but also in Eastern Europe, include "libertinism" and hedonism rather than domestic virtues; the denial of God rather than the conservative re-inscription of a spiritualized tradition; adultery and out-of-wedlock pregnancies rather than German-Jewish "angels in the house."[31] And rather than laying such sexual and religious transgression at the door of "colonial mimicry," or reading them (as earlier scholars did) within the still-intact religious architecture of "sin," Feiner implies that a similar cultural atmosphere in eighteenth-century Europe agitated the Jewish as the Christian worlds. The reflex of accounting for Jewish behaviors in the modern era by recourse to "foreign" influences – which provided shape to the field of Jewish gender modernization at the outset – has given way, with the host of new studies, to new methodologies, in which what holds interest is the particularity of Jewish historical phenomena, within a multi-directional web of influence and counter-influence, resistance, "invented tradition," and "hybridity" as well as "assimilation" and westernization.

Feiner has similarly brought attention to the larger picture of Jewish secularization in Eastern Europe beyond the overwhelmingly male

---

[30] Chava Turniansky, "Introduction," in *Glikl: Zikhronot 1691–1719*, ed. and trans. Chava Turniansky (Jerusalem: Zalman Shazar Institute, 2006), 28–32. Shmuel Feiner, *The Origins of Jewish Secularization in Eighteenth-Century Europe*, trans. Chaya Naor (Philadelphia: University of Pennsylvania, 2011), 37–38.

[31] Feiner, *The Origins of Jewish Secularization*, 56–57.

Haskalah. In an article that discerns important sociological trends from the negative mirror of maskilic excoriations of the "False Enlightenment," a term used most often for women's superficial acculturation – piano, easy romantic dalliances, and light French literature rather than the heavy lifting of Enlightenment philosophy or Hebrew poetry – Feiner demonstrates that the Haskalah westernization project explored by Hyman, David Biale, and others only tells half the story. Jewish modernization took shape in the midst of urban environments in which Jewish women explored modes of secularization that far outstripped those of their male counterparts in the maskilic intelligentsia; in these lights, the maskilim were a conservative cultural rear guard, and the Haskalah should be understood as an attempt to control and limit westernization rather than to unreservedly promote it. While the maskilim did indeed hope to modernize Jewish sex and gender by championing bourgeois models of gender and sexuality, their efforts were both preceded and outstripped by new, decidedly non-ideological and often non-bourgeois, forms of sexual behavior, often pioneered by young women. From the working-class young Jewish women who flooded the big cities in the 1860s and 1870s to the growing number of Jewish women studying in universities throughout Europe grew "the female revolutionaries, nihilists and socialists, who were attracted to radical ideologies and championed equality and free will."[32]

Perhaps the most fascinating reconsideration of the narrative of Jewish gender transformations in relation to emancipation, acculturation, and Enlightenment has been Ada Rapoport-Albert's recent work on women in the Sabbatian heresy. Rapoport-Alpert traces what she forthrightly calls the "egalitarian agenda" of Sabbatianism to both mystical and historical factors, both internal to Judaism: from the kabbalistic perspective, the equality and even prominence of women in the movement can be understood as an integral part of the larger heresy of Sabbatianism, in which the established order is abrogated, reversed or even overthrown with the advent of the messianic age. The historical hypothesis Rapoport-Albert offers for how Sabbatai Zevi's ideas about female equality might have developed also relies on internal Jewish conditions: the experience of the *conversos* on the Iberian Peninsula and as exiles in such regions as Sabbatai Zevi's Izmir. The pivotal role of women in maintaining clandestine Jewish practice after conversion is by now well-established among historians; Rapoport-Albert's contribution to this discussion is to suggest that once *conversos* returned to Jewish life, the historical memory and perhaps persistence of women's centrality in religious life, in combination with the family upheavals that

---

[32] Feiner, "Ha'isha hayehudiya hamodernit," 270.

accompanied the Iberian immigration, led to a cultural fluidity around questions of gender:

One of the legacies of the Converso experience may have been a shift in the perception of women's status within the Jewish faith. It follows that even if the Converso women had been integrated into Judaism, we need not assume that they were always and everywhere returned to the margins of religious life. And even where they were, the process of reintegrating the Conversos, which is known to have generated considerable tension over several other issues, might at the very least have prompted misgivings regarding the position of women in society. Sabbatai Zevi's liberationist promise to women had emerged against this historical background. His message was thus conceived in conditions that not only could inspire it, but may well have been particularly conducive to its reception and rapid propagation.[33]

Disruptions of the conventional gender order and notions of women's equality, then, might have indigenous Jewish religious and historical roots, finding direct expression many generations earlier than most scholars assume. Nevertheless, Rapoport-Albert makes no claim that these early expressions of gender equality created long-lasting change, except dialectically; skeptical of Scholem's controversial claim that Sabbatians and Frankists were instrumental in the Enlightenment, and arguing with earlier scholars who saw Hasidism as a continuation of the openness to female religious experience in Sabbatianism, Rapoport-Albert claims rather that the Jewish world – and particularly Hasidism – deliberately turned its back on such ideologies alongside its rejection of other antinomian aspects of Sabbatianism. Hasidism not only persisted in the traditional exclusion of women from religious life, but even developed new modes of such exclusion by offering male Hasidim "the spiritually invigorating experience of communal life within an emotionally charged, exclusively male fraternity, which functioned symbolically as an alternative to ordinary family life."[34]

Among the points of interest in this argument is that it reverses teleological assumptions about modernity as inevitably moving toward greater progress, in gender-equality as elsewhere. In the progression Rapoport-Alpert traces, an egalitarian form of Jewish religious enthusiasm (in the seventeenth century!) was followed by a movement in which such egalitarianism was decisively rejected – at least until, as Rapoport-Albert writes, "the entire Orthodox sector, Hasidic and non-Hasidic alike, woke up to the potential for engaging its womenfolk in the struggle against modernity and secularism."[35] The exclusion of women from participation in

---

[33] Ada Rapoport-Albert, *Women in the Messianic Heresy of Sabbatai Zevi: 1666–1816*, trans. Deborah Greniman (Oxford: Littman Library of Jewish Civilization, 2011), 113.

[34] Rapoport-Albert, *Women in the Messianic Heresy*, 1.

[35] Rapoport-Albert, *Women in the Messianic Heresy*, 4.

movements such as Hasidism (alongside other modern forms of traditionalism) may be understood, then, not as a "natural" feature of its traditionalizing impulses, or as an unconscious continuation of pre-modern
exclusions of women, but rather as a dimension of these movements inex-
tricable from their modernity.

In the light of these findings, Jewish modernity should be understood
as an arena for the development of both new secular gender models and
new traditionalizing systems. Modern Jewish culture was, for instance,
shaped both by the breakdown of traditional sexual segregation and by its
mobilization and reconfiguration in traditionalizing systems; indeed, we
should remember that the heyday of the Hasidic court and the Lithuanian
yeshivot was the nineteenth century, in which homosocial religious systems competed actively with such secularizing formations as the Haskalah
and secular Jewish culture. Traditionalizing sex-gender systems need not
be understood solely as a means of sexual repression or the suppression of
women. After Foucault, it is clear that such apparently "repressive" sexual systems are also culturally *productive* engines of social formation.[36] As
Rapoport-Albert shows, the exclusion of women from the Hasidic court
or from the yeshiva was instrumental in the construction of spaces for religious enthusiasm that were rivals not only with secular spaces (for instance
the theater), but also with other religious sites, for instance the traditional
family. The distinctive modernity of such traditionalizing religious formations as the yeshiva is explored by Shaul Stampfer in a study of the rise
of dormitories in the nineteenth century, which replaced older models of
boarding with families; in these dormitories, homosocial arrangements
were intensified rather than attenuated by the contributions of modern,
"rational" theories of adolescent pedagogy.[37]

Parallel homosocial arrangements for women in the religious world arose
only belatedly, with the new phenomenon of Orthodox girls' education, as
part of what Rapoport-Albert describes as the twentieth-century mobilization of women in "the struggle against modernity and secularism." In this
project, girls and women were not agents of modernization – as in Parush's
work on nineteenth-century women readers – or of *embourgeoisement* – as
in Hyman's German-Jewish wives. Rather, Jewish women became pioneers
and activists in the maintenance and revival of Orthodoxy. Nevertheless, it
can hardly be denied that the mobilization of women for traditionalist ends
was an eminently "modern" project: recent work by Shoshanah Bechofer

---

[36] Michel Foucault, *History of Sexuality: An Introduction*, Vol. 1 (New York: Vintage,
1990), 96.
[37] Shaul Stampfer, *Families, Rabbis and Education: Traditional Jewish Society in Nineteenth-
Century Europe* (Oxford: Littman Library of Jewish Civilization, 2010), 227.

and Agnieszka Oleszak has amply demonstrated the degree to which Sarah Schenirer, the founder of the Bais Yakov school system for girls, drew as fully from secular and even radical social movements (German pedagogy, Polish electoral politics, socialist youth movements) as she did from traditional sources.[38] Schenirer's adoption of progressive German pedagogical methods, emblematic perhaps of her "modern" approach, may well have been easier for rabbinical authorities to accept because of the limitation of such an educational culture to girls – a religious variation on Parush's "benefits of marginality." In Rapoport-Albert, Stampfer, Bechofer, and Oleszak, the assumption that modernity is defined by secularization, and that the transformation of Jewish gender in modernity should be sought primarily within the context of Europeanization, gives way to the recognition that religious impulses have shaped modernity as powerfully as secular ones, just as modernity has left its mark on Jewish religious formations.

This rethinking of the relationship between tradition and modernity, indigenous Jewish versus Western formations, inevitably also requires us to reconsider the assumption that tradition comprises those forms that preceded modernity and against which modernity should be measured. Stampfer, for instance, has also argued against the view that one of the central features of Jewish modernity was the critique and dissolution of the traditional practice of early, arranged marriage. Speaking of Eastern European Jews, Stampfer asserts that the "premature" arranged marriages against which maskilim and other modernizers militated were not, in fact, remnants of a long tradition, "medieval" in its character and history; rather, these arrangements were a new phenomenon, limited to the rabbinic elite, of the eighteenth and the first half of the nineteenth century – hardly the Middle Ages.[39]

Such work aligns with Talal Asad's more general insight that "tradition" has to be considered a primary product of and *effect* of modernization rather than its antecedent or target. In Asad's view, the very notion of an "enchanted" tradition that shapes the secularization thesis may arise in the nineteenth century with "the growing habit of reading imaginative literature – being enclosed within and by it – so that images of a 'pre-modern' past acquire in retrospect a quality of enchantment."[40] In the

---

[38] Shani Bechhofer, "Ongoing Constitution of Identity and Educational Mission of Bais Yaakov Schools: The Structuration of an Organizational Field as the Unfolding of Discursive Logics" (Ph.D. diss., Northwestern University, 2004); Agnieska Oleszak, "'The Borderland': The Beys Yaakov School in Kraków as a Symbolic Encounter between East and West," *Polin* 23 (2011): 277–290.

[39] Stampfer, *Families, Rabbis and Education*, 12.

[40] Talal Asad, *Formations of the Secular: Christianity, Islam, Modernity* (Stanford: Stanford University Press, 2003), 13–14.

case of arranged marriage, this "traditional" effect disguises the synchronic workings of class in modern society behind an invented, exalted – and modern! – discourse of tradition and of antiquity.[41] The diachronic narratives built into conceptions of modernity might more productively be considered as synchronic tensions *within* Jewish modernity. Modernity is the site of both secularization and religious revival, and both of these (and the infinite variations and gray area between them) are comprised of unpredictable combinations of "modern" and "traditional" elements, Jewish and non-Jewish influences. Modern Jewish culture, in this view, should be read not as what came later than, and in opposition to, traditional and premodern social formations, but as the very site of negotiation between the modern and the traditional, the Jewish and what lies beyond it.

Such hybrid formations as the movement for Orthodox girls' education are not limited to the traditionalizing sphere. Secular Jewish youth movements drew energy, as well, from "traditional" homosocial structures, and Michael Galchinsky has made the case that, in Victorian England, Jewish traditions of sexual segregation merged seamlessly into "the very different Victorian ideology of separate spheres."[42] Secular Jewish culture writ large might be considered such a hybrid phenomenon: in the "secular synagogue" of the Hebrew or Yiddish theater, sexual desegregation and the flouting of Jewish law (for instance in Friday evening performances) characterized the audience, while Hasidic settings, songs, and plots were ubiquitous onstage. While secular Jewish culture certainly adopted Western literary genres and conventions of romance, and their attendant ideologies of proper masculinity and femininity, these played a generative role in the transformation of modern Jewish attitudes toward courtship and marriage. Even at the height of the "westernizing" Haskalah, Jewish literature combined in syncretistic and unpredictable ways a veneration of European models of romance with a fondness for European self-critique of these same models: thus, S. Y. Abramovitsh's enormously popular nineteenth-century novella, *The Travels of Benjamin the Third*, is a parody of Cervantes's *Don Quixote*, itself a parody of earlier romances and a satire of readers besotted by these fantasies. Abramovitsh's choice of European literary models is no accident, and should remind us that "Western" or bourgeois culture is itself more various, less monolithic, in its view of sexuality than scholarship in this area has often assumed, containing trends and countertrends, romantic ideals and deflationary critiques.

[41] Stampfer, *Families, Rabbis and Education*, 14.
[42] Michael Galchinsky, *The Origin of the Modern Jewish Woman Writer: Romance and Reform in Victorian England* (Detroit: Wayne State University Press, 1996), 64.

Even literary artifacts that seem to wholeheartedly embrace Western romantic conventions often also reveal a kernel of indigenous Jewish approaches to sex. There are a remarkable number of Jewish literary works – most emblematically Avraham Mapu's 1853 biblical romance *Love of Zion* and Sh. An-sky's 1914 play *The Dybbuk* – that combine the romantic plot of young people falling in love against their parents' wishes with the more traditional notions of parental arranged marriage. In the double plot of erotic rebellion that is nevertheless underwritten by prior parental approval, Jewish writers had it both ways. In partnering a shepherd with a noble girl, they could reject the outdated notion that marriages should be made by a matchmaker; by revealing at the last minute that the shepherd actually possessed a distinguished pedigree (as happens, for instance, in Mapu), they could sidestep the consequences of erotic choice and class mixing. Somewhere in this conservative orientation – shared by the European bourgeoisie and the rabbinical classes from which the Jewish intelligentsia generally emerged – was a kind of native Jewish common sense, which recognized that while sexual attraction thrives on parental opposition, marriage itself probably benefits from parental approval.

Read more closely, Marion Kaplan's work already lays the groundwork for recognizing the distinctively Jewish character of apparently modern cultural formations: Kaplan makes the point that Jews did not, in fact, adopt wholesale the approach of their bourgeois neighbors to courtship and marriage, but rather developed distinctive Jewish practices within this context. The distance between romantic ideals and social realities, for instance, while common to all sectors of German society, expressed itself differently for Jews and non-Jews:

Ironically, anti-Semitism was also the cause of the overtly economic orientation of German Jews toward marriage. The Christian middle class, aping the nobility's hypocritical contempt of money, avoided talk of what it felt to be base, material motives by stressing the social status a marriage could offer. Jews could partake of no such camouflage. Non-Jewish families used dowries, ostensibly, to cement new social alliances. Jews, on the other hand, were ostracized from "good society" and could not pretend that social alliances took precedence over all else…. For them, money traditionally signified security in a hostile environment.[43]

Thus, a culturally determined directness about financial motivations for marriage (despite the "hypocritical" disdain in bourgeois circles for mercenary considerations) served to distinguish Jewish marriage arrangements from those of their neighbors. Such directness, however, was not everywhere operative: between parents and children, Jewish romance

---

[43] Kaplan, *The Making of the Jewish Middle Class*, 107–108.

was characterized rather by an obfuscation of the ratio between erotic choice and "baser" considerations. Thus, Kaplan describes "the fine art" of "coincidence," in which Jewish families camouflaged their allegiances to arranged matches: "Conscious of the growing contradictions between social ideology and social reality, some [Jewish] parents 'covered up' traditional, arranged marriages. Others arranged circumstances where certain young people could meet each other."[44] Such complex arrangements mirror, on the historical level, the cultural constructions that produce fictional Jewish marriages at the juncture of rebellious erotic choice and covert or forgotten parental approval. In these distinctively Jewish approaches to modernity, the "traditional Jewish" and "romantic bourgeois" are not so easily disentangled.

The study of modern Jewish sexual and gender culture, which began with the insight that Jewish modernity was generated by cultural borrowing, has also recognized that this borrowing was never unambiguous, or complete. But we might go further: if Jewish sexual modernity borrowed from European models at their inception, Western culture has also been profoundly shaped by modern Jewish cultural patterns. Scholarship on Freud has demonstrated the extent that the pressures of European ideals of proper masculinity shaped psychoanalysis, but it can hardly be denied that psychoanalysis has had at least as dramatic an effect on the meanings and conceptualizations of gender and sexuality in a post-Freudian world. And Jewish conceptions of sex and gender have been enormously influential in American popular culture, in which Lenny Bruce, Philip Roth, and Erica Jong are pivotal figures. So, too, does second-wave feminism owe an enormous debt to such Jewish women as Betty Friedan and Gloria Steinem. In the larger story of modernity as the arena for sexual and gender transformations, then, modernizing Jews play both a particularly anxious and enormously productive role.

SELECT BIBLIOGRAPHY

Biale, David. *Eros and the Jews: From Biblical Israel to Contemporary America.* New York: Basic, 1992.

Boyarin, Daniel. *Unheroic Conduct: The Rise of Heterosexuality and the Invention of the Jewish Man.* Berkeley: University of California, 1997.

Feiner, Shmuel. "Ha'isha hayehudiya hamodernit: Mikre mivkhan beyakhasei hahaskalah vehamoderna," in *Eros erusin ve-isurim: miniyut u-mishpaḥah ba-hisṭoryah,* ed. Israel Bartal and Isaiah Gafni. Jerusalem: Zalman Shazar Institute, 1998.

[44] Kaplan, *The Making of the Jewish Middle Class,* 109.

The Origins of Jewish Secularization in Eighteenth-Century Europe, trans. Chaya Naor. Philadelphia: University of Pennsylvania, 2011.

Freeze, ChaeRan Y. *Jewish Marriage and Divorce in Imperial Russia*. Hanover, NH: Brandeis University Press, 2002.

Galchinsky, Michael. *The Origin of the Modern Jewish Woman Writer: Romance and Reform in Victorian England*. Detroit: Wayne State University Press, 1996.

Gilman, Sander. *The Jew's Body*. New York: Routledge Press, 1991.

Gluzman, Michael. *Haguf hatsiyoni: le'umiyut, migdar, uminiut besifrut ha'avrit hahadashah*. Tel Aviv: Hakibbutz hameuchad, 2007.

Goldstein, Bluma. *Enforced Marginality: Jewish Narratives on Abandoned Wives*. Berkeley: University of California Press, 2007.

Hertz, Deborah. *How Jews Became Germans: The History of Conversion and Assimilation in Berlin*. New Haven: Yale University Press, 2007.

Hyman, Paula. *Gender and Assimilation in Modern Jewish History*. Seattle: University of Washington Press, 1995.

Kaplan, Marion. *The Making of the Jewish Middle Class: Women, Family, and Identity in Imperial Germany*. Oxford: Oxford University Press, 1991.

Oleszak, Agnieska. "'The Borderland': The Beys Yaakov School in Kraków as a Symbolic Encounter between East and West," *Polin* 23 (2011): 277–90.

Parush, Iris. *Reading Jewish Women: Marginality and Modernization in Nineteenth-Century Eastern European Jewish Society*, trans. Saadiya Sternberg. Waltham, MA: Brandeis University Press, 2004.

Pellegrini, Ann. *Performance Anxieties: Staging Psychoanalysis, Staging Race*. New York: Routledge, 1996.

Prell, Riv-Ellen. *Fighting to Become Americans: Assimilation and the Trouble between Jewish Women and Jewish Men*. Boston: Beacon Press, 1999.

Rodrigue, Aron. *Jews and Muslims: Images of Sephardi and Eastern Jewries in Modern Times*. Seattle: University of Washington Press, 2003.

Stampfer, Shaul. *Families, Rabbis and Education: Traditional Jewish Society in Nineteenth-Century Europe*. Oxford: Littman Library of Jewish Civilization, 2010.

Stein, Sarah Abrevaya. *Making Jews Modern: The Yiddish and Ladino Press in the Russian and Ottoman Empires*. Bloomington: Indiana University Press, 2003.

CHAPTER 36

JEWS AND SCIENCE

ULRICH CHARPA

INTRODUCTION

At a superficial glance, this topic appears to present itself as a meeting of ideal marriage partners. Concerning scientific research *itself*, there is a tremendous amount of evidence for the somewhat spectacular achievements associated with "Jewish success" in science, not only in the sense of societal acknowledgment through major prizes etc., but also through outstanding and relevant participation in scientific progress. As regards research *on* science, twentieth-century developments as well as recent work in history, sociology, and philosophy of science are closely linked to the names of Alexandre Koyré, Robert K. Merton, I. Bernard Cohen, Michael Polanyi, Ludvik Fleck, Thomas S. Kuhn, Joseph Ben-David, Hélène Metzger, Stephan Koerner, Gerd Buchdahl, Imre Lakatos, Edward Shils, and numerous other Jewish scholars.

Significantly, many of these authors and other scholars in science studies have had reasons not to pursue the topic of Jews and science. There are in fact two general tendencies in favor of the decision to exercise restraint. One tendency is the *rejection of particularism* with regard to science on the part of many scholars who were contemporary witnesses of "Deutsche Physik," Lyssenkoism and other peculiarities of twentieth-century ideologies. The other and quite opposite tendency, *against universalism*, is grounded in the acknowledgment of the importance of relativizing, especially "human" factors, to scientific change. Simply said, to the universalist it does not make sense to focus on *Jews*; to the particularist, it appears naive to accept the concept of *success* in a sense that goes beyond social esteem.

The divide between a universalist position and discussion of the Jewish side of a scientist is best illustrated by the example of Albert Einstein, the icon of twentieth-century science, through his own attitude towards science as "impersonal," and by two types of commentaries about him, even in one and the same volume and by the same Einstein scholar.[1]

[1] See, e.g., John Stachel, *Einstein from 'B' to 'Z'* (Boston: Birkhäuser, 2002).

One account presents the "human side," including his identity as a Jew, the other the scientific work. Authors such as Michael Polanyi, Thomas S. Kuhn, and others have drawn attention to the fact that speaking about science should not be limited to scientific theories, to their changing support by empirical evidence, and to each other. Conceding that commenting on science ought to be completed by considering processes of practical and theoretical learning, metaphysical and methodological preferences, personal as well as social factors, and a lot more, has opened the field for examining the role of certain groups without being clouded by ideological ideas on "Jüdische Physik" and related conceptions.[2]

Meanwhile, scholarly interest in the role of Jews in modern science, and the intersection of science and Judaism in the nineteenth and twentieth centuries, is advancing,[3] though still at the margins of science studies. The distinctly noticeable neglect over nearly a century as well as the cautious turn to the topic during the last two decades mirror the changing views on what science is, and to a minor degree also on what Judaism, and Jewish scientists are and/or ought to be.

[2] The distinction between "Jewish" and "German" (or "Aryan") Physics came into being as reaction to the revolutionary change in modern physics connected to the Principle of Relativity and to Quantum Theory. Its most influential advocates were the two experimental physicists and Noble Prize Laureates Philipp Lenard (1862–1947) and Johannes Stark (1874–1957). Their own approach to an "Aryan" physics was canonically enfolded in Lenard's *Deutsche Physik*, 4 vols (Munich: J. F. Lehmann, 1936–37) and has been promoted in the English-speaking world by Stark, "The Pragmatic and the Dogmatic Spirit in Physics," *Nature* 141, 30 April 1938, 770–772. This view is based on racist appraisals of the relevant physicists of all times, and additionally includes something like a characteristic of scientific styles with "Anschaulichkeit" (imageability) as criterion: the aim of working in the "Aryan" pragmatic style is reality, while "the goal of the dogmatic [Jewish] spirit is the formula" (Stark, "The Pragmatic and the Dogmatic Spirit," 771). Cf. below: The Antisemitic Explanation.

[3] See, e.g., the journal *Aleph. Historical Studies in Science and Judaism* 2001–; Geoffrey Cantor, *Quakers, Jews, and Science: Religious Responses to Modernity and the Sciences in Britain, 1650–1900* (Cambridge, Cambridge University Press, 2005); Geoffrey Cantor and Marc Swetlitz, eds, *Jewish Tradition and the Challenge of Darwinism* (Chicago: University of Chicago Press, 2006); Noah J. Efron, *Judaism and Science: A Historical Introduction* (Westport, CT: Greenwood, 2007); Ulrich Charpa and Ute Deichmann, eds, *Jews and Sciences in German Contexts* (Tübingen Mohr-Siebeck, 2007); Birgit Bergmann, Moritz Epple, and Ruti Ungar, *Transcending Tradition. Jewish Mathematicians in German-Speaking Academic Culture* (Heidelberg: Springer, 2012).

JEWISH HISTORY AND HISTORY OF
SCIENCE: CONCEPTUAL ISSUES

While the role of Jews in medieval and early-modern science is widely studied, dealing with Jews and modern science is an awkward topic. One reason
is the fact that – whatever most of the earlier Jewish scientists did or thought,
and however they may have irritated the communities of their time – it is
incontestably a part of the history of Judaism. The great Jewish figures in general medieval history of science were at the same time famous rabbis whose
acronyms are widely known. To a lesser extent, the same holds for some outstanding early modern scholars. They all defined themselves as authoritative
members of the Jewish community confronted with the task of reconciling
the traditions of their closely bound group with scientific advancement.

Compared to the early modern and pre-modern sceneries, the modern
situation is not well defined. Who is a Jewish scientist? What does the attribute "Jewish" mean here? Among successful scientists of the nineteenth and
twentieth centuries one comes across very different groups: there are incontrovertible Jews living in this or that respect as halachic individuals, among
them even rabbinically trained scientists; there are others, Jews according
to Jewish religious law, to whom Judaism is of no importance; and others
who are Jewish only according to a specific conception of Judaism. The list
can be continued. At the margins of the picture we find first and second
generation converts with ties to Judaism. The common distinction between
"legal" and mere "ethnic" Jews is burdened with the problem that the second category is too broad with regard to science studies. Taken on such a
basis it would magnify the number of people to be counted as Jewish scientists beyond reasonable limits. In contrast, historical investigations are not
bound to halachic decision making which has its own agenda and is focused
on singular cases in doubt. Historiography ought to integrate what appears
to be *thematically* significant. Therefore, while dealing with "Jews and science," it seems appropriate to distinguish the issue of the role of uncontroversial Jewish individuals in science from that of intersections between
Jewish history and history of science. As to the first topic, we need not
commit ourselves to the Orthodox strategy of rigid delineation to concede
the asymmetry between the Orthodox position and its liberal alternatives.

Without the Orthodox position as the starting point of determination,
all kinds of liberalizations would be empty. Taking this into consideration,
the philosopher Asa Kasher put forward the idea of a recursive definition
of being Jewish with the uncontroversial Orthodox as "core Jew."[4] Starting

---

[4] Asa Kasher, "Jewish Collective Identity," in *Jewish Identity*, ed. David T. Goldberg and
Michael Krausz (Philadelphia: Temple University Press, 1993), 56–78.

with the Orthodox appraisal, considering the (from an Orthodox point of view) less ideal but nevertheless inclusive individuals and their attitude towards others as the next step, one moves more and more towards peripheral individuals. The outcome is a pragmatic attitude with a marked preference for individuals like, e.g., the chemist and Darwinist Raphael Meldola (1849–1915),[5] grandson of a highly esteemed rabbi of London's Sephardic community, who took pride and interest in all matters of Jewish life. In some respects, such a figure appears more relevant to the history of Jews in science, than the far more prominent Einstein. Einstein is primarily viewed as a leading figure in general history of science and in general Jewish history.

To illustrate how rich and variegated the field is, we can take Heinrich Hertz (1857–1894) and his epoch-making work on electromagnetic waves. Hertz was the son of second generation converts to Protestantism, but he was often perceived as Jewish from authors as widely different as the Zionist lexicographer Salomon Winniger and antisemitic representatives of "Deutsche Physik."[6] To the latter, the idea of physical models was a result of the "rassische Gebundenheit" ("racial conditioning") of Hertz's physics. In addition to a proposal based on a pure empirical reconstruction of Hertz's approach, the racialists recommended intepreting *hz*, the unit of frequency, as standing for the "Aryan" and the more empirically oriented "Helmholtz." Such episodes do not make Heinrich Hertz a Jewish scientist, and there is no strict sense in which his personal story, his work, and his life belong to Jewish history, but there is no denying that they are interwoven with it. Other examples need not have ideological backgrounds as in Hertz's case. Sam Schweber has drawn attention to the fact that Hans Bethe (1906–2005), one of the outstanding figures of twentieth century physics, and a Protestant, was scientifically and privately shaped by the milieu of the German-Jewish *Bildungsbürgertum* (the culturally leading group of the bourgeoisie).[7] Logically speaking, in its historical and cultural usage "Jewish" is a vague predicate, which even encompasses relevant moments of such examples; as a halachic term it is classificatory and excluding.

[5] See Anthony S. Travis, "Raphael Meldola and the Nineteenth-Century Neo-Darwinism," *Journal for General Philosophy of Science* 41 (2010), 143–172; Cantor, *Quakers, Jews, and Science*, 340–345.
[6] Cf. Stefan Wolf, "Die Familie Hertz. Eine nichtjüdische Wissenschaftlerfamilie mit jüdischem Namen," in *Heinrich Hertz (1857–1894) and the Development of Communication*, ed. Gudrun Wolfschmidt (Norderstedt: Nuncius Hamburgensis, 2008), 253–273.
[7] Silvan S. Schweber, *Nuclear Forces. The Making of the Physicist Hans Bethe* (Cambridge: Harvard University Press, 2012).

In some respects corresponding to this opposition, the historian is confronted with two harshly contrasting intuitions. On one side, there is the proud narrative of an inconceivable Jewish success, externally visible by the number of Jews in prestigious academic posts, awardees of science prizes, and so forth. On the opposite side, the historian has to deal with the strong suspicion that there is no story of scientists *as Jews* worth telling at all. What would be left as a possible narrative would focus on the antisemitic construct of scientists as Jews. To meet these concerns, it seems appropriate not to confine the consideration to the "success-story" of Jews in science but to focus also on the relationship between science and Judaism with its own dynamics in the course of the nineteenth and twentieth centuries. It needs little deliberation, though, to see that an adequate outline of the "success-story" depends not unavoidably from a decisive determination of the "Jewishness" of one or the other scientist, but from an understanding as to how the relationship between being Jewish and being a scientist has been defined in modern times.

JUDAISM AND SCIENCE IN THE NINETEENTH AND TWENTIETH CENTURIES

Employing an a priori taxonomy to the possible relationships between science and Judaism, one can distinguish the following main options: indifference, conflict, separation, and one-sided or mutual support.[8] Admittedly, all such classifications suppress the dynamics of the relationship as well as factual overlappings, not to speak of explanatory contexts and motives. As a reminder of the fact that probably not one example, if examined in depth, would prove as simple as the taxonomy suggests, we will refer to the Einstein case under conflicting classificatory aspects. Regardless of such limitations, taxonomies facilitate access to fields whose abundance and complexity would otherwise overwhelm us.

---

[8] See partially overlapping Ian G. Barbour, *When Science Meets Religion: Enemies, Strangers or Partners?* (San Francisco: Harper Collins, 2000); idem, "On Typologies for Relating Science and Religion," *Zygon* 37 (2002): 345–359; critically Geoffrey Cantor and Chris Kenny, "Barbour's Fourfold Way: Problems with his Taxonomy of Science-Religion Relationships," *Zygon* 36 (2001): 765–781; see also the contributions by Noah Efron, Geoffrey Cantor, and R. L. Numbers, in Thomas Dixon, Geoffrey Cantor, and Stephen Pumphrey, eds, *Science and Religion: New Historical Perspectives* (Cambridge: Cambridge University Press, 2010).

INDIFFERENCE

Before exploring in greater detail the main options towards relating Jewish religion and science, one has to take into account the narrowness of religious scope when dealing with nineteenth- and twentieth-century science. Here, indifference towards this relationship is probably more common than all the other options put together. For a religious person, an encounter with modern science cannot be avoided. To most modern scientists, religion in general can be widely ignored, including its small Jewish ingredient. In contrast to their predecessors, many modern scientists did not and do not recognize any need to give much thought to this issue. Jewish scientists who do not live in religious contexts do not need to position themselves with regard to aspects of Jewish religion. Of course, the Israeli situation is specific.[9]

To people in a mainly secular environment, such as in twentieth-century Europe, indifference to religion does not essentially appear any different from indifference to philosophy, classical music, and other domains which certain groups acknowledge as valuable. A fitting anecdote concerns Einstein and his application to be appointed professor at Karl-Ferdinand-University, Prague: the authorities insisted on having his religious affiliation recorded. Because his spontaneous answer "none" was not permitted, he had to write "Mosaic."[10] In other words, at this time Einstein identified himself religiously as Jewish in order to satisfy a bureaucratic requirement. And such practice was typical of many scientists who lived in the large European cities around 1910.

Obviously, scientists living in Israel in their daily life do not have the same chance to stay indifferent towards Jewish religion in general and to certain interpretations of Judaism. Another example of how context determines attitudes is provided by Jewish scientists in twentieth-century America. Many of them constituted a certain group perceived as specifically Jewish because they were *free*-thinkers and *not* parochially integrated.[11] This view was mirrored by their self-appraisal (which resembled earlier tendencies in Europe[12]). The apparent paradox vanishes if one bears in mind that, in contrast to Europe, the United States was not and still is not

---

[9] Noah J. Efron, *Real Jews: Secular Versus Ultra-Orthodox: The Struggle for Jewish Identity* (New York: Basic Books, 2003).

[10] Abraham Pais, *Subtle is the Lord: The Science and Life of Albert Einstein* (Oxford: Oxford University Press, 1982), 192.

[11] David A. Hollinger, *Science, Jews, and Secular Culture*, second edition (Princeton: Princeton University Press, 1999), 17–41.

[12] David Kettler and Volker Meja, "Karl Mannheim's Jewish Question: History, Sociology, and the Epistemics of Reflexivity," *Simon Dubnow Institute Yearbook* 3 (2004): 325–347.

widely secularized. Its religious pluralism displays the same kind of tolerance as the Prague authorities did towards Einstein, and leads to creating something as a type of Jewishness that makes the difference to Christians by free-thinking and practicing no religion at all. A good example of how this category of the non-religious Jew has been accepted by the individuals concerned can be found in Stephen Jay Gould's frequently cited article on "Nonoverlapping Magisteria," which was inspired by his encounter with Christian debates on Darwinism in Rome. Advocating the thesis that science and religion comment on different realms, with no appropriate tools for a meaningful discourse in the other domain of professional expertise, he positions himself as a "Jewish agnostic."[13] In the context of his article, "Jewish" obviously stands for a "search for properly ethical values and the spiritual meaning of our lives."[14] Here, Judaism is reduced to something that, in principle, can be achieved by any orientation that provides moral judgment and uplifting feelings. Its function is not even confined to religion in a traditional sense. The currency of such orientation is an important historical fact that relativizes all discourse on Judaism and modern science. However, it does not affect this discourse itself. Since it does not do justice to science if we consider it free from aims and normative aspects, the conception of a personal quest for meaning falls far short of something as complex as Judaism.

CONFLICT

It is not by chance that Stephen Gould has formulated his NOMA principle confronting Christian problems with Evolutionary Theory and in a Catholic context overshadowed by the Galileo case. In line with the Enlightenment position, the mainstream of nineteenth- and twentieth-century Judaism has revived the project of Maimonides and other medieval thinkers to reconcile science and religion. Interestingly, the minor clashes that arise do not necessarily (an exception is, e.g., the Lubavitcher position[15]) correspond to confrontations of certain religious traditions with modernity, but are mainly struggles within modern approaches themselves. In a contribution to a Jewish Orthodox journal, R. Joseph B. Soloveitchik declares "I have never been seriously troubled by the problem of the biblical doctrine of creation vis-à-vis the scientific story of evolutionism at

---

[13] Stephen J. Gould, "Nonoverlapping Magisteria," *Natural History* 106 (March 1997): 16–22, here 16.

[14] Gould, "Nonoverlapping Magisteria," 17.

[15] Menachem M. Schneerson, *Emunah U-Madda* (Kfar Habad: Makhon Lubavitch Publishing House, 1977), 89–99.

both the cosmic and the organic levels, nor have I been perturbed by the confrontation of the mechanistic interpretation of the human mind with the Biblical spiritual concept of man."[16] With this he represents a broad tendency among traditional Jews trusting in the open and never-ending process of Torah interpretation. Conflicts are mainly due to philosophical "petrifications" of Judaism as belief system. Significantly, it was Abraham Geiger, one of the founders of the Reform movement, who on his way from Kantian "reason" to Jewish faith saw his project challenged by the Darwinian blurring of boundaries between humans and animals.[17] In contrast, Hermann Cohen and his more sophisticated Kantianism weakened the concept of the a priori in a way that excluded future conflicts with advancing science.[18]

SEPARATING

As a good starting point for examining deliberate separation, one may consider the following case from the late-nineteenth-century Dutch scene. Among the Jewish professors at Dutch universities at this time was Barend Joseph Stokvis (1834–1902), a distinguished physician. When Stokvis died, his academic colleagues praised him as "een goed Nederlander."[19] However, Stokvis was not only a good Dutchman. As chair of the Ashkenazi community's Poor Relief Council in his hometown of Amsterdam, he excelled as well as "a good Jew." In 1887, the same year that he succeeded his father in this post, Stokvis opened the First Dutch Congress of Science and Medicine with an address entitled "Nationaliteit en Naturweetenschap." To Stokvis, as to many other academics of his generation (one may think of Pierre Duhem's *La Théorie physique* (1906) and its distinction between British and French physics), it was a settled issue that there were different national styles of scientific research, not as a matter of citizenship but of mentality. In Stokvis's opinion, Hermann Boerhaave was a truly Dutch

---

[16] Joseph B. Soloveitchik, "The Lonely Man of Faith," *Tradition* 7 (1965): 2, 5–67, here 7.

[17] Shai Cherry, "Creation, Evolution and Jewish Thought" (Ph.D. diss. Brandeis University, 2001).

[18] Hermann Cohen, *Kants Theorie der Erfahrung* (Berlin: Bruno Cassirer, 1871); cf. the application to Judaism in Hermann Cohen, *[Die] Religion der Vernunft aus den Quellen des Judentums* (Berlin: Bruno Cassirer, 1919) (the definite article is a publisher's error).

[19] Quoted in Klaas van Berkel, "Het genootschap als spiegel van twee eeuwen wetenschaps-geschiedenis in Nederland," in *Spiegelbeeld der wetenschap. Het genootschap ter bevordering van Natuur-, Genees-, en Heelkunde, 1790–1990*, ed. idem (Rotterdam: Erasmus, 1991), 11–58, 39.

scientist, while Huygens was also a bit French, and Leeuwenhoek a bit German.

Seen against this background, the question suggests itself as to whether one could perhaps identify something like a Jewish style of research. The reason why Stockvis never dealt with this issue can be found easily, if we look closer at his description of the Dutch style. According to Stokvis, Dutch science is truth-oriented, guided by a skeptical attitude and the idea of open exchange with others, irrespective of their positions and backgrounds. In other words, Dutch science is in fact *universal* science, and other styles only make science deviate from the true path of ideal research.

As there is no arguable Jewish science that deviates from Dutch science, so too there is no scientific Judaism. Stokvis defines his role as an upstanding member of his Amsterdam community, not as a pioneer of the scientification of religion but as a selfless medical doctor and social benefactor. The region of *gemilut hasadim* is a neutral sphere apart from possible tensions between science and religion. In the realm of twentieth-century religious philosophy, Yeshayahu Leibowitz (1903–94) has put forward a philosophical thesis that matches Stokvis's practice of separating his parochial and his "Dutch" scientific identity. To Leibowitz, Judaism is a normative conception that neither collides nor harmonizes with science as a descriptive, explanative, and predictive project.[20]

As a practical counterpart to Leibowitz' position in twentieth-century science, Einstein was an influential public figure in many cases where he acted *in favor* of Jews, from individual help to the support of institutions, such as Hebrew University and Brandeis University. In contrast to his early years, he was far from being indifferent to Judaism. Nevertheless, his commitment to the separation of science from his "personal" attitudes never faltered. Whether his self-appraisal really corresponded to all aspects of his scientific work is another question, given that his metaphysics, his frequent usage of a certain type of thought experiments, and his style of popularizing Relativity Theory had a Reform Jewish source.[21]

---

[20] Menachem Kellner, "Torah and Science in Modern Jewish Thought: Steven Schwarzschild vs Yeshayahu Leibowitz," in *Torah et Science: perspectives historiques et théoriques, Études offertes à Ch. Touati*, ed. Gad Freudenthal (Leuven: Peeters, 2001), 229–237.

[21] Ulrich Charpa, "Aaron Bernstein's 'nächster großer Reformator'. Einstein, Reform Judaism, and the Fries School," in *Jews and Sciences in German Contexts*, ed. Charpa and Deichmann, 155–180.

ONE-SIDED AND MUTUAL SUPPORT

Compared to other religions, Judaism in general shows a distinctly positive tendency towards science and the idea that scientific research can improve religious life. When Norman Lamm, former president of Yeshiva University and one of the leading proponents of the conception *torah u-madda* (Torah and science), declares religious study and secular learning to exist in a "synergistic interrelation," he links himself to a respectable tradition: from Rabbi Yehuda ha-Nasi, who declared gentile cosmology "preferable to ours" (*Pesahim* 94b), over the great medieval and early modern figures like Maimonides and the Maharal of Prague, to his own teacher Joseph B. Soloveitchik.[22]

Science Supporting Judaism

It is a commonplace observation that technical devices can in many ways be helpful tools to religious observance. This does not necessarily include links to a tool's scientific preconditions, but such a connection was brought about in the case of electricity. More precisely, it was electrical light that confronted observant Jews with the scientific question about its physical character. In order to meet the rule of *Exodus* 53:3, it was necessary to decide whether or not switching on a lamp was something that would break the Sabbath. One early answer was given by William Crookes, who emphasized the difference between fire and the glowing of the filament encased in the glass bulb.[23] But this does not solve the problem of what type of an action switching on a lamp is; in other words, whether such an action is illicit work because it amounts to generation (*molid*) of something new or not. Obviously, by analogy with a philosophical approach, moving down from applied science to scientific foundations, such a Talmudic debate[24] leads from a technical construction to pure natural philosophy and fundamental questions of the following type: what does "change" in nature mean? In this case, science and natural philosophy support observant practice and religious decision making in situations which are triggered by new technical inventions.

Apart from such occasionally helpful science-based technology, there are mainly three domains that come into question as to where scientific

---

[22] Norman Lamm, *Torah Umadda. The Encounter of Religious Learning and Worldly Knowledge* (Northvale: Aronson, 1990), cf. idem, *The Shema. Spirituality and Law in Judaism as Identified in the Shema, the Most Important Passage in the Torah* (Philadelphia: The Jewish Publication Society, 2000), chap. 8.

[23] Cantor, *Quakers, Jews, and Science*, 298–300.

[24] Cf. the entry on electricity (*hashmal*) in the *Enzyklopediah Talmudit*, vol. 18, 155–190; 647–781.

support works. Here science and religion meet directly: the fields of the calendar, kashrut, and health. These three connections have been intensified with the emergence of modern science and are still relevant interventions. In all of them the conditions of religious observance become more and more favorable in the course of scientific progress. "[A] correct calendar is of imperative necessity to the descendants of that people, who are enjoined by Scripture authority to the performance of Rites and Ceremonies upon the periodical return of certain 'days, times, and seasons'."[25] This introductory remark from a nineteenth-century Jewish calendar, with its impressive accurateness attained with the help of advanced Victorian astronomy and its experts, is "atemporal." In principle, the objective was the same in Victorian England as in Jewish antiquity, or as it is today. While the rule remains stable, the chance to fulfill the "imperative necessity" advances simultaneously with the advancement of astronomical research.

The relationship between science and the dietary laws is of the same sort, but much more under debate. While collisions between the Jewish calendar and the time schedules of non-Jewish people can, at least in principle, be regulated (one might think of the *shabbes goy*) with relatively little effort, eating regulations have always been much more a matter of negotiation. Basically, this has to do with the clash between the fact of being surrounded by gentile customs on the one side and the objectives of kashrut – that is preserving the distinction between Jews and non-Jews (*Tobias* 1:10–11) – on the other. Science opens an additional perspective: accepting the dietary laws without caveat entails a commitment to *inform* oneself on the purity of the food available. From the nineteenth century, chemistry has been proposed as an aid in avoiding kashrut violations.[26] From the late eighteenth century there were also discussions on the outcomes of microscopy.[27] The microscopist faced a hitherto religiously unclassified and unseen world of living beings. Since the microscope caused the problem, this device was at the same time the only way out. It was the improvement of microscopical work that promised an aid to the appraisal of creatures that are invisible to the naked eye and resemble crustaceans and other animals that are not *kosher* within the range of normal vision.

A religious aspect of the dietary laws apart from the function of separating is that of sanctifying oneself (*Leviticus* 11:44). This conception is the starting point of connecting kashrut to health, as it found expression in Maimonides's

[25] Elias H. Lindo, *A Jewish Calender for Sixty-Four Years [...]*. London 1838, iii, quoted in Cantor, *Quakers, Jews, and Science*, 292.

[26] Cantor, *Quakers, Jews, and Science*, 300–301.

[27] David Ch. Kraemer, *Jewish Eating and Identity Through the Ages* (New York: Routledge, 2007), 157.

influential view that all food which is forbidden is unwholesome.[28] This idea had an interesting career even among non-Jews and encouraged anachronistic esteem of the medical wisdom of Jews from the days of Moses on.[29] There existed a time-honored and still wide-spread view of Jews as always having had privileged access to medical knowledge and conditions of healthy living, in full harmony with their religious tradition. But there is a contrasting discourse, which identified Jews as an unhealthy, degenerated population. This view became part of the nineteenth century antisemitic ideology at the same time when modern medicine turned itself into a scientifically based discipline which integrated laboratory and statistical research. The next step was to connect the antisemite's "Jewish Question" with eugenics and Social Darwinism, an essential strand of Nazi thinking.

As to scientific support of Judaism by biological arguments it was especially the exclusion of intermarriage that offered an ideal bridge to scientific thinking on heredity transmission and the possible distinctiveness of Jews. It is a historical fact that evolutionist anthropology combined with Mendelian genetics served as an inspiration for Jewish apologetics.[30] In this regard, it is important to differentiate what today would be appraised as quasi- or even pseudo-scientific discourses on Jewish race and its peculiarities (often with a focus on morphological characteristics) from adequate scientific discourse related to Jews and Judaism. One has to keep in mind that in contrast to Spencer's interpretation, for example, scientific Darwinism thematizes species which survived by features relevant to certain contexts. In alternative contexts such advantages can turn out to be counter-effective. In contrast, the social-Darwinist prefers the idea that there are superior or inferior features in an absolute sense. The attractiveness of such a view to social scientists, educationalists, politicians and so forth is at hand: it changes the perspective from a world of long-time, large-scale, and determining factors to a cosmos of human options for immediate action, such as the "transformation of Jewish life"[31] into modernity. Yet, evolution in a scientific Darwinian sense is not advancement, and even if one is inclined to count Jews as a genetically different population, they are, at the most, a slight variant. And this variant has come

---

[28] *Guide of the Perplexed* 3, 48.

[29] Cf. Mitchell B. Hart, *The Healthy Jew: The Symbiosis of Judaism and Modern Science* (Cambridge: Cambridge University Press, 2007).

[30] Cf. Hart, *The Healthy Jew*, 105–190; Dan Stone, "Of Peas, Potatoes, and Jews: Redcliffe N. Salaman and the British Debate over Racial Origins," *Simon Dubnow Institute Yearbook* 3 (2004): 221–240.

[31] Mitchell B. Hart, *Social Science and the Politics of Modern Jewish Identity* (Stanford: Stanford University Press, 2000), 100.

into being in a very short time-span, far beyond the duration that relevant evolutionary processes require.

As the controversy about the *y*-chromosome markers of the *kohanim* has shown, if there is anything significant with the biological features of Jews, it may be found in genetics and not in evolutionary theory. And even this perspective is not sufficient because it is due to the main tendencies of twentieth-century biological research with its neglect of developmental aspects of the path from the cell to the complete organism. Because the developmental view, in principle, integrates everything that has any impact on embryonic processes, the new "post-genomic" era of biology that has emerged in the 1990s promises to shed more light on "fine-structure" questions such as the characteristics of small sub-groups of modern mankind.

Judaism as a Support to Science

Since both science and medicine can be interpreted as means of religious practice, they themselves can benefit from religious norms. In the case of medicine, medical treatment in the hands of others as well as taking "good care of yourselves" (*Deuteronomy* 4:15) ranks as a religious duty. The emphasis on health and healing has far-reaching consequences with regard to Jewish attitudes towards reproductive genetics and other practical implementations of modern science into a modern society.[32] This aspect of medicine includes a general favorable condition of scientific work. If science functions as a means of good religious practice, the justification of the religious practice generates a justification of the subsidiary scientific practice. At the same time, the factual meanings of "healthiness," and "promptitude" with regard to religious relevant times, as well as of "kashrut," undergo a change in concrete contents. Along this line of thinking, halachic innovation and scientific advancement can, in principle, be related to each other as a feed-back-system.

The positive option was exercised by the Jewish representatives of the Enlightenment and their successors in the Jewish reform movements, from the nineteenth century right through to the present.[33] In its early

[32] See Yael Hashiloni-Dolev, *A Life (Un)Worthy of Living: Reproductive Genetics in Israel and Germany* (Berlin: Springer, 2007); idem, "German and Israeli Attitudes towards Reproductive Genetics and the Effect of Religion," in *Jews and Sciences in German Contexts*, ed. Charpa and Deichmann, 195–227; Shimon M. Glick, "A Jewish View of Genetic Enhancement," *Journal of Medical Ethics* 37 (2011): 415–419. The most prominent critic of the mainstream tendency is Leon Kass. See his "The Wisdom of Repugnance," *The New Republic*, June 2, 1997, 17–26.

[33] As standard information see Michael A. Meyer and Michael Brenner, *German-Jewish History in Modern Times*, vol. 2, *Emancipation and Acculturation* (New York: Columbia University Press, 1998).

beginnings it can be seen as a double change: on one side as mere secularization and accommodation, and on the other side an internal Jewish
effort to rebuild Judaism by retrieving neglected or partially forgotten practices of textual exegesis with the help of secular knowledge.[34]
Mathematics, modern languages, geography, and other subjects became
integral parts of Jewish education up to Rabbinical training. Not by
chance, the first director of the Jewish Free School for Impecunious
Children (Jüdische Freischule) in Berlin was an outstanding mathematician and secular philosopher, Lazarus Ben David (1762–1832). In its later
developments, the tendency to modernize Judaism itself became concre-
tized as disciplinary formation of the *Wissenschaft des Judentums* (and its
successors),[35] and as a broader movement in the shape of Reform Judaism
aimed at consistency between Jewish religious attitudes and all relevant
aspects of nineteenth -and twentieth -century sciences. Irrespective of
the agenda of central European Reform Judaism, science became also
widely recognized in Jewish cultures at the periphery of modern academic tendencies.[36] This is documented by the wide range of scientific
literature in Yiddish and Ladino which mainly provides basic information on scientific disciplines but also includes monographs on particular
outstanding topics.[37]

---

[34] Cf. David Sorkin, "Religious Reforms and Secular Trends in German-Jewish Life: An
Agenda for Reform," *Leo Baeck Institute Yearbook* 40 (1995): 169–184; Shmuel Feiner,
The Origins of Secularization in Eighteenth-Century Europe (Philadelphia: University of
Pennsylvania Press, 2010).

[35] The *Wissenschaft des Judentums* became institutionalized quasi-academically in Jewish
seminaries, but its results were also addressed to the lay public. Cf. Nils Roemer, *Jewish
Scholarship and Culture in 19th-Century Germany* (Madison: University of Wisconsin
Press, 2005); Shuly R. Schwartz, *The Emergence of Jewish Scholarship in America: The
Publication of the Jewish Encyclopedia* (Cincinnati: Hebrew Union College Press, 1991).

[36] Cf. Mordechai Zelkin, "Scientific Literature and Cultural Transformation in Nineteenth
Century East European Jewish Society," *Aleph. Historical Studies in Science and Judaism*
5 (2005): 249–271.

[37] As a general survey cf. Sarah A. Stein, *Making Jews Modern: The Yiddish and Ladino
Press in the Russian and Ottoman Empire* (Bloomington: Indiana University Press, 2004);
focused on science see Matthias B. Lehmann, *Ladino Rabbinic Literature and Ottoman
Sephardic Culture* (Bloomington: Indiana University Press, 2005), 187–201; Alexandre
Métraux, "Opening Remarks on the History of Science in Yiddish," *Science in Context*
20 (2007): 145–162; Stephen M. Cohen, "Chemical Literature in Yiddish: A Bridge
between the Shtetl and the Secular World," *Aleph. Historical Studies in Science and
Judaism* 7 (2007): 183–251; Roland Gruschka, "Tuvia Schalit's Di spetsyele relativitets-
teorye of 1927 and Other Introductions to the Theory of Relativity in Yiddish," *Science
in Context* 20 (2007): 317–339.

At a radical step further, Einstein's metaphysics exemplifies the conception of congruence in an uncompromised form: The physicist's thinking starts as that of a religious person's vague impressions of the world, with a certain "sensing" towards a relation of something supernatural and natural.[38] Seeing that nature is determined by strict laws, one is impelled to believe that there is a superior spirit who – as the famous dictum goes – "does not play dice." The scientist's task is to understand this deterministically regulated world, and his research work is a form of religious service.

Mutual Support of Science and Judaism

It is easy to see that such radical support of science by transforming in such a radical manner religion into science itself is unavoidably dependent on the idea that religion and science are instances of *belief*. In more moderate versions, Hermann Cohen and Steven Schwarzschild have developed conceptions that aim at uniting science and Judaism in other philosophical, especially Kantian terms. Here, the support of science by religion runs via common appraisals of the mental processes underlying science and religion. Both enterprises are seen as aiming at *true* conceptions of the world. The structure of the relationship is hierarchical in the same way as Kantian epistemology and philosophy of science are. In Kantian terms: Judaism (redefined in a pure, ideal form as truth-oriented) functions as a "regulative" idea on the scientific approach to the *noumenon*.

The result of activities guided by the principle of truth as the ultimate goal is progress. This basic idea has to be made more concrete with regard to science as well as to religion. To start with the latter, one has to keep in mind that the idea of progress is not without rivals. One could also argue that change in a Talmudic culture is either *mere change* due to the fact of never-ending rabbinical controversies and polemics, or even *decline* due to the superiority of former rabbis.[39] In contrast, science is seldom considered as stagnating or even declining; the most powerful intuition towards science is that it progresses. Not even the relativist denies the progressiveness of scientific change, and only confines each advancement to internal movements within merely changing conceptual frames.

---

[38] Max Jammer, *Einstein and Religion, Physics and Theology* (Princeton: Princeton University Press, 1999), 78–80; Charpa, "Aaron Bernstein's 'nächster großer Reformator'," 158–166.

[39] Compare the discussion of Maimonides's antithesis of progress and regress by Menachem Kellner, *Maimonides on the 'Decline of the Generations' and the Nature of Rabbinic Authority* (Albany: SUNY Press, 1996); tending towards "mere change" is Jonathan Sacks, "Creativity and Innovation in Halakhah," in *Rabbinic Authority and Personal Autonomy*, ed. Moshe Z. Sokol (Northvale, NJ: Jason Aronson, 1992), 123–168.

Menachem Fisch has made an interesting attempt to draw a parallel between a well-known model of scientific progress (which is also inspired by Kant) and a certain Talmudic tradition. To him, as science aims at true beliefs about the world, "the ultimate cognitive aim and purpose of Torah study is to approximate as closely as possible the only true, originally intended meaning of the holy Scriptures."[40] The method of coming closer to the truth, in science as in the interpretation of the Torah, is a critical dispute that occurs without a reliance on authority or inspiration. According to Fisch, the concurring "traditionalist" tendency is not generally "uncritical" but restricts the process of critical discussion to innovations that can be derived from already existing prominent conclusions. More radical Talmudic discussion is analogous to advancing scientifically by the exchange of striking arguments, and rabbinical training, which includes such a priority, could be considered favorable to entering the realm of science.

One of the problems with this, as with Hermann Cohen's and Steven Schwarzschild's views, results from its emphasis on beliefs as the core elements of Judaism. If we go back to the position that Judaism is essentially bound to adequate *action* – a traditional view renewed by Leibowitz[41] – the problem occurs that mere beliefs are too weak to guarantee the improvement of religious actions. It is *justified* beliefs that are needed. In science, the main justifying instances are empirical data. In a Talmudic environment justification arises from textual instances. In both realms progress is dependent on improving beliefs by mental attitudes that are superior to mere belief, in other words, religious and scientific *knowledge*. However, due to the rise of hypotheticism in theoretical physics from the nineteenth century on, and its philosophical commentaries, for decades the idea of knowledge in a strict sense has been assessed as naiveté. By now, in line with the shift of interest in science studies from Einstein's and Bohr's lofty spheres to tangible laboratory science, the epistemological perspective has changed.[42] With a focus on reliable procedures in experimental contexts, it

---

[40] Menachem Fisch, *Rational Rabbis. Science and Talmudic Culture* (Bloomington: Indiana University Press, 1997), 57. Fisch adopts a variant of Popperian methodology which – departing from Popper's original approach – is based on the concept of progressive beliefs in theories (Popper's own concern are theory shifts in a world separated from mental states).

[41] Yeshayahu Leibowitz, "Religion and Science in the Middle Ages and in the Modern Era" (1976), in *Judaism, Human Values, and the Jewish State*, ed. Eliezer Goldman (Cambridge: Harvard University Press, 1992), 132–142; cf. Kellner, "Torah and Science."

[42] See, e.g., Alvin Goldman, *Knowledge in a Social World* (Oxford: Oxford University Press, 1999).

no longer appears philosophically hazardous to speak of a scientist's and a rabbi's *justified* beliefs. In both domains, stable and well-grounded expert knowledge can be found, identified as familiarity with data and existing views; they may be represented in scientific textbooks or in the Talmud and other Jewish sources. It is not risky belief in other people's or one's own opinion that serves as condition of advancement, but *being acquainted* with the standard experts' views on the issues at stake.

Accepting the concept of knowledge rehabilitates the traditional ideas on learning, and scientific and religious institutions as cultures of it. Knowledge is uncontroversially an enabling factor, a cognitive "virtue," while mere belief is not. Focusing on the relevance of enabling factors (one may think also of skills, endurance, and other characteristics) rehabilitates the "folk" wisdom that the virtues of the learner are not only results but facilitate further cognitive progress. In this sense, the importance of enabling factors bridges Judaism to science.

The turn to "virtues" is not as new as may appear, not even if it is related to the specific topic of Judaism and science. Corresponding to some other nineteenth-century conceptions of science as research practice (e.g., Bernard and Helmholtz) the botanist Matthias Schleiden has outlined the assistance of Judaism to science based on the idea that an essential feature of both domains is the idea of acting with *competence*. This leads to the next step, that deliberate Jewish practices are a matter of training, expert knowledge, personality traits, and favorable institutional surroundings. It was R. Joseph B. Soloveitchik, the leader of Modern Orthodoxy, who (not without tensions to the Kantian tendencies he shares with Cohen, Schwarzschild, and others) has criticized the focus on belief and mere religious sense of something superior in favor of the methodological and content-based "virtues" of the trained expert (*lamdan*).[43] In principle, such competences count in all fields of demanding activities, in chess as well as in scientific research and religious practice.

ZIONISM AND SCIENCE

While relating Judaism to science has mainly been a matter of fundamental reflections and minor practical results, the impact of Zionism on science and vice versa is a comparatively simple relationship with gigantic practical outcomes. Israel is one of the world's scientifically leading countries, and a decisive part of the story of "Jewish success" in science (see below). But

---

[43] Joseph B. Soloveitchik, "The 'Common Sense' Rebellion against Torah Authority," in *Reflections of The Rav*, vol. 1, ed. Abraham R. Besdin, revised edition (New York: Ktav, 1993), 139–149.

one has to see that a great deal of Israel's scientific achievement today is less grounded in Zionist ideas than in the economic and military demands of the state. Nevertheless, it is partly due to aspects of Zionist ideology (and Jewish tradition) that Israel has not exclusively focused on applied science. Irrespective of its preferences to support technical innovations and a growing tendency to cut expenses for "pure" and at first sight "needless" scientific enterprises, Israel is still an eminent place for undertaking basic research. In his address at the opening ceremony of The Hebrew University of Jerusalem on April 1, 1925, Chaim Weizmann, the first president and himself an outstanding chemist, declared "the pursuit of *every* form of knowledge which the mind of man embraces"[44] as an objective of the Zionist project. That Weizmann's attitude was not only propagandistic is shown by the disciplinary history of The Hebrew University, for example by the fact that mathematics was first established as a "pure" discipline.[45]

Nevertheless, a priority for science connected to technical progress has been an essential part of the political Zionist vision from its early beginnings. Theodor Herzl's novel *Altneuland* has the character of a technological utopia, with large-scale electrification, chemical innovations in agriculture, and modern communication facilities, such as high speed electric railways and monorails.[46] To the Zionist project, science is primarily instrumental with regard to common welfare via the employment of technical devices. A less important Zionist utilization of science, which affected scientific methods, themata, and contents, was promoted by Zionist biologists. They aimed at establishing a biological basis for the Zionist project of nation building, a project which is still vivid, but in its earlier versions has been shown to be biased.[47]

---

[44] Chaim Weizmann, Barnet Litvinoff, *The Letters and Papers of Chaim Weizmann*, Series B: Papers, vol. I, August 1898–July 1931 (New Brunswick: Transaction, 1983), 442–445, here 443 (emphasis mine).

[45] See Shaul Katz, "Berlin Roots – Zionist Incarnation: The Ethos of Pure Mathematics and the Beginnings of the Einstein Institute of Mathematics at the Hebrew University of Jerusalem," *Science in Context* 17 (2004): 199–234.

[46] Anthony S. Travis, " 'The Jewish Jules Verne': Science, Technology and Theodor Herzl," (unpublished); idem, "2007 Edelstein Award Paper: What a Wonderful Empire is the Organic Chemistry," *Bulletin of the History of Chemistry*, 33, no. 1 (2008): 1–11.

[47] See Raphael Falk, *Ziyonut ve habiologia shel ha-yehudim* (Tel Aviv: Resling, 2006); Nurit Kirsh, "Population Genetics in Israel in the 1950s: The Unconscious Internalization of Ideology," *Isis* 94, no. 4 (2003): 631–655; idem, "Genetic Studies of Ethnic Communities in Israel: A Case of Values-Motivated Research Work," in *Jews and Sciences in German Contexts*, ed. Charpa and Deichmann, 181–194.

THE "SUCCESS-STORY"

In its simplest version, the success narrative runs like a group-oriented version of Cinderella's tale: In the beginnings of modern science, Jews were treated with contempt as outsiders. Due to great talent and ambition they freed themselves from this role, and, despite discrimination, in the end they became a superior group to all other groups from which scientific personnel was recruited. What does "Jewish success" in science stand for, if we try to describe the phenomenon that this narrative mirrors? Schematically seen, one can refer to the following: 1) *increase of participation*, as shown by the numbers of Jewish scientists; 2) *growth of scientific institutions* where many, most, or all of the scientists are Jews; 3) increase of the *relevance* of scientific work done by Jews; 4) *speed* of growth with regard to both participation and relevance; and 5) *efficiency* of participation.

To make this appraisal more concrete and at the same time to fix a starting point for discussing the issues at stake, one may refer to a contrasting story to the Cinderella tale, in which a talented young Jew did not participate in scientific research, never entered a scientific institution, never achieved anything relevant in a scientific domain and all this with an enormous waste of time and effort. This happened to Shlomo Ben Josua Haiman, who died in 1800. As a young man, living in Lithuania, he was fascinated by the natural sciences after reading David Gans's *Zemah David*, a work published two centuries earlier, in 1592. To get further into the questions of science, he left his home in deep winter around the year 1775 and marched about 150 miles in order to visit a rabbi who owned some more recent German books on science.[48] The greatest treasure that Shlomo brought back to his village was Johann Christoph Sturm's *Kurtzer Begriff der Physic*, a book written by a German scientist who died in 1703. It presented a merely qualitative approach to the study of nature, totally anachronistic in the age of Lagrange and artistic mathematical mechanics. Salomon Maimon, as Shlomo called himself later, never became a scientist. Not even an incomparably better informed and situated figure of his era, Moses Mendelssohn, became eminent as a scientist comparable to the leading names of the great scientific academies of the time.

To mark the span from Maimon's era to our own within the context of participation and relevance of Jews in science it may be noted that the authoritative *Encyclopédie* (1751–1780) discusses Spinoza and related thinkers but does not name a single Jew of modern times as a scientist. In one of the earliest works among the modern historiography of science, we find

---

[48] See *Salomon Maimon's Lebensgeschichte von ihm selbst geschrieben und herausgegeben von K. Ph. Moritz*, Teil I (Berlin: Vieweg, 1792), 120.

William Whewell's three-volume work, which mentions no more than two – today forgotten – Jews in science, two crystallographers with Sefardi names.[49]

In the course of the 160 years after Whewell's *History* the scene has spectacularly changed: Among the winners of Nobel Prizes for sciences, of the Fields medal for mathematics, and of the Turing Award by the Association for Computing Machinery are around 180 Jews. Jewish awardees account for about one quarter of a scientific population whose work is conceived as extremely relevant in their domains. Most of these successful researchers were not and are not members of a scientific institution one would consider Jewish. Today, many work at US universities, a situation that resembles the position of Jewish researchers in imperial and Weimar Germany. In pre-Nazi Europe we find outstanding Jewish scientists, most notably in Germany (some of them originally born in eastern countries such as Hungary). Helmholtz, the leading figure of science in imperial Germany, alone had a dozen prominent Jewish disciples, among them Eugen Goldstein, Fritz Haber, Gabriel Lippmann, Samuel Michelson and even such a colorful figure as Noah Bakst, the founder of the ORT-movement. This phenomenon was made possible by the successful entrance of Jews into German academia; this began with Moritz Abraham Stern, a mathematician, who was the first Jew appointed full professor at a German university (1859).[50] In the Netherlands, Reheul Lobatto became full Professor already in 1842. Although many Jews met obstacles as they tried to reach higher academic ranks, this did not exclude them from relevant scientific work. As often cited, around one-third of Germans who were awarded the Nobel Prize were Jewish. Even if one may have serious doubts about the meaning of "Jewish" in some cases, the phenomenon is worthy of note.

Intriguingly, it has been argued that remaining at the poorly paid position of "Privatdozenten" was a favorable incentive for innovative research.[51] Apart from the German-speaking scene, we come across high-ranking Jewish scientists in all European countries of the pre-Nazi era, e.g., Vito Volterra, Tullio Levi-Civita, Jacques Hadamard, Leonardo Salomon Ornstein, Paul Ehrenfest, and many others who were respected members of a transnational network of scientists.[52] Forced emigration brought some

[49] William Whewell, *History of the Inductive Science from the Earliest to the Present Time*, vol. 3 (London: Parker, 1847), 242.
[50] Cf. Bergmann, Epple, and Ungar, *Transcending Tradition*, 57.
[51] Shulamit Volkov, "Jewish Scientists in Imperial Germany (Part I and II)," *Aleph. Historical Studies in Science and Judaism*, 1 (2001): 215–281.
[52] For the Italian situation see Judith R. Goodstein, "The Rise and Fall of Vito Volterra's World," *Journal of the History of Ideas* 45 (1984), 607–617; Giuliano Pancaldi, "Vito

of them to countries such as the UK, Turkey, and Japan, but most went to the US, where they became citizens and contributed disproportionately, for their number, to the success of American research institutions.[53]

If we leave aside consideration of the individual level of participation and relevance, and define as Jewish scientific institutions universities in Israel, some specific US universities like Yeshiva University (with its two colleges),[54] and some smaller colleges in other countries, such as ORT Argentina, the performance of these institutions is impressive. According to the 2013 Shanghai Ranking, Israeli universities rank among the leading universities worldwide. Among the top 100, the *Weizmann Institute of Science* is ranked at 92, the *Technion* at 77, and *Hebrew University* at 59.[55] For an appreciation of this ranking it is relevant to point out that the numbers position the small state of Israel in the category of France (3 among the top 100). As to smaller countries, only Switzerland (3) compares to Israel in this regard.

Interestingly, the obvious efficiency of Israeli science is – in contrast to Switzerland and other successful small countries – not based on effective schooling.[56] This issue draws attention to a remarkable factor that was discussed after the publication of a comparative study on Israeli and Danish mathematics. Citation analysis showed that the impact of Israeli mathematics on the community of mathematicians exceeded that of Denmark (a comparable country with a highly developed educational system) by a factor 13.[57] Among the possible explanatory hypotheses concerning this bizarre ratio, it turned out that the simple distinction between Jewish and non-Jewish mathematicians tends to hide two relevant factors. One is the research orientation in Israeli mathematical higher education, whereas Danish instruction at the time of the survey followed the older German model with its distinct paucity of research seminars. The other and more

Volterra, Cosmopolitan Ideals and Nationality in the Italian Scientific Community between the Belle Époque and the First World War," *Minerva* 31 (1993) 31–37.

[53] Ute Deichmann, *Biologists under Hitler* (Cambridge: Harvard University Press, 1996); idem, *Flüchten, Mitmachen. Chemiker und Biochemiker im Nationalsozialismus* (Weinheim: Wiley, 2001).

[54] Gilbert Klapperman, *The Story of Yeshiva University* (New York: Macmillan, 1969).

[55] Institute of Higher Education Shanghai Jiao Tong University, shanghairanking.com/ARWU2013.html, retrieved July 20, 2014.

[56] "The level of achievement by Israeli pupils is 12 percent to 27 percent below (depending on the international exam) the average level of achievement in other (comparable) countries." Dan Ben David, "Education in Israel: A Problematic Present and a Hopeful Future," www.tau.ac.il/~danib/articles/EducFactsHopeEng.htm, retrieved July 20, 2014.

[57] Thomas Schøtt, "Scientific Productivity and International Integration of Small Countries: Mathematics in Denmark and Israel," *Minerva* 25 (1987): 3–20, here 8–12.

important factor is the integration of Israeli research activities into the international scientific community. Israeli mathematicians have much better contacts, especially to the leading American institutions in their field, than Danish researchers, as is documented by invitations and co-authoring. This suggests that the striking gap between the Israeli school and university systems is closed by the interaction of the higher-educational system with external systems, including through immigration from the United States and the former Soviet Union.

As to the *speed* of Jewish participation in modern science it appears remarkable that after lowering the institutional barriers in Europe from the mid-nineteenth century on it took not more than two generations for Jews to join academia broadly. The same thing happened with the successful children and grandchildren of those immigrants to the United States who were allegedly classified as underachievers in the first immigrant mental tests.[58] A US national survey showed that Jews, to a similar extent, were overrepresented in the top ranks of US science as they were in pre-NS-Germany.[59] Such speed of individual participation is as remarkable as that of the institutional ranking of Israeli universities. Nevertheless, neither development is unique. There is a parallel, on the level of the academic performance of first and second generation immigrants with an Asian and Hispanic background in the US,[60] and, institutionally, by the rapid emergence of modern Japan and more recently China and India as scientifically advancing countries. While it does not seem that the "success story" can be

[58] See the contentious account in Stephen J. Gould's *The Mismeasure of Man* (New York: Norton, New York 1981), 194–197, 230–232. Leading members of the British eugenic movement made similar attempts to determine the intelligence of Jewish immigrant children in 1925 (cf. Gavin Schaffer, "'Like a Baby with a Box of Matches'. British Scientists and the Concept of 'Race' in the Inter-War Period," *British Journal of the History of Science* 38 (2005): 307–324. The point of the matter here is that, however inadequate these tests may have been as measurements of intelligence, the results document a starting condition of the immigrants, especially the cultural barriers (including the language gap) between groups like the Anglo-Saxon testers and the newcomers from the continent.

[59] Martin Trow, *Aspects of American Higher Education, 1969–75* (Berkeley: Carnegie Council on Policy Studies in Higher Education, 1997); a historical overview on the development focused on one example is Dan Oren, *Joining the Club: A History of Jews and Yale* (New Haven: Yale University Press, 1986).

[60] Interestingly, their families' attitudes towards learning (also a classical Jewish topic) seem to play the key role in the success of these individuals. Cf. the monumental study of approximately 11,000 biographies by two sociologists Lingxin Hao and Han S. Woo, "Distinct Trajectories in the Transition to Adulthood: Are Children of Immigrants Advantaged?," *Children Development* 83 (2012): 1623–1639.

universally copied, providing an explanation for this development would be an inestimable contribution to the promotion of science.

EXPLANATORY ATTEMPTS

Local and social disparities within higher learning and scientific research are a common issue for analysis by sociologists and historians. Undeniably, science does not flourish everywhere, and dramatic successes should provoke an overwhelming demand for explanations. In fact, it does not. There are some attempts concerning certain groups, especially the tiny group of German-Jewish scientists before the Nazi-era.[61] As to the general phenomenon, not much explanatory progress has been made since Veblen's famous thesis of 1919 (see below). The main reasons are to be found in the development of science studies which were for a long time exclusively shaped by the "universalist" orientation and its "relativist" counterpart. If the division between a "Popperian" and a "Foucaultian" perspective on science is without alternatives, there is no room for dealing with "Jewish success." As already noted, modern social epistemology (Alvin I. Goldman and others) has changed the scene, but this recent development has not yet set out a new powerful explanatory approach.

In addition, the topic of Jewish success in science is an awkward one in certain notable ways. This, too, helps account for the relative weakness or lack of explanations for this phenomenon. Dealing with the success of one group indirectly includes dealing with the failure of others. Success is not a categorical phenomenon, but a comparative one, something in *contrast* to the achievements of others. Through commitment to the Enlightenment tradition, most modern historians and sociologists are intuitively egalitarian. Addressing the issue confronts them with the risk of challenging something that is – by moral standards – held in high esteem. In the specific case of the role of Jews in science, scholars face the additional problem that contrasting Jews to others seems deeply connected to antisemitism and its philo-Semitic counterpart. This is not merely a supposition, but in fact corresponds to the history of explanatory attempts. The first approaches to explaining the success story were motivated by antisemitic attitudes, and all antisemitic arguments were based on contrasting the situations of Jews and non-Jews. Among the responses to the antisemitic views we find many apologetic attempts, presenting the "Great Jews" in science

---

[61] Werner E. Mosse and others, eds, *Second Chance: Two-Centuries of German-Speaking Jews in The United Kingdom* (Tübingen: Mohr-Siebeck, 1991); Volkov, "Jewish Scientists"; Simone Wenkel, "Jewish Scientists in German-Speaking Academia: An Overview," in *Jews and Sciences in German Contexts*, ed. Charpa and Deichmann, 265–295.

and elsewhere,[62] often without taking the question of the Jewishness of these heroes too seriously. Considering this background, one cannot be surprised to find that the range of explanatory proposals towards "Jewish success" is rather restricted. Institutional success as well as speed and efficiency of participation are widely neglected, and the still most influential approach (Veblen's) is exclusively focused on individual mental conditions of academic success.

THE ANTISEMITIC EXPLANATION

The common definition of antisemitism as "discrimination against or hatred towards Jews"[63] is not very helpful in understanding the views relevant here. Academic antisemitism was a reaction that was first triggered when the participation of Jews in science became highly visible, that is in the second half of the nineteenth century; it unfolded in its ultimate form in the Nazi era. This type of antisemitism may also be motivated by primitive emotions, but in its presentation it is an explanatory mechanism consisting of three and sometimes four components: a comparative explanandum and a hierarchy of explanatory claims, starting with ascribing certain scientific practices to Jews and continued by assertions about them as explanations of these practices. The structure is probably borrowed from Richard Wagner's antisemitic "classic," *Das Judentum in der Musik* (1850), which left its mark even in the discussion of modern "Jewish" physics in the Nazi era.

The antisemite's explanandum exactly matches the success narrative contained, for example, in the following passage: "the hiring of Jews as full Professors reached an amount that was far beyond the percentage rate of Jews in Germany and other countries."[64] This was written in Germany in 1939. Half a century earlier, the Viennese surgeon Theodor Billroth had opened the door of academic antisemitism with his complaints about the number of Jewish doctors as compared to doctors of

---

[62] E.g., Siegmund Kaznelson, *Juden im deutschen Kulturbereich*, second edition (Berlin: Jüdischer Verlag, 1959); Ioan James, *Driven to Innovate. A Century of Jewish Mathematicians and Physicists* (Oxford: Lang, 2009).

[63] The US State Department, quoted in *Los Angeles Times*, May 12, 2009.

[64] "dass die Besetzung der Lehrstühle durch Juden schließlich einen Prozentsatz erreichte, der mit dem zahlenmäßigen Verhältnis des Judentums in Deutschland und anderen Ländern keinerlei Ähnlichkeit aufwies." Bruno Thüring, "Albert Einsteins Umsturzversuch der Physik und seine inneren Möglichkeiten und Ursachen," *Sitzungsberichte d. Münchener Arbeitstagung des Reichsinstituts f. Geschichte des neuen Deutschlands*, 4 (1939): 134–162, here 135.

"pure German blood."[65] The anti-Semite's explanation of this is that Jews meet with success because of certain practices that ought to be judged harshly and are not employed by non-Jews. On the next level, such practices are explained by the concreteness of Jews' attitudes, and on the following level by their inner "Jewishness." The anti-Semite mechanism works as well without one concrete Jew and only related to this imaginary "Jewishness" as fundamental explanatory factor. The weak point of this explanatory pattern is that those practices which the anti-Semite prefers are often employed by Jews, and what he rejects is often practiced by non-Jews. This is one of the reasons why the projects of "German Physics," "German Mathematics," etc. lost their attractiveness even to influential Nazis themselves. It could not be ignored that there were famous non-Jews who represented "Talmudic" science, and that there were Jews who had excelled in "German Science": For example, the classical treatise on "Anschauliche Mathematik" and many works on applied mathematics (the "German" alternatives to the "Jewish" project of practicing mathematics "foreign to reality" and "inimical to life"[66]) had to some extent been written by Jewish mathematicians (Stefan Cohn-Vossen, Theodor von Kármán, Leon Lichtenberg). Alternatively, in physics, it was the non-Jewish physicists Max Planck and Arnold Sommerfeld who forcefully promoted the new Theoretical Physics. Werner Heisenberg, the non-Jewish boy wonder of "Jewish Physics" who was hated by the leaders of "German Science," became the hope of Himmler and a key figure in German wartime fission research.[67]

In the cold light of day, "Jewish" practice was merely advanced scientific theorizing, and "Aryan Practices" were either simply older empirical strategies (Lenard, Stark) or normal practices of the applied sciences. Commonly, the successors to the chairs held by Jewish and non-Jewish practitioners of "Talmudic" science did not really practice something extraordinary; they were professors of hydrodynamics, technical mechanics and other applied domains with memberships in the Nazi Party.[68]

[65] "rein deutsches Blut." Theodor Billroth, *Ueber das Lehren und Lernen der medizinischen Wissenschaften an den Universitäten der deutschen Nation [...]* (Vienna: Gerold, 1876), 154
[66] Quoted in Sanford L. Segal, *Mathematicians under the Nazis* (Princeton: Princeton University Press, 2003), 362.
[67] See, e.g., Gordon Fraser, *The Quantum Exodus: Jewish Fugitives, the Atomic Bomb, and the Holocaust* (Oxford: Oxford University Press, 2012), 78–83.
[68] Cf. Freddy Litten, *Mechanik und Antisemitismus (Wilhelm Müller 1880–1968)* (Munich: Münchener Universitätsschriften, 2000).

THE VEBLEN-THESIS

The Veblen Thesis was put forward after World War I by the one of the twentieth century's most esteemed pioneers of social theory and economics, Thorstein Veblen, a son of Norwegian immigrants. The thesis itself mirrors his own fate as an individual who excelled academically in a life detached from his family background. To him, the Jewish success narrative corresponds to the academic participation of people who neither belonged to the social majority of their actual or adoptive country, nor were members of the societies of their family origins.[69] Being caught between two stools, they shaped themselves as independent intellectuals, "detached sceptics." Taking it for granted that relevance in science is due to "revolutionary" achievements, alienated Jews appear in an ideal position to embark on a scientific career.

There has been a great deal of discussion both in favor of and against this conception. The most fertile contribution is probably found in David Hollinger's argument that a large part of the intellectual Jews in the United States (similar to an earlier phenomenon in imperial Austro-Hungary) formed a group of its own which is academically successful on the basis of its way of life "in between."[70] Irrespective of Hollinger's group-perspective, the Veblen Thesis is primarily psychological and seems to appeal to those researchers who considered themselves as outsiders; in other words, scientists to whom the Einstein legend seems adequate. Criticisms of this view have emphasized that great science has also been done by people who went along faithfully with their institutions and their wider social contexts.[71]

But a criticism of Veblen's explanation can position itself more fundamentally: One may doubt whether the idea of the independent individual includes that of the creative scientist. The real Einstein case is the story of a young, highly talented physicist, who as a pupil had received private teaching, attended excellent schools, and received the chance to pursue his university studies. After being trained in one of the most respected universities of the time, he started his own project in close contact with his colleagues and never scorned their advice. He was always splendidly informed about the most recent developments in his domain, especially Poincaré's ideas on relativity theory. However Einstein as a private person may have felt or presented himself, as a scientist he was quite the opposite

---

[69] Thorstein Veblen, "The Intellectual Preeminence of Jews in Modern Europe," *Political Science Quarterly* 29 (1919): 33–43.

[70] Hollinger, *Science, Jews, and Secular Culture*; idem, "Why Are Jews Preeminent in Science and Scholarship? The Veblen Thesis Reconsidered," *Aleph. Historical Studies in Science and Judaism* 2 (2002): 145–163.

[71] See Volkov, "Jewish Scientists."

of a cognitively independent outsider. Creative scientists are primarily trained, informed *scientists*, in other words, persons who are to a large extent epistemically dependent. "No person can be creative without having access to a tradition, a craft, a knowledge base."[72] Veblen's thesis and its variants are deeply committed to the Romantic pattern of the autarkic, autonomous, and noble minded person, who creates the new. With this, we come back to the idea of learning as a condition of scientific success and its institutionalization.

EVERYMAN'S EXPLANATION

The first sympathetic attempt to explain the success of Jews in academia was a direct response to the first antisemitic explanation. The botanist Matthias Jakob Schleiden's rejoinders to Billroth's attack crystallize into the following argument: without the work of Jewish doctors (however they are religiously, genetically, morally, or otherwise judged) there would perhaps be no advanced medical science and no Professor Billroth.[73] To Schleiden, being a good doctor or scientist means to be a chain-link in the advancement of the discipline. This approach includes stressing the importance of being familiar with disciplinary concepts and principles, adopting scientific training, and establishing favorable relationships between the persons involved.[74]

Seen against this background, the Romantic pattern of the independent genius is an idealization that has nothing to do with the empirical conditions of scientific creativity. In more abstract terms, good science is not based on autarky, but on familiarity with the state of the art, on taking the criticism of others seriously (even facilitating it by clear exposition of one's own thoughts and communicating one's own strategies). This is what the real story of Einstein tells us. The creative scientist does not act and think as a private individual but as a professional persona,

---

[72] Mihaly Czikszentmihalyi, "Creativity," in *The MIT Encyclopedia of the Cognitive Sciences*, ed. Robert A. Wilson and Frank C. Keil (Cambridge: MIT Press, 1999), 205–206, here 205.

[73] "hat daher nicht bedacht, dass es ohne die Juden vielleicht nie einen Professor Billroth gegeben hätte." Matthias J. Schleiden, *Die Bedeutung der Juden für die Erhaltung und Wiederbelebung der Wissenschaften im Mittelalter*, third edition (Braunschweig: Baumgärtner, 1877), 66. Interestingly, this remark is omitted in the English translation (London: Gollancz, 1911).

[74] Ulrich Charpa, "Matthias Jakob Schleiden, 1804–1881: The History of Jewish Interest in Science and the Methodology of Microscopic Botany," *Aleph. Historical Studies in Science and Judaism* 3 (2003): 213–245.

belonging to the universal sphere of his discipline. In Schleiden's opinion, the traditional Jewish emphasis on learning and on informed dispute provides ideal conditions for participation in science. Of course, such a perspective is not without rivals. It is open to deliberation and historical comparison as to how similar results can be attained in contexts other than a Jewish one.

As to explaining the success of those with a Jewish background it does not require much effort to follow Schleiden's path of explanation by taking the reality of science, as a realm of knowledge acquisition and transmission, into account and focusing on favorable personal and institutional conditions of this complex endeavor. Such conditions favor *learning*, and learning opens the way to connecting oneself to other researchers and their contexts. Additionally, the neglected "folk" explanations of Jewish success, as they are proudly listed in popular books like Raphael Patai's *The Jewish Mind*,[75] provide a bulk of material in this regard. And if one feels encouraged by one of the biological, cultural, social, or other reasons which apologetic "folk" explanations presents, to add that being "a lojterer kop" (smart) is not an obstacle, the explanatory scene becomes more complete. The plausibility of Schleiden's and Everyman's view results from its strategy of explaining a *positivum* (success) *ex positivo* (enabling factors). Mere motives, including such negative feelings such as alienation, can explain why people develop fantasies about, e.g., being a successful scientist, but not why someone can realize such an intention. This is how modern action theory would declare Veblen-type approaches inferior to everyman's view. With the same result, Maimonides would have drawn our attention to the distinction between "mere" acting on one side, and on the other, "good" acting which presupposes advanced capabilities.[76] Scientific success is based on "good" acting. This apparently trivial insight into the roles of learning, learning conditions, and holding the activity of learning in high esteem provides the option to "demystify" the notable story of Jewish achievements in modern science:[77] The idea of competence-based action and its preconditions links the activities of Jewish researchers to the successful practices of Jews in other domains. At the same time, it connects such phenomena of Jewish history to the success stories of non-Jewish groups in academia and beyond.[78]

---

[75] Raphael Patai, *The Jewish Mind* (New York: Scribner, 1997).
[76] *Guide of the Perplexed*, III, 25; Soloveitchik, "'Common Sense' Rebellion."
[77] See Hollinger's postulates in "Why Are Jews Preeminent in Science and Scholarship?"
[78] Cf. Hao, "Distinct Trajectories."

SELECT BIBLIOGRAPHY

Berger, Yitzhak and David Shatz, eds, *Judaism, Science, and Moral Responsibility*, Lanham: Rowman & Littlefield, 2002.

Bergmann, Birgit, Moritz Epple, and Ruti Ungar, *Transcending Tradition. Jewish Mathematicians in German-Speaking Academic Culture*, Heidelberg: Springer, 2012.

Cantor, Geoffrey, *Quakers, Jews, and Science: Religious Responses to Modernity and the Sciences in Britain, 1650–1900*, Cambridge: Cambridge University Press, 2005.

Cantor, Geoffrey, and Marc Swetlitz, eds, *Jewish Tradition and the Challenge of Darwinism*, Chicago: University of Chicago Press, 2006.

Charpa, Ulrich and Ute Deichmann, eds, *Jews and Sciences in German Contexts*, Tübingen: Mohr Siebeck, 2007.

Diner, Dan, Ulrich Charpa, and Ute Deichmann, eds, "Wissenschaftsgeschichte / History of Science," *Simon Dubnow Institute Yearbook* 3 (2004): 149–312.

Dodick, Jeff and Raphael B. Shuchat, "Historical Interactions Between Judaism and Science and Their Influence on Science Teaching and Learning" in *International Handbook of Research in History, Philosophy and Science Teaching*, ed. Michael R. Matthews, New York: Springer, 2014.

Efron, Noah J., *A Chosen Calling: Jews in Science in the Twentieth Century*, Cincinnati: Hebrew Union College Press, 2014.

"Jews and the Study of Nature," in *The Routledge Companion to Religion and Science*, ed. J. W. Haag, G. R. Peterson, and M. L. Spezio, 79–89, New York: Routledge, 2012.

Judaism and Science: A Historical Introduction, Westport, CT: Greenwood Press, 2007.

Fraser, Gordon, *The Quantum Exodus. Jewish Fugitives, the Atomic Bomb, and the Holocaust*, Oxford: Oxford University Press, 2012.

Gimbel, Steven, *Einstein's Jewish Science. Physics at the Intersection of Politics and Religion*, Philadelphia: Johns Hopkins University Press, 2012.

Golan, Tal, ed., *Israel Studies*, 9, no. 2 (2004): Science, Technology and Israeli Society.

Hollinger, David A., *Science, Jews, and Secular Culture: Studies in Mid-Twentieth-Century American Intellectual History*, Princeton: Princeton University Press, 1996.

Sacks, Jonathan, *The Great Partnership: Science, Religion, and the Search for Meaning*, London: Hodder and Stoughton, 2011.

Samuelson, Norbert M., *Jewish Faith and Modern Science. On the Death and Rebirth of Jewish Philosophy*, Lanham: Rowman & Littlefield, 2008.

Sorkin, David, *The Religious Enlightenment: Protestants, Jews, and Catholics from London to Vienna*, Princeton: Princeton University Press, 2011.

CHAPTER 37

KABBALAH IN THE MODERN ERA

JODY MYERS

Kabbalah is the collective name for Jewish teachings, dating from the late twelfth century CE, that describe knowledge of God and the cosmos that is considered too special and subtle to be explicitly revealed in the written and oral Torah. Characteristic of kabbalistic theosophy is the axiom that God is essentially unknowable but that he has revealed aspects of divinity or a divine structure – the *sefirot*, the world of emanation – that is accessible to humanity. The physical world is the result of the dynamics within the divine world, and the two are parallel to and mirror each other. Armed with this knowledge of the divine structure and its relation to the lower world, kabbalists believed they could bring greater harmony to the upper divine realm – the term for this is theurgy – or participate in its drama. Others have sought ecstatic experiences of the divine or to achieve a state of *devekut*, adherence, to God. These objectives continue to be relevant to people who currently engage with Kabbalah.

The secrecy and power associated with Kabbalah means that people have yearned to learn it and share it with others. The cryptic style of kabbalistic writing and the frequent dependence on oral teaching resulted in multiple and diverse interpretations and vehement disagreement between kabbalists over the centuries. There were kabbalists who maintained that the era had been reached when kabbalistic texts were to be widely disseminated. Yet, most believed that it was meant to be esoteric and limited to Jews. In fact, since the thirteenth century, Christians – albeit, a very small number – have gained access to kabbalistic teachings and produced their own versions of it. While intense and specialized learning and rituals have generally been the province of an elite element in Jewish society, kabbalistic doctrines by the eighteenth century were considered authoritative in Jewish communities throughout the world and were integrated into daily practices and the liturgy. Kabbalists lived their lives within the framework of the Jewish community, generally punctilious in the observance of mitzvot and respected for their Talmudic learning. They were regarded as valuable community resources. Often serving as authorities in matters of halacha, they were also regarded as having the power to protect the community against evil or to intercede with God to confer blessings.

These older, elitist ideals are still voiced. They are most prevalent in Israel and among religious Jews who evince loyalty to halacha. Alongside the continuity, however, are the striking changes that have taken place since the late nineteenth century, and especially since the last third of the twentieth century. The ranks of those who advocate wider dissemination have swelled considerably. Far more than in the past, kabbalistic teachings are openly explicated, subject to piecemeal borrowing, and utilized by individuals and groups in novel ways.

FROM THE LATE EIGHTEENTH UNTIL THE MID-TWENTIETH CENTURY

At the beginning of the modern era, however, Kabbalah began to diminish in cultural importance in Jewish society. First, in reaction to what they regarded as the improper popularization and distortion of Kabbalah, European kabbalists in the late eighteenth century ruled against the publication of the teachings and against the study of some aspects of these teachings for men below the age of forty. While these strictures had been voiced for centuries, they began to be enforced.[1] Second, Kabbalah's legitimacy was attacked. Most followers of the European Enlightenment attacked Kabbalah in a multitude of ways – as a degenerate form of Jewish theology, as foreign to Judaism, as irrational, and the like – and they regarded the Hasidic movement as a particularly noxious expression of what they regarded as an unfortunate new phenomenon. There were also attacks on the authenticity of the Zohar and other kabbalistic writings by rabbinic opponents of Sabbateanism.[2] Most of the scholars of the *Wissenschaft des Judentums* concurred with this assessment. Of course, their collective disapproval was ignored by many religious Jews, even those in Western Europe. As late as the 1870s, for example, Jews from all over the region were making pilgrimages to the kabbalist Rabbi Elijah Guttmacher

---

[1] Moshe Idel, "On the History of the Interdiction against the Study of Kabbalah Before the Age of Forty," *AJS Review* 5 (1980): 1–20 (Hebrew).

[2] Shmuel Feiner, *Haskalah and History: The Emergence of a Modern Jewish Historical Consciousness* (Oxford, 2002) illustrates the consensus of the maskilim, with the exception of Eliezer Zweifel (1815–1888), who served as a bridge to a later appreciation of Hasidism and Kabbalah; Boaz Huss, *Like the Radiance of the Sky: Chapters in the Reception History of the Zohar and the Construction of its Symbolic Value* (Jerusalem, 2008).

of Graetz (1796–1874) to seek his blessings.[3] However, the pressures and educational reforms instituted by modernizing states seeking to culturally integrate Jews into their societies was one more factor weakening the cultural value of Kabbalah. In Western Europe by the end of the nineteenth century, kabbalists were no longer being produced or supported.

In parts of Central and Eastern Europe, where the acceptance of Enlightenment principles and the effort to integrate Jews were less intense, religious engagement with Kabbalah survived into the twentieth century. In Lithuania, the approach of Elijah ben Solomon Zalman, Gaon of Vilna (1720–1797) dominated among non-Hasidic circles known as the Mitnagdim. They insisted upon exact and rigorous Kabbalah scholarship in line with earlier theosophical teachings. Important disciples include Isaac Eisik (Haver) Wildmann (1789–1852) and Solomon Eliashiv (1841–1926), and they carried on their teacher's highly critical stance toward Hasidim and their approach to Kabbalah. Hasidic leaders tended to simplify kabbalistic concepts and incorporate them into homilies and stories. Theosophy for its own sake was not valued, but theosophical teachings were understood to correspond to the mind and emotions of the individual Hasid (or the tsaddik, and through him the individual Hasid) in order to facilitate the achievement of *devekut*. The Hasidic concern with the mystical performance of the commandments and with communal expressions of devotion moderated the potential individualism of ecstatic objectives. While the actual study of kabbalistic writings was not uniformly embraced or widely practiced, notable Kabbalah scholars appeared among the Breslov, Zhidochov, Chabad, and Izbica-Radzyn Hasidim; there were other Hasidic kabbalists who focused on intense devotional practices. Outside of Mitnagdic and Hasidic settings, traces of Kabbalah could be found in ethical, philosophical, and popular religious literature of the region.[4] The cultural suppression of Jewish studies in communist regimes and the devastation of the Holocaust ended the transmission of Jewish Kabbalah in Europe.

---

[3] Still unexamined are the kabbalistic writings and the veneration paid to this resident of Graetz in Prussia, to whom thousands of Jews streamed for amulets and personal guidance. See Jody Myers, *Seeking Zion: Modernity and Messianic Activism in the Writings of Tsevi Hirsch Kalischer* (Oxford and Portland, OR, 2004), 160, note 36.

[4] Moshe Idel, *Hasidism Between Ecstasy and Magic* (Albany, 1995); Allan Nadler, *The Faith of the Mitnagdim: Rabbinic Responses to Hasidic Rapture* (Baltimore, 1997); a short summary of the history of "The Kabbalah in Later Times" with references to kabbalists who have come to the attention of modern scholarship may be found in *Encyclopedia Judaica*, 2nd edition, ed. Michael Berenbaum and Fred Skolnik (Detroit, 2007), vol. 11, 619–622; see also "Kabbalah in the Late 20th Century," in ibid., 677–681.

Ironically, while engagement with Kabbalah was waning among European Jews, it was increasing among the non-Jewish population there. In the late eighteenth century, Western European critics of the religious establishment and religious orthodoxies who sought alternative approaches to religion and science found Kabbalah quite alluring. Christian Kabbalah mixed with alchemical symbolism passed into Freemasonry teachings and theosophical circles in England and France. The proliferation of European-language translations of Christian Knorr von Rosenroth's Latin compendium of kabbalistic writings, *Kabbalah Denudata*, led to the first scholarly investigations of Kabbalah as well as appropriations of it for alternative spiritualities. An example of the latter was Eliphas Levi (actually Alphonse Louis Constant, 1810–1875), whose many publications inspired the establishment of esoteric occult circles such as the Hermetic Order of the Golden Dawn and the Order of the Rosy Cross. Christian Kabbalah sources also found their way into the Theosophical Society, founded in 1875 by Helena Petrovna Blavatsky (1831–1891) and Henry Steel Olcott (1832–1907). Theosophists rejected the notion that the teachings found in Kabbalah originated in Jewish society and were the "possession" of the Jews; they taught, on the contrary, that Kabbalah was simply one particularized expression of the universal spiritual-scientific wisdom found among many authentic sacred traditions that had been suppressed and pronounced heretical for centuries. They blended Kabbalah with other occult traditions and elements of Hindu and Buddhist religious traditions. The Theosophical Society and its spin-off organizations established learning centers, held public lectures, and published books in Europe, India, and the United States.[5]

The study of Kabbalah as an academic discipline and as an aspect of secular Jewish culture began in late nineteenth-century Europe. The new academic methodologies, the popular interest in spiritual matters and in Kabbalah's inclusion in the occult, the growth of Jewish nationalism, the increasing antisemitism, and nostalgia prompted intellectuals to reassess Kabbalah and Hasidism and their potential in art, literature, politics, and alternate modes of Jewish spirituality. Shmuel Abba Horodezky (1871–1957), Ernst Mueller (1880–1954), and Gershom Scholem (1897–1982) pioneered the academic study of Jewish mysticism. As with all scientific research, this too was often shaped by or could be used to answer personal theological or ideologically driven dilemmas. Yet, it was a sharp break with

---

[5] Catherine L. Albanese, *A Republic of Mind and Spirit: A Cultural History of American Metaphysical Religion* (New Haven, 2007). On the history and teachings of the Theosophical Society, see Bruce F. Campbell, *Ancient Wisdom Revived: A History of the Theosophical Movement* (Berkeley, 1980).

Jewish tradition to assume that Kabbalah was a human construct whose prevalent expressions were no longer tenable.

In North Africa and the Middle East, Kabbalah remained a vital part of Jewish life well into the modern era. It was dominated by the teachings of the Yemenite Shalom Shar'abi (1720–1777), who established a new center of Kabbalah in Jerusalem called Beit El. He was known for his expertise in Lurianic Kabbalah, and especially his extensive system of meditations upon divine names (*kavvanot*). Shar'abi's *kavvanot* were included in prayerbooks and practiced by kabbalists throughout Muslim lands and beyond, and his disciples in Jerusalem were recognized as the supreme authorities in Kabbalah.[6] Outside of Palestine, from Baghdad to Morocco, Kabbalah scholars and practitioners continued to be productive and find followers. Yosef Hayyim ben Elijah of Baghdad (1835–1909) authored *Ben Ish Hai* (1898), a collection of homilies blended with Kabbalah and halacha that enjoyed great popularity and multiple publications. Through the twentieth century, Jewish communities continued to support Kabbalah scholars, promote the veneration of kabbalists and their tombs, and use kabbalistic symbols and texts in domestic and synagogue rites. The extent and intensity of these expressions diminished under the impact of westernization and the vicissitudes of war. The expulsions and mass migrations of Jews from these regions from the 1940s onward meant that these traditions might continue in the State of Israel.

During the first few decades of the twentieth century, Palestine grew as a center of Kabbalah, and some of this was accounted for by the relocation there of kabbalists from Muslim and Christian lands. Jerusalem became the center of kabbalistic yeshivot, congregations, and study circles representing previous traditions as well as new syntheses. In Palestine, one could become immersed in a Kabbalah-centered congregation. Participants described themselves during the 1920s and 1930s as in the midst of a renaissance of kabbalistic activity that included the formal study of Lurianic writings offered at all levels, literary productivity and publication of books, large gatherings of men to recite special midnight prayers, and prayer groups devoted to reciting the *kavvanot* of Shar'abi. The Shar'abi tradition was numerically the most significant. The most important center was the Beit El yeshiva, which was directed by Masud Ha-Cohen El-Haddad (until 1937) and thereafter by Shalom Haddaya (until 1945) and his son Ovadiah Haddaya (until 1969). Other important yeshivot dominated by but not exclusive to Sephardic Jews were Rehovot ha-Nahar (founded in 1898), led by Shaul Dwek Ha-Cohen, and Oz ve-Hadar (founded in 1923) within the Porat Yosef yeshiva. Indeed, the social commingling and the amalgamation

---

[6] Pinchas Giller, *Shalom Shar'abi and the Kabbalists of Beit El* (Oxford and New York, 2008).

of ideologies and practices are evident especially in Sha'ar Hashamayim yeshiva, founded in 1906. Led by rabbis representing the previously incompatible traditions of Mitnagdic and Polish Hasidic Kabbalah (Shimon Zvi Horowitz and Hayim Leib Yehuda Auerbach, respectively), the yeshiva mixed Hasidic, Mitnagdic, and Sephardic teachings.[7] In response to the national ingathering occurring at this time, Sha'ar Hashamayim yeshiva fostered the propagation of Kabbalah study among Torah scholars and supported the diffusion of kabbalistic teachings among the wider public. There were also kabbalists who operated outside of these yeshivot. Among these were Yehudah Ashlag (1885–1954) and Hillel Zeitlin (1871–1942), who were raised in Europe and educated in Hasidic Kabbalah. While their teachings were quite in contrast to one another, they both translated the Zohar into Hebrew, incorporated into their teachings a call for reshaping Jewish economic and political life, and – like many other kabbalists – regarded their era as on the brink of messianic redemption.[8] With the 1921 establishment of the Chief Rabbinate in the Yishuv, both the Ashkenazi chief rabbi, Abraham Isaac Kook (1865–1935) and the Sephardi chief rabbi Jacob Meir (1856–1939) were avid supporters of kabbalistic dissemination within religious society. In addition to the regular financial support from within the Yishuv, religious institutions raised money through emissaries who traveled through the Diaspora.

However, this cultural revival had dissipated by 1945. The large infusion of non-Orthodox Ashkenazim during the 1930s brought increasing strength to secular culture in the Yishuv. In this context, the academic study of Kabbalah was commenced at the Hebrew University under the guidance of Gershom Scholem. However, these academics were not interested in making links to, or even researching, the realm of Kabbalah among religious society. The Holocaust and the exodus of Jews from Muslim lands sundered the network of support and fertilization between Jerusalem and the Diaspora. Local Religious Zionists, even those who counted themselves among Kook's disciples, did not embrace Kabbalah or adopt Kook's desire to include it in the curriculum of the yeshiva. The socialist Zionists who dominated the leadership of the Jewish community in Palestine regarded the Ashkenazi Orthodox and Mizraḥi schools and circles that

---

[7] Jonatan Meir, "The Imagined Decline of Kabbalah: The Kabbalistic Yeshiva Sha'ar ha-Shamayim and Kabbalah in Jerusalem in the Beginning of the Twentieth Century," in *Kabbalah and Modernity: Interpretations, Transformations, Adaptations*, ed. Boaz Huss, Marco Pasi and Kocku von Stuckrad (Leiden, 2010).

[8] Jonathan Garb, *"The Chosen Will Become Herds": Studies in Twentieth Century Kabbalah* (New Haven & London, 2009), 23–30.

revered, studied and practiced Kabbalah as expressions of a way of life that was meant to disappear, and they directed scarce resources elsewhere.

MID-TWENTIETH-CENTURY RESURGENCE

The cultural value of Kabbalah noticeably surged in Israel and the United States at the beginning of the 1970s. There, and to a much lesser extent in Western Europe, Kabbalah acquired new stature within Jewish culture. Diversification and availability intensified in the 1990s to the extent that Kabbalah became a marketable commodity in the global economic system. The expansion and transformation occurred differently in each country, but the flow of teachers between the two largest centers of Jewish life after the Holocaust guaranteed that there would also be considerable overlap.

Crucial to the new interest in Kabbalah within the non-Orthodox population was the increased availability of writings that were not under the control of religious authorities and that were composed for an audience not yeshiva-trained. Academic articles, translations, and digests of and commentaries on kabbalistic texts were in print by the 1950s and relatively easy to find. For example, one could locate in the public libraries in large American cities the Soncino Press *Zohar* and Theosophical Society publications.[9] The New Age movement, which began in Great Britain after World War II and was evident in Israel and the United States by the late 1950s, also played a role in the diffusion of kabbalistic symbols and ideas, teaching that these were fundamental components of an ancient universal wisdom.[10] New Agers found evidence for their convictions in the recently published works on Kabbalah, and demand grew for books on Jewish mysticism written for the educated general reader.[11]

In North America, these idiosyncratic resources were utilized during the 1960s by Orthodox rabbis who devoted themselves to the task of "returning" assimilated college-aged Jews to Judaism. The first of these were Rabbi Zalman Schachter (later Schachter-Shalomi, 1924–2014) and Shlomo Carlebach (1924–1994). Active since shortly after World War II as Chabad

---

[9] *The Zohar*, translated by Harry Sperling and Maurice Simon (London, 1931–1934). In Israel, Yehuda Ashlag's Hebrew translation and commentary on the Zohar, published piecemeal from 1946 until 1965, was available.

[10] Wouter J. Hanegraaff, *New Age Religion and Western Culture: Esotericism in the Mirror of Secular Thought* (Albany, 1998).

[11] Examples of dissemination include a book written by Yehudah Ashlag's disciple Levi Isaac Krakovsky, *Kabbalah: The Light of Redemption* (Brooklyn, NY, 1950); see also Christine A. Meilicke, "Abulafianism among the Counterculture Kabbalists," *Jewish Studies Quarterly* 9 (2002): 71–101.

emissaries who traveled between American campuses, they grew bolder during the 1960s and established alternative Jewish communities featuring ecstatic worship, and – in the case of Schachter – encouraging engagement with Kabbalah and Judaism in conjunction with the spiritual resources of other religions. The social integration of the Jews in American society and the lack of constraints on religion facilitated such amalgamation. The early outreach activities of Rabbi Philip Berg (originally Gruberger, 1927–2013) also reflected a synthesis of disparate traditions. Based first in the United States and by 1971 in Israel, Berg presented a New Age version of Yehuda Ashlag's kabbalistic teachings to young, secular Jews looking for a spiritual outlook and practices free of the restrictions associated with Orthodox Judaism. Earlier, in partnership with Yehuda Zvi Brandwein (1903–1969), a disciple of Yehuda Ashlag, Berg founded a publishing house in Israel (1965) and New York (1969) for the purpose of disseminating the writings of Ashlag and other kabbalists.[12] Rabbi Aryeh Kaplan (1934–1983) was also involved in outreach work during the 1960s. His attraction to Breslov Hasidism, which was also engaged in its distinctive outreach, propelled Kaplan into work as a translator of Hasidic and kabbalistic books. Unlike Schachter and Berg, Kaplan remained faithful to Orthodox Judaism, though his publication of esoteric works for a mass readership certainly violated traditional Ashkenazic norms. All of these educational and cultural endeavors, designed to bring Jews toward a more exciting or contemplative Judaism than was then currently available, were nevertheless utilized by non-Jewish spiritual seekers. During the 1970s and 1980s, New Age, neo-pagan, "metaphysical," and Western adaptations of Asian religious traditions proliferated. North American campuses witnessed a tremendous growth of offerings in Jewish Studies and Jewish religious outreach organizations. Kabbalah as a subject of textual study occurred primarily in graduate schools and occasionally in the nascent Jewish Renewal and Havurah movements.

The popularity of Kabbalah in North America accelerated during the 1990s. It was spurred by publicity given to the activities of Philip Berg, who called his organization the Kabbalah Learning Centre. Incorporating popular themes like self-actualization, and erasing elements of Jewish particularism, Kabbalah Centre branches were established in major cities throughout the continent that included non-Jews as participants. The enthusiastic support of the popular celebrity Madonna was crucial to the spread of the organization and public awareness of Kabbalah.[13] Recognizing

---

[12] Jody Elizabeth Myers, *Kabbalah and the Spiritual Quest: The Kabbalah Centre in America* (Westport, CT, 2007).

[13] Ibid.

that people were flocking to Kabbalah Centres because there were few other options, American Jewish leaders from virtually all denominations developed what they deemed to be more acceptable modes of education in Kabbalah in synagogues, seminaries, and yeshivot. Academic study of Jewish mysticism expanded in colleges and universities. Publications of all types were produced for a wide audience, from popular astrology infused with kabbalistic symbols to commentaries designed for use in serious Torah study. With the growth of the Internet in the late 1990s, the available resources grew exponentially.

Israel during the 1970s also experienced increased interest in Kabbalah, though it primarily manifested in a revitalization of pre-existing kabbalistic communities and schools. As in America, in Israel there were efforts to use Kabbalah to bring non-observant or alienated Jews toward religious observance. During the early 1970s this was already apparent among Ashkenazic Jews with Chabad's intensified outreach efforts and Breslov Hasidism. The Orthodox rabbinate's control over funding religious institutions, and the greater popularity of more conservative kabbalistic communities, tended at this time to inhibit growth in Israel of the highly syncretistic groups that were appearing in America and Europe.[14] Since the beginning of the 1970s, kabbalistic yeshivot in the older Shar'abi tradition such as Beit El grew stronger, and new ones were established. The most prominent Kabbalah scholars were Rabbis Yehuda Meir Getz (1924–1995), Yaakov Moshe Hillel and David Batzri. The arrival in Israel of the North African kabbalist "holy man" Israel Abu Hazeira (known as the Baba Sali, 1890–1984) sparked an enthusiastic following. Most crucial for the resurgence of Kabbalah in the religious sector was the political sea change that occurred with the elections of 1977. A coalition of secular conservative nationalists, Mizrahim, and religious Israelis supplanted the secular socialist groups that had ruled the country for decades. From that time forward, financial resources have been invested in religious institutions and communities along traditional lines.

Since the 1990s, the production of kabbalistic resources in Israel and their export to the Diaspora have expanded tremendously. Israel continues to be the publishing center for classical kabbalistic works as well as modern commentaries produced for religious Jews. Hasidic, Mizrahi, and Haredi Torah scholars are using and creating these resources for their studies, and introductory, ethical, and reflective writings for a wider, religious readership. One such author is Daniel Frisch (1935–2005), a kabbalist who taught at Sha'ar Hashamayim yeshiva. His many Hebrew writings translate and

---

[14] For example, Philip Berg, who had arrived in Israel in 1971, pulled up stakes in 1982 and returned to North America. See ibid.

explain Zoharic literature, with a focus on personal ethical development.[15] Another kabbalist with an appeal across the Orthodox spectrum but with a greater Web presence is Itamar Schwartz, known by the name of his book *Bilvavi Mishkan Evneh*. A prolific writer, he has a website that provides free audio and video lessons.[16] For advanced students, as well, there is an abundance of classical and new works available, and the supply seems to be continually increasing.

Kabbalah as a tool of outreach continues in Ashkenazic circles, dominated by Breslov Hasidism. Photos of the Lubavitcher rebbe and slogans from Chabad and Breslov religious campaigns are ubiquitous in Israeli public spaces. Outreach with a kabbalistic tinge has gained new strength in North African and other Mizraḥi circles, where mass gatherings – often filmed and posted on the Internet – are presided over by preachers and teachers who stimulate the repentance of the audience. New kabbalistic holy men, who identify themselves as descendants of highly revered kabbalists stemming from Morocco, have generated a wide following. One of the more visible is Rabbi Yaakov Yisrael Ifergan (b. 1930) of Netivot, who has become popular on the basis of his reputation for diagnosing illnesses, predicting outcomes, and encouraging aspiring politicians.

While the Orthodox rabbinate still maintains control over publicly funded religious institutions, its ability to clamp down on forms of religious expression that reject Orthodoxy and halacha has diminished. Ashlagian Kabbalah gained a foothold in the 1990s through a number of different teachers claiming to be faithful to that legacy but rejecting Orthodoxy. Among these, Bnei Baruch, started in 1991 by Russian émigré Michael Laitman, has an international reach and following that at this point probably exceeds that of the Kabbalah Centre. Israeli New Age and neo-Hasidism can be found among individuals, institutes, and small movements. Like the more conventionally religious world, these non-Orthodox have a strong Web presence in online classes, broadcasts of lectures, and posted resources of all kinds.

DISTINCTIVE TRENDS IN CONTEMPORARY KABBALAH

One of the most striking features of the phenomenon that has been labeled "Kabbalah" is its variety. Kabbalistic symbols, words, and concepts may be found within a wide range of religious movements, from conventional Jewish congregations to non-denominational groups that worship the

---

[15] Daniel Frisch, *Matok MiDevash*, 22 vols (Jerusalem, 2003), includes the commentaries by Moses Cordovero, Isaac Luria, and others.

[16] www.bilvavi.net/ (Access July 6, 2010).

Goddess. Kabbalistic themes have made their way into contemporary art, song, dance, poetry, and literature produced by and for people of diverse backgrounds and which are to be used for multiple purposes. It is often unclear just what merits labeling something "kabbalistic." An image of the *sefirot*, a reference from the Zohar, or the evocation of inspiration from the holy men of Safed may be sufficient to earn the respectful awe, scornful smirk, confusion, or fear associated with the term Kabbalah. Among non-Jewish and non-Orthodox people who engage with Kabbalah in one form or another, it is typically one of a number of resources used in conjunction with others for spiritual, artistic, or healing purposes. It has not been established just how much of such content earns the designation kabbalistic or mystical.[17]

The term mysticism was applied during the nineteenth century at the outset of the academic study of religion to a specific Christian religious experience, and its appropriateness with regard to aspects of Jewish tradition has been questioned for decades. It was originally defined as an individual's direct experience of the divine, the result of an extraordinary mode of apprehension different from rational thinking or sensual perception. From the Christian perspective, the experience was a gift from God that felt like an infusion of immense joy and the sense of being completely filled up with or at one with God and the cosmos. Mysticism, then, was regarded as a mode of consciousness, private and psychological, seemingly unconnected to social and institutional contexts. While scholars did eventually accept that mystical experiences occur outside of Christianity, their consensus prior to the assertions by Gershom Scholem to the contrary was there was no mysticism in rabbinic Judaism. In his classic work, *Major Trends in Jewish Mysticism*, Scholem conceded that most kabbalists did not have as their main goal an ecstatic experience of God. He rejected, however, the too narrow definition of mysticism that then held sway among academics, and he pointed out that the theosophical and theurgical activities of the kabbalists merited their inclusion. He identified mysticism as irrational, antinomian, and anti-institutional, whereas "religion" is associated with concern for established rules and creeds, institutional longevity, and communal continuity. The creation of Kabbalah was, to him, a self-reflective effort of medieval rabbis to symbolically reinterpret the original myths so as to harness the power of the mystical impulse and keep it within the framework of halachic Judaism.[18]

---

[17] Boaz Huss, "The Mystification of Kabbalah and the Mythos of Jewish Mysticism," *Pe'amim* 110 (2007): 9–30 (Hebrew).

[18] Gershom Scholem, *Major Trends in Jewish Mysticism* (New York, 1941), 5–7. On the use of the term "mysticism" in academic discourse, see S. T. Katz, ed., *Mysticism and*

During the latter half of the twentieth century, it has been common to hear this romantic conception of mysticism and Kabbalah; indeed, this anti-institutional reputation has enhanced Kabbalah's attractiveness. Many among those engaged with Kabbalah, whether as academic scholars or as people who employ it in a spiritual pursuit (and sometimes the boundary between the two is blurred), have regarded it as the inner essence or "the heart" of Judaism. That this romantic notion was central to medieval kabbalists makes it that much easier to affirm what is, at bottom, a faith assertion. The recent renewal of interest in Kabbalah has to be regarded within the context of the Jewish spiritual revival that manifested itself in the last third of the twentieth century, a central theme of which has been the need to restore the vital feelings that had been neglected by or suppressed within mainstream Jewish religious institutions. Obviously, it is best to approach the subject without such assumptions and expectations.

Heated words about the authenticity of contemporary renderings of Kabbalah are also an expression of similar deeply felt needs. Who can determine the validity of a particular religious expression? There is no shortage of people who assert their expertise to determine "the real thing" from the superficial, erroneous, and unkosher varieties. Arguing for "originality" is problematic; if an updated teaching is necessarily less genuine than what scholars may regard as the original version, then Lurianic Kabbalah would have to be discarded, too. Today, some of the most ridiculed practices in the repertoire of kabbalist "holy men" are those which are replicas from the seventeenth century that are no longer palatable to many modern onlookers.[19] Academic methodologies can describe, explain, and compare; they may even be able to find evidence of financial scams, cruelty, and acts of fraud. But no academic should produce a definitive guide book or catalogue of genuine Kabbalah, any more than he or she should compose a list of legitimate forms of Judaism. Such judgments are highly subjective and emerge out of one's social context.

Perhaps the most important factor leading to the expanded, variegated realm of Kabbalah today is that the borders of the Jewish cultural tradition are far more porous than ever before. Jewish cultures in the modern period entered into a phase of greater openness as well, but strictures surrounding Kabbalah study and its irrelevance to many kept it sequestered for longer.

Philosophical Analysis (New York and Oxford, 1978); Martin S. Jaffee, "Inner-Worldly Monasticism: Towards a Model of Rabbinic-Halakhic Spirituality," a monograph supplement to *Orthodox Tradition* (Etna, CA, 2006). Suffice it to say here that later academic scholars of Kabbalah have challenged and far expanded Scholem's scholarship, and his should not be the final word on the subject.

[19] Matt Goldish, "Kabbalah, Academia, and Authenticity," *Tikkun* 20, no. 5 (2005): 63–67.

Engagement with Kabbalah occurs outside of Orthodox Jewish communities, and it occurs outside of Jewish society. Cross-cultural exchange and influence with regard to Kabbalah have probably never been as strong. At this juncture in the twenty-first century, eclecticism abounds. The cultural amalgamation is apparent in Israel as well as in the Diaspora, among the Orthodox as well as among New Agers. For Orthodox Jews interested in engaging with kabbalistic literature, there are an enormous number of new resources available at a very low cost. Israeli Orthodox Jews are especially active in publishing pre-modern writings, some of which were formerly considered heretical,[20] along with a multitude of commentaries in the vernacular in writing, in audio tapes, on the internet, on radio and television, in the synagogues, study houses, and public squares. It does not seem to be an ideal to teach purely from one school of thought. Rather, in this era in which concealed traditions are now so widely revealed, there is the alluring possibility of reconciling formerly disparate or unconnected schools of thought. The opportunity to harmonize may be regarded as part of God's design.[21] Of course, it is less likely than ever to teach purely from within one school of thought.

With such a proliferation of resources, it is obvious that the old prohibition against publishing and teaching esoteric teachings to unlearned men under the age of forty is no longer taken seriously. This had been a stricture only among the Ashkenazim. Recently, it has served as a handy tool for those opposed to the new and unconventional forms of Kabbalah. Yet, across the spectrum of Jewish religious denominations during the 1990s, Kabbalah was eventually regarded as too good a resource to ignore and too problematic to leave in the hands of other interpreters. Kabbalah has always been easy to adopt and adapt; the diversity within pre-modern kabbalistic writings and its characteristic cryptic expression permitted flexible readings. This has not changed. The added fact that Kabbalah today lacks an authoritative defender and is situated within a pluralistic, anti-authoritarian cultural milieu makes it all the easier to utilize it in a great variety of ways.

For Jews who affirm a loyalty to strict observance of halacha, Kabbalah is a most valuable aid. When scrutinized through the lens of kabbalists, all elements of Jewish ritual practice and the liturgy are invested with deep significance. They have the power to bring the *sefirot* into a harmonious

---

[20] Boaz Huss, "The Formation of Jewish Mysticism and Its Impact on the Reception of Rabbi Abraham Abulafia in Contemporary Kabbalah," in *Religion and Its Other*, ed. Heicke Bock, Jorg Feuchter, and Michi Knechts (Frankfurt & New York, 2008), 147–148, 156–162.

[21] Garb, *The Chosen Will Become Herds*, 31–36.

balance and ensure the smooth functioning of society and the world. Within Orthodox Jewish society, the infusion of Kabbalah into ritual observance tends to promote an exacting attention to traditional behaviors and the intentions with which they are practiced. Even where the commitment to halacha is not so strong or even a factor, performance of rituals and other practices may be given added importance and excitement. Kabbalists of the past provide an enhanced repertoire of special activities: contemplation of divine names, chants, tearful laments, pilgrimages to graves, writing amulets, wearing distinctive clothing, and the like. For example, a ritual from the Lurianic tradition designed to provide men with expiation for the sin of engaging in sexual relations with other men has found new life in the unorthodox setting of the Kabbalah Centre. Teacher Yehuda Berg recommends the practice as a way to break a person of habitual and destructive sexual behavior. A Kabbalah Centre member who testified to his experience enacting the old penitential ritual did not voice the concerns that apparently motivated pious Jews of the past, that is, the fear of suffering the wrath of God and a potentially painful reincarnation. Rather, he was pleased to have had such an adventure and delighted to discover that it had improved his behavior. Whether this person was male or female, Jew or Hindu, married or single, seems to matter very little.[22]

Indeed, Boaz Huss has pointed out that the emphasis on practices, rather than doctrines and theories, is characteristic of contemporary Hasidic and kabbalistic movements.[23] He argues that the pragmatic concern for the efficacy of a practice reflects the postmodern rejection of grand narratives. Within religion, this leads to the construction of shallow pastiches made of disparate cultural elements. Participants are not so concerned with the conceptual underpinnings of practices, which may actually contradict one another, but rather on whether they seem to have an effect. This may be most pervasive in the field of alternative medicine. A healer may attempt a therapy using Reiki or, if that does not work, try a visualization of the sefirotic Tree of Life. Furthermore, the attraction to modern kabbalistic saints such as the Baba Sali rests on his reputed ability to produce tangible results rather than his mastery of theoretical kabbalistic teachings. There has been a growing demand for kabbalistic healers, exorcists, business advisors, and political consultants, and such experts establish their credentials through testimonies of their success. A focus on kabbalistic practices is evident, however, even among those who subscribe to deeply layered doctrines and

---

[22] Yehuda Berg, *The Kabbalah Book of Sex and Other Mysteries of the Universe* (New York & Los Angeles, 2006), 251.

[23] Boaz Huss, "All You Need is LAV: Madonna and Postmodern Kabbalah," *The Jewish Quarterly Review* 95 (2005): 620–621.

remain primarily within a Jewish framework. This has led to the rejuvenation of rituals that had been previously marginal and the sharing of these across denominational boundaries. For example, dozens of sites on the internet, from Haredi to the other end of the range, are devoted to recommended behaviors for each of the forty-nine days of the counting of the Omer, based on the *sefirot* identified with each day.[24]

Connected to the focus on practices is the employment of kabbalistic symbols in the visual and plastic arts. Kabbalistic iconography has been granted new life in strange new settings. California Beat artist Wallace Berman (1926–1976) incorporated Hebrew letters into his illustrations after reading Gershom Scholem's *Major Trends in Jewish Mysticism*.[25] Years later, the German expressionist artist Anselm Kiefer (b. 1945) began to produce paintings and installations addressing themes of destruction, loss, and rebirth with titles such as Merkaba and Tzim-Tzum. Renderings of kabbalistic symbols are proliferating in religious objects – such as shevitis, amulets, and meditation guides – that are not perceived by their users as merely decorative. Commodification has become widespread. Far more than in the past, there is a thriving international market for kabbalistic objects and products associated with Kabbalah: jewelry, posters, clothing, amulets, and so on. The marketing of Kabbalah extends beyond the purchase of things with the purchase of courses and blessings.

Yet, Kabbalah has appeal for a wide array of people who pay attention to religious philosophy and who are seeking alternatives to conventional theism. The late twentieth century religious revival has been marked by a greater attraction to non-theistic conceptions of divinity. These have been regarded, rightly or wrongly, as leading to less coercive religiosity. Globalization, one facet of which is the migration of Asians to the West and Westerners' tourism in Asia, has fostered awareness of religious outlooks not predicated on monotheism or any personal deity. People who are inclined toward rationalism and find compelling modern secular critiques of religion may find non-theistic images of the sacred to be less primitive or childish. Whatever their motivations, they have configured kabbalistic concepts such as *Ein Sof, sefirot,* and the flux of energy between the *sefirot* and the upper and lower worlds to fit their preferences. The discovery of the concept Shekhinah has been particularly useful for people seeking a feminist spirituality. The astrological elements in Kabbalah teachings

[24] Even the Wikipedia entry on Counting of the Omer mentions the association of the *sefirot* with the days; http://en.wikipedia.org/wiki/Counting_of_the_Omer (Accessed July 15, 2010).
[25] Christine A. Meilicke, "The Forgotten History of David Meltzer's Journal *Tree*," *Studies in American Jewish Literature* 22 (2003): 52–71.

have found new enthusiasts, as have principles of reincarnation. Both have appeal among people with New Age and metaphysical outlooks, but also among religious Jews. These ideas provide new options. Kabbalistic teachings on evil provide specificity not generally available in rabbinic Judaism, which commonly explains it as a result of God's inscrutable will or "because of our many sins." Whether one believes evil or misfortune is the result of conflicting powers in the upper world, *kelipot* in the lower world, the relative position of the stars and planets, or the consequences of one's behavior in a previous life, one now has answers to nagging questions and actual methods for improving the future. Furthermore, kabbalistic renditions of the cosmos appear to have greater capacity for harmony with modern science. Both the "big bang" theory of creation and atomic physics have been compared to the concepts of *shevirat ha-kelim* and the sefirotic worlds within worlds. Similarity between kabbalistic ideas and Jungian views of the individual and collective unconscious, already noted in the 1930s, has been the foundation for new expertise in dream analysis.[26]

One of the key differences between contemporary Kabbalah in Israel and outside of it is the greater strength in the latter of a "universalized" Kabbalah, that is, kabbalistic teachings that address human beings as if they were of equal value. Kabbalistic texts produced by and for Jews in all periods prior to the late twentieth century present a very negative image of non-Jews. Non-Jews – usually designated as *ovdei avodah zarah*, or idol worshippers – are defined as ontologically distinct from and inferior to Jews, and more often than not are represented as powers of evil. Christian Kabbalists did not transmit these chauvinistic elements in their teachings. By the nineteenth century, the partisan Christian messages in their teachings gave way to "metaphysical" spirituality with an inclusive, ecumenical message. Today, non-Jewish purveyors of metaphysical religions continue to document a universalized Kabbalah. For example, the Rosicrucian Order, AMORC, regards Kabbalah as one of the sources contributing to the Rosicrucian wisdom that is available to all humanity.[27]

It was during the 1960s and 1970s, however, that there was a convergence between such non-Jewish universalized Kabbalah and the newer forms of Kabbalah promoted within the North American Jewish community. The rabbis who used kabbalistic teachings as vehicles for Jewish outreach were likely familiar with this other form of Kabbalah, because it was part of the

[26] Catherine Shainberg, *Kabbalah and the Power of Dreaming: Awakening the Visionary Life* (Rochester, VT, 2005).

[27] Dion Fortune, *Mystical Qabalah*, second edition (New York, 2000). The website of the organization includes a full journal issue and a listing of books devoted to Kabbalah; see www.rosicrucian.org/rosicrucian-digest-kabbalah (accessed April 7, 2017).

counterculture to which Jews were drawn. In any case, they would not have included the chauvinistic aspects and ethnic references from the original Aramaic and Hebrew texts into their teachings of Jewish Kabbalah; these would have been – and are still – unattractive to their audience. To this day, it is nearly impossible to find such ethnic references within Jewish mass-marketed books and web sites. For example, Daniel Matt's *The Essential Kabbalah: The Heart of Jewish Mysticism* contains no explicit statements differentiating Jews from non-Jews or statements that remove the latter from consideration.[28] Chabad Hasidism, which subscribes to the principle in *Tanya* that the non-Jew lacks a divine soul, does not publicly voice this.[29]

In the United States, individuals and groups that promote the incorporation of Kabbalah into Judaism do so without drawing attention to the traditional boundaries between Jews and non-Jews. Indeed, they are likelier to emphasize their openness toward other traditions. For example, ALEPH – The Alliance for Jewish Renewal, is the outgrowth of Zalman Schacter-Shalomi's outreach activities that sought to stimulate returnees to Judaism. Under his guidance, ALEPH trains rabbis, supports affiliated congregations, and provides educational resources for followers primarily in the US (there are international centers, and one in Israel). Jewish Renewal's idiosyncratic worship and ritual observance revolve around the kabbalistic concept of the four worlds of *atzilut, beriah, yetzirah*, and *assiyah* (emanation, creation, formation, and action); for example, participants regard the traditional system of prayer as a vehicle for rising from one level of reality to the next. Yet, this movement prides itself on combining Jewish tradition with "a modern consciousness that is politically progressive, egalitarian and environmentally aware," and on fostering communities that embrace interfaith families.[30]

Outside of Israel, where Jews are a minority within generally pluralistic societies, they interpret kabbalistic teachings with a weaker collective voice. The vast majority of teachers and organizations offering insight

---

[28] Daniel Matt, *The Essential Kabbalah: The Heart of Jewish Mysticism* (New York, 1994).

[29] Elliot R. Wolfson, *Open Secret: Postmessianic Messianism and the Mystical Revision of Menahem Mendel Schneerson* (New York, 2009), chap. 6. And when it is voiced, the leaders of the movement are very much on the defensive on this account. See "Chabad: 'We Vehemently Disagree' With Rabbi Manis Friedman," on FailedMessiah.com, http://failedmessiah.typepad.com/failed_messiahcom/2009/06/chabad-spins-we-vehemently-disagree-with-rabbi-manis-friedman.html (Accessed July 5, 2010) and "Kabbalah," on Chabad.org, www.chabad.org/kabbalah/article_cdo/aid/378741/jewish/Non-Jews.htm (Accessed July 5, 2010).

[30] See https://aleph.org (accessed June 20, 2010).

from Kabbalah tend to use it as one of a number of resources that an individual can utilize to create a more contemplative form of Judaism or a more meaningful individual practice. Much of this material, even that written by Jews for Jews, is cast in universalized terms and presented in the vernacular. People who are not Jewish are adding it to their potpourri of spiritual exercises and wisdom literature. Publishers are one force behind this expansion; the motto of the company producing the most titles on Judaism and spirituality, Jewish Lights Publishing, is "Jewish books that reflect the Jewish wisdom tradition for people of all faiths and all backgrounds."[31] When Kabbalah moves beyond the boundaries of Orthodox society, it tends to lose its connection to halacha. The Kabbalah Centre movement in North America was perhaps the first Jewish-led group to take this step. In the mid-1990s Kabbalah Centre leaders began to announce that authentic Kabbalah had nothing to do with Judaism or with the binding force of halacha, and they welcomed the participation of people of all religious backgrounds into their courses and communal events. Such openness would be far riskier in Israel. The Israel-based kabbalistic movement Bnei Baruch – whose leader also scorns organized religion, welcomes non-Jews into courses, and denies spiritual value to the observance of halacha – instructs his Jewish followers in Israel to adopt the external markers of Orthodoxy such as modest dress, head coverings, and Shabbat.

In Israel, the commitment to Jewish parochialism is stronger and to egalitarianism is weaker. Of course, New Agers are as universalistic in Israel as elsewhere, but they are a small minority among the many who are loyal to the well-established tenet that Jews are fundamentally different than and superior to non-Jews. Such ideas are more socially acceptable in Israel than in the Diaspora, and they align with Jewish nationalism. Fidelity to the negative depiction of non-Jews in kabbalistic writings is the norm within the religious sector in Israel. Some kabbalists have pointed out that these teachings are appropriate reasons for discriminatory laws.[32]

---

[31] See, for example, the book by Tamar Frankiel and Judy Greenfield, *Minding the Temple of the Soul: Balancing Body, Mind, and Spirit Through Traditional Jewish Prayer, Movement, and Meditation* (Woodstock, VT, 1997). According to the review in amazon.com by Caroline M. Myss, a "medical intuitive" who links the *sefirot* with the Christian sacraments and Hindu chakras, Frankiel and Greenfield's book belongs "in every health spa and at every retreat center in this country." www.amazon.com/Minding-Temple-Soul-Traditional-Meditation/dp/1879045648/ref=sr_1_3?ie=UTF8&s=books&qid=127838096 1&sr=1–3.

[32] Jonathan Garb, "'Kabbalah Outside the Walls': The Reaction of Rabbi Hadaya to the Rise of the State" (Hebrew), in *Rabbi Uziel and His Peers: Studies in the Religious Thought of Oriental Rabbis in 20th Century Israel*, ed. Z. Zohar, 13–27 (Tel Aviv, in press). Jody Myers, "Kabbalah for the Gentiles: Diverse Souls and Universalism in Contemporary

Yitzhak Ginsburgh (b. 1944 in the US), a kabbalist who is a follower of the Chabad rebbe, has been one of the most extreme. From his home in Israel, Ginsburgh directs Gal Einai Institute, an educational organization and publishing house that broadcasts knowledge of Kabbalah to non-Jews outside of Israel. This is in accordance with the charge issued by the Lubavitcher rebbe Menahem Mendel Schneersohn (1902–1994) to teach non-Jews to follow the seven commandments given to the offspring of Noah. Chabad teachers in America have been reluctant to take up this charge. Ginsburgh, however, uses kabbalistic texts to show non-Jews that their inferior souls will be improved by placing themselves under the authority of Jews and fulfilling the Noahide commandments. He finds kabbalistic sources to justify subservient political status for non-Jews in the Land of Israel and to kill those who evince violence against Jews.[33] While Ginsburgh's political activism is frowned upon, his understanding of Jewish teachings appears to be widely shared. With Hebrew as the vernacular, it is difficult to obscure the original terms used in classical kabbalistic writings; their sting must be removed through interpretation. Michael Laitman has made such an attempt through his version of Ashlagian Kabbalah by teaching that there is no spiritual value in the common designations "Jews" and "Nations of the World," and by including people of all backgrounds in the Bnei Baruch movement. However, Jews and Nations of the World are central to his teachings as designations for one's progress toward spiritual refinement, and the ethnic divisions persist in the social relations within the organization.[34]

In Israel Kabbalah is far more likely to be interpreted to support communal, political, and national causes. The Land of Israel in kabbalistic teachings is imbued with multiple sacred characteristics: it is sacred space most conducive for achieving higher states of consciousness, it is the earthly analogue to the upper world, and so on. Since the sixteenth century, kabbalists have depicted the migration of Jews from the Diaspora and the erection of Jewish institutions in the Yishuv as evidence of the "ingathering of sparks" or as advances toward cosmic harmony.[35] These correspondences have not diminished in recent years. The strengthening of

Kabbalah," in *Kabbalah and Contemporary Spiritual Revival: Historical, Sociological and Cultural Perspectives*, ed. Boaz Huss (Beer Sheva, 2010): 181–211.

[33] See www.inner.org/about/gal.htm (Accessed June 20, 2010).

[34] Myers, "Kabbalah for the Gentiles."

[35] Moshe Idel, "The Land of Israel in Medieval Kabbalah," in *The Land of Israel: Jewish Perspectives*, ed. Lawrence Hoffman (Bloomington, IN, 1986), 170–187; Arie Morgenstern, *Hastening Redemption: Messianism and the Resettlement of the Land of Israel*, translated by Joel A. Linsider (Oxford and New York, 2006).

corporate religious entities in the Land of Israel and, for some, the establishment of the state, were regarded as foreshadowing the Zoharic process "an awakening from below leads to an awakening from above." From the Mandatory era onward, Shalom Haddaya and his son Ovadiah, successive directors of the Beit El yeshiva, publicly described Zionist achievements as positive, kabbalistic processes that could bring unity within "the upper world." By the 1980s, members of the Religious Zionist camp adopted explicitly kabbalistic language for national military accomplishments, and the most extreme activists were reputed to regard such violence as hastening "an awakening from below."[36] By the turn of the twenty-first century, the most militant settler activists were those tutored and encouraged by Yitzhak Ginsburgh.[37] For the most part, however, leading kabbalists have not sanctioned such extremism and factionalism. They are more likely to be politically quiescent or to urge the electorate to vote for political parties that will strengthen and expand the power of religious authorities over Israeli society. Nevertheless, the drama, passion, and promises contained within kabbalistic narratives have added value and excitement to the Jews' return to the Land of Israel and to ancient messianic hopes.

Kabbalah has become an element in modern Jewish culture for myriad reasons. The tremendous variety of expressions in diverse social and cultural milieus and its widespread availability ensure that Kabbalah can no longer be regarded as a hidden tradition. Its malleability has enabled it to meet new challenges, and in turn it has been transformed in startling ways.

SELECT BIBLIOGRAPHY

Albanese, Catherine L. *A Republic of Mind and Spirit: A Cultural History of American Metaphysical Religion*, New Haven, 2007.

Ariel, Yaakov. "Hasidism in the Age of Aquarius: The House of Love and Prayer in San Francisco, 1967–1977," *Religion and American Culture* 13, no. 2 (2003): 139–165.

Bilu, Yoram. *The Saints' Impresarios: Dreamers, Healers and Holy Men in Israel's Urban Periphery*, Haifa, 2005 (Hebrew).

Campbell, Bruce F. *Ancient Wisdom Revived: A History of the Theosophical Movement*, Berkeley, 1980.

Dawson, Lorne L. *Comprehending Cults: The Sociology of New Religious Movements*, 2nd ed. Ontario, 2006.

[36] Garb, *The Chosen Will Become Herds*, 44–47.

[37] Yitzchak Ginsburgh, *Kabbalah and Meditation for the Nations* (Jerusalem, 2007); *Rectifying the State of Israel: A Political Platform based on Kabbalah* (Jerusalem, 2002); and "Baruch Hagever," in *Baruch Hagever: Sefer Zikaron Lakadosh Doktor Baruch Goldstein*, ed. Michael Ben-Horin and Netanel Ozri (Jerusalem, 1995) (Hebrew), 41–4.

Garb, Jonathan. "*The Chosen Will Become Herds*": Studies in Twentieth Century Kabbalah, New Haven & London, 2009.

"'Kabbalah Outside the Walls': The Reaction of Rabbi Haddaya to the Rise of the State" (Hebrew), in *Rabbi Uziel and His Peers: Studies in the Religious Thought of Oriental Rabbis in 20th Century Israel*, ed. Z. Zohar, Tel Aviv, in press.

"Mystical and Spiritual Discourse in the Contemporary Ashkenazi Haredi Worlds," *Journal of Modern Jewish Studies* 9 (2010), 17–36.

Giller, Pinchas. *Shalom Shar'abi and the Kabbalists of Beit El*, Oxford and New York, 2008.

Hanegraaff, Wouter J. *New Age Religion and Western Culture: Esotericism in the Mirror of Secular Thought*, Albany, 1998.

Huss, Boaz, ed. *Kabbalah and Contemporary Spiritual Revival*, Beer Sheva, 2011.

"The New Age of Kabbalah: Contemporary Kabbalah, the New Age, and Post- Modern Spirituality," *Journal of Modern Jewish Studies* 6, no. 2 (2007): 107–125.

Huss, Boaz, Marco Pasi and Kocku von Stuckrad, eds, *Kabbalah and Modernity: Interpretations, Transformations, Adaptations*, Leiden, 2010.

Idel, Moshe. "On the History of the Interdiction against the Study of Kabbalah Before the Age of Forty," *AJS Review* 5 (1980): 1–20 (Hebrew).

Kyle, Richard. *The New Age Movement in American Culture*, Lanham, MD, 1995.

Magid, Saul. "Rainbow Hassidism in America: The Maturation of Jewish Renewal," *The Reconstructionist* 68 (2004): 34–60.

Meilicke, Christine A. "Abulafianism among the Counterculture Kabbalists," *Jewish Studies Quarterly* 9 (2002): 71–101.

Meir, Jonatan. "The Revealed and the Revealed within the Concealed: On the Opposition to the 'Followers' of Rabbi Yehudah Ashlag and the Dissemination of Esoteric Literature," *Kabbalah* 16 (2007): 151–258.

Myers, Jody Elizabeth. *Kabbalah and the Spiritual Quest: The Kabbalah Centre in America*, Westport, CT, 2007.

Nadler, Allan. *The Faith of the Mithnagdim: Rabbinic Responses to Hasidic Rapture*, Baltimore, 1997.

Robinson, Ira. "Kabbalah and Science in *Sefer Ha-Berit*: A Modernization Strategy for Orthodox Jews," *Modern Judaism* 9, no. 3 (1989): 275–288.

Weissler, Chava. "Meanings of Shekhinah in the 'Jewish Renewal' Movement," *Nashim: A Journal of Jewish Women's Studies & Gender Issues*, 10 (Fall 2006): 53–83.

Wolfson, Elliot R. *Open Secret: Postmessianic Messianism and the Mystical Revision of Menahem Mendel Schneerson*, New York, 2009.

CHAPTER 38

ORTHODOXY AND ULTRA-ORTHODOXY AS FORCES IN MODERN JEWISH LIFE

JESS OLSON

On August 1, 2012, MetLife Stadium was filled to capacity with the unusual spectacle of over 90,000 (mostly male) Orthodox Jews. They had come to the new, state of the art, football stadium, home of the New York Jets and Giants, for reasons unrelated to sports; rather they were celebrating the twelfth Daf Yomi Siyyum ha-Shas, the completion of a seven-and-a-half-year, page-a-day reading of the Babylonian Talmud that has become a ritual for many thousands worldwide. On the field, a large dais was erected midfield, and over the course of the late afternoon and evening, several distinguished, black-clothed gentlemen offered words of congratulations and religious inspiration, among them leaders of communities, major Orthodox organizations, heads of yeshivot (advanced Talmudic academies) and leaders of Hasidic dynasties. The audience was mostly dressed the same, though scattered throughout were some from any number of different gradations of Orthodoxy; if one looked hard enough one could also find American street clothes and the small black suede and crocheted skullcaps that are the trappings of "modern" Orthodoxy. Participants were serenaded by the devotional songs of all-male musical groups in styles ranging from operatic cantorial music to electronica-infused pop. As the many figures who appeared on the dais spoke, mostly in English with occasional Yiddish, they emphasized themes of joy at the completion of the Talmud, triumph at the number of siyyum participants, and the memory of those lost in the Holocaust.

All of these accoutrements underscored the potent symbolism of the evening as a testament to the resilience of Orthodoxy. In fact, the official pamphlet announcing the siyyum made this sentiment explicit: "because this siyyum … will honor the memory of the Six Million *Kedoshim* [holy ones] who perished in the fires of Churban Europe [the Holocaust], it will be a powerful testament as well to the *nizichus* [victory] of Torah and the idea that it alone can preserve our past and ensure our future."[1] To participants it was proof that their worldview of fidelity to belief and

[1] Ticket order form, 12th Siyyum ha-Shas.

strict observance could not just survive in the secular culture of the United States, but was on the march. It was the triumph of a community once referred to in rabbinic parlance as the *sharit ha-plitah*, the surviving remnant of once-massive Orthodox communities that were ruthlessly wiped out in the ghettos and camps of the Nazi Holocaust.

To many, the form of Jewish identity represented at the siyyum is an unchanging one. Whether the event was judged with alarm for its tone of *ecclesia militens* or its marginalization of women (a controversial aspect that received significant press attention), or warmly as a unique manifestation of American religious diversity, most would agree with the participants that their Judaism is authentic in ways that other modern Jewish identities are not. The trappings of timelessness were all present, from the Babylonian Talmud that was the center of the event and of Orthodox identity, to the dark clothing that, even if modern, evokes Jewish garb worn for centuries (at least by Ashkenazim), to the old-world reverence shown for the rabbis and other leaders.

But though many of these aspects of identity are indeed at variance with mainstream Jewish and American society, they are as much a reflection of a modern negotiation of culture and society as an extension of a pre-modern identity. Indeed, a closer examination of the siyyum itself illustrates a fascinating amalgam of the modern and the traditional. The event celebrates an approach to traditional learning that dates back only to the early 1920s, when the daf yomi program was launched as an initiative of the decade-old Orthodox political party Agudat Yisrael. The siyyum's format and even language would have been shocking to an Orthodox Jew at the turn of the twentieth century, to say nothing of one at the turn of the nineteenth. Beyond the hyper-modernism of a twenty-first-century football stadium that broadcast the proceedings on massive Jumbotron screens, the use of English as the language of the proceedings would have been unthinkable less than a century ago by this community. Even the text itself, seemingly the most unimpeachably ancient element of the proceedings, was subject to modern treatment. The edition of choice for many, if not most of the participants was the *Schottenstein ArtScroll Talmud*, a contemporary English translation that for many of the participants is the only tool that allows them to keep up with the intense pace of the daf yomi year after year.

This chapter seeks to understand how the modern cultural negotiation of contemporary Orthodox Judaism developed historically. A complex but little-understood religious subculture, Orthodoxy has any number of forms and permutations, all of them fascinating, few of them adequately researched or understood. Although it is impossible in an essay such as this to provide an exhaustive description of every form Orthodoxy has taken, we can illuminate its essence by understanding how Jewish identity changed from an early modern, traditional religious culture shared by an overwhelming majority of Jews worldwide into a self-conscious, remarkably adaptable voluntary identity maintained by a motivated minority within a wider Jewish world whose members have long since embraced any number of alternative modern identities. This transformation, from traditional culture to self-conscious ideology, is the central theme in the story of Orthodoxy as a force in the modern evolution of both the Jewish people and the very idea of Judaism as a religious ideology.

THE IDEA OF ORTHODOXY: A TERM AND ITS ORIGINS

To begin analyzing this metamorphosis from "traditional" to "Orthodox" is not an easy or obvious process. The notion that Orthodox practice and belief are fundamentally timeless is dearly held both in the community and outside it, and with some reason. The trappings of Orthodoxy in the contemporary world are deeply informed by a sense of traditionalist precedence, even if the external social reality and internal ideological motivation have evolved over time. But the difficulties in understanding Orthodox identity are highlighted by as basic a problem as the very term "Orthodox." Most understand it as a description of any form of Judaism in the modern period (roughly 1500 to the present) characterized by devotion to strict belief and practice as the centerpiece of Jewish identity, derived from a rabbinic literature that dates back to the Second Temple.[2] Over time, the central text defining "Orthodox" Jewish practice, emerging out of several competing codifications, is the sixteenth-century *Shulhan Arukh*. But this usage includes a broad swath of historical communities, from the traditional kehillot that were the basic communal organizations of early modern Jews, to the plethora of contemporary groups engaged at various levels with non-Jewish culture who maintain strict religious observance. Added to this are other, even more recent designations such as "modern Orthodox," "ultra-Orthodox," and "haredi." But imprecise use of these terms has obscured their meaning to the point of incoherence. In fact, the word "Orthodox," defining a subset of the larger Jewish community, dates back no earlier than the early to mid-nineteenth century, where it was used both as a term of pride to defenders of tradition (for example, in the usage of American lay leader, cantor and Bible translator Isaac Leeser) and as a term of disparagement by those opposed to modernization of

[2] See Moshe Samet, "The Beginnings of Orthodoxy," *Modern Judaism* 8, no. 3 (1988): 249–269.

Jewish practice and theology.[3] It quickly gained currency as a term used indiscriminately for all Jews who identified self-consciously with a rigor of religious practice that set them apart as a recognizable faction of the larger Jewish community, regardless of communal, regional, or ideological variation. Complicating this even more, until very late the term "Orthodox" had little relevance for many, if not most Jewish communities. Outside of Ashkenazi Jewry, it has no historical relevance, and in Europe, because the term was coined to describe reaction to Jewish reform in Central Europe and North America, in places where this phenomenon was muted or non-existent it held little meaning beyond periodic use in polemic.[4] In these areas, religious belief and practice reflected a traditional mode of authority and identity that perceived religious belief and practice as timeless, a view buttressed by internal custom and external legal status that was ambiguous about the inclusion of Jews in broader society.

The appearance of a self-conscious Orthodoxy came first as a reaction to early, ad hoc attempts to reform Jewish religious practice.[5] These pioneering reform communities were almost entirely in German cities like Berlin and Hamburg, centers of the European Enlightenment and the Jewish Haskalah. Here, small, affluent, and acculturated communities faced a delayed grant of civic equality, and many believed that changing the form and content of Jewish worship was a solution to both complaints of backwardness by opponents of Jewish integration, and their own anxiety about what they perceived to be obscurantist aspects of traditional practice. In 1818, a conspicuously modern synagogue was dedicated in Hamburg to meet the needs of the growing community. In addition to aesthetic changes, the Hamburg Temple featured an organ to accompany prayer on the Sabbath and festivals (when playing musical instruments is prohibited by Jewish law) and a modernized prayerbook and liturgy.[6] This was one of the first drops in a flood of synagogue reforms throughout Central Europe, where various communities embraced changes that ranged from basic aesthetic improvements to expansive liturgical adjustments such as eliding references to the messianic redemption, the re-establishment of Jewish

[3] Samson Raphael Hirsch, "Religion Allied with Progress," *The Collected Writings*, Vol. 1 (Spring Valley, NY: Feldheim Publishers, 1990), 140.
[4] Jacob Katz, *Tradition and Crisis: Jewish Society at the End of the Middle Ages* (New York: Schocken, 1961).
[5] See Michael Meyer, *Response to Modernity, A History of the Reform Movement in Judaism* (Detroit: Wayne State University Press, 1988); Ismar Schorsch, *From Text to Context: The Turn to History in Modern Judaism* (Hanover, NH: Brandeis University Press, 2003).
[6] Jakob Josef Petukowski, *Prayerbook Reform in Europe: The Liturgy of Reform Judaism* (New York: World Union for Progressive Judaism, 1968).

sovereignty in Palestine, and cultic sacrifices. By the early 1840s, leaders of reform concluded that a critical mass of modern communities had been reached to necessitate formal guidelines, and three conferences between 1844–1846 laid the groundwork for the modern Reform movement.

The proto-Orthodox reaction by traditional rabbis opposed to this process appeared very early. Attitudes towards change in some aspects of worship were not uniformly negative at first; indeed, figures such as Isaac Bernays of Hamburg (1792–1849) adopted moderate aesthetic reforms without apology and little controversy (although he opposed the Hamburg Temple).[7] But the consecration of a modernized synagogue motivated several rabbis, including Moses Sofer of Pressburg (Bratislava; the Chatam Sofer, 1762–1839), Mordechai Benet of Moravia (1753–1829), Akiva Eger of Posen (1761–1837), Jacob ben Jacob of Lissa (Leszno; 1760–1832), to speak out decisively against its innovations in a booklet entitled *Eleh Divrei ha-Brit*. This, the first coordinated statement of rabbinic opposition to modern ritual changes, was the harbinger of an attitude towards modernization that would soon characterize self-conscious Orthodoxy.[8] Its authors denounced the credentials of those who advocated changes, used a polemical language that eschewed compromise and a wide variety of prooftexts outside of mainstream rabbinic legal literature to support positions they described as timeless. Those who advocated reforms, the pamphlet asserted, were "simple Jews, not learned in Torah," and the changes were contrary to the "laws of Moses and Israel." It was thus the duty of those "pious and holy ones" to "rise up and pronounce with one voice" the gravity of the violated prohibitions, which did no less than "endanger the Jewish soul." The rabbis condemned any changes made to the liturgy, public prayer in languages other than Hebrew, participation in congregations that used vernacular in the liturgy, and the introduction of musical instruments into the synagogue on the Sabbath or holidays.[9] Although severe, these sentiments did mirror the attitude of many Jews in early nineteenth-century Europe, in

---

[7] See Sid Leiman, "Rabbinic Responses to Modernity," *Judaic Studies* 5 (Fall, 2007): 35–50; Rivka Horowitz, "On Kabbala and Myth in 19th Century Germany: Isaac Bernays," *Proceedings of the American Academy of Jewish Research* 59 (1993): 137–183.

[8] The text *Eleh Divrei ha-Brit* is available at www.hebrewbooks.org/783. For a partial translation, see Paul Mendes-Flohr and Jehuda Reinharz, "These are the Words of the Covenant," in *The Jew in the Modern World*, 3rd edition (New York: Oxford University Press, 2011), 187–189. For detailed discussion of the text and the role of Mordechai Bennet in its creation, see Michael Miller, *Rabbis and Revolution: The Jews of Moravia in the Age of Emancipation* (Stanford: Stanford University Press, 2011), 76–80. Samet, "The Beginnings of Orthodoxy," 256–258.

[9] Eleh Divrei ha-brit, précis, 1819.

particular those still located in the dense Jewish communities of the former Polish-Lithuanian Commonwealth. Here rabbinic authority and prestige held much more sway, and reforms were often met with a strong reaction on the local and regional level, while ideologically motivated traditionalists presented a durable front against internal and external reforms.

ORTHODOXY AND JEWISH SOCIETY IN THE NINETEENTH CENTURY

But by the mid-nineteenth century, external governmental pressure and internal modernization had changed this dynamic dramatically, and Jewish traditionalism in Central Europe faced an existential challenge. To a casual observer, at the time of the revolutions of 1848 it already seemed in many communities that modernized religious practice and integrated Jewish communities were the future. Although still decades away from full acceptance and emancipation, many assumed that as Jews left behind traditional society, they would inevitably embrace "enlightened" religious practice as a matter of course. And where reform had succeeded in Central Europe, it often entirely co-opted the traditional kehillah, even in the face of traditionalist opposition. Rejecting communal schism, often because of government resistance and popular sentiment, reformers worked effectively for change within the official communities, in the process alienating remaining traditionalists.[10]

Contrary to a common perception, however, the erosion of traditionalist influence did not only benefit reformers. In fact, the period from 1848 to the end of the nineteenth century showed that where traditionalism was in decline, it also created a space for the emergence of a new model of self-conscious Orthodoxy. In Germany and Hungary, two new, competing expressions of this, both departures from receding traditionalism, came into their own between 1840–1870.[11] Each utilized a religious vocabulary and idealized past which claimed continuity with traditional society, rabbinic authority, and commitment to the full corpus of Jewish law and custom, which they understood to be hermetically transmitted since the divine revelation of the Torah at Sinai. They asserted exclusivity of authority to interpret and instruct in Jewish law and ritual, and

---

[10] Robert Liberles, *Religious Conflict in Social Context: The Resurgence of Orthodox Judaism in Frankfurt am Main* (Westport, CT: Greenwood, 1985), 167–68.

[11] Robert Liberles, "The Rabbinical Conferences of the 1850s and the Quest for Liturgical Unity," *Modern Judaism* 3, no. 3 (1983): 309–317; Jacob Katz, *A House Divided: Orthodoxy and Schism in Nineteenth Century Central European Jewry* (Waltham, MA: Brandeis University Press, 1998).

advocated the *Shulhan Arukh* as its definitive guide. Both emphasized the need to create new institutions to replace the eroded traditional kehillah – especially in education – to counter the incursion of external knowledge considered a threat to religious belief. Finally, both advocated strengthening, through internal and independent funding and private institutions if necessary, barriers that separated them from modernizers, even if it meant breaking with recognized communities. Together, these traits gave Central European Orthodoxy a new self-consciousness towards religious identity that is the hallmark of the transition from traditionalism to Orthodoxy.

Yet for all their similarities, these two intellectual forbears of most Orthodox communities today had contentious differences. In Germany, the neo-Orthodoxy of Samson Raphael Hirsch (1808–1888) and Esriel Hildesheimer (1820–1899) asserted itself as the corrective to Reform excess while embracing the acculturation of most German Jews.[12] Both rabbis were shaped by their own elite traditional and university education (both studied with Jacob Ettinger and Isaac Bernays; Hirsch attended university in Bonn, Hildesheimer in Berlin), and both placed high value on Jews receiving a sophisticated modern education as well as a firm grounding in traditional learning. This, the "Torah im derekh erets" model (a rabbinic phrase roughly translated in this context as "Torah and worldly knowledge"), was instrumental in their shared goal of expanding the traditional worldview to embrace the best of both Jewish and German intellectual worlds. Both Hirsch and Hildesheimer accepted engagement with German bourgeois culture as a harmonious counterpart to strict ritual observance, and did not reject moderate aesthetic changes to religious practice, such as wearing canonical garments, increasing the formality of religious services, and German sermons.[13] Like their teacher Jacob Ettlinger, an opponent of reform who pioneered the creation of a German Orthodox readership through his mid-century newspaper *Der treue Zionswächter* (The Faithful Guardian of Zion), both were outspoken opponents of Reform who embraced modern pastoral roles as leaders of their communities, activist political leadership in defense of Orthodoxy, and modern print media (Hirsch, for instance, edited the neo-Orthodox monthly, *Jeschurun*, for over thirty years).[14]

[12] See Miller, *Rabbis and Revolution*, 138–218; Liberles, *Religious Conflict in Social Context*; David Ellenson, *Rabbi Esriel Hildesheimer and the Creation of Modern Jewish Orthodoxy* (Tuskaloosa: University of Alabama Press, 1990).

[13] See Mordechai Breuer, *Modernity within Tradition: A Social History of Orthodox Jewry in Imperial Germany* (New York: Columbia University Press, 1992).

[14] For discussion of early German Orthodox press, see Judith Bleich, "The Emergence of an Orthodox Press in 19th Century Germany," *Jewish Social Studies* 42, nos. 3–4 (1980): 323–344.

This attitude towards engagement with non-Jewish society marked the most important fissure between the German neo-Orthodox and the flavor of Orthodoxy that emerged in the Hungarian and Galician regions of the Habsburg Empire. Here was a much larger and more densely concentrated traditionalist society, and many of its religious leaders were either the students of or heavily influenced by the thought of Moshe Sofer, leader of the Pressburg (Bratislava) community and its renowned yeshiva.[15] To the generation of Central European rabbis that emerged after Sofer's death in 1839, his image became synonymous with muscular opposition to ritual changes and admitting outside intellectual influence on Jewish society, a position summed up by the oft-referenced adage "*kol hadash asur min ha-Torah*," "all innovation is forbidden by the Torah."[16] Although detailed investigation into Sofer's long career as a community leader complicates his reputation as an uncompromising hardliner, his position towards religious reform was consistently antagonistic. As interpreted by his sympathizers, Sofer's ideology went far beyond challenging the aesthetics of worship in the synagogue to the basic presumption, shared by both Reform and neo-Orthodoxy, that European culture could be successfully accommodated within the framework of Judaism. They also opposed their German counterparts' educational symbiosis of general and religious studies. As the ideology of what would become broadly known as "ultra-Orthodoxy," it eschewed even modest changes to the customs and folkways that they considered authentic.[17]

During the tumultuous 1860s and 70s, these positions intensified. Final Jewish emancipation in Austria-Hungary (1867) and Germany (1871) sparked two conflicts that set the future trajectory for Orthodoxy and ultra-Orthodoxy. In the German Empire, Hirsch moved to sever the formal connection between his neo-Orthodox Israelitische Religionsgesellschaft (IRG) and the official Frankfurt Jewish community.[18] Having long been chafed by the liabilities of operating as a private religious society while

---

[15] See Jacob Katz, "Towards a Biography of the Hatam Sofer," trans. David Ellenson, in *Profiles in Diversity: Jews in a Changing Europe, 1750–1870*, ed. Francis Malino and David Sorkin (Detroit: Wayne State University Press, 1998), 223–266.

[16] This dictum appears in a responsa of the Hatam Sofer (*Sha'alot u-teshuvot Chatam Sofer, Orah Hayyim* 28; *Yoreh De'ah* 19), referring to the permissibility of eating "new" grain (hadash) before the offering of the Omer on the second day of Passover.

[17] For an important meditation on use of the term "ultra-Orthodoxy," see Michael Silber, "The Emergence of Ultra-Orthodoxy" in *The Uses of Tradition*, ed. Jack Wertheimer (New York: Jewish Theological Seminary Press, 1992), 23–84, here 26 note 4.

[18] See Michael Meyer, "Alienated Intellectuals in the Camp of Reform," *AJS Review* 6 (1981): 61–86.

being obliged by law to maintain membership in a Reform-dominated official community, Hirsch and several members of his community contended that Orthodox Jews had a right to separation from the official community for matters of conscience, a doctrine referred to as *Austritt*, or separation. He seized the opportunity presented by the German affirmation of communal secession for Catholic and Protestant communities to press for the same right for Jews, which was granted in 1876. In spite of provoking a backlash from those alarmed by the demise of "catholic Israel," Hirsch rallied enough members of the IRG in Frankfurt to formally secede, thus opening a new chapter in denominational identity which fundamentally transformed the historical nature of German Jewish communities.[19]

In Hungary, questions of secession and communal identity were even more fraught. Here, denominational conflict took a surprising turn that pitted two models of Orthodoxy against one another. The conflict began when Esriel Hildesheimer became rabbi of the influential Habsburg Jewish community of Eisenstadt. Unlike Germany, where Hirsch represented the far right of the denominational spectrum, Hildesheimer faced a powerful cohort of rabbis in Hungary that did not support even the moderate changes of neo-Orthodoxy. Some of these, including Akiva Joseph Schlessinger (1837–1922) and his father-in-law Hillel Lichtenstein (1814–1891), had earlier mobilized opposition to efforts of the Hungarian government to intervene in Jewish educational affairs, and they targeted Hildesheimer as an agent of unacceptable compromise and reform for his advocacy of a neo-Orthodox-style seminary in Eisenstadt. These and other like-minded rabbis undertook a vitriolic campaign to undermine Hildesheimer, tarring the German Orthodox rabbi as an opponent of "authentic" Judaism, culminating in 1865 with the *psak din* of Michalovce, a rabbinical decree that laid out a list of synagogue reforms they considered beyond the pale of Judaism – all of which targeted Hildesheimer and other neo-Orthodox leaders.[20] Utilizing extreme terminology (such as the sharply polemical term "beyt apikorusus," "house of heresy," to describe neo-Orthodox synagogues) and rulings on the impermissibility of clerical dress, of interior and exterior synagogue design, language not just of prayer but also of the rabbi's sermon, the *psak din* continued the precedent set decades earlier by *Eleh Divrei ha-Brit*, but with an even more radical ideology and re-reading of tradition.[21] Schlessinger and Lichtenstein's position

---

[19] Katz, *A House Divided*, and Liberles, *Religious Conflict in Social Context*.

[20] See Silber, "The Emergence of Ultra-Orthodoxy."

[21] The *psak din* of Michalovce may be found in *Lev Ha-ivri*, an extended commentary on the will of the Hatam Sofer penned by Schlessinger. See Akiva Joseph Schlessinger, *Lev ha-Ivri* (Lemberg: J. M. Stand, 1868).

did not ultimately prevail – among others, the influential Rabbi Moshe Shik (the Maharam Shik, 1807–1889) of Chust led the endorsement of a moderated response (although he still strictly rejected innovation). But the vitriolic document did ensure that the status-quo Orthodox position in Hungary epitomized a muscular Orthodox opposition to modernization, while Schlessinger's radicalism, and especially his strident polemics, became a fixture of discourse in segments of the Orthodox community.

East of the two Central European empires, the religious world of Russian Jewry evolved in directions that reflected a very different political and social reality. But even as they did so, the interests of emerging Russian Jewish Orthodoxy gradually dovetailed with those of their Central European counterparts. Jewish traditionalism in Russia faced a tumultuous process of government-directed modernization, centralization, and halting experiments in liberalization. Although many Russian Jews did partake in some form or another in aspects of modernization that targeted them, residual traditional communal structure, leadership, and institutions remained influential far longer than in Central Europe. Generally, the development of Russian religious patterns was driven less by reaction to fears of internal religious reform than in Central Europe. Rather, it grew out of a widespread sense that communities needed to develop means of preserving religious authority, belief, and practice threatened by broader Russian governmental policy that often employed (and exploited) Jewish advocates of modernization.

Those best equipped to thwart significant encroachment on their society and institutions were the numerous Hasidic groups present throughout Russian Ukraine, Belarus, and Poland. Hasidism had evolved in the late eighteenth and early nineteenth centuries from an upstart charismatic movement to remake huge swaths of the traditional community in its image. Its formidable social cohesion was based on the institution of the rebbe and principled suspicion of knowledge outside of traditional Jewish texts or the writings of Hasidic figures. The mystical initiation, charisma, and hereditary continuity of these rebbes made them both new foci of communal authority and producers of a new form of religious literature. Due to the general decline of the Russian kehillot (which were formally abolished in 1844) and the erosion of the status of the communal rabbi, Hasidim in many places created a new structure of religious community with authority to which even those not ideologically committed to Hasidism appealed.[22] Hasidic interpretation of traditional

---

[22] Shaul Stampfer, "The Missing Rabbis of Eastern Europe," in *Families, Rabbis and Education: Traditional Jewish Society in Nineteenth-Century Europe* (Oxford: Littman Library of Jewish Civilization, 2010), 277–302.

texts became a major field of literary production, primarily in the form of Torah commentary that folded nineteenth-century Hasidic concepts into the corpus of traditional exegesis, including the *Me ha-Shiloah* of Mordechai Yosef Leiner (1801–1854) of the Izhbits-Radzyn dynasty, and the *Sfat Emet* by Yehuda Aryeh-Leib Alter (1847–1905) of the Gerer dynasty. Other forms of Hasidic literature included legal tracts like the *Shulhan Arukh ha-Rav* of Shneur Zalman of Lyady (1745–1812), the first rebbe of the Chabad-Lubavitch dynasty. Additionally, Shneur Zalman's philosophical tract *Tanya*, and other texts like the *Likutei Amaraim* of Nachman of Breslov (first and last rebbe of the Breslov Hasidic movement), gave coherence to Hasidic theology. Finally, hagiographic literature about Hasidic leaders, beginning with (and modeled after) the *Shivhei ha-Besht* (Praise of the Ba'al Shem Tov), collections of oral traditions about the founder of Hasidism, bolstered the reputation and authority of the rebbe.

Non-Hasidic communities and institutions also evolved noticeably over the mid- to late nineteenth century. Perhaps most important was the modern yeshiva, which first emerged in Lithuania partly in response to the threat of modernization, partly to the success of Hasidism by students of Elijah ben Solomon, the Gaon of Vilna (GR"A, 1720–1797), an entrenched opponent of the charismatic movement. The exemplar of this institution was the Volozhin yeshiva (known in Orthodox circles as Yeshivat Eyts Hayyim) in Lithuania, established in 1803 by Hayyim ben Yitzkhok of Volozhin (1749–1821), a leading student of the Vilna Gaon. Along with the Mir yeshiva established around the same time, Volozhin featured important innovations that allowed it to thrive for most of the nineteenth century as a destination for advanced students. Unlike earlier yeshivot, Volozhin operated independently of the local community, had a leadership exemplified by Naftali Tsvi Yehudah Berlin (the Netziv, 1816–1893), and staff not under communal purview, supported by its own, independent fundraising efforts.[23] But the most marked difference from its traditional predecessors was a change in its mission of creating an idealized atmosphere of Torah study as a bulwark against encroaching modernization. By the second half of the nineteenth century the Volozhin model had spread to other Lithuanian yeshivot, each featuring different philosophical or exegetical styles. This "yeshiva world" produced an impressive array of literature, including glosses on the *Shulhan Arukh* such as the *Mishnah Berura* by Yisrael Meir Kagan of Radun (the Hafets Hayyim, 1838–1933), halachic compendia such as the *Arukh ha-Shulhan* of Yechiel Michel Epstein (1821–1908), which offered easily digested analyses of halacha that exerted

---

[23] See Shaul Stampfer, *The Lithuanian Yeshiva* (Portland: Littman Library of Jewish Civilization, 2011).

a strong influence over religious practice.[24] Yet another major intellectual development in Russian Orthodoxy that shared the agenda of stemming the inroads of modernization was the Musar movement. Musar, a genre of traditional literature concerned with the practical integration of ethics and morality into daily life, took on new life under the leadership of Israel Salanter (Lipkin, 1810–1883).[25] In its most radical form, the Musar movement was characterized by extensive study of Musar texts and extreme asceticism, often expressed as public critique and disruption of communal mores. Although extreme Musar asceticism was not widespread, general attentiveness to Musar as a tool of spiritual defense was eventually accepted widely, and today regular Musar lectures are a near-universal part of yeshiva curricula.

THE EMERGENCE OF ORTHODOX POLITICS

By the turn of the twentieth century, alarm in Orthodox circles about pervasive modernization, now far more entrenched among Russian Jews, became a unifying preoccupation for Orthodox Jews across Europe. But the greatest challenge to evolving Orthodoxy and the most important element in creating a unified Orthodox sense of purpose that transcended political borders was a new model of Jewish identity: nationalism, especially Zionism. Religious leaders were initially ambivalent about Zionism's emergence, which was predicated on a secular, national model of Jewish identity, to the extent that they were aware of it at all. Some rabbis including Shmuel Mohilever (1824–1898) and Naftali Tsvi Yehudah Berlin were involved with the Russian proto-nationalist Hibbat Zion; others, such as Tsvi Hirsch Kalisher (1795–1874) and Yehuda Alkali (1798–1878) figured among the movement's intellectual precursors. But as Zionism coalesced around a largely non- or anti-religious leadership and articulated an identity that sought in part to supplant religion with modern nationalism, increasing suspicion turned to outright opposition. Despite the potential for entente implicit in Zionism's religious overtones, few religious leaders were willing to explore it, most notably members of Mizrahi, the first Orthodox Zionist organization founded in 1902 by Yizkhok Yaakov Reines (1839–1915).[26] But even if Zionism was less controversial among the grass

---

[24] See Chaim Soloveitchik, "Rupture and Reconstruction: The Transformation of Contemporary Orthodoxy," *Tradition* 28 (1994): 64–130.

[25] See Immanuel Etkes, *Rabbi Israel Salanter and the Musar Movement* (Philadelphia: Jewish Publication Society, 1993); David Fishman, "Musar and Modernity: The Case of Novaredok," *Modern Judaism* 8, no. 1 (1988): 41–64.

[26] See Aviezer Ravitzky, *Messianism, Zionism and Jewish Religious Radicalism* (Chicago: University of Chicago Press, 1993).

roots regardless of religious identity, the overwhelming attitude from Orthodox religious leadership was opposition based on two objections. Doctrinally, thinking about Zionism among Orthodox leaders quickly gravitated towards endorsement of a Talmudic opinion that regarded human initiatives to re-settle the Land of Israel under Jewish sovereignty absent the messianic redemption to be a rebellion against the will of God. But more important was the basic challenge Zionism presented to a traditionalist monopoly on Jewish identity as a *religious* identity, one based not on modern romantic or ethnic notions of national cohesion, but on the historical, divine election of the Jewish people.[27]

It was this challenge that led to one of the most important innovations in early twentieth-century Orthodoxy: political organization. As Zionism continued to build support in the face of anti-Jewish violence and antisemitism throughout Europe, its increasingly bold model for the national reconstruction of a modern Jewish people led many Orthodox leaders to believe in the need for an emphatic response. In 1912 the Agudat Yisrael was created for this purpose.[28] Although not the first attempt of Orthodox leaders to become involved in European politics, as the movement expanded during the First World War it became an extremely effective mode of Orthodox political expression before the establishment of the State of Israel. Led by figures including Hayyim Ozer Grodzinsky (1863–1940) and Meir Shapira (1887–1933), an Agudah delegate to the Polish Sejm (and the initiator of the daf yomi program), the Agudah combined German-style neo-Orthodox ideology and organizational strategy with Eastern European charisma and demographics. After the First World War, and especially in the new Polish republic, the Agudah offered a robust electoral challenge to other Jewish political groups, including the older and more politically seasoned Zionists.

Most innovative about the Agudah was its role in subtly reorienting Orthodox models of rabbinic authority, represented by its executive leadership, a panel of rabbis known as the Council of Torah Sages (Moetset Gedolei ha-Torah). Inclusion on this council was based on the principle of *da'as Torah*, a model of clerical infallibility that considers certain rabbis to be possessed with transcendent insight into the Torah's view on matters

---

[27] For an interesting exception, see Joshua Shanes, "Ahron Marcus: Portrait of a Zionist Hasid," *Jewish Social Studies* 16, no. 3 (2010): 116–160.

[28] See Gershon Bacon, *The Politics of Tradition: Agudat Yisrael in Poland, 1916–1939* (Jerusalem: Magnes Press, 1996); Alan Mittleman, *The Politics of Torah: The Jewish Political Tradition and the Founding of the Agudat Israel* (Albany: SUNY Press, 1996); Jess Olson, *Nathan Birnbaum and Jewish Modernity* (Stanford: Stanford University Press, 2013).

including the mundane and political by dint of their engagement with Torah to the exclusion of other intellectual pursuits.[29] Even though the role of the council in directing Agudah strategy and tactics was largely symbolic, *da'as Torah* is an emphatic statement of rabbinic authority, a means of marking the boundaries of what was considered "Torah true" and what was excluded. In interwar Poland, the Agudah became a major social and political force replete with workers' and youth organizations offering an Orthodox response to Zionist and other modernist alternatives. Importantly, the Agudah also supported a network of schools for boys and girls; in the case of the latter, the Beys Yakov system introduced an Orthodox women's school system that was a true revolution in many communities.

ORTHODOXY AND ULTRA-ORTHODOXY AFTER WORLD WAR II

The physical destruction visited upon European Jewry by the Second World War is by now perhaps the most familiar exposition of the depths of human depravity and the evils of totalitarian ideology in contemporary culture. But as present as the tragedy of the Holocaust is in the broader culture, it is often overlooked that the Holocaust in the Orthodox world occupies a no less important role as a theological and pragmatic rallying point. As we have seen in something as innocuous and joyous as the celebration of the Siyyum ha-Shas, it is a trope that permeates the public culture of Orthodoxy, its many streams sharing a similar sense of profound loss while recognizing the power of the tragedy to preserve group cohesion. In Orthodox circles, the Holocaust represents in large part a lesson on the importance of eschewing engagement with the outside world while underscoring the centrality of Torah study to the increasing exclusion of other pursuits, and even adds a moral imperative to maintain high birth rates in Orthodox communities. Among the many reasons for these trends, the most important was the demography of destruction: East and Central Europe, the epicenter of the Nazi military conquest and genocide, was also the center of the largest traditional and Orthodox Jewish communities. The whole infrastructure of Orthodox Jewish life in Europe, including Hasidic courts, yeshivot, whole networks of primary and secondary schools for both boys and girls, Orthodox summer camps and youth groups which thrived as traditional communities but also used modern models to foster esprit de corps, all were wiped out between 1939 and 1945.

[29] See Jacob Katz, "*Da'at Torah*: The Unqualified Authority Claimed for Halakhists," *Jewish History* II, no. 1 (1997): 41–50.

Although several forms of Orthodox community served as an important source of morale and comfort in the ghettos and camps, in the aftermath of the defeat of Nazi Germany, almost nothing remained of these institutions in Central Europe.[30]

But aside from its role in post-war Orthodox identity formation, the most important consequence of the Holocaust was the bifurcation of European Orthodoxy into two new and different settings: North America and Israel. Most Holocaust survivors, regardless of ideological orientation, left Europe and arrived primarily in North America, territories of the British Commonwealth, and Palestine under the British Mandate. In North America, survivors from the camps of Europe invigorated the institutions and public presence of pre-war American Orthodoxy. Although often lost in the larger narrative of late nineteenth- and early twentieth-century American Jewish history, American Orthodoxy was a vital chapter even before the Second World War.[31] Among other unique features, pre-war American Orthodoxy was receptive to Zionism early on (the central offices of Mizraḥi were actually relocated to the US during the First World War).[32] It generally accommodated a more integrated identity, and in the densely populated Jewish neighborhoods of the greater New York area, Orthodox and traditionalist beliefs, cultural and social practices, as well as dozens of synagogues, battei midrash and yeshivot were a central part of the fabric of daily life. The origins of most major Orthodox institutions in America, including the Union of Orthodox Congregations of America (OU, established in 1898) and the Rabbinical Council of America (RCA, 1935) all date to the pre-World War II period. These institutions would, over time, help organize standards for the quality of kashrut supervision, rabbinical credentials, liturgy and other areas. An Orthodox institution of higher education, Yeshiva University, an amalgam of a Lithuanian-style yeshiva and a modern American university, grew under the guidance of figures such as Bernard Revel (1885–1940), and the later giant of post-war

---

[30] The thriving culture of Orthodox intellectual life and resistance in the ghettos and camps represent an understudied aspect of the Holocaust. Texts including *Sefer Esh Kodesh* of the Piasetzno rebbe, Kalonymus Kalman Szapira, continue to be printed and widely read today as a source of religious inspiration. See David Kranzler, *Thy Brother's Blood: The Orthodox Jewish Response During the Holocaust* (New York: Mesorah, 1987). See also Yaffa Eliach, *Hasidic Tales of the Holocaust* (New York: Vintage, 1982).

[31] See Jeffery Gurock, *Orthodox Jews in America* (Bloomington: Indiana University Press, 2009); Jenna Weissman Joselit, *New York's Jewish Jews: The Orthodox Community in the Interwar Years* (Bloomington: Indiana University Press, 1990).

[32] Yosef Salmon, "Mizrahi in America: A Belated but Sturdy Offshoot," *American Jewish Archives* XLVIII, no. 2 (1996): 161–175.

religious thought and philosophy, Joseph Ber Soloveitchik (1903–1993), to become a dynamic institution – including a modern campus and rabbinical seminary – in New York City's Washington Heights.[33]

The influx of Orthodox Holocaust survivors has had a major impact on the evolution and dynamism of American Orthodoxy. Whereas, in the pre-war period settlement in the United States was viewed with some suspicion by Orthodox leaders in Europe – some, including the Hafetz Hayyim, famously warned of its materialism and spiritual paucity – in the war's aftermath it became an ideal place to rebuild Orthodox communities.[34] Before the arrival of post-war immigrants, the dominant expression of Orthodoxy in North America was a diverse mode of identity known as "modern" Orthodoxy, as it remains today. It takes its cultural cues from a variety of sources, including the engaged Orthodoxy resembling that of Hirsch and Hildesheimer, a modified model of the Lithuanian yeshiva that allows for a range of openness to subjects outside of Torah study, and an ecumenical engagement with religious ideas from multiple streams of Orthodox thought. It maintains, more in practice than theory, a wide accommodation of modern American culture while maintaining a discreet distance from it.

But today, this identity is often on the defensive from more conservative communities, broadly referred to as "ultra-Orthodox," who are critical of most engagement with the non-Jewish world – and certainly modern American culture.[35] Although often indistinguishable to the outsider, these groups vary widely in their attitudes and cultural modes. In the Hasidic world, a whole spectrum of groups thrive. On one end are the visible and open Chabad Hasidim, who have flourished in the United States since 1951 under the leadership of Menachem Mendel Schneerson (1902–1994). Chabad is unique among Hasidic groups for its embrace of a proselytizing model of ultra-Orthodoxy, replete with a modern commercial sensibility, including a yearly fundraising telethon filmed in Los Angeles.[36] On the other end of the spectrum is Satmar Hasidism, established in

[33] See Jeffrey Gurock, *The Men and Women of Yeshiva: Higher Education, Orthodoxy, and American Judaism* (New York: Columbia University Press, 1988). Gilbert Klaperman, *The Story of Yeshiva University* (New York: Macmillan, 1969).

[34] See Arthur Hertzberg, "'Treifene Medina' – Learned Opposition to Emigration to the United States," *Proceedings of the Eight World Congress of Jewish Studies* (Jerusalem: World Congress of Jewish Studies, 1984), 1–30.

[35] See Samuel Heilman, *Sliding to the Right: The Contest for the Future of Jewish Orthodoxy* (Berkeley: University of California Press, 2006).

[36] See Maya Balakirsky Katz, *The Visual Culture of Chabad* (New York: Cambridge University Press, 2010); Samuel Heilman and Menachem Friedman, *The Rebbe: The Life and Afterlife of Menachem Mendel Schneerson* (Princeton: Princeton University Press, 2010); Elliot Wolfson, *Open Secret: Postmessianic Messianism and the Mystical Revision of Menahem Mendel Schneerson* (New York: Columbia University Press, 2009); and Sue

Hungary in the interwar period under the leadership of Joel Teitelbaum (1887–1979), which has grown to wield significant influence in American ultra-Orthodox enclaves. It is known for its opposition to any engagement with Jewish groups and organizations outside of its own, including other Orthodox and ultra-Orthodox groups, and is the most visible North American expression of the rejectionist stance of Hungarian anti-modernism discussed above.

Non-Hasidic conservative or ultra-Orthodox groups have also replicated their communities and institutions in North America, keeping some form of their earlier European identity intact. The descendants of German *Austritt* Orthodoxy, many of whom escaped Nazi Germany in the late 1930s, settled largely in the Washington Heights neighborhood of Manhattan.[37] Torn between discomfort with American culture, pressure from largely Eastern European-inflected Orthodoxy exerted from other urban American enclaves, and the more open posture of their predecessors such as Hirsch, they have oriented themselves along insular, ultra-Orthodox cultural patterns. A further evolution of the Lithuanian yeshiva model has also thrived in North America, in institutions like Ner Yisroel in Baltimore, established in 1933 by Ya'akov Yitzkhok Ruderman (1901–1987), the New Jersey Beth Medresh Govoha (or Lakewood Yeshiva) established by Aaron Kotler (1891–1962) in 1943, and the Hebrew Theological College (the Skokie Yeshiva) in Chicago founded by Hayyim Tsvi Rubenstein (1872–1944) in 1921. Some are self-contained on campuses that resemble small liberal arts colleges, and their students – including bachelors and married men along with their families – largely eschew engagement with the outside community aside from the bare minimum necessary to support their communities. The inner world of the yeshiva is a hermetic environment unencumbered by external concerns and dedicated solely to the study of rabbinic literature, usually in excess of ten hours a day.

All of these groups stress their continuity with pre-war European antecedents, but in fact they represent a significant social and cultural evolution. Dependent in large part on the financial success of Jews in the post-war United States and largely supported by donors, these communities enshrine an ideal of withdrawal by young men from the external society for the sake of full-time Torah study until well into their adult life,

Fishkoff, *The Rebbe's Army* (New York: Shocken Books, 2003). See also David Berger, *The Rebbe, the Messiah and the Scandal of Orthodox Indifference* (Portland: Littman Library of Jewish Civilization), 2001.

[37] See Steven Lowenstein, *Frankfurt on the Hudson: The German-Jewish Community of Washington Heights, its Structure and Culture* (Detroit: Wayne State University Press, 1991).

all the while placing significant pressure on families to have large numbers of children.[38] But the pursuit of the ideal of near-total devotion to Torah study has produced some economic and social tension. Long supported by internal institutions and private family money, the insularity, slowing financial growth, and pressure to have large families have led many within these communities to rely increasingly on public social services, stimulating, in turn, growing Orthodox involvement in local and regional politics.

The State of Israel, the other primary destination of post-war Orthodox refugees and immigrants, has experienced many of the same trends affecting North American Orthodoxy. But where the Orthodox in North America encountered another society in which they were a religious and ethnic minority that utilized strategies of identity roughly analogous to those in pre-war Europe, Israel is a modern, secular nation-state that defines itself as Jewish. As such, it represents the triumph of an identity from which a significant proportion of Orthodox Jews have long been alienated. While the six decades of Israel's existence have allowed time for the flowering of a whole spectrum of Israeli Orthodox identities and various attitudes towards the state, the basic tension of Zionism's insistence that it represents the exclusive successful form for the preservation of the Jewish people and the implication that religion has long outlived its utility has profoundly shaped not just the evolution of Orthodoxy, but of Israel itself.

Before the twentieth century, Jewish communities in Israel were overwhelmingly traditional. Sephardic communities had long been integrated into the larger apparatus of the Ottoman Empire as a *dhimmi* minority, while Ashkenazi Jews settled in the modern period primarily in the four "Holy Cities" of Jerusalem, Safed, Hebron, and Tiberias for devotional reasons. Ashkenazi communities of the "old yishuv" remained largely aloof from the broader Ottoman society, their men devoted almost entirely to Torah study and supported by charitable donations collected from Diaspora Jewish communities, the *halukah*. As nationalist-inspired Jewish immigration to the region began in the last decades of the nineteenth century, the arrival of modern, secular, and agrarian-minded settlers at first made little impact on these traditional communities. But as Zionist immigration rose in waves over the second (1905–14), third and fourth aliyot (1919–29), the increasingly bold assertions of hegemony over the Jewish community of non-Orthodox Jewish nationalists kept high a sense of mutual alienation, occasionally even resulting in violence, such as the

---

[38] See Samuel Heilman, *Defenders of the Faith: Inside Ultra-Orthodox Jewry* (Berkeley: University of California Press, 2000); William B. Helmreich, *The World of the Yeshiva: An Intimate Portrait of Orthodox Jewry* (Jersey City, NJ: KTAV, 2000).

Haganah-sanctioned assassination of Agudah activist Israël Jacob de Haan, in Jerusalem in 1924.[39]

When the new State of Israel was created in 1948, its founders recognized the need to address a latent Zionist–Orthodox identity conflict.[40] The Agudah and other groups critical of Zionism, despite their best efforts, had not effectively displaced its claim on the basic identity of the state, but were situated to have an impact on its basic political and cultural architecture. Led in Israel by some of the original founders and key figures of the movement in Europe, the Agudah and other Orthodox organizations and figures active in the transitional period from the mandate to statehood, such as Abraham Isaac Kook (1865–1935), gave voice to the concerns of the Orthodox community. David Ben-Gurion and other founders sought to mollify the then-small community of Orthodox citizens, and implementation of a "Status Quo Agreement," drafted in 1947, helped quash a secular constitution and granted Orthodox rabbinical courts oversight over several domestic matters, including marriage, divorce, and to some degree personal status (who is defined as Jewish). It also granted autonomy to Orthodox educational institutions (including an exemption from military service and stipends for young men engaged full time in yeshiva study that has become a source of much tension and controversy), even casting a religious structure to public observance of the Jewish calendar (the Sabbath as the official day of rest, including closure of government offices and public transportation).[41] The state also sought to create some place for Orthodoxy as a civic religion of Israel, under the auspices of an office of Chief Rabbinate (held by both a chief Ashkenazi and chief Sephardi rabbi), which oversaw the standards for the administration of laws under religious purview. The presence of a national chief rabbi has, in turn, had a significant impact on Israeli institutions; Shlomo Goren (1917–1994), for example, who headed the military rabbinate before ascending to the chief rabbinate in 1973, was instrumental in creating a culture conducive to religious observance in the Israeli military.

For parties like the Agudah, already experienced in political activism and parliamentary politics, these concessions gave adequate cover for arms-length engagement with state institutions. Protecting its interests by overseeing aspects of government that directly affected haredim was the

[39] See David Halevi, *Murder in Jerusalem* (Hebrew)(B'nei Brak: Tefutsah, 1987).
[40] See Ravitzky, *Messianism, Zionism and Jewish Religious Radicalism*; Charles Liebman, ed., *Religion, Democracy and Israeli Society* (Amsterdam: Harwood Press, 1997); Heilman, *Defenders of the Faith.*
[41] See Ilan Peleg, "Constitutional Order and *Kulturkampf*: The Role of Ben Gurion" *Israel Studies* 3, no. 1 (1998): 230–250.

near-exclusive platform of its engagement with the state; beyond that the community sought to separate and insulate itself from the influence of secular Israeli society. Politically, this has meant robust participation by haredi parties, such as United Torah Judaism, in the parliamentary process. Along with Shas, an ethno-religious Sephardic party with a leadership structure similar to the Agudah, haredi parties have proven remarkably adept at bringing the lock-step support of their constituencies to bear at the ballot box and remain a major consideration in domestic politics. Haredi enclaves have flourished, not dissimilar to neighborhoods and suburban towns in North America, keeping a tight grip on the insularity and social norms of the community, including in older communities such as Me'ah She'arim, as well as B'nei Brak (a suburb of Tel Aviv that became the home to numerous yeshivot and Hasidic communities in the post-1948 period), and more recent neighborhoods in Jerusalem and its surroundings (such as Beyt Shemesh). In these places numerous Hasidic groups have grown robustly, including groups such as Belz, whose Beyt ha-Midrash ha-Gadol in northern Jerusalem is the largest synagogue complex in Israel. Chabad, also a significant Hasidic presence in Israel as in North America, constructed a full-sized replica of Menachem Mendel Schneerson's Crown Heights residence in the Israeli town of Kfar Chabad.[42] Similarly, the re-establishment of European yeshivot of many stripes, from the Hungarian Erlau yeshiva established by Yohanan Sofer (1950), a direct descendant of the Hatam Sofer, to the Mir yeshiva, now the largest haredi yeshiva in Israel, are a robust and influential, non-Hasidic haredi presence. In addition to these institutions, a line of Lithuanian spiritual leaders, beginning with Avraham Yeshaya Karelitz (the Hazon Ish, 1878–1953), Elazar Menachem Man Shakh (1899–2001) and Yosef Shalom Elyashiv (1910–2012) have exerted significant influence over the belief and practice of haredim in Israel and the Diaspora.[43] Finally, the Edah Haredit and the Naturei Karta, groups representing a small minority of the Israeli Orthodox who derived their ideology from the extreme Hungarian position outlined above, reject all compromise with the Jewish State, including state funds which have, increasingly, been a major source of support for haredi communities in Israel.[44]

Although the most visible Orthodox segment of Israeli society, haredim are only one of the two major categories of Israeli Orthodox identity. As in the United States, large swaths of Orthodox Israelis are well-integrated

[42] See Ravitzky, *Messianism, Zionism and Jewish Religious Radicalism*, 181–206.
[43] Lawrence Kaplan, "The Hazan Ish: Haredi Critic of Contemporary Orthodoxy," *The Uses of Tradition*, ed. Wertheimer, 145–173.
[44] See Ravitzky, *Messianism, Zionism and Jewish Religious Radicalism*, 79–144.

into contemporary Israeli culture and society. They reflect the success of religious Zionism, evolved from the early theory of Yitzkhok Yaakov Reines but extensively developed by Abraham Isaac Kook (1865–1935), the first Ashkenazi chief rabbi of Mandate Palestine. Kook's religious ideology was shaped by an amalgam of the Lithuanian yeshiva, a fascination with Hasidic-oriented mysticism, and finally an intense, religiously driven devotion to the nation-building project of Zionism. His intellectual descendants are committed to a religious worldview no less strict in its commitment to observance than a haredi one. But like the modern Orthodox in America (and in the last few decades the ranks of Israeli religious Zionists have been augmented significantly by American Orthodox immigrants), they do not eschew modern dress, culture, or involvement in the daily life of modern Israel. What differentiates them from the haredim on the one side and secular Israel on the other is their understanding of the historical significance of the Jewish state.[45] Theirs is an eschatology diametrically opposed to the haredi view of the secular state of Israel as a basically illegitimate entity (even if it is one that may be engaged like a non-Jewish government for the sake of preserving communal interests). Rather, religious Zionism views modern Israel as the first stage in the extended unfolding of the messianic redemption. In the state's early years, this ideology was embraced by relatively few, buttressed by institutions such as the Merkaz ha-Rav yeshiva, established by Kook but deeply informed in its assertive religious nationalism by the leadership of his son, Zvi Yehudah Kook (1891–1982). But with the victories of the 1967 war that brought under direct Israeli control the former Jordanian West Bank (a region referred to in religious Zionist terminology by its biblical names of Judea and Samaria) and the whole of the city of Jerusalem including the site of the Temple Mount and other sites of great importance to the religious history of Judaism (including Hebron, traditionally understood to be the location of the burial place of the biblical patriarchs), religious Zionism has become an influential ideology across a wide swath of Israeli society. For Tsvi Yehudah Kook and his followers, the most extreme of which were organized under the name "Gush Emunim," the "bloc of the faithful," the conquests of 1967 were not mere military victories, they were a divine vindication of their belief that the creation of the State of Israel was instrumental in God's plan for the restoration of biblical Israel and the unfolding of the messianic redemption.

---

[45] See Ravitzky, *Messianism, Zionism and Jewish Religious Radicalism*; Shmuel Almog, Jehuda Reinharz and Anita Shapira, eds, *Zionism and Religion* (Hanover, NH: Brandeis University Press, 1998).

The impact of this worldview on Israeli society and politics is significant. Religious Zionists (in modern Hebrew they are referred to as "da'ati leumi" or national religious) are deeply patriotic, enthusiastic participants in the national institutions of Israel, including the Israeli Defense Forces (IDF).[46] They form the backbone of the settlement movement, especially in the West Bank. Although state policy since 1967 has prioritized the strategic growth of Jewish settlements in the West Bank, offering incentives for Israelis to reside in increasingly urban settlement blocs (such as Ariel, Gush Etzion, Beyt El, and Kiryat Arba among others, as well as several neighborhoods of East Jerusalem), and residents of settlements come from a variety of backgrounds and religious attitudes. But the national religious, those committed to the re-establishment of a greater Jewish commonwealth in the entirety of biblical Israel as part of a larger eschatology, are the most visible cohort. Many West Bank settlements, including some of the largest blocs such as the Etzion bloc, are almost entirely religious Zionist, as are an increasing number of new (and newly integrated) neighborhoods in Jerusalem. Institutions, including yeshivot such as Merkaz ha-Rav, Yeshivat Har Etzion, Yeshivat Sha'arei Mevasseret Zion, Yeshivat Kerem be-Yavneh, Yeshivat ha-Kotel, among others, have emerged in the last decades as important bastions of national religious thought, and offer their students, both Israeli and the increasingly dominant American modern Orthodox (who provide significant financial support through one or two-year "gap" programs for pre-college students) a variety of means to engage in Torah study along with military or other national service.

CONCLUSION

In the future, Orthodoxy in all its modern forms will likely continue to both evolve and play a significant role not just as an internal Jewish identity, but in North American and Israeli societies writ large. In the United States, the disappearance of barriers that once forced many to choose between an Orthodox religious identity and full participation in the broader economic and cultural life of the country has made isolation in segments of the Orthodox world a choice rather than a necessity. This has allowed Orthodox communities of all stripes to thrive. The American climate of religious tolerance of the practices and institutions of Orthodox communities has allowed their members to reach unprecedented levels of

---

[46] Military service in the most elite units of the IDF has become a point of pride for many in the national religious camp, and religious officers represent a growing segment of its upper ranks. See Stuart Cohen, "The Re-Discovery of Orthodox Jewish Laws Relating to the Military and War," *Israel Studies* 12, no. 2 (2007): 1–28.

civic engagement. Other factors of more recent development in American culture and politics dating from approximately the 1970s, such as the rise of a politically engaged evangelical Christianity and a general rise of visible religiosity in America in general, have also served as fertile soil for the growth of American Orthodoxy. Indeed, in one of the latest developments, American evangelical Christians and some Orthodox Jewish individuals and groups have established a congenial political and cultural partnership resting on a shared idealization of conservative religious values and robust defense of the State of Israel. On the other hand, the prevalence of ideas about multi-culturalism that has emerged during the same period, has also allowed increased levels of ethnic and religious difference to thrive in American culture. Modern Orthodox communities in cities like New York and Los Angeles figure regularly among the most affluent minority groups. More conservative Orthodox communities have similarly found the tolerance and independence allowed by contemporary American life to be a boon for their communal structures even in isolation.

In Israel, the public role of the Orthodox, both da'ati leumi and haredi communities, has only increased with each passing decade. The stress of a proportionately larger community of haredim, many of whom pursue Torah study full time with the aid of government support and exemptions from public service and the army, has fueled significantly tensions in Israeli society. This has only intensified with the increasing stridency of haredi groups, active and dynamic participants in the Israeli political process and increasingly willing to use their strength to pressure larger social conformity to their standards of modesty. Religious Zionists, also a growing segment of Israeli society, have come to represent a major force in public discourse and policy. As the peace process has faltered, various incarnations of religious Zionism including the National Religious Party and, most recently, Jewish Home (Beyt ha-Yehudi) have formed coalitions with other nationalist parties opposed to Israeli withdrawal from the Occupied Territories with profound implications for broader geopolitics.

"It will be a powerful testament ... to the *nizichus* [triumph] of Torah and the idea that it alone can preserve our past and ensure our future" wrote the publicists advertising the opportunity to take part in the twelfth Siyyum ha-Shas. Testimony, triumph, preservation, future – all through an idealized model of Torah: these are the catchwords of contemporary Orthodoxy. These words, although taken from just one Orthodox publication, are characteristic sentiments of the impassioned, often ebullient, sometimes histrionic public face of Orthodoxy. They are no less the central ideals that have informed the evolution of Orthodoxy from its early years as a response to the eroding traditional kehillah, through the conflicts of the nineteenth century and the trauma of the twentieth. Though the various shades of today's Orthodox identities continue to face profound internal and external challenges, it has continued to adapt and grow. And as dramatically demonstrated by some 90,000 enthusiasts of the *daf yomi* in August of 2012, this is in no small part thanks to a fascinating amalgam of modernity and tradition.

SELECT BIBLIOGRAPHY

Almog, Shmuel, Jehuda Reinharz and Anita Shapira, eds. *Zionism and Religion*. Hanover, NH: Brandeis University Press, 1998.

Bacon, Gershon. *The Politics of Tradition: Agudat Yisrael in Poland, 1916–1939*. Jerusalem: Magnes Press, 1996.

Biemann, Asher. "The Problem of Tradition and Reform in Jewish Renaissance and Renaissancism." *Jewish Social Studies* 8, no. 1 (2001): 58–67.

Bleich, Judith. "The Emergence of an Orthodox Press in 19th Century Germany." *Jewish Social Studies* 42, nos. 3–4 (1980): 323–344.

Breuer, Mordechai. *Modernity within Tradition: The Social History of Orthodox Jewry in Imperial Germany*. New York: Columbia University Press, 1992.

Cohen, Stuart. "The Re-Discovery of Orthodox Jewish Laws Relating to the Military and War." *Israel Studies* 12, no. 2 (2007): 1–28

Ellenson, David. *Rabbi Esriel Hildesheimer and the Creation of Modern Jewish Orthodoxy*. Tuscaloosa: University of Alabama Press, 1990.

Etkes, Immanuel. *The Gaon of Vilna: A Man and his Image*. Berkeley/Los Angeles: University of California Press, 2002.

  Rabbi Israel Salanter and the Mussar Movement: Seeking the Torah of Truth. Translated by Jonathan Chipman. Philadelphia: Jewish Publication Society, 1993.

Friedman, Menachem. *Hevra v'da'at: Ha-ortodoksia ha-lo-tsiyonit b'eretz yisrael, 1918–1936*. Jerusalem: Yad ben Tsvi Publications, 1977.

Gurock, Jeffrey. *Orthodox Jews in America*. Bloomington: Indiana University Press, 2009.

Heilman, Samuel. *Defenders of the Faith: Inside Ultra-Orthodox Jewry*. Berkeley: University of California Press, 1999.

Heilman, Samuel and Menachem Friedman. *The Rebbe: The Life and Afterlife of Menacham Mendel Schneerson*. Princeton: Princeton University Press, 2010.

Helmreich, William B. *The World of the Yeshiva: An Intimate Portrait of Orthodox Jewry*. Jersey City, NJ: KTAV, 2000.

Katz, Jacob. "Da'at Torah: The Unqualified Authority Claimed for Halakhists." *Jewish History* 11, no. 1 (1997): 41–50.

  A House Divided: Orthodoxy and Schism in Nineteenth Century Central European Jewry. Waltham, MA: Brandeis University Press, 1998.

  "Towards a Biography of the Hatam Sofer," trans. David Ellenson. In *Profiles in Diversity: Jews in a Changing Europe, 1750–1870*, ed. Francis Malino and David Sorkin, 223–266. Detroit: Wayne State University Press, 1998.

Liberles, Robert. *Religious Conflict in Social Context: The Resurgence of Orthodox Judaism in Frankfurt am Main, 1838–1877*. Westport, CT: Greenwood, 1985.

Lowenstein, Steven. *Frankfurt on the Hudson: The German-Jewish Community of Washington Heights, its Structure and Culture*. Detroit: Wayne State University Press, 1991.

Luz, Ehud. *Parallels Meet: Religion and Nationalism in the Early Zionist Movement (1882–1904)*. Philadelphia: Jewish Publication Society, 1988.

Manekin, Rachel. "Ha-brit ha-hadashah: Yehudim ortodoksiiim u-polanim katolim be-galitsiyah (1878–1883)." *Tsiyyon* 64, no. 2 (1999): 157–186.

Miller, Michael. *Rabbis and Revolution: The Jews of Moravia in the Age of Emancipation*. Stanford: Stanford University Press, 2011.

Mittleman, Alan L. *The Politics of Torah: The Jewish Political Tradition and the Founding of the Agudat Israel*. Albany: SUNY Press, 1996.

Ravitzky, Aviezer. *Messianism, Zionism and Jewish Religious Radicalism*. Chicago: University of Chicago Press, 1996.

Salmon, Yosef. "Mizrahi in America: A Belated but Sturdy Offshoot." *American Jewish Archives* 48, no. 2 (1996).

Samet, Moshe. "The Beginnings of Orthodoxy." *Modern Judaism* 8, no. 3 (1988): 249–269.

Silber, Michael. "The Emergence of Ultra-Orthodoxy." In *The Uses of Tradition*, ed. Jack Wertheimer, 23–84. New York: Jewish Theological Seminary Press, 1992.

Soloveitchik, Chaim. "Rupture and Reconstruction: The Transformation of Contemporary Orthodoxy," *Tradition*, 28 (1994): 64–130.

Stampfer, Shaul. *The Lithuanian Yeshiva*. Portland: Littman Library of Jewish Civilization, 2011.

CHAPTER 39

JEWS AND CHRISTIANITY

SUSANNAH HESCHEL

For two thousand years, Jews rejected the claim that Jesus fulfilled the messianic prophecies of the Hebrew Bible, as well as the dogmatic claims about him made by the Church Fathers – that he was born of a virgin, the son of God, part of a divine Trinity, and was resurrected after his death. Why Christians chose to form a religion about a Jewish preacher from the Galilee has long puzzled his fellow Jews, and the doctrines formed by Christians about him – the incarnation, Trinity, virgin birth, bodily resurrection – seemed to contradict the basic tenets of the Hebrew Bible, including its monotheism and the prophets' depiction of the messiah and the messianic era.

For two thousand years, a central wish of Christianity was to be the object of desire by Jews, whose baptism would affirm that Jesus had fulfilled the biblical prophecies of their own Scriptures. Christianity did not arise to eradicate Judaism, but to claim Jewish scriptures and teachings for Christian purposes, all the while claiming that Judaism was no longer in covenant with God. This supersessionism was a theological colonialism: that is, an annexation, subjugation, and appropriation of Judaism's Bible for Christian purposes – though not the destruction of either the Bible or the Jews. The dual quality marking supersessionism, in which the Old Testament is preserved as the record of a divine covenant, but one superseded by the New, is expressed in Romans 11:28, and informs Augustine's important definition of Jews as witnesses to Christian truth by living in a subservient status. Supersessionism guaranteed a centrality within Christianity of certain Jewish teachings, such as covenant, messiah, and the Old Testament itself, a Jewish presence that often discomfited Christian theologians even as they drew upon it for their own theological purposes.

While Judaism had no comparable theological need of Christianity, it was certainly influenced and even shaped by some Christian ideas over the course of the centuries. Jewish theology frequently found itself in a defensive posture, expressed in polemics against Christianity for its trinitarianism, which some Jews regarded as polytheistic idolatry, but Jews also experienced a fascination with Christianity that was not mirrored by a comparable fascination with other religions. Jews often adopted Christian motifs. For example, the medieval adoration of the Virgin Mary was translated in Jewish mysticism into its understanding of the Shekhinah, the divine presence, as female.

Yet Jewish views of Christianity in the pre-modern era tended to be explicitly negative. The great Jewish legal authority and philosopher Moses Maimonides, who lived in Egypt during the twelfth century, viewed Christianity as idolatrous because of its worship of the Trinity. On the other hand, many other rabbinical authorities recognized Christian claims that the Trinity was actually a unity and not idolatry. Maimonides was typical of a Jewish tradition of anti-Christian polemics that were often composed by Jews living in Muslim realms. Nonetheless, there also were Jews in the medieval and early modern eras who regarded Christians as handmaidens of Judaism, bringing the Bible and the God of Israel to the pagan world, thus preparing for the advent of the messiah.

Modern Judaism continued both postures, of polemic and fascination, but added new dimensions. New intellectual developments stemming from the European Enlightenment, historicism, emancipation, liberalism and antisemitism, and political movements such as nationalism and imperialism, all shaped modern theology, including Jewish self-understanding and Jewish views of Christianity. After World War II, Judaism and Christianity reconfigured their views of each other in light of the Holocaust, the blossoming of ecumenism, and the shift of the Jewish–Christian dialogue from Europe to America, with its political principles of democracy and its cultural commitment to religious tolerance.

Most significant in the modern period was the growing number of Jewish historians who examined the historical roots of Christianity within Judaism, with particular interest in the figure of the historical Jesus and the theology of Paul. In addition, some Jewish artists and poets began to use Christian symbols, particularly the crucifixion, to represent Jewish suffering under persecution and the Holocaust. Jewish scholars also began investigating examples of Christian influence on Judaism. Already in the nineteenth century, a new Jewish narrative of Christian origins developed: Jesus was a pious Jew who never intended to start a new religion, whereas Paul was the founder of Christianity, a religion *about* Jesus but not the faith *of* Jesus. Whereas Jesus taught Jewish monotheism and ethics, Paul mixed up those teachings with Greek pagan ideas, resulting in a non-biblical set of doctrines that became mandatory dogma for Christians. Jewish scholars further claimed that a proper understanding of the New Testament texts was only possible when its contents were examined in the context of early Judaism and its rabbinic writings.

Christianity became not only a topic in modern Judaism, but also a tool for Jewish theological reflection on the role of Judaism in Western civilization. Rather than a desiccated, discarded branch of Western, Christian civilization, Judaism was presented by Jewish historians such as Abraham Geiger (1810–1874) as the tree trunk of the West, with Christianity and Islam as two of its branches. Jewish history in Diaspora was not an experience of travail, but of mission: bringing Jewish monotheism to the pagan world, a task for which Christians and Muslims served as handmaidens.[1]

European Christianity of the eighteenth and nineteenth centuries served as the context in which Jews made their case for political and social emancipation, often by promoting the growing interest in religious tolerance and the similarities between Jewish and Christian faith. In Germany, Christian theologians engaged in the debates over Jewish emancipation, usually depicting Judaism in negative terms and Jews as unsuitable for full membership in German society. What Jewish thinkers came to recognize was that the "secularization" of Europe was a modernization of Christian commitments, not a repudiation of them. Debates over Jewish membership in the nations of Europe reiterated older Christian theological arguments regarding the trustworthiness of Jews. The Protestant biblical scholar Johann Michaelis, in the late eighteenth century, opposed emancipation, questioning whether Jews would demonstrate sufficient national loyalty to serve in the German armed forces, based on his reading of biblical claims to Jewish national exclusivity in relation to God. Over a hundred years later, the Jewish philosopher Hermann Cohen had to formulate defenses of Jewish national loyalty during the First World War.

Yet there were supporters. The philosopher Gotthold Lessing, one of the major figures of the German Enlightenment, presented an admirably wise, tolerant and gentle Jew in the figure of his friend, the Jewish philosopher Moses Mendelssohn (1729–1786), in an influential play entitled, Nathan the Wise. David Friedlaender, a disciple of Mendelssohn's, proposed a mass conversion of the Jews to Christianity – as long as Christianity gave up its doctrines and adopted Deism – a proposal Christians in early nineteenth-century Germany rejected.

Christianity was also the context that influenced Jewish reforms of their religious practices, synagogue liturgies, and identity as Jews. Organs were installed in synagogues, church music was used during services, and rabbis adopted the black robes and white collars worn by Protestant pastors and

---

[1] That view was already expressed by the medieval Jewish philosopher and legal expert Moses Maimonides in his "Epistle to Yemen."

began giving weekly hortatory sermons.[2] Yet this era was not simply about Jews assimilating into Europe, or synagogues becoming Christianized in their liturgies. Rather, Jews in Europe expressed a tone of rebellion in their insistence on Judaism as the "mother" religion of Christianity, which they portrayed as derivative and unoriginal.

During the long nineteenth century, Jews were gradually winning political acceptance in most of the Western and Central European countries in which they lived, while at the same time they witnessed the rise of racism and antisemitism on the intellectual as well as political level. In France, which was the first country to declare the Jews emancipated, integration seemed to proceed smoothly during the course of the nineteenth century, until the Dreyfus Affair of the 1890s turned France into a hotbed of anti-semitic, politicized discourse. Whereas Jews were given professorships in France, often engaging in research on Jewish history and philosophy, some noted German professors, such as Leopold von Ranke and Heinrich Treitschke, declared that scholarship was a Christian endeavor, and that Jewish Studies did not belong in the university.[3] Toward the end of the nineteenth century, with the rise of racial theory and its infiltration into academic disciplines, efforts to eradicate Jewishness began to be under-taken by some Christian theologians. Some theologians remained immune to Nazi antisemitism, while others sought to Nazify Christian theology by dejudaizing Christianity, and voices of Christian protest against Nazi antisemitism were rare and heard primarily outside Germany.[4] After the Holocaust, a nascent positive reevaluation of Judaism by some Christian theologians began to take shape, and a thoughtful dialogue began with some Jewish theologians, particularly in Germany, Britain, and the United States, who sought a more serious engagement with Christianity.

The eighteenth and nineteenth century debates over Jewish emancipa-tion raised the question of whether Judaism was a religion appropriate for integration into the modern nations and empires of Europe. Leora Batnitzky recently pointed out that the emergence of nation-states in Europe required a corresponding redefinition of Jewishness, from a com-plex of ethnic, cultural, and religious identities into a religion, Judaism, a set of beliefs and practices that would permit ethnic and cultural identifi-cation with a particular nation-state, whether France, Germany, England,

[2] Michael A. Meyer, *Response to Modernity: A History of the Reform Movement in Judaism* (New York: Oxford University Press, 1988).

[3] Christian Wiese, *Challenging Colonial Discourse: Jewish Studies and Protestant Discourse in Wilhelmine Germany*, trans. Barbara Harshav (Leiden: Brill, 2005).

[4] Susannah Heschel, *The Aryan Jesus: Christian Theologians and the Bible in Nazi Germany* (Princeton: Princeton University Press, 2008).

and so forth. For Jews, the redefinition meant they needed to win accept-ance from Christians and, at the same time, formulate a definition of Jewish identity that would discourage conversion to Christianity without denigrating Christianity. Discussions of Christianity by Jewish theologi-ans had to be cautious: calling attention to Jesus's Jewishness could arouse mockery or even anger from those Christians who viewed Judaism as an inferior religion. In an unpublished note written in 1770, Mendelssohn observed: "It is a disgrace that we should reproach Socrates and Plato because they were pagans! Was this a flaw in their morals? And Jesus a Jew? – And what if, as I believe, he never wanted to give up Judaism? One can only imagine where this remark would lead me." The answer: into dangerous waters, no doubt, given the generally negative views Christians at the time had of Judaism. The Jewishness of Jesus was known, but not to be publicized.

At the same time, the eighteenth-century Enlightenment saw the emer-gence of Christian critiques of the church, as well as new formulations of Christianity: not a rejection of Christianity, but a reformulation in what David Sorkin has termed a "religious enlightenment."[5] A broad movement of Unitarianism, under various guises, such as Deism and Socinianism, argued that Jesus was not a divine incarnation, but an inspiring religious teacher. In England, the Deist John Toland, whose work was known to Mendelssohn, denied the divinity of Jesus and insisted that he had had no intention of abolishing Jewish law.[6] In Germany, the quest for the his-torical Jesus was launched by Herman Samuel Reimarus (1694–1768), a Protestant theologian and teacher of Oriental languages at a high school in Hamburg. Reimarus, a Deist who rejected the miracles and revelatory sta-tus of the Bible in favor of a natural religion compatible with reason, left a long, unpublished manuscript at his death, fragments of which were pub-lished posthumously and anonymously by Gotthold Lessing from 1774 to 1778. In those so-called Wolfenbüttel Fragmente, Reimarus argued that Jesus was a Jewish reformer who sought nothing more than the revitaliza-tion of his Jewish faith, and that Christianity was invented after his death by his disciples in a deliberate and deceitful effort to serve their own ambi-tions.[7] The publication launched an outcry among conservative theologi-ans, for whom Jesus was not simply an inspiring religious leader but rather

[5] David Sorkin, *The Religious Enlightenment: Protestants, Jews, and Catholics from London to Vienna* (Princeton: Princeton University Press, 2008).

[6] Moshe Pelli, "The Impact of Deism on the Hebrew Literature of the Enlightenment in Germany," *Eighteenth-Century Studies* 6 (1972): 35–59.

[7] Hermann Samuel Reimarus, *Fragments*, trans. Ralph S. Fraser, ed. Charles H. Talbert (Philadelphia: Fortress Press, 1970).

the son of God, and it also launched, according to Albert Schweitzer, the movement known as the "quest for the historical Jesus," a scholarly effort to recover the historicity of Christian origins and the life and teachings of Jesus.

Christian reconsiderations of the historical Jesus found an echo among Jewish thinkers, from Orthodox rabbis to Reformers. Adam Ferziger has pointed out that some Orthodox rabbis of the eighteenth and nineteenth centuries expressed positive appreciation of Christianity even as they polemicized against the nascent movement of Reform Judaism.[8] Jacob Emden (1698–1776), a leading Orthodox rabbi in Germany in the late eighteenth century, expressed a positive appreciation of Jesus, stressing the commonalities between his teachings and those of other rabbis of antiquity, but also insisting on Jesus's human, non-divine character.[9] Emden's goal, however, was not to encourage Jews to take a more positive view of Christianity; rather, as the historian Maciejko has demonstrated, Emden's motivation was to curry favor with Catholic church authorities in Poland, in hopes they would collaborate with him in opposing Jewish heretical movements that were adopting Christian rituals, notably the Frankists.[10] As a harsh polemicist against liberal Jews and religious reforms, Emden, writes Maciejko, "deeply interiorized the Christian understanding of heresy and theological error and became for Judaism what Irenaeus and Hippolytus had become for Christianity: a chief heresiologist."[11]

That Jesus was a Jewish reformer, not a divine being, whose goal was the revitalization of Judaism, not the creation of a new religion, was the common view shared by most Jewish thinkers and liberal Protestant theologians. Mendelssohn insisted that Jesus taught nothing more than Judaism, and that there was no evidence to support claims to his divine incarnation. He wrote, in his widely known defense of Jewish emancipation, *Jerusalem: or, On Religious Power and Judaism* (1783), "Jesus of Nazareth himself observed not only the law of Moses, but also the ordinances of

---

[8] Adam Ferziger, *Exclusion and Hierarchy: Orthodoxy, Nonobservance, and the Emergence of Modern Jewish Identity* (Philadelphia: University of Pennsylvania Press, 2005).

[9] Blu Greenberg, "Jacob Emden: The Views of an Enlightened Traditionalist on Christianity," *Judaism* 27, no. 3 (1978): 351–363; Harvey Falk, "Rabbi Jacob Emden's Views on Christianity and The Noachide Commandments," *Journal of Ecumenical Studies* 19, no. 1 (Winter 1982): 105–111.

[10] See Pawel Maciejko, *The Mixed Multitude: Jacob Frank and the Frankist Movement, 1755–1816* (Philadelphia: University of Pennsylvania Press, 2011).

[11] Pawel Maciejko, "The Peril of Heresy, the Birth of a New Faith: The Quest for a Common Jewish–Christian Front against Franksim," in *Holy Dissent: Jewish and Christian Mystics in Eastern Europe*, ed. Glenn Dynner (Detroit: Wayne State University Press, 2011), 244.

the rabbis; and whatever seems to contradict this in the speeches and acts ascribed to him appears to do so only at first glance. Closely examined, everything is in complete agreement not only with Scripture, but also with the tradition." Mendelssohn not only viewed Jesus as a Jew, he also presented Judaism as the basis for Christianity: "Now Christianity, as you know, is built on Judaism, and if the latter falls, it must necessarily collapse with it into one heap of ruins."[12] The theological legitimacy of Christianity, he suggests in a motif that has continued among Jewish thinkers until the present day, depends upon the flourishing of Judaism.

Jewish views of Christianity in the modern era stressed the dependence of Christianity on Judaism: Judaism was described as the "mother" religion, Christianity as the "daughter" religion, Jesus as a Jew and Pharisaic religion as the context in which he was nurtured. When the metaphor was invoked in an address to Christian theologians in the 1960s by Abraham Joshua Heschel (1907–1972), the image was received warmly as an indication of religious intimacy. Heschel wrote, "The children did not arise to call the mother blessed; instead, they called the mother blind.... Judaism is the mother of the Christian faith. It has a stake in the destiny of Christianity. Should a mother ignore her child, even a wayward, rebellious one?"[13]

During the course of the modern era, however, the metaphor of Christianity as Judaism's daughter religion and the claim of Jesus's Jewish (not Christian!) identity shifted in implications and audience. Mendelssohn thought Jesus was not an original figure but a good Jew, yet kept his views mostly private to avoid debates with Christian theologians; some decades later, Geiger expressed similar views in public and was reviled by Christian theologians; a generation later, Martin Buber (1878–1965) claimed Jesus as his younger brother and was heralded, while Heschel avoided the topic of Jesus altogether and focused instead on commonalities between Jewish and Christian religious experiences, which he termed "depth theology."

The dilemma that haunted the modern period is the gauntlet Mendelssohn threw down: Jesus was a faithful Jew in every respect. What, then, is the purpose of Christianity? If it is the religion of Jesus, how is it distinguished from Judaism? And if the teachings of Jesus are those of liberal Pharisaic religion, what created the rigid legal system of the Talmud? Mendelssohn's comments emphasizing Jesus's adherence to Judaism seemed to be a way to build bridges to Christianity, but the claim also

---

[12] Michah Gottlieb, *Faith and Freedom: Moses Mendelssohn's Theological-Political Thought* (New York: Oxford University Press, 2011), 79.

[13] Abraham Joshua Heschel, "No Religion is an Island," in *Moral Grandeur and Spiritual Audacity: Essays of Abraham Joshua Heschel*, ed. Susannah Heschel (New York: Farrar, Straus and Giroux, 1966), 242.

suggested that Christianity itself was not the creation of Jesus, but a religion subsequently constructed about him. Judaism was the faith of Jesus, Christianity the religion about Jesus.

The next generation of Jewish thinkers, writing in the nineteenth century, used historicism as their method of understanding both Jewish identity and Christianity's dependence on Judaism. The *Wissenschaft des Judentums*, the historical study of Judaism, emphasized scholarship on the Second Temple period and early rabbinic Judaism. Participants in this movement sought not only to elucidate developments in Jewish history, but also to demonstrate how early Christian texts can best be clarified with reference to Jewish sources, particularly rabbinic texts. Scholars representing this movement include Abraham Geiger (1810–1874), Joseph Salvador (1796–1873), Heinrich Graetz (1817–1891), Levi Herzfeld (1810–1884), Joseph Derenbourg (1811–1895), Joseph Eschelbacher (1848–1916), and Felix Perles (1874–1933), among others. In arguing that Jesus can best be understood by studying the gospel texts in the context of Jewish sources, these scholars were engaging in a radical reversal of the gaze: instead of Christians examining Judaism and its history, Jews were now placing Christianity under the microscope of historicism and arriving at conclusions that frequently discomfited Christian theologians. Christian theologians, long accustomed to writing treatises dissecting the history and nature of Judaism, were unaccustomed to their own religion being placed for scrutiny under the gaze of a Jewish theologian. For them, this was the height of insolence and incivility.

Whereas the general Christian view portrayed late Second Temple Judaism as moribund, ossified, heartless, and spiritless, the *Wissenschaft des Judentums* presented a Judaism of depth and vitality. Instead of viewing the New Testament as a text that attempts to negate Judaism, they placed it within the context of ongoing, inner-Jewish religious debates. Jesus's arguments with Sadducees and Pharisees were not his effort to destroy those Jewish sects, but rather part of the heated controversies between them.

The most significant Jewish reevaluation of Christianity emerged with the groundbreaking work of Abraham Geiger, one of the most original and creative figures of the *Wissenschaft des Judentums* and a leader in the nineteenth-century movement of liberal (Reform) Judaism. Trained originally in Arabic studies at the University of Bonn, Geiger's first book, *What did Muhammad Take from Judaism?*, published in 1833, demonstrated the numerous parallels between Qur'anic and rabbinic texts. His study was the first to demonstrate the close affinities between Qur'anic readings of the Hebrew Bible and those of rabbinic (especially midrashic) literature, and the book was hailed all over Europe as opening a new way to understand the origins of Islam: its Jewish context. Almost thirty years later, when Geiger made similar arguments about the New Testament, however, his work – still widely read throughout Europe by Christian theologians – was reviled and condemned. Geiger was less interested in building bridges between Synagogue and Church than in changing the prevailing Christian view of Jewish history and religion. Nearly all subsequent Jewish thinkers followed his interpretation of Christian origins, but only in the second half of the twentieth century, after World War II, did his claims become accepted by Christians as well.

Geiger's argument began with his revisionist view of Jewish history during the Second Temple era, presented in his highly technical magnum opus, the *Urschrift und Übersetzungen der Bibel* (The Original Text and Translations of the Bible), published in 1857, one of the nineteenth century's most important works of Jewish scholarship. In that book, Geiger defined two tendencies in early Judaism: the liberal, progressive, democratizing movement led by the Pharisees, who struggled against the Sadducees, the conservative, aristocratic Temple priests who were anxious to preserve their prerogatives and authority. Geiger depicted the Pharisees with great sympathy as the reformers of Judaism of their day. Far from being the figures of hypocrisy and rigid adherence to religious law depicted in the New Testament, the Pharisees considered every Jew the equal of a priest, and the rabbinic literature that they began to compose eased the religious observances prescribed by the Bible and offered teachings that exhorted virtuous and pious behavior similar to those of the Gospels.

In his subsequent survey of Jewish history, *Das Judentum und seine Geschichte* (Judaism and its History), Geiger declared that while the Greeks had had a genius for philosophy, Jews have a genius for religion. In a passage that offended many contemporary Protestant theologians, Geiger wrote that Jesus

was a Jew, a Pharisaic Jew with Galilean coloring – a man who shared the hopes of his time and who believed that these hopes were fulfilled in him. He did not utter a new thought, nor did he break down the barriers of nationality.... He did not abolish any part of Judaism; he was a Pharisee who walked in the way of Hillel.[14]

Geiger's argument was radical: Jesus said nothing new or original, Paul invented a religion about him, and the true heirs of Jesus's own religious tradition – that of liberal, progressive Pharisaism – were modern-day Reform Jews, seeking to liberalize Judaism. Those wishing to follow the

---

[14] Abraham Geiger, *Das Judentum und seine Geschichte*, 3 volumes (Breslau, 1865–71); English translation, *Judaism and Its History*, trans. by Charles Newburgh (New York: Bloch Publishing, 1911), 131.

example of Jesus – the faith of Jesus, rather than the religion about him – ought to convert to liberal Judaism!

While classical Hellenic culture had ultimately deteriorated into an impure Hellenism, Geiger argued that Jewish monotheism was preserved by Jews, along with a strict adherence to ethics. Christianity and Islam had both started as monotheistic religions, but Christianity had incorporated Greek, pagan teachings that corrupted Jewish monotheism and transformed the faith of Jesus into a religion that demanded belief in irrational dogma. Such demands of dogmatic belief, in contrast to demands regarding ethical behavior, ran contrary to modernity's openness to science and the free exercise of reason. Since Judaism demanded only ethical behavior, rather than belief in dogma, Judaism was better suited to modernity, Geiger claimed, than was Christianity. Indeed, the faith of Jesus was precisely what liberal Protestants claimed they wanted as part of the purging of Christianity of dogma, miracles, and church doctrine. Reimarus had already noted the absence of significant difference between Jesus's teachings and those of Judaism

When the same kind of argument was put forward by Geiger, the Jewish theologian, a hundred years later, the hostile reactions of Christian theologians came swiftly and sharply. His work was widely read and discussed, and widely condemned by Christian theologians. While acknowledging the legitimacy of his historical studies, Christian scholars were discomfited by his conclusions. Franz Delitzsch (1813–1890), for example, a conservative theologian whose life's goal was winning Jewish love for Jesus, thought Geiger had misrepresented the Pharisees and defamed Jesus. Citing a Talmudic passage which reports that Hillel taught that one should always tell a bride she is beautiful, even if she is not, Delitzsch wrote that this shows that "Hillel sometimes transgressed the bounds of truth."[15] Geiger had elevated Hillel, Delitzsch wrote, "in order to rank Jesus below him … Hillel, however, left everything as he found it … All history, on the other hand, proclaims what Jesus has become."[16] "The tendencies of these two diverged as widely as heaven from earth. The teaching of Hillel is juristic, casuistic, and narrow-mindedly national, while that of Jesus is universally religious, moral, and humane."[17]

Probably the most important and lasting critique of Geiger's work came from the young Julius Wellhausen (1844–1918), who became one of the most influential biblical scholars of the modern era. Wellhausen devoted a

---

[15] Franz Delitzsch, *Jesus und Hillel: Mit Rücksicht auf Renan und Geiger* (Erlangen: Verlag von Andreas Deichert, 1866), 178; Talmud Bavli, tractate Ketubot, pages 16b–17a.

[16] Delitzsch, *Jesus und Hillel*, 178.

[17] Delitzsch, *Jesus und Hillel*, 161.

book to attacking Geiger's view of the Pharisees. He rejected out of hand Geiger's claim that Pharisaism constituted a liberalization of Jewish religious practice, and rejected Geiger's use of the sources. Even the early rabbinic texts, such as the Mishnah, were unacceptable sources, according to Wellhausen, for reconstructing first-century Judaism. Rather, he relied on the gospel polemics against the Pharisees, such as Matthew 23, as historically reliable representations of Pharisaic religion. What characterizes the Pharisees is their "religious materialism."[18] They "killed nature through the commandments. 613 written commandments and 1000 other laws and they leave no room for conscience. One forgot God and the way to him in the Torah."[19]

Despite Wellhausen's critique, affirming Jesus and Pharisaic religion while demoting Christianity became a popular Jewish formulation, reiterated in the work of numerous Jewish historians and rabbis well into the twentieth century, including Kaufmann Kohler, Samuel Hirsch, and Samuel Sandmel, among many others. Still another, contrasting viewpoint was developed by Heinrich Graetz, whose eleven-volume narrative, *History of the Jews*, tried to marginalize Jesus within first-century Judaism. Graetz argued that Jesus stemmed from the Galilee, a region dominated by simple, uneducated Jews not properly versed in rabbinic teachings. Furthermore, according to Graetz, Jesus was an Essene, and therefore uninvolved in the highly sophisticated, intellectual Pharisaic movement that ultimately developed into rabbinic Judaism. From the Essenes – or at least, the Essenes as described by the first-century Jewish historian Josephus – Jesus adopted baptism and promoted apocalypticism, which, Graetz claimed, was otherwise foreign to Judaism, though popular among the simple-minded Galilean Jews. It should be noted that Graetz's chapter on Jesus was withheld by the publisher of the first edition of volume three of his *History*, printed in 1856, out of fear that it would stimulate a hostile reaction, and it only appeared in the book's second printing, in 1863.[20] Apparently Mendelssohn's worries about speaking openly about Jesus retained validity nearly a century later.

[18] Julius Wellhausen, *Die Pharisäer und die Sadducäer. Eine Untersuchung zur inneren jüdischen Geschichte* (Greifswald/Bamberg 1874; Hannover ²1924; Göttingen ³1967), 19; *The Pharisees and the Sadducees: An Examination of Internal Jewish History*, trans. Mark E. Biddle (Macon, GA: Mercer University Press, 2001).

[19] Wellhausen, *Die Pharisäer und die Sadducäer*, 19.

[20] The chapter also appeared as an appendix to Moses Hess, *Rom und Jerusalem: Die letzte Nationalitätsfrage*, published in 1862. Hess had revised the manuscript of *Rom und Jerusalem*, a proto-Zionist work, while a guest in Graetz's home for several months in the spring and summer of 1862. See Susannah Heschel, *Abraham Geiger and the Jewish Jesus* (Chicago: University of Chicago Press, 1998), 136 and 273.

What were Jews permitted and expected to say about Jesus and Christianity? The concerns of Mendelssohn's and Graetz's publishers, and the many hostile reactions to Geiger's work from Christian theologians, indicate that Jews were treading on thin ice. Perhaps the Christian reactions perceived the radical nature of the Jewish assertions about Jesus. In writing their own version of Jesus and Christian origins, Jews were staking a radical political claim. Whereas Judaism had long been under Christian scrutiny, the gaze was now reversed: Jews were examining Christian texts and formulating their own conclusions regarding the origins of Christianity. Claiming there was nothing new or original in Jesus's teachings was not simply a denial or negation, but an attempt to overthrow Christian hegemony over Western culture; it was a revolt of the colonized.[21] Christianity was transformed into a daughter religion, serving Judaism's own interests by bringing Jewish monotheism to the pagan world.

Overarching claims to Judaism's superiority extended further, to a widespread insistence by modern Jewish thinkers that Judaism was better suited to modernity than was Christianity. Judaism, claimed Mendelssohn, Geiger, Cohen, and others, was a religion of reason, not dogma. Free to believe or not, and to arrive at religious beliefs through the exercise of reason, meant that Judaism did not seek intellectual constraints as did Christianity, which Paul had shaped into a set of dogma that often contradicted reason, yet were essential to defining Christian identity. These included the incarnation, Trinity, and virgin birth. Such Jewish claims that Christianity rested on beliefs contrary to reason were carried over from the Middle Ages, when Jews, sometimes in alliance with Muslims, painted Christianity as a religion of absurd doctrines.

Not all Jewish thinkers approached Christianity through a historicist lens. Nineteenth-century German-Jewish philosophers, such as Samuel Hirsch (1815–1889) and Salomon Formstecher (1808–1889), developed a theological model of incorporation, in which both Judaism and Christianity became components of a single whole. These philosophers transformed the contemporary philosophical methods of Schelling and Hegel that had been used to guarantee the dominance of Christianity over Judaism into systems in which, through the identical philosophical methods, Judaism emerged as theologically superior to Christianity. That superiority was identified primarily as Judaism's monotheism and its ethics, enshrined in religious law. Christianity's task was to spread Jewish monotheism to the Greco-Roman pagan world. The so-called 'mission theory'

---

[21] Susannah Heschel, "Revolt of the Colonized: Abraham Geiger's Wissenschaft des Judentums as a Challenge to Christian Hegemony in the Academy," *New German Critique* 77 (1999): 61–86.

of nineteenth-century liberal Jewish thought may well be, as Stephen Poppell has argued, a reinvestment of the contemporary understanding of the "Pauline" distinction between Jewish particularism and Christian universalism with a positive valuation: Christianity becomes the vehicle by which Judaism is able to reach the pagan world.[22] According to this mission theory, which has some precedents in pre-modern Jewish thought, Christianity, as a kind of Jewish messenger, inevitably fell victim to syncretism, developing rigid dogma alien to its Jewish roots, while Judaism retained itself pure of corrupt influences.

Other Jewish historians and theologians turned to the study of Islam and made similar arguments about its missionary function. Starting in the 1830s with the publication of Geiger's study of rabbinic influences on the Qur'an, Jewish philologists argued that Islam originated from Judaism. Whereas Christianity had corrupted Jewish monotheism with Greco-Roman pagan ideas, Islam remained closer to Judaism by preserving a strict monotheism, rejecting anthropomorphism, and proclaiming a religious law that enshrined a strict ethics. Ultimately, these arguments imply, it is Judaism that gave rise to all three monotheisms and, through them, to Western civilization. Rather than a religion that "died" with the birth of Christ, or a desiccated system of law, Judaism forms the tree trunk, with Christianity and Islam as two of its branches. Indeed, most modern Jewish thinkers favored Islam, claiming it remained closer to its roots in Judaism, but both religions depended on the health of the trunk of Judaism for their own survival. Such Jewish arguments incorporated both universalism with particularism: Judaism was the universal religion, giving birth to Christianity and Islam, but in its Jewish particularism preserved the true religion better than either of its daughters.

These well-developed tenets of modern Jewish thought managed to cross the boundaries between Liberal and Orthodox Judaism, and also crossed the ocean from Germany to the United States, as German-born liberal rabbis, such as Samuel Hirsch, David Einhorn, and Kaufmann Kohler, immigrated during the second half of the nineteenth century.[23] They

---

[22] Michael A. Meyer, "Universalism and Jewish Unity in the Thought of Abraham Geiger" and Stephen Poppell, "Response to Michael Meyer," both in *The Role of Religion in Modern Jewish History*, ed. Jacob Katz (Cambridge: Harvard University Press, 1975).

[23] Gershom Scholem has pointed out ways in which the *Wissenschaft vom Judentum* leveled many of the differences between liberal and Orthodox during the second half of the nineteenth century. See "Mi-Tokh Hirhurim 'al Hokhmat Yisra'el," *Luah ha-Ares 1944–45*; repr. *Devarim be-Go* 2 (Tel Aviv, 1982), 385–403; abbreviated trans. by the author, "Wissenschaft vom Judentum einst und jetzt," *Bulletin des Leo Baeck Instituts* 9 (1960): 10–20; repr. in *Judaica* 1 (Frankfurt am Main, 1963), 147–64. The American

popularized the argument that Jesus was a good Jew, Paul was a Jewish heretic and the real founder of Christianity, and Christianity had betrayed the teachings of Jesus and was really the religion of Paul. While focusing primarily on the Gospels, they tended to ignore the Pauline writings, and, as the historian Uriel Tal has noted, they presented Christianity as a religion of dogma even though most Protestants of their day had in fact renounced supernatural miracles and dogma in favor of a historical Jesus as a teacher and preacher.[24]

By the turn of the century, liberal Jews began to declare Jesus one of Judaism's great religious leaders as part of the ongoing effort to de-Christianize him. Martin Buber was representative of the tendency when he proclaimed:

From my youth onwards I have found in Jesus my great brother. That Christianity has regarded and does regard him as God and Saviour has always appeared to me a fact of the highest importance which, for his sake and my own, I must endeavor to understand ... I am more than certain that a great place belongs to him in Israel's history of faith and that this place cannot be described by any of the usual categories.[25]

Buber's impact on Jews in Europe during the years before and after World War I was enormous, and his influence extended to social theorists and Christian theologians as well. His books on Hasidism, written for a non-religious audience, presented that pietistic movement as engaged in the same existentialist quest as philosophers. His most famous work, *I and Thou*, published in 1922, de-exoticized religious experience and presented it as a relationship of profundity independent of religious doctrine, tradition, or even community. Buber's work was influential, wrote the Protestant theologian Paul Tillich, because he presented "mysticism as an element within prophetic religion," and maintained a "relation between prophetic religion and culture, especially in the social and political realms."[26] Indeed, Buber was an active member in the binational Zionist movement, Brit Shalom, and moved to Palestine after losing his position at the University of Frankfurt during the Third Reich.[27]

rabbinate attracted the more radical reformers within the German rabbinate, those who had difficulties securing a rabbinical post within Germany.

[24] Uriel Tal, *Christians and Jews in Germany*, trans. Noah Jacobs (Ithaca, NY: Cornell University Press, 1976).

[25] Martin Buber, *Two Types of Faith*, trans. Norman P. Goldhawk (New York: Collier Books, 1951), 12–13.

[26] Paul Tillich, "Martin Buber and Christian Thought," *Commentary* 5, no. 6 (1948): 516.

[27] Paul Mendes-Flohr, ed., *Martin Buber: A Land of Two Peoples* (New York: Oxford University Press, 1983).

While affirming the Jewishness of Jesus, Buber nonetheless was highly critical of Christianity. In his comparative study, *Two Types of Faith*, he distinguished between "emunah," the Hebrew word for faith that he said characterized biblical and Pharisaic religion, and "pistis," the Greek word for belief (in a proposition) that he claimed characterized Christian teaching as derived from the Pauline epistles and Greek philosophy. Jesus, he claimed, stood entirely within the Jewish context, an expression of Jewish religiosity. With frequent lectures to Protestant groups in post-war Germany, Buber became a highly acclaimed and influential figure in Christian circles, and radically altered the depiction of Judaism for his readers.[28]

Other Zionists also wrote in positive terms about Jesus. The American rabbi and Zionist leader Stephen Wise echoed Buber when he declared, "Jesus was a Jew, Hebrew of Hebrews ... Jesus did not teach or wish to teach a new religion."[29] Still others sought a more forthright diminution of Christianity. Arthur Marmorstein compared the New Testament with rabbinic texts, and concluded his study by claiming that Jesus said nothing new.[30] Claude Montefiore (1858–1938), a British scholar who served as one of the leaders of the liberal Jewish community in England, immersed himself in Christian scholarship on the New Testament. He concluded that Jesus may not have been original, but that he brought to the fore prophetic teachings of Judaism that had been neglected by other Jews. Montefiore sought to mitigate Paul's criticisms of the law by arguing that Paul misunderstood Judaism: "The early religion of Paul was more somber and gloomy than Rabbinic Judaism; the world was a more miserable and God-forsaken place."[31] Daniel Chwolson (1819–1911), a Jewish convert to Christianity who became a noted scholar of early Judaism and a professor in Russia, commented: "A Jew reading the gospels feels at home."[32]

Among Orthodox rabbis, similar views were also expressed, at least prior to World War I; they include Zwi Perez Chajes (1876–1927), and Elias Soloweyczyk (1801–1885), who echoed the kinds of arguments put forward

---

[28] Buber, *Two Types of Faith*.

[29] Stephen Wise, *Challenging Years: The Autobiography of Stephen Wise* (New York: Putnam, 1929), 281.

[30] Arthur Marmorstein, *Talmud und Neues Testament* (Jamnitz: Selbstverlag, 1908), 29.

[31] Claude Montefiore, *Judaism and St. Paul* (London: M. Goshen, 1914), 81f; cited by Walter Jacob, *Christianity through Jewish Eyes* (Cincinnati: Hebrew Union College Press, 1974).

[32] Daniel Chwolson, *Das letzte Passahmahl Christi und der Tag seines Todes nach den in Übereinstimmung gebrachten Berichten der Synoptiker und des Evangelium Johannis* (St. Petersburg: M. Eggers, 1892), 88.

by reformers such as Geiger.[33] Chajes, who served as chief rabbi of Vienna, and was also a Zionist leader and a Bible scholar, wrote his doctoral dissertation on the Gospel of Mark in 1899, and subsequently argued that "You have to be a rabbinical Jew, to know Midrash, if you wish to fathom the spirit of Christianity in its earliest years. Above all, you must read the Gospels in the Hebrew translation."[34] Soloweyczyk, a member of a distinguished Lithuanian rabbinical family, published a Hebrew translation and commentary on the Gospel of Matthew in 1869, later translated into French, German, and English, presenting verse-by-verse parallels with rabbinic literature and proclaiming: "Jesus had no other end in view than to animate men with faith in the one God and to urge them on to the practice of all the neighborly virtues and love for everyone, even enemies. May God grant us all, Jews and Christians, that we may follow the teaching of Jesus and his shining example, for our well-being in this world and our salvation in the next."[35]

The liberal rabbi and scholar Leo Baeck (1873–1956), writing in Germany during the 1920s, followed Geiger's lead on the Pharisees and Jesus, and emphasized the degeneracy that resulted from Paul's departure from Jesus's own adherence to rabbinic Judaism. The result, according to Baeck, is that Judaism maintained itself as a "classical religion" of ethics, but Christianity had deteriorated into a "romantic religion" of effeminate spirituality:

In this ecstatic abandonment, which wants so much to be seized and embraced and would like to pass away in the roaring ocean of the world, the distinctive character of romantic religion stands revealed – the feminine trait that marks it. There is something passive about its piety; it feels so touchingly helpless and weary; it wants to be seized and inspired from above, embraced by a flood of grace which should descend upon it to consecrate it and possess it – a will-less instrument of the wondrous ways of God.[36]

---

[33] Eliyahu Tsevi Soloweyczyk, *Kol Kore, o, Ha-Talmud veha-Berit ha-Hadashah* (Jerusalem: Jerusalem Center for Biblical Studies and Research, 1985; originally, Paris, 1869); Elias Soloweyczyk, *Die Bibel, der Talmud, und das Evangelium*, trans. Moritz Gruenwald (Leipzig: F.A. Brockhaus, 1877); Aron Kaminka, *Studien zur Geschichte Galiläas* (Berlin: H. Engel, 1890).

[34] Hirsch Peretz Chajes, "Jüdisches in den Evangelien," dated November 6, 1919, in *Reden und Vorträge*, ed. Moritz Rosenfeld (Vienna: Selbstverlag, 1932), 271. See also his *Markus-Studien* (Berlin: C. A. Schwetschke, 1899).

[35] Soloweyczyk, *Kol Kore*, 9.

[36] Leo Baeck "Romantic Religion," in *Judaism and Christianity: Essays by Leo Baeck*, trans. and ed. Walter Kaufmann (Philadelphia: Jewish Publication Society, 1958), 192, 189–292; originally Leo Baeck, "Romantische Religion," *Festschrift zum 50 jährigen Bestehen der Hochschule für die Wissenschaft des Judentums* (Berlin, 1922), 1–48.

Christianity is effeminate, Baeck argued, and therefore lacks ethics and moral responsibility, whereas Judaism is a masculine religion that places ethical commandments at the forefront and makes no demands that its adherents accept irrational dogma.

The efforts by Jews to demonstrate the affinities between the teachings of Jesus and those of the rabbis of his day led some Jews and Christians of liberal theological persuasion to recognize that the boundaries between the two religions had become blurred. Both liberal Jews and liberal Protestants were advocating a religion purified of the obligations of law and dogma, respectively, and were creating a set of religious teachings that sounded remarkably similar. The absence of a clear-cut boundary encouraged new efforts to disparage one another's religious claims in order to forge the distinctiveness of one's own.

The great German-Jewish philosopher Hermann Cohen (1842–1918) serves as an important transitional figure in Jewish views of Christianity. His work presents both a culmination of the historical arguments put forth by Geiger and those who followed his lead, and a strong philosophical argument that affirmed Christianity, but presented Judaism as ethically superior. Cohen acknowledged the influence of Protestantism on modern Reform Judaism, which "discarded the obligatory character of the Talmud as they [Protestants] have the traditions of the church.... We think and feel much more deeply in a Protestant spirit on all spiritual questions of religion."[37] In his study of Cohen's work, John C. Lyden sees incarnational elements in Cohen's critique of Christianity. Continuing in the tradition inaugurated by Geiger, Cohen viewed Christianity as the product of Greek polytheism combined with Jewish monotheism that resulted in non-rational doctrines such as the incarnation, God becoming man. By contrast, he emphasized Judaism's rejection of anthropomorphism, a position he viewed as philosophically superior. For ethical judgment to occur, Cohen argued, following Kantian principles, human autonomy was necessary. Yet the incarnation was both a humanization of God and a divinization of man. As Lyden writes, for Cohen Christianity has undermined moral autonomy: "Morality is then not based in our own freedom but in our dissolution into God in Christ."[38] The incarnation makes Jesus into a moral ideal that human beings

[37] Hermann Cohen, "Ein Bekenntnis in der Judenfrage," *Jüdische Schriften* (Berlin: C. A. Schwetschke, 1924), vol. II, 93. Cohen is here referring to the liberal Protestant rejection of numerous doctrines, such as the incarnation and virgin birth of Jesus, whom they affirmed as an ideal person with a unique and extraordinary religious subjectivity, rather than a divinely incarnate being.

[38] John C. Lyden, "Hermann Cohen's Relationship to Christian Thought," *Journal of Jewish Thought and Philosophy* 3, no. 2 (1994): 279–301.

can never achieve: "If Christ grounds morality as an historical person ... then there is a distinction made between the unique human and all other humans. This distinction becomes a new impediment to the idea of moral autonomy. Only if the unique human indicates the idea of humanity, only then will moral autonomy not be lost."[39]

The contamination of Jewish monotheism with Greek myth, then, not only was the founding moment of Christianity, but also a betrayal of Jesus's own faith and the compromise of human moral autonomy. The martyrdom of Jesus is a Jewish story, according to Cohen, a prefiguration of Jews suffering in Diaspora. The irony, writes Robert Erlewine, "is that if Christians charge that Jews were blind to the Messiah in their midst and killed him, Cohen is charging that Christians fail to see that Jesus is not only part and parcel of the Jewish testimony to the messianic ideal, but that it is the Christians who torture and kill those who bear witness in their assault on Jews in the name of the charge of deicide."[40] While critical of Christianity as a religion of myth that was therefore philosophically erroneous and incapable of morality, Cohen saw affinities between Judaism and Islam, writing, "The Jewish philosophy of the Middle Ages does not grow so much out of Islam as out of the original monotheism. The more intimate relationship between Judaism and Islam – more intimate than with other monotheistic religions – can be explained by the kinship that exists between the mother and daughter religion."[41] Perceived affinities between Judaism and Islam by Jewish thinkers functioned at times as tools for marking distinctions between Judaism and Christianity.

Other German Jews took a different approach. Franz Rosenzweig (1886–1929), one of the most complex philosophers of Judaism in Germany, had a complex relationship to Christianity. During the course of his close friendship with Eugen Rosenstock-Huessy (1888–1973), they debated the merits of Judaism and Christianity, and in 1913 Rosenzweig, at the age of 27, at

---

[39] Hermann Cohen, "Religion und Sittlichkeit," in *Jüdische Schriften*, vol. III, 156–157.

[40] Robert Erlewine, "From Exclusivity to Partnership: Abraham Joshua Heschel and the Legacy of Liberal Judaism," paper delivered at the American Academy of Religion meetings, San Francisco, CA, November 2011.

[41] Hermann Cohen, *Religion of Reason out of the Sources of Judaism*, trans. Simon Kaplan (New York: F. Ungar, 1972), 92; "Die jüdische Philosophie des Mittelalters erwächst nicht sowohl aus dem Monotheismus des Islam, als vielmehr aus dem ursprünglichen Monotheismus, und höchstens kann die Verwandtschaft, die zwischen dieser Tochterreligion und der der Mutter besteht, die innige Beziehung verständlich machen, welche intimer als sonstwo zwischen Judentum und Islam sich anbahnt." Hermann Cohen, *Die Religion der Vernunft aus den Quellen des Judentums* (Leipzig: G. Fock, 1919), 107–108.

first considered converting to Protestantism, then decided he would not. A variety of factors led him to change his mind and dedicate his life to the study of Judaism instead, and he even declined a prestigious professorship at a German university in the field of philosophy to pursue his Jewish interests. While undertaking military service during World War I, Rosenzweig continued his discussions with Rosenstock-Huessy via exchange of letters, later published, and also began what became his magnum opus, *The Star of Redemption*, published in 1921, a book that is often misunderstood as sympathetic to Christianity, according to Batnitzky.[42]

In *The Star of Redemption*, Rosenzweig argued that Judaism and Christianity were on separate but complementary and intertwined paths (without Islam), and that their ultimate truth could not be determined until the messianic era. Until then, they would remain enmeshed in a conflict and enmity that had been deliberately established between them by God. He writes, "Before God, then, Jew and Christian both labor at the same task. ... [However, God] has set enmity between the two for all time and has withal most intimately bound each to each."[43] Like Cohen, Rosenzweig affirmed Judaism's mission of preserving pure monotheism. That is, the rejection of Judaism is a necessary component of Christian theological self-affirmation, and it quickly develops into a hatred of the Jews.[44] As Batnitzky has pointed out, for Rosenzweig, relations between Judaism and Christianity are not constituted by mutuality and tolerance, but asymmetry and judgment.[45] Dialogue can only take place between positions that are different, and must maintain the differences if each participant is to retain its identity, so that identity is built on the negation of the other. While both Jews and Christians seek a relationship with God the Father, Jews are condescending toward Christians for thinking they need a third person, Jesus Christ, to mediate between them and God: "every Jew feels in the depths of his soul that the Christian relation to God, and so in a sense their religion, is particularly and extremely pitiful, poverty-stricken, and ceremonious."[46]

[42] Leora Batnitzky, "Dialogue as Judgment, Not Mutual Affirmation: A New Look at Franz Rosenzweig's Dialogical Philosophy," *Journal of Religion* 79, no. 4 (1999): 523–544.

[43] Franz Rosenzweig, *The Star of Redemption*, trans. William W. Hallo (New York: Holt, Rinehart and Winston, 1971), 415–416.

[44] Eugen Rosenstock-Huessy and Franz Rosenzweig, *Judaism Despite Christianity*, trans. Dorothy M. Emmet (New York: Schocken Books, 1971), 112.

[45] Batnitzky, "Dialogue as Judgment."

[46] Rosenzweig and Rosenstock-Huessy, *Judaism Despite Christianity*, 113. Gregory Kaplan, "In the End Shall Christians Become Jews and Jews, Christians? On Rosenzweig's Apocalyptic Eschatology," *Cross Currents* 53, no. 4 (2004): 511–529.

An example of a Jewish rejection of Christianity is Rosenzweig's claim that it is Judaism, not Christianity, that represents a theological universalism. The Jewish God is open to all people, without requiring access via Jesus, the church, or particular doctrines, as does Christianity. Jewish particularism, for Rosenzweig, has a protective, rather than exclusive, function. Yet Christianity also has a positive function for Judaism. Rosenzweig uses the image of the "star" to convey an inward force within Judaism and an outward force that drives Christianity that complement each other. Ultimately, which of the two is the true religion, preferred by God, will not be known until the messianic era.

Rosenzweig is a unique voice whose work appeared on the eve of doom, just a few years before Hitler came to power and Jews first in Germany, then throughout Europe, began to lose their rights, emigrate, and ultimately were deported and murdered. His work was revived after the war, and came into influence and prominence, among Christians as well as Jews, toward the end of the century. On the more popular level, however, Jews retained a primary focus on the older narrative, that Jesus was a loyal Jew, and Paul the founder of Christianity.

The dialogue of judgment, not tolerance, that Rosenzweig advocated, is implicit in modern Jewish discussions of Jesus. By divorcing Jesus from Christian understandings of him, and transforming him into a symbol of Jewish historical experience, Jews were attempting to reverse Christian supersessionist theology; theirs was a revolt of the colonized, a politicized theological engagement. Claiming a Jewish Jesus, then, is not a Christianization of Judaism, but more frequently stands in polemical relationship to that religion, and serves as an assertion of Jewish interests in a society dominated by (secularized) Christian culture. For that reason, it is not surprising to find positive statements about Jesus in the writings of Zionists, Reform and Orthodox rabbis, liberals and conservatives.

In their effort to recover a strong, vibrant Jewish history, Zionists sought to reclaim Jesus by arguing that he did not seek a dissolution of Jewish nationalism. Sweden's chief rabbi, Gottlieb Klein (1852–1914), wrote that in the gospels, "a Jew is speaking, no cult hero, but a Jew with a marked national consciousness."[47] In 1922, the Zionist Joseph Klausner (1874–1960) published his *Jesus of Nazareth*, the first book on Jesus written in modern Hebrew, both in order to make his contribution to the world of New Testament scholarship, and to affirm a central role for Jewish beliefs

---

[47] Gottlieb Klein, *Ist Jesus eine historische Persönlichkeit?* (Tübingen: J. C. B. Mohr (Paul Siebeck), 1910), 27; cf. "Zur Erläuterung der Evangelien aus Talmud und Midrasch," *Zeitschrift für neutestamentliche Wissenschaft* 5 (1904): 144–153.

in the course of Western history.[48] Klausner was well-versed in scholarly debates over Jesus and Second Temple Judaism, but his attempt at an original interpretation did not exert an influence in the scholarly community. Jesus, in his view, was a humble and pious Pharisee who had departed the boundaries of Jewish nationhood, making him unsuitable to Jews, while Paul was the real founder of Christianity.[49] The implication for modern Jews unsure of Zionism is clear: to reject Jewish nationalism is to end up like Jesus, as a Christian. Yehezkel Kaufmann (1889–1963), a Bible scholar and philosopher in the State of Israel who wrote a nationalist version of Jewish biblical history, attributed Christianity's success to the Jewishness of its message. That message could not be accepted by the pagan world directly from Judaism, because the Jews were in a state of exile and dispersion; "Christianity acted as the messenger of Judaism."[50] Kaufmann diverged somewhat from other Jewish writers on Jesus, arguing for apocalyptic elements in his teachings, but he drew no significant conclusions from that point.[51] While the claims of these Jewish historians regarding Jesus exerted little impact on the Christian New Testament scholarship of their day, they did ultimately become conventional understandings of the early Jesus movement by the late twentieth century.

Among Jews in Eastern Europe in the late nineteenth and early twentieth centuries, Jesus was often invoked as a figure of literary and artistic interest. During the 1880s, Eva-Maria Kaffanke has noted, German artistic representations of Jesus began to be criticized for being "too Jewish," so that artists made efforts to find "Oriental" models, at first Muslims and then Germans.[52] By contrast, Jewish artists emphasized visual identifications of Jesus as a Jew. The Jesus of "Ecce Homo," a sculpture by the Russian Jewish artist Mark Matveevich Antokol'skii (1841–1902), wears a skullcap and sidecurls, and Antokol'skii explained that Jesus "was and died a Jew for truth and brotherhood."[53] Drawing on the Gospel of John, the

[48] Joseph Klausner, *Jesus of Nazareth*, trans. by Herbert Danby (New York: Macmillan, 1925).
[49] Joseph Klausner, *From Jesus to Paul*, trans. W. F. Stinespring (New York: Macmillan, 1943).
[50] David Berger, "Religion, Nationalism, and Historiography: Yehezekel Kaufmann's Account of Jesus and Early Christianity," in *Scholars and Scholarship: The Interaction Between Judaism and Other Cultures*, ed. Leo Landmann (New York: Yeshiva University Press, 1990), 164.
[51] Yehezkel Kaufmann, *Golah VeNekhar* (Tel Aviv: Devir, 1929), 355–379.
[52] Eva-Maria Kaffanke, *Der deutsche Heiland Christusdarstellungen um 1900 im Kontext der völkischen Bewegung* (Frankfurt am Main: P. Lang, 2001), 192. Discussions of Jesus's appearance occurred during the 1930s in scholarly and pseudo-scholarly forums. See Hans F. K. Günther, "Wie sah Jesus aus?", *Volk und Rasse* 2 (1932): 118–119.
[53] Ziva Amishai-Maisels, "Origins of the Jewish Jesus," in *Complex Identities: Jewish Consciousness and Modern Art*, ed. Matthew Baigell and Milly Heyd (New

sculpture's title comes from the Roman procurator Pontius Pilate's presentation of a scourged Jesus to the Jewish community of Jerusalem just
before he was taken away to be crucified. Yet Antokol'skii's Jesus has no
crown of thorns or wounds, and is thus divorced from a Christian context,
as Olga Litvak has pointed out. He is not the suffering Christian savior,
but the dignified representative of the Jewish spirit. Litvak has explained
Antokol'skii's strategy as not so much about Jesus being Jewish as about
the viewers of the sculpture being forced to look at Jesus from a Jewish
viewpoint.[54] It was one of the first attempts at visualizing a Jesus figure that
would express what Jewish scholars, from Geiger to Baeck, had been suggesting. Similar depictions of Jesus as a Jew, best understood by Jews, are
also found in the paintings and sculptures of Jesus by other Jewish artists,
such as Maurycy Gottlieb.[55]

Not only is Jesus depicted as a Jew, he also came to be a symbol for
Jewish suffering. The 1909 story by the Yiddish writer Sholem Asch
(1880–1957), "In a Carnival Night," describes a papal procession in
sixteenth-century Rome that includes the beating of eight Jews. But then,
Asch writes, "Jesus climbs down from the cross in St. Peter's Cathedral
to become one of the Jewish martyrs persecuted by the Church. The
Virgin Mary joins Mother Rachel in sewing the shrouds."[56] In other
words, Jesus has remembered his Jewish roots, even if Christians have
forgotten them.

The artist Marc Chagall (1887–1985) frequently painted crucifixion
scenes, and his most famous, the 1938 "White Crucifixion," depicts Jesus
wrapped in a prayer shawl and nailed to the cross, while around him Jews
flee persecution. The death of Jesus does not bring a messianic end to
human suffering, but inaugurates a new era of misery for Jews. Chagall's
1944 "The Crucified" depicts a village with fully clothed Jews hanging from
a series of crosses. The Holocaust is the crucifixion, and the Crucifixion is
a mass murder of Jews.

Brunswick: Rutgers University Press, 2001), 51–86; here 58; idem, "Faith, Ethics, and the
Holocaust: Christological Symbolism of the Holocaust," *Holocaust and Genocide Studies*
3, no. 4 (1988): 457–481.

[54] Olga Litvak, "Rome and Jerusalem: The Figure of Jesus in the Creation of Mark
Antokol'skii," in *The Art of Being Jewish in Modern Times*, ed. Barbara Kirschenblatt-
Gimblett and Jonathan Karp (Philadelphia: University of Pennsylvania Press, 2008),
228–254.

[55] Ezra Mendelsohn, *Painting a People: Maurycy Gottlieb and Jewish Art* (Hanover,
NH: University Press of New England, 2002).

[56] See the discussion in David G. Roskies, *Against the Apocalypse: Responses to Catastrophe
in Modern Jewish Culture* (Syracuse: Syracuse University Press, 1999).

With the Holocaust, Jews move from affirming Jesus as a Jewish teacher, one of the many rabbis of his day, to viewing him in his crucifixion as the symbol for Jewish suffering. In the Holocaust memoir of Elie Wiesel, *Night*, writes David Roskies, "the Holocaust survivor was compared to Christ."[57] The central image of the book is Wiesel's description of three Jews hanging on the gallows at Auschwitz, the middle victim a young child who is too light to break his neck and so dies agonizingly slowly.[58] An anonymous voice asks, "Where is God now?" And another answers, "Where is He? Here He is. He is hanging here on this gallows." There is a kind of Christ envy that emerges from the image; the suffering of the Jews is explained by appeal to Christianity and by claiming superiority to it: the Jews are the greatest victims, and Jesus is a poor imitation. For Wiesel, Jesus was indeed a Jew, but his death suggested not the crucifixion of the first Christian at the hands of the Jews, but the crucifixion of all Jews at the hands of Christians.

Jesus could no longer serve simply as the signifier of Christian supremacy and Jewish subordination; now he represented, in Jewish art and literature, the degeneracy of the Christian religion and its wanton destruction of Jewish lives. Who was actually crucifying whom? As much as the religion about Jesus may have led to antisemitic pogroms, the faith of Jesus would have placed him, Asch, Chagall, and Wiesel imply, among the murdered Jews.

In the first decades after the Holocaust, Christians (theologians and historians) in Germany presented the German churches, both Protestant and Catholic, as victims of National Socialism. While many pastors and priests had been targets of Nazi wrath, others sought a compromise or even a theological synthesis with National Socialism. That most often took the form of a racial theology that rejected the Old Testament as a "Jewish" book inappropriate for Christians; proclaimed Jesus an Aryan, not a Jew; and sought a dejudaization of Christianity. Hitler was said to be avenging Jesus's death at the hands of the Jews, and one group of Protestant theologians even developed a synthesis of Nazism and Christianity. The political uses of this construction became particularly intense during the Third Reich: for example, the Jewishness of Jesus was used as an argument within Nazism against Christianity, at the same time that some Nazi-supported research institutions attempted to prove the Aryan purity of Jesus.[59]

---

[57] David G. Roskies, *Against the Apocalypse: Responses to Catastrophe in Modern Jewish Culture* (Cambridge, MA: Harvard University Press, 1984), 262.

[58] Elie Wiesel, *Night*, trans. Stella Rodway (New York, Hill and Wang, 1960).

[59] Susannah Heschel, *The Aryan Jesus: Christian Theologians and the Bible in Nazi Germany* (Princeton: Princeton University Press, 2008).

After the war, that history tended to be "forgotten" or denied by Christian theologians in Germany. The theologian Richard Rubenstein (b. 1924) was shocked when he met with Protestant pastor Heinrich Gruber in 1961. Gruber had been imprisoned during the Third Reich in Sachsenhausen and Dachau concentration camps for three years as punishment for having provided assistance to non-Aryan Christians and Jews seeking help escaping the Reich. Gruber told Rubenstein that in his understanding of Old Testament theology, Germany had simply served as the instrument of God's wrath toward the Jews; their murder was, he told Rubenstein, "part of God's plan."[60] Rubenstein, appalled by Gruber's statements, concluded that a radical reconsideration of theology, within both Jewish and Christian contexts, was necessary, and he also broke with earlier Jewish affirmations of Jesus: "At the heart of the problem is the fact that it may be impossible for Christians to remain Christians without regarding Jews in mythic, magic, and theological categories."[61]

Among Roman Catholics, as the historian John Connelly has demonstrated, recognition of the racism within the Catholic church that viewed baptized Jews as inferior Christians spurred efforts, led by John Oesterreicher, to make the Vatican reconsider Catholic teachings regarding Judaism.[62] Nostra Aetate, a 1965 declaration of the Second Vatican Council regarding the church's relations with other religions, presented Judaism as holding continued validity in the eyes of God, renounced charges of deicide against all Jews, and condemned antisemitism. That was the first and most radical Christian affirmation of Judaism in its day. Some years later, in 1980, a synod of the Protestant church of the Rhineland declared that it would no longer seek to missionize Jews, a radical shift in the history of Christianity, which had always prayed for the conversion of the Jews – and often sought their forced conversion.[63]

One of the most influential Jewish thinkers of the post-war era, whose work was widely read by Christians and who influenced Nostra Aetate, was Abraham Joshua Heschel (1907–1972). Born into a distinguished family of Hasidic leaders, a pietistic movement in Eastern Europe, he studied and

---

[60] Richard L. Rubenstein, "The Dean and the Chosen People," in *After Auschwitz: Radical Theology and Contemporary Judaism* (New York: Bobbs-Merrill, 1966), 54.

[61] Rubenstein, "The Dean and the Chosen People," 56.

[62] John Connelly, *From Enemy to Brother: The Revolution in Catholic Teaching on the Jews, 1933–1965* (Cambridge, MA: Harvard University Press, 2012).

[63] Susannah Heschel, "Confronting the Past: Post-1945 German Protestant Theology and the Fate of the Jews," in *The Protestant–Jewish Conundrum*, Studies in Contemporary Jewry 24, eds. Jonathan Frankel and Ezra Mendelsohn (Jerusalem: Hebrew University Press, 2010), 46–70.

taught in Berlin and Frankfurt from 1927 to 1938, where he witnessed Hitler's rise to power and Christian accommodations of National Socialism. Able to flee Nazi Europe in the summer of 1939, Heschel became an important theological voice in the United States, and was deeply engaged with Christian as well as Jewish colleagues; indeed, his work was initially received with greater acclaim by Christian theologians, such as Reinhold Niebuhr. Unlike his Jewish theological predecessors, from Mendelssohn to Buber, Heschel said virtually nothing about Jesus, and rarely discussed, in public, the history of Christian antisemitism, including the role of the churches and the Vatican during the Holocaust. At his meetings with Pope Paul VI, Cardinal Augustin Bea, and other leading Catholics during the Second Vatican Council, he focused on what he felt Jews and Christians share: the Hebrew Bible, experiences of prayer, belief in God's presence in their lives. When asked by the American Jewish Committee (AJC) in 1962 to help draft a memorandum that would alter the tone of discussions concerning Catholic-Jewish relations, he wrote:

"With humility and in the spirit of commitment to the prophets of Israel, let us consider the grave problems that confront us all as the children of God. Both Judaism and Christianity share the prophets' belief that God chooses agents through whom His will is made known and His work done throughout history. Both Judaism and Christianity live in the certainty that mankind is in need of ultimate redemption, that God is involved in human history, that in relations between man and man, God is at stake."[64]

In a remarkable statement that goes against the grain of modern Jewish views of Christianity, Heschel reminded his Jewish readers of the debt they owed to Christianity for preserving ancient Jewish texts, such as the apocrypha and the writings of Philo, and for the art and music that inspires all religious people. Insisting that "no religion is an island," Heschel noted that attacks against one religion ultimately undermine all religions: "Jews must realize that the spokesmen of the Enlightenment who attacked Christianity were no less negative in their attitude toward Judaism." Self-reliance, he wrote, has been replaced by interdependence: "sharing insights, confessing inadequacy."[65]

Heschel's engagement with Catholic theologians was repudiated in an article published in 1964 in the Orthodox Jewish journal, Tradition, by the leading Orthodox rabbi of the era, Joseph Soloveitchik.[66] A leading

---

[64] Quoted in Gary Spruch, *Wide Horizons: Abraham Joshua Heschel, AJC, and the Spirit of Nostra Aetate* (New York: American Jewish Committee, 2008), 10.

[65] Abraham Joshua Heschel, "No Religion is an Island," in *Moral Grandeur*, ed. Heschel, 236; 239.

[66] Joseph Soloveitchik, "Confrontation," *Tradition* (1964), 5–29.

authority on Jewish law and professor at Yeshiva University, Soloveitchik insisted that discussion between Jews and Christians must avoid theological exchange. Neither side should ask the other to change any of its beliefs, and the Vatican Council should only be asked to condemn antisemitism. Yet as Reuven Kimelman has pointed out in an article comparing the positions of Heschel and Soloveitchik, their positions concerning interfaith dialogue are not far apart.[67] Both insisted that Judaism's religious independence be recognized by Christians. Soloveitchik argued that Christians should not be asked to alter any doctrinal principles, whereas Heschel requested that antisemitism and charges of deicide against all Jews be condemned by the Church as a false teaching. Both met with cardinals and other church officials during the Second Vatican Council, both were widely read and influenced by Christian thought, and both delivered some of their most important lectures to Christian audiences. Nonetheless, many leading Orthodox rabbis and rabbinical organizations have concluded that Soloveitchik's position was a prohibition on theological dialogue with Christians, and have refused such engagement.

By contrast, Heschel argued that the modern era's emancipation of Jews has conveyed rights, but also obligations, including working with Christians to strengthen the faith of all people. By contrast, Michael Wyschogrod (1928–2015) has engaged Christian theologians on precisely the topics Heschel sought to avoid: Jesus, Paul, and Christian doctrine. Wyschogrod has been widely read by Christian theologians and deeply engaged in dialogue with what he has called "the Judaism of the Gentiles."[68] His work revives many of the themes present in classical and modern Jewish thought regarding Christianity, such as its role as a handmaiden, spreading Jewish monotheism to the Gentile world, and in rejecting Christian supersessionism. However, he departs radically in his affirmation of incarnation: "My claim is that the Christian teaching represents an intensification of the teaching of the in-dwelling God in Israel by concentrating that in-dwelling in one Jew rather than leaving it diffused in the people of Israel as a whole."[69]

---

[67] Reuven Kimelman, "Rabbi Joseph B. Soloveitchik and Abraham Joshua Heschel on Jewish–Christian Relations," *The Edah Journal* 4, no. 2 (2004): 1–21.

[68] Michael Wyschogrod, "A Jewish Perspective on Incarnation," *Modern Theology* 12, no. 2 (1996): 195–209.

[69] Michael Wyschogrod, *Abraham's Promise: Judaism and Jewish–Christian Relations*, ed. with an introduction by R. Kendall Soulen (Grand Rapids, MI: Eerdmans, 2004), 187. See also Michael Wyschogrod, *The Body of Faith: God and the People Israel* (Northvale, NJ: Jason Aronson, 2000).

By this, Wyschogrod means that God's indwelling in the community of Israel, God's entrance into human history, is analogous to the indwelling of the soul in the body, as he explains in his book, *The Body of Faith*. Jews as a people are not divine, but in preserving their existence as a people, a task Wyschogrod considers a central Jewish obligation, Jews embody the presence of God, a principle in tune with God's incarnation in the human body of Jesus. In contrast to many other Jewish thinkers, Wyschogrod does not see a link between Christianity and the Jewish people based on the historical Jesus's Jewish identity, but on a theological claim regarding Jesus's incarnation, a topic most other Jewish thinkers tend to avoid. What Wyschogrod expects is a Christian cessation of supersessionism, and its recognition of the continued and undiminished validity of Judaism. By contrast, the Jewish theologian David Novak argues that supersessionism need not be abandoned, but reformulated.[70] The effort to present a more tolerant Jewish approach to Christianity can also be found among Orthodox rabbinical figures. Rabbi Shlomo Riskin, chief rabbi of Efrat, Israel, has issued some highly positive statements about Jesus as a loyal Jew that became controversial within the Orthodox community. In an earlier generation, the distinguished expert on rabbinic law, Rabbi Jehiel Jacob Weinberg, expressed concern that "More than Christianity hates Judaism, Judaism hates Christianity."[71]

Wyschogrod's efforts to mitigate the negative judgment of Jewish theology concerning Christian doctrines, especially incarnation, are undertaken by him philosophically, but other Jewish scholars have used historical methods to demonstrate not that Christianity was derived from Judaism, but that Judaism was also shaped in significant ways through the ages by Christian belief and practice. In antiquity, historians such as Daniel Boyarin argue, both Judaism and Christianity emerge in a relationship of mutual influence, and that mutuality continues, as the medieval historian Israel Yuval has demonstrated, in their liturgies, festival celebrations, and self-understandings.[72] Such mutuality is central to the contemporary

---

[70] David Novak, *Jewish–Christian Dialogue: A Jewish Justification* (New York: Oxford University Press, 1989).

[71] Jehiel Jacob Weinberg, letter to Samuel Atlas, dated November 15, 1965; cited by Marc B. Shapiro, ed., "Scholars and Friends: Rabbi Jehiel Jacob Weinberg and Professor Samuel Atlas," *Torah U-Madda Journal* 7 (1997): 105–121; here 117.

[72] Daniel Boyarin, *Border Lines: The Partition of Judaeo-Christianity* (Philadelphia: University of Pennsylvania Press, 2004); Israel Yuval, *Two Nations in Your Womb: Perceptions of Jews and Christians in Late Antiquity and the Middle Ages*, trans. Barbara Harshav and Jonathan Chipman (Berkeley: University of California Press, 2008).

agenda of key figures studying Judaism and Christianity in antiquity, and increasingly scholars of medieval Jewish history are also turning away from a lachrymose account of persecutions toward narratives of coexistence and shared religious concerns.

In the year 2000, a small group of five Jewish scholars formulated a set of eight principles of Jewish views of Christianity, "Dabru Emet," (Speak the Truth) that was endorsed by over 200 Jewish intellectuals and rabbis. Some of the principles expressed classical liberal positions: Jews and Christians worship the same God, share the same moral principles, and seek justice and peace. Other principles sounded as though a bargain had been struck: "Christians can respect the claim of the Jews on the land of Israel" and "Nazism is a not a Christian phenomenon." "Dabru Emet" was welcomed primarily by Christian groups, especially in Europe, whereas its resonance among Jews was limited. Jon Levenson, for example, criticized the statement for asserting commonalities that are little more than platitudes, while ignoring serious theological differences.[73] Ultimately, the statement did not resolve disputes between Jewish and Christian groups over Zionism and the State of Israel, nor did it convince historians that Christianity was not central to the success of Nazi antisemitism and the Holocaust.

At the outset of the modern era, Jews still felt the conversionary pressures of Christians who believed Christianity was the sole path to heaven and the highest embodiment of religious truth. Jewish theologians such as Abraham Geiger recognized that it is not Jews who desire Christianity, but Christian theologians who require a myth of Jewish desire in order to legitimate Christianity. Yet Geiger's own scholarship awakened a Jewish desire for Jesus the Jew, and that desire, inchoate in his own work, eventually came to be a dominant mode of expressing modern Jewish identity in the writings of numerous theologians, writers, and artists, both before and after the Holocaust. In the second half of the twentieth century, as Jewish and Christian historians and theologians engaged in dialogue and joint research projects, and as the Holocaust loomed as an insistent rupture of past polemics, we see efforts at a new affirmation of one another's faith, a reliance on each other's scholarship, and a recognition that interfaith may be as important as faith itself.

---

[73] Jon D. Levenson, "How Not to Conduct Jewish–Christian Dialogue," *Commentary* 112, no. 5 (2001): 31–37; see also idem, "The Agenda of Dabru Emet," *Review of Rabbinic Judaism* 7 (2004): 1–26.

SELECT BIBLIOGRAPHY

Baeck, Leo. "Romantic Religion," in *Judaism and Christianity: Essays by Leo Baeck*, trans. and ed. Walter Kaufmann (Philadelphia: Jewish Publication Society, 1958).

Batnitzky, Leora. "Dialogue as Judgment, Not Mutual Affirmation: A New Look at Franz Rosenzweig's Dialogical Philosophy," *Journal of Religion* 79, no. 4 (1999): 523–544.

Buber, Martin. *Two Types of Faith*, trans. Norman P. Goldhawk (New York: Collier Books, 1951).

Cohen, Hermann. *"Ein Bekenntnis in der Judenfrage,"* in *Jüdische Schriften*, ed. Bruno Strauss (Berlin: C. A. Schwetschke, 1924).

Religion of Reason out of the Sources of Judaism, trans. Simon Kaplan (New York: F. Ungar, 1972).

Delitzsch, Franz. *Jesus und Hillel: Mit Rücksicht auf Renan und Geiger* (Erlangen: Verlag von Andreas Deichert, 1866).

Greenberg, Blu. "Jacob Emden: The Views of an Enlightened Traditionalist on Christianity," *Judaism* 27, no. 3 (1978): 351–363.

Gottlieb, Michah, ed., *Faith and Freedom: Moses Mendelssohn's Theological-Political Thought* (New York: Oxford University Press, 2011).

Heschel, Abraham Joshua. "No Religion is an Island," in *Moral Grandeur and Spiritual Audacity: Essays of Abraham Joshua Heschel*, ed. Susannah Heschel (New York: Farrar, Straus and Giroux, 1996), 235–250.

Heschel, Susannah. *Abraham Geiger and the Jewish Jesus* (Chicago: University of Chicago Press, 1998).

Jacob, Walter. *Christianity through Jewish Eyes* (Cincinnati: Hebrew Union College Press, 1974).

Klausner, Joseph. *From Jesus to Paul*, trans. W. F. Stinespring (New York: Macmillan, 1943).

Jesus of Nazareth, trans. by Herbert Danby (New York: Macmillan, 1925).

Maciejko, Pawel. *The Mixed Multitude: Jacob Frank and the Frankist Movement, 1755–1816* (Philadelphia: University of Pennsylvania Press, 2011).

Montefiore, Claude. *Judaism and St. Paul* (London: M. Goshen, 1914).

Novak, David. *Jewish–Christian Dialogue: A Jewish Justification* (New York: Oxford University Press, 1989).

Rosenstock-Huessy, Eugen and Franz Rosenzweig. *Judaism Despite Christianity*, trans. Dorothy M. Emmet (New York: Schocken Books, 1971).

Rosenzweig, Franz. *The Star of Redemption*, trans. William W. Hallo (New York: Holt, Rinehart and Winston, 1971).

Rubenstein, Richard L. "The Dean and the Chosen People," in *After Auschwitz: Radical Theology and Contemporary Judaism*, (New York: Bobbs-Merrill, 1966): 3–13.

Shapiro, Marc B., ed. "Scholars and Friends: Rabbi Jehiel Jacob Weinberg and Professor Samuel Atlas," *Torah U-Madda Journal* 7 (1997): 105–121.

Soloveitchik, Joseph. "Confrontation," *Tradition* 6, no. 2 (1964), 5–29.

Sorkin, David. *The Religious Enlightenment: Protestants, Jews, and Catholics from London to Vienna* (Princeton: Princeton University Press, 2008).

Tal, Uriel. *Christians and Jews in Germany*, trans. Noah Jacobs (Ithaca, NY: Cornell University Press, 1976).

Wellhausen, Julius. *The Pharisees and the Sadducees: An Examination of Internal Jewish History*, trans. Mark E. Biddle (Macon, GA: Mercer University Press, 2001).

Wyschogrod, Michael. "A Jewish Perspective on Incarnation," *Modern Theology* 12, no. 2 (1996): 195–209.

CHAPTER 40

JEWS AND MUSLIMS

IVAN KALMAR

From the close of the eighteenth to the middle of the last century, most European Jews and their descendants in the Americas knew little about flesh-and-blood Muslims. Yet their *ideas* about Muslims were central to how they imagined themselves as Jews. This was especially true of the "assimilated" Western Ashkenazim, who were very sensitive to their social and cultural surroundings. All around them, Muslims were a major issue. Scholarly research of the Muslim "Orient"[1] enjoyed high prestige. Popular fiction thrived on illustrated adventures involving clever harem girls and ferocious sheiks, set against a backdrop of fabulous palaces and desert oases. As the nineteenth century unfolded, it became ever more fashionable for high and petty bourgeois to decorate their interiors with images of Arab riders and alluring odalisques. At the hugely popular world exhibitions, whose vistas were dominated by mock-oriental palaces, exotic drummers and belly dancers performed, and sometimes real Arab farmers walked their cattle or steer. More permanent *arabisant* architecture included water towers that looked like minarets, movie theaters and Masonic Halls with horseshoe shaped doors and windows – and "Moorish" style synagogues, built not by the descendants of Jewish Sephardi but rather by "modern" Ashkenazi congregations of the most liberal sort.[2] The Jews, it was universally accepted, belonged to a nation whose roots were in the Orient. They were, as Wilhelm Dohm put it in 1781, Europe's "Asiatic refugees."[3]

Judaism was constructed as an oriental religion, the Jewish mind as an oriental mind and even the Jewish body as an oriental body.[4] This meant

---

[1] I am using the term "Orient" the old-fashioned way, as did Edward Said in *Orientalism* (New York: Vintage Books, 1978, 2003), with the focus not on China or Japan but on Muslim West Asia and North Africa.

[2] Ivan Davidson Kalmar, "Moorish Style: Orientalism, the Jews, and Synagogue Architecture," *Jewish Social Studies: History, Culture, and Society* 7 no. 3 (2001): 68–100.

[3] Christian Wilhelm von Dohm, *Concerning the Amelioration of the Civil Status of the Jews* (Cincinnati: Hebrew Union College, Jewish Institute of Religion, 1957), 1.

[4] Mitchell B. Hart, "Racial Science, Social Science, and the Politics of Jewish Assimilation," *Isis* 90, no. 2 (1999): 268–297.

that the Jewish religion, the Jewish mind and the Jewish body were seen as similar in important ways to their Muslim counterparts. At worst, they were attacked as an alien, noxious presence, foreign to both the soil and the spirit of the West. But at best they were appreciated as the living guardians of the West's religious and civilizational heritage, which stemmed from the East.

This essay explores the various facets of this imagined kinship between Muslim and Jew. The main historical and intellectual factors that contributed to the notion were biblical criticism at a time of secularization; the development of "race" as a concept in the context of Western imperial expansion; the Jewish effort to gain not only political equality but also admiration or at least respect; and the struggle over historic Palestine. This latter eventually robbed the concept of Jewish–Muslim kinship of its vitality and viability.

ORIENTALIZING THE BIBLE

The impulse to equate Jew and Muslim goes back to the very beginning of the Christian encounter with Islam. It stemmed from real and imagined similarities between Judaism and Islam, and from the fact that Jews and Muslims were Christianity's most familiar contemporary religious Others.[5]

With the increased interest in the Bible stimulated by the Renaissance and the Reformation, there appeared what might be called a biblical-ethnographic interest in the Orient. This considered the lifeways of contemporary Muslims to be a clue to the culture of ancient Israel. In a typically orientalist fashion, it was assumed that the Orient was ahistorical and monolithic. The current peoples of the Orient, it was thought, lived in the same kind of civilization as their "ancestors." And, as one oriental was like another, it mattered little if these ancestors had been Jews, Turks or Arabs. To see how ancient Israelites had lived, one could visit the Bedouin today, and not only in Palestine, but in Arabia or any other place they pitched their tents.

Many Christian artists in the West began to model biblical characters on what they knew of contemporary "Turks" (a rather generic term used more or less for all residents of the Ottoman Empire). The most striking,

---

[5] Jeremy Cohen, *Living Letters of the Law: Ideas of the Jew in Medieval Christianity* (Berkeley: University of California Press, 1999); Debra Higgs Strickland, *Saracens, Demons, & Jews: Making Monsters in Medieval Art* (Princeton: Princeton University Press, 2003); Suzanne Conklin Akbari, "Placing the Jews in Late Medieval English Literature" in *Orientalism and the Jews*, ed. Ivan Davidson Kalmar and Derek J. Penslar (Waltham, MA: Brandeis University Press, 2005).

and most enduring, iconographic expression of Orientalism in Western art was the use of turbans on biblical personages.[6] Rembrandt's biblical paintings, such as *Saul and David* or *David and Uriah*, sporting huge and prominently lit turbans, were neither the first nor nearly the last in this tradition. But they were among the most striking examples from the seventeenth century, when scholars as much as artists embraced the notion of learning about the Bible through the contemporary Orient.

Rembrandt's models had an appearance that contemporaries read as "Turkish" (a vague term referring to Muslims in general, but focusing on the Turkish speaking rulers of the Ottoman Empire). Biblical scholars were more interested in Arabs than Turks, because of the kinship between the Arabic and Hebrew languages that was already well known. The biblical text was examined in the light of Arabic and other Semitic documents as they were slowly becoming better known in the Christian West. Biblical studies were a major motivator of a resurgence in Arabic studies in the seventeenth and early eighteenth century. The first scholar to hold the new chair of Arabic at Oxford, Edward Pococke (1604–1691), was a Hebraist, who published commentaries on several books of the Bible.

In 1706, Rembrandt's countryman Albert Schultens would advocate explicitly the use of Arabic in interpreting Scripture. To him, it was not only Arabic language but also what we would now call Arabic culture that provided a key to the world of the Old Testament. Arabic philosophy and popular proverbs illustrated, to Schultens, facets of biblical thought.[7]

Eighteenth-century English scholars also believed that the Hebrew Scriptures embodied the spirit of a wider, oriental world. This attitude was in fact probably responsible for the introduction of the term "Orientalism" into the English language. If Joseph Spence, who used it in 1726 in his *Essay on Pope's Odyssey* is to be trusted, "Orientalism" was his own "new word."[8]

An important plea for reading the Bible as oriental poetry was the book *On the Sacred Poetry of the Hebrews* (1754), by the future Bishop of London, Robert Lowth.[9] Lowth had a direct influence on the German scholar Johann Gottfried Herder, author of *On the Spirit of Hebrew Poetry* (1782–83).[10] Even more importantly, Lowth influenced Johann David Michaelis

---

[6] Ivan Davidson Kalmar, "Jesus did Not Wear a Turban: Orientalism, the Jews, and Christian Art," in Kalmar and Penslar eds, *Orientalism and the Jews*.

[7] Albert Schultens, *Oratio De Linguæ Arabicæ Antiquissima Origine* (Franeker: Willem Coulon, 1729).

[8] Joseph Spence, *An Essay on Mr. Pope's Odyssey, in Five Dialogues* (London: Wilmot, 1737), 214–215; Brian Hepworth, *Robert Lowth* (Boston: Twayne Publishers, 1978).

[9] Robert Lowth, *Lectures on the Sacred Poetry of the Hebrews* (New York: Garland, 1971).

[10] Johann Gottfried Herder, *The Spirit of Hebrew Poetry* (Naperville, IL: Aleph Press, 1971).

(1717–1791), a teacher of Johann Gottfried Eichhorn (1753–1827). The latter was one of the major figures in the new "higher criticism" school of biblical philology.

Higher criticism had an enormous impact on modern scholarship. The association of Judaism with Islam and with pre-Islamic Semitic religion was crucial to it. The *Catholic Encyclopaedia* of 1908 was scarcely a partisan of this critical attitude to the biblical text, yet it was able to state its principles with precision and clarity:

A fundamental [principle] is that a literary work always betrays the imprint of the age and environment in which it was produced; another is that a plurality of authors is proved by well-marked differences of diction and style, at least when these coincide with distinctions in view-point or discrepancies in a double treatment of the same subject. A third received canon holds to a radical dissimilarity between ancient Semitic and modern Occidental, or Aryan, methods of composition.[11]

The first and the third "canons" are especially relevant. For the "higher" critics, the Bible was among other things a literary work, and it reflected what they considered an oriental, and not simply a Jewish, environment. This oriental environment, mental as well as physical (the two things were related in the mind of the critics, who often considered culture to be influenced by the climate), was radically different from that of "Aryan" Europe (or "Aryan" Persia and North India).

The intellectual excitement caused by the "higher criticism's" orientalist style of reading the Bible could not be overstated. The biblical critic Alexander Giddes wrote to his cousin after his European tour in 1783:

In Germany almost every man of learning is an Orientalist. In short, Sacred Criticism is everywhere the predominant study of the learned of all communions who seem to vie with one another which shall do most towards restoring the Scriptures to their primitive purity or as near to it as possible.[12]

Giddes's report notes the predominance of Germany in the biblical criticism of the time. Germany was also the major ground on which biblical criticism was united with a superficially secular "philosophy of history." This saw human history as a progressive replacement of one civilizational stage with another. Generally, such evolutionist schemes represented the

[11] "Biblical Criticism (Higher)," *The Catholic Encyclopedia* (New York: The Encyclopedia Press, 1907–14).
[12] Quoted by E. S. Shaffer, *"Kubla Khan" and the Fall of Jerusalem: The Mythological School in Biblical Criticism and Secular Literature, 1770–1880* (Cambridge: Cambridge University Press, 1980), 26.

civilization of the ascendant West, with its Christian heritage, as the pinnacle of lawful historical processes.

The weightiest example is the evolutionary scheme propounded by Hegel. In Hegel's philosophical "grand narrative," human history is identical to the history of the Spirit (*Geist*). When humanity lives in its most primitive stage, it is not yet able to discern the Spirit at all (which in the Hegelian scheme means that the Spirit has not yet begun to realize itself). The "spiritual" is then murkily fathomed as part of the "natural." Later, in its "abstract" form, the Spirit appears to humans *in contrast with* the concrete world. This was a step that, in the 1827 *Lectures on the Philosophy of History*, Hegel considered to be the unique achievement of Judaism, but within the broader religious landscape of the ancient Orient.[13] But for the Spirit to achieve its historical destiny, further development was necessary. *Geist* had to become concrete (and thus close to the actual lives of humanity) rather than remaining in the abstract isolation of a sublime creative force. This necessary step was taken with the incarnation of Christ. The concretization process then still had to undergo a lengthy history culminating in *Protestant* Christianity (or perhaps, as some readers of Hegel suggest, the process is still going on). Its goal was/is the moment when the Spirit is manifested not only in contrast to Nature but also in "union with it."[14]

In the earlier, "Jewish," stage of religion, thought Hegel, the *Geist* is apprehended in the form of a sublime, all-powerful God who is, however, entirely separated from the world: the One compared to whom the world is Nothing. (Even Spinoza, who could surely be read as imagining a God who dwells within the world, was still, according to Hegel, thinking "as a Jew."[15] Spinoza's philosophy of religion, Hegel said, was an "Oriental theory," an "echo from Eastern lands."[16]) Hegel termed Judaism a "Religion of the Sublime" (*Religion der Erhabenheit*).

Hegel believed that the worshipper's relation to divinity in this kind of religion was much the same as the oriental subject's relation to the tyrannical ruler represented by the evolving image of the "oriental despot." Islam was but a later revival, born in a dialectical tension with Christianity, of the oriental spirit of total submission to an aloof, remote and despotic

---

[13] Georg Wilhelm Friedrich Hegel, *The Philosophy of History* (New York: Dover Publications, 1956), 195.

[14] Hegel, *The Philosophy of History*.

[15] Georg Wilhelm Friedrich Hegel, *The Encyclopaedia Logic, with the Zusätze* (Indianapolis: Hackett, 1991), Paragraphs 151, 226.

[16] Georg Wilhelm Friedrich Hegel, *Lectures on the History of Philosophy* vol. 3 (London: Routledge & Kegan Paul, 1955), 252.

God. "It was first in the Jewish and then later in the Mohammedan religions," he wrote, "that God was interpreted as the Lord and essentially *only*
as the Lord."[17] So close was the relationship between the two religions to
Hegel, that he was even able to use the term "Arab religion" to include the
Jewish: he proposed that the idea that there is only one God and "he is a
jealous God who will have no other gods before him" is "the great thesis
of the Jewish, of overall Arab religion of the western Orient and Africa."[18]

Looked at specifically in the context of the relationship between
Christianity and Judaism, Hegel's scheme was a sort of secularization of
the classic Christian attitude to the difference between the two religions,
and between the Hebrew Old Testament and the Greek New, namely,
supersessionism. Just as Christianity was imagined as built upon and
superseding Judaism, so for Hegel the "Germanic" spirit was built upon
and superseded the Semitic. Hegel's Germanic *Volksgeist* (ethnic or racial
spirit) was to Semitic *Volksgeist* like Christianity was to the religion of the
Old Testament.

"SEMITES" AND "RACE"

The notion of the *Semite* resulted from this admixture of religion and
"race" (as well as the pseudo-scientific conflation, typical of the period, of
language family with descent group). "Race" was and is an extremely ill-
defined notion. Its nebulous nature was needed to allow it the flexibility
to function in all the very varied contexts that it was used in. There is one
thing, however, that all popular uses of "race" have in common. Race is
always imagined as the result of common descent.

Imagining the Jews as a descent group, and therefore, in the broadest definition of the term, as a "race," was the very cornerstone of the
Christian understanding of history, as it was of the Jewish. The Jews, after
all, were the Chosen People, the main actor on the stage of the biblical narrative. The biblical plot in fact moves ahead through the action of descent
groups – Israel and the *goyim* or "Nations." In fact, the late eighteenth
and early nineteenth century notion of race, including Hegel's, was recognizably similar to the biblical idea of a *goy*,[19] in spite of the significant
differences. The differences included the use of civilizational evolutionism
as well as the use of language families to define descent groups. They did

[17] Hegel, *Lectures on the History of Philosophy*, Paragraphs 112, 77.
[18] Georg Wilhelm Friedrich Hegel, *Philosophy of Religion* (Berkeley: University of California Press, 1984), 129.
[19] Related biblical terms with a slightly different nuance are *'am* and *le'om*.

not yet, until later in the nineteenth century, include biological notions of genetic inheritance.

That the Bible treats the Jews as a descent group is true even if, as is accepted by many scholars today, there has been significant conversion to Judaism through many periods of history, going back to antiquity. Most Jews today may in fact be the physical descendants of converts.[20] But the converts joined the imagined community and came to consider themselves as descended from the ancient Israelites. Their claim was legitimized by religious law, which did not and does not consider the children of properly converted mothers to be any different from those with an older Jewish pedigree.[21] From the late eighteenth century on, however, the partly fictive character of Jewish descent was largely though not entirely ignored. The default narrative became one of a large exodus from Roman-conquered Judea to Europe and elsewhere, where the Jews took on a few converts, yet maintained the character of a community of common descent. It could be said that the biblical, descent-based definition of "who is a Jew" was, *mutatis mutandis*, revived. The mainly religious notion of "Jew" inherited from the Middle Ages was now *racialized*.[22]

A racialization also took place among Muslims. In this case, however, the racially defined group was given a distinct name, and did not exactly coincide with the religiously defined one. "Arab" had rarely been used before the nineteenth century as a label for a human group (as opposed to a language). But now it became the label for a "race" to which the founder of Islam had belonged, and which spread Islam far and wide in the non-western world (there were relatively few Muslims in Europe and America). "Arab" became a racialization, informal and imprecise but still, of "Muslim."[23]

To identify Islam with only its Arabic-speaking followers is an error, as better informed westerners have always recognized, including in the

---

[20] The perennial claim that most Jews are descended from converts has recently been revived, with a critical examination of the claim's history, by Shlomo Sand, *The Invention of the Jewish People*, ed. Yael Lotan (New York: Verso, 2009); Ernest Renan, *On the Nation and the "Jewish People,"* ed. Shlomo Sand, trans. David Fernbach (New York: Verso, 2010).

[21] Menachem Finkelstein, *Conversion: Halakhah and Practice* (Ramat-Gan: Bar-Ilan University Press, 2006).

[22] On the relationship between Christian views of the Jews and the modern race concept, see J. Kameron Carter, *Race: A Theological Account* (New York: Oxford University Press, 2008); on that between theology and race see, for example, Craig R. Prentiss, ed. *Religion and the Creation of Race and Ethnicity: An Introduction* (New York: New York University, 2003).

[23] Youssef M. Choueiri, *Arab Nationalism, A History: Nation and State in the Arab World* (Malden, MA: Blackwell, 2000).

nineteenth century. But the popular near-equation of Muslim and Arab made good sense in the context of the evolutionist/supersessionist "philosophy of history" that we have just examined. It allowed observers in the Christian West to associate Qur'an and Torah with a common racial sensibility.

Indeed, in the early nineteenth century the term "Arab" could serve as the label for that wider race, later to be more commonly called "Semitic." This is how it was possible, as we have seen, for Hegel to speak in one breath "of the Jewish, of overall Arab religion of the western Orient and Africa."[24] "Let men doubt of unicorns," the main character is told in Benjamin Disraeli's *Tancred* (1847) by a "Jewish sheikh, "but of one thing there can be no doubt, that God never spoke except to an Arab."[25] The Jewish sheikh no doubt included Moses and the Prophets of Israel, and Disraeli, who was a baptized Anglican, presumably also included Jesus among the "Arabs."

The fuzzy ways in which the terms "Jew" and especially "Arab" were used reflected the lack of precision in such terms as "nation," "people," *Volk* and "race." "Semitic race" was introduced as a concept in the midst of an effort to reinvent "race" as a precise concept with definite biological and genetic connotations.

It is ironic that as far as the "Semitic race" is concerned, this far more precise and biologizing term for what Hegel or Disraeli called "Arab" was popularized by the major French orientalist and Bible scholar, Ernest Renan (1823–1892).[26] Renan is best known today, at least among English-speaking scholars, for his lecture, "What is a Nation?" (1882). In an oft-quoted passage, Renan declared that "A nation is thus a large-scale solidarity .... It presupposes a past, yet it is summed up in the present by a tangible fact: the clearly expressed consent and desire to continue a common life."[27] The whole essay is a strident polemic against biological (and geographic) theories of nationality, and indeed against confusing nation with race. And yet it was Renan who, in the expansive introduction to his *General History and Comparative System of the Semitic Languages* (1855), set the tone for the next hundred years, during which "Semitic race" under that label was considered an objectively given reality by most scholars and the public at large.

---

[24] Hegel, *Philosophy of Religion.*

[25] Benjamin Disraeli, *Tancred* (London: R. Brimley, 1904), 319.

[26] Renan was not the first to extend the term "Semite" from a language family to an imagined descent group. The *Jewish Encyclopedia* (New York: Funk and Wagnalls, 1901–06, "Anti-Semitism") suggested that Christian Lassen (1800–1876) had done so in 1844. But it seems to be Renan's work that made the usage widely familiar.

[27] Ernest Renan, "What is a Nation?" in Renan, *On the Nation and the "Jewish People,"* 64.

At times Renan seemed unsparing of his compliments. "It is the Semitic race," he would write, "which has the glory of having made the religion of humanity. Far beyond the confines of history, resting under his tent free from the taint of a corrupted world, the Bedouin patriarch prepared the faith of mankind."[28] Yet this must be taken in the usual supersessionist context: Semitic religion was a great contribution, but does not measure up to the Indo-European version:

Research that is reflexive, independent, rigorous, courageous, philosophical – in a word, the search for truth – seems to have been the heritage of that Indo-European race that has, from deep India to the northern extremities of the West and of the North, from the remotest centuries to modern times, sought to explain God, man and the world by a rational system, and left behind, like rungs to different levels (*echelonnées aux divers degrés*) of its history, philosophical creations that have always and everywhere been submitted to the laws of logical development. But to the Semitic race belong those firm and certain intuitions that have been first to free the divinity of its veils and, without reflection or reasoning, attained the most purified religious form that antiquity has known.[29]

Renan's *Histoire générale et système comparé des langues sémitiques* abounds with apparent insults such as "The Semitic people lack curiosity almost completely"; "In general, the perception of nuances is deeply absent among the Semitic peoples"; "polygamy, consequence of an original nomadic way of life, has blocked among the Semites the development of all that we call society, and has formed a race that is exclusively virile, without flexibility or *finesse*"; "The military inferiority of the Semites is due to this total lack of ability for discipline or subordination"; or "Morality has always been understood by this race in a manner very different from ours."[30] Obviously, the admirable qualities of the Semites do not compare with "ours." In politics, furthermore, the Semitic adoration of the One God corresponded to the notion of an absolute theocratic despotism.[31] With this last point, Renan managed to link Hegelian-style civilizational evolutionism, biblical philology and the deep orientalist tradition of depicting Asian governments as oriental despotisms.[32] (He was also attacking Christianity via its

---

[28] Ernest Renan, *The Life of Jesus* (New York: A. L. Burt, 1894), 70.

[29] Renan, *The Life of Jesus*, 3

[30] Ernest Renan, *Histoire générale et système comparé des langues sémitiques. Pt 1: Histoire générale des langues sémitiques*, fourth edition (Paris: Lévy, 1863). The quotations in this paragraph are on pages 10, 11, 14, and 15.

[31] Renan, *Histoire générale*; Ivan Kalmar, *Early Orientalism: Imagined Islam and the Notion of Sublime Power* (London: Routledge, 2012).

[32] Kalmar, *Early Orientalism*.

Jewish ancestor, a controversial maneuver for which Renan would become known.)

Shlomo Sand suggests that the young Renan, who wrote the *Histoire générale* with its negative judgments of the Semites, had a change of heart later, during the late 1880s when he produced "What is a Nation?" Here Renan insisted that in modern Western Europe "you can be French, English, or German while being Catholic, Protestant, Jewish or not practicing any religion."[33] Yet Renan never renounced the opinions made in his early tome. There is in fact no inconsistency between the racial concept of the Semites in the *Histoire générale* and the subjectivist conception of the nation in "What is a nation"? In 1882 Renan wrote that "In the ancient tribe and city the fact of race had, we admit, an importance of the first order. The ancient tribe and city were but an extension of the family. In Sparta, in Athens, all the citizens were relatives of a more or less close degree. The same was the case with the Beni-Israel[34] and," Renan adds in typical orientalist fashion "it is still so among the Arab tribes."[35] The point, in short, is not that he had been wrong about the Semites, including the ancient Israelites, as a race. Rather it is that because of conversion the *modern* Jews were not racial Semites, and even that perhaps only in *Western* Europe.[36] Therefore, presumably, they were not subject to the racial shortcomings of the ancient "Beni-Israel," or of the present-day Arab tribes.

JEWISH APOLOGISTS

The mature Renan's pronouncements on the modern Jews as a non-race were likely a response to the outrage that the *Histoire générale* excited among many Jews, including specific rejoinders by the major Jewish orientalists, Hajjim Steinthal and Daniel Chwolson.[37] While in the 1880s many

---

[33] Shlomo Sand, "The Unclassifiable Renan," introduction to Renan, *On the Nation and the "Jewish People";* Renan, "What is a Nation?" 61.

[34] The term "Beni-Israël" may be a mixture of Hebrew and Arabic: many of the Arab tribes, including at the time of Muhammad, had names beginning with *beni* ("sons" or "children of"). It may also be a misreading of the biblical *benei yisra'el* for "the Children of Israel." (Renan's comments are unrelated to the Indian Jewish community known as "Beni Israel.")

[35] The passage appears on p. 54 of Renan, "What is a Nation?" However, I am using my own translation, which is closer to the original (Ernest Renan, *Qu'est-ce qu'une nation?* (Paris: Mille et une nuits, 1997).

[36] Renan, "What is a Nation?," 46.

[37] Daniel Chwolson, "Zur Charakteristik der semitischen Völker," *Zeitschrift für Völkerpsychologie und Sprachwissenschaft* 1(1860); Heymann Steinthal, *Über Juden und Judentum: Vorträge und Aufsätze von H. Steinthal,* ed. Gustav Karpeles (Berlin: Poppelauer,

Jews would agree with Renan that they were either not racial Semites or if they were that their race played no role in their Jewish identity, this was not generally so earlier on, when being proud of one's Semitic heritage made more sense, as romantic philo-Semitism and philo-Orientalism among the Gentiles had not yet – as we will see – given up so much ground to antisemitic prejudice. A proud identification with the Semitic racial heritage developed then among many Jews. It was not universal then or ever, but it was a feeling that retained a presence for several generations, even in the face of increasing antisemitism later.

The strategy of the Jewish apologist for the Semitic race was *not* to deny or transcend the notion of history as the work of races, each with their own distinctive cultural capabilities and heritage. It was to recognize that supersessionism did permit a possible consensus on the value of Judaism as a "giver" of Christianity to the gentiles. Indeed, there were gentiles who stressed the importance of safeguarding the Old Testament heritage within an authentic Christianity. In England, this school of thought may be exemplified by writers such as Matthew Arnold and George Eliot,[38] by artists such as William Holman Hunt (1826–1910), who traveled to the Holy Land to create pious work that was true to what he saw as the historical setting of the Bible, and "restorationists of the Jews" including theologians, politicians and philologists, collectively known today as the early Christian Zionists.[39] This Semitic pride was not universal, but it would survive among many Jews until the mid-twentieth century even if, we shall see, it was losing steam steadily from the 1870s on.

Disraeli (1804–1881), was the earliest and possibly, in the public rather than the scholarly field, the most important among the apologists. Disraeli's parents arranged for him to be baptized while he was still a child but, as was normal at the time, he continued to be referred to as a Jew by others and, slightly less normal perhaps, by himself; for the popular definition of "Jew" was already based primarily on descent. Disraeli regarded Christianity as a popularization of Judaism designed to appeal to the

---

c. 1906); "Die Stellung der Semiten in der Weltgeschichte," *Jahrbuch für jüdische Geschichte und Literatur* (Berlin) 4 (1901), 46–69; Daniel Abramovich Chwolson, *Die Semitischen Völker, Versuch einer Charakteristik* (Berlin: F. Duncker, 1872), 64.

[38] David J. DeLaura, *Hebrew and Hellene in Victorian England: Newman, Arnold, and Pater* (Austin: University of Texas Press, 1969).

[39] Donald M. Lewis, *The Origins of Christian Zionism: Lord Shaftesbury and Evangelical Support for a Jewish Homeland* (New York: Cambridge University Press, 2010); Eitan Bar-Yosef, "Christian Zionism and Victorian Culture," *Israel Studies* 8 no. 2 (2003): 18–44; Michael Polowetzky, *Jerusalem Recovered: Victorian Intellectuals and the Birth of Modern Zionism* (Westport, CT: Praeger, 1995).

gentiles. In his view, the Church of England was in decline, and this was due mainly to "its deficiency of oriental knowledge."[40] The church, and the West in general, he argued in *Tancred*, must lose its spiritual foundations if it neglects "that oriental intellect to which they owed their civilization," i.e., the spirit of Judaism.[41]

In Germany among Disraeli's contemporaries, the most strident spokesman for Semitic racial pride was Moses Hess (1812–1875), among other things Marx's collaborator at the *Neue rheinische Zeitung*. As if in response to Marx (or was Marx replying to him?), in *Rome and Jerusalem: The Last Nationality Question* (1862) Hess claimed that "The race struggle is primary; the class struggle is secondary."[42] Those who battled in the "race struggle" were the Aryans and the Semites. Hess's "Rome" and "Jerusalem" were mere metaphors for these two "races."

A younger contemporary of Benjamin Disraeli, Emanuel Deutsch (also known as Immanuel, 1829–1873) articulated most effectively, within the scholarly world, the notion of Judaism as not only an ancient foundation for, but in fact an ancient equivalent of original Christianity. Deutsch was born in today's Poland and studied in Berlin, but spent most of his working life in Britain. He was an active Arabist and Islamist, and he died in Alexandria. However, he was and is most famous for his insistent argument that the Talmud embodied much of the same ethical and religious spirit as the New Testament. Such work was very well received by many contemporary readers, as had been Disraeli's racial philo-Semitic novels.[43] George Eliot, for example, was influenced by Deutsch to the extent that Deutsch appears to have inspired the character of Mordecai in *Daniel Deronda* (1876).[44]

In a famous essay first published in 1867, Deutsch established the notion that the Talmud contained the same ethical notions as did the New Testament, to which it was much closer than it was to the Torah:

That grand dictum, "Do unto others as thou wouldst be done by," against which Kant declared himself energetically from a philosophical point of view, is quoted by Hillel, the President, at whose death Jesus was ten years of age, not as anything new, but as an old and well-known dictum "that comprised the whole Law." (…) The Judaism of the time of Christ (to which that of our days, owing principally to

[40] Disraeli, *Tancred*, 83.

[41] Disraeli, *Tancred*, 202.

[42] Moses Hess, *Rom und Jerusalem, die letzte Nationalitätsfrage* (Prague, n.d.), 211.

[43] Ivan Davidson Kalmar, "Benjamin Disraeli: Romantic Orientalist," *Comparative Studies in History and Society* 4, no. 2 (2005): 348–371.

[44] Mary Kay Temple, "Emanuel Deutsch's Literary Remains: A New Source for George Eliot's 'Daniel Deronda'," *South Atlantic Review* 54, no. 2 (1989): 59–73.

the Talmud, stands very near), and that of the Pentateuch, are as like each other as our England is like that of William Rufus, or the Greece of Plato that of the Argonauts.[45]

Just like Disraeli, evidently, Deutsch considered Christianity to be but a Judaism for the gentiles, with the difference perhaps that what the scholar meant was *rabbinical* and by implication, modern Judaism, a distinction for which the less-academically inclined writer-politician had no eye.

And like for Disraeli, for Deutsch the Judaism celebrated as the living core of Christianity was completely oriental. To him, the students of the Talmudic academies were children of "the Orient."[46] The Talmud was an "utterly Eastern, antique, and thoroughly *sui generis*" work from "the gorgeous East …, where all things glow in brighter colors, and grow into more fantastic shapes."[47] Deutsch's argument for valuing the Jewish within the Christian religion was also one for valuing the oriental within the occidental. Deutsch stood not so much for the Judeo-Christian but for the Abrahamic common tradition.

Even more influential was the German-Jewish historian Heinrich Graetz (1817–1891). Graetz's *magnum opus*, *History of the Jews*, was written in several volumes between 1853 and 1870. He traveled to the Holy Land, like many others, in order to see for himself what was considered the enduring biblical character of the people and the scenery. Like Deutsch, Graetz stressed the primacy of Judaism in developing what others might consider Christian ethics.

Among the most enduring parts of Graetz's legacy is his assessment of Jewish history in Muslim-ruled medieval Spain. Graetz did record examples of persecution. However, readers were more likely to be struck by idyllic passages that described the Jews as living in "a garden, rich in odorous blossoms and luscious fruits, whose productions, though varied in color and taste, have their root in the same earth."[48] In this case, the fertile ground was that of Almoravid Spain, 1105–1148 CE, the period when the poet Yehudah ha-Levi flourished.

Largely under the influence of Graetz's instruction, liberal Jews learned to think of Muslim Spain as a worthy model for contemporary Germany and Europe.[49] They wished to show to their gentile neighbors that treating

---

[45] Emanuel Deutsch, *The Talmud* (Philadelphia: Jewish Publication Society, 1895).

[46] Deutsch, *The Talmud*, 42.

[47] Deutsch, *The Talmud*, 16, 18.

[48] Heinrich Graetz, *History of the Jews*, ed. Bella Löwy and Philipp Bloch (Philadelphia: Jewish Publication Society, c. 1891–98), vol. 3, 313.

[49] Ismar Schorsch, "The Myth of Sephardic Supremacy," *Leo Baeck Institute Year Book* 34 (1989): 47–66.

the Jews fairly and allowing them an important role in society would benefit modern European nations just as it had benefited medieval Muslim Spain.

It is understandable that, given this fact, many scholars interpret the so-called Moorish style synagogue as evoking Muslim Spain. Throughout the liberal Jewish communities of the world (many of whom were at least partly German-speaking), and to a much smaller extent even among the more modernizing Orthodox, synagogues of unprecedented size were built, often in conspicuous spaces in the city center, with domes, minarets, and horseshoe doors and windows borrowed from Islamic architecture. The earliest were built in the 1830s. But by the onset of the twentieth century, when the style began to fade in popularity, there were imposing Moorish style synagogues in New York, Manchester, Florence, Berlin, Prague, Vienna, Budapest, St. Petersburg, and countless other places in Europe, though they were most common in Germany and the Habsburg territories, and among German-speaking Jews in America.

The proper way to read the architecture of these buildings is not as nostalgia for Jewish Spain, however, but as indexing Western notions of the Jews as a Semitic people and the kinsfolk of the Arabs. Moorish style synagogues, which were mostly designed by gentile architects, make regular reference to building styles from the entire Islamic world. The Plum Street Temple of Cincinnati (1862), for example, still has America's tallest minarets, but there were no minarets – or domes – on Spanish synagogues or even on Spanish mosques. Documents recording the intent of various communities building Moorish style synagogues (which were at the time at least as often referred to as "Arabian" in style) also illustrate that the model was not just the Iberian but the wider Arab Muslim world.[50]

The interest that nineteenth- and early twentieth-century Jews had in their Semitic racial heritage extended to scholarship about the Semites and the Near East in general. The tradition of combining biblical study with that of oriental philology included major personalities from Emanuel Deutsch to perhaps the greatest orientalist of his time, Ignaz Goldziher (1850–1921), who like many Budapest Jews was bilingual and wrote mostly in German. In between the two, countless liberal rabbis wrote their semi-obligatory doctoral thesis, as did many secular Jewish scholars, on some aspect of oriental, often Arabic philology, often focusing on connections between Judaism and Islam. A good example is Abraham Geiger, who after studying Arabic wrote about Jewish-derived elements in the Qur'an.[51]

A minimal list of the great Jewish orientalist scholars from the early nineteenth to the late twentieth century might include, in addition to

[50] Kalmar, "Moorish Style."
[51] Abraham Geiger, *Judaism and Islám* (New York: KTAV, 1970).

the personalities already mentioned, David Samuel Margoliouth (1858–1940) in England and Armand Vambéry (1832–1912) in Austria-Hungary.[52] The tradition was only broken in the twentieth century, with Maxime Rodinson (1914–2004) in France and Bernard Lewis (1916–) in the United States, Jewish orientalists of major importance who have not written on the Talmud or the Bible.

Pride in being Semitic was still an explicit part of the ideology of certain Zionists in the early twentieth century, especially among German-speaking Jews. Members of the Bar Kokhba student association in Prague, who at times included Franz Kafka, were enthusiastic about the teachings of the philosopher and Zionist author Martin Buber (1878–1965). Buber unhesitatingly included himself and his Prague audience in Western Jewry, but contrary to the prevailing attitude among German-speaking Jews he did not despise, but rather romanticized, the "Eastern" – what we now call Eastern European – Jew. He ascribed to these *Ostjuden* (defined, to be sure, as much in terms of culture and language as of geography) some oriental characteristics that they, at least by implication, shared with Muslims. He saw living in them the pure oriental spirit that was the genuine heritage of the Jews, and was now being adulterated through misguided patterns of assimilation in the West. In fact, for Buber, these admirable oriental characteristics were shared even by orientals wider afield, such as the Chinese. In a lecture to the Bar Kokhba Association, he suggested that the occidental is a "motor man" (*motorischer Mensch*), who is unable to perceive "the undifferentiated base of organic life." But the latter is just what the oriental (Jewish, Arab, Chinese, etc.) excels at. In contrast to the Western "motor man," Buber classified the oriental as a "sensory man" (*sensorischer Mensch*).[53]

HARD ORIENTALISM

The Semitism of Buber and his early twentieth-century Prague audience was articulated during a period when antisemitism was gaining in popularity on philo-Semitism. Being called a Semite was, in the society at large,

---

[52] Many Jewish orientalists were discussed in Bernard Lewis, "The Pro-Islamic Jews," in *Islam in History: Ideas, People, and Events in the Middle East* (Chicago: Open Court, 1993), 142, 144. See also Martin S. Kramer and Bernard Lewis, *The Jewish Discovery of Islam: Studies in Honor of Bernard Lewis* (Tel Aviv: Moshe Dayan Center for Middle Eastern and African Studies, Tel Aviv University, 1999) and several articles in Kalmar and Penslar, eds, *Orientalism and the Jews*.

[53] Martin Buber, ed., "The Spirit of the Orient and Judaism" in *On Judaism* (New York: Schocken, 1967).

less than ever a compliment. Orientalism may be somewhat simplistically divided into a soft variety, which sincerely if often condescendingly admires the alleged spirituality, glittering splendor, and/or titillating sensuality of the East, and a hard variety, which condemns its irrationality, violence, and despotism. Philo-Semitism corresponds to the soft, and antisemitism to the hard variety of Orientalism in general.

Soft Orientalism is not really the opposite of hard Orientalism. These are, rather, dialectically joined aspects of one another. Streaks of each are generally found in the same author and the same period. The hard orientalist aspect, nevertheless, predominated between the Renaissance and the late eighteenth century, when a romantic sort of Orientalism appeared. Throughout the Western world during the long nineteenth century,[54] the imagined Orient had a profound influence on the Western imagination.[55] An Indophile Aryan mania, for instance, swept England in the early part of the nineteenth century.[56] True, Aryan pride always had the potential of opposing an alleged Aryan civilization, of which Europe was a part, to a Semitic one, which was alien to the West. But at first it mainly encouraged a general soft orientalist enthusiasm, which included the Arab and Jewish Orients as well. Probably this was because the West no longer felt threatened by the Muslim Orient, as its own imperial ascendance was clear.

The anti-Orient, hard aspect asserted itself more forcefully towards the end of the century, when most of the world was under Western colonial domination or influence (though most of the eastern Mediterranean had not been formally colonized). Although on the surface the job of bringing the world under the rule of the West was complete, increasingly the white man's reward felt like a burden. For while the late nineteenth century was the zenith of Western imperialism, it was also a period when Western power was seriously contested, through open rebellion, or through the simple non-cooperation of the "silent sullen peoples."[57]

This imperialist disappointment with the Orient helped to revive the frightening, "gothic" image of the Orient that had been in evidence even during Orientalism's romantic phase. The first well-known orientalist

---

[54] The phrase "long nineteenth century" is typically used to refer to the period between the French Revolution and World War I. Here it is extended to the middle of the twentieth century.

[55] Raymond Schwab, *The Oriental Renaissance: Europe's Rediscovery of India and the East, 1680–1880* (New York: Columbia University Press, 1984).

[56] Thomas R. Trautmann, *Aryans and British India* (Berkeley: University of California Press, 1997).

[57] Rudyard Kipling, "The White Man's Burden," in *The Five Nations* (London: Methuen, 1914).

novel, William Beckford's *Vathek* (1786), for example, was a thriller about a sexually perverted oriental despot. At the end of the nineteenth century, the gothic tinge of Orientalism developed into grotesque exotic entertainment. The characters were sometimes Jewish. A typical example was George du Maurier's 1894 novel *Trilby*, whose Jewish hypnotist, Svengali, became ever more oriental as the original was being reproduced and re-illustrated. Eventually the character acquired its stereotypical magician's turban, which du Maurier's Svengali did not wear.

The Jewish woman's image, in particular, underwent a change in focus from an ambiguously romantic soft Orientalism to a clearly condemnatory hard one. A heroine such as Scott's Rebecca in *Ivanhoe* (1819), and even partly Jewish Esther Gobseck, who appeared in several of Balzac's works including *The Splendors and Miseries of Courtesans* (1838–47) was still a sympathetic character, no matter that she led the immoral life of a high class prostitute. The "Jewess'" beauty and goodness were often identified with "oriental" features, especially her eyes. Balzac wrote that

Esther, excessively strong though apparently fragile, arrested attention by one feature that is conspicuous in the faces in which Raphael has shown his most artistic feeling, for Raphael is the painter who has most studied and best rendered Jewish beauty. (…) Esther's nationality proclaimed itself in this Oriental modeling of her eyes with their Turkish lids…. Only those races that are native to deserts have in the eye the power of fascinating everybody, for any woman can fascinate some one person. Their eyes preserve, no doubt, something of the infinitude they have gazed on.[58]

Esther embodied already many features of the Jewish *femme fatale* that became far more popular in the late nineteenth and early twentieth century, when increasing antisemitism coincided with a period of intense misogyny. This time, there was little tenderness in the dangerous woman's expression, and little sympathy in the author's portrayal of her. Still, the biblical tinge remained.

The most notorious example was the fashion in art, literature, and theater for the reinvented New Testament character of the "daughter of Herod." Unnamed in the Gospels, tradition based on Josephus identified her as "Salome." The New Testament image of the innocent dancing girl put up to no good by her scheming mother, was transformed in a series of portrayals into a seductive ogress. Of particular influence in this respect was Gustave Moreau's painting "Salome Dancing Before Herod" (1876). Moreau combined the biblical story, including echoes of the artistic

[58] Honoré de Balzac, *Scenes from a Courtesan's Life* (Gloucester, UK: Dodo Press, 2006), 35.

tradition of representing Esther appearing before Ahasuerus,[59] with references to a generalized Orient. Three sculpted faces behind Herod's throne recall the "Hindu Trinity": Brahma, Shiva, and Vishnu. But much of the interior architecture and the costuming recall the Muslim Orient. The biblical subject works for Moreau to fuse the fear and awe of sublime political power, associated with the Orient, with the fear and awe of woman. Oscar Wilde makes even more explicit the idea that woman's sadistic demand for love is even more powerful than that of the apparently dominant male. Wilde's Salome asks Herod for the head of John the Baptist because the handsome precursor of Christ had rejected her sexual advances. It was Wilde, too, who invented the exotic strip tease known as "the dance of veils" for his theatrical *Salome* of 1893, which was then adopted for a well-known operatic version by Richard Strauss (1905). Wilde wrote the play for Sarah Bernhardt (1844–1923), a celebrated actress who was, though baptized, also derided as the epitome of the Jewish and oriental *femme fatale*.[60]

It was amidst such phobic anxieties about things Jewish and oriental that the term "anti-Semite" was invented, presumably by Wilhelm Marr in 1879. Often, the pitch of antisemitic rhetoric was raised to the level that opposed the Semite and the Aryan as cosmic forces. Semites plotted to block the high destiny of the Aryans to lead the world to a better future. That destiny was expressed in the West's colonial domination over the planet.

Thus a pamphlet issued by the Austrian anthropologist Adolf Wahrmund, a founder of Austria's National Ethnographic Museum, systematically compared the Jews of the West to the Arabs of the desert, likening the caravan raids of the Bedouin to stock market raids by Jewish speculators at the bourses of Europe. In 1887 Wahrmund explicitly described Western power in sub-Saharan Africa and Central Asia as a barrier to Semitic (i.e., Arab) influence, and suggested that it be coupled with the removal of the Jews to isolated territories where they would be similarly surrounded.[61]

The term "anti-Semite" does literally imply anti-Jewish as well as anti-Arab feeling, the first in the context of Europe's internal struggle with ethnic nationality and religious identity, and the second in the context

---

[59] The image of Salome was connected to that of Esther, another orientalized image of a biblical female. Willy Hirdt, *Esther und Salome: zum Konnex von Malerei und Dichtung in Frankreich des 19. Jahrhunderts* (Tübingen: Francke, 2003).

[60] Karen Levitov, "The Divine Sarah and the Infernal Sally: Bernhardt in the Words of Her Contemporaries," in *Sarah Bernhardt: The Art of High Drama*, ed. Carol Ockman (New Haven: Yale University Press, 2005).

[61] Adolf Wahrmund, *Das Gesetz des Nomadenthums und die heutige Judenherrschaft* (Karlsruhe: H. Reuther, 1887).

of its efforts to dominate the rest of the world. The process of creating national and supra-national identities in Europe had the exclusion of the Jews as one of its byproducts and arguably even as one of its goals, and the development of a justificatory rhetoric of imperialism as another. The complex interaction between antisemitism and imperialism and colonialism has been explored by writers from Hannah Arendt to Aamir Mufti.[62] Mufti, in fact, claims that the modern Western preoccupation with the "Jewish Question," including the solution to it that required a departing of the Jews and the proposed partition of Palestine to accommodate them, served as a blueprint for subsequent colonial and post-colonial action such as the partition of India.

Yet the primary use of the term "antisemitism" was in a strictly Western context. Its target was the Jews. It was never directed primarily at the non-European Semites, the Arabs. A deprecating image of the Arab was not the end of the anti-Semites, but their beginning point. Taking for granted that the Arabs were inferior, they wished to argue that the Jews were no different. The Nazis would recognize this dynamic very well. Not wishing for strategic reasons to alienate certain Arab leaders, they preferred the term *anti-jüdisch* to *antisemitisch*.[63]

This is a good place to note that while the focus of this chapter is on imagining Jews and Muslims or Arabs in similar ways, the full picture – which would require more space – would need to place this near-equation in the context of a dialectic that includes how the *difference* between them was constructed. Even the most romantic admirers of the Jews as Semites generally considered the Jews to be the more westernized and therefore the more capable of progress.

This difference has been the almost exclusive focus of scholars who, with an ideological axe to grind, understand Zionism as historically little more than an imperialist tool aimed at controlling Arabs.[64] One major

[62] Aamir Mufti, *Enlightenment in the Colony: The Jewish Question and the Crisis of Postcolonial Culture* (Princeton: Princeton University Press, 2007); H. Arendt, *The Origins of Totalitarianism* (New York: Harcourt Brace Jovanovich, 1973), 527; Richard J. Bernstein, *Hannah Arendt and the Jewish Question* (Cambridge, MA: MIT Press, 1996). Part One of Arendt's book is entitled "Antisemitism." For a summary of the antisemitism/imperialism problem, see Kalmar, and Penslar, eds, *Orientalism and the Jews*.

[63] David Motadel, *Islam in Nazi Germany's War* (Cambridge, MA: Harvard University Press, 2014).

[64] See, for example, Gershon Shafir, "Zionism and Colonialism: A Comparative Approach," in *The Israel/Palestine Question: A Reader*, ed. Ilan Pappé, second edition (New York: Routledge, 2007); Nur Masalha, *The Bible and Zionism: Invented Traditions, Archaeology and Post-Colonialism in Palestine-Israel* (New York: Palgrave Macmillan, 2007).

scholar, however, who discussed the difference between the image of the Jew and the Arab *along with* the similarities was Jacques Derrida. Algerian-born Derrida, who understood himself as both Arab and Jewish, described Christian, Jewish *and* Muslim civilization as a unit, defined by the stated differences and the unstated (as he saw it) commonalities between them. It had been a cornerstone of his relatively ahistorical, "deconstructionist" method to regard all opposition as in a sense derived from an underlying but un-identifiable, un-expressed "trace" or *différance*. It is only through the difficult exercise of becoming conscious of the essentially unverbaliz-able trace that the whole system of visible oppositions can be properly "deconstructed." This allows one to retrace how the system had been "con-structed." Derrida suggested that Western civilization was constructed from the oppositions among Judaism, Christianity and Islam, on the foun-dations of the trace of commonality that he described as "the fold [*pli*] of this Abrahamic or Ibrahimic moment, folded over and again [*replié*] by the Gospels between the two other 'religions of the Book.' "[65]

Gil Anidjar developed Derrida's line of reasoning further in his *The Jew, the Arab: A Brief History of the Enemy*.[66] Here one of the premises was that, in the Christian West, Jew and Arab were connected as opposing but connected characters in the construction of the figure of the Enemy. Also significant is Anidjar's brief book, *Semites*, where the Arab/Jew opposition, united both under the label "Semite" and the label "Orient," is the figure of the opposition of "religion" to "the secular."[67]

In the present essay, however, the focus remains on the *conflation* of Jew and Muslim/Arab, lately much ignored, rather than their better studied difference, or even their *différance*. One reason is that understating the similarity may lead to falsely assuming that it was in some way a secret underlying force. "Read the incomparable," counsels Anidjar, "Shylock and Othello."[68] That is, consider the "incomparable" Jew and Muslim together, and you will be surprised to find that they can actually be com-pared. In fact, the historical record shows that not only were Jew and Arab/Muslim consistently and insistently compared at the surface, explicit level,

---

[65] Jacques Derrida, *Donner la mort* (Paris: Galilée, 1999), 149. See the translation and com-mentary by Gil Anidjar, "Introduction: 'Once More, Once More': Derrida, the Arab, the Jew," in *Acts of Religion*, eds, Jacques Derrida and Gil Anidjar (New York: Routledge, 2002), 10.

[66] Gil Anidjar, *The Jew, the Arab: A History of the Enemy* (Stanford: Standford University Press, 2003).

[67] Gil Anidjar, *Semites: Race, Religion, Literature* (Stanford: Standford University Press, 2008).

[68] Gil Anidjar, "Introduction: 'Once More, Once More'," 11.

but that in fact it is the *opposition* between them that was more subtle, and expressed at the level of what Said called "latent" as opposed to "manifest" Orientalism.[69] Shylock and Othello have been read together all the time.

If today the notion of imagining Jew and Muslim/Arab together seems odd to the extent that it is almost hard to imagine that it was once so pervasive, it is because we are looking back at it through the veil of long decades of relentless conflict in Israel/Palestine. The more the Zionist idea took hold, the more Arab objections to it gained prominence. The ideational forces that had created the near-equation of Jew and Arab were, at the end of the nineteenth century, already on the wane. They were weaker still when, in one of the last waves of imperialist border-drawing, in 1922, the Palestine Mandate was given to Britain in order to establish a Jewish homeland in the Holy Land. In spite of the "Weizmann-Faisal agreement" in which a major Jewish and a major Arab leader professed to be "mindful of the racial kinship and ancient bonds existing between the Arabs and the Jewish people,"[70] Palestinian and other Arab opposition to Jewish immigration was almost complete. Differences between the Jews and the Arabs began to seem much more important than similarities. They were increasingly articulated in terms of a contrast between a Western and an Oriental people. (Ironically, the contrast was also made along rather similar lines between the Western Ashkenazim and their Mizrahi, i.e., "oriental," coreligionists. The effort to make the *yishuv* more Western by acculturating the Mizrahim would continue in the State of Israel.[71])

Even so, at the founding of Israel there were still those who considered a state that gave the Jewish nation self-determination to be one of the fruits of the global anti-colonial liberation movement.[72] Such an attitude became

---

[69] Said, *Orientalism*.

[70] Quoted from the text as maintained online by the United Nations Information System on the Question of Palestine (UNISPAL), https://unispal.un.org/DPA/DPR/unispal.nsf/0/5BFF833964EDB9BF85256CED00673D1F (accessed January 3, 2012).

[71] See, for example, Adriana Kemp, ed., *Israelis in Conflict: Hegemonies, Identities, and Challenges* (Portland, OR: Sussex Academic Press, 2004); Rachel Shabi, *We Look Like the Enemy: The Hidden Story of Israel's Jews from Arab Lands*, first US edition (New York: Walker & Co., 2008); Yehouda A. Shenhav, *The Arab Jews: A Postcolonial Reading of Nationalism, Religion, and Ethnicity* (Stanford: Stanford University Press, 2006); As'ad Ganim, *Ethnic Politics in Israel: The Margins and the Ashkenazi Center* (New York: Routledge, 2010). Aziza Khazzoom, "The Great Chain of Orientalism: Jewish Identity, Stigma Management, and Ethnic Exclusion in Israel," *American Sociological Review* 68, no. 4 (2003): 481–510 captures orientalism towards Mizrahim in the context of the earlier philo-Semitic orientalism discussed in this chapter.

[72] Derek Penslar, "Zionism, Colonialism, and Postcolonialism," *Journal of Israeli History* 2, nos. 2–3 (2001): 84–98.

more and more rare after Israel conquered all of historic Palestine and more, in the Six Day War of 1967. The state of the Jews came to rule over a million Arab Palestinians beyond the 1949 armistice lines, which had enclosed a smaller State whose great majority was Jewish (even if the majority was gained in part by refusing to allow Arab refugees to come back). The occupation of new territory by Israel could and did appear to many as the reversal of a worldwide trend towards decolonization and as a throwback to the times of Western imperialism. At the time of the 1967 war, Israel's main enemy, Egypt, was led by its president, Gamal Abdel Nasser. Nasser was a major influence within the Non-Aligned Movement, an organization that led much of the post-colonial world in various degrees of opposition to the United States and the West. Widely admired in the recently liberated ex-colonies, Nasser passionately opposed the very existence of the Jewish State. In such an atmosphere, to consider Israel and the Jews together with the Arabs under the common label of "oriental races" was simply no longer possible.

Subsequent events are beyond the scope of this essay. Suffice it to say that the more radical anti-colonial and post-colonial rhetoric became, the more it was anti-Israeli, culminating in such events as the 1975 resolution by the United Nations General Assembly (later rescinded) that Zionism was "a form of racism and racial discrimination."[73] The large-scale immigration of Muslims to the West, many of them passionately opposed to Israel, the *intifadas* in Palestine, the continuing Jewish settlements beyond the internationally recognized borders of Israel and the suspension in 2010 of the "peace process," all belong on another page. The damage done to imagining Jew and Muslim together had been done earlier.

SELECT BIBLIOGRAPHY

Akbari, Suzanne Conklin. "Placing the Jews in Late Medieval English Literature," in *Orientalism and the Jews*, ed. Ivan Davidson Kalmar and Derek J. Penslar (Waltham, MA: Brandeis University Press, 2005): 32–50.

Anidjar, Gil. "Introduction: 'Once More, Once More': Derrida, the Arab, the Jew," in *Acts of Religion*, ed. Jacques Derrida and Gil Anidjar (New York: Routledge, 2002).

The Jew, the Arab: A History of the Enemy (Stanford: Stanford University Press, 2003).

Semites: Race, Religion, Literature (Stanford, CA: Stanford University Press, 2008).

Arendt, Hannah. *The Origins of Totalitarianism* (New York, NY: Harcourt Brace Jovanovich, 1973).

Balzac, Honoré de. *Scenes from a Courtesan's Life* (Gloucester, UK: Dodo Press, 2006).

---

[73] Resolution 3379, adopted November 10, 1975.

Bar-Yosef, Eitan. "Christian Zionism and Victorian Culture," *Israel Studies* 8, no. 2 (2003): 18–44.

Bernstein, Richard J. *Hannah Arendt and the Jewish Question* (Cambridge, MA: MIT Press, 1996).

"Biblical Criticism (Higher)." *The Catholic Encyclopedia* (New York: The Encyclopedia Press, 1907–14).

Buber, Martin. "The Spirit of the Orient and Judaism" in *On Judaism* (New York: Schocken, 1967).

Carter, J. Kameron. *Race: A Theological Account* (New York: Oxford University Press, 2008).

Choueiri, Youssef M. *Arab Nationalism, A History: Nation and State in the Arab World* (Malden, MA: Blackwell, 2000).

Chwolson, Daniel. "Zur Charakteristik der semitischen Völker," *Zeitschrift für Völkerpsychologie und Sprachwissenschaft* 1(1860).

Die Semitischen Völker, Versuch einer Charakteristik (Berlin: F. Duncker, 1872), 64.

Cohen, Jeremy. *Living Letters of the Law: Ideas of the Jew in Medieval Christianity* (Berkeley: University of California Press, 1999).

DeLaura, David J. *Hebrew and Hellene in Victorian England: Newman, Arnold, and Pater* (Austin: University of Texas Press, 1969).

Derrida, Jacques. *Donner la mort* (Paris, Galilée, 1999).

Deutsch, Emanuel. *The Talmud* (Philadelphia: Jewish Publication Socieity of America, 1895).

Finkelstein, Menachem. *Conversion: Halakhah and Practice* (Ramat-Gan: Bar-Ilan University Press, 2006).

Ganim, As'ad. *Ethnic Politics in Israel: The Margins and the Ashkenazi Center* (New York: Routledge, 2010).

Geiger, Abraham. *Judaism and Islám* (New York: KTAV, 1970).

Graetz, Heinrich. *History of the Jews* (Philadelphia, Jewish Publication Society, 1891–98), vol. 3.

Hegel, Georg Wilhelm Friedrich. *The Encyclopaedia of Logic, with the Zusätze* (Indianapolis: Hackett, 1991).

Lectures on the History of Philosophy, vol. 3 (London: Routledge & Kegan Paul, 1955).

The Philosophy of History (New York: Dover Publications, 1956).

Philosophy of Religion (Berkeley: University of California Press, 1984).

Herder, Johann Gottfried. *The Spirit of Hebrew Poetry* (Naperville, IL: Aleph Press, 1971).

Hess, Moses. *Rom und Jerusalem, die letzte Nationalitätsfrage* (Prague, n.d.).

Hirdt, Willy. *Esther und Salome: zum Konnex von Malerei und Dichtung in Frankreich des 19. Jahrhunderts* (Tübingen: Francke, 2003).

Kalmar, Ivan Davidson. "Benjamin Disraeli: Romantic Orientalist," *Comparative Studies of Society and History* 47, no. 2 (2005): 348–371.

Early Orientalism: Imagined Islam and the Notion of Sublime Power (London and New York: Routledge, 2012).

"Jesus did Not Wear a Turban: Orientalism, the Jews, and Christian Art," in *Orientalism and the Jews*, ed. Ivan Davidson Kalmar and Derek Penslar (Waltham, MA: Brandeis University Press, 2005): 3–31.

"Moorish Style: Orientalism, the Jews, and Synagogue Architecture," *Jewish Social Studies: History, Culture, and Society* 7, no. 3 (2001): 68–100.

Kemp, Adriana ed. *Israelis in Conflict: Hegemonies, Identities, and Challenges* (Portland, OR: Sussex Academic Press, 2004).

Khazzoom, Aziza. "The Great Chain of Orientalism: Jewish Identity, Stigma Management, and Ethnic Exclusion in Israel," *American Sociological Review* 68, no. 4 (2003): 481–510

Kipling, Rudyard. "The White Man's Burden," in *The Five Nations* (London: Methuen, 1914).

Kramer, Martin S. and Bernard Lewis. *The Jewish Discovery of Islam: Studies in Honor of Bernard Lewis* (Tel Aviv: Tel Aviv University, 1999).

Levitov, Karen. "The Divine Sarah and the Infernal Sally: Bernhardt in the Words of Her Contemporaries" in *Sarah Bernhardt: The Art of High Drama*, ed. Carol Ockman (New Haven: Yale University Press, 2005).

Lewis, Bernard, ed. "The Pro-Islamic Jews," in *Islam in History: Ideas, People, and Events in the Middle East* (Chicago: Open Court, 1993).

Lewis, Donald M. *The Origins of Christian Zionism: Lord Shaftesbury and Evangelical Support for a Jewish Homeland* (New York: Cambridge University Press, 2010).

Lowth, Robert. *Lectures on the Sacred Poetry of the Hebrews* (New York: Garland, 1971).

Masalha, Nur. *The Bible and Zionism: Invented Traditions, Archaeology and Post-Colonialism in Palestine-Israel* (New York: Palgrave Macmillan, 2007).

Mufti, Aamir. *Enlightenment in the Colony: The Jewish Question and the Crisis of Postcolonial Culture* (Princeton: Princeton University Press, 2007).

Penslar, Derek. "Zionism, Colonialism, and Postcolonialism," *Journal of Israeli History* 2, nos. 2–3 (2001): 84–98.

Polowetzky, Michael. *Jerusalem Recovered: Victorian Intellectuals and the Birth of Modern Zionism* (Westport, CT: Praeger, 1995).

Prentiss, Craig R., ed. *Religion and the Creation of Race and Ethnicity: An Introduction* (New York : New York University, 2003).

Renan, Ernest. *Histoire générale et système comparé des langues sémitiques. Pt 1: Histoire générale des langues sémitiques,* fourth edition (Paris: Lévy, 1863).

The Life of Jesus (New York: A.L. Burt, 1894).

On the Nation and the "Jewish People," ed. Shlomo Sand, trans. David Fernbach (New York: Verso, 2010).

Qu'est-ce qu'une nation? (Paris: Mille et une nuits, 1997).

Said, Edward. *Orientalism* (New York: Vintage Books, 1978, 2003).

Sand, Shlomo. *The Invention of the Jewish People*, ed. Yael Lotan (New York: Verso, 2009).

Schorsch, Ismar. "The Myth of Sephardic Supremacy," *Leo Baeck Institute Year Book* 34 (1989): 47–66.

Schultens, Albert. *Oratio De Linguæ Arabicæ Antiquissima Origine* (Franeker: Willem Coulon, 1729).

Schwab, Raymond. *The Oriental Renaissance: Europe's Rediscovery of India and the East, 1680–1880* (New York: Columbia University Press, 1984).

Shabi, Rachel. *We Look Like the Enemy: The Hidden Story of Israel's Jews from Arab Lands* (New York: Walker & Co., 2008).

Shaffer, E. S. *"Kubla Khan" and the Fall of Jerusalem: The Mythological School in Biblical Criticism and Secular Literature, 1770–1880* (Cambridge: Cambridge University Press, 1980).

Shafir, Gershon. "Zionism and Colonialism: A Comparative Approach," in *The Israel/Palestine Question: A Reader*, ed. Ilan Pappé (New York: Routledge, 2007): 78–94.

Shenhav, Yehouda A. *The Arab Jews: A Postcolonial Reading of Nationalism, Religion, and Ethnicity* (Stanford: Stanford University Press, 2006).

Spence, Joseph. *An Essay on Mr. Pope's Odyssey, in Five Dialogues* (London: Wilmot, 1737).

Steinthal,Heymann. "Die Stellung der Semiten in der Weltgeschichte," *Jahrbuch für jüdische Geschichte und Literatur* (Berlin) 4 (1901): 46–69.

Strickland, Debra Higgs. *Saracens, Demons, & Jews: Making Monsters in Medieval Art* (Princeton: Princeton University Press, 2003).

Temple, Mary Kay. "Emanuel Deutsch's Literary Remains: A New Source for George Eliot's 'Daniel Deronda,'" *South Atlantic Review* 54, no. 2 (1989): 59–73.

Trautmann, Thomas R. *Aryans and British India* (Berkeley: University of California Press, 1997).

Wahrmund, Adolf. *Das Gesetz des Nomadenthums und die heutige Judenherrschaft* (Karlsruhe and Leipzig: H. Reuther, 1887).

INDEX

CPSIA information can be obtained
at www.ICGtesting.com
Printed in the USA
LVHW081335250422
717153LV00014B/937